Lecture Notes in Computer Science 3290

Commenced Publication in 1973
Founding and Former Series Editors:
Gerhard Goos, Juris Hartmanis, and Jan van Leeuwen

Editorial Board

David Hutchison
 Lancaster University, UK
Takeo Kanade
 Carnegie Mellon University, Pittsburgh, PA, USA
Josef Kittler
 University of Surrey, Guildford, UK
Jon M. Kleinberg
 Cornell University, Ithaca, NY, USA
Friedemann Mattern
 ETH Zurich, Switzerland
John C. Mitchell
 Stanford University, CA, USA
Moni Naor
 Weizmann Institute of Science, Rehovot, Israel
Oscar Nierstrasz
 University of Bern, Switzerland
C. Pandu Rangan
 Indian Institute of Technology, Madras, India
Bernhard Steffen
 University of Dortmund, Germany
Madhu Sudan
 Massachusetts Institute of Technology, MA, USA
Demetri Terzopoulos
 New York University, NY, USA
Doug Tygar
 University of California, Berkeley, CA, USA
Moshe Y. Vardi
 Rice University, Houston, TX, USA
Gerhard Weikum
 Max-Planck Institute of Computer Science, Saarbruecken, Germany

Robert Meersman   Zahir Tari   Wil van der Aalst
Christoph Bussler   Avigdor Gal   Vinny Cahill
Steve Vinoski   Werner Vogels   Tiziana Catarci
Katia Sycara (Eds.)

On the Move to Meaningful Internet Systems 2004: CoopIS, DOA, and ODBASE

OTM Confederated International Conferences
CoopIS, DOA, and ODBASE 2004
Agia Napa, Cyprus, October 25-29, 2004
Proceedings, Part I

Springer

Volume Editors

Robert Meersman
Vrije Universiteit Brussel, STAR Lab
Pleinlaan 2, Bldg. G/10, 1050 Brussels, Belgium
E-mail: meersman@vub.ac.be

Zahir Tari
RMIT University, School of Computer Science and IT
City Campus, GPO Box 2476 V, Melbourne, Victoria 3001, Australia
E-mail: zahirt@cs.rmit.edu.au

Library of Congress Control Number: 2004113801

CR Subject Classification (1998): H.2, H.3, H.4, C.2, H.5, I.2, D.2.12, K.4

ISSN 0302-9743
ISBN 3-540-23663-5 Springer Berlin Heidelberg New York

This work is subject to copyright. All rights are reserved, whether the whole or part of the material is concerned, specifically the rights of translation, reprinting, re-use of illustrations, recitation, broadcasting, reproduction on microfilms or in any other way, and storage in data banks. Duplication of this publication or parts thereof is permitted only under the provisions of the German Copyright Law of September 9, 1965, in its current version, and permission for use must always be obtained from Springer. Violations are liable to prosecution under the German Copyright Law.

Springer is a part of Springer Science+Business Media

springeronline.com

© Springer-Verlag Berlin Heidelberg 2004
Printed in Germany

Typesetting: Camera-ready by author, data conversion by PTP-Berlin, Protago-TeX-Production GmbH
Printed on acid-free paper   SPIN: 11341079   06/3142   5 4 3 2 1 0

Volume Editors

Robert Meersman
Zahir Tari

CoopIS 2004

Wil van der Aalst
Christoph Bussler
Avigdor Gal

DOA 2004

Vinny Cahill
Steve Vinoski
Werner Vogels

ODBASE 2004

Tiziana Catarci
Katia Sycara

OTM 2004 General Co-chairs' Message

The General Chairs of OnTheMove 2004, Larnaca, Cyprus, are once more proud to observe that the conference series we started in Irvine, California in 2002, and continued in Catania, Sicily last year, has turned out to be a concept that attracts a representative selection of today's research in distributed, heterogeneous yet collaborative systems, of which the Internet and the WWW are its prime examples.

Indeed, as such large, complex and networked intelligent information systems become the focus and norm for computing, it is clear that one needs to address and discuss in a single forum the implied software and system issues as well as methodological, theoretical and application issues. This is why the OnTheMove (OTM) Federated Conferences series covers an increasingly wide yet closely knit range of topics such as data and Web semantics, distributed objects, Web services, databases, workflows, cooperation, ubiquity, interoperability, and mobility. OnTheMove wants to be a primary scientific forum where these aspects for the development of internet- and intranet-based systems in organizations and for e-business are addressed in a quality-controlled fundamental way. This third, 2004 edition of the OTM Federated Conferences event therefore again provided an opportunity for researchers and practitioners to understand and publish these developments within their respective as well as within their broader contexts.

OTM first of all co-locates three related, complementary and successful main conference series: DOA (Distributed Objects and Applications), covering the relevant infrastructure-enabling technologies, ODBASE (Ontologies, DataBases and Applications of SEmantics) covering Web semantics, XML databases and ontologies, and CoopIS (Cooperative Information Systems) covering the application of these technologies in an enterprise context through, for example, workflow systems and knowledge management. Each of these three conferences treats its specific topics within a framework of (a) theory, (b) conceptual design and development, and (c) applications, in particular case studies and industrial solutions.

Following and expanding the example set in 2003, we solicited and selected quality workshop proposals to complement the more "archival" nature of the main conferences, with research results in a number of selected and more "avant garde" areas related to the general topic of distributed computing. For instance, the so-called Semantic Web has given rise to several novel research areas combining linguistics, information systems technology, and artificial intelligence, such as the modeling of (legal) regulatory systems and the ubiquitous nature of their usage. We were glad to see that in 2004 several of the Catania workshops re-emerged with a second edition (notably WoRM and JTRES), and that four other workshops could be hosted and successfully organized by their respective proposers: GADA, MOIS, WOSE, and INTEROP. We trust that their audiences mutually productively and happily mingled with those of the main conferences.

A special mention for 2004 is in order for the new Doctoral Symposium Workshop where three young postdoc researchers organized an original setup and formula to bring PhD students together and allow them to submit their research proposals for selection. A limited number of the submissions and their approaches were independently evaluated by a panel of senior experts at the conference, and presented by the students in front of a wider audience. These students also got free access to all other parts of the OTM program, and only paid a heavily discounted fee for the Doctoral Symposium itself. (In fact their attendance was largely sponsored by the other participants!) If evaluated as successful, it is the intention of the General Chairs to expand this model in future editions of the OTM conferences and so draw in an audience of young researchers to the OnTheMove forum.

All three main conferences and the associated workshops share the distributed aspects of modern computing systems, and the resulting application-pull created by the Internet and the so-called Semantic Web. For DOA 2004, the primary emphasis stayed on the distributed object infrastructure; for ODBASE 2004, it was the knowledge bases and methods required for enabling the use of formal semantics; and for CoopIS 2004 the main topic was the interaction of such technologies and methods with management issues, such as occurs in networked organizations. These subject areas naturally overlap and many submissions in fact also treat envisaged mutual impacts among them. As for the earlier editions, the organizers wanted to stimulate this cross-pollination with a shared program of famous keynote speakers: this year we got no less than Roberto Cencioni of the EC, Umesh Dayal of HP Labs, Hans Gellersen of Lancaster University, and Nicola Guarino of the Italian CNR! As before we encouraged multiple-event attendance by providing authors with free access to other conferences or workshops of their choice.

We received a total of 350 submissions for the three conferences and approximately 170 in total for the workshops. Not only can we therefore again claim success in attracting a representative volume of scientific papers, but such a harvest allowed the program committees of course to compose a high-quality cross-section of worldwide research in the areas covered. In spite of the large number of submissions, the Program Chairs of each of the three main conferences decided to accept only approximately the same number of papers for presentation and publication as in 2002 and 2003 (i.e., an average of 1 paper out of 4 submitted, not counting posters). For the workshops, the acceptance rate varied but was stricter than before, about 1 in 2, to 1 in 3 for GADA and WoRM. Also, for this reason, we decided to separate the proceedings into two books with their own titles, with the main proceedings in two volumes and the workshop proceedings in a separate, third volume, and we are grateful to Springer for their suggestions and collaboration in producing these books. The reviewing process by the respective program committees as usual was performed very professionally and each paper in the main conferences was reviewed by at least three referees. It may be worthwhile to emphasize that it is an explicit OnTheMove policy that all conference program committees and chairs make their selections completely autonomously from the OTM organization. Continuing an equally nice (but admittedly costly) tradition, the OnTheMove Federated Event organizers decided again to make ALL (sizeable!) proceedings available to ALL participants of conferences and workshops, independent of their registrations.

The General Chairs really are especially grateful to all the many people who were directly or indirectly involved in the setup of these federated conferences and in doing so made them a success. Few people realize what a large number of people have to be involved, and what a huge amount of work, and, yes, risk organizing an event like OTM entails. In particular we therefore thank our eight main conference PC co-chairs (DOA 2004: Vinny Cahill, Steve Vinoski, and Werner Vogels; ODBASE 2004: Tiziana Catarci and Katia Sycara; CoopIS 2004: Wil van der Aalst, Christoph Bussler, and Avigdor Gal) and our 15 workshop PC co-chairs (Angelo Corsaro, Corrado Santoro, Mustafa Jarrar, Aldo Gangemi, Klaus Turowski, Antonia Albani [2x], Alexios Palinginis, Peter Spyns [2x], Erik Duval, Pilar Herrero, Maria S. Perez, Monica Scannapieco, Paola Velardi, Herve Panetto, Martin Zelm) who, together with their many PC members, did a superb and professional job in selecting the best papers from the large harvest of submissions. We also thank our Publicity Chair (Laura Bright) and Publication Chair (Kwong Yuen Lai), and of course our overall Workshops Chair (Angelo Corsaro).

We do hope that the results of this federated scientific event contribute to your research and your place in the scientific network. We look forward to seeing you at next year's edition!

August 2004   Robert Meersman, Vrije Universiteit Brussel, Belgium
                     Zahir Tari, RMIT University, Australia

Organization Committee

The OTM (On The Move) 2004 Federated Conferences, which involved CoopIS (Cooperative Information Systems), DOA (Distributed Objects and Applications) and ODBASE (Ontologies, Databases and Applications of Semantics), were proudly supported by RMIT University (School of Computer Science and Information Technology) and Vrije Universiteit Brussel (Department of Computer Science).

Executive Committee

OTM 2004 General Co-chairs	Robert Meersman (Vrije Universiteit Brussel, Belgium) and Zahir Tari (RMIT University, Australia)
CoopIS 2004 PC Co-chairs	Wil van der Aalst (Eindhoven University of Technology, The Netherlands), Christoph Bussler (Digital Enterprise Research Institute, National University of Ireland, Ireland) and Avigdor Gal (Technion – Israel Institute of Technology, Israel)
DOA 2004 PC Co-chairs	Vinny Cahill (Trinity College Dublin, Ireland), Steve Vinoski (IONA Technologies, USA) and Werner Vogels (Cornell University, Ithaca, NY, USA)
ODBASE 2004 PC Co-chairs	Tiziana Catarci (Università di Roma "La Sapienza", Italy) and Katia Sycara (Carnegie Mellon University, USA)
Publication Chair	Kwong Yuen Lai (RMIT University, Australia)
Organizing Chair	Skevos Evripidou (University of Cyprus, Cyprus)
Publicity Chair	Laura Bright (Oregon Graduate Institute, Oregon, USA)

CoopIS 2004 Program Committee

Dave Abel
Lefteris Angelis
Naveen Ashish
Alistair Barros
Boualem Benatallah
Salima Benbernou
Klemens Boehm

Athman Bouguettaya
Barbara Carminati
Fabio Casati
Barbara Catania
Tiziana Catarci
Bin Cui
Umesh Dayal

Alex Delis
Jorg Desel
Drew Devereux
Susanna Donatelli
Marie-Christine Fauvet
Elena Ferrari
Timothy Finin
Stephane Gancarski
Mohand-Said Hacid
Manfred Hauswirth
Geert-Jan Houben
Michael Huhns
Latifur Khan
Roger (Buzz) King
Akhil Kumar
Steven Laufmann
Qing Li
Fabien De Marchi
Maristella Matera
Massimo Mecella
Claudia Medeiros
Michael zur Muehlen
Andreas Oberweis
Beng Chin Ooi

Barbara Pernici
Jean-Marc Petit
Manfred Reichert
Tore Risch
Kai-Uwe Sattler
Monica Scannapieco
Ralf Schenkel
Cyrus Shahabi
Antonio Si
Peter Spyns
Nicolas Spyratos
Farouk Toumani
Susan Urban
Athena Vakali
Mathias Weske
Kyu-Young Whang
Mike Wooldridge
Jian Yang
Kokou Yetongnon
Ming Yung
Arkady Zaslavsky
Gang Zhao
Leon Zhao
Roger Zimmermann

ODBASE 2004 Program Committee

Karl Aberer
Sonia Bergamaschi
Alex Borgida
Chris Bussler
Mike Champion
Isabel Cruz
Mike Dean
Stefan Decker
Jerome Euzenat
Skevos Evripidou
Tim Finin
Avigdor Gal
Carole Goble
Nicola Guarino
Mohamed-Said Hacid
Ian Horrocks

Arantza Illaramendi
Vipul Kashyap
Michael Kifer
Roger (Buzz) King
Wolfgang Klas
Harumi Kuno
Yannis Labrou
Maurizio Lenzerini
Murali Mani
Leo Mark
David Martin
Michele Missikoff
Pavlos Moraitis
Maria Orlowska
Massimo Paolucci
Bijan Parsia

Adam Pease
Shazia Sadiq
Stefano Spaccapietra
Naveen Srinivasan
Steffen Staab
Rudi Studer

Sergio Tessaris
Paola Velardi
Guido Vetere
Kevin Wilkinson
Stuart Williams
Guizhen Yang

DOA 2004 Program Committee

Gul Agha
Matthias Anlauff
Egidio Astesiano
Ozalp Babaoglu
Sean Baker
Roberto Baldoni
Guruduth Banavar
Judith Bishop
Gordon Blair
Michel Chaudron
Shing-Chi Cheung
Geoff Coulson
Francisco Paco Curbera
Wolfgang Emmerich
Patrick Eugster
Pascal Felber
Mohand-Said Hacid
Doug Lea
Hong Va Leong
Peter Loehr
Joe Loyall

Frank Manola
Karim Mazouni
Keith Moore
Peter Pietzuch
Rajendra Raj
Andry Rakotonirainy
Timothy Roscoe
Douglas Schmidt
Heinz-W. Schmidt
Richard Soley
Jean-Bernard Stefani
Clemens Szyperski
Stefan Tai
Guatam Thaker
Nalini Venkatasubramanian
Norbert Voelker
Yi-Min Wang
Guijun Wang
Andrew Watson
Doug Wells
Albert Zomaya

Table of Contents, Part I

Part I

Cooperative Information Systems (CoopIS) 2004 International Conference

PC Co-chairs' Message 1
    Editors: Wil van der Aalst, Christoph Bussler, Avigdor Gal

Keynote

Business Process Optimization 2
    Umeshwar Dayal

Workflow/Process/Web Services, I

Discovering Workflow Transactional Behavior
from Event-Based Log 3
    Walid Gaaloul, Sami Bhiri, Claude Godart

A Flexible Mediation Process
for Large Distributed Information Systems 19
    Philippe Lamarre, Sylvie Cazalens, Sandra Lemp,
    Patrick Valduriez

Exception Handling Through a Workflow 37
    Hernâni Mourão, Pedro Antunes

Workflow/Process/Web Services, II

A Flexible and Composite Schema Matching Algorithm 55
    Shoujian Yu, Zhongming Han, Jiajin Le

Analysis, Transformation, and Improvements
of ebXML Choreographies Based on Workflow Patterns 66
    Ja-Hee Kim, Christian Huemer

The Notion of Business Process Revisited 85
    Jan L.G. Dietz, Nathalie Habing

Workflow/Process/Web Services, III

Disjoint and Overlapping Process Changes:
Challenges, Solutions, Applications 101
    Stefanie Rinderle, Manfred Reichert, Peter Dadam

Untangling Unstructured Cyclic Flows –
A Solution Based on Continuations..................................... 121
    Jana Koehler, Rainer Hauser

Making Workflow Models Sound
Using Petri Net Controller Synthesis 139
    Juliane Dehnert, Armin Zimmermann

Database Management/Transaction

Concurrent Undo Operations in Collaborative Environments
Using Operational Transformation 155
    Jean Ferrié, Nicolas Vidot, Michelle Cart

Refresco: Improving Query Performance Through Freshness Control
in a Database Cluster 174
    Cécile Le Pape, Stéphane Gançarski, Patrick Valduriez

Automated Supervision of Data Production –
Managing the Creation of Statistical Reports on Periodic Data 194
    Anja Schanzenberger, Dave R. Lawrence

Schema Integration/Agents

Deriving Sub-schema Similarities
from Semantically Heterogeneous XML Sources 209
    Pasquale De Meo, Giovanni Quattrone, Giorgio Terracina,
    Domenico Ursino

Supporting Similarity Operations
Based on Approximate String Matching on the Web 227
    Eike Schallehn, Ingolf Geist, Kai-Uwe Sattler

Managing Semantic Compensation in a Multi-agent System 245
    Amy Unruh, James Bailey, Kotagiri Ramamohanarao

Modelling with Ubiquitous Agents a Web-Based Information System
Accessed Through Mobile Devices...................................... 264
    Angela Carrillo-Ramos, Jérôme Gensel, Marlène Villanova-Oliver,
    Hervé Martin

Events

A Meta-service for Event Notification 283
  Doris Jung, Annika Hinze

Classification and Analysis of Distributed Event Filtering Algorithms 301
  Sven Bittner, Annika Hinze

P2P/Collaboration

A Collaborative Model for Agricultural Supply Chains 319
  Evandro Bacarin, Claudia B. Medeiros, Edmundo Madeira

FairNet – How to Counter Free Riding
in Peer-to-Peer Data Structures 337
  Erik Buchmann, Klemens Böhm

Supporting Collaborative Layouting in Word Processing 355
  Thomas B. Hodel, Dominik Businger, Klaus R. Dittrich

A Reliable Content-Based Routing Protocol
over Structured Peer-to-Peer Networks 373
  Jinling Wang, Beihong Jin, Jun Wei, Jing Li

Applications, I

Covering Your Back: Intelligent Virtual Agents
in Humanitarian Missions Providing Mutual Support 391
  Pilar Herrero

Dynamic Modelling of Demand Driven Value Networks 408
  Antonia Albani, Christian Winnewisser, Klaus Turowski

An E-marketplace for Auctions and Negotiations
in the Constructions Sector 422
  *Marina Bitsaki, Manos Dramitinos, George D. Stamoulis,
  George Antoniadis*

Applications, II

Managing Changes to Engineering Products
Through the Co-ordination of Human and Technical Activities 442
  Wendy K. Ivins, W. Alex Gray, John C. Miles

Towards Automatic Deployment in eHome Systems:
Description Language and Tool Support 460
  Michael Kirchhof, Ulrich Norbisrath, Christof Skrzypczyk

A Prototype of a Context-Based Architecture
for Intelligent Home Environments 477
    Pablo A. Haya, Germán Montoro, Xavier Alamán

Trust/Security/Contracts

Trust-Aware Collaborative Filtering for Recommender Systems 492
    Paolo Massa, Paolo Avesani

Service Graphs for Building Trust 509
    Pınar Yolum, Munindar P. Singh

Detecting Violators of Multi-party Contracts 526
    Lai Xu, Manfred A. Jeusfeld

Potpourri

Leadership Maintenance in Group-Based
Location Management Scheme 544
    Gary Hoi Kit Lam, Hong Va Leong, Stephen Chi Fai Chan

TLS: A Tree-Based DHT Lookup Service
for Highly Dynamic Networks 563
    Francesco Buccafurri, Gianluca Lax

Minimizing the Network Distance in Distributed Web Crawling 581
    Odysseas Papapetrou, George Samaras

Ontologies, Databases, and Applications of Semantics (ODBASE) 2004 International Conference

PC Co-chairs' Message 597
    Editors: Tiziana Catarci, Katia Sycara

Keynote

Helping People (and Machines) Understanding Each Other:
The Role of Formal Ontology 599
    Nicola Guarino

Knowledge Extraction

Automatic Initiation of an Ontology 600
    Marie-Laure Reinberger, Peter Spyns, A. Johannes Pretorius,
    Walter Daelemans

Knowledge Extraction from Classification Schemas 618
    Steffen Lamparter, Marc Ehrig, Christoph Tempich

Semantic Web in Practice

Generation and Management of a Medical Ontology
in a Semantic Web Retrieval System................................. 637
   Elena Paslaru Bontas, Sebastian Tietz, Robert Tolksdorf,
   Thomas Schrader

Semantic Web Based Content Enrichment and Knowledge Reuse
in E-science 654
   Feng Tao, Liming Chen, Nigel Shadbolt, Fenglian Xu, Simon Cox,
   Colin Puleston, Carole Goble

The Role of Foundational Ontologies
in Manufacturing Domain Applications 670
   Stefano Borgo, Paulo Leitão

Intellectual Property Rights Management
Using a Semantic Web Information System........................... 689
   Roberto García, Rosa Gil, Jaime Delgado

Ontologies and IR

Intelligent Retrieval of Digital Resources by Exploiting
Their Semantic Context 705
   Gábor M. Surányi, Gábor Nagypál, Andreas Schmidt

The Chrysostom Knowledge Base:
An Ontology of Historical Interactions 724
   Dan Corbett, Wendy Mayer

Text Simplification for Information-Seeking Applications 735
   Beata Beigman Klebanov, Kevin Knight, Daniel Marcu

Information Integration

Integration of Integrity Constraints in Federated Schemata
Based on Tight Constraining 748
   Herman Balsters, Engbert O. de Brock

Modal Query Language for Databases with Partial Orders 768
   Zoran Majkić

Composing Mappings Between Schemas Using a Reference Ontology..... 783
   Eduard Dragut, Ramon Lawrence

Assisting Ontology Integration with Existing Thesauri 801
   Jan De Bo, Peter Spyns, Robert Meersman

Author Index 819

Table of Contents, Part II

Part II

Ontologies, Databases, and Applications of Semantics (ODBASE) 2004 International Conference (continued)

Advanced Information Systems

Security Management Through Overloading Views 823
  Radosław Adamus, Kazimierz Subieta

Paradigms for Decentralized Social Filtering Exploiting Trust
Network Structure 840
  Cai-Nicolas Ziegler

A Necessary Condition for Semantic Interoperability in the Large 859
  Philippe Cudré-Mauroux, Karl Aberer

Information Mining

Mining the Meaningful Compound Terms
from Materialized Faceted Taxonomies............................. 873
  Yannis Tzitzikas, Anastasia Analyti

Heuristic Strategies for Inclusion Dependency Discovery 891
  Andreas Koeller, Elke A. Rundensteiner

Taming the Unstructured: Creating Structured Content
from Partially Labeled Schematic Text Sequences 909
  Saikat Mukherjee, I.V. Ramakrishnan

Querying

A Global-to-Local Rewriting Querying Mechanism
Using Semantic Mapping for XML Schema Integration................. 927
  Kalpdrum Passi, Eric Chaudhry, Sanjay Madria, Sourav Bhowmick

Querying Articulated Sources...................................... 945
  Carlo Meghini, Yannis Tzitzikas

Learning Classifiers from Semantically Heterogeneous Data............. 963
  Doina Caragea, Jyotishman Pathak, Vasant G. Honavar

Ontology Processing

A General Method for Pruning OWL Ontologies 981
  Jordi Conesa, Antoni Olivé

Finding Compromises Between Local and Global Ontology Querying
in Multiagent Systems 999
  Hector Ceballos, Ramon Brena

Aligning Ontologies and Evaluating Concept Similarities 1012
  Kleber Xavier Sampaio de Souza, Joseph Davis

Multimedia

EMMA – A Query Algebra for Enhanced Multimedia Meta Objects 1030
  Sonja Zillner, Utz Westermann, Werner Winiwarter

Ontology for Nature-Scene Image Retrieval 1050
  Song Liu, Liang-Tien Chia, Syin Chan

Semantic Web Services

Comparing Approaches for Semantic Service Description
and Matchmaking 1062
  *Sven Schade, Arnd Sahlmann, Michael Lutz, Florian Probst,
  Werner Kuhn*

On Managing Changes in the Ontology-Based E-government 1080
  *Ljiljana Stojanovic, Andreas Abecker, Nenad Stojanovic,
  Rudi Studer*

XML Processing

CLP(Flex): Constraint Logic Programming Applied
to XML Processing 1098
  Jorge Coelho, Mário Florido

VSM: Mapping XML Document to Relations with Constraint 1113
  Zhongming Han, Shoujian Yu, Jiajin Le

Distributed Objects and Applications (DOA) 2004 International Conference

PC Co-chairs' Message 1123
  Vinny Cahill, Steve Vinoski, Werner Vogels

Keynote

Cooperative Artefacts 1124
  Hans Gellersen

Performance

Performance Evaluation of JXTA Rendezvous 1125
  Emir Halepovic, Ralph Deters, Bernard Traversat

CORBA Components Collocation Optimization Enhanced
with Local ORB-Like Services Support 1143
  *Mohsen Sharifi, Adel Torkaman Rahmani, Vahid Rafe,
  Hossein Momeni*

Late Demarshalling: A Technique
for Efficient Multi-language Middleware for Embedded Systems 1155
  Gunar Schirner, Trevor Harmon, Raymond Klefstad

Quality of Service

Implementing QoS Aware Component-Based Applications 1173
  Avraam Chimaris, George A. Papadopoulos

A Framework for QoS-Aware Model Transformation,
Using a Pattern-Based Approach..................................... 1190
  Arnor Solberg, Jon Oldevik, Jan Øyvind Aagedal

Component-Based Dynamic QoS Adaptations in Distributed Real-Time
and Embedded Systems 1208
  *Praveen K. Sharma, Joseph P. Loyall, George T. Heineman,
  Richard E. Schantz, Richard Shapiro, Gary Duzan*

Adaptation

Dynamic Adaptation of Data Distribution Policies
in a Shared Data Space System 1225
  Giovanni Russello, Michel Chaudron, Maarten van Steen

TRAP/J: Transparent Generation of Adaptable Java Programs 1243
  *S. Masoud Sadjadi, Philip K. McKinley, Betty H.C. Cheng,
  R.E. Kurt Stirewalt*

Application Adaptation Through Transparent
and Portable Object Mobility in Java............................... 1262
  Caspar Ryan, Christopher Westhorpe

An Infrastructure for Development
of Dynamically Adaptable Distributed Components 1285
  Renato Maia, Renato Cerqueira, Noemi Rodriguez

Mobility

SATIN: A Component Model for Mobile Self Organisation 1303
  Stefanos Zachariadis, Cecilia Mascolo, Wolfgang Emmerich

Caching Components for Disconnection Management
in Mobile Environments 1322
    Nabil Kouici, Denis Conan, Guy Bernard

SPREE: Object Prefetching for Mobile Computers 1340
    Kristian Kvilekval, Ambuj Singh

Class Splitting as a Method to Reduce Migration Overhead
of Mobile Agents... 1358
    Steffen Kern, Peter Braun, Christian Fensch, Wilhelm Rossak

Replication

Eager Replication for Stateful J2EE Servers 1376
    Huaigu Wu, Bettina Kemme, Vance Maverick

Active Replication in CORBA: Standards, Protocols,
and Implementation Framework 1395
    Alysson Neves Bessani, Joni da Silva Fraga, Lau Cheuk Lung,
    Eduardo Adílio Pelinson Alchieri

A Framework for Prototyping J2EE Replication Algorithms 1413
    Özalp Babaoğlu, Alberto Bartoli, Vance Maverick,
    Simon Patarin, Jakša Vučković, Huaigu Wu

Scalability

A Distributed and Parallel Component Architecture
for Stream-Oriented Applications 1427
    P. Barthelmess, C.A. Ellis

An Architecture for Dynamic Scalable Self-Managed
Persistent Objects 1445
    Emmanuelle Anceaume, Roy Friedman, Maria Gradinariu,
    Matthieu Roy

GRIDKIT: Pluggable Overlay Networks for Grid Computing 1463
    Paul Grace, Geoff Coulson, Gordon Blair, Laurent Mathy,
    Wai Kit Yeung, Wei Cai, David Duce, Chris Cooper

Components

Enabling Rapid Feature Deployment on Embedded Platforms
with JeCOM Bridge 1482
    Jun Li, Keith Moore

Checking Asynchronously Communicating Components
Using Symbolic Transition Systems................................... 1502
    Olivier Maréchal, Pascal Poizat, Jean-Claude Royer

Configuring Real-Time Aspects in Component Middleware 1520
   Nanbor Wang, Chris Gill, Douglas C. Schmidt, Venkita Subramonian

Events and Groups

Programming Abstractions for Content-Based Publish/Subscribe
in Object-Oriented Languages 1538
   Andreas Ulbrich, Gero Mühl, Torben Weis, Kurt Geihs

A Practical Comparison Between the TAO Real-Time Event Service
and the Maestro/Ensemble Group Communication System 1558
   *Carlo Marchetti, Paolo Papa, Stefano Cimmino, Leonardo Querzoni,
   Roberto Baldoni, Emanuela Barbi*

Evaluation of a Group Communication Middleware
for Clustered J2EE Application Servers 1571
   Takoua Abdellatif, Emmanuel Cecchet, Renaud Lachaize

Ubiquity and Web

A Mobile Agent Infrastructure for QoS Negotiation
of Adaptive Distributed Applications 1590
   Roberto Speicys Cardoso, Fabio Kon

Model-Driven Dependability Analysis of WebServices 1608
   Apostolos Zarras, Panos Vassiliadis, Valérie Issarny

Dynamic Access Control for Ubiquitous Environments 1626
   Jehan Wickramasuriya, Nalini Venkatasubramanian

Author Index 1645

Cooperative Information Systems (CoopIS) 2004 International Conference PC Co-chairs' Message

We would like to welcome you to the Proceedings of the 12th International Conference on Cooperative Information Systems (CoopIS 2004). As in previous years, CoopIS was part of the federated conference On the Move (OTM) to Meaningful Internet Systems and Ubiquitous Computing, which this year took place in Agia Napa, Cyprus, together with the International Symposium on Distributed Objects and Applications (DOA) and the International Conference on Ontologies, Databases and Applications of Semantics for Large-Scale Information Systems (ODBASE).

In total, we received 142 submissions, out of which the program committee selected 34 as full papers for presentation and publication. In addition, 15 submissions were accepted as posters to be included in the proceedings.

The areas of interest continue to cover a wide variety of topics. Core topics like databases and workflow management are well represented as well as areas like security, peer-to-peer computing and schema integration. In addition, a significant number of papers cover applications indicating the continued interest of our community in the use of the research results.

We would like to thank all authors who submitted and presented papers at the conference for their hard work. Also, we would like to thank all conference attendees for their engagement at the conference as they together with the authors represent the CoopIS community. The PC members were terrific as they provided almost all reviews on time, excellent reviews that allowed the selection of the best submissions. The conference organizers provided professional management and a flawlessly working electronic conference submission management system. Thanks to all who were involved in the management for their support. We would like to thank in particular Zahir Tari and Kwong Yuen Lai for their professional help and guidance.

August 2004

Wil van der Aalst,
Eindhoven University of Technology, The Netherlands
Christoph Bussler,
Digital Enterprise Research Institute, National University of Ireland, Ireland
Avigdor Gal, Technion – Israel Institute of Technology, Israel
(CoopIS 2004 Program Committee Co-chairs)

Business Process Optimization

Umeshwar Dayal

Hewlett-Packard Labs, Palo Alto, California, USA

Abstract. Recently, we have seen increasing adoption of business process automation technologies (and emerging standards for business process orchestration) by enterprises, as a means of improving the efficiency and quality of their internal operations, as well as their interactions with other enterprises and customers as they engage in e-business transactions. The next phase of evolution is the rise of the intelligent enterprise, which is characterized by being able to adapt its business processes quickly to changes in its operating environment. The intelligent enterprise monitors its business processes and the surrounding environment, mines the data it collects about the processes to understand how it is meeting its business objectives, and it acts to control and optimize its operations to meet those business objectives. Decisions are made quickly and accurately to modify business processes on the fly, dynamically allocate resources, prioritize work, or select the best service providers. This talk will describe challenges in managing and optimizing the business processes of an intelligent enterprise. We will describe technology approaches that we are pursuing at HP Labs., the progress we have made, and some open research questions.

Brief Speaker Bio

Umeshwar Dayal is Director of the Intelligent Enterprise Technologies Laboratory at Hewlett-Packard Laboratories, Palo Alto, California. Umesh has over 25 years of research experience in data management. His current research interests are in data mining, business process management, and decision support technologies, especially as applied to e-business. Prior to joining HP Labs., he was a senior researcher at DEC's Cambridge Research Lab., Chief Scientist at Xerox Advanced Information Technology and Computer Corporation of America, and on the faculty at the University of Texas-Austin. he has published extensively and holds several patents in the areas of database systems, transaction management, workflow systems, and data mining. He is on the Editorial Board of four international journals, has co-edited two books, and has chaired and served on the Program Committees of numerous conferences. He is a member of the Board of the VLDB Endowment, a founding member of the Board of the International Foundation for Cooperative Information Systems, and a member of the Steering Committee of the SIAM Data Mining Conference. In 2001, Umesh and two co-authors received the VLDB 10-year Best Paper Award. You can reach him at umeshwar.dayal@hp.com.

Discovering Workflow Transactional Behavior from Event-Based Log

Walid Gaaloul, Sami Bhiri, and Claude Godart

LORIA - INRIA - CNRS - UMR 7503
BP 239, F-54506 Vandœuvre-lès-Nancy Cedex, France
{gaaloul,bhiri,godart}@loria.fr

Abstract. Previous workflow mining works have concentrated their efforts on process behavioral aspects. Although powerful, these proposals are found lacking in functionalities and performance when used to discover transactional workflow that cannot be seen at the level of behavioral aspects of workflow. Their limitations mainly come from their incapacity to discover the transactional dependencies between process activities, or activities transactional properties. In this paper, we describe mining techniques, which are able to discover a workflow model, and to improve its transactional behavior from event logs. We propose an algorithm to discover workflow patterns and workflow termination states (WTS). Then based on the discovered control flow and set of termination states, we use a set of rules to mine the workflow transactional behavior.

Keywords: Business intelligence, Workflow mining, transactional Workflows, Enterprize knowledge discovery, knowledge modelling.

1 Introduction

Current workflow management systems (WFMS) which are driven by explicit process models offer little aid for the acquisition of workflow models and their adaptation to changing requirements [1]. It is difficult for process engineers to validate a formal process model using by only a visual representation of the process. They often agree to a visual representation, but when they are confronted with the WFMS implementing the process, it often turns out that the system has a different interpretation of the process model than they had expected and the process model as it was modelled is rejected. The modelling errors are commonly not detected until the workflow model is performed. That is why **the workflow mining** approach proposes techniques to acquire workflow models from observations of enacted workflows instances (i.e. *workflow log*). All workflow activities are traced, and logs are passed to workflow mining component which (re)discover the workflow model.

Previous works on **workflow mining**[2,3,4,5] have restricted themselves to structural considerations with limited checks of transactional behavior. Especially, they have neglected transactional workflow properties [6], such as transactional dependencies between workflow activities, or activity transactional properties. We are convinced that the capability of **workflow mining** to discover workflows transactional features provides a significant improvement to WFMS understanding and design.

In this paper, we describe mining techniques which are able to discover a workflow model, and mine its transactional behavior from its event logs. We propose an algorithm to discover workflow patterns and workflow set of termination states (WTS). Then we extract from it the process transactional behavior using a set of rules.

The remainder of this paper is organized as follows. Section 2 presents a motivating example which shows the interest of mining workflow transactional behavior. Then in section 3 we introduce distinctive concepts and some needed prerequisites. Section 4 overviews our approach which we detail in the next four sections. Section 9 concludes and presents some future works.

2 Motivating Example

In this section we present a motivating example showing the need for discovering transactional behavior to detect design gaps and thereafter improve the workflow supporting the application. Let us suppose an application for on line purchase of personal computers (PC). This application is carried out by the workflow illustrated in the figure 1. Activities in the *online PC purchase* are described below.

Customer Requirements Specification (CRS): The first activity in the workflow is to receive a customer order. This activity allows to acquire the customer requirements and then creates a new instance of the workflow.

Customer Identity Check (CIC): The application checks the identity of the customer.

Payment (P): This activity ensures the payment process by credit card, cheques, ...

Command Items (CI): If the on line merchant have not all the computer components, he commands them.

Computer Assembly (CA): After receiving the required items, this activity ensures the computer assembly.

Send Item (SI): After payment and assembly, the computer is sent to the customer.

The application enhances its classical control flow by specifying an additional workflow transactional behavior to ensure failures handling. It specifies that (i) CRS, P, CI and CA are sure to complete, (ii) the work of CRS, CA and P can be semantically undone and (iii) the work of P and CA (respectively of CRS) will be semantically undone when SI (respectively CIC) fails.

Let suppose now that in reality (by observation of sufficient execution cases) SI never fails and P is not sure to complete. This means there is no need for P to be compensatable and CA have to be compensated when P fails.

Classical workflow mining is not able to detect such an anomaly and thereafter to improve the workflow model. To overcome this limitation, it is necessary to extend workflow mining in such a way to be able to discover workflow transactional behavior as a feed back loop to improve the transactional behavior of the workflow model.

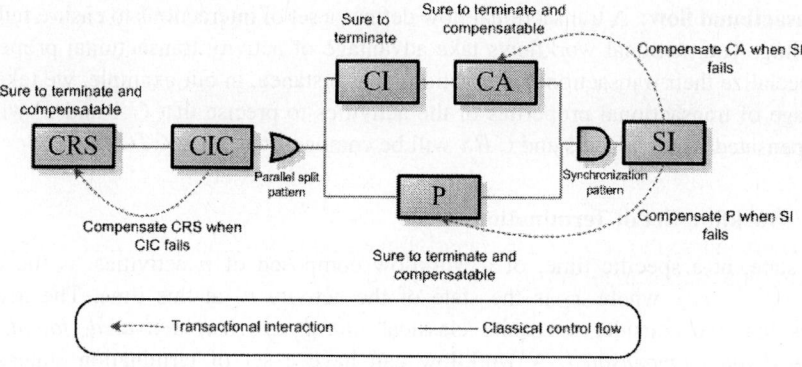

Fig. 1. An example of workflow involving transactional behavior.

3 Transactional Workflow

A transactional workflow, is a workflow that emphasizes transactional behavior for failures handling and recovery. Within transactional workflows, we distinguish between *the control flow* and *the transactional behavior*.

3.1 Control Flow

A Workflow process definition is composed of workflow activities. Activities are related together to form a control flow via transitions which can be guarded by a control flow operator. The control flow dimension is concerned with the partial ordering of activities. The activities that need to be executed are identified and the routing of cases along these activities is determined. Conditional, sequential, parallel and iterative routing are typical structures specified in the control flow dimension. We use workflow patterns [7] to express and implement the control flow dimension requirements and functionalities.

3.2 Transactional Behavior

Workflow transactional behavior specifies mechanisms for failures handling. It defines *activity transactional properties* and *transactional flow (interactions)*.

Activities transactional properties: Within transactional workflow, activities emphasizes transactional properties for its characterization and correct usage. The main transactional properties that we are considering are *retriable, compensatable* and *pivot*[8]. An activity a is said to be retriable (a^r) *iff* it is sure to complete. a is said to be compensatable (a^{cp}) *iff* its work can be semantically undone. Then, a is said to be pivot (a^p) *iff* its effect can not be compensated. Back to our example, we note that all activities except CIC and SI are specified as retriable, and activities CRS, P and CA are specified as compensatable.

Transactional flow: A transactional flow defines a set of interactions to ensure failures handling. Transactional workflows take advantage of activity transactional properties to specialize their transactional interactions. For instance, in our example, we take advantage of transactional properties of the activities to precise that CA and P will be compensated when SI fails and CRS will be compensated when CIC fails.

3.3 Workflow Set of Termination States

The state, at a specific time, of a workflow composed of n activities, is the tuple $(x_1, x_2, ..., x_n)$, where x_i is the state of the activity a_i at this time. The activity states that we consider are quite classical *initial, aborted, activated, failed, terminated and compensated*. A workflow can have a set of termination states. For instance the set of termination states of the workflow given in the section 2 is
{ *(CRS.terminated, CIC.terminated, P.terminated,CI.terminated, CA.terminated, SI.terminated); (CRS.compensated,CIC.failed, P.aborted,CI.aborted,CA.aborted, SI.aborted); (CRS.terminated,CIC.terminated, P.compensated, CI.terminated, A.compensated,SI.failed)*}.

4 Overview of Our Approach

Mining transactional workflow returns to discover control flow and transactional behavior. As illustrated in the figure 2, we mainly proceed in two steps. The first one consists in the mining of the control flow (section 6) and the set of termination states (section 7) from the workflow log. Then, based on the discovered control flow and set of termination states, we use a set of rules to mine the workflow transactional behavior (section 8). We illustrate the applicability of each one of these mining points through the previous example given in section 2. We show there how thanks to this mining we can improve the transactional workflow carrying out this application.

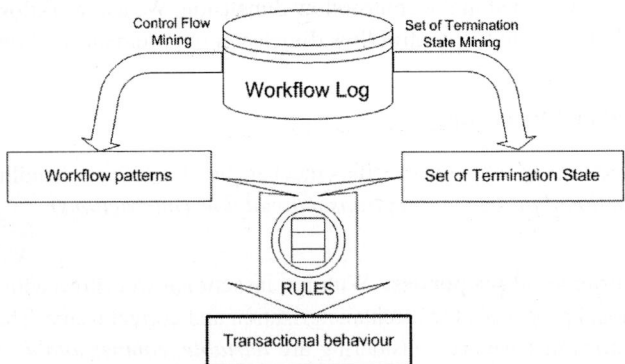

Fig. 2. Overview of our approach

5 Workflow Event Log

Workflows are defined as *case-based*, i.e., every piece of work is executed for a specific *case*. Many cases can be handled by following the same workflow process definition. Routing elements are used to describe sequential, conditional, parallel, and iterative routing thus specifying the appropriate route of a case [9,10]. To be completed, workflow log should cover all the possible cases (i.e. if a specific routing element can appear in the mined workflow model, the log should contain an example of this behavior in at least one case). Thus, the completeness of mined workflow model depends on how much the log covers all possible dependencies between its activities.

A workflow log is considered as a set of events streams. Each events stream represents a workflow execution. Each event is described by activity identifier, execution time and activity state (see Definition 1).

Definition 1 (Event log). *An event log is related to an activity.*

*Thus, an event is seen as a triplet **event**(activityId, occurTime, activityState), where:*

- *(activityId : int) is the ID of the activity concerned with the event,*
- *(occurTime : int) is the execution time,*
- *(activityState : symbol) is the activity state (initial, aborted, active, failed, terminated and compensated).*

A workflow log may contain information about thousands of events streams. Since there are no causal dependencies between events corresponding to different events streams, we can project the workflow log onto a separate events streams without loosing any information (see Definition 2).

Definition 2 (Workflow Event log). *A workflow log is considered as a set of events streams. Each events stream represents the execution of one case.*

*More formally, an events stream is defined as a quadruplet **stream**: (sequenceLog, workflowOccurence, beginTime, endTime) where:*

- *(sequenceLog: {event}): is an **ordered** Event log belonging to an execution of a workflow case,*
- *(wOccurence : int) is the workflow execution instance number,*
- *(beginTime: time) is the moment of log beginning,*
- *(endTime: time) is the moment of log end.*

*So, **workflowLog**: $\{wStream_i : \textbf{stream}; 0 \leq i \leq \text{number of workflow instantiations}\}$ is a Workflow Event log where: $\forall \ wStream_i \in \textbf{workflowLog}; \ wStream_i.wOccurence$ references the same workflow.*

We define $\mathcal{WL} = \{\textbf{workflowLog}\}$ as the set of all workflows logs.

An example of an events stream **stream** extracted from our workflow model example is given below:

L = **stream**(5, 16, [**event**(CRS,5,initial), **event**(CIC,5,initial), **event**(P,5,initial), **event**(CI,5,initial), **event**(CA,5,initial), **event**(SI,5,initial), **event**(CRS,8,terminated), **event**(CIC,10,terminated), **event**(CI,13,terminated), **event**(P,15,terminated), **event**(CA,16,failed), **event**(CA,18,terminated), **event**(SI,20,terminated)])

We are interesting in extracting workflow patterns that describe control flow within processes workflow. Statistical calculus used to discover these patterns (see section 6) extract control flow dependencies between workflow activities that are executed without "exceptions" (*i.e.* they reached successfully their **terminated** state). Because initial workflow log contains data relating to the whole life cycle of workflow activity (*i.e.* including all activity states), wee need to filter workflow log and take only the events that its state is exclusively **terminated** (see Definition 3). Note that this is the minimal information we assume to be present at this point. Any information system using transactional systems such as ERP, CRM, or workflow management systems offer this information in some form [5].

Definition 3 (**Log projection**). *Builds a Workflow Log state projection.*
$WorkflowLog_{state} : \mathcal{WL} \to \mathcal{WL}$
$wl = \{(sL, wO, beginTime, endTime)\} \to wl' = \{(sL', wO, beginTime, endTime\}$ where $sL' \subset sL$ and $\forall\ e{:}\{event\} \in sL'\ e.activityState = terminated$.

6 Control Flow Mining

In this present work, we are exclusively interested in discovering "elementary" workflow patterns: Sequence, Parallel split, Synchronization, Exclusive choice, Multiple choices, Simple merge and M-out-of-N Join pattern[7].

Discovering workflows patterns from event-based log basically involves determining the logical dependencies among its activities. *Activities dependence* is defined as an occurrence of one activity directly depending on another activity. We define three types of *Activities dependence*:

1. *Sequential dependence* captures the sequencing of activities (Sequence pattern) where one activity follows directly one other.
2. *Conditional dependence* captures selection, or a choice of one activity from a set of activities potentially following (*e.g.* exclusive choice pattern) or preceding (e.g. Simple Merge pattern) a given activity.
3. *Concurrent dependence* captures concurrency in terms of "fork" (e.g. Parallel Split pattern) and "join" (e.g. synchronization pattern).

The main challenge which we cope with is the discovery of the sequential or concurrent nature of joins and splits of these patterns. To reach our goal, we proceed with three steps: Step (i) the construction of statistical dependency table, Step (ii) the discovery of frequent episodes in log, and Step (iii) the mining of workflow patterns through a set of rules.

6.1 Construction of the the Statistical Dependency Table

Some numerical representations of event-log are needed for supporting analysis to be performed for discovering workflow patterns. The statistical dependency table based on a notion of frequency table [11] expresses activities dependencies. The size of this table is N*N, where N is the number of activities in mined workflow. The (m,n) table entry (notation P(*m/n*)) is the frequency of the *n* activity **preceding** the *m* activity. For example, let A and B two activities in mined workflow; P(B/A)=0.45 expresses that if B occurs, 45% of the time A is a previous activity. Note that the construction of statistical dependency table is done from terminated log event projection (this projection restrict log to executions without "exceptions").

If we assume that events stream is exactly correct (i.e., contains no noise) and derives from a sequential workflow, as well as the zero entries in statistical dependency table are interpreted as signifying independence, the non-zero frequencies frequency table directly represent probabilistic dependence relations, and so a causal dependency. But, due to the *concurrent dependence* as we can see in workflow patterns like Synchronization pattern, Parallel split pattern and Multiple choice pattern, the events streams represent interleaved events sequences from all of concurrent threads. As consequence, an activity might not, for some concurrency reasons, depend on the immediate predecessor, but on another "indirectly" preceding activity.

Thus, some entries in statistical dependency table indicates spurious or false dependencies. To unmask and correct this erroneous frequencies we calculate the frequency using a *concurrent window*, i.e. we will not only consider the events occurred immediately backwards but also the events covered by the *concurrent window*. Formally, a concurrent window defines a log slide over an events stream (see Definition 4).

Definition 4 (log window). *A log window defines a set of Event logs over an events stream S:**stream**(sLog, wOccurence, bStream, eStream).*

*Formally, we define a log window as a triplet **window**(wLog, bWin, eWin), where :*

- *(bWin : time) is the moment of the window beginning (with bStream $\leq$ bWin)*
- *(eWin : time) is the moment of the window end (with eWin $\leq$ eStream)*
- *wLog $\subset$ sLog and $\forall$ e: **event** where bWin $\leq$ e.occurTime $\leq$ bWin $\Rightarrow$ e: **event** $\in$ wLog.*

The time span eWin-bWin is called the width *of the window, and it is denoted* width(*window*).

The width of the *concurrent window* is the maximal duration that a concurrent execution can take. It depends on the studied workflow and is estimated by the user. Based on that, we construct an events stream partition (see Definition 5). This partition is formed by a set of overlapping windows. Each window is built by adding the next event log not included in the previous window. After that, we suppress events log which are not in concurrent window. Thus, the width of these windows can not be taller than the fixed concurrent duration.

Definition 5 (K-partition). *K-partition builds a set of partially overlapping windows partition over an events stream.*

*K-partition : **workflowLog** $\rightarrow$ ({ **window** })**
*S : **stream**(sLog, wOccurence, bStream, eStream) $\rightarrow$ $\{w_i :$ **window**; $1 \leq i \leq n\}$*
where:

- $w_1.bWin = bStream$ and $w_n.eWin=eStream$,
- $\forall w :$ **window** $\in$ **K-partition**, width(w)=k,

- $\forall i;\ 0 \leq i < n;\ w_{i+1}.wLog\{\text{the last } e\text{:}event\text{ in }w_{i+1}.wLog\} \subset w_i.wLog$ and $w_{i+1}.wLog \neq w_i.wLog$.

Based on this definition, we are now able to describe our mining algorithm. Algorithm 1 computes the activity frequency and algorithm 2 activity dependencies.

As starting point, we need to calculate, for each activity A in a mined workflow, its Statistic frequency (noted #A) from $WorkflowLog_{terminated}$. It is used then to calculate dependency frequency and to discover workflow patterns (see section 6.3). Algorithm 1 shows how it is computed from **workflowLog**. Each **stream** in **workflowLog** are read **event** by **event** and corresponding frequency activity are updated. Note that indentation is used in the algorithms below to specify the extent of loops and conditional statements.

Algorithm 1 : Statistic activity frequency algorithm

Input: Wlog : $WorkflowLog_{terminated}$(**workflowLog**), K :width(concurrent window)

  output: AFT : #[]

```
var
    t_id: int;
begin
    for all S:stream in Wlog
        for all e:event in S.sequenceLog
            t_id= e.activityId;
            AFT[t_id]++;
        endFor
    endFor
end
```

Algorithm 2 computes Statistic activity dependency. It scans the set **K-partition windows** over **workflowlog**, **window** by **window**, and for each **window** it computes for the last activity the frequencies of its preceded activities and the corresponding table is updated in consequence. The first **window** need a particular treatment. The statistic activity dependency will be found by dividing each row entry in the previous table by the frequency of activity computed in Algorithm 1.

Algorithm 2 : Statistic activity dependency algorithm

  Input: Wlog : $WorkflowLog_{terminated}$(**workflowLog**)
  output: SFD : Statistic activity Dependency Table

```
var
    t_reference: int;
    t_preceded : int;
    fWin : window;
    depFreq :int[][];
    freq :int
begin
    for all win:window in K-partition(Wlog)
```

```
            t_reference = last_activity(win)   /* the function
            last_activity(win) returns the activityId of the
            last event in win.wLog */
            win = preceded_Events(win); /* the function
            preceded_Events(win) returns win without
            the last event*/
            for all e:event in (win.wLog)
                t_preceded= e.activityId;
                depFreq[t_reference][t_preceded]++;
            endFor
        endFor
    /* particular case: first window*/
    fWin = firstwindow(K-partition(Wlog))  /* return the
    first window*/
    fwin=preceded_Events(fwin)
    While (fwin.wLog <> null)
        t_reference = last_activity(fwin)
        for all e:event in (fwin.wLog-{last_activity(fWin)})
            t_preceded= e.activityId;
            depFreq[t_reference][t_preceded]++;
        endFor
        fwin=preceded_Events(fwin)
    endWhile
    /*Final step: construction of statistical dependency
    table */
  for all freq=depFreq[t_reference][t_preceded] in depFreq
      P(t_reference/t_preceded]=freq/#t_reference;
  endFor
end
```

6.2 Discovering Episodes in Logs

The statistical dependency table is not sufficient. Some entries can indicate non-zero entries that do not correspond to dependencies. For example the events stream given in section 5 suggests a sequential dependency between CI and P activities which is incorrect. To deal with this issue, we will use episodes to eliminate this noise and to identify correctly workflow patterns.

Through the discovery of specific episodes in events stream, we can eliminate the confusion caused by the concurrency which produces spurious non-zero entries in the statistical dependency table. For this reason we are interested in finding recurrent combinations of events, which we call *frequent episodes*. Our definition of *frequent episode* is a variation of the one from [12]. Formally, an *episode* is a partially ordered collection of events occurring together. In our workflow mining technique we need to discover and identify K-Parallel and K-serial *episodes* in $WorkflowLog_{terminated}$ events streams projection. The calculus of K-Parallel and K-serial depends on *the width* of the *concurrent window* (see Definition 6 and 7). We have adapted an algorithm proposed in [12] to find such class of episodes.

Definition 6 (K-Parallel episodes). $\Pi(t_1, t_2)$ *denotes the K-Parallel relation on activities t_1 and t_2 and can be seen as a relation over workflow activities belonging to the same window.*

$\Pi(t_1, t_2)$ **iff** t_1 *and t_2 have (i) no time ordering constraints on their respective* **terminated** *events log and (ii) if t_1 and t_2 have events log in an event stream then these events log belongs to the same window W and K= width(W). Note that, there can be other events occurring between t_1 and t_2.*

Definition 7 (K-serial episodes). $\Gamma(t_1, t_2)$ *denotes the K-serial relation on activities t_1 and t_2 and can be seen as a relation over Workflow activity belonging to the same window.*

$\Gamma(t_1, t_2)$ **iff** *(i) the respective* **terminated** *events log of t_1 and t_2 in workflow log occur in this order and (ii) if they have events log in an event stream then these events log belong to the same window W and K= width(W). Note there can be other events occurring between t_1 and t_2.*

The K-Parallel and K-serial relations are easy to interpret and they can be discovered efficiently from log events stream [12]. Moreover, any complex partially ordered episode could be seen as a recursive combination of parallel and serial episodes.

6.3 Mining of Workflow Patterns

After the compute of the statistical dependency table and the discovery of episodes, the last step will be the identification of workflow patterns through a set a rules. In fact, each pattern will be identified by a particular episodes set and statistical tests. Each pattern has its own features, which represents its unique identifier. Our algorithm allows, if the execution log is completed, the discovery of the whole workflow patterns included in the mined workflow.

We divided the workflows patterns in three categories : sequence, fork and join patterns. In the following we will present rules to discover the most interesting workflow patterns belonging to these three categories.

Sequence pattern: In this category we find only the sequence pattern (c.f. table 1). In this pattern, the enactment of the activity B depends only on the completion of activity A. So we need, in besides of the discovery of $\Gamma(A,B)$ episode, statistical tests ($P(B/A) = 1 \wedge \#B = \#A$) that ensure the exclusive dependency linking B to A.

Fork patterns: This category (*c.f.* table 2) has a "fork" point where a single thread of control splits into multiple threads of control which can be, according to the used pattern, executed or not. In the following, we denote $\overline{p}(B_1, B_2, ..., B_n)$ the equivalency class of Π containing $\{B_i \,;\, 0 \leq i \leq n\}$.

Table 1. Rules of sequence workflow patterns mining

Rules : Episodes + Frequencies	Mining Workflow pattern
$\Gamma(A, B)$	Sequence pattern
$(P(B/A) = 1) \wedge (\#B = \#A)$	A — B

The causality between the activities A and B_i before and after "fork" point is shared by Exclusive Choice, Parallel Split and Multi-choice, the three patterns of this category. This causality is ensured by the statistical tests ($\forall 0 \leq i \leq n; P(B_i/A) = 1$). The Exclusive choice pattern, where one of several branches is chosen after "fork" point, has an episode different from Parallel Split and Multi-choice patterns which have the same episode. The non-parallelism between B_i, in the Exclusive choice pattern are ensured by ($\forall 0 \leq i, j \leq n; P(B_i/B_j) = 0$). Parallel Split and Multi-choice patterns differentiate themselves by the frequencies relation between the activity A and the activities B_i. Effectively, only a part of activities are executed in the Multi-choice pattern after "fork" point, while all the B_i activities are executed in Parallel Split pattern.

Join patterns: This category (*c.f.* table 3) has a "join" point where a single thread of control splits into multiple threads of control. The number of necessary branches for the activation of the activity B after the "join" point depends on the used pattern. In the following, we denote $\overline{p}(A_1, A_2, ..., A_n)$ the equivalency class of Π containing $\{A_i; 0 \leq i \leq n\}$.

The enactment of activity B after the "join" point in the Synchronization pattern requires the execution of all the A_i activities ($\forall 0 \leq i \leq n; P(B/A_i) = 1$). In contrary of Simple Merge and M-out-of-N-join pattern that have the same episodes different from the Synchronization pattern and where the parallelism between the Ai activities can be only seen in the M-out-of-N-join pattern ($\exists 0 \leq i, j \leq n; P(A_i/A_j) \neq 0$).

6.4 Example

As a working example, let the workflow model in section 2. We will focus on the discovery of the synchronization pattern formed by the given CA, P, SI activities. The width of the concurrence window infers the inclusion of the activity CI in our computing statistical dependency table and the discovery of episodes. This inclusion will allow us to remove any confusion or erroneous deductions. Table 4 presents a fraction of the statistical dependency table.

The episodes discovered in the log are:

$$\Gamma(\overline{p}(CA, P), SI)$$

Statistic dependency value (bold numbers) and discovered episodes bellow indicates that mined workflow contains a synchronization pattern formed by the given CA, P,

Table 2. Rules of fork workflow patterns mining

Rules : Episodes + Frequencies	Mining Workflow pattern
$\bigwedge_{i=0}^{n}(\Gamma(A,B_i))$	Exclusive choice pattern
$(\forall 0 \leq i \leq n; P(B_i/A) = 1) \bigwedge$ $(\forall 0 \leq i,j \leq n; P(B_i/B_j) = 0) \bigwedge$ $(\Sigma_{i=0}^{n} (\#B_i) = \#A)$	
$\Gamma(A,\overline{p}(B_1, B_2, ..., B_n))$	Parallel split pattern
$(\forall 0 \leq i \leq n; P(B_i/A) = 1) \bigwedge$ $(\forall 0 \leq i,j \leq n; P(B_i/B_j) \neq 0) \bigwedge$ $(\forall 0 \leq i \leq n \ \#B_i = \#A)$	
$\Gamma(A,\overline{p}(B_1, B_2, ..., B_n))$	Multi choice pattern
$(\forall 0 \leq i \leq n; P(B_i/A) = 1) \bigwedge$ $(\exists 0 \leq i,j \leq n; P(B_i/B_j) \neq 0) \bigwedge$ $(\#A \leq \Sigma_{i=0}^{n} (\#B_i)) \bigwedge (\#B_i \leq \#A)$	

SI activities. Note that the frequency $P(CA/CI)$ lets us think about the sequential pattern which can give an indication about the episodes class that we must find in order to identify this pattern.

7 Mining the Set of Termination States

In this section, we describe how to mine the set of termination states of a workflow from its log. First we give a formal definition of a workflow set of termination states denoted WTS (Definition 8). In this definition, we specify also the WTS format used in our mining approach. Then we present the algorithm used to mine the WTS from a given event log (Algorithm 3).

Definition 8 (Workflow Termination State WTS). *In a workflow execution case, each activity has its termination state. It is described by the activity identifier and the activity state. Thus, an activity Terminated State denoted ATS is seen as a couple:* **ATS** = *(activityid, state), where :*

- *(activityId : int) is the ID of the activity ,*
- *{(State: symbol)} is the **last** activity state*

Table 3. Rules of join workflow patterns mining

Rules : Episodes + Frequencies	Mining Workflow pattern
$\Gamma(\overline{p}(A_1, A_2, ..., A_n), B)$	Synchronization pattern
$(\forall 0 \leq i \leq n; P(B/A_i) = 1) \bigwedge$	
$(\forall 0 \leq i,j \leq n; P(A_i/A_j) \neq 0) \bigwedge$	
$(\forall 0 \leq i \leq n \; \#A_i = \#B)$	
$\bigwedge_{i=0}^{n}(\Gamma(A_i, B))$	Simple merge pattern
$(\Sigma_{i=0}^{n} P(B/A_i) = 1) \bigwedge$	
$(\exists 0 \leq i,j \leq n; P(A_i/A_j) = 0) \bigwedge$	
$(\Sigma_{i=0}^{n}(\#A_i) = \#B)$	
$\bigwedge_{i=0}^{n}(\Gamma(A_i, B))$	M-out-of-N Join pattern
$(n \geq \Sigma_{i=0}^{n} P(B/A_i) = 1 \geq m) \bigwedge$	
$(\exists 0 \leq i,j \leq n; P(A_i/A_j) \neq 0) \bigwedge$	
$(\forall 0 \leq i \leq n \; \#A_i \geq m*\#B)$	

*A Case Terminated State denoted CTS is a set of ATS corresponding to a workflow execution case; **CTS**={ATS}. The set of the workflow termination states denoted WTS contains all possible CTS without redundancy; **WTS**={CTS}.*

The algorithm build the WTS by proceeding as follows: each **stream** in the log is scanned and for each **event**, the **ATS** of its corresponding activity is updated by keeping only the last state. The Algorithm build for each **stream** its corresponding **CTS**. We can find many **stream**s with the same **CTS**. The algorithm build the **WTS** as a the set of all **CTS**s without redundancy.

Algorithm 3 : Mining Terminated States Set
 Input: Wlog : (**workflowLog**)
 output: WTS :(**workflow set of termination states**)

```
var
    activity : int;
    courantA : ATS;
    CourantC : CTS
    Resul    : WTS;
begin
    for all S:stream in Wlog
        CourantC=Null;
```

Table 4. Fraction of the statistical dependency table

P	CI	CA	P	SI
#CI = 100	0	0	0.36	0
#CA = 100	1	0	**0.41**	0
#P = 100	0.43	**0.29**	0	0
#SI = 100	1	**1**	**1**	0

```
        for all e:event in S.sequenceLog
            courantA.activityId = e.activityId;
            courantA.State= e.activityState;
            UpdateCTS(CourantC,courantA);
            /* the function UpdateCTS updates courantA
            in CourantC  */
        endFor
        WTS = WTS + CourantC;
    endFor
end
```

8 Mining Transactional Behavior

We define at this level a set of rules [13] allowing to mine workflow transactional behavior. These rules allow to tailor the activities transactional properties and the transactional flow according to the discovered control flow and set of termination states.

To illustrate the applicability of our rules we go back to the example of PC on line purchase. The control flow mining allows to discover the activities sequence order as illustrated in the figure 1. We suppose that the mining of the set of termination states allows to deduce the following WTS:
$\{[(CRS, \text{terminated}), (CIC, \text{terminated}), (P, \text{terminated}), (CI, \text{terminated}), (CA, \text{terminated}), (SI, \text{terminated})]; [(CRS, \text{terminated}), (CIC, \text{terminated}), (P, \text{failed}), (CI, \text{terminated}), (CA, \text{terminated}), (SI, \text{initial})]; [(CRS, \text{compensated}), (CIC, \text{failed}), (P, \text{aborted}), (CI, \text{aborted}), (CA, \text{aborted}), (SI, \text{aborted})]\}$.

Let a be an activity that can be compensated (what means $\exists ATS \in WTS \mid ATS.activityId = a \land ATS.state = compensated$), we extract from the discovered control flow and WTS the compensation condition of a denoted $cpCond(a)$. We can write $cpCond(a)$ in disjunctive normal form; $cpCond(a) = \bigvee cpCond_i(a)$. Then $cpCond_i(a)$ is one (and not necessary the) compensation condition of a. For instance for our example, the only activity that can be compensated is CRS and we have $cpCond(CRS) = CIC.failed$. Below, we introduce our rules to mine the workflow transactional behavior.

$\forall$ activity a

1. $\nexists ATS \in WTS \mid ATS.activityId = a \land ATS.state = failed \Longrightarrow$ **a is retriable**
2. $\exists ATS \in WTS \mid ATS.activityId = a \land ATS.state = failed \Longrightarrow$ **a is not retriable**

3. $\not\exists ATS \in WTS \mid ATS.activityId = a \wedge ATS.state = compensated \implies a$ **should be not compensatable and if it is not the case it will never be compensated.**
4. $\exists ATS \in WTS \mid ATS.activityId = a \wedge ATS.state = compensated \implies$
   a is compensatable
   $\wedge$ **a have to be compensated when one of its compensation conditions occurs**

The first (respectively the second) rule says that if a never fails (respectively can fail) then a is (respectively is not) retriable. The third and forth rules allows to deduce when an activity a is compensatable and when it will be compensated.

Back to our example, we can deduce by applying the above rules the following transactional behavior:

- by applying 1 to the all activities except CIC and P we obtain: CRS, CI, CA **and** SI **are retriable.**
- by applying 2 to CIC and P we obtain: CIC **and** P **are not retriable.**
- by applying 3 to the all activities except CRS we obtain: CIC, P, CI, CA **and** SI **should be not compensatable and if it is not the case, they will never be compensated.**
- by applying 4 to CRS we obtain:
  CRS **is compensatable**
  $\wedge$ CRS **have to be compensated when** CIC **fails**

Thanks to this transactional behavior mining, we are able to detect that contrary to what is specified, SI never fails and P can fail. These two information allow to improve the workflow by:

1. omitting the two compensation interaction when SI fails,
2. specifying that there is no need for P to be compensatable and
3. adding an interaction ensuring the compensation of CA when P fails

9 Conclusion and Future Work

In this paper we have introduced a new workflow mining approach that allows discovering workflow transactional behavior from event-Based Log. Previous works [2,3,4,5] have only been interested in discovering control flows. We proceed in two steps.

1. The first one consists in mining workflow patterns and the set of termination states. The mining of workflow patterns looks like the mining of control flows. But our approach is original regarding other proposed techniques:
   - It assumes a new approach never stated until now that it is characterized by a partial discovery of the workflow at its initial phase. Therefore, we can recover results of mining patterns workflows even if our log is incomplete;
   - It discovers more complex features with a better specification of "fork" point (Exclusive choice, Parallel split and Multi choice patterns) and "join" point (Synchronization, Simple merge and M-out-of-N Join patterns);
   - It deals better with concurrency through the introduction "*concurrent window*";

- It seems to be more simple in computing. This simplicity will not affect its efficiency in treating the concurrent aspect of workflow.
2. In the second step, based on the discovered control flow and set of termination states, we use a set of rules to mine the workflow transactional behavior.

Thus, our approach allows to detect transactional modelling anomalies and thereafter to improve the workflow model and then provides a significant improvement to WFMS understanding and design. However, the work described in this paper represents an initial investigation. In our future works, we hope to discover more complex patterns by using more metrics (*e.g.* entropy, periodicity, etc.) and by enriching the workflow log. We are also interested in the modelling and the discovery of more complex transactional characteristics of cooperative workflows (*e.g.*, workflows composition, compensate activity, roll-back, etc).

References

1. Joachim Herbst. Inducing workflow models from workflow instances. In *the Concurrent Engineering Europe Conference. Society for Computer Simulation (SCS)*, 1999.
2. Rakesh Agrawal, Dimitrios Gunopulos, and Frank Leymann. Mining process models from workflow logs. *Lecture Notes in Computer Science*, 1377:469–498, 1998.
3. Jonathan E. Cook and Alexander L. Wolf. Discovering models of software processes from event-based data. *ACM Transactions on Software Engineering and Methodology (TOSEM)*, 7(3):215–249, 1998.
4. Joachim Herbst. A machine learning approach to workflow management. In *Machine Learning: ECML 2000, 11th European Conference on Machine Learning, Barcelona, Catalonia, Spain*, volume 1810, pages 183–194. Springer, Berlin, May 2000.
5. W.M.P. van der Aalst and L. Maruster. Workflow mining: Discovering process models from event logs. In *QUT Technical report, FIT-TR-2003-03, Queensland University of Technology*, Brisbane, 2003.
6. Marek Rusinkiewicz and Amit Sheth. Specification and execution of transactional workflows. pages 592–620, 1995.
7. W. M. P. Van Der Aalst, A. H. M. Ter Hofstede, B. Kiepuszewski, and A. P. Barros. Workflow patterns. *Distrib. Parallel Databases*, 14(1):5–51, 2003.
8. A. Elmagarmid, Y. Leu, W. Litwin, and Marek Rusinkiewicz. A multidatabase transaction model for interbase. In *Proceedings of the sixteenth international conference on Very large databases*, pages 507–518. Morgan Kaufmann Publishers Inc., 1990.
9. S. Jablonski and C. Bussler. *Workflow Management: Modeling Concepts, Architecture, and Implementation*. International Thomson Computer Press, 1996.
10. Peter Lawrence. *Workflow handbook 1997*. John Wiley & Sons, Inc., 1997.
11. Jonathan E. Cook and Alexander L. Wolf. Automating process discovery through event-data analysis. In *Proceedings of the 17th international conference on Software engineering*, pages 73–82. ACM Press, 1995.
12. Heikki Mannila, Hannu Toivonen, and A. Inkeri Verkamo. Discovery of frequent episodes in event sequences. *Data Mining and Knowledge Discovery*, 1(3):259–289, 1997.
13. Sami Bhiri, Claude Godart, and Olivier Perrin. A transactional-oriented framework for composing transactional web services. To appear In *IEEE International Conference on Services Computing (SCC 2004)*. IEEE Computer Society, Shangai, september 2004.

A Flexible Mediation Process for Large Distributed Information Systems

Philippe Lamarre[1], Sylvie Cazalens[1], Sandra Lemp[1], and Patrick Valduriez[2]

[1] LINA,
University of Nantes, France
{cazalens|lamarre|lemp}@lina.univ-nantes.fr
[2] INRIA and LINA,
University of Nantes, France
Patrick.Valduriez@inria.fr

Abstract. We consider distributed information systems that are open, dynamic and provide access to large numbers of distributed, heterogeneous, autonomous information sources. Most of the work in data mediator systems has dealt with the problem of finding relevant information providers for a request. However, finding relevant requests for information providers is another important side of the mediation problem which has not received much attention. In this paper, we address these two sides of the problem with a flexible mediation process. Once the qualified information providers are identified, our process allows them to express their request interests via a bidding mechanism. It also requires to set up a requisition policy, because a request must always be answered if there are qualified providers. This work does not concern pure market mechanisms because we counter-balance the providers' bids by considering their quality wrt a request. We validated our process on a set of simulations. The results show that the mediation process supports the providers in adequacy with the user expectations, even if they are sometimes imposed.

1 Introduction

We consider distributed information systems that are open, dynamic and provide access to large numbers of distributed, heterogeneous, autonomous information sources. Information requesters and providers may come in or leave the system at any time, because of technical reasons but also because of their own choice. Entrance may be motivated by some expected benefits while exit may result from disappointment. On one hand, one can estimate that a requester satisfaction is a function of the quality of the answers it gets. On the other hand, the reasons of a provider's disapointment are more diverse. It may be for example because it never gets interesting requests while it is often solicited for uninteresting ones. Thus, it is important for the flexibility of the system to preserve the more possible diversity by avoiding the leave of requesters or providers.

In this context, most of the work in data mediator systems has dealt with the problem of finding relevant information providers for a request [20]. However, finding relevant requests for information providers is another important side of the mediation problem which has not received much attention. One way to proceed is to take the economical mechanisms as a starting point and to assume that the mediator asks providers to bid on requests like in an auction mechanism. In some way, a provider's bid on a request, which can be a simple real number, expresses its degree of interest in it. This gives a means to compare the providers, even if they have very different objectives or preferences.

However, the use of bids involves several questions. Firstly, should any provider bid on any request even if it is unable to answer it ? Obviously not. This is why providers capabilities should be taken into account. Secondly, only considering bids comes to attach a great importance to the providers and none to the requester. So how to get a more balanced view ? To answer this point, we introduce a notion of provider's quality with respect to a request. It represents an evaluation of how well the provider could perform and takes into account users' feed-backs. Finally, because bids express an interest, it might occur that no provider is interested in a given request. So, should we allow a request not to be treated even if some providers have the required capabilities? From our viewpoint, no. Some providers should be imposed the request, with an adequate counterpart.

Let us illustrate these underlying intuitions with a travelling problem example scenario. Assume that 1000 travel agencies, naturally competitive, are represented by 1000 providers which have advertised their capabilities at a mediator. They are free to switch from a mediator to another, or to leave the system. This may occur if they do not get the kind of request they want from the mediator or the system. Now consider a user who wants to arrange a travel to Alaska. She specifies the parameters (dates, departure town, amount of money allocated ...) to her user agent, called the requester in the following, and lets it look for possibilities. Considering its own capabilities, the requester asks the mediator to find 4 providers able to arrange travel and accommodation ... The first job of the mediator is to extract providers which can treat the request. This can be done using a matchmaking algorithm [12]. Let us say that the resulting list contains 40 providers (i.e. travel agencies). The next step is to choose 4 among these 40 which will be given in response to the requester. Here, it is the job of mediation. As a preliminary, the mediator has to obtain some pieces of information:

How well those providers might perform such request? In order to be able to answer this question, the mediator has to manage some database including information from previous users experiences, benchmarking results ... , and a method to merge all this information in order to obtain an evaluation of the quality, let us say a positive number.

How much those providers are interested in dealing with this request? Only providers can answer this question. So, the mediator asks them to make an offer. In order to bid, each provider is supposed to consider its objectives and current jobs, how well it expects to be dealing with this request ... , and to combine all those parameters using its own strategy. This could be a positive offer if it would like to be in the final selection, or a negative one if it considers that the fact of being selected would be prejudicial for it.

Going back to our scenario, let us assume that in our case, only 3 travel agencies wish to treat the request while the others consider it as "disturbing" for their own reasons. However the requester asked for four and it is possible to satisfy it. The problem is to choose the one over the 37 which will be imposed. To do so, the problem is to make "fair" balance between qualities and costs. Once the 4th provider has been chosen, the procedure can go on: sending this list to the requester, up to him to manage negotiations with those providers; or, sending the request to the selected providers; or anything else depending on the global architecture.

But the mediation process may not be completely over. Indeed, it would be unfair to let the requested provider support alone its imposition while the others got what they wished. As far as some kind of money is used by providers to bid on requests, it is possible to ask some financial participation to all the providers able to treat the request: everyone pays and the one which has been imposed gets something. This compensation increases the chance of the requested provider to obtain what it wishes in the next rounds.

The entire treatment of this scenario encompasses different aspects. Firstly, query planning processes may be required. This problem is adressed in different ways in the litterature [20,19]. Thus, we can indifferently assume that query planning is ensured by the mediator, or by the requesters or by any external module, without loss of generality. Secondly, the providers advertise their capabilities at the mediator which must support matchmaking techniques in order to match a given request with providers which are able to treat it. Matchmaking algorithms have been proposed by several groups [3,12,8,18]. Thus, we do not detail this point. Thirdly, the mediator has to evaluate how well the providers might perform a given request, under the form of a positive number, called quality. This aspect is related to reputation acquisition and several solutions have been proposed in the litterature. An overview is provided in [7]. Notice that, in order to validate the mediation process we have used some basic acquisition mechanisms.

The core of the problem and the focus of this paper is the definition of the mediation process and its validation. That is, given a request, bids and qualities, how to define which providers to select and what they have to pay. This problem has never been adressed before in this whole generality. There has been much work based on pure economics, dealing with bids only. But, to our knowledge, there is no work which combines both qualities of the providers and their bids and also introduces a requisition process.

Before going further, let us stress that the money we use is *virtual*. We could either talk of tokens or any other term indicating a mechanism to regulate the system. The difficulty is to define the selection of n providers and their invoicing in order to get some desired properties. Indeed the intuition is that there must be a kind of balance between bids and qualities, resulting in a balance between requesters and providers. But there must be also a balance between the different providers. This is why we use the term *mediation* (and thus mediator) with the Merriam-Webster dictionary meaning: *intervention between conflicting parties to promote reconciliation, settlement, or compromise.*

In this paper, we propose a flexible mediation process which takes into account the providers' interests via a bidding mechanism. The main contribution is the definition of the mediation process, within an overall mediation system architecture, and its validation through simulation. The paper is organized as follows. Section 2 describes the system overall mediation system architecture and the mediators main modules. Section 3 describes the mediation process. Section 4 describes our validation based on simulation. Section 5 discusses related works. Section 6 concludes.

2 Mediation System Architecture

The global system architecture is described in Figure 1. It is presented with a single mediator to process the requests, a number k of requesters and a number m of providers, which advertise their capabilities. Of course these two numbers vary in the course of time.

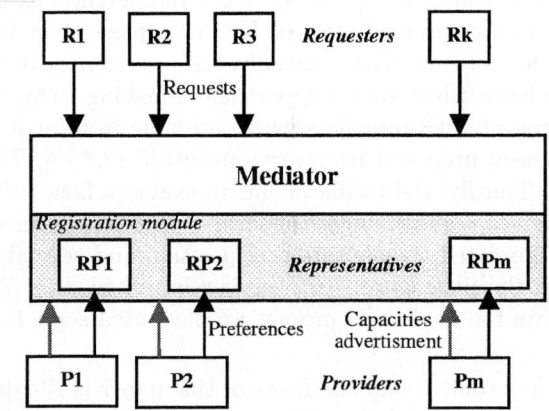

Fig. 1. Mediation system architecture.

An important point is the use of *provider representatives* in order to avoid a very significant network traffic. Indeed, request, bid and bill are exchanged between the mediator and each representative which are both located on the same computer The counterpart of this choice is that each provider has to regularly inform its representative of its *preferences* on the kind of requests it would like to get. If the number of requests is important, this choice makes the number of exchanged messages decrease.

The mediator uses a registration module, because at any time, it must be able to welcome a new provider and/or to accept a provider resignation. These changes are taken into account after the current mediation. When a new provider advertises its capabilities, its application is studied. If it is accepted, the registration module updates the capabilities database and it welcomes the provider's representative. Then, regularly, the provider has to update its preferences at its representative. When a provider deregisters (or after a long period of inactivity) the representative is removed.

Answers do not appear on Figure 1. In fact, as for querying the providers, different options exist, depending on the model of mediation that is needed [3, 17]. As a consequence, the querying and answers composition modules are placed on the requester side or on the mediator.

Figure 2, represents the mediator's inner architecture and focuses on the selection of providers relevant to a given request where a number n of providers is required. We do not mention some additional modules like those in charge of the query planning or of the payment, which are less central. The way quality is computed as well as the providers' strategies depend on the application. This is why the nature of feed-backs as well as the kind of information in the qualities database is not detailed.

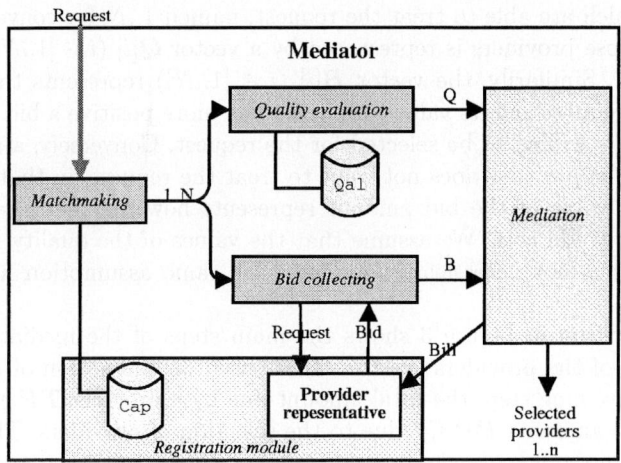

Fig. 2. Mediator's architecture.

Each incoming request is first submitted to the matchmaking module, which uses the capabilities database to match the request with the providers capabilities. It computes a set of N providers which are able to treat the request.

Then the quality evaluation module and the bidding module can be run in parallel. The quality evaluation module uses a qualities database which gathers feed-backs from providers or other mediators (feed-backs may come in at any time) as well as results from the mediator's own evaluation of providers (from benchmarks or analysis of answers). Given the incoming request, this module computes a quality for each of the N providers, and gives back a quality vector of positive real numbers. The bidding module is in charge of collecting the bids from the N provider representatives. It sends them the requests, waits for the bids until a given deadline and returns a bid vector of N real numbers.

The mediation module uses a two steps process. The first one selects the n required providers among the N possible ones. The second one determines the invoicing of each of the N providers. Both steps use the quality vector and the bid vector. A bill is sent to each representative. This procedure is the core of the mediator and is detailed in the next sections.

3 Mediation Process

We focus on the case where, from the mediation point of view, any given request can be viewed as a single "unit" of work called *task*. It includes a query together with additional information like the sender, the required number of providers (noted n) or even some meta-data which characterize the query. Notice that this information may be used by the representatives to determine their bids.

We assume that the matchmaking step has generated a number N of providers which are able to treat the request, named $1..N$ for convenience. The quality of those providers is represented by a vector $\boldsymbol{Q}[i]$ ($i \in [1..N]$) taking its values in $\mathbb{R}^+$. Similarily, the vector $\boldsymbol{B}[i]$ ($i \in [1..N]$) represents the providers' bids for the request and its values are in $\mathbb{R}$. The more positive a bid is, the more the provider is willing to be selected for the request. Conversely, a negative bid means that the provider does not want to treat the request; in that latter case, the absolute value of the bid amount represents how much the requisition of the provider would cost. We assume that the values of the quality function are comparable but not necessarily bounded. The same assumption holds for the bids.

The algorithm in Figure 3 shows the main steps of the mediation process. The ranking of the providers (vector $\boldsymbol{R}$) is based on the notion of *level* (vector $\boldsymbol{L}$). In the invoicing step, the total amount due by a provider $\boldsymbol{TP}[j]$ is the sum of the partial amounts $\boldsymbol{PP}[i,j]$ due to the selection of providers. The details of the different notions and calculations are given in the following and illustrated by Table 1.

3.1 Selection of the Providers

Definition 1. *Vector of providers' levels.*
$\forall i \in [1..N], \boldsymbol{L}[i] = \begin{vmatrix} (\boldsymbol{B}[i] + \varepsilon)^\omega \times (\boldsymbol{Q}[i] + \varepsilon)^{1-\omega} & \text{if } \boldsymbol{B}[i] \geq 0 \\ -(-\boldsymbol{B}[i] + \varepsilon)^\omega \times (\boldsymbol{Q}[i] + \varepsilon)^{\omega-1} & \text{otherwise.} \end{vmatrix}$
with $\omega \in [0..1]$ *and* $\varepsilon > 0$.

Intuitively, two different notions have to be considered: quality and bid. Whatever their values are, no one should be neglected. Hence a weighted sum is

```
{ IN  : [1..N], Q, B, n }
{ OUT : selection, TP }
begin
   for j in [1..N] do compute L[j]; { Levels of the providers }
   for k ← 1 to N do compute R[k]; { Rank the providers }
   selection ← R[1..min(n, N)];     { Select the n best ones }
                                    { Invoicing }
   for j in [1..N] do
       { compute j's total amount due in this mediation }
       TP[j] ← 0;
       for i in selection do
           { j's partial amount due to i's selection }
           compute PP[i,j];
           TP[j] ← TP[j] + PP[i,j]
end
```

Fig. 3. Mediation algorithm.

not appropriate. Moreover, the increase of the value of one or the other parameters should increase the level. This is why a product is used. Parameter ω ensures a balance between a provider's quality and bid. It reflects the relative importance that the mediator gives to the providers quality or to their preferences. In particular, if $\omega = 0$ (respectively 1) the mediator only takes into account the quality (respectively the bid) of a provider. Notice that in all our simulations, up to now, we have considered that ω is fixed by a human administrator. Parameter ε, usually set to 1, prevents the level from lowering downto 0 when the bid (resp., quality) is equal to 0 whatever the quality (resp. bid) is. In table 1, influence of the quality can be seen by comparing p_3 and p_{10} for example. Their bids are close, but p_{10} gets a higher level because its quality is greater. Conversely, the difference between p_4 and p_5 is obtained by the values of the bids.

Definition 2. Providers ordering.
Let r be a request. Relation $<_r$, is defined by : $\forall (i,j) \in [1..N]^2$, $i <_r j$ iff
1 - $L[i] < L[j]$, or
2 - $L[i] = L[j]$ and

- *if $\omega < 1 - \omega$ (i.e. the quality is more important than the bid)*
  - $Q[i] < Q[j]$, *or*
  - $Q[i] = Q[j]$ *and* ($B[i] < B[j]$, *or* $B[i] = B[j]$ *and* $i < j$)
- *if $\omega > 1 - \omega$ (i.e. the bid is more important than the quality)*
  - $B[i] < B[j]$, *or*
  - $B[i] = B[j]$ *and* ($Q[i] < Q[j]$, *or* $Q[i] = Q[j]$ *and* $i < j$)
- *if $\omega = 1 - \omega$: $i < j$*

Relation $\leq_r$, obtained from $<_r$ and where equality represents syntactical equality of names, is a total order on the set of N providers [6]. It always places the providers that want to treat the request before those who do not want to, independently of each other.

Definition 3. Providers ranking.
$\forall k \in [1..N] \boldsymbol{R}[k] = i$ iff $i \in [1..N]$ and $|\{j : j \in [1..N]$ and $j \leq_r i\}| = k$.

Intuitively, $\boldsymbol{R}[1]$ is the best provider according to ordering $<_r$, $\boldsymbol{R}[2]$ the second, and so on up to $\boldsymbol{R}[N]$ which is the last. The selection step selects all the n best providers, i.e. from $\boldsymbol{R}[1]$ to $\boldsymbol{R}[n]$. If there are less than n providers, all of them are selected. The complexity of the selection step is $\Theta(N \log_2(N))$ [6].

Table 1 shows the rank obtained by the ten providers. If request r asks for three providers ($n = 3$), p_2, p_1, p_{10} are selected (selection s_1). If $n = 8$, all the providers with a positive bid are selected as well as p_6 (selection s_2) even if its negative bid reflects that it does not want to treat this request. We say that p_6 is imposed the request.

Table 1. Two examples of selection with $\omega = 0.6$: s_1 ($n = 3$) and s_2 ($n = 8$)

	Q	B	L	R	s_1	TP	s_2	TP
p_1	8	2	4.655	2	*	1.201	*	0.485
p_2	2	10	6.542	1	*	3.579	*	0.485
p_3	3	2	3.366	5		0.0	*	0.485
p_4	1	5	3.866	4		0.0	*	0.485
p_5	1	1	1.999	6		0.0	*	0.485
p_6	10	-3	-0.880	8		0.0	*	-4.231
p_7	8	-4	-1.091	9		0.0		0.485
p_8	20	-8	-1.106	10		0.0		0.485
p_9	0	1	1.516	7		0.0	*	0.485
p_{10}	10	1	3.955	3	*	0.926	*	0.485

3.2 Invoicing

In usual auction mechanisms, invoicing is based on the comparison of the bids only. Here, the task is more complicated by the fact that each bid is balanced by a quality. Hence we cannot directly compare the bids. This is why a notion of *theoretical bid* of a provider is introduced.

Theoretical bid. It represents the bid that the provider should make in order to get a given level l. We do not consider the same question for the quality. Indeed, the provider cannot change its quality as it does for bids. It is the mediator who masters the estimated quality, and its judgement can only change in the course of time.

Proposition 1. *Let r be a request and let $i \in [1..N]$ be a provider. If the mediator uses a selection strategy such that $\omega \neq 0$ then, the theoretical bid with respect to r that i should make to reach level l is :*
$B^{Th}(i, l) = \alpha \; max(((\alpha \times l)^{\frac{1}{\omega}}(\boldsymbol{Q}[i] + \varepsilon)^{\frac{\alpha(\omega - 1)}{\omega}} - \varepsilon), 0)$
where $\alpha = 1$, if $l \geq 0$, and $\alpha = -1$ otherwise.

This formula is the result of the resolution of the equation $\boldsymbol{L}[i] = l$, $\boldsymbol{Q}[i]$ and ω and ε being fixed. With the data from Table 1, according to the Proposition 1, provider p_2 has to bid 3.579 in order to obtain the same level as p_4's one. Conversely, in order to come to p_2's level, p_4 must increase its bid up to 13.414. One should notice that the level grows as a function of l (all the other parameters being fixed). The definition of theoretical bid enables to specify the invoicing. Two cases are considered: competition and requisition. In this latter case, the cost of requisition is shared between *all the providers which are able to treat the request* (including those which have not been selected). In other words, when some provider is requisitioned, all the others may pay to support its effort. In case more than one provider are requested, the total amount due by a provider j ($\boldsymbol{TP}$ [j]) is the result of the addition of each requisition cost. To reflect this, the notation $\boldsymbol{PP}[i,j]$ (partial invoice corresponding to the selection of provider i) is introduced. To obtain an homogeneous notation this is used in case of requisition but also competition as well even if it is not useful in this latter case.

Partial invoice in the competitive case. In a competitive situation the selected provider has made positive bid. Competition is effective when more than n providers has done so. The calculation of the invoicing is carried out by comparing a selected provider with the best one which has not been selected. However, the amount of the invoice is not computed only from the bids. Instead, we consider the level of the providers which takes both offer and quality into account. Therefore, the partial invoicing of a selected provider corresponds to the bid which it should make to get the same level as the best unselected provider (theoretical bid). Note also, only selected providers have to pay something.

Definition 4. *The partial invoicing of a provider $j \in [1..N]$ concerning the selection of $i \in [1..N]$ in the case $\boldsymbol{B}[i] \geq 0$, is:*

$$\boldsymbol{PP}[i,j] = \begin{vmatrix} \boldsymbol{B}^{Th}(j, \boldsymbol{L}[\boldsymbol{R}[n+1]]) & \text{if } n < N \text{ and } i = j \text{ and } \boldsymbol{B}[\boldsymbol{R}[n+1]] \geq 0 \\ 0 & else \end{vmatrix}$$

Partial invoice in the requisition case. The situation is a requisition when at least a provider, having quoted negative, is selected. The idea is then to distribute the cost of the requisition on all the providers able to answer the request (and not only on those selected).

Definition 5. *The partial invoicing of a provider $j \in [1..N]$ concerning the selection of $i \in [1..N]$ in the case $\boldsymbol{B}[i] < 0$ is:*

$$\boldsymbol{PP}[i,j] = \begin{vmatrix} \frac{-\boldsymbol{B}^{Th}(i,\boldsymbol{L}[\boldsymbol{R}[min(n+2,N)]])}{N} & \text{if } i \neq j \\ \boldsymbol{B}^{Th}(i,\boldsymbol{L}[\boldsymbol{R}[min(n+1,N)]]) - \frac{\boldsymbol{B}^{Th}(i,\boldsymbol{L}[\boldsymbol{R}[min(n+2,N)]])}{N} & else \end{vmatrix}$$

In the first line, the provider, which is not selected, is required to support the selected one. In the second line, the amount allocated to the requisitioned provider is computed. Even if requisitioned, the provider is asked a given amount. In fact, that some provider p_a is imposed a request r is supported by all the providers.

Global invoicing. The total amount owed by each provider is obtained by adding the partial bills related to each selected provider. Of course, in the following, if i is not selected, $\boldsymbol{PP}[i,j] = 0$.

Definition 6. *The invoicing of every provider $j \in [1..N]$ is defined by:*

$$\boldsymbol{TP}[j] = \sum_{i \in [1..min(N,n)]} \boldsymbol{PP}[i,j]$$

The complexity of this calculation is $\Theta(N \times min(N,n))$.

Notice that in a competitive case, the provider never pays more than its own bid. In Table 1, selection s_1 corresponds to a competitive case. The selected providers p_1, p_2, p_{10} are the only ones to pay something. Selection s_2 corresponds to a requisition case (p_6). In that case, all the (ten) providers support the financial effort. If, under the same condition, n had been equal to 7, all the providers wanting the request would have got it and none of them would have been requisitioned. There would have been no invoicing because this is neither a competition nor a requisition.

4 Validation

We have simulated the mediation process and carried out a series of tests with two main objectives in mind. The first one is to evaluate the behaviour of the process in the course of time. That is, after several mediations, does the expected regulation phenomenon really occurs? The second objective is to evaluate the quality of the proposed solution, by comparing it with other selection methods.

We have already underlined in the paper that we use *virtual* money, as a means of regulation. For the simulations, we had to make some hypothesis about the way money circulates. Indeed, in the course of time, the providers spend their money in order to get requests and to support the providers which have been imposed. The process itself does not provide them any way to earn money. However a source of financing is necessary to them, because otherwise, after some time, they would become unable to bid positively, just because of a lack of credit. We have chosen to associate a bank with the mediator (if there were several mediators, there would be as many banks as mediators). Each bank has its own currency, and can create money if needed. This choice enables to measure the quality of the mediation with more accuracy and independently of the effects that a more general economic approach could have (for example, another choice could have been to reward any provider which treats a request. Hence each provider would have had its own financing source). Thus, in our simulations, in the case of a single mediator, the financing of each provider is ensured by the mediator in two ways:

- At the registration step, when the provider is accepted, the mediator's bank creates a given amount of money and gives it to this new participant. When a provider quits the system, the corresponding amount of money is progressively withdrawn by the bank. So, the total amount of money which circulates in the system is proportional to the number of registered providers.

– In the course of time, the mediator regularly redistributes the money which it gained to the providers. Indeed, it can be shown that the mediator never looses money in the mediation process, and even tends to earn some (even if the amounts are not that high) [6]. So, after some time, it would get all the money which it has itself put in circulation. This is why it redistributes it to all the providers, dividing equitably the money it has. Note that the amount of money that each provider can own is limited[1].

Given these assumptions, we have conducted two types of experiments. The first series is independent of any particular application. We compare the mediation process with a selection procedure that maximizes the system overall utility. The second series of tests focuses on a specific application, namely load balancing. It compares the mediation process with an optimal load balancing.

4.1 Comparison with a Selection Based on the System Global Utility Maximisation

Utility functions are commonly used to model the satisfaction of the participants in a system. The system global utility is then defined as the sum of the utilities of all the participants. Thus a way to select the providers for a given query is to choose the solution which maximizes this global utility: for each request, the Global Utility Maximisation selection (GUM selection) computes the sum of the utilities of all the participants for all the possible allocations and selects the one which gives the highest sum. However, maximizing this global utility does NOT mean that a majority of participants is satisfied. This is why our tests compare the individual utilities in the GUM selection and in the mediation process, expecting the latter to satisfy more participants.

To illustrate the differences between the two processes, we detail the results that have been obtained with the following hypothesis: a single requester, although there would be no change with several ones; a single mediator which allocates the requests to ten providers. We have conducted the experiments with much more providers, but the graphs rapidly become unreadable because of too many curves to represent. There are two kinds of requests (t_1 and t_2), each one requiring a single provider.

The utility function of a given provider i, noted $U[i]$, reflects how much it wants to treat a request. If it does not get it, the function returns zero. If it does get the request, the utility function returns a given number, which, in this series of tests, does not evolve in the course of time. The utility of the requester is directly function of the quality of the provider which has been selected to treat the request ($Q[i]$). Just as for the utility functions, the quality of the providers does not evolve. We do not consider the utility of the mediator because it does not have to be satisfied or unsatisfied. It just has to facilitate mediation. These parameters are fixed in order to highlight the differences between the two procedures. The values are given in Table 2.

---

[1] This is just to avoid a provider which does nothing, and so does not spend its money, to capitalize all the money.

Table 2. Providers' characteristics for comparison with the GUM selection.

		p_1	p_2	p_3	p_4	p_5	p_6	p_7	p_8	p_9	p_{10}
t1	Q	0.95	0.55	0.35	0.5	0.15	0.35	0.95	0.15	0.45	0.2
	U	-0.1	0.1	-0.4	0.1	0.6	0.4	-0.6	0.6	-0.1	0.5
t2	Q	0.45	0.65	0.55	0.1	0.6	0.35	0.05	0.15	0.6	0.45
	U	0.1	-0.5	0.5	-0.3	0.5	0.8	0.8	0.6	0.1	-0.5

The GUM selection maximizes $\sum_{i\in[1..N]} U[i] + U[requester]$. The mediation process is used with parameter $\omega = 0.5$ (which means that quality and bid are given the same importance). Each provider i's representative directly computes its bid ($B[i]$) from the provider's utility ($U[i]$) and from the money it has. For example, provider p_1 does not want to treat t_1 This is reflected by the value of the utility function. So, although p_1 has a good quality, its bid will be negative.

To compare the GUM selection and the mediation process, for each participant we measure the evolution of the difference between the participant's utility in the mediation process and its utility in the GUM selection, in function of the number of requests. Thus, in Figures 4 and 5, if the curve is positive, the participant's degree of satisfaction is higher in the mediation process.

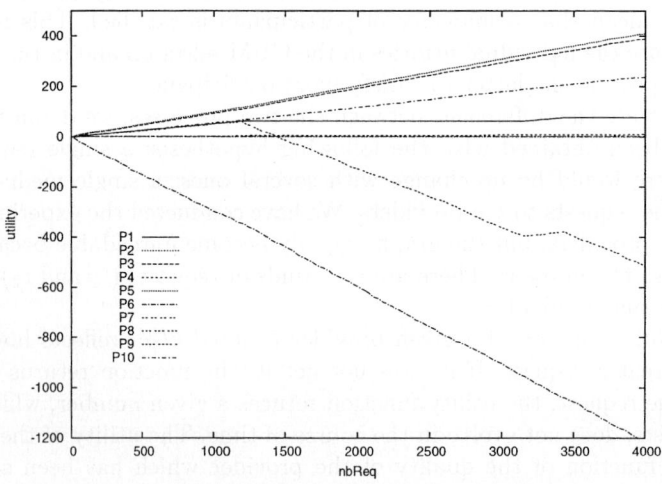

Fig. 4. Comparison with GUM selection: delta of utilities, providers case.

The two simulations treat the same requests in the same order. A glance at Figure 4 shows that a majority of providers is more satisfied with the mediation process than with the GUM selection. With our hypotheses, if provider j is selected, $\sum_{i \in [1..N]} U[i] + U[requester] = U[j] + U[requester] = U[j] + Q[j]$. Given the data of Table 2, provider p_1 (respectively p_6) maximizes the system global utility for request type t_1 (resp. t_2). So the GUM selection only selects p_1 and p_6, and, because they never change their utility function nor their quality, they monopolize all the requests. Provider p_6 is very satisfied with the GUM selection because it wants request type t_2 and gets all the requests of this type. This is why the corresponding curve in Figure 4 is the most negative one. On the contrary, provider p_1 does not want to treat request type t_1 despite its high quality. Thus, it is more satisfied with the mediation process, because the GUM selection imposes it to treat all the requests of this type until it decides to stop working with this mediator. Around 1200 requests after the begining of the mediation, p_1 indeed leaves the system because it has exceeded its tolerance threshold. This departure benefits to p_8 which was waiting to treat requests of type t_1. Accordingly, its curve starts decreasing after 1200 requests. Around 3500 requests, p_8's curve stops decreasing. This is due to p_1 which comes back just to check that it would still be imposed, and then leaves again.

The positive curves illustrate that the mediation process allocates the requests to several providers which have comparable qualities or utilities. This is important because, when coming to experiments where those parameters evolve, the GUM procedure will take into account those changes with much more difficulty because it always works with the providers it considered to be the best.

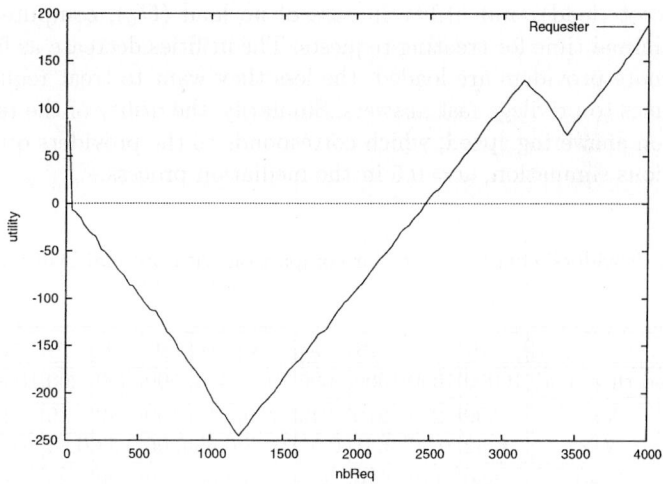

Fig. 5. Comparison with GUM selection: delta of utilities, requester case.

Figure 5 shows that while provider p_1 is selected by the GUM selection, the requester is more satisfied with this method than with the mediation process. Indeed, p_1 has a very good quality (0.95). As soon as p_1 has left the system with GUM selection and that p_1 has been replaced by p_8, the curve increases and even comes positive. Indeed, for requests of type t_1, the mediation process selects providers which have a better quality than p_8's which is very low (0.15). The changes in the curve around 3500 are due to p_1 temporary presence.

The results show that considering individual utilities, the mediation process is more interesting than the GUM selection for a majority of participants. An interesting point is to compare the system global utility in both cases, given that the GUM selection maximizes this value. The difference is measured by the ratio $= \frac{(\sum_{i \in [1..N]} u(i) + u[requester])_{medProc}}{(\sum_{i \in [1..N]} u(i) + u[requester])_{GUM}}$. The results show that the ratio varies between 80% and 92%. So the loss of global utility with the mediation process is not that important.

4.2 Comparison with an Optimal Load Balancing

This series of tests considers the same number of providers, requester and mediator, but it focuses more on the dynamics. There are still two types of requests, but the treatment times by the providers differ. Contrary to the preceeding simulation, all the providers want to treat all the types of requests, preferring the ones for which they perform the most rapidly. However they have a load threshold over which they do not ask for more requests.

Table 3 shows the providers characteristics: providers' load threshold, request treatment cost (load), and utility in case of no load (U_0), computed directly from the minimal time for treating requests. The utilities decrease as function of load. The more providers are loaded, the less they want to treat requests. This strategy comes to privilege fast answers. Similarily, the utility of the requester is also based on answering speed, which corresponds to the providers quality. Like in the previous simulation, $\omega = 0.5$ in the mediation process.

Table 3. Providers' characteristics for comparison with optimal load balancing.

		p_1	p_2	p_3	p_4	p_5	p_6	p_7	p_8	p_9	p_{10}
	load threshold	10000	1000	1000	1000	1000	400	500	300	200	1000
t_1	load	500	270	210	240	230	10	150	40	30	20
	U_0	0.52	0.39	0.51	0.56	0.48	0.95	0.06	0.33	0.54	0.67
t_2	load	550	170	220	300	210	200	10	20	35	40
	U_0	0.48	0.61	0.49	0.44	0.52	0.05	0.94	0.67	0.46	0.33

Like before, the curves in Figures 6 express the difference between the participant's utility in the mediation process and in the optimal load balancing solution; as before too, the difference takes into account past utility values.

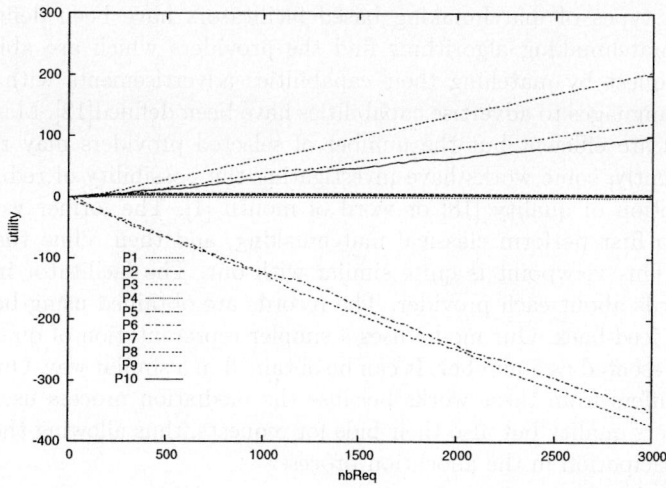

Fig. 6. Delta of utilities with optimal load balancing, providers case.

In this case too, there are more providers which are satisfied by the mediation process than by the optimal load balancing. Providers p_6 and p_7 are the only ones to prefer the optimal load balancing because they get the requests for which they perform best. In the mediation process, other providers with close qualities (p_8, p_9 and p_{10}) are more requested to treat those same requests, with their depends, but without major consequence for the requester.

Of course, the requester prefers an optimal balancing. However the ratio between the requester's utilities in both processes oscillate between 80% and 95%. So the degradation in the mediation process is not that important.

5 Related Work

In the context of distributed information systems, providing access to large numbers of distributed, heterogeneous information sources can be achieved by data mediators, matchmaking based facilitators or market approaches.

Data mediators rely on distributed database technology [19,20] to allow users to transparently query different data sources that are typically "wrapped" to provide a uniform interface to a mediator [15]. A mediator decomposes a user query into queries for the different data sources and integrates the results, much like a distributed database system. To work properly, data mediators require a global schema, typically relational or XML, to be designed over all data sources [13]. However, maintaining a global schema is difficult when source schemas change frequently or heterogeneity increases. Our solution does not require a common global schema. Furthermore, data sources are not passive since they can bid for requests provided by the mediator.

Several types of matchmaking based facilitators have been defined [5,3,8, 17]. The matchmaking algorithms find the providers which are able to treat a given request by matching their capabilities advertisements with the given request. Languages to advertise capabilities have been defined[12]. Matchmaking algorithms are efficient but the number of selected providers may remain too large. Recently, some works have investigating the possibility of reducing it by using a notion of quality [18] or word of mouth [1]. The former work clearly suggests to first perform classical matchmaking, and then refine the obtained selection. This viewpoint is quite similar with our. The facilitator in [18] uses track records about each provider. The records are obtained using benchmarks and users' feed-back. Our model uses a simpler representation of quality, which is just represented as a number. It can be obtained in a similar way. Our proposal strongly differs from these works because the mediation process uses not only the providers quality but also their bids for requests, thus allowing them a more active participation in the allocation process.

Mariposa [11] pioneered the use of a market approach for data mediators (then called distributed data manager). It uses an economical model for allocating queries to data sources based on a bidding process. The mediator broker selects a set of bids that corresponds to a set of relevant queries and has an aggregate price and delay under a bid curve provided by the user. However, the mediation procedure is simple and limited. It does not take into account providers' quality and some queries may not get processed although relevant data sources exist. The University of Michigan Digital Library (UMDL) project [4] also explores the use of auctions to treat requests. But there is no use of quality nor of requisition.

Auctions are widely recognized as a way to manage negotiation among participants. Several kinds of auctions mechanism exist [16,9]. For example, the generalized Vickrey auction selects the n best bidders who pay the price offered the $(n + 1)^{th}$ best bidder. In the purely competitive case our work looks like this generalized Vickrey auction, but it pushes generalization further because it takes into account the quality factor via ranking and theoretical bid. The mediation comes back to a generalized Vickrey auction when all the bids are positive, $\omega = 1$ (i.e. does not take quality into account), and $\varepsilon = 0$ (removing the technical parameter). If in addition, $n = 1$, it is a Vickrey auction.

Multi-attribute auctions [2,14] are another kind of generalization, which help finding goods suppliers, without considering requisition. The basic idea is that a good is not only qualified by a price but several other attributes like for instance quality. Obviously, in that case quality is attached to an item, while it is attached to the provider in our work. The technical consequence is that price and quality do not evolve the same way at all (for example, in multi-attribute auctions, the price increases if quality increases) leading to different formulas.

Imposition occurs any time a participant is obliged (required) to perform a task that it does not want to. The basic idea of fair imposition [10] is that all the participants must support the imposed one. The problem is tackled from a purely economical viewpoint, each participant sending their cost to perform the task. Fairness is obtained because the invoicing asks all participants to pay the same amount and gives a compensation to the imposed one. In the mediation, the requisition case generalizes the fair imposition mechanism, with the notion of quality and to n selected participants. It comes back to fair imposition [6] when $n = 1$ (only one selected provider), $\omega = 1$ (don't take quality into account), and $\varepsilon = 0$ (removing the technical parameter).

6 Conclusion

In this paper, we addressed the problem of mediation in large distributed information systems, considering that it does not only consist in finding relevant information providers for requests but also in finding relevant requests for providers. Our work brings several contributions: Firstly, we proposed a mediation system architecture where the mediator maintains databases about the providers capabilities and qualities, collects the providers bids for each request and uses a mediation module to select the required number of providers in a balanced way. Providers representatives were used to reduce the network load due to bidding.

Secondly, we proposed a mediation process and detailed both the selection and invoicing steps. The difficulty and the originality of this process is to take into account both the providers interest and qualities while ensuring that every request is satisfied as far as enough providers with the required capabilities are present.

Finally, we have conducted two series of tests, which have illustrated the process behaviour in the course of time. The process shows more flexibility because it avoids some providers to monopolize the requests, it gives medium quality providers the opportunity to get some requests and so give them some chance to improve their quality score. This is why the process can adapt faster to changes of the providers behaviour.

As future work, we plan to confront the mediation with a practical application, in which we can specify the obtention of the quality and the providers' strategies. We also plan to extend the mediation system architecture to several mediators, with auto-specialization according to requesters feed-backs, thus forming communities of providers and requesters sharing the same interests.

References

1. S. N. Chihiro Ono and al. Truth-based facilitator: Handling word-of-mouth trust for agent-based e-commerce. *Electronic Commerce Research*, 3, 2003.
2. E. David, R. Azoulay-Schwartz, and S. Kraus. Protocols and strategies for automated multi-attribute auctions. In *First International Conference on Autonomous Agents and Multiagent Systems (AAMAS'02)*. ACM Press, 2002.
3. K. Decker, K. Sycara, and M. Williamson. Middle-agents for the internet. In *Fifteenth International Joint Conference on Artificial Intelligence (IJCAI'97)*. Morgan Kaufmann, 1997.

4. E. Durfee, T. Mullen, S. Park, J. Vidal, and P. Weistein. *Intelligent Information Agents*, chapter Strategic Reasoning and Adaptation in an Information Economy. Springer, 1999.
5. D. Kuokka and L. Harada. Matchmaking for information agents. In *Fourteenth International Joint Conference on Artificial Intelligence (IJCAI'95)*. Morgan Kaufmann, 1995.
6. P. Lamarre and S. Cazalens. Médiation équitable dans un environnement ouvert d'agents compétitifs. In *Modèles Formels de l'Interaction*, 2003.
7. L. Mui, A. Halberstadt, and M. Mohtashemi. Notions of reputation in multi-agents systems : A review. In *First International Conference on Autonomous Agents and Multiagent Systems (AAMAS'02)*. ACM Press, 2002.
8. M. Nodine, W. Bohrer, and A. H. H. Ngu. Semantic brokering over dynamic heterogeneous data sources in infosleuth. In *International Conference on Data Engineering (ICDE)*, 1999.
9. T. W. Sandholm. *Multiagent Systems, a modern approach to Distributed Artificial Intelligence*, chapter Distributed Rational Decision Making. The MIT Press, 2001.
10. Y. Shoham and M. Tennenholtz. Fair imposition. In *Seventeenth International Joint Conference on Artificial Intelligence (IJCAI'01)*. Morgan Kaufmann, 2001.
11. M. Stonebraker, P. M. Aoki, R. Devine, W. Litwin, and M. A. Olson. Mariposa: a new architecture for distributed data. In *IEEE Int. Conf. on Data Engineering*, 1994.
12. K. Sycara, M. Klusch, and S. Widoff. Dynamic service machmaking among agents in open information environments. *ACM SIGMOD Record, Special Issue on Semantic Interoperability in Global Information Systems*, 28(1):47–53, 1999.
13. A. Tomasic, L. Raschid, and P. Valduriez. Scaling access to heterogeneous data sources with disco. *IEEE Trans. on Knowledge and Data Engineering*, 10(5), 1998.
14. N. Vulkan and N. R. Jennings. Efficient mechanisms for the supply of services in multi-agent environments. *Decision Support Systems*, 28:5–19, 2000.
15. G. Wiederhold. Mediators in the architecture of future information systems. *IEEE Computer*, 25(3), 1992.
16. E. Wolfstetter. Auctions: an introduction. *Journal of Economic Surveys*, 10(4):367–420, 1996.
17. H. C. Wong and K. Sycara. A taxonomy of middle-agents for the internet. In *Fourth International Conference on MultiAgent Systems (ICMAS 2000)*, pages 465–466, July 2000.
18. Z. Zhang and C. Zhang. An improvement to matchmaking algorithms for middle agents. In *First International Joint Conference on Autonomous Agents and Multiagent Systems (AAMAS'02)*. ACM Press, 2002.
19. T. Özsu and P. Valduriez. *Principles of Distributed Database Systems*. Prentice Hall, 2nd edition, 1999.
20. T. Özsu and P. Valduriez. *Handbook of Computer Science and Engineering*, chapter Distributed and Parallel Database Systems. CRC Press, 2nd edition, 2004.

Exception Handling Through a Workflow

Hernâni Mourão[1] and Pedro Antunes[2]

[1] Escola Superior de Ciências Empresariais, Instituto Politécnico de Setúbal, Campus do IPS –
Estefanilha, 2914-503 Setúbal, Portugal, and
LASIGE (Laboratory of Large Scale Information Systems)
hmourao@esce.ips.pt
[2] Faculdade de Ciências, Universidade de Lisboa, Departamento de Informática, Campo Grande
– Edifício C5, 1749-016 Lisboa, Portugal, and LASIGE (Laboratory of Large Scale
Information Systems)
paa@di.fc.ul.pt

Abstract. Exception handling is a fundamental functionality of workflow management systems (WfMS). User involvement in exception handling is recognized as critical in various situations due to the unpredictability nature of the exceptions that can occur in a running workflow (WF) engine. The problem however is how to orchestrate human ad hoc interventions with a minimum impact on system integrity. The control flow and data integrity dimensions of the impact are analyzed. Our perspective is to allow the maximum latitude possible to user interventions while keeping system correctness. We propose a solution that uses a WF to guide users handling WF exceptions. Furthermore, we extended the WF engine with a propagation mechanism allowing users to involve multiple members of the organization in the exception handling WF. This solution is implemented in the OpenSymphony (OS) platform. The implementation details of the proposed solution in the OS platform are also given in the paper.

1 Introduction

Exception handling in WfMS is fundamental to react to situations that differ from the normal behaviour of the designed processes and is critical to successful implementation in real world scenarios [1; 12; 24].

There are two types of events that require non-standard WF behaviour [29]: 1) some specific requirements of an instance running on the WFMS requiring special attention (*ad hoc* changes); and 2) due to new legislation, strategy or reengineering efforts the company has to change the business model (*dynamic or evolutionary change*). In the former situation, changes have an impact at the instance level, while in the later situation a new model is defined for all instances of a specific class.

Usually, the timing associated with dynamic changes allows proper planning [10]. This technique has been deeply studied [2; 4; 10; 15; 23; 25; 29].

Our work is focused on *ad hoc* interventions, where the change cannot be predicted in advance nor proper planning is usually feasible. In this type of situations the user involvement is carried out on a problem-solving basis [2; 6; 11; 14; 15; 31]. Moreover, a coordinated effort among all the persons involved in problem solving is crucial to overcome the situation.

The problem then is how to involve humans in exception identification and recovery while preserving the WF engine integrity. In this paper we developed an approach, introduced in [20], to support such human interventions. The basic solution consists in developing a toolkit of identification and recovery components. As a toolkit, this approach offers the flexibility, compositionality and extensibility necessary to allow humans handling exceptional situations. As a collection of individual components, each one must be developed to preserve the WF engine integrity. The toolkit exploitation is supported by a special WF dedicated to model and control the exception handling process (thus, exception handling is a process [10; 26]).

Two fundamental concerns have guided the implementation of this solution. One is that data describing the exceptional event is crucial to guide humans through the execution of recovery actions. The second issue is that an exception sometimes emerges as a series of events that travel throughout the organization, rather than one single exceptional event. As a consequence of these two concerns, the implemented solution also offers:

- A situation awareness component, gathering information about the exceptional events, implicated processes and engine status. This information may be gathered from the system (e.g. event types) and humans involved in the process (e.g. characterization of the exceptional event).
- An exception propagation component, allowing exceptions to propagate within the organization to a series of persons that may be involved in the identification and recovery actions. One human is always defined as being initially responsible for an exception, but can propagate the exception to other persons within the organization.

In the next section we identify and delimit the scope of our approach. Section 2 overviews related work. In section 3 we describe the concepts necessary to identify exceptions and define recovery actions. Section 4 begins with a brief introduction to the OS platform selected to implement the proposed solution and continues with a description of how the identification, situation awareness, propagation and recovery mechanisms are implemented in the platform. Finally, the last section presents the actual status of the project and indicates future work directions.

2 Scope and Limitations of Ad Hoc Interventions

Our approach is based on two fundamental assumptions: 1) the ad hoc interventions are carried out on a problem solving basis through a coordinated effort of all persons in the organization that are able to contribute; 2) the set of interventions permitted to users should be, in one way, sufficiently complete to solve the highest number of cases in the best possible way and, in the other way, sufficiently correct so that the process proceeds under engine control and without errors after the interventions.

Clearly, the first issue is a matter of Computer Supported Cooperative Work (CSCW) and will be critical to the implementation of our framework. Even though this matter is not the main objective of this paper, the work developed by [14] gives important guidelines on how to improve support to human interventions during exception recovery.

The second issue represents in some way a trade off: the higher the latitude of intervention, the higher the probability to have inconsistencies in the WF engine. Our approach was to study a large number of possible interventions and later verify their correctness. Before establishing the correctness criteria, we will discuss the various perspectives that should be taken into consideration when analyzing WfMS.

[27] identifies the following WF perspectives: 1) control flow; 2) resource or organization; 3) data or information; 4) task or function; and 5) operation or application. According to the author's arguments we will also abstract from resource, task and operation perspectives.

The data perspective will be discussed in more detail since it is a matter of some controversy. Our approach also abstracts from the control dimension. In fact, one of the primary objectives of WfMS was to remove control flow dependencies over data structures [17]. We advocate that any data inconsistencies should be identified and dealt within tasks. Moreover, the ad hoc interventions should not be constrained by data dependencies, as they can be dealt afterwards at the task level.

Our approach recognizes that a solid theoretical ground is needed to identify proper ad hoc interventions that keep the soundness (as defined in [27]) property of a WF. Therefore our focus is on the control perspective.

The concept of soundness assures that for any case the procedure terminates properly, i.e., termination is guaranteed, there are no dangling references, and deadlock and live lock are absent.

The adopted correctness criteria is slightly different from [23]:

The ad hoc interventions should not introduce any inconsistencies or errors in running instances (e.g., deadlocks or live locks). The process should be able to terminate without any other interventions under WfMS engine control after the interventions are carried out.

Finally, exceptions that can be anticipated can also be handled with some degree of planning and therefore are not the main objective of this work.

3 Related Work

Exception handling has been mainly approached with a systemic perspective. The foremost solutions were based on variations of the transactional mechanism used in database management systems. [32] has a good survey on the different methods used by this approach. Some recent solutions [3; 7; 16; 18] deal mainly with anticipated events. These approaches are very useful to increase the flexibility of WfMS by increasing their ability to adapt to different circumstances. However, a framework to support human involvement in solving exceptions has never been proposed in this context.

[14] presents an interaction framework for WF enactment. This framework is mostly important for unstructured processes and falls more on the CSCW area than on the systemic perspective. We believe that this framework is also important to guide human interventions during ad hoc operations.

[6] has one of the most complete studies of exceptions supporting human intervention. Although the cooperation of different users in solving exceptional situations is considered a critical issue, a conceptual framework to guide such approach is not proposed. We also do not see any evidence of the application of some correctness criteria.

In [26] a comprehensive model is proposed to deal with all possible types of exceptions but, again, a framework to involve the users is unavailable. The interventions dealing with unanticipated events are not presented as well.

4 Exception Handling

The exception handling process is divided in two phases: 1) exception identification; and 2) ad hoc interventions necessary to restore the system to a coherent state.

The next section describes the mechanisms necessary to identify the different classes of exceptions. The data structure that describes an exception is also detailed. The following section describes the exception recovery model and tools implemented to perform ad hoc interventions.

4.1 Exception Identification

There are several ways to identify exceptions in WF, according to different perspectives that one may apply to the problematic situation (the reader may find some orthogonal criteria for exceptions classification in the related literature [5; 8; 20; 24]). In particular, one may consider a system perspective and assume that an exception triggers an exceptional event in the system. On the other hand, some types of exceptions cannot be identified by the system and must be triggered by humans or external applications [5; 13]. The following classes of exceptional events are defined:

- Data events – Identified within the task that generates an error condition. Data events, even though identified within a particular instance, can affect a collection of instances (e.g., detection of the same trip being booked twice for the same client).
- Temporal events – Triggered on the occurrence of a given time stamp. Temporal events may be further classified into: timestamps, periodic and interval. Timestamps occur when a completion date associated with a task is not respected; periodic events occur on a determined periodical sequence (e.g., every morning at 9:00); and interval events are associated to time constraints between two tasks, e.g., the maximum time allowed after task 1 finishes before task n starts.
- WF events – Triggered during task or process start/end operations. Examples: a deadlock situation or a loop being executed more than expected.
- External events – These events are triggered from external sources. Example: a user cancels a given order.
- Noncompliance events – Triggered whenever the system cannot handle the process due to differences between modeled tasks and reality.
- System/application events – Triggered when the system is not able to recover from lower level failures, such as database or network failures (lower level failures are propagated as semantic failures [9]).

The post-functions defined by the WfMC [33] are used to identify the presence of data events upon completion of a given task. On the presence of a data error, the WF engine automatically triggers the event and instantiates the exception recovery WF.

We will now describe separately the identification mechanism for the three different classes of temporal events.

The method used to identify the *interval* class, is depicted in Figure 1 using the Petri net notation [28]. Assume that the WF designer would like to define a time interval constraint between tasks 1 and n in Figure 1.a. Figure 1.b shows how the WF specification has been changed to incorporate that constraint. If $task_n$ is executed before t1 fires, the constraint was respected and no temporal event is triggered. However, if t1 fires before $task_n$, a token is placed on p2 and the system triggers an exceptional event. The transition t2 implements the same task as $task_n$ and is inserted in the specification to assure that the WF execution will not stop on $task_n$ if a temporal event is triggered.

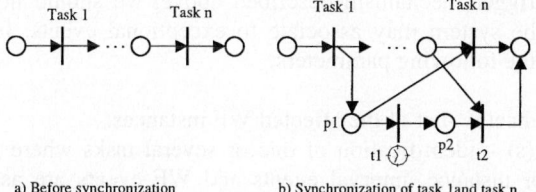

a) Before synchronization   b) Synchronization of task 1 and task n

Fig. 1. Identification mechanism for the interval class

The firing of t1 will instantiate the exception recovery WF. The running workflow can be suspended or allowed to continue depending on the specific application.

For the *timestamp* class we use a similar scheme, where $task_1$ is the initial task and $task_n$ is the task identified in the timestamp. In this situation the timer is fired when the predefined date/time is reached. The exception recovery WF is instantiated as in the above example.

Figure 2 shows the implementation of the trigger mechanism for the *periodical* class. The original model is shown at the top where $task_1$ is the first task of the WF and $task_n$ is the last one. The place p1 and transition t1 where inserted to implement the *periodical* class. While the WF instance is running, the timer is also running. When the timeout is reached, one periodical event is triggered and the timer is restarted. The timer stops with the firing of the last transition in the WF. Once again, the transition t1 instantiates the exception recovery WF.

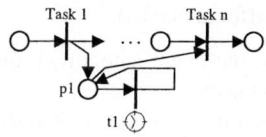

Fig. 2. Identification mechanism for the periodical class

To identify a WF event, a special condition must be inserted in the pre-functions or post-functions of every task that the WF modeler wants to monitor.

The external events are a particular category of events, because they cannot be detected by the system, as mentioned before. Thus, this type of event must be triggered by a human or external application.

The noncompliance events correspond to situations where the desired process either deviates from the model (by requiring some special treatment) or the model is not applicable to a particular context. In this type of situation the system requires some additional information regarding the model, i.e. additional tasks, tasks that should be modified or removed from the model, etc. Due to the intrinsic nature of these events, they are dependent of the specific context, which must be assessed by a human. Furthermore, these events may affect several tasks and processes.

Finally, the system/application events have characteristics similar to external events [19], although, in some circumstances, the exception may be automatically identified, e.g., the system is able to identify that a database server stopped without requiring human intervention.

Besides the trigger mechanism described above, we should now discuss the information that the system may associate to exceptional events. In this respect one should consider the following parameters:

1. Affected instance(s) –list of the affected WF instances.
2. Affected task(s) – identification of one or several tasks where the exception was identified. For instance, interval events and WF events are associated with one single task while data events may be associated with several tasks.
3. Data structures that characterize data events.
4. Expired timers, for temporal events in general.
5. Event categorization – classification of the event, as previously described.
6. A brief textual description of the event. This information applies to external events triggered by humans.
7. Model deviations – this applies to noncompliance events, and identifies a list of tasks that should be inserted, modified or removed.

We may also consider the following additional parameters:

8. Root cause – textual description, produced by a human, with the perceived root cause for an exception.
9. Person responsible – someone that may be responsible for the exception. This person may be selected by the system, from the list of persons associated to affected tasks, or selected by a human, as with the root cause mentioned above.
10. Impact – for every affected instance, the system may also provide information about deadlines and potential impact to the organization (based on metrics such as the diversity and number of affected tasks).

From the above list of items, the event categorization, affected tasks (at least one) and person responsible are mandatory.

It is now time to move forward from exception identification to recovery.

4.2 Exception Recovery

When an exceptional event is triggered, the system instantiates the WF recovery process modelled in Figure 3 and passes the several parameters identified in the previous section to the components described in this section.

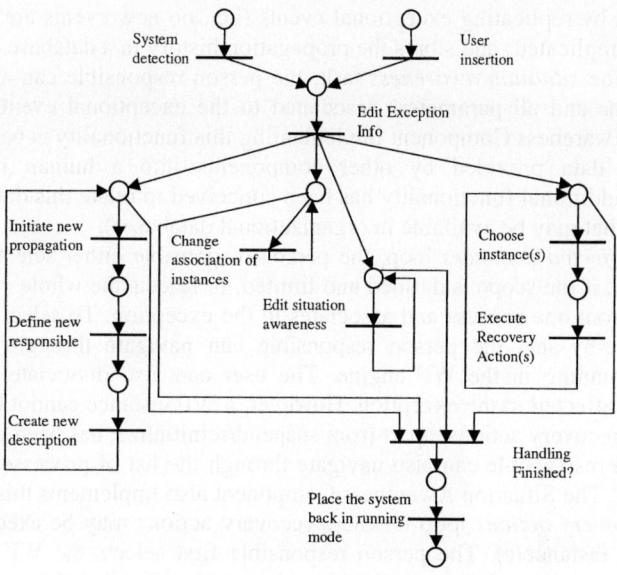

Fig. 3. Workflow Model for Exception Handling

There are two alternative ways to instantiate this process: either by *system detection* or by *user insertion*. They have been separated because these two tasks initialize the recovery process in different ways. The *system detection* task is used with the following event types: data, temporal, workflow, and system/application events. The *user insertion* task is used with external, noncompliance and system/application events (note that system/application events may be either identified by the system or by a human).

In both cases, the person responsible must have been identified, because that is the person who will be requested to execute the next action in the WF recovery process: *edit exception info*.

The purpose of this task is to specify some event parameters that the system was not able to specify, or should be redefined by a human (because human knows more about the context). E.g., the root cause falls in the first case, while the list of affected instances and person responsible fall in the second case. This task is supported by the Exception Information Component, which has a User Interface (UI) and implements the several mechanisms necessary to identify exceptional events and interface with the WF engine (e.g., access timers and process variables, or obtain the list of affected instances).

After this task the system enters in four parallel threads:
- *Exception propagation;*
- *Affected instances;*
- *Situation awareness; and*
- *Apply recovery actions.*

The *exception propagation* task allows the person responsible to propagate the event to one or several persons. This task is supported by the Exception Propagation Component, which besides other functionality, implements the propagation mechanism by replicating exceptional events (i.e., no new events are generated, they are simply replicated) and stores the propagation history in a database.

During the *situation awareness* task, the person responsible can analyze previous propagations and all parameters associated to the exceptional event. Currently, the Situation Awareness Component implementing this functionality is basically a UI that transforms data provided by other components into a human readable format (although additional functionality has been conceived to relate this data with other information that may be available in organizational databases).

In the *affected instances* loop, the person responsible either selects WF instances one-by-one, if the scope is defined and limited, or selects the whole collection of WF instances from one process and associates to the exception. To select the affected instances one-by-one, the person responsible can navigate through the list of WF instances running in the WF engine. The user can also dissociate WF instance(s) previously affected to the exception. However, a WF instance cannot be dissociated if one of the recovery actions, apart from suspend/reinitialize, has been executed over it. The person responsible can also navigate through the list of processes running in the WF engine. The Situation Awareness Component also implements this functionality.

The *recovery actions* loop is where recovery actions may be executed on the selected WF instance(s). The person responsible first selects the WF instance(s) and then chooses one of the available actions. The Toolkit Component currently implements the following list of actions:

- *Suspend/reinitialize instance(s);*
- *Ad hoc refinement;*
- *Forward and backward jumps;*
- *Terminate instance(s);*
- *Move operation; and*
- *Ad hoc extension.*

Using the *suspend/reinitialize* action, the person responsible can suspend the execution of a specific instance(s). Later on, by issuing another action, the instance(s) can be set to the running state. During the suspended state no tasks can be initiated. However, the tasks that already have started are not aborted by the system. The persons attached to those tasks are informed of the situation. These operations are not restricted since they do not affect the correctness criteria.

Using the *ad hoc refinement* action, the person responsible can perform a set of atomic activities from the list of standard WF activities, e.g., making a phone call, sending an email or writing a letter. The list of standard activities is currently small but expected to grow during system tests.

Still considering *ad hoc refinement*, another list is made available to the person responsible with all tasks defined in the affected process. The person responsible can then execute a task that was not yet executed, or repeat the execution of a task already executed. If a task is executed in advance and the user does not want to execute it twice, a marking mechanism is implemented that forces the task to be skipped when reached under model execution. The ad hoc refinement is not restricted. Based on [29], a parallel thread can be initiated, executing other tasks, while preserving the soundness of the final model. Furthermore, this is a valid transfer rule with no deadlocks and proper completion.

Backward jump skips to a previous step, while *forward jump* skips forward to another step in the WF instance.

As in [22], only *backward jumps* to actions in the history of the running instance will be allowed. However, since we advocate that the WF control evolution should be independent from WF data, we allow jumps to actions prior to loop iterations. We assume that tasks within and prior to the loop always assure the intended behavior of the loop control variables.

On the other hand, on the jump 1 in Figure 4, the system reaches a deadlock on S_5 because S_3 does not have any token. Only jump 2 is correct. To avoid this type of problem, the two rules of the following criteria must be satisfied: 1) the subnet starting at the destination place of the jump and finishing at the original place can be isolated (including every node in every branch leading from the start place to the end and every arc that finish or start on those nodes); 2) the isolated subnet is sound. The application of this rule follows from theorem 3, statement 3 in [27].

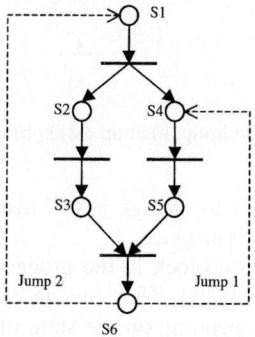

Fig. 4. Backward jump before AND-Splits

The two different ways to implement *forward jumps* are shown in figure 5. As in [22]: either the tasks in between are aborted (Figure 5.a) or executed in parallel with the tasks starting at the jump place (Figure 5.b).

If the tasks are aborted, the actual token is changed to the new place. A check must be done to assure that the system does not run into a deadlock or live lock situation. Like in backward jumps, we restrict the jump to the condition that the subnet from the origin of the jump to the target can be delimited and are sound.

On the other hand, if the tasks are executed in parallel, an AND-Split is inserted on the transition before S_1 (not show in Figure 5 for simplicity) and a task T_m (Figure 5.b) must be selected to synchronize the two parallel threads. The arc from T_n to S_n is removed and an AND-Join is inserted on task T_m with arcs from S_{m-1} and a newly created place S_k. This functionality requires modifying the model.

Figure 5 uses linear execution for simplicity. However, the operation will only be allowed if the subnets delimited from S_1 to S_{n-1} and S_n to S_{m-1} (subnets as defined above) are sound. This statement can be proved from the properties of soundness.

To implement forward task execution (as described in [22]), the person responsible can use *ad hoc refinement* to execute the task and mark the tasks to be skipped (as mentioned before). This way, the task is executed during exception handling and skipped whenever reached during standard execution of the model.

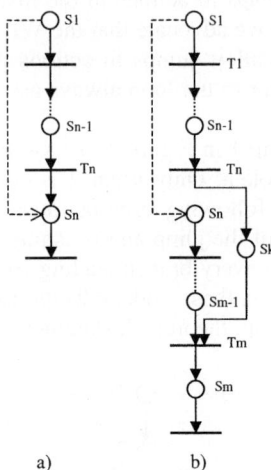

Fig. 5. Forward jump. a) abort tasks; b) parallel execution

To *terminate an instance* is to change a WF instance to the end state. No more actions will be executed on that instance.

The *move operation* moves a block in the process to a new location, keeping the remainder of the model unchanged. This change can only be executed if the final model is sound. Moreover, depending on the state of the instance, this operation can have different impact; hence, if there is more than 1 instance affected by this change, the dynamic change bug (as introduced in [11]) must be taken into consideration [29]. Our approach is to group instances according to their current state and apply different operations over each group.

Ad hoc extensions have a broader scope and a deeper impact on WF instance(s), since the person responsible can select an alternative path or choose a whole new model. On the alternative path scenario, we impose the restriction that only one thread is being executed on the instance. A check is made on the soundness property of the new path. If there is more than one instance affected, the change operation can be applied only to those instances with tokens on the same places. Our approach is to group instances as in the previous situation.

For the new model situation, a correspondence must be established between every place where the current instance has a token and a place in the new model (called destination places from now on). To check consistency, a new place is inserted in the new model with an arc to an AND-Split. This new AND-Split will have arcs for every destination place. If this model is sound, the operation can be carried out. As in the previous situations, the dynamic change bug must be taken into consideration when several instances are affected. If the change cannot be performed to all instances, different change operations (for different target models) will be carried out. Some special care will have to be taken on backward jumps after this operation: no further backward jumps to destinations in the old sub-model should be allowed.

Once the recovery actions are executed and the system is back to a coherent state, the system executes the last transition, *place the system back in running mode*, and the exception handling is complete.

5 Implementation in the OpenSymphony Platform

The adopted OS is an open source platform that implements a WF engine, user and role validation, a timer component, persistence store of WF application data and Web interfaces. All components are developed in Java and run over a Servlet container. WF models are stored in XML files.

The next section introduces the platform and the two following sections describe the implementation of exception identification and recovery.

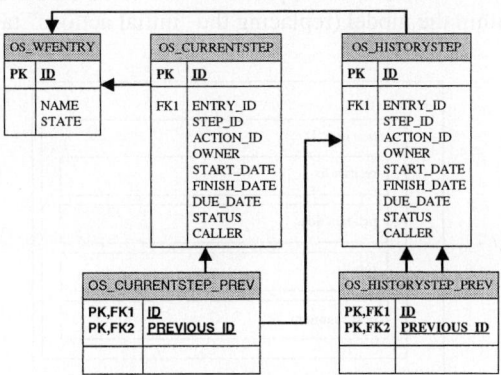

Fig. 6. OpenSymphony referential model

5.1 OpenSymphony Platform

The "osworkflow" component of the OS platform implements the WF engine. This component stores the WF relevant data in a RDBMS. Figure 6 represents the complete set of tables and their relationships in the OS referential model.

The main table, OS_WFENTRY, after the workflow instance has been initialized, is shown in Figure 7. The ID field is the key for the WF instance, the NAME is the file with the model, and STATE indicates whether this instance is activated, suspended or completed.

ID	NAME	STATE
...	...	...
32	example.xml	Activated
...	...	...

Fig. 7. OS_WFENTRY table after the example initialization

When a new instance is created, the WF engine inserts a new row in the table with a generated ID field and the file name selected by the caller. After successfully execution of the initialization tasks, the field STATE is set to *activated*.

An example of the sequence of methods to create a workflow instance is:
```
Workflow wf = new BasicWorkflow(username);
long id = wf.initialize("example", initAction, mapIs)
```

The first method initializes the class and sets an internal variable with the username of the user logged in the system. The second method creates and initializes the new instance. The first parameter is the name of the XML file with the model, the `initAction` variable indicates the number of the action to be executed, and `mapIs` is a set of key to value pairs used by the action.

In the OS platform states are named steps. For every step there is a list with the actions available for execution. Figure 8 shows the typical hierarchical organization of a step with a listing of actions 1 to n. The elements of action 1 are also shown. The step in Figure 8 is the initial step for the WF and is named "initial actions". For the remaining steps in an OS model, the upper element has a NAME and ID that uniquely identify the step within the model (replacing the "initial actions" tag in the Figure 8).

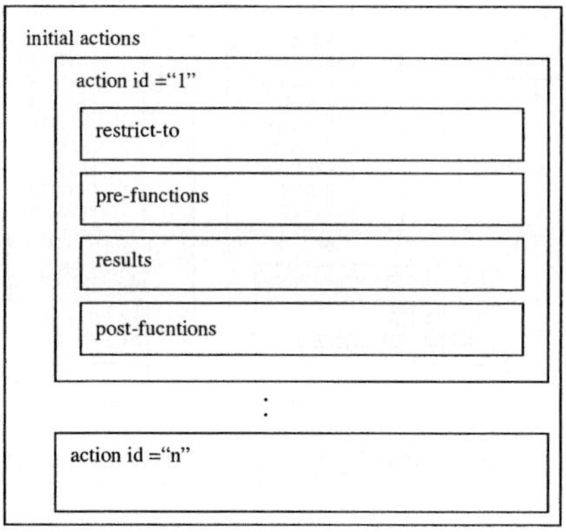

Fig. 8. Hierarchical organization of a step in the OS platform

To initialize the WF using action ID 1, the variable `initAction` must be equal to 1 in the `wf.initialize` method.

As represented in Figure 8, one action can contain four distinct elements: *restrict-to*, *pre-functions*, *results*, and *post-functions*.

The *restrict-to* element is composed by a series of conditions that must be evaluated to true to allow the execution of the action, e.g., only users that belong to a given role can execute that action.

After evaluating the conditions, the engine executes the *pre-functions*. They can implement tasks and set variables before the state transition takes place.

The next element is named *results* and is used to control the transition, i.e., the next step for the WF instance. Each element *results* can have 0 or more *conditional results* elements but must have at least one *unconditional result* element [21]. This structure can be compared to a "case" statement in a typical programming language where the element "case else" is mandatory. The first conditional element that is evaluated to true is executed. If none of the conditional elements is true the unconditional element is executed.

Let us assume that there are no conditional elements in action 1 and the unconditional element is:

```
<unconditional-result old-status="Finished"
        status="Run" step="1" owner="$(caller)"/>
```

The *unconditional result* indicates to the WF engine the number of the next step and a set of values to be stored in the database. This information is usually referred as WF relevant data [33] and will be described bellow.

After the transition takes place, the *post-functions* are executed (e.g., send an email to a user indicating that the action in the new step of the WF instance is ready to be executed).

To store the information about the current states of the various WF instances running on the system, the OS uses the table OS_CURRENTSTEP. Figure 9 lists the table field values after the successful initialization using action 1. The ID field is the key of this table that is automatically generated and ENTRY_ID is the foreign key to reference the WF entry table. The fields STEP_ID, OWNER, and STATUS reflect the attributes specified in the *unconditional result* element. The OWNER field is specified in the attribute owner and, assuming the username that triggered the initialization process was "Joao", is the value shown in Figure 9. The state assumed by the WF instance after the transition takes place is stored in the STEP_ID field and is defined in the attribute *step* (1 in the example). Finally, the attribute *status* specifies the field STATUS of the table and can assume any value.

ID	ENTRY_ID	STEP_ID	ACTION_ID	OWNER	START_DATE	FINISH_DATE	DUE_DATE	STATUS	CALLER
5	32	1		Joao	4/4/2004 11:50:33			Run	

Fig. 9. OS_CURRENTSTEP table after the example initialization

The fields ACTION_ID, FINISH_DATE, and CALLER are set to null because they will be used when the next action, executed on step 1, is performed. The DUE_DATE field could have been used to set the desired due date for this task.

The *conditional and unconditional results* correspond to an OR-Split, i.e., various conditional results being tested and only one defining the next step means that the direction of the flow is chosen by the executed element. The AND-Split has a slightly more difficult definition that is out of the scope of this document. Nevertheless, if an AND-Split is executed, the table OS_CURRENTSTEP will have 2 entries for this instance.

After the transition takes place, i.e., the entries in the database are changed, the WF engine executes the *post-functions*. Then, the instance becomes idle until another action is performed over it. In the example, the WF is on step ID 1 waiting for any user-triggered action or any automatic action (the OS platform has a special type of actions, called automatic actions, which are automatically fired when the engine reaches the step where they are defined). The XML model files must have entries for every reachable step.

Assume now, that action number 3 (defined in step 1 of example.xml) is later executed by username Joao on 6/4/2004 15:30:45. The row in Figure 9 is copied to the OS_HISTORYSTEP table and a new row is inserted in OS_CURRENTSTEP table reflecting the results of action 3. Figure 10 lists the table OS_HISTORYSTEP.

ID	ENTRY _ID	STEP _ID	ACTION _ID	OWNER	START_ DATE	FINISH _DATE	DUE _DATE	STATUS	CALLER
5	32	1	3	Joao	4/4/2004 11:50:33	6/4/2004 15:30:45		Run	Joao

Fig. 10. OS_HISTORYSTEP table after execution of action 2

Figure 10 shows the fields ACTION_ID, FINISH_DATE, and CALLER with the values already settled and defined by the execution of action 3.

Figure 11 displays the state transition diagram for the engine and summarizes the above description.

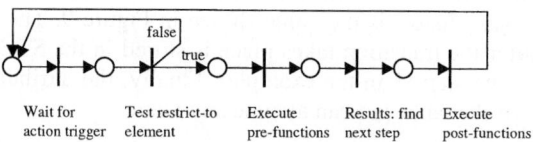

Fig. 11. State transition of the OS engine

To continue execution, the WF engine has methods to identify what are the available actions that a specific user can perform on a WF. These methods use the workflow ID to retrieve the actions defined in the model for the step.

Finally, the tables OS_CURRENTSTEP_PREV and OS_HISTORYSTEP_PREV identify the action executed before the current step and link the history of the tasks executed in the WF, respectively.

5.2 Exception Identification in the OS Platform

The process described in the previous section is used to create a new instance in the exception recovery WF, while the initialization of the exception related information is achieved through database utilities out of the scope of this paper. We will limit our description to the implementation of the exception triggering mechanisms.

The data events are implemented through the last pre-function element of the action. It identifies the presence of a data event and instantiates the exception recovery model. A post-function is also inserted to change the WF state to *suspended* if indicated in the data structure generated by the event. If the violated constraint is a generic rule, the other instance(s) that violates the constraint could also be identified and suspended if desired.

All temporal events are supported by the *Quartz* component provided by the OS platform, which implements a time triggering mechanism. Note also that a place in a Petri net is a step is OS and a transition is the set formed by the "pre-functions", "results" and "pos-functions. Their implementation in the OS platform is trivial, given the equivalence relation just mentioned, and therefore out of the scope of this paper.

In the case of an *end task*, a pre-function element is inserted in the action to identify the presence of an exceptional situation. For the *start task*, the functionality is implemented in a post-function. If the instance must be suspended, a post-function implements the functionality just after the transition takes place.

For the *start instance*, the test is carried out in the post-functions of the initial action and for the *end instance* a pre-function is inserted in the final action.

Finally, the system and application events are identified using the catch mechanism of programming languages. If during the execution of some code (condition, pre-functions, post-functions, or a user defined task) a non-caught exception construct from the program is raised, the code should instantiate the exception recovery WF. The decision whether the instance is suspended or not should depend on the code being executed, type of exception and application.

5.3 Exception Recovery in the OS Platform

To implement the exception recovery process, the model shown in Figure 3 was developed in an XML file, and the interfaces to propagate an exception, affect instances and edit descriptions were built using JSP to run over a Web environment.

As in the previous section, we will only describe the implementation of the various recovering tools used in the model.

The changes in the WF models of the OS platform are accomplished by editing the XML model file. A special method was developed to change the WF model used by a particular WF instance. This method will be used in various operations and changes the field NAME in the OS_WFENTRY table. A log entry is also generated for this operation. The description of the version system used in the new models is out of the scope of this paper.

In the tool *suspend/reinitialize instances(s)*, the field STATE of the WF OS_WFENTRY table is used. The *suspended* value in this field indicates that the WF instance cannot start any activity.

If a task started before the instance changes to the suspended state, a step transition can take place. The system should send messages to the person(s) executing manual tasks and to the supervisors of the automatic tasks.

In the *ad hoc refinement tool*, the list of standard actions is defined in a dedicated XML file. Some changes had to be made to the OS platform to support the execution of these actions within the scope of the instance. A WF model designer has to verify the modifications and inserts them in the model.

For the actions defined in the model of the running instance no special code was developed. These actions are listed to the user that can select the desired one.

To implement *forward and backward jumps* a new action is inserted in every step that uses the number of the destination step as a parameter.

To identify whether we are in the presence of a backward jump or a forward jump, the OS_HISTORYSTEP table is verified. If the destination step is in the table for this instance, we are in the presence of a backward jump, otherwise we must investigate the presence of a forward jump.

To allow a backward jump, the subnet, as defined in the exception recovery section, is identified. As this version of the system does not verify the soundness property of the models, we will restrict backward jumps to steps where the subnet only implements the sequence pattern, as defined in [30]. Later versions will implement the functionalities mentioned in the exception recovery section.

To investigate the presence of a forward jump, a simple algorithm is used to generate a tree of reachable steps from the current position. Once the destination step is found, we are in a presence of a forward jump. Any loop is iterated only once. A depth limit can be defined for complex models. If the step is reachable, the forward jump may be permitted. Again, as in backward jumps, only jumps in sequence patterns will be allowed.

If the user wants to implement a *forward jump* with parallel execution of the tasks between the actual step and the destination, the model must be changed. An AND-Split is inserted on the actual step and a task must be selected to synchronize the two parallel threads. An AND-Join is inserted on the task.

To *terminate an instance*, the field STATE of the OS_WFENTRY table is changed to *completed*.

The *move operation* requires model file modifications by a WF modeler to change the position of the task or block of tasks. Again, as the check for the soundness property is not implemented yet, this version will only allow changes of a block that only implements the sequence pattern and is moved in the limits of a branch that also implements the sequence pattern. If more than one instance with different step numbers are affected, the operation is divided into groups, as described in the exception recovery section. The change operation is implemented for every group. In some situations different models must be defined for different groups (when the instance state is between the previous position of the block and the new position), while in others only the matching between the original step number and the destination is different. E.g., assume a block was moved forward and there was no problem to execute the block twice. The instances that were executing a task in the middle of the block would become with the step number of the action that was positioned immediately after the block before the operation was carried out. This way it is assured that these instances do not skip the tasks that are between the old and the new positions of the block. All other instances keep the step number.

In the alternative path of the *ad hoc extension*, the user chooses another WF model from a list with a predefined new trajectory for the remaining steps. As described in the exception recovery section, the instances are grouped according to their actual step. The new model must have one step number equal to the present step in the instances. The correctness of the new model is based on the same assumption of every model in the system: the WF modeler has enough knowledge to construct sound models.

In an *ad hoc extension* every step number of every active thread in the affected instance(s) must have been defined. Again, to overcome the dynamic change bug, different models can be generated according to the different combination of steps in the different instances.

In the two previous cases, if there are no available models the user contacts the WF modeler to develop a new one.

6 Actual Status and Future Work

Two field tests and a simulation of the described system are in their initial phases. The field tests are being carried out in a Portuguese Port Authority and a design company, while the simulation tests are being carried out in a multinational automobile manufacturing company. The sizes of the two organizations involved in field tests are significantly different: the port authority has around 200 employees, while the design company has 10. By using different type of companies and different sizes we expect to understand how the system behaves in very different scenarios.

The completeness of the approach has to be validated, i.e., we have to test whether the implemented functionalities are complete enough to solve the exceptional situations that emerge in field tests. Some metrics used to evaluate the various ad hoc interventions will enable the selection of the most appropriate one for a given scenario in the future.

The impact on the number of models due to the number of instances affected by the exceptions will also be evaluated. The result of this evaluation will identify the need for the implementation of solutions for the dynamic change bug.

A test of the soundness property will increase the capability of the operations in various situations. This functionality will be developed in future versions.

On the other end, the growth of the standard list of actions used in ad hoc refinement will improve the system capability to deal with exceptions. The evolution of the list in the different scenarios will also be a matter of further research.

A log system that stores all the actions and propagations performed on every exception will be used to suggest strategies for similar situations. The mapping mechanism is a matter for later study.

We also expect to contribute to the development of the OS platform by increasing its flexibility to deal with exceptional situations.

References

1. Agostini, A., and De Michelis, G., 2000. Improving Flexibility of Workflow Management Systems. In: W.D. van der Aalst, J. Oberweis (Editor), BPM: Models, Techniques, and Empirical Studies. Springer-Verlag, pp. 218-234.
2. Agostini, A., and De Michelis, G., 2000. A light workflow management system using simple process models. Computer Supported Cooperative Work, 9(3): 335-363.
3. Casati, F., Ceri, S., Paraboschi, S., and Pozzi, G., 1999. Specification and Implementation of Exceptions in Workflow Management Systems. ACM Transactions on Database Systems, 24(3): 405-451. ACM Press.
4. Casati, F., Ceri, S., Pernici, B., and Pozzi, G., 1996. Workflow Evolution. Data and Knowledge Engineering, 24(3): 211-238.
5. Casati, F., and Pozzi, G., 1999. Modelling exceptional behaviors in commercial workflow management systems. Proc. IFCIS, CoopIS '99. UK, pp. 127-138.
6. Chiu, D.K., Li, Q., and Karlapalem, K., 2001. WEB Interface-Driven Cooperative Exception Handling in ADOME Workflow Management System. Information Systems, 26(2): 93-120. Elsevier Publishers.
7. Dayal, U., Hsu, M., and Ladin, R., 1991. A Transactional Model for Long-Running Activities. 17th VLDB'91. Barcelona, Spain.
8. Eder, J., and Liebhart, W., 1995. The Workflow Activity Model WAMO. Int. Conf. on Cooperative Information Systems. Vienna, Austria.
9. Eder, J., and Liebhart, W., 1996. Workflow Recovery. 1st CoopIS'96. IEEE International, Brussels, Belgium, pp. 124 - 134.
10. Ellis, C., and Keddara, K., 2000. A Workflow Change is a Workflow. In: W.D. van der Aalst, J. Oberweis (Editor), BPM: Models, Techniques, and Empirical Studies. Springer-Verlag, pp. 201-217.
11. Ellis, C., Keddara, K., and Rozenberg, G., 1995. Dynamic change within workflow systems. Proc. of Conf. on Organizational Computing Systems. ACM Press, Milpitas, CA, USA, pp. 10-21.

12. Ellis, C., and Nutt, G.J., 1993. Modeling and enactment of workflow systems. Application and Theory of Petri Nets. Springer-Verlag, USA, pp. 1-16.
13. Heinl, P., 1998. Exceptions During Workflow Execution. EDBT'98. Spain.
14. Jorgensen, H.D., 2001. Interaction as Framework for Flexible Workflow Modelling. Group '01. ACM Press, Boulder, Colorado, USA.
15. Kammer, P.J., Bolcer, G.A., Taylor, R.N., and Bergman, M., 2000. Techniques for Supporting Dynamic and Adaptive Workflow. Computer Supported Cooperative Work, 9(3): 269-292.
16. Klein, M., and Dellarocas, C., 2000. A Knowledge-Based Approach to Handling Exceptions in Workflow Systems. Computer Supported Cooperative Work, 9(3): 399-412. Kluwer Academic Publishers.
17. Leymann, F., 1997. Workflow-based applications. IBM Systems Journal, 36(1): 102-123.
18. Luo, Z., 2001. Knowledge sharing, Coordinated Exception Handling, and Intelligent Problem Solving for Cross-Organizational Business Processes. PhD Thesis, University of Georgia.
19. Mourão, H.R., and Antunes, P., 2003. Suporte à Intervenção de Operadores no Tratamento de Excepções em Fluxos de Trabalho. 4ª CAPSI. Porto, Portugal, pp. 29-42.
20. Mourão, H.R., and Antunes, P., 2003. Supporting Direct User Interventions in Exception Handling in Workflow Management Systems. 9th CRIWG 2003. Springer-Verlag, France, pp. 159-167.
21. The OpenSymphony project. Http://www.opensymphony.com2001, 20-04-2001.
22. Reichert, M., Dadam, P., and Bauer, T., 2003. Dealing with Forward and Backward Jumps in Workflow Management Systems. Software and Systems Modeling, 2(1): 37-58. Springer-Verlag.
23. Rinderle, S., Reichert, M., and Dadam, P., 2003. Evaluation of Correctness Criteria for Dynamic Workflow Changes. BPM '03. Springer-Verlag, Netherlands, pp. 41-57.
24. Saastamoinen, H., 1995. On the Handling of Exceptions in Information Systems. PhD Thesis, University of Jyväskylä.
25. Sadiq, S.W., 2000. Handling Dynamic Schema Change in Process Models. ADC 2000. 11th Australasian. IEEE International, pp. 120-126.
26. Sadiq, S.W., 2000. On Capturing Exceptions in Workflow Process Models. 4th International Conference on Business Information Systems. Poznan, Poland.
27. van der Aalst, W., 2000. Workflow Verification: Finding Control-Flow Errors using Petri-net-based Techniques. In: BPM: Models, Techniques, and Empirical Studies. Springer-Verlag, Berlin, pp. 161-183.
28. van der Aalst, W., 2002. Workflow Management. MIT Press, London, England.
29. van der Aalst, W., and Basten, T., 2002. Inheritance of workflows: an approach to tackling problems related to change. Theoretical Computer Science, 270(1): 125-203.
30. van der Aalst, W., Hofstede, A.H.T., Kiepuszewski, B., and Barros, A., 2002. Workflow Patterns, QUT Technical report, FIT-TR-2002-02.
31. Voorhoeve, M., and van der Aalst, W., 1997. Ad-hoc workflow: problems and solutions. Database and Expert Systems Applications, 1997, pp. 36-40.
32. Worah, D., and Sheth, A.P., 1997. Transactions in Transactional Workflows. In: S.K. Jajodia, Larry (Editor), Advanced Transaction Models and Architectures. Kluwer.
33. Workflow Management Coalition - Terminology & Glossary TC00-1011, 1999, Document Number WFMC-TC-1011, Issue 3.0. WFMC.

A Flexible and Composite Schema Matching Algorithm[*]

Shoujian Yu[1], Zhongming Han[1], and Jiajin Le[2]

College of Information Science and Technology, Donghua University,
1882 West Yan'an Road, Shanghai, China, 200051
[1] {Jackyysj, hx_zm}@mail.dhu.edu.cn
[2] Lejiajin@dhu.edu.cn

Abstract. Schema matching is a key operation in meta-information applications. In this paper, we propose a new efficient schema matching algorithm to find both direct element correspondences and indirect element correspondences. Our algorithm sufficiently exploits semantic, structure and instance information of two schemas. It has advantages of various kinds of algorithms and hence a learning methodism.

1 Introduction

Meta-information is a general approach to building large scale information systems and it is a management tool for information, the information representations include XML, relation and object, etc.. To efficiently integration and management different structural information is a challenge task, schema matching is crucial to this task. Meanwhile schema matching also is a key operation in many applications, e.g. data integration, information grid, data grid, schema integration, and semantic query processing, etc.. Nowadays, many schema matching tasks are done manually by domain experts. The schema matching problem at the most basic level refers to the problem of how to find the elements correspondences between source schema and target schema.

The elements matching result can be simple, direct 1:1 match or complex, indirect 1:n (n:1) match.. Recently, most researchers [4, 6, 11, 17] paid an attention to direct element match based on semantic and structure or based on a hybrid or composite match method. Such simplicity, however, is rarely efficient. Other researchers have thus proposed some new mechanisms to find indirect element correspondence. Most of automating schema algorithms can be cataloged into two classifications: *Instance* and *schema*. The first class of matching approaches takes instance data or data contents into account to find the element correspondence. On the other hand, the second class of matching approaches focuses on schema-level information including elements names, domains and schema structure, etc..

---

[*] This work has been partially supported by The National High Technology Research and Development Program of China (863 Program) under contract 2002AA4Z3430.

In our intuition, any single approach cannot fully exploit the information contained in a schema. To get better match results, the advantages of these two classes of approaches should be combined. Furthermore from some experimental results, we see that a good learning mechanism is effective in improving match results. Based on the above consideration, we proposed a new match algorithm with which we can discover both direct element correspondences and indirect element correspondences. In this paper, we make the following contributions: (1) Present an approach combining structure and instance schema matching; (2) Propose a new measure of match accuracy. (3) Conduct experiments to evaluate our algorithm.

The paper is structured as follows. In Section 2, we review related work. A general reference model for different schema representation is proposed in Section 3. Similarity matrix and a new measure are introduced in Section 4. A formula to compute similarity is proposed In Section 5. The matching process is discussed in Section 6. The experimental results of our matching algorithm are discussed in Section 7. Finally we have some concluding remarks in Section 8.

2 Related Work

Schema-based match algorithms take account of schema information and ignore instance data. The available information includes usual attributes of schema elements, such as name, description, data type, various relationships (part-of, is-a, etc.), constraints, and schema structure. Clio [1, 2], COMA [3], Cupid [4], Similarity Flooding (SF) [8], SKAT [9,10] fall into this category. Generally speaking, multiple match candidates can be found in this type of algorithms. For each candidate, it is customary to estimate the degree of similarity by using a number in [0,1], in order to identify the best match candidates.

When schema-based matching fails, the next logical step is to check the data stored in the schemas. The corresponding approaches are called instance-based match [11, 12]. Many researchers exploit machine-learning mechanism to match different schema. However these methods need the training phase and a lot of instances data to be found. Many algorithms including the above-mentioned algorithms are compared in the recent survey papers [12, 13, 14] of schema matching algorithms.

SemInt [5, 6, 7] represents a hybrid approach exploiting both schema and instance information to identify elements while neural-network is used in the learning process. However the method focuses on relational schemas. In [15], one novel approach is presented in which schemas are matched by combining schema-based matching and attribute context matching technology. This method can detect many indirect semantic correspondences between a source schema S and a target schema T besides the direct correspondences. However this approach uses regular expression of ontology made by domain experts to find indirect correspondences and it lacks an efficient learning mechanism. The algorithm in [16] is a mixed algorithm, which combines several methods with the emphasis on using the context provided by the way elements which are embedded in paths. The method developed in this paper tries to solve the n:m matching problem with the user manual input.

3 General Reference Model

Usually, each schemas has its own representation. In order to match different schemas under a uniform framework; many researchers use a medial representation, such as a tree [19], rooted directed graph [20] or RDF [18], etc.. We also use a general reference model to represent different schemas, and it is represented by a rooted directed graph. Nodes are the elements in the schema, and edges are relationships between elements. A general reference model (GRM) is a 4-tuple (E, DO, C, R), where: E is a finite set of elements. DO is the domain of elements. C is a finite set of constraints defined on elements. R is a finite set of relationships defined on elements.

An element of GRM can be an atomic element (e) or a composite element (ce). The former is of form $n_e = d_e$, where n_e is the name of the element and d_e is the domain of element. Unless the element is a key, elements may be single valued or multi valued. The latter contains other elements as sub-elements. We defer detail discussion of our model to the full paper.

We need some general types to serve as the domains of elements. The general types include char(n), integer, float, datetime, Boolean and binary object. In our opinion, these types represent most of the types defined in all models.

Structure relationships between elements can be divided into three categories:

Dependency/ Reference. This type of relationships reflects Dependency/ Reference links of two elements. In relational models, the foreign key or functional dependence is just this type of relation.

Is-Derived-From /Is-Type-Of. This type of relationship can be used to model the shared information. Schemas with them can be an arbitrary graph (e.g. cycles in recursive types). In OO models, Is-Derived-From connects a subtype to its supertype.

Containment. This is a basic hierarchal relation between elements in a general reference model. For example, a table contains its columns. An XML attribute is contained by an XML element.

4 Similarity Matrix and Measure

Firstly, we introduce the similarity matrix $(a_{ij})_{n \times m}$, it is a matrix representing the similarity of every pair of leaf elements, where n is the number of leaf elements in the source schema and m is the number of leaf elements in the target schema and a_{ij} equal to 1 if and only if source element e_i matches to target element e_j, otherwise its value is 0.

To provide a basis for assessing the quality of automatic match strategies, the match task has to be manually done by domain experts firstly. The obtained match results are used as the standard to assess the quality of the result automatically determined by the match system. With the similarity matrix, we can use the Hamming distance to measure the quality of schema matching. However, other usual measures, such as *Precision, Recall* and *Overall*, can also be computed.

Let A_1 and A_2 be similarity matrices formed by using our algorithm and by domain experts respectively (It means that A_2 is the real match results matrix). We denote the Hamming distance of the two matrices by $HD(A_1, A_2)$. Then we define our quality measure $H_{Measure}$ in the form

$$H_{Measure} = 1 - \frac{HD(A_1, A_2)}{n+m},$$

where n and m are the number of 1 in the similarity matrices A_1 and A_2 respectively.

If $A_1 = A_2$, which means that the match result obtained by our algorithm is the same as the match result determined by domain experts, then $H_{Measure} = 1$. If $HD(A_1, A_2) = 0$, then $H_{Measure} = 0$, which indicates that none of match results is true.

Unlike *Precision* and *Recall*, our measure takes both truth element match pairs and true negatives into account, it shows the trade-off between true positives and true negatives among all match pairs. Our measure get over the problem that *Recall* can easily be maximized at the expense of a poor *Precision* by returning all possible match pairs. In addition, a high *Precision* can be achieved at the expense of a poor *Recall* by returning only few (correct) match pairs. Meanwhile our measure doesn't have negative values, which the measure *Overall* could have. To some extent, another measure *F-Measure* is same to our measure, if every match pair is one 1:n match is viewed as one correspondence. However, to our knowledge, we do not how to compute *F-Measure* for 1:n match.

5 Computing Similarity Matrix

5.1 Linguistic Similarity

The linguistic similarity between two atomic elements is mainly related to element name, data type. In the absence of data instances, these conditions are probably the most useful source of information for matching. We use WordNet [21] to help us in evaluating the name similarity.

The linguistic similarity degree SI_l is computed by the formula.

$$SI_l(e_i, e_j) = w_{11} si_{l1}(e_i, e_j) + w_{12} si_{l2}(e_i, e_j)$$

where w_{11} and w_{12} are weights such that $0 \leq w_{11}, w_{12} \leq 1$ and $w_{11} + w_{12} = 1$, $si_{l_1}(e_i, e_j)$ is the similarity degree of (e_i, e_j) computed by means of WordNet and $si_{l_2}(e_i, e_j)$ is the similarity degree of the compatible coefficient of different data types defined by domain experts.

5.2 Path Similarity

A path of atomic element is a list of elements from root to the atomic element. In our reference data model, every atomic element is reachable from the root element.

The path similarity is computed by the formula:

$$SI_p(e_i, e_j) = \frac{\sum_{k=1}^{m} w_k SI_l(e_{i_k}, e_{j_k})}{m}$$

where e_{i_k} and e_{j_k} are ancestor of e_i and e_j respectively, w_k is the weight such that $0 \leq w_k \leq 1, k = 1, 2, \cdots m$ and $\sum_{k=1}^{m} w_k = 1$, $m = \min(N_s, N_t)$ with N_s and N_t being the length of paths of e_i and e_j respectively.

Usually, one element could have more than one path. Then path similarity for each path is computed, so path similarity of one element pair could have more than one value, we choose the maximum value as the last path similarity.

5.3 Structure Similarity

To compute structure similarity is a challenging task, many researchers exploit the similarity of surrounding elements, e.g. parent and child elements, to compute the similarity. It is certainly reasonable. However, all kinds of dependencies are more important in evaluating similarity and should be considered.

For any atomic element, it could be an element that (1) some elements are dependent on it, we call it K-element; (2) it is dependent on other element, we name it D-element; (3) it is an isolated element. We call it I-element. Usually, one element could be an element that satisfies (1) and (2), then we deal with it as a D-element. If one element is a K-element, then we denoted the set of elements that are dependent on it by $[e] = \{e_j \mid e \rightarrow e_j\}$. We call this set equivalent class of element e.

Now, we can compute structure similarity. Let se, te be source element and target element respectively, then we have the following cases.

If one of se and te is a I-element, then $SI_s(se, te) = SI_l(se, te)$.

If both se and te are D-element, then we have

$$SI_s(se,te) = w_1 SI_l(se,te) + w_2 SI_l(se',te')$$

where se, te are dependent on se' and te' respectively. w_1 and w_2 are weights such that $0 \le w_1, w_2 \le 1$ and $w_1 + w_2 = 1$

If one of se and te is a K-element and other is a D-element. Without loss of generality we can let se be a K-element and te be a D-element. Then

$$SI_s(se,te) = w_1 SI_l(se,te) + w_2 SI_l(se,te')$$

where te are dependent on element te'. w_1 and w_2 are weights such that $0 \le w_1, w_2 \le 1$ and $w_1 + w_2 = 1$

The most difficult match case is that both se and te are K-element. We use the following intuition to treat this case.

(I) If two elements belong to two equivalent classes of two similar K-elements, they could be similar.

(II) If most of members in two equivalent classes are similar, then two K-elements are similar.

Based on our intuition, we calculate the structure similarity of every pair (se, te) by the formula:

$$SI_s(se,te) = \begin{cases} SI_s(se,te) + |SI_s(se,te) - AV(i)| & AV(i) \ge TH_s \\ SI_s(se,te) - |SI_s(se,te) - AV(i)| & AV(i) < TH_s \end{cases}$$

$$SI_s(se_i,te_i) = \begin{cases} SI_s(se_i,te_i) + |SI_s(se,te) - AV(i)| & SI_s(se,te) \ge AV(i) \\ SI_s(se_i,te_i) - |SI_s(se,te) - AV(i)| & SI_s(se,te) < AV(i), AV(i) < TH_s \\ SI_s(se_i,te_i) & SI_s(se,te) < AV(i), AV(i) \ge TH_s \end{cases}$$

where $se_i \in [se], te_i \in [te]$, m is the number of element pairs, and TH_s is a threshold of structure similarity. $AV(i) = \dfrac{\sum_{i=1}^{m} SI_l(se_i, te_i)}{m}$.

5.4 Knowledge Similarity

In our opinion, knowledge is very efficient tool for complex matching such as 1:n or n:1 or general n:m matching, because it is difficult to find out relationships between one element and multiple other elements according to the semantic and structure analysis.

We construct a knowledge repository for a complex object, which consists of complex objects. Usually, an object could have more than one type of combination. We define a knowledge similarity for each combination. Once we find one element with a higher similarity to more than one element, then we will check knowledge similarity.

5.5 Combination of Similarity

By now, we have similarity of linguistic similarity, path similarity, structure similarity and knowledge similarity. To obtain the integrated similarity, we should take some certain operation to aggregate them. Max, Min, Average and Weighted sum, etc. are usual choice for combining similarity. In order to get a more accurate match result, we use both weighted sum and threshold technology.

6 Matching Process

The matching algorithm proposed in this paper is a composite algorithm. The Figure 1 is the matching process of our method.

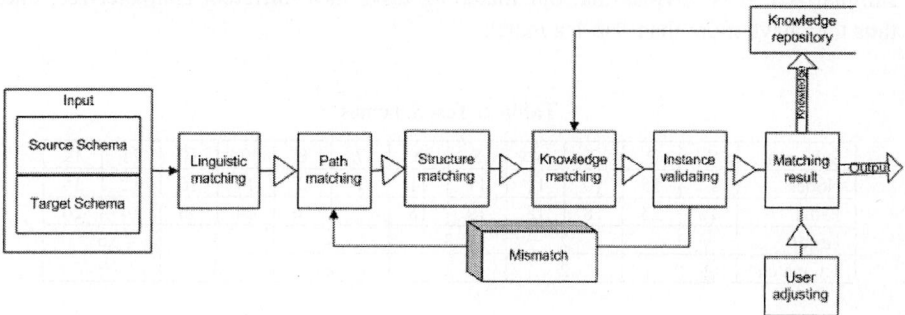

Fig. 1. Matching Process

It is obvious that the matching process has five steps. Two schemas, source schema and target schema, are input into our prototype system, and represented by our general reference model. Firstly, we perform the linguistic matching for elements of two schemas. The following steps are path matching, structure matching and knowledge matching. After these steps, we will check match results based on data instance. Afterwards, we get the final match result. Then the user can check it, and make a feedback. If some matches are false or missing, then return to the path matching to restart the matching process.

In instances validating phase, in order to data/instance validating, we define some data patterns based on those in [5] to check the matching result. The data patterns can be divided into three catalogues: Character, Numeric and Datetime.

After the user checks matching result, we will perform knowledge indentation and extraction. Usually, we count for one element matching more than one target element. The knowledge will be reused for the matching in the future.

7 Experimental Results

We have made a comprehensive assessment of our prototype system by several complex real world schemas. The main goal is to investigate the effect of our method with data validating and without data validating.

In the test, we used both structure and terminological relationships considering that, given any two schemas, these techniques always apply even though no data are available. Thus, we tested our approach with two steps on each source-target pair. In the first step, we consider merely terminological relationships and structure. In the second step, we take characteristics of numerical value into account.

For our evaluation, 12 schemas are employed, which are taken from different practical application areas, including purchase orders, student management and customers. These schemas are represented by XSD and relations. For short, we refer to them as 1, 2, etc., respectively. In Table 1, the characteristics of the test schemas are summarized. It is obvious that our matching tasks have different characterizes, and thus they have more than one 1:n match.

Table 1. Test Schemas

Schemas	1	2	3	4	5	6	7	8	9	10	11	12
Nodes	13	15	10	11	11	11	7	8	14	16	12	15
Paths	16	25	18	18	19	18	7	10	24	30	14	26
Group	1		2		3		4		5		6	
1:n match	0		2		1		2		3		3	

We then have the results for the first step in which we consider merely terminological relationships and structure. Figure 2 shows the quality of the matching result without data validating evaluated by our $H_{Measure}$. Figure 3 shows the quality of the matching result with data validating.

Now we analyze the matching results. In the first step, the third task is well performed with the accuracy 1 and the fourth task is badly performed with the accuracy 0.67 because this the schemas in this task include some elements with same name but different meaning and numerical values. However we also know that most of 1:n matches in the task 2, 5, 6 are discovered in the first step. It indicates that our algorithm is efficient. The most difficult match in the first step is the match with the same element name but different meaning and numerical values such as, in the task 1. The element Office of source schema means a telephone of office. On the other hand, just Phone is used in target schema. Obviously, this problem could be solved in the

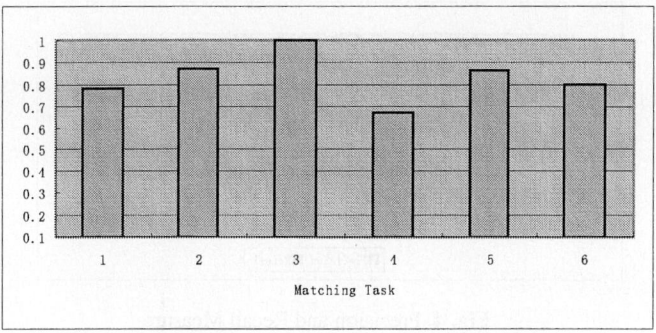

Fig. 2. Matching Result without Data Validating

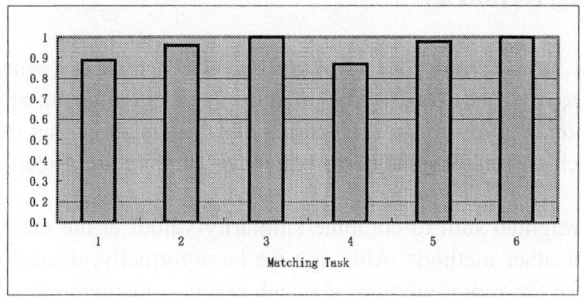

Fig. 3. Matching Result with Data Validating

second step. The use of characteristics of numerical values improves the performance. By analyzing and checking data patterns, we overcome most of the difficulties of match tasks, particularly those with the same name but different meaning or with different names but the same data value.

Evidently, most of different schema matching tasks, including XML XSD, DTD and Relation matching, could achieve about 0.9 or greater accuracy after the data invalidating step. This shows that our algorithm can deal with various schema matches with complex match types.

The next figure shows measure *Precision*, and *Recall*, we get these results without data validating process, the result with data validating is also can be computed, due to space limitation, we omit it.

From Figure 4, we can know that all values of measure *Precision* are great than values of our measure, on the opposite, all values of measure *Recall* are lesser than values of our measure, explaining this is easy: because that measure *Precision* just take the true passive match into account and measure *Recall* do not take the true negatives into account. So our can adjust two measures and it represents harmonic mean of *Precision* and *Recall*. So it is easily seen that our measure is better than other measure.

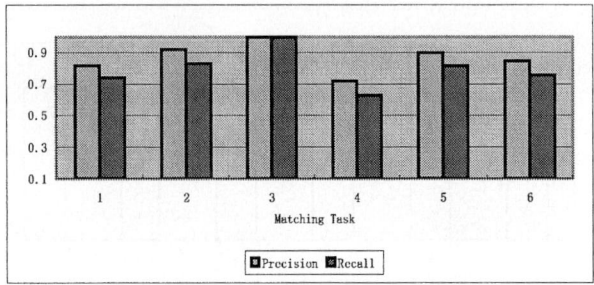

Fig. 4. Precision and Recall Measure

8 Concluding Remarks

In this paper, we have developed a new approach with which two schemas input into our prototype are matched. Our algorithm fully exploits semantic, structure and instance information of two schemas. Experimental results show that our algorithm is efficient to match direct element correspondences and indirect element correspondences.

We use the weighted sum to combine similarity values at the moment. In the future, we will test other methods. Although we have formally given the match types, we do not discuss the representation of match result----mapping. Now, we use relations to store and access the match result. In future, we will develop more expressive representation of mapping to satisfy other model management operations, say merge, diff and combination, etc.

References

1. Yan, L.L., R.J. Miller, L.M. Haas, R. Fagin: Data-Driven Understanding and Refinement of Schema Mappings. SIGMOD (2001)
2. Miller, R.J. et al: The Clio Project: Managing Heterogeneity. SIGMOD Record 30:1. (2001) 78–83
3. Do, H.H., E. Rahm: COMA – A System for Flexible Combination of Schema Matching Approach. VLDB (2002)
4. Madhavan, J., P.A. Bernstein, E. Rahm: Generic Schema Matching with Cupid. VLDB (2001) 49 – 58.
5. Li, W.S., C. Clifton: Semantic Integration in Heterogeneous Databases Using Neural Networks. VLDB (1994)
6. Li, W.S., C. Clifton: SemInt: A Tool for Identifying Attribute Correspondences in Heterogeneous Databases Using Neural Network. Data and Knowledge Engineering. (2000) 49–84
7. Li, W.S., C. Clifton, S.Y. Liu: Database Integration Using Neural Networks: Implementation and Experiences. Knowledge and Information Systems. (2000)

8. Melnik, S., H. Garcia-Molina, E. Rahm: Similarity Flooding: A Versatile Graph Matching Algorithm. ICDE (2002)
9. Mitra P, Wiederhold G, Jannink J: Semiautomatic integration of knowledge sources. Proceeding of Fusion '99, Sunnyvale, USA
10. Mitra P, Wiederhold G, Kersten M: A graph oriented model for articulation of ontology interdependencies. In Proc Extending DataBase Technologies, LNCS, vol. 1777. Springer, (2000) 86–100.
11. An Hai Doan, Pedro Domingos, Alon Y. Halevy: Reconciling Schemas of Disparate Data Sources: A Machine-Learning Approach. SIGMOD Conference (2001)
12. Jaewoo Kang Jeffrey F. Naughton: On schema matching with opaque column names and data values. International Conference on Management of Data and Symposium on Principles of Database Systems and Proceedings of the 2003 ACM SIGMOD international conference on Management of data San Diego, California.
13. Rahm, E., P.A. Bernstein: A Survey of Approaches to Automatic Schema Matching. VLDB Journal. (2001)
14. Hong-Hai Do, Sergey Melnik, Erhard Rahm: Comparison of Schema Matching Evaluations. evaluations. Proceedings of the 2nd Int. Workshop on Web Databases (German Informatics Society) (2002)
15. Li Xu and David W. Embley: Discovering Direct and Indirect Matches for Schema Elements. Eigthth International Conference on Database Systems for Advanced Applications (DASFAA '03). (2003)
16. Guilian Wang, Joseph Goguen, Young-Kwang Nam and Kai Lin: Critical Points for Interactive Schema Matching. Proceedings of the Sixth Asia Pacific Web Conference, Hangzhou, China (2004)
17. L. Palopoli, G. Teracina, and D. Ursino: The system DIKE: Towards the semi-automatic synthesis of cooperative information systems and data warehouses. Proceedings of ADBIS-DASFAA (2000) 108 – 117
18. http://www.w3.org/TR/rdf-concepts/
19. Anhai Doan, Jayant Madhavan, Pedro Domingos, and Alon Y. Halevy: Learning to Map between Ontologies on the Semantic Web. Proceedings of the 11th International World Wide Web Conference (WWW) (2002)
20. Milo, T., S. Zohar: Using Schema Matching to Simplify Heterogeneous Data Translation. VLDB. (1998) 122–133
21. Wordnet 2.0, http://www.cogsci.princeton.edu/~wn/

Analysis, Transformation, and Improvements of ebXML Choreographies Based on Workflow Patterns

Ja-Hee Kim* and Christian Huemer

Research Studios Austria Studio Digital Memory Engineering
ARC Seibersdorf research GmbH Thurngasse 8/20, A-1090 Wien
Department of Computer Science and Business Informatics, University of Vienna,
at Liebiggasse 4/3-4, 1010 Vienna, Austria.
kim@mminf.univie.ac.at, christian.huemer@univie.ac.at

Abstract. In ebXML the choreography of a business process should be modeled by UMM (UN/CEFACT Modeling Methodology) and is finally expressed in BPSS (Business Process Specification Schema). Our analysis of UMM and BPSS by workflow patterns shows that their expression power is not always equivalent. We use the workflow patterns to specify the transformation from UMM to BPSS where possible. Furthermore, the workflow patterns help to show the limitations of UMM and BPSS and to propose improvements.

1 Introduction

The trend towards service-oriented architectures resulted in a growing interest in the choreography of B2B business processes, which is in the focus of this paper. The most prominent example of an service-oriented architecture is Web Services [1]. Web Services are defined as a software application identified by a URI, whose interfaces and bindings are capable of being defined, described, and discovered as XML artifacts. A Web Service supports direct interactions with other software agents using XML-based messages exchanged via Internet-based protocols [2]. The Web Services base standards are WSDL, UDDI and SOAP. However, Web Services are isolated and opaque. Business processes require collections of Web Services jointly used to realize more complex functionality [3]. This lead to the development of the Business Process Execution Language for Web Services (BPEL). BPEL's primarily focuses on the orchestration of executable business processes. In addition, BPEL supports so-called abstract processes for specifying a choreography of business protocols between business partners [4].

Apart from Web Services, the ebXML framework is another important approach. In contrast to Web Services, ebXML has been developed specifically for e-business. ebXML is also based on a service-oriented architecture. ebXML provides a set of loosely coupled specifications that enable so-called business service

---

* This work was partially supported by the Post-doctoral Fellowship Program of Korea Science & Engineering Foundation (KOSEF).

interfaces (BSI) of different business partners to interoperate. These specifications span over the topics of messaging, registries, profiles & agreements, business processes, and core (data) components. Accordingly, business serves interfaces are expected to carry out standardized business processes. The ebXML architecture specification recommends to use the UML-based UN/CEFACT Modeling Methodology (UMM) for analyzing and designing the inter-organizational business processes. Those aspects that are relevant for configuring the business service interfaces are mapped to the XML-based business process specification schema (BPSS). BPSS instances are stored in a registry and are referenced by the profiles of companies supporting the corresponding business process.

As mentioned above, interoperability requires that collaborating business partners implement a shared business logic. BPEL and UMM/BPSS provide languages describing a share business logic with respect to the choreography of a business process. Thus, it is important that these languages lead to unambiguous definitions of business processes. Furthermore, these languages must be able to capture choreography requirements that appear in any B2B business process. Inasmuch it is important to systematically evaluate the capabilities of these languages. There does not exist a special metric for evaluating B2B processes. However, a B2B business process might be considered as an inter-organizational workflow. Aalst et al. developed workflow patterns to analyze executable workflows [5]. An evaluation of BPEL according to these patterns is provided in Wohed et al. [6]. In our paper we use the same patterns to evaluate ebXML processes. In other words, we analyze UMM version 12 [7] and BPSS 1.1 [8]. Both UMM and BPSS describe a choreography rather than an executable process orchestration. An ebXML process flow consists of collaborative activities that are decomposed in a way that each of the two collaborating partners perform exactly one activity (c.f. Section 2). From a specific partner's view the process flow is still the same, but instead of the collaborative activities the flow consists only of the activities assigned to the corresponding partner. Thus, we feel that the patterns are relevant even to analyze a choreography.

We demonstrate how the workflow patterns are realized in UMM and BPSS. Patterns that cannot be realized usually indicate limitations of the current versions and give hints for improvements in future revisions. Showing how a pattern is expressed in both standards, helps to identify mapping rules between the standards. This is important for automatically deriving a BPSS specification from a UMM model, but also for reverse engineering.

The remainder of this paper is structured as follows. Section 2 gives an introduction into the two standards of interest: UMM and BPSS. In Section 3 we show how the 20 patterns, which are organized in 6 categories, are expressed in both UMM and BPSS. Each pattern supported by the standards is demonstrated by means of a practical example. The summary in Section 4 gives an overview of the patterns supported and of the derived mapping rules.

2 Overview of UMM and BPSS

Since 1997 the United Nations's Centre for Trade Facilitation and Electronic Business (UN/CEFACT) has been developing it modeling methodology UMM. UMM concentrates on the business operational view (BOV) of the Open-edi reference model [9]. The BOV is limited to those aspects regarding the making of business decisions and commitments among organizations. This means that UMM is independent of the technology - e.g. Web Services or ebXML - used to implement a B2B partnership. UMM is based on UML. It defines a UML profile for modeling the business aspects of inter-organizational business processes. The UMM methodology covers 4 views: The business domain view (BDV) is used to gather existing knowledge. It collects information about existing business processes and does not construct new ones. The goal of the business requirements view (BRV) is to identify possible business collaborations in the considered domain and to detail the requirements of these collaborations. The business transaction view (BTV) defines the choreography of the business collaboration and structures the business information exchanged. The fundamental principle of the business service view (BSV) is to describe the interactions between network components.

The most important view for our evaluation is the BTV, since it deals with the choreography of the inter-organizational business process called business collaboration in UMM. A business collaboration is performed by two (= binary collaboration) or more (multi-party collaboration) business partners. A business collaboration might be complex involving a lot of activities between business partners. However, the most basic business collaboration is a binary collaboration realized by a request from one side and an optional response from the other side. This simple collaboration is a unit of work that allows roll back to a defined state before it was initiated. Therefore, this special type of collaboration is called business transaction.

Consequently, a business transaction consists always of two collaborating activities. Each activity is performed by one business partner. The initiating business activity outputs information that is sent to the reacting business activity. In case of a simple information distribution or notification the reacting business activity processes the information and the transaction is completed. If a response is expected the reacting business activity outputs the business information and returns it to the initiating business activity. Note, that acknowledgments are not explicitly modeled in the BTV, but time values assigned to a business activity signify that they expect an acknowledgment from the collaborating activity in a given time frame.

In UMM a business transaction is modeled by an activity graph. Fig.1 shows the example of an *authorize payment* business transaction in UMM. Owing to the strict well-formedness rules described above, a business transaction follows always the same pattern as shown in Fig.1. In case of information distribution and notification the object flow returning a business document is omitted. Due to the strict choreography of the activities within a business transaction, our

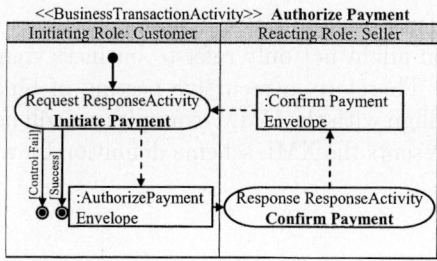

Fig. 1. An example of a business transaction.

pattern based analysis in the following section does not consider the activities within a business transaction.

A business collaboration is built by more business transactions. It is important that the business collaboration defines an execution order for the business transactions. In UMM, this choreography is defined by an activity graph called business collaboration protocol. In the current version 12 of UMM all activities of the business collaboration protocol must be stereotyped as business transaction activities. A business transaction activity must be refined by the activity graph of a business transaction. This means that recursively nesting business collaborations is not possible in UMM. A business collaboration protocol is able to model a multi-party collaboration. However, each business transaction involves exactly two partners by definition. Our pattern-based analysis evaluates the choreography of the business collaboration protocol. It checks whether a certain pattern is supported by the business collaboration protocol or not. All the examples illustrated in Fig.3 to Fig.10 are business collaboration protocols. It is important to note that UMM is based on UML 1.4. Therefore some limitations are a result of limitations of UML 1.4. We will point out if they are solved by UML 2.0.

The work on BPSS was based on the UMM meta model. However, it is not mandatory to use UMM in order to create an BPSS instance. The goal of the BPSS is to provide the bridge between e-business process modeling and specification of e-business software components [8]. It provides an XML schema to specify a collaboration between business partners, and to provide configuration parameters for the partners' runtime systems in order to execute that collaboration between a set of e-business software components. BPSS identified those UMM modeling elements that are relevant for the runtime systems and discarded the rest. The relevant modeling elements have been expressed in XML schema.

The UMM artefacts that are considered by BPSS are more or less the business transaction and the business collaboration protocol. Nevertheless, the mapping is not always straight forward as we will recognize in the next section. Again, our analysis will not evaluate the activities within a business transaction due to its strict choreography. Therefore, the analysis considers the business collaboration protocol equivalent called binary collaboration. As the name indicates, BPSS supports only the definition of collaborations between two partners. Multi-party collaborations were deprecated in BPSS 1.1. In contrast to UMM, the activities within a collaboration might not only refer to business transactions, but also to other collaborations. Therefore, a recursive nesting of binary collaborations is possible. In order to align with the UMM examples we will not use this concept in our analysis. Fig.2 presents the XML schema definition for a binary collaboration in BPSS.

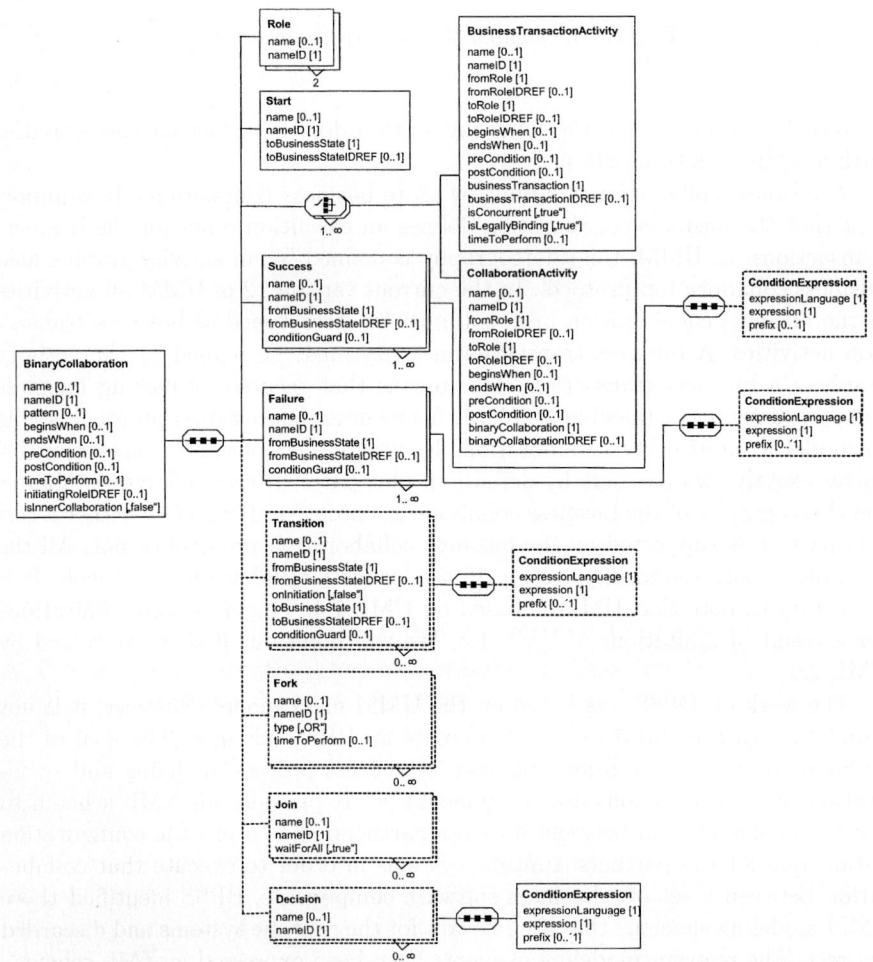

Fig. 2. BPSS 1.1 binary collaboration element.

3 Workflow Pattern Based Transformation

In this section we analyze UMM and BPSS based on well-known workflow patterns proposed by Aalst et al. [5]. Since UMM is based on UML, analyzing UMM is very similar to UML [10]. However, UMM's meta model defines B2B-specific tagged values. Sometimes a pattern is realized by these tagged values - which is marked 't' in Table 1 at the end of the paper. Furthermore, UMM does not use all features of UML activity graphs due to a more restrictive meta model. These workflow patterns are categorized into six classes - basic control patterns, advanced branching and synchronization patterns, structural patterns, patterns involving multiple instances, state-based patterns, and cancelation patterns. The UMM and BPSS analysis for each class of patterns is presented in a separate subsection. This analysis shows the expression power and the limitations both of UMM and BPSS. It gives hints to improve the expression power of UMM and BPSS. Furthermore, the analysis helps to derive the transformation rules between UMM model and BPSS.

3.1 Basic Control Flow Patterns

Aalst et al categorize basic control patterns into *sequence, parallel split, synchronization, exclusive choice,* and *simple merge*. They are similar to definitions of elementary control flow concepts provided by WfMC [11]. Both of UMM and BPSS support all theses patterns.

Sequence. A sequence pattern means all activities are executed one by one. Each subactivity state of UMM represents *business transaction activity* or *collaboration transaction activity* of BPSS and the state is connected to other state by *transition*. Fig.3 illustrates a very simple *binary collaboration* for ordering products. In this example, a request quote transaction is followed by the order products transaction.

The UMM *business collaboration protocol* is based on a UML 1.4 activity graph. BPSS was developed by mapping the UMM meta model of the *business collaboration protocol* into an XML representation. However, not all UMM concepts are represented one-to-one in BPSS. Therefore, a transformation from UMM models to BPSS is not straightforward. A very significant difference between UMM and BPSS is the handling of final states. A *final* state of UMM should be transformed to either *success* or *failure* element of BPSS. A *single* UMM final state representing both a successful and an unsuccessful result must be mapped to both a *success* and a *failure* element in BPSS. User input or naming convention of *final* state of UMM may be able to help the decision. Moreover, UMM needs two concepts for a transition to a *final* state: The transition and the state. However, the two concepts are merged into a single BPSS element, representing both a transition and a state. The same concept applies to initial states.

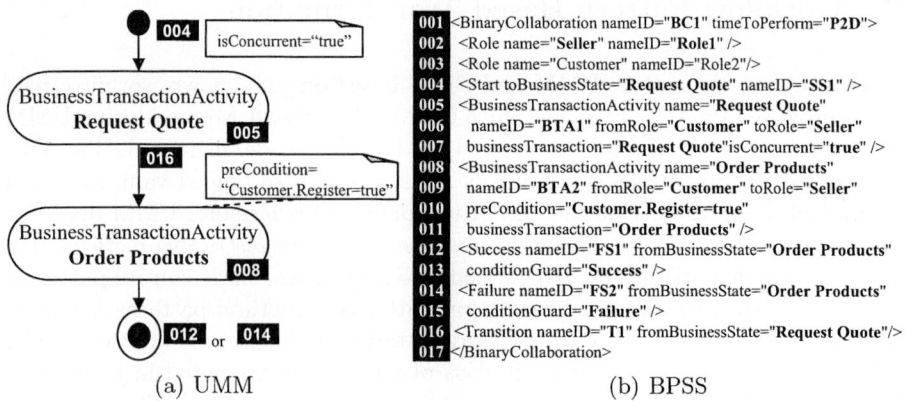

Fig. 3. An example of a sequence pattern.

Parallel split and synchronization. A parallel split pattern is a kind of AND-fork, after which multiple succeeding threads are executed in parallel. For example, after *ordering products*, the customer should *authorize the payment*. In parallel to this authorization, the *planning schedule* and a subsequent *shipping schedule is defined*. In UMM this parallel split pattern is modeled using pseudo state *fork* depicted by a bar (c.f. in Fig. 4a). BPSS uses a *fork* element of type *or* (see line 041 in Fig. 4b). This means that its attribute *type* is set to *or*. This is in opposite to *xor* which is discussed in the *deferred choice* pattern.

A synchronization pattern, a synonym for an AND-join, forms an antithesis to the parallel split pattern. A successor of a synchronization pattern starts if all its predecessors are completed. In Fig. 4a the seller ships the products after the completion of both activities *authorized payment* and *define shipping schedule*. This means that the *notify shipment* transaction must wait for the completion of both preceding activities. In UMM the synchronization pattern is realized by a *synchronization* pseudo state. Similarly to a *fork* state, the synchronization is depicted as a bar. BPSS realizes this pattern using a *join* element whose *wait for all* attribute is *true* (line 042 in Fig. 4b). This is in opposite to an OR-join where the the *wait for all* attribute is set to *false*.

Exclusive choice and simple merge. After an exclusive choice pattern one execution path is chosen from many alternative branches based on a decision. UMM uses a *decision* pseudo state which is depicted as a diamond. Usually, the decision is based on the state of a business object. For example, after *requesting quote* the customer may want to *order products*. If the customer is registered, the customer can *order products* right away. Otherwise the customer should register himself before ordering. In 5a the decision is based on the state of the *customer information*. If it is confirmed the next transaction is *order products*, and *register customers* otherwise. BPSS realizes the exclusive choice pattern by a *decision* element (line 028 in Fig. 5b). The decision element specifies a *condition*

Analysis, Transformation, and Improvements of ebXML Choreographies   73

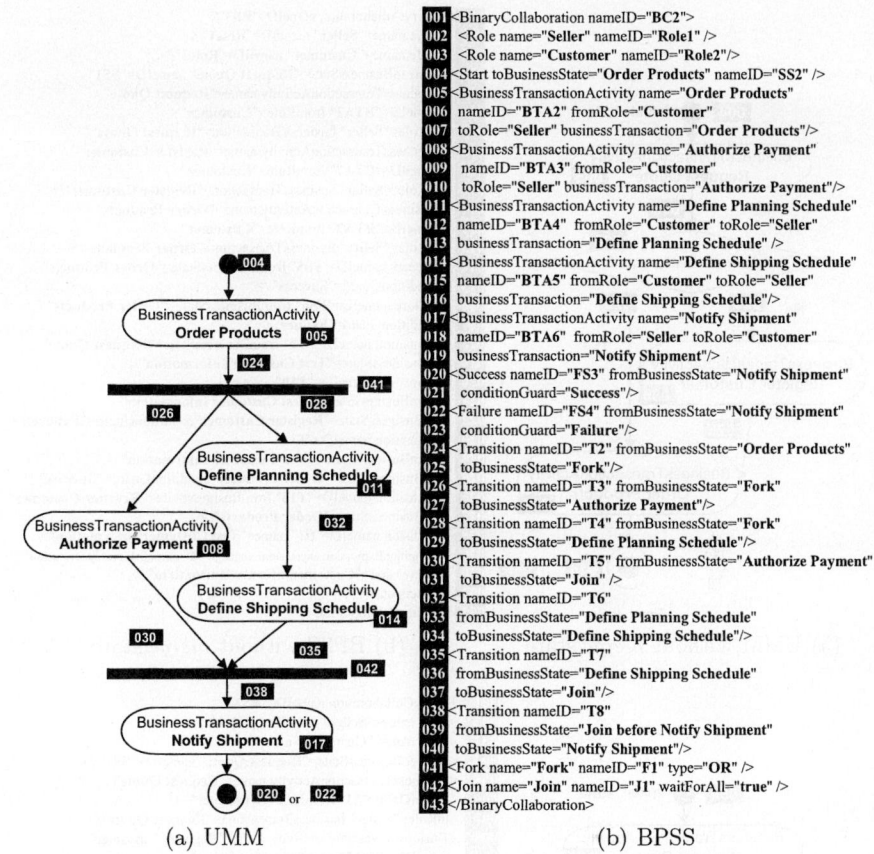

Fig. 4. An example of a parallel split and a synchronization pattern

expression (line 020). All transitions starting from the decision (line 020 and 023) carry mutually exclusive condition guards with respect to the *condition expression*. Another realization of an exclusive choice is using the result of *binary transaction activity*. We detail this realization in arbitrary cycle.

A simple merge pattern, an antithesis of the exclusive choice pattern, merges several alternative branches. For a simple merge pattern, neither any special pseudo state nor any element is mandatory. Multiple transitions leading to one state (*business transaction activity order products*) represent the pattern like Fig.5a (line 023 and 026 in Fig. 5b). However, UMM also supports a *merge* state depicted by a diamond as illustrated in Fig.5c. In this case, a *merge* state is transformed to a *join* element (line 030 in Fig.5d) whose attribute *wait for all* is *false*.

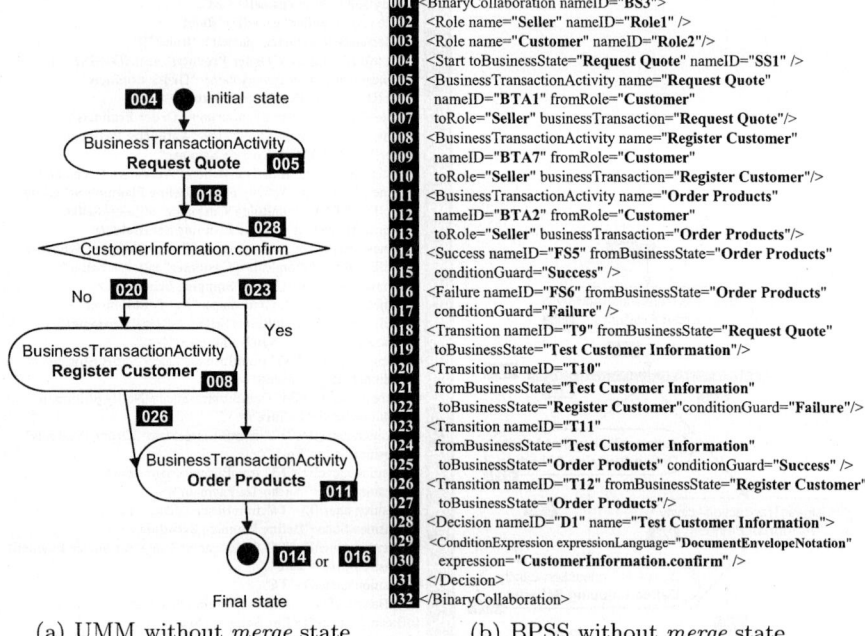

(a) UMM without *merge* state (b) BPSS without *merge* state

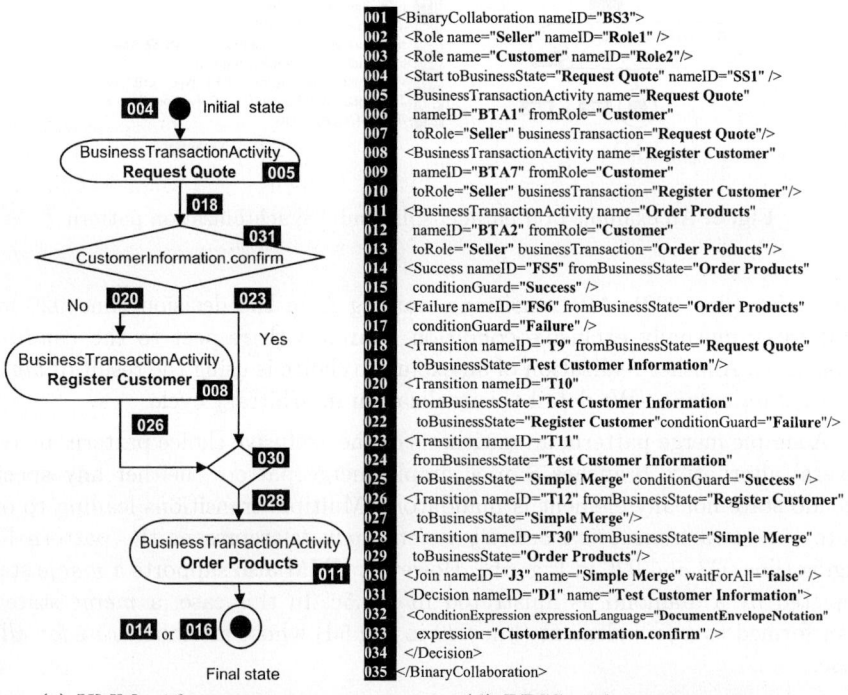

(c) UMM with *merge* state (d) BPSS with *merge* state

Fig. 5. An example of an exclusive choice and a simple merge pattern.

3.2 Advanced Branching and Synchronization Patterns

In this subsection we examine more advanced patterns for branching and merge. This category includes *multi choice, synchronizing merge, multi merge,* and *discriminator*.

Multi choice and synchronizing merge. After a multi choice pattern several execution paths are chosen from many alternative threads based on a decision. For example, after *ordering products*, the seller usually initiates both the *issue invoice* transaction and the *notify shipment* transaction. Both must be completed in order to *authorize payment*. However, notify shipment makes only sense if the seller ships the products. If the customer collects the products this transaction is not necessary. Therefore, its execution is based on the party accomplishing the shipment. UMM supports this pattern by placing guards on the outgoing transitions from a *conditional fork*. In Fig.6a the *transition* from a *fork* pseudo state to *activity* state, *notify shipment*, is guarded by the decision on whether *the shipper is the seller* or not. In BPSS the transitions (line 025 in Fig.6b) from the *fork* element (line 011) with condition expressions (line 027) realize this pattern. A *fork* pseudo state may have several guarded outgoing transitions. All decisions must be evaluated before the first business transaction preceding the multi choice is executed. The order of evaluating these condition expressions is not important.

A synchronizing merge, an antithesis of the multiple choice, converges into one continuing activity. UMM realizes this pattern in exactly the same way as the *synchronization* pattern. By definition, the synchronization pseudo state does not wait for threads that have not been started. Since BPSS does not support this pattern directly, we need a work around to realize this pattern. This work around uses a *join* element whose attribute *wait for all* is *true* like in the case of the synchronization pattern (line 036 in Fig.6b). However the *join* element cannot be executed since *wait for all* attribute indicates that the *join* element must wait for all incoming threads to finish. Hence, the *fork* element (line 035) includes an attribute *time to perform*. After the specified time is exceeded, all the not executed transactions are skipped and the collaboration continues from the corresponding join. Although a *time to perform* attribute makes this pattern possible, this realization wastes time. Moreover, it is dangerous since we can ignore not only pruned threads by guarded transitions but also *binary transaction activities* that must be executed. For example, we assume the customer has a responsibility of collecting the products in Fig.6. Even if the invoice is issued in one hour, the *authorize payment* should wait for two days. More dangerous is the case of not issuing the invoice for two days after *ordering products*, because the customer should *authorize payment* anyway. For avoiding this problem, UML 2.0 recommends a *decision* node instead of a guarded transition like Fig.6c and Fig.6d. A circle with a cross in Fig.6d is a *flow final* node. This node is supported by UML 2.0 and means the termination of only a thread. The representation of Fig.6c can be directly transformed to BPSS. If a *type* of a *fork* is *xor* and the cor-

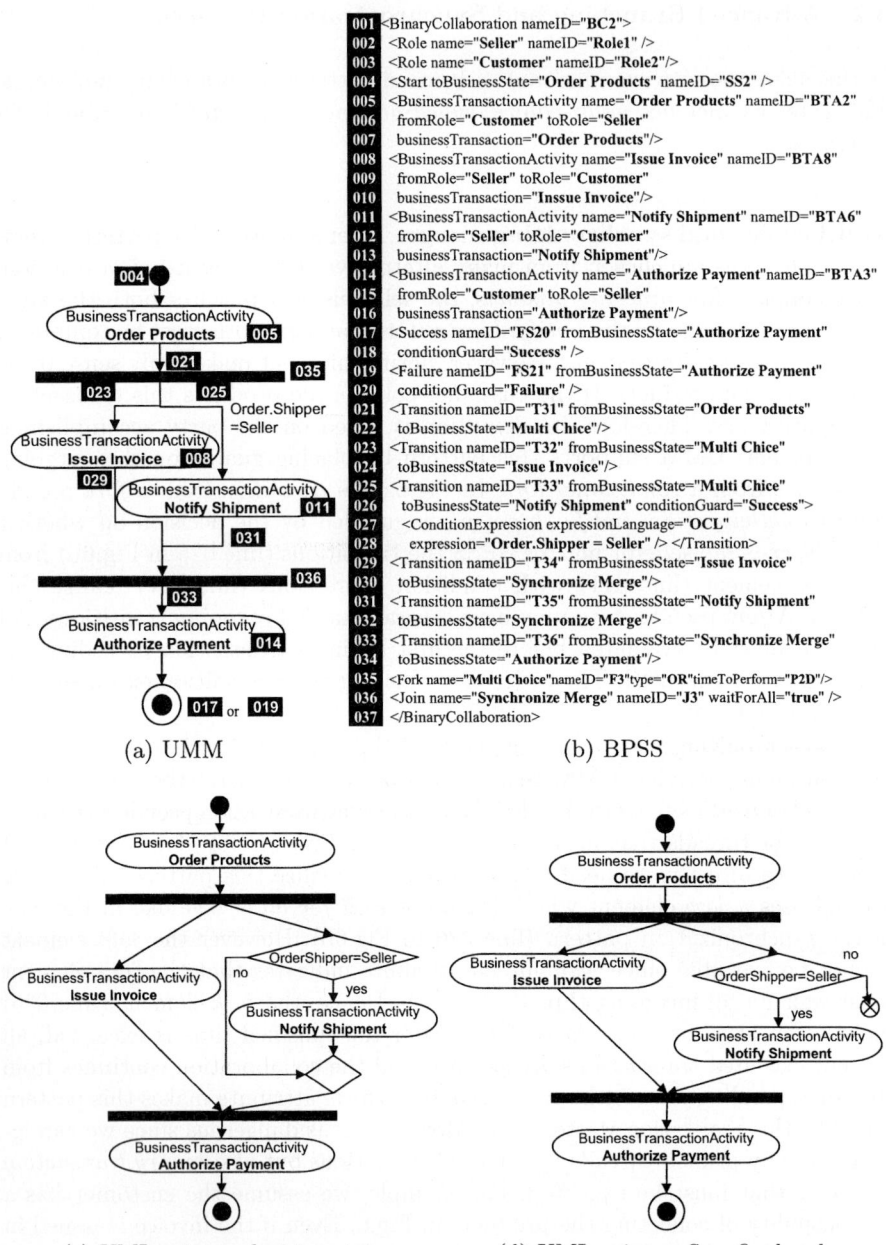

Fig. 6. An example of a multi choice and a synchronizing merge pattern.

responding *join* element is not reached in *time to perform*, a timeout exception is generated.

Discriminator. A discriminator pattern is similar to the synchronization pattern since multiple threads converge to one thread and the following thread is executed only once. However, the continuing activity starts after the first preceding thread finishes. We consider an example similar to the one used for explaining multi choice and a synchronizing merge. The seller is always responsible for the shipment. The customer authorizes the payment either if the invoice is issued or if the seller notifies the shipment. UMM does not support this pattern, since there is no semantically equivalent pseudo state. In UML 2.0, a join specification might be assigned to a join node. This join specification decides when the continuing thread is started (see Fig.7a). BPSS realizes the pattern by a *join* element (line 034 in Fig.7b), whose *wait for all*'s value is *false*.

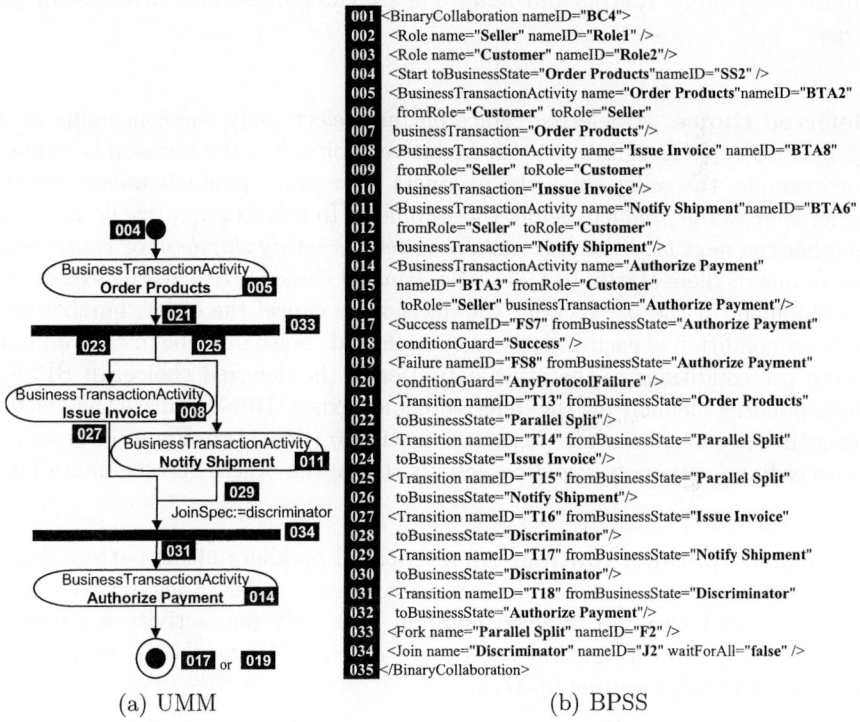

Fig. 7. An example of a discriminator pattern.

Multi merge. After a multi merge pattern multiple threads are merged into one continuing activity, which is executed whenever a precedence thread reaches the multi merge pattern. UMM does not support it now, since the current UMM is based on UML 1.4, which forces forks and joins to be well-nested. However, in UML 2.0 this constraint disappears and a *merge* node following a *fork* node realizes this pattern. BPSS does not support the multi merge pattern either. Future versions of BPSS need improvements to support this pattern. We recommend to adopt the concept of UML 2.0. In UML 2.0 there exist both a pseudo state merge node - depicted as a diamond - and a synchronization node - depicted as bar. Currently, in BPSS there exists a single element *join* to realize simple merge, synchronization and discriminator. We prefer a new element similar to the UML diamond to realize simple merge and multi merge.

3.3 State-Based Patterns

If the execution of one activity depends on the state of another activity, the pattern is categorized into the class of state-based patterns. *Deferred choice, interleaved parallel routing* and *milestone* are categorized into this class of patterns.

Deferred choice. A deferred choice pattern selects only one continuing activity from several candidates like an exclusive choice, but the decision is implicit. For example, the seller ships the products after *order products* unless the customer *cancels the products* before the shipment. In this example, we do not know whether the next *business transaction activity* is *notify shipment* or *cancel order* before one of them starts. In UMM the deferred choice is realized by events, e.g. the shipment of the products or the decision to cancel the order. Furthermore, the post condition of each activity in the deferred choice must be in contradiction to the pre conditions of the other activities in the deferred choice. In BPSS, a corresponding element for the deferred choice exists. BPSS realizes this pattern using the element *fork* whose *type* attribute is *xor* (line 022 in Fig.8b). As soon as a succeeding *business transaction activity* starts, the others become unavailable.

Interleaved parallel routing. An interleaved parallel routing pattern defines the execution of a set of activities in an arbitrary order. Each activity of the set is executed once. At a given point in time only one activity is executed. The execution order is fixed at run time. Neither UMM nor BPSS supports the interleaved parallel routing pattern.

Milestone. A milestone pattern is the start of an activity depends on the state of one or more other activities. For example, *order products* in Fig.3 can be only initiated after *register customer* and before *unregistered customer* in Fig.9. UMM uses tagged values, *pre condition* and *post condition* for this pattern. The *pre condition* and *post condition* are transformed as attributes of a *business transaction activity* in BPSS. Before initializing *order products*, (line 008 in Fig.3b), its *pre condition* "Customer.Register=true" is checked (line 010 in Fig.3b). This value is modified in *register customer* and *unregister customer* of another *binary collaboration* using *post condition* (line 008 and 011 in Fig.9b).

Analysis, Transformation, and Improvements of ebXML Choreographies

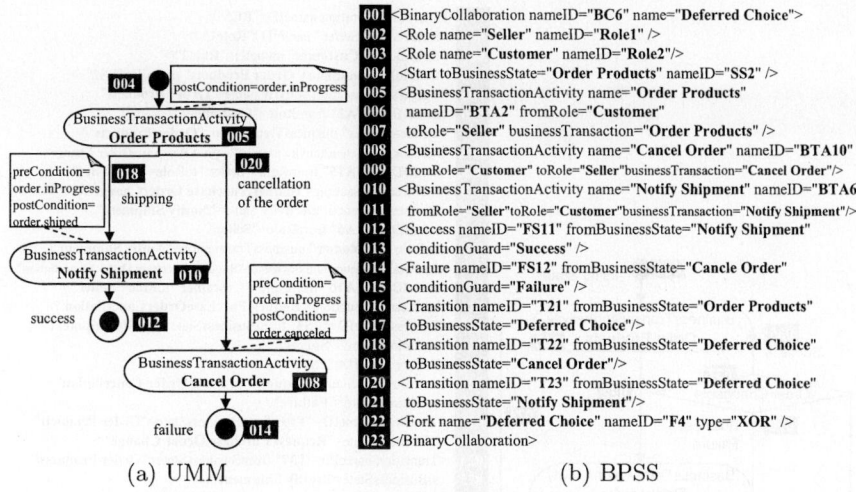

Fig. 8. An example of a deferred choice pattern.

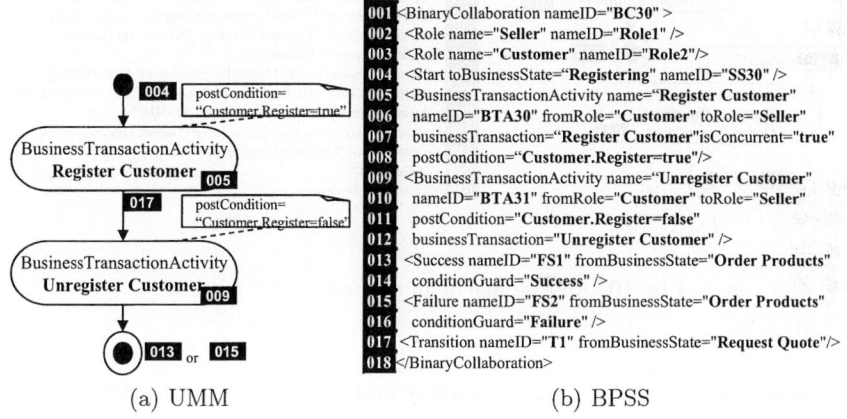

Fig. 9. An example of a milestone pattern.

3.4 Structural Patterns

In this subsection we examine the structural patterns *arbitrary cycle* and *implicit termination*. Preventing these patterns improves the readability and makes the interpretation easier. However, neither UMM nor BPSS imposes structural restrictions on the model.

Arbitrary cycles. A structural cycle pattern is a loop that has only one entry and only one exit point. The *while* and *for* statements of C language are examples of structural cycles. Contrary to a structural cycle, an arbitrary cycle pattern

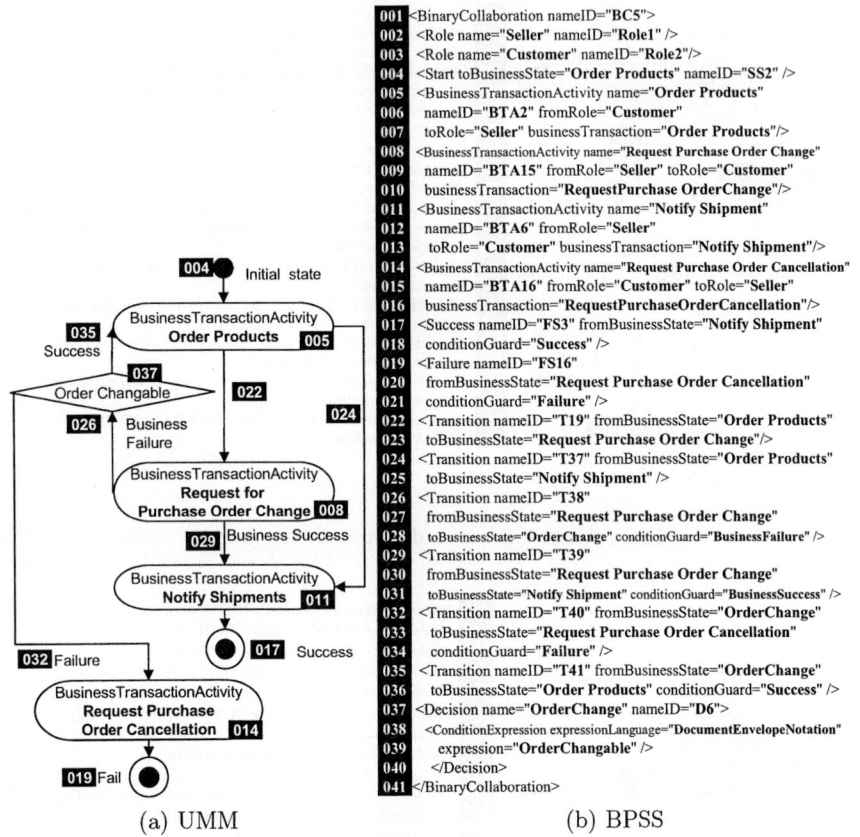

Fig. 10. An example of an arbitrary cycle pattern.

has no restriction on the number of entry and exit point. Some arbitrary cycles are constructed by the combination of multiple *decisions, xor-typed forks* and *transitions*. In this case UMM and BPSS are able to realize the arbitrary cycle. However, arbitrary cycles might involve forks and joins as well. Since each fork has a corresponding join, transitions can not cross the boundary of the fork-join-block, UMM does not fully support the arbitrary cycle pattern. Since BPSS does not include a similar well-formedness rule it fully supports the arbitrary cycle.

Fig.10 offers an example of an arbitrary cycle pattern. An undesirable situation, such as a lack of raw material, a natural disaster, or a strike, can prevent the seller from shipping the exact number of products in time. In this case, the seller should inform the customer about the situation and *request for purchase order change*. The choice between *request for purchase order change* and *notify shipment* is realized by a deferred choice pattern. If the customer accepts the request, the seller ships the products. Otherwise, the customer decides whether he changes the order or cancels the order. If he decides to change the order, the *binary collaboration* restarts from *order products*. Since the cycle (*order products* → *request for purchase order change* → *order changable* → *order products*) has three exit points, this example includes an arbitrary cycle pattern.

Implicit termination. Both UMM and BPSS have an explicit final state (a *final* state of UMM and a *success* and a *failure* element of BPSS) but they also support a special kind of implicit termination pattern. An implicit termination pattern means a situation where there is no activity to be done even if a final state is not reached and at the same time the workflow is not in deadlock. For example, *binary collaboration* has an attribute, *time to perform* (line 001 in Fig.3b). That is, the *binary collaboration* is forced to terminate in two days although the final state has not been reached.

3.5 Patterns Involving Multiple Instance

We examine patterns involving multiple instances in this subsection. These patterns are categorized by the ability to launch multiple instances of activities and synchronization among the instances. The patterns are *multiple instances without synchronization*, *multiple instances with a priori design time knowledge*, *multiple instances with a priori run time knowledge*, and *multiple instances without a priori run time knowledge*.

Multiple instances with a priori design time knowledge and *multiple instances with a priori run time knowledge* restrict the number of instances at design time and run time, respectively. In contrast, *multiple instances without synchronization* and *multiple instances without a priori run time knowledge* have no limitation on the number of instances. While UML supports *multiple instances with a priori design time knowledge* and *multiple instances with a priori run time knowledge* [10], UMM does not use this feature.

Multiple instances without a priori run time knowledge can manage the relationship among instances such as synchronization differently from *multiple instances without synchronization*. BPSS supports only the *multiple instances without synchronization* by assigning *true* to a *business transaction activity*'s attribute *is concurrent* (line 007 in Fig.3b). Since the activity diagram of UML does not support this pattern, *is concurrent* is expressed as a tag value of an activity in UMM.

3.6 Cancelation Patterns

Both *cancel activity* pattern and *cancel case* pattern are cancelation patterns. By performing activities of the cancelation patterns other activities are withdrawn.

Cancel activity. A cancel activity pattern cancels an enabled activity. UML supports through transition with triggers. However, UMM does not use this feature and BPSS does not support this pattern directly, either. This pattern can be supported by a deferred choice pattern [5]. However, a *business transaction* *activity* is composed of other activities in the *business transaction* view and each activity of *business transaction* corresponds to other workflow in the company. Moreover, we cannot interrupt the *business transaction activity* even using a deferred choice. In Fig. 11 if *define planning schedule* fails, we do not need to *authorize payment* any more. However, even if *define planning schedule* fails before the customer sends the *authorize payment envelope*, BPSS does not provide a pattern to cancel the authorize payment transaction. The only workaround is a milestone pattern using pre- and post-conditions.

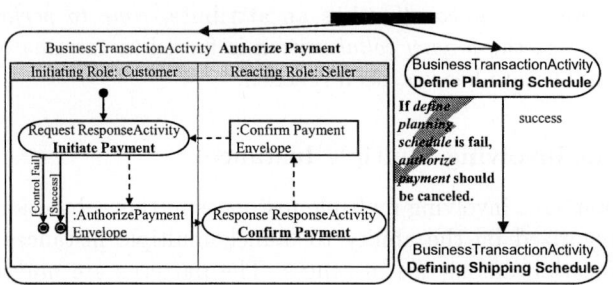

Fig. 11. A problem of a cancel activity pattern.

Cancel case. A cancel case patterns terminates a *binary collaboration*. In UMM (BPSS), as soon as a *final* state (a *success* or a *failure* element) is reached, the *binary collaboration* is terminated. Even if other *business transaction activities* remain, they do not open any more. In this case, a timeout exception can be generated. Therefore, although a *binary collaboration* has several *final* states, they should be mutually exclusive.

4 Conclusion

In this paper, we analyze the expression power of UMM and BPSS by workflow patterns. We summarize the analysis in Table 1. A '+' and a '-' in a cell of the table refer to direct support and no support, respectively. Even if a pattern is rated as a '-', we can realize the pattern partially by the combination of other patterns [5]. A 't' means that the pattern is realized as a tag value in UMM not by a feature of an activity graph in UML. A '2' indicates that the pattern can be supported if UMM will adapt UML 2.0.

According to the presentations of each pattern in both UMM and BPSS, we are able to derive the transformation rules listed below. This list covers all known rules necessary to transform a UMM business collaboration protocol to a BPSS binary collaboration. Our future work includes representation of these rules in a formal syntax and an implementation of the mapping from UMM business processes represented in XMI [12] to BPSS.

Table 1. Comparison of UMM and BPSS

	UMM v. 12	BPSS v. 1.10
Sequence	+	+
Parallel Split	+	+
Synchronization	+	+
Exclusive Choice	+	+
Simple Merge	+	+
Multi Choice	+	+
Synchronizing Merge	+	-
Multi Merge	2	-
Discriminator	2	+
Arbitrary Cycles	-	+
Implicit Termination	t	+
MI without Synchronization	t	+
MI with a Priori Design Time Knowledge	-	-
MI with a Priori Runtime Knowledge	-	-
MI without a Priori Runtime Knowledge	-	-
Deferred Choice	+	+
Interleaved Parallel Routing	-	-
Milestone	t	+
Cancel Activity	-	-
Cancel Case	+	+

– An *initial* state and an *activity* state are transformed to a *start* element and a *business transaction activity*, respectively.
– A *final* state is transformed to a *success* or a *failure* element. We need some convention for deciding whether *final* state is transformed to a *success* or a *failure* element.
– A *transition* of UMM is transformed to a *transition* of BPSS. However, if the transition leads to a *final* state, the transition becomes an attribute of a *success* or a *failure* element. The same exception applies to transitions from the initial state.
– A *synchronization* state with multiple incoming transitions is transformed to a *fork* element whose *type* attribute is *or*. If some outgoing transitions are guarded, the *fork* element needs a *time to perform* attribute.
– A *synchronization* state with multiple outgoing transitions is transformed to a *join* element whose *wait for all* attribute is *true*.
– A *decision* state with multiple incoming transitions is transformed to a *decision* element.
– A *decision* state with multiple outgoing transitions is transformed to a *join* element whose *wait for all* attribute is *false*.
– If an *business transaction activity* has multiple outgoing transitions and each transition is triggered by event, a *fork* element is inserted between *business transaction activity* and its outgoing transitions. The *type* of the *fork* is *xor* if triggering events are not concurrent.

- Tagged values, *is concurrent* and *time to perform*, are transformed to the same named attributes of *business transaction activity* and *binary collaboration*, respectively.

Our research resulted in the need for improvements for both UMM and BPSS. Some patterns like an implicit termination and an arbitrary cycle are supported by both. For reasons of readability these patterns should be avoided. Therefore, we need to study well-formedness rules for prohibiting these patterns.

In spite of their similarity, the transformation between UMM and BPSS is not straightforward since the sets of workflow patterns that the two languages support are not exactly the same. For example, while BPSS realizes a discriminator pattern, a BPSS instance derived from UMM will never use this pattern since UMM cannot support the pattern yet. If a new UMM version adopts UML 2.0, the gap between UMM model and BPSS is reduced since the new UMM supports more workflow patterns including a discriminator.

We can also apply the workflow pattern to transformations between other heterogeneous business process modeling languages such as BPEL4WS and XPDL.

References

1. Ferris, C., Farrell, J.: What are web services. Communications of the ACM **46** (2003) 31 – 35
2. W3C Web Services Architecture Working Group: Web services architecture requirements; W3C working draft (2002) http://www.w3.org/TR/2002/WD-wsa-reqs-20021114.
3. Leymann, F., Roller, D.: Modeling Business Processes with BPEL4WS. In: Proceedings of the 1st GI Workshop XML4BPM. (2004) 7–24
4. Peltz, C.: Web services orchestration and choreography. IEEE Computer **36** (2003) 46 – 52
5. Van der Aalst, A., Hofsteded, A.T., Kiepuszewski, B., Barros, A.: Workflow patterns. Distributed and Parallel Databases **14** (2003) 5 – 51
6. Wohed, P., van der Aalst, W.M., Dumas, M., ter Hofstede, A.H.: Analysis of web services composition languages: The case of bpel4ws. Lecture notes in computer science **2813** (2003) 200–215
7. UN/CEFACT TMG: UN/CEFACT modeling methodology, revision 12 (2003) http://www.untmg.org.
8. UN/CEFACT TMG: ebXML business process specification version 1.10 (2003)
9. ISO: Open-edi Reference Model. ISO/IEC JTC 1/SC30 ISO Standard 14662. ISO (1995)
10. Dumas, M., ter Hofstede, A.H.: UML activity diagrams as a workflow specification language. Lecture notes in computer science **2185** (2001) 76 – 90
11. WfMC: Workflow management coalition terminology & glossary. Technical Report WFMC-TC-1011, WfMC (1999)
12. Jeckle, M.: OMG's XML Metadata Interchange XMI. In: Proceedings of the 1st GI Workshop XML4BPM. (2004) 25–42

The Notion of Business Process Revisited

Jan L.G. Dietz and Nathalie Habing

Delft University of Technology
P.O. Box 5031, NL-2600GA Delft
j.l.g.dietz@ewi.tudelft.nl, nhabing@worldonline.nl

Abstract. The notion of business process is becoming increasingly important in all business and information/communication technology related disciplines, and therefore gets a lot of attention. Consequently, there is a variety of definitions as well as a variety in preciseness of definition. The research reported in this paper aims at clarifying the different understandings and unifying them in a common conceptual framework. Three fundamental questions concerning business processes are investigated: about the difference between business process and information process, about the distinction between the 'deep' structure and the 'surface' structure of a business process, and about the difference between system and process. These questions are discussed within the framework of the Ψ-theory and the DEMO methodology.

1 Introduction

Since the early 90's the term 'business process' has become widely accepted within the areas of business process and information systems engineering, particularly through the publications of Hammer, Champy and Davenport [11, 12, 6]. Numerous publications have followed upon these pioneering ones. At the same time a number of other disciplines have incorporated the notion of business process, like e.g. workflow and quality management. This has lead to a likewise diverse set of definitions, ranging from rather informal ones, like in [19], to quite formal definitions, like in [1].

It is the purpose of this paper to clarify this diversity and to try to unify the different understandings. In particular, the next research questions are addressed:

1. Is the notion of business process a really new notion or can it be defined, e.g. by means of specialization and/or aggregation, on the basis of existing notions? If so, how? If not so, how should it be understood and how should it be related to existing notions in information systems engineering?
2. The way in which business processes present themselves to us, may change while some 'essence' in it remains stable. Apparently there is a 'deep' structure behind the 'surface' structures that people observe and change. What is this deep structure and how can it be extracted from a surface structure?
3. What is precisely meant by 'process' in contrast to 'system'? To exemplify this question: it is quite common to speak of 'business *process*' and of 'information *system*'. Do people mean really different notions by these different terms or is 'process' in business process more like 'system' in information system?

We will seek answers to these questions within the conceptual framework of the Ψ-theory (Ψ is pronounced as PSI which is an acronym for Performance in Social Interaction). This theory has emerged from over ten years of practical experience and corresponding scientific research concerning the DEMO methodology (Design & Engineering Methodology for Organizations) [7, 8, 22, 22]. The Ψ-theory has its theoretical roots in three existing branches of philosophy: semiotics, language philosophy, and systemic ontology. Semiotics is the general study of signs, based on the seminal work of Peirce [18]. It has been elaborated by e.g. Morris [16] and Nauta [17]. In the last decade, a sub field has emerged, called organizational semiotics, which addresses in particular the use of signs by people in organizations [24]. Language philosophy starts with Austin [2] but has been brought to the public particularly through the Speech Act Theory of Searle [21] and the Communicative Action Theory of Habermas [9]. Systemic ontology is the more precise and more formal alternative for general systems theory [3]. It has been developed by Bunge [4, 5]. The outline of the paper is as follows. In section 2 a summary of the underlying Ψ-theory is provided, and in section 3 the DEMO methodology is briefly introduced. In section 4 an example case from health care is modeled and discussed. Section 5 contains the conclusions. Particular attention is given to the generalizability of the findings. Answers to the research questions as formulated above are developed, and conclusions of the whole study are drawn.

2 The Ψ-Theory

There exist two different system notions, each with its own value, its own purpose, and its own type of model: the function-oriented or teleological and the construction-oriented or ontological system notion. The *teleological system* notion is about the (external) function and behavior of a system. The corresponding type of model is the *black-box model*. Ideally, such a model is a (mathematical) relation between a set of input variables and a set of output variables, called the transfer function. Knowing the transfer function means knowing how the system responds to variations in the values of the input variables by changing the values of the output variables. Otherwise said, through manipulating the input variables, one is able to control the behavior.

The *ontological system* notion is about the (internal) construction and operation of a system. The relationship with function and behavior is that these are brought forward, and consequently explained, by the construction and the operation of a system. The ontological definition of a system, based on the one that is provided in [5], is as follows. Something is a system if and only if it has the next properties:
- *Composition*: a set of elements of some category (physical, biological, social etc.).
- *Environment*: a set of elements of the same category. The composition and the environment are disjoint.
- *Production*: the elements in the composition produce things (products or services) that are delivered to the elements in the environment.
- *Structure*: a set of interaction relationships among the elements in the composition and between these and the elements in the environment.

An important characteristic is the category to which the elements of a system belong. Therefore, we prefer to call a system according to the definition above a *homogeneous* system. As will be shown later, homogeneous systems can be integrated to constitute heterogeneous systems. The corresponding type of model is the *white-box model*, which is a direct conceptualization of this ontological system definition.

The teleological system notion is adequate for the purpose of using or controlling a system. It is therefore the dominant system concept in e.g. the social sciences, including the organizational sciences. If the transfer function is too complicated to understand, the technique of *functional decomposition* can be applied through which the black-box model of a system is replaced by a structure of sub models of which the transfer functions are more readily understandable. One has to bear in mind however that the knowledge acquired about the system is still functional or behavioral knowledge, in other words, it does not reveal anything about its construction. It is a widely spread misunderstanding to think that if the technique of functional decomposition is applied down to some elementary level, one has revealed the construction of the system. This is not true and can never be true. Moreover, one can make virtually any functional decomposition of a black-box model one likes. Instead, for the purpose of building and changing a system, one needs to adopt the ontological system notion. It is therefore the dominant system notion in all engineering sciences.

The ontological definition of an *organization* is that it is a system in the category of social systems. This means that the elements are social individuals, i.e. human beings in their ability of entering into and complying with commitments about the things that are produced in collaboration. The Ψ-theory provides an explanation of the construction and the operation of organizations, regardless their particular kind or branch (like industry or government, or manufacturing or service). It is based on several axioms, of which the relevant ones for this paper are presented hereafter.

The Construction Axiom

An organization consists of *actors* (human beings fulfilling an actor role) who perform two kinds of acts. By performing *production acts*, the actors bring about the mission of the organization. A production act (P-act for short) may be material (e.g. a manufacturing or transportation act) or immaterial (e.g. deciding, judging, diagnosing). By performing *coordination acts* (C-acts for short), actors enter into and comply with commitments. In doing so, they initiate and coordinate the execution of production acts. An *actor role* is defined as a particular, atomic 'amount' of authority, viz. the authority needed to perform precisely one kind of production act. The result of successfully performing a P-act is a *production fact* or P-fact. P-facts in a library, for example, include "membership M has started to exist" and "the late return fine for loan L is paid". The variables M and L denote an instance of membership and loan respectively. Examples of C-acts are requesting and promising a P-fact (e.g. requesting to become member of the library).

The result of successfully performing a C-act is a *coordination fact* or C-fact (e.g. the being requested of the production fact "membership #387 has started to exist"). Just as we distinguish between P-acts and C-acts, we also distinguish between two worlds in which these kinds of acts have effect: the *production world* or P-world and the *coordination world* or C-world respectively (see Figure 1). At any moment, the C-world and the P-world are in a particular state, simply defined as a set of C-facts or P-facts respectively created up to that moment. When active, actors take the current state of the P-world and the C-world into account (indicated by the dotted arrows in Figure 1). C-facts serve as agenda for actors, which they constantly try to deal with. Otherwise said, actors interact by means of creating and dealing with C-facts.

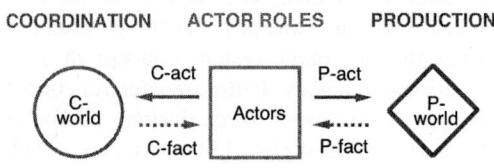

Fig. 1. The white-box model of an organization

The Transaction Axiom

P-acts and C-acts appear to occur in generic recurrent patterns, called *transactions* [8]. The genericity of this pattern has turned out to be so omnipresent and persistent that we consider it to be a socionomic law. A transaction goes off in three phases: the order phase (O-phase), the execution phase (E-phase), and the result phase (R-phase). It is carried through by two actors, who alternately perform acts. The actor who starts the transaction and eventually completes it, is called the *initiator*. The other one, who actually performs the production act, is called the *executor*. The O-phase is a conversation that starts with a request by the initiator and ends (if successfully) with a promise by the executor. The R-phase is a conversation that starts with a statement by the executor and ends (if successfully) with an acceptance by the initiator. In between these two conversations there is the E-phase in which the executor performs the P-act.

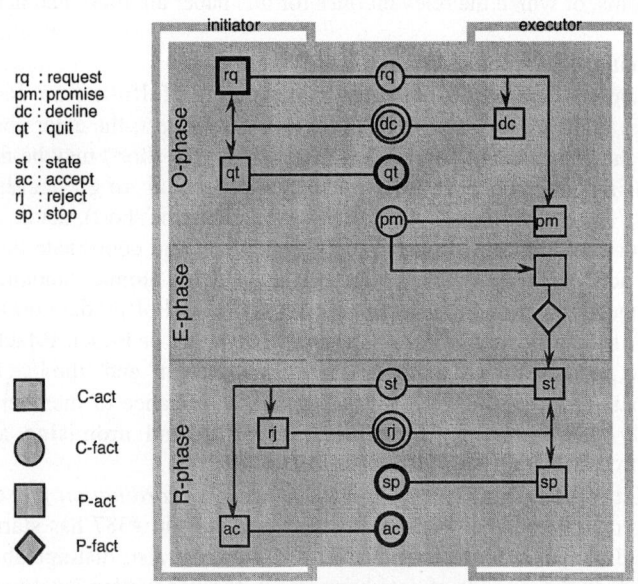

Fig. 2. The standard pattern of a transaction

Figure 2 exhibits the standard pattern of a transaction. A white box represents a C-act (type) and a white disk represents a C-fact (type). A gray box represents a P-act (type) and a gray diamond a P-fact (type). The initial C-act is drawn with a bold line, as is every terminal C-fact. The gray colored frames, denoted by "initiator" and "executor" represent the *responsibility areas* of the two partaking actor roles.

The standard pattern must always be passed through for establishing a new P-fact. A few comments are in place however. First, performing a C-act does not necessarily mean that there is oral or written communication. Every (physical) act may count as a C-act. Second, C-acts may be performed *tacitly*, i.e. without any signs being produced. In particular the promise and the acceptance are often performed tacitly (according to the rule "no news is good news"). Third, next to the standard transaction pattern, four cancellations patterns are identified. Together with the standard pattern they constitute the complete transaction pattern. Every *transaction process* is some path through this complete pattern, and every *business process* in every organization is a connected collection of such transaction processes. This holds also for processes across organizations, like in supply chains and networks. Therefore, the transaction pattern must be taken as a *socionomic law*: people always and everywhere conduct business (of whatever kind) along this pattern.

The Abstraction Axiom

Three human abilities play a significant role in performing C-acts [7]. They are called forma, informa and performa respectively. The *forma* ability concerns being able to produce and perceive sentences (Note. By sentence is meant the atomic unit of information). The forma ability coincides with the semiotic layers syntactics and empirics [24]. The *informa* ability concerns being able to formulate thoughts into sentences and to interpret sentences. The term 'thought' is used in the most general sense. It may be a fact, a wish, an emotion etc. The informa ability coincides with the semiotic layers semantics and pragmatics. The *performa* ability concerns being able to engage into commitments, either as performer or as addressee of a coordination act. It coincides with the (organizational) semiotic layer socialics. This ability may be considered as the *essential* human ability for doing business (of any kind). A similar distinction in three levels of abstraction can be made on the production side. The *forma* ability now concerns being able to deal with recorded sentences, called documents (Note. The term 'document' is used here to refer in a most general sense to the forma aspect of information). The *informa* ability on the production side concerns being able to reason, to compute, derive etc. Lastly, the *performa* ability concerns being able to establish original new things, like creating material products or making decisions. Because this is at the core of doing business (on the production side), it is called the *essential* production.

Looked upon from the production side, the abstraction levels may be understood as 'glasses' for viewing an organization (see Figure 3). Looking through the *essential* glasses, one observes the essential business actors, who perform P-acts that result in original (non-derivable) facts, and who directly contribute to the organization's function. These essential acts and facts are collectively called *B-things* (from Business). Looking through the *informational* glasses, one observes intellectual actors, who execute informational acts like collecting, providing, recalling and computing knowledge about business facts. Informational acts and facts are collectively called *I-things* (from Information and Intellect).

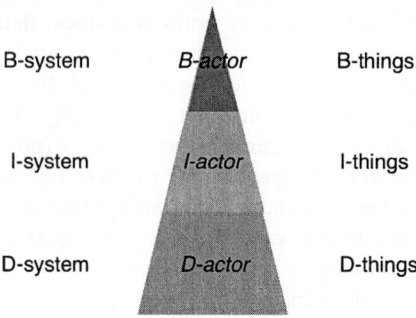

Fig. 3. The three aspect systems of an organization

Looking through the *documental* glasses, one observes documental actors, who execute documental acts like gathering, distributing, storing, and copying documents containing the knowledge mentioned above. Documental acts and facts are collectively called *D-things* (from Document and Data). Recall that an actor is a person fulfilling an actor role. So, for example, a person may simultaneously fulfill a B-actor role, an I-actor role and a D-actor role: if you receive a customer order, you may perform some documental acts (like copying and archiving), you may need to perform some informational acts (like inquiring about the customer) and you will actually deal with the request for delivery.

The abstraction levels as distinguished in the Ψ-theory are an example of a *layered nesting* of (sub) systems. Generally spoken, a system in some layer *supports* (the operation of) a system in the next higher layer. Conversely, a system in a layer *uses* systems in the next lower layer. So, B-systems use I-systems and I-systems use D-systems. Conversely, D-systems support I-systems and I-systems support B-systems. If a system X supports a system Y, it means that the function of system X is expressed in terms of the construction and operation of system Y. For example, the actor in the B-system of a library who registers new members, needs to know the age of a candidate member. This information can by definition only asked for in the I-system. In order to get the information, the subject who fulfills the B-actor role has to take his 'shape' of I-actor and initiate an (informational) transaction resulting in the provision of the needed knowledge by the executor of this transaction (the I-actor who is the proprietor of this piece of knowledge). Usually, this I-actor will not know the requested knowledge by heart and thus has to initiate, in his 'shape' of D-actor, a (documental) transaction of which the executor is a D-actor who keeps record of the requested knowledge. A copy of the record (a document) is sent to the initiator who, in his shape of I-actor, is able to interpret the document and lastly, in his shape of B-actor, is able to take the appropriate action based on the acquired knowledge. What the layered nesting constitutes is an intrinsically solid integration of three homogeneous systems into one *heterogeneous* system, which is the (complete) organization. The integration is solid because it builds on the inseparability of the three human abilities.

3 The DEMO Methodology

DEMO is a methodology for (re)designing and (re)engineering organizations that takes full advantage of the Ψ-theory. The model of an organization in DEMO consists of four aspect models. Together they constitute the complete white-box model of one of the aspect systems of an organization: the B-system, the I-system or the D-system. Figure 4 exhibits the aspect models and their interrelationships. The Construction Model (CM) specifies the composition, the environment and the structure of a system: the identified transaction types and the associated actor roles. The Process Model (PM) specifies the lawful sequences of events in the Coordination World and the Production World: the (atomic) process steps and their causal and conditional relationships. The State Model (SM) specifies the lawful states of the Coordination World and the Production World: the object classes, the fact types and the ontological coexistence rules. Lastly, the Action Model (AM) specifies the action rules that serve as guidelines for the actors in dealing with their agenda: there is an action rule for every type of agendum.

The models are expressed in diagrams, tables and pseudo algorithms. In this paper, only the Actor Transaction Diagram, the Transaction Result Table, and the Process Step Diagram are presented, and only the B-system is modeled. The subsequent modeling of the I-system and the D-system goes rather straightforward. The general procedure to arrive at a correct and complete set of models of the B-system of an organization consists of three analysis and three synthesis steps:

1. The *Perfoma-Informa-Forma* Analysis. In this step all available pieces of knowledge (from documents, interviews etc.) are divided in three sets, according to the distinction between the three human abilities. Normally the relative sizes of these sets (amount of text) is about 1:2:4.
2. The *Coordination-Actors-Production* Analysis. The Performa things are divided into C-acts/facts, P-acts/facts and actor roles. This step goes rather straightforward since the three kinds are well distinguished.
3. The *Product Structure* Analysis. Every transaction type of which an actor in the environment is the initiator may be conceived as delivering and 'end product' to the environment. Generally, the (internal) executor of this transaction type is initiator of one or more other transaction types, and so on. The results of these cascaded transactions are 'components' of the 'end product'.
4. The *Transaction Pattern* Synthesis. The transaction pattern is put 'over' the results so far, as a template in order to cluster the things found into transaction types. Next, for every transaction type, the resulting P-event type is correctly and precisely formulated. The Transaction Result Table can now be produced.
5. The *Construction* Synthesis. For every transaction type, the initiating actor role(s) and the executing actor role are identified. This is the first step in producing the Actor Transaction Diagram.
6. The *Organization* Synthesis. A definite choice has to be made as to what part of the construction will be taken as the organization to be studied and which part becomes the environment. The Actor Transaction Diagram can now be finalized.

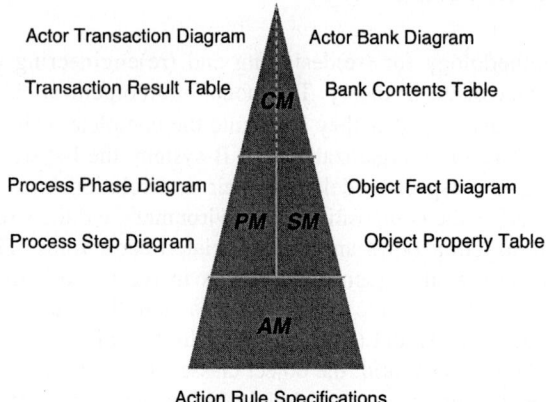

Fig. 4. The four aspect models

The model of the B-system of an organization, also called the *essential* model of the organization, is concise but very comprehensible, particularly for managers; the construction model (CM) of most middle-sized or corporate divisions can be represented on an A1-size sheet of paper. The model of a B-system is also complete and coherent. Because of these properties and because of the abstraction from all implementation issues, it is a candidate reference model, applying to all organizations in a particular branch or industry.

4   The Health Care Reference Model

The health care model as discussed in this section is one of the outcomes of the research that has been reported in [10]. To identify generic transactions in care processes, we investigated four different care processes or patient groups: patients with (or suspected of) breast cancer, patients with a tumor in the head-neck area, patients with (or suspected of) Schizophrenia and patients with rheumatism. We consider the identified commonalities in these processes sufficiently representative for calling the presented common model a health care reference model.

The research was carried out in four phases. In the first phase we identified all the care-clusters involved in the care for each patient group and drew up an inventory of the activities performed in these care-clusters. In the second phase we identified from the inventory the core activities performed in each care-cluster and described them in a structured and generic way. In the third phase we compared the core activities of one care-cluster with the core activities of other care-clusters to identify generic transactions types. The generic transactions found were used to construct a generic Actor Transaction Diagram, Transaction Result Table and Process Step Diagram. The fourth phase was concerned with the evaluation of our results. Several care providers reviewed the results and tested them against real-life examples of clinical situations.

Transaction Result Table		
T#	Transaction Type Name	Resulting Production-fact
T01	(Re)establish patient problem	Patient problem PP is (re)established
T02	Execute clinical examination	Clinical examination CE regarding patient problem PP is executed
T03	Secure patient availability	The patient is available for performing a CE or a PA.
T04	Provide expert opinion on PP	Expert opinion EO regarding (re)establishing PP is provided
T05	Establish policy options	The policy options for PP are established
T06	Provide expert opinion on PO	Expert opinion EO regarding establishing policy option P is provided
T07	Execute policy	Policy P for patient problem PP is executed
T08	Execute policy activity	Policy activity PA in policy P is executed
T09	Secure material availability	Patient material PM is available for performing PA

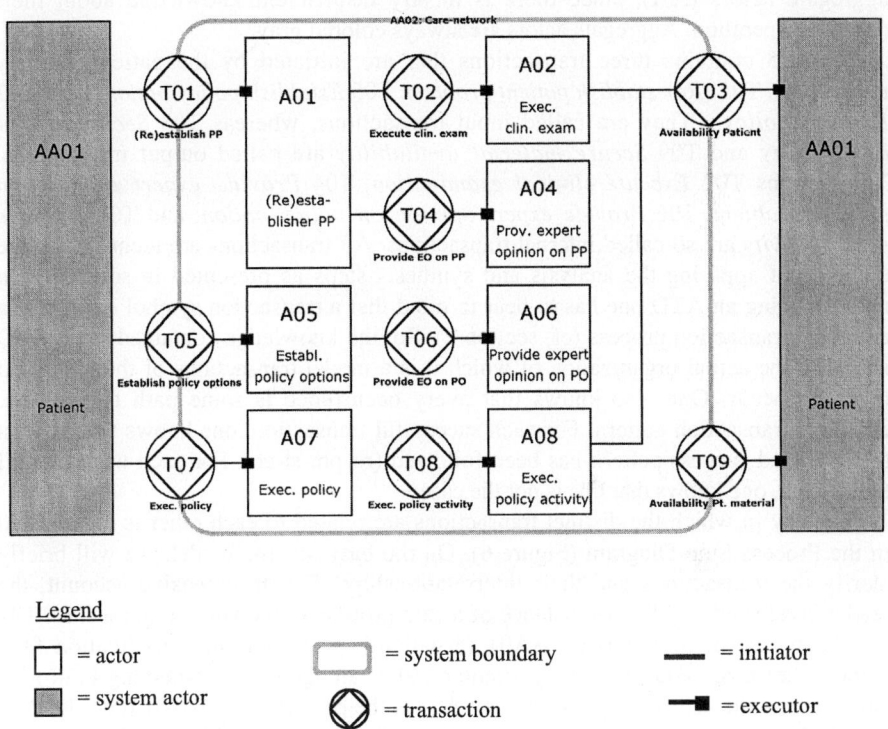

Fig. 5. Generic Actor Transaction Diagram (ATD) for Care Processes

The generic Actor Transaction Diagram (ATD) for Care Processes as presented in Figure 5 shows the identified transaction types and the involved actor roles. In the ATD a transaction is represented by a circle (the generic symbol for coordination) in which a diamond is drawn (the generic symbol for production). Actors are displayed as rectangles. The small box on the edge of an actor symbol at the conjunction with the transaction link indicates that the actor is the executor of the transaction. The scope of the model (system boundary) is represented by a gray-lined rectangle. The table on top of the figure is the Transaction result Table. It specifies the facts that are created as the result of successfully carrying through a transaction of the corresponding type. Words in capitals (like P, PP and PA) denote variables that have to be instantiated. They serve to uniquely identify the core entities. Examples are patient problem (PP) and policy activity (PA).

The actor roles A01, A02, A04, A05, A06, A07, and A08 constitute the composition of the modeled system. They are elementary, i.e. they are executor of exactly one transaction type. The environment consists only of actor role AA01. Actor roles in the environment are generally modeled as non-elementary, so-called aggregate actors (AA), since there is mostly insufficient knowledge about their (internal) operation. Aggregate actors are always colored gray.

Figure 5 contains three transactions that are initiated by the patient, namely transactions T01 *(Re)establish patient problem*, T05 *Establish policy options*, and T07 *Execute policy*. They are called input transactions, whereas T03 *Secure patient availability* and T09 *Secure material availability* are called output transactions. Transactions T02 *Execute clinical examination*, T04 *Provide expert opinion on patient problem*, T06 *Provide expert opinion on policy option*, and T08 *Execute policy activity* are so-called internal transactions. All transactions are identified as the outcome of applying the analysis and synthesis steps as presented in section 3. In understanding an ATD one has to bear in mind that a transaction symbol stands for a complete transaction process (cf. section 2). So, the knowledge contained in an ATD is that in the actual organization of which it is a model transactions of the identified types do occur. One also knows that every occurrence is some path through the complete transaction pattern. For each successful transaction, one knows that at least the so-called success pattern has been followed (rq-pm-st-ac). For each unsuccessful transaction, one knows that this is not the case.

The way in which the distinct transactions are related to each other is represented in the Process Step Diagram (Figure 6). On the basis of this model, we will briefly clarify the transactions and their interrelationships. For an extensive account, the reader is referred to [10]. An instance of a care process starts with a request for a T01 (establish patient problem) by AA01 (a patient). The resulting coordination fact, namely the being requested of a particular T01 is an agendum (something to do) for A01. One of the acts to be performed by A01 is the promise of this T01 (coordination step T01/pr). However, there exists a wait condition (wc) for this step, indicated by the dotted arrow from T02/pr to T01/pr. It means that actor A01 has to wait until the fact T02/pr is created before she is able to perform T01/pr (promising to the patient that she will establish his problem). The state T02/pr can be reached if A01 performs the T02/rq, i.e. the request for a clinical examination, which is directed to A02. This causal relation (cr) between T01 and T02 is optional. Accordingly, the wait condition on T01/pr is also optional (if no clinical examination is needed, A01 does not have to wait for promising T01). If the act T02/rq is performed, the coordination fact T02/rq is created (a clinical examination is requested). This fact is an agendum for A02. There is a (non-optional) causal relation from T02/rq to T03/rq, meaning that the first thing to do for A02 is to request to AA01 (the patient) for the execution of a T03 (becoming physically available for a clinical examination).

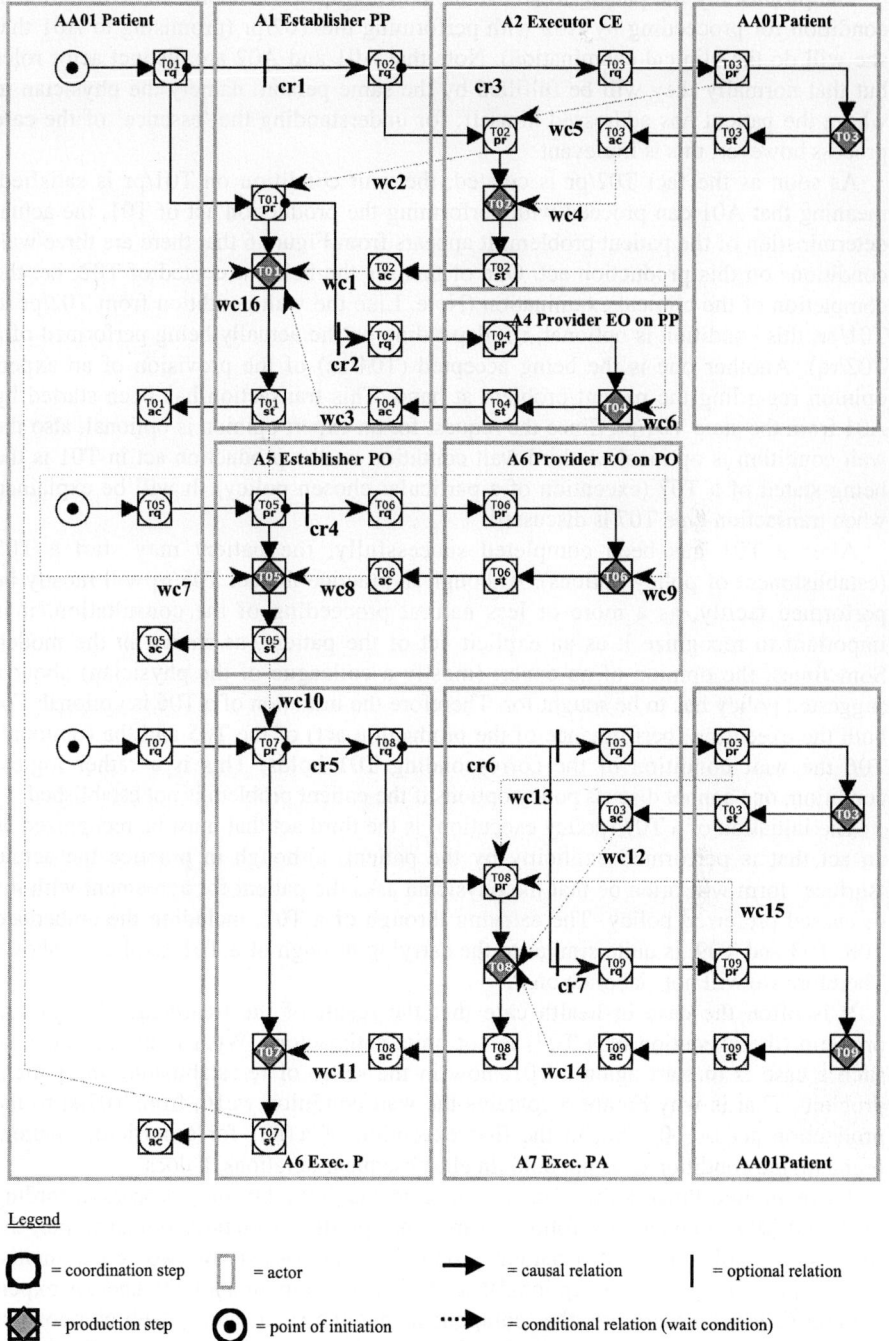

Fig. 6. Generic Process Step Diagram (PSD) for Care Processes

The promise by the patient to be available (T03/pr) is considered to be a sufficient condition for proceeding by A02 with performing the T02/pr (promising to A01 that she will do the clinical examination). Note that A01 and A02 are distinct actor roles but that normally they will be fulfilled by the same person, namely the physician to whom the patient has addressed himself; for understanding the 'essence' of the care process however, this is irrelevant.

As soon as the fact T02/pr is created, the wait condition on T01/pr is satisfied, meaning that A01 can proceed with performing the production act of T01, the actual determination of the patient problem. It appears from Figure 6 that there are three wait conditions on this production act. One of them is the being accepted of T02, i.e. the completion of the clinical examination (Note. Like the wait condition from T02/pr to T01/pr, this condition is optional, i.e. depending on the actually being performed of a T02/rq). Another one is the being accepted (T04/ac) of the provision of an expert opinion regarding the patient problem at hand. This transaction has been started by A01 from the state T01/pr. Since the request for an expert opinion is optional, also the wait condition is optional. A third wait condition on the production act in T01 is the being stated of a T07 (execution of a particular chosen policy). It will be explained when transaction type T07 is discussed.

After a T01 has been completed successfully, the patient may start a T05 (establishment of policy options). Although in practice the act T05/rq will mostly be performed tacitly, as a more or less natural proceeding of the consultation, it is important to recognize it as an explicit act of the patient, as shown in the model. Sometimes, the opinion of an expert (mostly a colleague of the physician) about a suggested policy has to be sought for. Therefore the initiation of a T06 is optional. For both the execution (performance of the production act) of the T05 and the (optional) T06 the wait condition of the corresponding T01 holds. This is a rather logical condition; one cannot discuss policy options if the patient problem is not established.

The initiation of a T07 (policy execution) is the third act that must be recognized as an act that is performed explicitly by the patient, although in practice the actual 'surface' form will often be that the physician asks the patient for agreement with the discussed preferred policy. The carrying through of a T07, including the embedded T08, T03 and T09, is quite similar to the carrying through of a T01, explained above. Therefore we will not elaborate on it.

It is often the case in health care that the result of the treatment of a patient problem (the execution of a T07) is not quite satisfactory. What is usually done in such a case is to start again a T01, now in the sense of re-establishing the patient problem. That is why Figure 6 contains the wait condition wc16, from T07/st to the production act of T01. So, in the first execution of a T01 for a particular patient problem, the condition does not hold. In all subsequent iterations, it does.

The exhibited Process Step Diagram also shows that a business process according to the DEMO methodology follows a tree-like product structure. For example, the 'product' establishment of a patient problem (T01) consists of two 'components' (which both happen to be optional): a clinical examination (T02) and an expert opinion (T04). Furthermore, the 'component' has the (mandatory) 'sub component' patient availability (T03). In DEMO, a *business process* is defined as a collection of causally related transactions. So, the Process Step Diagram in Figure 6 contains three business processes, each of them initiated by the patient.

5 Discussion and Conclusions

We will successively address now the three research questions as formulated in section 1. Before proceeding to do this, we like to discuss once more the important distinction between the teleological (function-oriented) and the ontological (construction-oriented) notion of system, as well as between the corresponding model types: the black-box model and the white-box model. This distinction appears to be recognized rarely, both in theory and in practice. It can also scarcely be recognized in the various modeling techniques that are currently in use. The point is that the two perspectives are complementary and that both are needed for a full understanding of a system. To be more precise, only a black-box model is helpful for understanding the function and the behavior of a system, and only a white-box model is helpful for understanding the construction and the operation of a system. Moreover, these two kinds of models cannot replace each other. If one has to deal with the usage or the control of a system, only a black-box model is appropriate. When one has to deal with building or changing a system, only a white-box model is appropriate. A good and pure example of a black-box model is the value chain model [19]. Good and pure examples of white-box models are the Petri Net [1] and the EPC [13]. There exists a quite large amount of model types that we would like to call black-grey models, indicating that they are not purely black but derivatives of the black-box model; anyhow, they are not white-box models. Examples of this class of model are the DFD in all its variants (cf. e.g. [28]), and IDEF0 [20]. Although widely applied in systems engineering, they are just not suited for it, as we have made clear.

From the Ψ-theory as explained in section 2, it follows that a business process or business system (the B-system of an organization) is fundamentally different from an information system (the I-system of an organization). The difference is strongly related to the social character of the interactions between actors. Only the B-system is able to produce original new facts, like decisions and judgements. It is important that they can be held responsible for these decisions and judgements. The I-system is only capable of computing or deriving facts from existing ones. There is no point in holding someone responsible for the rightness of mathematical or logical operations. Therefore, the production acts in the I-system can easily be replaced by acts of artifacts (computer applications, intelligent agents etc.), whereas the production acts in the B-system can only be produced by human beings. Consequently, business processes cannot be addressed appropriately if modeling techniques are used that consider decisions and judgments to be similar to computation or derivation and to data or document handling. Examples of such techniques, taken from the information systems area, are DFD, IDEF, UML, Petri Net and EPC. These techniques just lack the appropriate notions. So, the answer to question 1 is that the notion of business process is a really new notion and that it can only be dealt with correctly if it is taken as really different from information processes. Consequently, new theories and new methodologies are needed. Examples are the Ψ-theory and the DEMO methodology as presented in this paper. Other examples can be found in [14], [25], [26] and [27].

The Ψ-theory also provides the clue to answering question 2, about the distinction between a 'deep' structure and a 'surface' structure of business processes. As the 'deep' structure of a business process we propose to take the (white-box model of the)

B-system of an organization. As the 'surface' structure of a business process we propose to take the implementations of the B-system, the I-system and the D-system. We like to emphasize that the relationship between 'deep' and 'surface' is not simply a matter of generalization-specialization, as e.g. suggested in [15]. Instead it is both about the layered nesting of the three aspect systems and about the way these are implemented. An additional element in the 'deep' structure of a business process is the generic transaction pattern. As discussed in [7], a business process is a fiber of molecules (the transaction processes) that are composed of atoms (the C-acts/facts and the corresponding P-acts/facts). The generic transaction pattern is nothing less than a socionomic given. People all over the world, whether consciously or unconsciously, and in all organizations follow this pattern when doing business.

As we have also shown, a clear distinction can be made between system and process. It is also worthwhile to do it. To illustrate this, the Actor Transaction Diagram models the *business system* of an organization (the B-system), whereas the Process Step Diagram models its *business processes*. Note that both are white-box models, while in practice these terms 'system' and 'process' are also used to denote black-box models; this contributes of course to the current confusion. It is common practice however not to be so exact in distinguishing between these meanings. As a consequence, the term 'business process' must sometimes be understood as a teleological notion and sometimes as an ontological one. Moreover, sometimes it has to be taken as business system instead of business process. This answers question 3.

The analysis of the four different care processes has provided substantial practical evidence for the rightness of our conclusions. Regarding question 1, rather continuous discussions have taken place about the authority and responsibility of the actor roles in the B-system. It has led to the clarification of the various actor roles in these care processes. For example, the actor roles A01 and A02 (cf. Figure 5) are usually fulfilled by the same person (the physician). In discussing the model one has become aware of the distinct roles and the possible other ways of organizing the care process. Another important discussion was about the role of initiator of the patient in the transactions T01, T05 and T07. Normally, T01 and T05 are carried through during one consultation. Before we started our analysis and modeling activities, the two roles of the patient were not distinguished, and it was generally not clear who asked for establishing the policy options, it was even mostly not considered to be a separate transaction. Moreover, in many cases the physician thought he or she was the initiator of T05. As a general conclusion, it was appreciated that that these matters have been clarified and it was agreed that no one else than the patient could be the initiator of T05. So, as the overall result, the people in the care processes were pleased by the clarification of the way the patient's roles were modeled and they also considered it right in the context of the modern legal position of the patient in his/her relationship to care providers.

Regarding question 2, the conciseness of the essential model, together with a very clear abstraction from implementation issues, was very much appreciated. In one case (the breast cancer care process) we also have gone through a re-engineering project of the various business processes. The distinction between the three aspect systems has proven to be very helpful. None of the proposed changes appeared to be at the B-level, and most were at the D-level (new forms, new flows of forms, other archiving procedures etc.). The insight that these changes would not have a deep impact and thus could not be very risky, while still improving the efficiency considerably, have been beneficial. At the same time, the deep structure has been very helpful in checking the effects of the I-level and D-level changes. Next, after the analyses of the four care processes, the idea of there being one common reference model popped up spontaneously. In first instance there were four different DEMO-models, however containing a large common core. The differences were analyzed and common solutions were proposed to each of the health care institutions. This has not only lead to the conception of the reference model, as presented in this paper, but also to an improved appreciation of this model as the valid model in all four institutions.

With these answers to the questions in section 1 we have shed a different light on the notion of business process. In the discussions we hope to have contributed to the clarification of the different understandings as well as to their possible unification. An implicit outcome of the Ψ-theory is that only social individuals are able to bear responsibility. Consequently, the usage of this term in the context of intelligent agents can only be metaphorical, as long as human beings are considered to be the only social individuals (as is currently the case). Lastly, the example of the health care processes that we have presented shows that the DEMO methodology is capable to deal with one of the most complicated existing kinds of business processes in an appropriate, concise but still very comprehensible way.

References

1. Aalst, W.M.P. van der, Hee, K.M. van, *Workflow Management: Models, Methods and Systems*, MIT Press, MA, 2001
2. Austin, J.L., *How to do things with words*, Harvard University Press, Cambridge MA, 1962
3. Bertalanffy, L. von (1968), *General Systems Theory*, Braziller, New York.
4. Bunge, M.A., *Treatise on Basic Philosophy*, vol.3, *The Furniture of the World*, D. Reidel Publishing Company, Dordrecht, The Netherlands, 1977
5. Bunge, M.A., Treatise on Basic Philosophy, vol.4, A World of Systems, D. Reidel Publishing Company, Dordrecht, The Netherlands, 1979
6. Davenport, T.H., 1993. *Process Innovation*. Harvard Business School Press, Boston.
7. Dietz, J.L.G., The Atoms, Molecules and Fibers of Organizations, *Data and Knowledge Engineering*, vol. 47, pp 301-325, 2003
8. Dietz, J. L. G., Generic recurrent patterns in business processes. In: Aalst, W. van der, Hofstede, A. ter, & Weske, M. (Eds.), *Business Process Management*, LNCS 2678. Springer-Verlag, 2003.
9. Habermas, J., *Theorie des Kommunikatives Handelns*, Erster Band, Suhrkamp Verlag, Frankfurt am Main, 1981
10. Habing, N., J.L.G. Dietz, P.J. Toussaint, J.H.M. Zwetsloot-Schonk, A transaction-based generic model of care processes, *Methods of Information in Medicine* (forthcoming)
11. Hammer, M., 1990. Reengineering Work: Don't Automate, Obliterate. *Harvard Business Review*. July-August, pp. 104-112.
12. Hammer, M., J.A. Champy, 1993. Reengineering the Corporation: A Manifesto for Business Revolution, Nicholas Brealy, London.
13. Keller, G., M. Nüttgens, A.-W. Scheer. Semantische Prozessmodellierung auf der Grundlage „Ereignisgesteuerte Prozessketten (EPK)". Veröffentlichung des Institut für Wirtschaftsinformatik, Paper 089, Saarbrücken, 1991 (http://www.iwi.uni-sb.de/iwi-hefte/heft089.ps).

14. Lind, M., G. Goldkuhl, The constituents of business interactions – generic layerd patterns, *Data and Knowledge Engineering*, vol. 47 no. 3, pp 327-348, 2003
15. Malone, T.W., K. Crowston, G.A. Herman, *Organizing business knowledge: the MIT process handbook*, chapter 12, MIT Press 2003
16. Morris, C.W., *Signs, Language and Behavior*, George Braziller, New York, 1955
17. Nauta Jr., D., *The Meaning of Information*, Mouton & Co, The Netherlands, 1972
18. Peirce, C., 1958, *Collected Papers of Charles Sanders Peirce*, Cambridge Mass.
19. Porter, M.E., V.E. Millar, 1985, How information gives you competitive advantages, Harvard Business Review.
20. Rico, D., *IDEF0 methodology*, J. Ross Publishing, 2004
21. Searle, J.R., *Speech Acts, an Essay in the Philosophy of Language*, Cambridge University Press, Cambridge MA, 1969
22. Reijswoud, V.E. van, 1996. *The Structure of Business Communication: Theory, model and application*. PhD Thesis Delft University of Technology, Delft.
23. Reijswoud, V.E. van, J.B.F. Mulder, J.L.G. Dietz, Speech Act Based Business Process and Information Modeling with DEMO, *Information Systems Journal*, 1999
24. Stamper, R., Liu, K., Hafkamp, M. & Ades, Y. (2000) "Understanding the Roles of Signs and Norms in Organizations", *Journal of Behavior and Information Technology*.
25. Taylor, J.R., E.J. van Every, *The emergent organization – Communication as Its Site and Surface*, Lawrence Erlbaum Associates, 2000
26. Weigand, H, A. de Moor, workflow analysis with communication norms, *Data and Knowledge Engineering*, vol. 47 no. 3, pp 349-369, 2003
27. Winograd, T, F. Flores, *Understanding Computers and Cognition: A New Foundation for Design*. Ablex, Norwood NJ, 1986
28. Yourdon, E., *Modern Structured Analysis*, Prentice-Hall, Inc., 1989

Disjoint and Overlapping Process Changes: Challenges, Solutions, Applications*

Stefanie Rinderle, Manfred Reichert, and Peter Dadam

University of Ulm, Faculty of Computer Science,
Dept. Databases and Information Systems
{rinderle, reichert, dadam}@informatik.uni-ulm.de

Abstract. Adaptive process–aware information systems must be able to support ad–hoc changes of single process instances as well as schema modifications at the process type level and their propagation to a collection of related process instances. So far these two kinds of (dynamic) process changes have been mainly considered in an isolated fashion. Especially for long-running processes, however, it must be possible to adequately handle the interplay between type and instance changes as well. One challenge in this context is to determine whether concurrent process type and process instance changes have the same or overlapping effects on the original process schema or not. Information about the degree of overlap is needed, for example, to determine whether and – if yes – how a process type change can be propagated to individually modified process instances as well. This paper provides a formal framework for dealing with overlapping and disjoint process changes and presents adequate migration strategies depending on the particular degree of overlap. In order to obtain a canonical representation of changes an algorithm is introduced which purges change logs from noisy information. Finally, a powerful proof-of-concept prototype exists.

1 Introduction

To stay competitive at the market for companies it becomes more and more important to adequately support their business by process–aware information systems (PAIS) [1]. Doing so it is not sufficient to implement business processes only once and to let the PAIS then run eternally without any adaptations. In fact the ability to quickly react to market changes or exceptional situations by appropriate process changes is key to success [2,3,4,5,6,7]. Basically, in a PAIS changes can take place at two levels – the *process type* or the *process instance* level. Process type changes become necessary, for example, to adapt the PAIS to optimized business processes or to new laws [8,9]. In particular, applications supporting long-running processes (e.g., handling of leasing contracts or medical treatments) and the process instances controlled by them are affected by such type changes [8,9]. As opposed to this, changes of single process instances have

---

* This work was done within the research project "Change management in adaptive workflow systems", which is funded by the German Research Community (DFG).

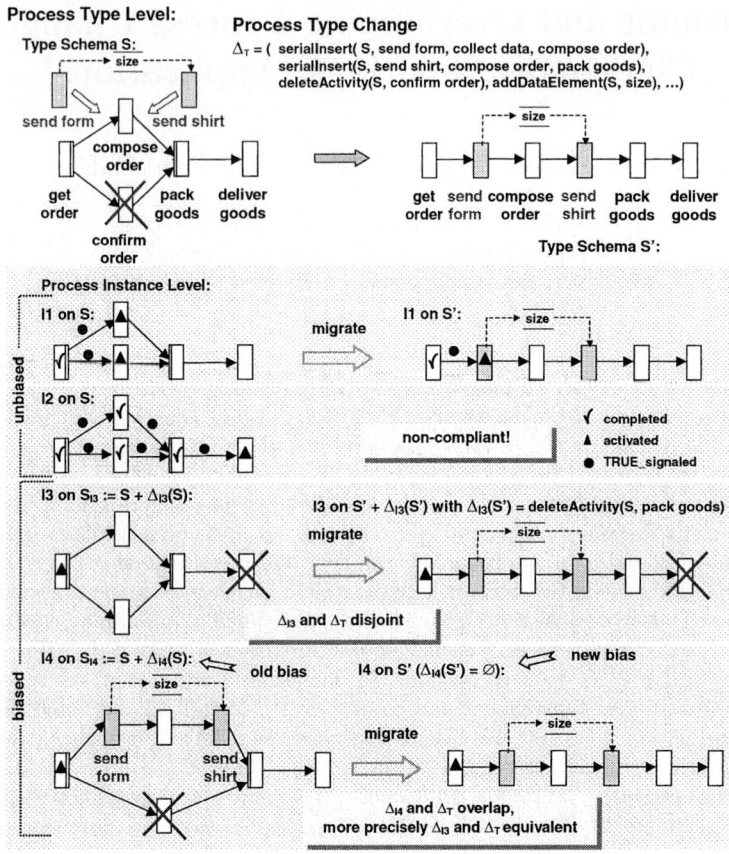

Fig. 1. Process Type and Instance Changes (Example)

often to be carried out in an ad-hoc manner in order to deal with an exceptional situation or evolving process requirements [8,9].

Process type changes are handled by modifying the respective *process schema*. Very often it is desired to *propagate* a process type change to related process instances as well. Process instances for which this is possible are called *compliant*, i.e., they can be *migrated* to the new process schema [3,10]. Adapting a single process instance during runtime, in turn, logically results in an instance-specific schema (i.e., a *process instance schema* differing from the original schema this instance was created from). In the following, we call such individually modified process instances *biased* (e.g., instances I_3 and I_4 in Fig. 1).

Currently there are only few adaptive process management systems (PMS) which support both kinds of changes in one system [7,11]. All these PMS have in common that once an instance has been individually modified (i.e., it possesses an instance-specific process schema due to an ad–hoc change), it can no longer benefit from process type changes; i.e., changes of the schema they were originally created from. However, doing so is not sufficient in many cases, especially in connection with long-running processes as we have learned from several case studies within medical and automotive environments. In order to come to a complete solution, therefore, it must be possible to propagate process schema changes are carried out at the type level to biased instances as well.

When analyzing the interplay between process type and process instance changes we are faced with several challenges. In [8] we have already discussed the problem of *structural and state–related* conflicts that may arise when propagating a process type change to a biased process instance. Structural conflicts between type and instance changes, for example, may lead to deadlock–causing cycles or incomplete input data for activity executions [8].

Another fundamental issue not treated so far concerns the handling of overlapping type and instance changes; i.e., the handling of concurrent changes[1] on a process schema that partially have the same effects on this schema. In this paper we give insights into fundamental challenges and solution approaches for coping with such *overlapping* changes. One example is depicted in Fig. 1 where process type change Δ_T and process instance change Δ_{I_4} (of instance I_4) both insert activities *send form* and *send shirt* (into schema S). Propagating type change Δ_T to instance–specific schema S_{I_4} would therefore lead to multiple insertion of the same activities. Usually, this would not correspond to the user's intention who, for example, has already anticipated a process optimization by an ad–hoc modification at the instance level. Furthermore Δ_T and Δ_{I_4} both delete the same activity *confirm order*. As a consequence Δ_T actually could not be applied to S_{I_4} since *confirm order* is not longer present.

One prerequisite to adequately deal with such cases is to effectively detect whether (concurrent) process type and process instance changes overlap. Another challenge is to correctly migrate biased process instances to a modified type schema even if the instance–specific changes overlap with the process type change. Basically the problem is that the current representation of the instance–specific schema, which is based on original schema S plus bias $\Delta_I(S)$, must be transformed into a representation based new schema S' plus bias $\Delta_I(S')$. Doing so offers several advantages: If I is actually re–linked to S' it can benefit from further process optimizations of S'. Furthermore, reassigning instances to their actual schema version contributes to an optimal management and redundancy–free storage of process schemes and instances. Looking again at instance I_4 from Fig. 1 we can observe that Δ_T and Δ_I do exactly the same, i.e., they have the same effects on the original process schema S. We therefore call them *equivalent*. For the above reasons, for equivalent changes a desired *migration strategy* would be to abstain from any propagation of Δ_T on I_4 but to re–link or migrate I_4 to S'. In the latter case, representation of I_4 on S' would no longer require maintenance of an instance–specific change, i.e., $\Delta_I(S') = \emptyset$ (cf. instance I_4 on S' in Fig. 1). Assume now that an additional activity *send reminder* has been

---

[1] In the following, we assume that certain instance–specific changes took place before the process type change occurs. Nevertheless, we call such changes concurrent since they work on the same original process schema.

inserted into I_4. Then Δ_T and Δ_{I_4} would no longer be equivalent but Δ_T be subsumed by Δ_{I_4}. For this case an adequate migration strategy is to migrate I_4 to S' (i.e., to re–link I_4 to S') but to further maintain the insertion of *send reminder* as instance–specific change Δ'_{I_4} based on S'. We conclude that for any adaptive PMS it becomes necessary to detect whether process type and process instance changes overlap, and to also determine the *degree of overlap*. This, in turn, is fundamental in order to apply adequate migration strategies.

In this paper we provide fundamental definitions for *disjoint, overlapping*, and *equivalent* process changes. Doing so is important in order to be able to provide adequate migration strategies. We illustrate this by means of selected scenarios. Based on formal definitions for disjoint and overlapping process changes we discuss different approaches for detecting them. Thereby *structural, operational*, and *hybrid* approaches are presented and estimated along their specific strengths and limitations. We derive an adequate approach to detect to which degree concurrent process changes overlap. This approach comprises a sophisticated method to *purge* unnecessary information (*noise*) from change transaction logs, i.e., we aim at finding a canonical respresentation of change transaction logs. Such noise within change logs, for example, may result from mutually compensating changes. Furthermore, taking purged change transaction logs the necessary information to decide on the degree of overlap between concurrent changes is extracted. Altogether, this method provides the basis for being able to apply adequate migration strategies for any kind of biased instance.

The remainder of this paper is organized as follows: In Section 2.1 we shortly introduce WSM Nets as the process meta model taken to illustrate the presented results. The formal framework – definitions for disjoint, overlapping and equivalent changes – as well as migration strategies are provided in Section 2.2. In Section 3 we discuss different approaches for detecting the degree of overlap between process type and process instance changes and a method to purge noise from change transaction logs in Section 4. We close with a discussion of related work in Section 5 and a summary in Section 6.

2 Disjoint and Overlapping Process Changes

In this paper, we exemplarily use WSM Nets (as for example applied in ADEPT [9]) and the change operations based on them. However, most of the presented results are independent of the used process meta model. Section 2.1 gives background information on WSM Nets necessary for further understanding of the paper. Based on this, Section 2.2 introduces definitions for diesjoint an overlapping changes and exemplarily presents migration strategies for selected scenarios.

2.1 Background Information

A process schema is represented by attributed, serial-parallel process graphs with additional links for synchronizing parallel paths [6].

Definition 1 (WSM Net). *A tuple $S = (N, D, NT, CtrlE, SyncE, LoopE, DataE)$ is called a WSM Net if the following holds:*

- *N is a set (bag) of activities and D a set of process data elements*
- *$NT: N \mapsto \{$StartFlow, EndFlow, Activity, AndSplit, AndJoin, XOrSplit, XOrJoin, StartLoop, EndLoop$\}$
  NT assigns to each node of the WSM Net a respective node type.*
- *$CtrlE \subset N \times N$ is a precedence relation*
- *$SyncE \subset N \times N$ is a precedence relation between activities of parallel branches*
- *$LoopE \subset N \times N$ is a set of loop backward edges*
- *$DataE \subseteq N \times D \times \{read, write\}$ is a set of read/write data links between activities and data elements*

A WSM Net S is *structurally correct* if the following constraints hold:

1. S has a unique start node *Start* and a unique end node *End*.
2. Except for nodes *Start* and *End* each activity node of S has at least one incoming and one outgoing control edge $e \in CtrlE$.
3. $S_{block} := (N, CtrlE, LoopE)$ is structured following a block concept, for which control blocks (sequences, branchings, loops) can be nested but must not overlap.
4. $S_{fwd} = (N, CtrlE, SyncE)$ is an acyclic graph, i.e., the use of control and sync edges must not lead to deadlock-causing cycles.
5. Sync links must not cross the boundary of a loop block; i.e., an activity from a loop block must not be connected with an activity from outside the loop block via a sync link (and vice versa).
6. For activities with mandatory input parameters linked to global data elements it has to be ensured that respective data elements will be always written by a preceding activity at runtime.
7. Parallel write accesses on data elements (and consequently lost updates on them) have to be avoided.

Taking a WSM Net S new process instances can be created and started. Logically, each instance I is associated with an instance-specific schema $S_I := S + \Delta_I$ (for unbiased instances $\Delta_I(S) = \emptyset$ and consequently $S_I = S$ holds). The execution state of I is captured by marking function $M^{S_I} = (NS^{S_I}, ES^{S_I})$. It assigns to each activity n its current status $NS(n)$ and to each control edge its marking $ES(e)$. Markings are determined according to well defined marking rules [6], whereas markings of already passed regions and skipped branches are preserved (except loop backs). Concerning data elements, different versions of a data object may be stored, which is important for the context-dependent reading of data elements and the handling of (partial) rollback operations. Formally:

Definition 2 (Process Instance). *A process instance I is defined by a tuple $(S, \Delta_I, M^{S_I}, Val^{S_I}, \Pi_I^S)$ where*

- $S = (N, D, NT, CtrlE, SyncE, ...)$ denotes the process schema I was derived from. We call S the <u>original schema</u> of I.
- Δ_I comprises instance-specific changes $op_1^I, \ldots, op_m^I$ that have been applied to I so far. We call Δ_I the <u>bias</u> of I. Schema $S_I := S + \Delta_I$ (with $S_I = (N_I, D_I, NT, CtrlE_I, \ldots)$) which results from the application of Δ_I to S, is called the <u>instance–specific schema</u> of I.
- $M^{S_I} = (NS^{S_I}, ES^{S_I})$ describes node and edge markings of I:
  $NS^{S_I}: \quad N_I \quad \mapsto \quad$ {NotActivated, Activated, Running, Completed, Skipped}
  $ES^{S_I}: (CtrlE_I \cup SyncE_I \cup LoopE_I) \mapsto$
  {NotSignaled, TrueSignaled, FalseSignaled}
- Val^{S_I} is a function on D_I. It reflects for each data element $d \in D_I$ either its current value or the value UNDEFINED (if d has not been written yet).
- $\Pi_I^S = <e_0, \ldots, e_k>$ is the execution history of I. $e_0, \ldots, e_k$ denote the start <u>and</u> end events of activity executions.

Activities marked as Activated are ready to fire and can be worked on. Their status then changes to Running. As an example take instance I_1 from Fig. 1: Activity *get order* is completed whereas activity *compose order* is activated. Activities with marking Skipped cannot be longer selected for execution.

Table 1 presents a selection of *high-level change operations* which can be used to define or modify WSM Nets. These change operations include formal pre- and post-conditions. They automatically perform the necessary schema transformations whereas schema correctness (cf. correctness constraints 1. – 7. for WSM Nets) is ensured. One typical example of such a change operation is the insertion of an activity and its embedding into the process context.

When applying a series of connected change operations op_i $(i = 1, \ldots, n)$, e.g., when inserting two activities and a data dependency between them, it is often desired to apply either all of these change operations or none of them (atomicity). In order to achieve this, change operations $op_1, \ldots, op_n$ must be carried out within same *change transaction* $\Delta = (op_1, \ldots, op_n)$ (*change* for short).

2.2 Formal Framework

In Sect. 1 we have already introduced the notions of *disjoint* and *overlapping* changes informally. In this section we give formal definitions of these concepts which serve as theoretical underpinning for the following considerations. First of all, we abstract from whether changes are carried out at the type or at the instance level. More precisely, we base our considerations on two arbitrary changes (or change sets) Δ_1 and Δ_2 concurrently applied on the same schema S.

Let S be a (correct) process schema and Δ_1 and Δ_2 two changes which transform S into another (correct) process schema S_1 and S_2 respectively (notation: $S_1 := S + \Delta_1$ and $S_2 := S + \Delta_2$). Generally, disjointness and overlapping are special relations between two changes of the same schema. The challenging question is how to define a relation on changes. Either this can be done by directly

Table 1. A Selection of High-Level Change Operations on WSM Nets

Change Operation op Applied to Schema S	Effects on Schema S
Additive Change Operations	
serialInsert(S, X, A, B)	insertion of activity X between two directly succeeding activities A and B
parallelInsert(S, X, (A, B))	insertion of activity X parallel to control block with start activity A and end activity B
insertSyncEdge(S, src, dest)	insertion of sync edge linking two activities src and dest from parallel execution paths
Subtractive Change Operations	
deleteActivity(S, X)	deletes activity X from schema S
deleteSyncEdge(S, edge)	deletes synchronization edge $\in$ SyncE from schema S
Order-Changing Operations	
serialMove(S, X, A, B)	moves activity X from current position to position between directly succeeding activities A and B
Attribute Changing Operations	
changeActivityAttribute(S, X, attr, nV)	changes value of attribute attr of activity X to nV
changeEdgeAttribute(S, edge, attr, nV)	changes value of attribute attr of edge $\in$ CtrlE $\cup$ SyncE to nV
Data Flow Change Operations	
addDataElement(S, d, dom, defVal)	adds data element d with domain dom and default value defVal to S
deleteDataElement(S, d)	deletes data element d from S
addDataEdge(S, (X, d, mode))	adds data edge (X, d, mode) linking activity X with data element d (mode $\in$ {read, write})
deleteDataEdge(S, dataEdge)	deletes data edge dataEdge from S

comparing Δ_1 and Δ_2 or by correlating their effects on the original schema S. Effects of Δ_1 and Δ_2 on S, in turn, are reflected by resulting process schemes S_1 and S_2. Consequently, a relation between changes Δ_1 and Δ_2 can be determined by finding a relation between S_1 and S_2. – In the workflow literature several (equivalence) relations for process schemes have been discussed [2,12, 13]. In the context of this work, the relation between concurrent changes affects the *behavior* of the resulting process schemes. Therefore, we base our further considerations on a behavioral equivalence relation for process schemes which is known as *trace equivalence* [10,13].

Definition 3 (Trace Equivalence Between Process Schemes). *Let S_1 and S_2 be two process schemes. S_1 and S_2 are equivalent with respect to their possible traces (formally: $S_1 \equiv_{trace} S_2$) iff each execution history $\Pi_I^{S_1}$ producible on S_1 can be generated on S_2 as well and vice versa.*

Intuitively, two process schemes S_1 and S_2 are trace equivalent if each possible behavior of S_1 (represented by its execution histories) can be simulated by process schema S_2 and vice versa. Based on trace equivalence we now introduce an adequate definition for overlapping and disjoint changes. Intuitively, two change transactions Δ_1 and Δ_2 overlap if they have (partially) the same effects on the underlying process schema S. This is the case if Δ_1 and Δ_2 manipulate the same – already existing – elements of S or insert the same activities into S.

Overlapping effects on already existing elements of a process schema may result from subtractive, order–changing, or attribute–changing operations (cf. Table 1). Subtractive changes that overlap may affect the applicability of Δ_1 on S_2 and vice versa (cf. Fig. 1). Overlapping order–changing and attribute–changing operations may mutually *override* the effects of each other. Assume, for example, that change Δ_1 moves an activity X to position A (resulting in S_1) and Δ_2 moves X to position B (resulting in S_2). Then applying Δ_1 to S_2 would override the effects of Δ_1 and vice versa. Both problems – change applicability and overriding of change effects – can be avoided if Δ_1 and Δ_2 are *commutative*, i.e., applying Δ_2 on S_1 leads to a process schema which is trace equivalent to the process schema that results when applying Δ_1 on S_2. Formally:

Definition 4 (Commutativity of Changes). *Let S be a (correct) schema and Δ_1 and Δ_2 be two changes transforming S into (correct) schema S_1 and S_2 respectively. We call Δ_1 and Δ_2 commutative if the application of Δ_1 to S_2 and the application of Δ_2 to S_1 result in trace equivalent schemes, formally:*
$$\Delta_1, \Delta_2 \text{ commutative} \iff (S + \Delta_1) + \Delta_2 \equiv_{trace} (S + \Delta_2) + \Delta_1$$

Thus commutativity is a first property for characterizing disjoint changes. However, it is not strong enough to cover disjointness of additive changes (e.g., insertions of new activities) as well. In particular, commutativity does not exclude the (undesired) multiple insertion of the same activity (cf. Fig. 1). In order to avoid this effect, we additionally claim that the sets of activities which are newly inserted by Δ_1 and Δ_2 respectively have to be disjoint. Formally:

Definition 5 (Disjoint and Overlapping Changes). *Let $S = (N, D, CtrlE, SyncE, DataE, ...)$ be a WSM Net and Δ_1 and Δ_2 be two change transactions which transform S into WSM Nets S_1 and S_2 with $S_i = (N_i, D_i, CtrlE_i, SyncE_i, ...), i = 1, 2$*
I) We denote Δ_1 and Δ_2 as disjoint (notation: $\Delta_1 \cap \Delta_2 = \emptyset$) iff the following properties hold:
(1) Δ_1 and Δ_2 are commutative (cf. Def. 4)
(2) $(N_1 \setminus N) \cap (N_2 \setminus N) = \emptyset$[2]
II) We denote Δ_1 and Δ_2 as overlapping (notation: $\Delta_1 \cap \Delta_2 \neq \emptyset$) if they are not disjoint.

As it can be seen from Def. 5 the notion of overlapping concurrent changes is still relatively rough. As indicated in the introduction it is possible to further classify overlapping changes according to their degree of overlap. One of these subclasses is formed by *equivalent* changes, i.e., changes which have exactly the same effects on original schema S. Formally:

Definition 6 (Equivalent Change Transactions). *Let S be a WSM Net and Δ_1 and Δ_2 be two change transactions which transform S into WSM Nets S_1*

---

[2] We abstract from realization details regarding the concurrent insertion of the same activity. Informally, two process activities are considered as equal iff they use the same activity template and the same semantic identifier.

and S_2. Then Δ_1 and Δ_2 are equivalent, i.e., $\Delta_1 \equiv \Delta_2$ iff S_1 and S_2 are trace equivalent (cf. Def. 3). Formally:

$$\Delta_1 \equiv \Delta_2 \iff S_1 \equiv_{trace} S_2$$

A very interesting application of Def. 5 and Def. 6 is the correct handling of concurrent process type and process instance changes as described in Section 1. More precisely, based on the particular degree of overlap between process type change Δ_T and process instance change Δ_I (which can be determined based on Def. 5 and 6) different migration strategies have to be applied. To illustrate this, in the following, we present the migration strategies for disjoint and equivalent process type and instance changes.

Policy 1 (Migrating Instances With Disjoint Bias). *Let S be a (correct) process type schema and Δ_T be a process type change which transforms S into another (correct) type schema S'. Let further $I = (S, \Delta_I, \ldots)$ be a process instance on S with instance-specific schema $S_I := S + \Delta_I$. Finally, let Δ_T and Δ_I be disjoint changes (cf. Def. 5), i.e., $\Delta_T \cap \Delta_I = \emptyset$. Then:*
I can correctly migrate to S' preserving Δ_I on S', i.e., $I = (S', \Delta_I, \ldots) :\iff$

1. $S_I^* := (S + \Delta_I) + \Delta_T$ *is a correct schema (according to the structural correctness constraints 1. – 7. set out for the used process meta model); i.e., Δ_T can be correctly applied to $S_I = S + \Delta_I$* **(Structural Correctness)**.
2. *I is compliant with S_I^*; i.e., the (reduced) execution history Π_I^S of I on S_I can be produced on S_I^* as well* **(State-Related Correctness)**.[3]

We call the migration strategy introduced in Policy 1 the *standard migration case*. When applying it to an instance I, which is both structurally and state-related compliant with S', we actually propagate Δ_T to I and migrate I to S' preserving instance-specific change Δ_I on S'. Generally, migrating a process instance I for which instance change Δ_I overlaps with type change Δ_T is called the *advanced migration case*. As discussed above, adequate strategies for this case depend on the *degree of overlap* between process type and instance changes. It ranges from *equivalence* of the changes (cf. Def. 6) to minor overlapping between them. To give an idea of these advanced strategies we sketch the one for dealing with *equivalent* process type and process instance changes.

Policy 2 (Migrating Instances With Equivalent Bias).
Let S be a (correct) process type schema and Δ_T be a process type change which transforms S into another (correct) type schema S'. Let further $I = (S, \Delta_I, \ldots)$ be a process instance on S with instance execution schema $S_I := S + \Delta_I$. Finally let Δ_T and Δ_I be equivalent changes, i.e., $\Delta_T \equiv \Delta_I$. Then I can correctly migrate to S' with resulting bias $\Delta_I = \emptyset$ on S', i.e., $I = (S', \emptyset, \ldots)$.

---

[3] How to efficiently ensure compliance and how to automatically adapt instance markings when migrating them to the changed process type schema is extensively discussed in [14].

If an instance change Δ_I is equivalent with process type change Δ_T the advanced migration strategy is to re–link instance I to the new process type schema S' without applying any further changes or checks. In the sequel, instance change Δ_I is nullified due to the application of Δ_T, i.e., $\Delta_I(S') = \emptyset$.

An example is depicted in Fig. 1 where instance change Δ_{I_4} is equivalent with type change Δ_T (obviously S' and S_{I_4} are trace equivalent). Consequently, we can re–link I_4 to S' and we can set $\Delta_{I_4}(S') = \emptyset$. Due to lack of space, for dealing with further degrees of overlap we refer to [15].

3 Detecting the Degree of Overlap Between Concurrent Process Changes

Let S be a (correct) process schema and let $I = (S, \Delta_I, \ldots)$ be a (biased) process instance on S (with bias Δ_I). Let further Δ_T be a type change transforming S into another (correct) process schema S'. Then the challenging question arises whether Δ_T and Δ_I are disjoint or whether they are overlapping each other (cf. Def. 5). A naive solution would be to directly check Def. 5. Doing so would require materialization of resulting process schemes $S_{(\Delta_T, \Delta_I)} := (S + \Delta_T) + \Delta_I$ and $S_{(\Delta_I, \Delta_T)} := (S + \Delta_I) + \Delta_T$ and explicit verification of trace equivalence between $S_{(\Delta_T, \Delta_I)}$ and $S_{(\Delta_I, \Delta_T)}$. However, this approach is not applicable in practice for three reasons:

1. Δ_T cannot be always applied to $S_I := S + \Delta_I$ and vice versa Δ_I to $S' := S + \Delta_T$ (e.g., if Δ_T and Δ_I delete the same activities). Consequently, $S_{(\Delta_T, \Delta_I)}$ and $S_{(\Delta_I, \Delta_T)}$ respectively cannot be materialized.
2. Even if $S_{(\Delta_T, \Delta_I)}$ and $S_{(\Delta_I, \Delta_T)}$ can be materialized the verification of trace equivalence would require to determine all execution histories producible on $S_{(\Delta_T, \Delta_I)}$ and $S_{(\Delta_I, \Delta_T)}$. This, in turn, would demand reachability analyses for both schemes resulting in exponential complexity.
3. Assume that we can materialize both $S_{(\Delta_T, \Delta_I)}$ and $S_{(\Delta_I, \Delta_T)}$ and determine all possible execution histories. Nevertheless we would have to replay all these execution histories on the mutually other process schema. Due to the possibly large number of creatable execution histories and their large volume a severe performance penalty can be caused.

For these reasons we have to find better suited approaches to verify Def. 5 for Δ_T and Δ_I. The information we can use for this purpose comprises process schemes $S, S_I,$ and S' and changes Δ_T and Δ_I. Intuitively, taking this information we come to the following three kinds of approaches (cf. Fig. 2): *(1) structural approaches* which directly compare process schemes $S, S_I,$ and S', *(2) operational approaches* directly contrasting changes Δ_I and Δ_T (i.e., looking at the two sets of applied change operations), and *(3) hybrid approaches* (cf. Sect. 4) combining approaches (1) and (2). In the following we present these variants and systematically rate their particular stenghts and limitations.

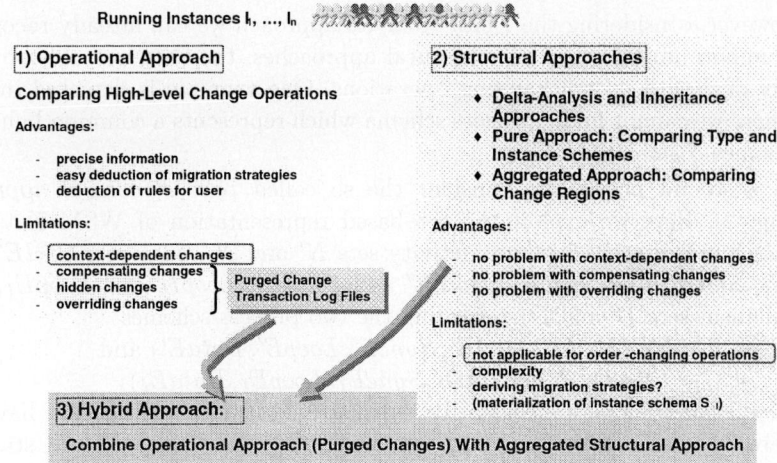

Fig. 2. Approach Overview to Detect Overlapping of Changes

3.1 Structural Approaches

The essence of all structural approaches is to compare process type schema $S' := S + \Delta_T$ with process instance schema $S_I := S + \Delta_I$ in order to gain information about the degree of overlap between Δ_T and Δ_I. A promising approach to analyze the difference between two process schemes, the so called *Delta Analysis*, has been presented in [16] and used by v.d. Aalst and Basten in [12]. In [12] Delta Analysis is based on four inheritance relations on process schemes. Roughly speaking a process schema S_1 is a subclass of process schema S_2 if it can do everything S_2 can do and more. With this, for example, v.d. Aalst and Basten determine the *Greatest Common Divisor (GCD)* for process schemes S_1 and S_2 which represents the common superclass of S_1 and S_2. Though this approach is very promising it cannot be adopted to the problem described in this paper since it shows the reverse line of attack as the following example illustrates:

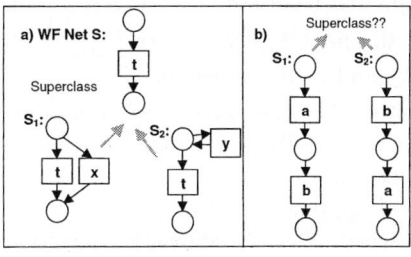

Fig. 3. Determining the Greatest Common Divisor (Examples)

Consider process schemes S_1 and S_2 (represented by WF Nets [2] – a Petri Net based formalism) as depicted in Fig. 3a). Applying the approach presented by v.d. Aalst and Basten [12] we start from process schemes S_1 and S_2 and determine the common superclass S. By contrast, in our approach we already have common divisor S and derive process type schema S' and process instance schema S_I by applying Δ_T and Δ_I respectively.

However, considering the Delta Analysis approach we can already recognize one common limitation of all structural approaches: they are not able to adequately deal with order–changing operations. One example is depicted in Fig. 3b) where we cannot find a process schema which represents a common behavior for schemes S_1 and S_2.

As a second possibility, consider the so called *pure structural approach* (cf. Fig. 2). Here we exploit the set–based representation of WSM Nets (cf. Sect. 2.1) and directly compare activity sets N' and N_I, edge sets $CtrlE'$ and $CtrlE_I$, $SyncE'$ and $SyncE_I$, $DataE'$ and $DataE_I$, $LoopE'$ and $LoopE_I$, and data element sets D' and D_I regarding the two process schemes

- $S' = (N', D', NT, CtrlE', SyncE', LoopE', DataE')$ and
- $S_I = (N_I, D_I, NT, CtrlE_I, SyncE_I, LoopE_I, DataE_I)$.

However, doing so is unnecessarily expensive. Actually we do not have to compare "whole" activity and edge sets since they have been derived starting with same original schema S, i.e., starting with the same activity and edge sets. In other words we already know a common divisor $S = (N, D, ...)$ for S' and S_I. Therefore we can reduce complexity by exploiting the common ancestry of S' and S_I what results in a third method which we call *aggregated structural approach* (cf. Fig. 2). More precisely, the aggregated structural approach works by comparing differences between process type schema S' and original schema S and between process instance schema S_I and original schema S. These differences can be easily determined by building the following difference sets:

- $N^{add}_{\Delta_T} := N' \setminus N$ and $N^{add}_{\Delta_I} := N_I \setminus N$
- $N^{del}_{\Delta_T} := N \setminus N'$ and $N^{del}_{\Delta_I} := N \setminus N_I$
- $CtrlE^{add}_{\Delta_T} := CtrlE' \setminus CtrlE$ and $CtrlE^{add}_{\Delta_I} := CtrlE_I \setminus CtrlE$
- and so on (cf. [17])

A first example is depicted in Fig. 4a). Both Δ_T and Δ_{I_1} serially insert activity X at the same position ("between B and C") into S_1 whereas Δ_{I_2} serially inserts another activity Y between A and B. Obviously, Δ_T and Δ_{I_1} overlap since they offend against claim (2) for disjoint changes (cf. Def. 5). Using the aggregated structural approach, we obtain $N^{add}_{\Delta_T} = N^{add}_{\Delta_{I_1}} = \{X\}$. This corresponds to the expected result, i.e., the multiple insertion of same activity X. Regarding instance I_2 on S_1, Δ_T and Δ_{I_2} are disjoint according to Def. 5. Application of the aggregated structural approach results in $N^{add}_{\Delta_T} \cap N^{add}_{\Delta_{I_2}} = \emptyset$, $N^{del}_{\Delta_T} \cap N^{del}_{\Delta_{I_2}} = \emptyset$, $CtrlE^{add}_{\Delta_T} \cap CtrlE^{add}_{\Delta_{I_2}} = \emptyset$, and $CtrlE^{del}_{\Delta_T} \cap CtrlE^{del}_{\Delta_{I_2}} = \emptyset$. Interpreting this result, we can state that Δ_T and Δ_{I_2} are disjoint.

These first two examples from Fig. 4a) show that the aggregated structural approach works fine for insert (and delete) operations. Reason is that we are able to precisely determine which activities have been inserted or deleted. In contrast, for move operations the aggregated structural approach (and consequently the pure structural approach) may be too imprecise[4]. Fig. 4b) shows a respective

---

[4] It is not sufficient to map a move operation onto respective delete and insert operations. Since activities are not really deleted or inserted structural approaches fail.

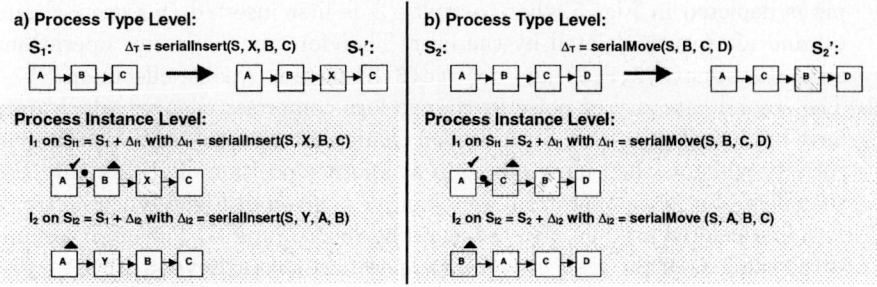

Fig. 4. Inserting and Moving Activities (Examples)

example: For all three changes on schema S_2, $N^{add}_{\Delta_T} = N^{add}_{\Delta_{I_1}} = N^{add}_{\Delta_{I_2}} = \emptyset$ and $N^{del}_{\Delta_T} = N^{del}_{\Delta_{I_1}} = N^{del}_{\Delta_{I_2}} = \emptyset$ holds (no activity has actually been inserted or deleted). Determining the sets of newly inserted and deleted control edges for Δ_T and Δ_{I_1} yields $CtrlE^{add}_{\Delta_T} = CtrlE^{add}_{\Delta_{I_1}} = \{(A,C),(C,B),(B,D)\}$ and $CtrlE^{del}_{\Delta_T} = CtrlE^{del}_{\Delta_{I_1}} = \{(A,B),(B,C),(C,D)\}$ respectively. From this result we can conclude that $\Delta_T \cap \Delta_{I_1} \neq \emptyset$. Comparing the respective edge sets for Δ_T and Δ_{I_2} again we obtain: $CtrlE^{add}_{\Delta_T} \cap CtrlE^{add}_{\Delta_{I_2}} \neq \emptyset$ and $CtrlE^{del}_{\Delta_T} \cap CtrlE^{del}_{\Delta_{I_2}} \neq \emptyset$. This indicates that $\Delta_T \cap \Delta_{I_2} \neq \emptyset$ holds. However, these results are too imprecise since in both cases we cannot exactly determine which activity has been actually moved. In case Δ_T and Δ_{I_1} are solely based on structural considerations, activity C as well as activity B could have been moved. When comparing Δ_T with Δ_{I_2} we can only conclude that these changes actually overlap but we are not able to make further statements. Both effects – not knowing which activities have been moved and imprecise statements about overlapping – are aggravated if change transactions comprise several move operations. In summary, taking this imprecise information it is not possible to derive adequate migration strategies.

3.2 Operational Approach

A solution to overcome the drawback of structural approaches in conjunction with order–changing operations – not knowing which activities have been actually moved – may be to directly compare applied changes Δ_T and Δ_I. Obviously, Δ_T and Δ_I contain precise information about applied changes in general and about actually moved activities in particular. However, this operational approach also shows limitations. As summarized in Fig. 2 change transaction logs may contain information about change operations which actually have no or only hidden effects on the underlying process schema. Reason is that the users who define changes (i.e., the process designer or the end user) do not always act in a goal–oriented way when modifying a process schema. In fact they may try out the best solution resulting in noisy information within the change logs:

1. The first group of changes without any effects on S' are *compensating changes*, i.e., changes mutually compensating their effects. A simple exam-

ple is depicted in Fig. 5 where activity Z is first inserted (between F and G) and afterwards deleted by the user. Therefore the respective operations serialInsert(S,Z,F,G) and delete(S,Z) have no visible effects on S'.
2. The second category of noise in change logs comprises changes which only have hidden effects on S'. Such *hidden changes* always arise from deleting an activity which is then inserted again at another position. This actually has the effect of a move operation. An example is given in Fig. 5 where activity E is first deleted an then inserted again between Y and G. The effect behind is the same as of the respective move operation serialMove(S, E, Y, G).
3. There are changes overriding effects of predeceding changes (note that a change transaction is an <u>ordered</u> series of single change operations). Again consider Fig. 5 where the effect of the hidden move operation serialMove(S, E, Y, G) (cf. 2.) is overwritten by move operation serialMove(S, E, F, G), i.e., in S' activity E is finally placed between F and G.

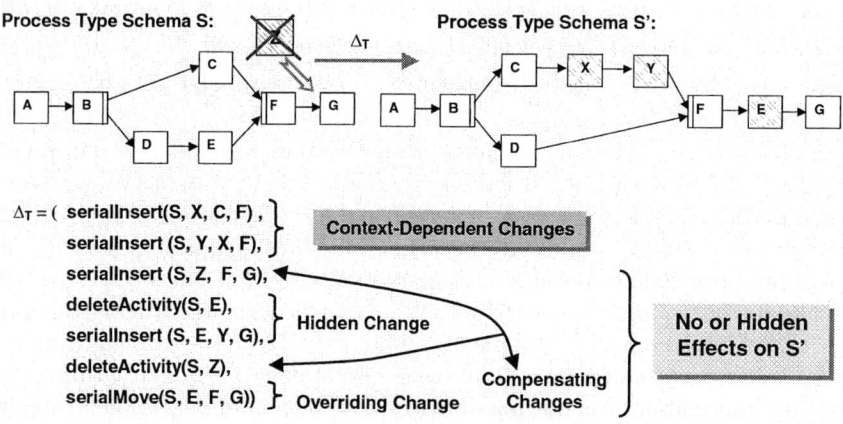

Fig. 5. Process Type Change Transaction (Example)

However, the presence of compensating, hidden, or overriding changes within a change transaction is a cumbersome but conquerable problem. Reason is that we can find methods to *purge* a change transaction from these kinds of changes (cf. Alg. 1). Doing so is essential in order to find a canonical and minimal view on change logs. This, in turn, is necessary to be able to determine which activities actually have been moved by a change.

A much more severe limitation of the operational approach is its disability to adequately deal with *context–dependent changes*, i.e., changes which are mutually based on each other. An example is depicted in Fig. 5: First, activity X is inserted serially between C and F. Based on this a second activity Y is inserted between $\underline{X}$ and F. Obviously, the second insertion uses the newly added activity of the first insertion as change context.

Why are such context–dependent process type and process instance changes critical when applying the operational approach? Fig. 6 illustrates the underlying problem. Obviously, Δ_T and Δ_I are equivalent since S' and S_I are trace equivalent. Unfortunately, this equivalence relation cannot be determined based on the depicted change transaction logs since Δ_T and Δ_I have inserted activities X, Y and Z in different orders. Therefore the operational approach sketched so far would only detect an overlapping (multiple insertion of same activities) but not be able to determine the degree of overlap, i.e., the total equivalence between Δ_T and Δ_I.

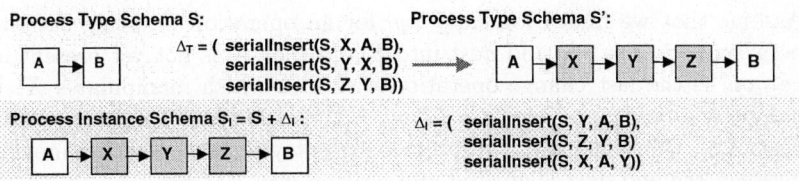

Fig. 6. Equivalent Process Type and Instance Changes (Example)

At this point an important conclusion is that structural approaches have no problems with context–dependent changes. Consider again Fig. 6. Applying the aggregated structural approach (cf. Sect. 3.1) we get $N^{add}_{\Delta_T} = N^{add}_{\Delta_I}$, $N^{del}_{\Delta_T} = N^{del}_{\Delta_I}$, $CtrlE^{add}_{\Delta_T} = CtrlE^{add}_{\Delta_I}$, and $CtrlE^{del}_{\Delta_T} = CtrlE^{del}_{\Delta_I}$ and therefore $\Delta_T \equiv \Delta_I$ holds.

In summary, at this point we have the following situation (cf. Fig. 2): Structural approaches are able to cope with context–dependent changes as well as with compensating, hidden and overriding changes. Reason is that structural approaches are based on the actual effects on a process schema. However, they are unable to adequately deal with order–changing operations. In contrast, when applying the operational approach we are able to precisely determine which activities have been moved but we are not able to handle context–dependent changes. Altogether, in the following section we combine both methods to a *hybrid approach* in order to exploit the particular strengths and to overcome the particular limitations.

4 The Hybrid Approach

The hybrid approach presented in the following combines elements of structural and operational approaches (cf. Sect. 3). How this approach works in general is presented in Sect. 4.1. How we can apply the hybrid approach to concurrent process type and instance changes is illustrated in Sect. 4.2.

4.1 Purging Change Logs and Consolidated Activity Sets

Let S be a (correct) process schema and let Δ be a change which transforms S into another correct process schema $S' := S + \Delta$. Informally, the hybrid approach works as follows: First, the activity sets actually inserted into and deleted from $S - N_\Delta^{add}$ and N_Δ^{del} (cf. Sect. 3.1) – are determined (*structural approach*). Taking this information the change log capturing Δ is *purged*. More precisely, this purging is accomplished by scanning the log of change $\Delta = (op_1, \ldots, op_n)$ in reverse order and by determining for each change operation op_i ($i = 1, \ldots, n$) whether it actually has any effects on S. If so we incorporate op_i into a new – intially empty – change log Δ^{purged}. Finally, in order to reduce the number of necessary change log scans to one we use an auxiliary set A to memorize which activities have been already handled. In detail, the following considerations are made when determining Δ^{purged}:

- Assume that we find a log entry op_i for an operation inserting activity X between activities src and $dest$ into S and that X is not yet present in A, i.e., op_i is the last change operation within Δ which manipulates X. If X has been already present in S ($X \notin N_\Delta^{add}$) a *hidden change* is found (cf. Sect. 3.2). Consequently, a respective log entry for an operation moving X between src and $dest$ is created and written into Δ^{purged}.

- If log entry op_i denotes an operation deleting activity X from S and $X \notin A$ but X is still present in S' ($X \notin N_\Delta^{del}$) then we have found a *compensating change*. Therefore op_i (and the respective insert operation) are left outside Δ^{purged}.

- If log entry op_i denotes an operation moving activity X to a position between activities src and $dest$ and op_i is the last operation within Δ which has effects regarding X ($X \notin A$) we have to distinguish between two cases: If X has been inserted before op_i ($X \in N_\Delta^{add}$) we write a new log entry in Δ^{purged} denoting an operation inserting X between src and $dest$. If X has been also present in S ($X \notin N_\Delta^{add}$) we write op_i unalteredly into Δ^{purged}.

In the following, the *consolidated activity sets* ($N_\Delta^{add}, N_\Delta^{del}, N_\Delta^{move}$) (cf. Def. 7) will serve as the basis for determining the degree of overlap between changes. Note that N_Δ^{add} and N_Δ^{del} can be determined using the aggregated structural approach (cf. Sect. 3.1) but we have to use purged change logs (operational approach) in order to obtain N_Δ^{move}.

A formalization of the method described above is given in Alg. 1. For the sake of simplicity we restrict this description to serial insert operations. However adopting parallel and branch insertions runs analogously.

Definition 7 (Purged Change Transaction; Consolidated Activity Sets). *Let $S = (N, D, \ldots)$ be a (correct) process schema. Let further Δ be a change which transforms S into another (correct) process schema $S' = (N', S', \ldots)$. Then the purged representation of Δ, Δ^{purged} and the consolidated activity sets ($N_\Delta^{add}, N_\Delta^{del}, N_\Delta^{move}$) can be determined by applying Algorithm 1.*

Algorithm 1. PurgeConsolidate(S, N, N', $\Delta = (op_1, \ldots, op_n)$) $\longrightarrow$
$(\Delta^{purged}, (N_\Delta^{add}, N_\Delta^{del}, N_\Delta^{move}))$

```
A:=∅; Δ^purged = ∅;
N_Δ^add := N' \ N;  N_Δ^del := N \ N';
for i = n to 1 do {
  if (op_i = serialInsert(S, X, src, dest)) {
    if (X ∉ A) {
      A := A ∪ {X}; //X not considered so far
      if(X ∉ N_Δ^add){ //X actually not inserted ⟶ hidden move
        if (src ≠ c_pred(S, X) ∧ dest ≠ c_succ(S, X)^5){ //X moved to another position?
          Δ^purged.addFirst(serialMove(S, X, src, dest))//adds entry at beginning of Δ^purged;
          N_Δ^move := N_Δ^move ∪ {X};}} else {
        Δ^purged.addFirst(serialInsert(S, X, src, dest));}} continue};
  if (op_i = serialMove(S, X, src, dest)) {
    if (X ∉ A) {
      A := A ∪ {X};
      if (X ∈ N_Δ^add) {
        Δ^purged.addFirst(serialInsert(S, X, src, dest)); } else {
        if (src ≠ c_pred(S, X) ∧ dest ≠ c_succ(S, X)) {
          Δ^purged.addFirst(serialMove(S, X, src, dest));
          N_Δ^move := N_Δ^move ∪ {X};}} continue;}
  if (op_i = delete(S, X)) {
    if (X ∉ A) {
      A := A ∪ {X};
      if(X ∈ N_Δ^del){
        Δ^purged.addFirst(delete(S, X));}}}
  Δ^purged.addFirst(op_i);
}
return (Δ^purged, (N_Δ^add, N_Δ^del, N_Δ^move));
```

4.2 Application to Concurrent Process Type and Instance Changes

A practically relevant application of the hybrid approach introduced in Sect. 4.1 is to determine the degree of overlap between concurrent process type and process instance changes. We illustrate this by the following example:

Fig. 7 shows the mode of operation of Alg. 1 applied to the log of change Δ_T in Fig. 5. Initially, Alg. 1 determines the sets of newly inserted and deleted activities regarding schema S, i.e., $N_{\Delta_T}^{add} = \{X, Y\}$ and $N_{\Delta_T}^{del} = \emptyset$. Based on this information change log Δ_T is traversed once (in reverse direction) and purged from noisy operations op_6, op_5, op_4, op_3. Algorithm 1 finishes with purged change transaction $\Delta_T^{purged} =$ (serialInsert(S, X, C, G), serialInsert(S, Y, X, G), serialMove(S, E, F, G)) (cf. Fig. 7). Based on this purged change log the set of activities actually moved by Δ_T can be determined as $N_{\Delta_T}^{move} = \{E\}$. Together with the set of newly inserted and deleted activities we obtain consolidated activity sets $(N_{\Delta_T}^{add}, N_{\Delta_T}^{del}, N_{\Delta_T}^{move}) = (\{X, Y\}, \emptyset, \{E\})$.

Purging change logs from noisy information has several advantages: First, the purged form of a change log can be used as the canonical representation of this change, i.e., if we have to compare changes (what we actually have to do when determining the degree of overlap between them) we can use the purged form as an adequate basis. Furthermore, purged change logs are also sufficient to determine the difference between changes. This, for example, is necessary if we want to calculate the instance bias after migration to the changed schema (if

---

[5] c_pred(S, X) (c_succ(S, X)) denotes all direct predecessors (successors) of X in S.

Change Log (in reverse order):	Initialization: $A = \emptyset$; $N_{\Delta T}^{add} = \{X, Y\}$; $N_{\Delta T}^{del} = \emptyset$;	Purged Change Log
$\Delta_T = ($		$\Delta^{purged}_T = ($
op_7 = serialMove(S, E, F, G),	$E \notin A \Rightarrow A = \{E\}$;	
	$E \notin N_{\Delta T}^{add} \wedge$ new pos. $\Rightarrow$	op_3 = serialMove(S, E, F, G),
op_6 = deleteActivity(S, Z),	$Z \notin A \Rightarrow A = \{E, Z\}$; $Z \notin N_{\Delta T}^{del}$;	
op_5 = serialInsert (S, E, Y, G),	$E \in A$;	
op_4 = deleteActivity(S, E),	$E \in A$;	
op_3 = serialInsert (S, Z, F, G),	$Z \in A$;	
op_2 = serialInsert (S, Y, X, F),	$Y \notin A \Rightarrow A = \{E, Z, Y\}$;	
	$Y \in N_{\Delta T}^{add} \Rightarrow$	op_2 = serialInsert(S, Y, X, F),
op_1 = serialInsert(S, X, C, F))	$X \notin A \Rightarrow A = \{E, Z, Y, X\}$;	
	$X \in N_{\Delta T}^{add} \Rightarrow$	op_1 = serialInsert(S, X, C, F),

Fig. 7. Purging A Change Log (Example)

bias and respective type change are not disjoint or equivalent). A more detailed treatment of these issues can be found in [17].

5 Discussion

In the workflow literature, there are many approaches either dealing with process type changes ("schema evolution") or single process instance changes [11,7,2,3,4,5]. Thereby, main focus has been put on providing appropriate correctness criteria for deciding about compliance of <u>unbiased</u> instances. Although there are some approaches [7,11] that provide common support for process type and instance changes there is no **interplay** between them. WASA$_2$ [7], for example, realizes changes of single process instances by deriving a new schema version with exactly one running instance. Consequently, individually modified instances are excluded from further process type changes.

Commutativity (cf. Sect. 2.2) is an important property in the context of concurrent changes in cooperative applications. In [18], operations commute if the state changes on an object as well as the values returned by the operations are independent of the order in which they are executed. Wäsch and Klas claim that concurrent changes on complex objects can be correctly carried out if they are commutative followed by a *history merge* of the respective changes [19]. In this paper, we use commutativity to define disjointness of changes. However, we do not restrict correctness of concurrent changes on commutativity but we provide advanced solutions for non commutative and therefore overlapping changes.

As discussed in Section 3.1 an interesting structural approach to compare process schemes is the Delta Analysis based on inheritance relations [12]. The used inheritance relations as well as our definition of disjointness and overlapping are based on equivalence notions between process schemes. V.d. Aalst and Basten use *branching bisimilarity* as equivalence relation [12,2,20,21]. There are

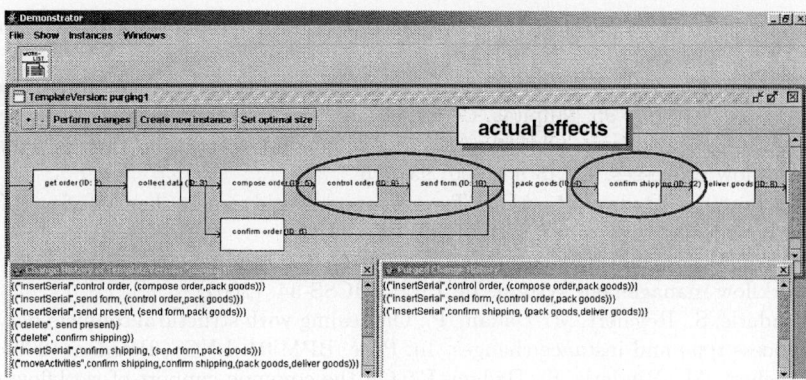

Fig. 8. Purging A Change Log (Prototype)

several other notions of equivalence between process schemes [13]. In [22], for example, v. Glabbeek and Goltz provide a very nice classification of semantic equivalences based on the basic notions of *bisimulation* and *trace equivalence*. Another approach to provide semantic equivalence of process schemes is given [23]. This work offers interesting methods to maintain the semantical meaning of a process schema before and after the change by applying semantics–preserving transformations.

6 Summary

In this paper, we have established a formal framework for dealing with concurrent process changes. An important application of this results is the propagation of process type changes to biased process instances. Based on the particular degree of overlap between process type and instance change we have to choose different migration strategies. To be able to decide to which degree process changes overlap we have presented an advanced approach which comprises structural aspects as well as operational solutions like purging change transactions.

We have implemented the presented concepts within a proof–of–concept prototype. Within this prototype migration of unbiased process instances as well as migration of biased instances with disjoint bias can be correctly and efficiently carried out. Furthermore, it can be precisely determined to which degree process type and instance changes overlap. Alg. 1 for purging change logs has been implemented. Fig. 8 depicts the example change log from Fig. 7 and the resulting purged change log.

References

1. v.d. Aalst, W., van Hee, K.: Workflow Management. MIT Press (2002)
2. v.d. Aalst, W., Basten, T.: Inheritance of workflows: An approach to tackling problems related to change. Theoret. Comp. Science **270** (2002) 125–203

3. Casati, F., Ceri, S., Pernici, B., Pozzi, G.: Workflow evolution. Data and Knowledge Engineering **24** (1998) 211–238
4. Ellis, C., Keddara, K., Rozenberg, G.: Dynamic change within workflow systems. In: Proc. COOCS'95, Milpitas, CA (1995) 10–21
5. Sadiq, S., Marjanovic, O., Orlowska, M.: Managing change and time in dynamic workflow processes. IJCIS **9** (2000) 93–116
6. Reichert, M., Dadam, P.: $ADEPT_{flex}$ - supporting dynamic changes of workflows without losing control. JIIS **10** (1998) 93–129
7. Weske, M.: Formal foundation and conceptual design of dynamic adaptations in a workflow management system. In: Proc. HICSS-34. (2001)
8. Rinderle, S., Reichert, M., Dadam, P.: On dealing with structural conflicts between process type and instance changes. In: Proc. BPM'04. LNCS, Potsdam (2004)
9. Reichert, M., Rinderle, S., Dadam, P.: On the common support of workflow type and instance changes under correctness constraints. In: Proc. CoopIS '03, Catania, Italy (2003) 407–425
10. Rinderle, S., Reichert, M., Dadam, P.: Correctness criteria for dynamic changes in workflow systems – a survey. Data and Knowledge Engineering, Special Issue on Advances in Business Process Management **50** (2004) 9–34
11. Kochut, K., Arnold, J., Sheth, A., Miller, J., Kraemer, E., Arpinar, B., Cardoso, J.: IntelliGEN: A distributed workflow system for discovering protein-protein interactions. Distributed and Parallel Databases **13** (2003) 43–72
12. v.d. Aalst, W., Basten, T.: Identifying commonalities and differences in object life cycles using behavorial inheritance. In: Proc. ICATPN '01, Newcastle, UK (2001) 32 – 52
13. Kiepuszewski, B.: Expressiveness and Suitability of Languages for Control Flow Modelling in Workflows. PhD thesis, Queensland University of Technology, Brisbane (2002) (available via http://www.tm.tue.nl/it/research/patterns).
14. Rinderle, S., Reichert, M., Dadam, P.: Flexible support of team processes by adaptive workflow systems. Distributed and Parallel Databases **16** (2004) 91–116
15. Rinderle, S., Reichert, M., Dadam, P.: On dealing with semantically conflicting business process changes. Technical Report UIB-2003-04, University of Ulm (2003)
16. Guth, V., Oberweis, A.: Delta analysis of petri net based models for business processes. In: Proc. Applied Informatics. (1997) 23–32
17. Rinderle, S.: Schema Evolution In Process Management Systems. PhD thesis, University of Ulm (2004) (to appear).
18. Badrinath, B., Ramamritham, K.: Semantics-based concurrency control: Beyond commutativity. ACM Transactions on Database Systems **17** (1992) 163–199
19. Wäsch, J., Klas, W.: History merging as a mechanism for concurrency control in cooperative environments. In: Proc. RIDE'96, New Orleans (1996) 76–85
20. Basten, T.: Branching bisimilarity is an equivalence indeed! Information Processing Letters **58** (1996) 141–147
21. Verbeek, E.: Verification of WF–Nets. PhD thesis, Technical University of Eindhoven (2004)
22. v. Glabbeek, R., Goltz, U.: Refinement of actions and equivalence notions for concurrent systems. Acta Informatica **37** (2001) 229–327
23. Frank, H., Eder, J.: Equivalence transformations on statecharts. In: Proc. SEKE'00, Chicago (2000) 150–158

Untangling Unstructured Cyclic Flows – A Solution Based on Continuations

Jana Koehler and Rainer Hauser

IBM Zurich Research Laboratory
CH-8803 Rueschlikon
Switzerland
{koe|rfh}@zurich.ibm.com

Abstract. We present a novel transformation method that allows us to map unstructured cyclic business process models to functionally equivalent workflow specifications that support structured cycles only. Our solution is based on a continuation semantics, which we developed for the graphical representation of a process model. By using a rule-based transformation method originally developed in compiler theory, we can untangle the unstructured flow while solving a set of abstract continuation equations. The generated workflow code can be optimized by controlling the order in which the transformation rules are applied.

We then present an implementation of the transformation method that directly manipulates an object-oriented model of the Business Process Execution Language for Web Services BPEL4WS. The implementation maps abstract continuation equations to the BPEL4WS control-flow graph. The transformation rules manipulate the links in the graph such that all cycles are removed and replaced by equivalent structured activities. A byproduct of this work is that, if a continuation semantics is adopted for BPEL4WS, its restriction to acyclic links can be dropped.

1 Introduction

Unstructured cycles in business process modeling usually cause hot debates. Do business consultants and customers really need to express cyclic business process flows? What do they try to express and specify with these cycles? Isn't it the case that different people interpret these cycles differently and that this is not good? Isn't a good business consultant able to resolve these problems when reviewing the process model with the customer and map it to a process model that has controlled, well-structured cycles only?

We do not know the best answer to all these questions and we can easily imagine that different needs and points of view may lead to very different answers. Rather, we are interested in the technical problems behind the discussion:

– Is there a formal semantics for graphically represented business process models containing unstructured cycles, which facilitates their transformation into a structured representation?
– Given a business process model containing unstructured cycles, can it be transformed into an equivalent specification in the Business Process Execution Language for Web Services (BPEL4WS) [1] that supports only structured cycles?

An answer to these questions is important for our work, where we investigate the suitability of graphical business process models as a means for requirement specification and develop methods that allow us to automatically generate executable workflow code from such models. On the one hand, we are interested in models that allow users to express business requirements without being constrained by the limitations of IT systems. On the other hand, we need automatic algorithms that can transform such models into performant code tailored to a specific IT platform.

In this paper, we describe a method that we developed to synthesize BPEL4WS code from business process models containing unstructured cycles. Section 2 introduces an example of an electronic purchasing process that contains unstructured cycles. A *continuation semantics* is proposed to capture the intended meaning of the cycles. Section 3 presents an efficient rule-based transformation method originating from compiler theory that takes a model with unstructured cycles and transforms it into a *functionally equivalent* model with structured cycles only. Section 4 discusses the possibilities to optimize the generated workflow code by controlling the application order of the transformation rules. In Section 5, we discuss how this transformation method can be implemented as an update transformation that manipulates an initially invalid BPEL4WS model. We conclude in Section 6 with a summary and outlook on future work.

2 Unstructured Cyclic Flows

We start with the graphical representation of a business process model that describes the possible flow of activities by adopting a UML Activity Diagram-like notation [2]. The choice of the representation language does not matter as long as we can assign the semantics to its graphical elements that we introduce below. Figure 1 shows the example of an electronic purchasing business process, which we will use throughout this paper. The process describes how a user buys products via an online purchasing system.[1]

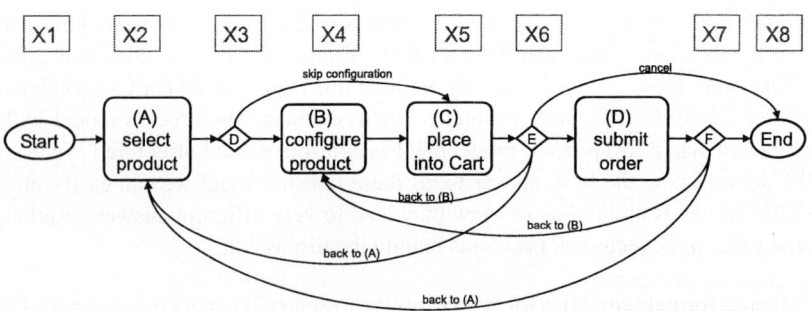

Fig. 1. Purchasing business process showing unstructured cycles.

---

[1] The role of the boxed variables, which are vertically aligned with selected nodes in the process model, will become clear in the next section.

Once the process has started, activity *(A) select product* is executed. After the *select product* activity has been completed, the process branches. The user can either decide to configure the product executing activity *(B) configure product* or to place the product directly into the shopping cart using activity *(C) place into Cart*. Note that we consider a nonconcurrent process model in which the branching is *exhaustive* and *disjoint*, i.e. after each decision exactly one of the possible branches is selected. After these activities have been completed, the user submits the order by executing activity *(D) submit order*. This sequence of activities describes the "normal" purchasing process. For a successful implementation, however, this process must allow the user to navigate freely between the various activities. For example, after a product is placed into the cart, the user may want to revisit its configuration and perhaps change it. Furthermore, a user may want to select several products before submitting an order. After an order has been submitted, the user may also want to revisit the configuration of the ordered product and/or change the set of selected products. Finally, a user may want to delay or cancel the placement of an order and leave the process without executing the *submit order* activity. This freedom in the process execution is described by the various back links from decisions E and F to one of the possible activities A or B.

The example illustrates that arbitrary, unstructured cycles may easily occur in the graphical representation of business processes. *Unstructured* cycles are characterized by *more than one entry or exit* point. Consider the example above and the cycle containing A, B, C, and D. This cycle can be entered in A by coming from *Start*, E, or F. It can also be entered in B by coming from E or F, and left via F and E. These multiple entry and exit points are the characteristic features of unstructured (sometimes also called wild or arbitrarily nested) cycles. In contrast to unstructured cycles, a *structured* cycle has *exactly one entry and one exit* point. On the one hand, unstructured cycles have even been identified as a pattern that frequently occurs in a business process model [3]. On the other hand, they are often the source of semantic problems [4], which explains why commercial workflow systems usually only implement structured cycles.

2.1 Continuation Semantics for Unstructured Graphical Flows

In order to transform a business process model with unstructured cycles into workflow code, which supports structured cycles with uniquely defined entry and exit points only, we assign a *continuation semantics* to the graphical model. Continuation semantics is a special form of a denotational semantics for programs with jumps. It has its origins in the Theory of Computation, where it has been discussed extensively in the context of functional and imperative languages [5]. A *continuation* describes "the rest of the program that has yet to be evaluated".

> *The key to achieving such a semantics is to make the meaning of every command a function whose result is the final result of the entire program, and to provide an extra argument to the command meaning, called a* continuation, *that is a function from states to final results describing the behavior of the "rest of the program" that will occur if the command relinquishes control.* [6], page 116.

The continuation semantics partitions the graphical flow into the past, present, and future and allows us to describe the intended execution of a process model. For example, given the activity A, we consider A the present state of the process, Start as its past and B or C as its future. We developed a method that assigns a continuation semantics to graphical models describing sequential flows. First, we assign continuation variables to the Start and End nodes as well as to all other nodes, in which sequential flows branch or merge, i.e., each activity or decision node in the flow that has more than one incoming or outgoing link is assigned a continuation variable. The resulting assignment is shown in Figure 1, which vertically aligns the boxed continuation variables with their corresponding nodes in the flow model.

Second, we have developed a method that allows us to extract *continuation equations* from the graphical process model. On the left-hand side of the equation symbol, we put the continuation variable that we consider the present. On the right-hand side of the equation, we describe the possible continuations that can follow this variable. A continuation can either be another variable or it can be an activity, which we denote by *invoke A*, *invoke B*, etc. A linear continuation can be described using the sequence operator ";". A branching of the continuation is described using a conditional statement *if* ⟨*condition*⟩ *then x*. Each link leaving a decision node in the process model is mapped to a branching. The ⟨*condition*⟩ can be derived from the process model if its graphical representation is annotated by branching conditions for the decision nodes. We introduce fresh Boolean variables to capture these conditions, but abstract from any concrete value in the following. For example, the condition that drives the continuation from process step A to process step B is denoted by the variable AB, the condition to continue from A to C is denoted by AC. Once a continuation variable has been added to each branch at the right-hand side of an equation, this equation is complete and a new equation begins. For the example under consideration, we obtain the following eight equations.

(1) x_1 = Start; x_2;
(2) x_2 = invoke A; x_3;
(3) x_3 = if AB then x_4;
    if AC then x_5;
(4) x_4 = invoke B; x_5
(5) x_5 = invoke C; x_6

(6) x_6 = if CD then invoke D; x_7 endif;
    if CEnd then x_8;
    if CA then x_2;
    if CB then x_4;
(7) x_7 = if DB then x_4;
    if DA then x_2;
    if DEnd then x_8;
(8) x_8 = End ;

The ordering of the conditional statements in the equations is arbitrary, because we consider nonconcurrent business process models with exhaustive and disjoint branching that do not need to specify an explicit ordering in which the branches are tried.

3 Transformation Method

We are now in the position to answer our second question: can a graphical model containing unstructured cycles be mapped into an equivalent program permitting structured cycles only? The answer was given almost forty years ago [7]: any concurrent or sequential *flow diagram* can be translated into a functionally equivalent program containing a single while-loop and new conditional statements. Unfortunately, the proof in [7] is nonconstructive, i.e., it does not give us a method of computation. Soon after this fundamental result, the problem of transforming unstructured loops into a well-structured form became known as the *GOTO-elimination problem* in compiler theory. Several algorithmic solutions, which permit an arbitrary number of well-structured loops but also focus on the optimization of the transformed code [8,9,10], have been developed based on the famous T1-T2 transformations [11]. We describe the application of these techniques to the problem of business-to-IT model transformation in more detail in the next section.

3.1 Solving the System of Equations

Our transformation method is based on the transformation rules presented in [8]. Whereas Ammarguellat presents her transformation rules using a Lisp-like notation, we have developed a representation based on the abstract mathematical equations introduced above, from which implementations for very different model representations can be easily derived. A derived implementation, which works on an object-oriented model of the Business Process Execution Language for Web services [1] is discussed in the second part of this paper. The soundness of the rules follows from the observation that each of them preserves the possible continuations in the encoded flow model.

Substitution: This rule reduces the number of variables and thereby also the number of equations. Given the occurrence of a variable on the right-hand side of an equation, it replaces this variable with its defining equation.

$$\begin{array}{l} x_0 = \textit{invoke A}; \boxed{x_1}; \\ \boxed{x_1} = \textit{invoke B}; \end{array} \longrightarrow \begin{array}{l} x_0 = \textit{invoke A}; \\ \textit{invoke B}; \end{array}$$

Factorization: This rule is applied to a continuation equation that contains several disjoint and exhaustive branches, which all lead to the same continuation x. The multiple occurrences of x are replaced by a single occurrence of x at the end of the equation, which is guarded by a new Boolean condition assembled from the governing conditions of the various branches. Fresh variables have to be used to capture the "state" of governing conditions in the case that different executions of the flow can modify their value in different ways, cf. [12] for more details. In the following, we will omit these variables in order to keep the example transformations more easily readable.

$$\begin{array}{l} x_0 = \textit{invoke A}; \\ \quad \textit{if c then invoke B}; \boxed{x_1} \\ \quad \textit{else if d then } \boxed{x_1}; \\ \textit{endif}; \end{array} \longrightarrow \begin{array}{l} x_0 = \textit{invoke A}; \\ \quad \textit{if c then invoke B}; \\ \quad \textit{pred} := c \vee (\neg c \wedge d); \\ \quad \textit{if pred then } \boxed{x_1}; \end{array}$$

Derecursivation: This rule eliminates cycles. It is applied to equations that mention the same continuation variable x at their left-hand and right-hand sides. The occurrence of x in the right-hand side is eliminated by a repeat-while statement ranging from the beginning of the right-hand side until x occurs. The termination condition for the loop is obtained from the conditions on the execution path that leads to the continuation variable. This rule can be applied if no other continuation variables occur between the equation sign and the recursive continuation variable. Otherwise, the continuations have to be reordered first using a variant of the if-distribution rule below.

$$\begin{array}{c} \boxed{x_0} = invoke\ A; \\ if\ c\ then\ \boxed{x_0}; \end{array} \longrightarrow \begin{array}{c} x_0 = repeat \\ invoke\ A; \\ while\ c; \end{array}$$

If-Distribution: This rule rewrites nested branching continuations into a sequence of branches that can be arbitrarily ordered. This rule may occur in many different forms. A variant used in this paper is shown below:

$$\begin{array}{c} x_0 = if\ \boxed{c1}\ then\ x_1 \\ else\ if\ \boxed{c2}\ then\ x_2; \\ endif; \end{array} \longrightarrow \begin{array}{c} x_0 = if\ \boxed{\neg c1 \wedge c2}\ then\ x_2; \\ if\ c1\ then\ x_1; \end{array}$$

These rules are maintained and organized by a transformation engine that operates in the following steps:

1. Select a rule that is applicable to an equation;
2. Apply the rule and compute the modified set of equations;
3. Goto step 1 until only a single equation remains in the set.

3.2 Solving the Example

In the following, we describe how the example equations are solved. The order in which the rules are selected for application determines the quality of the generated workflow code. For our purposes, we developed various application orders that enable our transformation engine to produce code of different quality. We discuss our optimization heuristics in Section 4.

Pass 1: Only the substitution rule is applicable. The derecursivation rule is not applicable, because no equation contains the same variable on both sides. The factorization rule is not applicable, because no equation contains multiple occurrences of the same continuation variable on the right-hand side. The transformation engine decides to apply the substitution rule to variable x_3 in Equation (2), then to variable x_6 in Equation (5), and finally to variable x_7 in the (transformed) Equation (5).

(1) x_1 = Start; x_2;
(2) x_2 = invoke A;
    if AB then x_4;
    if AC then x_5;
(4) x_4 = invoke B; x_5
(8) x_8 = End;

(5) x_5 = invoke C;
    if CD then invoke D;
        if DB then x_4;
        if DA then x_2;
        if DEnd then x_8;
    endif ;
    if CEnd then x_8;
    if CA then x_2;
    if CB then x_4;

Pass 2: The transformation engine works on the complex Equation (5) by applying the factorization rule to the continuation variables x_2, x_4, x_8, which each occur twice on the right-hand side of this equation. Then, the variable x_8 is eliminated by substituting Equation (8).

(5) x_5 = invoke C;
  if CD then invoke D;
  if CA $\vee$ (CD $\wedge$ DA) then x_2;
  if CB $\vee$ (CD $\wedge$ DB) then x_4;
  if CEnd $\vee$ (CD $\wedge$ DEnd) then End;

Pass 3: The variable x_4 is substituted in Equations (2) and (5). Then, multiple occurrences of x_5 in Equation (2) are eliminated by applying the factorization rule again.

(2) x_2 = invoke A;
  if AB then invoke B;
  if AB $\vee$ AC then x_5;

(5) x_5 = invoke C;
  if CD then invoke D;
  if CA $\vee$ (CD $\wedge$ DA) then x_2;
  if CB $\vee$ (CD $\wedge$ DB) then invoke B; x_5
  if CEnd $\vee$ (CD $\wedge$ DEnd) then End;

Pass 4: The transformation engine eliminates the recursion in Equation (5). Variable x_2 occurs inside the continuation that the repeat-while loop will spawn, i.e., x_2 has to be moved using if-distribution prior to creating the loop such that it succeeds x_5.

(5) x_5 = repeat
    invoke C;
    if CD then invoke D;
    if CB $\vee$ (CD $\wedge$ DB) then invoke B;
  while CB $\vee$ (CD $\wedge$ DB);
  if CA $\vee$ (CD $\wedge$ DA) then x_2;
  if CEnd $\vee$ (CD $\wedge$ DEnd) then End;

Pass 5: Variable x_5 is substituted in Equation (2).

(2) x_2 = invoke A;
  if AB then invoke B;
  if AB $\vee$ AC then
      repeat
        invoke C;
        if CD then invoke D;
        if CB $\vee$ (CD $\wedge$ DB) then invoke B;
      while CB $\vee$ (CD $\wedge$ DB);
      if CA $\vee$ (CD $\wedge$ DA) then x_2;
      if CEnd $\vee$ (CD $\wedge$ DEnd) then End;
  endif;

Pass 6: The transformed Equation (2) is recursive. Variable x_2 occurs inside the conditional branch governed by AB $\vee$ AC, which would be incorrectly interrupted if derecursivation were applied immediately. Therefore if-distribution is applied first to rearrange the branching continuations. The transformed Equation (2) is inserted into Equation (1) to replace the last remaining occurrence of x_2. These last transformation steps solve the equational system. Only a single equation defining the variable x_1 is left, which contains no other continuation variables on its right-hand side.

(1) x_1 = Start;
 repeat
  invoke A;
  if AB then invoke B;
  if AB $\vee$ AC then
   repeat
    invoke C;
    if CD then invoke D;
    if CB $\vee$ (CD $\wedge$ DB) then invoke B;
   while CB $\vee$ (CD $\wedge$ DB);
  endif;
 while (AB $\vee$ AC) $\wedge$ (CA $\vee$ (CD $\wedge$ DA));
 if (AB $\vee$ AC) $\wedge$ (CEnd $\vee$ (CD $\wedge$ DEnd)) then End;

Any applied transformation rule preserves the possible continuations of the process model. The flows described by the business process model and the flow described by the remaining equation (or any intermediate form of the equation set) are functionally equivalent, i.e., when invoked on the same input, both flows will produce exactly the same output.

4 Optimizing the Generated Workflow

We have developed two techniques to further simplify and optimize the generated workflow code, which we describe in the following:

1. The resulting normalized process model, in particular the governing conditions, can be simplified by exploiting the fact that the branching is disjoint and exhaustive.
2. The transformation engine can influence various structural properties of the generated code by applying the transformation rules in a specific order.

4.1 Simplifying the Normalized Process Model

Several of the governing transitions in the solved equation form a tautology, because they describe all possible paths to reach a particular continuation. Activity C has to be executed in any possible execution path. It will either follow activity A directly or it will follow activity B, but it cannot be skipped. This means that (AB $\vee$ AC) is a tautology, because the transitions to B or C are the only ones possible from A. Thus, the condition that governs the inner loop is unnecessary. From B, only a single, unguarded transition to C is possible. The same argumentation applies to (CEnd $\vee$ (CD $\wedge$ DEnd)). It follows that the condition governing the reachability of End can be skipped.

Furthermore, the Start and End activities can be removed from the equational representation, because they do not describe business-relevant data manipulations. In the flow model, these nodes indicate where the business process starts and ends. They determine the initial entrance into the flow and how the continuation equations are systematically built from the graphical model. The variable assigned to the start node also determines which continuation variable is left after the equational system has been solved. The result of these simplification steps is:

x_1 = repeat
　　　invoke A;
　　　if AB then invoke B;
　　　repeat
　　　　　invoke C;
　　　　　if CD then invoke D;
　　　　　if CB ∨ (CD ∧ DB) then invoke B;
　　　while CB ∨ (CD ∧ DB);
　　while CA ∨ (CD ∧ DA);

We observe that this equation contains two properly nested loops. The inner loop captures the forward and backward flow between the activities B, C, and D. The outer loop captures the backward flow to activity A from either C or D.

4.2 Controlling Rule Application Order

The second opportunity for optimizing the generated code lies in computing the "correct" order for the application of rules by the transformation engine. We note that each transformation rule guarantees that the transformation will *terminate*, but the rule application is *not confluent*, i.e., different application orders produce syntactically different transformation results. The method in [8] uses a topological sorting of the nodes in the control-flow graph to determine the order in which variables should be eliminated from the equations. We found this method to be insufficient for our purposes. Instead, we developed a control scheme that keeps information about how often variables occur on the right-hand side of the equations. We also added rule priorities. Factorization has a higher priority than derecursivation. Derecursivation is only applied directly prior to a substitution step or as a last step of the transformation if the remaining equation is recursive. If-distribution is only applied if required, which happens in two situations: First, to move any continuation of the flow towards the end activity to the very end of an equation. Second, to move continuation variables outside the scope of applicability of the derecursivation rule. To explain how the rule application order is controlled, let us revisit the example.

In the first pass, only the substitution rule was applicable. The following occurrences of continuation variables on the right-hand side of the equations are counted: $x_2 = 3, x_3 = 1, x_4 = 3, x_5 = 2, x_6 = 1, x_7 = 1$, and $x_8 = 2$. We note that the variables x_3, x_6, x_7 occur only once. Whenever such single-occurrence variables exist, the transformation engine will apply the substitution rule to eliminate them from the equation set. In the second pass, the factorization rule was applicable, because the variables x_2, x_4, and x_8 occured twice in the same right-hand side of an equation. Owing to its higher priority, this rule was applied. Then the substitution rule was considered again, controlled by the occurrence of the continuation variables: $x_2 = 2, x_4 = 2, x_5 = 2, x_8 = 1$. Only the variable x_8 occurs a single time and thus the substitution rule was applied to it.

For the third pass, all remaining continuation variables occur exactly two times. Only the substitution rule is applicable. The transformation engine has no unique choice to continue. This phenomenon reflects the fact that the flow graph encoded in the business process model is *non-reducible*, which is a widely studied phenomenon in compiler theory [13]. Using the transformation rules from [8], code duplication is unavoidable, e.g., variable x_4 is substituted in Equations (2) and (5) in Pass 3. In contrast to programming languages, non-reducibility of the underlying flow graph seems to be quite common for business process models. To avoid code duplication for such non-reducible flows, we have developed an alternative code generation method that synthesizes a state-machine encoded in BPEL4WS, cf. [12].

The transformation engine selects the variable that occurs the minimum number of times. If no such choice exists (as is the case in our example), it selects the variable that has the *smallest* right-hand side in its equation. *Small* can be defined in different ways depending on the goal of the code optimization. It can be the number of *invoke* statements, the number of conditions tested or any other user-defined criterion or combination thereof. In our case, we try to minimize the number of *invoke* statements followed by the number of tested conditions, because we want to minimize the number of Web service invocations generated for the workflow code, and we want to keep the branching logic as simple as possible. Consequently, the transformation engine selects variable x_4 in the third pass. Eliminating x_4 transforms Equation (5) into a recursive equation and thus, in Pass 5, the derecursivation rule is applied. It requires applying the if-distribution rule first, because another continuation variable occurs in the scope for applying this rule. In Pass 5, the only variables left are x_2 (which occurs twice) and x_5 (which occurs once). Consequently, x_5 is substituted first. In Pass 6, derecursivation preceded by if-distribution is applied because of the higher rule priority. Finally, in Pass 7, a last application of the substitution rule is possible.

4.3 Mapping to BPEL4WS

The single equation computed by the transformation engine contains only two well-structured cycles in the form of repeat-while statements as well as a few conditional branches. It can be directly mapped to an XML representation of the standardized language BPEL4WS. Each invocation of an activity is mapped to the invocation of a Web service. A repeat-while loop is mapped to a while-do loop combined with an assignment:

```
<sequence>
  <assign newcondition := true />
  <while newcondition>
    <assign newcondition := condition/>
  </while>
</sequence>
```

A conditional statement is mapped to a `<switch>`:

```
<switch>
  <case condition = guard-expression/>
</switch>
```

We show an abstract specification in simplified BPEL4WS syntax that defines the control-flow for the workflow, but omits all details that relate to partners, messages, and Web services as well as fresh variables that may have been introduced during the transformation to capture the values of guard conditions.

```
<process>
  <sequence>
    <assign cond1: = 'true'/>
    <while cond1>
      <sequence>
        <invoke A/>
        <switch>
          <case condition = 'AB'>
            <invoke B>
          </case>
        </switch>
        <assign cond2 := 'true'/>
        <while cond2>
          <sequence>
            <invoke C/>
            <switch>
              <case condition = 'CD'>
                <invoke D/>
              </case>
            </switch>
            <switch>
              <case cond = '(CD & DB) or CB'/>
                <invoke B>
              </case>
            </switch>
            <assign cond2 := '((CD & DB) or CB)'/>
          </sequence>
        <while/>
      </sequence>
    </while>
        <assign cond1 := '(((CD & DA) or CA) & (AB or AC))'/>
  </sequence>
</process>
```

The XML representation can also be graphically displayed by mapping it, for example, to the UML Profile for BPEL [14], which is sketched in Figure 2.

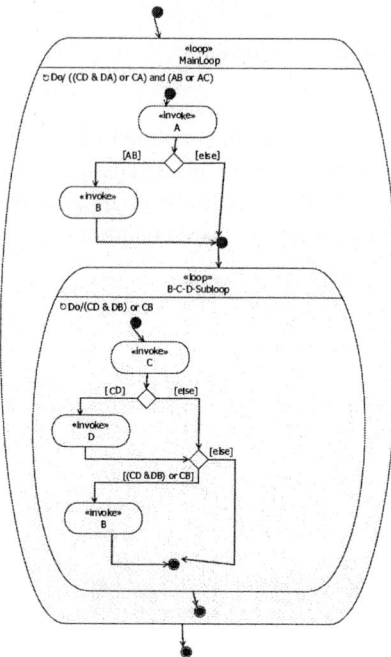

Fig. 2. Resulting BPEL4WS diagram.

5 Working Directly on a BPEL4WS Model

Based on the abstract description of the transformation rules, very different implementations can be imagined. First, one can refactor the graphical business process model, e.g., by replacing cyclic links with appropriate loop nodes in UML 2. The advantage of this approach is that different, but equivalent views on the process model can be offered to the modeler and that a view of the process model is available, which is structurally very similar to the generated code. The disadvantage lies in the need to add many additional variants to the four basic transformation rules that deal with the various graphical modeling elements. Second, one can map an unstructured cyclic flow directly to an executable specification in some workflow language, which supports unstructured cycles or refactor the workflow specification until it contains only structured cycles. In the following, we discuss an implementation that maps an unstructured cyclic business process model directly into BPEL4WS. The process model can also contain concurrency, which may be introduced by fork or join activities in UML 2, for example.

Figure 3 gives a more complete overview of the BPEL4WS language in the form of an object-oriented model, which we have developed. We adopt the view of a model as a containment hierarchy, starting with one root object, where each node may have any number of property settings in the form of name-value pairs. A property value is either a simple data value or a reference to another object in the same model. A convenient way to represent such models is the UML class diagram [2]. Objects are represented as classes, properties are represented as attributes, and references to other objects that express non-simple values can be expressed with the help of associations.

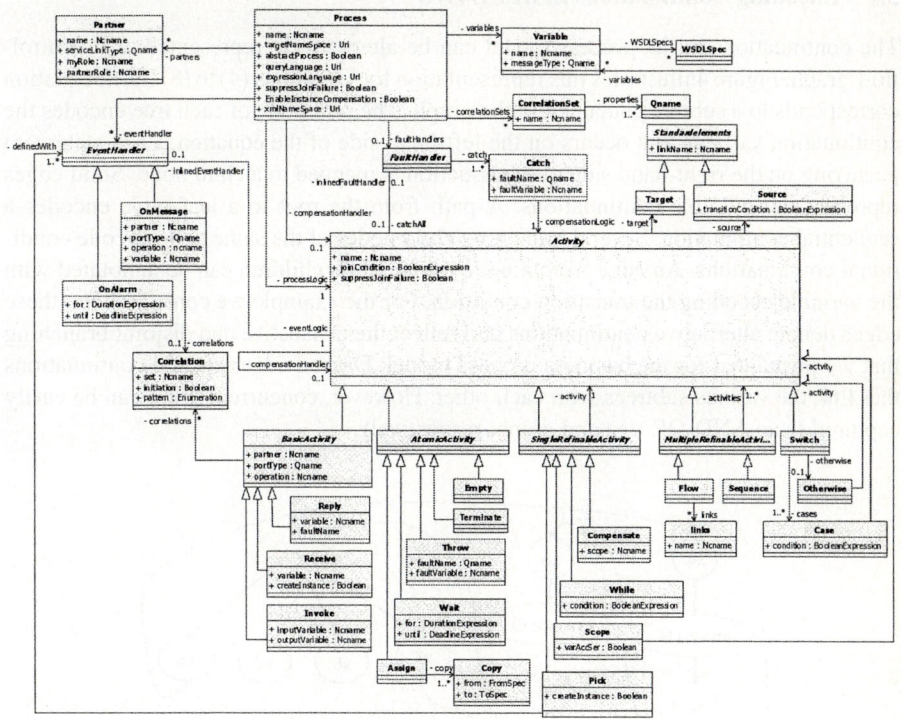

Fig. 3. Class diagram for the BPEL4WS language.

Some details of the BPEL4WS language have been omitted from this class diagram: We have not further refined the definitions of the types used for the *From* and *To* attributes, which we simply called *FromSpec* and *ToSpec*. Similarly, the types *Ncname*, *Qname*, *BooleanExpression*, *DurationExpression*, and *Deadline Expression* remain undefined. We do not (yet) care about the visibility of associations, which is simply set to *private*. Furthermore, we do not make explicit whether certain associations are aggregations or compositions. Some attributes may not occur together. For example, the *for* and *until* attributes of a *Wait* activity occur exclusively. We have again abstracted from this detail and assume that in this case, an attribute may be set to *unknown* or the Object Constraint Language OCL [15] would be used to add constraints to our model. As for associations, we have not made a distinction between whether a set of associated classes is ordered or unordered, which distinguishes a *sequence* activity from a *flow*. The multiplicity of the associations has been derived from the BPEL schema definitions. For example, a process may define 0 to n event handlers. However, if the *EventHandler* element is used in the XML definition, at least one *OnMessage* or *OnAlarm* handler should be present.

Again, this is best expressed with the help of OCL constraints that are added to the class diagram.

5.1 Encoding Continuations in BPEL4WS

The continuations in the process model can be alternatively represented as a control-flow graph. Figure 4 illustrates this representation for Equations (4) to (8). Each equation corresponds to a subtree contained in the graph. The root node of each tree encodes the continuation variable that occurs on the left-hand side of the equation. Each statement occurring on the right-hand side of the equation is mapped to a child node. Solid edges represent the possible continuations. A path from the root to a leaf node encodes a sequential continuation. Several branching child nodes of the same node encode conditional continuations. An edge from a node to one of its children can be annotated with the variable encoding the transition condition. For the example we consider here, these edges denote alternative continuations and reflect the exhaustive and disjoint branching that we postulated for the business process model. Dashed edges encode continuations that link the various subtrees with each other. However, concurrent flows can be easily captured in an AND-OR tree and graph, respectively.

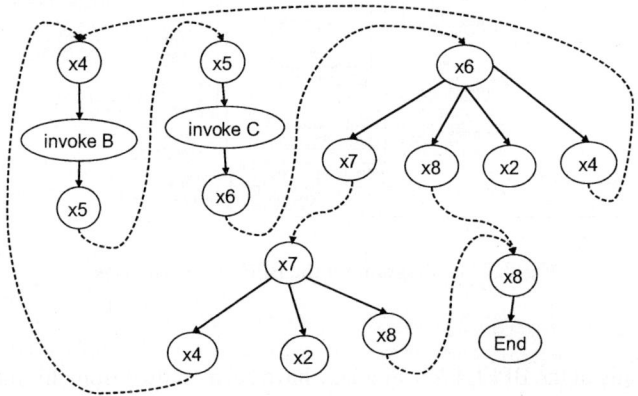

Fig. 4. Forest of trees capturing the semantics of continuation equations.

The encoding in BPEL4WS works as follows: The control-flow graph is mapped to a BPEL4WS flow containing a sequence for each subtree. Tree nodes, which contain continuation variables, are mapped to empty BPEL4WS activities. Tree nodes, which contain activity invocations, are mapped to invoke activities. Depending on the semantics of Start and End nodes in the business process model, these nodes are either mapped to empty or invoke activities. The names of the empty activities are set to the names of the continuation variables they encode, the names of the invoke activities are set to the names of the activities. The edges between the tree nodes are mapped to links and the activities define whether they are the source or target of a link. The transition conditions are captured in the transitionCondition attribute of a source element.

If a node has more than one child node, another flow is introduced. Alternatively, we could map these alternative, nonconcurrent branches to a switch, but in using a flow we adopt a unique encoding for all edges and can immediately capture concurrent branching. The example encoding for the control flow that was captured in Equations (4) and (6) is sketched below.

```
<flow>
  <links>
    <link name='x2link'>
    <link name='x3link'>
    <link name='x4link1'>
    <link name='x4link2'>
    ...
  </links>

  <sequence>
    <empty name='x4'/>
      <target linkName='x4link1'/>
      <target linkName='x4link2'/>
    </empty>
    <invoke name='B'/>
    <empty name ='x5'>
      <source linkName='x5link'/>
    </empty>
  </sequence>

  <sequence>
    <empty name='x6'/>
      <target linkName='x6link'/>
      <source linkName='x6-x7link'
        transitionCondition='CD'/>
      <source linkName='x6-x8link'
        transitionCondition='CEnd'/>
      <source linkName='x6-x2link'
        transitionCondition='CA'/>
      <source linkName='x6-x4link'
        transitionCondition='CB'/>
    </empty>
    <flow>
      <empty name='x7'>
        <target linkName='x6-x7link'/>
      </empty>
      <empty name='x8'>
        <target linkName='x6-x8link'/>
      </empty>
      <empty name='x2'>
        <target linkName='x6-x2link'/>
      </empty>
      <empty name='x4'>
        <target linkName='x6-x4link'/>
```

```
      </empty>
    </flow>
  </sequence>
</flow>
```

We could almost hand over this BPEL4WS specification to a BPEL4WS engine. Unfortunately, our process definition violates a major constraint of the specification, namely that the `links` must form an acyclic graph. As we can see in Figure 4, the encoding links form a control cycle.

We observe that the continuation semantics paves the way to allowing cyclic links between activities in BPEL4WS, because the semantics clearly defines which instructions in the BPEL4WS program should be executed next, and rescheduling activities for another execution has a clear meaning. This is in contrast to the current semantics of BPEL4WS links, where cyclic links cause activities to wait for each other to complete execution, while none of them can start. Although the current limitation in the specification can be overcome and an execution semantics for cyclic BPEL4WS flows is within reach, such an extension would make it easy to write BPEL4WS programs that contain runtime errors such deadlocks and livelocks, which require verification technology for detection.

5.2 Transforming the BPEL4WS Model

The cyclic, concurrent BPEL4WS model can be transformed into valid acyclic BPEL 1.1 code if all control cycles encoded in the links are sequential and properly nested within a single concurrent execution branch, i.e., there should be no control link from one sequential cycle to another running in a different concurrent thread. Each sequential cycle can be transformed by replacing cyclic links with appropriate BPEL4WS `while` activities. However, no links are allowed between two different `while` activities in the BPEL4WS specification, i.e., the language forbids any form of synchronization of concurrent cyclic processes in order to avoid problems of possible deadlocks or livelocks, etc. We do not propose the sequentialization of concurrent BPEL4WS as a possible solution to transform unstructured concurrent cycles, although it is a theoretical possibility [7], because we do not consider it to be practically relevant. Instead, the direct execution of cyclic BPEL4WS, as sketched above, seems to make more sense.

The transformation rules can be reformulated as a manipulation of links and their sources and targets.

Substitution works on `empty` activities that are the target of exactly one link. Consider the trees for Equations (4) and (5). The substitution deletes the root node x_5 of tree (5) and the leaf node x_5 of tree (4). A new link (or associated activity in our class model) is created from the parent node of the deleted leaf node in tree (4) (`invoke B`) to the child node of the deleted root node (`invoke C`) in tree (5).

Factorization is applied to trees (BPEL4WS `flows`) that contain multiple occurrences of an `empty` activity with the same name. No additional Boolean variables are required, but instead the transition conditions are assembled from the links when multiple occurrences of the same node are merged. Consider the substitution of x_7, for example. This requires joining the transition condition CD of the link to x_7 with the transition conditions $DB, DA, DEnd$ of the links <u>from</u> x_7. We obtain $CD \wedge (DB \vee DA \vee DEnd)$, which is transformed into disjunctive normal form and leads to three new links with transition conditions $CD \wedge DB$, $CD \wedge DA$, and $CD \wedge DEnd$, which replace the old links. Multiple paths to the same leaf node can be merged by disjunctively joining their transition conditions. For example, when merging the two empty activities labeled x_8, we obtain the new transition condition $CEnd \vee (DEnd \wedge CD)$. Figure 5 illustrates this transformation.

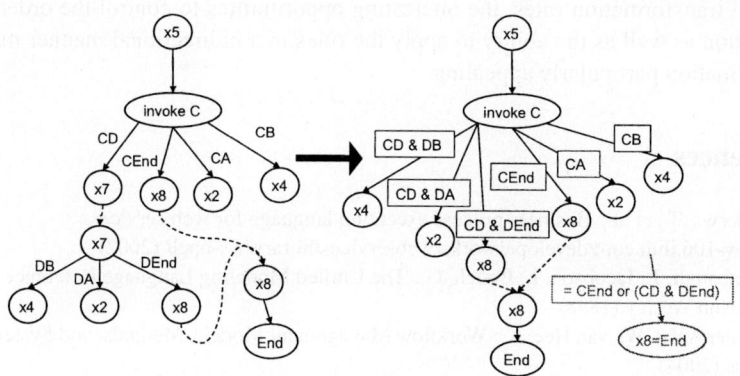

Fig. 5. Factorization working on links.

Derecursivation directly introduces a new while activity instead of a repeat-while loop. It is applied to trees that contain links from an empty activity node back to the root of the same tree.

One can imagine using OCL [15] or any other expression language to describe the pre- and postconditions of the transformation rules by using the types, associations, and attributes of the BPEL4WS class diagram. The precondition of a rule describes when the rule is applicable to the model, whereas the postcondition describes the required update. The computation of the update, often called *model reconciliation*, is a nontrivial computation that goes beyond the focus of this paper and is the subject of our current work. Expressions in the postcondition should be limited such that the update is unique and can be computed efficiently, i.e., they must be functional. This requirement translates into restrictions on the expression language, which we are currently investigating. Furthermore, our transformation rules all have a natural inverse interpretation, although we only described them in an unidirectional and not in a bidirectional way. In the case of bidirectional transformations, the pre- and postconditions must be limited such that the reconciliation of the model is computable in both directions.

6 Conclusion

We discuss the transformation of business process models with unstructured cycles into workflow languages that support only well-structured cycles based on a continuation semantics. We present a rule-based transformation method that works on a set of continuations that captures the semantics of cyclic models. From this abstract representation, various implementations of the transformation method, which can be tailored to different model representations, can be derived. For example, we discuss the implementation of the transformation as an update of an object-oriented model for the Business Process Execution Language BPEL4WS. A byproduct of our work is that we can show that, if a continuation semantics is defined for BPEL4WS links, the requirement of acyclicity can be dropped and executable cyclic workflows could be permitted. The small set of required transformation rules, the interesting opportunities to control the order of rule application as well as the ability to apply the rules in a bidirectional manner make this transformation particularly appealing.

References

1. Andrews, T., et al.: Business process execution language for web services. www-106.ibm.com/developerworks/webservices/library/ws-bpel/ (2002)
2. Rumbaugh, J., Jacobson, I., Booch, G.: The Unified Modeling Language Reference Manual. Addison Wesley (1898)
3. van der Aalst, W., van Hee, K.: Workflow Management Models, Methods, and Systems. MIT Press (2004)
4. van der Aalst, W., Desel, J., Kindler, E.: On the semantics of EPCs: A vicious circle. In: Proceedings of the Workshop on EPK. (2003) 7–18
5. Reynolds, J.: The discoveries of continuations. LISP and Symbolic Computation **6** (1993) 233–247
6. Reynolds, J.: Theories of Programming Languages. Cambridge University Press (1998)
7. Böhm, C., Jacopini, G.: Flow diagrams, turing machines and languages with only two formation rules. Communications of the ACM **9** (1966) 366–371
8. Ammarguellat, Z.: A control-flow normalization algorithm and its complexity. Software Engineering **13** (1992) 237–251
9. Erosa, A., Hendren, L.: Taming control flow: A structured approach to eliminating goto statements. In: Proceedings of the International Conference on Computer Languages (ICCL, IEEE Press (1994) 229–240
10. Peterson, W., Kasami, T., Tokura, N.: On the capabilities of while, repeat, and exit statements. Communications of the ACM **16** (1973) 503–512
11. Hecht, M., Ullman, J.: Flow graph reducibility. SIAM Journal of Computing **1** (1972) 188–202
12. Hauser, R., Koehler, J.: Compiling process graphs into executable code. In: Third International Conference on Generative Programming and Component Engineering. LNCS, Springer (2004) forthcoming.
13. Aho, A., Sethi, R., Ullman, J.: Compilers–Principles, Techniques, and Tools. Addison-Wesley (1986)
14. Amsden, J., Gardner, T., Griffin, C., Iyengar, S., Knapman, J.: UML profile for automated business processes with a mapping to BPEL 1.0. IBM Alphaworks http://dwdemos.alphaworks.ibm.com/ wstk/ common/ wstkdoc/ services/ demos/ uml2bpel/ docs/ UMLProfileForBusinessProcesses1.0.pdf (2003)
15. Warmer, J., Kleppe, A.: The Object Constraint Language – Precise Modeling with UML. Addison-Wesley (1999)

Making Workflow Models Sound Using Petri Net Controller Synthesis

Juliane Dehnert[1] and Armin Zimmermann[2]

[1] Fraunhofer ISST, Mollstr. 1, 10178 Berlin, Germany
juliane.dehnert@isst.fraunhofer.de
[2] Technische Universität Berlin, Einsteinufer 17, 10587 Berlin, Germany
azi@cs.tu-berlin.de

Abstract. More and more companies use "process aware" information systems to make their business processes more efficient. To do this, workflow definitions must be formulated in a formal specification language, as they represent executable derivates of business process descriptions. Both for the less formal descriptions of business processes as well as the workflow definitions, Petri-net based approaches are used successfully. In the literature the business process descriptions are required to be well-structured, leading to a sound workflow definition. We argue that in many cases well-structuredness is too restrictive for practitioners. Relaxed soundness has been introduced previously as a more suitable requirement. The paper presents how methods from controller synthesis for Petri nets can be used to automatically make this type of models sound. For this reason we adopt the idea of controllability for Petri net workflow models.

1 Introduction

Over the last decade more and more companies work with "process aware" information systems. These systems are configured on the basis of explicit process descriptions. Examples are dedicated Workflow Management systems (WfMS), such as Staffware, but also normal ERP systems which became enhanced by a workflow module. Prerequisite for their use is the specification of workflow, the computer-supported parts of the company's business processes.

Both for the descriptions of business processes as well as the workflow definitions, Petri-net based approaches are used successfully. For the definition of workflow Petri nets are particularly suitable, as they have a formal syntax and an unambiguous, operational semantics. The operational semantics offers the possibility to use the process descriptions right away as input format for a WF-engine. Examples of WfMS using Petri net based process descriptions are COSA (Software Ley/COSA Solutions/Transflow [SL99]) and Income (Get Process AG). Moreover, their formal foundation allows to validate the derived process description prior to their use within a WfMS. This helps to avoid faulty situations at run-time and therefore saves costs and raises customer satisfaction. An important property that every workflow definition should satisfy is soundness [Aal98]. Soundness guarantees that there are no faulty executions at run-time.

A workflow definition describes a business process in a machine readable manner. As their modeling requires a deep inside into the application context, domain experts are often put in charge of the modeling, although they do not necessarily have high modeling expertise.

Well-structuredness has been proposed [Aal98,LSW98,MR00] as a property that assists non expert modelers in formalizing their business processes. It requires a strict block structuring of the process descriptions. The restriction to well-structuredness is also present in UML v1.4 activity diagrams [UML02]. Strict block structuring conditions are relaxed by allowing control-links (resp. synchronization edges) to synchronize tasks belonging to different parallel control flow paths in BPEL4WS [BEA03] and ADEPT [RD98].

The advantage of this structural property is purely technical and lies in its close relationship to soundness. It has been shown that well-structured process descriptions are sound, provided they are life.

Well-structuredness has its shortcomings. We will argue in the paper that modeling in a well-structured manner requires: 1) to have a comprehensive insight into the whole process, possibly spanning different organizational units, 2) to implement efficiency aspects via the ordering of tasks, and 3) to accept redundancy.

This paper uses relaxed soundness [DvdA04] as a different property which is better suited to assist the modeler. We show that relaxed soundness meets the intuition of the modelers, not requiring expertise beyond their own organizational unit. However, because relaxed soundness is weaker than soundness, an additional step is required to achieve a sound WF-net. One contribution of the paper is to show how methods from Petri net controller synthesis can be adopted to automatically make this type of models sound. For this reason we apply the idea of task controllability to Petri net workflow models.

The paper presents an algorithm for the generation of the robust subgraph, i.e. the part of the behavior of a workflow model that can be controlled to avoid faulty situations. This algorithm is a refined version of the one presented in [Deh02].

An advantage of the approach proposed here is that the result of the automatic transformation can be used to detect potential for a process optimization. The separation between business process modeling and soundness transformation enables the modeler to adapt the model easily if business process requirements change.

The remainder of the paper is organized as follows: In the next section an application example is used to introduce the chosen modeling technique, namely WF-nets. The suitability of possible properties is compared in addition. In Section 4 relevant methods from Petri net controller synthesis are briefly introduced and their application to the area of workflow modeling is described. In Section 4.2 we broaden the scope of the proposed methods to reactive workflow systems. This is done by representing the interaction with the environment within the process descriptions. Section 5 focuses on process optimization based on the prior computations. Finally, the results are summarized.

2 An Application Example

As modeling technique for the specification of workflow we use Petri nets. We refer to the class of Place/Transition nets and more in particular to Workflow nets (WF-nets). This net class was introduced in [Aal98,Aal00]. WF-nets were tuned to fit the requirements within the domain of workflow management. Petri net theory was exploited to develop adequate properties and efficient algorithms for that Petri net class [Aal00,VBA01].

A WF-net is a Petri net which has a unique source place (i) and a unique sink place (o). This corresponds to the fact that any case handled by the process description is created if it enters the WfMS and is deleted once it is completely handled by the WfMS. In such a net, a task is modeled by a transition and intermediate states are modeled by places. A token in the source place i corresponds to a "fresh" case which needs to be handled, a token in the sink place o corresponds to a case that has been handled. The process state is defined by the marking. In addition, a WF-net requires all transitions and places to be on some path from i to o. This ensures that every task (transition) or condition (place) contributes to the processing of cases.

Figure 1 shows two WF-nets modeling the process "Handling of incoming order". Both process descriptions cover the ordering of a product which involves two departments: the accounting department handling the payment and the sales department handling the distribution.

In Figure 1a) the distributed organizational assignment is visible. The process starts by splitting the control-flow into two threads (AND_process_order), where the right one models the tasks of the accountancy and the left one models the tasks of the sales.

In accounting the customer's credit-worthiness is checked first (c.f. transition check_credit). The result of this task is either ok or not_ok. In case the result is positive the payment is arranged (arrange_payment), otherwise the instance is canceled and the customer is notified (notify_customer). On the sales side the order is recorded (record_order) and then either assembled (pick), wrapped (wrap), and delivered (deliver); or else canceled (cancel).

The threads of the two parallel departments are joined again in the transitions AND_cancel and AND_accept. The process "Handling of incoming order" is completed by archiving information on that instance (archive).

The WF-net in Figure 1b) describes the behavior of the same business process in a slightly different manner. The assignment of tasks to organizational units is neglected here. The tasks are ordered such that the net is well-structured instead (details see below). The two model variants are used in the following to show the differences and advantages between relaxed soundness and well-structuredness.

3 Basic Properties of Workflow Models

This section recalls and compares some properties of process descriptions.

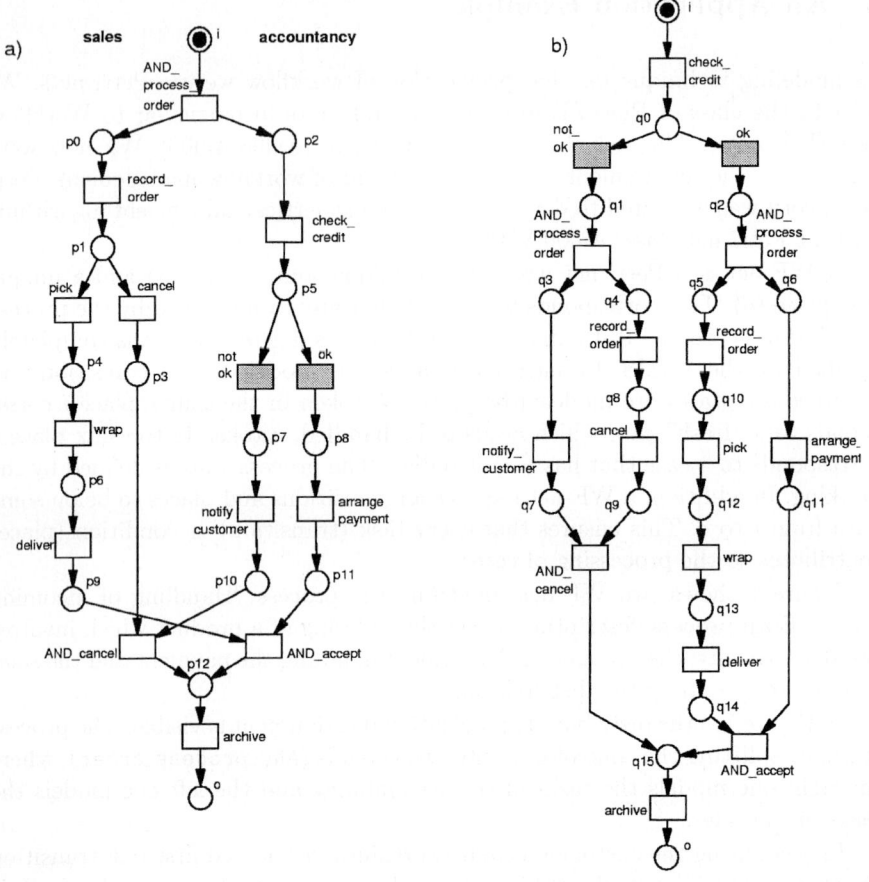

Fig. 1. WF-nets for process "Handling of incoming order"

3.1 Soundness

In [Aal98] *soundness* was introduced as a correctness criterion for WF-nets. A WF-net is sound if all its firing sequences are sound. A firing sequence is sound if it can terminate properly, which means that eventually there is a token in place o and at that moment there are no other tokens left in the net. Soundness of a WF-net excludes dead transitions, deadlocks and livelocks.

The WF-net in Figure 1b) is sound, while the one in Figure 1a) is not. This is caused by firing sequences that do not terminate properly in the left model, e.g.

- AND_process_order, record_order, pick, wrap, deliver, check_credit, not_ok, notify_customer.

In this firing sequence the case deadlocked having tokens in place p9 and p10.

It is clear that a WF-net which shall be used as input for a WfMS must be sound. Serving as a scheduling basis, soundness of the workflow definition is necessary to guarantee a smooth processing of the supported business process at runtime. Things are different for the modeling phase of a workflow, because it is not obvious for a modeler to see whether a complex workflow model is sound or not. To support the domain experts in formalizing their business processes, different properties are therefore required. In the literature *well-structuredness* [Aal98, LSW98,MR00] and *relaxed soundness* [DR01] have been considered helpful.

Well-Structuredness

A WF-net is well-structured[1], if every split is complemented by a corresponding join. In terms of Petri-net theory this property is characterized by the absence of *handles*[2] [ES90]. Note that the WF-net in Figure 1b) is well-structured, whereas the other WF-net is not. An example for a handle is the place-transition pair (AND_process_order, p12).

Well-structuredness is a structural property, whose validity can be easily reviewed. This and the close relationship to soundness[3] motivated its use as a requirement during workflow modeling. There are however sound WF-nets which are not well-structured. These WF-nets would be disregarded although suitable for the use within WfMSs. This shortcoming of well-structuredness was also addressed in [CWBH+03]. Providing refinement rules for the generation of sound WF-nets the authors propose some conditions under which well-structuredness can be relaxed while keeping soundness.

There are other disadvantages imposed by well-structuredness. Modeling in a well-structured manner requires a deep insight into the whole process. The tasks of the process must all be organized in well-structured blocks which may be combined again only in a well-structured manner. Such a hierarchical design ignores the organizational assignment of tasks and therefore requires overview of the whole process. This can hardly be assumed if the process to be described is spanning different organizational units of the company, involving various modelers. A further disadvantage is that the modeler might be forced to implement efficiency aspects at an early design state. The modeler might be restricted by imposing well-structuredness in a way that induces him/her into coming up with process descriptions such as the WF-net from Figure 1b). Determined through the ordering, the tasks of the sales can only start after the customer check of the accountancy was performed. Parallel execution of sales and accountancy is then restricted. Last but not least, redundancy was introduced. Some tasks (AND_process_order and record_order) had to be represented by multiple transitions.

---

[1] In the context of Event-driven Process Chains the terms hierarchical modeling and well-formedness [LSW98,MR00] were used synonymously.

[2] A handle is a pair of two different nodes (a place and a transition) that are connected via two elementary paths sharing only these two nodes.

[3] A well-structured net is structurally bound and structurally life [ES90]. Liveness and boundedness of a WF-net imply soundness.

Relaxed Soundness

An alternative property was introduced with relaxed soundness [DR01]. This property has been adapted from soundness with the intention to represent a more pragmatic view of correctness. It is weaker (in a formal sense) than soundness and therefore easier to accomplish.

Modeling business processes domain experts record the tasks and their order as they observe them to happen (or as they wish them to happen). This means they gather the desired behavior. Domain experts are no Petri net specialists. It may therefore happen that they overlook side effects of their model, i.e. firing sequences that do not express desired behavior. Relaxed soundness reflects this process understanding as it requires only that all relevant behavior is described correctly. It does neither forbid situations with residual tokens nor livelocks/deadlocks. A relaxed sound WF-net should be interpreted as follows: it specifies all business processes in terms of sequences of tasks for which a firing sequence from the initial state i to the final state o exists such that the transitions for these tasks occur in the order of a sound firing sequence.

Whereas in a sound WF-net *all* firing sequences are sound, relaxed soundness only requires that there are so many sound firing sequences that each transition is contained in one of them. A relaxed sound WF-net may have other firing sequences which do not terminate properly, e.g. by a deadlock or with tokens left in the net.

The process specification shown in Figure 1a) is relaxed sound. The following sound firing sequences contain all transitions:

- AND_process_order, record_order, pick, wrap, check_credit, ok, deliver, arrange_payment, AND_accept, archive,
- AND_process_order, check_credit, not_ok, notify_customer, record_order, cancel, AND_cancel, archive,

This definition still leaves room for ambiguities since it does not demand the precision of workflow definitions as they are required for their execution within a WfMS. Compared to well-structuredness, relaxed soundness does not make any assumptions on the structure of the WF-net. A relaxed sound WF-net may contain cycles and/or choices that do not satisfy the free-choice property. In contrast to soundness, it does not require all firing sequences to be sound, but only requires all tasks to be covered by at least one sound firing sequence.

Tests checking relaxed soundness have been implemented within Petri net tools such as LoLA [Sch99] (Low Level Petri Net Analyzer) and Woflan [VBA01]. Both algorithms parse the reachability graph, to decide whether a given WF-system is relaxed sound or not. To guarantee termination, the WF-systems must have been checked for boundedness before. This is a drawback of the proposed approach, as this requires the construction of the coverability graph, with a theoretical worst-case complexity of non-primitive recursive space [EN94].

4 Synthesis of Sound WF-Nets

We already stated that a process description which will be used as input for a WfMS must be sound. This corresponds to the requirement that supporting a business process at run-time, any faulty execution should be precluded. We will now describe how a relaxed sound WF-net can be made sound. The proposed transformation is automated.

Making a relaxed sound WF-net sound means to restrict the set of all possible firing sequences to a subset of sound ones. Looking at the reachability graph RG of the relaxed sound WF-net, this comes down to finding a WF-net with a behavior equal to a sound subgraph of RG. Naturally it would be nice not to generate a new net, but to change the primary WF-net such that it implements the restricted behavior. Both the generation of a new WF-net as well as the change of the primary WF-net are feasible methods.

The first possible approach uses methods from Petri net synthesis [CKLY98]. Based on a subgraph of the reachability graph containing only sound firing sequences, a WF-net is synthesized. The behavior of the synthesized net is isomorphic to the sound subgraph. A disadvantage of this method is that the derived WF-net does not necessarily look like the primary WF-net. As the net is generated on the basis of the reachability graph, information such as place names, layout, and ordering of transitions are ignored. The new net therefore only coincides with the primary WF-net in the names of the transitions.

We therefore favor a different method, which applies methods from Petri net controller synthesis. The idea is to compute and introduce places that supervise or control the behavior of the Petri net. These places, called *controller places* [YMLA96] or *monitors* [GDS92], avoid entering a set of *forbidden states*[4]. The information needed for their computation can be gained in various ways, e.g. from place invariants [YMLA96], general mutual exclusion conditions (GMECs) [GDS92], or sets of forbidden markings [GRX03]. Because the original net is kept and enhanced with additional elements, the resulting net will be easily recognized by the modelers.

4.1 Applying Petri Net Controller Synthesis for Workflow Modeling

We favor the computation of the controller places based on a set of forbidden markings [GRX03], because the prerequisites (set of forbidden markings, state transitions to be prevented) can be directly mapped to our approach. Starting from a sound subgraph, the forbidden markings correspond to all states that are beyond the sound subgraph. State transitions to be prevented correspond to state transitions leaving the sound subgraph. For every one of these instances an equation system is established which is used to compute a controller place inhibiting this forbidden state transition. The equation system consists of three

---

[4] An additional place can only restrict the behavior because the place can block transitions but it cannot enable transitions which are not enabled in the net without the place.

equations: 1) the event separation condition — an equation which in terms of the incidence matrix describes the interdiction of the corresponding state transition — 2) the *marking equation lemma*, and 3) the general property of T-invariants[5]. All three equations should hold in the resulting net. The first represents the new requirements: state transitions leaving the subgraph become disabled. The latter two represent the behavior described by the sound subgraph, which should be maintained independently from the introduction of new places.

The equation systems of different instances may have common solutions. As a result, the number of needed controller places is generally much smaller than the number of forbidden state transitions. The set of controller places together with the associated arcs determine, what was called the *synchronization pattern*. Adding the pattern to the primary WF-net a new WF-net is generated, that supports a subset of the primary behavior.

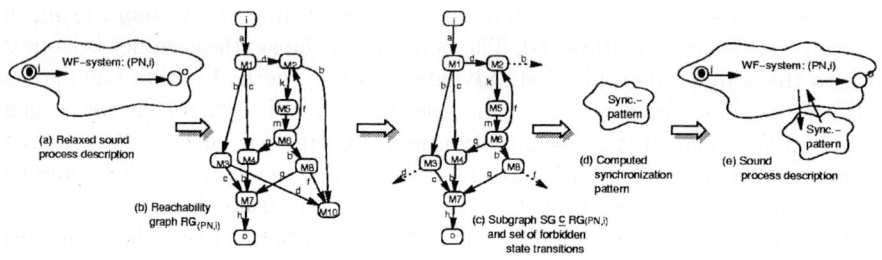

Fig. 2. Applying controller synthesis for workflow modeling.

Figure 2 illustrates the application of controller synthesis to workflow modeling.

Applying either one of the synthesis methods, all firing sequences supported by the resulting net are sound, as they are covered by a sound subgraph. Moreover, the calculated net again satisfies the properties of a WF-net: from the construction it can be concluded that it is strongly connected, having one source and one sink place [DvdA04].

Still, the subgraph given by assembling all sound sequences does not necessarily provide a reasonable base for the computation of the sound WF-net. Remember that the resulting WF-net does not support state transitions leaving the sound subgraph. Corresponding transitions of the resulting WF-net become disabled in markings, where they could fire in the primary net. In the following we will argue that prevention from firing is only reasonable if the task, modeled by the affected transition, represents *controllable* behavior.

---

[5] A (short-circuited) relaxed sound WF-net is covered with T-invariants [Deh03].

4.2 WF-Systems Are Reactive Systems

We consider a WF-system to be a reactive system [Deh02]. They run in parallel with their environment, respond to inputs from the environment and produce output events which in turn influence the environment.

The interaction with the environment takes place via incoming external events or via the evaluation of external information. The reactive system has to respond to external events and to incorporate the possible outcomes of the information evaluation.

An external event could be an incoming query, an acknowledgment from a customer, a message from another company, information from a business partner, or just a timeout. Examples for the evaluation of external information are questions about available capacities, the check for credit-worthiness of a customer, and the identity check of a co-operating partner.

Reflecting the interaction with the environment, we distinguish controllable and non-controllable tasks. In the process description this is reflected in a corresponding classification of the transitions. *Controllable transitions* model internal tasks, i.e. tasks whose execution is covered by the local workflow control. In contrast to that, *non-controllable transitions* represent the behavior of the environment. Their firing cannot be forced by the local workflow control but depend either on the evaluation of external data or on an incoming external event.

Throughout this paper we represent non-controllable transitions by gray boxes. We assume that non-controllable transitions are free-choice and do not conflict with controllable transitions. This reflects the fact that the behavior of the environment cannot become disabled through the local control. In the remainder we will consider only WF-nets which satisfy these restrictions.

4.3 Impact of Controllability upon the Generation of Sound WF-Nets

Applying methods from Petri net (Controller) Synthesis, the resulting WF-net does not support state transitions leaving the sound subgraph. Corresponding transitions of the resulting WF-net become disabled in markings, where they could fire in the original net. It is obvious that the state transitions to be prevented must not reflect uncontrollable behavior, as this would exceed the capabilities of the local workflow control.

Consider the sound subgraph in Figure 3a). It contains all sound firing sequences of the WF-net "Handling an incoming order", which are highlighted in the figure. Enforcement of this desired behavior is not possible, as there are non-controllable state transitions (depicted by a bow) leaving the subgraph. The corresponding transitions (ok and not_ok) reflect the outcome of a decision based on an evaluation of external data, and is not left to the discretion of a local workflow control.

Consequently, the subgraph must be restricted furthermore until all state transitions leaving the subgraph reflect controllable, and therefore preventable, behavior.

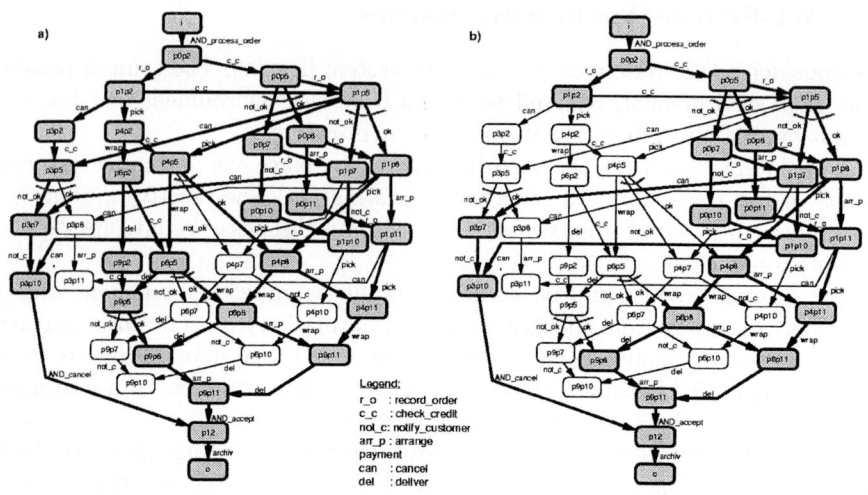

Fig. 3. Reachability graph with highlighted sound subgraph a) robust subgraph b)

Such a subgraph exists if the WF-net is not only relaxed sound but also *non-controllable choice robust* (short: robust). This criterion provides a means to describe robustness of a WF-system against all possible requests from the environment. A WF-system is robust if 1) there is a sound subgraph of the reachability graph which starting in i ends in o, 2) contains at least one t-labeled state transition for any non-controllable transitions, and 3) has only controllable state transitions leading out of the subgraph.

Assuming progress for non-controllable transitions, the existence of such a subgraph guarantees that it is possible to terminate properly independent from the influence of the environment. While all non-controllable transitions are covered by the subgraph, there is always a way to react and to terminate properly. Hence, if a WF-system is robust, the workflow controller can guarantee proper termination independently from all possible influences of the environment.

The robustness criterion together with an algorithm constructing the maximal robust fragment were introduced in [Deh02]. The algorithm decides whether a given bounded WF-system is robust, and if so, returns the maximum robust subgraph $SG = (SG\_Nodes, SG\_Edges)$ of the system's reachability graph RG. The algorithm otherwise aborts with the result "not robust", displaying the set of non-controllable transitions which may inhibit proper termination. Figure 4 shows an improved variant of the algorithm using an informal notation. Sets frequently used in the algorithm are the sets of all direct and indirect predecessors $Pred(n, G)$ (successors $Succ(n, G)$) of a node n within a graph G. These sets contain all nodes that lie on any path that lead to (start at) this node.

The algorithm mainly works as follows. It initially marks all states that potentially belong to the desired fragment and then progressively removes mistaken candidates. Potential states are all lying on a path from state i to state o. Illegal

Initialization:
SG_Nodes := Pred(o, RG);
SG_Edges := all edges of RG that connect nodes in SG_nodes;
Illegal_states:= nodes in SG_Nodes from where
       non-controllable state transitions leave the subgraph SG;

Body:
while Illegal_states $\neq \emptyset$ **do**
   SG_Nodes:= SG_Nodes \ Illegal_states;
   SG_Edges:= edges of RG that connect nodes in SG_nodes;
   (cut illegal states and state transitions *)*
   SG_Nodes:= Succ(i, SG) $\cap$ Pred(o, SG);
   SG_Edges:= edges of RG that connect nodes in SG_nodes;
   (recompute strongly connected component *)*
   Illegal_states:= nodes in SG_Nodes from where
         non-controllable state transitions leave the subgraph SG;
   (recompute current set of illegal states *)*
od

Test and output
if all non-controllable transitions are represented in the robust subgraph
  then print (The WF-system is robust); return SG:=(SG_Nodes,SG_Edges);
  else print (The WF-system is not robust);
     return not covered non-controllable transitions;
fi

Fig. 4. Robustness algorithm

states are states from where non-controllable state transitions leave the fragment. The algorithm stops if the iteration of this procedure does not identify any more illegal states.

An algorithm similar to the presented one has been introduced in the context of manufacturing systems recently [GRX03]. This algorithm computes a maximally permissive behavior, starting from a reachability graph and avoiding a set of forbidden states. Our algorithm differs in the computation of the strongly connected component, because the existence of i and o states in a WF-net can be exploited. In our algorithm an additional robustness check is performed on the resulting subnet, requiring that all non-controllable transitions are covered. This guarantees that none of the possible behavior of the environment is neglected. In [GRX03] it is proved that the algorithm is of polynomial complexity in the number of states of the reachability graph. The complexity of our algorithm is the same because the additional robustness check is only polynomial in the number of transitions.

The application of the algorithm shows that the example WF-net "Handling an incoming order" is robust. The resulting subgraph is shown in Figure 3b).

Thereby the WF-net reflects a set of accepted (sound) executions which can be enforced independently from the moves of the environment. Applying the Petri net controller synthesis algorithm to the robust subgraph, two controller places $Pc1$ and $Pc2$ are computed. Adding the places and corresponding arcs to the original WF-net, the process description shown in Figure 5 is derived.

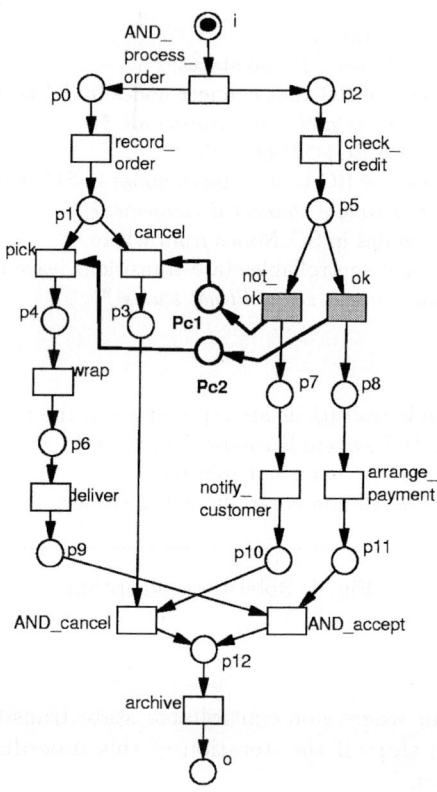

Fig. 5. Sound WF-net "Handling an incoming order" with controller places

The resulting WF-net is per construction sound. Using the enhanced process description as a workflow specification, i.e. as input for a WfMS, it can now be guaranteed that only sound executions will occur.

5 Interactive Process Improvement

Implementing the robust subgraph, the set of sound firing sequences has been restricted. This is done to avoid executions which are not sound, but could otherwise not be prevented due to the behavior of the environment.

Consider again the relaxed sound process description of the example "Handling of incoming order" (Figure 1a)). The firing sequence

- AND_process_order, record_order, pick, wrap, check_credit, ok, deliver, arrange_payment, AND_accept, archive.

is sound but became forbidden in the enhanced process description. The reason can be found in the non-controllable outcome of the check for credit-worthiness, which represents a choice of the environment.

Before using the enhanced process description as input for a WfMS, the restrictions with respect to the original specification should be communicated to the modeler. As the whole set of sound firing sequences were specified, she should approve the reduced set of accepted executions. The evaluation could either be done based on the revised, sound WF-net or on the reachability graph.

Approval based on the revised WF-net. This method could be used if the sound WF-net was computed applying the Petri net controller synthesis method. Only then it can be assumed that there is a high similarity between the primary and the resulting process description. Looking at the introduced places the modeler has to evaluate whether the thereby introduced synchronization is acceptable to be supported at run-time.

Approval based on the reachability graph. Looking at the difference between the relaxed sound subgraph and the robust subgraph, all those firing sequences are described which have been specified in the primary relaxed sound WF-net, but will not be supported in the resulting sound WF-net. The domain expert should decide whether it is acceptable to disregard these executions at run-time.

The idea to use the reachability graph as supplementary interface to the domain experts was introduced in [AdM00] first. The authors propose to use both the Petri net and the corresponding reachability graph as interface to the modeler and to use the basic synthesis algorithm [NRT92] to transfer between both descriptions. Adequate for their modeling approach is the Petri net class of *Elementary Net Systems*. In contrast to our approach all process models are assumed to be acyclic, free-choice and sound. Interaction with the environment is not considered.

Both methods point at executions which might have been considered useful originally, but were eliminated to make the model sound. However, these disregarded executions might express desirable behavior. If so, the process description must be revised. The sound but prevented firing sequences can be enabled, if some recovery behavior is added. This is necessary if the behavior of the environment would lead to deadlocks otherwise. Recovery behavior can be added by integrating new transitions into the WF-net. By firing of one of these transitions it is possible to escape a former deadlock state – leading to a state where proper termination is again possible. Clearly, these transitions should only then be implemented if the corresponding tasks are reversible in reality.

We will consider again our running example. Applying the synthesis method to the robust fragment from Figure 3b), a pessimistic strategy was implemented.

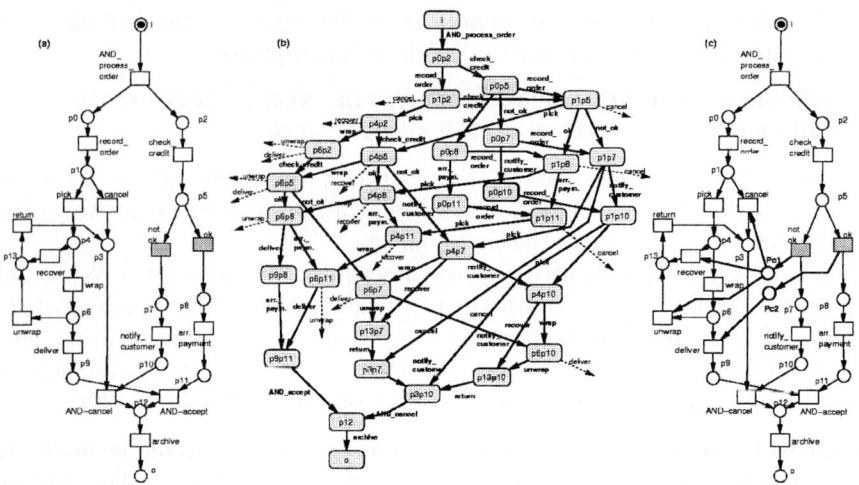

Fig. 6. Optimized sound WF-net "Handling of incoming order" with controller places

In favor of avoiding deadlocks only sequentialized executions are supported. In the derived WF-net (c.f. Figure 5) the customer check is always executed before the sales department may start the delivery process. All sound executions covering parallel execution of sales and accountancy have been precluded.

The domain experts may reject this process description. They know that the customer check and the delivery process both take a long time. Furthermore, the probability that the customer check is not ok, is very small. Therefore they want to support the parallel execution of sales department and accountancy. A more optimistic approach should thus be implemented. The delivery of the order to the customer should be started already, hoping that the customer check will be ok. Only in the rare case that the decision not_ok was taken, the order should be returned to stock and canceled finally.

For the specification of the necessary recovery behavior, we assume that all tasks within the sales department that occur before the delivery can be reset without extraordinary charges. This affects tasks pick and wrap. Corresponding recovery tasks are return and unwrap. After the item has been returned to stock, the instance should be canceled. Task deliver is considered to be non-reversible. The revised WF-net is shown in Figure 6 a). Notice that the integrated tasks only show one possible way of modeling the recovery behavior.

The resulting WF-net is again relaxed sound and robust. The robust subgraph is shown in Figure 6b). All sound firing sequences of the initial, relaxed sound WF-system (c.f. Figure 1a)) are maintained. Some additional, but less efficient executions are accepted too. Implementing the computed synchronization pattern results in the sound WF-system shown in Figure 6c).

6 Summary

This paper showed that relaxed soundness as a property for workflow modeling is better suited than well-structuredness. The gap between the resulting process description and a sound workflow definition is bridged by an automatic transformation. Methods from Petri net controller synthesis are adopted for this task. Thereby, a synchronization pattern is added to the original WF-net, installing a certain task ordering. Thus only in this second step efficiency aspects become determined. We showed that the results of the computation point out optimization potential. The advantages of the proposed approach are obvious. Modelers, normally domain experts, are not required to possess highly developed modeling skills and are relieved of thinking about efficiency aspects during the modeling. Moreover, the concept of task controllability is transferred to the domain of workflow modeling. This is a necessary prerequisite for the application of controller synthesis, and enables the description and analysis of workflow systems as reactive systems.

References

[Aal98] W.M.P. van der Aalst. The Application of Petri Nets to Workflow Management. *The Journal of Circuits, Systems and Computers*, 8(1):21–66, 1998.

[Aal00] W.M.P. van der Aalst. Workflow Verification: Finding Control-Flow Errors using Petri-net based Techniques. In *Business Process Mangement: Models, techniques, and Empirical Studie*, volume 1806 of *LNCS*, pages 161–183. Springer Verlag, 2000.

[AdM00] A. Agostini and G. de Michelis. A Light Workflow Management System Using Simple Process Models. *Computer Supported Cooperative Work*, 9(3/4):335–363, 2000.

[BEA03] BEA Systems, IBM Corporation, Microsoft Corporation, SAP AG, Siebel Systems. *Business Process Execution Language for Web Services (Version 1.1*, 2003.

[CKLY98] J. Cortadella, M. Kishinevsky, L. Lavagno, and A. Yakovlev. Deriving Petri Nets from Finite Transition Systems. *IEEE Transactions on Computers*, 47(8):859–882, 1998.

[CWBH+03] P. Chrzastowski-Wachtel, B. Benatallah, R. Hamadi, M. O'Dell, and A. Susanto. A top-down petri net-based approach for dynamic workflow modeling. In W. van der Aalst, A. ter Hofstede, and M. Weske, editors, *1st International Conference on Business Process Management (BPM)*, volume 2678 of *LNCS*, pages 336–353. Springer, 2003.

[Deh02] J. Dehnert. Non-controllable choice robustness: Expressing the controllability of workflow processes. In J. Esparza and C. Lakos, editors, *23rd Int. Conf. on Application and Theory of Petri Nets*, volume 2360 of *LNCS*, pages 121–141. Springer, 2002.

[Deh03] J. Dehnert. *A Methodology for Workflow Modeling - From business process modeling towards sound workflow specification*. PhD thesis, TU Berlin, 2003.

[DR01] J. Dehnert and P. Rittgen. Relaxed Soundness of Business Processes. In K.L. Dittrich, A. Geppert, and M.C. Norrie, editors, *Advanced Information System Engineering, CAISE 2001*, volume 2068 of *LNCS*, pages 157–170. Springer, 2001.

[DvdA04] J. Dehnert and W. van der Aalst. Bridging the Gap Between Business Models and Workflow Specifications. *International Journal of Cooperative Information Systems (IJCIS)*, 3(3), 2004. to appear.

[EN94] J. Esparza and M. Nielsen. Decidability Issues for Petri Nets: A Survey. *Journal of Information Processing and Cybernetics*, 30:143–160, 1994.

[ES90] J. Esparza and M. Silva. Circuits, Handles, Bridges and Nets. In G. Rozenberg, editor, *Advances in Petri Nets 1990*, volume 483 of *LNCS*, pages 210–242. Springer, 1990.

[GDS92] A. Giua, F. DiCesare, and M. Silva. Generalized mutual exclusion constraints on nets with uncontrollable transitions. In *Proc. IEEE Int. Conf. on Systems, Man, and Cybernetics*, pages 974–979, Chicago, IL, 1992.

[GRX03] A. Ghaffari, N. Rezg, and X. Xie. Design of a live and maximally permissive petri net controller using the theory of regions. *IEEE Transactions on Robotics and Automation*, 19(1):137–142, 2003.

[LSW98] P. Langner, C. Schneider, and J. Wehler. Petri Net Based Certification of Event-driven Process Chains. In J. Desel and M. Silva, editors, *Application and Theory of Petri nets*, volume 1420 of *LNCS*, pages 286–305. Springer, Berlin, 1998.

[MR00] D. Moldt and J. Rodenhagen. Ereignisgesteuerte Prozessketten und Petrinetze zur Modellierung von Workflows. In *Visuelle Verhaltensmodellierung verteilter und nebenläufiger Software-Systeme*, volume 24/00-I of *Fachberichte Informatik*, pages 57–63, 2000.

[NRT92] M. Nielsen, G. Rozenberg, and P. S. Thiagarajan. Elementary transition systems. *Theoretical Computer Science*, 96(1):3–33, April 1992.

[RD98] M. Reichert and P. Dadam. ADEPTflex: Supporting Dynamic Changes of Workflow without Loosing Control. *Journal of Intelligent Information Systems*, 10(2):93–129, 1998.

[Sch99] K. Schmidt. LoLA: A Low Level Analyser. In *Proc. Int. Conf. Application and Theory of Petri net*, volume 1825 of *LNCS*, pages 465–474, 1999.

[SL99] Software-Ley. *COSA 3.0 User Manual*. Software-Ley GmbH, Pullheim, Germany, 1999.

[UML02] Unified Modeling Language: version 1.4.2, ISO, 2002.

[VBA01] H.M.W. Verbeek, T. Basten, and W.M.P. van der Aalst. Diagnosing Workflow Processes using Woflan. *The Computer Journal*, 44(4):246–279, 2001.

[YMLA96] K. Yamalidou, J. Moody, M. Lemmon, and P. Antsakli. Feedback control of Petri nets based on place invariants. *Automatica*, 32(1):15–28, 1996.

Concurrent Undo Operations in Collaborative Environments Using Operational Transformation

Jean Ferrié[1], Nicolas Vidot[2], and Michelle Cart[1]

[1] LIRMM, Montpellier II University
161, rue Ada, 34392 Montpellier (France)
{ferrie, cart}@lirmm.fr
[2] GRIMAAG, Université des Antilles et de la Guyane
B.P. 7209, 97275 Schœlcher Cedex, Martinique (France)
http://www.martinique.univ-ag.fr

Abstract. In distributed collaborative systems, replicated objects, shared by users, are subject to concurrency constraints. All methods [4, 13, 18, 15, 16, 19, 22] proposed to serialize concurrent operations and achieve copies convergence of replicated objects are based on the use of *Operational Transformations*. In this context, giving the user the ability to undo an operation has been recognized as a difficult problem [1, 2, 3, 12, 14, 20, 21]. The few general propositions to solve the problem sometimes compromise copies convergence and/or users' intention, insofar as the Operational Transformations used are unsuitable for undo. This paper has a twofold objective. Firstly, it aims to highlight two general conditions (named C3 and C4) that need to be satisfied by any transformation adapted to undo. Secondly, it presents a general undo algorithm based on the definition of a generic undo-fitted transformation, which automatically verifies these conditions. The interest of the proposed method is that the undoing of an operation obeys to the same processing as the one used for regular operations in collaborative systems such as [15,19].

Keywords: Distributed collaborative systems, copies consistency, operational transformations, concurrent undo

1 Introduction

The purpose of a collaborative system is to facilitate team working and, in particular, to enable the manipulation of shared objects by members of a team whilst making them evolve in a coherent way. Usually, a shared object involved in a collaborative activity (shared text edition, shared CAD, electronic conferences, etc.) is subject to concurrent accesses and real-time constraints. The real-time aspect necessitates every user seeing the effects of his own actions on the object immediately, and the effects resulting from the actions of other users as soon as possible. In a distributed system when assuming non-negligible network latency, this high reactivity cannot be achieved unless each object is replicated on every site. Consequently, the problem is to conciliate both real-time constraint and consistency preservation of object copies, as they can be modified concurrently by many users.

In this context, various algorithms [4, 13, 18, 15, 16, 19, 22], which exploit the semantic properties of the operations on the objects, have been proposed to serialize concurrent operations and thus ensure the convergence of all copies of an object. All these algorithms, which are based on Operational Transformations, exploit a transposition function to transform an operation before integrating it into the history associated with an object copy so as to respect user intention in case of concurrency. The same problem is found in configuration management [9]. In these contexts, giving the user the ability to undo an operation has been recognized as a difficult problem [1, 2, 3, 12, 14, 20, 21], when taking concurrency between operations into account. In [20] an undo algorithm ANYUNDO was proposed to enable a user to undo any operation (local or remote) that has been executed on the object. The action of undoing an operation is based on the generation of the inverse operation and the transformation of the latter to take concurrent operations into account. Unfortunately, some critical situations can compromise the convergence of the copies and/or the user intention. In a recent paper [21], corrections to ANYUNDO algorithm are made in order to remedy some critical situations. Such situations are avoided in adOPTed [14], at the expense of a restrictive undo policy which only allows local operations to be undone in the reverse execution order. The lack of generality of these algorithms is due to the fact that the Operational Transformations used are not well suited to undo. To obtain a correct result, the transposition function would have to satisfy two conditions (called C3 and C4) highlighted by our study. These conditions are difficult to check in practice. In this context, our approach proposes a general undo algorithm which automatically satisfies conditions C3 and C4 thanks to the definition of a generic Operational Transformation adapted to undo.

The paper is organized as follows. Section 2 describes the model used along with the use of the Operational Transformations to ensure the consistency of the copies of an object in distributed collaborative environments. Section 3 describes the problems presented by the undo of an operation and the conditions that must be met by the inverse operation to ensure that the action of undoing an operation is carried out correctly. Section 4 details the principles of the general undo algorithm. Section 5 illustrates how it works with an example. Section 6 compares it with the other known algorithms.

2 Operational Transformations

A distributed collaborative system is constituted from a set of sites interconnected by a supposed reliable network. Each object shared by the users is replicated so that a copy of the object exists on every site and it can be handled using definite operations. In order to maintain consistency between copies, every operation generated and executed on a site must be executed on all other copies as well. This requires every operation *generated* on a site to be *broadcast* to the other sites; after *reception* on a site, the operation is *executed* on the local copy of the object. Given a site, a *local* operation is an operation generated on this site whereas a *remote* operation is one that has been generated on another site. In order to guarantee users a minimum response time, operations generated on a site (i.e. local operations) are executed immediately on this site.

This section reviews the three constraints encountered when trying to achieve consistency maintenance of object copies and outlines the principles of their solutions: (1) causality preservation, (2) user intention preservation and (3) convergence. A collaborative text editor will be used as an example. Let us assume a text is an ordered collection of sentences, each one being an object represented by a string of characters. The operations defined on this object are:

insert(p, c): inserts character c at position p in the string,
delete(p): deletes character at position p in the string.

In the following, we suppose that users are working concurrently and are modifying the same sentence.

2.1 Causality Preservation

An operation op_1 is said to *causally precede* op_2 (noted op_1 *precedes$_c$* op_2) iff op_2 was generated on a site after op_1 has been executed on this site. Consequently, op_2 is supposed to depend on the effects of operation op_1. *Causality preservation* ensures that all operations related by a causality relation are executed in the same order on every copy. It is achieved in the majority of the methods [4, 13, 18, 15, 19], by using a state vector associated with each site and each object and by timestamping each operation. Instead of state vectors, method [22] uses continuous timestamps delivered by a sequencer which, when associated with a differed broadcast, makes it possible to ensure a sequential reception compatible with the causal reception.

2.2 User Intention Preservation

Operations that are not causally related are said to be concurrent. In other words op_1 and op_2 are *concurrent* iff neither (op_1 *precedes$_c$* op_2) nor (op_2 *precedes$_c$* op_1). In this case, neither one depends on the effects of the other. Thus, they can be executed in any order on the different sites. Nevertheless, if a site executes op_1 before op_2, it must take into account the changes made by op_1 when it executes op_2 so as the *intention* of the user who generated op_2 to be respected. The intention of a user may be for instance to add 's' at the end of a word or to double a letter in a word. This intention is achieved by the execution of an operation which is relative to a specific state of the object. In the example of Figure 1-a, two users work simultaneously on the same object whose state is "efect". The intention of user 1 is to add 'f' to obtain "effect". This is achieved by operation insert(2, 'f'). The intention of user 2 is to add 's' at the end of the word which is achieved by the operation insert(6, 's'). When this operation is delivered and executed on site 1, the new state is "effecst" which is not what user 2 expected. To respect his intention, operation insert(6, 's') needs to be transformed on site 1 in order to execute insert(7, 's') instead of insert(6, 's') (see Figure 1-b).

User intention preservation ensures that the execution of an operation op on each copy has an effect that achieves the intention of the user at the time when op was generated. The problem of user intention preservation is due to the fact that an operation generated on a site achieves user intention depending on the state of the copy on this site. If this operation were to be executed on a remote site after the execution of a concurrent operation, it might no longer achieve the initial intention in the case of the state of the copy not being the same. The solution to this problem is based on the use of Operational Transformations. This consists of transforming every remote operation to be executed so that it takes into account the modifications made by all the concurrent operations serialized before it. This transformation is possible provided that a function specific to the semantics of the operations is defined which gives for all pairs of operations (op_1, op_2) an operation written as $op_2^{op_1}$, which is defined for the state resulting from the execution of op_1 and which achieves the same intention as op_2. This transformation function introduced in [4] is also used in other systems [13, 18, 16, 19, 22] under various denominations. We call it *forward transposition*.

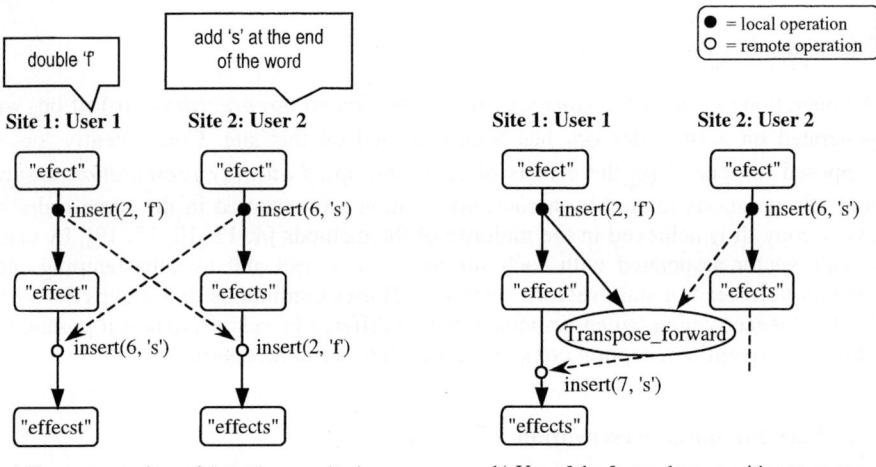

a) Non-respect of user 2 intention, on site 1   b) Use of the forward transposition to ensure the respect of user 2 intention, on site 1

Fig. 1. Respecting the intention of the user

Let O_i be the initial state of the object, $O_i.op$ the state obtained after the execution of op and Intention(op, O_i), the intention which is achieved by operation op on object state O_i. The forward transposition is then formally defined as follows:

$$\text{Transpose\_forward}(op_1, op_2) = op_2^{op_1}$$
$$\text{with: } \forall\ O_i, \text{Intention}(op_2^{op_1}, O_i.op_1) = \text{Intention}(op_2, O_i).$$

Figure 1-b depicts the effect of the forward transposition for the pair of operations (insert(2, 'f'), insert(6, 's')). More generally, let seq_n be a sequence of n operations; the forward transposition of operation op with seq_n, noted op^{seq_n}, is defined recursively by: $op^{seq_n} = \text{Transpose\_forward}(op_n, op^{seq_{n-1}})$ with $seq_n = op_1.op_2....op_n = seq_{n-1}.op_n$ and $op^{seq_0} = op$, where $op_i.op_j$ represents the execution of op_i followed by the execution of op_j.

It is important to note that the forward transposition requires both operations to be defined with the object in the same state. To satisfy this requirement in all situations, different solutions have been proposed in order to apply forward transposition in the right way.

In [18] operation op_1 is transformed using the reverse function of forward transposition (called Exclusion_Transformation), so that it is defined for the same state as op_2 and enables the use of the forward transposition. In [13] several equivalent histories which respect the causal order are kept on each site so that the intermediate states of the object can be retrieved on each site. In [11, 15, 19] a new transformation is defined. This function [11] which we call *backward transposition* makes it possible to change the execution order of a pair of operations while respecting user intention. More accurately, the backward transposition of a couple of operations (op_1, op_2), executed in this order, gives as a result the couple (op_2', op_1') corresponding to their execution in reverse order which leads to the same state, and is compatible with the forward transposition. Formally:

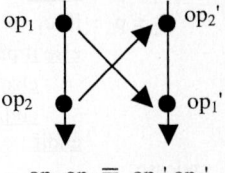

$$op_1.op_2 \equiv op_2'.op_1'$$

Transpose_backward (op_1, op_2) = (op_2', op_1')
with: op_2 = Transpose_forward (op_1, op_2') and
op_1' = Transpose_forward (op_2', op_1)

The backward transposition is only defined for a sequence of operations (op_1, op_2) obtained from concurrent operations (op_1, op_2'). Both forward and backward transpositions are examples of what is called *Operational Transformation*. In the following, these Operational Transformations are applied to objects of the type "string of characters". They are applied to XML objects in [9], and spreadsheets objects in [10]. They are also applied recursively over the different levels of a tree representation of documents in [6].

2.3 Copies Convergence

Taking into account causality as well as user intention is not always sufficient to achieve executions that guarantee the convergence of the copies on all sites. Indeed, as concurrent operations can be executed in any order on different sites, the forward transposition needs to verify two conditions [4, 13]. The first condition C1, ensures that, starting from the same state, the execution of op_1 followed by the execution of $op_2^{op_1}$ produces the same state as the execution of op_2 followed by the execution of $op_1^{op_2}$. It is formally defined as:

Condition C1. Let op_1 and op_2 be two concurrent operations defined on the same state. The forward transposition verifies C1 iff:
$$O_i.op_1.op_2^{op_1} \equiv O_i.op_2.op_1^{op_2}$$
where $\equiv$ denotes the equivalence of states obtained after applying both sequences from the same state O_i.

Figure 2 gives an example of a forward transposition verifying condition C1. In the case of concurrent insertions of different characters at the same position ($p_1=p_2$), the alphabetical order (noted pr()) is arbitrarily privileged. In the case of concurrent insertions of the same character, only one character is inserted, and the returned operation is identity (id).

Transpose_forward (*insert (p_1,c_1), insert (p_2,c_2)*) =
  case p_1 ? p_2 of
    $p_1 < p_2$: return *insert ($p_2 +1, c_2$)* ;
    $p_1 > p_2$: return *insert (p_2, c_2)* ;
    $p_1 = p_2$: if $c_1 = c_2$ then return *id*
            else if pr(c_2) > pr(c_1) then return *insert (p_2, c_2)*
                else return insert *(p_2+1, c_2)* ;
                endif ;
            endif ;
  endcase

Fig. 2. Example of a forward transposition verifying C1

The second condition C2, ensures that the forward transposition of an operation with a sequence of two or more concurrent operations does not depend on the order used to serialize these operations. It is formally defined as follows:

Condition C2. Whatever operations op_1, op_2 and op_3 are, the forward transposition verifies C2 iff:

$$op_3^{op_1:\,op_2} = op_3^{op_2:\,op_1}$$

where the notation $op_i:op_j$ denotes $op_i.op_j^{op_i}$.

Most methods, adOPTed [13], SOCT2 [15, 16] and GOTO [19] are based on satisfying conditions C1 and C2. In [18] conditions C1 and C2 are not required but a unique serialization order which complies with the causal order is imposed for the operations on all the sites; unfortunately, it may be necessary to Undo/Redo some operations to conform to this order. In [4], condition C2 is not required to the detriment of the convergence of the copies. In [22], condition C2 is not needed thanks to the implementation of a unique and continuous serialization order, given by a sequencer.

2.4 Principles of Collaborative Algorithms

Generally speaking, the principle of collaborative algorithms capable of ensuring the consistency of the copies involves memorizing the history of the operations executed from the initial state to the current state for each copy of object. Any operation generated locally is executed immediately before being added to the history. The reception of a remote operation OP requires a phase of integration to determine the operation OP' achieving the same intention as OP, to be executed on the current state. The difference between the algorithms lies in how they transform the received operation OP. For instance, in the algorithms such as SOCT2 [15, 16] or GOTO [19], when a site receives a remote operation OP, it determines the sequence seqconc of concurrent operations, then executes the processing shown in Figure 3.

1.	Forward transpose OP with the sequence of concurrent operations, noted seqconc, to obtain operation OP' such that: Transpose_forward (seqconc, OP) = OP'
2.	Execute OP' on the current state
3.	Append OP' to the local history

Fig. 3. Processing of a remote operation once received by a site

In the following, we show how to undo any operation (do or undo) so that the undo operation is processed in the same way as any other operation OP, while respecting the three constraints: (1) causality preservation, (2) user intention preservation and (3) copies convergence.

3 Undo Problems

Let op be the operation to achieve intention I, executed on the object O from the initial state O_i. Let us consider the sequence seq of (n-1) operations (with seq = $op_1.op_2....op_{n-1}$), respectively, to achieve the intentions $I_1, I_2,...I_{n-1}$ executed in this order starting from the state O_i.op.

Undoing operation op consists of generating and executing, at the current state O_i.op.seq, the operation op_{n+1} that cancels the effects of op without modifying the intentions of the other operations. This operation must lead the object to the same state as the sequence seq' of the (n-1) operations (with seq' = $op_1'.op_2'....op_{n-1}'$), where these operations achieve the *same* intentions $I_1, I_2,...I_{n-1}$ and are executed in this order starting from the initial state O_i. In other words: $O_i.op.seq.op_{n+1} = O_i.seq'$.

The operation op_{n+1} can be obtained using two different strategies.

Strategy 1. It consists in generating operation $\overline{op}$, the inverse operation of op, from state O_i.op and considering it as an operation concurrent with the sequence of operations seq. Thus $\overline{op}$ must be forward transposed with seq; the operation obtained $\overline{op}^{seq}$ can then be executed on the current state. This strategy and the algorithm called naïve algorithm of undo which implements it are illustrated by Figure 4. The algorithm is executed on the site where a decision is made to undo; the operation $\overline{op}^{seq}$, which is broadcast to the other sites, is processed on these sites like a regular operation.

Strategy 2. It consists in backward transposing the pair (op, seq) so as to obtain an equivalent history (seq', op') in which the operation op' (i.e. $op^{seq'}$) to be undone is the last one executed. To undo op, it then suffices to generate operation $\overline{op}'$, the inverse operation of op', and to execute it on the current state. This strategy and the algorithm which implements it are illustrated by Figure 5.

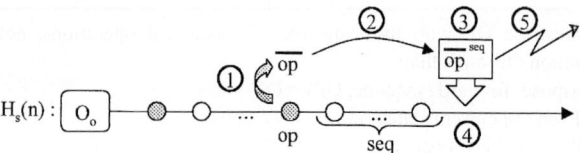

1. Generate the *inverse of op*, noted $\overline{op}$, on the state O_i.op such that: $O_i.op.\overline{op} = O_i$
2. Calculate $\overline{op}^{seq}$ = Transpose_forward (seq, $\overline{op}$)
3. Execute $\overline{op}^{seq}$ on the current state O_i.op.seq
4. Append $\overline{op}^{seq}$ to local history
5. Broadcast $\overline{op}^{seq}$ to other sites

Fig. 4. Undoing op according to Strategy 1

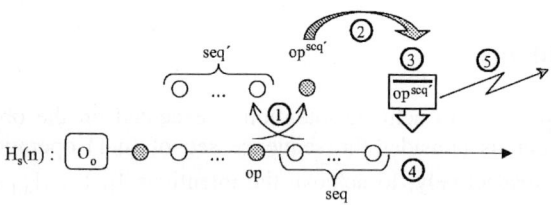

1. Calculate (seq', op') = Transpose_backward (op, seq) with op' = $op^{seq'}$
2. Generate the *inverse of $op^{seq'}$*, i.e. $\overline{op}^{seq'}$
3. Execute $\overline{op}^{seq'}$ on the current state O_i.op.seq
4. Append $\overline{op}^{seq'}$ to the local history
5. Broadcast $\overline{op}^{seq'}$ to other sites

Fig. 5. Undoing op according to Strategy 2

Strategy 2 was first proposed and used in [12]. All other existing systems in which it is possible to undo and which are based on the Operational Transformations [14, 20, 21] use Strategy 1. They consider the undoing of an operation op as the generation of the inverse operation $\overline{op}$ Insofar as the inverse operation is regarded as a *regular* operation, this process ignores the specificity of undo and fails to observe the conditions needed to ensure the correction of the undo algorithm.

3.1 Neutrality of the Do/Undo Pair for the Transposition (Condition C3)

To ensure the preservation of user intention when undoing operation, constraints on the forward transposition must be satisfied. This is illustrated by the example in Figure 6. To undo op_1 on site 1, the naïve algorithm based on Strategy 1 leads to generation and execution of $op_2 = \overline{op_1}$, which is then broadcast to site 2. When operation op_3 = insert(2, 'a'), which carries out the intention to insert 'a' *after* 'b', is received on site 1 it is regarded as being concurrent with op_1 and op_2. As a result, it is forward transposed successively with op_1 and op_2 to give the operation $op_3 \circ p_1 \cdot op_2$ = insert(1, 'a') whose execution leads to the state "ab". In this example, the copies converge towards the same state "ab" and the undoing of op_1 strictly respects the intention of user 1 since 'b' was not removed. However, the intention of user 2 was not respected insofar as 'a' was inserted *before* 'b'. In fact, the transposition of op_3 with the sequence seq = $op_1.op_2$ = $op_1.\overline{op_1}$ should have resulted in op_3. In other words, the sequence $op_1.op_2$ and more generally the do/undo pair, should have acted as a neutral element for the transposition of op_3.

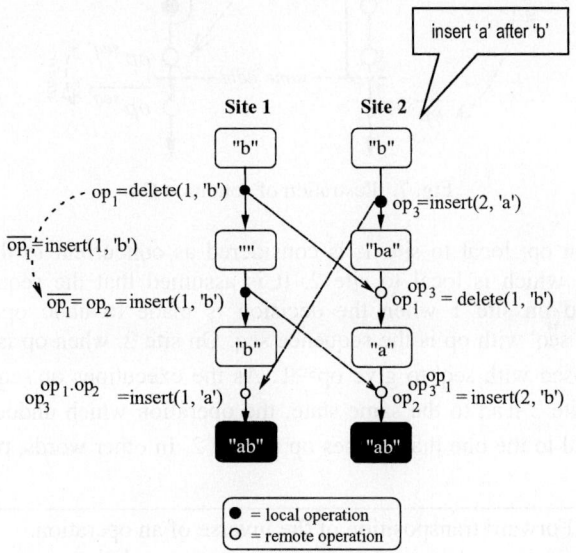

Fig. 6. Situation caused by the failure to respect condition C3

To ensure that the intention is respected, the forward transposition with an undo operation must verify the general condition C3.

Condition C3. Neutrality of do/undo pair for the transposition.
Let seq = $op_i.op_{i+1}....op_{j-1}.op_j$ and seq' = $op_{i+1}'....op_{j-1}'$ be two sequences such that:
- $\forall k \in [i+1..j-1]$, op_k and op_k' achieve the same intention I_k,
- op_j is the operation which undoes op_i,

then, the forward transposition verifies C3, iff :
$\forall op_k$, $op_k^{seq} = op_k^{seq'}$

3.2 Forward Transposition of the Inverse of an Operation (Condition C4)

When an operation is undone by using the inverse operation, the forward transposition of this inverse operation must verify the condition C4 which is illustrated by Figure 7.

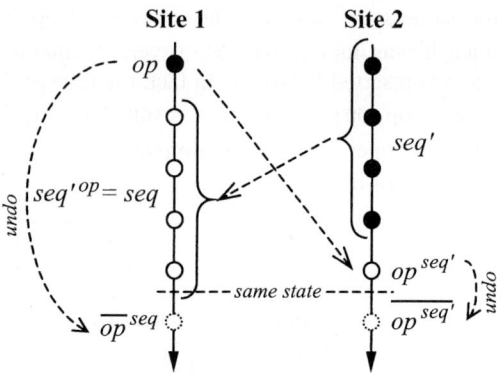

Fig. 7. Illustration of condition C4

The operation op, local to site 1, is considered as concurrent to the sequence of operations seq', which is local to site 2. It is assumed that the sequence seq' was already received on site 1 when the decision is made to undo op. The forward transposition of seq' with op is the sequence seq. On site 2, when op is received, it is forward transposed with seq' to give op$^{seq'}$. As the executions op.seq on site 1 and seq'.op$^{seq'}$ on site 2 lead to the same state, the operation which undoes op on site 1 must be identical to the one that undoes op on site 2. In other words, $\overline{op}^{seq} = \overline{op^{seq'}}$ must hold.

Condition C4. Forward transposition of the inverse of an operation.
Let op be an operation and seq and seq' two sequences such that:
- Transpose_forward (op, seq') = seq,

then the forward transposition verifies C4, iff:
$$\overline{op}^{seq} = \overline{op^{seq'}}.$$

3.3 Critical Cases Analysis

Examples of critical situations were presented in [2, 14, 20]. In these examples, undo is problematic insofar as the use of the naïve algorithm based on Strategy 1 leads to an incorrect result. In fact, as we show in [23], it appears that conditions C3 and/or C4 are not respected.

Therefore, these conditions are necessary to preserve the intentions of all operations. They are also sufficient to preserve intention since C4 ensures that the intention of undo operations is respected while C3 ensures that the intention of any operation is respected in presence of undo operations.

4 Undo Algorithm

4.1 Principle

As previously seen with the undo algorithm based on Strategy 1, the fact of using the inverse operation and forward transposing it with the operations that follow, makes it necessary to verify condition C4. In practice, it may be very difficult to verify C4 because an unspecified number of operations is involved. The method that we propose ensures that conditions C3 and C4 are automatically verified. In order to achieve this, an undo operation has to be distinguished from a *regular* operation. We thus introduce the operation *undo(op)* which expresses the intention to undo operation op. More accurately, a regular operation is specified by its name op, whereas an undo operation is specified by the name *undo( )* along with the name of the operation to be undone. Using the notations established in the definition of undo problems, we have:

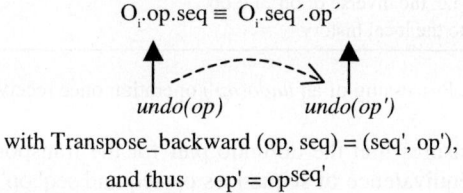

with Transpose_backward (op, seq) = (seq', op'),

and thus op' = op$^{seq'}$

So, generating the operation *undo(op)*, defined on the O_i.op state, and forward transposing it with seq, must be equivalent to generating operation *undo(op')* defined for the current state O_i.seq'.op' where op' is the last operation executed and achieves the same intention as op. In our method, this is obtained thanks to the definition of forward transposition functions specific to undo, which are such that, $\forall$op and $\forall$seq :

$$\text{Transpose\_forward(seq, undo(op))} = \text{undo(op')}$$

The execution of *undo(op')* will then consist of executing the inverse operation $\overline{op'}$ on the current state O_i.op.seq. The use of the specific operation *undo(op)* and the definition of specific transposition functions ensure that C4 is automatically verified by construction because:

as op' = op$^{seq'}$, the inverse operations actually verify

$$\overline{op'} = \overline{op^{seq'}} = \overline{op}^{seq}.$$

In practice, the operation *undo(op')* is obtained by successively forward transposing *undo(op)* with each operation in the sequence seq. The final undo algorithm executed on the site where the decision is made to cancel the operation op is shown in Figure 8-a. Before being appended to the history and broadcast, *undo(op')* is timestamped with the current state vector of the site as a regular operation [15, 16, 19].

The other sites which receive the operation *undo(op')* execute the algorithm shown in Figure 8-b. On these sites, the sequence seqconc of the operations which are concurrent to *undo(op')* is determined thanks to state vectors associated to each operation (see section 2.1).

1. Generate *undo(op)*
2. Forward transpose *undo(op)* with the operations in sequence seq to obtain operation *undo(op')* such that:
   Transpose_forward (seq, *undo(op)*) = *undo(op')*
   with op' such that: O_i.op.seq ≡ O_i.seq'.op'
3. Execute *undo(op')*, i.e. the inverse of op', i.e. $\overline{op'}$
4. Timestamp *undo(op')* by using state vector
5. Append *undo(op')* to the local history
6. Broadcast *undo(op')* to other sites

Fig. 8-a. Final Undo Algorithm on the site where the decision is made to cancel op

Forward transpose *undo(op')* with the sequence of concurrent operations, noted seqconc, to obtain operation *undo(op")* such that:
$$\text{Transpose\_forward (seqconc, } undo(op')) = undo(op")$$
Execute *undo(op")*, i.e. the inverse of op", i.e $\overline{op"}$
Append *undo(op")* to the local history

Fig. 8-b. Processing of an *undo(op')* operation once received by a site

The algorithm ensures that the do/undo pair for the transposition remains neutral. Indeed, taking the equivalence of sequences op.seq and seq'.op' into account, forward transposing an operation op_j with the sequence op.seq.undo(op') amounts to successively forward transposing op_j with the operations in sequence seq', then with op' and finally with undo(op'). Achieving this last forward transposition amounts to achieving the inverse of the forward transposition of op_j with op', as shown thereafter. The end result is that the forward transposition of op_j with the sequence op.seq.undo(op'), which contains the do/undo pair, is reduced to the forward transposition of op_j with seq', which ensures that condition C3 is verified. Let us note that the Undo Algorithm works even when the operation op itself is an *undo* operation. The proof of the Undo Algorithm can be found in [23].

An advantage of our approach lies in the fact that an *undo(op')* operation, received by a site, can be processed in the same way as a regular operation. According to Figure 3, when OP represents a regular operation op, then OP' is obtained by forward transposing op with the sequence seqconc. Let us imagine that OP represents an undo operation, *undo(op')*, then OP' would be obtained by forward transposing *undo(op')* with seqconc. That exactly matches the processing shown in Figure 8-b. Finally, the processing of a remote operation, whether it is an undo operation or a regular one, received by a site, obeys to the *same* algorithm.

In a sense, we can say that our method is based on Strategy 2, insofar as operation op' is calculated as if the operation to be undone were the last one to be executed. On another hand, it is also related to Strategy 1 insofar as operation op' is obtained by using forward transposition applied to *undo(op)* (instead of $\overline{op}$ as in Strategy 1). The advantage of our approach is that backward transposition is not needed anymore. The *only* adaptation to be done consists in determining the forward transpositions specific to *undo*.

4.2 Transpositions Specific to Undo

The method supposes that the forward transpositions written by the programmer are completed to take undo into account. In other words, the Transpose_forward (op_1, op_2) function must be specified for the cases where either op_1 or op_2 (or both) are *undo* operations. This section shows how the forward transposition can be written in generic form, taking undo into account; this generic form specific to undo does not require any work on behalf of the programmer because it only uses the operations to be undone, their forward transposition and the corresponding inverse operations which have already been defined.

Forward Transposition with an Undo Operation. This section specifies Transpose_forward (op_1, op_2) when op_1 = undo(op_3). In this case op_2 and undo(op_3) are both defined for the same state (see Figure 9-a). Thus, one can consider that the operation to be undone op_3, was executed right before undo(op_3) (see Figure 9-b).

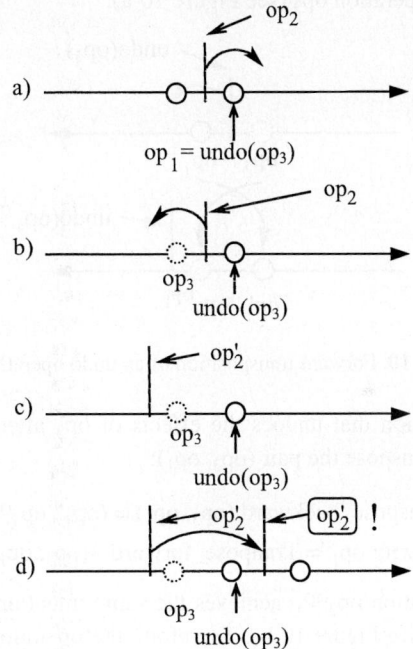

Fig. 9. Forward transposition with an undo operation

As undo(op_3) amounts to undoing the effect of op_3, forward transposing op_2 with undo(op_3) amounts to undoing the effect due to the forward transposition of the operation op_2' (to be determined) with op_3. For this we need the function which delivers op_2' such that Transpose_forward (op_3, op_2') = op_2, where op_2 and op_3 are known. This function is the inverse of the forward transposition. It is written as Transpose_forward^{-1} and formally defined by:

Transpose_forward^{-1}(op_i, Transpose_forward(op_i, op_j)) = op_j.

By applying this function to operations op_3 and op_2 (see Figure 9-b|c) operation op_2' can be obtained by: Transpose_forward^{-1}(op_3, op_2) = op_2'. From its definition, operation op_2' achieves the same intention as op_2 but is defined for the same state as op_3. According to the condition C3, as the forward transposition of an operation with the pair op/undo(op) must not modify this operation, the forward transposition of op_2' with the pair op_3/undo(op_3) is quite simply op_2' (see Figure 9-d). To summarize:

$$\text{Transpose\_forward (undo}(op_3), op_2) = \text{Transpose\_forward}^{-1}(op_3, op_2)$$

Forward Transposition of an Undo Operation. The specification of Transpose_forward (op_1, op_2) in the case where op_2 = undo(op_3) proceeds from the same method. It supposes that undo(op_3) and op_1 are defined for the same state, i.e. the state produced by operation op_3 (see Figure 10-a).

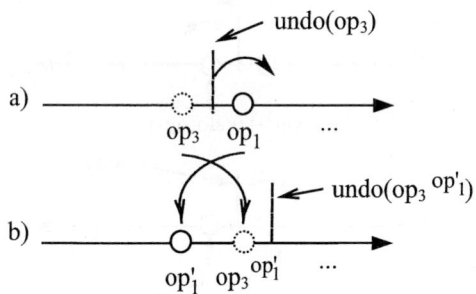

Fig. 10. Forward transposition of an undo operation

To obtain the operation that undoes the effects of op_3 after op_1 was executed, it suffices to backward transpose the pair (op_3, op_1):

$$\text{Transpose\_backward }(op_3, op_1) = (op_1', op_3{}^{op_1}),$$
$$\text{with } op_1' = \text{Tranpose\_forward}^{-1}(op_3, op_1).$$

The transposed operation $op_3{}^{op_1'}$ achieves the same intention as op_3 if it had been executed just after op_1 (see Figure 10-b). Therefore, the operation we need in order to undo the effect of op_3 is undo($op_3{}^{op_1'}$). To summarize:

$$\text{Transpose\_forward }(op_1, \text{undo}(op_3)) = \text{undo }(\text{Transpose\_forward}$$
$$(\text{Transpose\_forward}^{-1}(op_3, op_1), op_3))$$

The complete generic function of the forward transposition which takes undo into account is given in Figure 11. It uses the inverse of the forward transposition. The following specifies how to obtain it when one of the operations in the couple is also an undo operation.

```
Transpose_forward (op₁,op₂) =
case (op₁ = undo(op₃))
    if (op₂ = undo(op₄)) and op₃ = op₄
        return id(op₂)
    else
        return Transpose_forward⁻¹(op₃,op₂)
    endif ;
case (op₂ = undo(op₄))
    return undo (Transpose_forward (Transpose_forward ⁻¹(op₄,op₁), op₄)) ;
case {op₁ and op₂ are regular operations}
endcase
```

Fig. 11. Forward transposition adapted to undo

Inverse of the Forward Transposition with an Undo Operation. When op_1 is an undo operation, the inverse of the forward transposition, i.e. Transpose_forward^{-1}(op_1, op_2) can be obtained by the same logic [23]. It is written:

$$\text{Transpose\_forward}^{-1}(\text{undo}(op), op_2) = op_2 \circ p$$

Inverse of the Forward Transposition of an Undo Operation. The inverse of the forward transposition, Transpose_forward^{-1}(op_1, op_2), when op_2 is an undo operation is difficult to obtain. Given that we know op_1 and op_2, this amounts to finding op_2' such that Transpose_forward (op_1, op_2') = op_2. As op_2 is an undo operation, written as undo(op_3), then op_2' is also an undo operation, written as undo(op_3'). Thus, finding op_2' amounts to finding op_3'. When considering the relation previously established to calculate the forward transposition of an undo operation, operation op_2 is given by the following:

op_2 = undo (Transpose_forward (Transpose_forward^{-1}(op_3', op_1), op_3')).

In addition, when considering op_2 = undo(op_3), given that we know op_2, so we know op_3. As op_3 is given by op_3 = Transpose_forward (Transpose_forward^{-1}(op_3', op_1), op_3'), finding op_3' would be necessary before knowing Transpose_forward^{-1}(op_3', op_1). This evaluation is impossible using operation op_1 alone. In fact, in order to obtain the result, we need to refer to the history of the site [23] and to reorder the operations to obtain an equivalent history containing the operation op_2', i.e. undo(op_3').

5 Illustration of the Undo Algorithm

In this section we show on an example how our Undo Algorithm works. The example, referred as *Insert-Insert-Tie Dilemma* [20], corresponds to a situation illustrated in Figure 12-a. User 1 on site 1 deletes the character 'b', while user 2 on site 2 inserts 'a'

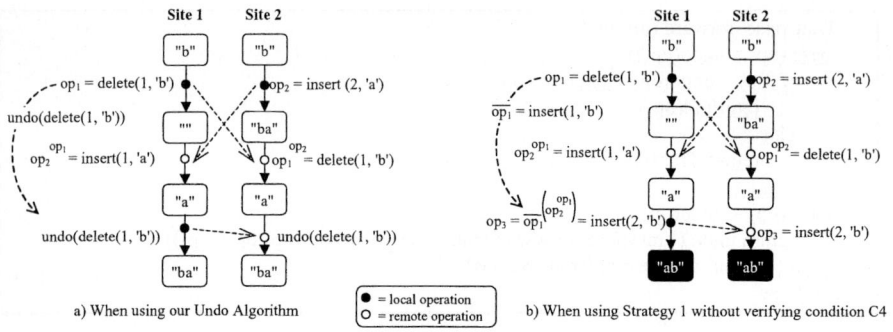

Fig. 12. Insert-Insert-Tie example

after 'b'. When op_2 (resp. op_1) is received on site 1 (resp. site 2), it is forward transposed with op_1 (resp. op_2) before being executed. Respecting condition C1 ensures that the copies converge towards the same state "a". Let us suppose that user 1 then decides to cancel operation op_1. The application of our Undo Algorithm (see Figure 8-a), with operation op corresponding to *delete(1, 'b')*, gives the following statements:

Step 1. Generate *undo(delete(1, 'b'))*.
Step 2. Seeing that seq = insert(1, 'a'), thus compute:
Transpose_forward (insert(1, 'a'), *undo(delete(1, 'b'))*).
Referring to Figure 11, insert(1, 'a') corresponds to op_1 and *undo(delete(1,'b'))* to op_2, which leads to the case where op_2 = undo(op_4), with op_4 = delete(1, 'b'). According to these notations, the result to be computed is:
undo (Transpose_forward(Transpose_forward $^{-1}$(op_4,op_1), op_4))
which needs to compute:
i) the inverse of Transpose_forward(delete(1, 'b'), insert(1, 'a')); the result is insert(2, 'a');
ii) Transpose_forward (insert(2, 'a'), delete(1, 'b')); the result is delete(1, 'b').
The final result of step 2 is *undo(delete(1, 'b'))*.
Step 3. Execute the inverse of delete(1, 'b'), that is insert(1, 'b'), which leads to the final state "ba".

After being timestamped and appended to the history, the resulting operation of step 2, *undo(delete(1, 'b'))*, is broadcast to site 2. When it is received on this site, the algorithm shown in Figure 8-b is applied. As there is no concurrent operation, the inverse of delete(1, 'b'), that is insert(1, 'b'), is directly executed and leads to the same state "ba".

The application of the naïve algorithm based on Strategy 1 (see Figure 4) and illustrated in Figure 12-b would lead to a wrong result. The operation $\overline{op_1}$ = insert(1, 'b') would be generated then forward transposed with $op_2 op_1$ to obtain $op_3 = \overline{op_1}\ op_2 op_1$ = insert(2, 'b') whose execution would lead to state "ab". Operation op_3, broadcast to site 2 would be executed as it is on this site. Although the copies would converge towards the same state, the undoing of op_1 would lead to an incorrect state since the intention of user 2, namely 'a' placed *after* 'b', would not be respected in the final state. The reason for this anomaly is due to the failure to respect condition C4. The operation executed on site 2 to undo operation $op_1{}^{op_2} = delete(1, \text{'b'})$, should be identical to the inverse operation $\overline{op_1}{}^{op_2} = insert(1, \text{'b'})$, which is not the case here.

It results that, when using our Undo Algorithm, the example referred as *Insert-Insert-Tie Dilemma* [20], is not a critical situation anymore.

6 Comparison with Existing Approaches

The adOPTed algorithm [13] is based on the use of Operational Transformations and on a multidimensional history associated with each copy. This history is represented by a graph where each dimension relates to the operations generated by a given user. An extension to the adOPTed algorithm, based on the naïve algorithm, is proposed in [14] to enable a user to undo operations. However, the extension restricts undo to local operations only on condition that they are undone according to the inverse chronological order. As a result of these limitations an operation $\overline{op}$ that undoes op can only be separated from the operation op in a given dimension by a sequence containing do/undo pairs only. This characteristic facilitates the adaptation of the forward transposition function (called *translateRequest*) so that it can take the do/undo pairs into account and ensure that condition C3 is verified. Moreover, thanks to the multidimensional history, for any operation op concurrent to a sequence seq, the operation op^{seq} is directly available. Therefore, the verification of condition C4 is unnecessary because the undoing of op is achieved by generating and executing $\overline{op}^{seq}$. However, the undoing of local operations according to their inverse chronological order remains a restrictive solution.

The DistEdit Selective Undo algorithm [12] implements Strategy 2 and only ensures that a condition equivalent to C3 is met, since condition C4 is automatically satisfied by this Strategy.

The REDUCE system [19] is based on Operational Transformations and on a linear history associated with each copy of the object. The principle of the undo algorithm, called ANYUNDO [20, 21], is a naïve algorithm adaptation obtained by grouping an operation and the corresponding undo in the history. This adaptation makes it possible to ensure the neutrality of the do/undo pairs during the transposition of an operation and, therefore, to ensure that condition C3 is met. More precisely, undoing op is achieved by: generating $\overline{op}$, transposing it forward with the sequence seq of the operations executed after op; and executing and broadcasting the operation obtained $\overline{op}^{seq}$. Grouping op and the corresponding undo operation to obtain the do/undo pair, written as op^*, is achieved by backward transposing the pair (seq, $\overline{op}^{seq}$). In [20], the lack of a timestamp for an undo operation makes it impossible to distinguish between concurrent operations and causally dependent operations; that may result in violating user intention and lead to the divergence of the copies. In [21], this mistake is corrected and conditions IP1, IP2 and IP3 equivalent to conditions C3 and C4 are retrieved. However, the correction is obtained by extending the ANYUNDO algorithm with undo specific additive treatments. The interest of our approach lies in the generality of the processing of a remote operation whether it is an undo operation or a regular one. This generality is obtained thanks to the introduction of a specific undo operation which obeys to the same processing as a regular operation.

7 Conclusion

This article reviews the problems arising from the cancellation of an operation in distributed collaborative environments that use Operational Transformations. Traditionally, undo operations were often limited to the handling of the inverse operation. However, we show that when concurrency occurs, this approach is insufficient to ensure that the copies converge and it fails to respect user intention. Moreover, the forward transposition function must verify two conditions, which we have highlighted. However, these conditions are difficult to check in practice. In this context, we proposed a general undo algorithm for which these conditions are automatically met. Its originality lies in its capacity to consider undo as a specific operation that requires the adaptation of the Operational Transformations, an adaptation for which we give a generic specification. This algorithm makes it possible to undo any operation, local or remote, in all situations of concurrency, including those that are widely considered as problems. The paper concludes with a comparison with existing algorithms.

References

[1] Abowd G. D. , Dix A. J.; "Giving Undo Attention"; Interacting with Computers, vol. 4, n° 3, pp. 317-342, 1992.
[2] Berlage T.; "A Selective Undo Mechanism for Graphical User Interfaces Based on Command Objects"; ACM Transactions on Computer-Human Interaction, vol. 1, n° 3, pp. 269-294, 1994.
[3] Choudhary R., Dewan P.; "A general Multi-User Undo/Redo Model"; Proc. of European Conference on Computer Supported Work (ECSCW'95), Stockholm, October 1995, pp. 231-246.
[4] Ellis C.A., Gibbs S.J.; "Concurrency Control in Groupware Systems"; Proc. ACM Int. Conf. on Management of Data (SIGMOD'89), Seattle, May 1989, pp.399-407.
[5] Ellis C.A., Gibbs S.J., Rein G.L.; "Groupware: Some issues and experiences"; Commun. ACM, January 1991, vol.34, n° 1, pp.39-59.
[6] Ignat C., Norrie M.C.; "Customizable Collaborative Editor Relying on the treeOPT Algorithm"; Proc. 8th European Conf. on Computer Supported Cooperative Work (ECSCW'03), Helsinki, September 2003.
[7] Li D., Zhou L., Muntz R. R.; "A new paradigm of user intention preservation in realtime collaborative editing systems"; Proc. 7th Int. Conf. on Parallel and Distributed Systems (PADS'00), Iwate, Japan, July 2000.
[8] Mancini R., Dix A., Levialdi S.; "Reflections on Undo"; Technical report, University of Hudders eld, 1996.
[9] Molli P., Skaf-Molli H., Oster G.; "Divergence Awarenes for Virtual Team through the Web"; Proc 6th Int. Conf. on Integrated Design and Process Technology (IDPT'02), June 2002
[10] Palmer C.R., Cormack G.V.; "Operation Transforms for a Distributed Shared Spreadsheet"; Proc. ACM Int. Conf. on Computer Supported Cooperative Work (CSCW'98), Seattle, November 1998, pp. 69-78, 1998.
[11] Prakash A., Knister M.J.; "Undoing Actions in Collaborative Work"; Proc. ACM Int. Conf. on Computer Supported Cooperative Work (CSCW'92), November 1992, pp. 273-280.
[12] Prakash A., Knister M.J.; "A Framework for Undoing Actions in Collaborative Systems"; ACM Transactions on Computer-Human Interaction, vol. 1, n° 4, pp. 295-330, 1994.

[13] Ressel M., Nitssche-Ruhland D., Gunzenhäuser R.; "An Integrating, Transformation-oriented Approach to Concurrency Control and Undo in Group Editors"; Proc. ACM Int. Conf. on Computer Supported Cooperative Work (CSCW'96), Boston, November 1996, pp. 288-297.
[14] Ressel M., Gunzenhäuser R.; "Reducing the Problems of Group Undo"; Proc. ACM Int. Conf. on Supporting Group Work (GROUP'99), Phoenix, November 1999, pp.131-139.
[15] Suleiman M., Cart M., Ferrié J.; "Serialization of Concurrent Operations in a Distributed Collaborative Environment"; Proc. ACM Int. Conf. on Supporting Group Work (GROUP'97), Phoenix, November 1997, pp. 435-445.
[16] Suleiman M., Cart M., Ferrié J.; "Concurrent Operations in a Distributed and Mobile Collaborative Environment"; Proc. 14th IEEE Int. Conf. on Data Engineering (IEEE / ICDE'98), Orlando, February 1998, pp. 36-45.
[17] Suleiman M.; "Sérialisation des opérations concurrentes dans les systèmes collaboratifs répartis"; Doctoral thesis, Université de Montpellier 2, July 1998.
[18] Sun C., Jia X., Yang Y., Zhang Y.; "A generic operation transformation schema for consistency maintenance in real-time cooperative editing systems"; Proc. ACM Int. Conf. on Supporting Group Work (GROUP'97), Phoenix, November 1997, pp.425-434.
[19] Sun C., Ellis C.S.; "Operational Transformation in Real-Time Group Editors : Issues, Algorithms and Achievements"; Proc. ACM Int. Conf. on Computer Supported Cooperative Work (CSCW'98), Seattle, November 1998, pp. 59-68.
[20] Sun C.; "Undo Any Operation at Any Time in Group Editors "; Proc. ACM Conf. on Computer Supported Cooperative Work (CSCW'00), Philadelphia, Pennsylvania, December 2-6, 2000, pp. 191-200.
[21] Sun C.; "Undo as Concurrent Inverse in Group Editors"; ACM Transactions on Computer-Human Interaction, vol. 9, n° 4, pp. 309-361, December 2002.
[22] Vidot N., Cart M., Ferrié J., Suleiman M.; "Copies convergence in a distributed real-time collaborative environment"; Proc. ACM Int. Conf. on Computer Supported Cooperative Work (CSCW'00), Philadelphia, Pennsylvania, December 2-6, 2000, pp. 171-180.
[23] Vidot N.; "Convergence des Copies dans les Environnements Collaboratifs Répartis"; Doctoral thesis, Université de Montpellier 2, September 2002.

Refresco: Improving Query Performance Through Freshness Control in a Database Cluster

Cécile Le Pape[1], Stéphane Gançarski[1], and Patrick Valduriez[2]

[1] Laboratoire d'Informatique de Paris 6, Paris, France
`Firstname.Lastname@lip6.fr`
[2] INRIA and LINA, Nantes, France
`Patrick.Valduriez@inria.fr`

Abstract. We consider the use of a cluster system for managing autonomous databases. In order to improve the performance of read-only queries, we strive to exploit user requirements on replica freshness. Assuming mono-master lazy replication, we propose a freshness model to help specifying the required freshness level for queries. We propose an algorithm to optimize the routing of queries on slave nodes based on the freshness requirements. Our approach uses non intrusive techniques that preserve application and database autonomy. We provide an experimental validation based on our prototype *Refresco*. The results show that freshness control can help increase query throughput significantly. They also show significant improvement when freshness requirements are specified at the relation level rather than at the database level.

1 Introduction

Recently, the database cluster approach [4,8,9], *i.e.* cluster systems with off-the-shelf (black-box) DBMS nodes, has gained much interest for various applications such as Application Service Provider (ASP). In the ASP model, applications and databases are hosted at the provider site and accessed by customers, typically through the Internet, who are no longer concerned with data and application maintenance tasks. Through replication of customers' databases at several nodes, a database cluster can yield high-availability and high-performance at a much lower cost than with a DBMS on a tightly-coupled multiprocessor. In the Leg@net project[1], the objective is to demonstrate the viability of the ASP model using a database cluster for pharmacy applications in France. In particular, we must support mixed workloads composed of front-office update-intensive transactions (e.g. drug sales) and back-office read-intensive queries (e.g. statistics on drugs sold). In practice, front-office processing has priority over back-office processing which usually has to be performed during closing hours. Preserving

---
[1] Project sponsored by the RNTL between LIP6, Prologue Software and ASPLine.

autonomy is often of major importance in a database cluster. In the ASP context, autonomy means that applications and databases must remain unchanged when hosted at the provider site, in order to avoid high costs in migration and maintenance. Thus, our challenge is to exploit the cluster's parallelism to allow both front-office and back-office to be performed on-line, as efficiently as if they were local to the pharmacy site. Our approach is to capture application semantics for optimizing load balancing within the cluster system.

In [4], we discussed the architectural issues underlying our approach. We showed that using a transaction processing monitor or a parallel DBMS does not address the autonomy requirements. We also showed that synchronous (eager) replication is not appropriate for the ASP model, and we proposed an asynchronous (lazy) replication scheme. In order to avoid consistency problems, we use a mono-master (primary copy) replication scheme: *update transactions* (or *transactions* for short) are all sent to a single master node while *read-only queries* (or *queries* for short) may be sent to any node. Slave nodes are updated asynchronously through *refresh transactions* and may contain *stale data* until the refresh process is completed. However, as the serialization order of refresh transactions on any slave node is the same as the serialization order of the corresponding transactions on the master node, we guarantee that queries always read a consistent state, though maybe stale, on slave nodes. This is obtained by sending refresh transactions sequentially to each slave node, according to the serialization (commit) order obtained on the master node. Mono-master replication has the advantage of simplicity and is sufficient in many cases where most of the conflicts occur between OLTP transactions and OLAP queries, as in our pharmacy application and most of ASP potential applications. In mono-master replication, one main dimension for data quality is *freshness* which is defined through *freshness level*. The data at a slave node is totally fresh if it has the same value as that at the master node, *i.e.* all the corresponding refresh transactions have been propagated to the slave nodes. Otherwise, the freshness level reflects the distance between the data value at the slave node and that at the master node.

In this paper, we address the problem of expressing and exploiting freshness requirements in order to optimize the execution of queries. An obvious observation is that queries do not always require perfectly fresh data and may tolerate to read some stale data. For instance, assume a query Q computing the average quantity sold per product and per day over the last six months, on a table $SALE$ containing the sales history. As it covers a large time interval, computing Q may be acceptable even if it misses the last tuples inserted in table $SALE$. In this case, application semantics is modelled by freshness requirements which express how many missing tuples in $SALE$ are tolerated in order to compute Q. Another observation is that a slave node does not always need to be refreshed in order to comply with the freshness requirements of a query, even if the query requires perfect freshness. For instance, if all the transactions executed on the master node and waiting for refresh on a slave node S_i do not access table $SALE$, *e.g.* they access table $PRODUCT$, S_i is still perfectly fresh for Q, but may be not fresh enough for a query accessing table *PRODUCT*. In this case, detecting potential conflicts between transactions and queries helps reducing the refresh sequence to apply to a node to get it fresh enough for a query. Hence, application semantics is also modelled by the potential conflicts between queries and transactions. In this context, we want to increase efficiency by allowing queries to be sent to slave nodes even if they are not up-to-date, according to application requirements on data freshness. The problem can be stated as follows: given an autonomous database replicated in mono-master mode, evaluate the level of copy freshness of slave nodes to route a query to and select a node such that (1) the copy freshness level guarantees that the query result will satisfy the query freshness requirements and (2) the choice of the node optimizes query response time.

There are several projects close to our approach [1,2,7,12,5,8,9,6]. However, they all have one or more of the following limitations: are specific to some kind of data (*e.g.* XML documents), do not allow to model several kinds of freshness level, do not take updates into account, require substantial modification of the DBMS transaction manager, or do not model conflicts between OLAP and OLTP loads at a granularity finer than the entire database.

In this paper, we make three main contributions. First, we define a freshness model for users to specify freshness requirements for queries. This model allows capturing conflicts between queries and transactions. Second, we propose an algorithm to optimize the routing of queries on slave nodes based on the freshness requirements and the conflicts. Third, we provide an experimental validation using *Refresco* (*Routing Enhancer through FREShness COntrol*), a middleware prototype which implements our approach.

The paper is organized as follows. Section 2 gives an overview of our database cluster architecture. Section 3 defines the freshness model. Section 4 gives the algorithms to optimize query routing. Section 5 presents our experimental validation. Section 6 compares our approach with related work. Section 7 concludes.

2 Database Cluster Architecture

Figure 1 gives an overview of our database cluster architecture, derived from [4]. As shown, our middleware preserves the autonomy constraint because it interfers neither with client's applications nor with existing databases and DBMS: it receives requests from the application and sends them to nodes. Results are returned from nodes to the load balancer which forwards them to clients. The database is fully replicated on nodes $S_1, S_2, \ldots, S_N$. S_0 is the *master node* which is used to perform transactions and queries. The other nodes are *slave nodes* used for queries. They are updated only through *refresh transactions*. Refresh transactions are sent sequentially, according to the serialization (commit) order obtained on the master node, in order to guarantee the same serialization order on slave nodes. Metadata useful for the load balancer is provided and managed by the DBA using the metadata repository. It includes for instance the default level of freshness required by a query. It also includes information about which

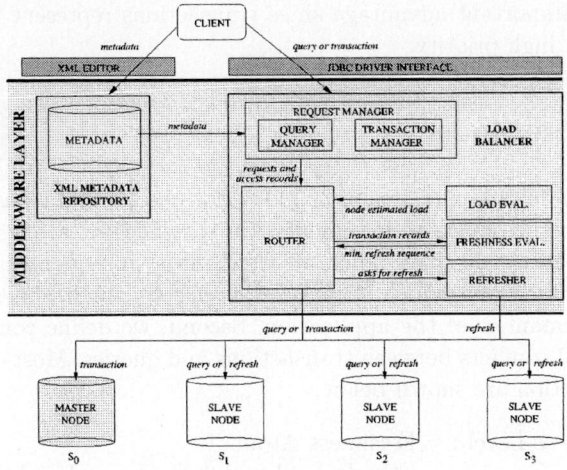

Fig. 1. Mono-master replicated database architecture

part of the database is updated by the transactions and read by the queries, enabling the detection of potential conflicts between updates and queries.

The load balancer which receives clients' requests performs two main functions: request management and routing. The request manager prepares specific *access records* for transactions and queries: the transaction manager and the query manager prepare respectively *transaction records* and *query records*. Access records are built using metadata and dynamic information provided by the clients (*e.g.* parameters for SQL programs) or resulting from the execution of transactions on the master node or obtained by parsing application code when available.

The router uses access records to send requests to nodes. Whenever a request is sent to a slave node, its estimated duration is maintained by the load evaluation module. Transactions are sent to the master node. Transaction records are enriched with dynamic information about the transaction execution on the master node (commit time of the transaction, number of tuples changed, ...). They are stored by the freshness evaluation module until every node has executed the corresponding refresh transaction and then removed.

When the router receives a query Q, it asks the freshness evaluation module to compute the corresponding minimum refresh sequence for every node. It also asks the load evaluation module to compute the current node's load. Then, it computes a cost function for Q for every slave node, including the cost of the possible execution of refresh transactions in order to make the slave node fresh enough for Q. Then the router sends the query and possible refresh transactions to the slave node which minimizes the cost function, thus minimizing the query response time. Since queries are only sent to slave nodes, they do not interfer with the transaction stream on the master node. In our application example, this yields an important advantage since transactions represent front-office applications with high priority.

3 Freshness Model

In this section, we present a freshness model for queries and transactions. First, we describe how freshness requirements are specified for a query. Based on a definition of transaction precedence, we define refresh sequences. Then we give three freshness measures which allow users to specify the freshness of data that matches the semantics of the application. Second, we define conflict classes to model potential conflicts between transactions and queries. Most of the concepts used in this section are shown below.

$$
\begin{aligned}
\text{Freshness Level} &::= \text{Freshness Atom} \\
&\mid \text{Freshness Level} \lor \text{Freshness Level} \\
&\mid \text{Freshness Level} \land \text{Freshness Level} \\
\text{Freshness Atom} &::= (\text{Access Atom, Freshness Measure, Threshold}) \\
\text{Freshness Measure} &::= \text{Age} \mid \text{Order} \mid \text{Card} \\
\text{Access Atom} &::= \text{Database} \mid \text{Relation} \mid \text{Attribute} \\
\text{Conflict Class} &::= \{\text{Access Atom}\}
\end{aligned}
$$

3.1 Freshness Requirements

Freshness requirements of queries are specified through a flexible model which allows the user (database programmer or DBA) to define the staleness allowed for each part of the database read by the query depending on the desired granularity and freshness measure. First, the user determines the *access atoms* of the query, *i.e.* the parts of the database accessed by the query. Depending on the granularity desired, an access atom can be the entire database, a relation or even a relation attribute. For each access atom a, the user gives a condition on a which bounds the staleness of a under a certain threshold t for a given *freshness measure* μ, *i.e.* such as $\mu(a) < t$. The *freshness level* of a query Q is then defined as a logical formula composed of every freshness atom and denoted by $Fresh(Q, S_i)$: the results of Q at a slave node S_i are fresh enough if $Fresh(Q, S_i)$ is satisfied, *i.e.* if it returns *true*.

3.2 Precedence Order and Refresh Sequences

We now define a precedence order among requests, in order to define the freshness on slave nodes. This order reflects the global serialization order among transactions over the cluster, *i.e.* the serialization order obtained on the master node and reproduced on the slave nodes. It is used to define refresh sequences for a node, which contain the refresh transactions necessary to make the copy of the node fresh enough. First, we define state sequences for requests (transactions or queries) : *accepted, running, done* and *notified*. A request is *accepted* when the connection between the client and the system is successful. The request is given a global identifier i and is denoted by r_i. Request r_i is *running* if its beginning is recorded in the DBMS log, at the master node if r_i is a transaction, at a slave node if it is a query. If r_i is a transaction, it is *done* when its commit or abort is recorded in the DBMS log. If r_i is a query, it is done when it has committed at a slave node and returned a result with a satisfying level of freshness. Finally, a request is *notified* when its results are returned to the client.

As said in Section 1, we must ensure that queries always read a consistent (possibly stale) state of the database. In a mono-master configuration, the local concurrency control at the master node always produces consistent states. Thus, ensuring global consistency is equivalent to ensuring that refresh transactions are executed on a slave node in the serialization order of the master node, which we obtain by sending refresh transactions sequentially, according to this order. In practice, retrieving the serialization order on the master node depends on the isolation protocol used by the local DBMS. If it provides commit-order serializability, this is straightforward by reading commit log records[2]. We base our precedence order and thus our freshness computation on the commit log record of a transaction for two main reasons. First, since this information is available in most existing DBMS, this makes our approach generic. Second, reading a log is a non-intrusive method, which is important to preserve autonomy.

The *precedence order among transactions* is defined as follows: let T and T' be two transactions, we say that T precedes T', denoted by $T \prec T'$, if T and T' have committed on the master node, and T is done before T' is done. Note that, as it is based on commit time, $\prec$ is a *total order* among transactions.

The *precedence order between transactions and queries* is defined as follows: let T be a transaction and Q be a query, we say that T precedes Q, denoted by $T \prec Q$, if T is done before Q starts running. Note that there is no need of an order among queries.

Let seq be a transaction sequence. $Head(seq)$ denotes seq without its last element, $Apply(seq, S_i)$ denotes the state of node S_i after applying the transactions of seq on S_i. We define $MinRefresh(S_i, Q)$ the minimal refresh sequence to apply on S_i according to the $\prec$ order defined above, in order to make it fresh enough for query Q as the sequence of transactions t such as:

$\forall t \in MinRefresh(S_i, Q)$, t has committed on S_0, and
$Fresh(Q, Apply(MinRefresh(S_i, Q), S_i))$, and
$\neg Fresh(Q, Apply(Head(MinRefresh(S_i, Q)), S_i))$

We also define $PerfectRefresh(S_i)$ the refresh sequence to apply on S_i according to the $\prec$ order defined above, in order to make it perfectly fresh for any query. It is the sequence of transactions t such as:
$\forall t \in PerfectRefresh(S_i)$, t has committed on $S_0 \wedge \neg(t$ is done on $S_i)$

---

[2] We use the Oracle's SERIALIZABLE ISOLATION_LEVEL.

3.3 Freshness Measures

Classifications of freshness measures can be found in [1,2,3,11,12]. We adapt these measures to our context because we cannot use internal information of the DBMS transaction manager to evaluate them.

Let a be an access atom. We consider different measures μ and define them, at a given instant t, for a being either an attribute, a relation or the entire database. First, we define $U(a_i)$ as the set of transactions updating an access atom a_i, $U(a_i) = \{T \in PerfectRefresh(S_i) \wedge T\ updates\ a_i\}$, where T updates a_i is defined as follows:

- if a_i is an attribute $R.att$, T updates a_i if it inserts or deletes at least one tuple in R_i, or modifies att in at least one tuple of R_i,
- if a_i is a relation R_i, T updates a_i if it inserts, deletes or modifies at least one tuple in R_i,
- if a_i is the database, T updates a_i if it inserts, deletes or modifies at least one tuple.

We define three freshness measures *Order*, *Age* and *Card* as follows:

Order(a_i): the ordering measure of a_i is the number of transactions updating a which have committed on the master node and have not yet been propagated on slave node S_i at instant t, i.e.
$$Order(a_i) = |U|\ \text{(the cardinal of } U\text{)}$$

Age(a_i): the age of a_i is the maximum time since at least one transaction updating a has committed on the master node and has not yet been propagated on slave node S_i at instant t, i.e.
$$Age(a_i) = Max(t - T.commit\_time), T \in U$$

Card(a_i): this measure reflects the number of stale elements in a_i. If a_i is an attribute $R.att$, $Card(a_i)$ is the number of tuples in R_i inserted, deleted or having att being modified by all the transactions in U. If a_i is a relation R, $Card(a_i)$ is the number of tuples in R_i inserted, deleted or updated by all the transactions in U. If a_i is the database, $Card(a_i)$ is the number of tuples inserted, deleted or updated by all the transactions in U.

These different measures correspond to different user requirements. Measure *Order* is useful, for instance, for queries involving history relations, since it can estimate the number of missing inserted tuples. Measure *Age* allows modelling queries such as "Give the value of X as it was no later than Y minutes ago". It is also useful for queries accessing history relations. For instance, if a query wants data as of last week, the results will be correct if computed on a node stale since one hour. Measure *Card* is more relevant for estimating the accuracy of a query result, since it is able to count the number of individual updates missing to get a copy perfectly fresh. These measures can also be combined to define complex measures. Note that, by definition, freshness is computed just before a query is sent to the best node: transactions sent to the master node after this moment are not taken into account.

3.4 Conflict Classes

Conflict classes are used to detect potential conflicts between transactions and queries, before query execution. They are stored in the metadata repository. They may be given by the user or inferred by parsing the transactions' source code (when available). They can also be deduced from the access atoms used to model transactions and queries.

Let r be a request. The *conflict class* of r, denoted by $CC(r)$, is defined as a set of access atoms potentially accessed by r. The conflict class of a request r is a superset of the data set which the request will actually access. As transactions are serialized at the master node, we are not interested in the data read transactions. Thus, $CC(r)$ is the data which r will potentially write (resp. read) if r is a transaction (resp. a query). Conflict classes may be defined in different ways, depending on the granularity needed by applications. Consider transaction T_1, and queries Q_1 and Q_2 defined as follow:

T_1: *update PRODUCT set price=price*1.1 where id=1234;*
Q_1: *select   id,   avg(quantity)   from   SALE   where   date   between to_date('07/01/2003')*
 and to_date('12/31/2003') group by id;
Q_2: *select id from PRODUCT where type='Lotion';*

The table below shows the conflict classes for T_1, Q_1 and Q_2 according to the selected granularity level. When specified at the database level, T_1 and Q_1 potentially conflict. But they do not potentially conflict when specified at the relation level because Q_1 reads data from table $SALE$ when T_1 updates data in table $PRODUCT$. Q_2 and T_1 potentially conflict at the relation level when they do not conflit at the attribute level. This example shows that the choice of the granularity level impacts potential conflicts: the finer the granularity, the less potential conflicts exist.

granularity	CC(Q_1)	CC(T_1)	CC(Q_2)
database	{database}	{database}	{database}
relation	{SALE}	{PRODUCT}	{PRODUCT}
attribute	{SALE.id, SALE.quantity, SALE.date}	{PRODUCT.price}	{PRODUCT.id, PRODUCT.type}

Conflict classes allow defining *potential conflicts* between requests. Since transactions are serialized on the master node, there is no need for our middleware to handle write/write conflicts. Thus, since a query cannot conflict with another query, we only need to define potential conflicts between a transaction and a query. A query Q and a transaction T potentially conflict if a least one access atom of $CC(Q)$ conflicts with one of $CC(T)$ conflicts, according to the following rules:

  ⋄ the database potentially conflicts with any other access atom
  ⋄ a relation R_i potentially conflicts with a relation R_j iff $R_i = R_j$

⋄ a relation R_i potentially conflicts with an attribute $R_j.col_k$ iff $R_i = R_j$
⋄ an attribute $R_i.att_k$ potentially conflicts with an attribute $R_j.att_l$ iff $R_i = R_j \wedge att_k = att_l$

In other words, an access atom potentially conflicts with another one if they are the same or if one is included in the other. Potential conflicts include real conflicts, *i.e.* conflicts at execution time. This means that whenever a transaction and a query actually conflict, a potential conflict has been detected *a priori*. The reverse is not true. Consider query Q_3: *select * from PRODUCT where id=4567;*. Even at the finest granularity of our model (attribute), a potential conflict is detected on *PRODUCT.id* between Q_3 and transaction T_1 defined above. However, at execution time, T_1 and Q_3 do not access the same tuple and will not actually conflict. This problem could be solved in some cases by defining conflict classes at finer granularity levels (*e.g.* tuple), but this would make freshness evaluation much more complex and costly in terms of metadata management.

4 Trading Freshness for Load Balancing

In this section, we show how freshness can be evaluated and give an algorithm that use the freshness model to optimize query load balancing.

4.1 Evaluating Freshness

Computing the measures defined above is relatively straightforward. *Order* is evaluated by counting the number of transactions necessary to get an access atom copy perfectly fresh. *Age* is evaluated using the commit time of transactions. *Card* evaluation uses the number of tuples modified by a transaction returned by the database driver after the transaction commit on the master node. However, freshness atoms can not be evaluated with a perfect precision. The main reason is that we must evaluate them before the query is sent to a given slave node. At that time, we do not know which tuples will be accessed by the query. As discussed in Section 3.4, it is thus impossible to determine which transactions not already propagated on the node will really conflict with the query. Our solution to this problem is to compute an upper bound for freshness atoms, called *confidence level*. The confidence level of a freshness atom (a, μ, t), denoted by $conf(a, \mu)$, is a value which guarantees that $\mu(a) \leq conf(a, \mu)$. Therefore the following holds: $(conf(a, \mu) \leq t) \Rightarrow (\mu(a) \leq t)$.

Confidence levels are computed using potential conflicts between queries and transactions, as defined in Section 3.4, based on the conflict classes stored in the metadata repository. As potential conflicts include real conflicts, this guarantees that freshness atom evaluation is over-estimated. Note however that transactions which do not potentially conflict with the access atoms included in the freshness atom are not considered in the computation.

4.2 Computing the Minimum Refresh Sequence for a Query $MinRefresh(S_i, Q)$

A query is sent to a slave node only if the node satisfies the freshness level of the query. Therefore, when choosing an execution node, the router needs to know for every slave node which refresh transactions must be sent to the node if it is not fresh enough. To this end, it asks the freshness evaluation module to compute the corresponding minimum refresh sequence for every node. Figure 2 shows the queue managed by the freshness evaluation module where incoming transactions are stored until every slave node has executed it. They are placed in the queue in the global serialization order, i.e. the serialization order on the master node. The refresh level of a slave node S_i is represented by a "stack pointer" $level_i$: all transactions preceding the transaction pointed by $level_i$ have already been executed at S_i. Node S_i is perfectly fresh when $level_i$ meets the master node pointer, $master\_level$.

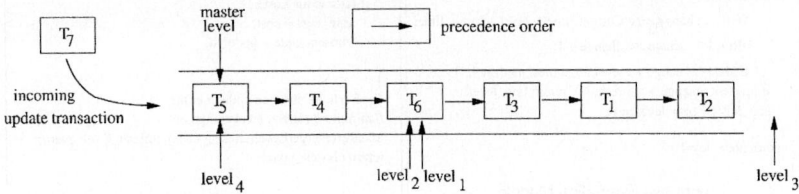

Fig. 2. Transactions global ordering.

In this example, the set of running transactions is $T_1, T_2, ..., T_6$ while an incoming transaction T_7 is about to be inserted. The global execution order is $(T_2, T_1, T_3, T_6, T_4, T_5)$. There are four slave nodes: S_1 and S_2 have processed transactions (T_2, T_1, T_3, T_6), S_3 has not been updated since the beginning may be due to a network failure and S_4 is the only slave node perfectly fresh.

This data structure minimizes memory utilization. First, since there is only one queue for all the slave nodes, adding a node to the cluster only implies adding a new pointer. Second, as soon as an transaction has been propagated to all slave nodes, it is deleted from the queue. Based on this queue, function $getMinRefresh$ (see Figure 3.a) computes the minimum refresh sequence of a slave node S_i for the freshness level f of a given query, which is available in the query record. It returns a pointer to a level between the node current level and the master node level. This means that the sequence of transactions between the node current level and the level computed must be applied to the slave node in order to make it fresh enough for the query. If the freshness level is a freshness atom, the algorithm tries to decrease the refresh level needed, from the master level to the lowest possible level. The best case is to reach the current node level: no refresh is necessary for this query on this node. For each level reached, the confidence level of this freshness atom is updated when some potential conflict is detected with the corresponding transaction. The process ends when the threshold for the freshness measure is exceeded.

```
getMinRefresh(f, i){
  // f : freshness level of a query
  // i : slave node identifier
  if (f.type == "AND")
    return max(getMinRefresh(f.left_op, i),
               getMinRefresh(f.right_op, i));
  if (f.type == "OR")
    return min(getMinRefresh(f.left_op,i),
               getMinRefresh(f.right_op, i));
  // the freshness level is a freshness atom
  m = f.freshness_measure;
  t = f.threshold;
  a = f.access_atom;
  node_level = getLevel(i);
  master_level = getLevel(master_node);
  tmp_level = master_level;
  current_change=0;
  // find the first transaction over the threshold
  while (tmp_level != node_level) {
    if (conflicts(f,tmp_level)) {
      switch (m) {
        "AGE" : change = getCurrentTime()-level.commit_time;
        "ORDER" : change = change + 1;
        "CARD": change += level.nb_tuples_modified; }
      if (current_change > a.threshold) return tmp_level;  }
    tmp_level = tmp_level.next;
  }
  return node_level;
}
```
Freshness Evaluation Module

```
route (query){
  // compute the best node for this query
  min_cost=+infinity;
  for (node_id in slave nodes) {
    cost = getNodeLoad(node_id);
    refresh_level = minRefresh(query.fresh_level, node_id);
    refresh_cost = refreshCost(refresh_level, node_id);
    cost += refresh_cost;
    if (cost<min_cost) {
      min_cost = cost;
      chosen_node = node_id;
    }
  }
  // refresh the choosen node until the
  // minimum refresh level computed
  asksRefresh(getLevel(chosen_node), refresh_level, query);
  return chosen_node;
}
```
Router

Fig. 3. Computing the minimum refresh sequence and routing algorithm for a query

4.3 Routing Algorithm

Figure 3.b shows the routing algorithm which evaluates query refreshment and execution cost on every slave node in order to choose the best node. First, based on previous executions of the query, function *getAvgTime(query)* evaluates the query execution time on the node. Then the current load of the node is added. It is estimated by the load evaluation module which sums the remaining execution time of all the running transactions on the node. Finally, the total cost is increased with the refresh cost, given by expression *refreshLoad(getMinRefresh(Q.freshness_level,node),node)* which evaluates the execution time of the minimum refresh sequence for the query Q on this node. The best node is the one minimizing the total cost. If more than one node have the same cost, we make a random choice. Before the function *route()* returns, it calls function *asksRefresh()* which asynchronously sends a refresh demand to the refresher. The query execution starts on the node when the refreshment is done.

In our approach, routing is a multi-criteria decision. It takes into account simultaneously the query freshness criterion, but also the current nodes load criterion and the refreshment cost criterion. Hence, the router may decide that refreshing a stale node is better than choosing a node fresh enough, for example when the refresh sequence is small and the node sligthly loaded. All these criteria are considered at the same time, which is more efficient than optimizing one criterion after each other. Our refresh strategy is embedded in the routing process. It is different from [9], where routing is independent from the refresh strategy. The strategy in [9] proceeds as follows. It first selects the nodes which are fresh enough and then elects the least loaded node. If there is no node fresh enough for a query, the query waits until refresh is activated upon time-out. Thus, it does not take into account, as we do, cases when the refreshment cost is lower than sending the query to a node fresh enough but very loaded.

5 Experimental Validation

In order to validate our approach, we developped a prototype, called *Refresco*, which implements our architecture and routing algorithm. We evaluate the influence of freshness on global performance, with different freshness measures. Then we focus on the impact of freshness threshold. Finally, we study the impact of different cluster sizes to show significant benefits even with small numbers of nodes.

5.1 Prototype Environment

The prototype is implemented in Java (jdk 1.4). The database is fully replicated on four nodes, each running the Oracle 8i server under Linux. The middleware layer runs on a fifth node. All nodes (Pentium IV 2Ghz, 512 Mb RAM) are interconnected by a switched 1 GBit/s Fast-Ethernet local area network. We generated the database according to the TPC-R benchmark [10] with a scaling factor of 1. The workload contains OLTP transactions and OLAP queries sending one SQL request (transaction or query) every 5 ms. The transactions correspond to the TPC-R refresh function RF1 while the queries are randomized TPC-R queries. The workload is composed of six transaction streams and six query streams. The average response time, obtained by executing transactions on a load-free single Oracle Server node is about 4ms for OLTP transactions while it is more than two minutes for OLAP queries. Each experiment has a duration of 20 minutes.

5.2 Experiment Parameters and Performance Measures

Experiment parameters are described in the table below. Within the same experiment, every query has the same freshness policy: the freshness level is a logical AND formula and access atoms are defined by the same freshness measure, the same freshness threshold and the same granularity.

Threshold	0, ..., $+\infty$
Granularity	database / relation
Freshness measure	age / order / card
Number of nodes	1, 2, 3, 4

For every experiment, we made the following measurements:

- *Query throughput*: the number of queries executed per hour.
- *QMRT*: the mean response time per query in seconds.
- *Transaction throughput*: the number of transactions executed on the master node per minute.
- *TMRT*: the mean response time per transaction on the master node in milliseconds.

The total response time of a query is detailed as the time to choose the best node (routing time), the time to refresh the node (refresh time) and the time to execute the query on the selected node (DB time).

5.3 Impact of Freshness Threshold

In these experiments, we focus on how the freshness policy influences transaction and query performance. We use measures *Age*, *Order* and *Card*. We ran these experiments on 4 nodes using the database granularity. We vary the freshness threshold from 0 to 1200s for measure *Age*, from 0 to 160000 transactions for measure *Order* and from 0 to 240000 tuples for measure *Card*. Maximum limits for the threshold are defined according to the experiment duration (20 minutes). Over this limit, freshness thresholds become so high that even the most obsolete slave node would be fresh enough to satisfy the query. Any higher threshold will give the same results.

Figure 4(a) shows that varying freshness does not impact transaction throughput on the master node, as one could expect. More interesting, it also shows that transaction mean response time is almost the same than the reference time, when no queries are sent to slave nodes. This mean that transactions are not slowed down by queries. This result is a direct consequence of choosing a mono master configuration where the master node does not perform queries. Though obvious, this result is important if we remember that in our context, we must guarantee that transactions, generated by front-office applications, are interactive.

Figure 4(b) shows that relaxing data freshness improves query throughput significantly. For instance, with a freshness threshold of 300s for measure *Age* (*i.e.* data may be out-of-date since at most 5 minutes), twice as many queries are performed within the same time as when the freshness threshold is 0 (*i.e.* data must be perfectly fresh). The query throughput is 70% percent as good as the reference throughput, obtained when no transaction is applied on the master node (last column on the right). This is important in pharmacy applications where statistics on stocks may be computed on-line but are usually acceptable even if computed with data stale since hours or even days.

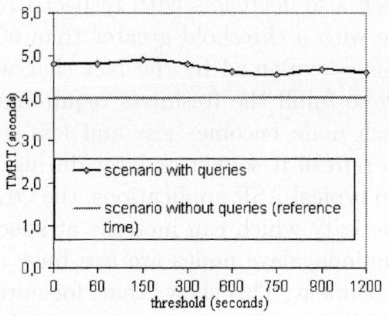
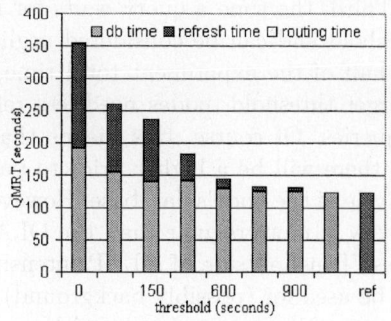

(a) Influence of freshness (measure Age) on transaction mean response time

(c) Influence of freshness (measure Age) on query response time

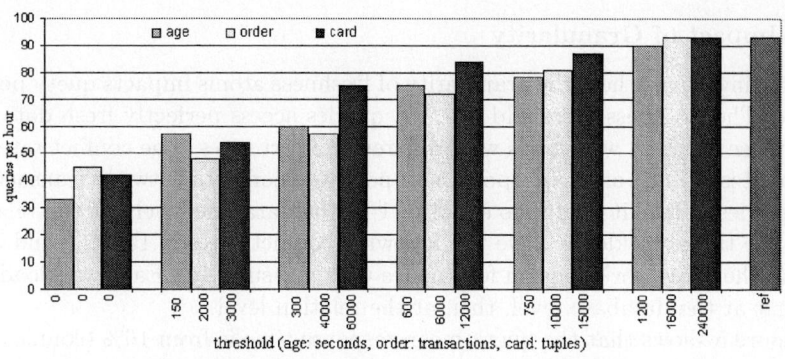

(b) Influence of freshness on query throughput

Fig. 4.

Figure 4(c) shows how relaxing data freshness decreases query response time. For instance, with a freshness threshold of 300s (measure Age), the user obtains the query results 50% faster compared to a freshness threshold of 0. Results for other measures are very similar and we omit them to keep the figure readable. The decomposition of response time in routing time, refresh time and database time helps explaining these results. First, the database time decreases with respect to the threshold. This is purely due to experimental conditions: queries wait less time for refresh, thus more queries are sent to each node during the same time and the local DBMS remains less idle. With a more intensive workload and the same number of nodes, the local DBMS would be overloaded and the database time would no longer decrease. Second, we see that the routing time used by the router to choose the best node is negligible[3]. In fact, it decreases as the threshold increases since the router reaches faster the required freshness level.

---

[3] It is even too small to be seen on the figure

Third, the time a query waits for refresh also decreases with respect to the threshold and can be considered negligible with a threshold greater than 600s, *i.e.* half of the experiment total time. This is explained by the fact that with a larger threshold, nodes need less refresh to fulfill the freshness requirements of queries. Of course, this means that each node becomes less and less fresh and there will be a higher price to pay to refresh it sooner or later during the lifecycle of the node's database. However, in typical ASP applications, the OLTP activity is more regular than the OLAP activity which can increase at specific times. Thus, outside of OLAP intensive periods, slave nodes are less busy and can be used for (possibly background) refreshment. This shows that, for normal use cases, the overhead induced by our middleware, i.e. routing time + refresh time, remains acceptable and can be considered negligible when users accept to read data stale since a reasonable time.

5.4 Impact of Granularity

We now investigate how the granularity of freshness atoms impacts query performance. The freshness threshold is 0, *i.e.* queries access perfectly fresh data. We built three different workloads with different conflict rates. The conflict rate of a workload is defined as the proportion of potential conflicts between transactions and queries. Thus, it is always equal to 1 at the database level. At the relation level, the three workloads have the following conflict rates: 0.15, 0.50 and 0.80. We ran the three workloads on four nodes with measure *Age*. Each workload was run first at the database level, then at the relation level.

Figure 5 shows that the query mean response time is from 16% (conflict rate of 0.8) to 70% (conflict rate of 0.15) better when the freshness requirements are specified at the relation level. At the database level, every query must wait until its execution node is perfectly fresh. At the relation level, the router knows when a query asks for data belonging to a relation which has not yet been updated on the master node. Hence, queries without conflicts do not have to wait for refresh (see section 5.3). The benefits depend on the conflict rate since the more queries conflict with transactions, the more slave nodes must be refreshed before query execution.

Figure 6 shows for conflict rate of 0.15 how queries are balanced on the slave nodes at the database and relation levels. We model the quantity of work done on a slave node as the total execution time of all the queries executed on the node. We distinguish between queries conflicting (resp. non conflicting) with transactions at the relation level. At the database level, queries are simply balanced on the slave nodes depending on the load, in a classical way. But even queries without conflict must wait until their execution node is perfectly fresh because the router cannot detect it since their freshness is specified at the database level. At the relation level, slave nodes appear to get specialized: node 2 gets non conflicting queries while other queries are balanced between node 1 and node 3. Queries without conflict are executed without waiting because they need not refresh. Since conflicting queries need refresh, they require more resources so two nodes are used. The percentage of slave nodes used by conflicting queries

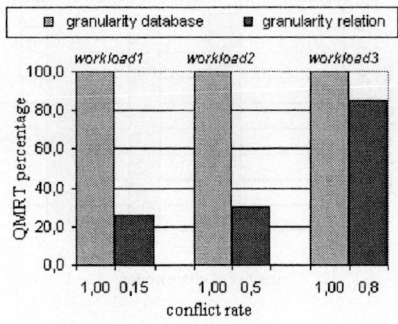
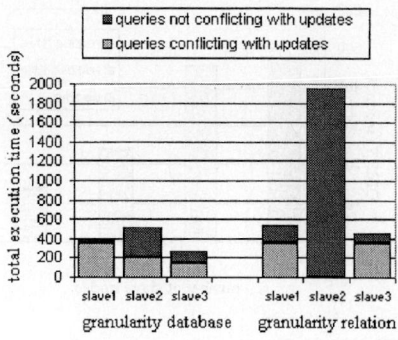

Fig. 5. Influence of granularity on query mean response time

Fig. 6. Load balancing of queries on slave nodes

decreases with the conflict rate. This locality-oriented phenomenon stems from the routing algorithm behavior, because refreshment cost is one criterion. Nodes where conflicting queries have been executed are fresher than nodes with only queries without conflict. Thus, these fresh nodes are better candidates for the next conflicting queries because their refreshment cost is low. As time goes on, the freshness divergence of slave nodes increases and this phenomenon is amplified. This behavior of our router satisfyes the requirements of applications where many queries asks for data which are not updated very often. It is particularly efficient when the conflict rate is low. In the pharmacy application case, it is true for instance for queries computing incompatibilities among drugs sold to the same customers. The table which contains such information is only updated whenever a new product is put on the market, which is less than one time per day.

5.5 Impact of the Number of Cluster Nodes

We now focus on the impact of the number of cluster nodes on performance. We want to demonstrate the benefits we can expect, even with a small number of nodes in order to keep the cost of hosting an application reasonable. The same experiment (freshness measure is *Age*, threshold is 600 and granularity is the database) has been executed successively on one up to four nodes. Other measures and thresholds give similar results and are omitted due to space limitations.

Figure 7 shows that with only 2 slave nodes, the query mean response time is twice better than with only one node. The explanation is simply that the router balances the queries between the two slave nodes. Adding another node decreases significantly the mean response time. This is obtained by a large gain in database time. It appears that the refresh time increases with the number of nodes, but remains acceptable (less than 10%). This is mainly due to the fact that when many nodes are used, each one receives less queries in average.

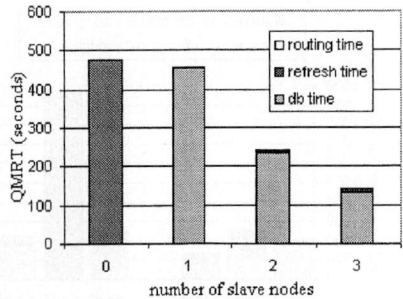 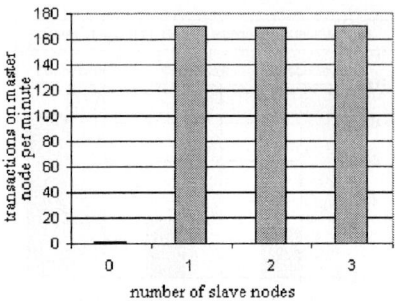

Fig. 7. Influence of number of nodes on query response time

Fig. 8. Influence of number of nodes on transaction throughput

Whenever a query is sent to such a node, it takes less advantage from the refresh already performed on the node for preceding queries.

Figure 8 justifies our choice of dedicating the master node to transactions, taking into account that our workload is rather transaction intensive. The first column on the left shows that the transaction throughput would be dramatically poor if queries where all sent to the master node. With more than one node, we can route queries only on slave nodes and the number of nodes does not impact the transaction throughput, since slave nodes are refreshed in a lazy mode.

6 Related Work

There are several interesting projects related to our work. The PowerDB project at ETH Zurich deals with the coordination of cluster nodes in order to provide a consistent view to the clients. Their authors give a specific solution to XML document management in [5] and to cache evaluation for OLAP queries in [8], without taking updates into account. More recently, they addressed issues similar to the ones addressed in this paper [9]. With a similar architecture, they show how trading freshness for query performance leads to substantial gains in query response time and make a nice comparison of various refresh strategies. However, their freshness model is very simple, with only one freshness measure, equivalent to our measure *Age*. Furthermore, they do not model conflict classes to detect potential conflicts, *i.e.* they only consider one level of granularity for access atoms : the entire database. As mentionned in Section 4.3, their routing is independent of their refresh strategy and they do not take into account, as we do, cases when the refreshment cost is lower than sending the query to a node fresh enough but very loaded. Furthermore, they model freshness as the ratio between the commit time of the last transaction propagated on a slave node and the commit time of the most recent update transaction on the master node. This definition does not reflect any real-world measure. It is also difficult to interpret, except when freshness is equal to 1, since it depends on the clock origin. The Trapp Project at

Stanford [7] adresses the problem of precision/performance trade-off, but focuses on optimizing the computation of aggregate queries by reducing the cost of wide-area network communications. The TACT middleware layer [12] implements the continous consistency model. However, reads and writes are mediated individually, not at the transaction level, which is not appropriate for the management of legacy database application in an ASP cluster. Quasi-copies [1] can be seen as materialized views with limited inconsistency, but the fressness model is not as complete as ours, and it is not clear how queries coming from legacy applications may be seamlessly integrated into their system. Epsilon transactions [2] provide a nice theoretical framework for divergence control, with different consistency metrics. However, it requires to alter the concurrency control, since divergence control is done at the lock manager level. Thus, it hurts the DBMS autonomy constraint.

7 Conclusion

In this paper, we addressed the problem of query performance in a database cluster with optimistic replication. Based on the observation that many queries do not need to access perfectly fresh data, which is the case in our ASP context with pharmacy applications, we strived to exploit user requirements on data freshness to improve query performance.

Assuming mono-master replication, we proposed a freshness model for users to specify the required freshness level for queries. The model is flexible since it allows users defining composite freshness formulas, with different freshness measures and at different levels of granularity. We proposed algorithms to evaluate data freshness and compute the minimum set of refresh transactions needed to guarantee that a node is fresh enough with respect to a given query. Our refresh strategy is embedded in the load balancing process: a node is selected to execute a query based on its current load as well as on the cost of refreshing it enough to comply with the query freshness requirements.

To validate our approach, we developed the *Refresco* prototype on LIP6's cluster running Oracle 8i under Linux. Through experimentation with the TPC-R benchmark, we showed that significant benefits can be obtained by relaxing freshness with a reasonable threshold, whatever the freshness measure and even with few nodes. We also showed that the overhead induced by computing nodes' freshness is negligible in the routing process. Finally, we showed the major impact of granularity levels on load balancing when defining conflict classes. It appears that, if freshness requirements are defined at a fine level of granularity (*e.g.* relation), our routing strategy is self-adaptable. It routes queries that read update-intensive data to some nodes which remain always fresh, while queries that read data with low update frequency are routed to other nodes which can remain stale longer. This yields significant gains in response time for workloads where the conflict rate is low (*e.g.* a 70% gain for a conflict rate of 0.15). Our choice of mono-master replication was motivated by its simplicity advantage (to maintain copy consistency) and by the fact that it is sufficient to many applications like in our ASP context. However, a remaining issue is that the master node is a single point of failure and a potential bottleneck for heavy transactional workloads. A solution is multi-master replication which provides high-availability and allows for transaction parallelism (using several master nodes). But multi-master replication is more involved since parallel updates may produce inconsistent copies. In [4], we introduced a preventive solution to this problem. The preventive replication method provides strong consistency without the overhead of synchronous replication, by exploiting the cluster's high speed network. Thus, to exploit the solution proposed in this paper with multi-master replication, we can use preventive replication between masters and optimistic replication between each master and its slaves.

There are several interesting directions for future work. First, we want to investigate other freshness measures, such as the euclidian distance for numerical data. We also want to study the impact on performance induced by finer levels of granularity such as tuple or relation subset. It is not clear yet if the added overhead for metadata management will be amortized by performance gains. Second, we plan to improve our refresh strategy. As mentionned in Section 5.3, our approach fits well with OLAP intensive sessions of limited duration so that refreshment may be performed during idle periods. In order to limit staleness of some nodes, we plan to include autonomous refresh capabilities in our system, for instance, active rules implemented through triggers. Finally, despite our purpose was to demonstrate that the ASP mode is viable with few nodes dedicated to each application, we want to how our approach scales up with the number of nodes by running experiments on larger clusters.

References

1. R. Alonso, D. Barbará, and H. Garcia-Molina. Data caching issues in an information retrieval system. *ACM TODS*, 15(3):359–384, 1990.
2. D. Barbará and H. Garcia-Molina. The demarcation protocol: A technique for maintaining constraints in distributed database systems. *VLDB Journal*, 3(3):325–353, 1994.
3. R. Gallersdörfer and M. Nicola. Improving performance in replicated databases through relaxed coherency. In *Int. Conf. on VLDB*, 1995.
4. S. Gançarski, H. Naacke, E. Pacitti, and P. Valduriez. Parallel processing with autonomous databases in a cluster system. In *Int. Conf. On Cooperative Information Systems (CoopIS)*, 2002.
5. T. Grabs, K. Böhm, and H.-J. Schek. Scalable distributed query and update service implementations for XML document elements. In *Workshop on Research Issues in Data Engineering*, 2001.
6. A. Labrinidis and N. Roussopoulos. Balancing performance and data freshness in web database servers. In *Int. Conf. on VLDB*, 2003.
7. C. Olston and J. Widom. Offering a precision-performance tradeoff for aggregation queries over replicated data. In *Int. Conf. on VLDB*, 2000.
8. U. Röhm, K. Böhm, and H.-J. Schek. Cache-aware query routing in a cluster of databases. In *Int. Conf. On Data Engineering (ICDE)*, 2001.

9. U. Röhm, K. Böhm, H.-J. Schek, and H. Schuldt. Fas - a freshness-sensitive coordination middleware for a cluster of olap components. In *Int. Conf. on VLDB*, 2002.
10. Transaction Processing Performance Council. Tpc-r : a business reporting, decision support benchmark. http://www.tpc.org/tpcr/default.asp.
11. K.-L. Wu, P. S. Yu, and C. Pu. Divergence control for epsilon-serializability. In *Int. Conf. On Data Engineering (ICDE)*, 1992.
12. H. Yu and A. Vahdat. Design and evaluation of a conit-based continuous consistency model for replicated services. *ACM TOCS*, 20(3):239–282, 2002.

Automated Supervision of Data Production – Managing the Creation of Statistical Reports on Periodic Data

Anja Schanzenberger[1,2] and Dave R. Lawrence[1]

[1] Middlesex University, School of Computing Science
Trend Park, London, N11 2NQ, United Kingdom
{anja1, dave7}@mdx.ac.uk
2 GfK Marketing Services GmbH & Co. KG
Nordwestring 101, 90319 Nuremberg, Germany
anja.schanzenberger@gfk.de

Abstract. Data production systems are generally very large, distributed and complex systems used for creating advanced (mainly statistical) reports. Typically, data is gathered periodically and then subsequently aggregated and separated during numerous production steps. These production steps are arranged in a specific sequence (workflow or production chain), and can be located worldwide. Today, a need for improving and automating methods of supervision for data production systems has been recognised. Supervision in this context entails planning, monitoring and controlling data production. Since there are usually alternate solutions, it makes good sense to consider several approaches. The two most significant approaches are introduced here for improving this supervision, the 'closely coupled –' and the 'loosely coupled approach'. In either situation, dates, costs, resources, and system health information is made available to management, production operators and administrators to support a timely and smooth production of periodic data. Both approaches are theoretically described and compared. The main finding is that both are useful, but in different cases. The main advantages of the 'closely coupled approach' are the large production optimisation potential and a production overview in the form of a job execution plan, whereas the 'loosely coupled approach' mainly supports unhindered job execution without adapting legacy components and offers a sophisticated production overview in form of a milestone schedule. Ideas for further research include investigation of other potential approaches and theoretical and practical comparison.

1 Introduction

This research focuses on effective improvements to automated supervision of distributed data production systems. Two of these enhancements are introduced and compared in this paper. Data production systems are specialised data processing systems. They typically comprise multiple production steps. Their goal is to periodically process and analyse large quantities of data and report pertinent statistics. They are be deployed in such areas as government, administration, market research, and other businesses with an interest in statistical analysis based on periodic data observation. It is important to note that data production is periodic, i.e. data is observed continually. Automated planning takes advantage of this periodic behaviour. The approach to modelling 'goods' production is a useful reference when considering the supervision of data production systems, but there are also some important differences. For example, no parts-lists can be used. Many aggregations and separations of the produced data-packages are normal. Data packages are mixed together or are divided into other data packages and thus are not constant (i.e. changing primary keys). Moreover, there is a need to control the many deviations which are normal at run time in data production. Deviations can arise from the dynamic time scheduling of data (e.g. delayed deliveries), or they can arise out of dynamic changes of input data (statistical principle: different samples can lead to the same statistical result). This report focuses on the supervision and management of data production rather than on the data production techniques themselves. Thus, how the data production process is carried out will only be briefly described. Automated supervision means planning, controlling and monitoring of data production processes to enable all participating contributors (manager, operators and administrators) to control production and provide IT-aided tools for decision support in every production situation.

1.1 A Typical Scenario

The GfK Group is a leading market researcher. GfK Marketing Services [9], one of four main divisions of GfK Group, produces reports from periodical observation of retailers world-wide (e.g. periodic reports concerning competition, demographic evaluation of subsidiaries or product 'hit'-lists). Local branches are available in more than 35 countries. Each country has a branch where the data is collected. GfK MS have established a very large distributed, component-based data production system as in figure 1.

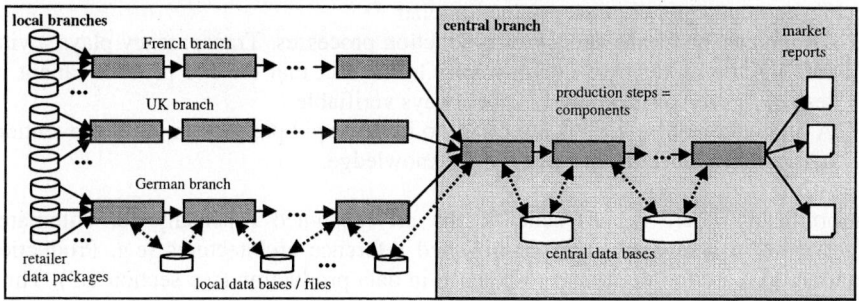

Fig. 1. Simplified Workflow of a Distributed Data Production System

Approximately twenty sequenced components (i.e. production steps) are located in each country's branch. This workflow is continued at the central branch and involves roughly forty additional components to proceed production. Data sources are the roughly 30,000 different data packages per month delivered from an appropriate sample of retailers (ca. 10,000). Several local and central databases serve as storage for the periodically incoming data. Data is gathered, classified and formatted into a GfK internal uniformed format. After transmission to the central branch (ca. 750 GB p.a.) the extrapolation to statistical reports follows (ca. 5000 different report types per month). This extrapolation is accomplished via data warehouse technology and will be briefly described. Although the process begins local, it ends centralised, so that reports can be provided at the international level. All the centralised data and processes are observed and processed by local staff through the use of web based tools. Although the majority of the local operators are just responsible for local reports, some international departments have been established to produce worldwide reports and use local data to do so. There are approximately 10,000 jobs per day involved, whereas a job is defined as processing one single data package (or a data definition package) at one component. The duration time of a job can last from few seconds to several hours. An analysis of GfK's processes demonstrates justification for research into appropriate supervisory methods. Today, the majority of supervision is conducted manually for each production step by permanent polling logs. Production planning is not automated and is prepared manually. Costs, dates and resources are only planned manually and can not be checked. Thus, management has no proven evidence with reference to the optimisation potential of data production. However, for GfK, the conclusion is that continued business success can not be reached sufficiently without automated supervision.

1.2 Aims and Objectives

There are various reasons as to why it is important to introduce automated supervision to data production. The main objectives are:

- To automatically achieve a *measurable* process. This is important for gathering information for calculating operating figures needed in managing data production (e.g. a return of investment, productivity, optimisation potential etc.).
- To automatically obtain a production plan.
- To increase the transparency of production processes. Transparency plays a vital role in data production, due primarily to the fact that the end product cannot be tested. A good or bad report is not always verifiable.
- A high automation level is important to insure rapid production, error prevention, and independence from staff's expert knowledge.

Unfortunately, there is no 'state of the art' designed especially for automated supervision in data production. Established reference architectures (e.g. Production Planning [5]) are too dissimilar to be used in data production (see section 1.3). Thus, diverse self-created, potential system architectures that obtain these objectives have been investigated. The two main approaches are discussed here and their differences are shown through theoretical evaluation by using the following comparison criteria:

- Which reference architecture is used? It is usually recommended to use proven and established reference architectures when searching for a system architecture.
- Which level of supervision is best? For example, appropriate supervision might consider each activity in the data production system or might only deliver aggregated overviews.

- What type of IT-aided supervision is used? Is planning, controlling and monitoring supported in full? Has the approach strengths or weaknesses regarding planning, controlling or monitoring functionalities?
- How is the degree of optimisation reached? Is it achieved manually by staff members who must continuously be engaged in their work or through automation?
- How responsive are the different approaches in relation to production and to supervision? For example, is it possible that data production is delayed through reactively planning methods or is it the other way around? Is the supervision inhibited by too many manual tasks?
- How large is the effort and expenditure to conduct supervision, implement it and to develop the needed user interfaces?
- What types of control is used in an approach? Which parts of it are to be conducted manually and which automated? For example, can each activity have a priority or is activity re-planning the strategy?
- What kind of support is given for organisational levels? (E.g. statistics for management, production overview for operators, etc.)
- Does the approach work with legacy applications?

Through examinations of these comparisons, the advantages or disadvantages of each approach, as well as their most suitable environments, will be discussed.

1.3 Academic Literature Discussion

It should always be a goal to use academic or commercial representations when the intention is to implement a new system architecture. The following methods have been discussed but have all been rejected with preference given to "real-world" implementation in data production.. Nevertheless research has shown that they are all very useful as reference architectures.

Data warehouse technology [10] can be used to extrapolate statistical reports as investigated in [15] for data production (e.g. included in production components), but as the majority of this report focuses on supervision and management of data production, data warehouses will not be considered.

In [5] Production Planning (PPS) and Shop Floor Planning System (SFP) concepts are introduced, but the majority are not notably eligible since they are exclusively made for goods production (e.g. [11]). As previously discussed, data production is not similar enough to these concepts to justify the needed modifications in commercial representatives. Moreover, SFP systems are often made for small to medium sized organisations due to rapidly growing planning problems with high job volumes.

The processing of jobs could be conducted by Job Scheduling Systems (e.g. [7]). However, the question is whether or not such a concept has a chance to evolve its efficiency. The necessary re-synchronisation of the supervisory tool to its plan (after each step), in order to remark delays at once, is not advisable, as this would lead to a loss of performance. Thus, in such a case, job scheduling is not really economical.

Workflow Management [1] and Business Process Management Systems [8] have also been discussed. For instance, in [3] integrated workflow planning is introduced and in [14], workflow instance scheduling with project management tools is investigated. A representation for a workflow management system is distributed by

SAP [13]. However, the underlying concepts usually lack automated supervision except of controlling the data and control flow [1]. A production overview is not sufficiently supported.

Finally, traditional project management [6] includes a project overview, but lacks support for an advanced periodically repeated data production.

2 Supervisory Approaches

Sophisticated approaches appropriate for automated supervision in data production were to be determined. Although some initial drafts have been considered (e.g. a system architecture based on web services can be found in [2] [16] [17], other ideas were to use Petri Nets (e.g. similar to [12]), etc.)), this research shows that there are two key concepts worth serious consideration in real-world systems. These key concepts are introduced here (section 2.1 the 'closely coupled approach', section 2.2 the 'loosely coupled approach'). In both these cases, the same distributed data production system is assumed to be the observation base (i.e. the supervised object that has to be managed).

2.1 Closely Coupled Approach – Shop Floor Planning and Scheduling

This approach is an interesting concept for a close coupling of the jobs to a plan. The plan must be continuously compared with the actual process. The plan can be remodelled through reactive planning if variances are recognized. Strict planning of jobs allows to reach a high optimisation potential. For example, less important jobs can be rescheduled to less production critical times. Only planning enables the estimation of differences between the current states and the planned states within any system. Without a plan, no comparison of objectives is possible except comparisons with former production periods. Additionally, with detailed planning resources can be planned much more accurately.

The System Architecture
Research of related work basically illustrates two tactics for supervising goods production: Production Planning Systems (economic based gross-planning) and Shop Floor Planning (detailed job planning) [5]. Both well-known technologies are role models for the following system architecture (see figure 2).

> A) **Management Information System (MIS) of the Supervisory Tool**
> This user interface offers detailed views into the production processes in form of a MIS and a planning tool. The MIS includes overviews like GANTT and Pert diagrams (e.g. interrelationships and critical paths). Resource management can be conducted. The detailed planning possibilities of Shop Floor Planning allow for the correlation of humans and machines to current orders. This enables the management to plan and to react directly on load and personnel situations. Thus, capacity utilisation can be displayed correctly. As it is not recommended to create fully automatic plans, (e.g. unforeseen events, necessary manual inspection of the

plans, rearrangement of jobs, etc.), the production managers must have a tool to enable reactive planning.

B) Supervisory Tool Functions

The functional level can be divided into segment-oriented and centralized functions. 'Customer orders' are requested reports from customers, and must be completely produced by a defined date. 'Data orders' are derived from customer orders, and contain due dates and information about data which has to be produced to fulfil the customer orders. If data orders are backwards propagated to each process segment, then they can be used to inform former process segments of what data has to be available when. Production operators are responsible for controlling the progress of data orders. Centralised functions are partially automated plan creations and calculation of production status, (difference between plan and current states). Differences are displayed as progress degrees. In addition to data orders, customer orders and data packages can have a progress degree. Resource functions are needed for planning human resources and PC loads

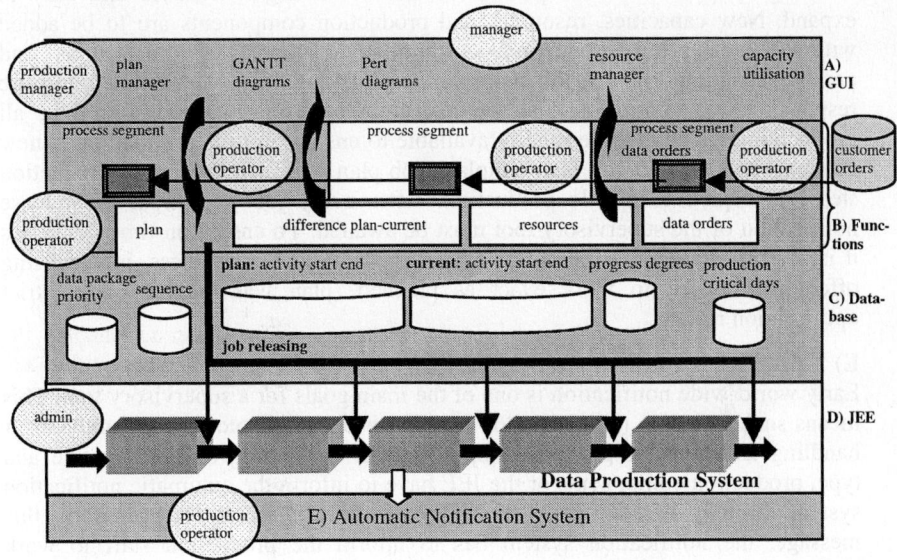

Fig. 2. Supervisory Tool as Shop Floor Planning Combined With Job Scheduling

When using this approach, it is essential that production (as often as possible) will be conducted as planned. Plan-creation must be carefully and accurately arranged to meet optimisation goals. After completing a job, the job execution environment must notify the supervisory tool about its state and duration times. The supervisory tool must then release the next job. This entire process demands coordination and communication between job execution environment and the supervisory tool. If delays or errors are recognised, staff must be notified to change the plan if necessary.

C) The Supervisory Tool's Database

The control information storage is a centralised database where world-wide access can be provided using web technology. Tables are needed for the plan, current states, the data packages and their priorities. These priorities are essentially important to separate high prior jobs from other jobs, and thus effectively enable demand driven production. The flow sequence (workflow definition) is necessary to determine the sequence of events and for job releasing. For calculations of the difference, two pools for planned and current activities are available. Production critical days (days with high work load) can also be monitored and included in planning decisions.

D)   Job Execution Environment - Closely Coupled to the Supervisory Tool
A job execution environment (JEE) administrates and controls the execution of all production steps. It is responsible for a smooth load balancing of resources and considers dependencies between certain jobs. Jobs must run parallel and job execution is thus very dynamic. Production components can be decoupled through using job queuing technology. Dependencies between data packages must be considered to support the special needs in data production. Such an environment has to support different platforms and to use open standards to be able to work with legacy production components. It has to be highly reliable and easy to expand. New capacities, resources and production components are to be added without interrupting production. Additionally, support of transactions and persistence is important. A job history allows tracking the past. Administrators are responsible for controlling the job execution environment, and within it, all production PCs have to be readily available to ensure on-time production. If new data package arrive, a job plan template (job plan = sequence of more production steps) is copied to enable production. After every job execution, the release notification of the supervisory tool must be awaited. To ensure on-time deliveries it is always necessary to avoid delays in production. Nevertheless, job realising offers the chance to work exact as planned (plan was created under strict optimisation rules).

E)   Automatic Notification System
Early world-wide notification is one of the main goals for a supervisory tool. This means such a system (e.g. based on e-mails) is a good choice for proactive error handling and thus for production optimisation. Depending on error source and type, production components or the JEE have to inform the automatic notification system through messaging whenever jobs end with errors. Triggered by this message, the notification system has to inform the production staff to work accordingly and handle the errors.

Beside all of the positive factors contained in this system architecture, there are some disadvantages. In short, criticisms of the closely coupled approach, is the high level of planning effort, the problem to determine strong planning algorithms, (e.g. heuristics, artificial intelligence or operational research algorithms, etc.) [4], a slow down in production, caused by the need for releasing each job and usually an extraordinarily high effort to control workflows (see figure 5).

2.2 Loosely Coupled Approach – The Milestone Architecture

The loosely coupled approach (see figure 3) is a different suggestion to automatically supervise data production. One of the most appealing ideas was to discard plans totally. Not following a plan means there is no need for job releases, and also no need to control the whole workflow. Thus, some of the most significant problems (recognized in the closely coupled approach) can be avoided. However, the absence of traditional and concrete plans inhibits an ideal optimisation of data production, due to the fact that jobs would usually run whenever they came in. Thus, other supervisory mechanisms must be invented to fulfil the requirement for a high-quality production control. Proven traditional project management delivers the guiding ideas for the loosely coupled concept.

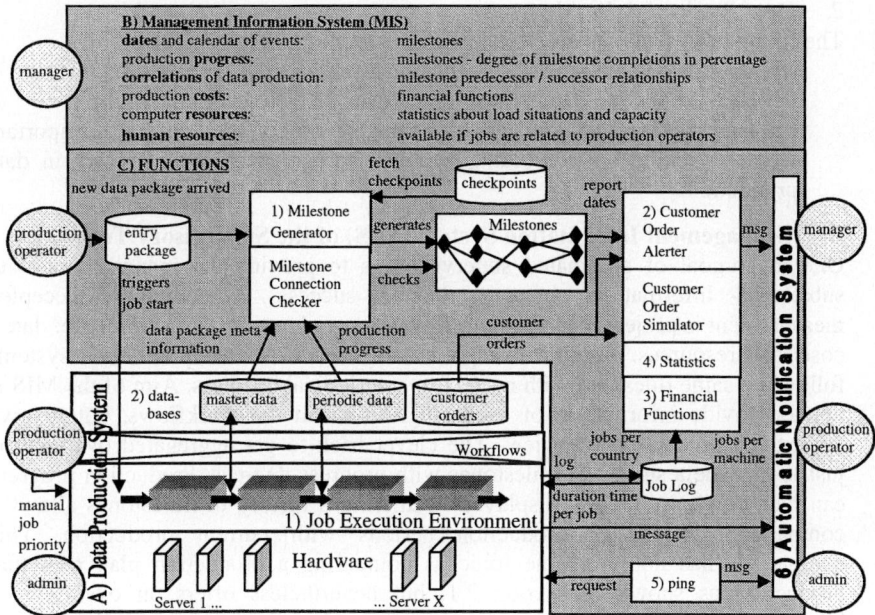

Fig. 3. The Milestone Architecture

A) The Data Production System

The Data Production System consists of production servers, an environment to execute the production processes (job execution environment: JEE) and databases containing all production data. Noticeable is that no workflow level exists within this loosely coupled method. Forwarding of data and executing the next jobs has to be provided totally within the JEE. The JEE works without any connections to the supervisory tool.

1. Job Execution Environment (JEE)

Main focus of the JEE is a well-controlled and reliable job execution. The throughput can only be optimised by working with priorities and load-balancing. However, human intervention is supported through allocation of manual priorities to data packages to enable a faster flow through the production system. For example, the JEE can consist of message queues where jobs are inserted to wait for their execution. It has to support different platforms and to use open standards to be able to work with legacy production components. New capacities, resources and production components are to be added without interrupting production. Additionally, support of transactions and persistence is important. A job history allows tracking the past. Duration times of jobs have to be logged to support clues for future production cycles and evaluation of load situations. Moreover, in case of components which need interactions, the assignment of human resources could be gathered and thus considered. The JEE has also to cope with controlling the health of the production system (e.g. recognising hanging components). Errors in job execution have to be reported immediately to the automatic notification system to inform production operators early.

2. *Data Production Databases*

The following data types are needed for data production in general.
- Master data: Reference data for information about the observed data.
- Periodic production data: All observed data delivered periodically.
- Customer orders: Due dates of customer orders are the most important elements to meet for avoiding penalties and unsatisfied customers in data production.

B) Management Information System (MIS) of the Supervisory Tool

One main goal of automated supervision is to provide the management with substantial information about production success. A commonly accepted measurement is project management. Key points to be controlled with it are: dates, costs and resources. Without exception, supervision of data production systems follow the same rules, but with respect to a periodical business. Aim of the MIS is not to provide information of each single job and the workflows, but to give aggregated production overview. The clever trick to get aggregated overview is just to provide a survey of milestones with progress degrees. Production progress can then be measured and displayed. Gathering a history of milestones allows a comparison of former production periods with current production. This comparison has not the same force as comparing a production plan to actual production as shown in section 2.1, but nevertheless offers an overview of historical operational development regarding duration times and throughput. Moreover, a look-ahead of milestones can predict the production situation in the near future. Other important benchmark data are costs, which can be calculated exactly by assessing the job log. Thus all jobs have to be logged, analysed and summarised through appropriate financial functions. The history of jobs is also the basis for statistics about resources, load situations, capacities, bottlenecks or production critical days. Summarised, the MIS offers the management a well-founded base for decisions.

C) Supervisory Tool Functions

1. *Milestone Module*

A popular and well established tool for project management are milestones. Traditional milestones are activities with no duration time, but with a due date. Milestones for data production have to be enriched with data content information and a progress degree. Data content can be distinctly differentiated through its primary keys. Content-oriented milestones thus deliver status information about production. To simplify the implementation, checkpoints are introduced. They represent the different points of interest in the production process and are templates for the content-oriented milestones. All production data must pass these checkpoints. The checkpoints as well as the milestones have predecessor-successor relationships. They form a directed acyclic graph and can thus easily be mapped and stored in a database. This enables displaying content-based relationships based on time-oriented milestones states. Current production situations ('what' is produced now, and how is the progress), can be easily supervised. Information about 'what' is produced 'when' can be estimated by creating milestones with look-ahead. The look-ahead can be created if the times between related milestones are gathered. The milestone history can then be used to estimate the milestones due dates in future. Milestones can be created automatically if the event of a new data packages arrives at the systems entrance is recognised. A look-ahead can be created if planned dates of arriving data packages are gathered.

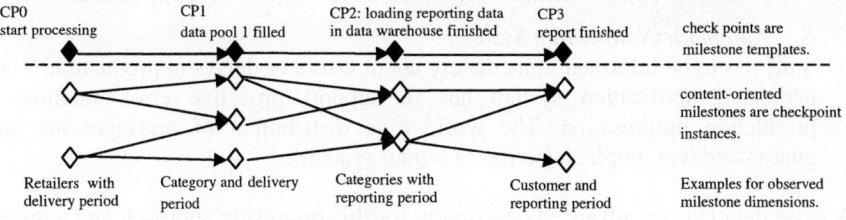

Fig. 4. Simplified Example of Content-oriented Milestones

Figure 4 shows the checkpoints and their instantiated milestones. Each milestone consists of observed dimensions (i.e. its primary keys). At Checkpoint CP0, two milestones are shown. Since Checkpoint 0 has two dimensions (retailer and delivery period), one milestone could be, for example, 'Dixons Jan2004' and the other 'Marks & Spencers Jan2004'. Both would then have one common predecessor at checkpoint level CP1 since both retailers would have provided data for the category 'Color TVs' and for the delivery period 'Jan2004'. If it were now assumed that the category 'Color TVs' must be reported bimonthly, the reporting period, a dimension of checkpoint 2, would then be 'Jan-Feb2004'. Then, after extrapolation in CP3, the end product 'statistical report over Colour TVs' would be delivered to a Customer (e.g. 'Sony') based on the reporting period 'Jan-Feb2004'. Since all milestones have due dates and progress states, production operators can be informed about content, delays, and the progress in their data production.

2. Customer Order Tools

Warnings of current upcoming customer orders given from an alerter could help to identify production critical data. Recognising delayed or critical data early allows timely to increase the priorities of the implicated jobs to fasten the production process. Often it is difficult for management to answer questions about the customer order coverage. A simulator based on information of former production cycles can be set up for this estimation.

3. Financial Functions
For calculating production costs financial functions based on the job log are useful. Costs can be divided per participating segments, departments or countries to fulfil the requirements of a smart accounting. Additionally, taking job priorities and quantity of jobs into account for cost calculation increases the fairness of accounting and the explanatory power of the calculated total.

4. Statistics
A job log is the history of all processed jobs. The benefit of a job log is the possibility to analyse the production process in detail. For example, especially Business Process Management System vendors offer often functionalities to query exactly those process logs [8]. Identified benefits are the possibilities to track operations, to detect inefficiencies and thus to gain business insights. For surveying production in detail, those analyses are essentially important.

5. Hardware Surveillance
Surveillance of system health is essential to keep production processes alive. Hardware surveillance means to control PCs (ping) and network reliability.

6. Automatic Notification System
Staff has to be informed immediately about errors or delays in production. Thus, a dedicated notification system has to support proactive error handling and production optimisation. The world-wide distribution of messages has to be guaranteed (e.g. implementation as e-mail system).

A more detailed and advanced description for this promising approach and a report of ongoing work can be found in [18].

3 Early Experiments and Implementation Results

This report deals with the adoption and customisation of data production rather than with the usage and comparison of the role models since these are discussed in detail in the literature PPS [5], WFMS [1], Project Management [6], etc. Until now, there has been no detailed investigation into the consequences and effects of supervising data production. One must cope with problems such as changing primary keys, immense volumes of distributed data and jobs, tracking the manifold aggregations and separations, and the frequent instability of the data packages. All these problems are not fully dealt with if one uses the traditional role models.

Due to the immenseness of data production systems, the enormous effort involved in establishing automated supervision, and the restrictions imposed on the resources available for implementation, the decision was made to concentrate only on one of the architectural approaches rather than prototyping them both. Today, GfK Marketing Services, have started to implement the loosely-coupled approach due to their large data production system with countless deviations. The initial results are discussed as follows:

- Milestones are created automatically when new data packages arrive (i.e. semi automation). As data entrances are distributed, messages associated with data

package arrivals are sent to the centrally located milestone database. Thus, the supervision information is centralised in order to give all participants the same state information (e.g. important for gaining international reports).
- GANTT or Pert diagrams were deemed to be insufficient in the case of low data aggregation because the numerous correlations that exist between the data packages prohibit a quick and accurate overview from being produced. High data aggregations do not lend themselves to exactness and explanatory power (e.g. a traffic-light is always yellow, but never green or red).
- An interactive management system for milestones was generated. The interface displays a list of milestones all belonging to a single checkpoint-level. The trick to keep the overview is, only one milestone can be selected at any one time and the predecessors and successors of the selected milestone are shown in accompanying lists. These predecessors and successors can be, in turn, selected, so that their corresponding predecessors and successors can be viewed, and so on. This enables very fast navigation throughout the milestone chain.
- Production operators cannot work without planned due dates. Thus, each Milestone has a planned due date and a history due date (which is the average of the last X pre-periods). In order to determine planned due dates, a Due Date Editor was developed, whereby due date rules that are specific to particular milestones can be managed.
- Since data production is ever changing (e.g. deviations), generating connections between milestones cannot simply be done once. Thus, milestone connections were divided into 'planned' (these are based on the connections in the last X pre-periods) and 'latest' connections, which are the actual connections.
- The arrival of new data packages (which triggers milestone generation), milestone states (e.g. complete or incomplete) and the connections between milestones are checked at regular intervals, in order to keep information up-to-date.
- So as to reduce the number of emails sent via the automatic notification tool, responsibilities were clearly set and how one reacts to an error message was clearly defined.

4 Conclusion – Comparing Both Approaches

The complexity and possible varieties of data production systems has a likely consequence that there will never be only one single correct solution for automated supervision. Industry is extremely multi-faceted. The study of all reference architectures, the study of automated supervision for data production systems and early experiments made with the discussed approaches shows that theoretical research is very useful towards informative categorisation of high-quality approaches (see figure 5).

Category	Closely Coupled Approach – Shop Floor Planning Architecture	Loosely Coupled Approach – Milestone Architecture
basis (role-model)	Production planning systems - Supervisory tool is strongly coupled to Job Execution Environment	Project management - Supervisory tool is NOT coupled to Job Execution Environment
level of supervision	Lowest level of surveillance (job level); Needs a lot of control data;	Aggregated level of surveillance (milestones): detailed job information is

Category	Closely Coupled Approach – Shop Floor Planning Architecture	Loosely Coupled Approach – Milestone Architecture
	Delivers exact data for surveillance;	not used for heavy surveillance; Needs less control data than closely coupled approach; Delivers inexact data for surveillance because of aggregation;
type of IT-aided supervision		
degree and type of planning	(high) Creation of production plans; Comparing plan with actual production; Comparing former production periods; Backwards propagated Data orders;	(medium) Creating a look-ahead of milestones; Comparing former production periods Look-ahead of Milestones
type of monitoring	Planned activities – current activities and history; Progress degrees of activities;	Job log; milestone history (including progress degrees);
type of controlling	Planning tool (part manual, part automated planning); Planning and replanning of activities; Deadline surveillance: data orders, plan of activities and customer order alerter; Setting breakpoints depends on support in the Job Execution Environment; Resource management Capacity management	Automated look-ahead creation of milestones; Changing job priorities (within the JEE); Deadline surveillance: milestone due dates and customer order alerter; Setting breakpoints depends on support in the Job Execution Environment; Resource monitoring Capacity monitoring
degree of optimisation	(very high) Every single job can be optimally planned; no bottlenecks;	(medium) Jobs are processed with priorities; sometimes bottlenecks;
manual	A lot of work time for reactive planning must be invested;	Adjustment of job priorities: less work time must be invested;
automated	(less) Problem with good optimisation algorithms (can be an NP-hard Problem)	(high) Jobs are processed with priorities
Responsiveness		
of production	Delays through resource conflicts - reactive planning is needed; Automated releasing jobs can cause delays; High communication effort between supervisory tool and data production system;	No delays in production due to supervision;
of supervision	Exhausting manual planning may cause delays	No delays in production due to supervision;
Effort and expenditure		
to conduct supervision	A planner is permanently occupied with planning; Future and past resource bottlenecks are identifiable through provable plans; Just interventions if problems occur; Permanent checking management overviews;	A production operator can change job priorities if needed exceptional; Only past resource problems are identifiable, due to check functions only assess current situations (no plans); Just interventions if problems occur; Permanent checking management overviews;
of concept implementation	A plan manager software is needed: effort high; workflows have to be considered: effort high;	No planning software is needed: effort low; No workflows: effort low;
GUIs	All GUIs must be aggregated views; A drill-down to job level is possible;	Less aggregation effort due to milestones are aggregated; Drill-down to job level is not possible;
Contingent and type of control		
manual control	Re-planning; Reaction on automatic notifications; Setting breakpoints if supported;	Changing job priorities exceptional; Reaction on automatic notifications; Setting breakpoints if supported;
automated control	Plan creation; Comparison plan-current production; Comparison former production periods;	Creation of Milestones with look-ahead; Anticipating job aging through changing job priorities;

Category	Closely Coupled Approach – Shop Floor Planning Architecture	Loosely Coupled Approach – Milestone Architecture
	Statistics;	Comparison former production periods; Statistics;
Support for organisational levels		
management	Plan, Gantt-Pert diagrams, resource and capacity manager, customer order alerter and simulator, financial functions, statistics;	Milestones, resource and capacity monitoring, customer order alerter and simulator, financial functions and statistics (logged by JEE);
production operators	Plan, automatic notification	Milestones, automatic notification
administrators	Ping	Ping (logged by JEE)
management	Plan, Gantt-Pert diagrams, resource and capacity manager, customer order alerter and simulator, financial functions, statistics;	Milestones, resource and capacity monitoring, customer order alerter and simulator, financial functions and statistics (logged by JEE);
Works without changing legacy applications	no	yes

Fig. 5. Categorisation of Automated Supervision Approaches

The summarised conclusions which can be derived from the described research results can be found in figure 6.

Conclusion	Closely Coupled Approach – Shop Floor Planning Architecture	Loosely Coupled Approach – Milestone Architecture
Main advantages	Very high optimisation potential; Differences in plan – current production; Future resource problems identifiable; Oriented at proven production planning systems;	Not workflow oriented – easy to implement; freely acting job execution environment; Oriented at proven project management
Main disadvantages	Workflow orientation to strong: supervisory tool must have knowledge about the production sequence; critic on excessive planning; implementation and execution effort for data production is high (e.g. finding robust planning algorithms and communication between supervisory tool and data production system)	Optimisation potential not as big as with close coupled approach; Future resource problems not identifiable;
Recommended for	Small to medium-sized data production systems, with a small number of data packages and few deviations; For data production with strongly restricted resources;	Large-sized data production systems, with a high number of data packages and many deviations; Data Production where optional data deliveries are allowed. For data production with tolerably restricted resources;

Fig. 6. Comparison of Automated Supervision for Data Production

Finally, as discussed in section 3, it is not possible to implement all approaches and ideas in the near future. Nevertheless, future work for this research will continue to be prototyped using the loosely-coupled approach. More information of the ongoing work can be found in [18]. The experiments made with the prototype are still in their infancy, but look promising. Thousands of dynamic jobs can presently be handled through the job execution environment without problems and the milestone database is already filled with a first half year of production data. Currently, the initial users are becoming familiar with the new supervisory tools. Their experiences with the system will ultimately affect the initial concepts. Through gathering information related to their experiences, the outcomes can be refined, evaluated and categorised for this most promising approach. Based on the milestone database it is expected to provide additional and more aggregated production meta information for higher management, to calculate and evaluate the return of investment of data production.

References

1. Frank Leymann, Dieter Roller: Production Workflow - Concepts and Techniques. Prentice Hall, New Jersey (2000).
2. Anja Schanzenberger, D.R.Lawrence: A Web Service Based Approach to Monitor and Control a Distributed Component Execution Environment. EuroMedia-WEBTEC Conference 2003, Plymouth, (2003)
3. Hilmar Schuschel, Mathias Weske: Integrated Workflow Planning and Coordination. DEXA 2003, Lecture Notes in Computer Science, Vol. 2736, Ed. V.Markik, W.Retschitzegger, O.Stepankova, Springer-Verlag, Berlin Heidelberg New York (2003)
4. eter Brucker: Scheduling Algorithms, Third Edition, Springer-Verlag, Berlin Heidelberg New York (2001)
5. K. Kurbel: Produktionsplanung und –steuerung, Methodische Grundlagen von PPS-Systemen und Erweiterungen. 5.Ed., Oldenburg Verlag München Wien (2003)
6. Walker Royce, Software Project Management - A unified framework. Addison Wesley Professional (1998)
7. UC4: UC4 global - job scheduling system. [Online], http://www.uc4.com, [2.Nov.2003]
8. F. Casati, M. Shan: Semantic Analysis of Business Process Executions. Lecture Notes in Computer Science, Vol. 2287, Ed. C.S. Jensen et al., EDBT 2002, Springer-Verlag, Berlin Heidelberg New York (2002)
9. GfK Marketing Services: [Online], http://www.gfkms.com, [2004, Jun., 15]
10. Lusti, Markus: Data Warehousing und Data Mining. Sec. Ed., Springer-Verlag, Berlin Heidelberg New York, Springer-Lehrbuch (2001)
11. Chin-Yin Huang: Distributed manufacturing execution systems: A workflow perspective. Journal of Intelligent Manufacturing, Vol. 13, 485-497, Kluwer Academic Publishers Netherland (2002)
12. H.M.W. Verbeek, T.Basten, W.M.P van der Aalst: Diagnosing Workflow Processes using Woflan. The Computer Journal, Vol.44, No.4. BCS The British Computer Society (2001)
13. SAP AG: R/3. [Online]: http://www.sap.de, [2003, Jul., 02]
14. Christoph Bussler: Workflow Instance Scheduling with Project Management Tools. Database and Expert Systems Applications, Proceedings 9th. Int. Workshop IEEE, 753-758, IEEE Press (1998)
15. Jens Albrecht, Wolfgang Lehner, Michael Teschke, Thomas Kirsche: Building a Real Data Warehouse for Market Research. Database and Expert Systems Applications, Proceedings 8.th Int. Workshop IEEE, 651-656. IEEE Press (1997)
16. Anja Schanzenberger, Colin Tully, Dave R. Lawrence: Ueberwachung von Aggregationszustaenden in verteilten komponentenbasierten Datenproduktionssystemen. BTW 2003: 10th Conference on Database Systems for Business, Technology and Web. Ed. G. Weikum et. al. GI-Editon, Lecture Notes in Informatics, 544 -558, Koelln Druck+Verlag GmbH Bonn (2003)
17. Anja Schanzenberger, Wolfgang Lehner: Einsatz von WebServices in daten-intensiven Umgegungen. Gesellschaft für Informatik FG 2.5.2, Workshop: Entwicklung von Anwendungen auf der Basis der XML Web-Service Technologie (2002)
18. Anja Schanzenberger, Dave Lawrence: E-Project Management in Data Production. working paper, [Available]: anja.schanzenberger@gfk.de, (2004)

Deriving Sub-schema Similarities from Semantically Heterogeneous XML Sources

Pasquale De Meo[1], Giovanni Quattrone[1],
Giorgio Terracina[2], and Domenico Ursino[1]*

[1] DIMET, Università Mediterranea di Reggio Calabria, Via Graziella,
Località Feo di Vito, 89060 Reggio Calabria, Italy,
[2] Dipartimento di Matematica, Università della Calabria, Via Pietro Bucci,
87036 Rende (CS), Italy
{demeo, quattrone}@ing.unirc.it
terracina@mat.unical.it, ursino@unirc.it

Abstract. In this paper we propose a semi-automatic technique for deriving similarities between XML sub-schemas. The proposed technique is specific for XML, almost automatic and light. It consists of two phases: the former one selects the most promising pairs of sub-schemas; the latter one examines them and returns only the similar ones. In the paper we discuss some possible applications that can benefit of derived sub-schema similarities and we illustrate some experiments we have conducted for testing the validity of our approach. Finally, a comparison of the proposed approach with some related ones already presented in the literature, as well as a real example case aiming at better clarifying it, are presented.

1 Introduction

The derivation of semantic mappings among concepts of different sources is becoming a challenging issue in the field of Information Systems; as a matter of fact, their knowledge allows the improvement of source interoperability and plays a key role in various applications, such as source integration, ontology matching, e-commerce, semantic query processing, data warehouse, source clustering and cataloguing, and so on.

In the past, most of the proposed approaches for deriving mappings were manual [1]; nowadays, due to the enormous number of available sources, it is widely recognized the need of semi-automatic techniques [2,3,9,10,13]. Moreover, most of the mapping derivation theory has been *developed to operate on databases* [16] and the main focus has been on deriving similarities and dissimilarities between *single classes of objects* (e.g., two entities, two relationships, an entity and a relationship, and so on).

However, nowadays, the Web is becoming the reference infrastructure for many applications conceived to handle the partner interoperability. Web sources

---
* Corresponding author

are quite different from databases, since they are semi-structured. In the last years, in order to make Web activities easier, World Wide Web Consortium (W3C) proposed XML (eXtensible Markup Language) as a new standard information exchange language, that unifies representation capabilities, typical of HTML, and data management features, typical of classical DBMS. In order to improve the capability of representing and handling the intensional component of XML sources, W3C proposed to associate XML Schemas with XML documents. An XML Schema can be considered as a catalogue of the information that can be found in the corresponding XML documents.

The exploitation of the semi-structured paradigm in general, and of XML in particular, makes it evident the necessity to develop new approaches for deriving semantic mappings; these approaches are quite different from the traditional ones. As a matter of fact, in semi-structured information sources, a concept is not generally expressed by a single class of objects but it is represented by a group of them; as an example, in XML, concepts are expressed by elements which can be, in their turn, described by sub-elements. In such a situation, the emphasis shifts away from the extraction of semantic *correspondences between object classes* to the derivation of semantic *correspondences between groups of object classes*, each being, in practice, a little portion of information source (i.e., a little sub-source). As an example, consider two XML Schemas S_1 and S_2, storing tourist information. Assume that S_1 contains an element hotel whereas S_2 stores the three elements boarding_house, youth_hostel and bed_&_breakfast. A classic schema mapping approach does not derive any similarity among these elements because neither boarding_house nor youth_hostel nor bed_&_breakfast are similar with hotel. However, it is possible to recognize a similarity between the element hotel and the group of elements boarding_house, youth_hostel and bed_&_breakfast and this is a similarity between portions of schemas, i.e., a sub-schema similarity. This clearly shows that the sub-schema similarity extraction problem goes beyond the classic schema mapping derivation problem and allows more refined results to be obtained. Generalizing this line of reasoning, it is also interesting to analyze semantic correspondences holding amongst larger portions of information sources.

This paper aims at providing a contribution in this setting; indeed, it presents a technique for extracting similarities between XML sub-schemas, i.e., portions of semantically heterogenous XML Schemas. Our approach is characterized by the following features:

- *It is almost automatic*, in that it requires the user intervention only for validating obtained results; the present overwhelming amount of available information sources on the Web makes such a feature particularly relevant.
- *It has been specifically conceived for operating on XML Schemas*; with regard to this, we point out that XML source interoperability will play a more and more relevant role in the future; as a consequence, it will be more and more common the necessity to handle the interoperability of a group of information sources that are all XML-based. In this particular application context, the exploitation of generic approaches, designed to operate on information

sources with different formats, is unnecessarily expensive; indeed, these approaches generally translate all involved information sources into a common format and, only after, perform the interoperability management activities. In addition, they have not been designed to exploit the specificities of the XML language.
– *It is light*, since it does not exploit any threshold or weight; as a consequence, it does not need any tuning activity; in spite of this, obtained results are satisfactory, as pointed out in Section 4.

Our approach assumes the existence of an *Interschema Property Dictionary* (IPD), i.e., a catalogue storing relationships between concepts represented in the involved XML Schemas. More specifically, it assumes that IPD stores the following properties: *(i) Synonymies*: a synonymy indicates that two concepts have the same meaning; *(ii) Hyponymies/Hypernymies*: given two concepts c_1 and c_2, c_1 is a hyponym of c_2 (which is, in its turn, the hypernym of c_1) if c_1 has a more specific meaning than c_2; *(iii) Overlappings*: an overlapping exists between two concepts if they are neither synonyms nor one hyponym of the other but share a non-empty set of properties.

In the literature, many approaches for deriving synonymies, hyponymies and overlappings have been proposed (see, for example, [2,3,9,10,13]); any of them could be exploited for constructing IPD. However, in our experiments, we have adopted the synonymy derivation approach proposed in [4] and the hyponymy and overlapping extraction technique illustrated in [5]. The reason of these choices is that these techniques have the same features and adopt the same philosophy as the approach we are describing here. In our opinion this fact is particularly important because, in the whole, we obtain a *unified*, almost automatic, XML-specific and light approach for deriving similarities and dissimilarities among concepts and groups of concepts represented in a set of semantically heterogeneous XML Schemas. In our opinion this fact is extremely interesting because: *(i)* we are proposing an approach for deriving a property typology (i.e., sub-schema similarity) which is seldom considered by approaches proposed in the literature (which, often, aim at deriving similarities and dissimilarities between *single concepts*); *(ii)* the approach proposed here is part of a more general framework whose purpose is the *uniform derivation* of various kinds of terminological and structural properties (namely synonymies, homonymies, hyponymies, overlappings between single concepts and similarities between sub-schemas). It is worth pointing out that the exploitation of IPD does not introduce scalability problems; indeed, even if IPD must be computed for each pairs of schemas into consideration, the worst case time complexity of its derivation is smaller than that relative to the extraction of sub-schema similarities (see [4,5] and Theorems 2, 4 and 5)

Given an XML Schema, the number of possible sub-schemas that could be derived from it is exponential against the number of its elements and attributes. In order to avoid huge numbers of sub-schema pairs to be handled, we propose a heuristic technique for singling out only the most promising ones. A pair of sub-schemas is considered "promising" if the sub-schemas at hand include a large number of pairs of concepts whose similarity has been already stated (i.e., a large number of pairs of concepts for which a synonymy, an hyponymy or an overlapping has been already derived). In this way it is probable that the overall similarity of the promising pair of sub-schemas will be high. After that the most promising pairs of sub-schemas have been selected, they must be examined for detecting those ones that are really similar.

The similarity degree relative to each pair of sub-schemas is determined by applying suitable functions associated with matchings defined on a suitable bipartite graph, constructed from the components of the sub-schemas of the pair (see below). The idea underlying the adoption of graph matching algorithms as the core step for "measuring" the similarity of two sub-schemas is motivated by the following reasoning: two sub-schemas can be detected to be similar only if it is possible to verify that, for many of their elements, there exists a form of similarity (e.g., a synonymy, a hyponymy or an overlapping). The graph matching algorithm is, thus, used to carry out such a verification.

This paper is to be considered as a part of a more complex research effort on the extraction and the exploitation of intensional knowledge from heterogeneous sources that we are conducting from several years. The main contributions of the approach presented in this paper to this research framework are: *(i)* it is specific for XML sources whereas the other sub-schema similarity extraction approaches we have proposed in the past were generic; *(ii)* it focuses on sub-schema similarities whereas the other approaches specific for XML we have proposed in the past considered only the derivation of synonymies, homonymies, hyponymies and overlappings between *single objects*.

2 Preliminaries

In this section we introduce some preliminary concepts that will be exploited in our approach. The first of them is the concept of x-component that allows both elements and attributes of an XML document to be uniformly handled.

Let S be an XML Schema; an *x-component* of S is either an element or an attribute of S. An x-component is characterized by its name, its typology (indicating if it is either a simple element, a complex element or an attribute) and its data type. The set of x-components of S is denoted as $XCompSet(S)$.

We introduce now some boolean functions that allow the strength of the relationship existing between two x-components x_S and x_T of an XML Schema S to be determined. These functions are:

- *veryclose*(x_S, x_T), that returns *true* if and only if: *(i)* $x_T = x_S$, or *(ii)* x_T is an attribute of x_S, or *(iii)* x_T is a simple sub-element of x_S. In all the other cases it returns *false*.
- *close*(x_S, x_T), that returns *true* if and only if x_T is a complex sub-element of x_S. In all the other cases it returns *false*.
- *near*(x_S, x_T), that returns *true* if and only if either *veryclose*$(x_S, x_T) = true$ or *close*$(x_S, x_T) = true$. In all the other cases it returns *false*.

– $reachable(x_S, x_T)$, that returns $true$ if and only if there exists a sequence of k $distinct$ x-components $x_1, x_2, \ldots, x_k$ such that $x_S = x_1, near(x_1, x_2) = near(x_2, x_3) = \ldots = near(x_{k-1}, x_k) = true, x_k = x_T$. In all the other cases it returns $false$.

We are now able to introduce the concept of $connection\ cost$ from an x-component x_S to an x-component x_T. It is denoted by $CC(x_S, x_T)$ and is defined as:

$$CC(x_S, x_T) = \begin{cases} 0 & \text{if } veryclose(x_S, x_T) = true \\ 1 & \text{if } close(x_S, x_T) = true \\ \mathcal{C}_{ST} & \text{if } reachable(x_S, x_T) = true \text{ and } near(x_S, x_T) = false \\ +\infty & \text{if } reachable(x_S, x_T) = false \end{cases}$$

Here $\mathcal{C}_{ST} = min_{x_A}(CC(x_S, x_A) + CC(x_A, x_T))$ for each x_A such that $reachable(x_S, x_A) = reachable(x_A, x_T) = true$.

The next proposition provides an estimation of the maximum value the connection cost from x_S to x_T can assume, if it is finite. Due to space constraints we cannot show here the proof of the propositions and theorems we present in this paper; the interested reader can find them at the address:
http://www.mat.unical.it/terracina/coopis2004/proofs.pdf.

Proposition 1. Let S be an XML Schema; let x_S and x_T be two x-components of S; let m be the number of complex elements of S. If $CC(x_S, x_T) \neq +\infty$, then $CC(x_S, x_T) < m$. □

We now introduce the concept of neighborhood of an x-component. This concept plays a key role in our approach.

Definition 1. Let S be an XML Schema and let x_S be an x-component of S. The dth $neighborhood$ of x_S is defined as:

$$nbh(x_S, d) = \{x_T |\ x_T \in XCompSet(S), CC(x_S, x_T) \leq d\} \qquad \square$$

Proposition 2. Let S be an XML Schema; let x_S be an x-component of S; let m be the number of complex elements of S; then $nbh(x_S, d) = nbh(x_S, m-1)$ for each d such that $d \geq m$. □

We call $significant\ neighborhoods$ of x_S all neighborhoods $nbh(x_S, d)$ such that $nbh(x_S, d) \neq nbh(x_S, d-1)$.

The following theorem states the worst case computational complexity for deriving all neighborhoods of all x-components in an XML Schema S.

Theorem 1. Let S be an XML Schema; let n be the number of x-components of S. The worst case time complexity for constructing all neighborhoods of all x-components of S is $O(n^3)$. □

Theorem 1 is particularly important since it guarantees that our approach is polynomial (see, below, Theorems 2 and 4). It could appear that a polynomial complexity to the degree of three for neighborhood derivation causes scalability problems for the whole approach. Actually, this is not the case. Indeed, in an XML source exploited as a database, the intensional component (i.e., the XML Schema) is generally much smaller than the extensional one (i.e., the XML document); as a consequence, the number of involved x-components (i.e., n) is generally very small. Moreover, the derivation of the neighborhoods of a Schema S must be carried out once and for all when S is examined for the first time; derived neighborhoods can be, then, exploited each time a sub-schema similarity extraction task involving S is performed. Only a change in the intensional component of S requires to update the corresponding neighborhoods; such a task, however, is infrequent and, in any case, it does not imply to re-compute, but simply to incrementally update, them.

A case example. Consider the XML Schema S_1, shown in Figure 1, representing a university. Here *professor* is an x-component and its typology is "complex element" since it is a `complexType` element. Analogously *identifier* is an x-component, its typology is "attribute" and its data type is ID.

In S_1, $veryclose(professor, identifier) = true$ because *identifier* is an attribute of *professor*; analogously, $close(university, professor) = true$ because *professor* is a complex sub-element of *university*. Moreover, we have that $near(professor, identifier) = true$ because $veryclose(professor, identifier) = true$; finally, $reachable(university, identifier) = true$ because $near(university, professor) = true$ and $near(professor, identifier) = true$. As for neighborhoods, we have that:

$nbh(university, 1) = \{university,$ *professor, phd-student, paper, course, student, identifier, name, cultural_area, courses, papers, advisor, thesis, authors, research_interests, type, volumes, pages, argument, duration, attended_by, program, teached_by, students, enrollment_year, attends*$\}$

For instance, *professor* belongs to *neighborhood(university, 1)* because $CC(university, professor) = 1$. All the other neighborhoods can be determined analogously.

3 Approach Description

3.1 Selection of the Most Promising Sub-schemas

Overview. The first problem our approach must face is the extremely high number of possible sub-schemas that could be derived from an XML Schema S; this number, indeed, is exponential against the number of x-components of S.

In order to avoid huge numbers of pairs of sub-schemas to be examined, we have designed a heuristic technique for singling out only the most promising ones. This technique receives two XML Schemas S_1 and S_2 and a Dictionary IPD of Interschema Properties relating complex elements of S_1 and S_2. Interschema Properties it considers are synonymies, hyponymies and overlappings.

```xml
<?xml version="1.0" encoding="UTF-8"?>
<xs:schema xmlns:xs="http://www.w3.org/2001/XMLSchema">
    <!-- Decaration of attributes -->
    <xs:attribute name="identifier" type="xs:ID"/>
    <xs:attribute name="name" type="xs:string"/>
    <xs:attribute name="cultural_area" type="xs:string"/>
    <xs:attribute name="courses" type="xs:IDREFS"/>
    <xs:attribute name="papers" type="xs:IDREFS"/>
    <xs:attribute name="advisor" type="xs:IDREF"/>
    <xs:attribute name="thesis" type="xs:string"/>
    <xs:attribute name="research_interests" type="xs:string"/>
    <xs:attribute name="authors" type="xs:IDREFS"/>
    <xs:attribute name="type" type="xs:string"/>
    <xs:attribute name="volumes" type="xs:integer"/>
    <xs:attribute name="pages" type="xs:integer"/>
    <xs:attribute name="argument" type="xs:string"/>
    <xs:attribute name="duration" type="xs:duration"/>
    <xs:attribute name="attended_by" type="xs:IDREFS"/>
    <xs:attribute name="teached_by" type="xs:IDREFS"/>
    <xs:attribute name="program" type="xs:string"/>
    <xs:attribute name="students" type="xs:IDREFS"/>
    <xs:attribute name="enrollment_year" type="xs:date"/>
    <xs:attribute name="attends" type="xs:IDREFS"/>
    <xs:element name="professor">
        <xs:complexType>
            <xs:attribute ref="identifier"/>
            <xs:attribute ref="name"/>
            <xs:attribute ref="cultural_area"/>
            <xs:attribute ref="courses"/>
            <xs:attribute ref="papers"/>
        </xs:complexType>
    </xs:element>
    <xs:element name="phd-student">
        <xs:complexType>
            <xs:attribute ref="identifier"/>
            <xs:attribute ref="advisor"/>
            <xs:attribute ref="thesis"/>
            <xs:attribute ref="research_interests"/>
            <xs:attribute ref="papers"/>
        </xs:complexType>
    </xs:element>
    <xs:element name="paper">
        <xs:complexType>
            <xs:attribute ref="identifier"/>
            <xs:attribute ref="authors"/>
            <xs:attribute ref="type"/>
            <xs:attribute ref="volumes"/>
            <xs:attribute ref="pages"/>
        </xs:complexType>
    </xs:element>
    <xs:element name="course">
        <xs:complexType>
            <xs:attribute ref="identifier"/>
            <xs:attribute ref="name"/>
            <xs:attribute ref="argument"/>
            <xs:attribute ref="duration"/>
            <xs:attribute ref="attended_by"/>
            <xs:attribute ref="teached_by"/>
            <xs:attribute ref="program"/>
            <xs:attribute ref="students"/>
        </xs:complexType>
    </xs:element>
    <xs:element name="student">
        <xs:complexType>
            <xs:attribute ref="identifier"/>
            <xs:attribute ref="name"/>
            <xs:attribute ref="enrollment_year"/>
            <xs:attribute ref="attends"/>
        </xs:complexType>
    </xs:element>
    <!-- Decaration of root -->
    <xs:element name="university">
        <xs:complexType>
            <xs:sequence>
                <xs:element ref="professor" maxOccurs="unbounded"/>
                <xs:element ref="phd-student" maxOccurs="unbounded"/>
                <xs:element ref="paper" maxOccurs="unbounded"/>
                <xs:element ref="course" maxOccurs="unbounded"/>
                <xs:element ref="student" maxOccurs="unbounded"/>
            </xs:sequence>
        </xs:complexType>
    </xs:element>
</xs:schema>
```

Fig. 1. The XML Schema S_1

The most promising pairs of sub-schemas are derived as follows: for each tuple $\langle x_{1_j}, x_{2_k} \rangle \in IPD$, such that $x_{1_j} \in S_1$ and $x_{2_k} \in S_2$, x_{1_j} and x_{2_k} are taken as the "seeds" for the construction of the most promising pairs of sub-schemas. More specifically, our technique:

- considers all pairs $\langle nbh(x_{1_j}, \delta), nbh(x_{2_k}, \gamma) \rangle$, such that $nbh(x_{1_j}, \delta)$, (resp., $nbh(x_{2_k}, \gamma)$) is a *significant neighborhood* (see Section 2) of x_{1_j} (resp., x_{2_k});
- from each pair $\langle nbh(x_{1_j}, \delta), nbh(x_{2_k}, \gamma) \rangle$, it derives a pair $\langle prosub_{1j_\delta}, prosub_{2k_\gamma} \rangle$ such that $prosub_{1j_\delta}$ (resp., $prosub_{2k_\gamma}$) is obtained from $nbh(x_{1_j}, \delta)$ (resp., $nbh(x_{2_k}, \gamma)$) by pruning it in such a way to remove the portions of $nbh(x_{1_j}, \delta)$ (resp., $nbh(x_{2_k}, \gamma)$) that are dissimilar with $nbh(x_{2_k}, \gamma)$ (resp., $nbh(x_{1_j}, \delta)$), i.e., those x-components of $nbh(x_{1_j}, \delta)$ not involved in similarities with x-components of $nbh(x_{2_k}, \gamma)$ - see below for more details.

Technical Details. In this section we formalize our technique for selecting the most promising pairs of sub-schemas. In particular, given two XML Schemas S_1 and S_2, the set SPS of the most promising pairs of sub-schemas associated with them, is obtained by calling a suitable function Φ as follows:

$$SPS = \Phi(S_1, S_2, IPD)$$

For each tuple $\langle x_{1_j}, x_{2_k}\rangle \in IPD$, Φ calls a function Ψ for deriving the set of the most promising pairs of sub-schemas having x_{1_j} and x_{2_k} as their seeds. The formal definition of Φ is:

$$\Phi(S_1, S_2, IPD) = \bigcup\nolimits_{\langle x_{1_j}, x_{2_k}\rangle \in IPD} \Psi(S_1, S_2, x_{1_j}, x_{2_k}, IPD)$$

The function Ψ receives two XML Schemas S_1 and S_2, two complex elements $x_{1_j} \in S_1$ and $x_{2_k} \in S_2$ and an Interschema Property Dictionary IPD; for each pair of significant neighborhoods $nbh(x_{1_j}, \delta)$ and $nbh(x_{2_k}, \gamma)$, Ψ calls a function ξ which extracts the most promising pair of sub-schemas $\langle prosub_{1j_\delta}, prosub_{2k_\gamma}\rangle$ associated with it. Ψ can be defined as follows:

$$\Psi(S_1, S_2, x_{1_j}, x_{2_k}, IPD) =$$
$$\bigcup\nolimits_{\substack{0 \leq \delta < \mu(S_1)\\ 0 \leq \gamma < \mu(S_2)}} \xi\left(S_1, S_2, nbh(x_{1_j}, \delta), nbh(x_{2_k}, \gamma), \nu\left(IPD, nbh(x_{1_j}, \delta), nbh(x_{2_k}, \gamma)\right)\right)$$

Here, the function μ receives an XML Schema and returns the number of its complex elements. The function ν receives an Interschema Property Dictionary IPD and two neighborhoods $nbh(x_{1_j}, \delta)$ and $nbh(x_{2_k}, \gamma)$; it returns the set $IPD_{\delta\gamma} \subseteq IPD$ of interschema properties involving only pairs of x-components belonging to $nbh(x_{1_j}, \delta)$ and $nbh(x_{2_k}, \gamma)$.

The function ξ receives two XML Schemas S_1 and S_2, two neighborhoods $nbh(x_{1_j}, \delta)$ and $nbh(x_{2_k}, \gamma)$ and the set $IPD_{\delta\gamma}$ as constructed by ν; in order to extract the most promising pair of sub-schemas $\langle prosub_{1j_\delta}, prosub_{2k_\gamma}\rangle$ associated with $nbh(x_{1_j}, \delta)$ and $nbh(x_{2_k}, \gamma)$, ξ activates a function θ for pruning $nbh(x_{1_j}, \delta)$ and $nbh(x_{2_k}, \gamma)$ in such a way to eliminate the most dissimilar portions. ξ can be formalized as follows:

$$\xi\left(S_1, S_2, nbh(x_{1_j}, \delta), nbh(x_{2_k}, \gamma), IPD_{\delta\gamma}\right) =$$
$$\langle \theta\left(nbh(x_{1_j}, \delta), \pi(S_1, IPD_{\delta\gamma})\right), \theta\left(nbh(x_{2_k}, \gamma), \pi(S_2, IPD_{\delta\gamma})\right)\rangle$$

Here, the function π receives a schema S_h, $h \in \{1, 2\}$, and the set $IPD_{\delta\gamma}$ computed by ν and returns the complex elements belonging to S_h and involved in at least one property of $IPD_{\delta\gamma}$.

The function θ receives a neighborhood $nbh(x_S, d)$, relative to a schema S, and the set $IPDInvolvedOne$ of complex elements of S involved in at least one interschema property of $IPD_{\delta\gamma}$. It constructs a sub-schema $prosub_{S_d} \subseteq nbh(x_S, d)$ by removing from $nbh(x_S, d)$ each complex element x_R, along with all its sub-elements and attributes, such that both the following conditions hold: (i) $x_R \notin IPDInvolvedOne$; (ii) for each complex element x_{R_i} such that $x_{R_i} \in nbh(x_S, d)$ and $reachable(x_R, x_{R_i}) = true$, $x_{R_i} \notin IPDInvolvedOne$.

In other words a complex element x_R is not inserted in $prosub_{S_d}$ if both it and all complex elements in $nbh(x_S, d)$ reachable from it are not involved in any interschema property of $IPD_{\delta\gamma}$. Note that the two conditions above guarantee that if x_R is removed then all x-components reachable from it are removed too. Indeed, if the two conditions above are valid for x_R then they must be also valid for all x-components reachable from it.

The next theorem states the worst case time complexity for computing the most promising pairs of sub-schemas.

Table 1. The Interschema Property Dictionary IPD relative to S_1 and S_2

x-component of S_1	x-component of S_2	interschema property typology
university	university	synonymy
professor	researcher	overlapping
phd-student	researcher	overlapping
paper	article	synonymy
paper	journal	hyponymy
paper	conference	hyponymy

Theorem 2. Let S_1 and S_2 be two XML Schemas. Let IPD be the Interschema Property Dictionary relative to S_1 and S_2; let m be the maximum between the number of complex elements of S_1 and S_2; let n be the maximum between the number of x-components of S_1 and S_2. The worst case time complexity for computing, by means of the function Φ, the set SPS of the most promising pairs of sub-schemas associated with S_1 and S_2 is $O(m^6 \times n)$. □

The next theorem states an upper bound to the number of promising pairs of sub-schemas returned by the function Φ.

Theorem 3. Let S_1 and S_2 be two XML Schemas; let IPD be the corresponding Interschema Property Dictionary; let m be the maximum between the number of complex elements of S_1 and S_2. The maximum cardinality of SPS is $O(m^4)$. □

As for these two theorems all considerations about the value of n that we have drawn after Theorem 1 are still valid. Moreover, since in an XML document the number of attributes and simple elements is generally much greater than the number of complex elements, the value of m is even smaller than that of n.

A case example (cnt'd). Consider the XML Schemas S_1 and S_2, relative to a University and illustrated in Figures 1 and 2. Consider the corresponding Interschema Property Dictionary shown in Table 1[1].

In order to construct SPS, first the function Φ is activated. For each tuple of IPD, Φ calls the function Ψ. In order to show the behaviour of Ψ, we consider its application to the pair of complex elements $\langle university_{[S_1]}, university_{[S_2]}\rangle$[2]. For each pair of significant neighborhoods $nbh(university_{[S_1]}, \delta)$ and $nbh(university_{[S_2]}, \gamma)$, Ψ activates the function ξ. In order to illustrate the behaviour of ξ, we consider its application to $nbh(university_{[S_1]}, 1)$ and $nbh(university_{[S_2]}, 2)$. $nbh(university_{[S_1]}, 1)$ has been shown in the previous section; $nbh(university_{[S_2]}, 2)$ is as follows:

---

[1] As previously pointed out, we have chosen to construct IPD by applying the approaches described in [4,5]; however, any other approach presented in the literature for deriving synonymies, hyponymies and overlappings among elements of different XML Schemas could be exploited.

[2] Here and in the following, whenever necessary, we use the notation $x_{[S]}$ for indicating the x-component x of an XML Schema S.

```
<?xml version="1.0" encoding="UTF-8"?>
<xs:schema xmlns:xs="http://www.w3.org/2001/XMLSchema">
    <!-- Decaration of attributes -->
    <xs:attribute name="identifier" type="xs:ID"/>
    <xs:attribute name="responsibles" type="xs:IDREFS"/>
    <xs:attribute name="authors" type="xs:IDREFS"/>
    <xs:attribute name="chief" type="xs:IDREF"/>
    <xs:attribute name="people" type="xs:IDREF"/>
    <xs:attribute name="projects" type="xs:IDREFS"/>
    <xs:attribute name="name" type="xs:string"/>
    <xs:attribute name="type" type="xs:string"/>
    <xs:attribute name="cultural_area" type="xs:string"/>
    <xs:attribute name="roles" type="xs:string"/>
    <xs:attribute name="research" type="xs:string"/>
    <xs:attribute name="title" type="xs:string"/>
    <xs:attribute name="volume" type="xs:integer"/>
    <xs:attribute name="year" type="xs:date"/>
    <xs:attribute name="argument" type="xs:string"/>
    <xs:attribute name="budget" type="xs:string"/>
    <xs:attribute name="funds" type="xs:string"/>
    <xs:attribute name="termination" type="xs:date"/>
    <xs:attribute name="pages" type="xs:integer"/>
    <xs:attribute name="booktitle" type="xs:string"/>
    <xs:attribute name="address" type="xs:string"/>
    <xs:attribute name="publisher" type="xs:string"/>
    <xs:attribute name="locations" type="xs:string"/>
    <xs:attribute name="labs" type="xs:string"/>
    <!-- Decaration of complex elements -->
    <xs:element name="article">
        <xs:complexType>
            <xs:choice>
                <xs:element ref="journal"/>
                <xs:element ref="conference"/>
            </xs:choice>
        </xs:complexType>
    </xs:element>
    <xs:element name="researcher">
        <xs:complexType>
            <xs:attribute ref="identifier"/>
            <xs:attribute ref="name"/>
            <xs:attribute ref="type"/>
            <xs:attribute ref="cultural_area"/>
            <xs:attribute ref="roles"/>
            <xs:attribute ref="research"/>
        </xs:complexType>
    </xs:element>
    <xs:element name="project">
        <xs:complexType>
            <xs:attribute ref="identifier"/>
            <xs:attribute ref="argument"/>
            <xs:attribute ref="budget"/>
            <xs:attribute ref="funds"/>
            <xs:attribute ref="responsibles"/>
            <xs:attribute ref="termination"/>
        </xs:complexType>
    </xs:element>
    <xs:element name="journal">
        <xs:complexType>
            <xs:attribute ref="identifier"/>
            <xs:attribute ref="authors"/>
            <xs:attribute ref="title"/>
            <xs:attribute ref="volume"/>
            <xs:attribute ref="pages"/>
            <xs:attribute ref="year"/>
        </xs:complexType>
    </xs:element>
    <xs:element name="conference">
        <xs:complexType>
            <xs:attribute ref="identifier"/>
            <xs:attribute ref="authors"/>
            <xs:attribute ref="title"/>
            <xs:attribute ref="booktitle"/>
            <xs:attribute ref="address"/>
            <xs:attribute ref="year"/>
            <xs:attribute ref="pages"/>
            <xs:attribute ref="publisher"/>
        </xs:complexType>
    </xs:element>
    <xs:element name="department">
        <xs:complexType>
            <xs:attribute name="identifier"/>
            <xs:attribute name="chief"/>
            <xs:attribute name="people"/>
            <xs:attribute name="projects"/>
            <xs:attribute name="locations"/>
            <xs:attribute name="labs"/>
        </xs:complexType>
    </xs:element>
    <!-- Decaration of root -->
    <xs:element name="university">
        <xs:complexType>
            <xs:sequence>
                <xs:element ref="article" maxOccurs="unbounded"/>
                <xs:element ref="project" maxOccurs="unbounded"/>
                <xs:element ref="researcher" maxOccurs="unbounded"/>
                <xs:element ref="department" maxOccurs="unbounded"/>
            </xs:sequence>
        </xs:complexType>
    </xs:element>
</xs:schema>
```

Fig. 2. The XML Schema S_2

$nbh(university_{[S_2]}, 2) = \{university, article, project, researcher, department,$
$journal, conference, identifier, argument, budget, funds, responsibles, termina-$
$tion, name, type, cultural\_area, roles, research, chief, people, projects, locations,$
$labs, authors, title, volume, pages, year, booktitle, address, publisher\}$

For this pair of neighborhoods the set $IPD_{\delta\gamma}$ returned by the function ν is equal to IPD. ξ activates θ for pruning $nbh(university_{[S_1]}, 1)$ and $nbh(university_{[S_2]}, 2)$ in such a way to remove the most dissimilar portions. As an example, the complex element $student_{[S_1]}$ is pruned from $nbh(university_{[S_1]}, 1)$ because: (i) $student_{[S_1]}$ is not involved in any interschema property of $IPD_{\delta\gamma}$; (ii) there does not exist any complex element x_{R_i} such that $x_{R_i} \in nbh(university_{[S_1]}, 1)$, $reachable(student_{[S_1]}, x_{R_i}) = true$ and x_{R_i} is involved in some interschema property of $IPD_{\delta\gamma}$.

The final promising pair of sub-schemas returned by ξ, when applied on $nbh(university_{[S_1]}, 1)$ and $nbh(university_{[S_2]}, 2)$, is illustrated in Figure 3. All the other promising pairs of sub-schemas can be determined analogously.

```xml
<?xml version="1.0" encoding="UTF-8"?>
<xs:schema xmlns:xs="http://www.w3.org/2001/XMLSchema">
  <!-- Decaration of attributes -->
  <xs:attribute name="identifier" type="xs:ID"/>
  <xs:attribute name="courses" type="xs:IDREFS"/>
  <xs:attribute name="papers" type="xs:IDREFS"/>
  <xs:attribute name="advisor" type="xs:IDREF"/>
  <xs:attribute name="authors" type="xs:IDREFS"/>
  <xs:attribute name="cultural_area" type="xs:string"/>
  <xs:attribute name="name" type="xs:string"/>
  <xs:attribute name="thesis" type="xs:string"/>
  <xs:attribute name="research_interests" type="xs:string"/>
  <xs:attribute name="type" type="xs:string"/>
  <xs:attribute name="volumes" type="xs:integer"/>
  <xs:attribute name="pages" type="xs:integer"/>
  <xs:element name="professor">
    <xs:complexType>
      <xs:attribute ref="identifier"/>
      <xs:attribute ref="name"/>
      <xs:attribute ref="cultural_area"/>
      <xs:attribute ref="courses"/>
      <xs:attribute ref="papers"/>
    </xs:complexType>
  </xs:element>
  <xs:element name="phd-student">
    <xs:complexType>
      <xs:attribute ref="identifier"/>
      <xs:attribute ref="advisor"/>
      <xs:attribute ref="thesis"/>
      <xs:attribute ref="research_interests"/>
      <xs:attribute ref="papers"/>
    </xs:complexType>
  </xs:element>
  <xs:element name="paper">
    <xs:complexType>
      <xs:attribute ref="identifier"/>
      <xs:attribute ref="authors"/>
      <xs:attribute ref="type"/>
      <xs:attribute ref="volumes"/>
      <xs:attribute ref="pages"/>
    </xs:complexType>
  </xs:element>
  <!-- Decaration of root -->
  <xs:element name="university">
    <xs:complexType>
      <xs:sequence>
        <xs:element ref="professor" maxOccurs="unbounded"/>
        <xs:element ref="phd-student" maxOccurs="unbounded"/>
        <xs:element ref="paper" maxOccurs="unbounded"/>
      </xs:sequence>
    </xs:complexType>
  </xs:element>
</xs:schema>

<xs:schema xmlns:xs="http://www.w3.org/2001/XMLSchema">
  <!-- Decaration of attributes -->
  <xs:attribute name="identifier" type="xs:ID"/>
  <xs:attribute name="authors" type="xs:IDREFS"/>
  <xs:attribute name="name" type="xs:string"/>
  <xs:attribute name="type" type="xs:string"/>
  <xs:attribute name="cultural_area" type="xs:string"/>
  <xs:attribute name="roles" type="xs:string"/>
  <xs:attribute name="research" type="xs:string"/>
  <xs:attribute name="title" type="xs:string"/>
  <xs:attribute name="volume" type="xs:integer"/>
  <xs:attribute name="year" type="xs:date"/>
  <xs:attribute name="pages" type="xs:integer"/>
  <xs:attribute name="booktitle" type="xs:string"/>
  <xs:attribute name="address" type="xs:string"/>
  <xs:attribute name="publisher" type="xs:string"/>
  <!-- Decaration of complex elements -->
  <xs:element name="article">
    <xs:complexType>
      <xs:choice>
        <xs:element ref="journal"/>
        <xs:element ref="conference"/>
      </xs:choice>
    </xs:complexType>
  </xs:element>
  <xs:element name="researcher">
    <xs:complexType>
      <xs:attribute ref="identifier"/>
      <xs:attribute ref="name"/>
      <xs:attribute ref="type"/>
      <xs:attribute ref="cultural_area"/>
      <xs:attribute ref="roles"/>
      <xs:attribute ref="research"/>
    </xs:complexType>
  </xs:element>
  <xs:element name="journal">
    <xs:complexType>
      <xs:attribute ref="identifier"/>
      <xs:attribute ref="authors"/>
      <xs:attribute ref="title"/>
      <xs:attribute ref="volume"/>
      <xs:attribute ref="pages"/>
      <xs:attribute ref="year"/>
    </xs:complexType>
  </xs:element>
  <xs:element name="conference">
    <xs:complexType>
      <xs:attribute ref="identifier"/>
      <xs:attribute ref="authors"/>
      <xs:attribute ref="title"/>
      <xs:attribute ref="booktitle"/>
      <xs:attribute ref="address"/>
      <xs:attribute ref="year"/>
      <xs:attribute ref="pages"/>
      <xs:attribute ref="publisher"/>
    </xs:complexType>
  </xs:element>
  <!-- Decaration of root -->
  <xs:element name="university">
    <xs:complexType>
      <xs:sequence>
        <xs:element ref="article" maxOccurs="unbounded"/>
        <xs:element ref="researcher" maxOccurs="unbounded"/>
      </xs:sequence>
    </xs:complexType>
  </xs:element>
</xs:schema>
```

Fig. 3. The promising pair of sub-schemas relative to $nbh(university_{[S_1]}, 1)$ and $nbh(university_{[S_2]}, 2)$

3.2 Derivation of Sub-schema Similarities

Our technique for deriving sub-schema similarities between two XML Schemas S_1 and S_2 receives the set SPS of the most promising pairs of sub-schemas and the Interschema Property Dictionary IPD relative to S_1 and S_2 and selects the most similar pairs of sub-schemas.

Actually, two levels of sub-schema similarities can be defined, depending on the typology and the strength of the similarities existing among x-components belonging to the sub-schemas into examination. *Strong sub-schema similarities* are directly derived by taking into account only synonymies. *Weak sub-schema similarities* cannot be derived with the only support of synonymies but need the contribution of hyponymies and overlappings.

More specifically, the two sets of pairs of similar sub-schemas can be defined as:

$$SSS_{strong} = \rho_{strong}(SPS, IPD) \qquad SSS_{weak} = \rho_{weak}(SPS, IPD)$$

Here, the function ρ_{strong} derives the strong sub-schema similarities whereas the function ρ_{weak} extracts the weak ones.

ρ_{strong} operates by computing the objective function associated with a maximum weight matching defined on a suitable bipartite graph. More specifically, let $\langle prosub_{1j_\delta}, prosub_{2k_\gamma} \rangle \in SPS$ be a promising pair of sub-schemas; let $BG_{\delta\gamma} = \langle NSet, ESet \rangle$ be the bipartite graph associated with $prosub_{1j_\delta}$ and $prosub_{2k_\gamma}$. $NSet = PSet \cup QSet$ is the set of nodes of $BG_{\delta\gamma}$; there is a node in $PSet$ (resp., $QSet$) for each complex element of $prosub_{1j_\delta}$ (resp., $prosub_{2k_\gamma}$). $ESet$ is the set of edges of $BG_{\delta\gamma}$; in $ESet$ there exists an edge $\langle p, q \rangle$ between two nodes $p \in PSet$ and $q \in QSet$ if and only if, in IPD, there exists a synonymy between the element corresponding to p and the element corresponding to q.

The maximum weight matching on $BG_{\delta\gamma}$ is the set $ESet^* \subseteq ESet$ such that, for each node $x \in PSet \cup QSet$, there exists at most one edge of $ESet^*$ incident onto x and $|ESet^*|$ is maximum (the interested reader is referred to [11] for details about the maximum weight matching). The objective function we associate with the maximum weight matching is $\chi_{BG} = \frac{2|ESet^*|}{|PSet|+|QSet|}$. Here $|ESet^*|$ represents the number of matches relative to $BG_{\delta\gamma}$, as well as the number of synonymies involving $prosub_{1j_\delta}$ and $prosub_{2k_\gamma}$. $2|ESet^*|$ indicates the number of matching nodes in $BG_{\delta\gamma}$, as well as the number of similar complex elements present in $prosub_{1j_\delta}$ and $prosub_{2k_\gamma}$. $|PSet| + |QSet|$ denotes the total number of nodes in $BG_{\delta\gamma}$ as well as the total number of complex elements relative to $prosub_{1j_\delta}$ and $prosub_{2k_\gamma}$. Finally, χ_{BG} represents the share of matching nodes in $BG_{\delta\gamma}$ as well as the share of similar complex elements present in $prosub_{1j_\delta}$ and $prosub_{2k_\gamma}$.

We assume that $prosub_{1j_\delta}$ and $prosub_{2k_\gamma}$ are similar if $\chi_{BG} > \frac{1}{2}$. Such an assumption derives from the consideration that two sets of objects can be considered similar if the number of similar elements is greater than the number of the dissimilar ones or, in other words, if the number of similar elements is greater than half of the total number of elements.

Theorem 4. *Let S_1 and S_2 be two XML Schemas; let IPD be the corresponding Interschema Property Dictionary; let m be the maximum between the number of complex elements of S_1 and S_2. The worst case time complexity for computing SSS_{strong} is $O(m^7)$.* □

With regard to this result, the same reasoning about the extremely small number of complex elements in an XML Schema, that we have introduced after Theorems 2 and 3, is still valid.

ρ_{weak} receives SPS and IPD and returns weak sub-schema similarities. We call them "weak" because, differently from ρ_{strong}, which takes only synonymies into account, ρ_{weak} considers also overlappings and hyponymies, that are weaker properties than synonymies, for representing concept similarities.

When we introduce hyponymies and overlappings in the computation of sub-schema similarities we must consider that, often, more than one element of a schema is hyponymous or overlapping with an element of the other schema.

As an example, consider the element *house* of one XML Schema, having four attributes, namely *bedroom*, *bathroom*, *kitchen* and *garden*. Consider, also, a second XML Schema having the element *firstfloor*, characterized by the attributes *garden*, *kitchen* and *lounge*, and the element *secondfloor*, characterized by the attributes *bedroom*, *bathroom* and *garret*. Both *firstfloor* and *secondfloor* are overlapping with *house* because they share some of its attributes, and the information content of *house* is distributed over *firstfloor* and *secondfloor*. Clearly, in this case, it would be wrong to select just one of these overlapping properties to characterize the relationship among *house*, *firstfloor* and *secondfloor* and, consequently, to represent the similarity between the corresponding sub-schemas. A consequence of this reasoning is that, in order to derive weak sub-schema similarities, it is not possible to apply maximum weight matching techniques; indeed, they would associate an element of a schema with at most one element of the other schema.

ρ_{weak} works as follows. Let $\langle prosub_{1j_\delta}, prosub_{2k_\gamma}\rangle \in SPS$ be a promising pair of sub-schemas; let $BG'_{\delta\gamma} = \langle NSet', ESet'\rangle$ be a bipartite graph associated with $prosub_{1j_\delta}$ and $prosub_{2k_\gamma}$. Here, $NSet' = PSet' \cup QSet'$ is the set of nodes of $BG'_{\delta\gamma}$; there is a node in $PSet'$ (resp., $QSet'$) for each complex element of $prosub_{1j_\delta}$ (resp., $prosub_{2k_\gamma}$). $ESet'$ is the set of edges of $BG'_{\delta\gamma}$; in $ESet'$ there exists an edge $\langle p, q\rangle$ between two nodes $p \in PSet'$ and $q \in QSet'$ if and only if, in IPD, a synonymy, an hyponymy or an overlapping holds between the element corresponding to p and the element corresponding to q.

Let $\eta_p = \{p \in PSet'$ such that at least one edge of $BG'_{\delta\gamma}$ is incident onto it$\}$ and $\eta_q = \{q \in QSet'$ such that at least one edge of $BG'_{\delta\gamma}$ is incident onto it$\}$ be the set of nodes of $PSet'$ and $QSet'$ involved in at least one interschema property; we assume that $prosub_{1j_\delta}$ and $prosub_{2k_\gamma}$ are weakly similar if $\chi'_{BG} = \frac{|\eta_p|+|\eta_q|}{|PSet'|+|QSet'|} > \frac{1}{2}$. Such an assumption indicates that two sub-schemas are weakly similar if at least half of their elements are someway related by an interschema property. The justification underlying such an assumption is analogous to that we have seen for strong similarities.

Theorem 5. Let S_1 and S_2 be two XML Schemas; let IPD be the corresponding Interschema Property Dictionary; let m be the maximum between the number of complex elements of S_1 and S_2. The worst case time complexity for computing SSS_{weak} is $O(m^6)$. □

A case example (cnt'd). Let us consider the XML Schemas illustrated in Figures 1 and 2. In Section 3.1 we have shown how the corresponding set SPS of promising pairs of sub-schemas can be derived. In this section we show how the sets SSS_{strong} and SSS_{weak} can be constructed. In particular, due to space constraints, we shall concentrate our attention on the promising pair of sub-schemas illustrated in Figure 3.

For this pair, the objective function χ_{BG} computed on it is equal to $\frac{4}{9} < \frac{1}{2}$; as a consequence, we can conclude that the promising pair of sub-schemas into consideration is not strongly similar. The value of χ'_{BG}, computed by ρ_{weak} when applied on the same pair of sub-schemas, is equal to $\frac{9}{9} > \frac{1}{2}$, which allows us to conclude that a weak similarity holds between the two sub-schemas into consideration.

4 Experimental Results

The approach proposed in this paper has been implemented in a prototype. In order to evaluate its performances, we have carried out various tests on several XML Schemas.

In our evaluation campaign we applied the following methodology: *(i)* a set of test schemas has been selected; *(ii)* a group of experts has been asked to identify the sub-schema similarities holding for the involved schemas; *(iii)* sub-schema similarities relative to the same schemas have been detected by applying the approach to evaluate; *(iv)* the similarities provided by the experts and those returned by the approach to test have been compared to compute two widely accepted measures, namely Precision and Recall [7]. *Precision* specifies the share of correct properties detected by the system among those it derived. *Recall* indicates the share of correct properties detected by the system among those the experts provided. Both Precision and Recall fall within the interval [0, 1]. In the ideal case they are both equal to 1; as a consequence, it is possible to state that the greater Precision (resp., Recall) is, the better the system under evaluation works.

In our experimental tests we have exploited a set of XML Schemas relative to various application contexts. More specifically, a first group of Schemas concerned the management of projects financed by European Union; a second group was relative to land and urban property registers; finally, a third group handled financial information. All these Schemas can be found at the address http://www.mat.unical.it/terracina/coopis2004/tests.html. Such a variety of Schemas, derived from disparate application contexts, is justified by our desire to test the behaviour of our approach in many application environments. We have considered 10 XML Schemas; their size, i.e., the number of their elements and attributes, ranged from 16 to 75; the average size was 40; this number of schemas and these sizes are quite close to those generally exploited in the literature for evaluating interschema property extraction approaches (see [7] for details about this).

Average values of Precision and Recall obtained in our experiments are 0.90 and 0.82, resp. In our opinion, the value of Precision is very satisfactory; the smaller value of Recall is justified by considering that: *(i)* the possible number of sub-schema similarities is exponential against the number of x-components of the corresponding schemas; *(ii)* we have used a heuristics for selecting the most

Table 2. Variation of Precision and Recall w.r.t. possible errors in the IPD

Case	Precision	Recall	Case	Precision	Recall
No errors	0.90	0.82	(d)	0.84	0.83
(a)	0.92	0.71	(e)	0.76	0.83
(b)	0.93	0.68	(f)	0.69	0.85
(c)	0.93	0.61			

promising pairs of sub-schemas for guaranteeing a polynomial complexity to our approach.

A second experiment has been carried out for testing the effects of errors and inaccuracies in the IPD received in input by our approach. In this experiment we have asked an expert to validate the IPD returned by the approaches described in [4,5] in such a way to remove any possible error. After this, we have performed some variations on the correct IPD and, for each of them, we have computed Precision and Recall of our system. Variations we have carried out on IPD are: (a) 10% of correct properties have been filtered out; (b) 20% of correct properties have been filtered out; (c) 30% of correct properties have been filtered out; (d) 10% of wrong properties have been added; (e) 20% of wrong properties have been added; (f) 30% of wrong properties have been added.

Table 2 presents the values of Precision and Recall we have obtained in all these tests. These results show that our system is quite robust w.r.t. errors and inaccuracies in IPD. A further, interesting, quite intuitive, conclusion that can be drawn from these experiments is that the lack of correct interschema properties in IPD causes a decrease of Recall and a slight increase of Precision. Vice versa, if wrong interschema properties are inserted in IPD, we can notice a slight increase of Recall and a decrease of Precision.

5 Related Work

In the literature the extraction of sub-schema similarities received less attention than the derivation of other, more common, interschema properties, such as synonymies, homonymies and hyponymies. In this section we examine some of the sub-schema similarity derivation approaches and highlight their similarities and differences w.r.t. our own. Preliminarily, we point out that our approach is specialized for XML information sources whereas, to the best of our knowledge, the related approaches proposed in the literature are either specific for databases or operate on generic data sources.

In [15], the authors propose $SKAT$ that exploits a set of *first-order logic rules* to determine the semantic relationships existing between two ontologies/schemas. There are important differences between $SKAT$ and our approach. First, $SKAT$ is logic-based whereas our approach is graph-based. Moreover, $SKAT$ initially requires the human expert to provide some basic matching and mismatching relationships relative to the schemas into consideration. On the contrary, our approach initially requires the presence of an Interschema Property

Dictionary to be constructed by applying any approach for deriving synonymies, hyponymies and overlappings previously proposed in the literature. As for similarities between the two approaches, we point out that both of them require the human expert to validate obtained results.

[14] proposes *Similarity Flooding (SF)*, a technique for carrying out schema matching activities. *SF* operates on a large variety of data sources. First it converts input schemas into labelled graphs; then, it uses a *fixpoint computation* to determine semantic matchings between the nodes of the graphs. These matchings are refined by means of specific software modules called *filters*. Both *SF* and our approach are graph-based; moreover, in both of them structural information associated with input schemas plays quite an important role. As for differences between them, our approach is based on an Interschema Property Dictionary received in input whereas *SF* initially requires a lexical similarity dictionary. Finally, in *SF*, human experts must check the generated matchings at each iteration of the fixpoint computation whereas, in our approach, the human validation is required only at the end.

In [13] Cupid, a system for deriving interschema properties among heterogeneous information sources, is presented. Cupid takes an external thesaurus in input; its approach consists of two phases, named *linguistic* and *structural*. Our approach and Cupid share some similarities; indeed, both of them *(i)* require an initial dictionary; *(ii)* exploit structural information about the input schemas and *(iii)* are graph-based. As for differences between them, we observe that Cupid exploits sophisticated techniques taking into account various characteristics of involved schemas; as a consequence, it is an excellent choice when the precision of results is compulsory and the involved schemas are not numerous. On the contrary, our approach is less sophisticated, does not exploit thresholds and weights (that, conversely, play an important role in Cupid) and, consequently, does not need a tuning phase. As a consequence, it is particularly suited when the involved sources are numerous and large, that is a typical situation in Web scenarios.

In [6] the authors propose the iMAP prototype. iMAP operates in two phases: the first one exploits Artificial Intelligence techniques, like *Bayesian Network* or *beam search*, to generate a set of rough matchings; the second one uses auxiliary information (like domain constraints, graph matchings, etc.) for refining these matchings. Interesting properties of iMAP are its *modularity* and its *extensibility*, since new matching algorithms might be easily included in it; however, since it exploits Artificial Intelligence techniques, it needs quite a long training phase and this negatively influences its scalability.

In [12] the system *SemInt*, exploiting machine learning techniques to identify semantic matchings between the attributes of two relational schemas, is presented. Some similarities can be recognized between our approach and *SemInt*; indeed, both of them *(i)* require human intervention only for validating obtained results; *(ii)* have been conceived and optimized for operating on a specific data model. As for differences between them, we have that: *(i) SemInt* takes into account both intensional and extensional information whereas our approach exploits only the intensional one; *(ii)* SemInt exploits machine learning techniques; as a consequence it might achieve very satisfactory results but it might exhibit substantial performance problems for large schemas; *(iii)* SemInt operates on relational databases whereas our approach works on XML Schemas.

In [8] the authors propose COMA (COmbining MAtch). It provides an *extensible* library of different schema matching algorithms and allows the users to specify a *matching strategy*, stating the algorithms to exploit and the way to combine their results. As a consequence, COMA appears a complex software infrastructure rather than a specific matching algorithm; hence, it might combine the various algorithms discussed in this section to obtain more sophisticated results.

6 Conclusions

In this paper we have presented a semi-automatic approach for deriving sub-schema similarities between XML Schemas; we have shown that our approach is specialized for XML sources, is almost automatic, semantic and "light". It consists of two steps: the first one selects a set of promising pairs of sub-schemas, whereas the second one computes sub-schema similarities. We have pointed out that our approach is part of a more general framework that allows a unified derivation of similarities and dissimilarities among concepts and groups of concepts represented in heterogeneous XML Schemas. We have also presented the experimental results obtained by applying our approach on some, quite variegate, XML Schemas. Finally, we have examined various other related approaches previously proposed in the literature and we have compared them with ours by pointing out similarities and differences.

Presently we are working for the development of an XML Schema integration approach taking sub-schema similarities into account. In the future, we plan to study the possibility to make our sub-schema similarity derivation technique more refined by taking into account the "context" of the involved sub-schemas when computing their similarity; in addition, we plan to develop techniques exploiting sub-schema similarities in the other application contexts we have mentioned in the Introduction. Finally, we argue that several other terminological and structural properties already studied for single concepts, such as hyponymies and overlappings, could be extended to sub-schemas. In the future, we plan to verify if this intuition is really feasible and, in the affirmative case, to define corresponding techniques.

References

1. C. Batini and M. Lenzerini. A methodology for data schema integration in the entity relationship model. *IEEE Transactions on Software Engineering*, 10(6):650–664, 1984.
2. S. Castano, V. De Antonellis, and S. De Capitani di Vimercati. Global viewing of heterogeneous data sources. *Transactions on Data and Knowledge Engineering*, 13(2):277–297, 2001.

3. C.E.H. Chua, R.H.L. Chiang, and E.P. Lim. Instance-based attribute identification in database integration. *The International Journal on Very Large Databases*, 12(3):228–243, 2003.
4. P. De Meo, G. Quattrone, G. Terracina, and D. Ursino. "Almost automatic" and semantic integration of XML Schemas at various "severity levels". In *Proc. of the International Conference on Cooperative Information Systems (CoopIS 2003)*, pages 4–21, Taormina, Italy, 2003. Lecture Notes in Computer Science, Springer.
5. P. De Meo, G. Quattrone, G. Terracina, and D. Ursino. Extraction of synonymies, hyponymies, overlappings and homonymies from XML Schemas at various "severity" levels. In *Proc. of the International Database Engineering and Applications Symposium (IDEAS 2004)*, Coimbra, Portugal, 2004. Forthcoming.
6. R. Dhamankar, Y. Lee, A. Doan, A. Halevy, and P. Domingos. iMAP: Discovering complex semantic matches between database schemas. In *Proc. of the ACM International Conference on Management of Data (SIGMOD 2004)*, Paris, France, 2004. ACM Press-Forthcoming.
7. H. Do, S. Melnik, and E. Rahm. Comparison of schema matching evaluations. In *Proc. of the International Workshop on Web, Web-Services, and Database Systems*, pages 221–237, Erfurt, Germany, 2002. Lecture Notes in Computer Science, Springer.
8. H. Do and E. Rahm. COMA- a system for flexible combination of schema matching approaches. In *Proc. of the International Conference on Very Large Databases (VLDB 2002)*, pages 610–621, Hong Kong, China, 2002. VLDB Endowment.
9. A. Doan, J. Madhavan, R. Dhamankar, P. Domingos, and A. Halevy. Learning to match ontologies on the Semantic Web. *The International Journal on Very Large Databases*, 12(4):303–319, 2003.
10. A. Gal, A. Anaby-Tavor, A. Trombetta, and D. Montesi. A framework for modeling and evaluating automatic semantic reconciliation. *The International Journal on Very Large Databases*, (Forthcoming), 2004.
11. Z. Galil. Efficient algorithms for finding maximum matching in graphs. *ACM Computing Surveys*, 18:23–38, 1986.
12. W. Li and C. Clifton. SEMINT: A tool for identifying attribute correspondences in heterogeneous databases using neural networks. *Data and Knowledge Engineering*, 33(1):49–84, 2000.
13. J. Madhavan, P.A. Bernstein, and E. Rahm. Generic schema matching with Cupid. In *Proc. of the International Conference on Very Large Data Bases (VLDB 2001)*, pages 49–58, Roma, Italy, 2001. Morgan Kaufmann.
14. S. Melnik, H. Garcia-Molina, and E. Rahm. Similarity Flooding: A versatile graph matching algorithm and its application to schema matching. In *Proc. of the International Conference on Data Engineering (ICDE 2002)*, pages 117–128, San Jose, California, USA, 2002. IEEE Computer Society Press.
15. P. Mitra, G. Wiederhold, and J. Jannink. Semi-automatic integration of knowledge sources. In *Proc. of Fusion'99*, Sunnyvale, California, USA, 1999.
16. E. Rahm and P.A. Bernstein. A survey of approaches to automatic schema matching. *VLDB Journal*, 10(4):334–350, 2001.

Supporting Similarity Operations Based on Approximate String Matching on the Web

Eike Schallehn[1], Ingolf Geist[1], and Kai-Uwe Sattler[2]

[1] Dpt. of Computer Science, University of Magdeburg
P.O. Box 4120, 39106 Magdeburg, Germany
{schallehn|geist}@iti.cs.uni-magdeburg.de

[2] Dpt. of Computer Science and Automation, Technical University of Ilmenau
P.O. Box 100565, 98684 Ilmenau, Germany
k.sattler@computer.org

Abstract. Querying and integrating sources of structured data from the Web in most cases requires similarity-based concepts to deal with data level conflicts. This is due to the often erroneous and imprecise nature of the data and diverging conventions for their representation. On the other hand, Web databases offer only limited interfaces and almost no support for similarity queries. The approach presented in this paper maps string similarity predicates to standard predicates like substring and keyword search as offered by many of the mentioned systems. To minimize the local processing costs and the required network traffic, the mapping uses materialized information on the selectivity of string samples such as q-samples, substrings, and keywords. Based on the predicate mapping similarity selections and joins are described and the quality and required effort of the operations is evaluated experimentally.

1 Introduction

The growing amount of information publicly or locally available from a growing number of databases and other informations systems in networks raises the need for an integrated or mediated access to this information. Among the many problems to be solved is the resolution of data level conflicts in weakly related or overlapping data sets from different sources. Similarity-based operations became one way to address this problem in data integration scenarios. Unfortunately, the support for such operations in current data management solutions is rather limited. And worse, interfaces provided over the Web are even more limited and almost always do not allow any similarity-based lookup of information. The principal idea of the presented approach is to provide a pre-selection for string similarity operations by using string containment operations as provided by most information systems. Regarding the pre-selection this approach is similar to those by Gravano et al. introduced in [5]. Contrary to their pre-selection strategy, the one presented here is not only applicable in a scenario were integrated data sets or data sets in general are materialized in one database, but allows re-writing string similarity queries for the virtual integration of autonomous sources. This way, it is applicable in Web integration scenarios.

The proposed pre-selection is based on the edit or Levenshtein distance, which expresses the dissimilarity of two strings by the minimal number k of operations necessary to transform a string to a comparison string. A basic observation described by Navarro et al. in [15] is, that if we pick any $k + 1$ non-overlapping substrings of one string, at least one of them must be fully contained in the comparison string. This corresponds to *Count Filtering* as introduced by Gravano, where the number of common q-grams (substrings of fixed length q) in two strings is used as a criterion.

The problem is, we can not use additional filtering techniques like described in [5] to further refine the pre-selection, because we can not access the necessary information in a non-materialized scenario. And, if we choose inappropriate substrings, the candidate sets can be huge. In this case, the question is: which substrings are appropriate? Obviously, we can minimize the size of the intermediate result by finding the $k + 1$ non-overlapping substrings having the best selectivity when combined in one disjunctive query. Then, processing a string similarity predicate requires the following steps:

1. Transform the similarity predicate to an optimal disjunctive substring pre-selection query considering selectivity information
2. Process the pre-selection using standard functionality of the information system yielding a candidate set
3. Process the actual similarity predicate within a mediator or implemented as a user defined function in standard DBMS

While this sketches only a simple selection, we will describe later on, how for instance similarity joins over diverse sources can be executed.

The remainder of this paper is structured as follows. After giving an overview of related work in Section 2 we will describe the mapping of string similarity predicates in Section 3. Based on the described mapping we outline how similarity selections and joins can be performed in an integration scenario in Section 4. Section 5 describes necessary data structures and algorithms for maintaining information on substring selectivity required for the predicate mapping. Finally, we present experimental results in Section 6 and conclude with a short summary and outlook in Section 7.

2 Related Work

The roots of this research stem from similarity operations in Information Retrieval and probabilistic data processing. Spatial and similarity joins were first addressed for materialized scenarios and data values that either represented points in a mutidimensional metric space or could be mapped to such a space. A recent overview is given by Koudas and Sevcik in [12]. Though searching and performing more complex operations in multidimensional spaces is well researched, string data would have to be mapped to such a space of fixed dimensionality to apply the previously mentioned approaches. This can be done using for instance FastMap introduced by Faloutsos and Lin in [3], which is based on metric multidimensional scaling, and was actually used for this purpose by Jin et al. as described in [10]. Nevertheless, this approach requires a fully materialized data set, the full domain of string values to define the mapping, and according interfaces to perform a similarity search based on a vector representation of a string. Based on Fuhr's probabibilistic datalog ([4]) in [2] Cohen described a related approach for performing joins based on textual similarity, contrary to shorter strings used here. For this purpose he applied document vector representations as known from Information Retrieval. Our approach is based on the edit or Levenshtein distance for string values. A short overview of similarity measures in general is included in [18] by Santini and Jain, while Navarro gives an overview of approximate string matching in [14]. Based on distance and similarity measures for string values according similarity operations were introduced in recent research, such as the previously mentioned approach by Jin et al. in [10]. In [5] and [6] Gravano et al. present and refine an approach to perform joins based on similarity of string attributes through efficient pre-selections of materialized q-grams. Schallehn and Sattler in [19] use temporarily created Tries for similarity operations based on string similarity research by Shang and Merret ([20]). Nevertheless, all these approaches are only applicable if the data sets to be joined are locally materialized or the source systems do not have to process the similarity predicates.

In addition to the previously mentioned research, the approach presented here builds on [15] by Navarro and Baeza-Yates. They use q-gram indexes for approximate searches within texts and q-samples chosen by their selectivity for querying in an information retrieval context. An overview of indexing techniques for approximate string matching is given for instance in [16]. Possible index structures are suffix trees, suffix arrays as well as q-gram and q-sample indexes.

The count-suffix tree was proposed by Krishnan et al. [13] and refined by Jagadish et al. in [9]. Especially, the pruned version of a count-suffix tree is useful for substring selectivity estimation with tight space requirements. Pruned q-gram tables are very similar to end-biased histograms [7]. The highest frequency information are maintained and all lower frequencies are put into one bucket and estimated with one frequency. Because a q-gram index contains only strings with a fixed length q the problem that shorter and longer strings are estimated with the same selectivity does not occur. In our approach count-tries are used for storing information about q-grams of varying lengths q. These tries can be seen as count-suffix trees as described in [13,9], which contain only prefixes of the suffix of a supported lengths, i.e. the number of levels is pruned. Query-based sampling [1,8] is a method to obtain source descriptions from text-databases, i.e. tokens and their corresponding frequency information. Based on this idea we adapted the general approach to q-grams and substring queries.

Other work related to our approach deals with the implementation of data integration operators (mainly joins) in the presence of sources with limited query capabilities. The specification of query capabilities is addressed e.g. in [21], where the set of queries accepted by a source (or wrapper) is described using Datalog variants and is used for a capbilities-based rewriting. For the implementation of join operations on sources with limited capabilities the bind join was introduced in [17], where tuples from the results of one relation are used to fetch the corresponding tuples from the second relation even if this source does not support a full table scan.

3 Mapping Similarity Predicates

We consider a predicate like $edist(x, y) \leq k$ as part of a join condition, where x and y represent attribute names, or of a selection criterion, where one may represent a literal search string. We use the classic definition of the edit distance, which includes only insertion, deletion, and replacement. In this case, for a threshold k the number of required non-overlapping substrings is $n = k + 1$, because all of the above mentioned operations can only modify one substring each. A common derivative in addition allows transpositions of characters and increases the number of sub-strings to be considered to $n = 2k + 1$, because every transposition can modify two substrings. Considering what kind of substring is most suitable, let us assume a predicate $edist('Vincent\ van\ Gogh', stringAttribute) \leq 1$. Assuming we have selectivity information $sel(a)$ about any substring $a = s[i,j], 0 \leq i < j < length(s)$ of $s \in \Sigma^*$ over an alphabet Σ available as discussed later in Section 5, we may choose the following substrings for pre-selection predicates:

- **Arbitrary Substrings:** 'Vincent van' ∨ ' Gogh'
- **Fixed length substrings (q-samples):** 'Vinc' ∨ 'Gogh' (here $q = 4$)
- **Tokens:** 'Vincent' ∨ 'Gogh'

All three obviously must yield a candidate set including the correct result, but they differ largely regarding their selectivity. Intuitively, longer strings have a better selectivity, because every additional character refines the query. This consideration would render the transformation to q-samples as the least effective one. On the other hand, there is an overhead for managing and using selectivity information. Storing such information for arbitrary strings requires complex data structures to be efficient and considerable memory resources. In general, choosing a suitable substring paradigm implies a trade-off between several aspects.

Selectivity: as mentioned above, the selectivity of longer substrings is always better than or, in the unlikely worst case, equal to a shorter substring, $sel(s[i,j]) \geq sel(s[k,l]), 0 \leq k \leq i \leq j \leq l < length(s)$. Choosing a small q as for instance 3 or 4 will likely return more intermediate results and this way introduce a high overhead for transfer and local processing.

Maintenance: independently of what data structure we use for maintaining selectivity information, the required data volume grows dramatically with the (possible) length of the substrings due to a combinatoric effect for each additional position. Hence, a greater q increases the necessary overhead for global processing and the global resource consumption.

Applicability: we run into problems if a comparison string is not long enough to derive the necessary number of substrings such as tokens or q-samples. For instance, if the allowed edit distance is $k = 3$ and $q = 5$ a disjunctive pre-selection must contain $n = k + 1 = 4$ q-samples of length 5, i.e. the minimal required length of the mapped search string is $l_{min} = n * q = 20$. Obviously, it is not possible to derive the necessary 5-samples from the string 'Vincent van Gogh'.

Source capabilities: we consider two kinds of sources regarding the query capabilities, those allowing substring and those allowing keyword searches. For the latter, only tokens are suitable for composing pre-selection queries.

3.1 Substring Decomposition

The optimal solution to the addressed problem regarding selectivity performs the mapping *map_substring* in terms of a complete decomposition of the search string s into $n = k + 1$ non-overlapping substrings. The decomposition consists of positions $pos[0] \ldots pos[n]$ with $pos[0] = 0$ and $pos[n] = length(s)$ such that the concatenation $s = s[pos[0], pos[1] - 1]s[pos[1], pos[2] - 1] \ldots s[pos[n-1], pos[n] - 1]$ of the substrings is equal to the search string. An optimal decomposition would yield the minimal selectivity $1 - \Pi_{i=0}^{n-1}(1 - sel(s[pos[i], pos[i+1] - 1]))$. Here we assume independence between the selected query strings.

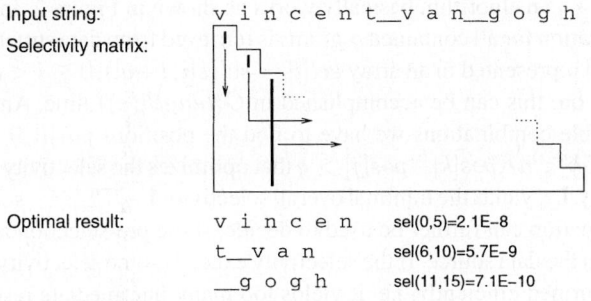

Fig. 1. Finding selective substrings for $k = 2$, hence $n = k + 1 = 3$

The algorithm sketched in Figure 1 uses a lower triangular matrix A where a_{ij} represents the selectivity of substring $s[i, j]$, hence, $0 \leq i \leq j < length(s)$. If a count suffix trie is used for storing selectivity information, as shown in Section 5, this matrix can be generated from $length(s)$ path traversals in the trie. An exhaustive search is quite expensive for long strings, but it can be tuned by skipping high selectivities in the upper region of the triangular matrix. Furthermore, starting with a decomposition of equal length substrings and stepwise adjusting this decomposition by moving adjacent cut positions represents a greedy approach yielding sufficient results regarding the selectivity quickly. The disadvantage here is that we need selectivity information on the variable length substrings $s[pos[i], pos[i+1]-1]$. Possible solutions and problems for the storage and retrieval of this information is outlined in Section 5, but obviously it requires much more resources than managing the same information for q-samples as introduced in the following.

3.2 q-Samples

The main advantage of using q-samples, i.e. non-overlapping q-grams of fixed length q, for a mapping *map_qgram* of an edit distance predicate to a disjunctive source query results from the straightforward maintenance of according selectivity information, as shown later on in Section 5.

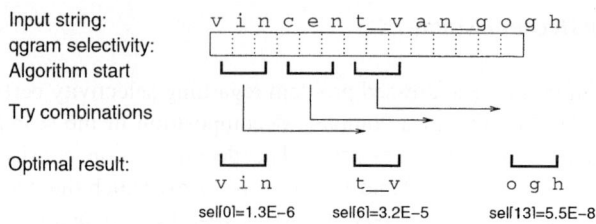

Fig. 2. Finding selective 3-samples for $k = 2$, hence $n = k + 1 = 3$

To find the best possible combination of n q-samples from a single string s with $length(s) \geq n * q$ an algorithm basically works as shown in Figure 2. In a first step selectivity information for all contained q-grams is retrieved from data structures described in Section 5 and represented in an array $sel[i] = sel(s[i, i+q]), 0 \leq i < length(s) - q$. As shown later on, this can be accomplished in $O(length(s))$ time. Among the number of all possible combinations we have to find the positions $pos[i], 0 \leq i < n$ with $\forall j, k : 0 \leq j < k < n \wedge pos[k] - pos[j] > q$ that optimizes the selectivity of the disjunctive source query, i.e. yields the minimal overall selectivity $1 - \Pi_{i=1}^{n}(1 - sel[pos[i]])$. This selectivity estimation can further be used to decide, if the pre-selection actually should be performed on the data source. If the selectivity exceeds some selectivity threshold and can not be performed efficiently, i.e. it yields too many intermediate results, the query can be rejected. As the number of possible combinations is $\Pi_{i=1}^{n}(length(s) - (n * q))$ an exhaustive search can become very expensive, especially if the mapping has to be applied during a bind-join on a great number of long strings as shown in Section 4. Alternatively, a greedy algorithm with $O(length(s))$ was implemented yielding sufficiently selective combinations, in most cases equal to the result of the exhaustive search.

The selectivity of the resulting pre-selection

$$\sigma_{\bigvee_{i=1}^{n} substring(s[pos[i], pos[i]+q], stringAttribute)}$$

can further be improved by not only considering the retrieved q-samples at $pos[i]$, but also the bounding substring, resulting in a complete decomposition of s. In the given example this may be 'vincen' and 't_van_g' and 'ogh', which can easily be derived. Though we can not estimate the selectivity of this query based on the given information, unless we move to the approach presented in the previous subsection, it must be better or at least equal to our estimation made based on q-gram selectivity. Another refinement of the presented approach would be to dynamically determine q based on the string length and the number of required q-samples, e.g. $q := \lfloor length(s)/n \rfloor$. This would solve the problem of applicability for shorter strings mentioned above, and improve the selectivity of the pre-selection for longer strings. The disadvantage is that we would need selectivity information for various length q-grams. Finally, if q is fixed and the applicability condition $length(s) \geq n * q$ does not hold, we may decide to nevertheless send a disjunctive query to the source, containing $m = \lfloor length(s)/q \rfloor < n$ substrings. Though this may not yield all results to the query, it still yields the subset containing $k - (n - m)$ differences in the string representations. Of course, the source query should only be executed, if the estimated selectivity $1 - \Pi_{i=1}^{m}(1 - sel[pos[i]])$ is below a threshold granting efficient processing and transfer of the pre-selection.

3.3 Tokens

Considering only substrings of a fixed or variable length would neglect the query capabilities of a great number of sources providing keyword search instead of substring search. To support such interfaces we can apply a mapping *map_token* to choose a set of tokens $T = \{t\}$ derived from our search string s using common delimiters like spaces, commas, etc. Managing and retrieving selectivity information for keywords can be based on standard approaches from information retrieval like the $TF * IDF$ norm. Therefore, it is quite straightforward as outlined in Section 5. Finding an optimal combination is also easier than with *q*-samples or substrings. The disadvantages of the approach are the in general worse selectivity of keywords compared to the other approaches, a relatively big space overhead for managing selectivity information compared to *q*-grams, and problems with the applicability. The latter results from the fact that $k + 1$ tokens have to be derived, which often may not be possible, e.g. it is impossible to derive a pre-selection for a query like

$$\sigma_{edist('ErnestHemingway', authorName) \leq 2}$$

because the threshold $k = 2$ implies the need of $n = 3$ tokens, which are not available. The selectivity problems occur because we can not take advantage of longer substrings, we can not take advantage of token-spanning substrings, and a probability growing with n of having one or more relatively un-selective keywords in our pre-selection.

4 Similarity-Based Operations

The selectivity-based mapping of similarity predicates can be used for rewriting and executing similarity queries on Web sources. In this way we can support approximate string matching in global queries even if the source systems support only primitive predicates such as *substring(a, b)*, e.g. in form of SQL's "a like '%b%'" predicate or *keyword(a, b)* representing an IR-like keyword containment of phrase *b* in string *a*. In the following we use a generalized form *contains(a, b)* that has to be replaced by the specific predicate supported by the source system. With regard to approximate string matching in Web queries we focus on two operations: the similarity selection returning tuples satisfying a string similarity condition, the similarity join combining tuples from two relations based on an approximate matching criterion. In the following we describe strategies for implementing these operators using selectivity-based mapping.

4.1 Similarity-Based Selections

Intuitively, a similarity selection $\tilde{\sigma}_{SIM(s,attr)} r(R)$ is an operation returning all tuples satisfying a similarity condition $SIM(s, attr)$ where $attr \in R$ with a similarity value greater or equal than a given threshold:

$$\tilde{\sigma}_{SIM(s,attr)} r(R) = \{t \mid t \in r(R) \wedge SIM(s, t.attr) \geq threshold\}$$

A particular variant of such a similarity predicate considered here is the edit distance:

$$\tilde{\sigma}_{edist(s,attr) \leq k} r(R) = \{t \mid t \in r(R) \land edist(s, t.attr) \leq k\}$$

Without loss of generality we focus on simple predicates only. Complex predicates, e.g. connected by $\lor$ or $\land$ can be handled by applying the following steps to each atomic predicate and taking into account query capabilities of the sources. However, query capability issues are addressed in other works (see Sect. 2). Furthermore, we assume that source systems do not support such predicates but only the primitive predicate *contains(a, b)* introduced above. Now, the problem is to rewrite a query containing $\tilde{\sigma}_{SIM}$ in the following form:

$$\tilde{\sigma}_{SIM} \rightarrow \tilde{\sigma}_{SIM}(\sigma_{PRESIM}(r(R)))$$

where σ_{PRESIM} is pushed to the source system and $\tilde{\sigma}_{SIM}$ is performed in the mediator.

Assuming *SIM* is an atomic predicate of the form $edist(s, attr) \leq k$ the selection condition *PRESIM* can be derived using the mapping functions *map_qgram*, *map_substring*, *map_token* from Section 3 which we consider in the generalized form *map*. This mapping function returns a set $\{q\}$ of q-samples, substrings, or keywords according to the mappings described in Section 3. The disjunctive query represented by this set in general contains $k + 1$ strings, unless the length of s does not allow to retrieve this number of substrings. In this case, the next possible smaller set is returned, representing a query returning a partial result as described before. In any case, the estimated selectivity of the represented query must be better than a given selectivity threshold.

Based on this we can derive the expression *PRESIM* from the similarity predicate as follows:

$$PRESIM := \bigvee_{\forall q \in map(s)} contains(q, attr)$$

In case of using the edit distance as similarity predicate we can further optimize the query expression by applying length filtering. This means, we can omit the expensive computation of the edit distance between two strings s_1 and s_2 if $|\text{length}(s_1) - \text{length}(s_2)| \geq k$ for a given maximum distance values k. This holds, because in this case the edit distance value is already $\geq k$. Thus, the final query expression is

$$\tilde{\sigma}_{edist(s,attr) < k}(\sigma_{|\text{length}(s) - \text{length}(attr)| \leq k}(\sigma_{PRESIM}(r(R))))$$

where the placement of the length filtering selection depends on the query capabilities of the source. A second optimization rule deals with complex disjunctively connected similarity conditions of the form $SIM(s_1, attr) \lor SIM(s_2, attr)$. In this case the pre-selection condition can be simplified to

$$\bigvee_{\forall q_1 \in map(s_1)} contains(q_1, attr) \lor \bigvee_{\forall q_2 \in map(s_2)} contains(q_2, attr)$$

A general problem that can occur in this context are query strings exceeding the length limit for query strings given by the source system. This has to be handled by splitting the query condition into two or more parts $PRESIM_1 \ldots PRESIM_n$ and building the union of the partial results afterwards:

$$\tilde{\sigma}_{SIM}(\sigma_{PRESIM_1}(r(R)) \cup \cdots \cup \sigma_{PRESIM_n}(r(R)))$$

Obviously, the above mentioned optimization of applying length filtering can be used here, too.

4.2 Similarity Join

Based on the idea of implementing similarity operations by introducing a pre-selection we can realize similarity join operations, too. A similarity join $r_1(R_1) \bowtie_{SIM} r_2(R_2)$ where the join condition is a approximate string criterion of the form $SIM(R_1.attr_1, R_2.attr_2) > threshold$ or $edist(R_1.attr_1, R_2.attr_2) \leq k$. As in the previous sections we consider in the following only simple edit distance predicates.

A first approach for computing the join is to use a bind join implementation. Here, we assume that one relation is either restricted by a selection criterion or can be scanned completely. Then, the bind join works as follows (Fig. 3). For each tuple of the outer relation r_1 we take the (string) value of the join attribute $attr_1$ and perform a similarity selection on the inner relation. This is performed in the same way as described in Section 4.1 by mapping the string to a set of q-grams, sending the selection to the source and post-process the result by applying the similarity predicate. Next, each tuple of this selection result is combined with the current tuple of the outer relation.

foreach $t_1 \in r_1(R_1)$ **do**
  $s := t(R_1.attr_1)$
  foreach $t_2 \in \tilde{\sigma}_{edist(s, attr_2)}(\sigma_{PRESIM}(r_2(R_2)))$ **do**
    output $t_1 \circ t_2$

Fig. 3. Bind join

The roles of the participating relations (inner or outer relation) are determined by taking into account relation cardinalities as well as the query capabilities. If a relation is not restricted using a selection condition and does not support a full table scan it has to be used as inner relation. Otherwise, the smaller relation is chosen as the outer relation in order to reduce the number of source queries. Obviously, a bind join implementation requires $|r_1| + 1$ source queries if no constraint on the result from r_1 exists.

A significant reduction of the number of the source queries can be achieved by using a semi-join variant. Here, one of the relations is first processed completely. The string values of the join attribute are collected and the *map* function is applied to each of them. The resulting set S of q-grams, tokens or substrings is used to build a single pre-selection condition. Next, this pre-selection is sent to the source. Finally, the result is joined with the tuples from the first relation using the similarity condition (Fig. 4).

If the pre-selection condition exceeds the query string limit of the source, the pre-selection has to be performed in multiple steps. In the best case, this approach requires

$\mathcal{S} := \emptyset$
foreach $t_1 \in r_1(R_1)$ **do**
    $\mathcal{S} := \mathcal{S} \cup map(t(R_1.attr_1))$
$r_{tmp} := \sigma_{\bigvee_{s \in \mathcal{S}} contains(s, attr_2)}(r_2(R_2))$
foreach $t_1 \in r_1(R_1)$ **do**
    foreach $t_2 \in r_{tmp}$ **do**
        if $edist(t_1(R_1.attr_1), t_2(R_2.attr_2)) < k$
            output $t_1 \circ t_2$

Fig. 4. Semi join

only 2 source queries assuming that the first relation is cached in the mediator or 3 source queries otherwise. The worst case depends on the query length limit as well as the number of derived q-grams. However, if the number of queries is greater than $|r_1|+1$ one can switch always to the bind join implementation.

5 Managing Selectivity Information

In the previous sections we described the mapping of similarity-based predicates to substring and keyword queries. In this section we shortly review and adapt data structures to store selectivity information and algorithms to extract these information.

5.1 Data Structures

There are various kinds of data structures to store information for approximate string matching, for instance described by Navarro in [16]. For the purpose of matching, these structures hold pointers to the occurrences of substrings in the text. As for selectivity estimation the number of occurrences are interesting, and not the positions themselves, the data structures were adapted to hold counts instead of pointers. Based on the kind of string decomposition possible data structures are

- full count-suffix trees (FST) or pruned count-suffix trees (PST) for arbitrary length substrings,
- hash tables or pruned hash tables which store fixed length q-grams or tokens and their corresponding counts, and
- count tries (CT) or pruned count tries (PCT), that store count information of tokens or q-grams of variable length q.

Count-Suffix tree: a suffix tree is a trie that stores not only all strings s of a database but also all suffixes $s[i, length(s) - 1], 0 \leq i < length(s)$ of s. The count-suffix tree is a variant of a suffix tree which does not store pointers to the occurrences of the substrings $s[i, j]$ but maintains the count of substrings $C_{s[i,j]}$. As each node corresponds to a substring $s[i, j]$ the count value $C_{s[i,j]}$ can have two meanings: (i) $C_{s[i,j]}$ describes the number of strings in which $s[i, j]$ is contained or (ii) $C_{s[i,j]}$ denotes the number of occurrences of the substring $s[i,j]$. In our further investigations we assume the second case. The count assigned to the root node N is the number of all suffixes in the database.

The space requirements of a full count-suffix tree can be prohibitive for estimating substring selectivity because of limited available space and high costs for substring selectivity estimation, especially if we assume the operations presented in Sec. 4. Therefore, the pruned count-suffix tree was presented by Krishnan et al. in [13]. This data structure maintains only the counts of substrings that satisfy a certain pruning rule. Examples for a rule are: maintain only the top-n levels of the suffix-tree, i.e. retain only substrings with a length $length(a) \leq l_{max}$, or retain all nodes that have a count $C_a > p_{min}$, where p_{min} is the pruning threshold. A pruned count-suffix tree can be used to summarize the selectivity information of arbitrary substrings, which is the first kind of the pre-selection predicates.

q-gram hash table: The second kind of substring decomposition uses q-samples that allow cheaper storage and computation costs. The selectivity information are stored in hash tables, which contain q-grams extracted from the string in the database. Each entry in a hash table $\mathcal{H}_q$ consists of a q-gram with length q as key and the assigned count information C_{qgram}. To access the information efficiently the address is computed by a hash function, similar to Karp-Rabin [11], i.e. the hash value of a q-gram can be computed from the hash value of the previous q-gram in a string in a time of $O(1)$. These kind of hash functions are useful in constructing as well as in searching for selectivity information. In order to reduce the storage costs the hash table can be pruned using a pruning rule. A typical pruning rule is based on the count: maintain only those q-gram entries with a count greater than a given threshold, i.e. $C_{qgram} > p_{min}$. To support q-samples of varying length selectivity information of q-grams with differnt length has to be maintained. A straightforward solution can use several hash tables for different length q. However, this approach causes a considerable redundancy addressed in the next paragraph.

Count trie (CT): as mentioned in [9] a count-suffix tree can be pruned by different rules apart from minimum counts. In order to find a compressed representation of q-grams of different lengths by the maximum height of the count-suffix tree a pruning rule $p \leq q$ means, for each suffix s_i of a string s only the part $s_i[0,q]$ is stored in the count-suffix tree. For each suffix, which now represents a q-gram, the count of occurrences is maintained. Furthermore, if only q-grams of a certain minimum length p_{min} should be maintained, the pruning rule can be extended to $p_{min} \leq q \leq p_{max}$. As almost all q-grams are a prefix of $(q+i)$-grams, the compression rate is very high. Additional pruning based on the counts can be performed corresponding to the q-gram hash tables. Thus, the data structure can hold information for the selectivity estimation for q-grams. The structure is not supposed to help estimating the selectivity information for arbitrary substrings like the count-suffix tree described above. Corresponding to pruned count-suffix trees and pruned hash tables, it is possible to construct pruned count tries. In a pruned count trie only nodes that have a count greater than a threshold $p_{mincount}$ are maintained.

5.2 Estimation of Selectivity Values

Count suffix-trees: decomposition into arbitrary substrings requires selectivity information for each substring in the query string. These information are stored in a full count-suffix tree or in a pruned count-suffix tree. To efficiently retrieve all selectivity information from an FST, a suffix-tree is constructed from the query string s, called ST_s. Subsequently, the tree ST_s is traversed in pre-order and each traversal step is repeated immediately in the FST. Thus, in each step the selectivity is assigned to the corresponding position in the lower triangular matrix (see Sec. 3.1). The selectivity of a substring $s[i,j]$ $0 \leq i < j \leq length(s)$ itself is computed by $sel(s[i,j]) = \frac{C_{s[i,j]}}{N}$ with $C_{s[i,j]}$ the count value associated to the node of the FST which represents the substring, and N the count value associated to the root node. Traversing the suffix-tree of query string s and the count-suffix tree in parallel reduces the search costs compared to querying each substring separately. If a substring is not found, its selectivity is assumed to be 0.

q-gram hash table: the decomposition of the query string s into q-samples requires the selectivity information of all q-grams of s. The cost for computing the selectivity information is $O(length(s))$. If a q-gram is contained in a hash table $\mathcal{H}_q$, the estimated selectivity is $sel(qgram) = \frac{C_{qgram}}{N}$ with C_{gram} the associated count value and N the number of all q-grams in the database. Using a pruned hash table some q-grams might not appear in the table. In this case, the estimated selectivity is simply the pruning selectivity $sel_p = \frac{p-1}{N}$ with p the minimum count. This kind of strategy works well for low pruning limits. Token tables are used in a straightforward way. To each token t the token count C_t in the complete database is stored. The selectivity of the token is defined as $sel(t) = \frac{C_t}{N}$ with N sum of all token counts in the database. In a pruned token table not found tokens are estimated with $sel(t) = \frac{p-1}{N}$ with p the pruning limit.

Count trie: a count tries can be used to estimate selectivity information for q-grams of a length q with $p_{min} \leq q \leq p_{max}$. For each q-gram $s[i, i+q]$ with $0 \leq i < length(s) - q$ of a query string s the count trie CT has to traversed from the root node to a node on level q to find the associated count information $C_{s[i,i+q]}$. Thus, the costs of obtaining selectivity information are $O(length(s) * q)$. The selectivity is computed by $sel(s[i, i+q]) = \frac{C_{s[i,i+q]}}{N}$ with N the number of q-grams assigned to root of the count trie.

5.3 Building and Maintaining Selectivity Information

In this paper we assume uncooperative Web sources, i.e. sources provide only limited query capabilities, e.g. via a Web interface or a restricted Web service. However, either a substring or a keyword search has to be supported.

First, an initial description of the substring distribution is needed. If this can not be retrieved from a cooperative source or some kind of vocabulary, a possible approach uses *query-based sampling* as described in [1]. There, query-based sampling is used for the construction of source descriptions of text databases. The obtained descriptions allow the selection of relevant sources in distributed text retrieval. The general approach can be described by the following steps:

1. Select an initial query string
2. Send the query string to the source and execute it
3. Retrieve top (first or sample) k results (tuples)
    a) extract substrings according the selected type
    b) update the statistic information of the summary structure

4. while no exit condition is reached, randomly select a new query string from the learned substrings and continue with step 2.

A query string is either an arbitrary substring, a q-gram, or a token. The corresponding query is a substring query for the former two cases and a keyword query for the latter case. As substring queries do not rank the results, there are two approaches in step 3: select the first k or sample k results. Selecting only the first k returned tuples allows a fast computation for the sample tuples. If the results are ordered, the extracted frequency information and substrings are too biased. This problem can be solved by using the sample k approach. The sample can be drawn from the arriving results by applying a reservoir sampling algorithm. The randomly selected tuples are used to build the summary structure. The disadvantage is the retrieval of the complete query results necessary to sample the data.

The ideas behind query-based sampling are the following. At first, the selectivity information can be seen as an ordered "stop word list", i.e. we want to avoid substrings with a bad selectivity. But, substrings occuring with a high frequency are extremely well approximated with query based sampling, as shown in the evaluation in Section 6. This way we can avoid big result sets even with a relatively small ratio of sampled tuples.

6 Evaluation

For evaluation purposes we used a real-life data set containing detailed information about cultural assets lost or stolen from private persons and museums in Europe during and after the Nazi regime. Because the gathered data is often imprecise or erroneous, similarity based operations are important in this application scenario and are already part of the application. This current research targets the integration with similar databases available over the Web. The experiments dealt with a collection of approximately 60000 titles of cultural assets. The data set contains a great number of duplicates with identical and similar values, e.g. 14% of the tuples have identical duplicates, 2.2% of the tuples have duplicates with an edit distance of 1, and 1.8% of the tuples have duplicates with an edit distance of 2. To evaluate the key criteria described in the following, this data set as well as necessary index structures were materialized in one local Oracle 9i database and queries were mapped to SQL substring queries for pre-selection. The required mapping and further evaluation was implemented in a mediator on top of the database system using Java. The considered queries were similarity self-joins on this one table. The key criteria considered during evaluation are the selectivity of generated pre-selections, the quality of our selectivity estimation, and the applicability to actual data values. Figure 5 shows the average selectivity we achieved with the proposed q-samples approach for a varying maximum edit distance k and varying q. The size of the candidate sets retrieved from the database were reasonable, especially for $q = 4$ and $q = 5$, 100 to 300 of the approximate 60000 original titles.

To answer the question, how many queries provide a good selectivity, beneath a given threshold, which also can be used to reject a query if the intermediate result would exceed a reasonable limit, we investigated the selectivity distribution of queries created from every tuple in the data set. The results are shown in Figure 6 for varying q and k. For example, in Figure 6(c) where $k = 3$, if we set the selectivity threshold to 5%,

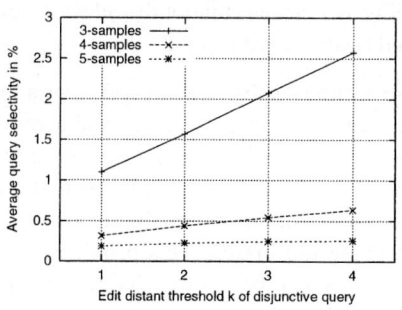

Fig. 5. Average selectivity for varying q and k

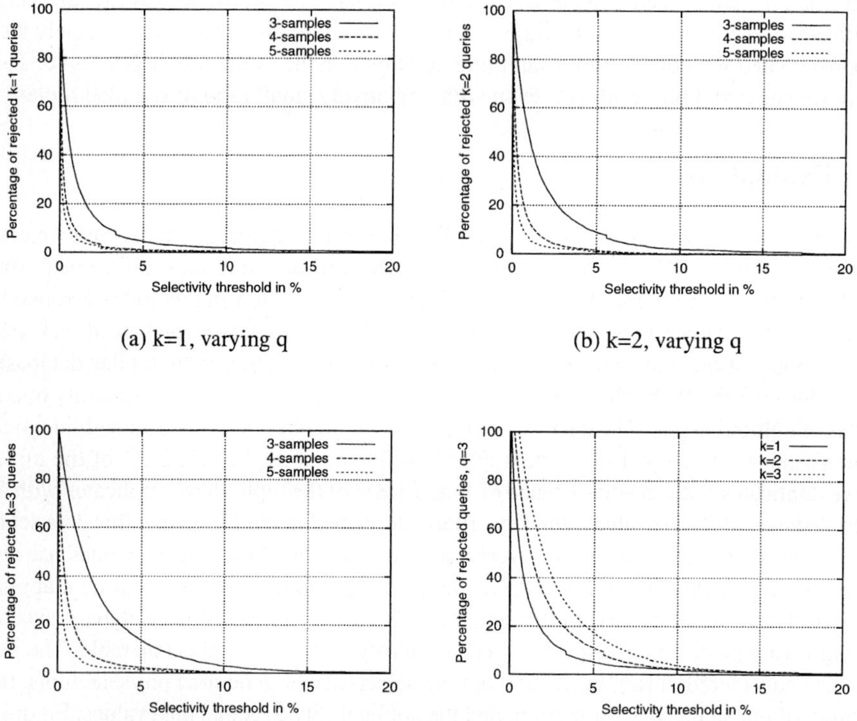

(a) k=1, varying q

(b) k=2, varying q

(c) k=3, varying q

(d) varying k, q=3

Fig. 6. Cumulative selectivity distribution for varying q and k

we have to reject approximately 3% of the queries using 4-samples and 5-samples and approximately 14% of queries using 3-samples. Though the former observation may seem quite bad, actually the edit distance threshold of $k = 3$ is not realistic for most applications, where real duplicates often have a distance of 1 or 2. The effect improves for smaller k as shown in Figure 6(d), where for the the same selectivity threshold we see that for $k = 2$ we only have to reject 10% and for $k = 1$ only 5% of our queries. Again, for longer substrings with $q = 4$ and $q = 5$ the queries perform far better, as seen in Figures 6(a) and 6(b).

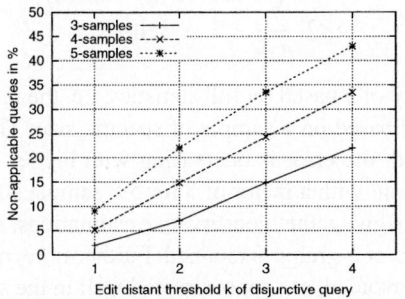

Fig. 7. Applicability for varying q and k

A problem with the presented approach occurs, if the number of required q-samples can not be retrieved from a given search string, because the latter is not long enough for the decomposition. Figure 7 shows how often this was the case with our data set and for varying q and k, i.e. the query strings s did not fulfill the condition $length(s) \leq q*(k+1)$. Though, in this case we can still step back instead of reject and send a query containing less than $k + 1$ q-samples providing at least a subset of the result as mentioned before. Nevertheless, while greater q benefit the selectivity they hinder the applicability when many short query strings exist. Therefore, the parameters q, k, and a possible selectivity threshold have to be chosen carefully based on characteristics of a given application.

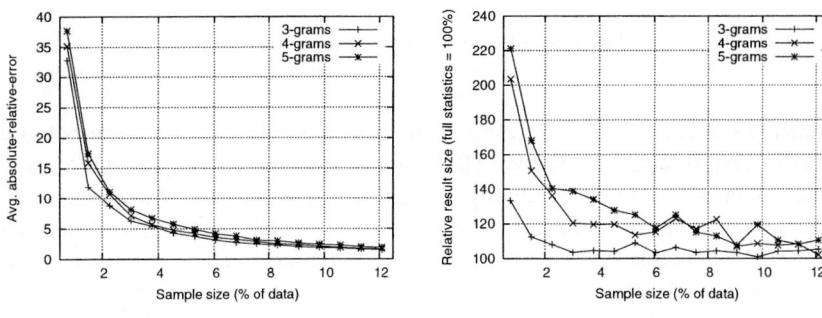

(a) Sample size estimation errors (b) Quality of the pre-selection decisions

Fig. 8. Sample size vs. Quality

In Sec. 5.3 we described the usage of query-based sampling in order to build selectivity summaries for uncooperative sources. Now we have to evaluate the quality of these information and the impact on the pre-selection predicates. First, the differences between full scan estimation and estimation based on a certain sample size are investigated. From all possible q-grams 2000 were selected into a query set $\mathcal{Q}$. Subsequently, we computed the average of the absolute-relative-errors defined as

$$e = \frac{1}{|\mathcal{Q}|} \sum_{q \in \mathcal{Q}} \frac{\text{abs}(\text{sel}(q) - \text{est}(q))}{\text{sel}(q)},$$

with $\text{sel}(q)$ the selectivity of q based on full statistics, i.e. the real selectivity, and $\text{est}(q)$ the estimated selectivity based on a sample of specific size. The results are illustrated in Fig. 8(a). As expected, the error is decreasing with bigger sample sizes. However, the error is quite significant with a factor of 5 for 5% sample size. But that only means, that for small samples we give rather conservative estimations. And, the most important thing is, the relative order of q-grams is retained. Furthermore, high ranked q-grams, i.e. those, which have to be avoided, are approximated well in the sample.

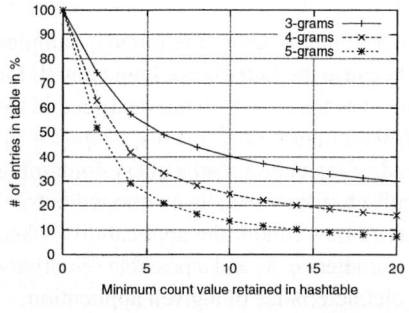 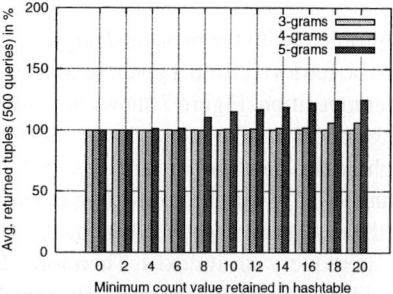

(a) q-gram table sizes vs. pruning limits

(b) Quality of pre-selection vs. pruning limits

Fig. 9. Results for pruned q-gram tables

Following the evaluation of the estimation errors the influence of the errors to the pre-selection results have to be shown. Therefore, we generated a sample set of queries $\mathcal{Q}_2$ which contains 500 strings randomly selected from the database. We measured the average number of tuples returned by the pre-selection condition for an edit distance $k = 2$, i.e. a disjunction of three q-sample substring queries. Here, we assumed the average result size of substring queries created with full statistics as 100%. Fig. 8(b) shows the result sizes of pre-selection queries created using selectivity information from different sample sizes. Even the precision of query based sampling selectivity estimation is not very high, the query results are close to full statistics. That has several reasons. The selectivity estimation of high ranked q-grams is rather high and ranking similarity is high. Thus, even if the selectivity estimation is not perfect, the relative order of the q-grams is good.

Finally, we evaluated the influence of the pruning limit on sizes of the storage structures as well as on the quality of pre-selection. The results are illustrated in Figures 9(a) and 9(b) respectively. Especially for 4- and 5-grams pruning reduces the storage costs decisively, e.g. with a pruning limit $p_{min} = 15$ the size of the 5-gram table reduces to 10% of the original size. Nevertheless, the quality of the estimations and result set sizes based on the estimations are very good as seen in Figure 9(b).

7 Conclusions and Outlook

In this paper we presented an approach for querying based on string similarity in a virtually integrated and heterogeneous environment. String similarity is expressed in terms of the edit distance, and global queries are re-written to a source query using standard interfaces to efficiently select a candidate set and a global part of the query that actually computes the correct result within a mediator. To grant efficiency, queries are re-written to disjunctive source queries based on selectivity information for q-samples, arbitrary substrings, or tokens. As the approach in general is quite new, there is of course a great number of open questions, which require further research or could not be discussed here in detail due to space limitations. The currently achieved results of fetching only a small fraction of a percent of the original data in most scenarios may be suitable for many applications, but for large data volumes this already may be prohibitive. On the other hand, while a complete decomposition of a search string to substrings is optimal regarding the selectivity, the necessary overhead seems impractical in most applications. We pointed toward mixed approaches and are currently researching further ways for selectivity estimation.

Using the string edit distance for similarity operations does not fully reflect real-world requirements, were similarity is most often specific to attribute semantics of the given application, e.g. the similarity of presentations of a persons name can be judged much better using a specific similarity measure. Nevertheless, the general principle of pre-selection by query re-writing remains applicable, as well as many aspects of mapping a given value based on selectivity. A framework for query processing should provide generalized operations clearly separated from application-specific aspects.

References

1. J. Callan and M. Connell. Query-based sampling of text databases. *ACM Trans. Inf. Syst.*, 19(2):97–130, 2001.
2. W. Cohen. Integration of heterogeneous databases without common domains using queries based on textual similarity. In L. M. Haas and A. Tiwary, editors, *Proceedings ACM SIGMOD, 1998, Seattle, Washington, USA*, pages 201–212. ACM Press, 1998.
3. C. Faloutsos and K.-I. Lin. FastMap: A fast algorithm for indexing, data-mining and visualization of traditional and multimedia datasets. In *ACM SIGMOD 1995*, pages 163–174, 1995.

4. N. Fuhr. Probabilistic datalog – A logic for powerful retrieval methods. In *Proceedings of the Eighteenth Annual International ACM SIGIR Conference on Research and Development in Information Retrieval*, Retrieval Logic, pages 282–290, 1995.
5. L. Gravano, P. G. Ipeirotis, H. V. Jagadish, N. Koudas, S. Muthukrishnan, and D. Srivastava. Approximate string joins in a database (almost) for free. In *VLDB 2001*, pages 491–500, 2001.
6. L. Gravano, P. G. Ipeirotis, N. Koudas, and D. Srivastava. Text joins in an RDBMS for web data integration. In *WWW 2003*, pages 90–101, 2003.
7. Y.E. Ioannidis and V. Poosala. Balancing histogram optimality and practicality for query result size estimation. In M.J. Carey and D.A. Schneider, editors, *ACM SIGMOD 1995*, pages 233–244, 1995.
8. P.G. Ipeirotis and L. Gravano. Distributed search over the hidden web: Hierarchical database sampling and selection. In *VLDB 2002*, pages 394–405, 2002.
9. H.V. Jagadish, O. Kapitskaia, R.T. Ng, and D. Srivastava. One-dimensional and multi-dimensional substring selectivity estimation. *The VLDB Journal*, 9(3):214 – 230, dec 2000.
10. L. Jin, C. Li, and S. Mehrotra. Efficient record linkage in large data sets. In *Eighth International Conference on Database Systems for Advanced Applications (DASFAA '03), March 26-28, 2003, Kyoto, Japan*, 2003.
11. R.M Karp and M.O. Rabin. Efficient randomized pattern-matching algorithms. *IBM Journal of Research Developments*, 31(2), mar 1987.
12. N. Koudas and K. C. Sevcik. High dimensional similarity joins: Algorithms and performance evaluation. *IEEETKDE: IEEE Transactions on Knowledge and Data Engineering*, 12, 2000.
13. P. Krishnan, J.S. Vitter, and B.R. Iyer. Estimating Alphanumeric Selectivity in the Presence of Wildcards. In H.V. Jagadish and I.S. Mumick, editors, *ACM SIGMOD 1996*, pages 282–293, 1996.
14. G. Navarro. A guided tour to approximate string matching. *ACM Computing Surveys*, 33(1):31–88, 2001.
15. G. Navarro and R. Baeza-Yates. A practical q-gram index for text retrieval allowing errors. *CLEI Electonic Journal*, 1(2), 1998.
16. G. Navarro, R.A. Baeza-Yates, E. Sutinen, and J. Tarhio. Indexing Methods for Approximate String Matching. *IEEE Data Engineering Bulletin*, 24(4):19 – 27, dec 2001.
17. M.T. Roth and P.M. Schwarz. Don't scrap it, wrap it! a wrapper architecture for legacy data sources. In M. Jarke, M.J. Carey, K.R. Dittrich, F.H. Lochovsky, P. Loucopoulos, and M.A. Jeusfeld, editors, *VLDB 1997*, pages 266–275, 1997.
18. S. Santini and R. Jain. Similarity measures. *IEEE Transactions on Pattern Analysis and Machine Intelligence*, 21(9):871–883, 1999.
19. E. Schallehn, K. Sattler, and G. Saake. Efficient Similarity-based Operations for Data Integration. *Data and Knowledge Engineering Journal*, 48(3):361–387, 2004.
20. H. Shang and T. H. Merrett. Tries for approximate string matching. *IEEE Transactions on Knowledge and Data Engineering*, 8(4):540–547, 1996.
21. V. Vassalos and Y. Papakonstantinou. Describing and using query capabilities of heterogeneous sources. In M. Jarke, M.J. Carey, K.R. Dittrich, F.H. Lochovsky, P. Loucopoulos, and M.A. Jeusfeld, editors, *VLDB 1997*, pages 256–265, 1997.

Managing Semantic Compensation in a Multi-agent System

Amy Unruh, James Bailey, and Kotagiri Ramamohanarao

Dept. of Computer Science and Software Engineering
The University of Melbourne, VIC 3010, Australia
{unruh,jbailey,rao}@cs.mu.oz.au

Abstract. Recovery in agent systems is an important and complex problem. This paper describes an approach to improving the robustness of an agent system by augmenting its failure-handling capabilities. The approach is based on the concept of semantic compensation: "cleaning up" failed or canceled tasks can help agents behave more robustly and predictably at both an individual and system level. However, in complex and dynamic domains it is difficult to define useful specific compensations ahead of time. This paper presents an approach to defining semantic compensations abstractly, then implementing them in a situation-specific manner at time of failure. The paper describes a methodology for decoupling failure-handling from normative agent logic so that the semantic compensation knowledge can be applied in a predictable and consistent way– with respect to both individual agent reaction to failure, and handling failure-related interactions between agents– without requiring the agent application designer to implement the details of the failure-handling model. In particular, in a multi-agent system, robust handling of compensations for delegated tasks requires flexible protocols to support management of compensation-related activities. The ability to decouple the failure-handling conversations allows these protocols to be developed independently of the agent application logic.

1 Introduction

The design of reliable agent systems is a complex and important problem. One aspect of that problem is making a system more robust to failure. The work described in this paper is part of a Department of CSSE, University of Melbourne project to develop methodologies for building more robust multi-agent systems, in which we investigate ways to apply transactional semantics to improve the robustness of agent problem-solving and interaction. Traditional transaction processing systems prevent inconsistency and integrity problems by satisfying the so-called ACID properties of transactions: Atomicity, Consistency, Isolation, and Durability [1]. These properties define an abstract computational model in which each transaction runs as if it were alone and there were no failure. The programmer can focus on developing correct, consistent transactions, while the handling of concurrency and failure is delegated to the underlying engine.

Our research is motivated by this principle: we would like to make a system of interacting agents more robust, by improving its failure-handling behavior. We would also like agent designers to be able to define failure-handling information in a way that is easy to understand and which does not require them to make tweaks to a given agent's existing domain logic; and by providing an underlying support mechanism which takes care of the details of the failure-handling.

However, in most multi-agent domains, principles of transaction management can not be directly applied. The effects of many actions may not be delayed: such actions "always commit", and thus correction of problems must be implemented by "forward recovery", or failure *compensation* [1]– that is, by performing additional actions to correct the problem, instead of a transaction rollback. In addition, actions may not be "undoable" nor repeatable. Further, it is often not possible to enumerate how the tasks in a dynamic agent system might unfold ahead of time: it is not computationally feasible, nor do we have enough information about the possible "states of the world" to do so.

In this paper, we focus on one aspect of behavior motivated by transactional semantics, that of approximating failure atomicity by *semantic compensation*: improving the ability of an agent system to recover from task problems by "cleaning up after" or "undoing" its problematic actions. The use of semantic compensation in an agent context has several benefits:

– It helps leave an agent in a state from which future actions– such as retries, or alternate methods of task achievement– are more likely to be successful;
– it helps maintain an agent system in a more predictable state: agent interactions are more robust; and unneeded resources are not tied up;
– it can often be applied more generally than methods which attempt to "patch" a failed activity;
– and (in the context of our longer-term project goals) it allows a long "transaction" to be split up into shorter ones, with less chance of deadlocks, and higher concurrency.

We introduce the concept of semantic compensation by presenting an example in a "dinner party" domain. (We use this domain because it has a rich semantics and is easily understandable; its issues can be mapped to analogous problems in more conventional domains). Consider two related scenarios, where a group of agents must carry out the activities necessary to prepare for holding a party. First, consider an example where the party will be held at a rented hall, e.g. for a business-related event. Fig. 1A shows one task decomposition for such an activity. The figure uses an informal notation, where subtasks that may be executed concurrently are connected by a double bar; otherwise they are executed sequentially. The subtasks include planning the menu, scheduling the party and arranging to reserve a hall, inviting the guests and arranging for catering. The figure indicates that some of the subtasks (such as inviting the guests) may be delegated to other agents in the system.

Next, consider a scenario which differs in that the party will be held at the host's house. In this case, while the party must be scheduled, a hall does not

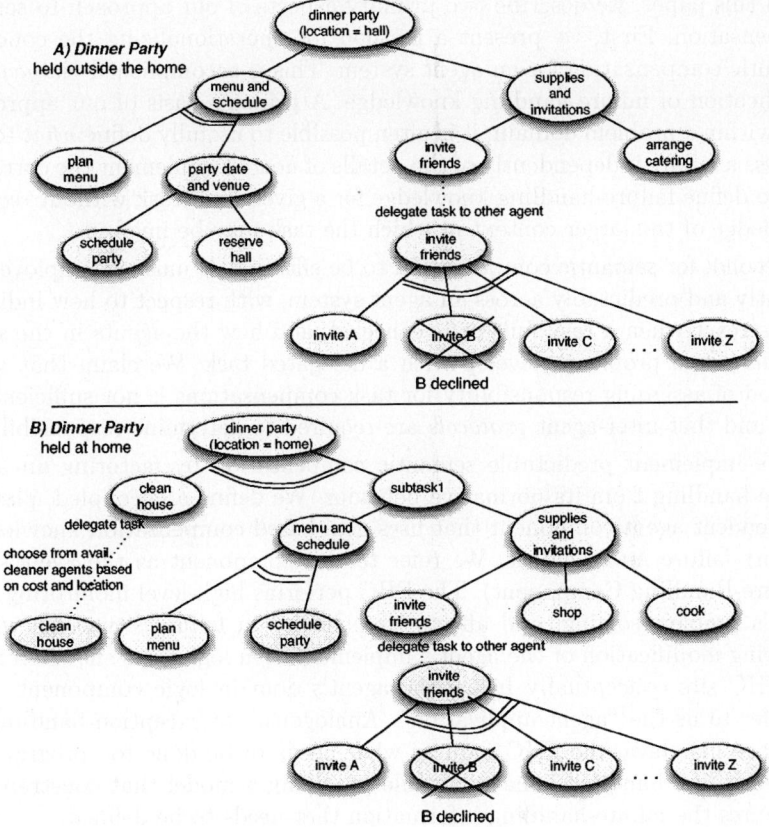

Fig. 1. Planning a dinner party.

need to be reserved. In addition, the hosts will not have the party catered and will shop themselves. Fig. 1B shows a task decomposition for this scenario.

If the party planning fails or the event must be canceled, then a number of things might need to be done to properly take care of the cancellation– that is, to "compensate for" the party planning. However, the specifics of these activities will be different depending upon what has been accomplished prior to cancellation. In the first case (Fig. 1A) we may have to cancel some reservations, but if we have used caterers, then we will not have to deal with any extra food; in the second case (Fig. 1B), we have no reservations to cancel, but we will likely have unused food. In either event, the party cancellation activities can be viewed as accomplishing a *semantic compensation*; clearly, compensation activities must address agent task semantics. An exact 'undo' is not always desirable– even if possible. Further, compensations are both context-dependent and usually infeasible to enumerate ahead of time, and employing a composition of subtask compensations is almost always too simplistic.

In this paper, we describe two primary aspects of our approach to semantic compensation. First, we present a method for operationalizing the concept of semantic compensation for an agent system. This is accomplished via *goal-based* specification of failure-handling knowledge. A primary basis of our approach is that within a problem domain, it is often possible to usefully define *what* to do to address a failure independently of the details of *how* to implement the correction; and to define failure-handling knowledge for a given (sub)task without requiring knowledge of the larger context in which the task may be invoked.

Second, for semantic compensation to be effective, it must be employed consistently and predictably across an agent system, with respect to how individual agents react when a task fails or is canceled, and how the agents in the system *interact* when problems develop with a delegated task. We claim that a fixed method of assigning responsibility for task compensations is not sufficiently robust, and that inter-agent *protocols* are required to determine responsibility.

We implement predictable semantic compensation by factoring an agent's failure-handling from its normative behavior. We define a decoupled, platform-independent agent component that uses goal-based compensation knowledge to support failure management. We refer to this component as the agent's FHC (Failure-Handling Component). The FHC performs high-level monitoring of the agent's problem-solving, and affects its behavior in failure situations without requiring modification of the agent's implementation logic[1]. As shown in Fig. 2, the FHC sits conceptually below the agent's domain logic component, which we refer to as the "agent application". Analogously to exception-handling in a language like Java, the FHC reduces what needs to be done to "program" the agent's failure-handling behavior, while providing a model that constrains and structures the failure-handling information that needs to be defined.

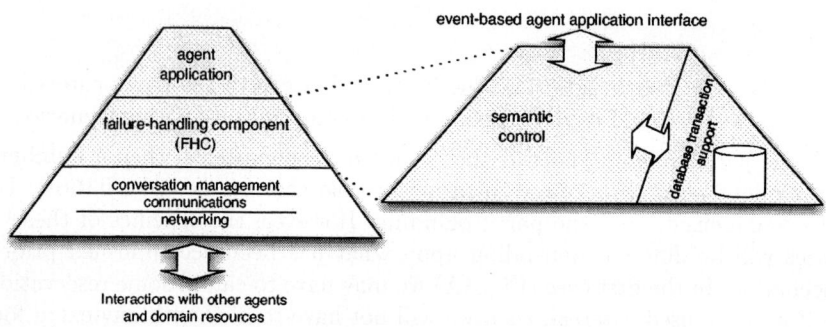

Fig. 2. An agent's FHC. We refer to the domain logic part of the agent, above the failure-handling component, as the "agent application".

---

[1] With respect to our larger project goals, this framework will also support other aspects of our intended transactional semantics, such as logging, recovery from crashes, and task concurrency management.

In Section 2, we describe our approach to goal-based definition of failure-handling knowledge. Section 3 outlines how the FHC uses this knowledge to provide robust and well-specified reactions to task failures and cancellations, and to support predictable and consistent failure-handling-related interactions between the agents in the system, independent of changes in the 'core' agent application logic. In Sections 4 and 5 we finish with a discussion of related work, and conclude.

2 Goal-Based Semantic Compensation

The example of Section 1 suggested how compensation of a high-level task can typically be achieved in different ways depending upon context. It is often difficult to identify prior to working on a task the context-specific details of how a task failure should be addressed or a compensation performed. It can be effectively impossible to define all semantic compensations prior to runtime in terms of specific actions that must be performed.

Instead, we claim it is more useful to define semantic compensations *declaratively*, in terms of the *goals* that the agent system needs to achieve in order to accomplish the compensation, thus making these definitions more widely applicable. We associate *failure-handling goal definitions* with some or all of the tasks (goals) that an agent can perform. These definitions specify at a goal[2]– rather than plan– level *what* to do in certain failure situations, and we then rely on the agents in the system to determine *how* a goal is accomplished. The way in which these goals are achieved, for a specific scenario, will depend upon context.

Figures 3A and 3B illustrate this idea. Suppose that in the party-planning examples of Section 1, the host falls ill and the party needs to be canceled. Let the compensation goals for the party-planning task be the following:
- all party-related reservations should be canceled;
- extra food used elsewhere if possible; and
- guests notified and 'apologies' made.

The figures show the resulting implementations of these compensation goals for the activities in Figs 1A and 1B. Note that the compensation goals for the high-level party-planning task *are the same in both cases*, and indicate what needs to be made true in order for the compensation to be achieved. However, the *implementations* of these goals will differ in the two cases, due to the different contexts in which the agent works to achieve them. When the party was to be held at home (Fig. 3B), extra food must be disposed of, and (due to the more personal nature of the party) gifts are sent to the guests. In the case where the party was to be held in a meeting hall (Fig. 3A), there are reservations that need to be canceled. However, there is no need to deal with extra food (the caterers will handle it) nor to send gifts. Some compensation goals may be already satisfied

---

[2] In this paper, we use 'goal' and 'task' interchangeably; as distinguished from plans, action steps, or task execution. In our usage, goals describe conditions to be achieved, not actions or decompositions.

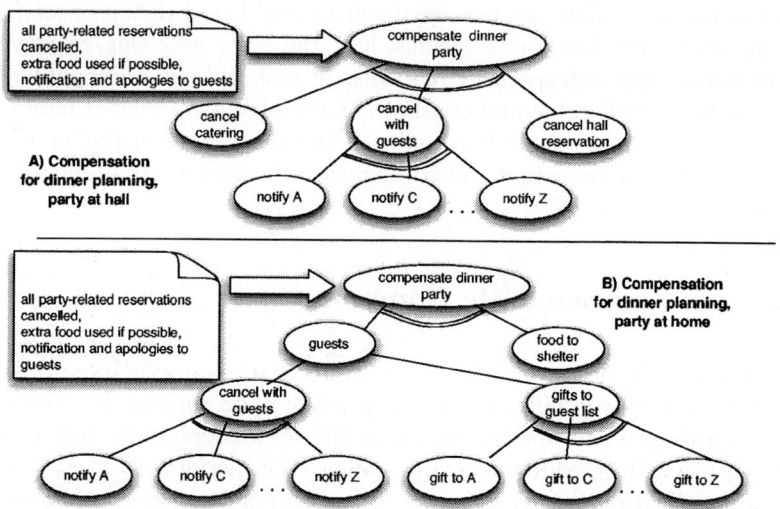

Fig. 3. Compensation of dinner party planning.

and need no action, and some tasks may be only partly completed at time of cancellation (e.g. not all guests may be yet invited).

Note that a semantic compensation may include goals that do not address any of the (sub)tasks of the original task, such as the gift-giving in the first example. Some compensation activities may "reverse" the effects of previous actions (e.g. canceling the reservation of a meeting hall), but other previous effects may be ignored (no effort is made to "undo" the effects of the house-cleaning) or partially compensatable (dealing with the extra food) depending upon context. The definition of such a semantic compensation is task- and domain-specific.

A goal-based formulation of failure-handling knowledge has several benefits:
- it allows an abstraction of knowledge that can be hard to express in full detail;
- its use is not tied to a specific agent architecture; and
- it allows the compensations to be employed in dynamic domains in which it is not possible to pre-specify all relevant failure-handling plans.

In order to use goal-based compensation in an agent context, the agent developer must provide domain-dependent information prior to runtime. For each (sub)task of an agent's for which failure-handling will be enabled, a set of parameterized failure-handling goals– not plans– must be associated with the task. Our model allows two types of failure-handling knowledge to be associated with each task: goals whose achievement is triggered by the task's failure (*stabilization* goals, which perform immediate local "cleanup"); and *compensation* goals triggered by cancellation. (Cancellation may but need not result from failure).

The goal-based definitions are then instantiated (bound) and used at runtime by the agent's FHC to direct the agent's behavior in failure situations. As will be further described in Section 3, the FHC can present new compensation goals to its agent application, which implements the goals according to context[3]. Failure handling is triggered in the FHC by the agent application's problem-solving and/or task cancellation.

Default failure-management is top-down: when a high-level task is canceled, the agent is given that task's (high-level) compensation goals to achieve. However, the agent's FHC may additionally be provided with information about when to directly employ compensations for subtasks of a canceled task; when to *retry* a failed task (allowing other alternatives to be tried by the agent application); and when not to compensate a failed task; in the form of a set of event-driven, domain-dependent *strategy rules*. The strategy rules refine the FHC's default failure-handling behavior, and allow localized compensations and retries to be spawned.

We view the process of constructing these definitions, and associated strategy rules, as "assisted knowledge engineering"; we can examine and leverage the agent's domain knowledge to support the definition process. (We are researching ways to provide semi-automated support for this process). Because the FHC enforces an explicit and straightforward use of this failure-handling knowledge, the developer need not replicate equivalent behavior in the agent application; thus "domain logic" and failure-handling knowledge may be largely separated, making each easier to modify.

Such failure-handling knowledge can be added to an agent system *incrementally*, allowing a progressive refinement of its knowledge about how to react in failure situations, which it takes advantage of when applicable– otherwise, its behavior is as before. The failure-handling knowledge augments, not overrides, the agent's domain logic.

This section provided an overview of a foundation of our approach: the employment of goal-based– rather than plan- or action-based– definitions of semantic compensations. More details are provided in [2]. Our methodology separates the definition of task failure-handling knowledge from the agents' implementation of that knowledge, allowing the compensations to leverage runtime context in a way that makes them both more robust and more widely applicable.

3 Managing Compensations of Delegated Tasks

The previous section described a method for defining compensations in dynamic and complex agent environments. In this section, we describe a methodology for supporting consistent and predictable system behaviour on failure, while reducing what needs to be done by the agent developer to "program" the agent system to handle failure. To accomplish these goals, we separate each agent's "normative" from failure-handling knowledge by means of a decoupled component that:

---

[3] If an agent application is given a compensation goal to achieve, this does not necessarily mean that direct work on the goal will be immediately initiated: it may have unmet preconditions.

- is not tied to a specific agent architecture, but leverages the agent's problem-solving knowledge
- determines *when* to invoke task compensation goals or retries based on the agent's activities and task status
- determines *what* goals to initiate, based on failure-handling knowledge; and
- provides support for multi-agent task compensation scenarios

As introduced in Fig. 2, we label this component the agent's FHC. The FHC maintains an abstraction of the agent's problem-solving history to support its failure management. In this paper we focus on one aspect of that failure handling: the agent's interactions, and how the FHC allows compensation-related interaction protocols to be factored from normative agent conversations.

The need for failure-handling protocols as a core part of the failure-handling methodology can be illustrated by considering compensation scenarios. A task delegation generates an implicit compensation scope for a task; potentially, either the delegator or the 'delegatee'– the agent to which the task was assigned– could be in charge of a compensation if it is later required. Most approaches suggest that a specific 'failure handler' agent/service be used for each activity [3], or that the agent/service that performed the original task will be responsible for its compensation should the need arise [4]. However, no fixed approach for determining which agent should be responsible for compensation, is appropriate all of the time. The agent that performed the original task may be too busy to perform the compensation, unable to perform the compensation, or currently offline/unreachable. If the agent failed at the original task, it should perhaps not take on the compensation of that task. However, we do not want to automatically target a separate failure-handling agent: often the agent that performed the 'forward' task will be the best suited to implement its compensation. Any approach should also accommodate situations where the *delegating* agent is offline.

Consider again the "dinner party" example of Section 2. The `invite guests` task is delegated by the primary "party planning" agent to an "invitation" agent. If the party needs to be canceled, then as part of the compensation process, the `invite guests` task will be compensated by canceling with all confirmed/pending guests. As a default, it makes sense for the invitation agent to contact the guests again– it may have retained internal state useful to the task– but not if it is overloaded or offline. Alternatively, the invitation agent might have failed (and contributed to the failure of the party planning task). In this case, the delegating agent (if online) prefers that the original invitation agent *not* be responsible for the invitation cancellations.

Before compensation for a task can proceed, *responsibility* for the compensation needs to be assigned to one of the agents in the compensation scope. Such an assignment does *not* indicate which agent will actually perform the task; once an agent is responsible for a compensation, it may delegate it. The example above illustrates that a fixed method for assigning compensation responsibility will not always be appropriate. It is more robust to require the relevant agents in the scope of the compensation activity to mutually determine which will be responsible. For this, an interaction *protocol*– supporting a conversation between the agents– is required.

Below, we describe the agent's FHC, and then detail the way in which it is used to support a set of factored compensation-related agent interaction protocols. We describe one of the protocols used by our system, which allows delegated compensations to be robustly managed.

3.1 The Agent's Failure-Handling Component (FHC)

A key aspect of our failure-handling model is the use of an abstract, goal-level representation of the agent's activities. This allows us to support a decoupled and architecture-independent mechanism for managing goal-based compensations. As suggested in Fig. 2, we define a model in which an agent application (the agent's domain logic) sits upon its FHC. The FHC supports a platform-independent API based on a goal-level failure-handling *ontology*, which allows goal instantiation and status information to be exchanged with the agent application. The agent application provides notifications on new goals and goal achievement/failure (with failure modes) to the FHC, and the FHC may introduce new goals to the agent application, to initiate both compensations and retries. In addition, all messages to/from the agent are filtered through its FHC, as will be further described below.

Based on the information from the agent, the FHC maintains a goal-level history of task/subtask information for currently relevant agent tasks: for each such task, a tree structure is built in the FHC to syntactically track the goals and subgoals generated as the agent application's problem-solving progresses. We call such a tree a *task-monitoring tree*. The monitored information does not include task details, only goal information. Each node in an FHC task-monitoring tree corresponds to a task subgoal. A node may be in one of the states shown in Fig. 4. The FHC uses this task structure in conjunction with the goal-level failure-handling knowledge described in Section 2, and domain events, to support compensations, task retries/alternatives, and management of task failure and cancellation events. (When a task is canceled, the agent application is instructed to halt all work on it). Compensations cause new task nodes to be created, and compensation tasks may themselves support compensations or retries.

Achievement or *failure* information is reported by the agent application; a task may be explicitly moved to a *canceled* state or reinvoked (retried) by the FHC.

Fig. 4. FHC task node states. 'Canceled' indicates the state of the associated task node only; *not* the status of any corresponding compensation or stabilization activities.

Any agent application which correctly supports this API, and for which failure-handling knowledge is provided, may be "plugged into" the FHC; it is not architecture-specific. The agent application performs planning, task decomposition and execution. The FHC tracks task decomposition and reacts to task failures– reported via the API– by instructing agents to achieve repair goals. That is, an agent's FHC makes decisions about *what* failure-handling goals should be achieved, and *when* they will be requested of the agent. The agent's application logic is then invoked to implement the tasks and determine the details of how to correct for the failures. The FHC's failure-handling augments, not overrides, the agent application's.

The use of the FHC reduces the agent developer's implementation requirements, by providing a model that structures and supports the failure-handling information that needs to be defined. The motivation behind the use of the FHC is analogous to that of the exception-handling mechanism in a language like Java; the developer is assisted in generating desired agent failure-handling behavior, and the result is easier to understand and predict than if the knowledge were added in an ad-hoc fashion.

[2] provides additional detail, describes the API, and discusses the requirements on an agent application to correctly support the interface with the FHC. In particular, the agent must utilize a goal/subgoal representation of its task problem solving, and communicate changes in this information to its FHC. It must also be able to determine whether or not a given goal is already achieved, and support instructions to start/halt work on a goal.

Below, we focus on one specific aspect of the FHC. Its representation and maintenance of goal-level agent information allows failure-handling interaction protocols to be specified and implemented orthogonally from the agent application logic, to the benefit of system robustness and behavioral consistency. In the following, we assume that, as shown in Fig. 2, the agent architecture includes a "conversation" layer, which ensures that the agent's incoming/outgoing messages adhere to the system's prescribed interaction protocols [5,6]. We assume that this layer supports 'are you alive' pings to the agent(s) participating in active conversations, and generates error events if these other agents are not reachable.

3.2 Compensation Interaction Protocols

The agent application's 'regular' interaction protocols will determine how subtasks are allocated and delegated. These protocols may involve negotiation or bidding [5] or market mechanisms [7], as well as direct sub-task assignments or subscriptions, and typically include the reporting of error/task results.

We do not require the FHC to understand the semantics of these conversations. We separate failure-handling conversations the agent's 'regular' protocols, and implement them in the FHC. Based on the way in which we decouple the FHC from the agent application, and the way in which the FHC represents and maintains high-level task information as communicated from the agent, we are able to support failure-handling protocols in a manner transparent to the agent application. This factoring obviates the need for the agent application to implement handling the compensation-related protocols itself. The agent application developer does not have to build the agent applications to support these protocols, and as long as the agent's implementation of its FHC API is correct, the protocol's correct implementation is *independent of changes* to the agent logic. Similarly, the compensation-related interaction protocols may be changed without impacting the agent application.

To implement robust compensation-related interactions via the agent's FHCs, we have two requirements. First, the FHC must be able to explicitly detect conversation 'timeout' events, when an agent is offline (down or unreachable). As described above, we assume this information is provided by the agent's underlying conversation layer. Second, we must be able to associate, or "connect" the pair of task nodes– one in the delegating agent's FHC task tree structure and one in the delegatee's– that correspond to the same delegated task, without requiring the FHCs to parse the conversations that led to the delegation. With this, compensation information can propagate from one agent's FHC to another using the associated nodes.

"Connecting" delegated tasks across agents. To connect FHC task nodes across delegations, we make three requirements of the agent application as part of its implementation of the FHC API. First, we require that agents represent a task to be allocated explicitly *as* a task, so that they can communicate the creation of such tasks to their FHC. Second, we require that the agents 'know' when they are sending out messages related to assigning or allocating a task, and can associate those messages with their local representation of the task. Third, we require that receiving agents know when they are creating a task *based on* an incoming message, and are able to associate this new task with the relevant message ID (MID). This level of awareness on the part of the agent application is necessary to allow the FHC to operate independently of any specific agent delegation protocols. We then require the agent to implement the following aspects of the FHC API to support task node association:

1. When an agent begins a task delegation activity for which communication will be required, it notifies the FHC of the new task (goal). The FHC will build a new task node associated with the task.
2. When the agent sends out messages related to delegation of that task, it associates these messages– which are passed via the FHC– with the UID of the new goal. The FHC annotates the outgoing message information with the UID of the corresponding FHC task node (TNID).
3. The FHCs of the receiving agent(s) process the message envelope to record MID/TNID associations.
4. If an agent is assigned a delegated task (either directly or after an exchange), the delegating agent informs its FHC of the assignment, and the receiving agent annotates its `new task` notification to its FHC with the MID of the message by which the task was assigned. Based on its MID/TNID bookkeeping, the FHC of the receiving agent will create a new task node with an ID that links it to the parent task node in the delegating agent.

Fig. 5 illustrates this process with an example ContractNet-like delegation protocol. The FHC is not required to parse the agent's messages; it is only necessary for the agent application to implement the interface correctly with respect to indicating associated task/delegation message correspondences. It is this bookkeeping that allows compensation-related protocols to be factored from the agent's regular conversations. The agent's normal conversations take care of any task delegation for a given scenario, but the FHCs of the agent involved ensure that the delegator/delegatee relationship for a task is made explicit. If a task later needs to be compensated, both delegator and delegatee can can be involved in determining responsibility.

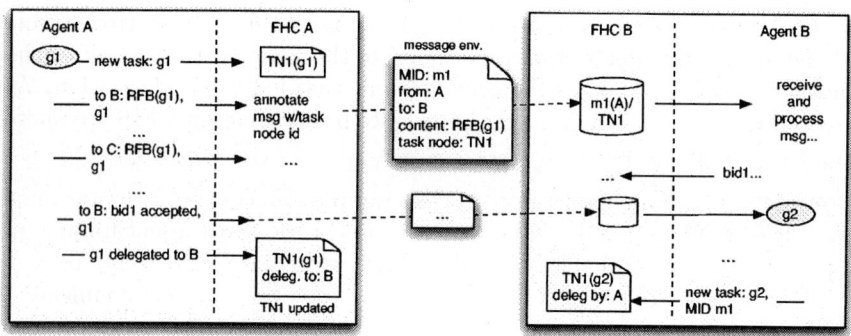

Fig. 5. "Connecting" a related task nodes in two agent's FHCs, with an example bid delegation protocol. Agent A's application logic associates RFB (request for bid) messages with their associated subtask ID (g1), and communicates this to its FHC. Agent A's FHC annotates these outgoing messages with g1's task node ID (TN1). When B's bid is accepted, A's FHC notes the delegation, and B's FHC uses the request MID to associate the new task with TN1.

Failure-Handling Protocols. The protocols related to compensation scope utilize inter-agent FHC task node associations, and must encompass several related types of communications necessary to support predictable failure-handling in delegated task contexts. These include:

1. When a canceled task is to be compensated, determination of which agent will be responsible for the compensation.
2. Propagation of a task cancellation notification to a sub-task delegatee and collection of the cancellation results by the parent task. (Cancellation requires task 'halt'; sub-task agents report if cancellation was successful. Recall that "canceled" refers to the FHC task node for the original task, not the status of any subsequent compensation tasks).
3. Notification of sub-task failure and failure mode from delegatee to delegator. (The agents' "regular" protocols may support exchange of sub-task failure information as well; but the respective agents' FHCs ensure that this information is always exchanged regardless of other prescribed interactions).

We require that these protocols encompass situations where a participating agent has crashed or gone offline. In addition, we would like them to support 'reasonable' autonomy of agents while enforcing predictability of behavior. In defining the protocols, we assume that reliable message delivery and acknowledgment is supported by the agents' underlying communication layers.

We define our protocols using Petri nets [8]. A Petri net consists of *places* (depicted as ovals) and *transitions* (depicted as rectangles), which are linked by arrows. A transition in a Petri net is enabled if each incoming place has at least one token. An enabled transition can be fired by removing a token from each incoming place and placing a token on each outgoing place. We follow the notation used in [9], which may be mapped to FIPA AUML [10] diagrams: we have two types of places, one corresponding to protocol states and the other to messages and events[4]. An exchange of messages adheres to a given protocol if each successive message, when activated by a token, enables a transition to a new (protocol state) place. In our semantics, for all protocol states with subsequent transition(s), one and only one of the transitions must occur.

Fig. 6 shows Protocol 1 above: *determination of compensation responsibility*. This protocol is a pairwise conversation between a delegator and delegatee. It can only be initiated from a system state in which the "forward" task has been successfully canceled, and cancellation information propagated, as supported by Protocol 2. From Protocol 1's start states (s0 and s1), if the delegator (parent) is offline, the delegatee (child) must take responsibility. Otherwise, the delegatee is given autonomy to decide independently of the delegator whether it will take responsibility for the compensation, *unless* it has itself failed. If the delegatee rejects the compensation responsibility, is offline, or fails in the compensation, the delegator must take responsibility[5]. If a delegated task has failed, then is subsequently canceled and compensation required, the delegating agent (if online) must decide whether or not the delegatee will be allowed to make decisions about the compensation. As long as at most one of the agents are offline, the protocol ensures that *one and only one agent in the compensation scope* will take responsibility for the compensation.

For example, suppose in Fig. 6 that the delegatee (C) is offline when the protocol is initiated at state s1– a completed task is canceled. C's "offline" event causes a transition to s3. Because one and only one transition from a protocol state must occur, the delegator (P) must take responsibility for the compensation, and indicates this to C (message (1)). If/when C comes back online, it will retrieve this message and will not address the compensation. Alternatively, suppose that C is online and declines the compensation responsibility (2), but

---

[4] The protocol below includes agent communication timeouts; other compensation-related events are cancel and failure.

[5] The protocol in the figure is simplified for readability: the compensation information is not parameterized, and it does not include the case where the delegatee, based on its local knowledge, does not believe that the cancellation needs to be compensated. Note also that in this protocol, the delegator is not required to report on compensation results to the delegatee. An alternate protocol could require this as well.

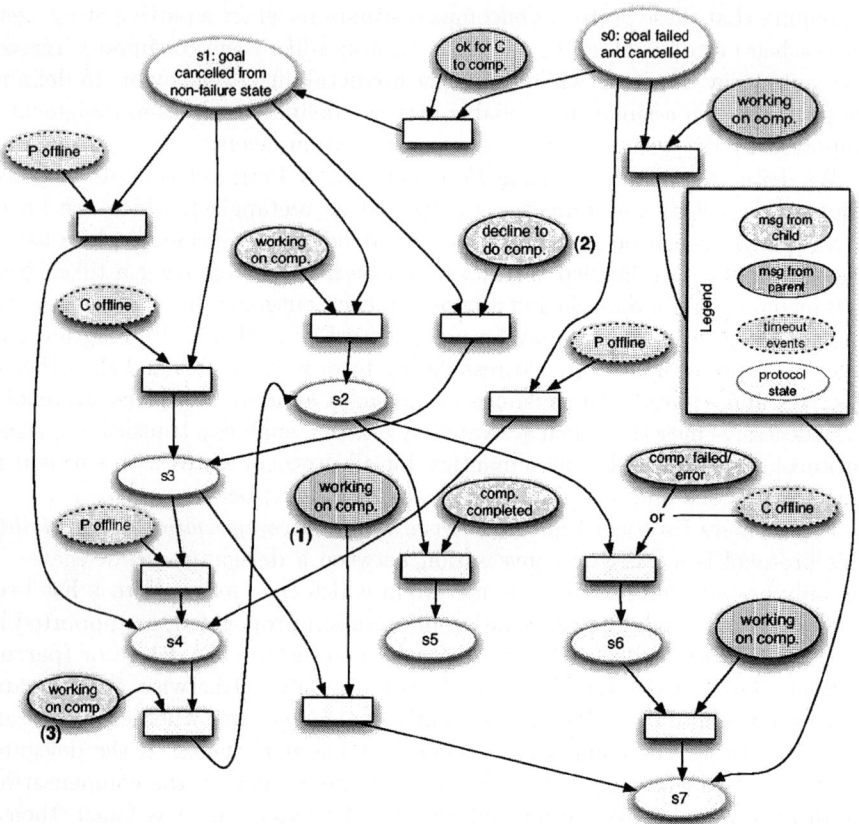

Fig. 6. The protocol to determine compensation responsibility. 'P' is the delegating ("parent") agent, and 'C' is the delegatee ("child") agent, with respect to the given canceled goal. The 'protocol state' labels are used only to distinguish the states. The numbered messages are referenced in the example.

then receives notification that P is offline. From this state (s4), C must now take on the compensation (3), if possible.

A compensation is treated by the agent application as a new task like any other, though the FHC of the responsible agent logs the association with its original task. The protocol described above does not determine task delegation. The FHC-based interactions determine only which agent is initially *responsible* for the new compensation task; then, as is possible with any task, the responsible agent may decide to delegate it.

3.3 Prototype Implementation and Initial Experiments

We have implemented a prototype multi-agent system in which for each agent, an FHC interfaces with an agent application logic layer. The agents are implemented in Java, and the FHC of each agent is implemented using a Jess core[11]. The agent-application components of our prototype are simple goal-based problem-solvers to which an implementation of the FHC interface was added. Currently, the interface uses Jess "fact" syntax to communicate goal-based events.

The prototype implements the goal-based semantic compensation model described here. The protocols it uses, while not yet specified declaratively, are implemented as described here with respect to the messages that must be exchanged by the delegating and delegatee agents. However, the current prototype is more limited than the model in that it does not yet support pings/timeout events, and its means of "connecting" delegated task nodes across agents is hardwired to a specific delegation protocol.

We have performed initial experiments in several relatively simple problem domains. Our prototype has helped us to conclude that this approach is feasible, and suggests that our approach to defining and employing goal-based failure-handling information generates useful behavior in a range of situations. Work is ongoing to define failure-handling knowledge and strategy rules for more complex problem domains in which agent interaction will feature prominently.

4 Related Work

Our approach is motivated by a number of transaction management techniques in which sub-transactions may commit, and for which forward recovery mechanisms must therefore be specified. Examples include open nested transactions [1], flexible transaction [12], SAGAs, [13], and ConTracts [14]. Earlier related project work has explored models for the implementation of transactional plans in BDI agents [15,16,17,18], and a proof-of-concept system using a BDI agent architecture with a closed nested transaction model was constructed [19].

In [20], Greenfield et al. discuss a number of issues that can arise when employing "traditional" compensation models, similar to those raised here. In Nagi et al. [21,22] an agent's problem-solving drives 'transaction structure' in a manner similar to that of our approach (though the maintenance of the transaction structure is incorporated into their agents, not decoupled). However, they define specific compensation plans for (leaf) actions, which are then invoked automatically on failure. Thus, their method will not be appropriate in domains where compensation details must be more dynamically determined.

Parsons and Klein et al. [23,24] describe an approach to MAS exception-handling utilizing sentinels associated with each agent. For a given domain, "sentinels" are developed that intercept the communications to/from each agent and handle certain coordination exceptions for the agent. The exception-detecting and -handling knowledge for that shared model resides in their sentinels. Entwisle et al.[25] take a related approach in which decoupled exception-handling agents utilize a knowledge base to monitor, diagnose, and handle problems in a system. In our approach, while we decouple high-level handling knowledge, the agents retain the logic for failure detection and task implementation; some agents may be designed to handle certain compensations.

Chen and Dayal [26] describe a model for multi-agent cooperative transactions. Their model does not directly map to ours, as they assume domains where commit control is possible. However, the way in which they map nested transactions to a distributed agent model has many similarities to our approach. They describe a peer-to-peer protocol for failure recovery in which failure notifications can be propagated between separate 'root' transaction hierarchies (as with cooperating transactions representing different enterprises).

[27] describe a model for implementing compensations via system ECA rules in a web service environment– the rules fire on various 'transaction events' to define and store an appropriate compensating action for an activity, and the stored compensations are later activated if required. Their event- and context-based handling of compensations have some similarities to our use of strategy rules. However, in their model, the ECA rules must specify the compensations directly at an action/operation level prior to activation (and be defined by a central authority). WSTx [4] addresses transactional web services support by providing an ontology in which to specify *transactional attitudes* for both a service's capabilities and a client's requirements. WSTx-enabled 'middleware' may then intercept and manage transactional interactions based on this service information. In separating transactional properties from implementation details, and in the development of a transaction-related capability ontology, their approach has similar motivations. However, their current implementation does not support parameterized or multiple compensations.

Workflow systems encounter many of the same issues as agent systems in trying to utilize transactional semantics: advanced transactional models can be supported [28], but do not provide enough flexibility for most 'real-world' workflow applications. Existing approaches typically allow user- or application-defined support for semantic failure atomicity, where potential exceptions and problems may be detected via domain rules or workflow 'event nodes', and application-specific fixes enacted [29,30].

We are not aware of existing work which explicitly uses protocols for flexibly managing compensation responsibility. Recently, there have been efforts to specify languages for web service composition and coordination. For example, BPEL4WS and WS-Coordination/Transaction [3,31] provide a way to specify business process composition, scoped failure-handling logic, and coordination contexts and protocols. Each BPEL activity may have a compensation handler, which may be invoked by the activity's failure handler. Compensation and fault handlers may be arbitrary processes. Our approach to semantic compensation has some similarities to the BPEL model, with strategy rules (Section 2) and protocols serving to coordinate "inner scope" compensation. However, our model pushes the implementation of failure handling to the agent application logic.

5 Conclusion

We have described an approach to increasing robustness in a multi-agent system. The approach is motivated by transactional semantics, in that its objective is to support *semantic compensations* for tasks in a given domain; we assume environments in which we cannot wait to "commit" actions. We augment an agent's failure-handling capabilities by improving its ability to "clean up after" and undo its failures, and to support retries. This behavior makes the semantics of an agent system more predictable, both with respect to the individual agent and with respect to its interactions with other agents; thus the system becomes more robust in its reaction to unexpected events.

Our approach is goal-based, both with respect to defining failure-handling knowledge for agent tasks, and in determining when to employ it. By abstracting the agent's failure-handling knowledge to a goal level, it can be decoupled from agent domain implementations and employed via the use of a failure-handling component with which the agent application interfaces, supporting predictable behavior and decreasing the requirements on the agent developer. Our methodology separates the definition of failure-handling knowledge from the agents' implementation of that knowledge, allowing the compensations to leverage runtime context in a way that makes them both more robust and more widely applicable.

For semantic compensation to be effective and predictable, it is necessary to control not only how individual agents react when a task fails or is canceled, but how the agents in the system *interact* when problems develop with a task assigned by one agent to another. Flexible interaction protocols are necessary to achieve a useful degree of control. We have described a method for factoring compensation-related protocols from the agent application to its failure-handling component, allowing them to be developed independently, and have described one key such protocol used by our system.

Project work will continue in evaluating our failure-handling methodologies, and to further develop our prototype. Evaluation will include development of scenarios in additional domains– with emphasis on scenarios that require multi-agent interaction; analysis and characterization of failure-handling strategies (including strategies for dealing with cascading failures and analysis of the overhead incurred by the use of the FHC infrastructure); and will also include tests in which we "plug in" different application agent architectures on top of the FHC, e.g. a BDI agent [15]. Our experiments will also help us to evaluate the ways in which a failure-handling strategy is tied to the problem representation.

Acknowledgments. This research is funded by an Australian Research Council Discovery Grant.

References

1. Gray, J., Reuter, A.: Transaction Processing: Concepts and Techniques. Morgan Kaufmann (1993)
2. Unruh, A., Bailey, J., Ramamohanarao, K.: A framework for goal-based semantic compensation in agent systems. In: 1st International Workshop on Safety and Security in Multi-Agent Systems, AAMAS '04. (2004)

3. Business Process Execution Language for Web Services (BPEL4WS): http://www-106.ibm.com/developerworks/webservices/library/ws-bpel (2003)
4. Mikalsen, T., Tai, S., Rouvellou, I.: Transactional attitudes: Reliable composition of autonomous web services. In: Workshop on Dependable Middleware-based Systems. (2002)
5. FIPA: http://fipa.org, http://www.fipa.org/specs/fipa00029/
6. Nodine, M., Unruh, A.: Facilitating open communication in agent systems. In Singh, M., Rao, A., Wooldridge, M., eds.: Intelligent Agents IV: Agent Theories, Architectures, and Languages. Springer-Verlag (1998)
7. Walsh, W., Wellman, M.: Decentralized supply chain formation: A market protocol and competitive equilibrium analysis. JAIR **Vol. 19** (2003) 513–567
8. Reisig, W.: Petri nets: An introduction. EATCS Monographs on Theoretical Computer Science (1985)
9. Poutakidis, D., Padgham, L., Winikoff, M.: Debugging multi-agent systems using design artifacts: The case of interaction protocols. In: First International Joint Conference on Autonomous Agents and Multi-Agent Systems. (2002)
10. Odell, J., Parunak, H., Bauer, B.: Extending uml for agents. In: Agent-Oriented Information Systems Workshop at the 17th National conference on Artificial Intelligence. (2000)
11. Friedman-Hill, E.: Jess in Action. Manning Publications Company (2003)
12. Zhang, A., Nodine, M., Bhargava, B., Bukhres, O.: Ensuring relaxed atomicity for flexible transactions in multidatabase systems. In: Proceedings of the 1994 ACM SIGMOD international conference on Management of data, Minneapolis, Minnesota, United States, ACM Press (1994) 67–78
13. Garcia-Molina, H., Salem, K.: SAGAs. In: ACM SIGMOD Conference on Management of Data. (1987)
14. Reuter, A., Schwenkreis, F.: Contracts - a low-level mechanism for building general-purpose workflow management-systems. Data Engineering Bulletin **18** (1995) 4–10
15. Rao, A.S., Georgeff, M.P.: An abstract architecture for rational agents. In: *Third International Conference on Principles of Knowledge Representation and Reasoning*, Morgan Kaufmann (1992)
16. Busetta, P., Bailey, J., Ramamohanarao, K.: A reliable computational model for BDI agents. In: 1st International Workshop on Safe Agents. Held in conjunction with AAMAS2003. (2003)
17. Ramamohanarao, K., Bailey, J., Busetta, P.: Transaction oriented computational models for multi-agent systems. In: 13th IEEE International Conference on Tools with Artificial Intelligence, Dallas, IEEE Press (2001) 11–17
18. Smith, V.: Transaction oriented computational models for multi-agent systems. Internal Report, University of Melbourne (2003)
19. Busetta, P., Ramamohanarao, K.: An architecture for mobile BDI agents. In: 1998 ACM Symposium on Applied Computing. (1998)
20. Greenfield, P., Fekete, A., Kuo, D.: Compensation is not enough. In: 7th IEEE International Enterprise Distributed Object Computing Conference (EDOC'03), Brisbane, Australia (2003)
21. Nagi, K., Nimis, J., Lockemann, P.: Transactional support for cooperation in multiagent-based information systems. In: Proceedings of the Joint Conference on Distributed Information Systems on the basis of Objects, Components and Agents, Bamberg (2001)
22. Nagi, K., Lockemann, P.: Implementation model for agents with layered architecture in a transactional database environment. In: AOIS '99. (1999)

23. Parsons, S., Klein, M.: Towards robust multi-agent systems: Handling communication exceptions in double auctions. In: Submitted to The 2004 Conference on Autonomous Agents and Multi-Agent Systems. (2004)
24. Klein, M., Rodriguez-Aguilar, J.A., Dellarocas, C.: Using domain-independent exception handling services to enable robust open multi-agent systems: The case of agent death. Autonomous Agents and Multi-Agent Systems **7** (2003) 179–189
25. Entwisle, S., Loke, S., Krishnaswamy, S.: Aoex: An agent-based exception handling framework for building reliable, distributed, open software systems. In: Submitted to IAT2004. (2004)
26. Chen, Q., Dayal, U.: Multi-agent cooperative transactions for e-commerce. In: Conference on Cooperative Information Systems. (2000) 311–322
27. T. Strandens, R.K.: Transaction compensation in web services. In: Norsk Informatikkonferanse. (2002)
28. Alonso, G., Agrawal, D., El Abbadi, A., Kamath, M., Gunthor, R., Mohan, C.: Advanced transaction models in workflow contexts. In: ICDE. (1996)
29. Casati, F.: A discussion on approaches to handling exceptions in workflows. SIGGROUP Bulletin **Vol 20. No. 3** (1999)
30. Rusinkiewicz, M., Sheth, A.P.: Specification and execution of transactional workflows. Modern Database Systems: The Object Model, Interoperability, and Beyond (1995) 592–620
31. Curbera, F., Khalaf, R., Mukhi, N., Tai, S., Weerawarana, S.: The next step in web services. Communications of the ACM **Vol. 46, No. 10** (2003)

Modelling with Ubiquitous Agents a Web-Based Information System Accessed Through Mobile Devices

Angela Carrillo-Ramos, Jérôme Gensel, Marlène Villanova-Oliver, and Hervé Martin

Laboratory LSR – IMAG. B.P. 72
38402 Saint Martin d'Hères Cedex, France
{carrillo, gensel, villanov, martin}@imag.fr

Abstract. This paper describes *PUMAS*, our proposal of architecture which uses ubiquitous agents in order to give to nomadic users (users who often change of location) access to a *Web Information System* (*WIS*) through their *Mobile Devices (MDs)*. *PUMAS* focuses on the exchange of information between *MDs* seen as peer ubiquitous agents and takes into account the user's needs, location and the limited configuration of her/his *MD* for displaying the information. *PUMAS* also handles two important aspects of a nomadic use of a *WIS*: *user location* (provided by a *GPS* device) and *information distribution among several heterogeneous MDs* (controlled by a *Peer to Peer* approach). In addition, we present the Agent Class Diagram and the Interaction Diagrams of *PUMAS* in the *Agent UML (AUML)* notation [8]. An application relying on *PUMAS* is described.

1 Introduction

Nowadays, Internet is extensively used to access and exchange information. Ideally, users should have the effective information (i.e. *"the right information in the right place at the right time"*). However, when a nomadic user (users who often change of location) searches for information, she/he could get in response a too large quantity of information which is not always relevant for her/him and which is not always supported by her/him *Mobile Device* (*MD*). In the last years, information access for *Web Information Systems* (*WIS*) have changed a lot because of technical advances in *MD* (e.g. PDA, phones, laptop...), of the multimedia nature of exchanged data, of the inherent mobility of nomadic user, of the characteristics of the *MD* (e.g., reduced capacities like small size of screen, memory, hard disk...), etc.

Additionally, many functional and technical issues have to be considered when modelling a *WIS*. Not only the system is supposed to answer user requests but it should also ideally provide them with information adapted to their needs, constraints and preferences. The underlying challenge for *WIS* designers is to provide *WIS* users with useful information based on an intelligent research and a suitable display of the information delivered by the system. In order to reach this goal, an interesting approach could be the *Multi-Agent Systems (MAS)*.

Carabelea et al [2] have defined a *MAS* as "a federation of software agents interacting in a shared environment that cooperate and coordinate their actions given their own goals and plans". A *MAS* can be a useful tool for modelling a *WIS* due to the properties of agents like knowledge (defined, own and acquired), communication with users or other agents, mobility, etc. Ramparany [11] has shown the interest of *MAS* when Internet is used to access and exchange information through new *MDs* (*"smart devices"* like PDA, phones, laptops...). In this case, agents can be useful to represent the user's characteristics inside the system and *MDs* can work like *"cooperative devices"*. Agents can be executed on the *MD* and/or migrate through the net for searching information on different servers in order to satisfy the user's requests.

Agents may be *mobiles* and/or *ubiquitous*. A *Mobile Agent* [10] is a software entity that can migrate autonomously throughout a network from host to host. It is not bounded to the platform where it has begun its execution. Mobile agents are emerging as an alternative programming concept for the development of distributed application. An *Ubiquitous Agent* [15] is an intelligent system that allows users to consult data at any time from any place. Moreover, De Carolis *et al.* expose in [3] that these agents must have autonomy of execution and the capability to communicate with other agents in order to share and interchange information for accomplishing individual or collaborative tasks. If an ubiquitous agent needs to migrate through the net for carrying out the tasks assigned to it, this agent becomes a *Mobile Ubiquitous Agent*.

Some architectures like *KODAMA* [13] and *MIA* [1] use agents and define general components and communication features for a *WIS* accessed through *MDs*. However, these architectures are too generic and they do not make explicit the relations between agents (agent roles, activities, possible migration...) for accomplishing their tasks. The *CONSORTS* [6] architecture proposes a mechanism for defining the relations that hold between agents (communication, hierarchy, role definition...), with the purpose of satisfying user requests. However, *CONSORTS* does not consider aspects like the distribution of information between *MDs* (which could improve response time).

Moreover, an agent could behave independently from the server and other agents. This is the foundation of *Peer to Peer Systems* (*P2P System*) which we apply here to *MAS*. *P2P systems* are characterized by a direct communication between the peers with no communication needed with a specific server, and by the autonomy that a peer has for accomplishing some assigned tasks. We call an *Agent-Based Web Information System* (*ABWIS*) a *WIS* developed using an agent approach and accessed by users through *MDs*. Following the *P2P* approach, an *ABWIS* has to represent knowledge required by each agent for accomplishing tasks associated with their different roles (client, server, coordinator...). The work in [9] is an example of *Peer Multi-Agent System* whose characteristics are used in our approach.

In this paper, we propose an architecture called *PUMAS (Peer Ubiquitous Multi-Agent Systems)* for designing, developing and deploying *Agent-Based Web Information System (ABWIS)*. Each *MD* informs the system about the user's location (using a *GPS* device), stores information and integrates agents having the ability of performing tasks. These agents can on the one hand, migrate to different servers (or other *MDs*) in order to find the one(s) that will help to answer the user requests or, on the other hand, use a central platform in order to communicate to others agents and to ask them the information for satisfying their requests. An *ABWIS* could represent different systems like a guided tourist visit, a supply chain, the global traffic control, etc. [6]

Our approach focuses on the definition of an architecture based on agents for an *effective* access to *WIS* using *MDs* and makes use of ubiquitous agents which are in charge of filtering information. This process is performed by two filters: the *Content Filter* performs the selection of the relevant information for the user according to her/his constraints and preferences (e.g. profile, location, last requests) and, the *Display Filter* transforms the information provided by the *content filter* according to the technical capabilities of her/his *MD*.

The paper is structured as follows: in section 2, we describe general architectures for modelling *WIS* accessed using *MDs*. Section 3 presents the characteristics of a *Peer Multi-Agent System*. Then, in section 4, we describe *PUMAS*, our architecture whose goal is to provide an *effective access* to information in a *WIS* using peer ubiquitous *MAS*. Section 5 gives an application example before we conclude in section 6.

2 Architectures for Modelling MAS

This section presents the principles of three architectures based on agents which model *WIS* accessed through *MDs*. Some ideas borrowed from these architectures will be used in Section 4 in order to define our approach *PUMAS*.

KODAMA [13] (*Kyushu University Open and Distributed Autonomous Multi-Agent Architecture*) is a multi-level architecture for modelling distributed systems based on agents. It is composed of four levels: *i)* the *Application Level* defines the tasks assigned to each agent by a set of rules. Each rule has a priority and an interpretation policy which is a method for interpreting messages sent by other agents. *ii)* The *Agent Communication Level* establishes the mechanism of communication between agents. The agents are organized in a hierarchical structure which defines how they can communicate and the agents to whom an agent provides services. *iii)* The *Infrastructure Agent level* connects the two previous levels and simulates a network layer in which agents are nodes and their relations/communications are arcs. It is in charge of adapting the exchange of messages between agents. *iv)* The *Transport Level* supplies a transport service to send data between source and target machines through the network using protocols like *TCP/IP*.

In *KODAMA*, the concept of *community* refers to a set of agents organized in a hierarchical way. This hierarchy distinguishes between a *portal agent* (which plays both the roles of coordinator and profile controller) and *ordinary agents*.

KODAMA has been implemented in a system delivering advertisement information to customers of the shopping malls in Nagoya (Japan). Each customer has a cellular phone with a transmitter which sends signals to receivers located in the mall. The nearest receiver to the customer's phone activates the agents of the advertisement system (for searching information about stores which are close to the customer) and sends messages to the customer's phone through e-mails.

MIA [1] (*Mobile Information Agent*) is a *WIS* represented as a *MAS* whose purpose is to search specific data at any time through *MDs* (PDAs, phones equipped with a *GPS* device, or cellular *WAP* phones). *MIA* uses the following ubiquitous computing characteristics: user's location, continuous and permanent information access and *PDA* technology. *MIA* is composed of: *i)* Some *Mobile Agents* which are *MDs* that allow the system to estimate their geographic location (given by a *GPS* device or by the user) and a wireless communication with a server located on the Internet. *ii) A Server* which allows communication between application and mobile agents. It uses the *HTTP* protocol in order to communicate with the mobile agents and sends query results through *HTML* and *WML* pages. *iii) Agents* which represent the Information System Model and are classified into: *user agents* (model and check user), *localization agents, spider agents* (Web intelligent agents in charge of searching for information according to user's needs) and *Matchmaker* (a portal agent which is an intermediate between the server and the other agents. It activates the *spider agents* for starting the information research).

The information is classified by Beuster *et al.* [1] in *topics* and *extracts*. *Topics* are web pages containing information related to the user's preferences and location (for instance, the user is a lover of Renoir's paintings or that the user is in the room which is dedicated to Renoir's paintings) while *extracts* are information about the topic itself (for example, addresses of museum where an exhibition of Renoir takes place).

Although *KODAMA* and *MIA* are generic architectures for modelling *ABWIS*, they do not specify how the agents do communicate with each other and do not describe each component and the services of the agents inside the *Information* System. Our work aims at providing a description of each of these aspects.

CONSORTS [6] (*architecture for* **CO**g**N**itive **ReSO**urce management with physically-g**R**ounding agen**TS**) is an architecture of ubiquitous agents designed for a massive support of *MDs*. It detects the user's location and defines the user's profile through a *Spatio-Temporal Reasoner (STR)* which manages the *Spatio-Temporal Inference Engine* and the *Spatial Information Database*[6]. *CONSORTS* uses the location and the profile of the user in order to adapt the information (content) to her/him. Each *MD* communicates with the application through a *Device Wrapper Agents (DWAs)*. Each *DWA* has a communication interface with the system and renders transparent the communication between the agents and the system without considering the kind of *MD* used (PDA, phone...). The other agents of *CONSORTS* are: First, the *User Model Manager (UMM)* which manages users profile using a set of inference rules defined in the *STR*. These rules are defined according to the functional requirements of the system. The *UMM* communicates with the *STR* in order to get the user's location which is used as a criterion for defining the user's profile. Second, the *Service Agent (SA)*[1] is the system coordinator and stays in permanent communication with the *UMM*. It knows which agents are active in the system, their services, constraints and profiles. Profiles are defined according to rules specified in the *STR* (for instance, if the user is in a museum room, the *SA* gives her/his information about the exhibitions, adapting it to her/his *MD* constraints). Third, the *Personal Agent (PA)*[2] is the representation of each user in the system. Interacting with the *DWA*, it allows users to connect themselves to the system. A *PA* knows the user's location; it is in charge of

---

[1] In the third version of *CONSORTS, SA* is called *Service Provider Agent* [6]
[2] *Personal Agent* is also called *Service Requester Agent* [6].

interpreting the user's requests and communicates with the *SA* which provides the information hold by the system. For defining a user profile, the *UMM* considers three features: *Intentions, Preferences and Attributes*. The *Intention* is the set of tasks a user can perform during a period of time (e.g., if a picture is taken, the user could send it to a friend). The *Preference* is the set of tasks the user would like to do during a period of time (e.g., whenever she/he takes a picture, the user sends it to a friend). The *Attribute* describes the personal user's information and other characteristics about her/him in the system (e.g., the user who takes picture is a photographer).

The third version of *CONSORTS* [6] introduces the *mass user support* like a service provided through the coordination of the agents based on the *social coordination* concept. *Social Coordination* is an automatic negotiation between proxy agents (*Personal Agents*) with a language that replaces the verbal requests of users. *CONSORTS* provides four new services [6]: *i*) the *Service Adaptation* which adapts the services of the system according to the user's situation (location, profiles, current activities ...), *ii*) the *Service Combination* which provides common languages for services (i.e. an ontology) that are implemented in different contexts, *iii*) the *Service Composition* which provides new services from available ones (i.e. a new service can be defined as the connection between two available services) and *iv*) the *Agent Security* provides a framework which manages the computational resources for the agents, controls their behaviour in the system and eliminates them when they present abnormal behaviours (i.e. when an agent performs illegal tasks which do not concern its roles).

CONSORTS [6] also introduces the *Location-Aware Middle Agent* which helps the *STR* to locate other agents and is the mediator between the *Service Provider Agent* (*SA*) and the *Service Requester Agents* (*PAs*) in the *Social Coordination Process*.

The Table 1 summarizes the principal characteristics of theses architectures.

Table 1. Architectures for modelling MAS.

	KODAMA	MIA	CONSORTS
Data Distribution	Several servers	Several Servers	Content Server
Type of MD	Cellular phone	PDA, Cellular phone, Cellular WAP phone	PDA, Cellular phone, Laptop
Multimedia Data	Text	Text	Text, Images
Communication protocols	TCP/IP	HTTP, WAP	HTTP
Rules Definition for agents	Yes	Unknown	Rules in the STR
Mechanism of Profile Definition	Yes but it is not precisely described	Preference and location of user	Preferences, Intentions and Attributes
Mechanism of location detection	Transmitter in the MD and receivers in the places	GPS or location introduced by the user	Sensors: camera or Wireless LAN
Coordinator Agent	Portal Agent	Server and Matchmaker	Service Agent
Portal Agent	Portal Agent	Matchmaker	Device Wrapper Agent
Type of agents	Agents organized in hierarchical way	Mobile, user, localization, spider and Matchmaker	Spatio-Temporal, User Model Manager, Service, Personal, and Mobile

From the architectures *KODAMA, MIA* and *CONSORTS*, we identify three common levels which should form the classical architecture of an *ABWIS*. These levels have been integrated into our architecture *PUMAS* as presented in section 4: *i*) a *Mobile Agent Level* which is composed of the *MDs* and the *Mobile Agents*. The user accesses the system through her/his *MD* and there are *Mobile Agents* which are executed on her/his *MDs. ii)* an *Intermediate Level* which offers services (connection, communication, etc.) in order to communicate with the *Information System. iii)* an *Information System Level* which represents the services (functional requirements) that the system offers to users.

3 Peer Multi-agent Systems

CONSORTS proposes ideas about different roles agents can play in a *MAS*. Nevertheless, it is necessary to precise how an agent can be aware of the other agents which could help it to solve problems such as how to define strategies for satisfying user requests and how to assign roles, activities and responsibilities to each agent for a specific system. Panti *et al.* [9] describes a *Peer Multi-Agent System* based on the *"peer"* concept which is exploited by *PUMAS*. A *peer* represents a person or an organization and has an associated agent that manages information about her/him, and has the capability to manage and control a simple *"workflow"*. A *workflow* refers here to a sequence of actions to be performed in the system and describes the abilities that this agent must have for managing assigned tasks, for exchanging information, for interpreting the behaviour rules of the other peer agents, and for proposing the coordination and collaboration services that each agent could provide to the system.

Panti *et al.* introduce the concept of *peer agent* whose goal is to communicate and share tasks and resources with other peer agents in a dynamic environment without the help of an explicit server. Moreover, a *peer agent* manages its own knowledge base for carrying out its tasks. This knowledge is also used for representing a client or for playing the server role according to the required work. In general, a *peer agent* can play the role of the server because it has the knowledge for doing so: it has an address service (*yellow pages*) for searching and founding its peers and it can adapt itself to changes in the network. Also, if some network problems occur, a *peer agent* executes its assigned tasks without the collaboration of other agents and informs them about it when these problems are solved (using the mechanism of *yellow pages*).

The internal architecture of a *peer agent* and the steps for defining the strategy in order to answer user information requests are: *i)* the Wrap*ping Component (W)* which is a communication interface between users and the system or, with other agents, *ii)* the *Searching/Representation Component (S/R)* which allows to store and exploit a list of all the agents that it knows (e.g., because it has previously worked with them) and their services, *iii)* the *Reformulation/Coordination Component (R/C)* which defines tasks and services that the agent offers to the system in order to process an information request. They are parts of its knowledge. In addition, the agent knows tasks and services of the other agents which can help it to reach a common goal. This knowledge allows to define the workflow for allocating responsibilities to the other agents (it plays the coordinator role) for accomplishing its tasks in a collaborative/cooperative way, and *iv)* the *Strategy Generation Component (SG)* which describes the strategy used for solving a problem or for satisfying an information request.

The existing tools for implementing peer *MAS* have limitations and problems: especially, they suffer from a lack of expressiveness of the languages used for describing and defining data and services. Moreover, they do not consider distributed systems problems like heterogeneity, data inconsistency, etc. Our approach aims at taking into account those aspects.

4 PUMAS Architecture

In the previous sections, we have exposed general and specific architectures (*MIA, KODAMA* and *CONSORTS*) for modelling *ABWIS* with their advantages and their problems. In spite of the contributions of each architecture, there are many aspects which are not considered for modelling and implementing an *ABWIS:* knowledge representation, Communication, Coordination, Control, Cooperation and Negotiation mechanisms *(CCCN)* for the cooperative work of the agents, migration of the agents, protocols and language of communication between them, etc.

Some characteristics of *PUMAS* are based on *CONSORTS*. It also relies on the three classical levels of an *ABWIS* (section 2) each being modelled as a *Multi-Agent System (MAS)* whose characteristics are exposed in the following subsections. The inherent mobility of the user and of the agents is supported by ubiquitous agents which can be transmitted through the network to get some needed information and which can communicate with other agents for performing tasks. In *PUMAS*, the *Ubiquitous Agents* are organized in a *Hybrid Peer to Peer Architecture* which addresses security in the applications (security problems inherent to the agents mobility), communication between agents in a point to point or in a broadcast way, management of the agent's states (connected, disconnected, killed, etc.) and the services provided by them.

4.1 Objective

The main objective of *PUMAS* is to integrate the access through *MD* and ubiquitous agents into *WIS* developed using the *KIWIS* platform [14]. *KIWIS* is an environment dedicated to the automatic generation of *WIS* given some conceptual specifications. It is a tool for *WIS* developers which puts the emphasis on adaptability to users by focusing on data access and presentation. It offers guidelines for the design steps of a *WIS* and is in charge of the automatic deployment of this *WIS*. We use these guidelines for modelling the *Information System Level* in an *ABWIS*.

A *WIS* developed using *KIWIS* is composed of five models [14]: *i)* a *User Model* which describes the users (individuals or groups) needs and profiles, *ii)* a *Data Model* which describes the application domain supported by the *WIS, iii)* a *Progressive Access Model* which describes the progressive access modalities, iv) a *Functionality Model* which describes the functionalities of the *WIS* (consultation, modification, etc.) and the related security aspects, and *v)* The *Hypermedia Model* which describes the presentation features in terms of Web pages composition and graphical aspects specified by a charter.

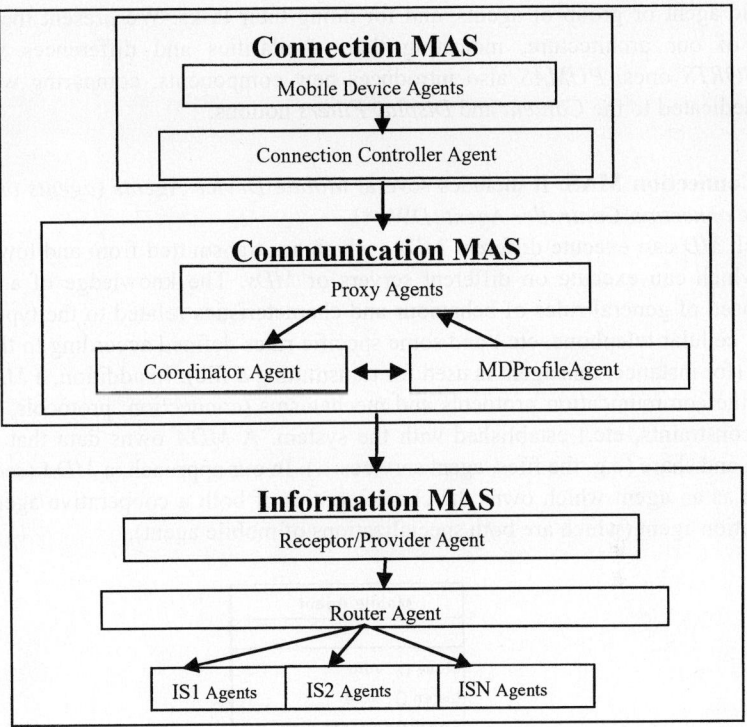

Fig. 1. The *PUMAS* Architecture.

The *Progressive Access* (*PA*) notion is an access process which relies on the fact that the user of a *WIS* does not need to access all the information all the time. The *PA* is then used to build a *WIS* which has the capacity to give access to its resources (i.e. information and functionalities) gradually and in an adapted way. First, resources considered as essential for a user are provided, and then, some complementary ones, if needed, are proposed through a guided navigation [14]. Considering a nomadic user, she/he will get first only the relevant resources (taking into account her/his location, but also her/his needs, etc.). In *PUMAS*, we use the *Progressive Access Model* (*PAM*) in order to define the *Content Filter* which aims at selecting the *effective information*. Moreover, the system must consider the technical constraints of the user's *MD*. In *PUMAS*, also the *Display Filter* is related to the *Hypermedia Model* which allows to organize the delivered information in a way supported by the *MD*.

4.2 PUMAS: An Architecture Based on Three Multi-agent Systems

The *PUMAS* architecture (see Fig. 1) is composed of three *MAS: Connection, Communication and Information* (each one represents one level of an *ABWIS*) into which each agent is a peer ubiquitous agent. The agents are connected to a central platform in order to know about them, their services and for managing their communications, but they are autonomous for connecting and disconnecting, for sending messages to a specific agent or group of agents, and for doing their tasks. We present the components of our architecture, indicating their similarities and differences with the *CONSORTS* ones. *PUMAS* also introduces new components, comparing which the ones dedicated to the *Content* and *Display Filters* notions.

The Connection MAS. It includes several *Mobile Device Agents (agents on MD*)*[3] and a *Connection Controller Agent (DWA*)*.

Each *MD* can execute different *MDAs* which are transmitted from and towards the *WIS* which can execute on different servers or *MDs*. The knowledge of a *MDA* is composed of general rules of behaviour and characteristics related to the type of *MD* (PDA, cellular telephone, etc.) and some specific rules defined according to the application (for instance, this agent is used for transmitting a file). In addition, a *MDA* must know the communication protocols and mechanisms (connection, protocols, network type, constraints, etc.) established with the system. A *MDA* owns data that it could handle and share (e.g. the files, agent services...). In our approach, a *MDA* (see Fig. 2) is seen as an agent which owns the characteristics of both a cooperative agent and a connection agent (which are both specializations of mobile agent).

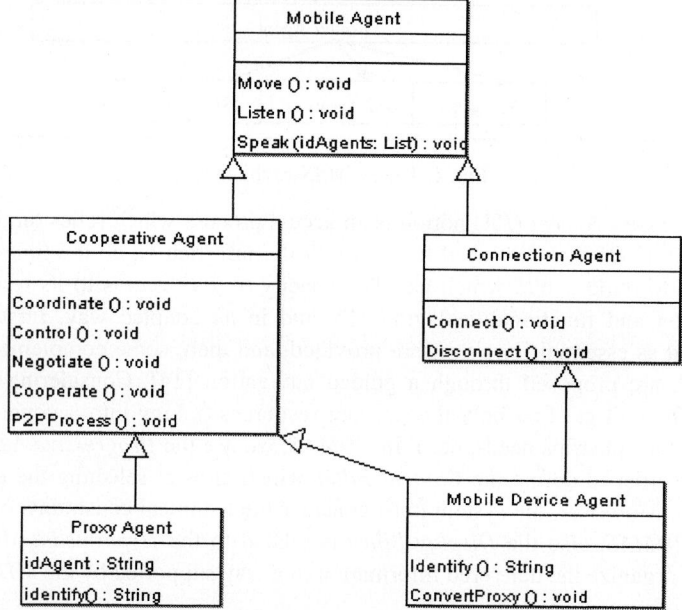

Fig. 2. Class Diagram for a *Mobile Device Agent*. This kind of agent has the characteristics and operations of a *Mobile Agent*, a *Cooperative Agent* and a *Connection Agent*.

---

[3] In the remainder of the section, we indicate in brackets and with "*" the expressions used in *CONSORTS* to designate equivalent components.

The *Connection Controller Agent (CCA)* detects the *MD type* (PDA, cellular phones...) using *CC/PP[4]* files and facilitates its connection taking into account the connection protocol. The *CCA* is the intermediate between the *Connection MAS* and the *Communication MAS*. *CCA* also checks the connections established by the users through their *MDs* and relates each *MDA* with its corresponding *Proxy Agent* in the *Communication MAS* (see next paragraph). For implementing the *Connection MAS*, it is necessary to define the communication and infrastructure levels between *Mobile Device Agents (MDA)* and the *Connection Controller Agent (CCA)* in order to make transparent the connection to the system for the *MDs* and to display the information (answers to information requests) according to the specific technical restrictions of the *MDs*. We also need to define the *User Model* which stores information about specific technical characteristics of the *MD* (specified in the *CC/PP file*, located in the MD and that can be transmitted and analysed by the *MDA* and the *Connection Controller Agent*) and to adapt the presentations to the physical constraints of the *MD* connected to the *WIS*. This has to be done with respect to the principles of *KIWIS* [14].

The *CCA* introduced by *PUMAS* allows to check if the user is still connected. If not, it checks if she/he has voluntarily disconnected or if the disconnection has been caused by a fault (e.g. system or network problem). The *CCA* checks out if the user wants to continue with her/his last session (she/he would be represented by the same *Proxy Agent*) or open a new one (she/he would be represented by a new *Proxy Agent*).

The Communication MAS. It offers an interface which makes the communication transparent between users. There is one *Proxy Agent* representing the connection of each *MDA* (two different users can connect themselves to the system through the same *MD* and there would be two different *Proxy Agents*). The *MDProfile Agent (UMM*)* has to check the user's profile (according her/his *MD*) and her/his information needs. In addition, this agent together with the *Coordinator Agent (DWA*)* checks and establishes the mechanism for interchanging hypermedia data with the user (*Display Filter*). The *Coordinator Agent* is in permanent communication with the *Connection Controller Agent* in order to verify the connection state of the agent which needs the information. The *CCA* has the knowledge of all the agents in the system (yellow pages for the agents with their connections, states, services ...) and their profiles according to the technical restrictions, location and connection time (for the communication with the *MDProfile Agent* and *Connection Controller Agent*).

Each *Personal Agent* in *CONSORTS* provides only identification properties and methods. The contribution of *PUMAS* is to represent and specify in the equivalent of the *Personal Agent*, the *Proxy Agent (PA)*, and in the *Mobile Device Agent (MDA)* some additional knowledge and behaviour which are inherited from the *Cooperative*

---

[4] http://www.w3.org/Mobile/CCPP/. The *W3C* proposes *CC/PP (Composite Capability/ Preference Profiles)* which is a description of device capabilities and user preferences. "A *CC/PP profile* contains a number of *CC/PP attribute names* and *associated values* that are used by a server to determine the most appropriate form of a resource to deliver to a client". *CC/PP* uses *RDF (Resource Description Framework)* for describing the profiles.

Agent (See Fig. 2). First, *PA* and *MDA* are able to perform the *Coordination, Cooperation, Control and Negotiation (CCCN) tasks* in the *MAS*. Second, they adopt the *P2P process* (explained in Section 3) in order to define the strategy to apply for achieving the assigned tasks (*CCCN* or another) and for finding out the peers which can cooperate and work with them.

On the one hand, the *Proxy Agent* could be a representation of the *MDA* within the system. In this case, there are two agents, one *MDA* on the *MD* and one *Proxy Agent* in the system (located on the server or on another *MD*). On the other hand, a *MDA* can play itself the role of *Proxy Agent*. This *MDA* is then transmitted to the system and is executed on the server. It is worth noting that if the *Proxy Agent* is a representation of the *MDA*, it has the same properties and behaviours of the *MDA* except the Connection ones (which are useless as it stands inside the system).

We define the selection and implementation of communication mechanisms between the *Proxy Agents*, the *Coordinator Agent* and the *MDProfile Agent* according to *KODAMA* [13]. For the *Display Filter*, we define the *functionality and hypermedia models* according to users profiles, users requests and physical restrictions associated the *MDs*, by exploiting principles integrated in *KIWIS* [14]. We consider that the *Coordinator Agent* performs a first filter according to profile defined by *MDProfile Agent* (location of the agent, time of connection, etc) and that the *Connection Controller Agent* performs a second filter according the characteristics and technical restriction of the *MD* which has connected. In Fig. 3 we present how to embed (and adapt) the *CONSORTS* architecture within *PUMAS*:

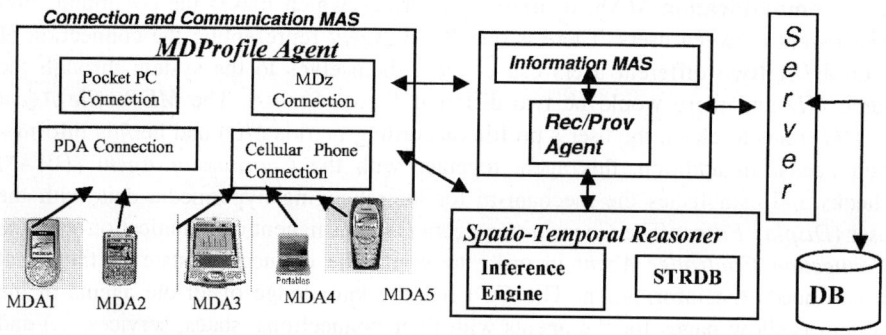

Fig. 3. Multi-Agents Systems Integration with *CONSORTS*

The Information MAS. The internal structure of the *Information MAS* (see Fig. 1) is composed of *Agents* associated with the different *WIS* (which can be represented as *MAS* or not), the *Router Agent (UMM*)* which defines the profiles of the users and/or agents and their preferences or history inside the system and, the *Receptor/Provider Agent (Service Agent*)* which has a general view of the whole system (it knows the agents of the *Communication and Information MAS*, their services, their locations, their profiles ...). Generally, the *Receptor/Provider Agent* receives all the requests that are transmitted from the *Communication MAS* and redirects them to the right *Information System* by means of the *Router Agent (RA)*. This *RA also* applies the *Content Filter* according to both the user's profile (preferences, user history, intentions, etc) and/or to information included in the request (user's location, connection time, specific parameters, etc).

The *Information System (IS)* can be executed on a server or on a *MD* (for example, we could consider that the information system of a *MD* consists in its stored files like pictures, XML files, etc). Let us now introduce a possible scenario of communication between two different agents which are executed on two different *MDs, MD1 and MD2*. Let us assume that *MD1* (a *PDA*) asks for information stored in *MD2* (a Cellular phone). The request is propagated through *PUMAS* core: it is first transmitted through the *Connection Controller Agent*, then to the *Communication MAS* agents, then to the *Receptor/Provider Agent (R/PA)* and finally to the *Router Agent (RA)*. The latter redirects the request to the *IS* agent located in *MD2* which searches for the information. The retrieved information is returned to *MD1* following the inverse path. Please note that during this process, the *Content and Display* filters are respectively applied by the *Router Agent* and by the *MDProfile Agent*. Through this example, we can observe the *Hybrid Peer to Peer Architecture* of *PUMAS*. The core of *PUMAS* centralizes the requests: on the one hand, it is in charge of the process of obtaining the effective information (which satisfies the user information needs) and, on the other hand, it is in charge of applying the *Content and Display Filters* for adapting the answers. The main *peer* characteristics are: *i*) A *MD* can communicate with a specific *Information System* (located on a server or on a *MD*) passing this information like a parameter of the request and the *Router Agent (RA)* transmits the request to this specific *Information System* (communication agent to agent), and *ii*) the agents have the autonomy of connecting to and disconnecting from the system. An advantage that *PUMAS* offers is that it can also help a user who does not know which specific *Information System* to interrogate for needed information by using the process just explained (this process has like main agents the *R/PA*, the *RA* and the different *Information Systems Agents* which are executed on several *Information Systems*).

4.3 General Agent Issues

In this section, we present the issues related to the agents in the *PUMAS* architecture and some solutions about the modelling principles we have adapted for the information management, agent rules, user profiles and the implementation of our architecture.

Information Management. According to Kothari [5], an agent must have the knowledge and the information to be shared with others, information about its state and the knowledge of its context. For this, *PUMAS* considers that the server stores its own data (knowledge, interchanges with the system coordinator, the agents and their services ...), its rules and its context. Also, each agent must store its knowledge (own, acquired, of context) and its rules (what it can do and/or what has learned to do), its services and the roles it can play within the system. Finally, each agent must store its life cycle (when it has been created, the execution of its tasks and when it must be destroyed). We can represent the information distribution between the *MDs* and/or the server but we must consider the problems with the data that this distribution involves (atomicity, consistency, integrity, etc.).

Definition of Profiles and Agent Rules. For defining user profiles, we can use the *CONSORTS* scheme of *preferences, intentions and attributes* according to the functional application requirements (see section 2). But according to Nagendra *et al.* [7], this definition can be more general: it must consider a mechanism for detecting users and their activities in the system, a representation of criteria that are used to define the profile (user location, intentions...) and an algorithm to implement this representation. For this, we use the extension of *CC/PP* proposed in [4] for defining the general profiles of the *MDs* which could be connected to the system like a service offered by the *MDProfileAgent*. These extensions of *CC/PP* concern the specific features of a nomadic user when defining her/his profile. (e.g. Location, network characteristics, etc.). For defining the agents (behaviours and activities), ontologies can be used. The *W3C* recommends *OWL (Web Ontology Language)*, a language for defining Web Ontologies. *OWL* can be used to describe a *MAS* like a set of classes (agents) and relations (communications and knowledge representation) between them as *XML* files. The *OWL* components are classes, attributes, instances of classes and relations of classes.

4.4 Design of PUMAS Agent Interactions

We use here *Agent UML (AUML)* [8, 10] as a formalism for modelling the interaction between the agents and for explaining how the *PUMAS* agents can access the *ABWIS* for getting the *effective information*. *AUML* is a set of *UML (Unified Modelling Language)* idioms and extensions. It has a representation of three layers for agent interaction protocols. First, *templates and packages* represent the protocol as a whole. Second, *sequence and collaboration diagrams* capture inter-agent dynamics. Finally, *activity diagrams* and *state charts* capture both intra-agent and inter-agent dynamics. An example of each diagram is shown below. Fig. 4 shows the *AUML* package diagram (with its classes and relations) which represents *PUMAS*.

In the Interaction Diagrams of *AUML,* messages between the agents are called *Communication Acts* (e.g., confirm, disconfirm, inform, not-understand, propose, refuse, request, subscribe, propagate ...). In this kind of diagrams, there are messages that could involve a condition. They can as well represent the concurrency between agents. Let us explain by using the following example (see Fig. 5): several *MDAs* could simultaneously send their messages of request to the *Connection Controller Agent*. Then, the decision box reflects that a *MDA* can simultaneously send different messages, according to a condition. In the example shown in Fig. 5, a *MDA* can send a message of *"propose"* (e.g., to propose to be represented by the same *Proxy Agent* in each connection), or a message of *"subscribe"* (e.g., to subscribe like a valid user in the system) or a message of *"query-if"* (e.g., a request if this agent can represent a valid user in the system), according to the condition.

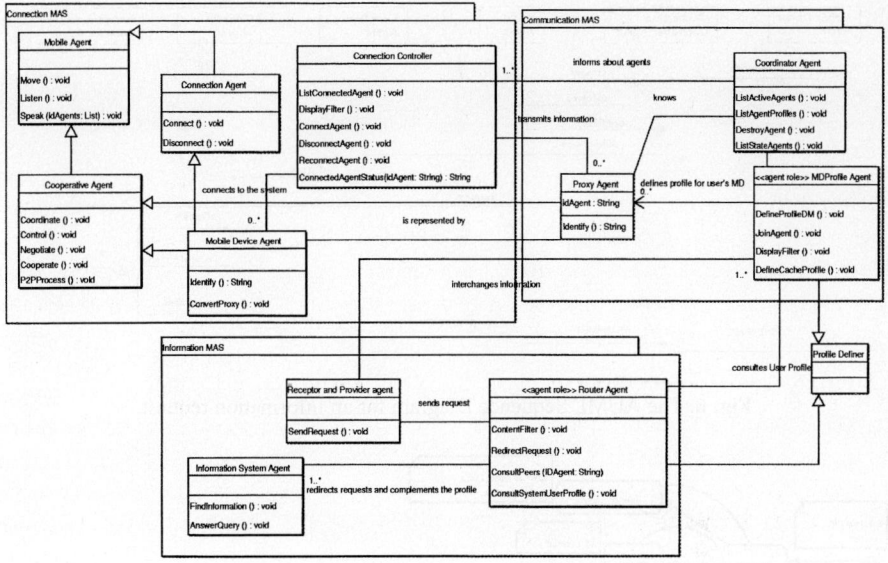

Fig. 4. Package Diagram of *PUMAS*

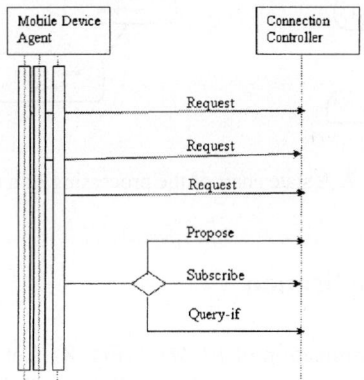

Fig. 5. Example of concurrent sending of messages between Agents.

The Fig. 6 shows an *AUML Sequence Diagram* which represents the interactions between the agents when a *MDA* asks for information. The state chart which establishes the valid states of the processing of a request is shown in Fig. 7.

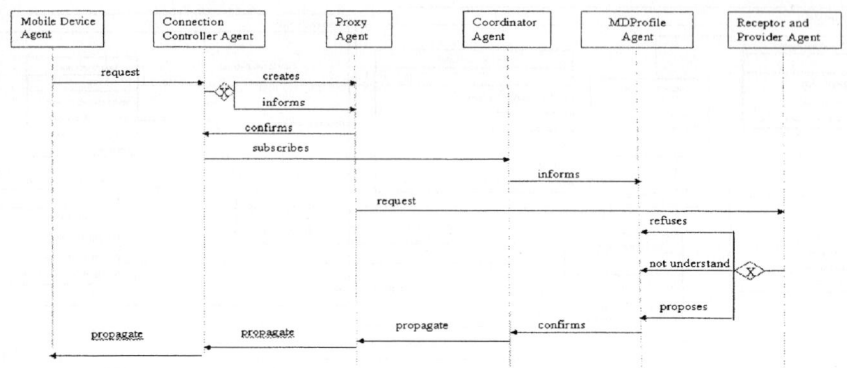

Fig. 6. The AUML Sequence Diagram for an information request.

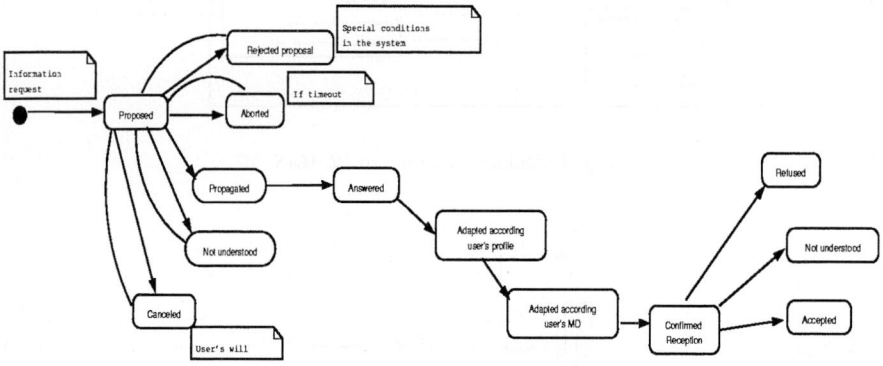

Fig. 7. A state chart of the processing of a request.

5   Example of Application

This section shows an application of *PUMAS* (Fig. 8). Let us assume that an External Audit company gives *MDs* of different types (PDA, cellular, laptop, etc.) to its auditors for doing their work at several client companies. Every day, for documenting their work, the auditors must prepare the audit documents which contain the recording of tests results (tests for the different systems of the client company), tests, reports, etc.

An auditor can ask for information in order to complete her/his work. Initially, the *MDA* which executes on her/his *MD* could ask for information to the other agents which execute on the *MDs* of auditors who work at the same company (or the auditors who participate in the same auditory). If the information obtained satisfies the present request(s), the *MDA* and the agents interchange it. Otherwise, the auditor communicates through her/his *MD* with the general audit system (the application) using, for example, a *WebService* (*Communication MAS*). This latter checks the user profile,

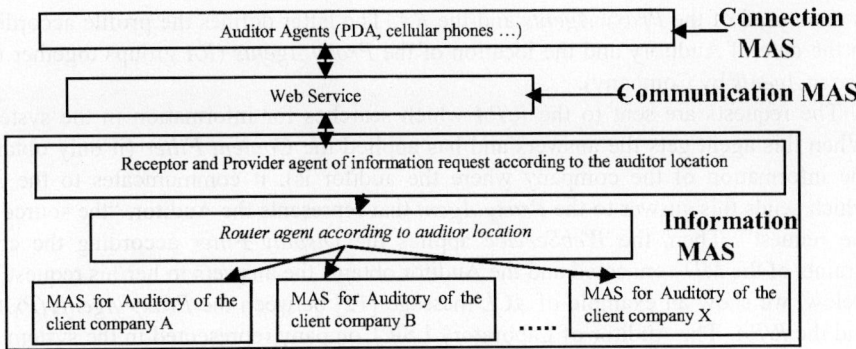

Fig. 8. An auditory system modelled with *PUMAS*

her/his permissions in the system and the type of her/his *MD*. The *WebService* passes the information request to the *Information MAS*. The *Rec/Prov Agent (R/PA)* gets the information query. Depending on the auditor location (criterion chosen for the routing), the *Router Agent (RA)* identifies the company where the auditor is and then, sends her/his request to the *Information MAS* which handles the client company auditory. Once the information is available, the *Information MAS* gives the retrieved information to the *WebService* which checks the type of this information (e.g., image, audio, video) and, together with the *Connection Controller Agent (CCA)*, defines how to display it to the auditor according to the characteristics of her/his *MD* (*Display Filter*). Each auditor (A_i) has a *MD* (in this example, there is one *MDA* per *MD*: *MDA1*, *MDA2*, *MDA3* and *MDA4*, see Fig. 9). The *Spatio-Temporal Reasoner (STR)* gets the location of each *MD* and assigns to it an *ID* inside the system (*AxCy*: Auditor *x* of Company *y*). When an auditor needs information, she/he connects to the system through the *WebService* (*CCA and Coordinator Agent*) which controls the different connections.

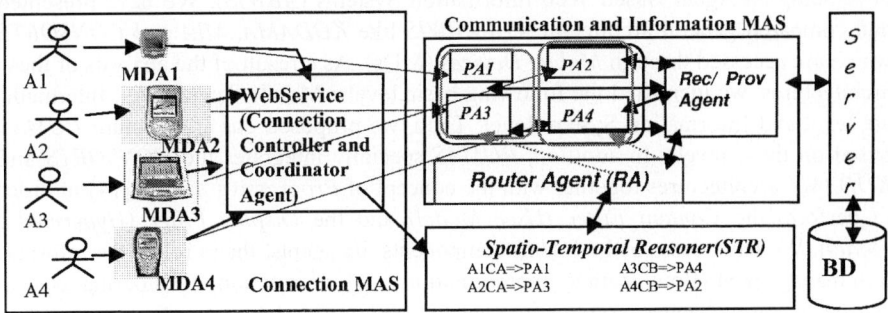

Fig. 9. Connection, Communication and Information MAS

A *Proxy Agent* is created per connection (*PA1, PA2, PA3* and *PA4*). Using established rules in the *STR*, and verifying both the location and existence in the system of each *PAs*, the *RA* defines the profiles, (in this case, the profiles of the Auditors of Company A and the one of the Auditors of Company B). The profile is defined as a group which is composed of the *Proxy Agents* and the *RA*. The latter defines the profile according to the date of Auditory and the location of the *Proxy Agents* (*RA* groups together the *Proxy Agents* by Company).

The requests are sent to the *R/PA* which searches for information in the system. When this agent gets the answers and has applied the *Content Filter* (it only obtains the information of the company where the auditor is), it communicates to the *RA* which sends this answer to the *Proxy Agent* that represents the Auditor, "the source of the request". Then, the *WebService* applies the *Display Filter* according the constraints of the *MD* connected and the Auditor obtains the answers to her/his request(s). Below, we show an example of *ACL* message [12] between the *Proxy Agent1(PxA1)* and the *R/PA*. The Auditor of Laboratory LSR Company represented in the system by *PxA1* asks for her/his Auditory documents to the system. The information about her/his physical location, connection time and language is given by the *WebService* and it is appended in each message whose sender is *PxA1*. The agent in charge of receiving and providing the information is the *R/PA*:

```
(REQUEST
        : sender     PxA1         : receiver Receptor/Provider Agent
        : content    " ( (provide (caption
                     : content "JADE-LEAP Tests - Auditory Papers, Laboratory LSR-IMAG, France,
                     Saint Martin D'Heres, 38402, Friday, June 21 2004, 12:00 )
                     : langage: English")
                     (service
                            :name AuditoryPapersRequest;
                            : provider Receptor/Provider Agent)))"
        :langage    fipa-sl      :ontology     auditory-companies )
```

6   Conclusions and Future Work

In this paper, we have proposed *PUMAS*, an architecture for modelling, designing and developing an Agent Based Web Information Systems (*ABWIS*). We have presented and compared general architectures of *ABWIS* like *KODAMA, MIA* and *CONSORTS* which are accessed through *Mobile Devices* (MDs). As a result of the analysis of these architectures, we identified the following basic levels: Mobile Agent level, Intermediate level and Information System level. Then, we proposed our architecture *PUMAS* based on these levels. In addition, *PUMAS* specially integrates the *CONSORTS* and *KODAMA* architectures together with the concept of *Progressive Access* [14] in order to perform the *Content Filter (User Model)* and the *Display Filter (Hypermedia Model)*. We have described *PUMAS* components, its agents, theirs roles, the information management (flow, storage, representation ... of information) considering aspects as user location changes, communications between users, definition of user's profiles, etc. We have used *AUML* models as a formalism for representing the interaction between the agents of an *ABWIS* modelled with *PUMAS*. Finally, we have presented a scenario for using *PUMAS* (the general model of an application for an External Auditing company). For implementing *PUMAS*, we have chosen *JADE-LEAP* for its independence of execution platform on several *MDs*. We have tested on the *MDs* of our team (some Pocket PC with Windows CE, using crème – *kVM* which is personal

Java compliant, and some *PDA* with *PalmOS* using an implementation *MIDP 1.0)*, the examples which come with it and we have introduced some changes in these examples. However, since a *Stand-Alone* execution *JADE-LEAP* has shown to be instable on our *Pocket PC*, we succeed in the implementation having recourse to a *Split Execution* which simulates a *Hybrid P2P Architecture*.

Our future work concerns the aspects related to the implementation of this kind of systems such as selecting the language for communicating the agents *(ACL)*, producing an *API* for communicating the agents (temporal and spatial information availability), distributing the information between *MDs* and establishing the mechanism for coordinating and controlling theirs activities.

Acknowledgements. The author Angela Carrillo-Ramos is partially supported by Universidad de los Andes (Bogotá, Colombia). She also thanks Fernando De la Rosa for his comments.

References

1. Beuster G., Thomas B., Wolff C.: Ubiquitous Web Information Agents. In: Workshop on Artificial Intelligence In Mobile Systems and European Conference on Artificial Intelligence (ECAI'2000). Berlin, Germany, August 20-25, 2000. (2000). http://www.uni-koblenz.de/~gb/papers/aims2000/paper.pdf. (January 2004).
2. Carabelea, C., Boissier, O.: Multi-Agent Platform on Smart Devices: Dream or Reality? In: Proceedings of the Smart Objects Conference (sOc'2003). Grenoble, France, May 15-17, 2003. (2003) 126-129.
3. De Carolis, B., Pizzutilo, S., Palmisano, I.: D-ME: Personal Interaction in MAS Environments. In: Proc. of 9th International Conference of User Modeling (UM 2003). Johnstown, PA, USA, June 22-26, 2003. Heidelberg. (ed.): UM 2003. LNCS, Vol. 2702. Springer-Verlag, Berlin Heidelberg New York (2003) 388-392.
4. Indulska, J., Robinson, R., Rakotonirainy, A., Henricksen, K.: Experiences in Using CC/PP in Context-Aware Systems. In: M.-S.Chen, P.K.Chrysanthis, M.Sloman, A.Zaslavsky (eds.): Mobile Data Management: 4th Int. Conference, MDM 2003 Melbourne, Australia, January 21-24, 2003. LNCS, Vol. 2574. Springer-Verlag, Berlin Heidelberg (2003) 247-261.
5. Kothari, N.: AGENTOS – A Java Based Mobile Agent System. ICS Honors Project Final Report. Information and Computer Science, University of California, Irvine. (1997). http://netresearch.ics.uci.edu/Previous_research_projects/agentos/doc/nikhil-final-report.pdf. (Last review: January 2004).
6. Kurumatani, K.: Mass User Support by Social Coordination among Citizen in a Real Environment. In: Chen, Shu-Heng; Ohuchi, Azuma (eds.): Multi-Agent for Mass User Support. International Workshop (MAMUS 2003). Acapulco, Mexico, August 10, 2003. LNAI, Vol. 3012. Springer-Verlag, Berlin Heidelberg (2004) 1–16.
7. Nagendra Prasad, M.V, McCarthy, J.: A Multi-Agent System for Meting Out Influence in an Intelligent Environment. In: Proc. of the Eleventh Conference on Innovation Applications of Artificial Intelligence (IAAI' 99). Orlando, Florida, USA, July 18-22, 1999. AAAI Press / The MIT Press (eds.) (1999) 884-890. http://seattleweb.intel-research.net/people/mccarthy/MusicFX-IAAI99.PDF. (January 2004).

8. Odell, J., Van Dyke Parunak, H., Bauer, B.: Representing Agent Interaction Protocols in UML. In: P. Ciancarini and M.J. Wooldridge (eds.): Agent Oriented Software Engineering: First International Workshop AOSE 2000. Limerick, Ireland, June 10, 2000. LNCS, Vol. 1957. Springer-Verlag Berlin Heidelberg (2001) Online Date July 2003. 121-140.
9. Panti, M., Penserini, L., Spalazzi, L.: A Multi-Agent System based on the P2P model to Information Integration. In: Proc. of First International joint Conferences on Autonomous Agents and Multi-Agent Systems (AAMAS 2002). Bologna, Italy. 2002.
http://www.agentcities.org/EUNET/Projects/acnet_proj_38.pdf (January 2004)
10. Poggi, A., Rimassa, G., Turci, P., Odell, J., Mouratidis, H., Manson, G.: Modelling Deployment and Mobility Issues in Multiagent Systems Using AUML. In: P. Giorgini, J.P. Mûller, J.Odell (eds.): Agent Oriented Software Engineering: Fourth International Workshop AOSE 2003. Melbourne, Australia - July 15, 2003. LNCS, Vol. 2935. Springer-Verlag Berlin Heidelberg (2004). 69-84.
11. Ramparany, F., Boissier, O., Brouchoud H.: Cooperating Autonomous Smart Devices. In: Proceedings of the Smart Objects Conference (sOc'2003). Grenoble, France, May 15-17, 2003. (2003) 182-185.
12. Sashima, A., Izumi, N., Kurumatani, K.: CONSORTS: A Multiagent Architecture for Service Coordination in Ubiquitous Computing. In: Chen, Shu-Heng; Ohuchi, Azuma (eds.): Multi-Agent for Mass User Support. Int. Workshop (MAMUS 2003). Acapulco, Mexico, August 10, 2003. LNAI, Vol. 3012. Springer-Verlag, Berlin Heidelberg (2004) 190–216.
13. Takahashi, K., Amamiya, S., Iwao, T.: An Agent-based Framework for Ubiquitous Systems. In: Challenges in Open Agent Systems '03 Workshop (Challenge03). Melbourne, Australia, July 14-15 2003. (2003)
http://www.agentcities.org/Challenge03/papers.php (Janvier 2004).
14. Villanova, M.: Adaptabilité dans les systèmes d'information sur le web : Modélisation et mise en œuvre de l'accès progressif. Thèse Doctorale (In French). INPG, France. (2002).
15. Wenyin, L., Chen, Z., Li, M.,Zhang, H.: A Media Agent for Automatically Building a Personalized Semantic Index of Web Media Objects. Journal of the American Society for Information Science, Vol. 52, No.10 (2001) 853-855.

A Meta-service for Event Notification

Doris Jung and Annika Hinze

University of Waikato, New Zealand
{d.jung,hinze}@cs.waikato.ac.nz

Abstract. The integration of event information from diverse event notification sources is, as with meta-searching over heterogeneous search engines, a challenging task. Due to the complexity of event filter languages, known solutions for heterogeneous searching cannot be applied for event notification
In this paper, we propose the concept and design of a Meta Service for Event Notification. We define transformation rules for exchanging event filter definitions and event notifications between various event services and sources. We transform each filter defined at a meta-service into a filter expressed in the language of each event notification source. Due to unavoidable asymmetry in the semantics of different langues, some superfluous information may be delivered to the meta-service. These notifications are then post-processed to reduce the number of spurious messages. We present a survey and classification of filter languages for event notification, which serves as basis for the transformation rules. The proposed rules are implemented in a prototype transformation module for a Meta Service for Event Notification.

1 Introduction

Alerting Services or Event Notification Services (ENS) inform their users about changes that have occurred at information objects. These changes are called events. Information objects can be, e.g., documents in a digital library or temperature sensors in a facility management system; events can be caused, e.g., by new, changed or deleted objects. The service actively or passively observes the information objects at the providers sites (e.g., documents in digital libraries or sensors in buildings). Users describe their interest in form of personal profiles that define filter conditions for the information delivery. In a widely distributed application context, each of the considered applications may employ their own alerting services (e.g., as done for digital libraries provided by different publishing houses or as currently available for tourist information). Users on the other hand, are interested in combined information from diverse and heterogeneous sources. Similar to the problem of information querying over widely distributed information sources, here we encounter the problem of distributed filtering over heterogeneous event sources.

Unfortunately, the results known from research in meta-searching [12] and query rewriting for search over heterogeneous sources [3,21] cannot simply be applied to the new context of event notification. Advanced filter conditions are more complex than search queries; in fact, they can be seen as extensions of search queries: A simple filter expression can be seen as a standing search query. Additionally, filter expressions can contain sophisticated event pattern descriptions referring to temporal succession of events, such as sequences and disjunction of events [11,19,20].

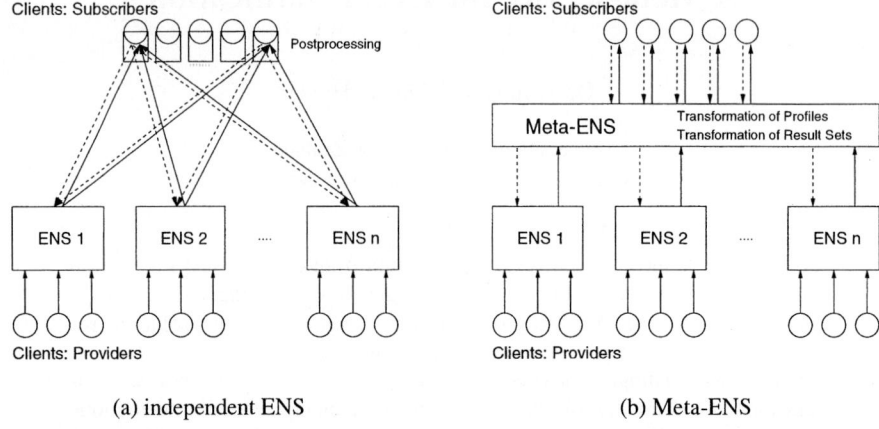

Fig. 1. Communication of clients with several independent ENS vs with a Meta-ENS

1.1 Problem Statement and Contribution of the Paper

The existence of several independent event notification services causes a number of problems, see Figure 1(a) for illustration:

1. Subscribers are forced to subscribe the same profile to a number of services; these use different filter languages (i.e., the profiles have to be expressed differently) with differing expressiveness. In Figure 1(a), the large number of dashed arrows from each subscriber indicates the repeated subscriptions.
2. Composite events combining events from different providers that are handled by different services cannot be directly subscribed to. In consequence, the client has to subscribe to (several) separate services and implement post-filtering locally. In Figure 1(a), the arrows from each ENS indicate the notifications that have to be post-filtered at the subscribers' sides.
3. If providers serve several services, the duplicates have to be removed in a post-filter process at the client side. In Figure 1(a), the postfiltering is depicted as boxes at the subscribers' sides.

An umbrella service could combine all providers but would force a flat homogenization of the providers, while ignoring the existing heterogeneity of the providers and services. Moreover, there are the issues of trust, downwards compatibility, company strategy, and required integration of legacy systems.

As a solution to the three problems we propose the equivalent of a Meta-Search Engine: a *Meta Event Notification Service* (Meta-ENS), see Figure 1(b). Our solution allows for and supports the heterogeneity of services and providers. It integrates services while accepting their differences and diversity. The advantages are evident: Subscribers can have a uniform access for profile definition, having access to several event sources. Users are not repeatedly notified about the same event, i.e., duplicate recognition can be implemented on the meta-service level. In addition, security and privacy issues are easier to address. A number of research questions emerge as a result of the analysis given above, which have to be answered for the design of the meta-service:

1. Which event patterns for composite events are typically supported in profile and filter languages for event notification services? Are there categories of languages?
2. How to translate the event patterns in one language into the patterns of a target language such that profile definitions can be converted between languages? How are the result sets influenced by the transformation? What postprocessing is necessary for re-transforming the result sets to match the initial profile query?
3. How to detect duplicates of event messages that refer to the same event? How to detect messages referring to the same event?

1.2 Focus and Organization of the Paper

In this paper, we will address the first two questions, which we believe to be essential for the implementation of a Meta-ENS. For the elimination of duplicates, existing techniques from information retrieval and information dissemination may be employed (see, e.g., [23]). Note that we do not make assumptions abut the nature of the services, e.g., distributed or centralized services. We abstract from the problems of event detection and ordering in a distributed environment.

In the remainder of the paper, we propose the detailed design of a *Meta Service for Event Notification* that translates filter expressions for heterogeneous event notification services. After a brief introduction of the concepts of filter languages (Section 2), we first analyze the filter languages of existing alerting services in order to identify typical event patterns (Section 3). In Section 3.2, the services will be ordered into groups based on the expressiveness of their filter languages. Based on this classification, we propose a set of transformation rules for the translation of filter expressions between these groups (Section 4). We conclude the paper by a summary and an outlook towards further research and challenges to be addressed.

2 Concepts

In this section, we introduce the basic concepts of event notification services. A more detailed discussion of models and terms can be found in [9]. Event notification services inform its users about events that occurred on a given set of objects. Events are reported to the service by means of event messages. Objects have certain states, defined by their properties at a certain time, e.g., the state of a database, the content of a web-page.

Definition 1 (Event). *An event is the occurrence of a state transition of an object of interest at a certain point in time. Events are reported by means of event messages (or notifications), which contain a timestamp referring to the event's occurrence time.*

Events have no duration. Events may be state changes in databases, signals in message systems. We consider *primitive events* and *composite events*, which are formed by combining primitive and composite events. The set of composite events $\mathbb{E}_C$ detectable by a certain system is defined by its system event algebra, i.e, by its filter and profile semantics. Composite events are created based on an event algebra. Event composition defines new event instances. The new (composite) event instances inherit the characteristics of all contributing events; the event occurrence time is defined by the composition operator. We denote the fact that a set of event instances contributes to a composite event by the $\succ$ operator:

Definition 2 (Composition Contribution $\succ$). *Let $e_1, ..., e_n \in \mathbb{E}$ be event instances that contribute to the composite event $e \in \mathbb{E}_C$. This relation is expressed as $\{e_1, ..., e_n\} \succ e$. The $e_1, ..., e_n$ can be primitive or composite event instances.*

One of the central terms of an event notification service is the user profile:

Definition 3 (Profile). *A profile is a query q_{exp} that is periodically evaluated by the Event Notification Service against incoming events, i.e., a query that is evaluated against the trace of events reported to the service.*

We distinguish *event instances* from *event classes*. An event class is a set of events specified by a profile while an event instance relates to the actual occurrence of an event. In the following, we simply use the term *event* whenever the distinction is clear from the context. Events (instances) are denoted by lower Latin e with indices, i.e., $e_1, e_2, \ldots$, while event classes are denoted by upper Latin E with indices, i.e., $E_1, E_2, \ldots$. The fact that an event e_i is an instance of an event class E_j is denoted *membership*, i.e., $e_i \in E_j$. This relationship is non-exclusive, i.e., $e_i \in E_j$ and $e_i \in E_k$ is possible even with $E_j \neq E_k$. Event classes may also have subclasses, so that $e_i \in E_j \subset E_k$. The timestamp of an event $e \in E_1$ is denoted $t(e)$.

Definition 4 (Duplicate). *Duplicates of events are event instances that belong to the same event class.*

Note that duplicate events refer to separate event instances – in contrast, the same event instance might be reported twice to the service, leading to duplicate event messages. Duplicate events could be subsequent changes of the same document in a digital library, but also all events referring to a certain document collection. Note that duplicates need not necessarily have identical event types or identical timestamps.

In a ENS, query profiles are evaluated against the history of all observed events.

Composite Event Pattern Operators. This section informally describes the concepts of the most common operators for composite events. Event composition defines new event instances that inherit the characteristics of all contributing events. The occurrence time of the composite event is defined by the composition operator. The events e_1 and e_2 used in the definitions below can be any primitive or composite event; E_1 and E_2 refer to event classes with $E_1 \neq E_2$. $t(.)$ refers to occurrence times defined based on a reference time system, T denotes time spans in reference time units. We use the contribution operator $\succ$ (cf. Definition 2) to identify the events that contribute to a composite event. Note that temporal operators are defined on event instances as well as on event classes, resulting in event instances and event classes, respectively.

Disjunction: The *disjunction* $(E_1|E_2)$ of events occurs if either $e_1 \in E_1$ or $e_2 \in E_2$ occurs. The occurrence time of the composite event $e_3 \in (E_1|E_2)$ is defined as the time of the occurrence of either e_1 or e_2 respectively: $t(e_3) := t(e_1)$ with $\{e_1\} \succ e_3$ or $t(e_3) := t(e_2)$ with $\{e_2\} \succ e_3$.

Conjunction: The *conjunction* $(E_1, E_2)_T$ occurs if both $e_1 \in E_1$ and $e_2 \in E_2$ occur, regardless of the order. The conjunction constructor has a temporal parameter that describes the maximal length of the interval between e_1 and e_2.[1] The time of the composite event $e_3 \in (E_1, E_2)_T$ with $\{e_1, e_2\} \succ e_3$ is the time of the last event: $t(e_3) := max\{t(e_1), t(e_2)\}$.

Sequence: The *sequence* $(E_1; E_2)_T$ occurs when first $e_1 \in E_1$ and afterwards $e_2 \in E_2$ occurs. T defines the maximal temporal distance of the events. The time of the event $e_3 \in (E_1; E_2)_T$ with $\{e_1, e_2\} \succ e_3$ is equal to the time of e_2: $t(e_3) := t(e_2)$.

Negation: The *negation* $\overline{E}_T$ defines a "passive" event; it means that no $e \in E$ occurs for an interval $[t_{start}, t_{end}]$ with $t_{end} = t_{start} + T$ of time. The occurrence time of $\overline{e}_T \in \overline{E}_T$ is the point of time at the end of the period, $t(\overline{e}_T) := t_{end}$ When clear from the context, we write $\overline{e}_T$ when referring to a passive event.

Simultaneity: The *simultaneity* $(E_1 : E_2)_T$ occurs when both events $e_1 \in E_1$ and afterwards $e_2 \in E_2$ happen it the same time: $t(e_1) = t(e_2)$.

Selection: The *selection* $E^{[i]}$ defines the occurrence of the ith event $e \in E$ of a sequence of events of class E, $i \in \mathbb{N}$.

The model of composite events consists of (primitive or composite) events combined through event constructors. Note that temporal operators are defined on event instances as well as on event classes, resulting in instances and classes, respectively. This means that operators on event classes form profiles, i.e. queries, whereas operators on event instances describe certain composite event instances.

Composite Event Pattern Parameters. In addition to the event operators, we define the two parameters of consumption mode and duplicate handling. Consumption mode is a concept concerning the strategy of evaluation in respect to the event history. When specifying a profile it is necessary to define whether event instances should be disposed of after matching or whether they should be considered again for a new filtering process. if disposed, there are two possibilities to do so: 'delete' and 'delete and reapply'. For 'delete', all event instances which occurred before the matched event instance are deleted. The other option is to delete only those event which have taken part in the matched event instance. If no event instances are deleted this is called 'keep'.

Duplicate handling describes which event instances out of a list of identical duplicates are regarded for the filtering process. The following possibilities are relevant for our analysis: first, last, all, n^{th}, and n to m. The values refer to the ordering number of the duplicate events.

3 Survey of Profile Definition Languages in ENS

This section addresses the first problem that we identified in the introduction (Problem 1): Which event patterns for composite events are typically supported in profile and filter languages for ENS and are there categories of languages? We have analyzed filter languages of several event-based systems. This section presents the initial results of our analysis, which has been carried out in three steps.

---

[1] $(E_1, E_2)_\infty$ refers to an event composition without temporal restrictions.

1. *The overview*: For each system, we list the supported operators, support of time frames, consumption mode, and duplicate handling. These analyses are based on the available literature, i.e., we refer to the operators and their parameters the way the initial publication does. Consequently, there are differences in the semantics and symbols compared to the ones introduced in Section 2. This overview is given subsequently in Section 3.1.
2. *Comparative Study*: For each filter language, the filter operators are translated into the terminology used here. Based on this, we perform a uniform comparison of the approaches. This comparative study is presented in Section 3.2.
3. *Language Groups*: Based on the comparative study, we identified five groups (types) of filter languages for event-based services. Section 3.3 presents the definition of the language groups. These language groups form the basis for the design of the meta-service for event notification and event-based communication.

3.1 Overview of Systems and Supported Event Patterns

Our overview of filter languages is presented ordered by system type; we analyzed the following types[2]: Event Notification Services (see Table 1), Event-based Infrastructures (see Table 2), Event-based Infrastructures (see Table 2) and Hybrid systems (see Table 3). An extended analysis that also covers active database systems and event actin systems can be found in [13]. For each of the systems, we analyzed the following characteristics of the profile languages: operators for building event patterns, support of time frames in the patterns, the consumption modes and the supported duplicate handling.

Event Notification Services We analyzed a selection of eight typical event notification services: A-MediAS [9], an adaptive and integrating event notification service; the Corba Notification Service [8], Elvin [22]; Hermes [4], an event notification service for digital libraries; Keryx [1], which is designed to distribute notifications in the internet; READY [7], the sequel of the event-action system YEAST; and Siena [2]. The results are shown in Table 1. Most ENS still only support primitive events, with research focussing on efficient filter algorithms.

Event-based Infrastructures In the category of event-based Infrastructures, we analyzed Cobea [16], which is used e.g. for the management of networks; Rebeca [5], an event-based architecture for electronic commerce; Regis [17], a development environment for distributed systems that has been extended by the pattern language GEM [19]; and Salamander [18], a system for the distribution of web-applications. The results are shown in Table 2.

Hybrid Systems Hybrid systems are able to handle a variety of event sources: web-documents, databases and files. We examined the systems Conquer [15] and OpenCQ [14] from the Continual Queries project, and Eve [6]. Eve combines characteristics of active databases and event-based architectures to execute event driven workflows. The result of the analysis is shown in Table 3. Hybrid systems combine events from different sources, supporting a variety of event patterns.

As illustrated in this section, the analyzed systems support a variety of event patterns, using various operators and auxiliary parameters. Note, that the list of analyzed systems cannot be exhaustive, but considers a representative set of selected systems and

---

[2] Note that the exact distinction between the types may be arguable.

Table 1. Composite event operators in Event Notification Services

System	Operators	Time frame	Consumption Mode	Duplicate handling
A-mediAS	Conjunction: $(E_1 \& E_2)$ Disjunction: $(E_1 \| E_2)$ Sequence: $(E_1; E_2)$ Negation: $(E_1 - E_2)$ Selection: $First(E_1)$	yes	keep, delete, delete and reapply	first, last, all, n^{th}, n to m
CORBA notification service	only primitive events	–	–	–
Elvin	only primitive events	–	–	–
Hermes	only primitive events	–	–	–
Keryx	only primitive events	–	–	–
Ready	Conjunction: $(E_1 \&\& E_2)$ Disjunction: $(E_1 \| E_2)$ Sequence: $(E_1; E_2)$ Negation: $(not\ E_1)$			first, last, all, n^{th}, n to m
Siena	Sequence: $(E_1.E_2)$	–	delete	first

Table 2. Composite event operators in Event-based Infrastructures

System	Operators	Time frame	Consumption Mode	Duplicate handling
Cobea	Conjunction: $(E_1 \& E_2)$ Disjunction: $(E_1 \| E_2)$ Sequence: $(E_1; E_2)$ Whenever: $(\$E_1)$ Without: $(E_1 - E_2)$	Duration	Keep events	all
Rebeca	Conjunction: Disjunction: Sequence: Negation:	yes	Delete and reapply, (recent, chronicle)	–
Regis	Conjunction: $(E_1 \& E_2)$ Disjunction: $(E_1 \| E_2)$ Sequence: (E_1, E_2) Negation: $(\{E_1; E_2\}!E_3)$ Time: $(E_1 + timeperiod)$	Duration-window	Delete all events	first
Salamander	only primitive events	–	–	–

languages. In the next section, we introduce our classification of filter languages, which allows to identify language groups that support typical subsets of event patterns.

Table 3. Composite event operators in Hybrid Systems

System	Operators	Time frame	Consumption Mode	Duplicate handling
CQ: Conquer and OpenCQ	Conjunction Disjunction Sequence: $(E_1; E_2)$ Negation: Simultaneity: $(E_1 \| E_2)$	yes	–	–
Eve	Conjunction: $(CON(E_1, E_2, sw))$ Disjunction: $(DEX(E_1, E_2))$ Sequence: $(SEQ(E_1, E_2, sw))$ Simultaneity: $(CCR(E_1, E_2, sw))$ Negation: $(NEG(E_1, (E_2, E_3, sw), sw))$ Repetition: $REP(E_1, times, sw)$	yes	delete and reapply (chronicle)	first, n^{th}

3.2 Classification of Filter Languages – A Comparative Study

This section presents our *comparative study* of filter languages: This is the second step in our approach to answer the question for common patterns and groups of filter languages (Problem 1). We translate each system's operators into the terminology used here, in order to allow for a uniform comparison of the approaches. We first introduce our classification methodology and then present the actual classification. This classification shall be the basis for identifying typical language groups in the next section.

Extending the survey presented in the last section, we have classified the profile languages of selected event systems. We developed a set of classification criteria, which are a combination of the semantic language characteristics defined by Hinze/Voisard [10] and Zimmer/Unland [24]. Both works describe the semantics of filter languages. Both use operators for event patterns and additional parameters.

Composite Event Pattern Operators. As shown in the previous section, the systems use different operators for event patterns. Additionally, equally named operators do not necessarily have the same semantics while similar semantics might be expressed using different operators. Moreover, the exact semantic description of these operators is rarely given in literature. Here, we will translate all systems' operators into the following schema: conjunction, disjunction, negation, selection, sequence and simultaneity (see Table 4).

Event Pattern Parameters. Considering the analyzed systems, it becomes clear that to simply consider the operators is not sufficient in order to convey the full semantic meaning. Each system offers parameters, which further define/change the operators semantics. We shall briefly describe the different parameters proposed in the two schemas.

Hinze/Voisard define two parameters: event instance selection and event instance consumption (see left column in Table 4). 'Event instance selection' describes which events qualify for a composite event and how duplicated events handled. Examples are to select the first event in a list of duplicates, the last one or a particular n^{th} one. 'Event instance consumption' defines which events are consumed by composite events, i.e., removed from the matching trace. Options are to keep the selected event instances, to remove them, or to remove them and reapply the event pattern (similar to our definition in Section 2). In [10], only two of the three options are formally defined. Both event pattern parameters can be combined freely.

Unland/Zimmer defined separate parameters for concurrency, consumption, selection, traversion, and coupling (see middle column in Table 4). Concurrency can be 'overlapping' or 'non-overlapping', allowing for components of different event-instances to overlap each other or not. Consumption may be 'shared', 'exclusive parameter', or 'exclusive': Either no event-instance is deleted, or all event-instances which have taken part in the matching of a composite event are deleted, or all event-instances before the terminating event-instance of a composite event are deleted. These parameters are similar to the Event instance consumption, but not identical. The selection parameter is similar to and can be expressed via Hinze/Voisard's Event Instance selection.

The parameters are partially interdependent: Shared consumption mode requires overlapping concurrency and an exclusive consumption mode is only logical in combination with a non-overlapping concurrency. The concurrency mode for the exclusive consumption is undefined. This interdependence of parameters is our main reason for primarily following Hinze/Voisard's classification.

Not all parameters are applicable for the systems we are interested in, e.g., the concurrency mode and the traversion mode. The traversion mode, which describes the direction of traversing composite events is irrelevant here, since systems filter their events in the timely order and not backwards. This parameter will not be included in our classification. The coupling mode defines whether the components of different event-instances may be interleaving. These modes are expressed by Hinze/Voisard using negation and wildcards. We therefore exclude this parameter from our classifications.

We followed a hybrid approach and use a combination of both schemas, which is shown in the right column of Table 4. Our *combined classification schema* combines the operators proposed in the two schemas and also uses a combination of the proposed event pattern parameters. We use the characteristics from Unland/Zimmer's consumption mode; the duplicate handling is based on Hinze/Voisard's Event Instance Selection.

We now use the combined classification schema for our comparative study of filter languages in event-based systems. The results of the study are presented as a language classification in Table 5. This table serves three purposes: It gives an overview of event-based filter languages, provides a uniform analysis of the languages (i.e., translated into a common schema), and gives a first impression of the operators and parameters typically supported in event-based systems.

Based on the language classification, we make the following observations in the comparative study: If composite events are supported, all[3] of these systems implement conjunction and disjunction (i.e., operators without ordering). Some implement the sequence operators (requires ordering), fewer the negation (required observation). Selection and simultaneity are rarely supported: Selection is a special case of duplicate handling and simultaneity is difficult to determine for distributed systems - it can be expressed by conjunction with a small ϵ-time frame. Time frames are not always supported, requiring a time handling strategy for distributed systems. Consumption mode

---

[3] With the exception of Siena that only supports a single operator for research purposes.

Table 4. Comparison of the two schemas for semantic classification and our combined schema.

Hinze/Voisard	Unland/Zimmer	Combined Classification
Composite Event Pattern Operators		
conjunction	conjunction	conjunction
disjunction	disjunction	disjunction
sequence	sequence	sequence
negation	negation	negation
selection	-	selection
-	simultaneity	simultaneity
Time frames		
Event Instance Consumption	Consumption Mode	Consumption Mode
Event Instance Selection	Parameter Selection	Duplicate Handling
-	Concurrency Mode	-
(above parameter/operators combination)	Coupling Mode	-
(above parameter combination)	Traversion Mode	-

and duplicate handling are rarely made explicit. If they are explicit, several options are supported, otherwise they are hard coded in the system and difficult to determine.

3.3 Language Groups

Based on the observations from our comparative study of languages in the previous section, we identify *language groups* (types) of filter languages for event-based systems. This is the third and final step in answering the question for typical event patterns and groups of filter languages for ENS (Problem 1).

These language groups form the basis for the design of the meta-service for event notification and event-based communication. In the next section, we address the second problem (as identified in the introduction) and define rules for profile transformations between these language groups. Parameters for Consumption Mode and Duplicate Handling (cf. Section 2) are very rarely explicitly described in the literature. For this reason, we did not include the parameters in the definition of groups – they will be consider separately. Thus, the languages are classified into groups based on their support for time frames and by their support for pattern operators.

We define five groups as shown in Table 6. There are two groups without time frame support: CEs support conjunction, disjunction and negation; a group member is PLAN. SCEs support conjunction, disjunction, negation, and sequences. Members are READY, Rebeca, and Active House (CEA).

There are three groups with time frame support: TCE offer conjunction, disjunction and sequence. Members of this group are Yeast and Sentinel (language Snoop). The OTCEs support conjunction, disjunction, sequence and negation; members of this group are Samos, Cobea, and GEM. STCE offer conjunction, disjunction, sequence, negation, and simultaneity. Members of this group are Eve, Conquer, and OpenCQ. The disequilibrium of the group assignment of negation and sequence is due to the different effect of time-frames on the operators.

Table 5. Comparison of Profile Definition Languages = Filter Languages, alphabetically ordered by system/language name. Characteristics are derived directly from the literature (whenever possible) or inferred from given examples

Systems	Composite Events	Operators						Time frame	Consumption Mode			Duplicate handling			
		Conjunction	Disjunction	Sequence	Negation	Simultan.	Selection		keep	delete	delete & reapply	first	last	all	detailed
Active House	×	×	×	×								×			
A-mediAS	×	×	×	×							×		×	×	
Cobea	×	×	×	×						×						
Corba NS	–									×						
Elvin	–															
Eve	×	×	×	×	×	×			×		×		×			
GEM (Regis, Darwin)	×	×	×	×	×				×		×		×			
Hermes	–															
Keryx	–															
OpenCQ	×	×	×	×	×				×							
PLAN	×	×	×	×	×				×				×	×		
Ready	×	×	×	×	×								×	×		
Rebeca	×	×	×	×	×								×	×		
Salamander	–											×				
Samos	×	×	×	×		×			×		×		×			
Siena	×	×	×		×						×		×			
Snoop (Sentinel)	×	×	×	×					×		×			×	×	
Yeast	×	×	×	×					×				×		×	×

Table 6. Groups of Filter Languages

Time-frame-less Composite Events	Time-framed Composite Events
CE: Simple Composite Events *(conjunction, disjunction and negation)*	**TCE**: Simple Time-framed Composite Events *(conjunction, disjunction and sequence)*
	OTCE: Ordinary Time-framed Composite Events *(TCE and negation)*
SCE: Sophisticated Composite Events *(CE and sequence)*	**STCE**: Sophisticated Time-framed Composite Events *(OTCE and simultaneity)*

3.4 Summary of Findings Regarding a Classification of Filter Languages

The three steps of analyzing profile languages presented in this section are our answer to the first research question stated in the introduction of this paper (identification of typical event patterns and language groups). Firstly, we analyzed typical patterns for composite events in filter languages. Secondly, we compared the filter languages based on a classification schema. Thirdly, we used the classification to identify typical groups of filter languages. The findings of this section shall serve as a foundation for answering the second problem of finding transformation rules between languages from different groups. The second problem is addressed in the next section.

4 Profile and Result Transformations

We now address the problem of translating filter expressions between languages that use different operators and semantics (Problem 2). The answer to this problem shall provide a set of transformation rules that form the core of the proposed Meta-ENS for integrating heterogeneous event notification services. Here, we therefore especially consider the challenge of translating a filter expression of the meta-service in to the target language of other systems. The meta-service is assumed to support all of the composite event/profile concepts (operators and parameters) introduced in Section 2.

4.1 Transformation Methodology

For each language group, we introduce transformation rules for translating filter expressions defined at the Meta-ENS into equivalent filter expressions using a language of the group. As can be derived from the group definitions, a simple translation of filter expressions between groups is not possible. Instead, for different semantic concepts in two distinct groups, we have to find expressions that are semantically close. Additionally, auxiliary profiles and post-filtering may be required.

Profile Transformations. If a certain operator does not exist in one language a transcription expression has to be used. These transcriptions may be more or less expressive than the source expression. We define therefore four types of transformations: equivalent, positive, negative, and transferring transformation. We denote these transformations with the arrow-notation that is shown in Table 7. It is an extension of the notation used for Boolean transformations [3]. Equivalent transformations lead to expressions that have identical result sets. Positive transformations result in expressions that are less selective than the original - potentially creating larger result sets; negative transformations result in more selective expressions compared to the original filter expression (creating smaller result sets). Larger result sets without subsequent postfiltering lead to false positives in client notifications. Smaller result sets lead to missed event notifications. Transferring transformations (when omitting event patterns) use postfiltering and auxiliary profiles.

Post-filtering and Auxiliary profiles. For the considered transformations between languages groups, not all of the original operations can be expressed in the languages of less powerful groups. In order to use weaker systems in cooperation with stronger ones, auxiliary profiles (i.e., additional filter expressions) have to be defined at the services. The filter results are delivered to the stronger system which then needs to perform additional simple filter operations (post-filtering).

Notification Transformation. Differing from query transformation, the result set obtained in an event notification service is not simply a set of tuples or documents. For ENS, the result reflects the filter expression, i.e., the temporal connection between the events is reported. If for two communicating systems, the less expressive system receives a message from a more expressive one, the notification might not be comprehensible to the less expressive filter language. Lets consider the following example: Consider two systems A and B, where the filter language of A supports only sequences and disjunction, the filter language of B supports only conjunction. The systems cannot cooperate directly, since their set of filter operators are disjunct. In order to cooperate, system A defines a profile p_A at the Meta-ENS ($p_A = ((E_1; E_2)|(E_2; E_1))$). Meta-ENS transforms this expression into a profile p_B that is defined at system B: $p_B = (E1, E_2)$ with $p_A \longleftrightarrow p_B$. When system B sends a notification $n_B = (e1, e_2)$ to the Meta-ENS, the system A is notified by the transformed message $n_A = ((e_1; e_2)|(e_2; e_1))$. Thus, not only the filter expressions have to be transformed for the cooperation but also the notifications.

The contributions of this section are (1) a set of profile transformation rules for the interaction of the meta-service with other ENS, (2) auxiliary profile definitions and rules for post-filtering, and (3) notification transformation rules. In this section, firstly we introduce the transformations for composite operators together with auxiliary profiles and post-filtering. Secondly we define transformation rules for event pattern parameters which form the basic building block for our Meta-ENS.

Table 7. Types of Transformations

Transformation	Notation
Equivalent Transformation	$\longleftrightarrow$
Positive Transformation	$\xrightarrow{+}$
Negative Transformation	$\xrightarrow{-}$
Transferring Transformation	$\xleftrightarrow{\#}$

Table 8. Target system without time frames: CE - Meta-ENS: E refers to event classes, $N(E)$ to notifications regarding an event in class E, $t(N(E))$ to the time of the event notification

Operators	Target Group CE — Meta-ENS timeless	timed
Conjunction	$(E_1, E_2) \longleftrightarrow (E_1, E_2)_\infty$	$(E_1, E_2) \xleftarrow{\pm} (E_1, E_2)_T$
Disjunction	$(E_1 \vert E_2) \longleftrightarrow (E_1 \vert E_2)$	—
Sequence	$(E_1, E_2) \xleftarrow{\#} (E_1; E_2)_\infty, t(N(E_1)) < t(N(e_2))$	$(E_1, E_2) \xleftarrow{\pm} (E_1; E_2)_T$
Negation	—	$(E_1) \xleftarrow{\pm} (E_1)_T$
Simultaneity	$(E_1, E_2) \xleftarrow{\#} (E_1 : E_2), t(N(E_1)) = t(N(E_2))$	—
Selection	$(E_1) \xleftarrow{\pm} (E_1)^{[1]}, (E_1, E_1) \xleftarrow{\pm} (E_1)^{[2]}, \ldots$	—

4.2 Profile Transformation of Composite Operators

This section defines the transformation rules for composite operators. The rules are presented for the transformation of filter expressions defined at the Meta-ENS towards expressions of a target system within a given group (as identified in Section 3.2). We assume the Meta-ENS supports all concepts and event patters introduced in this paper. We now iterate through the five target groups and show the necessary transformations. Due to limitations of space not all refinements of every rule are given in this paper. For further details please contact the authors.

Simple time-frame-less composite events (CE): We give the transformation between the event operators expressed for the Meta-ENS into the target group CE (see Table 8). In the Meta-ENS, the operators can be timed (subscript T) or time-frame-less (subscript ∞). If necessary, we also define auxiliary profiles and post-filtering of notifications. The filter expressions of the Meta-ENS are given on the right-hand side, the ones of the source group on the left-hand side of the transformations.

Conjunction, Disjunction, and Negation are almost identical; the transformation is based on the change of time frames. Towards the Meta-ENS, the missing time frame has to be set to ∞. Towards the target system the time frame of the Meta-ENS is lost, which leads to less expressive filter expressions. Negation does not exist without a time frame. Sequence and simultaneity do not exist in this group and have to be simulated. For each $i \in \mathbb{N}$ in selection $E_1^{[i]}$, a separate transformation has to be defined. Alternative transformations for negation and selection are given in Table 10. Note that disjunction, simultaneity, and selection are undefined as timed operators and the negation is undefined as a timeless operators (cf. Section 2).

Sophisticated time-frame-less composite events (SCE): Conjunction, Disjunction, and Negation are similar to the simple time-frame-less version (see Table 9). The sequence operator is now supported and is transformed analogous to the conjunction. For simultaneity, a combination of conjunction, sequence and negation can be used.

Simple time-framed composite events (TCE): Conjunction, Disjunction, and Sequence are directly supported (see Table 10). The selection is realized using transferring trans-

Table 9. Target system without time frames: SCE - Meta-ENS: E refers to event classes, $N(E)$ to notifications regarding an event in class E, $t(N(E))$ to the time of the event notification

Operators	Target Group SCE — Meta-ENS timeless	timed
Conjunction	see CE in Table 8	
Disjunction		
Sequence	$(E_1, E_2) \longleftrightarrow (E_1; E_2)_\infty$	see CE in Table 8
Negation		
Simultaneity	see CE in Table 8	
Selection		

formation. Negation can only be implemented in systems with a time concept; it then uses a transferring transformation.

Ordinary time-framed composite events (OTCE): Conjunction, Disjunction, Sequence, and Simultaneity are similar to TCE (see Table 11). Negation is directly supported. Simultaneity has to be constructed; Selection requires additional filtering in the meta-service.

Sophisticated time-framed composite events (STCE): Almost all operators are supported (see Table 12), only the selection requires a transformation for each $i \in \mathbb{N}$ in selection $E_1^{[i]}$.

4.3 Transformation of Operator Parameters

The group definitions given in Section 3.3 abstracted from the parameters of consumption mode and duplicate handling strategy since these parameters are rarely explicitly supported in the considered systems. In Table 13, we show the influence of considering parameter transformations on operator transformations (as introduced in the previous

Table 10. Target system with time frame support: TCE - Meta-ENS: E refers to event classes, $N(E)$ to notifications regarding an event in class E, $t(N(E))$ to the time of the event notification

Operators	Target Group TCE — Meta-ENS timeless	timed
Conjunction	$(E_1, E_2)_\infty \longleftrightarrow (E_1, E_2)_\infty$	$(E_1, E_2)_T \longleftrightarrow (E_1, E_2)_T$
Disjunction	$(E_1|E_2) \longleftrightarrow (E_1|E_2)$	—
Sequence	$(E_1; E_2)_\infty \longleftrightarrow (E_1; E_2)_\infty$	$(E_1; E_2)_T \longleftrightarrow (E_1; E_2)_T$
Negation	—	$(E_1)_T \xleftrightarrow{\#} (\overline{E_1})_T$, $N = \overline{N(E_1)_T}$
Simultaneity	$(E_1, E_2) \xleftrightarrow{\#} (E_1 : E_2), t(N(E_1)) = t(N(E_2))$	—
Selection	$(E_1) \xleftrightarrow{\#} (E_1)^{[i]}, N = (N(E_1))^{[i]}$	—

Table 11. Source system with time frame support: OTCE - Meta-ENS: E refers to event classes, $N(E)$ to notifications regarding an event in class E, $t(N(E))$ to the time of the event notification

Operators	Target Group OTCE — Meta-ENS	
	timeless	timed
Conjunction	see TCE in Table 10	
Disjunction		
Sequence		
Negation	—	$(E_1)_T \longleftrightarrow (E_1)_T$
Simultaneity	see TCE in Table 10	
Selection	see TCE in Table 10	

Table 12. Source system with time frame support: STCE - Meta-ENS: E refers to event classes, $N(E)$ to notifications regarding an event in class E, $t(N(E))$ to the time of the event notification

Operators	Target Group STCE — Meta-ENS	
	timeless	timed
Conjunction	see TCE in Table 10	
Disjunction		
Sequence		
Negation	see OTCE in Table 11	
Simultaneity	$(E_1 : E_2) \longleftrightarrow (E_1 : E_2)$	—
Selection	see TCE in Table 10	

Table 13. Parameter transformations: Duplicate handling and consumption mode parameter

		first		last		all		i-th	
		all	unique	all	unique	all	unique	all	unique
first	all	$\longleftrightarrow$							
	unique	$\rightleftarrows^\pm$	$\longleftrightarrow$						
last	all	-	-	$\longleftrightarrow$					
	unique	-	-	$\rightleftarrows^\pm$	$\longleftrightarrow$				
all	all	$\xrightarrow{\pm}$	$\xrightarrow{\pm}$	$\xrightarrow{\pm}$	$\xrightarrow{\pm}$	$\longleftrightarrow$			
	unique	-	-	-	-	$\rightleftarrows^\pm$	$\longleftrightarrow$		
i-th	all	$\xrightarrow{\pm}$	$\xrightarrow{\pm}$	-	-	$\rightleftarrows^\pm$	-	$\longleftrightarrow$	
	unique	-	$\xrightarrow{\pm}$	-	-	$\rightleftarrows^\pm$	$\rightleftarrows^\pm$	$\rightleftarrows^\pm$	$\longleftrightarrow$
Duplicate Parameter	Selection	first		last		all		i-th	
		all	unique	all	unique	all	unique	all	unique

section). We show which transformation are possible when translating the parameter set of one system (y-axis in Table 13) into the parameter set of another system (x-axis in Table 13). That is, for all possible combinations of the duplicate and selection parameter we state whether the transformation is not possible (indicated by a dash) or equivalent (indicated by $\longleftrightarrow$) or only possible in one of the given directions while creating a larger result set (indicated by $\rightleftarrows^\pm$ and $\xrightarrow{\pm}$, where the arrow orientation defines the direction of the possible transformation).

This section presented our answer to the second problem stated in the introduction: translating filter expressions between languages that use different operators and semantics (Problem 2). We provided a set of transformation rules that form the core of the proposed Meta-ENS for integrating heterogeneous event notification services. The transformation rules presented here have also been implemented in a prototype transformation component that can be used with any given ENS .

5 Conclusion and Outlook

In this paper, we proposed the concept and design of a Meta Service for Event Notification. In detail, we presented the answers to the following two research problems: Firstly, subscribers of heterogeneous event notifications services are forced to subscribe the same profile to a number of services using different filter languages. Secondly, composite events combining events from different providers that are handled by different services have to be identified by a subscriber-based post-filtering.

As a solution to these two problems we proposed the detailed design of a Meta-Event Notification Service based on transformation rules. In particular, this paper presented the following contributions: Firstly, we presented a survey of filter languages for event notification. Secondly, we introduced a classification schema for profile definition languages. Thirdly, we identified five categories of profile languages. Fourthly, we proposed detailed transformation rules for translating profiles defined at the Meta-ENS into languages of system from the five categories (and vice versa for notifications). An extended description of our findings can be found in [13].

As proof of concept, we have implemented a transformation component for the proposed language transformations. The implementation was carried out using Prolog. The transformation component currently supports the operator transformations. The next version of the transformation component will incorporate the proposed parameter transformation. Future research will see the close integration of the transformation component into our prototypical event notification system A-mediAS [9]. The transformation can be used for the role of a Meta-ENS in the communication with other ENS (as providers) and for the mediation between ENS (as providers and subscribers).

References

1. S. Brandt and A. Kristensen. Keryx: Internet notification service for dynamic web applications. (slide presentation), presented to W3C, 1997.
2. A. Carzaniga, D. Rosenblum, and A. Wolf. Interfaces and algorithms for a wide-area event notification service. Technical Report CU-CS-888-99, University of Colorado, Department of Computer Science, 1999.
3. C. K. Chang, H. Garcia-Molina, and A. Paepcke. Predicate rewriting for translating boolean queries in a heterogeneous information system. *ACM Transactions on Information Systems (TOIS)*, 17(1):1–39, 1999.
4. D. Faensen, L. Faulstich, H. Schweppe, A. Hinze, and A. Steidinger. Hermes - A notification service for digital libraries. In *Proc. of the ACM JCDL*, Roanoke, VA, 2001.
5. L. Fiege, G. Mühl, and F. C. Gärtner. A modular approach to build structured event-based systems. In *Proc. of the ACM SAC Symposium on Applied Computing*, Madrid, Spain, 2002.

6. A. Geppert and D. Tombros. Event-based distributed workflow execution with EVE. Technical Report ifi-96.05, University Zurich, Computer Science Department, 1996.
7. R. Gruber, B. Krishnamurthy, and E. Panagos. The architecture of the READY event notification service. In *Proc. of the IEEE ICDC Middleware Workshop*, Austin, TX, 1999.
8. R. Gruber, B. Krishnamurthy, and E. Panagos. CORBA notification service: Design challenges and scalable solutions. In *Proc. of the IEEE ICDE*, Heidelberg, Germany, 2001.
9. A. Hinze. *A-MEDIAS: Concept and Design of an Adaptive Integrating Event Notification Service*. PhD thesis, Freie Universitaet Berlin, Department of Computer Science, July 2003.
10. A. Hinze and A. Voisard. Composite events in notification services with application to logistics support. Technical Report tr-B-02-10, Freie Universität Berlin, Department of Computer Science, 2002.
11. A. Hinze and A. Voisard. A parameterized algebra for event notification services. In *Proc. of Symposium on Temporal Representation and Reasoning*, Manchester, UK, 2002.
12. Adele E. Howe and Daniel Dreilinger. SAVVYSEARCH: A metasearch engine that learns which search engines to query. *AI Magazine*, 18(2):19–25, 1997.
13. D. Jung and A. Hinze. Analysis and transformation of profile definition languages for event notification services. Technical Report 12/2004, Computer Science Department, University of Waikato, New Zealand, August 2004.
14. L. Liu, C. Pu, and W. Tang. Continual queries for internet scale event-driven information delivery. *IEEE Transactions on Knowledge and Data Engineering*, 11(4):610–628, 1999.
15. L. Liu, C. Pu, W. Tang, and W. Han. Conquer: A continual query system for update monitoring in the WWW. *International Journal of Computer Systems, Science and Engineering*, 14(2):99–112, 1999.
16. C. Ma and J. Bacon. COBEA: A CORBA-based event architecture. In *Proc. of the COOTS Conference on Object-Oriented Technologies and Systems*, Berkeley, CA, 1998.
17. Jeff Magee, Naranker Dulay, and Jeff Kramer. A Constructive Development Environment for Parallel and Distributed Programs. In *In Proc. of the International Workshop on Configurable Distributed Systems*, Pittsburgh, March 1994.
18. G. R. Malan, F. Jahanian, and S. Subramanian. Salamander: A push-based distribution substrate for internet applications. In *Proc. of the USENIX Symposium on Internet Technologies and Systems*, Monterey, California, 1997.
19. M. Mansouri Samani and M. Sloman. GEM: A generalised event monitoring language for distributed systems. *IEE/IOP/BSC Distributed Engineering Journal*, 4(2):96–108, 1997.
20. D. Mishra. *Snoop: Am Event Specification Llanguage for Active Database Systems*. Masters thesis, University of Florida, 1991.
21. Douglas W. Oard. A comparative study of query and document translation for cross-language information retrieval. In *AMTA*, pages 472–483, 1998.
22. B. Segall and D. Arnold. Elvin has left the building: A publish/subscribe notification service with quenching. In *Proc. of the AUUG Australian UNIX and Open Systems User Group Conference*, Queensland, Australia, 1997.
23. T. W. Yan and H. Garcia-Molina. Duplicate removal in information dissemination. In *Proc. of the VLDB*, Zurich, Switzerland, 1995.
24. D. Zimmer and R. Unland. On the semantics of complex events in active database management systems. In *Proc. of the IEEE ICDE*, Sydney, Australia, 1999.

Classification and Analysis of Distributed Event Filtering Algorithms

Sven Bittner and Annika Hinze

University of Waikato, New Zealand,
{s.bittner, hinze}@cs.waikato.ac.nz

Abstract. Publish/subscribe middleware provides efficient support for loosely coupled communication in distributed systems. A number of different distributed message-filtering algorithms have been proposed. So far, a systematic comparison and analysis of these filter algorithms is still missing.

This paper proposes a classification scheme for distributed filter algorithms that supports the theoretical and practical analysis of these algorithms. We present a first cut theoretical evaluation and a subsequent practical evaluation of promising candidate algorithms. Factors that are considered include the characteristics of the underlying network and application-related constraints.

Based on the findings of these evaluations, we conclude with a summary of the strengths and weaknesses of the algorithms that we have studied.

1 Introduction

Large scale distributed systems increasingly rely on middleware-level publish/subscribe services to implement loosely coupled communication between components. The exchanged messages are filtered and forwarded to the appropriate components. This paper proposes a classification of distributed filter algorithms and provides an extensive theoretical and experimental analysis of selected algorithms.

An event notification system or publish/subscribe system is a middleware implementing the event-based communication paradigm. A *publisher* component sends *event messages* that announce the occurrence of events, i.e., the occurrence of something of interest within the distributed system. *Subscriber* components can subscribe to events that are of interest to them; these subscriptions are called *profiles*. Components can act as publishers and/or subscribers. The publish/subscribe system filters the incoming messages according to the subscribers' profiles and forwards matched messages to the respective subscribers. The distributed components of the publish/subscribe system are referred to as *brokers*.

We now briefly describe the current situation from which we will derive the research questions that are addressed in this paper. Several distributed algorithms have been proposed for the efficient filtering of event messages based on the context of the messages [1,3,7,9,10,11,12,14]. Rendezvous nodes [11,12] are particular brokers that specialize in the filtering of selected event types and act as meeting points for profiles and event messages. Rendezvous nodes are a combination of a centralized and a distributed filtering strategy, because brokers are responsible for a predefined set of profiles.

Distributed filter algorithms employed in hierarchical networks exploit the hierarchical system structure [1,3,14]. Either every broker knows all profiles and event information is propagated down the tree starting at the root node [1], or each broker only knows the profiles registered by its children [3,14]. Events are forwarded first up to the root and then down to the leaves. In point-to-point networks, each broker knows about its neighbor nodes and either events or profiles are forwarded within the network [3].

Several optimizations [3,7,9,10] have been proposed to minimize the number of profiles that have to be forwarded to directly connected brokers. Covering uses the selectivity among profiles to decrease filtering overhead; merging unites several profiles to one profile for filtering [9,10]. In [3], immediate computation of real covering is suggested, which results in costly computation. In [7], computation of coverings on request is proposed, which results in more network traffic, since all covered profiles are computed and forwarded if necessary.

From this brief survey of algorithms, one key problem becomes apparent: Which is the most efficient algorithm for a given network topology and application? So far, most of the algorithms have only been analyzed based on simulations of network topologies. In consequence, the results obtained in these evaluations do not consider several influential factors. In addition, most analyses have been carried out independently for single algorithms and, thus, have been performed under differing evaluation boundary conditions. As a consequence, we identify two open issues: (1) the definition of a classification scheme for distributed filter algorithms; and (2) a uniform performance analysis of filter algorithms that allows for a comparison of the algorithms' efficiency. Both issues are addressed in this paper. The contributions of this paper are as follows:

1. The introduction of a concise classification scheme for distributed filter algorithms.
2. A classification of existing filter algorithms according to the proposed scheme.
3. A theoretical performance analysis of filter algorithms.
4. An experimental performance analysis of selected filter algorithms.
5. Algorithm recommendations based on the applications and network topologies.

The remainder of the paper is organized as follows: Section 2 proposes a classification scheme for distributed filter algorithms. Section 3 briefly introduces our test system DAS. Section 4 presents the results and analysis of the experiments. The paper is rounded off by a conclusion and directions for future research.

2 Classification of Filter Algorithms

Several algorithms for distributed filtering have been proposed. A comparison of these algorithms and a general evaluation of filter approaches is difficult due to the diversity of the approaches. What is needed is a concise classification scheme for distributed filtering algorithms.

In this section, we propose such a classification scheme for distributed event filtering algorithms. This scheme provides a fundament for comparing the properties of the different types of algorithms. We classify existing filter algorithms with regard to the proposed scheme. Additionally, we introduce the results of a theoretical evaluation of the algorithms in the proposed classification space. Finally, we identify the most promising filter algorithms to be evaluated in an experimental analysis.

Our classification scheme uses the following dimensions (see Table 1) that are subsequently explained in detail: (1) location of filtering, (2) spreading of filter complexity and memory strategy, and (3) communication with subscribers. We briefly present a description of each dimension and provide a theoretical evaluation of conceivable combinations of alternatives in all dimensions.

1. **Location of filtering:** Filtering can be performed close to the subscribers (flooding of events) or providers (flooding of profiles) [4], or at certain broker nodes [11,12]. Flooding of events results in high network traffic, but less memory usage. Flooding of profiles results in the opposite: less network traffic and high memory consumption. Filtering at fixed (arbitrary) brokers gives the advantage of having control of the filtering according to available resources, but has the disadvantage of high load at filtering brokers in both network and computation.

2a. **Spreading of filter complexity:** The filter complexity can be spread over several brokers by exclusive filtering at certain brokers or by distributed filtering. Exclusive filtering can be implemented with little control overhead [12]. A disadvantage is the danger of multiple notifications for a single event, because the event information may be forwarded to several neighbour brokers. For distributed filtering, each broker accomplishes the filtering steps necessary to find all neighbor brokers with matching profiles [4,11]. Beneficially, filter overhead is divided and the network traffic is minimized (only brokers with matching profiles are involved in filtering). The necessity of repeated filtering while forwarding the event message (to determine the appropriate neighbour) is a drawback. For distributed filtering, different memory strategies may be applied (see 2b).

2b. **Memory strategy:** Preventive storing refers to the storage of all available profiles, even duplicate and covered ones; this is beneficial in case of unsubscriptions. The resulting higher memory usage is a disadvantage. Optimistic storing minimizes the numbers of stored profiles (e.g. by discarding covered ones). In this case, unsubscriptions produce high network load, but less memory is used.

3. **Communication with subscribers:** We distinguish three alternatives: direct communication, forwarding via the network, and delivery via broker proxies (transparent communication). In direct communication, only the filtering broker and the subscriber are involved in communication [4]. A disadvantage is that either a connectionless protocol has to be used (resulting in unreliable communications) or new connections have to be established over time. When forwarding messages via the network of brokers, only neighbor brokers and local clients are communicating directly [12]. Local clients are publishers and subscribers that are directly connected to a broker. A drawback is the higher memory consumption: Information about the location of clients is needed, either by following the reverse path of the subscriptions, indexing all clients, or flooding notifications. When using brokers as proxies, brokers act as subscribers to their neighbor nodes [4,11] and thus limit the number of subscribers each broker node has to deal with. Exploiting covering between profiles of several subscribers is possible and beneficial. A disadvantage is the necessity of post-filtering to notify client subscribers.

Table 1. Classification and theoretical evaluation of Distributed Filter Algorithms (EF - event forwarding, PF_x - profile forwarding, RN_x - rendezvous nodes, × = feature is supported, Evaluation: -- to ++ = poor to excellent results)

Algorithm	Filter Location			Spreading of Complexity (Memory Strategy)			Communication			Theor. Evaluation			
	Subscribers	Publishers	Arbitrary	Exclusive	Distributed Preventive Storing	Distributed Optimistic Storing	Direct	Forwarding	Transparent	Network Traffic	Memory Usage	Efficiency	Scalability
EF	×			×			×			--	++	+-	-
PF_1		×		×			×			+	--	+-	--
PF_2		×		×				×		+-	--	+-	--
PF_3		×			×		×			+	-	+	-
PF_4		×			×			×		+-	-	+	-
PF_5		×			×				×	+	+-	++	+-
PF_6		×				×	×			+	+-	+	+-
PF_7		×				×		×		+-	+-	+	+-
PF_8		×				×			×	+	+	++	+
RN_1			×	×			×			-	--	-	--
RN_2			×	×				×		-	--	-	--
RN_3			×		×		×			+-	--	+-	-
RN_4			×		×			×		-	--	+-	-
RN_5			×		×				×	+-	-	+	+-
RN_6			×			×	×			+-	-	+-	-
RN_7			×			×		×		-	-	-	-
RN_8			×			×			×	+-	+	+	+-

From the previous characteristics, we categorize filter algorithms as shown in Table 1. Columns 2–4 refer to the introduced dimensions. Our evaluation can be found in Column 5. Unfortunately, the available literature is not detailed enough to allow for a full classification of existing systems. Moreover, not all 17 variations may be implemented in existing systems. We identify three types of algorithms based on the filter location (distinguished by their names in Column 1): event forwarding (EF), profile forwarding (PF) and rendezvous nodes (RN).

Except in EF, we can find several subtypes of the algorithms. In EF each broker only filters for local subscribers; this implies exclusive filtering and direct communication. From the subtypes, we consider PF_8 and RN_8 as most promising because they have the least memory requirements due to use of coverings between profiles of several subscribers and an optimistic storage strategy. Our conclusion results from a combination of the evaluations shown above. We select one of each group for experimental analysis in our middleware: EF, PF_8, RN_8.

3 The Testbed: DAS – Distributed Alerting Service

We used the event notification service DAS as a flexible architecture with exchangeable filter components in order to evaluate different filter approaches. In this section, we first

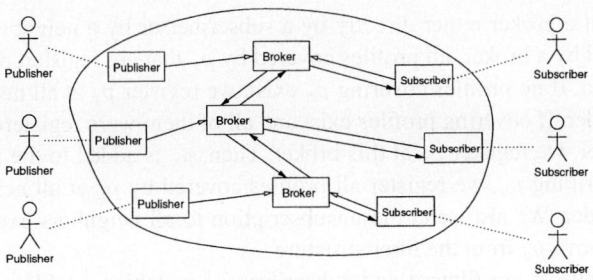

Fig. 1. Architecture of the distributed system DAS

describe DAS's architecture and then give details about the implementation of the three algorithms selected based on our theoretical analysis.

3.1 Architecture

Our distributed system DAS consists of three component types: brokers, subscribers and publishers, see Figure 1. To abstract from the physical network we use an acyclic overlay network to exchange profiles and event messages. Here, problems such as circulating messages and duplicates are displaced to lower communication layers. The acyclicity is no restriction in case of link errors, since a path between two nodes is found as long as any physical connection exists. Our reference implementation in DAS uses communication via TCP/IP. DAS is implemented in Java.

Within each broker, profiles and events are processed according to the chosen algorithm (EF, PF or RN), i.e., they are filtered or forwarded to neighbor nodes. Each broker's filter component maintains a profile repository; events are filtered against the repository. This centralized filtering uses a tree-based algorithm [6]. After the filtering, notifications are created from the processed event messages.

3.2 Implementation of the Distributed Filter Algorithms

We used three specialized implementations of the broker class for implementing the distributed filter algorithms. This section describes the algorithms' implementations in DAS. Similar algorithms have been discussed in Section 1.

Event Forwarding (EF). This is the simplest algorithm, since events are flooded through the network and brokers only filter for local subscribers. Subscriptions are added to and removed from a broker's filter structure. Profiles are registered only directly by subscribers. Events are flooded to all neighbor brokers except the sender. Events are filtered and on match, the profiles' subscribers are notified.

Profile Forwarding (PF). Profile forwarding uses covering among profiles, therefore, subscribing profile p_x and unsubscribing profile p_y are complex tasks. A profile p_x can be registered at a broker either directly by a subscriber or by a neighboring broker. If p_x is registered by a broker, all profiles covered by p_x that are registered by this broker can be removed. If no profiles covering p_x exist, we register p_x at all neighbor brokers except the sender. If covering profiles exist and all of them were registered by the same neighbor broker, we register p_x at this broker. Then, p_x is added to the filter structure. When unsubscribing p_y, we register all profiles covered by p_y at all neighbor brokers except the sender. We also send the unsubscription to all neighbors except its sender. Finally we remove p_y from the filter structure.

Published events are filtered and subscribers of matching profiles are notified. If a subscriber is a broker, it is notified exactly once about each event even if several profiles match. When notifications arrive at a broker, the contained event is filtered and all subscribers except the sender are notified. Again, brokers are notified only once.

Rendezvous Nodes (RN). Rendezvous nodes are specified when configuring the network. When brokers connect to each other to build up the overlay network they also exchange information about known rendezvous nodes. Therefore, each broker knows which neighbor to contact to reach the rendezvous node for specific event types.

RN also uses coverings among profiles. For subscribing p_x at a rendezvous node, all covered profiles registered by the subscribing broker are removed. For subscribing p_x at a non-rendezvous node, p_x is sent towards its rendezvous node. Finally, p_x is added to the filter structure. When unsubscribing p_y at a non-rendezvous node, all covered profiles are sent towards the respective rendezvous node. Then, the unsubscription p_y is sent towards the rendezvous node. Finally, p_y is removed from the filter structure.

Events are filtered and in case of a match the neighbor brokers (except the sender) are notified exactly once. Then, the event is forwarded towards the rendezvous node. When a broker receives a notification, it filters the contained event and in turn notifies all subscribers excluding the sender. Again, brokers are notified only once per event.

Computation of Covering. We used an interval-based computation of the profile covering. Our local filtering holds a separate profile tree for each attribute (a variation of [6]). The coverings are computed by analyzing the profiles in the leaves of the filter structure. For example, if a predicate contains the greater-than operator, all profiles that only occur in subsequent edges are covered. By intersecting the results from all attributes we can derive the coverings of profiles.

4 Experimental Analysis

In this section, we present the an overview of the results of our experimental analysis. A detailed discussion of the results can be found in [2].

We used our prototype in a realistic setting in a LAN with 100 mbps bandwidth, and machines with 1GHz and 256 MB main memory running under Linux. We evaluated the influence of different system parameters, namely:

1. Proportion of matching events over all events (see Section 4.1),
2. Portion of matching profiles per events (see Section 4.1),

3. Number of brokers (see Section 4.2),
4. Number of profile coverings (see Section 4.3),
5. Number of event types (see Section 4.4),
6. Locality of profiles and events (see Section 4.5), and
7. Number of profiles (see Section 4.6).

Our analysis uses the following units of measurement:

Filter efficiency: This measure refers to the system's performance, i.e., the number of events per second that can be processed by the system. We computed the filter time in the broker nodes and exclude the network forwarding time: The efficiency (i.e, the number of filtered events processed per second) is computed by dividing the number of published events by the time that the brokers took for the filtering of these events. We also evaluated parallel efficiency e, which refers to the speedup achieved by distributing the event filtering over several brokers; it is given as speedup per broker. Parallel efficiency gives an indication of the scalability of the algorithms.

Network load per event: The network load per event was computed by totaling the size of event data received by all brokers and dividing by the number of published events.

Duplication of profiles: This measure refers to the average number of brokers at which a profile is registered. For example, the value 2.0 states that each profile is registered on average by 2 brokers. The system's performance is influenced by duplication, since more memory is needed to store the same number of profiles. This memory consumption results in page swaps and less efficiency. Duplication is computed by dividing the total number of registered profiles by the number of profiles registered by clients.

We additionally use the following terms: the proportion of matching events over all events is referred to by p^e. The portion of matching profiles per event is referred to by p^p; it is computed by the number of profile notifications divided by the number of events published. The utilization of events σ is defined by $\sigma = \frac{p^p}{p^e}$. The utilization σ states how many profiles are notified by a matching event on average.

In the following experiments we only used event types with one attribute — we can easily derive the behavior of our algorithms in cases of more attributes. Figure 2 shows the filter time for the filtering of 100,000 events against 10,000 profiles with different numbers of attributes and values of p^e ($p^e = p^p$ since only unique profiles are used). Here, we assumed that non-matching events are recognized after the evaluation of half of the type's attributes in average (mean value of recognition after each attribute). Our filter algorithm minimizes the number of attributes evaluated to recognize non-matching events, for details see [6].

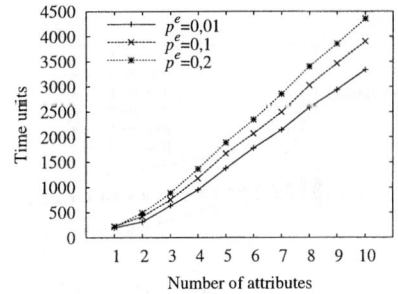

Fig. 2. Filter time depending on #attributes

Another restriction is the connection of only one publisher and one subscriber to each broker (see Figure 1). In realistic scenarios we expect more clients with individually fewer profiles and events, which leads to the same overall quantity. Our results can be generalized, because only the overall number of profiles and events influence efficiency and scalability. For example, more clients would increase the costs for synchronization, but the use of proxies that handle connections to clients would decrease the communication overhead with brokers. If not explicitly stated otherwise, events and profiles are unique, i.e., they do not overlap. In the following subsections, we describe our experimental results in detail. All experiments were performed with a standard deviation under 1% regarding efficiency.

4.1 Influence of Matching Events and Profiles

Here, we analyze the influence of the proportion of matching events p^e and the average number of matching profiles p^p on efficiency and network load. Duplication of profiles is not considered here, because it remains stable over the experiments. We used 4 brokers connected as a linear bus. The rendezvous node is located at an inner broker. Each broker managed 50,000 local profiles. We also analyzed different values of the utilization σ.

Hypotheses: Extending our theoretical analysis (see Section 2), we expect the following behavior: With increasing p^e and p^p, the algorithms are less efficient (i.e., fewer events are filtered per second). With small p^p and p^e, PF should be more efficient than the other two algorithms. The network load is expected to be lowest in PF, followed by RN and EF. For EF we expect the maximum network load regardless of p^p and p^e.

Results: Figure 3(a) shows efficiency in number of processed events per second over the proportion of matching events p^e. As expected, PF is very efficient in case of small p^e. With increasing p^e, a strong decline in efficiency is caused by costly notifications and the post-filtering. The efficiency of EF changes less with increasing p^e, because no post-filtering is necessary. The number of created notifications increases, which results in a linear efficiency decrease. The influence of increasing p^e on RN is greater than on EF but less than for PF. The reasons are both the use of post-filtering and the creation of more notifications.

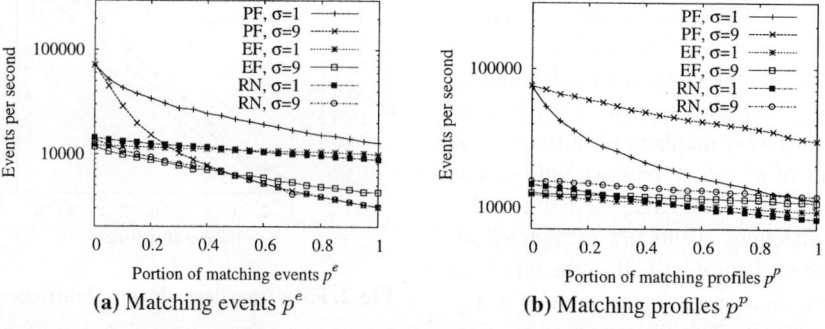

Fig. 3. Filter efficiency depending on the on the portion of matching events p^e and profiles per event p^p.

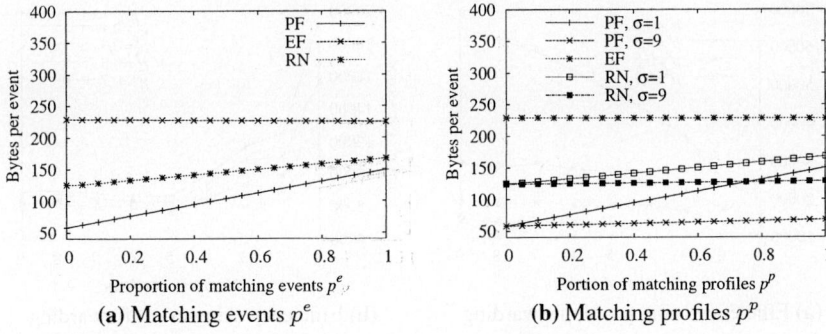

Fig. 4. Network load depending on the proportion of matching events p^e and matching profiles p^p

Figure 3(b) shows the influence of increasing p^p on the filtered events per second. Again, PF shows the best efficiency. With increasing σ (i.e., increasing utilization of events) efficiency increases, since less post-filtering is needed while the number of notifications remains constant. EF is less influenced by changing p^p — the event flooding causes non-matching events to be rejected earlier. The efficiency of RN lies between EF and PF for the same reasons as described above (post-filtering in rendezvous nodes and more notifications).

The network load for the three algorithms is shown in Fig. 4 as bytes per event over p^e and p^p. EF shows the highest load due to the flooding of all events. RN's forwarding of all events to the rendezvous nodes leads to less network load. The least load is caused by PF, because only matching events are forwarded. With constant p^e, the utilization of events σ does not influence the network load (leading to identical graphs in Fig. 4(a), not shown for the sake of clarity in the diagram). With constant p^p, the network load is influenced by σ (except for EF, which floods all events). Increasing σ (see Fig. 4(b) with $\sigma = 1$ and $\sigma = 9$) results in decreasing network load, because fewer events notify the same number of profiles (i.e., decreasing p^e).

4.2 Influence of Number of Brokers

In this subsection, we analyze the influence of the number of brokers on efficiency, parallel efficiency, duplication of profiles, and network load. For the experiments, we used the network topology as shown in Fig. 5.[1] The network size was varied between 1 and 9 brokers. We used a single event type; Broker 2 acts as rendezvous node. 200,000 unique profiles were used.

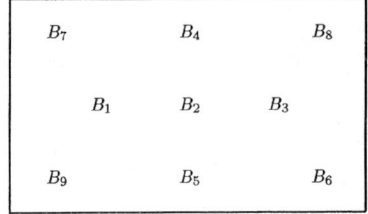

Fig. 5. Network topology for brokers

Hypotheses: Extending the theoretical evaluation from Section 2, we state the following hypotheses: When using more brokers, we expect improved efficiency for PF and less

---
[1] Many other topologies could have been tested. This is a first cut evaluation not using a simulation. Further large scale tests with more general and larger topologies are advised.

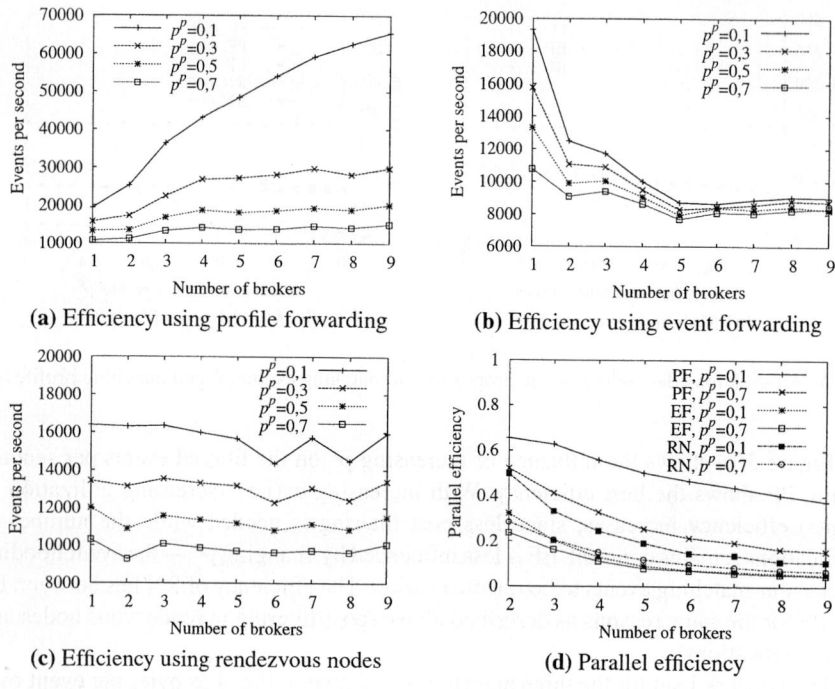

Fig. 6. Filter efficiency and parallel efficiency depending on number of brokers

efficiency improvement for RN. The efficiency of EF should not change. PF is expected to show the best parallel efficiency and EF the worst one. The network load is expected to increase for all three algorithms, most in PF, followed by RN and EF. For profile duplication, we expect the opposite effect: EF duplicates no profiles, PF all profiles and RN is a compromise between the two.

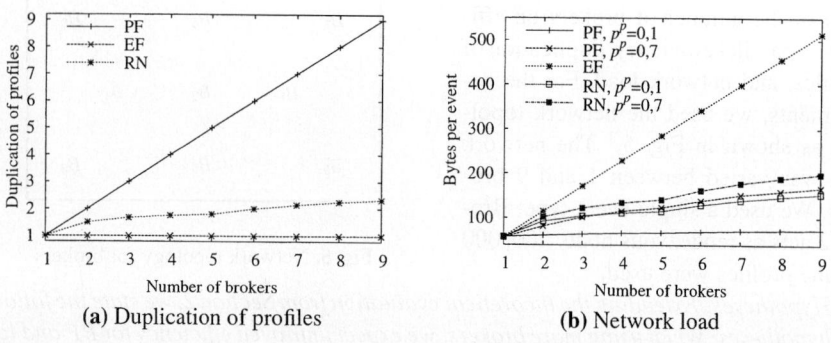

Fig. 7. Duplication of profiles and network load depending on the number of brokers

Results: Figure 6 shows the results for filter efficiency and parallel efficiency; both are given as events per second over the number of brokers. PF has a steep increase in efficiency when adding brokers (see Fig. 6(a)). The increase is highest for $p^p = 0.1$; lower p^p lowers the filter efficiency. Here, the main load is caused by the notifications. EF's efficiency is decreasing when adding more brokers (Fig. 6(b)), which is due to increased communication overhead. The influence of p^p when adding brokers is small, because the additional overhead due to notifications is small compared to the overall communication complexity. The efficiency is lowest when using five brokers, because Broker 2 (which is the system's bottleneck) is overloaded. RN's efficiency is nearly unchanged when adding brokers (see Fig. 6(c)). Here, the system's bottleneck is the rendezvous node, which performs the same amount of filtering steps regardless of the network size. The filter efficiency decreases when reaching a certain number of brokers. The reason is the asymmetrical network of brokers – some brokers encounter greater load than others.

The results for parallel efficiency are shown in Fig. 6(d). Parallel efficiency e is measured in speed increase per broker over the number of brokers. The measure is computed as $e = \frac{f_{sat}^n}{n * f_{sat}^1}$ where f_{sat}^i refers to the maximal event frequency that can be processed in i brokers and n is the number of brokers in the network. The best results are recorded for PF due to its good load distribution. Overall, the parallel efficiency decreases as the number of brokers increases. The results are disappointing; the main reason for this behavior is the high communication overhead between the brokers.

The results for the duplication of profiles are shown in Fig. 7(a)). When using PF, the duplication increases linearly. Since the profiles are unique (i.e., have no overlap), each broker stores all profiles. EF shows a constant duplication value of 1.0. Results for RN lie between PF and EF with duplication values lower than 2.5.

The results for the network load are shown in Fig. 7(b); compared to the profile duplication, the order of the algorithms is reversed. EF shows a constant increase of network load. Using PF, only matching events are distributed, which results in low network load. For high values of p^p, the network loads for RN and PF are very similar. Events are always forwarded to the rendezvous node, causing little additional expense.

4.3 Influence of Covering

In this subsection, we discuss the influence of coverings. Only equality operators are used, so the utilization of events σ is equivalent to coverings (e.g., $\sigma = 5$ stands for 5 covered profiles per profile). Coverings appear only between local profiles at the brokers. We used the same network of brokers as described in Section 4.1, one event type and $200,000$ profiles. We analyzed efficiency, duplication of profiles and network load.

Hypotheses: We expect decreasing efficiency with increasing coverings using constant p^e (more load because of more notifications). Using constant p^p, the result should be the opposite (fewer forwarding and filtering steps). The duplication of profiles is expected to decrease when using higher covering (exploiting the covering feature). The network load should remain unchanged under constant p^e and changing σ. With constant p^p and increasing σ, the network load is expected to decrease, since fewer events are forwarded (except when using EF).

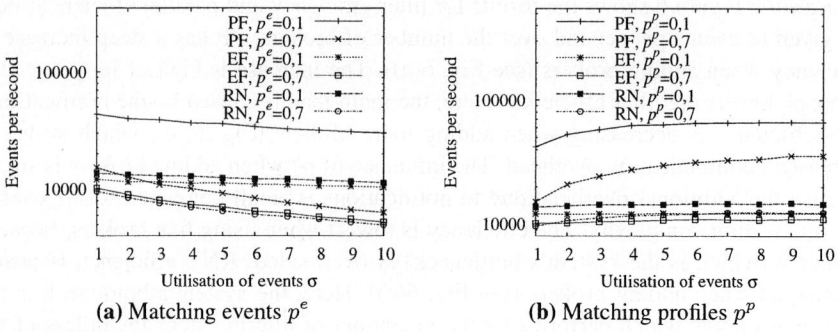

Fig. 8. Efficiency depending on the utilization of events σ and varying p^e and p^p

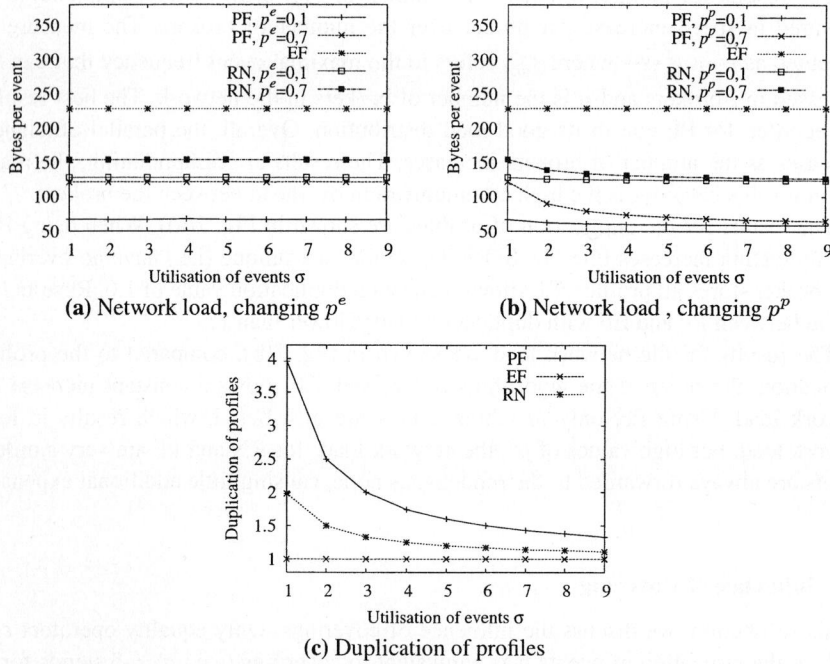

Fig. 9. Network load and duplication of profiles depending on the utilization of events σ with various portions of matching events p^e and profiles p^p

Results: Figure 8(a) shows the efficiency over the covering under changing proportion of matching events p^e. All three algorithms show decreasing efficiency when using more coverings, since more notifications are generated. With a high value of p^e, the differences among the algorithms are marginal, since nearly all events have to be flooded. With small p^e, PF is by far the most efficient algorithm. With higher p^e, efficiency decreases less (changing the proportion of complexity of notifications to all-over complexity). Using EF and RN, the decrease in efficiency is reduced.

Figure 8(b) shows the efficiency over the covering under changing proportion of matching profiles p^p. Increasing σ and constant p^p lead to higher efficiency. The reason is the constant number of notifications while filtering fewer events. PF shows the highest efficiency increase, since only events with matching profiles are forwarded. In contrast to the behavior for matching events p^e as seen in Fig. 8(a), the differences for the algorithms grow with increasing σ. RN's efficiency improves more slowly, because events are always forwarded to the rendezvous node. EF is independent of σ, because events are always forwarded to all brokers.

The network load remains constant with unmodified p^e (Fig. 9(a)), because the same number of events is forwarded (but there are more notifications). As expected, a high p^e increases the network load and EF causes the highest load. Constant p^p (Fig. 9(b)) results in decreasing network load because each event matches multiple profiles (which decreases communication among brokers). With growing σ, this effect becomes less influential. High p^p increases the network load (except for EF). The duplication of profiles (Fig. 9(c)) decreases with growing coverings. PF shows the largest duplication, followed by RN and EF (which never distributes profiles). For high coverings, the duplication graphs of PF and RN converge to the graph of EF.

4.4 Influence of Event Types

In this subsection, we analyze the influence of the number of event types on efficiency, duplication of profiles and network load. We used the network topology illustrated in Fig. 5 with each broker being rendezvous node for at most one event type. 180,000 unique profiles were registered, which were evenly distributed between the event types.

Hypotheses: We expect that the number of event types will have little effect on efficiency. PF and EF should be almost independent. RN's efficiency should increase when arranging rendezvous nodes well. Duplication of profiles and network load should be independent of the number of event types, except when using RN. There, the paths to the rendezvous nodes affect the duplication of profiles and the network load.

Results: The filter efficiency is illustrated in Fig. 10 (note the different scales). PF shows nearly constant values (see Fig. 10(a)). The small performance increase is due to our central filter algorithm, which builds a separate filter structure per event type. Increasing p^p decreases performance because more notifications are created. EF behaves similarly (see Fig. 10(b)), except that p^p has almost no influence, because the flooding overhead dominates over the processing of notifications. RN's efficiency depends on the location of the rendezvous nodes in the network (see Fig. 10(c)). For up to three nodes, if the rendezvous nodes are central nodes, the efficiency increases. The rendezvous nodes have lower burden, because fewer events have to be filtered. The efficiency decreases when using more than four event types. The reason is that some of the rendezvous nodes are outer nodes of the network – inner nodes have to forward all events and become a bottleneck.

The duplication of profiles is independent of the number of event types (Fig. 11(a)). Since only unique profiles are used, the duplication is 9.0 using PF and 1.0 using EF. Using more than two event types in RN increases the duplication based on the position of

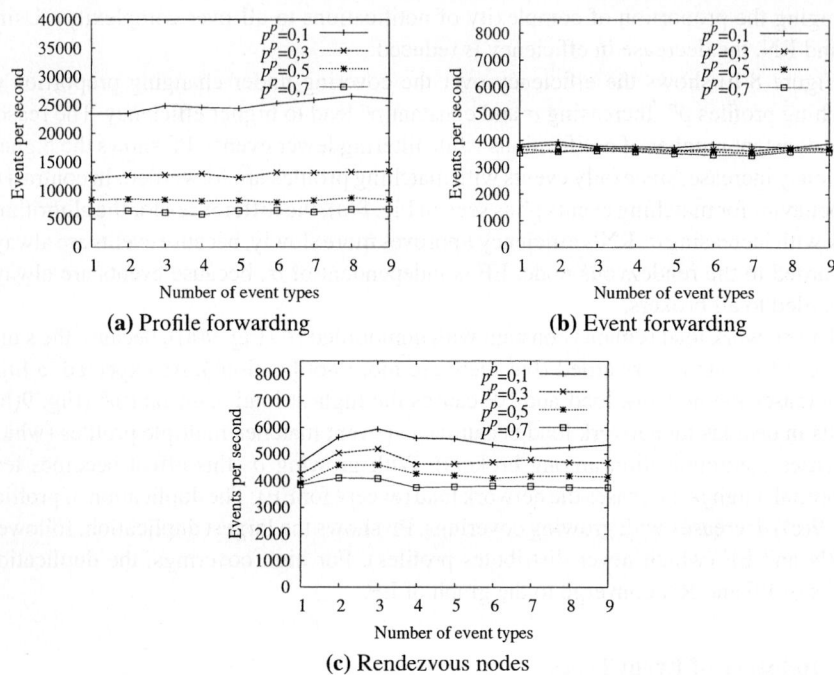

Fig. 10. Efficiency depending on number of event types and various p^p

the rendezvous nodes. The results for network load are similar (see Fig. 11(b), logarithmic ordinate). PF and EF cause stable network load. Using RN causes an increase of network load after an initial decrease (longer paths to rendezvous nodes). Increasing p^p increases the network load for PF and RN. Here, RN is less influenced due to the superfluous forwarding to the rendezvous nodes.

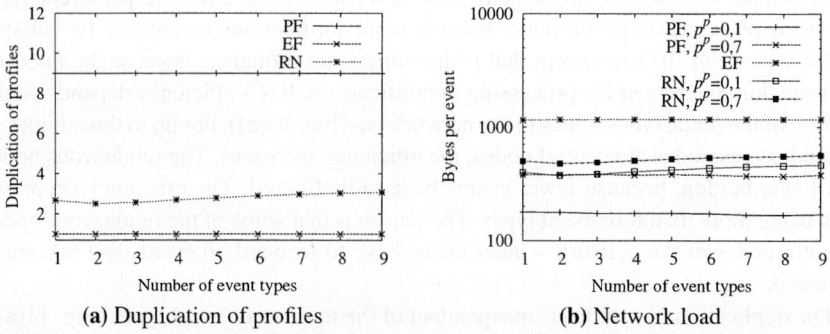

Fig. 11. Duplication of profiles and network load depending on number of event types

4.5 Influence of Locality

In this subsection, we analyze the influence of locality of profiles and events on efficiency and network load. Locality refers to the fact that events from a broker's local publishers only match profiles from local subscribers. We used four brokers as a linear bus, as described in Sect. 4.1. 160,000 profiles referred to a single event type. We increased the number of matching profiles per event per broker (p^p per broker = locality). The duplication of profiles is not considered, since profiles remained unchanged.

Hypotheses: We expect an efficiency increase based on higher locality between profiles and events for PF (since fewer notifications are forwarded to neighbors). When using RN a small increase should occur: Due to the overall event forwarding to the rendezvous node only a smaller part of communication complexity is saved. For EF, we expect independence between locality and efficiency. Analogous results are expected for the network load: Less load for PF and RN, independence for EF.

Results: Figure 12 shows the efficiency depending on locality. PF's efficiency increases by a factor of 2 to 3.5 when increasing locality from 0 to 1. The reason is the early rejection of events at their local brokers. As expected, EF is independent of the locality; all events are flooded. RN is less influenced by locality than PF; the efficiency improves only by a factor of 1.25. The reason is the overall forwarding of events to rendezvous nodes. PF shows a better adaptation to locality than the other two algorithms. RN does not support the hypothesis due to the communication overhead between brokers on the path to the rendezvous node (overcomes the advantage of filtering in fewer brokers). The network load is shown in Fig. 13: EF is not influenced by the locality due to flooding. PF and RN show decreasing load due to early rejection of unmatched events.

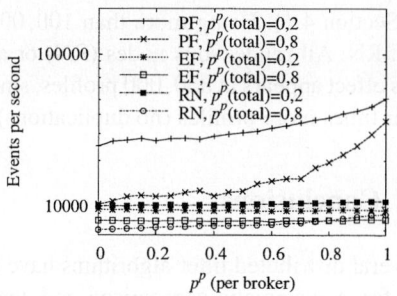

Fig. 12. Efficiency depending on locality and different p^p

4.6 Influence of Number of Profiles

In this subsection, we discuss the influence of the total number of profiles on the efficiency. We used four brokers connected as a linear bus. We subscribed different numbers of unique profiles ($\sigma = 1$). The proportion of matching events was set to $p^e = 0.8$.

Hypotheses: Efficiency is expected to decrease rapidly with increasing number of profiles. Using PF and RN, the main memory is expected to quickly be fully loaded and swapped out to secondary memory. EF should be more stable when using large numbers of profiles, since they are not duplicated.

Results: Figure 14 shows the efficiency over increasing number of profiles. As can be seen in the figure, PF and RN can process up to 100,000 unique profiles and EP can process up to 350,000 unique profiles in main memory (not shown in the graph: this value increases for PF or RN when using coverings). PF shows the best efficiency as

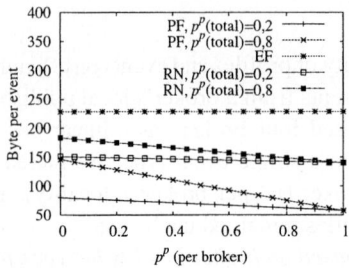
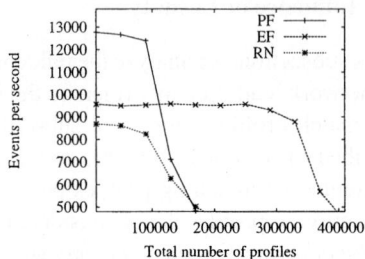

Fig. 13. Network load depending on locality   **Fig. 14.** Efficiency over number of profiles

long as the profiles are stored in main memory, followed by EF and RN. Due to the large proportion of matching events ($p^e = 0.8$), RN is less efficient than EF (as discussed in Section 4.1). Using more than 100,000 profiles causes an efficiency plunge for PF and RN: All rendezvous nodes (RN) or all brokers (PF) create bottlenecks. Using EF, this effect appears at 350,000 profiles, since the four brokers can process approximately four times more profiles (no duplications).

5 Conclusions

Several distributed filter algorithms have been proposed for publish/subscribe systems. So far, a systematic comparison and analysis of these filter algorithms had not been achieved. In this paper, we proposed the first classification scheme for distributed filtering algorithms for publish/subscribe systems. In a second step, we classified existing filter algorithms according to the proposed concise scheme. As a third step, we analytically evaluated 17 algorithms based on their features according to the classification dimensions. Out of the 17 algorithms, we selected the 3 most promising ones: event forwarding (EF), profile forwarding (PF), and rendezvous nodes (RN). In an extensive experimental analysis, we evaluated these three algorithms. The results of the experimental analysis support the findings of the theoretical analysis and yield a finer grained insight into the behavior of each algorithm under different conditions. A detailed discussion of the results can be found in [2]. Many existing evaluations have used simulated data, e.g., in [4,12,13]; others have measured different factors [8]. We used no simulation data nor a simulated network topology. The real publish/subscribe system DAS was used throughout upon real data sets. DAS has been developed for event monitoring in facility management systems.

We conclude our experimental analysis of algorithms with the following recommendations based on the underlying applications and network topologies. We refer to our key measurements filter efficiency, network load, and duplication of profiles:

Filter efficiency: For most applications, profile forwarding (PF) is the most efficient algorithm. Especially if there is a low proportion of matching profiles or events, PF is significantly more efficient than EF or RN. For a high proportion of matching profiles, the three algorithms converge, since all events have to be flooded. In rare cases with high proportions of matching profiles, EF is the most efficient algorithm. The reason is the simplicity of the filter protocol with its low overhead. Rendezvous nodes show mediocre results for all applications and topologies: They prove to be of no benefit, as inner nodes always have to forward all events.

Network load per event: The network load in event forwarding (EF) is independent from any other system parameters (except the number of brokers), since all events are always flooded. PF causes the least network load because only matching events are forwarded. Rendezvous nodes show mediocre results, since events are always forwarded to the rendezvous nodes. When increasing p^e or p^p, the network load also increases for PF and RN, but never reaches that of EF.

Duplication of profiles: Duplication is highest when using PF. For unique profiles, the duplication is especially high, because each broker filters each profile – this implies high memory usage. The same picture holds for RN but in a smaller degree. Coverings eliminate duplications for PF and RN. In EF, profiles are not duplicated and therefore the highest number of profiles can be filtered.

Due to this dependency of the filter algorithms on the system's parameters, a publish/subscribe system should support different filter algorithms. According to the system load and application, the system can choose an optimal algorithm:

If many profiles match an event we should choose event forwarding (EF) with its simple protocol. Event forwarding does not cause significant network load since the events have to be forwarded through the network anyway. We should also use EF in case of high numbers of subscribed profiles (profile duplication and memory use are lowest). In most of the other cases (fewer profiles, small portions of matching events, coverings), profile forwarding (PF) should be used. This algorithm causes less network load and the filtering is significantly more efficient than for EF and RN. Unfortunately, rendezvous nodes (RN) have not been advantageous in any tested system configuration. One of the reasons is the limited size and variation of the used broker topology. This first cut analysis is scheduled to be extended using larger and more general topologies in computer grids.

The idea of an adaptive system that uses the appropriate filter algorithm depending on the applications parameters has been implemented in A-mediAS, an adaptable mediating event notification system [5]. A-mediAS uses adaptation only for local filtering of primitive and composite events. We plan to integrate DAS's adaptable distributed filter algorithms within A-mediAS. Another step for future research is the use of distributed filter algorithms for composite events in grid topologies and mobile environments, imposing advanced requirements on the algorithms and the system's adaptability.

References

1. G. Banavar, T. Chandra, B. Mukherjee, J. Nagarajarao, R. E. Strom, and D. C. Sturman. An Efficient Multicast Protocol for Content-based Publish-Subscribe Systems. In *Proceedings of the 19th IEEE International Conference on Distributed Computing Systems (ICDCS '99)*, pages 262–272, Austin, USA, June 1999.
2. S. Bittner and A. Hinze. Design and analysis of an efficient distributed event notification service. Technical Report 11/2004, Computer Science Department, University of Waikato, New Zealand, August 2004.

3. A. Carzaniga, D. S. Rosenblum, and A. L. Wolf. Interfaces and Algorithms for a Wide-Area Event Notification Service. Technical Report CU-CS-888-99, Computer Science Department, University of Colorado, October 1999.
4. A. Carzaniga, D. S. Rosenblum, and A. L Wolf. Design and evaluation of a wide-area event notification service. *ACM Transactions on Computer Systems*, 19(3):332–383, August 2001.
5. A. Hinze. *A-MEDIAS: Concept and Design of an Adaptive Integrating Event Notification Service*. PhD thesis, Freie Universität Berlin, July 2003.
6. A. Hinze and S. Bittner. Efficient Distribution-based Event Filtering. In *Proceedings of the 22nd IEEE International Conference on Distributed Computing Systems Workshops (ICDCSW '02)*, pages 525–532, Vienna, Austria, July 2002.
7. G. Mühl. Generic Constraints for Content-Based Publish/Subscribe Systems. In *Proceedings of the 6th International Conference on Cooperative Information Systems (CoopIS '01)*, pages 211–225, Trento, Italy, September 2001.
8. G. Mühl. *Large-Scale Content-Based Publish/Subscribe Systems*. PhD thesis, Technische Universität Darmstadt, September 2002.
9. G. Mühl and L. Fiege. Supporting Covering and Merging in Content-Based Publish/Subscribe Systems: Beyond Name/Value Pairs. *IEEE Distributed Systems Online (DSOnline)*, 2(7), July 2001.
10. G. Mühl, L. Fiege, and A. Buchmann. Filter Similarities in Content-Based Publish/Subscribe Systems. In *Proceedings of the International Conference on Architecture of Computing Systems (ARCS '02)*, pages 224–238, Karlsruhe, Germany, April 2002.
11. P. Pietzuch and J. Bacon. Hermes: A Distributed Event-Based Middleware Architecture. In *Proceedings of the 22nd IEEE International Conference on Distributed Computing Systems Workshops (ICDCSW '02)*, pages 611–618, Vienna, Austria, July 2002.
12. A. I. T. Rowstron, A.-M. Kermarrec, M. Castro, and P. Druschel. SCRIBE: The Design of a Large-Scale Event Notification Infrastructure. In *Proceedings of the 3rd International Workshop on Networked Group Communications (NGC 2001)*, pages 30–43, London, UK, November 2001.
13. D. Tam, R. Azimi, and H. Jacobsen. Building Content-Based Publish/Subscribe Systems with Distributed Hash Tables. In *Proceedings of the First International Workshop on Databases, Information Systems, and Peer-to-Peer Computing (DBISP2P), LNCS 2944*, pages 138–152, Berlin, Germany, September 2003.
14. H. Yu, D. Estrin, and R. Govindan. A Hierarchical Proxy Architecture for Internet-scale Event Services. In *Proceedings of IEEE 8th International Workshops on Enabling Technologies: Infrastructure for Collaborative Enterprises (WET ICE '99)*, pages 78–83, Stanford, USA, June 1999.

A Collaborative Model for Agricultural Supply Chains*

Evandro Bacarin[1], Claudia B. Medeiros[2], and Edmundo Madeira[2]

[1] Departament of Computer Science - UEL - CP 6001
86051-990 Londrina PR Brazil
bacarin@uel.br

[2] Institute of Computing - UNICAMP - CP 6176
13081-970 Campinas SP Brazil
{cmbm,edmundo}@ic.unicamp.br

Abstract. This paper presents a collaborative model for agricultural supply chains that supports negotiation, renegotiation, coordination and documentation mechanisms, adapted to situations found in this kind of supply chain – such as return flows and composite regulations. This model comprises basic building blocks and elements to support a chain's dynamic execution. The model is supported by an architecture where chain elements are mapped to Web Services and their dynamics to service orchestration. Model and architecture are motivated by a real case study, for dairy supply chains.

1 Introduction

A supply chain is a network of retailers, distributors, transporters, storage facilities and suppliers that participate in the sale, delivery and production of a particular product [1,2]. It is composed of distributed, heterogeneous and autonomous elements, whose relationships are dynamic, and change while the chain is activated. Supply chains present several research challenges, such as recording and tracking B2B and e-commerce transactions, designing appropriate negotiation protocols, providing cooperative work environments among enterprises, or coordinating loosely coupled business processes [3].

This paper is concerned with modeling, supervising and coordinating processes in agricultural supply chains, a specific kind of chain that has a large economic impact all over the world. These chains present new challenges in their specification and management, which so far have been mostly ignored by Computer Science researchers.

To start with, the flow within a chain is subject to a wide range of controls. Besides the economic and delivery schedule limitations found in B2B negotiations, agricultural supply chains are sensitive to geographic location, season, climate and product perishability. Examples of concerns are, for instance, whether

---

* The research reported in this paper was partially financed by CNPq (ORION project), the PRONEX/FINEP/CNPq SAI project and CNPq WEBMaps and Agro-Flow projects.

the production process is harmful to the environment or whether it uses genetically modified substances. This requires setting up strict monitoring at all stages, as well as enforcing a large set of rules, which may be product, region or season-sensitive. A parallel concern is the quality of the final product, which involves auditing all production and distribution stages.

Another peculiarity is the so-called "return flow" within such chains, in which the refuse of a given stage of the chain may be recycled and re-enter the chain at another stage. Recycling is not a problem restricted to agricultural chains, but the constraints imposed on these cycles are. Finally, the number and kinds of actors encountered allow limitless possibilities of chain configurations, and the same kind of raw material may originate a large set of interrelated chains.

Our solution combines research in databases, computer networks, and distributed systems and is based on tackling the problem in several stages and levels. The first stage involves *modeling the chain's components* and *dynamics*. Subsequent stages consist in *mapping* the chain to our architecture, whose elements are seen as Web Services.

For each of these stages, the chain's elements and flow have to be considered at two levels: within and across enterprises. Furthermore, service coordination also considers two levels: global dynamics, treated by Coordination Plans; and inter-element dynamics, treated via Contracts negotiated between trading partners.

The main contributions are the following: (i) a general model for specification of agricultural supply chains, which takes into consideration cross organizational collaboration aspects; (ii) an architecture for its implementation, which emphasizes coordination and service flow composition issues; (iii) the validation of the model via a real life case study in agriculture, stressing the peculiarities of this kind of application domain.

The rest of this paper is organized as follows. Section 2 provides an example that will be used throughout the paper to illustrate our work. Section 3 describes the model. Section 4 specifies the architecture and shows how it supports dynamic behaviour. Section 5 outlines an implementation of a chain via Web services. Section 6 contains related work and section 7 concludes the paper.

2   Agricultural Supply Chains

This section presents a simple agriculture supply chain that will be used throughout the paper to illustrate our solution. Figure 1 shows this example – the *dairy cattle supply chain*. The goal of this dairy chain is to process milk, producing and commercializing its products – such as bottled milk, butter, or cheese. The starting point is a "Milk Producer" – a farm that has milk-cows. The farmer gathers milk at given periods. Next, milk is delivered by some sort of transportation means "Transport 1" to a Dairy (production). It can only be processed if it obeys certain constraints stated in "Regulation 1". At the "Dairy", it is processed to create products, which are then transported for wholesale and finally retail commercialization, reaching the end consumer. Products and inputs may be stored at different storage facilities throughout the chain – e.g., warehouses. At each stage, various actors – humans or software – may intervene: lawyers, commodity brokers, quality certifiers or software agents.

Some of the chain's refuse may provide feedback to it, in terms of return flows – such as from the Dairy back to the Producer. For instance, milk that overflows from vats returns to the farms to be used in cattle feed.

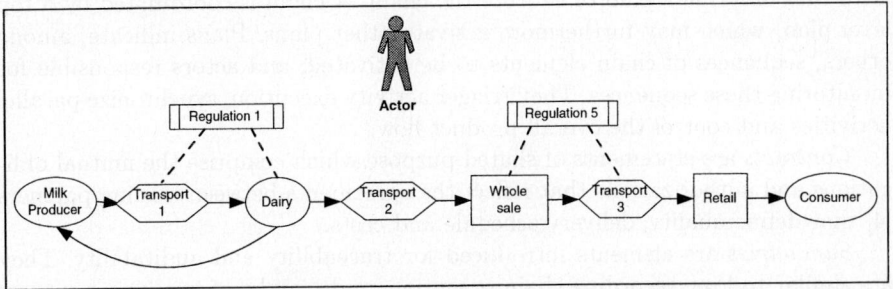

Fig. 1. The Dairy Supply Chain

Even though the diagram in Fig. 1 shows a sequential execution, this is seldom the case. Each chain component may moreover encapsulate other chains. Negotiation, cooperation and coordination issues occur at all levels. Coordination may be centralized – such as in the milk cooperative – or distributed among several coordination centers, that negotiate with each other.

3 A Model for Supply Chains

3.1 Basic Elements

The model's basic elements are Actors, Production, Storage and Transportation. Chain dynamics are furthermore supported by elements Regulation, Contract, Coordination Plan and Summary.

A *Production Element* encapsulates a productive process that uses raw material extracted from its own environment or inputs obtained from other components and produces a product that is passed on to the chain. It is represented graphically by an ellipsis.

A *Storage Element* stores products or raw material and a *Transportation Element* moves products and raw material between production and storage components. They are represented by rectangles and diamonds respectively.

Actors are software or human agents that act in the chain. They may be directly or indirectly involved in the execution of activities A *Regulation Certifier* is an actor that is responsible for certifying that activities or products within the chain obey a set of constraints – such as sanitary regulations or quality specifications.

Regulations are sets of rules that regulate a product's evolution within the chain. These rules specify constraints imposed at distinct execution stages, such as government regulations, quality criteria, or conditions determined by a region's social, cultural, economic or even religious context. Regulations may be atomic or complex, containing other regulations within them.

Interactions among chain components are organized by means of *Coordination plans* and negotiated via *Contracts*. A *Coordination plan* is a set of directives that describe a plan to execute the chain. A chain is coordinated by a top level plan, which may furthermore activate other plans. Plans indicate, among others, sequences of chain elements to be activated, and actors responsible for monitoring these sequences. They trigger activity execution, synchronize parallel activities and control the overall product flow.

Contracts are statements of shared purpose which comprise the mutual obligations and authorizations that reflect the agreements between trading partners [4] that define quality, delivery schedule and costs.

Summaries are elements introduced for traceability and auditability. They are similar to logs, recording chain execution, and may be of two kinds: process and product summaries. A *process summary* contains information about the execution of a production process. A *product summary* stores information on how, when and where a product went through each chain step. It also includes information on certification "stamps" received throughout chain execution.

Dynamics and execution depend on coordination plans, which specify valid element interactions in a very high level. During execution of a specific chain instance, elements are instantiated, contracts negotiated, and the Coordination plan is refined. A Coordination Plan is completely specified only at the end of the execution of a chain, since real-time contract negotiations will dynamically change the chain's configuration, as well as the partners involved.

3.2 Element Composition and Encapsulation

Production, Storage and Transportation elements can be simple or complex. Complex elements are those that can be decomposed into other elements. A complex Production element must include other productive processes, while Transportation and Storage elements cannot encapsulate production elements.

The degree of composition of the elements depends on the level of detail desired. Figure 2 shows how the Dairy Production element of Fig. 1 can encapsulate other production chains. Composition and encapsulation of other elements can be likewise exemplified. Raw milk that arrives at the dairy is pasteurized and stored at the "Milk Warehouse". It may subsequently be bottled within the "Bottling of milk" production element, or be transported via the "Transport 6" element to the "Cheese Production" element.

The placement of a Regulation element within a chain indicates when and where it is applied. "Regulation 1" represents conditions established by the Dairy to accept Raw Milk. They include parameters such as: milk acidity or fat content as well as milk region provenance - e.g., for sanitary reasons. Thus, it is location-sensitive. "Regulation 2" defines rules that determine whether the milk is suitable

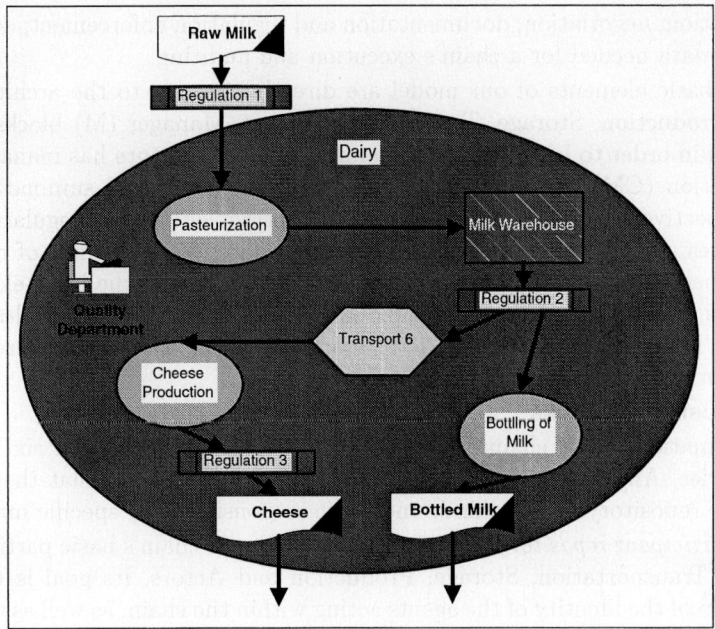

Fig. 2. Breaking down Dairy production element

for cheese or bottling and "Regulation 3" represents quality conditions for cheese comercialization.

Actor "Quality Department" is a sector within the Dairy to check some of the conditions expressed within Regulations 2 and 3. It is within the Dairy element denoting that it can only enforce regulations within it.

3.3 Return Flows

Most supply chain studies ignore return flows, unless they model products returned by a consumer. Waste reuse is seldom considered. Environmental concerns are forcing producers to consider residues. Thus, harmful waste is now being returned to its producer or reprocessed, creating *return flows* in the supply chain. Return flow constraints are modeled within regulations and the flow is modeled by backward or forward links between a chain's components.

4 The Architecture

4.1 Building Blocks

The architecture supports the model described in section 3. It is composed of blocks that encapsulate data and/or services. These blocks can be classified into: those that represent the model's basic elements; those used to support coordination, negotiation, documentation and regulation enforcement; and those used for data needed for a chain's execution and auditing.

The basic elements of our model are directly mapped to the architecture's blocks Production, Storage, Transport and Actor. Manager (M) blocks are introduced in order to handle chain dynamics. The architecture has managers for: coordination (CM), negotiation (NM), regulations (RM) and summaries(SM), that respectively handle coordination plans, contract settlement, regulations and summaries, all mentioned in section 3. Furthermore, distinct kinds of repositories are needed to store information on: chain Participants (the basic elements), Products, Regulations, Contracts and Summaries. The contents and roles of Production, Transport, Storage and Actor blocks are straightforward. There follows a description of manager and repository blocks.

Repository Blocks

Information about chains' elements and execution is stored in six kinds of repositories. Any implementation of the architecture requires that there be at least one repository of each kind, under the responsibility of specific managers.

A *Participant repository* stores cadastral data on a chain's basic participants, namely: Transportation, Storage, Production and Actors. Its goal is to allow validation of the identity of the agents acting within the chain, as well as the roles played by them. It also helps the process of chain instantiation, by supporting the selection of actual businesses to play a given role within a chain.

A *Product repository* contains data on all products and materials used within a supply chain. Its goal is to allow verification of product properties, as well as supporting cross-references within and across chains.

A *Regulation repository* stores regulations for contract negotiation and quality control. Such regulations include global rules (e.g., government level) and local rules (e.g. within a production process).

A *Contract repository* stores contracts established among chain components. More details on these contracts are provided in the next section. A *Coordination plan repository* contains coordination plans specified at distinct granularity levels. The coordination plan repository also contains information about plan execution (e.g., instantiation, validity).

All these repositories support composition of their elements. Thus, composite contracts can be built by aggregating other contracts, plans can be built from the composition of previously stored plans, and so on. Summaries, on the other hand, record the execution of a chain and thus cannot be created from past summaries.

A *Summary Repository* stores product and process summaries, for documentation and auditing. Thus, they can be controlled by government agencies, such as health or sanitation departments, to check on the quality of products and of the production process.

Manager Blocks

The chain's elements and flow have to be considered at two levels: within and across enterprises. Furthermore, service coordination also considers two levels: global dynamics, treated by a Coordination Plan; and inter-element dynamics, treated via the negotiation of Contracts between trading partners. Cooperation, collaboration and negotiation within a chain and the documentation of its activities are handled by manager blocks. Managers may be totally automated or require human Actor intervention.

A *Coordination manager* is in charge of Coordination Plans, interpreting, controling and coordinating them. It is also responsible for managing the Coordination plan Repository. Therefore, these managers trigger and coordinate all processes within the chain. In particular, they are responsible for starting negotiation among components, and may also start regulation enforcement procedures.

A *Negotiation manager* is responsible for handling contracts and coordinating negotiation among distinct chain elements. It also controls Contract Repositories.

A *Summary manager* controls access to a Summary Repository. A *Regulation Manager* encapsulates the access to a Regulation Repository and is also used to verify regulations using information from all repositories. It informs to the Coordination and Negotiation managers whether a regulation has been obeyed or not. Thus, it does not play an active role in regulation enforcement.

4.2 Orchestration of the Supply Chain

The backbone of all orchestration interactions within a chain is formed by a hierarchy of Coordination Managers, that communicate along specific protocols based on a coordination plan. A coordination manager CM at a given hierachical level can only communicate with its parent and its children (levels immediately above and below).

All other interactions among managers are described in terms of this coordination hierarchy background. Each coordination manager CM in the hierarchy may be associated with at most one regulation manager RM, one summary manager SM and one negotiation manager NM. These three managers (RM, SM and NM) are said to be *within the scope* of that coordination manager.

A coordination manager, furthermore, interacts with: the negotiation and summary managers within its scope; and with all regulation managers above its level, and the regulation manager within its scope.

Consider again the "Milk Producer" and "Dairy" elements of figure 1. Suppose that the milk producer is, in fact, a cooperative that agregates several milk farms and the dairy is composed of three production units (for butter, bottled milk and cheese). Figure 3 depicts the block arrangement for those elements and some of their interactions. This example details only production elements, but similar arrangements may also be done for transportation or storage elements. The figure shows a 2-level hierarchy, rooted at CM3.

NM1, RM1 and SM1 are within the scope of CM1 (the cooperative's coordination manager). CM1 can communicate with CM3 (its parent in the coordination hierarchy), with the farms (its children), NM1, RM1 and SM1 (the managers within its scope).

A Negotiation Manager can interact with any other negotiation manager, and with regulation managers of the same scope or above. Negotiation is always triggered by a coordination manager interacting with a negotiation manager.

A Regulation Manager may interact with regulation managers at any level above it. They may also respond to requests from any negotiation manager within the same scope or below its level, and to the coordination manager within the same scope or below its level.

Summary Managers only interact with coordination managers and with any other SM.

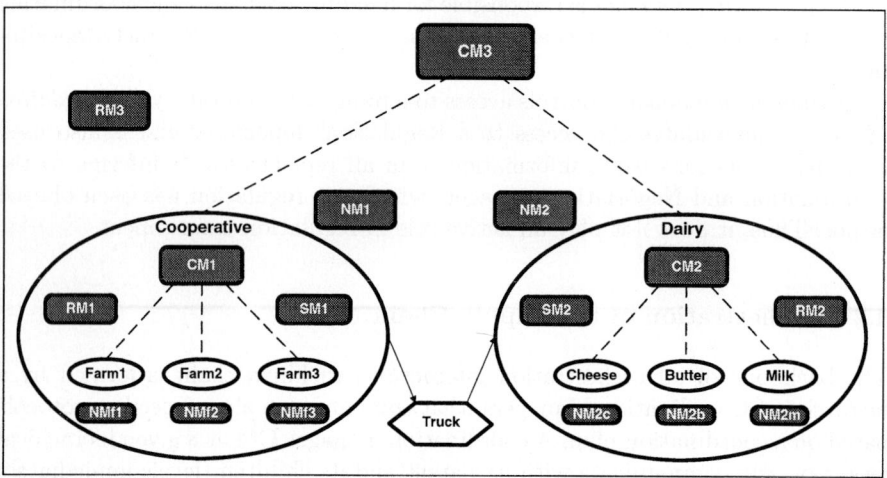

Fig. 3. Illustrating scope and manager hierarchies

4.3 Revisiting the Case Study Using the Architecture

This section illustrates how chain dynamics are supported within the architecture. It starts by discussing coordination aspects, followed by negotiation aspects.

Coordination

The first step in chain execution is its instantiation – this means that a plan's components are instantiated – e.g., Farm 3, registered in the Participant Repository, is a specific farm in Fig. 3. Farms 1, 2 and 3 are furthermore production elements. Each farm has its own negotiation manager (NMf1, NMf2, NMf3). Once the elements start being instantiated, they can agree to establish collaboration, according to coordination plans written and ran by a coordination manager (e.g., CM3). This begins chain execution, started by some coordination manager "higher-up" in the manager hierarchy (CM3) or by actor intervention.

The cooperative and the dairy may undergo several negotiation processes. Those negotiation processes are led by negotiation managers NM1 (for the cooperative) and NM2 (for the dairy). Negotiation is triggered by CM3. In this example, the cooperative and the dairy have their own regulation managers, namely RM1 and RM2. RM3 is responsible for handling regulations within the scope of CM3, and external to the scope of the dairy and cooperative.

Suppose now that CM3, as part of its plan, asks the cooperative to supply 5000 liters of milk the next day. None of the farms can singly afford that volume. Thus, CM1 coordinates this production. It may demand 1000 liters of one farm; 1500 liters of another; and 2500 liters of the last one. As soon as a farm gets the request ready, it reports to CM1. When all farms have reported, CM1 reports to CM3. This kind of communication and execution protocol is similar to that found in management of nested complex transactions in distributed systems [5].

Now, CM3 will ask some transportation agent (Truck) to collect the milk at the cooperative and deliver it to the dairy. When the milk arrives, Truck will notify CM3. CM3 will then ask the dairy to produce 100 liters of bottled milk, 50Kg of butter and 200Kg of cheese. CM2 takes care of this assignment, by coordinating the activities of butter, cheese and bottled milk units. Each unit reports the completion of its task to CM2. When all units have accomplished their tasks, CM2 reports to CM3, and so on.

In this scenario, CM1 and CM2 are subordinated to CM3, but they can coordinate plans that do not depend on CM3, for instance, related to their internal activities.

Negotiation

The relationships among cooperative, farms, dairy (and the respective production units) is governed by contracts. The establishment of a contract is started by a coordination manager that requests intervention from negotiation managers. Consider, again, that CM3 asks the cooperative for a daily production of 5000 liters of milk for the next three months to be delivered to the dairy, but there is not any predefined quota for each farm. The negotiation happens at two distinct levels: the cooperative negotiates with the dairy through NM1 and NM2; the farms negotiate among themselves through NMf1, NMf2 and NMf3.

The negotiation sequence covering both negotiation levels is depicted in Fig. 4. First, CM3 asks the cooperative to deploy a contract negotiation with the dairy. This figure shows that, as soon as CM1 receives a negotiation request from CM3 (edge 1), CM1 starts two activities: a) It asks NM1 (edge 2) to negotiate the contract with the dairy's NM (NM2); b) It asks (edge 3) Farm 1's CM (CMf1) to start milk quotas negotiation among the farms.

As a consequence of CM1's request, NM1 and NM2 develop a negotiation process. NM1 proposes contract clauses to NM2 (edge 4). The latter considers each clause individually and may accept it, reject it or propose an alternative (edge 5). The cycle proposal X alternative runs until they agree to or reject the clause. Eventually, NM1 and NM2 agree to the contract. At the same time, CMf1 asks NMf1 (edge 6) to begin quota negotiation with NMf2 and NMf3 (edges 7 and 8, 9 and 10).

When quota negotiation is finished, NMf1 reports this to CMf1 (edge 11), which in turn relays this information to CM1 (edge 12). Eventually, NM1 and NM2 agree on the deployment contract and NM1 reports the agreement to CM1 (edge 13). As soon as both negotiation processes (milk quotas and deployment contract) are finished, CM1 reports to CM3 (edge 14). Note that eventually NM1 might ask the Cooperative or NM2 might ask the Dairy about some negotiation parameters during a negotiation process. This kind of request is not depicted in this figure.

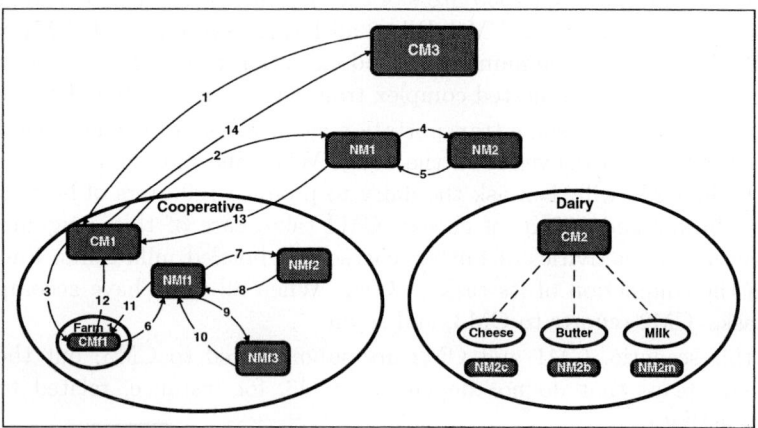

Fig. 4. Coordination and negotiation relationship

A contract is executed and renegotiated on a clause-by-clause basis by the initiative of a coordination manager. For instance, the supply chain may have to be dynamically reconfigured due to a new factor (e.g. a new law, some natural disaster or animal epidemics in a region). Considering the managers illustrated in the Fig. 4, CM3 asks CM1 and CM2 to negotiate new parameters via the suitable negotiation managers NM1 and NM2. These, in turn, verify their contracts in order to determine which contracts and which clauses were affected. The affected clauses are renegotiated individually, again under the proposal X alternative cycle. Negotiation and renegotiation may need human intervention. Each new contract is stored in a Contract Repository by some negotiation manager.

Documentation

The chain execution is documented into summaries that follow products along the chain. Summaries are in fact composed of sequences of local process and product summaries. They are updated at each chain step, and can be merged or subdivided.

Documentation proceeds along the chain. For instance, when the butter unit starts, a new process summary is created for its production process. At the end of this process, the butter unit's CM asks its summary manager to create a summary for the butter produced. This new butter summary is composed of a description of the butter fabrication process, appended to the input milk summary. Eventually, the dairy will output the butter to the next chain step, and this butter will be accompanied by its summary.

Regulation Upholding

Coordination and negotiation involve regulation checking and upholding. For instance, at the end of butter production, CM2 may ask its regulation manager RM2 to check if the product satisfies the suitable restrictions. In order to do this, it will inform RM2 which constraints must be checked. Next, RM2 will combine information from Participant and Product repositories, plus data from the product summary to check these regulations, and return a verdict on regulation compliance, which is also stored in the summary.

5 Implementation

5.1 Mapping into Classes

Implementation of our architecture can be specified in terms of classes in an object-oriented system. Figure 5 uses UML and shows a high level specification of some of the topmost classes needed. The basic elements are in grey, managers are in black, repositories are in white. It shows that basic components include Storage, Transportation and Production, and also the possible compositions among them (Actors are not shown). Note the closed arrowheads from Production, Transport and Storage to Element. This indicates that Element generalizes the other classes, whereas black diamonds indicate composition – e.g., a Production element can encapsulate any other element, whereas Transportation and Storage elements cannot contain Production components.

Black arrows indicate responsibility relationships – e.g., a NM handles contracts, or a SM handles summaries. These classes are implemented in Java. The next section presents highlights of these classes.

5.2 Class Specification

CoordinationManager Class. This class implements the CM block of Fig. 5. A Coordination Manager executes coordination plans. A coordination plan is composed by a set of activities. The coordination plan is a XML file that can be mapped to a BPEL4WS script. The values transferred to and from activities are also XML files. Each activity has an identification and may yield a result after completion. These activities include: execution of another coordination plan, execution of a clause of a contract, verification of a regulation, execution of a Web service operation, and execution of local operations. Activities may be executed sequentially or in parallel and may be synchronized by synchronization primitives.

A given plan can have more than one instance executing at the same time. Thus each plan execution has a unique instance identification. Each plan execution may also receive parameters from the environment.

A CM communicates with a CM within its scope (e.g., CM3 and CM1) via interfaces *CoordinationIF* (Fig. 6) and *ActivityReportIF* (Fig. 7). Orchestration is performed through these interfaces. The lower level CM receives the request

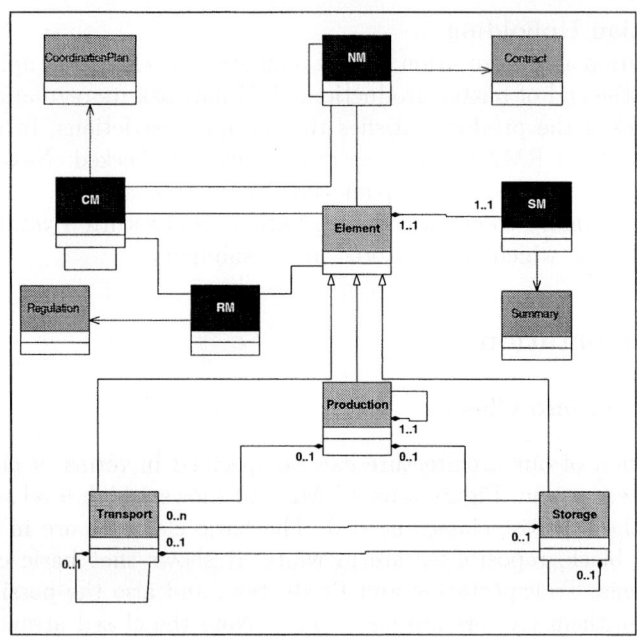

Fig. 5. Class diagram with emphasis in model components and management

```
public interface CoordinationIF {

        public void executeStoredPlan(CoordinationManagerAddress caller,
                             ActivityIdentification activityId,
                             PlanIdentification planId,
                             CoordinationPlanAddress planAddr,
                             Properties pars);
}
```

Fig. 6. CoordinationIF interface

through its *CoordinationIF* interface and reports the result to the parent's *ActivityReportIF* interface.

Figure 6 shows that the request for plan execution contains parameter *planAddr* that informs the address of the repository where the demanded plan is stored, *planId* is a key that identifies the plan inside the repository, *pars* are environmental parameters, *caller* is the address of the higher Coordination Manager, and *activityId* keeps both the activity and the instance identification of the higher activity that demanded the plan execution. The parameters *caller* and *activityId* are used to report the execution status to the higher manager.

Eventually, the lower manager reports the execution status to the parent manager. Using the received *caller* parameter, it can reach the higher manager and execute *reportPlanStatus* operation of the higher manager (Fig. 7). The parameter *st* informs the status (DONE, ACTIVE, SUSPENDED, RESUMED, CANCELED) and may convey some value produced by the plan's execution, and *activityId* received previously is assigned to *id*.

```
public interface ActivityReportIF {
  public void reportPlanStatus(ActivityIdentification id, PlanStatus st);
}
```

Fig. 7. ActivityReportIF interface

The Coordination Manager has another interface called *OwnerComponentIF* that is quite similar to *CoordinationIF* interface. This new interface is used by a component to demand an inner Coordination Manager the execution of a plan. The execution may be synchronous or asynchronous, and there is an operation to ask the status of an asynchronous plan execution.

ActivityReportIF interface also receives reports from other kind of activities in a similar way.

RegulationManager Class. This class implements the RM block of Fig. 5. An instance of this class verifies regulations. A regulation is evaluated against a summary of a product to verify if that product satisfies the constraints expressed in the regulation.

A Regulation is specified in an XML file (Fig. 8). It contains a section (tag *verify*) with the conditions that must hold for the regulation to be satisfied (the regulation is said to be satisfied). The evaluation of this condition may produce a certificate stamp - another XML file.

```
<regulation id=''unique_id'' type=''CategoryName''>
    <parameters> ... </parameters>
    <enforce>
        <reg var=''VarName'' id=''RegulationIdentification''
            address=''RegulationRepositoryAddress'' >
            <par name=''Parameter1Name''> Parameter1Value</par>
        </reg>
    </enforce>
    <verify> </verify>
    <action>
        <ifok>
            <mark m=''all|alltrue|allfalse|#VarName|##''/ >
        </ifok>
    </action>
</regulation>
```

Fig. 8. Regulation XML file

Complex Regulations embed other regulations to be verified (tag *enforce*). The value produced by the evaluation of an enforced regulation is assigned to *VarName*. A complex regulation is satisfied iff its condition holds and so do all the enforced regulations.

The *action* tag indicates whether to store the certification stamps in the summary or not. The *mark* tag will instruct which mark is appended to the summary; e.g, *all* means that all stamps will be appended; *alltrue* appends the stamps whose value is yes; *allfalse* is the opposite; #*VarName*, appends the stamp contained in variable *VarName*; ##, appends only the stamp produced by the composite regulation.

5.3 Implementation as Web Services

All architecture elements can be seen as implemented through or encapsulated by Web Services. The only exception is the coordination plan, which is mapped to a workflow.

In more detail, repositories and contracts are static entities encapsulated by Services that provide access to them. Actors can be either Services (e.g., a broker) or Service clients. All managers correspond to services, and the remaining architecture elements – Production, Transportation and Storage – are atomic services or the result of service composition via coordination plans.

The workflow that describes a coordination plan is constructed just as any workflow described in the literature [6], i.e.:

- totally predefined before execution; or
- constructed in an *ad hoc* manner by the CM responsible for the orchestration, while the chain is executed, typical of scientific workflows (e.g., [7,8]); or
- a combination of both.

Each workflow activity references a service responsible for its execution. For instance, in figure 3, a coordination plan executed by CM2 is a workflow that contains an activity that starts cheese production. This activity must refer to the cheese unit (a Service), the desired kind of cheese (a Service for a Product Repository) and the regulations (a Service to a Regulation Repository) that must be verified during the production process in order to ensure cheese quality.

There follows the ennumeration of the interfaces of these Services, which can also be depicted as WSDL specification. Most of these blocks also implement an administration interface, used to configure the corresponding Web Service. The main interfaces of Transportation, Production and Storage Services are:

- *Interfaces for specific/business services:* each element represents a chain partner (e.g., business, enterprise, industry), and therefore can have one or more interfaces for its specific services.
- *Contract Negotiation interface:* receives requests from the Negotiation Manager about negotiation and contract parameters.
- *Contract Execution interface:* accepts requests from other components (or Coordination Manager) to execute a specific contract clause.

- *Sumary Management interface:* responsible for exchange and certification of summaries, via communication with the Summary Manager.

A Coordination Manager Service implements at least the following interfaces. The Java specifications of some of them are shown in section 5.2:

- *Coordination interface:* receives requests from a higher Coordination Managers. Orchestration happens through this interface.
- *Activity Report interface:* receives status reports about the activities demanded from another Service.
- *Owner Component interface:* the interface by which a Coordination Manager receives requests from the component that owns it.

The interfaces implemented by a Negotiation Manager Service include:

- *Negotiation Coordination interface:* accepts requests from the Coordination Manager.
- *Peer Negotiation interface:* for negotiation with another Negotiation Manager Service.

A Summary Manager Service has one *Exchange interface* for exchange of summaries among summary managers.

Finally, a Regulation Manager Service has one interface *Regulation Verifying interface*. It is responsible for checking all rules within a regulation against the chain's state. This may require requesting information from all repositories. It may be invoked by one or more chain components. The component that invoked it is responsible for enforcing the corresponding regulation.

All repositories are encapsulated by Services. The interfaces of these Services offer access to these data for retrieval and update. These interfaces can be accessed by the Managers of a chain and also by external services and systems that have no connection with a chain, but want to perform queries on products, participants, contracts and plans.

6 Related Work

There are several issues that can be analyzed under the umbrella of supply chains - e.g., concerning algorithms adopted, logistics, placement strategies, partner choice. One particular trend, called by [2] IT-related supply chains, concerns information technology tools and techniques to specify and implement such chains. In particular, a recent direction concerns the communication technologies adopted. Problems encountered in electronic commerce and B2B applications and interactions are the same as those faced by supply chain interactions [9].

Though there are many proposals for combining workflows and Web Services (e.g., [10] on agriculture) proposals for supply chains combining these mechanisms are still preliminary. The closest is the research on e-business using Web services, but for other goals – e.g., see [11]. [12] even states that the main reason for the lack of practical implementation of strategic supply chain development can be found in the high degree of complexity that is connected with the identification of supply chain entities and the modelling of the chain structure, as well as the high coordination effort.

Our goal is to contribute to solving these issues. Most researchers do not examine the entire chain, focusing only on some aspects. Auditing structures and log maintenance are ignored. Agricultural chains are mostly examined under a business or logistics framework.

Examples of such approaches are the work of [13] or [14]. The first categorizes integrated supply chains into three models, namely: channel master, chain web, and chain organism. The author states that the predominant model in agricultural supply chain is the channel master. In this model, a dominant firm specifies the terms of trade across the entire supply chain and the coordinated behaviour is based on specification contracts. [14] discusses the usage of information technology in the american cattle-beef supply chain. The paper emphasizes the need for better information integration and well-defined means for describing and enforcing activitites coordination, negotiation and execution of contracts.

Since our proposal is based on Web services implementation, we also examine a few related issues. Two aspects have to be considered: mapping a chain's components to Web services and composition of these services.

[15] analyzes issues in service composition and comments on various standards for orchestration and choreography, such as BPEL4WS, WSCI and BPML. Important concerns in service execution in this context are long running transactions and exception handling. The actions in those standards are undone by compensation actions. This affects documentation of chain execution, since all performed actions are logged in summaries and in repositories. [16], in turn, overviews several proto-patterns for architecting and managing composite Web services, while [17] is more concerned with service semantics.

[18] proposes a mechanism for service definition and coordination. Their architecture is based on a 2-level workflow. At the highest level, a workflow orchestrator controls execution, while at the lowest level service execution can be controlled by a regular workflow engine. This is done through entry points placed between activities. In contrast, the work of [19] uses statecharts for defining service composition, and is based on a distributed orchestration engine.

[20] proposes a service-oriented architecture built upon the Web services proposals for inter-enterprise and cross-enterprise integration. Using this architecture, process managers can compose and choreograph business processes based on exposed enterprise and Web services.

Several other authors are concerned with organizational and modeling aspects of supply chains, as indicated by the classification proposed by [2] to analyze efforts in supply chain modeling. This includes for instance work on partner coordination [1], logistics [21] or business contract languages [4].

7 Conclusions

This paper presented a framework for modeling, supervising and coordinating processes in agricultural supply chains. This framework is comprised of two parts: (i) a model for these production chains, that covers both declarative and dynamic aspects; and (ii) an architecture to support the model, based on Web Services and their interfaces.

The model takes into account the fact that agricultural chains are inherently heterogeneous, and sensitive to different kinds of constraints. Chain definition using this model involves specifying its basic components (Actors, Transportation, Process and Storage) and the components needed for cooperation, collaboration, negotiation and documentation (Contracts, Coordination plans, Policies and Summaries). The model provides rules for composition and construction of these elements, thereby allowing *ad hoc* chain construction and execution. The model is mapped into an architecture of Web Services that provides support for contract negotiation, plan coordination, regulation enforcement and summary management. These services also encapsulate access to distinct repositories, that contain data on the chain's partners, processes, policies, constraints, contracts and execution documentation. This architecture supports flow execution at two dimensions: within and across enterprises, for a multiple hierarchy of coordination levels, under service orchestration. Service coordination encompasses global and local dynamics, enforceable by communication protocols established among and across coordination levels.

The main contributions are thus the following: (1) an information technology-based model for specification of agricultural supply chains, which takes into consideration scope, structure and goals, and supports coordination, cooperation and documentation; (2) an architecture for its implementation, which emphasizes negotiation, regulation management, coordination and service flow issues; (3) validation of the model via a real life case study in agriculture.

Current work includes refining the object model of the framework, which will in turn allow implementation and testing of the architecture. This includes testing the suitability of scientific workflows to support the dynamics of ad-hoc coordination plan construction. The implementation will be tested against case studies provided by Brazil's agriculture ministry research corporation.

References

1. Kumar, K.: Technology for supporting supply chain management. Communications of the ACM **44** (2001) 58–61
2. Min, H., Zhou, G.: Supply chain modeling: past, present and future. Computer & Industrial Engineering **43** (2002) 231–249
3. Arsanjani, A.: Developing and Integrating Enterprise Componentes and Services. Communications of the ACM **45** (2002) 31–34
4. Weigand, H., Heuvel, W.: Cross-organizational workflow integration using contracts. Decision Support Systems **33** (2002) 247–265

5. Oszu, T., Valduriez, P.: Principles of Distributed Database Systems. Prentice Hall (1991)
6. Gal, A., Montesi, D.: Inter-enterprise workflow management systems. In: Proc. 10th International Conference and Workshop on Database and Expert Systems Applications (DEXA '99). (1999) 623–627
7. Weske, M., Vossen, G., Medeiros, C.B., Pires, F.: Workflow Management in Geoprocessing Applications. In: Proc. 6th ACM International Symposium Geographic Information Systems – ACMGIS98. (1998) 88–93
8. Cavalcanti, M., Mattoso, M., Campos, M., Llirbat, F., Simon, E.: Sharing Scientific Models in Environmental Applications. In: Proc ACM Symposium Applied Computing - SAC. (2002)
9. Medjahed, B., Benatallah, B., Bouguettaya, A., Ngu, A., Elmagarmid, A.: Business-to-business interactions: issues and enabling technologies. The VLDB Journal **12** (2003) 59–85
10. Fileto, R., Liu, L., Pu, C., Assad, E., Medeiros, C.B.: POESIA: An Ontological Workflow Approach for Composing Web Se rvices in Agriculture. VLDB Journal **12** (2003)
11. Rust, R., Kannan, P.: E-Service: a New Paradigm for Business in the Electronic Environment. Communications of the ACM **46** (2003) 36–42
12. Albani, A., Keiblinge, A., Turowski, K., Winnewisser, C.: Identification and modelling of web services for inter-enterprise collaboration exemplified for the domain of strategic supply chain development. In Meersman, R. e.a., ed.: CoopIS/DOA/ODBASE 2003. (2003) 74–92
13. Peterson, H.: The "learning" supply chain: Pipeline or pipedream? American J. Agr. Econ. **84** (2002) 1329–1336
14. Salin, V.: Information technology and cattle-beef supply chains. American J. Agr. Econ. **82** (2000) 1105–1111
15. Peltz, C.: Web services orchestration: a review of emerging technologies, tools, and standards. Technical report, Hewlett Packard, Co. (2003)
16. Benatallah, B., Dumas, M., Fauvet, M., Rahbi, F., Sheng, Q.: Overview of some patterns for architecting and managing composite web services. ACM SIGecom Exchange **3** (2002) 9–16
17. Bussler, C., Fensel, D., Maedche, A.: A Conceptual Architecture for Semantic Web enabled Web Services. ACM Sigmod Record **31** (2002) 24–30
18. Belhajjame, K., Vargas-Solar, G., Collet, C.: Defining and coordinating openservices using workflows. In et al., R.M., ed.: CoopIS/DOA/ODBASE 2003. (2003) 110–128
19. B. Benatallah, Q.Z. Sheng, M.D.: Environment for web services composition. IEEE Internet Computing (2003) 40–48
20. P. Fremantle, Weerawarana, S., Khalaf, R.: Enterprise Services. Communications of the ACM **45** (2002) 77–82
21. Simon, S.: The art of military logistics – moving to dynamic supply chain. Communications of the ACM **44** (2001) 62–66

FairNet – How to Counter Free Riding in Peer-to-Peer Data Structures

Erik Buchmann and Klemens Böhm

Otto-von-Guericke Universität, Magdeburg, Germany
{buchmann|kboehm}@iti.cs.uni-magdeburg.de

Abstract. Content-Addressable Networks (CAN) manage huge sets of (key, value)-pairs and cope with very high workloads. They follow the peer-to-peer paradigm: They consist of nodes that are autonomous. This means that peers may be uncooperative, i.e., not carrying out their share of the work while trying to benefit from the network. This article deals with this kind of adverse behavior in CAN, e.g., not answering queries and not forwarding messages. It is challenging to design a forwarding protocol for large CAN of more than 100,000 nodes that bypasses and excludes uncooperative nodes. We have designed such a protocol, with the following characteristics: It establishes logical networks of peers within the CAN. Nodes give positive feedback on peers that have performed useful work. Feedback is distributed in a swarm-like fashion and expires after a certain period of time. In extreme situations, the CAN asks nodes to perform a proof of work. Results of experiments with 100,000 peers are positive: In particular, cooperative peers fare significantly better than uncooperative ones.

1 Introduction

Content-Addressable Networks (CAN [1]) manage huge sets of (key, value)-pairs and cope with very high workloads. A CAN is an example of the peer-to-peer (P2P) paradigm: it consists of *nodes*, a.k.a. *peers*. Peers are autonomous programs connected to the Internet. Nodes participate in the work, i.e., data storage and message processing in the context of CAN. At the same time they also make use of the system. In CAN this means that they may issue queries. As with any P2P system, the owners of the nodes bear the infrastructure costs.

Autonomy of the peers implies that there is no coordinator that checks the identity or intentions of nodes. Doing without a coordinator has important advantages, such as scalability and no single point of failure. But it also implies that peers may try to reduce the costs of participation. With conventional CAN protocols, nodes actually do take part in the work voluntarily, and a node can reduce its infrastructure dues by not carrying out its share of the work. In economic terms, the dominant behavior is free riding [2], and the situation is an instance of the Prisoner's Dilemma [3]. In the context of CAN, free riding means ignoring incoming messages that relate to queries issued by other nodes. This can be achieved by tampering the program, blocking the communication, etc. In our terminology, such nodes are *unreliable* or *uncooperative*. It is very important to rule out this kind of behavior. The motivation of the owners of cooperative nodes will decline rapidly otherwise. From a technical perspective, the CAN might fall apart if some peers do not cooperate, and it might not be able to evaluate many queries.

Existing work does not solve these problems. Related work in mobile ad-hoc networks [4,5,6,7] assumes that adjacent nodes can eavesdrop traffic – detecting uncooperative behavior is easy. Others have proposed micropayments, public-key infrastructures, and certified code in similar contexts [8,9]. But infrastructure costs would be unreasonably high, and the resulting system would not be P2P any more. Related work on trust management in P2P systems does not scale to many nodes ($>$ 100,000), or does not deal with message forwarding [10,11].

This article proposes a CAN protocol that renders free riding unattractive, and focuses on the evaluation of queries. The protocol envisioned has the following objectives: (1) Nodes deliver the results of queries of another node only as long as it is cooperative. (2) At the same time, they should not rely on a node that has not proven its cooperativeness. (3) All this should not affect cooperative nodes, except for some moderate overhead.

Designing such a protocol is not obvious: There is no central 'trusted authority', so nodes must rely solely on past interactions of their own or of reliable nodes they know. Further, CAN are supposed to work with large numbers of nodes, e.g., 100,000 or more. Finally, the behavior of peers may change over time. Our solution is a CAN protocol that establishes logical networks of peers within the CAN. Nodes give positive feedback on nodes that have performed useful work. Feedback is distributed piggybacked on 'regular' messages in a swarm-like fashion and expires after a certain period of time. Query results are sent via chains of reliable nodes only. The effect is that the logical networks do not answer queries from uncooperative nodes.

Our evaluation is experimental and is directed towards one main question: Are the mechanisms proposed here effective, i.e., do they rule out uncooperative behavior, with moderate overhead? Our experiments show that the mechanisms do serve the intended purpose, and we have obtained these results for large CAN. In a network of 100,000 nodes, cooperative peers fare significantly better than partly or fully uncooperative ones.

Enforcing cooperation in distributed systems whose components are autonomous is a broad and difficult issue, and we readily admit that this article is only a first stab at the problem. Aspects not explicitly addressed include spoof feedback, spoof query results, and malicious behavior and application-specific issues. However, we think that our lightweight approach for reputation management is extensible, e.g., with negative feedback. This would allow to counter those kinds of adverse behavior effectively.

The remainder of this article has the following structure: After reviewing CAN in Section 2, Section 3 provides a discussion of cooperativeness in CAN. Section 4 introduces our reliability-aware forwarding protocol. Section 5 features an experimental evaluation. Related work is discussed in Section 6, and Section 7 concludes.

2 Content-Addressable Networks

Content-Addressable Networks (CAN [1]) are a variant of *Distributed Hash Tables (DHT)*. Alternatives to CAN differ primarily in the topology of the key space [12,13,14].

Each CAN node is responsible for a part of the key space, its *zone*. I.e., the node stores all (key, value)-pairs whose keys fall into its zone. This space is a torus of Cartesian coordinates in multiple dimensions, and is independent from the underlying physical network topology. In other words, a CAN is a virtual overlay network on top of a large physical network. In addition to its (key, value)-pairs, a CAN node also knows its neighbors, i.e., nodes responsible for adjacent parts of the key space.

A query in CAN is simply a key in the key space, its result is the corresponding value. I.e., a query is a message addressed by the query key. A node answers a query if the key is in its zone. Otherwise, it forwards the query to another node, the *target peer*. To do so, the peer uses *Greedy Forwarding*. I.e., given a query that it cannot answer, a peer chooses the target from its neighbors according to the following criteria: (1) The (Euclidean) distance of the key to the target in question is minimal. (2) The target node is closer to the key than the current peer. In what follows, we refer to the protocol described so far as *classic CAN*.

CAN, as well as any other DHT, are useful as dictionaries. In a file-sharing scenario, the CAN would store the locations of the files, and the files remain at their original locations. Other applications for DHT are annotation services which allow users to rate and comment web pages, or push services for event notification.

2.1 Enhancements to the Classic CAN

Greedy Forwarding in classic CAN sends messages from neighbor to neighbor. This causes a problem, at least when the key space is low-dimensional: The number of peers forwarding a certain message (*message hops*) is unnecessarily large. We have proposed in [15] that a peer does not only know its neighbors, but some remote peers as well. The so-called *contact cache* of the peer contains these remote peers. The contact cache is limited in size. In contrast to the neighbors, contacts may be out of date, and a peer may replace a contact by another one at any time. Furthermore, messages have an attachment. It contains contact information of the peers that have forwarded the message and of the peer that has answered it. A peer that receives such a message uses this information to update its contact cache. No additional messages are necessary to maintain the contact cache. Greedy Forwarding does not only take the neighbors into account, but the ones in the contact cache as well. Finally, Greedy Forwarding also works if information in the contact cache is outdated. In what follows, we refer to this variant of CAN as *enhanced CAN*.

[15] shows that even a small number of additional contacts decreases the average number of message hops significantly. For instance, a contact cache of size 20 (i.e., 20 peers in addition to the neighbors) reduces the number of hops in a CAN of 100,000 peers by more than $2/3$, assuming a real-world distribution of the keys of the queries and of the (key, value)-pairs.

Example 1: Peer S in Figure 1 is responsible for zone (0.3, 0.3 : 0.5, 0.5). Assume that it has issued a query with the key $(0.9, 0.9)$, i.e., it wants to retrieve the corresponding value. Since S is not responsible for this key, it uses Greedy Forwarding and sends the message to P_1. P_1 in turn is not responsible either and forwards the message to P_2, etc. Once the right peer R is reached, it returns the query result to S. In the enhanced CAN, the result is directly returned to the issuer of the query. □

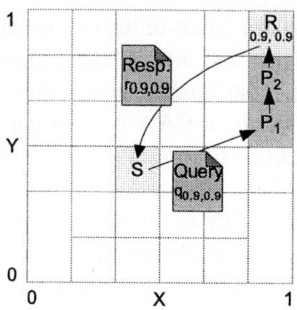

Fig. 1. Forwarding in Enhanced CAN.

3 Cooperation in CAN

In our terminology, a node that handles all incoming messages as expected is *cooperative*. A cooperative node answers the query if the key falls into its zone, or forwards it to another node that seems to be appropriate. From the point of view of another peer, the node is *reliable*. *Uncooperative* nodes in turn try to benefit from the network in a selfish way. In our context, uncooperative behavior is ignoring incoming messages that have to do with queries issued by other nodes.

Since uncooperative nodes hide their intentions and do not come up with statements like "Connection Refused" or "Host Unreachable", repair mechanisms like Expanding Ring Search or Flooding [1] will not work. Furthermore, such nodes may spread falsified information to improve their standing. This implies that classic CAN might fall apart in the presence of uncooperative nodes.

Example 2: In a classic CAN with a percentage u of uncooperative peers that are not explicitly known, the probability p of forwarding a message via n peers is $p = (1-u)^n$. For example, in a network with 5% uncooperative peers, the probability to send a message via 10 nodes is less than 60%. The average path length in a network with a d-dimensional key space and c nodes is $l = (d/4)(c^{1/d})$ (see [1]). Given a key space with $d = 4, l = 10$ for 10,000 peers.

Now think of a CAN protocol that bypasses uncooperative peers when forwarding a query. Then the only peer that it cannot bypass is the peer responsible for the key of the query, so $p = 1 - u = 95\%$. Replication may improve the situation further, but this is beyond this article. □

A peer can estimate the reliability of a certain other peer if it has observed its behavior a couple of times. But frequently this is not the case. For instance, think of a new peer that has issued a query before it had a chance to prove its reliability. Therefore our protocol incorporates a *proof of work (ProW) protocol*: a node proves to another node that it has invested a certain amount of resources by providing some "certificate" of resources spent [16,17]. ProW can be seen as *entry fees* for the CAN, paid to one peer. A ProW is a mathematical problem that is hard to solve, but the solution is easy to verify. The ProW has nothing to do with the operations performed by the CAN. We for our part are not concerned with the design of ProW; we just deploy the concept. – The rationale behind

ProW is determent: With our protocol, an uncooperative peer will be more likely to carry out an expensive ProW. Hence, it is more economic to behave cooperatively.

The design of a reliability-aware CAN protocol depends on the attributes of the nodes and the characteristics of the applications. We make the following assumptions. These assumptions are quite similar to the ones behind other P2P protocols.

Application profile with frequent queries, small results. This article focuses on an application profile for P2P data sharing with the following characteristics: Peers remain connected to the network for a long time. They issue queries frequently and regularly. Query results are typically small, thus their delivery is not much more expensive in terms of infrastructure costs than query routing. It is acceptable if some (very few) queries remain unanswered. – Example applications are object lookup systems, annotation services, push services etc. These assumptions imply that sophisticated and expensive countermeasures [10,9] against free riders are not applicable in our settings. We strive for lightweight mechanisms that must cope with a high rate of parallel queries and that make cooperation the *dominant* behavior.

Timely query results. Query results are needed in time, so it is infeasible to batch queries and issue them at once. – If we allowed peers to issue batches of queries, they could get by by behaving cooperatively from time to time only. Note that the sample applications mentioned in the previous paragraph fulfill this assumption as well.

Equal private costs. A general problem is that the cost of a node, regarding memory, network or CPU consumption, is private information. E.g., a peer connected with a dial-up modem is more interested in saving network bandwidth than one using a leased line. But observing the capabilities of other nodes is difficult. We leave this aside for the time being and assume equal private costs for all nodes. Our protocol could be extended to address different costs by using ProW of different extents.

Messages are not modified during forwarding. We assume that only the issuer of information can have falsified it. For example, a peer may create falsified feedback. But it is unable to intercept a response message and claim to be the peer who has provided the query results. In the presence of cryptographic signatures and the unlimited connectivity of the Internet, this is a realistic assumption: Each peer can ask the issuer of a message to verify its integrity. – This assumption allows us to come up with a protocol that rejects feedback from unknown or uncooperative sources.

No uncooperative behavior at application level. This article leaves aside misbehavior from the application perspective. For example, a node may want to prevent other nodes from obtaining access to a certain (key, value)-pair containing unfavorable information. It might try to accomplish this by running a DoS attack on nodes responsible for the pair. When looking at the storage level in isolation, such an attack consumes resources without providing any benefit. While uncooperative behavior at the application level is an important problem, it is beyond the scope of this article. The problem of free riding at the storage level has to be solved first. In other words, our protocol does not deal with nodes that spend their resources for attacking the network, or that try to discredit a single peer, but behave reliably otherwise.

Verifiability of query results. The issuer of a query must be able to verify the correctness of the result. Otherwise, a node could send back a spoof query result and save the cost for data storage. Verification of query results can take place in two ways. (1) In the case of replication, the node collects the query result from more than one node and forms a quorum. (2) In some applications, any peer can verify the correctness of the query result. For instance, if the CAN is used as a directory for object lookup or web-page annotations, a peer could always check if directory entries are valid. We do not expect any major difficulties when extending our protocol in this direction.

4 A Reliability-Aware CAN Protocol

In the context of our protocol, each peer decides individually if it deems another peer reliable, based on a set of observations from the past. We refer to such observations as *feedback*. Each node can only make observations on operations it is involved in. In our context, a peer accepts another peer as reliable or not – there are no shades in between. We settled for a simple reliability model because a sophisticated one (cf. [18]) would lead to a binary decision just as well. In addition, information about other nodes are always imperfect, hence a rich model would only mock a degree of accuracy that is not achievable in reality.

Our protocol has four aspects:
- Peers observe nodes and generate feedback (Subsection 4.2),
- share feedback with others (Subsection 4.3),
- administer feedback in their repository (Subsection 4.4),
- use feedback to bypass unreliable peers (Subsection 4.5).

4.1 Data Structures

Our implementation contains two classes *FeedbackRepository* and *Feedback*. They refer to classes already used in enhanced CAN, notably *ContactCache* and *Message*. Feedback objects bear feedback information. The node a Feedback object refers to is the *feedback subject*. Further, a Feedback object contains a *timestamp* and the ID of the peer that has generated the feedback, the *feedback originator*. Each node has one private Feedback-Repository object that implements its feedback repository. It stores t Feedback objects, for s_r peers each. It has methods for checking the reliability of a peer and for selecting Feedback objects to be shipped to other peers. Table 1 lists all relevant parameters. We discuss their default values in Subsection 5.1.

4.2 Generating Feedback

A peer assumes that another peer is reliable if its feedback repository contains at least t Feedback objects referring to that peer. Because peers may change their behavior, Feedback objects expire after a period of time (e). Thus, only a continuing stream of positive feedback lets a peer be reliable in the eye of others. Feedback is generated in the following situations:

Table 1. Relevant Parameters.

Protocol-related Parameters

Symbol	Description	Default Value
t	reliability threshold; unit: number of Feedback objects	3
q	number of feedback objects generated for one forward	0.1
e	Feedback object lifetime; unit: experiment clock time units	100,000
b	maximum number of Feedback objects per message	20
s_r	size of feedback repository; unit: number of peers	100
s_c	size of contact cache; unit: number of peers	20

Experiment-related Parameters

Symbol	Description	Default Value
n	number of peers	100,000
d	dimensionality of the key space	2
u	percentage of uncooperative peers	5%

F1 *After joining the CAN, the new peer generates t Feedback objects for the peer who handed over the zone.*

F2 *After receiving an answer to a query, a peer generates one Feedback object for the node that has answered.*

F3 *After observing a message forward, the current peer generates one Feedback object with probability q.*

F4 *After having obtained a ProW, the receiver creates t Feedback objects for the peer that has delivered it.*

F2 acknowledges answering queries. Because forwarding messages consumes less resources than answering queries, F3 generates feedback only with probability q. Finally, providing a ProW (F4) or helping a new peer join the CAN (F1) are strong indications that the peer is cooperative. Because at least t Feedback objects are needed to deem a peer reliable, this is the number of Feedback objects created. In each case, the timestamp of the Feedback object is the current time, and the feedback originator is the current peer. The Feedback object is stored in the feedback repository of the current peer.

Example 3: Consider the situation depicted in Figure 2. Peer R answers a query issued by S. Because T_1 is the peer closest to S that R deems reliable, R sends it the

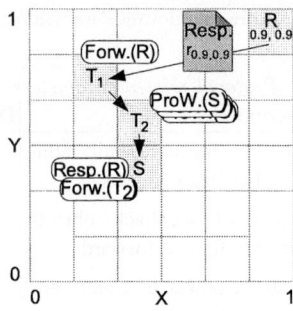

Fig. 2. Sources of feedback.

message. According to F3, T_1 decides to create a Feedback object[1] with subject R, in order to acknowledge that R has forwarded the message. T_1 then forwards the message to T_2. In our example, T_2 does not generate feedback with subject T_1 because this only happens with probability q. The only next peer possible is S, but T_2 does not know if it is reliable or not. Therefore, T_2 asks for a proof of work. S returns this proof, so T_2 creates t Feedback objects with subject S and forwards the message to it. Finally S obtains its answer. It creates one Feedback object with subject R for answering, and one with subject T_2 for forwarding. □

4.3 Disseminating Feedback Information

Sharing feedback between peers results in logical networks of peers that are *transitive*: one peer sees that another one performs useful work and spreads this information to others. To bound the overhead of our protocol, a node appends a small set of b Feedback objects to messages that it sends out anyhow.

Method *generateFeedbackAttachment* (Figure 3) determines an adequate set of Feedback objects to be attached. It is invoked with the outgoing message and the peer the message will be forwarded to. objectives of our feedback dissemination algorithm. Subsection 2.1 has pointed out that each peer needs a well-balanced set of *reliable* contacts to forward messages to. Each peer must be provided with a good set of feedback objects on peers in its contact cache. There are two locations where feedback is helpful:
(1) peers far away from the feedback subject who have the feedback subject in their contact caches, and
(2) neighbors of the feedback subject.

According to (1), method generateFeedbackAttachment first selects Feedback objects whose subjects have forwarded the current message. It starts with the node that has forwarded the message directly to it, and selects all feedback from its repository regarding that node. The procedure recurs with the next peer in the chain of the last forwarders, until there are $b/2$ feedback objects in the attachment, or the issuer of the message is reached. Regarding (2), the current peer then looks at the peer it intends to

---
[1] Rounded rectangles stand for Feedback objects, located next to their originator, with the feedback subject in parentheses.

```
1  generateFeedbackAttachment(Message m, TargetPeer P_t) {
2      FeedbackAttachment F := ∅;
3      // (1) get Feedback objects about the last forwarders
4      forall (p ∈ m.lastForwarders in chronological order) {
5          Feedback F' := {f | p = f.subject ∧ f ∈
6      this.FeedbackRepository };
7          add F' to F;
8          if (|F| > b/2) break;
9      }
10     // (2) get feedback objects close to P_t
11     sort this.FeedbackRepository by dist(P_t, f.subject) with f ∈
12     this.FeedbackRepository;
13     forall (f ∈ this.FeedbackRepository ∧ f.subject ≠ P_t) {
14         add f to F;
15         if (|F| > b) break;
16     }
17     return F;
18 }
```

Fig. 3. Feedback Dissemination

forward the message to. It orders the feedback objects in its repository by the distance of the subject and the target peer. It then adds objects from the top of the list to the attachment of the message until its size is b.

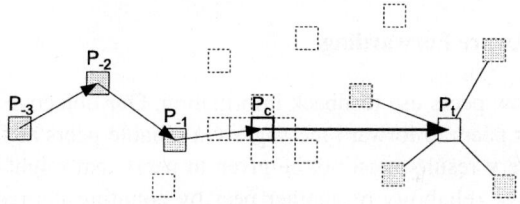

Fig. 4. Forwarding Feedback.

Example 4: Suppose the peer P_c in Figure 4 is about to forward a message to P_t. Peers that have forwarded the message in the past are labeled with P_{-1}, P_{-2}, P_{-3}. Other peers known by P_c are shown as dashed boxes. Assume P_c has feedback available about all peers depicted in the figure. It has to determine b objects to be attached to the message. Following our protocol, P_c will select Feedback objects whose subjects are the nodes in light grey. □

4.4 Managing Local Feedback Objects

Each peer administers a repository of Feedback objects. It must decide which objects should be inserted into or removed from the repository. Some rules for removal are simple – feedback that has expired can be discarded. Insertion is more complex: with the protocol described so far, the number of incoming or newly generated Feedback objects is very large. Thus, when obtaining feedback, a node works off the following rules:

R1 *If a Feedback object is part of a message from a peer that the current peer does not deem reliable, then discard it.*
R2 *If the timestamp of a Feedback object is older than e, then discard it.*
R3 *If the repository contains a Feedback object s.t.*
  - *both the originators and the subjects of the incoming Feedback object and the one in the feedback repository are identical, and*
  - *the originator of the feedback is different from the current peer,*

  then keep the object whose timestamp is newer, and discard the other one.
R4 *If the feedback repository already contains at least t Feedback objects about the same feedback subject, append the incoming one, and remove the Feedback object with the oldest timestamp.*

R1–R3 ensure that the feedback repository contains up-to-date feedback from reliable sources. R3 prevents from perceiving a peer as reliable based on observations of a single node only. An exception is feedback from the current node itself. R4 avoids unnecessarily large numbers of Feedback objects. Since t objects are already sufficient for reliability, more feedback does not provide any further value. Having survived Rules R1–R4, a Feedback object is added to the feedback repository. If the size of the repository exceeds $s_r \times t$, all Feedback objects regarding one peer are removed. That peer is the one with the smallest number of valid Feedback objects. This is natural, because peers can set unreliable peers aside, but want to keep useful ones.

4.5 Reliability-Aware Forwarding

We now explain how peers use feedback information. Our objective is twofold: on the one hand, we want peers to forward messages via reliable peers as far as possible. On the other hand, query results must not be given to peers that might be uncooperative. A peer estimates the reliability of another peer by counting the respective Feedback objects in its feedback repository. If the number is at least threshold t, it is reliable. A valid Feedback object is one that has passed the rules from Subsection 4.4.

Method *forwardMessage* (Figure 5) is responsible for sending messages to appropriate peers. Note that Message m, which is parameter of *forwardMessage*, always contains a key to determine the target of the message in the key space. If the message is not a query, the key is the center of the zone of the target peer. Reliability-aware greedy forwarding now works as follows: each peer wants to find not only a close, but a close *reliable* node that is nearer to the target of the message than itself. If the peer has such a node in its contact cache, it sends it the message. If not, it makes a distinction between query results and other messages.

Query Results: If the current peer wants to forward a query result, it does so to one of its (possibly unreliable) neighbors in the right direction, but asks for a ProW before doing so. If the ProW arrives in time, it forwards the message to the neighbor. Otherwise, the peer tries another neighbor. In the extreme situation that there is no further contact, the current peer drops the message. [19] tells us that a P2P system must not provide any service to nodes that have not yet proven their willingness to cooperate. Therefore such messages must not go to unknown peers until they have proven their reliability.

FairNet – How to Counter Free Riding in Peer-to-Peer Data Structures   347

```
 1  forwardMessage(Message m) {
 2      // determine candidates to forward the message to
 3      CandidatePeers C := {p | dist(p, m.key) < dist(this, m.key) ∧ p
 4      ∈ this.ContactCache };
 5      sort C by dist(m.key, p) with p ∈ C;
 6
 7      // search for a reliable addressee
 8      forall (p ∈ C) {
 9          Feedback F := {f | f.subject = p ∧ f.type = positive ∧ f
10          ∈ this.FeedbackRepository};
11          if (|F| ≥ t) {
12              m.attachment = generateFeedbackAttachment(m, p);
13              send(m, p);
14              return;
15          }
16      }
17      // the current peer does not know a reliable node
18      if (m.type = query result) {
19          Neighbors N := all neighbors of this in C;
20          forall (p ∈ N) {
21              requestProW(p);
22              waitForProWAnswer (timeout);
23              if (ProW answer returned in time) {
24                  generateFeedback(p);
25                  m.attachment = generateFeedbackAttachment(m, p);
26                  send(m, p);
27                  break;
28              }
29          }
30      } else {
31          Peer p := first element in C;
32          m.attachment = generateFeedbackAttachment(m, p);
33          send(m, p);
34      }
35  }
```

Fig. 5. Reliability-Aware Forwarding in CAN.

The ProW is limited to neighbors for security reasons: this prevents peers from asking random other ones for a ProW in order to perform DoS attacks.

At first sight, carrying out ProW in the context of evaluation of queries issued by other peers is not dominant. However, recall our assumption that peers issue queries at a steady rate. A peer with a poor standing would have to carry out a ProW insignificantly later anyhow, when issuing a query itself. Besides that, doing a ProW now does not delay the evaluation of its own query later on. – Further, ProW might seem to be a disincentive to join the network. But the issue is application-specific, i.e., is the benefit from joining the CAN higher than the ProW cost plus the cost of processing queries? Our experiments in Section 5 indicate that the number of ProW is rather small, so the answer to the question should be affirmative in most scenarios.

Other Messages: If a message is not a query result, an uncooperative node cannot benefit from it. So the current peer selects the peer closest to the message key from its contact list and sends it the message. A node that is not reliable in the eye of others is either uncooperative or did not yet have a chance to prove its cooperativeness. The hope is that the second case is true.

4.6 Discussion

So far, we have described a protocol that detects and excludes uncooperative nodes. Let us say why this is the case: Recall that a node is uncooperative if it tries to benefit from the network with little effort. There are two ways to do so: (1) suppress messages, by not answering or not forwarding them, (2) propagate spoof feedback, be it with the peer in question as subject, be it with another peer. Both variants do not result in any benefit: Namely, messages travel via chains of reliable peers, whenever possible. Only messages containing no query results are sent to unknown, but not necessarily uncooperative peers. Integration of peers depends on observations made by reliable peers. Every peer discards incoming feedback from a peer that it does not deems reliable. Since feedback expires after some of time, peers have to keep proving their reliability.

Applicability of the protocol is important as well. Because our protocol bypasses not only uncooperative peers, but also suspicious ones, the number of peers forwarding a message increases. On the other hand, many lost messages have to be repeated in conventional CAN protocols in the presence of free riders. So their costs are not as low as it seems at first sight. Furthermore, peers do not send out messages only to share feedback information with our protocol, and all information attached to a message is strictly limited in size. Finally, logical networks of peers make it unnecessary that a peer stores feedback about all other peers.

Our protocol gives rise to many questions. The effectiveness of our selection policy of Feedback objects to be forwarded is unclear. Next, small contact caches ($s_c < 0.02\%$ of all peers) have turned out to be surprisingly efficient for enhanced CAN [15]. We wonder if small contact caches and feedback repositories, together with a small number of Feedback objects appended, is effective as well. Here, effectiveness means 'good differentiation between cooperative and uncooperative peers, with moderate overhead'. We will now address these questions experimentally.

5 Experimental Evaluation

We have evaluated our reliability-aware CAN protocol by means of extensive experiments. The most important question is as follows: How well does the protocol detect uncooperative behavior (Subsection 5.3)? Put differently, does it pay to be cooperative from the perspective of an individual node? Subsection 5.2 addresses another question: What is the overhead of our reliability-aware CAN protocol, as opposed to the other protocols from this article?

Our cost measure is the number of message hops, i.e., the number of peers involved in a single CAN operation. This is in line with other research on DHT [20]. This article leaves aside characteristics of the physical network, such as total latency. We have an implementation of CAN that is fully operational, and our experiments use it as a platform. All experiments ran on a cluster of 32 loosely coupled PC, equipped with 2 GHz CPU, 2 GB RAM and 100 MBit Ethernet each. [21] provides more information on our experimental framework.

5.1 Determining Parameter Values

For the evaluation, we must come up with meaningful parameter values (cf. Table 1).

n, d: The claim behind CAN is web scalability. However, with existing CAN protocols where free riders remain unknown, scalability is bounded. The longer the paths, the larger the probability that a message is lost (cf. Example 2). To verify that this is not the case with our protocol, we have a large number of peers (100,000) and a small dimensionality (2), in order to have long paths. Real applications would use a larger d.

s_c: [15] has shown that a contact cache of size 20 is adequate, even for large networks.

u: In P2P networks without sanctions against free riders, their number is large [22]. In our setting in turn, cooperative behavior is expected to dominate. Hence, a fraction of 5% of uncooperative peers is a highly conservative value.

s_r, b: Feedback objects are small, i.e., a few bytes for the identifiers of feedback subject and object and the timestamp. However, their number should be limited, because processing them is resource-consuming. We estimate that 20 Feedback objects attached to a message and a feedback repository size of 100 are viable, even for mobile devices.

q: The number of Feedback objects generated for each forward depends on the application on top of the CAN. We assume that storing data and answering queries is ten times as expensive as forwarding messages. So we set q to 0.1.

t, e: Threshold t and lifetime[2] e are security-relevant parameters. A low threshold t and a high value for e allow uncooperative peers to get by with processing only few incoming messages. The opposite case, i.e., large t and small e, would burden cooperative peers with ProW requests. We use values $t = 3$ and $e = 100,000$, obtained from previous experiments (not described here for lack of space).

5.2 Performance Aspects

We anticipate that the number of hops per message is higher with the reliability-aware CAN protocol, than with the enhanced CAN. The reason is that the target node of a message is not the node that is closest to the destination, but the closest *reliable* node. An experiment examines these issues quantitatively. Next to the number of hops, we are also interested in the number of proofs of work requested. A proof of work[3] also leads to an additional pair of messages.

This experiment uses 2,000,000 queries whose keys are uniformly distributed. We also have carried out experiments with real data, but they do not provide any further insight. We omit them here for lack of space. In order to compare the overhead of our protocol with the enhanced CAN running on optimal conditions, we use cooperative nodes only. In the presence of free riders, enhanced CAN would loose many messages,

---

[2] Here the unit of time is given in experiment clock cycles, i.e., this is the number of queries issued.

[3] We are interested in general characteristics of the reliability-aware CAN. To this end, it is sufficient to simulate the proof of work. The advantage is that this does not slow down the experiments.

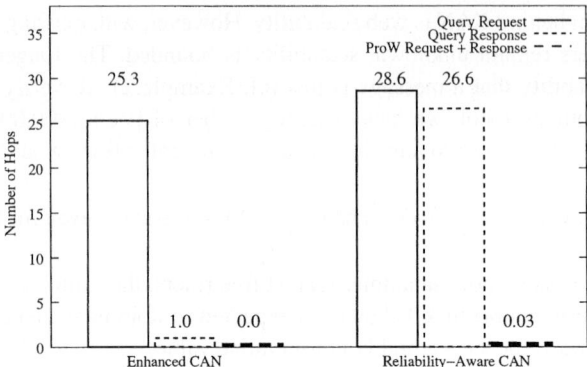

Fig. 6. Total number of hops.

distorting the measurement results. In other words, the setup lets enhanced CAN looks better.

After an initialization period of 500,000 queries, we counted the message hops for each query. We distinguish between message hops necessary to deliver the query itself, those necessary to return the result, and those necessary to request and to return a ProW. Figure 6 graphs the number of hops per query. The figure tells us that the overhead (number of message hops) of the reliability-aware protocol for cooperative nodes is reasonable. Delivering queries only takes slightly more hops in the reliability-aware CAN than in the enhanced CAN. Clearly, our protocol must forward query results between reliable nodes instead of returning them directly to the issuer. So the number of hops is now around twice as large, which we deem acceptable. Finally, the number of proofs of work is tolerable as well.

5.3 Effectiveness

Uncooperative peers try to reach their goals with minimal effort. A peer may try to trick the feedback mechanism by processing only a fraction of incoming messages, hoping that this is sufficient to become cooperative in the eyes of other peers. In what follows, we examine if this kind of uncooperative behavior may be successful. To do so, we have refined the uncooperative peers. First, they never return proofs of work requested. This is natural because these are the most costly requests. Second, they react to some, but not all incoming messages. The percentage of messages reacted to is a parameter that we adjust in our experiments. In what follows, 50 peers are reacting with 0% probability, another 50 with 1% and so on up to 99%. The remaining peers are fully cooperative. Our objective is to block all uncooperative peers, independent of the degree of uncooperativeness, and serve only fully cooperative ones.

Each peer corresponds to a point in the xy-plane in Figure 7. The x-coordinate of a peer is the percentage of the messages it reacts to. Its y-coordinate is the rate of its queries that are successful. In other words, a fully cooperative peer that does not obtain any result to its queries corresponds to Point B. A fully uncooperative peer that obtains results to all of its queries corresponds to Point D. There should not be any such peers; and our

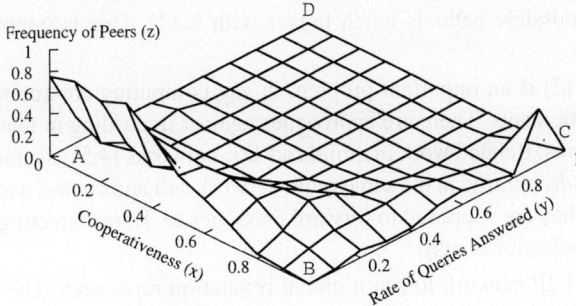

Fig. 7. Behavior vs. Benefits

protocol works well if uncooperative peers have a low rate of 'successful' queries. Note that we can already 'declare success' if a lower degree of cooperation leads to a much lower rate of 'successful' queries *on average*. The reason is that this is sufficient to deter uncooperative behavior.

The z-axis is the number of peers that correspond to the point in the xy-plane. For instance, consider the z-values corresponding to points on the y-axis, i.e., fully uncooperative peers. There are no fully uncooperative peers that benefit much from the CAN, since $z = 0$ for $y > 0.3$. This is a positive result. Analogously, consider the z-values corresponding to points with $x = 1$, i.e., fully cooperative peers. The y-coordinate of most of these points falls into the interval $[0.8; 1.0]$. In other words, cooperative peers have most of their queries answered. This is again positive. Note that the values on the z-axis are scaled to 1 in the direction of peers with the same degree of cooperativeness. That is, the sum of all peers with the same behavior equals 1. This is why the elevation at the bottom left of the figure is very high. Finally, the figure tells us that the CAN more or less blocks all peers that are uncooperative and serves only cooperative ones. This is in line with our objective mentioned above. Our main result is that the protocol levels up to our objectives. Cooperative behavior actually pays off.

6 Related Work

Distributed Hash Tables administer a large number of (key, value)-pairs in a distributed manner, with high scalability. The variants, next to CAN, differ primarily in the topology of the key space. *LH** [23] determines nodes responsible for a certain key statically by its hash function. *Chord* [12] organizes the data in a circular one-dimensional data space. Messages travel from peer to peer in one direction through the cycle, until the peer whose ID is closest to the key of the query has been found. *Pastry, Tapestry* [13,14] use a Plaxton Mesh to store and locate its data. The forwarding algorithm is similar to the one of Chord. Pastry and Tapestry forward to peers such that the common prefix of the ID and the query key becomes longer with each hop. Because of the organization as a Plaxton Mesh, multiple routes to the addressed position in the data space are possible. With CAN in turn, the number of possible alternative routes for forwarding messages increases with the number of neighbors, i.e., with the dimensionality of the key space.

The choice of possible paths is much bigger with CAN. This is important to bypass unreliable peers.

Free riding [2] is an important problem in any computing environment with many anonymous participants. There are approaches against free riding in many different application scenarios. Related work in mobile ad-hoc networks [4,5] assumes that adjacent nodes can eavesdrop traffic in the same radio network cell and control access to the parts of the network they are supposed to forward messages to. Here, detecting and punishing uncooperative behavior is easy.

[10] uses a P2P network to run a global reputation repository. The approach does not address most of the questions that are relevant in our context, e.g.: Who should be allowed to give feedback? What to do with feedback that comes from untrusted peers? What happens if the originator of a feedback item becomes malicious? From a different perspective, our contribution is a tight coupling of reliability management and message forwarding in P2P networks. [10] in turn deals with trust management on top of such a network.

Another approach to rule out uncooperative behavior is based on micropayments [9, 24]. But while monetary schemes provide a clean economic model, infrastructure costs may simply be too high in a setting such as ours. A further disadvantage is that they require a central bank. This is not in line with our design rationale.

[11] offers a direct way of sharing reputation information without intermediaries. Every peer describes each other node with a rating coefficient, i.e., a numeric value. The coefficients are shared after every transaction between nodes involved. A node updates its coefficients by adding the new value weighted by the coefficient of the sender. This is not applicable to large networks because the way of updating coefficients limits reputational information to nodes next to the rated node.

Banning uncooperative nodes may also be the result of using Public Key Cryptography. Public Key Certificates signed by a large number of peers provide verifiable identities [8]. The idea is that groups of peers are mutually verifying and signing their identities. Unfortunately, whenever such a group recognizes that one of their members became uncooperative, certificates must be revoked. In other words, an individual uncooperative peer may break its entire group.

7 Conclusions

This article has presented a CAN protocol that deals with one of the biggest obstacles in P2P systems, namely free riding. In CAN, uncooperative peers basically are those that do not process incoming messages related to queries issued by other nodes. Our protocol explicitly acknowledges work carried out by peers. This facilitates the emergence of self-organized virtual networks within the CAN. The protocol ensures that unreliable peers do not obtain any benefits. Uncooperative behavior is unattractive. The 'downside' of the protocol are slightly longer message paths, in order to bypass unreliable peers, and a number of proofs of work that seemingly unreliable nodes must perform. Several issues remain open for future research. We for our part want to address security issues.

References

1. Ratnasamy et al., S.: A Scalable Content-Addressable Network. In: Proceedings of the ACM SIGCOMM 2001 Conference, New York, ACM Press (2001) 161–172
2. Ramaswamy, L., Liu, L.: Free riding: A new challenge to peer-to-peer file sharing systems (2003)
3. Axelrod, R.: The Evolution of Cooperation. Basic Books, New York (1984)
4. Buchegger, S., Boudec, J.Y.L.: Coping with False Accusations in Misbehavior Reputation Systems for Mobile Ad-hoc Networks. Technical Report IC/2003/31, EPFL, EPFL-IC-LCA CH-1015 Lausanne, Switzerland (2003)
5. Buttyan, L., Hubaux, J.P.: Enforcing Service Availability in Mobile Ad-Hoc WANs. In: Proceedings of the 1st ACM International Symposium on Mobile Ad Hoc Networking & Computing, IEEE Press (2000) 87–96
6. Marti et al., S.: Mitigating Routing Misbehavior in Mobile Ad Hoc Networks. In: Mobile Computing and Networking. (2000) 255–265
7. Srinivasan et al., V.: Cooperation in Wireless Ad Hoc Networks. In: Proceedings of the IEEE INFOCOM. (2003)
8. Gokhale, S., Dasgupta, P.: Distributed Authentication for Peer-to-Peer Networks. Workshop on Security and Assurance in Ad hoc Networks. (2003)
9. Golle et al., P.: Incentives for Sharing in Peer-to-Peer Networks. LNCS **2232** (2001) 75ff.
10. Aberer, K., Despotovic, Z.: Managing Trust in a Peer-2-Peer Information System. In: Proceedings of the CIKM-01, New York (2001) 310–317
11. Padovan et al., B.: A Prototype for an Agent based Secure Electronic Marketplace Including Reputation Tracking Mechanisms. In: HICSS. (2001)
12. Stoica et al., I.: Chord: A Scalable Peer-To-Peer Lookup Service for Internet Applications. In: Proceedings of the ACM SIGCOMM 2001 Conference. (2001) 149–160
13. Rowstron, A., Druschel, P.: Pastry: Scalable, Decentralized Object Location, and Routing for Large-Scale Peer-to-Peer Systems. In: IFIP/ACM International Conference on Distributed Systems Platforms. (2001) 329–350
14. Zhao, B.Y., Kubiatowicz, J., Joseph, A.D.: Tapestry: an infrastructure for fault-resilient wide-area location and routing. Technical Report UCB//CSD-01-1141, University of California at Berkeley (2001)
15. Buchmann, E., Böhm, K.: Efficient Routing in Distributed Scalable Data Structures (in German). In: Proceedings of the 10th Conference on Database Systems for Business, Technology and Web. (2003)
16. Back, A.: Hashcash – A Denial of Service Counter-Measure. http://www.cypherspace.org/~adam/hashcash/ (2002)
17. Jakobsson, M., Juels, A.: Proofs of work and bread pudding protocols. In: In Proceedings of the IFIP TC6 and TC11 Joint Working Conference on Communications and Multimedia Security (CMS '99), Leuven, Belgium. (1999)
18. Xiong, L., Liu, L.: A Reputation-Based Trust Model For Peer-To-Peer Ecommerce Communities. In: IEEE Conference on E-Commerce (CEC'03). (2003)
19. Friedman, E., Resnick, P.: The Social Cost of Cheap Pseudonyms. Journal of Economics and Management Strategy **10** (1998) 173–199
20. Kleinberg, J.: The Small-World Phenomenon: An Algorithmic Perspective. In: Proceedings of the 32nd ACM Symposium on Theory of Computing. (2000)
21. Buchmann, E., Böhm, K.: How to Run Experiments with Large Peer-to-Peer Data Structures. In: Proceedings of the 18th International Parallel and Distributed Processing Symposium, Santa Fe, USA. (2004)
22. Adar, E., Huberman, B.: Free Riding on Gnutella. First Monday **5** (2000)

23. Litwin, W., Neimat, M.A., Schneider, D.A.: LH* - Linear Hashing for Distributed Files. In Buneman, P., Jajodia, S., eds.: Proceedings of the 1993 ACM SIGMOD International Conference on Management of Data, Washington, D.C., May 26-28, 1993, ACM Press (1993) 327–336
24. Yang, B., Garcia-Molina, H.: PPay: micropayments for peer-to-peer systems. In Atluri, V., Liu, P., eds.: Proceedings of the 10th ACM Conference on Computer and Communication Security (CCS-03), New York, ACM Press (2003) 300–310

Supporting Collaborative Layouting in Word Processing

Thomas B. Hodel, Dominik Businger, and Klaus R. Dittrich

University of Zurich, Department of Informatics
Winterthurerstr. 190, CH-8057 Zürich, Switzerland
{hodel, dittrich}@ifi.unizh.ch, businger@isb.unizh.ch,
http://www.ifi.unizh.ch/

Abstract. Collaborative layouting occurs when a group of people simultaneously defines the layout of a document at the same time into a coherent set of meaningful styles. This activity is characterized by emergence, where the participants' shared understanding develops gradually as they interact with each other and the source material. Our goal is to support collaborative layouting in a distributed environment. To achieve this, we first observed how face-to-face groups perform collaborative layouting in a particular work context. We report about the design and evaluation of a system which provides a large workspace and several objects that encourage emergence in collaboration conflicts. People edit documents that contain the raw text and they enhance the readability by layouting this content.

1 Introduction

A significant gap lies between the handling of business data (customer, product, finance, etc.) and text data (documents). Documents are not treated as a product even though a lot of companies' knowledge is stored within this structure. For a large-scale document management environment, local copies of remote data sources are often made. However, it is often difficult to monitor the sources in order to check for changes and to download changed data items to the copies. Very often, text documents are stored somewhere within a confusing file structure with an inscrutable hierarchy and low security. On the other hand, for operational functional data the infrastructure and the data are highly secure, multi-user capable and available to several other tools for compiling reports, data provenance, content and knowledge. Collaborative processes can be defined and applied to such data.

In this paper, we focus on the database-based collaborative layouting problem within documents. Based on a database-based collaborative editor, collaborative layouting processes are developed. The presented algorithms enable collaborative structuring of text for layout-, styles-, flows-, notes-, or security purposes, with a fast and constant transaction time, independent of the amount of the affected objects. In part two, we present approaches for multidimensional structuring of text. Then, in part three, we evaluate the chosen approach and describe the developed collaborative database-based algorithms. Part four discusses collaboration conflicts and concludes the paper.

1.1 Problem Description

Numerous word processing systems exist for documents, but no accurate collaborative layouting system is available (and no database-based text editor). According to our knowledge (see also part 1.3), no standard word processing application provides this functionality. Under a collaborative layouting system we understand the possibility to define the layout or to apply styles/templates simultaneously.

Implementing such functionalities involves several aspects. The layouting system has to be designed in such a way that it is collaborative, i.e. that several people can define, add, delete and change the layout or apply templates simultaneously within the same document, and can immediately see actions carried out by other people. The defined layout, or part of it, should be dynamically changeable, as long as only a certain person has the permission to apply modification to it, and the consistency of the whole style can be guaranteed.

1.2 Underlying Concepts

The concept of dynamic, collaborative layouting requires an appropriate architectural foundation. The lowest level is a collaborative editing / document management system. Our concept and implementation is based on the TeNDaX [6] collaborative editing system, which we briefly introduce.

TeNDaX is a **T**ext **N**ative **Da**tabase e**X**tension and makes use of such a philosophy for texts. It enables the storage of text in databases in a native form so that editing text is finally represented as real-time transactions. Under the term 'text editing' we understand the following: writing and deleting text (characters), copying & pasting text, defining text layout & structure, inserting tables, pictures, and so on i.e. all the actions regularly carried out by word processing users. With 'real-time transaction' we mean that editing text (e.g. writing a character/word, setting the font for a paragraph, or pasting a section of text) invokes one or several database transactions so that everything which is typed appears within the editor as soon as these objects are stored persistently. Instead of creating files and storing them in a file system, the content of documents is stored in a special way in the database, which enables very fast real-time transactions for all editing processes [7].

The database schema and the above-mentioned transactions are created in such a way that everything can be done within a multi-user environment, as approved by database technology. As a consequence, many of the achievements (with respect to data organization and querying, recovery, integrity and security enforcement, multi-user operation, distribution management, uniform tool access, etc.) are now, by means of this approach, also available for word processing.

TeNDaX proposes a radically different approach, centered on natively representing text in fully-fledged databases, and incorporating all necessary collaboration support. Under collaboration support we understand functions such as editing, awareness, fine-grained security, sophisticated document management, versioning, business processes, text structure, data lineage, metadata mining, and multi-channel publishing - all within a collaborative, real-time and multi-user environment.

TeNDaX creates an extension of DBMS to manage text. This addition is carried out 'cleanly' and the responding data type represents a 'first-class citizen' [1] of a DBMS (e.g. integers, character strings, etc.).

1.3 Related Work

Only very little is available in the literature concerning the storage of layout and structure information of text documents in databases for collaborative applications work.

[8] discusses various mechanisms for storing multimedia content in databases. It focuses on the handling of object types, DTDs and automatic object type creation, whereas the main goal of this paper is not only to show ways of storing structure information about text documents, but also how to maintain the integrity of this information in a collaborative multi-user word processor application.

The Reduce project [13] implements a word processor that enables users to edit any part of a text document at any time in a collaborative way. The prototype CoWord [12] works as a plug-in for Microsoft Word, enhancing it with those collaboration features. The basis of documents that can be edited with CoWord are files, whereas this paper introduces data structures and algorithms for storing and editing text documents and their layout and structure information in a database. Unfortunately, hardly anything has been published about the internal mechanisms and data structures used by CoWord, thus making it impossible to compare it with the work done in TeNDaX. Apart from CoWord, no other collaborative word processor has been found which can handle layout information, and the editor from the TeNDaX project seems to be the only one to store all its data in a database.

[2,3,9,10,14] describe approaches used in the well-known document formats MS-Word-Doc, Adobe PDF and the Rich Text Format. All those documents describe how complex layout and structure information can be stored in files, but the mechanisms described are neither applicable for storing such information in databases nor do they account for collaborative issues, which are the two main subjects in this paper. Nonetheless concepts from these papers helped in finding an efficient way of storing layout information in databases for collaborative applications, as described in this paper.

Further important resources for ideas concerning how to maintain and synchronize layout and structuring information for text documents both in databases and other applications, were taken from the documentation of the javax.swing.text classes [11].

2 Approaches for Multidimensional Structuring of Text

To use the following terminology: Whenever the term '**text document**' is used here, it refers to the digital representation of a text, either in memory or, on storage. A '**TextBlockElement**' is a logical entity that represents a section of a text document between a start and an end point in a document. Both, the start and the end point of such a TextBlockElement will be called '**borders**' of a TextBlockElement. An arbitrary number of visible or invisible characters, paragraph and page properties together define a '**style**' with a style name. Such a style can be applied to a

TextBlockElement. One or more styles together build a so-called **'style sheet'** that can be assigned to a text document. Each style's name in a style sheet is unique for that particular style sheet. Assuming that style sheet A and style sheet B have styles with the same defined names, the layout of the text document can be changed by changing the style sheet assigned to it.

2.1 Multidimensional Structuring of Text

A text document's main purpose is to represent text. To increase the benefits and the readability of text documents, one can structure them in multiple dimensions. Most obviously, the text can be split into sentences, paragraphs, pages, chapters and so on. In addition to that, the readability can be further enhanced by using different styles to display the letters, e.g. bold, italic, underlined, different fonts and font sizes, and so forth.

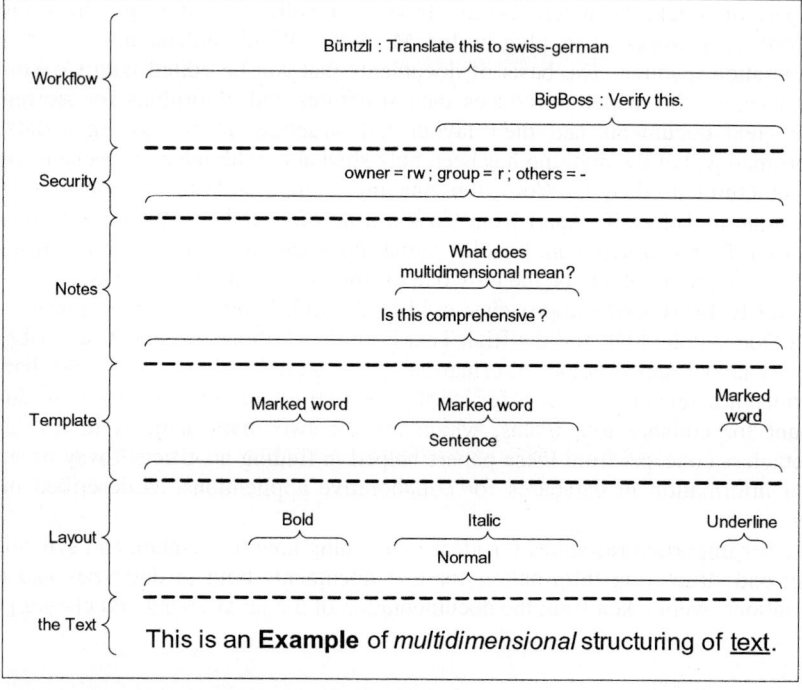

Fig. 1. Example for multidimensional structuring of text

When working together on a text document, other features have proven to be very useful too, such as having a possibility to add comments to a certain section in the text, to limit the read-write access on text, or to specify tasks that someone has to do with a certain part of the text. All of these applications depend on the fact that one can define a number of consequent characters as an entity or element in the text and can link such an element with the data defining its properties. Such a TextBlockElement could then define a logical block of the text (line, paragraph, chapter or book) or contain any data assigned to that section of text, as for example a comment or security information on it. In this way, a text document can be structured in multiple dimensions (see Fig. 1.).

As the layout of a text is one of the most complicated dimensions of such a structured text, the rest of the paper will mainly be focused on issues concerning the storage and handling of layout information in a collaborative database-driven application. All of the conclusions drawn from that can equally be applied to any of the other dimensions.

2.2 Categories of Layout Information

The main reason for applying layout to a text, is to structure a text to enhance its read- and understandability. Such a structure most likely originates from a logical structure that the author sees behind the text. It can be - but doesn't have to be - visually expressed.

There are different ways to structure a text. The simplest way is to use punctuation and line breaks. This can be accomplished by just adding the punctuation characters or invisible line break characters into the string that represents the text document. With these two tools the readability of a text can already be enhanced dramatically.

Furthermore, one can apply different text attributes to any number of consequent characters to mark them or to divide long texts into titles, subtitles lists and normal text. This is a bit more complicated than simply adding punctuation and line breaks, since a whole section of characters has to be defined as one logical entity, in this case represented by a TextBlockElement. This shall be done in a memory saving manner and the TextBlockElements integrity shall be maintainable at a minimum number of operations when altering the text document before, inside or after the section represented by the TextBlockElement.

Those TextBlockElements can either have an arbitrary set of properties or a predefined set of properties as defined in a logical style. Such a logical style is preferably defined in one central location, as for example in a style sheet (e.g. a CSS file, Cascading Style Sheet), together with all the other styles available in the text document to separate layout information from the text as far as possible. Each TextBlockElement represents a section of text in the document and has to move, shrink and grow as the text in the document is being edited. The combination of all the TextBlockElements comprises the logical structures of the document and these have to be stored together with the text.

2.3 Common Practices for Storing Layout Information in Files

All word processors that can handle layout information have implemented a way of handling and storing the text and the layout information of a document together. There are several different approaches from which different concepts can be adapted and enhanced in a database solution.
- Define a TextBlockElement as an object and assign layout and logical information to it. In this case, the text is internally represented not as one string of characters,

but rather as a collection of objects containing parts of the text as strings of characters.
- Blend in the definition of the TextBlockElements as a sequence of normal characters into the string of characters that build up the actual text. When loading such a document, the encoded information has to be parsed out of the string of characters and then visualized accordingly. Any mark-up language such as HTML or XML, works like that. Even compound documents in Rich Text Format (RTF) function this way.
- Define TextBlockElements as objects separate from the string of characters that build up the text, and give TextBlockElements pointers to the first and last characters which are represented by the TextBlockElements.

For supporting multidimensional structuring of text, the third option proved to be the most efficient one.

2.4 SGML and Markup

Markup languages, like HTML, have proven to be very powerful in their ability to layout text and those such as XML, in representing machine readable data. Both are Standard Generalized Markup Languages (SGMLs) and share the concept that a string stored in a text file is recursively divided into sections by SGML tags to represent the structure of the data stored in the string in a tree manner. The tree only emerges from the string when it is parsed for the according tags.

2.5 Storing of Text and TextBlockElements in TeNDaX

In TeNDaX no text files are used to represent the text, but on the server side a chain of CChar objects is stored in the database, and on the client side there is an array of character objects. The reasons why this structure is the best choice and offers a high level of performance are described in [4,5]. To add structuring information like the SGML-Structure of an HTML document to a file stored in TeNDaX, many different methods are available. In the following section some of these are presented and discussed.

2.5.1 As Attributes of Each Character
When every character is stored as a character object, the most "simple" way of storing layout information on text might appear to be storing it as additional attributes on every character (see Fig. 2.). This sounds very straight forward but brings considerable disadvantages with it. First, there's a serious performance issue, both when it comes to the used memory and to necessary operations on changes. The space issue can be solved by using pointers to additional objects storing all the layout data for one or more sections of identically formatted text.

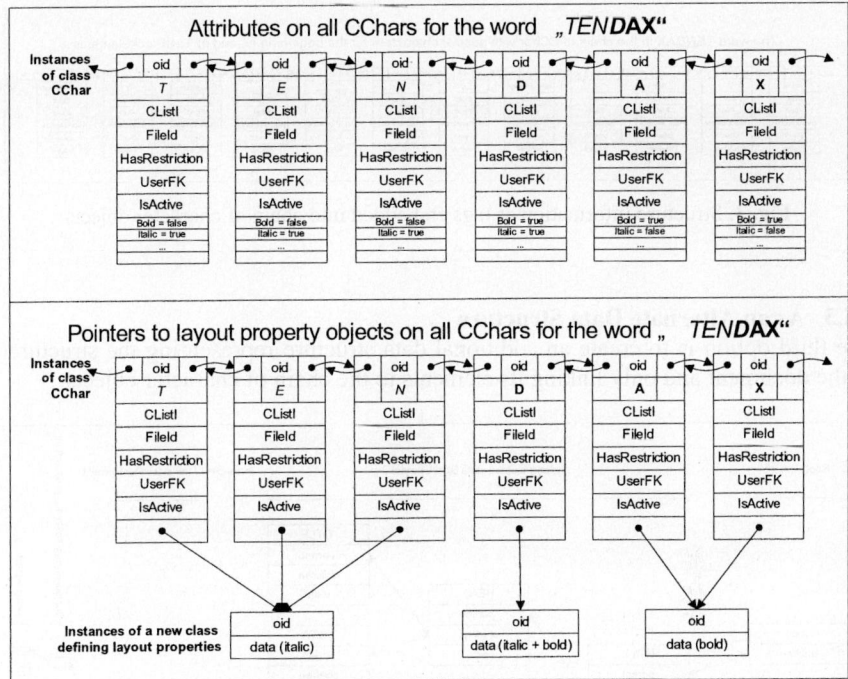

Fig. 2. Structure information on each character object

However that still leaves us with the transactional performance issue. For every change in the formatting, each of the concerned character objects has to be altered; in the worst case scenario, this would mean that if someone wanted to change the font size of an entire document, then every single character of the document would first have to be altered, both in the client and in the database.

2.5.2 As Tags of One or Multiple Characters

As shown above, defining structural information on every single character is far too expensive. To decrease these costs the text could be split up into sections and the layout information could be assigned to that section instead of to every single character inside the section (see Fig. 3.). Such sections are also used in HTML, XML or any other SGML, and are defined with so-called tags. The idea is to mark the beginning and the end of a section with a tag. In HTML and XML this is done with a series of predefined characters which are embedded into the text. As in TeNDaX, the characters are stored as objects that can have multiple properties. It would even be possible to use only one single character object to represent such a start- or end-tag.

Either way, there are still serious limitations to that technique. The Client and Database need to be equipped with mechanisms to efficiently insert, find, edit and delete the tags. Furthermore, multidimensional structuring of text becomes very complicated if tags are used, which are inserted into the text.

Fig. 3. Structure information as tags embedded into chain of character objects

2.5.3 As an Alternate Data Structure
The third option is to create an additional data structure representing the structure(s) of the document and only linking its elements to the chain of character objects.

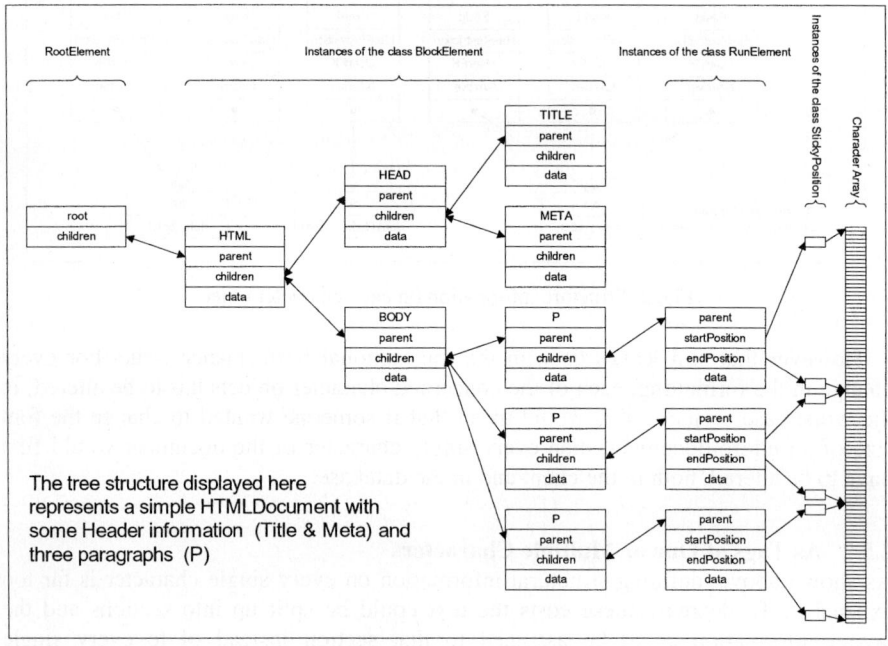

Fig. 4. SGML tree structure in java

In the TeNDaX java client the java classes from the package javax.swing.text can be used to implement this functionality (see Fig. 4.). The HTMLDocument (javax.swing.text.html.HTMLDocument) stores the text internally in an array of characters, and the SGML - Tree that represents the layout of the HTML document which is being stored as a tree consisting of BlockElements and RunElements. Each instance of BlockElement represents a subsection of the text which can in turn be divided into subsections. The leaf of such a branch is then represented by a RunElement which has a pointer to the beginning and to the end of the section in the text.

On the database side there is no need to follow the suggestions made by the java implementation, which is why a simpler but similarly efficient implementation is possible. The question which we had to ask ourselves was: is it really necessary to store the required information in the form of a tree structure, or would a collection of TextBlockElement objects be sufficient? It turned out that a non-hierarchically ordered collection of TextBlockElements on the database side is sufficient for reconstructing the complete tree structure on the client side, as long as certain precautions are taken when synchronizing the client and database.

In the following section of this paper, the newly constructed data structure on the database side will be explained, together with its advantages and disadvantages.

3 Evaluation

Corresponding to the RunElements in java, CTextBlockElements in the database represent a selection of text and contain data that applies to that section. To keep the position and the size of such a section efficiently up-to-date and synchronous with the clients, the start and end borders of the section must somehow be marked in the text. In Java, this is accomplished with instances of the class StickyPosition. A StickyPosition represents the offset of a character in the text and moves together with the character whenever text is inserted or deleted before the StickyPosition. This is done by increasing and decreasing a counter every time text is inserted, depending on the position of the insertion. In the database, with potentially thousands of positions in thousands of documents, this solution would not be efficient enough. A far more efficient way is to add a pointer from the character object after the desired position of the border to the TextBlockElement that starts or ends there. When text is then inserted or deleted before, inside or after the section, the borders are still always before the same character. It's only when deleting the character which actually links the pointer to a border, that care must be taken that the pointer is moved to the next character on the right.

This now enables the definition of sections of text which are unaffected by insert or delete actions. However if one would like to be able to have multiple sections start at the same position (for example, the sections "book 1", "chapter 1" and "paragraph 1" start at the same positions), another data structure is needed.

Instead of having pointers which point directly from the character object to the TextBlockElement object, TextBlockElementBorder objects can be used as an intermediate to implement this 1:n relationship. To simplify things even more, these TextBlockElementBorders don't even need instantiated objects, but only virtual borders represented by a unique identifier. The first character object inside a TextBlockElement has a pointer to such a virtual TextBlockElementBorder, and the TextBlockElement object has as it's start attribute a pointer to the same virtual TextBlockElementBorder. The same applies accordingly to the first character object appearing after the end of the TextBlockElement. A simple example is shown in Fig. 5.

With this data structure it is not only possible to structure a text in one dimension, but rather in multiple dimensions, merely by using a different value for the BlockType attribute in the TextBlockElements in the database and a separate RootElement for the tree structure in the java client.

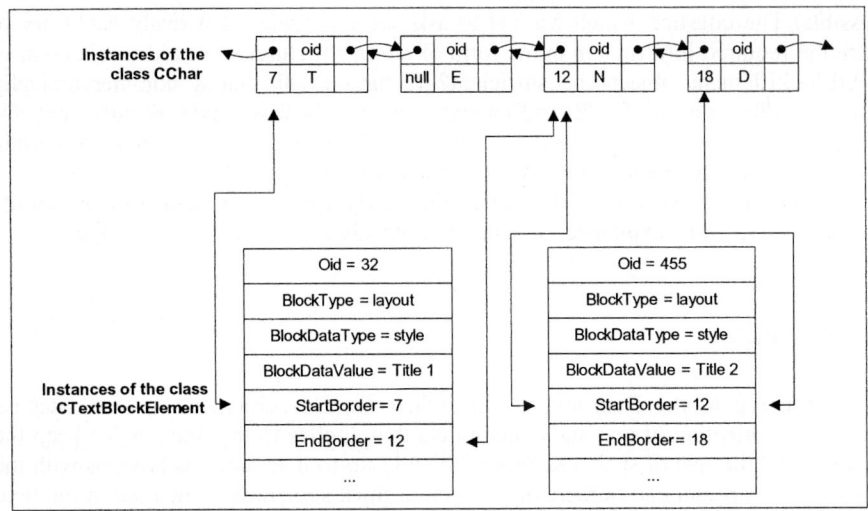

Fig. 5. TextBlockElements on virtual borders

3.1 Loading and Synchronization of Structure Information

As stated earlier, it is not necessary to store the complete SGML tree in the database in order to restore it in or to synchronize it with the clients. As line breaks are already embedded into the chain of character objects in the database, the system doesn't have to take care of splitting other TextBlockElements when a line break is inserted into the text. All other changes in the TextBlockElement tree of the client are directly coupled to the layout and formatting actions taken by the user.

3.1.1 Loading of a Document

When a document is loaded from the database, first the complete set of characters, including all the line breaks, is loaded into the client. Then all the TextBlockElements of the document are loaded, and depending on the type of TextBlockElement used, an action is taken. For layout TextBlockElements this action would be to apply the properties defined in the TextBlockElement object to the section of text it represents. Since all the TextBlockElements have a unique object identifier and since it is always true that a TextBlockElement A, with an identifier higher than TextBlockElement B, is younger than TextBlockElement A, the TextBlockElements of a document can be loaded in a chronological order. This again makes it possible for the java class that manages the tree structure (javax.swing.text.DefaultStyledDocument.ElementBuffer) in the client to reconstruct the tree, so that it then looks identical to any other instance in any other client that currently has the same document open.

3.1.2 Propagating Changes

Whenever a user now initiates a change in the clients TextBlockElement tree, only the action that initialized this change has to be stored and propagated accordingly to the database and to the other clients. The insertion or deletion of one or more characters in the client does not affect the TextBlockElement structure, neither in the client nor in the database.

The only action that has to be taken when deleting a character object from the database, is to check whether or not it carries a pointer to a virtual TextBlockElementBorder A. If this is the case, the pointer to A has to be moved to the next character object on the right that is not being deleted. If this character object already carries a pointer to a virtual TextBlockElementBorder B, the pointer to A can be dismissed and all references to A within the TextBlockElements of this document have to be replaced with references to B.

Whenever the function is being called to locally create a TextBlockElement in the client, either the TextBlockElements OID is already known, which means that the same Element already exists on the database, or its OID is not yet known, which means that the action creating the TextBlockElement has been initiated in the local client and that the new element has to be created in the database as well. The creation of the new TextBlockElement in the database will then be propagated to all but the initiating client. When the TextBlockElement has been created on the database, the returned OID from the database is assigned to the Element in the client.

If the OID for the TextBlockElement to be created is already given, the Element has already been created in the database and the creation of the Element in the client is due to a propagation action from the database or from another client.

If a TextBlockElement with the specified OID already exists locally in the client, this means that an already existing Element has been altered in the database and therefore must also be altered in the client.

To delete a TextBlockElement, the initiating client only has to call the according function in the database. If the deletion is successful, it is propagated to all clients whereupon they also locally delete the TextBlockElement.

3.2 Database Schema

In the following section of the paper, we describe the used data structure that implements the structures of a document on the database side, and later we move on to discuss the algorithms.

To define a TextBlockElement in a document, a pointer to a virtual border has to be set on the first CChar inside and the first CChar after the TextBlock. Pointers to the same virtual border then have to be set in the new CTextBlockElement. Depending on the type of TextBlockElement, the data for the TextBlock must then be set accordingly. In Fig. 6, the example of a TextBlockElement is shown, that defines that the letters "TEN" have the style "Title 1", assigned from the style sheet with the name "Classic1", and a second TextBlockElement defines that the letters "TENDA" have the workflow task assigned to them that the user "theBoss" should complete the action "Sign this!".

Splitting up the information contained in a TextBlockElement into three parts, makes it possible to structure a document in multiple dimensions, to assign simple data type - value pairs to a TextBlock or even to make references to complex database objects, as, for example, styles from a style sheet, simple tasks or complete workflows.

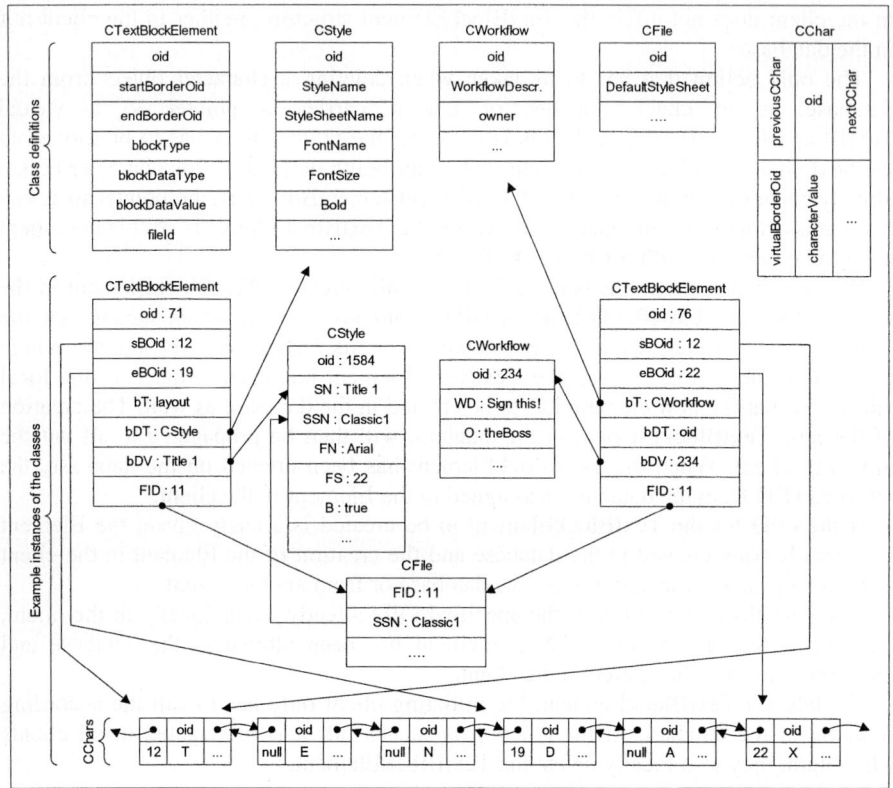

Fig. 6. Database schema and samples

To speed up the searches for CTextBlockElements with a reference to a given virtual border, a two dimensional index is maintained on CTextBlockElement.FileId and CTextBlockElement.startBorder, and another one on CTextBlockElement.FileId and CTextBlockElement.endBorder. These indices are guaranteed to have almost linear performance no matter how many documents are stored in the database.

3.3 Description of the Algorithms Used

In the following section the algorithms for storing and manipulating layout and structure information in a database-driven collaborative word processing application are described.

o is he symbol for an object in the system.
$$o = object$$

The elementary function (Elementary functions are assumed given. Their implementation varies with the programming language used.) *delete(o)* removes the object o from the system.
$$delete(o) = deletes\ o$$

3.3.1 TextBlockElements

The symbol c represents a character in the chain of characters of a text document stored in the database or the client.

$$c = character\ in\ the\ text$$

The elementary function $index(c)$ returns the offset of c in the text.

$$index(c) = offset\ of\ c$$

The elementary function $border(c)$ returns a reference to the (virtual) border at the position between $index(c)-1$ and $index(c)$, if there is no reference defined to a virtual border at this position it returns the null value.

$$border(c) = reference\ to\ border\ between\ index(c)-1\ and\ index(c)$$

The symbol b represents a border of a TextBlock between two consequent characters c_1 and c_2.

$$b = border\ /\ index\ position\ between\ c_1\ and\ c_2$$

whereas

$$index(c_1) + 1 = index(c_2)$$

Any number of consequent character objects in the text document can be defined as a logical entity or a TextBlockElement. The symbol e represents a TextBlockElement.

$$e = textBlockElement\ of\ the\ text$$

The elementary function $newElement()$ creates a new object of the type TextBlockElement.

$$newElement() = the\ new\ element\ e$$

The elementary functions $start(e)$ and $end(e)$ respectively return references to the virtual borders $b1$ and $b2$, at the beginning and at the end of the TextBlockElement e respectively.

$$start(e) = starting\ border\ of\ e$$

$$end(e) = ending\ border\ of\ e$$

Does the TextBlockElement start and end at the same position, it is an empty but valid TextBlockElement of a text section with the length zero. In this case the $start(e)$ equals $end(e)$.

To access the attribute values of a TextBlockElement e the elementary Functions $blockType(e)$, $dataType(e)$ and $dataValue(e)$ can be used. These return for example "layout", "Integer" and "12".

$$blockType(e) = e's\ type\ of\ block$$

$$dataType(e) = e's\ type\ of\ data$$

$$dataValue(e) = the\ stored\ value$$

The function *createTextBlock(c_1, c_2, blockType, dataType, value)* inserts a new TextBlockElement, which represents the text section from character c_1 to character c_2.

The function *createTextBlock* first checks if a TextBlockElement *e* with the given specifications already exists, that has to be given a new data value. Is this the case, the new value is being assigned to the TextBlockElement *e*. If not, it is being checked if on the character objects c_1 and c_2 a border is defined. If a border is already defined it fetches its border identifier. Else it creates a new border on the respective character object and then fetches its border identifier. Then a new TextBlockElement *e* is being created and its *start, end, blockType, dataType* and *dataValue* are being set. At the end the new or edited TextBlockElement *e* is being returned.

$$createTextBlock(c_1, c_2, blockType, dataType, value) \rightarrow e \text{ whereas}$$
$$\text{if } \exists e'\ (\ start(e') = border(c_1) \land end(e') = border(c_2) \land$$
$$blockType(e') = blockType \land dataType(e') = dataType\ )$$
$$e \leftarrow e'$$
$$\text{else}$$
$$e \leftarrow newElement()$$
$$start(e) \leftarrow createElementBorder(c_1)$$
$$end(e) \leftarrow createElementBorder(c_2)$$
$$blockType(e) \leftarrow blockType$$
$$dataType(e) \leftarrow dataType$$
$$dataValue(e) \leftarrow value$$
$$fi$$
$$dataValue(e) \leftarrow value$$

The function *createElementBorder(c)* is defined as:

$$createElementBorder(c) \rightarrow b \text{ whereas}$$
$$\text{if } !\ border(c) = null$$
$$b \leftarrow border(c)$$
$$\text{else}$$
$$b \leftarrow newBorder(c)$$
$$fi$$

In *createElementBorder(c)* it might be necessary to define a new virtual border, which can be accomplished by using the elementary function *newBorder(c)*. It defines a virtual border *b* which represents the index positioned between *index(c)-1* and *index(c)*.

$$newBorder(c) = \text{the new border, positioned between } index(c)\text{-}1 \text{ and}$$
$$index(c)$$

The merging of two borders, as described in this paper, is defined as follows:

$mergeBorders(b_1, b_2)$

$\quad$ while $\exists e\ (start(e) = b_1 \vee end(e) = b_1)$
$\quad\quad \forall c\ (border(c) = b_1)\ border(c) \leftarrow null$
$\quad\quad \forall e\ (start(e) = b_1)\ start(e) \leftarrow b_2$
$\quad\quad \forall e\ (end(e) = b_1)\ end(e) \leftarrow b_2$
end while

All references to b_1 in all the TextBlockElements are being replaced with references to b_2. As it is possible that this function is being called at the same time by multiple users, it has to be ensured that at the end the function really all references to b_1 have been replaced with references to b_2. This assurance is being made by using the while-loop.

3.3.2 Styles und Style Sheets

To store styles and style sheets in the database and in the client the symbol s is introduced for a style, e.g. "Title 1" with font Arial und font size 22.

$$s = style$$

A style defines values for an arbitrary set of character, paragraph or page properties. Each property consists of an attribute name and an attribute value. The symbol a represents a collection of such attribute name - value combinations, e.g. "Font = Arial" or "Font size = 22". Such a collection can consist of an arbitrary number of attribute names - value pairs.

$$a = \{attribute\ name\ -\ value\ paris\ \}$$

To access the attributeSet a of a style s the elementary function $data(s)$ can be used. It returns a reference to the collection of attribute-value pairs a of the style s.

$$data(s) = attributeSet\ a\ of\ s$$

The value of the style- and the styleSheet- attribute together build the unique identifier of the defined style in the database. The elementary function $name(s)$ returns a reference to the value of the attribute "StyleName" of the style s, e.g. "Title 1"

$$name(s) = name\ of\ the\ style\ s$$

Assuming styleSheet s_1 has styles defined with the same names as styleSheet s_2, the two styleSheets s_1 and s_2 can define two different layout visualisations of the same document. The elementary function $styleSheet(s)$ returns a reference to the value of the attribute "StyleSheetName" of the style s.

$$styleSheet(s) = name\ of\ the\ StyleSheet\ s\ belongs\ to$$

The elementary function $newStyle()$ creates a new empty style object s.

$$newStyle\ () = the\ new\ empty\ style\ s$$

To create a new style s or replace an existing style s, the function *editStyle(styleName, styleSheetName, a)* is defined as follows:

$\quad$ *editStyle(styleName, styleSheetName, a)* $\rightarrow s$ *wheras*

$\qquad$ if $\exists s'$ *(name(s')* = *styleName* $\wedge$ *styleSheet(s')* = *styleSheetName*)

$\qquad\qquad s \leftarrow s'$

$\quad$ else

$\qquad\qquad s \leftarrow newStyle$ *()*

$\qquad\qquad name(s) \leftarrow styleName$

$\qquad\qquad styleSheet(s) \leftarrow styleSheetName$

$\quad$ *fi*

$\qquad\qquad data(s) \leftarrow a$

As a certain combination of styleName and styleSheetName values are by definition unique within the database, *editStyle* replaces the attributeSet of an existing style with the same styleName and styleSheetName attributes or creates a new style with the given names and attributeSet.

The function removeStyle(styleName, styleSheetName) is defined as:

$\quad removeStyle(styleName, styleSheetName)$ *whereas*

$\qquad \forall s$ *(name(s)* = *styleName* $\wedge$ *styleSheet(s)* = *styleSheetName*)

$\qquad delete(s)$

To delete a complete StyleSheet from the system the function *removeStyleSheet(styleSheetName)* is defined as follows:

$\quad removeStyleSheet(styleSheetName)$ *wheras*

$\qquad \forall s$ *(styleSheet(s)* = *styleSheetName*)

$\qquad delete(s)$

4 Conclusion, Collaboration Conflicts

Since TeNDaX was built to support multiple users editing the same text document simultaneously, it has to be possible not only to insert and delete characters, but also to define TextBlockElements at the same time. To define a TextBlockElement, a reference to the start and to the end of the TextBlock as well as the TextBlockElement data have to be available. As the data of a TextBlockElement is created in one client only and cannot be accessed by any other, no collaboration conflicts can be expected here. However in order to be able to create a TextBlockElement on the database and then propagate it to the clients, the references to the start and to the end of the

TextBlockElement have to remain valid until the TextBlockElements creation has been completed.

If, for example, client A tries to create a TextBlockElement "E" starting at character object "2e49" and ending at character object "6a02", and, at exactly the same time client B deletes the character object "2e49" from its local character array and from the database, then by the time the TextBlockElement "E" should be created on the database, one of its borders no longer exists in the database, as it has been deleted just previously. As a consequence, the TextBlockElement cannot be created and the initiating user will receive an error message asking him/her to try again.

This is one of three possible collaboration conflicts. The start character object or the end character object, or even both the start and the end character object of the TextBlockElement have been deleted. Everything else that is initiated by two or more different users affecting the same area in a text document does not really represent a technical conflict, as things down in the database and thus also in the clients happen sequentially, but probably just too fast for a user to realise the time shift between the actions. This might result in a situation where one user marks a word bold, for example, and another user marks the whole sentence to be the style "Title 1"; depending on who's transaction is executed first on the database, the appearance of the sentence will look different, but technically spoken that's not a conflict and therefore doesn't have to be handled by the system.

References

[1] S. Abiteboul, R. Agrawal, P. Bernstein, M. Carey, S. Ceri, B. Croft, D. DeWitt, M. Franklin, H. G. Molina, D. Gawlick, J. Gray, L. Haas, A. Halevy, J. Hellerstein, Y. Ioannidis, M. Kersten, M. Pazzani, M. Lesk, D. Maier, J. Naughton, H. Schek, T. Sellis, A. Silberschatz, M. Stonebraker, R. Snodgrass, J. Ullman, G. Weikum, Widom, and J. Stan Zdonik, "The Lowell Database Research Self Assessment," Massachusetts 2003.

[2] S. M. Burke, "The_RTF_Cookbook," vol. 2004, 2003.
http://search.cpan.org/~sburke/RTF-Writer/lib/RTF/Cookbook.pod

[3] S. Haigh, "A Glossary of Digital Library Standards, Protocols and Formats," Information Technology Services National Library of Canada, 1998.
http://www.nlc-bnc.ca/9/1/p1-253-e.html

[4] T. B. Hodel and K. R. Dittrich, "A collaborative, real-time insert transaction for a native text database system," presented at Information Resources Management Association (IRMA 2004), New Orleans (USA), 2004.

[5] T. B. Hodel and K. R. Dittrich, "A native text database: What for?," presented at Information Resources Management Association (IRMA 2004), New Orleans (USA), 2004.

[6] T. B. Hodel and K. R. Dittrich, "Concept and prototype of a collaborative business process environment for document processing," Data & Knowledge Engineering, vol. Special Issue: Collaborative Business Process Technologies, 2004.

[7] T. B. Hodel, M. Dubacher, and K. R. Dittrich, "Using Database Management Systems for Collaborative Text Editing," presented at European Conference of Computer-supported Cooperative Work (ECSCW CEW 2003), Helsinki (Finnland), 2003.

[8] P. Iglinski, "An Object-Oriented SGML/HyTime Compliant Multimedia Database Management System," 1997.
http://www.acm.org/sigmm/MM97/papers/iglinski/ACMMM97.html

[9] Microsoft, "Microsoft Word 97 Binary File Format," Microsoft, 1998.
http://www.google.ch/search?hl=en&ie=UTF-8&oe=UTF-8&q=%22Microsoft+Word+97+Binary+File+Format%22&btnG=Google+Search&meta=
[10] Microsoft, "Rich Text Format (RTF) Specification, version 1.6," Microsoft, 1999.
http://msdn.microsoft.com/library/default.asp?url=/library/en.us/dnrtfspec/html/rtfspec.asp
[11] Sun, "JavaTM 2 Platform, Standard Edition, v 1.4.2 API Specification," Sun Microsystems, 2003.
http://java.sun.com/j2se/1.4.2/docs/api/
[12] C. Sun, "CoWord Prototype," 2004.
http://www.cit.gu.edu.au/~scz/projects/coword/
[13] C. Sun, X. Jia, Y. Zhang, and Y. Yang, "REDUCE: a prototypical cooperative editing system," ACM Transactions on Computer-Human Interaction, pp. 89 - 92, 1997.
[14] C. G. a. J. Warnock, "Adobe® Portable Document Format Reference 1.5," Adobe Systems Incorporated, 2003.
http://partners.adobe.com/asn/acrobat/sdk/public/docs/PDFReference15_v6.pdf

A Reliable Content-Based Routing Protocol over Structured Peer-to-Peer Networks*

Jinling Wang[1,2], Beihong Jin[1], Jun Wei[1], and Jing Li[1]

[1] Institute of Software, Chinese Academy of Sciences, Beijing, China
{jlwang, jbh, wj, lij}@otcaix.iscas.ac.cn
[2] Graduate School of the Chinese Academy of Sciences, Beijing, China

Abstract. Much work has been done on building content-based publish/subscribe systems over structured P2P networks, so that the two technologies can be combined together to better support large-scale and highly dynamic systems. However, existing content-based routing protocols can only provide weak reliability guarantee over structured P2P networks. We designed a new type of content-based routing protocol over structured P2P networks — Identifier Range Based Routing (IRBR) protocol, which organizes subscriptions on the basis of the identifier range of subscribers. It provides strong reliability guarantee and is more efficient in event delivery. Experimental results demonstrate the routing efficiency of the protocol.

1 Introduction

Publish/subscribe (pub/sub) is a loosely coupled communication paradigm for distributed computing environments. In pub/sub systems, publishers publish information to event brokers in the form of *events*, subscribers subscribe to a particular category of events within the system, and event brokers ensure the timely and reliable delivery of published events to all interested subscribers. The advantage of pub/sub paradigm is that information producers and consumers are full decoupled in time, space and flow [1], so it is well suitable for large-scale and highly dynamic distributed systems.

Publish/subscribe systems can be generally divided into two categories: *subject-based* and *content-based*. In *subject-based* systems, each event belongs to one of a fixed set of *subjects* (also called *topics*, *channels*, or *groups*). Publishers are required to label each event with a subject name; subscribers subscribe to all events under a particular subject. In *content-based* systems, events are no longer divided into different subjects. Each subscriber defines a filter according to the internal structure of events; all events that meet the filter will be sent to the subscriber. Compared with subject-based pub/sub systems, content-based systems are more expressive and flexible; they enable subscribers to express their interests in a finer level of granularity.

---

* This work was supported by the National Grand Fundamental Research 973 Program of China under Grant No. 2002CB312005; the National Hi-Tech Research and Development 863 Program of China under Grant No. 2001AA113010; and the National Natural Science Foundation of China under Grant No. 60173023.

A large-scale content-based publish/subscribe system usually contains many event brokers; each broker serves a certain number of clients (publishers or subscribers). In such systems, one of the key technical problems is the routing protocol for messages (usually called *content-based routing* protocol [2, 3]), i.e., how to route messages (subscriptions, events, etc.) from the sending nodes to destination nodes. Content-based routing protocols significantly affect the efficiency, reliability and scalability of the content-based pub/sub systems.

Although a lot of content-based routing protocols have been proposed, almost all these protocols are based on static network topology and lack the adaptive ability to node failures or changing of topology. In recent years, there have been some works on the research of failure recovery and routing reconfiguration in content-based pub/sub systems [4, 5, 6], but building a reliable content-based pub/sub system still remains a challenge.

On the other hand, structured P2P networks such as Pastry [7], Tapestry [8], Chord [9] and CAN [10] have recently gained popularity as a platform for the construction of large-scale distributed systems. The nodes in these networks are organized into a directed graph with a specific structure, so that the length of path between any two nodes are usually no more than $log_k(N)$, in which k is a pre-defined parameter, and N is the max number of nodes in the networks. Structured P2P networks have many advantages such as decentralization (no central control points are needed) and self-organization (nodes can dynamically arrive or depart). Since there are multiple paths between any two nodes, the networks provide a high level of fault-tolerance for message delivery. Unless numerous neighbors of a node fail simultaneously, the node can always find a path to deliver a message a step further to the destination address.

Therefore, many people have tried to build content-based pub/sub systems over structured P2P networks, hoping to improve the fault-tolerant ability of pub/sub systems by the advantages of structured P2P networks. However, existing content-based pub/sub systems over structured P2P networks all use the traditional content-based routing protocols (or with minor improvements), which can hardly be integrated with the highly dynamic P2P networks. As a result, all these systems weaken the reliability guarantee of event delivery. What's more, many systems require the existence of some special nodes (i.e., rendezvous points) in the networks. These rendezvous points provide centralized services for the pub/sub system, whose loads are much more heavy than the average nodes. As a result, these systems also lose the decentralization and load-sharing features of the structured P2P network.

Based on the characteristics of structured P2P networks, we design a new type of content-based routing protocol for pub/sub systems — Identifier Range Based Routing (IRBR) protocol. It can be naturally integrated with the routing protocol of structured P2P networks, and make use of the fault-tolerance mechanism of structured P2P networks to provide a high level of reliability guarantee for event delivery. As long as the message from publishing nodes to subscribing nodes is arrivable in the P2P network, the subscribers can always receive the subscribed events exactly once.

At the same time, the IRBR protocol also has a high efficiency in event routing. Compared with existing content-based routing protocols over structured P2P networks, the IRBR protocol can disseminate an event to all interested subscribers with less network traffic.

The IRBR protocol can be implemented on structured P2P networks using prefix-based routing protocols, such as Pastry and Tapestry. We have developed a prototype pub/sub system on Pastry to implement the IRBR protocol. Experimental results demonstrate the routing efficiency and fault-tolerance of the protocol.

The remainder of the paper is organized as follows. In Section 2, we briefly introduce the content-based routing protocols and the routing protocol of Pastry. In section 3, we discuss related work. In Section 4, we give some preliminaries. In Section 5, we introduce the IRBR protocol. In Section 6, we present and analyze the experimental results. Finally, in Section 7, we conclude the paper with a summary.

2 Background

2.1 Content-Based Routing Protocols

Content-based routing protocols can be divided into two categories: *precise routing* and *imprecise routing*. Precise routing protocols (such as [11, 12, 13]) aim at minimize the network traffic among event brokers, while imprecise routing protocols (such as [14, 15, 16]) aim at lessening the processing load on event brokers with the sacrifice of some network efficiency. In this paper, we mainly focus on the precise routing protocols.

Typically, there are an uncertain number of receivers for a message (event, subscription, etc.) in the content-based pub/sub systems. As a result, all precise content-based routing protocols are based on a certain type of application-level broadcast protocol, and use some optimization methods to avoid unnecessary message delivery. For the dissemination of events, the main optimization method is to detect whether there are interested subscribers in the destination subnet. For the dissemination of subscriptions, the main optimization method is to calculate the *covering* relations [11] among filters.

According to the underlying broadcast protocols, there are traditionally two types of precise content-based routing protocols: *spanning tree forwarding* and *reverse path forwarding*.

1. Spanning tree forwarding

In this type of protocol, all event brokers in the system are organized into a tree structure. When a broker receives a subscription from its clients, the subscription is forwarded from the current broker to the root broker, and the message delivery is optimized with the covering relation among filters. When a broker receives a published event from its clients, the event is disseminated with the *spanning tree forwarding* broadcast algorithm [17], i.e., the event is forwarded from the current broker to the root broker, each broker along the path forwarding the event to its children that are interested in the event.

The disadvantages of the protocol include the single points of failure and performance bottleneck on the root node in the tree structure.

SIENA [11] and JEDI [18] have proposed the hierarchical topology for event brokers, in which the routing protocols belong to this type.

2. Reverse path forwarding

This protocol uses the *source-based forwarding* broadcast algorithm [17] to disseminate subscriptions, and the *reverse path forwarding* broadcast algorithm [17] to disseminate events. Each event broker knows a spanning tree rooting at itself in advance. When a broker receives a subscription from its clients, it forwards the subscription to other brokers through its own spanning tree, and the message delivery is optimized with the covering relation among filters. Each event broker then builds an event dissemination tree rooting at itself according to the reverse paths of subscriptions. When a broker receives a published event from its clients, the event is then forwarded to other brokers through its own event dissemination tree.

The advantage of the protocol is that it equally distributes the workload among all brokers. Its main disadvantage is that each broker in the network simultaneously belongs to multiple event dissemination trees, so the routing information in each broker can hardly been replaced by that of other brokers. Once a broker fails, the routing reconfigure of the whole system will be very complex.

The routing protocols in Gryphon [12], Rebeca [19] and the peer-to-peer structure of SIENA all belong to this type.

To further decrease the network traffic resulting from a subscribing operation, some systems (such as SIENA, Hermes [20]) confine the clients' ability to publish events, requiring each client send out an *advertise* message before it actually publishes events. The *advertise* message states the constraints that the published events will meet, and it is disseminated to other brokers with the *source-based forwarding* algorithm. The *subscription* message is then disseminated with the *reverse path forwarding* algorithm, following the reverse paths of advertise messages to reach the corresponding brokers. In such a way, the network traffic caused by a subscribing operation can be decreased, but with the cost of extra *advertise* message delivery. Therefore, this method is applicable for applications where just a few clients can publish events, the events meet certain constraints, and the publishing ability of clients don't change frequently.

2.2 Routing Protocol of Pastry

Pastry is a simple and efficient structured P2P network. In Pastry, each node has a unique identifier, which is an l-digit number with Base k. Pastry divides the whole identifier space into different identifier ranges according to the prefix of identifiers; each outgoing edge of a node takes charge of a certain identifier range. For every node, all of its outgoing edges and the corresponding identifier ranges constitute its routing table. Suppose there is a node with identifier n, and its routing table is RT^n. We can view RT^n as the following set:

$$RT^n = \{(prefix, nodeId, address)\}$$

Each entry in the routing table means that the current node will use *nodeId* as the next hop to all destination nodes whose identifier begins with *prefix*, and the IP address of *nodeId* is *address*. The node with identifier *nodeId* is like the *representative* of all nodes in the identifier range with the given prefix. For example, suppose $k=4$, $l=3$, the routing table of the node with identifier 213 is shown in Figure 1(a). If there is no node with given prefix in the whole network, then there is no corresponding routing entry in the routing table.

Figure 1(b) shows the division of whole identifier space for node 213. Each rectangle in the tree means an identifier range, and the root rectangle means the whole identifier space. Each leaf rectangle (except the identifier 213) has a corresponding item in the routing table. For each prefix in the routing table, if its length is k, then it shares the first k-1 digits with the identifier of the current node, and has a different number in the k-th digit.

Suppose node 213 wants to send a message to node 201. Node 213 first looks up the routing entry with prefix 20 in its routing table, and gets the next hop 202, so it sends the message to node 202. Node 202 then looks up the routing entry with prefix 201 in its own routing table, and sends the message to the corresponding address. The total number of hops is 2 for the message.

Pastry provides a high level of fault-tolerance. During the forwarding of message, if the current node finds that the next hop has failed, it will forward the message with the idea of *greedy method*, i.e., it will choose a node in the routing table whose identifier is closest to the destination identifier, and forward the message to the node. At the same time, it will try to find another node in the corresponding identifier range to repair the routing table.

prefix	nodeId	address
0	031	192.168.2.1
1	102	192.168.5.5
3	320	...
20	202	...
22	221	...
23	233	...
210	210	...
211	211	...
212	212	...

(a) Routing table of node 213

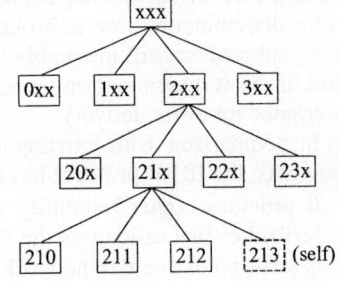

(b) Identifier space division for node 213

Fig. 1. An example of routing table in a Pastry node

3 Related Work

In recent years, many content-based pub/sub systems have been built on structured P2P networks. There are mainly two types of routing protocols in these systems:
1. Scribe-Based

Scribe [21] is a subject-based pub/sub system built on Pastry. There is a special node (called *rendezvous*) in the network for each subject. When a node creates a subscription, the subscription message is forwarded to the corresponding rendezvous. Each rendezvous then builds an event dissemination tree rooting at itself according to the reverse paths of all subscription messages. When a node publishes an event, the event is first forwarded to the corresponding rendezvous, and then it is disseminated to all interested nodes through the event dissemination tree. To detect failures in the event dissemination tree, each node will periodically send out heartbeat messages to its children in the tree. If a node has not received the heartbeat message after a given time, it will suspect its parent node have failed, and send a message in another path to the rendezvous to repair the event dissemination tree. Scribe can just provide weak reliability guarantee on event routing; during the failure and repairing period of event dissemination trees, some nodes may not get the events they have subscribed. Furthermore, the protocol has the disadvantages of performance bottlenecks and single points of failure on the rendezvous nodes.

Hermes [20] and the work of D. Tam et al. [22] are both based on the routing protocol of Scribe, with some extension to provide content-based subscriptions. But such hybrid systems (the combination of subject-based system and content-based system) are less expressive and flexible than the pure content-based system. At the same time, they cannot provide a higher level of reliability guarantee than Scribe.

2. Reverse Path Forwarding

W. W. Terpstra et al. [23] have built a pure content-based pub/sub system on Chord, with the traditional reverse path forwarding protocol. It also weakens the semantic of event delivery and cannot guarantee the delivery of events to all interested subscribers.

In both of the above routing protocols, the event dissemination tree has already been built before an event is published. However, in a structured P2P network, due to the dynamic arrival and departure of nodes, there is every possibility that the pre-built event dissemination tree is broken when an event is actually published. As a result, some subscribers will inevitably lose some events during the failure and repairing period of event dissemination trees, so these protocols can just provide weak reliability guarantee for event delivery.

In comparison with existing content-based routing protocols on structured P2P networks, the IRBR protocol has the following advantages:

- It provides higher reliability guarantee; subscribers can always receive the subscribed events as long as the message from publishing nodes to subscribing nodes is arrivable in the P2P network;
- It is more efficient in event dissemination; a published event can arrive at all subscribed nodes with less network traffic;
- It supports pure content-based pub/sub systems rather than hybrid pub/sub systems.

The routing protocol in Bayeux [24] is somewhat similar with the IRBR protocol. Bayeux is a subject-based pub/sub system built on Tapestry, in which each subject has a corresponding rendezvous node in the network. When a node creates a subscription, the subscription message is forwarded to the corresponding rendezvous, and then the rendezvous sends back a *response* message to the subscribing node. The paths of all *response* messages form an event dissemination tree rooting at the rendezvous. Bayeux is efficient in event delivery and can provide a high level of fault-tolerance, but each node in the event dissemination tree has to maintain a subscriber list, which records all subscribers that the current node should forward events to. The subscriber list may be very large and take up a lot of resources on each node. Furthermore, the cost of matching an incoming event with subscriptions is largely determined by the size of the subscription list. Compared with the routing protocol in Bayeux, the IRBR protocol can support pure content-based pub/sub system, and each node needs to maintain less information, so the workload on each node is decreased.

P. Triantafillou et al. [25] have also proposed a content-based pub/sub system on Chord, but the paper just discussed a distributed matching algorithm and did not touch the routing protocol issues.

4 Preliminaries

4.1 Architecture Overview

A pub/sub system over structured P2P network can be described as a layered architecture, as shown in Figure 2. The peer-to-peer layer connects the event brokers into a structured P2P network, the event notification layer takes charge of the event dissemination among brokers, and the application layer is the application that actually publishes and subscribes events. Our IRBR protocol is the routing protocol for the event notification layer, which is built on the top of the peer-to-peer layer.

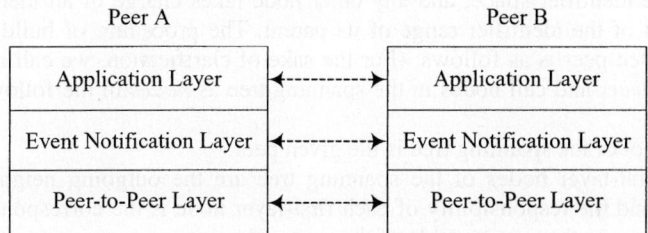

Fig. 2. Architecture overview

The topology of pub/sub systems over structured P2P networks can be further divided into two categories: *super-peer* and *pure-peer*. In the super-peer structure (such as Hermes), each node in the P2P network just works as event broker, each broker connecting to several clients that are outside of the P2P network. In the pure-peer structure (such as Scribe and Bayeux), each node in the P2P network works as both event broker and client. The two structures have no substantial differences; we can see the super-peer structure as a special form of pure-peer structure, in which there are multiple application instances in the application layer of each node. For the sake of simplicity, in the following discussion we suppose the pub/sub system is built on the pure-peer structure, and there is just one instance in the application layer of each node.

The event notification layer interacts with other two layers by means of *operations*; each operation may include some parameters. The event notification layers of different nodes interact with each other by means of *messages*; each message may also include some parameters. To differentiate operations from messages, we denote operations by the following form: *operation_type(parameter_lists)*, such as *subscribe(f_1)*, and denote messages by the following form: *(message_type: parameter_lists)*, such as *(subscription: sp_1, f_1, dp_1)*.

Generally speaking, the event notification layer should provide at least following operations to the upper layer:

- *subscribe(filter)*: the application layer is interested in all events that meet the constraint of *filter*.
- *unsubscribe(filter)*: the application layer is no longer interested in all events that meet the constraint of *filter*.
- *publish(event)*: the application layer publishes a new event.

The application layer should also provide the following operation to the event notification layer:
- *notify(event)*: the event notification layer notifies the application layer of the arrival of a subscribed event.

4.2 Protocol Overview

According to the characteristics of structured P2P networks, we can easily build a spanning tree for each node with the idea of *responsibility delegation*. Each node in the spanning tree takes charge of a certain identifier range. The root node takes charge of the whole identifier space, and any other node takes charge of an identifier range that is a part of the identifier range of its parent. The procedure of build a spanning tree for a given peer is as follows: (For the sake of clarification, we call nodes in the network as *peers* and call nodes in the spanning tree as *nodes* in the following of this subsection)

1) The root of the spanning tree is the given peer.
2) The first-layer nodes of the spanning tree are the outgoing neighbors of the peer, and the responsibility of each first-layer node is the corresponding identifier range in the routing table of the root node.
3) For each first-layer node, its children in the spanning tree are its outgoing neighbors whose corresponding identifier ranges overlapped the responsibility of the first-layer node, and the responsibility of each child is the overlapped part of the identifier range.
4) Build the other layers of the spanning tree in the same way.

Therefore, the most straightforward broadcast algorithm for structured P2P networks is the *source-based forwarding* algorithm. S. El-Ansary et al. [26] have already implemented a broadcast algorithm on Chord with this idea.

In the IRBR protocol, subscriptions and events are all disseminated with the *source-based forwarding* broadcast algorithm. When an event broker receives a subscription from its clients, it will send out the subscription through the spanning tree rooting at itself. The message delivery is also optimized with the covering relation among filters. When a broker receives a subscription, it is not concerned about which incoming edge the message comes from, but the identifier range that the subscriber belongs to (i.e., through which outgoing edge the peer will reach the subscriber). In such a way, the spanning tree of each peer also becomes its event dissemination tree. When a broker receives a published event from its clients, it will send out the event through the same spanning tree.

From the construction procedure of the spanning tree we can see that the path from the root node to any other node in the tree is actually the ideal path between the two peers in the network. However, the event dissemination trees in the *Scribe-based* protocol and the *reverse path forwarding* protocol are built on the *reverse* paths of subscription messages. As the structured P2P network is a direct graph, if the number of hops from peer A to peer B is 1, then the number of hops is usually larger than 1 from peer B to peer A. Therefore, the IRBR protocol is certainly more efficient in event delivery than the other protocols.

As the event dissemination tree in the IRBR protocol is built dynamically at the time of event publishing, the change of neighbors between the time of subscribing and publishing has no influence on event delivery. What's more, a message just needs to be sent to any node in the destination identifier range rather than a specific node, which further improves the reliability guarantee of the protocol.

4.3 Data Structure

Suppose there is a filter f. Let $f(e)$ denote the predicate "event e matches the filter f". Let E_f denote the set $\{e \mid f(e)\}$, i.e., all events that match the filter f.
For two filters f_1 and f_2, let $f_1 \sqsupseteq f_2$ denote the predicate "f_1 covers f_2", i.e.:
$$f_1 \sqsupseteq f_2 \Leftrightarrow E_{f_1} \supseteq E_{f_2}$$
We say f_1 has larger *scope* than f_2 if f_1 covers f_2.

The event notification layer of each node maintains a filter table, which is the only data structure needed by the IRBR protocol. Suppose the filter table of node n is FT^n, we can abstractly represent it as the following set:
$$FT^n = \{(prefix, filter)\}$$

Each entry (called *filter entry*) in the filter table means that in the identifier range with the given prefix, there is at least one node interested in E_{filter}. Different entries in the table can have the same prefix.

The prefix in the filter entries can be equal to the identifier of the current node, meaning the application layer of the current node is interested in certain events. All prefixes other than the identifier of the current node must have a corresponding entry in the routing table of Pastry.

For different event models and matching algorithms, there can be different implementations of the filter table. For example, filters are organized into a parallel searching tree in Gryphon, while they are organized into a Trie structure in XTrie [27]. Our IRBR protocol does not rely on the specific implementation of filter table.

5 The IRBR Protocol

5.1 Basic Operations

Subscribing

Suppose there is a node with identifier n_1. When its application layer executes the operation $subscribe(f_1)$, the event notification layer first saves the filter entry (n_1, f_1) into its filter table, and then sends out the *subscription* message to other nodes.

The format of the *subscription* message is as follows: *(subscription: subscriber_prefix, filter, destine_prefix)*, in which *subscriber_prefix* means the identifier range of the subscriber, *filter* means the filter of the subscription, and *destine_prefix* means the destination identifier range of the message. If node X sends a *subscription* message to node Y, then node Y should forward the message to all nodes with prefix *destine_prefix*.

When the application layer of node n_1 executes $subscribe(f_1)$, the event notification layer will send message $(subscription: sp_i, f_1, re_i.prefix)$ to node $re_i.nodeId$ for each entry re_i in the routing table, in which sp_i is the prefix of n_1 and has the same length as $re_i.prefix$. For example, suppose the application layer of node 213 executes *sub-*

$scribe(f_1)$. The event notification layer of the node will send message *(subscription: 213, f_1, 210)* to node 210, message *(subscription: 21, f_1, 20)* to node 202, message *(subscription: 2, f_1, 0)* to node 031, etc.

When the event notification layer of a node receives a message *(subscription: sp_1, f_1, dp_1)*, it will perform the following steps:
1) Save the filter entry (sp_1, f_1) into its filter table. If there has been a filter entry $fe = (sp_1, f_2)$ and $f_1 \sqsupseteq f_2$, then fe becomes unnecessary and should be deleted.
2) For each entry re_j in the routing table, send message *(subscription: sp_1, f_1, $re_j.prefix$)* to node $re_j.nodeId$ if $re_j.prefix$ begins with dp_1.

In such a way, the *subscription* message will arrive at all nodes in the network after several hops.

The above algorithm is essentially the *source-based forwarding* broadcast algorithm. As we know, it would be very inefficient if a message is broadcasted among the whole network for each subscribing operation, so some form of optimization mechanism is a must. The *reverse path forwarding* protocol optimizes the dissemination of subscription messages according to the covering relation of subscriptions from the same neighbors, i.e., if a new subscription can be covered by another subscription from the same neighbor node, the subscription message does not need to be forwarded any further. But due to the dynamic nature of the structured P2P networks, the neighbors of a node are varying from time to time, which makes the idea inapplicable in the environment.

However, for each node in the structured P2P network, the way it divides the global identifier space is unchangeable. In other words, the total entries and the identifier range of each entry in the routing table are fixed; what is changeful is just the *representative* of each identifier range. In the IRBR protocol, as the filter table of every node is organized on the basis of identifier ranges, we can optimize the message delivery according to the covering relation of filters from the neighboring identifier ranges. When the application layer executes $subscribe(f_1)$, the event notification layer first checks its filter table to find which identifier ranges have already defined filters with scope larger than f_1, and then uses this information to reduce the destination identifier ranges of the *subscription* message.

For example, suppose the application layer of node 213 executes the operation $subscribe(f_1)$. First, node 213 sends a *subscription* message to each entry in the routing table with 3-digit prefix (i.e., 210, 211, 212). In the filter table of node 213, if there is a 3-digit prefix (such as 210) with a filter f_2, and $f_1 \sqsubseteq f_2$, then every node in the network has already known that a node with prefix 21 is interested in E_{f2}, and $E_{f1} \subseteq E_{f2}$, so the current node does not need to send the *subscription* message to all nodes without prefix 21. The change of the filter tables of all nodes is shown in Figure 3.

If there is not such entry in the filter table of node 213, but there is a 2-digit prefix (such as 22) with a filter f_3, and $f_1 \sqsubseteq f_3$, then every node in the network has already known that a node with prefix 2 is interested in E_{f3}, and $E_{f1} \subseteq E_{f3}$, so the current node does not need to send the *subscription* message to all nodes without prefix 2. In such a way, we can greatly decrease the network traffic caused by a subscribing operation. With the increasing of subscriptions, the messages exchanged for a subscribing operation will be less and less.

node Id	filter table
011	$(2, f_2)$
...	...
201	$(21, f_2)$
...	...
210	$(210, f_2)$
211	$(210, f_2)$
212	$(210, f_2)$
213	$(210, f_2)$
...	...

a) The initial state: node 210 has a filter f_2

node Id	filter table
011	$(2, f_2)$
...	...
201	$(21, f_2)$
...	...
210	$(210, f_2), (213, f_1)$
211	$(210, f_2), (213, f_1)$
212	$(210, f_2), (213, f_1)$
213	$(210, f_2), (213, f_1)$
...	...

b) Node 213 executing $subscribe(f_1)$; $f_1 \sqsubseteq f_2$

Fig. 3. The change of filter tables resulting from the subscribing operation

Unsubscribing

When the application layer of a node executes the operation *unsubscribe(filter)*, the event notification layer should inform other nodes that it is no longer interested in E_{filter}. At the same time, since the canceled filter may have covered other filters in the neighboring identifier ranges, the event notification layer should also send out these covered filters to certain identifier ranges.

We define a message type *updateSubscription* to serve the unsubscribing operation. An *updateSubscription* message indicates the given identifier range will cancel a filter and add some other filters. The format of the message is as follows: *(updateSubscription: subscriber_prefix, canceled_filter, added_filters, destine_prefix)*, in which *subscriber_prefix* means the identifier range of the requester, *canceled_filter* means the canceled filters, *added_filters* means the added filters, and *destine_prefix* means the destination identifier range of the message.

When the application layer of node n_1 executes $unsubscribe(f_1)$, the event notification layer will perform the following steps:
1) $FT^{n1} = FT^{n1} - \{(n_1, f_1)\}$;
2) Set *add_filters* = Φ, *len* = length(n_1);
3) For each $re_i \in RT^{n1} \wedge$ length($re_i.prefix$) = *len*, send message (*updateSubscription: sp_i, f_1, add_filters, $re_i.prefix$*) to $re_i.nodeId$, in which sp_i is the prefix of n_1 and has the same length as $re_i.prefix$;
4) If $\exists fe$ ($fe \in FT^{n1} \wedge$ length($fe.prefix$) = *len* $\wedge$ $fe.filter \sqsupseteq f_1$), then there is no need to send *updateSubscription* message to other identifier ranges; the procedure finishes.
5) Otherwise, *add_filters* = *add_filters* $\cup$ { $fe.filter$ | $fe \in FT^{n1} \wedge$ length($fe.prefix$) = *len* $\wedge$ $fe.filter \sqsubseteq f_1$ }, *len* = *len* – 1; repeat the procedure from step 3 to step 5.

For example, suppose the application layer of node 213 executes $unsubscribe(f_1)$. First, node 213 sends a message (*updateSubscription: 213, f_1, Φ, destine_prefix*) to each entry in the routing table with 3-digit prefixes (i.e., 210, 211, 212). In the filter table of node 213, if there is a 3-digit prefix (such as 210) with a filter f_2, and $f_1 \sqsubseteq f_2$, then the identifier range with prefix 21 is still interested in E_{f2}, and $E_{f1} \subseteq E_{f2}$, so node 213 does not need to send the *updateSubscription* message to all nodes without prefix 21. As a result, the states of filter tables of all nodes return from Figure 3(b) to Figure 3(a).

If there is not such entry in the filter table of node 213, and there is a 3-digit prefix (suppose it to be 211) with a filter f_3, $f_1 \sqsupseteq f_3$, then node 213 should send message (*updateSubscription*: 21, f_1, {f_3}, *destine_prefix*) to each entry in the routing table with 2-digit prefixes. If no filter entry with 2-digit prefixes could cover f_1, then node 213 should also send the *updateSubscription* message to each entry in the routing table with 1-digit prefixes. The change of filter tables of all nodes is shown in Figure 4.

node Id	filter table
011	(2, f_1)
...	...
201	(21, f_1)
...	...
210	(211, f_3), (213, f_1)
211	(211, f_3), (213, f_1)
212	(211, f_3), (213, f_1)
213	(211, f_3), (213, f_1)
...	...

a) The initial state; $f_1 \sqsupseteq f_3$

node Id	filter table
011	(2, f_3)
...	...
201	(21, f_3)
...	...
210	(211, f_3)
211	(211, f_3)
212	(211, f_3)
213	(211, f_3)
...	...

b) Node 213 executing *unsubscribe(f_1)*

Fig. 4. The change of filter tables resulting from the unsubscribing operation

When a node receives an *updateSubscription* message from other nodes, it first updates its own filter table, and then forwards the message to all nodes with prefix *destine_prefix*.

Publishing

When the application layer of a node executes the operation *publish(event)*, the event notification layer should send out the *notification* messages to inform other nodes. The format of the *notification* message is as follows: (*notification: event, destine_prefix*), in which *event* means the published event and *destine_prefix* means the destination identifier range of the message.

When the application layer of node n_1 executes *publish(e_1)*, the event notification layer will check the filter table to get the destination identifier ranges for the *notification* messages. For each entry re_i in the routing table, if there exists a filter entry $fe = (re_i.prefix, f_i)$ in the filter table and $f_i(e_1)$ holds, then the event notification layer should send message (*notification: e_1, $re_i.prefix$*) to node $re_i.nodeId$.

When a node (suppose its identifier to be n_2) receives a message *(notification: e_1, dp_1)*, its event notification layer will work as follows:
1) If there is a filter entry (n_2, f) in its filter table and $f(e_1)$ holds, notify the application layer of the arrival of the event.
2) For each routing entry re_j in the routing table, if $re_j.prefix$ begins with dp_1, and there is a filter entry $fe = (re_j.prefix, f_j)$ in the filter table so that $f_j(e_1)$ holds, send message *(notification: e_1, $re_j.prefix$)* to the node $re_j.nodeId$.

After several hops, the *notification* message can arrive at all nodes that are interested in the event.

Figure 5 shows the dissemination tree for an event e published by node 213. In the figure, the rectangle besides each node means the filter table of the node. We suppose node 023 has already executed *subscribe(f_a)*, node 201 has already executed *subscribe(f_b)*, and $f_a(e)$ and $f_b(e)$ both hold.

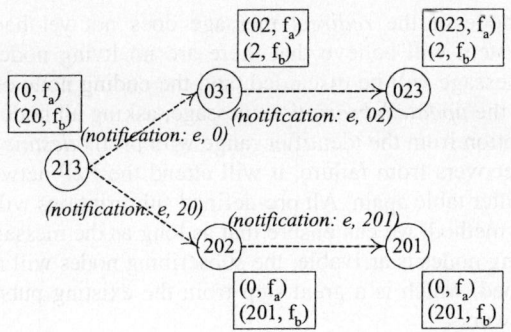

Fig. 5. The dissemination tree of event e when $f_a(e)$ and $f_b(e)$ hold

5.2 Fault-Tolerance Mechanism

Unlike the Scribe-based protocol and reverse path forwarding protocol, the event dissemination tree in the IRBR protocol is built dynamically at the time of event publishing. When a node receives a subscription, it will update the filter table according to the identifier range of the subscriber. When a node receives an event, it will match it with the entries in the filter table, and forward the event to its current neighbors according to the matched identifier ranges. Therefore, the change of neighbors between the time of subscribing and the time of publishing has no influence on event delivery.

On the other hand, in the IRBR protocol, a given message (event, subscriptions, etc.) can be sent to any node in the given identifier range rather than a specific node, and the receiving node will forward the message to other nodes in the identifier range. Therefore, the failure of a specific node or link will not prevent the message from reaching other nodes, which further improves the reliability guarantee of the protocol.

Due to node failure or link failure, a node may fail to send a message to its neighbor for a given identifier range. The IRBR protocol makes use of the fault-tolerant mechanism of structured P2P networks to deal with such failures. We define a message type *redirect*, which encapsulates the original message and routes the message to any other node in the given identifier range. The format of the *redirect* message is as follows: *(redirect: middle_id, destine_prefix, original_message)*, in which *middle_id* means the destination identifier of the *redirect* message, *destine_prefix* means the destination identifier range of the original message, and *original_message* means the content of the original message. The value of *middle_id* is the middle identifier value in the identifier range with prefix *destine_prefix*. For example, if the identifier is a 3-digit number with base 4, then the value of *middle_id* for prefix 21 is 211.

During the forwarding of *subscription*, *updateSubscription* and *notification* messages, if a node fails to send the message to its neighbor for a given identifier range, the event notification layer will encapsulates the original message with a *redirect* message, and use the routing mechanism of the P2P network to send the *redirect* message to *middle_id*. The P2P network will find a proper path to forward the *redirect* message, so that each node along the path has a closer identifier to *middle_id* than the last node. During the forwarding process of the *redirect* message, if the current node has the prefix *destine_prefix*, then the message will not be forwarded any further; it is transformed into the original message and processed at the current node.

If the ending node of the *redirect* message does not yet have the prefix *destine_prefix*, the system will believe that there are no living nodes with prefix *destine_prefix*. The message will be discarded, and the ending node of the *redirect* message will send out the *updateSubscription* message, asking all nodes in the network to cancel the subscription from the identifier range with prefix *destine_prefix*.

When a node recovers from failure, it will attend the P2P network as a new node and initialize the filter table again. All pre-defined subscriptions will be defined again.

With the above method, we can ensure that as long as the message from publishing nodes to subscribing nodes is arrivable, the subscribing nodes will not lose any events they have subscribed, which is a great step from the existing pub/sub system on the structured P2P networks.

6 Performance Evaluation

6.1 Experimental Setup

We have developed a prototype pub/sub system to implement the IRBR protocol. The performance of the prototype system is evaluated with a variety of simulated workloads. The experiments discussed below were performed on a common Notebook PC with an Intel Pentium IV CPU at 1.6GHz and 512MB RAM running Windows XP Professional and JDK 1.4.1.

The prototype system is built on an open source implementation of Pastry — FreePastry 1.3.2 [28]. FreePastry provides a network simulator, which can simulate large numbers of nodes with one physical computer. In our experiments, the number of nodes in the P2P network is 1000.

In the experiments, the identifier of each node is an 8-digit number with Base 4, i.e., the whole system can contain at most 2^{16} nodes.

To evaluate the routing efficiency of the IRBR protocol, we also implement two other content-based routing protocols over structured P2P networks: Scribe-based protocol and reverse path forwarding protocol (we call it the *RPF* protocol in the follows), so that we can compare the routing efficiency of the three protocols under the same environment and workloads. In the experiments for the Scribed-based protocol, we suppose there were only one rendezvous in the network.

Since the main operations of a pub/sub system is *subscribe* and *publish*, we mainly observe the following values under different numbers of subscriptions:
- The average number of messages exchanged for a subscribing operation, which reflects the routing efficiency for subscribing operations;
- The average number of messages exchanged for a publishing operation, which reflects the routing efficiency for publishing operations.

For the subscribing operation, the three protocols all use the covering relation among filters to optimize the message delivery, so the number of messages exchanged are largely influenced by the probability of covering relations among filters. Therefore, we define a parameter *covering rate*, meaning the probability of $f_1 \sqsubseteq f_2$, in which f_1 and f_2 are both randomly selected from all filters.

For the publishing operation, the number of messages exchanged is largely influenced by the number of nodes that are actually interested in the event. If there are k

nodes (exclude the publishing node) interested in the event, then there are at least k messages exchanged in the event delivery. Therefore, we define a parameter *matching rate*, meaning the probability of e_i matching f_j, in which e_i is randomly selected from all events, and f_j is randomly selected from all filters.

In the experiments, we randomly generated the events and filters, so that they meet the given covering rate and matching rate. The content of each event is a set of "attribute=value" pairs. Each attribute is of a *double* data type, and the value is randomly generated in the zone of (0, 10). The content of each subscription is a set of "attribute<value" pairs, in which the values are also randomly generated in the zone of (0, 10).

Suppose the number of total attributes is a_n, the number of attributes in each subscription is a_s, and the number of attributes in each event is a_e. Then:

$$\text{Covering rate} = C_{a_n}^{a_s} \times (1/2)^{a_s}$$

$$\text{Matching rate} = C_{a_n}^{a_e} \times (1/2)^{a_e}$$

6.2 Experimental Results

Figure 6(a) shows the average number of messages exchanged for a subscribing operation when $a_n=4$ and $a_s=4$ (the corresponding covering rate is 6.25%). Figure 6(b) shows the average number of messages exchanged for a subscribing operation when $a_n=5$ and $a_s=4$ (the corresponding covering rate is 1.25%). In the Scribe-based protocol, the subscription message just needs to be sent to a given node (rendezvous), so it certainly needs to exchange the least number of messages. From the figures we can see the IRBR protocol has the higher routing efficiency than the RPF protocol. The reason is that the RPF protocol aggregates filters on the basis of neighbor nodes, while the IRBR protocol aggregates filters on the basis of identifier ranges, so a filter is more likely to be covered by other filters in the IRBR protocol.

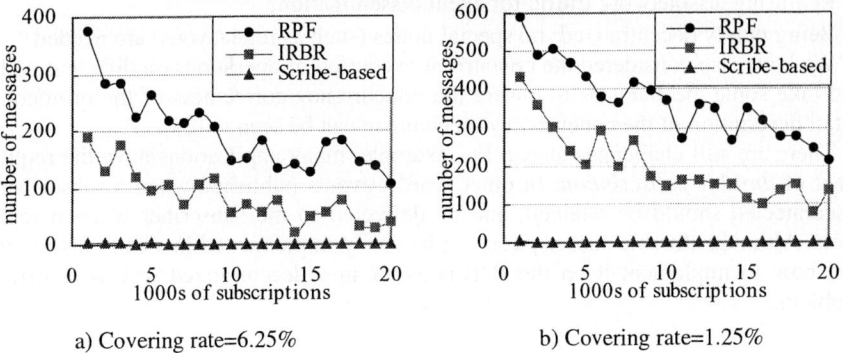

Fig. 6. The average number of messages exchanged for a subscribing operation

Figure 7(a) shows the average number of messages exchanged for a publishing operation when $a_n=4$ and $a_e=4$ (the corresponding matching rate is 6.25%). Figure 7(b)

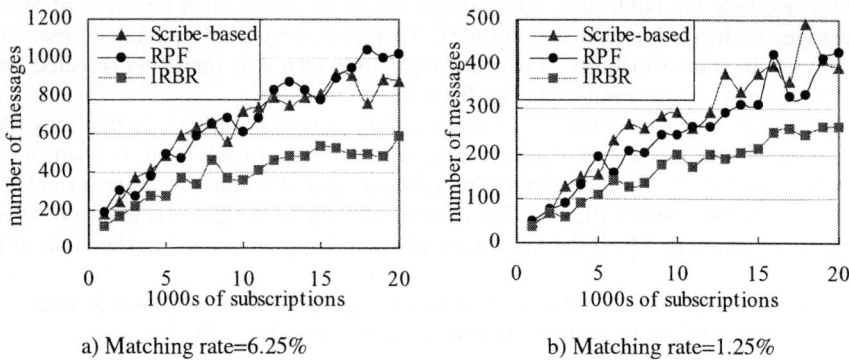

a) Matching rate=6.25% b) Matching rate=1.25%

Fig. 7. The average number of messages exchanged for a publishing operation

shows the average number of messages exchanged for a publishing operation when $a_n=5$ and $a_e=4$ (the corresponding matching rate is 1.25%). From the figures we can see the IRBR protocol is more efficient in event delivery than the other two protocols.

7 Conclusion

In this paper, we propose a new type of content-based routing protocol over structured P2P networks — Identifier Range Based Routing (IRBR) protocol. It can be naturally integrated with the routing protocol of the structured P2P networks, and has the following advantages in comparison with existing pub/sub systems over structured P2P networks:
- Supporting pure content-based pub/sub systems;
- Providing a higher level of reliability guarantee;
- Requiring less network traffic for event dissemination;
- Being purely decentralized; no special nodes (such as rendezvous) are needed.

We have also considered the concurrent execution of operations on different nodes, and take some mechanisms to ensure the concurrency correctness of the protocol. A detail description of the concurrency mechanism can be seen in [29].

There are still challenges ahead. For example, many applications have the requirement of *durable subscription*. In other words, events published when a subscriber is disconnected should be retained, and be delivered to the subscriber when it reconnects. Although durable subscription can be easily implemented in a centralized manner, how to implement it on the P2P network in a decentralized way is a difficult problem.

References

1. P. Th. Eugster, P. A. Felber, R. Guerraoui, A.-M. Kermarrec. The many faces of publish/subscribe. ACM Computing Surveys, 35(2) (2003) 114 – 131

2. A. Carzaniga, D. S. Rosenblum and A. L. Wolf: Content-Based Addressing and Routing: A General Model and its Application. Technical Report CU-CS-902-00, Department of Computer Science, University of Colorado at Boulder (2000)
3. B. Segall, D. Arnold, J. Boot, M. Henderson, and T. Phelps: Content based routing with elvin4. In: Proceedings of AUUG2K. (2000)
4. G. Cugola, G. Picco, and A. Murphy: Towards dynamic reconfiguration of distributed publish-subscribe middleware. In: Proceedings of 3rd International Workshop on Software Engineering and Middleware. (2002)
5. Z. Shen and S. Tirthapura: Self-stabilizing routing in publish-subscribe systems. In: Proceedings of the Third International Workshop on Distributed Event-Based Systems (DEBS'04). (2004)
6. P. Costa, M. Migliavacca, G. P. Picco, and G. Cugola: Introducing reliability in content-based publish-subscribe through epidemic algorithms. In: Proceedings of the 2nd International Workshop on Distributed Event-Based Systems (DEBS'03). (2003)
7. A. Rowstron and P. Druschel: Pastry: Scalable, distributed object location and routing for large-scale peer-to-peer systems. In: Proceedings of IFIP/ACM Middleware Conference. (2001)
8. B. Zhao, J. Kubiatowicz, and A. Joseph: Tapestry: An Infrastructure for Fault-Tolerant Wide-area Location and Routing. Technical Report No. UCB/CSD-01-1141, Computer Science Division, University of California, Berkeley (2001)
9. I. Stoica, R. Morris, D. Karger, F. Kaashoek, and H. Balakrishnan: Chord: A Scalable Peer-to-peer Lookup Service for Internet Applications. In: Proceedings of the SIGCOMM (2001) 149-160
10. S. Ratnasamy, P. Francis, M. Handley, R. Karp, and S. Shenker: A Scalable Content-Addressable Network. Proceedings of the SIGCOMM (2001) 161-172
11. A. Carzaniga, D. S. Rosenblum, and A. L. Wolf: Design and evaluation of a wide-area event notification service. ACM Trans. on Computer Systems 19(3) (2001) 332-383
12. G. Banavar, T. D. Chandra, B. Mukherjee, J. Nagarajarao, R. E. Strom, and D. C. Sturman: An efficient multicast protocol for content-based publish-subscribe systems. In: Proceedings of 19th IEEE International Conference on Distributed Computing Systems. (1999)
13. R. Chand and P. A. Felber: A Scalable Protocol for Content-Based Routing in Overlay Networks. In: Proceedings of 2nd IEEE International Symposium on Network Computing and Applications (2003) 123-130
14. A. Riabov, Z. Liu, J. Wolf, P. Yu and L. Zhang: Clustering algorithms for content-based publication-subscription systems. In: Proceedings of 22nd IEEE International Conference on Distributed Computing Systems (2002)
15. Y. Wang, L. Qiu, D. Achlioptas, G. Das, P. Larson, and H. Wang: Subscription partitioning and routing in content-based publish/subscribe networks. In: Proceedings of 16th International Symposium on Distributed Computing (2002)
16. F. Cao and J. P. Singh. Efficient event routing in content-based publish-subscribe service networks. In: Proceedings of the 23rd Conference of the IEEE Communications Society (Infocom) (2004)
17. Y. K. Dalal and R. Metcalfe: Reverse path forwarding of broadcast packets. Communications of the ACM 21(12) (1978) 1040-1048
18. G. Cugola, E. D. Nitto, and A. Fuggetta: The JEDI event-based infrastructure and its application to the development of the OPSS WFMS. IEEE Trans. on Software Engineering 27(9) (2001) 827-850
19. G. Muhl: Large-Scale Content-Based Publish/Subscribe Systems. PhD thesis. Darmstadt University of Technology, Germany. (2002)
20. P. Pietzuch and J. Bacon: Hermes: A distributed event-based middleware architecture. In: Proceedings of the 1st International Workshop on Distributed Event-Based Systems (DEBS'02). (2002)

21. M. Castro, P. Druschel, A.-M. Kermarrec and A. Rowstron: SCRIBE: A large-scale and decentralised application-level multicast infrastructure. IEEE Journal on Selected Areas in Communications 20 (2002)
22. D. Tam, R. Azimi, and H.-A. Jacobsen: Building Content-Based Publish/Subscribe Systems with Distributed Hash Tables. In: Proceedings of 1st International Workshop on Databases, Information Systems, and Peer-to-Peer Computing (DBISP2P 2003). (2003) 138-152
23. W. W. Terpstra, S. Behnel, L. Fiege, A. Zeidler, and A. P. Buchmann: A peer-to-peer approach to content-based publish/subscribe. In: Proceedings of the 2nd international workshop on Distributed event-based systems (DEBS'03). (2003)
24. S. Q. Zhuang, B. Y. Zhao, A. D. Joseph, R. H. Katz, and J. Kubiatowicz: Bayeux: An Architecture for Scalable and Fault-tolerant Wide-Area Data Dissemination. In: Proceedings of the 11th International Workshop on Network and Operating System Support for Digital Audio and Video (NOSSDAV 2001). (2001)
25. P. Triantafillou and I. Aekaterinidis. Content-Based Publish-Subscribe Over Structured P2P Networks. In: Proceedings of the 3rd international workshop on Distributed event-based systems (DEBS'04). (2004)
26. S. El-Ansary, L. O. Alima, P. Brand, and S. Haridi: Efficient broadcast in structured P2P networks. In: Proceedings of the 2nd International Workshop on Peer-to-Peer Systems (IPTPS'03) (2003)
27. C.-Y. Chan, P. Felber, M. Garofalakis, and R. Rastogi: Efficient Filtering of XML Documents with XPath Expressions. The VLDB Journal 11(4) (2002) 354-379
28. Rice University: FreePastry Project. http://freepastry.rice.edu/FreePastry. (2004)
29. J. Wang, B. Jin, J. Wei, and J. Li: An Efficient Fault-tolerant Content-based Routing Protocol over Structured Peer-to-Peer Networks. Technical report, TCSE, Institute of Software, Chinese Academy of Sciences. (2004)

Covering Your Back: Intelligent Virtual Agents in Humanitarian Missions Providing Mutual Support

Pilar Herrero

Facultad de Informática. Universidad Politécnica de Madrid.
Campus de Montegancedo S/N.
28.660 Boadilla del Monte. Madrid. Spain
pherrero@fi.upm.es

Abstract. One of the first areas where virtual reality found a practical application was military training. Two fairly obvious reasons have driven the army to explore and employ this kind of technique in their training; to reduce exposure to hazards and to increase stealth. Many aspects of military operations are very hazardous, and they become even more dangerous if the soldier seeks to improve his performance. Intelligent Virtual Agents (IVAs) are used to simulate a wide variety of high fidelity simulation scenarios like the one we have described above. The work described in this paper focuses on military humanitarian assistance and disaster relief in Co-operative Information System (CIS), emphasising on how important it is for IVAs inhabiting this kind of scenarios to be aware of their surrounding before interacting with it. We also highlight the importance of increasing the psychological "coherence" between the real life and the virtual environment experience in order to reflect human perception, behaviour and reactions.

1 Introduction

Imagine yourself as a young soldier agent (A1) who has been assigned to humanitarian missions for keeping the peace in a country in military conflict. You are on night patrol with your comrade (A2) when you make out a suspicious movement in the parking of one of the buildings.

At the distance at which you are located it is almost impossible to distinguish clearly what is going on there and therefore you decide to get out of the patrol car to be closer of the scene of the incident and find out what is exactly happening.

The closer is the soldier A1 to the scene the clear is the perception that the agent has from the scene and therefore the bigger is the awareness that the agent has of the situation.

The agent A1 realises that there is a struggle between two people but some details – such as the female/male sex - are not visible from a distance.

When the soldier A1 hears a scream of a young female voice asking for help, he becomes conscious of the situation: a man is struggling a young lady.

The soldier A1 wants to move towards the scene but he needs a wise and sensible strategy before making the approaching movement. He decides to alert to his comrade (A2), sending him to surround the parking.

While the soldier A2 goes towards the back of the parking, the soldier A1 approaches to the crime scene, perceiving more details: the struggler has a gun and he is aiming to the woman head while he is trying to take advantage of her.

In that moment the soldier agent A2 screams: "Halt!", the struggler turns around to see what is going on and then the soldier agent A1 shoot him, liberating the young lady.

In the above scenario, the collaboration between the soldiers agents plays a very important role as well as the combination of visual and hearing perception.

The research that we present in this paper is precisely oriented towards endowing IVAs with perceptual mechanisms that allow them to be "realistically *aware*" of their surroundings. We propose a perceptual model, which seeks to introduce more coherence between IVA perception and human being perception. This will increment the psychological "*coherence*" between the real life and the virtual environment experience. This coherence is especially important in order to simulate realistic situations as, for example, the scenarios described above. A useful training would involve endowing soldier agents with a human-like perceptual model, so that they would react to the same stimuli as a human soldier. Agents lacking this perceptual model could react in a non-realistic way, hearing or seeing things that are too far away or hidden behind other objects. The perceptual model we propose in this paper introduces human limitations inside the agent's perceptual model with the aim of reflecting human perception.

In this paper, we firstly give an overview of how we have designed and formalised our perceptual model: analysing the factors that can make the perceptual model more realistic; re-defining and reinterpreting a set of concepts - introduced by an awareness model, known as the Spatial Model of Interaction- to be used as our perceptual model key concepts. We also explain how our perceptual model has been implemented and we describe some scenarios where our perceptual model has found a practical application: military training in humanitarian assistance and disaster relief in Co-operative Information System (CIS).

2 Designing and Formalising Our Perceptual Model

Many approaches have been employed to implement the visual process of perception in IVAs, oriented to different kind of applications, such as artificial creatures [Blumberg 97], [Terzopoulos 97] or virtual humans [Chopra-Khullar 01], [Hill 02a], [Hill 02b], [Noser 97], [Thalmann 01]. Perception in those agents has been modelled in diverse ways, depending on what they were designed for. Basically, the implementation of perception can be focussed on the processing of sensory inputs [Terzopoulos 97] or on the cognitive process of perception [Hill 02a]. In this paper we have focused on the sensory inputs of the perceptual model. A classification of current approaches can be found in [Herrero 03].

Perception can be understood as the first level of a situational awareness model. Endsley [Endsley 88], [Endsley 93] defines situational awareness -or situational assessment-as "The perception of the elements in the environment within a volume of space and time, the comprehension of their meaning, the projection of their status into the near future, and the prediction of how various actions will affect the fulfilment of one's goals" [Endsley 95]. So, the critical factors in the process of situation assessment are (Figure 1): Perception of elements in current situation; Comprehension of current situations, and Projection of future.

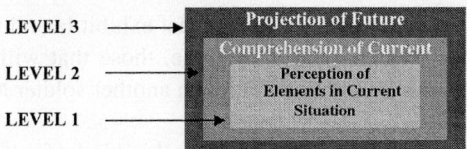

Fig. 1. Situational Awareness

Bearing in mind the previous definition, sensitive perception can be understood as the first level of awareness, and therefore, taking into account our own experience on Computer Supported Collaborative Work (CSCW) applications, we have decided to develop our perceptual model based on one of the most successful CSCW awareness models, known as the "Spatial Model of Interaction" (SMI) [Benford 93]. This awareness model introduces a set of key awareness concepts - which have been extended to introduce some human factors - and uses the properties of the space to mediate interaction.

There are many factors that contribute to our ability as humans to perceive an object, some of which are directly working on the mental processes, being not easily modelled or reproduced in a virtual world.

In order to carry out this research we have analysed separately those human factors which are relevant for visual and auditory [Herrero 03] perception. Then, we have selected some of them to be introduced in our perceptual model: This concepts are the perceptual acuity, the transitory region as well as some physical factors.

The perceptual acuity is a measure of the sense's ability to resolve fine detail and is dependent upon the person itself, its perceptual capabilities, the item's surroundings and the person's surroundings. While in a visual medium it is known as *Visual Acuity*, in a hearing medium it is known as *Auditory Acuity*.

The transitory region is the interval in the space between perfect and null perception. This factor plays an important role in a visual medium where it is known as *Lateral Vision*. In a hearing medium this concept can be understood as the cone in the space known as *Cone of confusion* (a cone extending outwards from each ear where sound events are subject to ambiguity)

These human factors are strongly related to some physical factors such as the distance between the item (object or sound) and the position of the agent's sense ($d_{sense\text{-}item}$) and some *Item's Factors* such as the object's size (for a visual medium) or the sound intensity (in a hearing medium).

In a hearing medium it is also important to take into account some factors associated to the sound source propagation, as the directivity of sound, introducing the directional characteristic of a sound source.

Intelligent soldier agents that exhibit visual acuity would be able, for instance, to perceive a message, wrote on a notice board, only if the distance from the agent to that notice board is within the visual range of perception. In a hearing medium, Intelligent soldier agents that exhibit auditory acuity would be able, for instance, to detect a sound only if its frequency is within the usual human audible range, and only if it is not too far.

In the same way, intelligent soldier agents that exhibit lateral vision would be able to avoid anomalous behaviours as, for example, those that will happen if a soldier agent A is not aware of and can not interact with another soldier agent B who is inside its Lateral Vision area.

Finally, intelligent soldier agents inhabiting this kind of environments would be able to address verbally their messages if they exhibit the directivity of sound property.

3 Key Concepts in the Spatial Model of Interaction

As we mentioned in previous sections, the key concepts of our perceptual model are based on the main concepts of a CSCW awareness model known as *The Spatial Model of Interaction (SMI)* [Benford 93].

The spatial model, as its name suggests, uses the properties of space as the basis for mediating interaction. It was proposed as a way to control the flow of information of the environment in CVEs (Collaborative Virtual Environments). It allows objects in a virtual world to govern their interaction through some key concepts: medium, aura, awareness, focus, nimbus, adapters and boundaries.

Aura is the sub-space which effectively bounds the presence of an object within a given medium and which acts as an enabler of potential interaction. In each particular medium, it is also possible to delimit the observing object's interest; this area is called *focus:* "The more an object is within your focus the more aware you are of it". The focus concept has been implemented in the SMI as a circular sector limited by the object's aura.

In the same way, it is possible to represent the observed object's projection in a particular medium; this area is called *nimbus*: "The more an object is within your nimbus the more aware it is of you". The nimbus concept, as it was defined in the Spatial Model of Interaction, has always been implemented as a circumference in a visual medium. The radio of this circumference has an "ideal" infinite value, although in practice, it is limited by the object's aura.

The implementations of these concepts – aura, focus and nimbus- in the SMI didn't have in mind human aspects. Therefore, if our perceptual model for IVAs had taken these concepts as they were defined, then it would have reduced the level of coherence between the real and the virtual agent behaviour.

An additional concept was involved in controlling interaction between objects in the SMI, *awareness*. One object's awareness of another object quantifies the subjective importance or relevance of that object. The awareness relationship between every pair of objects is achieved on the basis of quantifiable *levels* of awareness between them and it is unidirectional and specific to each medium. Awareness between objects in a given medium is manipulated via *focus* and *nimbus*. Moreover, an object's aura, focus, nimbus, and hence awareness, can be modified through *boundaries* and some artefacts called *adapters*.

4 Reinterpreting the SMI's Key Concepts

Neither the SMI nor its implementations considered aspects of human perception. Therefore, we decided to introduce into the SMI some factors concerning human perception. In this section, we are going to describe how the key concepts defining the SMI have been modified to introduce these human factors.

A. Focus

In our perceptual model, the focus notion is the area within which the agent perceives the environment.

a) Visual Focus

Taking into account two human factors - the *Visual Acuity* and the *Lateral Vision* – and the *object's size*, in [Herrero 03] a new mathematical function has been defined to represent the human-like visual focus as a double cone delimited by two angles: one of them associated to the human foveal field of vision and the other one associated to human lateral field of vision (see figure 2).

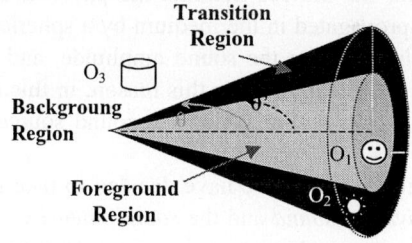

Fig. 2. IVAs Visual Focus in the Perceptual Model

An IVA endowed with this perceptual model and a focus as the showed in the figure 2 could be able of perceiving an object as O1, could be able of perceiving some details – as for example the movement- of an object as O2 and will not be able of perceiving an object as O3.

b) Hearing Focus

Taking into account two human perceptual factors - the *Auditory Acuity* and the *Cone of Confusion* -, a new mathematical function has been defined to represent the human-like hearing focus as an sphere which center is located in between both ears (see figure 3).

Fig. 3. IVAs Hearing Focus in the Perceptual Model

An IVA endowed with this perceptual model and a focus as the showed in the figure 3 could be able of detecting a sound only if the propagated sound reaches the agent's ear within its audible range.

B. Nimbus

Just as with the above-mentioned focus concept, the nimbus concept in the Spatial Model of Interaction does not consider any human factors, thus hypothetically reducing the level of coherence between real and virtual agent behaviour.

a) Visual Nimbus

Taking into account the object's physical constraints – such as the object's shape and size-, in [Herrero 03] some mathematical functions have been defined to represent the object's nimbus as an ellipsoid or a sphere depending on the conic by which it is circumscribed.

b) Hearing Nimbus

In a hearing medium, the nimbus delimits the physical area of projection of a sound source. Sound is propagated in the medium by a spherical wavefront, but even if this occurs, it could happen that the sound amplitude, and therefore its intensity, weren't the same in all the directions. For this reason, in this model we interpret the nimbus concept as the region within which the sound source is projected with the same intensity.

Starting from this interpretation, we have decided to take into account some factors –such as the *directivity of sound* and the *sound intensity* – and their influence on nimbus and its representation within an environment, leaving the rest of the factors, as for example, the presence of non-linear effects or the homogeneity of the medium, for future research and extensions to this work.

Taking into account these factors, in [Herrero 03] we have centred our research in the projection of human voice, giving a new mathematical function to represent the human-like hearing nimbus as a cardioid (Figure 4).

This figure represents the perimeter within which the human being projects its voice (human voice nimbus) with a given intensity. For any other sound source (different to human voice), it would be necessary to calculate the pattern of directivity before formulating nimbus.

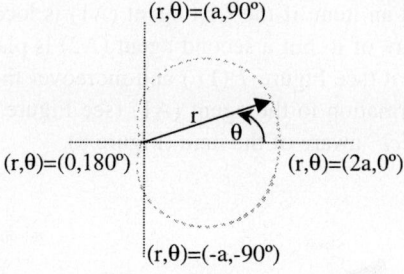

Fig. 4. Auditory Nimbus

C. Awareness

Awareness is a very broad concept with many different meanings in many different areas. In fact, we have reinterpreted the concept of "awareness" introduced by the SMI from the agent perception point of view.

In our perceptual model *awareness* represents whether an agent perceive an object or a sound as to be aware of it.

In this way, in our visual perceptual model, awareness represents the overlap between the focus and the nimbus. If this overlap is not null, it means that the agent is aware of the item's presence (Figure 5).

Fig. 5. Visual Awareness

In the same way, in our hearing perceptual model, awareness represents whether the item (the sound in this case) "effectively" projects inside the agent's focus. If so, it means that the agent is aware of the sound's projection (Figure 6).

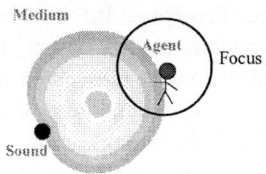

Fig. 6. Hearing Awareness

In Co-operative Information System (CIS), the awareness that an agent has of an item could be associated to the presence of a third agent. In this way, giving two agents (A1 and A2) and an item, if the first agent (A1) is located far away from the item as to be visual aware of it, but a second agent (A2) is placed closer to that item as to be visual aware of it (see Figure 7 (1)) and moreover the agent (A2) passes on verbally the item's information to the agent (A1) (see Figure 7 (2)), then the agent (A1) could be an *"indirect"* aware of the item (Figure 8).

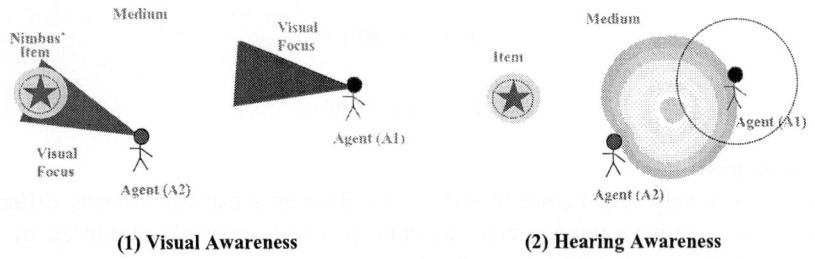

(1) Visual Awareness **(2) Hearing Awareness**

Fig. 7. "Indirect" Awareness in CIS

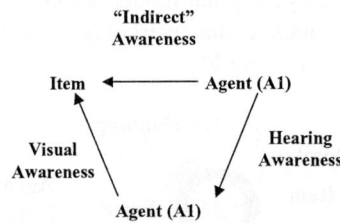

Fig. 8. An Scheme of "Indirect" Awareness in CIS

In CIS, the awareness that an agent has of an item could also be distorted by the presence of an additional agent/item. In this way, let's imagine a hearing medium where an agent A1 is having awareness of an item (a sound in this case). If while the agent (A1) is having a direct hearing awareness of this sound another agent (A2) starts speaking, the hearing awareness that the agent (A1) has of the sound could be distorted by the propagation of the agent (A2)'s voice (Figure 9).

The distorted awareness could be classify as: *High*, *Medium* and *Low* depending on the *distortion factor* (see the "Perceptual Information" section)

Taking into account the previous considerations, the perceptual information that an agent has of an "item"(object/sound) in a given medium must be more reliable when the agent has a *direct awareness* of the item than when the agent has a *indirect awareness* of the later must be more reliable than when the agent has a *distorted awareness* of the item. In the following section we are going to describe in detail how this perceptual information should be.

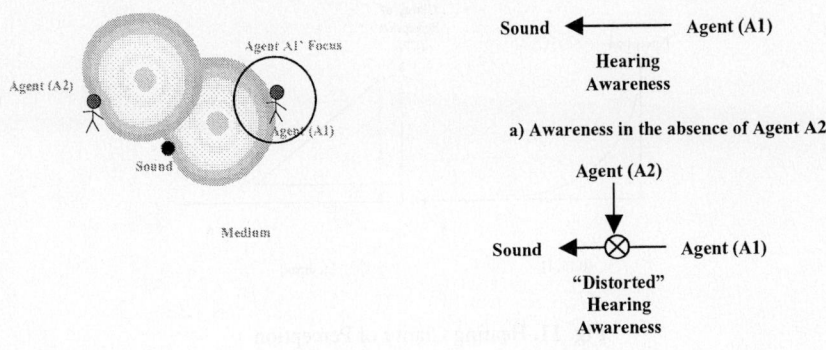

Fig. 9. "Distorted" Awareness in CIS

5 Perceptual Information

In the previous sections we have introduced the key concepts of our perceptual model as well as the awareness classification to determine what kind of awareness can have an agent of an object in CIS. In this section we are going to concentrate on the information that each an every agent can perceive from the environment.

The IVA's perceptual module will be in charge of calculating what in [Herrero 03] we have called *Clarity of Perception*.

Clarity of Perception is a measurement of the ability to perceive clearly an item (an object or a sound) inside the agent's visual or hearing focus. Once the awareness calculated for an item with respect to an agent is not null, the agent's perceptual module will calculate the clarity of perception for this item.

In [Herrero 03], and taking into account some perceptual studies introduced by [Howarth 97], [Levi, 02a] and [Levi 03b], we propose a set of Gaussians as the functions to describe the variation in the clarity of perception with the eye-object distance for a fixed object's size in the foreground and lateral region of perception, respectively (Figure 10).

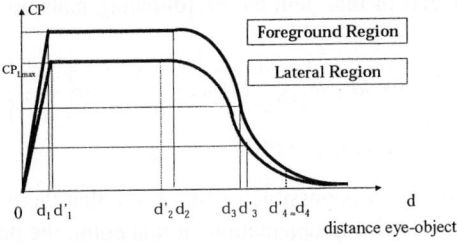

Fig. 10. Visual Clarity of Perception

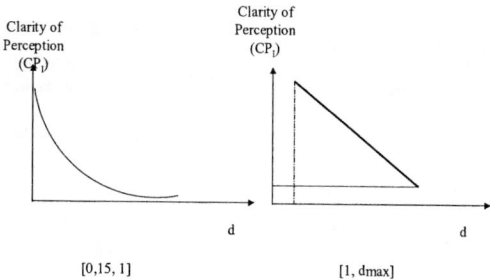

Fig. 11. Hearing Clarity of Perception

In the same way, in [Herrero 03] and mixing the theoretical studies introduced by [Zahorik 02] with the experimental results introduced by [Shinn-Cunningham 00], we also propose a set of functions to describe the binaural auditory calrity of perception versus the ear-sound distance (Figure 11).

As we have already introduced in the previous sections, the awareness of interaction between an agent and an item (object or sound) could be classified as "Direct Awareness", "Indirect Awareness" and "Distorted Awareness".

When a soldier agent is having a direct awareness of an item, the clarity of perception with which it is perceiving the item would be given by the set of visual (or hearing) functions introduced in [Herrero 03] (Figures 10 and 11).

However, when the soldier agent (A) is having an *indirect awareness* of an item – by an agent (B)-, the perceptual information that the agent A can get from the item could be given by explicit or implicit request. If the soldier agent A wants to know some specifics details of the item, then the agent A will ask to the soldier agent B for those specific details of the observed item that it wants to know, having therefore an "explicit indirect awareness". However, if the soldier agent A doesn't ask to the soldier agent B for any kind of specific details of the observed item, then the agent B could provide the agent A with that perceptual information that it consider useful for it, having therefore an "implicit indirect awareness". In both cases, the perceptual information could not be as precise as if the agent A would be perceiving the item by himself.

We propose to model the perceptual information that an agent – having an indirect awareness of an item- has of that item by the following mathematical function (equation 1, figure 12):

$$0 < Id < Id_{max} \quad PI(Id) = \frac{1}{\sigma\sqrt{2\pi}} \exp\left(\frac{id^2}{2\sigma^2}\right) \quad (1)$$

$$Id > Id_{max} \quad PI(Id) = PI_{max}$$

Having a look to figure 12, it is possible to appreciate that there is a transition at (Id_t, PI_t). In our perceptual model implementation, at this point, the perceptual information increases form a "low" to "medium". In the same way, the perceptual information will get its maximum value at (Id_{max}, PI_{max}). If later the agent's transmitter is working as the agent's own perceptual senses.

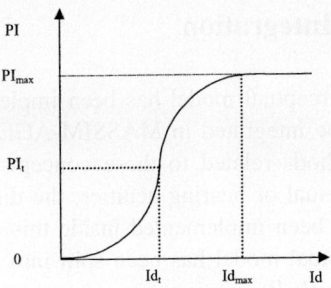

Fig. 12. Indirect Awareness: Perceptual information (PI) vs. the item's details (Id)

When the soldier agent (A) is having an *direct awareness* of an item – for example a sound (S1)- which is been propagated in the medium with an intensity (I1), if while the agent A is perceiving the sound a second sound source (S2) starts propagating in the same medium with an intensity (I2), the perceptual information that the agent A has of the sound (S1) could be distorted by the interference with the propagation of the sound S2, being the level of distortion dependent on the distance between the sound source S1 and the sound source S2 d_{S1S2} as well as the intensity associated to the sound source S2.

We propose a mathematical function (equation 2) to formalise the perceptual information that a agent (A) has of an item (Item) distorted by the presence of a second item (Item'):

$$PI_{(A->Item)Item'} = f(d_{Item-Item'}, Item')PI_{(A->Item)} \qquad (2)$$

where:

$PI_{A->Item}$: Represents the perceptual information that an agent has of an item in direct awareness.

$f(d_{Item-Item'}, Item')$: Represents the *distortion factor* associated to the presence of the item "Item' " in the medium. This factor depends on the distance between both items as well as on the physical details of the item "Item' "- such as the item's intensity when the item is a sound.

In our perceptual model, where we have classified the perceptual information as *High*, *Medium* and *Low*, the factor of distortion could modify the perceptual information from *High* to *Medium* - or even *Low* and from *Medium* into *Low*.

In this way, A *High* distortion factor (*high distorted awareness*) will change *high* perceptual information into *low* perceptual information while a *Medium* distortion factor (*medium distorted awareness*) will change *High* perceptual information into *Medium* perceptual information,

In the following section we are going to describe how we have implemented our perceptual model and where we have integrated it in order to obtain the perceptual model validation.

6 Perceptual Model Integration

The human-like agent's perceptual model has been implemented as an independent object-oriented library to be integrated in MASSIM-AGENT, and most of the key human concepts (and methods related to these concepts) defined in this research work, like, for example, visual or hearing acuities, the distance of resolution or the clarity of perception, have been implemented inside this library. Moreover, the implementation of our perceptual model has been split into two different components: *Perceptual Engine* and *Agent's Perception*.

The perceptual engine implements concepts, such as focus, nimbus and awareness for all the agents, objects and sound sources in the environment.

The agent's perception implements concepts, such as the agent's clarity of perception, as well as the specific agent's perceptual information.

The perceptual engine is in charge of getting the physical details, such as position size or sound source intensity, of all the objects/agents (in general we will call them items) that are in the environment and calculating their nimbus. The perceptual engine also asks each agent's about its perceptual details –such as its sense acuity or which is the angle delimiting its field of vision-, calculating the agent's focus and outputting a list of all those items that can be perceived by this agent according to these physical and perceptual details.

This library has been integrated with MASSIM_AGENT, a prototype system built using the MASSIVE-3 CVE system and the SIM_AGENT toolkit for developing agents, but the design of this library has been done to make it independent on any VE system or agent platform. In fact, we have also integrated it with an intelligent tutoring system in a project called MAEVIF (Model for the Application of Intelligent Virtual Environments to Education and Training). This project is part of the Spanish National R&D Plan.

MASSIM_AGENT is the first prototype resulting of the integration of the MASSIVE-3 system and the SIM_AGENT toolkit. MASSIM_AGENT was the result of a collaboration established between the Mixed Reality Laboratory (MRL) at the University of Nottingham and the Universidad Politécnica de Madrid (UPM).

In the figure 13, it is possible to appreciate how the perceptual engine triggers a sequence of interactions across the *agent's perception* component, *MASSIM_AGENT*, *MASSIVE-3* and all the existing agents in *SIM_AGENT*.

First, the *perceptual engine* interacts with *MASSIVE-3* to join an environment (*joinMassive()*), introducing some objects inside this environment (*massiveObjectNew()*) and making a list of these objects (*massiveCreateList()*).

Then the *perceptual engine* calculates the nimbus for all the objects that have been created inside the environment. Once it has associated a nimbus with each of these objects, the *perceptual engine* also has to calculate the agent's focus for all the agents created by SIM_AGENT. Before calculating the agent's focus, the *perceptual engine* needs to ask the *agent's perception* component about the perceptual details of every agent that inhabits the environment. The required details depend on the human sense to be simulated.

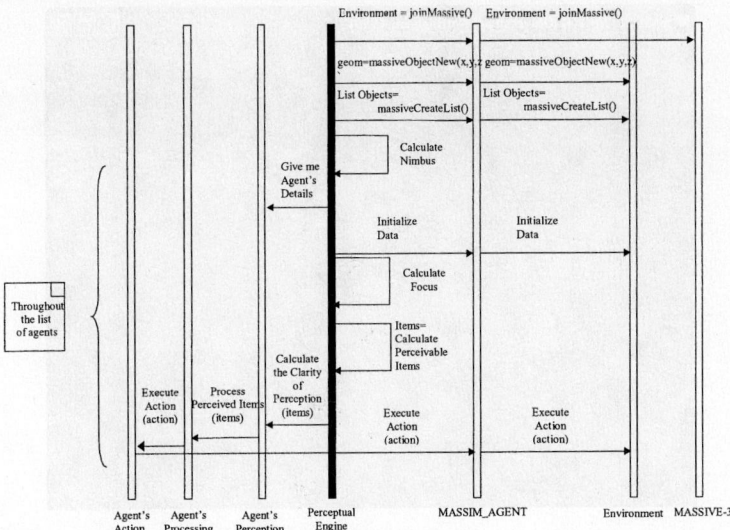

Fig. 13. Sequence Diagram

Once the *perceptual engine* has calculated the foci and nimbi shapes, it determines the perceivable items, and, from then onwards, the *agent's perception* block will just concentrate on determining the perceptual information for these items.

This perceptual information is sent to *SIM_AGENT* for a decision to be made on the actions to be executed by the agent. These decisions are made by the *agent's central processing* component, which contains a set of pre-established rules.

A special situation will arise if there is a boundary between the agent and the object to be perceived. If this happens, the *agent's perception* needs to ask to the *perceptual engine* about the boundaries before calculating how the clarity of perception is modified by their presence.

7 Some Scenarios for Human-Like Perception

In order to prove the usefulness of the proposed perception model, lets consider that, as it was previously mentioned, mIVAS systems can be used to simulate military operations, as for example, humanitarian missions, where the soldiers' training plays a very important role.

In this kind of systems, soldiers can be trained for living and surviving the worse real-life situations. To get a useful training, it is important to endow soldier agents with a human-like perceptual model.

Fig. 14. The military scenario

Different scenarios and situations can be raised where human-like perception plays a very important role. In this section we are going to describe some of them.

To understand the results presented in this section, the reader has to take into account the classification of visual and hearing perceptual information established to implement the perceptual model. This classification determines that the agent's perceptual information can be: *High*, *Medium* and *Low*.

Lets imagine that a soldier agent (A1) is on patrol with its comrade (A2). The patrol (P1) is placed at a physical position given by the co-ordinates (x,y,z)= (1,0,0) in the space, in meters, with an orientation of 90° related to the x axis of co-ordinates.

Lets also imagine a citizen that lies down on the ground at co-ordinates (10,25,0), remaining immobile.

Each of the agents soldiers is endowed with a visual acuity (in Snellen notation) equivalent to 20/20 and his foreground angle of vision is $\theta=30°$ while his lateral angle of vision is $\theta'=65°$.

Introducing all these values in the implemented perceptual model, we get the foreground and lateral soldier's cone of vision [Herrero 03]. In the same way, we get the nimbus geometry associated to the citizen, which in this case is an ellipsoid, and the citizen's nimbus, following the set of equations introduced in [Herrero 03], the perceptual model calculates the maximum distance of resolution at which each of the soldiers could perceive the citizen's details.

As the patrol is located at a position farther than this distance, none of the s soldiers agents can perceive clearly what is the object that is lying on the floor.

As another patrol (P2) is close to the scene, the soldier agent A1 in the patrol P1 ask to the patrol P2 to go to there. When the patrol P2 arrives to the object's position, they realise that the object is a human body and, immediately, one the agents assigned to the patrol P2 (A3) start make body gestures while the other (A4) asks for assistance by radio, -the men needs urgently medical attendance.

Although the patrol P1 could not be aware of the object on the floor due to the physical distance, the patrol P1 can be aware of the body gestures made by the soldier agent (A3) having therefore and "implicit indirect awareness".

In this moment, the patrol P2 has a *high direct awareness* of the citizen, the patrol P1 has a *medium direct awareness* of the patrol P2 and the patrol P1 has a *low indirect awareness* of the citizen.

Lets now imagine that the patrol P1 moves toward the patrol P2 and while the patrol P1 is located at co-ordinates (0.5,6,0) the soldier agent A3 start screaming to explain verbally the citizen situation. The voice of the agent A3 propagates into the medium arriving to the ear of the agents inside the patrol P1 with an intensity close to 60dB. This intensity is within the agent's audible range, and therefore, in this moment, the patrol P2 has a *high direct awareness* of the citizen, the patrol P1 has a *high direct awareness* of the patrol P2 and the patrol P1 has a *medium indirect awareness* of the citizen.

And finally, when the patrol P1 arrives to the scene, both patrols will have *high direct awareness* of the citizen.

Lets also imagine that while the two patrols are in the scene, the soldier agents A2 and A4 are chatting pleasantly, having a *high direct awareness* of each other. In that moment, a medical helicopter arrives to pick the citizen up. The helicopter interfere in the agents conversation and, starting from that moment, the soldier agent A2 will have a *distorted awareness* of the soldier agent A4, being the factor of distortion dependent on the helicopter's physical details (such as its engine intensity or its position). While the helicopter is placed at co-ordinates (x,y,z)=(-40,25,25) the perceptual information that the agent A2 has of the agent A4 is *medium*, having therefore a *medium distorted awareness*. However when the helicopter moves to co-ordinates (x,y,z)=(1,25,0), the helicopter's distortion factor increases and the perceptual information that the agent A2 can get from the agent A4 decreases to *low*, having therefore a *high distorted awareness*.

8 Conclusions

We have developed a human-like perceptual model for Intelligent Virtual Agents (IVAs) based on one of the most successful awareness models in Computer Supported Cooperative Work (CSCW), called the Spatial Model of Interaction (SMI) [Benford 93]. Our perceptual model extends the key concepts of the SMI to IVAs and makes a reinterpretation of the SMI key concepts in the context of human-like perception.

The work described in this paper focuses on military humanitarian assistance and disaster relief in Co-operative Information System (CIS), emphasising on how important it is for IVAs inhabiting this kind of scenarios to be aware of their surrounding before interacting with it.

Based on previous works [Herrero 03], we have introduced a new awareness classification as a way of having a measurement of the perceptual information that a soldier agent can get from the environment in a specific situation.

We also highlight the importance of increasing the psychological "coherence" between the real life and the virtual environment experience in order to reflect human perception, behaviour and reactions.

Acknowledgements. The work presented in this paper has been supported by the Communication Research Group (CRG), led by Steve Benford and Chris Greenhalgh at the School of Computer Science and Information Technology in the University of Nottingham, in UK.

References

[Benford 93]   Benford, S.D., and Fahlén, L.E. A spatial Model of Interaction in Large Virtual Environments. Proc. Third European Conference on Computer Supported Cooperative Work (ECSCW'93), Milano, Italy. Kluwer Academic Publishers, 1993.

[Blumberg 97]   Blumberg, B. Go with the Flow: Synthetic Vision for Autonomous Animated Creatures. Proceedings of the First International Conference on Autonomous Agents (Agents'97), Marina del Rey, CA, 1997.

[Chopra-Khullar 01]   Chopra-Khullar, S. and Badler, N. Where to look? Automating attending behaviors of virtual human characters. Autonomous Agents and Multi-agent Systems 4(1/2), pp. 9-23, , 2001.

[Endsley 88]   Endsley. M., *Design and evaluation for situation awareness enhancement*. Proceedings of Human Factors Society and Annual Meeting, volume 1, 1988.

[Endsley 93]   Endsley. M. *Towards a theory of situation awareness*. Technical report, Texas Technical University, Department of Industrial Engineering, 1993.

[Endsley 95]   Endsley. M. Toward a Theory of Situation Awareness in Dynamic Systems. Human Factors, 37(1), 65-84, 1995.

[Herrero 03]   Herrero P. A Human.Like Perceptual Model for Intelligent Virtual Agents. Ph.D. Thesis. Universidad Politécnica de Madrid, Jun. 2003.

[Hill 02]   Hill, R. Han, C. van Lent, M. Applying Perceptually Driven Cognitive Mapping To Virtual Urban Environments. Conference on Innovative Applications of Artificial Intelligence (IAAI-2002) in Edmonton, Canada.2002.

[Hill 02]   Hill, R. Han, C. van Lent, M. Perceptually Driven Cognitive Mapping of Urban Environments. Proceedings of the First International Joint Conference on Autonomous Agents and Multiagent Systems, Bologna, Italy, July, 2002.

[Howarth 97]   Howarth, P. A. and Costello P.J., Contemporary Ergonomics 1997, Ed. S.A.Robertson, Taylor and Francis London,, pp 109-116, 1997.

[Levi 02]   Levi, D.M., Klein, S.A. & Hariharan, S. Suppressive and Facilitatory Spatial Interactions in Foveal Vision: Foveal Crowding is simple contrast masking. Journal of Vision, 2, 140-166. 2002. http://journalofvision.org/2/2/2/

[Levi 02]   Levi, D.M., Hariharan, S. & Klein, S.A. Suppressive and Facilitatory Spatial Interactions in Peripheral Vision: Peripheral Crowding is neither size invariant nor simple contrast masking. Journal of Vision, 2, 167-177.2002. http://www.journalofvision.org/2/2/3/

[Noser 97]   Noser, H., A Behavioral Animation System Based on L-systems and Synthetic Sensors for Actors. PhD Thesis. École Polytechnique Fédérale De Lausanne. 1997

[Shinn-Cunningham 00] Shinn-Cunningham, BG. Distance cues for virtual auditory space Proceedings of the IEEE 2000 International Symposium on Multimedia Information Processing. Sydney, Australia. December 2000.

[Terzopoulos 97] Terzopoulos D. and Rabie, T.F. Animat Vision: Active Vision in Artificial Animals. Published in Videre: Journal of Computer Vision Research, 1(1):2-19, 1997.

[Thalmann 01] Thalmann, D. The Foundations to Build a Virtual Human Society. Proc. Intelligent Virtual Actors (IVA'01), Madrid, Spain. 2001.

[Zahorik 02]   Zahorik, P. Assessing auditory distance perception using virtual acoustics J. Acoust. Soc. Am., 111, 1832-1846. 2002.

Dynamic Modelling of Demand Driven Value Networks

Antonia Albani, Christian Winnewisser, and Klaus Turowski

Business Informatics and Systems Engineering
Business Faculty, University of Augsburg,
Universitätsstraße 16, 86135 Augsburg, Germany
{antonia.albani, christian.winnewisser, klaus.turowski}
@wiwi.uni-augsburg.de

Abstract. Companies are more and more focusing on their core competencies and therefore are increasingly collaborating with partners, forming value networks in order to better react to fast changing market requirements. Value networks for complex products and services are exposed to dynamic changes making it very difficult for a requestor of a product or service to keep track on all suppliers or service providers contributing to a specific request. The modelling of such networks becomes very complex and therefore often diminishes the practical impact of supply network management approaches. This paper proposes a concept for the dynamic modelling of supply networks, introducing the concept of self modelling demand driven value networks. The concept has been proven by applying it to the business domain of strategic supply network development and by implementing a prototype application for the domain mentioned. Apart from introducing the concept, technical issues and design aspects of the implementation are discussed in this paper and the prototype is introduced.

1 Introduction

Innovations in information and communication technologies, primarily the emergence of the Internet, combined with drastic changes in the competitive landscape (e.g., globalisation of sales- and sourcing-markets, shortened product lifecycles, innovative pressure on processes), shifted managerial attention towards the use of information technologies to increase flexibility of the business system and to improve inter-company collaboration in value networks, often referred to as inter-organisational systems (IOS), e-collaboration and collaborative commerce [12, 17]. The concept of value networks itself with companies flexibly collaborating to design, produce, market and distribute products and services had been well established, e.g., by [14, 26], even before the above mentioned technologies had become available. One of the most important theoretical foundations of those works are the new institutional economics, most notably the transaction cost theory, as established and advanced, among others, by [7, 8, 27], who extend the neoclassical theory by analysing the influence of property-rights structures and transaction costs on incentives and economic behaviour. Part of the transaction cost theory is the notion that transaction cost occur when goods or services are transferred over a clear identifiable interface within an institution or between institutions and include the cost of information, negotiation and enforcement [9].

Apparently, technological innovations such as global, web-based infrastructures, standards and distributed systems can lead to a substantial reduction in transaction cost. E.g., electronic market places generally reduce the cost of information and negotiation, whereas advanced planning, controlling and management systems in the field of supply chain management could positively impact the cost of enforcement. As a consequence, sinking transaction cost can influence decisions about vertical integration resulting in changes in the structure of institutions, which might lead to the disintegration of value-chains. As a result, with the application of advanced information technology, value networks should emerge rapidly [18]. However, at present IT-enabled value networks can be largely found in the form of rather small, flexible alliances of professionalized participants, whereas the IT support of large value networks with multiple tiers of suppliers, as they can be found in many traditional production oriented industries, still causes considerable difficulties.

This is largely attributed to the fact that a key pre-requisite for IT-enabling large value networks is simply knowing all participants of the respective network. In large supply networks, which extend to tier-8 or even further with several hundred participants in industries such as automotive, this cannot be taken for granted, especially with respect to the fact that there is a constant churn of participants in such large networks. Therefore, the problem of modelling complex supply networks has to be solved before the necessary IT support for key business processes such as supply chain management, development, production planning and scheduling, fulfilment and customer relationship management can be introduced to transform those networks to operating, flexible value networks. In fact, [13] point out that the main reason for the lack of practical implementation of supply chain management systems in complex supply networks can be found in the high degree of complexity that is connected with the identification of supply chain entities and the modelling of the supply chain structure, as well as the high coordination effort.

To propose a solution for the above-described modelling problem for the IT-support of value networks, the concept of *self modelling demand driven networks* is introduced in chapter 2 of this article. To illustrate the concept of self modelling demand driven networks the business domain of strategic supply network development is introduced. This business domain serves as basis for the modelling, design and practical implementation of a prototype application for self modelling demand driven networks. The functional requirements and technical aspects of the application of strategic supply network development mentioned before are presented in chapter 3, whereas a description of the design issues and implementation of the prototype system is given in chapter 4.

2 Self Modelling Demand Driven Networks and the Domain of Strategic Supply Network Development

At the core of the concept of self modelling demand driven networks is the notion, that network nodes of a supply network can be identified by applying the pull principle. With the pull principle, a network node at the beginning of a (sub-)network can identify potential nodes, i.e. suppliers, in a subsequent tier by performing a bill of materials explosion. With this information, primary requirements and dependent requirements can be identified and the respective information can be communicated – sending a *demand* – to the respective network nodes, i.e. potential suppliers for dependent requirements, in the subsequent tier, as these suppliers are generally known by the initiating lot.

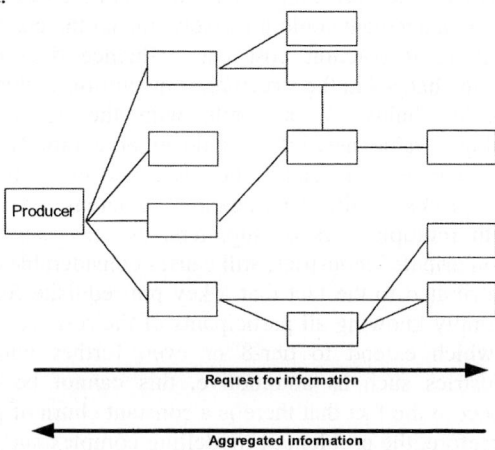

Fig. 1. Concept of self modelling networks

This procedure is repeated by the nodes in the respective tiers until the final tier is reached. Then, the information from the nodes further upstream is aggregated and split-lot transferred to the initiating node (see Fig. 1). Every node in tier-x receives demands from clients in tier-(x-1) and communicates sub-demands, depending on the demand received, to relevant suppliers in tier-(x+1). Since every node repeats the same procedure, a requestor receives back aggregated information from the whole dynamically built network based on a specific demand sent at a specific time. Having the fact that requestor-supplier relationship may change over time, new dynamically modelled supply networks – which may differ from the actual ones – are build whenever sending out new demands to the suppliers in the subsequent tiers. The practical application of this concept will be explained further in the subsequent chapters.

In order to illustrate the concept of self modelling demand driven networks and to develop a prototype application, a suitable business domain for practical implementation has to be identified. Most potential domains, such as supply chain management, require real-time interaction in the network, thereby considerably increasing the level of complexity for dynamic modelling of networks. Therefore, the domain of strategic purchasing has been chosen. Strategic purchasing deals with long-term supplier relationships, but is nowadays still focusing on the suppliers in tier-1, without taking advantages of information available in the whole supply network. Therefore strategic purchasing has to be put in a network perspective first before being suitable to serve as basis for a prototype application of self modelling networks.

2.1 From Strategic Sourcing to Strategic Supply Network Development

Purchasing has become a core function in enterprises in the 90ies. Current empiric research shows a significant correlation between the establishment of a strategic purchasing function and the financial success of an enterprise, independent from the industry surveyed [6]. One of the most important factors in this connection is the buyer-supplier-relationship. At many of the surveyed companies, a close cooperation between buyer and supplier in areas such as long-term planning, product development and coordination of production processes led to process improvements and resulting cost reductions that were shared between buyer and suppliers [6].

In practice, supplier development is widely limited to suppliers in tier-1. With respect to the above demonstrated, superior importance of supplier development we postulate the extension of the traditional frame of reference in strategic sourcing from a supplier-centric to a supply-network-scope [3] i.e., the further development of the strategic supplier development to a strategic supply network development. This refocuses the object of reference in the field of strategic sourcing by analysing supplier networks instead of single suppliers. Embedded in this paradigm shift is the concept of the value network that has been described in the introduction.

2.2 Description of the Functional Tasks of Strategic Supply Network Development

To design a prototype for self modelling demand driven networks based on the domain of strategic supply network development, the respective functional tasks have to be defined. Those tasks will be derived from the main tasks of strategic sourcing. The most evident changes are expected for functions with cross-company focus. The functional tasks of strategic supply network development have been illustrated in a function decomposition diagram [3, 2] (see Fig. 2).

Processes and tasks that will be automated have been shaded. Following, only the task of *"Model strategic supply networks"* is described being the only part of the process that leads to the modelling of strategic supply networks. The focus is set on changes to current tasks of strategic purchasing. For detailed information about the other tasks we refer to [3, 2].

Task „Model strategic supply networks": The process "identification of strategic supply networks" from strategic purchasing undergoes the most evident changes in the shift to a supply network centric perspective. The expansion of the traditional frame of reference in strategic sourcing requires more information than merely data on existing and potential suppliers in tier-1. Instead, the supply networks connected with those suppliers have to be identified and evaluated, e.g., by comparing alternative supply networks in the production network. Requirements and technical issues of this functionality will be illustrated in more detail in chapter 3, whereas the design and development of the application implementing that functionality will be explained in chapter 4.

According to the assumptions described above, the rating of supply networks requires the evaluation of networks instead of single suppliers. There has been preparatory work on evaluation methods for business networks (e.g., [20, 18]) on

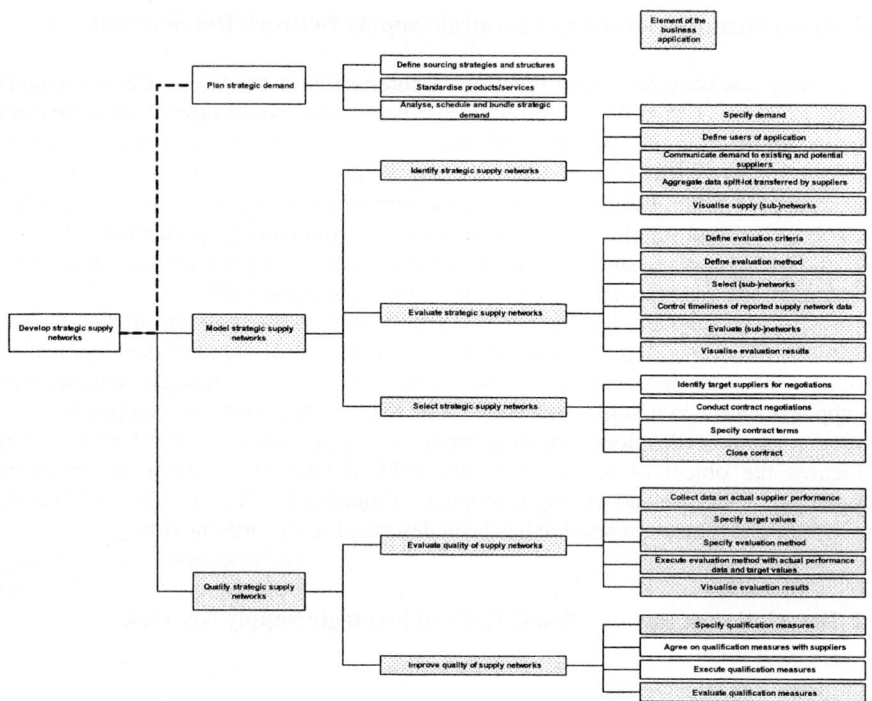

Fig. 2. Functional decomposition diagram for the supply network development [3, 2]

which we have based initial methods for the described application. However, there is need for further research, especially in the area of aggregation of incomplete information. For the time being, the problem has been tackled by identifying strategic, "mission critical" suppliers through a multi-dimensional mix of evaluation criteria (e.g., in the area of volume, quality, service levels, processes) and by aggregating the evaluation results for these suppliers as representatives for the whole supply network.

In the first prototype implementation, the selection of suppliers will not be automated by the application. Strategic supply network development deals with long-term supplier relationships. An automation of respective fundamental contract negations seems neither feasible nor desirable in the short term. In fact, the results from automated supply network identification and evaluation should be used as decision support for supplier selection.

3 Functional Requirements and Technological Issues of Self Modelling Demand Driven Value Networks

Having explained the concept of self modelling demand driven value networks constituting the basis for the development of the strategic supply network development (SSND) application, the functional requirements and the technical issues of the application need to be analysed in more detail.

3.1 Functional Requirements for the SSND System

The SSND system supports companies in identifying and developing their strategic networks, in order to improve their productivity and to compete on the daily market. Fig. 3 shows a sample network with the nodes representing companies, being either producers or suppliers depending on the context.

Fig. 3 on the left shows the complete demand driven network constituted of existing (nodes highlighted) and alternative supply sub-networks. Existing sub-networks are those with whom the producer already collaborates. Alternative sub-networks are networks which are built by sending a demand for a specific product to new chosen suppliers, with yet no relation to the producer. The whole network is demand driven since the producer communicates a specific strategic demand, by performing a bill of materials explosion, to existing and selected alternative suppliers in tier-1. Subsequently, the suppliers in tier-1 perform themselves a bill of materials explosion reporting the corresponding sub-demands to their own respective suppliers. E.g., for supplier 1-2, these are the suppliers 2-2, 2-3 and 2-4 in tier-2. In the following, these suppliers report the newly defined sub-demands to their related suppliers in tier-3, which split-lot transfer the requested information including e.g. ability of delivery for the requested product, capacity per day, minimum volume to be ordered, time of delivery. The requestors aggregate the information received from all suppliers contacted for a specific request with the own information and send it back to the supplier 1-2 in tier-1. Having aggregated the information of all suppliers, the supplier 1-2 adds its own information before split-lot transferring it to the producer.

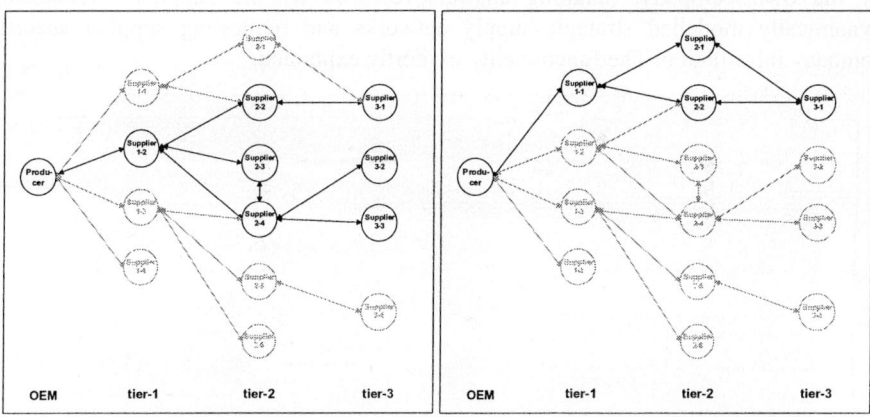

Fig. 3. Left: Supplier Network. Right: Alternative Supplier Network

With the suppliers' data locally available, the producer can visualise the selected sub-network, in which each participant constitutes a network hub. Based on that data, the producer is able to evaluate the performance of that selected sub-network by self defined benchmarks. In order to optimise sub-networks, alternative demand driven sub-networks can be visualised and modelled by applying the same concept as described above to new defined suppliers. Fig. 3 on the right highlights an alternative virtual supply sub-network fulfilling the requirements for a product of the specific demand sent. In the event of this alternative supply sub-network being the best performing one in the whole network, the existing supply sub-network can be modified, substituting supplier 1-2 in tier-1 with the new supplier 1-1, while keeping supplier 2-2 in tier-2 and supplier 3-1 in tier-3.

To illustrate the functionality which needs to be implemented and provided for each network node Use Cases [16] have been defined and documented. The most important use cases are shown exemplary in Fig. 4.

Looking at the system running on one node, there are different actors interacting with that system. The actor *user* is the responsible person of the company running the system on the node focusing on. The actor *client* represents clients who potentially send demands for a specific product to the company. The actor *supplier* represents actual or potential suppliers which are requested to collaborate in order to fulfil a specific demand requested by a client. Additionally there is an actor called *yellow pages* which is a central registration system allowing new companies, not yet known in the system, to make them publicly available in the SSND network. The yellow pages platform is the entry point to the SSND network for companies not yet collaborating with or known by an existing network node. The possibility of integrating new nodes (unknown companies for the SSND system) to the supply network by registering at a central platform (yellow pages) provides companies with an additional value of modelling alternative supply networks with potential suppliers in tier-1 not yet known by the companies and eventually performing better in order to fulfil requested demands.

The functionality provided by the SSND system is made up of tasks for registering to the network, handling, specifying and sending demands received by clients or defined by the own company, handling answers received by the suppliers, visualising dynamically modelled strategic supply networks and requesting supplier specific company information. The functionality is shortly explained.

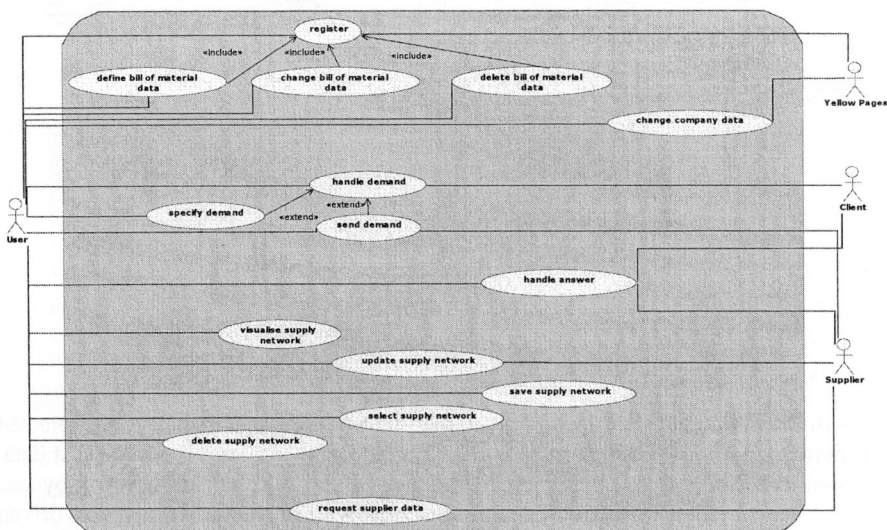

Fig. 4. Use cases for the domain of strategic supply network development

In order to become a member of the network, not only general information about a company, like name, address, branch, transaction volume, etc. is necessary to be made available over the yellow pages in the SSND system, but also information about products a company is producing. Therefore a user of the SSND system needs to be able to *define*, *change* and *delete bill of material data* in addition to the general *company data* which all together is then made available at the yellow pages system.

For dealing with demands, the system needs to provide functionality to *handle demands* received from a client. That means that products which are not produced directly by the company need to be *specified* and the sub-demands for those products need to be *sent* to existing or potential suppliers. A company can also specify own demands when modelling the own supply network for own products.

When sending out demands to existing or potential suppliers, answers are expected and *handled* when arriving. While handling answers, information received from the different suppliers is aggregated and added to the own information. The result is a dynamically generated supply network containing detailed information for each node about ability of delivery. The resulting supply network is sent back to the client requesting the information.

Having received the dynamically generated network for a demand sent for a specific product, the network can be *visualised* and *saved* or *deleted* if e.g. a better supply network exists already. Older supply networks can be *updated* in order to receive newest information of the suppliers collaborating in order to deliver the requested product. That means that the same demand is sent out to the suppliers once again receiving back an actual and new modelled supply network.

Apart from sending demands in order to develop a strategic product-specific supply network the system provides also functionality to request general information about any specific company being part of the SSND network by *requesting supplier data*.

3.2 Technological Issues for the SSND System

For the development of such a self modelling demand driven supply network different design aspects and technological issues need to be discussed, since the concept described above poses multiple technological challenges which have implications on the system design. Technological and design issues regard e.g., distributed systems with nodes playing different roles (e.g. user, supplier), asynchronous communication, consistency of data and synchronisation. The challenges of distributed systems and asynchronous communication will be described exemplary in the following and rationales for the chosen technologies in the design model of strategic supply network development will be given.

Distributed Systems: As defined by [19], the network of independent systems that constitute the strategic supply network appears to the user of a single node inside that network as a single system and therefore represents a distributed system. It is an open peer group of loosely coupled systems. There are no server or directory infrastructures and apart from the fact, that every node is autonomous and implements functions for its own view of the network, no hierarchy exists. Regarding the different roles a node can play – e.g. being the *producer* sending a demand to known suppliers or being a *supplier* receiving demands from a client and either sending the related sub-demands to the known suppliers or sending the answer back the client – each node in its context of the application is able to store data, to send and receive demands or answers from other nodes in the network. The communication takes place between peers without guaranty that a node is always online and contributing to the network. Regarding all those aspects mentioned, the application for strategic supply network development can be considered as a peer-to-peer application having all main features – client-server functionality, direct communication between peers and autonomy of the single nodes – of today's peer-to-peer applications as defined by [4] and [15]. The only difference of the SSND system to today's understanding of peer-to-peer applications is the initialisation of new nodes in such a peer-to-peer network. In a peer-to-peer network a new node can contact any other node of the network in order to become a member. In the SSND network a new node does always have to contact a specific node, namely the yellow pages node. The advantage of such a solution is that the companies building new strategic networks can request information about new companies from the yellow pages node and alternatively send a demand to a new member in tier-1 additionally to the known nodes. Therefore a node has the possibility to extend the number of directly collaborating nodes and perform better to the network when new requests arrive.

Asynchronous Communication: To enable such loosely coupled networks, messaging can be used as transport constituting communication channels. Messaging systems encapsulate sending and receiving of messages and allow multiple transport mechanisms, e.g. SOAP/XML, JMS or even SMTP. By using the concept of conversations [11] based on messaging, pre-programmed patterns (conversational policies inside conversational contexts) can be implemented for flexible transactions of information between nodes. Conversation policies are used in the agent community for coupling internal states of agents but are used in this context to couple business processes. Conversation policies are machine readable patterns of message exchange in a conversation between systems and are composed of a message schema, sequence and timing information. To support the direct conversation with suppliers in the different tiers of the network or with filtered groups of them, unicast and multicast methods of addressing peers or groups of peers are needed. The client-server paradigm, using synchronous invoke/return schemes would create unnecessary dependencies between systems and could lead to deadlock situations. A higher level of robustness can be achieved by applying peer-to-peer approaches and using conversation.

In the following it is shown how those technical issues have been addressed in the business application of strategic supply network development.

Looking at the business logic running on the autonomous nodes for implementing the SSND system, similar functionality can be identified, e.g. receiving demands, generating new sub-demands, sending sub-demands, receiving answers, elaborating answers and responding to demands received. Additionally, the software composing the functionality of nodes has to be scalable to the companies needs. For the implementation of such a system the business component technology [22] has been chosen as a possible solution to build such a distributed network. The underlying idea of business components combines components from different vendors to an application which is individual to each customer. This principle of modular black-box design has been used in this system allowing different configurations of the system – by combining different components regarding the need of the specific node – ranging from a very simple configuration of the system – e.g. having only a visualisation component and no evaluation component of the supply network – to a very complex and integrated solution of the system – e.g. with an evaluation component integrated and the system being coupled with an enterprise integration system.

For the issues of asynchronous communication between nodes communication channels that support the message exchange between business components, and therefore between communication components of each participating node of the strategic supply chain network, are proposed. They act as a coordination instance and decrease the coupling between components. Potential technologies are software busses, event channels or tuple spaces [10, 19]. Tuple spaces support the data driven communication according to the pull-principle where an interested party has to request data, filtered by specific restrictions configured by the requesting party. Tuple spaces act as message buffer, allowing asynchronous communication by storing messages until they are explicitly deleted or fetched. Therefore they decouple sender and receiver of messages in a temporal manner. To implement the pull technology of the SSND network, the concept of tuple spaces has therefore been implemented in the prototype application and has been combined with the Web Service technology responsible for the exchange of messages between components distributed on different nodes of the SSND network. Web services are a new promising paradigm for the development of modular applications accessible over the Web and running on a variety of platforms. The Web service standards are SOAP [24] – supporting platform independency – WSDL [25] – specifying the interfaces and services offered – and UDDI [23]– used for the publication of the Web services offered by a specific company. All standards are based on the eXtensible Markup Language (XML) [5]. An overview of standards and related technologies for Web services is given in [21].

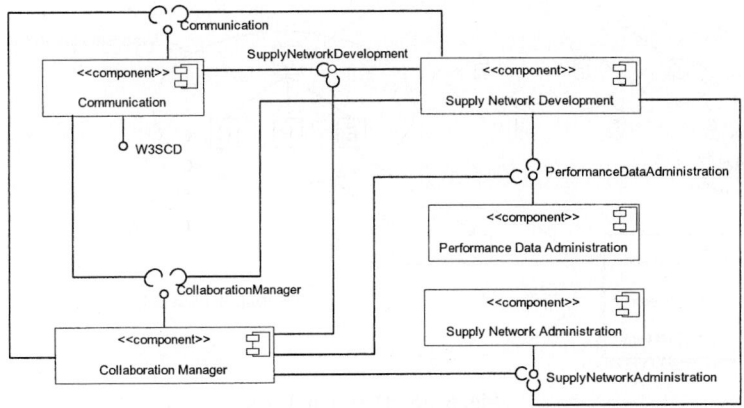

Fig. 5. Component model for the domain of strategic supply chain development

4 Design and Implementation of the Strategic Supply Network Development System

To illustrate the feasibility of the concepts described above, a business component model for the domain of strategic supply network development has been derived, based on the Business Component Modelling (BCM) process [1]. The business component model is shown in Fig. 5 in accordance with the notation of the Unified Modelling Language [16]. Five components have been identified, designed and implemented for the SSND system. For a detailed description of the different components we refer to [3, 1]. The component *supply network development* is the main component responsible for dynamically modelling of strategic supply networks. The component implements an interface providing services for specifying demands, updating strategic supply networks etc. All communication between the SSND systems located on different network hubs is executed by the *communication component*. The communication component implements the Web Service interface W3SCD in order to provide access to the component as a Web Service. The services offered are e.g. process a request, process a reply. The Web Service interface with the services offered are described and made publicly available in a WSDL document over a directory service (UDDI). That means that all services provided by the communication component are globally available and accessible by any other node in the SSND network, allowing the exchange of messages between the network nodes. The exchange of messages using the Web Service technology is shown in Fig. 6.

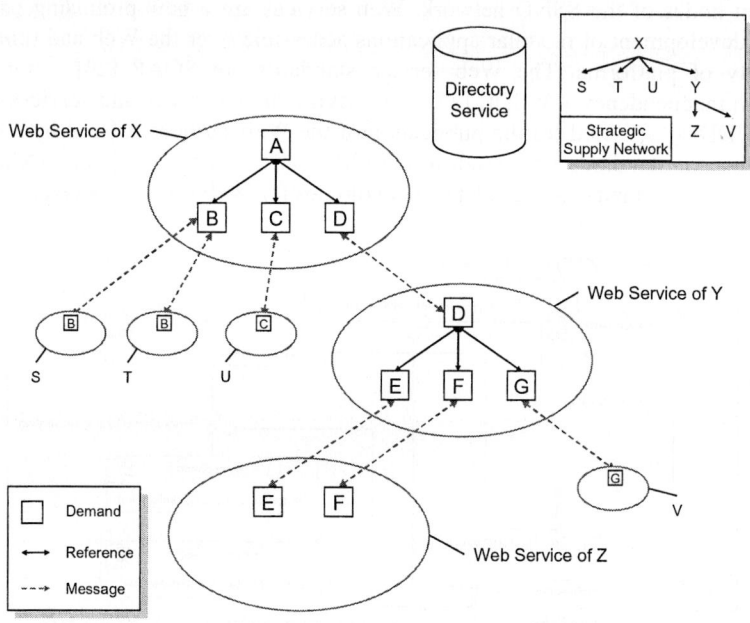

Fig. 6. SSND System Logic

The ovals in the picture represent company nodes in the network of SSND. Each company has the SSND system installed, containing all components shown in Fig. 5. Every node offers therefore services provided by the communication component as Web Service, which are made publicly available over the UDDI directory service (see Fig. 6). A company defines sub-demands which are required from companies contributing in the network by a bill of material explosion, e.g. the sub-demands required from company X for the product A are B, C and D. The sub-demands B and C are communicated by messages to the companies S, T, U and Y, calling the service *process request* provided as Web Service. The companies S, T and U send back the information about ability of delivery calling the Web Service *process reply* of company X. Company Y instead identifies the products needed from the own suppliers by a bill of material explosion, resulting in sub-demands E, F and G which again are communicated to the own suppliers by calling their Web Services. Receiving back the information about delivery abilities, the company Y aggregates the information and returns the own supply network for that specific demand to the company X by calling the corresponding Web Service. Company X, aggregating the information from all suppliers, is then able to visualise the suppliers' network (top-right in Fig. 6) for further evaluation.

For prove of concept, the prototype tool SSND has been implemented and a short description of the tool is given in this section. The SSND prototype supports the dynamic modelling of strategic supply networks in implementing all functionality defined in the use-cases introduced in Fig. 4. Companies can define new or update existing demands and send them to existing or potential suppliers receiving back as a result a supply network with detailed information about every supplier contributing to that demand. An example view of a supply network for the production of an electronic motor executed by the SSND system is shown in Fig. 7. Only a selected area of the whole supply network is shown.

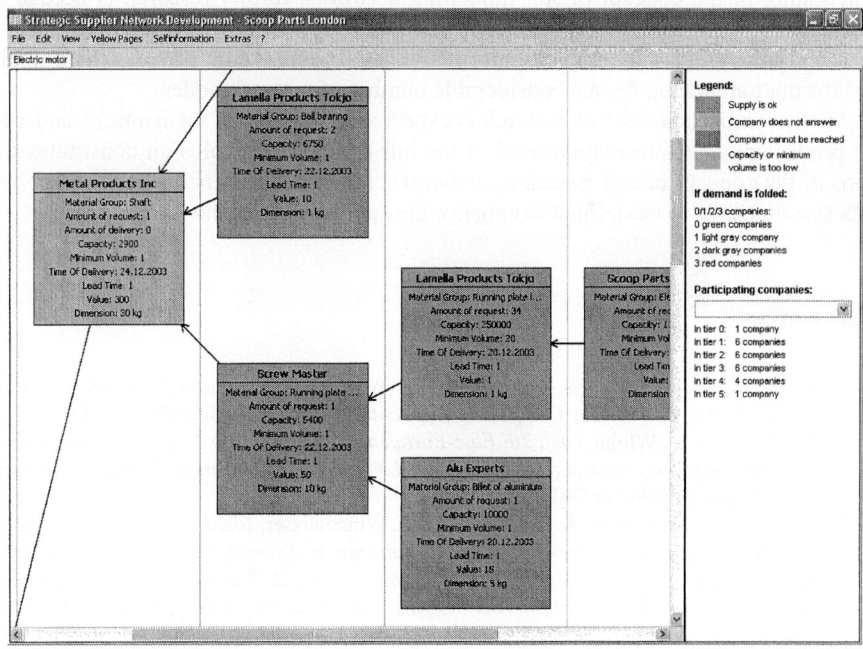

Fig. 7. SSND Supply Network for an Electronic Motor

The rectangles represent the different companies of the supply network visualised with important information about the node contributing to the supply network of the electronic motor. Relevant information for the requestor about the suppliers is e.g.

name of the company, material group the supplier is producing, minimum volume necessary to be ordered and capacity per day. The companies are visualised in the SSND prototype in different colours, differentiating between a) suppliers which are able to deliver the product and amount requested b) suppliers which are not answering to the demand sent c) suppliers which are not online or where a communication problem exists and therefore can not be reached and d) suppliers which do not have enough capacity for producing the required product, or where the volume required by the client is too low. The tool provides different modes of visualising the network – adding more detailed information to the nodes, showing just parts of the network, etc – in order to support the client with all necessary information for developing the strategic supply networks. A detailed description of the tool would go beyond the scope of this paper.

5 Conclusion

In this article, the concept of self modelling networks has been introduced and the practical applicability of the concept has been illustrated with the business domain of strategic supply network development. While the prototype demonstrates the basic functioning of the concept of self modelling networks, further research is needed to enhance the applicability of the concept. For large supply networks, methods have to be found to aggregate incomplete information, as it seems quite obvious there might be information lacking from a considerable number of network nodes.

Another important field of research is expected in the area of (semantic) standards. As product related information used in the bill of material explosion constitutes the basis of the concept of self modelling networks, interfaces to existing PDM, ERP and PPS systems have to be defined to enhance the applicability of the prototype.

References

[1] A. Albani, A. Keiblinger, K. Turowski and C. Winnewisser, *Domain Based Identification and Modelling of Business Component Applications*, in L. Kalinichenko, R. Manthey, B. Thalheim and U. Wloka, eds., *7th East-European Conference on Advances in Databases and Informations Systems (ADBIS-03), LNCS 2798*, Springer Verlag, Dresden, Deutschland, September 2003, pp. 30-45.

[2] A. Albani, A. Keiblinger, K. Turowski and C. Winnewisser, *Identification and Modelling of Web Services for Inter-enterprise Collaboration Exemplified for the Domain of Strategic Supply Chain Development*, in R. Meersmann, Z. Tari and D. C. Schmidt, eds., *On The Move to Meaningful Internet Systems 2003: CoopIS, DOA, and ODBASE - OTM Confederated International Conferences CoopIS, DOA, and ODBASE 2003, LNCS 2888*, Springer Verlag, Catania, Sicily, Italy, November 2003 2003, pp. 74-92.

[3] A. Albani, A. Keiblinger, K. Turowski and C. Winnewisser, *Komponentenmodell für die Strategische Lieferkettenentwicklung*, in W. Uhr, W. Esswein and E. Schoop, eds., *6. Internationale Tagung Wirtschaftsinformatik (WI-03) Medien - Märkte - Mobilität*, Physica-Verlag, Dresden, Deutschland, September 2003, pp. 61-80.

[4]   D. Barkai, *Peer-to-Peer Computing*, Technologies for Sharing and Collaboration on the Net. Intel Press (2001).
[5]   T. Bray, J. Paoli, C. M. Sperberg-McQueen, E. Maler, F. Yergeau and J. Cowan, *Extensible Markup Language (XML) 1.1*, Recommendation, World Wide Web Consortium (W3C), 04.02.2004.
[6]   A. S. Carr and J. N. Pearson, *Strategically managed buyer - supplier relationships and performance outcomes*, Journal of Operations Management, 17 (1999), pp. 497 - 519.
[7]   R. H. Coase, *The Nature of the Firm*, Economica, 4 (1937), pp. 386-405.
[8]   R. H. Coase, *The New Institutional Economics*, The American Economic Review, 88 (1998), pp. 72-74.
[9]   E. G. Furubotn and R. Richter, *Institutions and Economic Theory: The Contribution of the New Institutional Economics*, The University of Michigan Press (1997), pp. 40.
[10] D. Gelernter, *Multiple tuple spaces in Linda*, Proc. of PARLE '89, Springer Verlag (1989), pp. 20-27.
[11] J. E. Hanson, P. Nandi and S. Kumaran, *Conversation support for Business Process Integration*, Proceedings 6th IEEE International Enterprise Distributed Object Computing Conference (EDOC-2002), IEEE Press, 2002, pp. 65-74.
[12] E. Kopanaki, S. Smithson, P. Kanellis and D. Martakos, *The Impact of Interorganizational Information Systems on the Flexibility of Organizations*, Proceedings of the Sixth Americas Conference on Information Systems (AMCIS), Long Beach, CA, 2000, pp. 1434 - 1437.
[13] D. M. Lambert and M. C. Cooper, *Issues in Supply Chain Management*, Industrial Marketing Management, 29 (2000), pp. 65-83.
[14] T. W. Malone and R. J. Lautbacher, *The Dawn of the E-Lance Economy*, Harvard Business Review (1998), pp. 145 - 152.
[15] M. Miller, *Discovering P2P*, Sybex, San Francisco (2001).
[16] OMG, *OMG Unified Modelling Language Spezifikation Version 2.0*, (2003).
[17] A. Picot, R. Reichwald and R. Wiegand, *Die grenzenlose Unternehmung - Information, Organisation und Management*, Wiesbaden, 2001.
[18] M. Sawhney and J. Zabin, *The Seven Steps to Nirvana: Strategic Insights into eBusiness Transformation*, New York, 2001.
[19] A. S. Tanenbaum, *Distributed Operating Systems*, Prentice Hall, 1995.
[20] D. Tapscott, D. Ticoll and A. Lowy, *Digital Capital: Harnessing the Power of Business Webs*, Boston, 2000.
[21] A. Tsalgatidou and T. Pilioura, *An Overview of Standards and Related Technology in Web Services - Special Issue on E-Services*, International Journal of Distributed and Parallel Databases (2002), pp. 135-162.
[22] K. Turowski, ed., *Standardized Specification of Business Components*, Gesellschaft für Informatik, Working Group 5.10.3 - Component Oriented Business Application Systems, Augsburg, 2002.
[23] *UDDI Version 3.0*, http://uddi.org/pubs/uddi-v3.00-published-20020719.htm, accessed 22.06.2004.
[24] W3C, *SOAP Specification, Version 1.2*, http://www.w3.org/TR/SOAP/, accessed 22.06.2004.
[25] W3C, *Web Services Description Language (WSDL) Version 2.0*, http://www.w3.org/TR/wsdl12/, accessed 22.06.2004.
[26] H.-J. Warnecke, *Vom Fraktal zum Produktionsnetzwerk. Unternehmenskooperationen erfolgreich gestalten*, Berlin, 1999.
[27] O. E. Williamson and S. G. e. Winter, *The Nature of the Firm: Origins, Evolution, and Development*, Oxford University Press (1993).

An E-marketplace for Auctions and Negotiations in the Constructions Sector

Marina Bitsaki[1], Manos Dramitinos[1], George D. Stamoulis[1], and George Antoniadis[2]

[1] Department of Informatics, Athens University of Economics and Business,
76 Patision Str. Athens, GR-10434, Greece
Tel: +30 210 8203693, Fax: +30 210 8203686
{marina, mdramit, gstamoul}@aueb.gr
[2] Content Delivery Systems
INTRACOM S.A.,
19,5 Km Markopoulou Ave., 190 02 Peania, Attika, Greece
gant@intracom.gr

Abstract. Project e-Sharing has developed an e-marketplace that supports the efficient sharing of resources among companies of the constructions sector (primarily) according to their time-varying needs. In this paper, we present the e-Sharing Trader system, which supports the leasing of resources by means of electronic auctions and negotiations. The Trader auction-related part supports a wide variety of single- and multi-object auctions together with innovative bidding agents for the English and the ascending clock auctions; these agents place bids on behalf of the users according to their specified preferences. The Trader negotiation-related part supports direct multi-attribute negotiations between users by means of a semi-structured negotiation protocol, automated agent-aided price negotiation, and two-object multi-attribute negotiations so that a user leases either two complementary resources or none, or exactly one out of two substitute resources. We also compare the e-Sharing Trader with existing e-marketplaces and discuss the advantages of our work.

1 Introduction

E-sharing[1] is an EU-funded IST project that has implemented an innovative electronic web-based marketplace.

It is based on the innovative business idea of facilitating the sharing of equipment, personnel and other resources among companies. The project is motivated by the fact that some of the resources of one company may remain idle for long periods of time (e.g. due to a drop in the company's business cycle), while at the same time other companies may need additional resources and hence are interested in leasing them in order to fulfill their own projects' increased obligations.

---

[1] e-Sharing [9] (e-Sharing-IST-2001-33325) is partly funded by the European Commission within the IST Programme (key action II.3 "Management systems for suppliers and consumers" and sub-key action II.3.1 "Dynamic Value Constellations").

The constructions sector is a prominent example and constitutes the focus field of the project. In order for the e-Sharing approach to be successful, the support of trading mechanisms that are well suited in the e-Sharing context is of great importance. In this paper, we present the e-Sharing Trader system, which supports the leasing of resources by means of electronic auctions and negotiations.

The main motivation for the Trader functionality is that the constructions sector is characterized by high investment cost of certain equipment and by difficulty in maintaining a higher usage level of this equipment. These features leave a wide space for benefits to both lessors[2] (by earning revenue from idle equipment) and lessees (lower investment requirements). The Trader's goal is to increase the overall market efficiency by supporting trading mechanisms for fast, transparent and efficient sharing of resources by means of electronic auctions and negotiations.

The auction-related part of the Trader supports a variety of popular auction mechanisms, both simple and multi-object, as opposed to most existing e-marketplaces. The selection and adaptation of these mechanisms are strongly motivated by the project's context. The simple auctions supported are First Price Sealed Bid, Vickrey and English auction and are conducted within a pre-defined time period which is publicly announced. Innovative bidding agents that are constituent part of the Trader are also available for the users to choose from: these can represent users in simple English auctions and bid on their behalf in an automated way. It is worth noting that the e-Sharing users' control over the agents' behavior is greater than that of similar approaches in other e-marketplaces. The multi-object auctions supported are the combinatorial sealed auction for 2-3 items, the uniform and pay-your-bid multi-unit sealed auctions and the ascending clock auction. An agent for bidding on users' behalf in ascending clock auctions is also provided by e-Sharing. The aforementioned multi-object mechanisms are useful in the e-Sharing context, where demand for and supply of multiple objects are very common.

The negotiation-related part of the Trader enables users to exchange negotiation messages in order to reach a deal for the leasing of a resource. The e-Sharing approach is the support of a semi-structured negotiation protocol that facilitates bargaining among the e-Sharing users. Adaptation of other researchers' work regarding agent-aided price negotiation agents has also been carried out. The resulting negotiation agents are offered as part of the Trader. Moreover, two-object negotiations are supported: this allows a user to lease a) two complementary resources or none of them or b) exactly one of two substitute resources. The coexistence of electronic auctions and negotiations under the same platform is also an original feature of the Trader. We also compare the e-Sharing Trader with existing e-marketplaces and discuss the advantages of our work.

The remainder of this paper is organized as follows: In Sect. 2 we give an overview of the e-Sharing platform. In Sect. 3, we present the Trader auctions and bidding agents while in Sect. 4 we present the Trader negotiation protocol

---

[2] We use henceforth the term "lessor" to denote the user who offers idle resources for leasing and the term "lessee" to denote the user who attempts to lease resources.

and price-negotiation agents. In Sect. 5 we compare the Trader with existing e-marketplaces. Finally, in Sect. 6 we provide some concluding remarks.

1.1 Background on Auctions and Negotiations in Existing E-marketplaces

Business activity on the Internet is expanding rapidly and e-commerce is considered at least as important as traditional commerce. A very popular method of allocating goods within this competitive economic context is the use of auctions. Auctions offer the advantage of transparency and simplicity in determining market-based prices and economic efficiency (i.e. social welfare maximization), since certain auction designs can guarantee that goods are acquired by those that value them the most. Furthermore, auctions may lead to higher revenues for the providers compared to traditional methods of selling goods, due to the competition arising. Auctions' popularity has also increased due to their good performance - in terms of economic efficiency and revenue for the state - when applied in regulation; spectrum auctions are a prominent example of a successful application [5]. Commercial sites that run user-initiated auctions such as eBay [12], uBid [14] and onSale [11] report to be transacting millions of dollars daily. Besides retail, niche market wholesale e-marketplaces employ auctions too. The most prominent example is the electronic marketplace for Dutch Flowers Auctions [4]. However, there is very recent use of bidding agents available within the aforementioned e-marketplaces, while users can choose from other commercial bidding agents to bid on their behalf in eBay auctions. Indeed, the large number of these commercial bidding agents constitutes a significant indication of users' increased interest in bidding agents. We discuss this phenomenon in Sect. 5.

Electronic negotiations have also been studied thoroughly. However, despite their many advantages, their applicability is very limited in electronic markets, especially if compared to that of auctions. A survey of electronic negotiations, their main advantages and applications, as well as a discussion of the main reasons for their absence in commercial e-marketplaces is provided in [1]. The most important reason is that user strategies are very hard to predict due to the multi-attribute nature of negotiations and the various trade-offs among them. Thus, analysis of electronic negotiations requires an inter-disciplinary approach involving socio-economic factors. This implies that e-negotiations cannot be applied successfully in "general" retail e-marketplaces, though they perform well in context-specific markets where analysis of user behavior is tractable. Raiffa's "science and art of negotiations" depicts the fact that the design of electronic negotiations is often a "trial-and-error" process [1]. Some other efforts in applying e-negotiations in niche e-marketplaces are currently in progress [8]. The absence of e-negotiations from most e-marketplaces is also justified by the fact that the cost of supporting e-negotiations is higher than auctions (due to the more demanding analysis and implementation of accurate information representation) while the logistic gains are less. Last but not least, the limited "know-how" in supporting e-negotiations prohibits their widespread applicability.

2 The E-sharing Platform

The e-Sharing physical architecture represents the way the physical components, such as the e-Sharing servers and the clients, are placed and how they are connected to and interact with each other. It also represents and specifies the network through which the physical components are connected. The physical architecture of e-Sharing is depicted in Fig. 1. Although the physical architecture described here is a solution designed to work as a prototype network, future scalability needs have also been taken under consideration in its design.

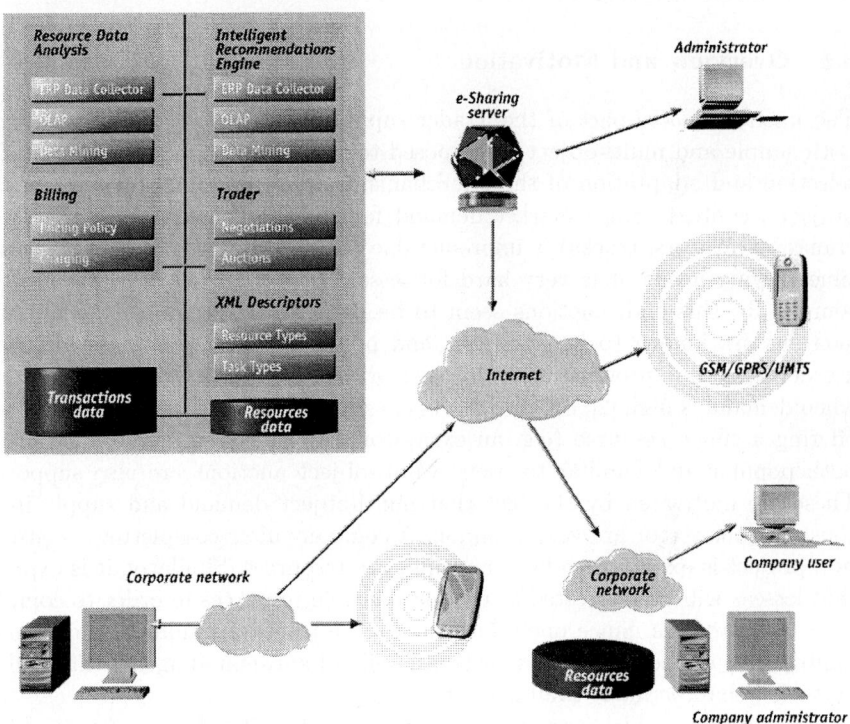

Fig. 1. The e-Sharing Architecture

e-Sharing platform has been implemented over J2EE: the application server used is JBoss 3.0.4 with integrated web container Apache Tomcat 4.1.12 and Oracle 9i was chosen as the project's database. Conceptually, the J2EE architecture meets the project's goals regarding scalability, easy code maintenance and security due to the J2EE tiers depicted in Fig. 1. Data (Persistence Storage Tier) are separate from the session Enterprise Java Beans implementing the operations that can be performed by e-Sharing users (Business Logic Tier). These tiers are also separate from the web-based Interface Tier that makes the e-Sharing functionality accessible to end users (Client Tier). The Trader system supports the leasing of resources by means of electronic auctions and negotiations. Since the focus field of the project is primarily the constructions sector, the end users are employees of constructions companies who access e-Sharing from their corporate networks. They may also use PDAs and WLANs or telephones and GSM/GPRS/UMTS networks to obtain immediate access to the e-Sharing functionality whenever this is needed. For example, a user can access Trader from one of his company's construction sites in order to negotiate the leasing of an excavator which is needed for the construction project.

3 Trader Auctions

3.1 Overview and Motivation

The *auction-related* part of the Trader supports a variety of popular auctions, both simple and multi-object, as opposed to most existing e-marketplaces. The selection and adaptation of these mechanisms are strongly motivated from the project's context. Since market demand for specific types of equipment (e.g. cranes, excavators, trucks) is unpredictable due to the constructions companies time-varying needs, it is very hard for lessors to set a fixed price for their resources. To this end, auctions seem to be the proper means of trade. Indeed, auctions are known to be fast, fair, and possibly efficient. By revealing market demand they produce market-based prices and sellers attain high revenue when demand is high [2]. Single-object (i.e. simple) auctions are useful for lessors offering a single resource (e.g. an excavator) in the system. Such auctions are both popular and familiar to users. Multi-object auctions are also supported. These are motivated by the fact that multi-object demand and supply in the constructions sector are very common. A company after completing a construction project is expected to have multiple idle resources. Similarly, it is expected that lessees will be interested in renting multiple resources in order to complete their own projects. Since open auctions can be time consuming and due to the limited time of the e-Sharing's users, a family of automated agents that will bid on their behalf, is made available for them.

The Trader enables users to create single- and multi- object auctions, bid in them either manually or by means of automated agents, search and view auctions hosted by Trader, as well as view details about them. The simple auctions supported are First Price Sealed Bid, Vickrey and English auctions. The multi-object auctions supported are the combinatorial sealed auction for 2-3 items, the uniform and pay-your-bid multi-unit sealed auction and the ascending clock. All the aforementioned auctions except the ascending clock auction are conducted within a predefined known time period. Innovative original bidding agents that are constituent part of the Trader are also available for the users to choose from: these are presented in Sect. 3.5.

There is an extensive literature on auctions. Below we briefly overview the mechanisms supported by the Trader, based on [2].

3.2 Single-Object Auctions

When a single unit is to be traded, the respective mechanisms are defined as *single-object auctions* or *simple auctions*. The e-Sharing system provides the following simple auction mechanisms:

First Price Sealed-bid auction: each bidder submits a sealed bid without knowing others' bids. The object is awarded to the highest bidder. The winner pays his own bid. It is beneficial for each bidder to shade his bid, i.e. submit a bid lower than his maximum willingness-to-pay, in order to acquire a positive net benefit in case of winning.

Second Price Sealed-bid (Vickrey) auction: each bidder submits a sealed bid without knowing others' bids. The object is awarded to the highest bidder. However, contrary to the first price sealed-bid auction, the winner pays the second-highest bid. It is a dominant strategy for each bidder to reveal his true willingness-to-pay since his payment in case of winning is determined exclusively by his rivals' bids.

English auction: it is an open process, with price ascending progressively. In particular, the price starts from the lowest acceptable level i.e., the reserve price set by the auctioneer and proceeds to solicit higher bids from the bidders until no one is willing to increase the bid. The object is awarded to the highest bidder, who pays his bid. Each bidder raises his bid by a small increment until his willingness-to-pay is reached.

3.3 Multi-object Auctions

When multiple *identical* items or multiple units of a divisible quantity are to be traded, the respective mechanisms are defined as *multi-unit auction mechanisms*. A bid in the context of multi-unit auctions is defined to be a set of pairs of the form (p, q) of the per unit expressed willingness-to-pay p for a quantity q of units. For each player there can be awarded multiple quantities of units corresponding to different pairs (p, q). From this set one can reconstruct the user's demand curve in an acceptable range of quantities. Equivalently, a bid may comprise a set of values, each declaring the willingness-to-pay for each extra unit desired. The e-Sharing system provides the following multi-unit auction mechanisms:

Sealed bid auction: bids are submitted in sealed envelopes. The K units available are allocated to the K highest bids. The following payment rules apply:

- *Uniform payment rule:* all winners are charged with the per unit price of the lowest winning bid for each of the units they are awarded. Alternatively, winners can be charged with the per unit price of the highest losing bid for each of the units they are awarded.
- *Pay-your- bid payment rule:* each user pays for every unit he is awarded the per unit price p that he has declared in his respective bid.

This type of auction gives bidders incentives to shade their bids. If the bid is very low, the payments will be lower too but the number of won units will also decrease.

Ascending clock auction: this is a progressive auction mechanism; hence it is conducted in rounds. A clock indicates the current per unit price, and bidders report the quantity demanded for this price; the clock price is then raised again. Bidders gradually reduce their demand (they are not allowed to increase it) and units are awarded to bidders when demand matches supply. The per unit charge of the winners is the clock's last indication. Each bidder shades his bids in order to acquire a higher benefit.

When *heterogeneous* objects are to be traded, combinatorial auctions allow users express their preferences on groups of complementary or supplementary goods. The e-Sharing system provides the following combinatorial auction:

Combinatorial sealed-bid auction for 2-3 objects: bidders are allowed to submit any combination of units they wish at a single price. Winner determination is performed by examining all possible overall allocations and finding the most profitable one. Each user pays his own bid. Users may shade bids, although it is now more risky due to the large number of possible allocations examined by the auctioneer.

3.4 Auction Management Functionality

The Trader functionality regarding auctions management is presented here. This functionality comprises a wide set of capabilities, including the typical ones present in any e-marketplace of practical importance. The lessee may perform one of the following tasks:

- "Monitor Auctions": The lessee sets criteria specifying the auctions that are of interest to him. For example, a lessee may define that he is interested only in English auctions for trucks. After storing these criteria, the system will "hide" from this user all the auctions that do not match his criteria. In the example above, these could be a Vickrey auction for trucks or an English auction for an excavator. This way, the Trader is customized and tailored to its users' specific interests and needs. If the lessee decides not to set any monitor criteria, then no "filtering" of information is done by the system and he is informed about all the auctions that are stored in the system.
- "View Running Auctions": The lessee views the auctions that are in progress and that match his preferences.
- "View Running Auctions I Have Bidded": The lessee views all the running auctions where he has placed a bid.
- "Bid": The lessee either places a bid or creates a bidding agent that bids on his behalf in an auction.
- "Change Monitor Criteria": The lessee changes the criteria about the auctions he is interested in.
- "View Future Auctions": The lessee views all auctions of interest that are scheduled in the (near) future.
- "View Past Auctions": The lessee views auctions that were conducted in the past.

- "Search All Auctions": The lessee searches all auctions, both current and future ones, given a set of search criteria, e.g. the time when these auctions occur, their type, the type of resources traded etc. The system displays the results that match the given search criteria, regardless whether there is conflict with lessee's monitor criteria or not.
- "Add/Remove From Monitored Auctions": The lessee manually adds or removes an auction from those that are of interest to him. For example, he may select to monitor a specific auction for an excavator, despite the fact that he has declared that he is generally interested in auctions for trucks.
- "View Auction Details": The lessee views details about a specific auction, such as the auction's start and end date, its starting price, the minimum bid increment, etc.
- "View Auction Bids": The lessee views the bids submitted in an open auction. Moreover, he can view the bids submitted to a past auction, regardless of its type.

The lessor may perform one of the following tasks:

- "Organize Auction": The lessor creates an auction for one or some of his idle resources.
- "View Running Auctions": The lessor views the auctions that are in progress and that he has organized.
- "View Future Auctions": The lessor views all his auctions that are scheduled in the future.
- "Update Future Auction": The lessor updates the parameters of a future auction.
- "Cancel auction": The lessor cancels one of his future auctions
- "View Auction Details": The lessor views details about a specific auction. This functionality complements the aforementioned options provided to the lessee.
- "View Auction Bids": The lessor views the bids submitted in one of his auctions.

The Trader's users can easily perform the aforementioned tasks by means of accessing from their respective browsers user-friendly Java Server Pages that provide this functionality.

3.5 Trader Bidding Agents

Bidding Agents for Simple English Auction
English auctions with bidders participating remotely (e.g. users accessing the auction site through Internet) are in general performed during predefined time periods, in which the user should monitor the auction and bid accordingly. This complicates user strategies, compared to the traditional English auction, in which all bidders are present in the auction house from the beginning, and there is no time limit. In particular, it is possible that a bidder does not manage to place a

bid higher than the standing one, due to the time limit, thus not winning in an auction where he could have possibly won otherwise.

e-Sharing enables users to select among various types of bidding agents to participate in the auction on their behalf. Users' presence in the system is not necessary during the auction any more. The agents developed by e-Sharing are based on input of certain parameters given by the user. They pertain to auctions taking place for a predefined time period. In particular, three types of agents have been defined and implemented:

- The "Simple Agent", which increases the bid up to the user's maximum willingness-to-pay without taking any special care if the auction is nearing its completion.
- The "Smart Agent", which increases the bid by a small increment until he realizes that the auction is nearing its completion. It then places one last bid, which is computed according to a formula giving the *optimal* such bid under certain assumptions.
- The "Adaptive Agent", which is applicable when the user's willingness-to-pay is not accurately known, or can be influenced by the bids of the other players/agents.

Below we provide a formal description about these types of bidding agents for an English auction that takes place in a predefined time period $[T_1, T_2]$.

Simple Agent

Agents' Input: the user feeds the agent with: his maximum willingness-to-pay u, the bid increment d, and the estimated expected number of bids to be placed n. Agents' Bidding Strategy: if there have been placed no bids in the auction when the agent joins it, then it bids an amount of d. After a delay Dt_1 from its last bid (or from its joining the auction), the agent examines whether another user (or the agent of another user) has submitted a bid that is higher than its recent-most own bid. If this is indeed the case, then the agent submits a new bid, which is the standing bid b increased by d, provided that $b + d \leq u$ and time has not expired. If $b + d > u > b$ and time has not expired, then the submitted bid equals u. (If no bid is to be placed, due to lack of activity by the opponents, then Dt_1 is computed again, and the above step is repeated.) Delay Dt_1 is selected randomly each time. Note that randomization of delays avoids simultaneous bids by different agents. In particular, for each bid, delay Dt_1 it is drawn from a uniform distribution in the range $[0, 2 \cdot \frac{T_2 - T_1}{n}]$. This also motivates the interpretation of n as an approximate estimate of the expected number of bids to be placed by this agent in the worst case that its opponents respond immediately to its own bids. The above procedure is repeated until the end of the auction or until the agent's bid has reached the maximum value u that is permissible by the user.

Motivation: The above strategy mostly pertains to the case where users have pure private values, which means that each of them knows only its own valuation and has no information on the valuations of its opponents which do not affect his own valuation. The strategy of bidding a small amount above the standing bid each time this is raised by one of its opponents is optimal for a user participating in a traditional English auction with no time limits. The present agent implements this strategy, yet in an auction with a predefined time limit. Each time the agent is about to place a new bid, it suffices to bid for a price higher than the minimum acceptable increment from the observed standing bid, provided that it will submit at least another bid in the future. In that case it would raise the bid, thus increasing its charge in case of winning, without increasing its probability of winning. The present agent does not take any special care close to the end of the auction and this is why it is referred to as Simple Agent. Below, we propose another agent that also includes such a feature.

Smart Agent
Agents' Input: the user feeds the agent with: his maximum willingness-to-pay u, the bid increment d, and the expected number of bids to be placed n.
Agents' Bidding Strategy: As long as termination of the auction has not been approached yet, bidding is performed as in the case of the Simple Agent, except for the fact that delay Dt is now calculated as follows: After a delay Dt_1 from its last bid (calculated as in the case of the Simple Agent), the agent counts the time Dt_2 that has elapsed since the last standing bid was placed, by one of its opponents. The agent waits more for an extra time Dt_2 and submits its new bid; that is $Dt = Dt_l + Dt_2$. (This implies that Dt depends on the activity level; see below.) This procedure is repeated until either the agent's bid has reached the maximum value u permissible by the user or the time Dt_{last} left until the end of the auction is less than the maximum possible value of the delay Dt_l; namely $2 \cdot \frac{(T_2-T_1)}{n}$. This implies that the agent "realizes" that the auction is nearing its completion. In this case, the agent's bidding process terminates with a last bid called "jump-bid" b_j, which is given by: $b_j = \frac{b+u}{2}$, where b is the standing bid. This bid is placed even if the current standing bid was one previously placed by this same agent.
Motivation: The above strategy mostly pertains to the case where users have pure private values. As in case of the Simple Agent, the agent increases its bid slightly above the standing bid, until termination of the auction has been approached. Since the auction terminates at a predefined time, if the agent would keep on applying the strategy of the Simple Agent towards the end of the auction, it might lose by a user with lower valuation than its own, due to a conservative last bid. Instead, the agent submits a "jump-bid" to balance the gain from a lower than its valuation bid and the risk of losing. The "jump-bid" proposed above maximizes the expected profit of the user in a certain case of a model for the competition. The proof of this result is innovative, and is presented in Appendix A. Compared to the Simple Agent, the present agent also includes some additional intelligence regarding computation of the time it places a bid too. If there is low activity (respectively high activity), then Dt_2 is large (respectively small), which implies limited (respectively high) interest for the object auctioned. The agent decides to remain inactive accordingly, for a time duration that depends on the last inactive period.

Adaptive Agent
Agents' Input: the user feeds the agent with: his first estimate of maximum willingness-to-pay u_0, the bid increment d, the expected number of bids to be placed n, the ultimately permissible maximum bid u_{max} (where $u_{max} > u_0$).
Strategy: before submitting a bid, the agent estimates the value u_i at time t_i given the standing bid b, where $t_1, t_2, \cdots$ are the times when this agent previously placed its bids:

$$u_i = \begin{cases} u_{i-1} & \text{if } u_{i-1} \geq b \\ \min\{u_{max}, \frac{b+u_{max}}{2}\} & \text{if } u_{i-1} < b \end{cases}$$

The rest of the bidding strategy is the same as in the first case. The process terminates when the auction has come to completion or the standing bid exceeds the last update of the valuation.
Motivation: The above strategy mostly pertains to the case where users have either a common valuation for the object auctioned (but this common values is not entirely known to them) or correlated values. After each opponent's bid is observed, the adaptive agent receives extra information about the valuation of the object and uses it to update this valuation, up to the level u_{max}. In order for both values b and u_{max} to be taken equivalently into account, u_i is updated as above. The agent employs the strategy of the Simple Agent, but its next bid is calculated according to this new update as well.

Bidding Agent for Ascending Clock

The e-Sharing system provides a bidding agent that places bids on behalf of users in the context of ascending clock auctions. Recall that in the ascending clock auction the bid represents the desired quantity of the user at the current price, that is a certain point in the bidders' demand schedule (curve). Thus, in order to bid on the user's behalf, the agent is to provide a number of choices for demand schedules: each such schedule is a parameterized curve; the associated parameter is also to be provided by the user. The e-Sharing system provides three choices for demand curves depicted in Fig. 2. In each such curve, quantity decreases as price increases: in Fig. 2a quantity decreases with constant rate as price increases (linear demand curve), in Fig. 2b quantity decreases faster at low prices than at higher prices, as price increases (convex demand curve) and in Fig. 2c quantity decreases slower at low prices than at higher prices, as price increases (concave demand curve).

For each of the aforementioned curves, the user should specify the parameters a, b and c for the non-linear curves. Since this is hard for the user, the user will have to specify a number of more meaningful parameters: the highest quantity, the highest price and for the non-linear curves the quantity corresponding to half the highest price; see the points depicted with bullets in the figures. The curve parameters can be derived uniquely from these above. These curves correspond to the bids that will be submitted by the agents.

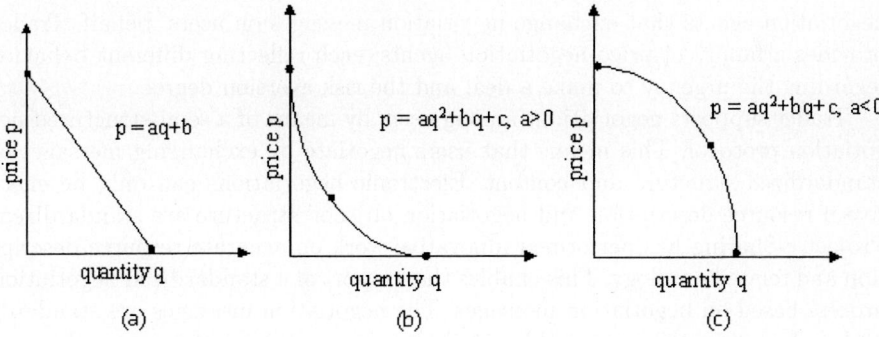

Fig. 2. a) Linear demand curve b) Convex demand curve c) Concave demand curve

4 Trader Negotiations

4.1 Overview and Motivation

The Trader also supports electronic *negotiations*. Inclusion of this functionality is primarily motivated by the fact that in the constructions sector, negotiations are very common. This implies that Trader's users are familiar with the basic principles of negotiations. Moreover, other researchers' studies [1] also agree that electronic negotiations are very promising. E-negotiations promise higher levels of process efficiency and faster emergence of higher quality (i.e. accurate and mutually profitable) agreements. This potential economic impact leads to an increased demand for supporting appropriate e-negotiations for specific situations. Supporting e-negotiations for a wide variety of resources is impossible, mainly because e-negotiations imply the existence of a well-defined structure of the negotiation messages that can be exchanged. The latter relies on the accurate and rich description of the traded resources and their respective attributes that determine their market value, which is feasible only for specific contexts. Hence, well-structured e-negotiations enable bargaining for a rich set of attributes, eliminate misunderstandings and save time and money for the parties involved. This should be contrasted with traditional negotiations that are conducted either face-to-face or by using the telephone, or simplified electronic negotiations that are conducted by means of exchanging unstructured emails. The latter type of negotiations suffer from limited transparency of the negotiated issues, due to the absence of accurate resource description and a negotiation objects' schema. They also suffer from high transaction costs and limited number of negotiation parties since negotiations among a lessee and many lessors for the leasing of a resource is impossible over the phone. e-Sharing lessors can use negotiations for the leasing of their resources either if there is significant trade-off among their offer's attributes or if they believe that the market demand for their resources is minimal, hence an auction would not attain high revenues. The former case is well served by the Trader semi-structured negotiation protocol; this is fully described in Sect. 4.2. The latter case motivates the use of automated price negotiation agents that exchange negotiation messages on users' behalf. Trader provides a family of price negotiation agents, each reflecting different behavior regarding the urgency to make a deal and the risk aversion degree.

Trader supports negotiations among users by means of a semi-structured negotiation protocol. This means that users negotiate by exchanging messages of standardized structure and content. Electronic negotiations can only be effective if resource description and negotiation objects' structure are standardized. Project e-Sharing has performed innovative work on accurate resource description and related ontology. This enables the support of a standardized negotiation process based on negotiation messages. The negotiation messages are standardized and contain the permissible attributes for which negotiation can be performed, and their corresponding proposed values from the users that created them. The negotiation is in general multi-attribute; e.g., it may concern the price, the leasing period, and the potential for human operators for an excavator. Price negotiation agents that operate on behalf of the users enhance the Trader negotiation-related functionality, which is overviewed here.

4.2 Trader Negotiation Protocol

The Trader negotiation protocol, i.e. the way for lessees to negotiate with lessors for their respective resources, is briefly presented here. Since none of the existing e-marketplaces support negotiations (see Sect. 5) both this protocol and its implementation are innovative.

The lessee may perform one of the following tasks:

- "Negotiate": The lessee submits a negotiation offer to a lessor for a resource that the latter has offered for negotiation. User comments may be attached to the negotiation request in order to facilitate bargaining. The lessee who "responds" to the lessors' offers for his idle resources - presented to him by the Offers Management system - always initiates the negotiation process. After this, an arbitrary amount of negotiation objects are exchanged between the two parties until a deal is reached or the negotiation fails.
- "View Pending Requests": The lessee views all negotiation requests he has submitted to various lessors and the answers that the respective lessors have sent to him.
- "Accept Negotiation Counter-offer": The lessee accepts a negotiation counter-offer that a lessor has submitted as a response to his request, hence a deal is made. Charging is instantly performed due to the integration of the Trader with the e-Sharing Accounting/Billing system.
- "Deny Negotiation Counter-offer": The lessee denies a negotiation counter-offer that a lessor has submitted as a response to his request.
- "Create New Quotation": The lessee answers to a counter-negotiation offer that has been submitted by a lessor as a response to his request.

The lessor may perform one of the following tasks:

- "View Pending Requests": The lessee views all negotiation requests that lessees have sent to him, as well as the answers he has sent to him.

- "Accept Negotiation Request": The lessor accepts a negotiation request that a lessee has submitted for one of his offers, hence a deal is made. Again, charging is performed instantly.
- "Deny Negotiation Request": The lessor denies a negotiation request that a lessee has sent to him.
- "Create New Quotation": The lessor replies to a negotiation request that has been submitted by a lessee for one of his offered resources, by placing a counter-offer. User comments can be attached to the negotiation request in order to facilitate the negotiation process.

4.3 Two-Object Negotiations

The Trader also supports two-object negotiations: this feature allows a lessee to lease a) two complementary resources that are offered by generally different lessors or none of them, e.g. both an excavator and a truck that are needed for a construction project (AND-type negotiation) or b) exactly one of two substitute resources, e.g. one of two cranes that are offered by two different lessors (OR-type negotiation). The support of this functionality is strongly motivated from the needs of the constructions sector, where the existence of such complementarities or substitutions among resources is common. In order to initiate such a "two-object" negotiation process, a lessee creates a two-object negotiation request for two offers of two lessors. Subsequently, each lessor receives the part of the two-object request that is related to his offer. Though the lessors know that they have received a part of a two-object negotiation request, they ignore its type; i.e. whether it is an AND-type or an OR-type negotiation. Moreover, the Trader business logic ensures that the respective lessors can only accept or deny these requests; no counter offers are allowed. This is done in order to prevent the lessors from maliciously blocking a two-object request. Indeed, since it would likely that the lessee request would concern two complementary resources, the lessors would have the incentive to never accept this request, even if it were profitable for them to do so. Instead, they would create counter offers in order to get the most money out of the lessee's valuation for the bundle of the two resources. The Trader guarantees that a deal is achieved, and lessee is charged, if and only if a) both lessors accept an AND-type lessee two-object request or b) one of the lessors accepts an OR-type lessee's request. The latter is achieved due to the Trader business logic and the serialization that the application server performs on the business logic session beans' methods: Even if two lessors simultaneously accept their respective part of the lessee's two-object request, access to the bean's method is serialized. Hence, only the first acceptance of the lessee request will be admitted to the system; the second will be discarded.

4.4 Trader Negotiation Agents for a Single Resource

The e-Sharing Trader provides negotiation agents that perform the process of leasing an object at an acceptable price on behalf of users. A user might be either a lessor or a lessee. We concentrate on the model of a two-party, single-issue negotiation proposed by Faratin et al in [3]: two agents negotiate for the leasing price of an object. Every agent is initialized with the following set of parameters:

- Acceptable range for the price. The least preferred acceptable price is defined to be the reservation value.
- Time of negotiation completion.
- A scoring function that gives the score that the agent assigns to each acceptable price. For lessors, higher prices are preferred to lower ones. On the contrary, lessees prefer lower prices than higher ones. The Trader supports three types of such scoring functions, for the user to choose from:
  - *Impartial*: scores increase constantly at the whole acceptable range of prices.
  - *Aggressive*: scores increase faster towards most preferred prices (convex function).
  - *Conservative:* scores increase slower towards most preferred prices (concave function).

To simplify matters for the user, these functions are fully specified. That is, there is no parameter value to be submitted by the user. At each step, the opposing agent rejects his opponent's offer if a time limit has passed, accepts his opponent's offer if it gives a higher score than the score of the new counter-offer he intends to make, or makes a new counter-offer. Several types of agents can be defined depending on the tactics they use to compute the next offer. The Trader supports three types of agents for the user to choose from:

- *Impatient agents* that approach (or even reach) their reservation value very quickly.
- *Patient agents* that reveal their reservation value when time is almost exhausted.
- *Regular agents* that approach steadily the reservation value until time is exhausted.

A formal description of the negotiation agents is presented in Appendix B.

5 Comparison of the Trader with Existing E-marketplaces

In this section, we summarize the Trader innovative features and we compare the Trader with existing e-marketplaces. The Trader supports both single- and multi- object auctions, as opposed to existing e-marketplaces (e.g. eBay) that support solely single-object auctions. Multi-unit auctions promote the fast and easy sharing of resources and are motivated by the e-Sharing focus on the constructions sector where multi-object demand and supply are common. For example, under the eBay approach, a lessor of 5 trucks would have to organize 5 separate auctions; the lessees interested in 2 or more trucks would have to bid in multiple auctions. On the contrary, in the Trader approach, this lessor would organize just one multi-unit auction and the lessees would offer various amounts of money for the respective quantities of trucks in that auction. Hence, significant logistic gains are attained and the whole trading process is facilitated. The bidding agent for ascending clock auction is an additional innovative feature of Trader that saves valuable time to its users: Users' presence in the system is not necessary during the auction; automated bidding agents represent lessees instead. Moreover, the support of the combinatorial sealed auction for 2-3 items is also an innovative feature of the Trader, which is well suited in the e-Sharing context. This auction exploits complementarities that apply to the constructions sector and enables the lessees interested in leasing bundles of complementary resources to do so without facing the exposure problem. This means that lessees can place different bids for different bundles that are of different value to them and be sure that they will never be awarded a subset of resources at a charge that exceeds the corresponding maximum willingness to pay of the user. Also, winner determination in this auction compares all the possible outcomes of the auction and chooses the outcome that attains the highest revenue; hence the lessor's profits are maximized. For example, a lessor aiming to take advantage of the aforementioned complementarities could create such an auction for an excavator and two trucks. Lessees that would be interested in different bundles of resources, (e.g. an excavator and a truck, or just one truck or both resources) would declare their willingness to pay for each desired bundle. Upon completion of the auction the resources would be awarded to the lessees that value them the most, by choosing the allocation of highest value, while the lessor would have attained the highest feasible revenue. Note that due to the fact that winner determination is NP-complete, the restriction of auctioning at most 3 resources has been imposed; this restriction does not apply to the other multi-unit - auctions.

Regarding the support of single-object auctions, both Trader and existing e-marketplaces support the same popular mechanisms. However, the presence of bidding agents for simple English auctions that are constituent part of the aforementioned e-marketplaces is limited. Recently, eBay has offered to its users a bidding agent for its simple English auctions; its strategy is described in [12], and is much simpler to that of the Simple Agent described in Sect. 3.5. The main argument for the lack of bidding agents is that users do not trust agents and refuse to use them in practice. They prefer to manually bid towards the closing time of the auction (sniping), thus raising concerns on the use of agents. We believe that indeed users do not trust the eBay agent as opposed to all agents in general, simply because the strategy of these agents is considered by users as more beneficial for the seller and due to the limited control that users have over the agents' behavior (see below). This is also why the same users prefer to use other commercial bidding agents to bid on their behalf in eBay auctions. Indeed, the recently developed variety of commercial bidding agents for eBay auctions is a significant indication of users' increased interest in bidding agents [7], [13], [10].

eBay's bidding agent has a fixed strategy, which is to place a new bid whenever a rival tops his own bid. The user just declares his willingness to pay and has no other way to influence the agent's behavior. Since multiple instances of this agent may represent multiple users and compete against each other in the same auction, it is clear that this agent's strategy drives prices up and limits the winner's profits. On the contrary, Trader enables users to select among various types of bidding agents and to affect the respective agent's behavior by setting its input parameters. Besides the willingness to pay, another very important parameter, namely the expected number of bids that are to be submitted by the agent on user's behalf (this is the n parameter, see Sect. 3.5). This enables the user to decide on the tradeoff between discouraging of new rivals by submitting multiple bids and attaining a higher final discount by limiting the number of submitted bids. Hence, the *user* controls the bidding agent's strategy and actions. This is an innovative feature of the Trader that makes its bidding agents attractive for users, as opposed to eBay.

The negotiation-related functionality of the Trader is also innovative, since, to the best of our knowledge, existing e-marketplaces support only auctions. By supporting negotiations, that are very popular in the constructions sector as a means of conducting business, the Trader has a competitive advantage over existing e-marketplaces. Due to the generic and accurate resource description, the Trader reduces users' search and transaction costs and facilitates the emergence of fast, highly beneficial deals, thus serving market's needs and resulting in lower prices. Agent-aided price negotiation and two-object negotiations complement this functionality, contribute to meeting users' needs and constitute advanced features of our work that are not supported in any of the existing e-marketplaces.

6 Conclusions

The e-Sharing system has implemented an innovative e- marketplace for the leasing of resources, primarily pertaining to the constructions sector. In this paper, we present the e-Sharing Trader system, which implements electronic auctions and negotiations for fast, transparent and efficient sharing of resources. The Trader supports a variety of popular auction mechanisms, both simple and multi-object. The selection and adaptation of these mechanisms are strongly motivated by the project's context. Innovative bidding agents have also been defined and implemented. The Trader also enables users to negotiate in order to reach a deal for the leasing of a resource. Adaptation of other researchers' work regarding agent-aided price negotiation agents has also been carried out and these negotiation agents are offered as part of the Trader too. Moreover, the innovative functionality of two-object negotiations is supported. By comparing the e-Sharing Trader with existing e-marketplaces and demonstrating the advantages of our work, we have argued that the Trader is rather innovative and could be applied to other context-specific e-marketplaces as well.

References

1. M. Bichler, G. Kersten, S. Strecker. Towards a Structured Design of Electronic Negotiations. Group Decision and Negotiation, Vol. 12, No. 4, (311-335), 2003.
2. C. Courcoubetis and R. Weber. Pricing Communication Networks : Economics, Technology and Modelling. John Wiley & Sons, 2003, ISBN 0470851309.
3. P. Faratin, C. Sierra, N. Jennings. Negotiation Decision Functions for Autonomous Agents. Preprint submitted to Elsevier Science, October 1997.
4. A. Kambil and E. Heck. Making Markets, How Firms Can Design and Profit from Online Auctions and Exchanges. Harvard Business School Press, Boston, ISBN 1-57851-658-7.
5. D. Salant. Auctions and Regulation: Reengineering of Regulatory Mechanisms. Journal of Regulatory Economics, 17:3, pp.195-204, 2000.
6. http://www.agentlink.org/agents-barcelona/presentations.
7. http://www.auction-sentry.com
8. http://www.cn.bizipoint.com/en/member_benefits.php
9. http://esharing.intranet.gr/docs1.htm
10. http://www.esnipe.com
11. http://www.onsale.com
12. http://pages.ebay.co.uk/help/buyerguide/bidding-prxy.html
13. http://www.sniperight.com
14. http://www.ubid.com

Appendix A: Derivation of the "Jump-Bid"

The "jump-bid" proposed in Sect. 3.5 maximizes the expected profit of the user under the following assumptions: Two users compete for the object. The valuations of the two users for the item to be auctioned are drawn from the uniform distribution in $[0,1]^3$ whose cumulative distribution function is denoted as $F(x)$, where $F(x) = x$. This information and the standing bid is common knowledge to the users. The opponent user's "jump-bid" is taken to be its own valuation (truthful bidding). Therefore, when considering the opponent's bid as a parameter, the "jump-bid" to be derived is essentially the most conservative (w.r.t. that parameter) optimized "jump-bid". The proof of the formula of the "jump bid" is as follows: Let U_i be the random variable that denotes the valuation of user i. We assume that we have reached the point at which the two users will place their "jump-bids" and that the standing bid b is placed by user 2. We want to calculate the "jump-bid" b_1 of user 1 provided that user's 2 "jump-bid" will be its valuation (the value of which is not known to user 1). Then the probability

---

[3] The jump-bid to be derived applies also if the support interval of the uniform distribution is any interval of the form $[0, C]$. Assuming a uniform distribution for valuations is a standard way of work in auction theory [2].

of winning for user 1 is given by:

$$\Pr[\text{user 1 wins}] = \Pr[b_1 > U_2 | U_2 \geq b]$$

$$= \frac{\Pr[b_1 > U_2 \text{ and } U_2 \geq b]}{\Pr[U_2 \geq b]}$$

$$= \begin{cases} \frac{F(b_1) - F(b)}{1 - F(b)} & \text{for } b_1 > b \\ 0 & \text{otherwise} \end{cases}$$

$$= \begin{cases} \frac{b_1 - b}{1 - b} & \text{for } b_1 > b \\ 0 & \text{otherwise} \end{cases}$$

The expected payoff of user 1 with valuation u_1 is given by:

$$E_1 = \Pr[\text{user 1 wins}] \cdot (u_1 - b_1) = \left(\frac{b_1 - b}{1 - b}\right) \cdot (u_1 - b_1)$$

(Recall that $u_1 > b$, otherwise the agent has completed its bidding.) The optimal "jump-bid" for user 1 is the solution of the following maximization problem:

$$\max_{b_1 \in [b, u_1]} \left\{ \frac{b_1 - b}{1 - b} \cdot (u_1 - b_1) \right\},$$

which gives $b_1 = \frac{b + u_1}{2}$. In the general case of N users, the derivation of the "jump-bid" is rather complicated and an approximation could be considered. For example, if the number of users N is large, an approximation of the optimal "jump-bid" b_1^N for user 1 is as follows: $b_1^N = \frac{(2N-1)u_1}{2N} - \frac{b}{2N}$, where u_1 is user's 1 valuation for the object and b is the current standing bid.

Appendix B: Negotiation Agents for a Single Resource

Below we present a formal description of the negotiation agents based on [3]. We formulate a bilateral negotiation model between the lessor's and the lessee's agent that negotiate for a single-issue object, namely for the price p of an object. For each agent the following hold:
Input:

- Acceptable range for the price $[\underline{p}_i, \overline{p}_i]$.
- Time of negotiation completion t^i_{max}.
- A scoring function $V_i : [\underline{p}_i, \overline{p}_i] \to [0, 1]$ that gives the score agent i assigns to each price in $[\underline{p}_i, \overline{p}_i]$. V_i is monotonically increasing if the agent represents the lessor and monotonically decreasing if the agent represents the lessee. We define three different scoring functions among which the user has to select, according to his own preferences:

- Impartial: $V_i(p) = ap + b$.
- Aggressive: $V_i(p) = ap^2 + bp + c, a > 0$.
- Conservative: $V_i(p) = ap^2 + bp + c, a < 0$.

Strategy: Let $p^t_{i \to j}$ denote the offer agent i makes to agent j at time t. The whole negotiation procedure is described by a finite sequence of such offers starting at time $t = 0$. Next, we will describe how agent j decides to reject, accept or make a counter offer to agent i, and in the latter case how the agent computes a counter offer. When agent j receives an offer $p^t_{i \to j}$ from agent i at time t, it rates the offer according to the scoring function. The decision that agent j makes at time t', is given by the interpretation function

$$I^j : I^j(t', p^t_{i \to j}) = \begin{cases} \text{reject} & \text{if } t' > t^j_{max} \\ \text{accept} & \text{if } V_j(p^t_{i \to j}) \geq V_j(p^{t'}_{j \to i}) \\ \text{offer } p^{t'}_{j \to i} & \text{otherwise} \end{cases}$$

where $p^{t'}_{j \to i}$ is the potential next offer of agent j to agent i at time t' and is computed according to the selected type of agent. That is, the offer is rejected when time has been completed and the offer is accepted when it gives a higher score than the score of the new counter-offer he intends to make. Otherwise, the agent makes a new counter-offer. We restrict attention to three types of agents:

Impatient agent: The offer of agent i to agent j at time t' is given by the formula:

$$p^t_{i \to j} = \begin{cases} \underline{p}_i + (\frac{\min\{t, t_{max}\}}{t_{max}})^{0.1} \cdot (\overline{p}_i - \underline{p}_i) & \text{if } V_i \text{ decreasing} \\ \underline{p}_i + 1 - (\frac{\min\{t, t_{max}\}}{t_{max}})^{0.1} \cdot (\overline{p}_i - \underline{p}_i) & \text{if } V_i \text{ increasing} \end{cases}$$

This agent approaches its reservation value very quickly.

Patient agent:

$$p^t_{i \to j} = \begin{cases} \underline{p}_i + (\frac{\min\{t, t_{max}\}}{t_{max}})^{10} \cdot (\overline{p}_i - \underline{p}_i) & \text{if } V_i \text{ decreasing} \\ \underline{p}_i + 1 - (\frac{\min\{t, t_{max}\}}{t_{max}})^{10} \cdot (\overline{p}_i - \underline{p}_i) & \text{if } V_i \text{ increasing} \end{cases}$$

This agent reveals its reservation value when time is almost exhausted.

Regular agent:

$$p^t_{i \to j} = \begin{cases} \underline{p}_i + (\frac{\min\{t, t_{max}\}}{t_{max}}) \cdot (\overline{p}_i - \underline{p}_i) & \text{if } V_i \text{ decreasing} \\ \underline{p}_i + 1 - (\frac{\min\{t, t_{max}\}}{t_{max}}) \cdot (\overline{p}_i - \underline{p}_i) & \text{if } V_i \text{ increasing} \end{cases}$$

This agent increases/decreases gradually the price towards its reservation value throughout the entire negotiation interval.

Managing Changes to Engineering Products Through the Co-ordination of Human and Technical Activities

Wendy K. Ivins[1], W. Alex Gray[1], and John C. Miles[2]

[1] School of Computer Science, Cardiff University, Queen's Buildings, Newport Road, PO Box 916, Cardiff U.K. CF24 3XF
{W.K.Ivins, W.A.Gray}@cs.cf.ac.uk
[2] School of Engineering, Cardiff University, Queen's Buildings, The Parade, PO Box 925, Cardiff, U.K. CF24 0YF - MilesJC@Cardiff.ac.uk

Abstract. Changes to engineering products need to be effectively co-ordinated with other members in the development team. Current approaches to managing change have limitations and often require further manual, ad-hoc activities to co-ordinate each change. This results in an inconsistent approach to change management. Our approach uses change processes to manage changes to products. Change processes are modelled using UML Activity Diagrams, which clearly show how human and technical activities are co-ordinated for each type of change operation. Change process enactment has been achieved in a research prototype by integrating workflow technology with a development system that supports versioning. This process-based approach to change management provides standardised, auditable change processes, which support change throughout the product development lifecycle. This negates the need for manual, ad-hoc activities to co-ordinate changes, resulting in a more consistent approach to managing change.

1 Introduction

The development of engineering products is a complex process that usually involves co-operation between participants from different disciplines and functions, often working in teams that are distributed across different sites. A large number of artefacts are generated during the development of a complex engineering product. A significant number of these artefacts will be generated and managed using computer-based systems. The development process is iterative and the product and its artefacts will be subject to many changes during the development lifecycle. These changes need to be effectively managed to ensure that they are co-ordinated with the work of other team members.

Problems with co-ordination can lead to a significant increase in delays and costs in development projects [1, 2, 3]. Co-ordination is a complex problem, which is compounded by a number of factors, which include: the size and structure of the development team; the size and complexity of the engineering product; the complexity of the development process; support for different development systems and tools; and the sharing and reuse of artefacts.

Engineering organisations currently use quality standards such as ISO 10007 [4] for configuration management and/or computer-based mechanisms such as versioning systems to control changes to products. These approaches have limitations and are often supplemented with manual, ad-hoc activities for co-ordinating change, which results in an inconsistent approach to managing change. A process-based approach to change management is proposed to overcome these limitations. Changes to engineering products are managed by change processes, which provide explicit support for the co-ordination of the human and technical activities involved in each type of change operation.

The paper is organised as follows: Section 2 considers the need for co-ordination and identifies the key activities for managing change; Section 3 looks at the limitations of the current approaches to managing change; Section 4 introduces the process-based approach to managing change and discusses the modelling and enactment of change processes; Section 5 concludes the paper and outlines future work.

2 The Need for Co-ordination

Co-ordination is an integral part of teamwork. As Mintzberg [5] observes: *"Every organized human activity – from the making of pottery to the placing of a man on the moon – gives rise to two fundamental and opposing requirements: the **division of labour** into various tasks to be performed and the **coordination** of those tasks to accomplish the activity."*

This is true for the development of most complex engineering products. One of the key functions of project management is to break down the overall effort of developing a complex product into tasks, which can then be assigned to team members. For engineering products this is commonly achieved using a work breakdown structure that provides tasks for the development of all of the components in the product structure. Team members may spend much of their time working independently on their allocated tasks and their work will involve the creation and modification of artefacts, which will change the current state of the product. Each change needs to be effectively co-ordinated with the work of other developers in the team, particularly if their work is affected by this change. This implies that managing changes to engineering products is a co-ordination problem.

Managing changes to an engineering product requires support for co-ordinating both the technical and human activities involved in each type of change operation. A UML Use Case Diagram (see Fig. 1) has been developed to show the key activities that are required for changing a product. It shows that a developer can change a product either by changing an artefact or by changing the configuration. In team-based development this change needs to be co-ordinated with the work with other developers. This includes running constraint checks to make sure the change activity is allowable, finding the developers affected by the change, obtaining permission for the change to go ahead, notifying relevant users that the change has occurred and propagating the change to other affected configurations. The agreed approval procedure should be followed before a product is released.

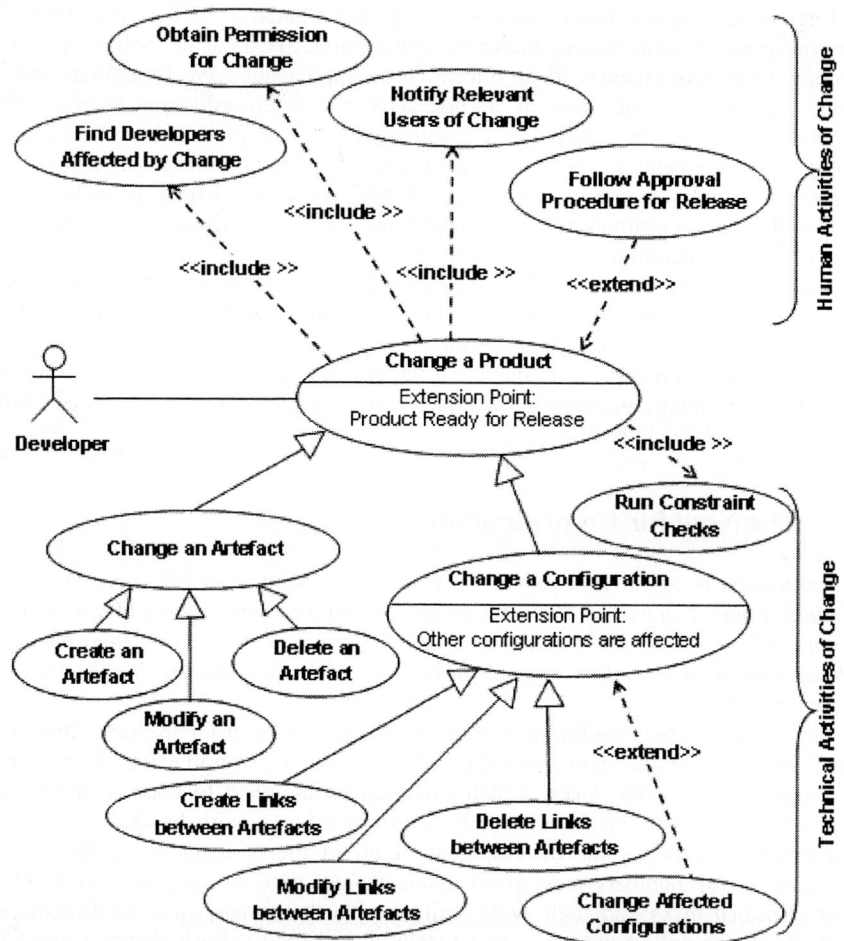

Fig. 1. Key Activities of Managing Changes to a Product

The human activities of change are often co-ordinated in a manual, ad-hoc manner, where it is left to the originator of the change to co-ordinate their activities with other team members. There can be problems with change notification if the originator of the change needs to inform the developers affected by the change. He/she may be unaware of the impact of a change, how it affects related artefacts, and who needs to be notified. He/she may intend to notify all affected parties but gets distracted with other responsibilities or may accidentally leave out certain affected users.

If developers are unaware of changes that affect their work then the product development lifecycle can be adversely affected. This can result in much time being wasted in having to redo work or solving a product problem, caused by using an outdated artefact because the affected person was not notified of the relevant changes. It may be preferable to seek permission for a change from affected parties when there is an obvious dependency between artefacts, such as when an artefact is a component of one or more composite artefacts.

3 Current Approaches to Managing Change

Approaches have been developed to help engineering organisations manage the changes to products and artefacts. We have classified the two most commonly used approaches to managing changes to products as a quality-based approach and a technology-based approach.

3.1 Quality-Based Approach to Managing Change

The **quality-based approach** is addressed through quality standards, such as the ISO 10007 [4] standard for configuration management. These involve the development of formal change control procedures, which define the actions that should be followed by people with particular roles when changes are made to baselined products. Change control is often implemented in organisations as a paper-based procedure, which can result in problems in keeping others informed of the change and keeping the change procedure consistent [6]. Systems have been developed to automate change control procedures (e.g. [7,8]) to provide a more consistent change procedure and improve communication. These provide support the *Follow Approval Procedure for Release Use Case*.

The main limitation with the quality-based approach is it only considers change to a product after the release of a configuration baseline. Artefacts that have not yet been released are not subject to formal change procedures, which may delay development by introducing unacceptable delays. However, a product's state changes most often in the early stages of development before the product and its artefacts are baselined. Therefore, the quality-based approach does not address the required human activities for change during the most dynamic period of a product's development.

3.2 Technology-Based Approach to Managing Change

Versioning systems are an example of a **technology-based approach** to managing change. They provide support for change through computer-based mechanisms to control the engineering product data and capture changes to a product and its artefacts. Versioning operations can be applied to artefacts to control changes at any point in the development lifecycle. The literature on versioning systems used in engineering product development has been reviewed to identify the level of support for the use cases given in Fig. 1. The results of the review are summarised in Table 1. It shows that the versioning systems in the review provide good support for most of the use cases that address the technical activities of change:

- The *Change an Artefact Use Cases* are supported with mechanisms to create, modify and delete versions of artefacts in a product. All but one of these systems [27] supports versioning to the artefact level. Developers capture changes to artefacts in versions. An initial version is generated when an artefact is created. Subsequent versions are generated each time a developer captures a change to the artefact. Katz [33] emphasises that versions:- *"are not simply data that change over time"* but:- *"represent a significant, semantically meaningful change"*.

Table 1. Support for Use Cases in Versioning Systems

Versioning System	Human Activities				Technical Activities							
					Change an Artefact			Change a Configuration				
	Find Developers Affected by Change	Obtain Permission for Change	Notify Relevant Users of Change	Follow Approval Procedure for	Create an Artefact	Modify an Artefact	Delete an Artefact	Create Links between Artefacts	Modify Links between Artefacts	Delete Links between Artefacts	Change Affected Configurations	Run Constraint
Version Server [9]					●	●	●	●	●	●	●	●
DOSS [10]	O		O		●	●	●	O	O	O		O
ORION [11]	O		O		●	●	●	●	●	●	O	O
DVSS [12]	●		●		●	●	●	O	O	O		O
Iris [13]					●	●	●	O	O	O	O	●
NELSIS [14]					●	●	●	O	O	O		●
IBM Version Model [15]					●	●	●	O	O	O		O
Version Model [16]					●	●	●	O	O	O		O
PLAYOUT [17]					●	●	●	●	●	●		O
Data Model [18]	O		O		●	●	●	●	●	●	O	O
Cadence [19]					●	●	●	●	●	●		O
Version Model [20]					●	●	●	O	O	O		O
IC Design Environment [21]					●	●	●	●	●	●		O
Valid Design Data Management [22]					●	●	●	●	●	●		O
GARDEN [23]					●	●	●	●	●	●		O
OVM [24]	O	O	O		●	●	●	●	●	●		O
Data Management Model [25]					●	●	●	●	●	●		O
Version Model [26]	O		O		●	●	●	O	O	O	●	O
EDICS [27]	●		●		O	O	O	●	●	●		O
COMMIT [28]	O		O		●	●	●	●	●	●	●	●
VSDCE [29]					●	●	●	●	●	●		O
CIMS/EDBMS [30]	O		O		●	●	●	●	●	●	●	O
Agent System for Version Control [31]	O	O	O		●	●	●	●	●	●	●	●
CoDVS [32]	O		O		●	●	●	O	O	O	O	O

Key: ● - Good Support for Use Case   O - Some Support for Use Case

- The *Change a Configuration Use Cases* are supported through mechanisms to develop composite artefacts, which are provided by all reviewed systems. A composite artefact is one that is hierarchically composed of component artefacts. Fifteen of these systems provide more sophisticated support for configurations by capturing the versions of each component artefact in composite artefacts.
- The *Change Affected Configurations Use Case* is supported by nine of the systems through mechanisms for change propagation. This allows new versions of artefacts to be automatically incorporated into configurations. For example, a new version of a composite artefact is automatically created if one of its components changes and the configuration is updated accordingly. This spawns further change if the composite artefact is itself a component of another artefact and so on. Four of these systems limit change propagation to the next level only.
- The *Run Constraint Checks Use Case* is supported by most systems through versioning constraint checks. For example, not being able to delete an artefact if it is a component of a composite artefact. Five of the systems also enforce development process constraints such as checking interface constraints to ensure that components can be successfully integrated and/or complying with restrictions imposed by application tools or manufacturing equipment

Most of the systems in Table 1 give poor support for the use cases that support the human activities of change:

- Change notification is provided by less than half of the systems. This supports the *Find Developers Affected by Change Use Case* and the *Notify Relevant Users of Change Use Case*. Most of these systems support flag-based and message-based notification. The flag-based approach notifies users only when they explicitly access a changed artefact. The message-based approach notifies users of artefacts that directly reference a changed artefact when a change occurs. Two systems [12,27] also allow users to register an interest in an artefact.
- Two systems [24,31] provide mechanisms for requesting changes. These could provide some support for the *Obtain Permission for Change Use Case*.

The reviewed systems constrain the developers to using the change management approach imposed in the versioning system, which is embedded in the code that implements each of the change operations. This approach is not visible to developers, which makes it difficult for them to understand the interactions between the mechanisms and to predict the effect of the changes. It also imposes a "one-size-fits-all" approach to managing changes, which cannot be easily adapted to meet the current or future needs of the development team. These systems have concentrated on supporting the technical activities of managing changes and have little or no provision for co-ordinating the activities of the team members who are involved in the change.

Table 1 does not include versioning systems used in Software Configuration Management (SCM), which have largely evolved independently from versioning systems for engineering product development. Comparisons of the approaches to versioning in these two areas can be found in [34, 35, 36, 37]. These highlight a lack of support for complex product configurations in most SCM tools.

Many engineering organisations use both quality-based and technology-based approaches to manage changes to their products. However, these approaches are not tightly integrated and often require further manual, ad-hoc activities to co-ordinate the changes. This can result in an inconsistent approach to change management.

4 The Process-Based Approach to Managing Change

The Use Case Diagram in Fig.1 shows that managing change to engineering products requires both human and technical activities. The proposed process-based approach combines concepts from both the quality-based and technology-based approaches to overcome their main limitations. The approach is achieved through the modelling and enactment of change processes, which provide explicit support for co-ordinating the human and technical activities involved in each type of change operation.

Developers use operations provided by a versioning system to make changes to the products. Versioning is an integral part of the change process as it captures the point where a change is instigated. A model of the change process is developed for each type of versioning operation to explicitly define the required co-ordination of human and technical activities involved in the change. Change process enactment automates the co-ordination of the human and technical activities to ensure a consistent approach to managing change each time a developer selects a versioning operation.

Joeris [38] also advocates a process-based approach to change management in software development. He observes that the technical view of Software Configuration Management (SCM) has concentrated on providing mechanisms to support versions and configurations and the management view of SCM has focused on providing procedures for handling change requests and performing changes to a well-defined change process. However, he identifies a gap of process support between the technical and management view of SCM. Joeris's work is similar in concept to our research. However, the work is presented at a high level of abstraction and, unlike our process-based approach, there are no detailed processes for managing change.

4.1 Change Process Modelling

A model of the change process is required for each operation provided by the chosen versioning system. The versioning model used in our work is largely based on VSDCE [29], which was developed as part of the DESCRIBE project. The versioning model was extended in [39] to support reuse and sharing of artefacts. This extended model offers many useful features to support engineering product development:

- It can model the complexity of the structure of a product and its composite artefacts and supports versioning artefacts and creating configurations.
- It provides workspaces similar to those proposed by Katz et al. [9]. Each developer has a private **Developer Workspace** for each product he or she is working on. This holds artefacts that are under development. Each product has a public **Product Workspace** which holds artefacts that are stable but not approved. Approved artefacts are stored in a public **Release Workspace.**
- It supports version states similar to those proposed by Chou and Kim [11]. A **Transient Version** (TV), represents an artefact that a designer is currently working on. It is considered unstable and may be updated or deleted. A **Working Version** (WV) is used for artefacts that are considered stable, but need to be checked against the work of other developers or other artefacts. A **Released Version** (RV) is an approved artefact.

The versioning operations provided by the model are summarised in Table 2.

Table 2. Versioning Operations Provided by the Extended Model of VSDCE

Versioning Operation	Transient Version	Working Version	Released Version
Create New Artefact	Created as an initial version in developer's workspace	Not applicable	Not applicable
Create New Version	From existing artefact in any version state. Stored in developer's workspace	By promoting a TV. Stored in product workspace	By promoting a WV. Stored in release workspace
Update Version	Yes	No	No
Delete Version	Yes - if not in a configuration	No	No
Promote Version (Component)	Yes	Yes	Not applicable
Promote Version (Composite)	Yes – but remove unpromoted component TVs	Yes –but remove unpromoted component WVs	Not applicable
Create a Configuration	Create a composite TV by linking to components in any version state	Create a composite WV by linking to component WVs and RVs	No – composite RVs come from promoted composite WVs
Update a Configuration	Yes	Yes	No
Delete a Configuration	Yes- deletes links but not versions	Yes- deletes links but not versions	No

The versioning system provides technical mechanisms to store and control a product's artefacts but it gives no support for the human activities of managing change. This is addressed in our research by change processes.

A set of change process models were developed to cover all of the versioning operations shown in Table 2. Each change process model should clearly illustrate how change for a particular versioning operation is managed by providing a visual representation of the co-ordination of technical activities performed by the versioning system and the human activities performed by the team members involved in the change. This includes explicit support for change notification, seeking permission for changes and constraint checking. A UML Statechart Diagram is provided in Fig. 2, to show how the processes for the versioning operations given in Table 2, change the state of the artefacts of engineering products under development.

The technique chosen for process modelling needed to explicitly show the co-ordination of the human and technical activities involved in each change. It was therefore important that the change process models were transparent. A behavioural model was required to clearly show the sequence of activities in a process. It needed to be capable of representing sequential and concurrent activities, alternative paths and iteration. It also needed to clearly differentiate between human and technical activities in the process. Support for sub-processes was desirable for modelling activities at different levels of abstraction and for representing common, repetitive sequences of activities. UML Activity Diagrams were chosen to model the change processes as this modelling technique met all of the above requirements.

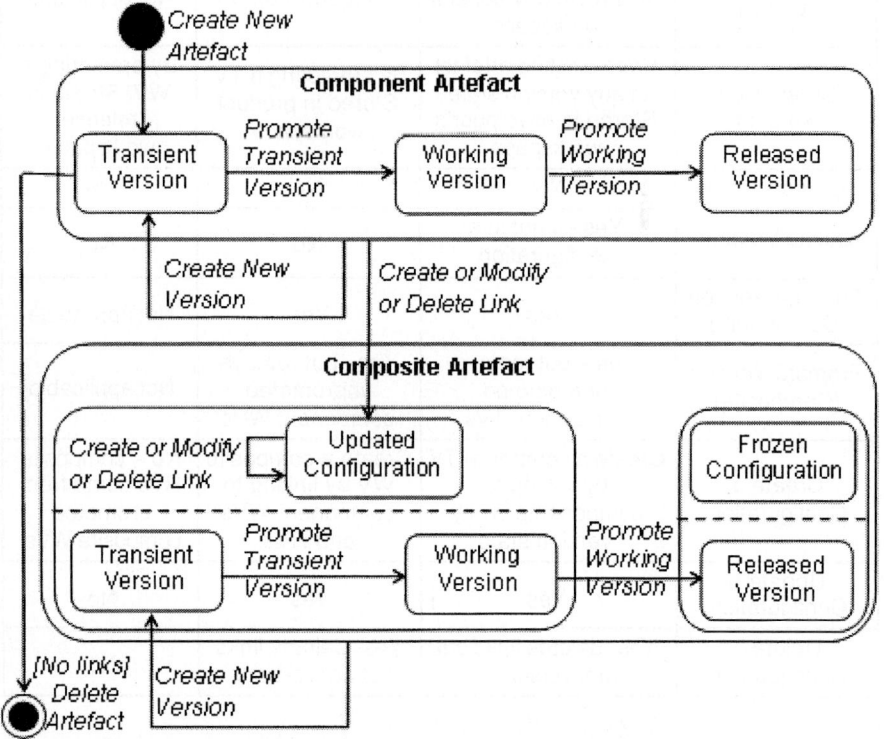

Fig. 2. Statechart Diagram Showing How Artefacts are Changed by Processes

An example change process model is given in Fig. 3. It shows the sequence of activities involved in promoting a transient version (TV) of a composite artefact to a working version (WV). The operation involves moving the artefact from the developer's private workspace to the project workspace and changing its version state. The change process shows a range of technical and human activities, including:
- running external constraint checks by calling a sub-process,
- notifying the developer who instigated the process of any problems,
- concurrently co-ordinating with the owners of component artefacts that are TVs to see if they agree to promote their artefacts, providing the option to link the composite artefact into the configurations of more complex artefacts by calling further sub-processes,
- notifying all relevant users of the successful promotion of the composite artefact.

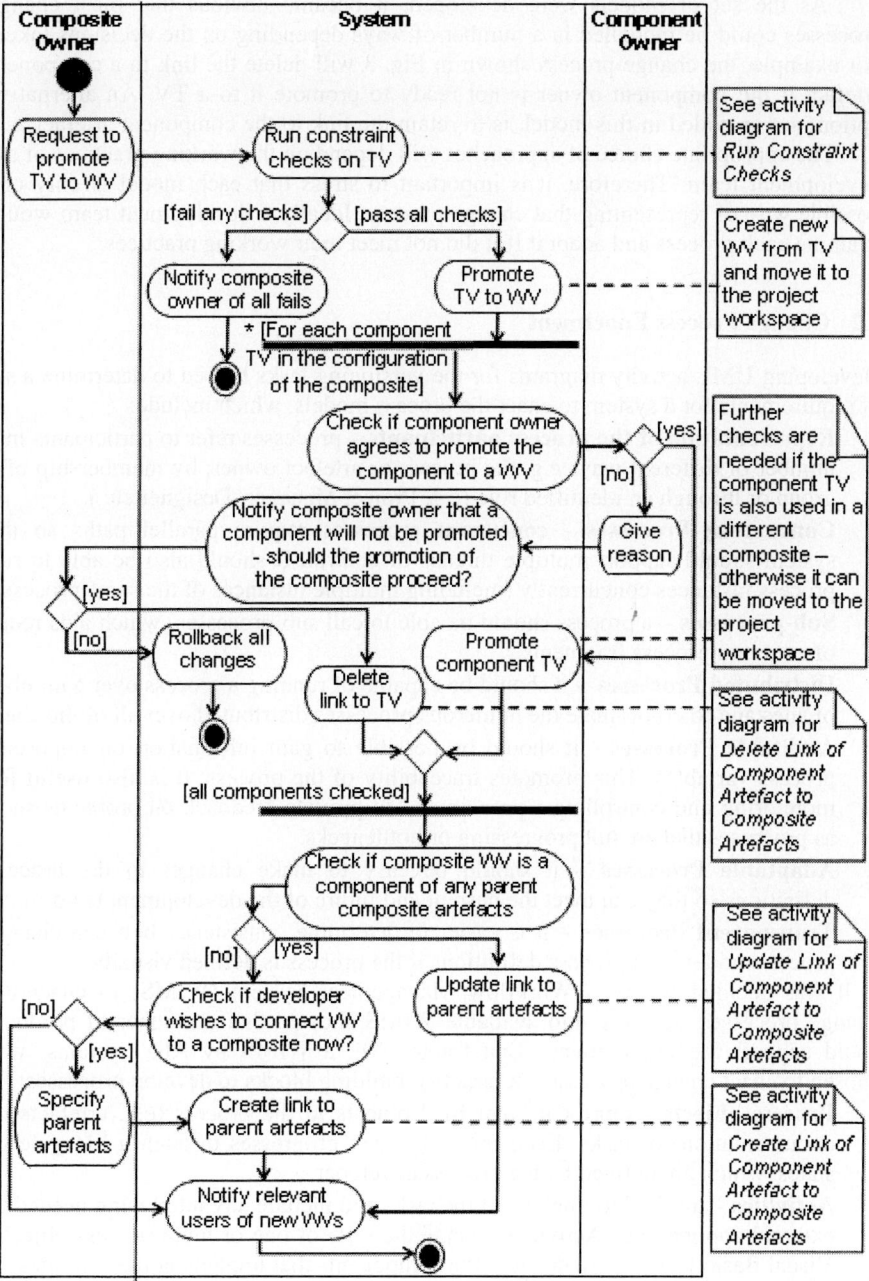

Fig. 3. Activity Diagram Showing the Change Process to Promote a TV of a Composite Artefact to a WV.

As the set of models were developed, it became obvious that most change processes could be modelled in a number of ways depending on the decisions taken. For example, the change process shown in Fig. 3 will delete the link to a component artefact if the component owner is not ready to promote it to a TV. An alternative option, not provided in this model, is to retain the link to the component artefact as a TV. The appropriate choice of approaches will depend on the working practices of the development team. Therefore, it is important to stress that each model is only one possible way of representing that change process. Ideally a development team would examine each process and adapt it if it did not meet their working practices.

4.2 Change Process Enactment

Developing UML activity diagrams for the versioning tasks helped to determine a set of requirements for a system to enact the process models, which include:

- **Representation of the process participants** – processes refer to participants in a number of different ways e.g. the process or artefact owner; by membership of a group or through an identified role (e.g. Project Manager, Designer etc.).
- **Concurrent Processes** - concurrent processes require parallel paths so the system should support multiple threads of control. It should also be able to run process instances concurrently (including multiple instances of the same process).
- **Sub-processes** – a process should be able to call sub-processes, which aids reuse of common process fragments.
- **Distributed Processes** - it should be capable of running a process over a number of sites and to co-ordinate the numerous processes distributed over all of the sites.
- **Auditable Processes** - it should be possible to gain information on important process variables. This promotes traceability of the process. It is also useful for monitoring and controlling a process and to provide feedback on problems such as processes that are not progressing or bottlenecks.
- **Adaptable Processes** – it should be easy to make changes to the process definitions so they can meet the current and future of the development team.
- **Transparent Processes** – it is easier to determine consistency between change process models and process definitions if the process is defined visually.

It was decided to use a Workflow Management System (WfMS) to enact the change processes. A study into available WfMS showed that a number of products could support the requirements. Stateframe [40], a WfMS by Alia Systems, was chosen to enact change processes. It uses two building blocks to develop processes:

- **Process objects** - represent "real life" objects in the process (e.g. artefacts or documentation) or tasks. Each process object progresses through a lifecycle of states, which are defined by the process developer.
- **Activities** - are used to implement the tasks and include any interfacing needed to external applications. Activities change the state of one or more process objects. Visual Basic was used to develop the components that implement the activities.

A research prototype has been developed to demonstrate the feasibility of enacting change processes in a suitable engineering application domain. One of the authors has extensive experience in developing software to test semiconductors so this was the chosen domain. The prototype integrates a versioning system with workflow technology to enact the change processes. The prototype has two key sub-systems:

- **Test Software Development Environment (TSDE)** - to provide mechanisms to support the versioning operations in Table 2. Its initial data set has a number of interdependencies: A set of test modules, created by a small team of developers, are assembled to make test programs with many of modules shared across different test programs; Composite modules have a number of different components; Many of the component modules are linked to several different composites. An example developer's workspace is shown in Fig. 4.
- **Change Process Enactment System (CPES)** - which uses Stateframe to enact the change processes for the versioning operations provided by TSDE.

Process definitions for the versioning processes are developed using a mapping tool, which is part of the StateFrame toolset. An example process map is given in Fig. 5 to show the process for creating a new version of an artefact. The map shows two

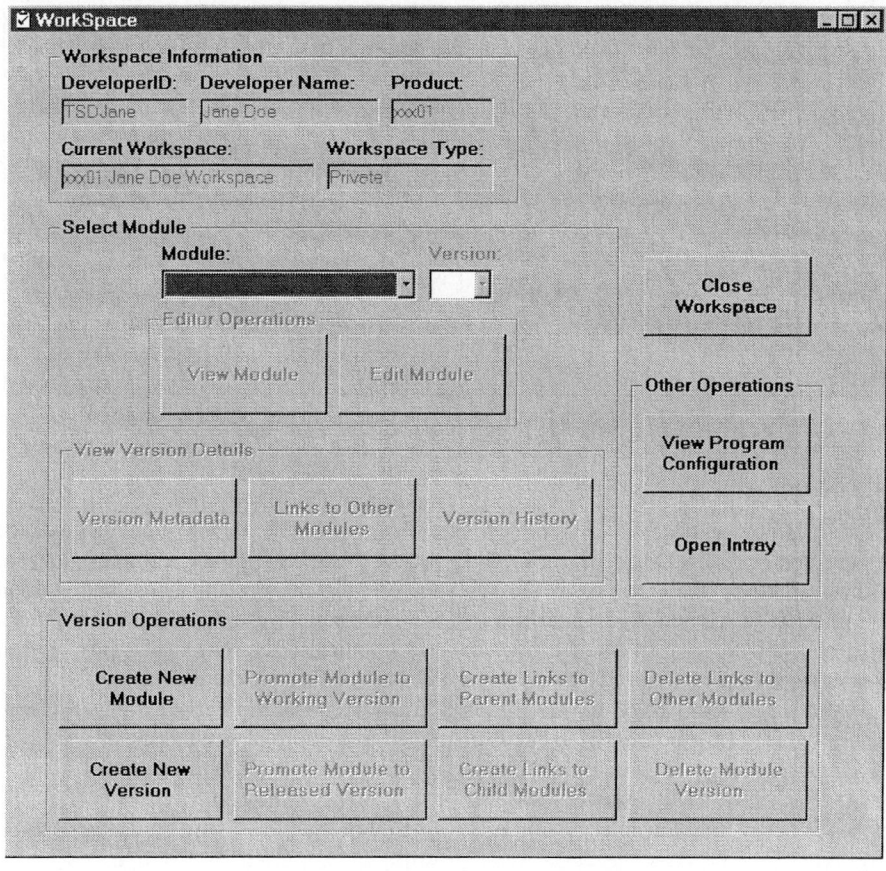

Fig. 4. A Developer's Workspace in TSDE

kinds of activity: automatic activities (denoted by the gears icon), which interface with TSDE to provide the technical activities required by the change process; and GUI activities (denoted with the computer icon), which interface with developers to provide the human activities required by the change process.

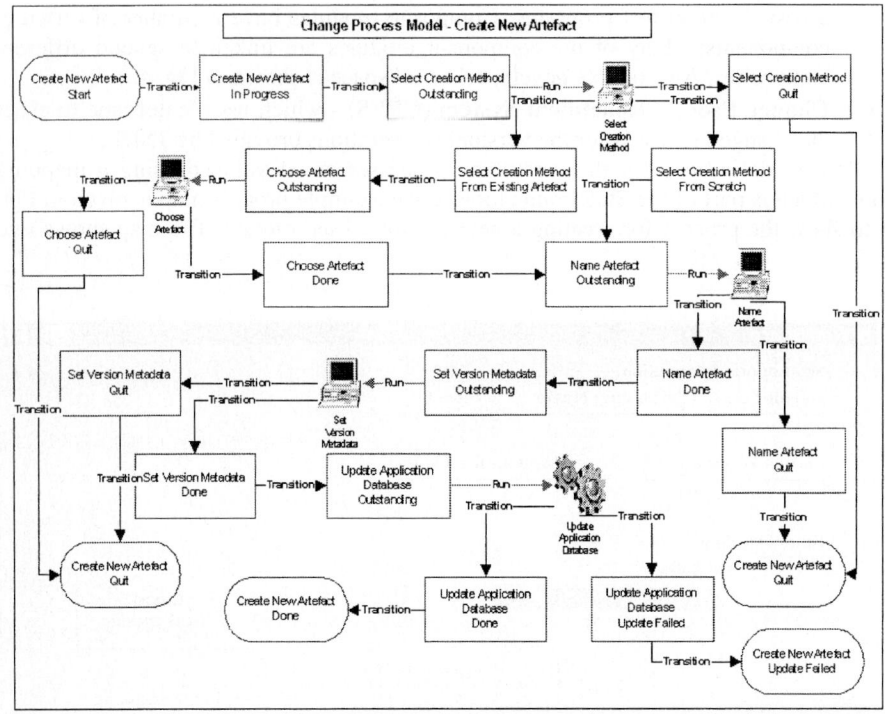

Fig. 5. Create New Version Process Description

A developer chooses a versioning operation from TSDE, which starts an instance of the appropriate change process. The process instance triggers activities that are either placed in the in-trays of the relevant participants or call tasks that are run automatically. Activities can interface to TSDE to run queries and operations. When a user chooses a task from their in-tray then a Graphical User Interface is provided to guide the user's actions. Fig. 6 shows the Stateframe client displaying a GUI in its right-hand window, which allows the user to enter information about a new version. The progress of the process instance is displayed in the left hand window.

Each change process was tested using scenario-based tests to cover all process paths. Each activity in a process was also tested to check the behaviour of each of the possible events that the activity supports.

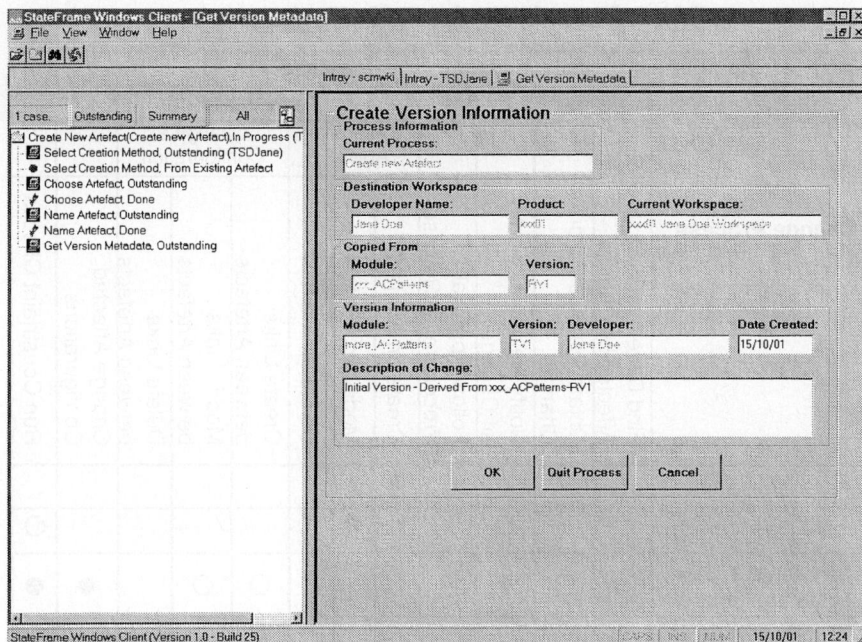

Fig. 6. Providing Interaction with the User

Implementation of the change processes has lead to some important considerations:
- The number of tasks in an activity should be minimised. Initially tasks that could be done by one person were grouped into a single activity. This resulted in processes that are program-centric rather than process-centric as much of the process logic is locked into the activity code and is not visible in the process map. Separating each task into its own activity improves the flexibility and transparency of the process.
- Reusing tasks and sub-processes cuts down on the process development time. An investigation in the tasks that make up versioning shows that about 60% of the tasks were used in two or more processes. Developing activities with small task granularity helps with reuse but process dependencies need to be checked to ensure the correct sequencing of tasks.
- Process variables were set up to support information flow between the process activities and provide traceability of the process. Process variables can store information for each process instance such as developer name, product name, artefact name and version.

Other research projects such as CRISTAL [41], MOKASSIN [42] and P_PROCE [43] include mechanisms for versioning and workflow to support engineering applications. However, unlike the process-based approach, these do not provide explicit change processes to co-ordinate the required human and technical activities for each versioning operation.

Table 3. Support for Use Cases in the Change Processses

Change Process	Human Activities				Technical Activities							
					Change an Artefact			Change a Configuration				
	Find Developers Affected by Change	Obtain Permission for Change	Notify Relevant Users of Change	Follow Approval Procedure for Release	Create an Artefact	Modify an Artefact	Delete an Artefact	Create Links between Artefacts	Modify Links between Artefacts	Delete Links between Artefacts	Change Affected Configurations	Run Constraint Checks
Create New Artefact					●							
Create New Version	O		O			●						O
Promote a TV (Component)	●	O	●					O	O		●	●
Promote a TV (Composite)	●	●	●					O	O	O	●	●
Promote a WV (Component)	●	●	●	●					O		●	●
Promote a WV (Composite)	●	●	●	●					O		●	●
Delete a TV	●	●	●				●			O	O	●
Create Links to Composites	●	●	●					●				
Create Links to Components	●	●	●					●				

Key: ● - Is included in change process   O - May be included in change process

5 Conclusions

The process-based approach provides a set of change processes to manage changes during engineering product development. Table 3 shows how each of the change processes provides support for the use cases identified in Fig. 1. Some of the change processes in Table 4 could be supported using the current approaches:
- The *Create New Artefact Change Process* requires no co-ordination with other developers and so could be supported using the versioning systems in Table 1.
- The *Create New Version Change Process* and the *Delete Link to a Component Change Process* require that other developers need only be notified of a change.

These could be supported with versioning systems that provide change notification mechanisms.

However, all other change processes require more complex co-ordination of technical and human activities. They are not adequately supported using the existing technology-based and quality-based approaches, even when engineering organisations use both approaches for managing change. Developers therefore require further manual ad-hoc activities to co-ordinate each change with the work of other developers. This can result in an inconsistent approach to managing change.

The process-based approach to managing change provides a set of change processes to explicitly support the co-ordination of the technical and human activities required in each type of change operation. These include activities that co-ordinate each change with the work of other developers. The process-based approach is therefore more comprehensive in supporting the use cases identified in Fig. 1 than the existing quality-based and technology-based approaches.

The process-based approach allows teams to develop separate processes, under different levels of control depending on the version state of an artefact. Artefacts that are not considered stable enough for release have less formal change processes, which co-ordinate the activities of developers involved in the change without imposing an inappropriate administrative burden. Formal change control procedures are included in processes to control the release of artefacts. Therefore, the process-based approach provides change processes for artefacts at all stages of the development lifecycle. This overcomes the main limitation of the quality-based approach, which only considers controlling changes to a product after the release of a configuration baseline.

The process-based approach extends the scope of the technology-based approach to change management by providing clearly defined and enactable change processes, which provide explicit support for co-ordinating both the technical activities provided by the versioning system and the human activities performed by team members who are involved in a change. These processes are transparent and the process definitions can be adapted to reflect the current and future needs of a development team. The appropriate change process is triggered when a developer chooses a versioning operation from the workspace of their development environment. This provides consistent and traceable processes for all developers who use these change processes, which is an improvement over the technology-based approach to managing change.

The current research prototype has been developed as a proof of concept system. It has shown that versioning and workflow can be integrated to enact processes that manage changes to engineering products for a single phase of the semiconductor development process. Further work is needed to integrate change processes into a commercial development system that provides versioning capabilities. This would provide a more realistic environment for evaluating the system using field trials. The scope of the system should be extended to support teams from different disciplines working on different phases of the product development lifecycle. It should support teams distributed over several sites, working on more complex artefacts with a large number of artefacts. This would be much closer to its expected usage in commercial development environments.

Our research group has also been looking at mechanisms to help collaborative teams overcome consistency problems associated with the dynamic evolution of configurations [44] and to provide integrity checking to ensure consistency of artefact versions with design constraints [45].

References

1. Bailetti, A.J., Callahan, J.R., DiPetro, P.: A Coordination Structure Approach to the Management of Projects. IEEE Trans. on Engineering Management, 41(4) (1994) 394-403
2. Crabtree, R.A., Fox, M.S., Baid, N.K.: Case Studies of Coordination Activities and Problems in Collaborative Design. Research in Engineering Design, 9 (1997) 70-84
3. Klein, M., Faratin, P., Sayama, H., Bar-Yam, Y.: What Complex Systems Research Can Teach Us About Collaborative Design. Proc. 6th Int. Conf. Computer Supported Cooperative Work in Design (2001) 5-12
4. BS EN ISO 10007 - Quality Management Guidelines for Configuration Management (1997)
5. Mintzberg, H.: The Structuring of Organizations, Prentice Hall (1979).
6. Chapin, N.: Changes in Change Control. Proc. 1989 Conf. on Software Maintenance (1989) 246-253
7. Crnkovic, I.: A Change Process Model in an SCM Tool. Proc. 24th Euromicro Conf. (1998) 794-799
8. Huang, G.Q., Lee, W.Y., Mak, K.L.: Development of a Web-based System for Engineering Change Management. Robotics and Computer Integrated Manufacturing, 17 (2001) 225-267
9. Katz, R.H., Chang, E., Anwarrudia, M.: A Version server for Computer-Aided Design Data. In: Proc. 23rd Design Automation Conf. (1986) 27-33
10. Weiss, S., Rotzell, K., Rhyne, T., Goldfein, A.: DOSS: A Storage System for Design Data. In: Proc. 23rd Design Automation Conf. (1986) 41-47
11. Chou, H.T., Kim, W.: A Unifying Framework for Version Control in a CAD Environment. In: Proc. 12th Int. Conf. on Very Large Databases (1986) 336-344
12. Ecklund, D. J., Ecklund, E.F., Eifrig, R.O., Tonge, F.M.: DVSS - A Distributed Version Storage Server for CAD Applications. Proc. 13th Int. Conf. on Very Large Databases (1987) 443-454
13. Beech, D., Mahbod B.: Generalised Version Control in an Object-Oriented Database. Proc. 4th Int. Conf. on Data Engineering (1988) 14-22
14. van der Wolf, P., van Leuken, T.G.R.: Object Type Oriented Data Modelling for VLSI Data Management. Proc. 25th Design Automation Conf. (1988).351-356
15. Dittrich, K.R., Lorie, R.A.. Version Support for Engineering Database Systems. IEEE Trans. on Software Engineering, 14(4), (1988) 429-437
16. Biliris, A.: Database Support for Evolving Design Objects. Proc. 26th Design Automation Conf. (1989) 258-263
17. Seipmann E., Zimmermann, G.: An Object-Oriented Datamodel for VLSI Design System PLAYOUT. Proc. 26th Design Automation Conf. (1989) 814-817
18. Kitagawa, H., Ohbo, N.: Design Data Modeling with Versioned Conceptual Configuration. Proc. .13th Int. Computer and Software Conf. (1989) 225-233
19. Liu, L.C.: Design Data Management in a CAD Framework Environment. Proc. 27th Design Automation Conf. (1990) 156-161
20. Ahmed, R., Navathe, S.: Version Management of Composite Objects in CAD Databases. Proc. Conf. on Management of Data (1991) 218-227
21. Milo, A., Nehab, S.: Data Framework for VLSI Design. Proc. Int. Conf. on Computer Aided Design (1991) 140-143
22. Banks, S., Bunting, C., Edwards, R., Fleming, L., Hackett, P.: A Configuration Management System in a Data Management Framework. Proc. 28th Design Automation Conf. (1991) 699-703
23. Wagner, F.R., Veigas de Lima, A.H.: Design Version Management in the GARDEN Framework. Proc. 28th Design Automation Conf. (1991) 704-709

24. Hübel, C., Käfer, W., Sutter, B.: Controlling Cooperation Through Design-Object Specification – A Database-oriented Approach. Proc. 3rd Euro. Conf. on Design Automation (1992) 30-35
25. Krishnamurthy, K., Law, K.H.: A Data Management Model for Design Change Control. Concurrent Engineering: Research and Applications, 3(4) (1995) 329-343
26. Ramakrishnan, R. Janaki Ram, D.: Modeling Design Versions. Proc. 22nd Int. Conf. on Very Large Databases (1996) 556-566
27. Machura, M.: Managing Information in a Co-operative Object Database System. Software – Practice and Experience, 26(5) (1996) 545-579
28. Rezgui, Y., Brown, A., Cooper, G., Yip, J., Brandon, P., Kirkham. J.: An Information Management Model for Concurrent Construction Engineering. Automation in Construction, 5 (1996) 343-355
29. Santoyridis, I., Carnduff, T.W., Gray, W.A., Miles, J.C.: An Object Versioning System to Support Collaborative Design within a Concurrent Engineering Context. Proc. 15th British Nat. Conf. on Databases (1997) 184-199
30. Zhang, Y., Gong, L.: Version Support and Management in CIMS/ EDBMS. Int. Conf. on Intelligent Processing Systems (1997) 843-847
31. Florida_James, B., Rossiter, N., Chao, K.M.: An Agent System for Collaborative Version Control in Engineering. Integrated Manufacturing Systems, 11(4) (2000) 258-266
32. Delinchant, B., Gerbaud, L., Wurtz, F., Atienza, E.: Concurrent Design Versioning System, Based on XML File. Proc. 28th Conf. Industrial Electronics Society (2002) 2485-2490
33. Katz, R.H: Toward a Unified Framework for Version Modeling in Engineering Databases. ACM Computer Surveys, 22(4) (1990) 375-408
34. Dart, S.A. Parallels in Computer-Aided Design Frameworks and Software Development Environment Efforts. IFIP Transactions, 16 (1992) 175-189
35. Estublier, J., Favre, J. M., Morat, P.: Toward SCM/PDM Integration? Proc. 8th Int. Symp. on Systems Configuration Management (1998) 75-94.
36. Wesfechtel, B., Conradi, R.: Software Configuration Management and Engineering Data Management: Differences and Similarities. Proc. 8th Int. Symp. on Systems Configuration Management (1998) 96-106
37. Dahlqvist, A.P., Crnkovic, I., Larsson, M.: Managing Complex Systems - Challenges for PDM and SCM. Proc. 10th Int. Symp. on Software Configuration Management (2001)
38. Joeris, G: Change Management Needs Integrated Process and Configuration Management. SIGSOFT Software Engineering Notes, 22(6) (1997) 125-141
39. Ivins, W.K., Miles, J.C., Gray, W.A.: Versioning Support for Design Reuse. Proc. 2nd Int. Conf. on Engineering Computational Technology (2000) 9-15
40. Stateframe Product Overview, Alia Systems (2003).
41. McClatchey, R., Baker, N.,. Harris, W,. Le Goff, J.M, Kovacs, Z., Estrella, F., Bazan, A., Le Flour, T.: Version Management in a Distributed Workflow Application. Proc. 8th Int. Workshop on Database and Expert Systems Applications (1997) 10-15
42. Joeris, G.: Cooperative and Integrated Workflow and Document Management for Engineering Applications. Proc. 8th Int. Workshop on Database and Expert Systems Applications (1997) 68-73
43. Qian, F., Shensheng, Z.: Product Development Process Management System Based on P_PROCE Model. Concurrent Engineering: Research & Applications, 10(3) (2002) 203-211
44. Al-Khudair, A., Gray, W.A., Miles, J.C.: Dynamic Evolution and Consistency of Collaborative Configurations in Object-Oriented Databases. Proc. 39th Int. Conf. on Technology of Object-Oriented Languages and Systems (2001), 207-218
45. Goonetillake, J.S., Carnduff, T.W., Gray, W.A.: An Integrity Constraint Management Framework in Engineering Design. Computers in Industry, 48 (2002), 29-44.

Towards Automatic Deployment in eHome Systems: Description Language and Tool Support

Michael Kirchhof, Ulrich Norbisrath, and Christof Skrzypczyk

Department of Computer Science III, Aachen University of Technology,
Ahornstr. 55, 52074 Aachen, Germany,
{kirchhof|uno|christof}@i3.informatik.rwth-aachen.de

Abstract. eHome systems are essentially component-based systems. One of the main reasons preventing a wide application of eHome systems in practice is the effort needed to interconnect all appliances, necessary controller and infrastructure components to benefit from derived value-added services. In the area of software engineering, this problem is addressed by configuration management and software deployment. In this paper, we introduce a language, which forms a basis for describing coarse-grained and abstract scenario defaults up to complete deployment information to carry out the actual installation in an eHome. We present a tool supporting the automatic transformation of an abstract input document into a complete deployment document adapted to a specific eHome environment. The tool is based on the description language.

1 Introduction

Home automation promises new comfort and useful services in everyday life. These services will become manifest in ubiquitous appliances. From users' point of view, services should be at least as easy in use. From developers' point of view, different *appliances and technologies* exist, which have to be integrated.

Connecting home area networks with communication and data networks provides potential for many service ideas. So far, remote control of services is most popular. Furthermore, users may access their eHome using different communication and data networks. Appliances can be controlled from any place (e.g., the office) using a browser and the Internet. The owner of an eHome may determine and change state of the alarm equipment with the Wireless Application Protocol (WAP [1]) and mobile communication networks using a mobile phone. In case of an alarm, the security equipment sends a multimedia message (e.g., MMS [2] or eMail) to the owner of an eHome, who will receive the message with the mobile phone. But eHome Services may also interact on their behalf with other data and communication network services making value-added services possible.

Decoupling of services from the underlying infrastructure is based on abstraction from the infrastructure itself. An eHome Service should rely on the types of devices, instead of specific devices and their proprietary implementation. For example, an alarm system should be able to integrate any motion detector or device, which is able to detect motion (e.g., cameras), instead of being tightly bound to a vendor-specific motion detector. Taking the back-end systems into account, an eHome Service is not only a piece of software executed on the service gateway. An *eHome Service* is the *wholeness of services a user experiences*.

Home automation aims at mass markets. Therefore, a technical background can not be expected from the users. Mainly users will expect trivial *plug-and-play* from home automation appliances as they do from their legacy pendants. This leads to the demand for *self-configuring* and *maintenance-free* systems. Home automation can not require technicians come to the user's home to integrate any kind of devices to home networks. Hence, there is a need for automatic configuration management and software deployment. Current approaches deal with manual configuration management and software deployment [3,4]. The solution has to ease the realization, the configuration, and the deployment of distributed eHome systems, which do not impose any further burdens to users.

To ease and automate this *configuration and deployment process*, we will introduce a language, which forms a basis for describing coarse-grained and abstract scenario defaults up to complete deployment information to carry out the actual installation in an eHome. Furthermore, we will introduce an ontology and tools to support the automatic transformation of a very abstract input document into the complete deployment document adapted to a specific eHome environment.

This paper is structured as follows: In the following section, the scenario of our eHome system is described. In section 3, we will discuss related languages and frameworks capable of describing and processing various aspects of component-based systems in the face of automation. In section 4, we will introduce our proposed description language and in section 5, the tool support is described. Finally, we give a summary and a conclusion of this paper.

2 Scenario

The scenario is illustrated in figure 1: The connected home on the right-hand side of the drawing is equipped with a *residential gateway*, a hardware device, which provides access to communication infrastructures via different protocols (e.g., X.10, EHS, Lon, Jini) and acts as a runtime environment for the *service gateway*. The service gateway manages and runs certain software components. In our work, we focus on the domains of Security, Consumption, and Infotainment. The services in these domains are based on certain equipment, as some examples are shown in the figure: an alarm system depends on cameras, motion detectors, and lamps or sirens. Monitoring and optimization of energy consumption can be realized by the use of ammeters, photo sensors, thermometers, or the heating systems. Elements of the infotainment domain can be incorporated for audio-based and video-based interaction. The communication backbone is an IP-based platform, including a distributed extension. With this extension, internal and external communication can be handled equivalently. Beside direct interaction with devices in the house, interaction with the eHome system based on personal computers, PDAs, and mobile phones is realized. Service providers are connected to the systems via the distributed IP-based platform to provide digital content, applications, and services.

eHome systems are built on top of integrable net-aware devices in households. Applicable devices, communication techniques, and infrastructures vary in several dimen-

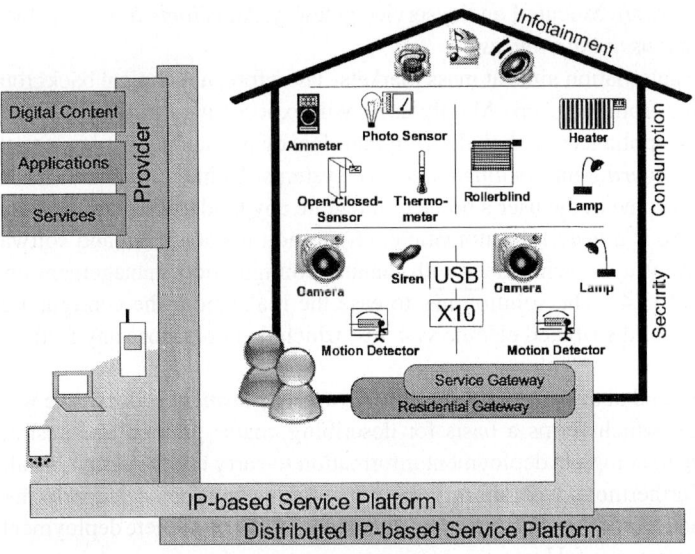

Fig. 1. Scenario

sions: Devices vary with respect to interfaces, features, locations, and range. Important differences in communication are protocols, bridges, name spaces, and through-put. The applied infrastructure is centralized, because current development in gateway technology provides sufficient computational power for eHomes and allows to reduce the complexity of system design in contrast to decentralized or mixed approaches. Distribution aspects of gateway technology and service execution are to be observed in a later phase. Last but not least, the integration of external service providers is an unanswered question. Until now, just hardware-specific problem fields have been dealt with. Hence, suitable and reasonable models and structures for this new application domain still need to be developed.

In contrast to traditional distributed systems, one very important fact in eHome Systems is that the expected potential of market penetration is extremely high (in terms of million households), but the variety in terms of the underlying ontology is relatively small. To solve the configuration and deployment problem in eHome systems, we introduce configuration documents on three levels. We describe transformations on these documents, as well as tools supporting the different levels. Further improvement with respect to the automatic handling of such documents should be possible by the incorporation of knowledge-based systems. Resulting from the expected high penetration and the extremely large amount of expected variants, a manual adaption of systems for each customer is neither possible nor affordable. Thus, there must be a possibility to automate this adaption process. On the one hand the configuration has to be automated and on the other hand the deployment has to be automated. To ease the configuration and deployment task, we rely on the layered approach to OSGi-based gateways described in [5]. To abstract from communication details in terms of provider-ehome-connectivity, we make use of the Distributed Services Framework (DSF) [6].

3 Related Work

As we want to define a language capable of describing both configuration and deployment information, we studied other frameworks offering such descriptions or forming a base for automatable deployment of components. The most important ones and their benefits are described below.

xADL 2.0 [7] is an XML-based description language for software architectures. Inheriting XML's schema-based mechanisms, it is flexible and highly extensible. The default schemes for xADL 2.0 based on xArch [8] provide definitions for elements typically found in architecture description languages (ADL). The creation, management, and manipulation of xADL 2.0 documents and schemes is well supported by tools from the xADL 2.0 community. However, there are no tools supporting automatic configuration or deployment processes.

The *Openwings* [9,10] consortium was founded as an open community. Its objective is to specify a framework for component-based systems independent of database, architecture, and operating system. Openwings defines its own component model and component programming model. It has a strong focus on the application in loosely coupled distributed networks. In Openwings, every component has to be started separately or via batch support. There is no mechanism defined to automate the instantiation process of a complete component-based system.

RIO [11] is an extension of the Jini-framework [12]. It adds a component model and a component programming model to the Jini-framework. In RIO, components are called Jini Service Beans (JSB). They are described in an XML-based notation called *Operational String*. Operational Strings may include further Operational Strings and Service Bean Elements. Service Bean Elements include all information necessary to install a JSB. Hence, it is sufficient to specify Operational Strings to instantiate a complete component-based system by one operation.

The *Open Services Gateway Initiative* (OSGi) [13,14] specifies a set of software application interfaces (APIs) for building open-service gateways on top of *residential gateways* [5]. The residential gateway describes a universal appliance that interfaces with internal home networks and external communication and data networks. Similar to a data network gateway, a residential gateway is equipped with interfaces to different physical media and provides conversion between protocols. It represents a concept, which lets different networks communicate transparently. This leads to a wide support of various standardized technologies. In the OSGi context components are called *bundles*. Each bundle may provide its own configuration[1] user interface (UI) utilizing the (specified) HTTP-service. Additionally, for configuration data get- and set-methods are provided in order to be directly accessible from other bundles and components. The configuration

---

[1] The meaning of configuration in OSGi in this context differs from our understanding of configuration. In OSGi configuration is the setting of properties. In our context a configuration is a document, which also includes the collection and combination of components. For a more precise definition see [15].

data is isolated within the bundle. A third way for the realization of configuration tasks is implementing the interface ManagedService. Bundles can be remotely configured by the module Configuration Admin, which is specified by OSGi, too. Configuration data are encapsulated in Property objects. The Configuration Admin acts as a mediator. With that, basic configuration in terms of adjustments of properties can be realized. OSGi is widely used in white goods and has the potential to be established as a standard framework for household appliances.

The OSGi gateway (see figure 2) resides within a Java runtime environment, which offers the well-known features of Java [16]. The core component is specified as the *OSGi service framework*, which acts as a container for service implementations. This environment includes a Java runtime with life cycle management, persistent data storage, version management and a service registry. Services are Java objects implementing a concisely defined interface. Services are packaged within *bundles*, which register zero, one or more services within the framework's service registry. Bundles contain services implemented in the Java programming language, a manifest file describing import and export aspects, and additional implementation-specific libraries. Bundles can be deployed and undeployed during runtime, while the information in the manifest file ensures the integrity of the system. Security aspects are handled as well. As the figure shows, a bundle is not restricted to rely on functionality offered by the framework, it can profit from every layer below, i.e. native functionality offered by the operating system and the hardware. This stands in contrast to layered approaches in software engineering, but allows the realization of bundles for any protocol. To ensure a minimal common set of functionality, certain bundles are standardized (e.g., the Log bundle for logging and the HTTP bundle for user interface purposes).

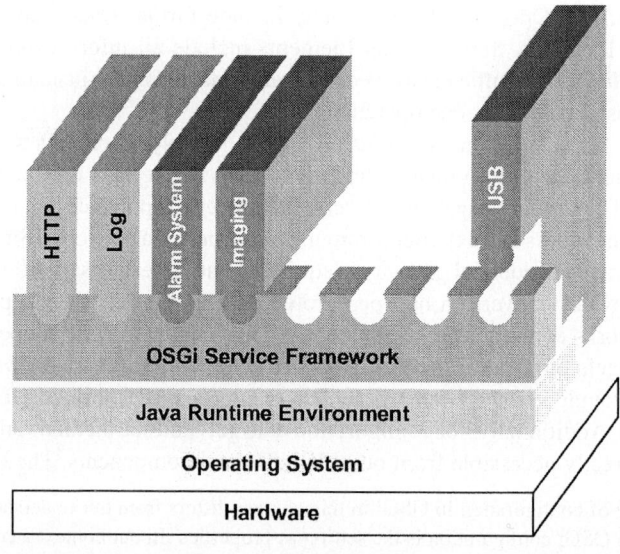

Fig. 2. OSGi System Structure

Central to the OSGi specification [17] is the *service framework* with a service registry. Components register their services at the service registry where other applications may retrieve and use them. Based on the concept of residential gateways [18,19], the open services gateway specification describes an approach that permits coexistence of and integration with multiple network and device access technologies. In addition, components may be added implementing new technologies as these emerge. Interaction is enabled via Java interfaces, without relying on proxy objects. While other systems -like Jini- are decentralized, the OSGi approach is a centralized system, which simplifies the maintenance of the system to the disadvantage of distribution aspects.

To make eHome systems affordable for the masses far-reaching automation is needed. A requirement for tool support to achieve the automatisms is the existence of an extensible language describing abstract scenario requirements up to complete deployment configurations. Hence, it is highly desirable to combine the extensibility and basic properties of xADL 2.0 with the possibility of automatic deployment of RIO's operational strings. Furthermore, the language should allow the usage of frameworks like Openwings with a strong focus on distribution. To support OSGi as an established eHome framework, the necessary information for the deployment on this platform have to be integrated and a tool to support automatic deployment has to be developed.

Whereas the specification languages mentioned above (like xADL 2.0 or RIO's Operational Strings) are intended to describe software components and their dependencies, our goal is to cover also the physical architecture of eHome systems. This allows us to extend the simplification of the configuration process beyond software issues and discloses automatic generation of complete system solutions including all involved products.

4 Description Language

Our approach is process-oriented. So, we examine the life cycle of a newly ordered service. For the relations between configuration document levels, the supporting tools, and the knowledge base compare figure 3. The customer (i.e., the eHome owner) triggers this process, by requesting the provider portal to display available services. After authentication and authorization, the suitable services are identified. Of course there is a large amount of general knowledge (like platform specific drivers for appliances, interface descriptions, controller components, and dependencies), which has to be acquired and specified by the provider or its subprovider in beforehand to allow the determination of these services. We distinguish three different levels of a configuration document: If the customer decides to subscribe to one of the offered services, this choice, which we will call *scenario configuration document* (1), is transferred to the provider. Then, this document is enriched with necessary information to do the actual software installation at the customer's home. The tool supporting this step is called Deployment Producer and the resulting document is called the *deployment configuration document* (2). After installation of the necessary hardware, a tool called Runtime Instancer instantiates the deployment configuration and brings the functionality specified in the scenario configuration document to life. While the service is maintained, the Runtime Instancer is used to save the current configuration, deployment data, and status information of the eHome in an *runtime configuration document* (3). After a phase of usage, maintenance, or in-

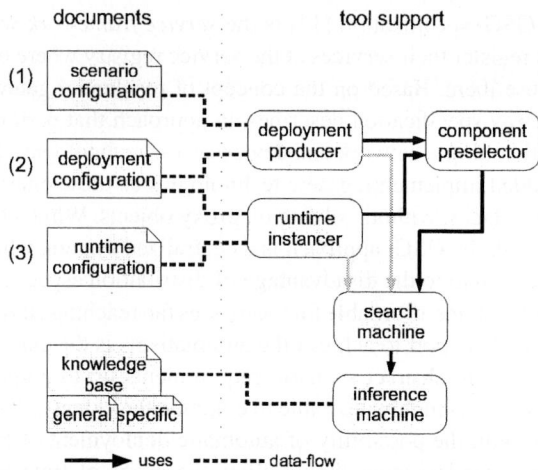

Fig. 3. Configuration Document Levels, Tools, and Knowledge Base

stalling further services the service is stopped and deactivated via the Runtime Instancer. We emphasize that this process should also hold for upgrading a service. Upgrading is either extending a service with new devices or adding services, which could depend on already installed services. Hence, we demand that the scenario configuration document is able to include a previous deployment configuration.

According to the life cycle described above, there exist three levels of a configuration document. Our language describes all three corresponding configuration types starting with very simple and abstract scenario configurations up to complete runtime configurations including the current states of the already installed devices. Apart from software components, the language also describes all devices and platforms used in the system. The term *platform* stands for a combination of a framework and the device it is executed on. Software components, devices and platforms are called *units*. An important part of the model is the knowledge base, which classifies all known unit types. Figure 4 shows such a simplified device classification. The type attributes in the hierarchy are passed down to further type specifications. A description of a unit should always name its type to specify its functional context and include the corresponding attributes.

The language also describes the dependencies between units. In our context, these are called *connections*. Together, units and connections form a configuration graph where units are represented by nodes and connections by edges. There are three main types of connections:

Logical connections. A *logical connection* indicates where a software component is being executed on and is always directed towards a framework.
Physical connections. *Physical connections* give information on the kind of the communication medium and the protocols used by the devices.
Usability connections. All other dependencies are described by the *usability connections*.

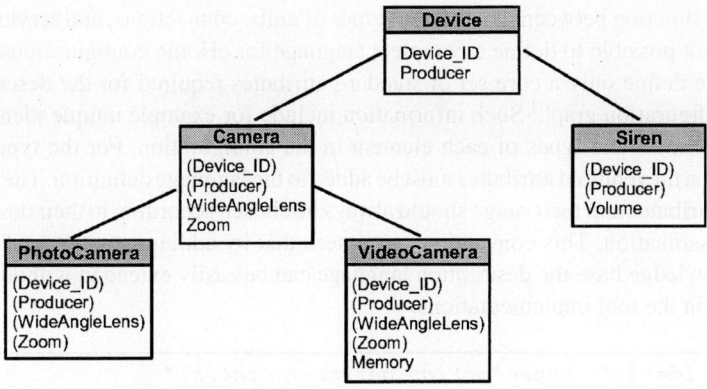

Fig. 4. Classification of Different Device Types

The connection types are also classified in the ontology and there exist many further specializations for each of the three main types. For example special types for USB, Infrared and Bluetooth connections are possible. There are also special types of usability connections, for instance to indicate driver and control components of devices. In addition, the ontology can be extended if any new types with new attributes are required.

Finally, a service itself must be described. On the one hand, all units and connections have to be assigned to the service they are used by, so the service also needs a name and an identifier. On the other hand, more specific attributes of the service are required. Often it is important to know what priorities the service has while accessing shared resources. A good example are loudspeakers, which can be used by surveillance, infotainment and communication services at the same time. Other service attributes can describe functional behavior of a service. However, sometimes it seems more sensible to use special formalisms to describe such kinds of information and place them in an extra file. In this case, a corresponding link to the external data and some meta information should be provided within the service description. In our implemented examples we use rule-based descriptions for the service behaviors, which are managed by a rule engine [20, 21] after the installation. But also in the descriptions of units and connections, the use of special formalisms seems sensible, for example to specify the geographic locations of the devices. In this context, it is also important to observe that it is not possible to achieve a complete description of really all aspects of the eHome system.

```
<?xml version="1.0" encoding="ISO-8859-1"?>
<eHome xmlns="x-schema:eHomeSchema.xml">
  <Units> ... </Units>
  <Connections> ... </Connections>
  <Services> ... </Services>
</eHome>
```

Listing 1.1. Structure of a Configuration Description

The distinction between the different types of units, connections, and services shows that it is not possible to define a complete language for eHome configurations. For this reason, we define only a core set of standard attributes required for the description of every configuration graph. Such information include for example unique identification numbers, names and types of each element in the configuration. For the type specific information the required attributes must be added to the language definition. The names of the new attributes and their range should always be chosen according to their descriptions in the classification. This convention guarantees that by adding new types of products to the knowledge base the description language can be easily extended without causing problems in the tool implementations.

```xml
<Unit    id="56"   type="motion_detector_control"
    supertype="component" status="ready">
  <Attributes>
      <Producer value="Philips"/>
      <Platform>
         <OS value="DebianLinux3.0"/>
         <Framework value="rio"/>
         <MinPlatformCPU value="2"/>
         <MinPlatformMemory value="16"/>
      </Platform>
  </Attributes>
  <Resources>
      <DriverFile value="sensor_driver"/>
      <Component>
         <InterfaceFile value="sensor65-dl.jar"/>
         <ImplFile value="sensor65.jar"/>
         <DataFile value="action_sensor.xml"/>
      </Component>
  </Resources>
  <Instances> ... </Instances>
  <States>...</States>
</Unit>
```

Listing 1.2. Component Description

For the realization of the language we define an XML document class [22]. It includes all core elements needed for the description of the graph structure and also some standard attributes of the most usual unit, connection and service types. Listing 1.1 shows the skeleton of a typical XML document describing an eHome system. Depending on the product types used in the house different XML elements must be added to the schema definition (or DTD) of the language. It is the task of the Runtime Instancer to extract the required information and use them during the deployment and installation process. Listing 1.2 shows the specific description of a component for the RIO framework [11]. If describing components for other frameworks, the attributes can vary. Correspondingly, listing 1.3 presents the structure of a connection description and listing 1.4 shows an example of a simple service description.

```
<Connection  id="6" type="physical_USB" supertype="physical"
      source_unit_id="58"  target_unit_id="62"
      scenario="simple_security" status="ready">
  <Attributes>
     <Bidirectional value="false"/>
  </Attributes>
  <Resources>...</Resources> ...
  <States>...</States>
</Connection>
```

Listing 1.3. Connection Description

```
<Scenario  id="100" type="simple_security"
      supertype="security"  status="ready">
  <Attributes>
     <Description value="a very simple security scenario"/>
     <PriorityAudio value="5"/>
  </Attributes>
  <Resources>...</Resources> ...
  <States>...</States>
</Scenario>
```

Listing 1.4. Service Description

5 Tool Support

The configuration process can be simplified by using several tools. The main goal of the Deployment Producer is the automatic creation of deployable deployment configurations containing all relevant information about the eHome services. Especially, the data required for the installation of the software components is important. The user should provide an abstract description of the wanted future eHome system, specifying its devices and services only as far as desired. The tool should then be able to generate descriptions of possible deployment configurations, to estimate their values and to present the best solutions to the user. The descriptions should be based on the XML language introduced above. In order to provide the semantic information required for the configuration process an appropriate knowledge base has to be provided. We propose an algorithm for the automatic search of runnable configurations. A simplified version of this algorithm is described in this section. We also present its first implementation.

It is easy to show that the creation of deployable configurations is a NP-hard problem and that excessive search is needed to find all existing solutions. For all units in the original configuration, the implemented algorithm examines recursively all combinations of possible products. Of course, not all arrangements of devices and components are possible. The products cannot be regarded independently from the service context and from their dependencies to the other products. On each level of the recursive search one more unit will be specified. The Deployment Producer tests all possible product choices for this unit and for each choice creates a new configuration containing the product's specification. These new configurations are then passed in succession to the next recursion level, where the new added information can be taken into account while processing the other still not processed units. Hence, regarding a single search path of the tree, for the units from the lower recursion levels the number of the possible product choices is narrowing by each new added product specification. By using depth-first-search, the algorithm traverses such a tree of different configurations and tries to find a solution with all units successfully specified (see figure 5).

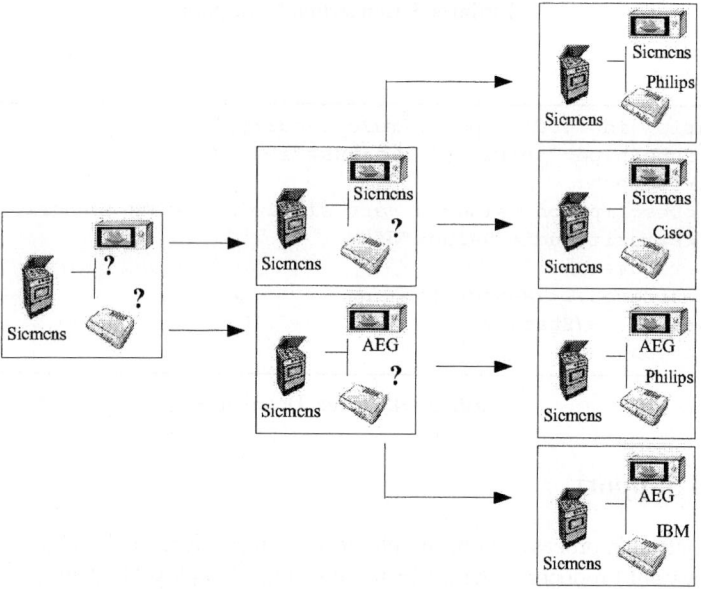

Fig. 5. Building the Search Tree (Recursive Search)

To decide, which devices and components can work together, the tool has to analyze the possible product combinations in the context of the given services. The required data is stored in the knowledge base. It contains both a hierarchy of all unit, connection and service types with their attributes and states, and the semantic dependencies between them and their requirements. By using this knowledge base, the program can process each pair of connected units and depending on their already fixed attributes determine their other properties. Every already fixed unit attributes narrows the number of product choices for the other connected units. So in order to allow all possible configurations on each recursion level only the necessary attributes should be set.

To access the knowledge base, the Deployment Producer uses the tool *Component Preselector*. The development of the interface between these two programs is one of the main challenges of the project. In order to use the semantic information of the knowledge base we define the communication procedures between them. For this reason we define several *request types* for accessing the knowledge base. As described above in the first request type the Deployment Producer passes the attributes of the two connected units in order to receive more complete specifications of both. In certain situations, depending on the attribute values of the units no connection is possible at all. Such situations are called *conflicts*. If a connection can be found , the configuration on the current recursion level will be filled with the new attribute values and the search can proceed, either with the next connection of the current unit or the first connection of the following unit on the next recursion level. Two further request types of the interface will be mentioned later in this text.

It is important to remark that the original input configuration can be rather abstract and it will usually never consist of all devices and components needed for the realization of the final eHome system. In case of an upgrade there will be at least one deployable part in the configuration in addition to the abstract description of new devices and services. That is why the Component Preselector not only confirms and specifies a possible interaction of two units standing in a certain relation, but also returns a small subconfiguration containing all the other units needed for their connection. For example a house security control component, which should be connected with a motion detector device will always need at least a driver component for the device and a platform where the component can be executed. Hence, the answer of the Component Preselector will also contain these two new units and the connections between them. The Deployment Producer adds this subconfiguration to the current eHome configuration replacing the two old units and their connection. After all units and connections from the original input file were processed, the found configuration finally contains all information required for the deployment of the system. All relevant attributes of the units are fixed and all missing parts of the configuration are added. That is why this first phase of the search is called *completion phase*.

A found configuration already contains the information required for the deployment. All element attributes are specified and all missing units added. However, now the configuration can contain several units of the same type, which are also equivalent in their functions. The second phase of the search is called *merging phase*. Now the program must try to find all equivalent units in the configuration graph and merge their nodes if all dependencies with the other involved units allow the transformation. This is not only necessary to generate sensible and cheap configurations but also to guarantee the actual realization of the system. The reason is that during the completion phase all missing units are added to the configuration without regarding any physical limits of the existing resources, like the amount of the available connection slots or the disc memory capacities of the platforms. The aim is to reach the smallest possible amount of units, but at the same time guarantee that all limits are respected. To find out if two units of the same type can be merged the program has once again to consult the knowledge base of the Component Preselector. Here the tool uses the second request type. During this procedure the tool must check the available resources and all the other assumed characteristics of the units, like their geographical positions and their functions. Usually several merging transformations are possible and one transformation can make other possible transformations impossible, which could lead to much better configurations later. In order to find the best solution all these possibilities should be examined. It is necessary to recursively test all possible merging transformations for all configurations found in the completion phase. The chance of losing better merging transformations is a further reason why it is not possible to look for double units already during the completion phase and add only units, which really do not exist so far. Configurations with missing merging possibilities, which still contain some units not respecting their resource limits will be rejected. Figure 6 presents an example of a simple search tree showing the two phases of the search. As already described above, the nodes in the tree represent configuration graphs consisting of many units. Each child node of such a configuration graph specifies a configuration graph with further attributes of the units, connections or services set.

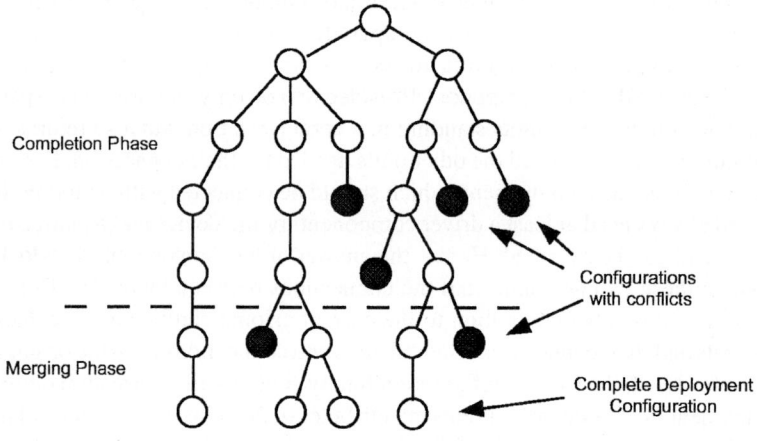

Fig. 6. Search Tree

If no single path without conflicts can be found an appropriate message will be shown to the user. The message will also state the reasons for the failure of the search, usually naming the products causing the problems. To get this information the third request type of the Component Preselector is used. In this case the user can either add new products to the knowledge base or review the original configuration file. Each change requires a new start of the search afterwards. The program valuates all successfully completed and merged configurations according to the amount and the costs of all new devices and software components. Then it offers the best solutions to the user. If there are still some attributes of the units left unspecified the user will be asked to choose between all products suiting the properties. In the final description of the eHome system all devices and software components are specified by concrete products. The Runtime Instancer can find all information needed for the deployment of the services on the framework.

The tool shown in figure 7 implements the described algorithm. The user interface integrates some features of a simple XML viewer, which allow to manage and to navigate through the configuration files. During the configuration process the tool interacts with a simple Component Preselector whose implementation is based on the Jess [20] rule engine and on a knowledge base represented in an OWL file [23]. Unavoidable conflicts during the search are reported and finally the remaining choices for equivalent products

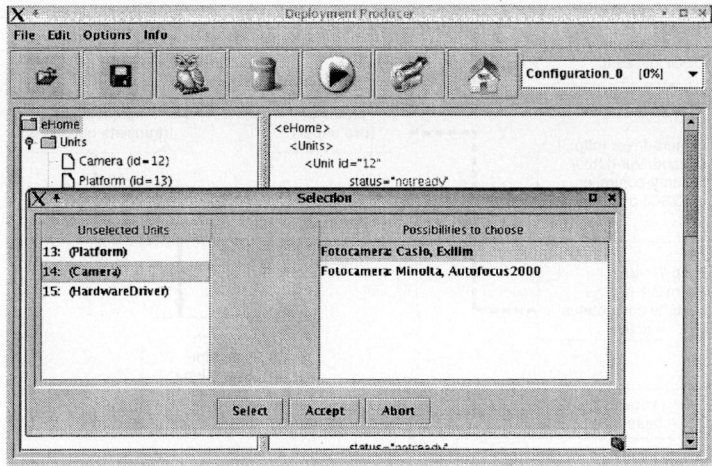

Fig. 7. DeploymentProducer

are offered to the user. If a conflict is caused by a missing description of units, this description has to be developed manually. This is a major task and handled in another paper [24]. If all software components are already available it is also possible to test the found configuration by deploying it on the given framework.

Figure 8 shows small cutouts of a successful automatic configuration process for a security scenario on the basis of figure 3. In this example, the scenario configuration consists of the request for a security service and the fact that 2 cameras are already installed on an OSGi gateway. This is translated by the Deployment Producer with the specific information of the destination house (here depicted with a floor plan) and general information (driver, dependency, platform and service descriptions) from an OWL-based knowledge base into a customized deployment configuration document. This document includes all information, which is needed by the Runtime Instancer to load and startup all software components to run the security service. These are on the one hand the OSGi capable security controller and on the other hand the drivers to control the alarm, the sensors, and the cameras. Furthermore, the sequence of starting the components is coded in this document. The Runtime Instancer can generate a document, which stores current states in addition to the former mentioned information. The Component Preselector translates questions like "What's the OSGi driver for this camera?" or "Which components are needed at least for this security service?" in queries for the knowledge base, which can be operated by the Search Machine and the Inference Machine.

The process was evaluated with some simple examples from the security domain with up to 40 units. In this case, the computation time for producing a deployment configuration document was less than a minute on a usual desktop computer. However, we know that this time heavily benefits from the small knowledge base we used. Additionally, the intended scenario was predefined and thus the specification of the necessary dependencies and attributes could easily be derived. Tests in more realistic environments are

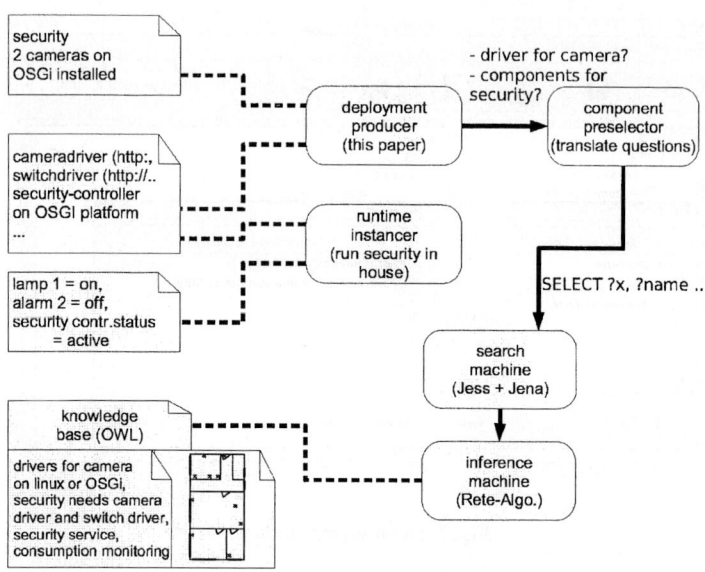

Fig. 8. Example Applied to Configuration Document Levels

current work with our cooperation partner inHaus [25]. Realistic environments require tests with bigger knowledge bases, more devices, and more complex services.

6 Summary and Outlook

One of the major problems hindering broad application of eHome systems is the expected variance of different configurations. To cope with these problems, applying methods from configuration management and software deployment combined with process automation seems to lead to reasonable solutions, because the restriction to the eHome application domain enables the usage of a clear-cut and comprehensive ontology. Automation requires a uniform description language for all configuration and deployment steps. Languages partly capable of fulfilling our requirements are widely used in the area of architecture description languages and component frameworks. The proposed language combines the features required for an automated eHome configuration and deployment process, as discussed in section 3. We developed a tool to automate one step of the configuration and deployment process. The developed Deployment Producer is able to create service configurations based on rather abstract system descriptions. Promising tests with our cooperation partner inHaus [25] show the applicability of our approach in a realistic environment.

However, a great number of units is expected in future eHome systems. The development of more efficient, heuristic search algorithms will be necessary due to computational complexity. Strategies for keeping the knowledge base up-to-date must be found. The more available products are taken into consideration, the better the results arc the tool can offer. Further integrative work has to be done: The interoperability of the Component Preselector, Deployment Producer, and the Runtime Instancer has to be extended. Tight integration in the underlying frameworks like the Distributed Service Framework (DSF) [6] and the Layered Approach to OSGi (PowerArchitecture) [5] has to be further investigated, in order to ease the realization of Web-enabled eHome systems.

References

1. Lee, W.M., Foo, S.M., Watson, K.: Beginning WAP, WML, and WMLScript. Wrox Press Ltd (2000)
2. 3GPP: Multimedia Messaging Service, TS 22.140. http://www.3gpp.org (2002)
3. Westfechtel, B., Conradi, R.: Version Models for Software Configuration Management. ACM Computing Surveys **30** (1998)
4. van der Hoek, A.: (Integrating Configuration Management and Software Deployment)
5. Kirchhof, M., Linz, S.: Component-based Development of Web-enabled eHome Services. In: Proceedings of Ubiquitous Mobile Information and Collaboration Systems Workshop 2004 (UMICS 2004). Lecture Notes in Computer Science, Springer (2004) to appear.
6. Kirchhof, M.: Distributed and Heterogeneous eHome Systems in Volatile Environments (2004)
7. Dashofy, E.M., van der Hoek, A., Taylor, R.N.: A Highly-Extensible, XML-Based Architecture Description Language. In Kazman, R., Kruchten, P., Verhoef, C., van Vliet, H., eds.: Proceedings of the Working IEEE/IFIP Conference on Software Architecture (WICSA'01). Volume ix., IEEE Computer Society, Washington, DC, USA (2001)
8. Dashofy, E., Garlan, D., van der Hoek, A., Schmerl, B.: xARCH. http://www.isr.uci.edu/architecture/xarch/ (17.06.2004) (2002)
9. General Dynamics Decision Systems: Openwings. (http://www.openwings.org (10.05.2004))
10. Smith, M., Carpenter, J.: Openwings Policy Service Specification Ver. 1.0 Final. General Dynamics Decision Systems, INC. (2003)
11. Dennis Reedy: Project Rio. (http://rio.jini.org (10.05.2004))
12. Sun Microsystems, Inc.: The Community Resource for Jini Technology. (http://www.jini.org (8.5.2004))
13. Open Services Gateway Initiative: OSGi Service Platform. http://www.osgi.org (13.11.2003) (2003) Release 3.
14. Prosyst Software AG: mBedded Server 5.x. (http://www.prosyst.de/solution_html/mbeddedserver.html (22.6.2004))
15. Kirchhof, M., Norbisrath, U.: Configuration and Deployment in eHome-Systems. In: Proceedings of Information Systems: New Generations (ISNG 2004). (2004) to appear.
16. Sun Microsystems, Inc.: Java. http://java.sun.com (06.05.2004) (2004)
17. Open Services Gateway Initiative: OSGi Service Platform. (http://www.osgi.org (13.11.2003))
18. Waring, D.L., Kerpez, K.J., Ungar, S.G.: A newly emerging customer premises paradigm for delivery of network-based services. In: Computer Networks. (1999) 411–424
19. Saito, T., Tomoda, I., Takabatake, Y., Ami, J., Teramoto, K.: Home Gateway Architecture and Its Implementation. IEEE Transactions on Consumer Electronics 46 (2000) 1161–1166
20. Friedman-Hill, E.: Jess, The Rule Engine for the Java Platform. (2003) Version 6.1.
21. Kirchhof, M., Stinauer, P.: Service Composition for eHome Systems: A Rule-based Approach. (2004)

22. World Wide Web Consortium (W3C): XML - Extensible Markup Language. (http://www.w3.org/XML/ (06.05.2004))
23. Bechhofer, S., van Harmelen, F., Hendler, J., Horrocks, I., McGuinness, D.L., Patel- Schneider, P.F., Stein, L.A.: OWL Web Ontologie Language Reference. http://www.w3c.org/TR/2003/PR-owl-ref-20031215/ (2003)
24. Norbisrath, U., Salumaa, P., Schultchen, E., Kraft, B.: Fujaba based tool development for eHome systems. In: Proceedings of the International Workshop on Graph-Based Tools (GraBaTs 2004). Electronic Notes in Theoretical Computer Science, Elsevier (2004) to appear.
25. inHaus Duisburg: Innovationszentrum Intelligentes Haus Duisburg. (http://www.inhaus-duisburg.de (22.6.2004))

A Prototype of a Context-Based Architecture for Intelligent Home Environments

Pablo A. Haya, Germán Montoro, and Xavier Alamán

Universidad Autónoma de Madrid
Dpto. Ingeniería Informática
Ctra. Colmenar Viejo km 15.
Madrid 28049 – SPAIN
{Pablo.Haya, German.Montoro, Xavier.Alaman}@uam.es

Abstract. This paper presents a proposal of a context-based architecture to achieve the required synergy among the ubiquitous computing devices of an intelligent environment. These devices produce context information that models the behaviour of the environment. This context information is the glue among the devices and the context-aware applications. The generated context information provides a common view of the world. A blackboard architecture allows to share this context information and a context model is proposed to represent it. A prototype of such a smart room has been developed, including several devices as well as a set of context-aware demonstrators. They work together employing the context information stored on the blackboard.

1 Introduction

In the last years, numerous research groups have been working in different technologies related with what Weiser defined as "Ubiquitous Computing" [1]. Weiser's vision[1] stands on three key points: Firstly, the proliferation of computing devices beyond the desktop computer. These include hundreds of devices with different sizes and shapes interconnected by wireless communication. Secondly, the physical environment as a main part of his approach, since the user activity is not limited to work in front of a desktop computer. And lastly, the seamless interaction between user and computing devices, doing computers invisible to users. Nowadays, these three points have been summarized into the challenge that users can demand computation capabilities everywhere and anytime.

Ubiquitous computing, also-called pervasive computing, has appeared as a new research branch for mobile computing and distributed systems, and, it has raised new opportunities and challenges in computer science [2]. From a hardware point of view, wireless technologies, processing capabilities and the storage capacity are some of the responsible actors to do computing more pervasive [3, 4]. Original approaches in operating systems, file systems and middlewares have been developed, novel user interfaces paradigms [5] applied, and new application models proposed [6].

---

[1] "Ubiquitous computing enhances computer use by making many computers available throughout the physical environment, while making them effectively invisible to the user."

Moreover, intelligent environments and context-aware computing have run in parallel with ubiquitous computing (see Background section). The first ones provide a framework to support ubiquitous computing applications. The second ones have demonstrated the important role that context plays in ubiquitous computing. Context-awareness and intelligent environment initiatives merge in the current Ambient Intelligence paradigm.

Our work focuses on intelligent home environments. It aims to lead to better computing device interoperability. We believe that a global view of the world, shared by every computing device, is necessary to reach efficient device cooperation. Context information guides the structure of this model and provides a better understanding of the relevant information and its relationships. This context model is built from the contributions of every component, and it is dynamically modified as new components appear and disappear.

This paper is organized as follows: first, background work on context and intelligent environments is described. In the next two sections, a context model and a context layer are proposed. After, the results of the previous sections are reflected in a smart room prototype and several context-aware applications. Finally, the future work and the conclusions are explained.

2 Background

2.1 Context and Context-Aware Application

Context has been tied to ubiquitous computing, although the term has had several meanings that differ subtly. The first definitions of context consisted of a list of properties that applications had to be aware of. Schilit [7] highlights that three important aspects of context are: where you are, who you are with, and what resources are nearby.

Pascoe [8] states that "context is a subjective concept that is defined by the entity that perceives it". Thus, context can be any information, depending on the interest of a particular entity. Winograd [9] reinforces the previous statement asserting that "something is context because of the way it is used in interpretation, not due to its inherent properties".

Dey [10] defines context as any information that can be used to characterize the situation of an entity, where an entity is a person, place, or object that is considered relevant to the interaction among a user and an application, including themselves.

Recently, Coutaz and Rey [11] propose an operational definition that relates context to a user involved in a particular task, where context is a composition of a variable state vector over a period of time. The importance of the relationships between the context information is revealed by Henricksen et al [12]. In addition, there are several groups researching in modelling context as a semantic web, such as the Cobra project [13], Aire project [14] and the initiative pervasive semantic web [15].

2.2 Intelligent Environments

An intelligent environment consists of an infrastructure shared by applications, devices and people constrained by physical boundaries. Intelligent environments bring computation into physical world [16]. They are common places where smart devices can interact in a meaningful way.

Research on home automation has focused on hiding computational devices and providing transparent interaction to accommodate to non-technical users. A leading project is The Aware Home [17] from the Future Computing Environments group at Georgia Tech. A real smart house designed to assist elderly people.

There is a great interest in having unencumbered and non-invasive interfaces. One of the first works in this area was the Intelligent Room [18] from the Artificial Intelligence group of the MIT. This room, also-called HAL, consisted of a highly interactive environment which uses multimodal interfaces and embedded computation to allow people to interact with the environment in a natural way. Recently, this work is going on in the Project Aire from the same group [19]. Other related projects are Interactive Workspaces [20], Roomware [21] and SmartOffice [22].

Industry has also shown its interest in this area. The Microsoft Research Vision Group is developing the basic technology to build intelligent environments. The result of this work is EasyLiving [23].

2.3 Our Proposal

According to the previous sections, developing a ubiquitous computing system is a task that should take into account numerous topics. We have centered in two issues:

- To accomplish a seamless integration among pervasive components. There are different and heterogeneous technologies [24]. Moreover, the environment configuration is highly dynamic.
- To obtain a natural interaction that allows to deploy these systems into everyday spaces. User interaction has to keep as flexible as possible. Besides, user preferences and capabilities can change over time and the environment response should adapt to these changes.

As we have pointed out, this heterogeneous mix of software and hardware entities imposes some requirements. In agreement with other works [9, 22, 25] we believe that a global "world model" combined with an asynchronous communication mechanism, is the best approach to achieve complex interactions among components. We propose a context model as a world model (see section 3) and a blackboard architecture [26] (see section 4) as context repository and communication mechanism. Our blackboard implementation differs from other architectures based on tuples where receivers find the information making a pattern-matching mechanism (as Linda [27] or IBM TSpace [28]). In our case, information is stored in a relationship graph, and it is retrieved after traversing through it, as we will show below.

The blackboard allows communicating context changes, finding available resources, and revealing if an entity is added or removed. Information from the blackboard is used by pervasive devices to understand the context and adapt to it. For example, the people in the room and the status of several physical devices (lights, heating, speakers, etc.) are represented in the context layer, and used to automatically generate a spoken-dialogue interface [29].

3 Context Model

Context is a fundamental part in human communication [9]. This way, it should incorporate into the design of computer systems if we want the human-computer interaction to be more human than computer-like. We propose a context centric approach that deals with context information representation and distribution. We focus on what is the relevant information that the applications require, without considering how the context is obtained and processed. This facilitates the integration of new components. Next, we will determine what context is and how it can be modelled, and finally, we will describe its distribution mechanism.

As we have seen above, information does not present intrinsic features that allow us to define it as context, but it acquires this category depending on how applications interpret it. In other words, information is transformed into context when it is used. So, any information, independently what it represents, can be understood by an entity as context. According to this, a context model should include all the possible information. Obviously, there is no model that can embrace this complexity. This makes that context models focus on those features which have more probabilities to be required by context-aware applications. Nevertheless, the model should also provide flexible mechanisms to incorporate new information that can become relevant.

The model building has been divided in two steps: firstly, we shall determine on which entities we will acquire context information. People, places, objects, applications and devices are the most common. Secondly, we shall decide which properties of these entities will be measured. As the background section shows, there are several approaches to find the type of information that is frequently used as context. We focus on Dey's two-tiered categorization [10]. He distinguishes between primary and secondary context types.

3.1 Primary Context Type

We have adopted Dey's approach to develop our intelligent environment context model. There are three different main entities. The first one is the place, given that the concept of physical space plays a central role in smart environment. The second one is the person, as the final user of the system. And the last one is the resource, which comprises both physical devices and applications.

Depending on each entity, the primary context varies. For instance, the context of a room is determined by its environmental variables (lighting, noise level, temperature ...), of a person by her/his location, identity and activity, and of a resource by its location, handler and state. In order to represent the previous context information, we have distinguished internal context from external context. On the one hand, internal context describes stand-alone properties, on the other hand external context models relationships among context information sources.

Thus, location is represented as a bidirectional relation among a place and a user. This relation is defined in both directions. This way, to ask for who is inside a room is as easy as to know the room where a person is located. For the same reason, relations among places and resources are established. In contrast, mobile resources, such as PDAs or laptops, are not directly tied to a room, but they are related to the person who wears them. In order to know which resources are being used on a certain time, a relationship between the resource and its handler is defined. This handler can be a user or a resource.

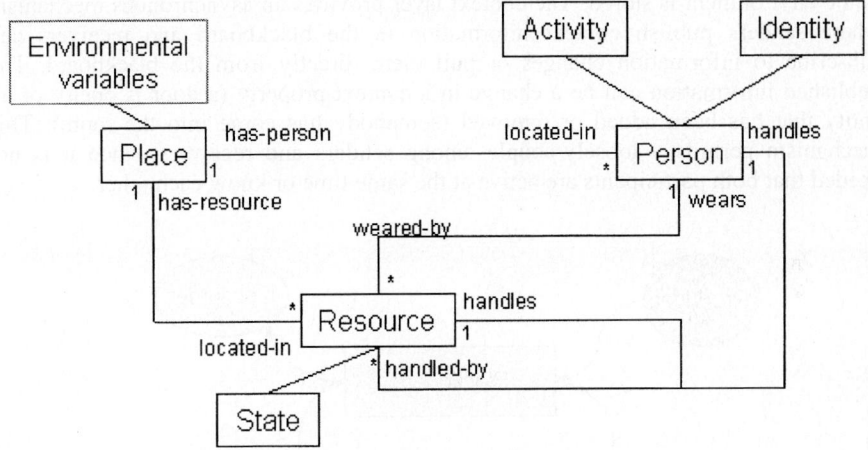

Fig. 1. Primary context relationships and properties

Figure 1 schematically shows the primary context relationships and properties. Notice that context changes dynamically along time, so it is not explicitly included as a part of the model.

3.2 Secondary Context Type

Secondary context types are related with useful but not so frequently used information. This information extends the model described above adding new properties and new relationships. Besides, new entities can be included. This information depends on the domain of context-aware applications. For instance, a contextual audio player application could require that songs would be an entity of the model. This application could necessitate the user's list of favourite songs and which type of song fits with each activity. Then, when a random play is requested, the model information helps to decide which song will be the next.

Our model leads to a semantic network where primary context is the main part. As we will describe, secondary context information is accessible (see namespace section) from primary context information entities since these entities are implemented as indices to any other model information.

4 Context Layer

We have presented the basic context model of our intelligent environment. This section deals with how context-aware applications benefit from it. We propose a middleware, also-called context layer, which allows to notify changes in the context model, discover new context information sources and add them to the model. The context layer implementation lies on a global data structure, called blackboard [26]. This blackboard is a model of the world, where all the prominent information related to the environment is stored. The context layer provides an asynchronous mechanism where senders publish context information in the blackboard and receivers can subscribe to information changes or pull them directly from the blackboard. The published information can be a change in a context property (a door is open), or an entity that has been added or removed (somebody has come into the room). This mechanism permits a loosely-couple among senders and receivers, since it is not needed that both participants are active at the same time or know each other.

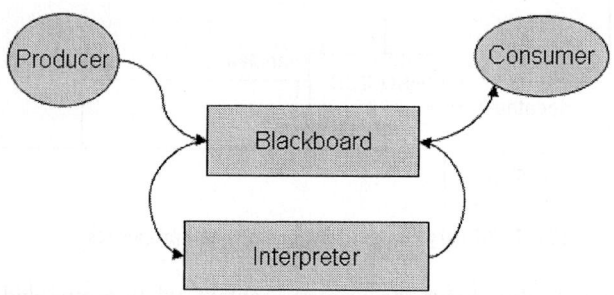

Fig. 2. Interaction between main components of the context layer

Figure 2 illustrates a generic interaction between the main components of the context layer. Producers publish the information gathered from context information sources. Interpreters refine this information and leave it again in the blackboard, and final consumers recover it. Producers measure context directly from real world, providing high-resolution information but with a poor level of abstraction. Interpreters make good this lack by deducing new context properties and relations. Finally, consumers are the context-aware applications.

Components of very different kinds can be found within an intelligent environment. They can be very close to the physical world like sensors, switches, appliances, screens, microphones, speakers, etc. Or they can be related to any kind of software components, such as dialogue managers, intelligent agents, user interfaces, etc.

4.1 Context Representation

Our main goal is to find a structure that can represent not only the relationships among primary types of context but also their properties. The model should also be easily extensible. For these reasons, an undirected graph structure has been chosen to represent context information. This graph is a data structure composed by a set of nodes and a set of edges. There are two types of nodes: the first one represents an entity and is defined by a name, a type (room, person, resource ...) and a list of properties. The second one represents a property. Each property is a name-value pair, where a value can be a literal or another property. There are also two types of edges, those that correspond to the relationships among entities, and those that link entities and properties. It is guaranteed that relations only exist among entities. Thus, the blackboard is composed by an entity graph, where each entity is a tree of properties. This graph is stored in the blackboard and represents a snapshot of the environment context at any moment.

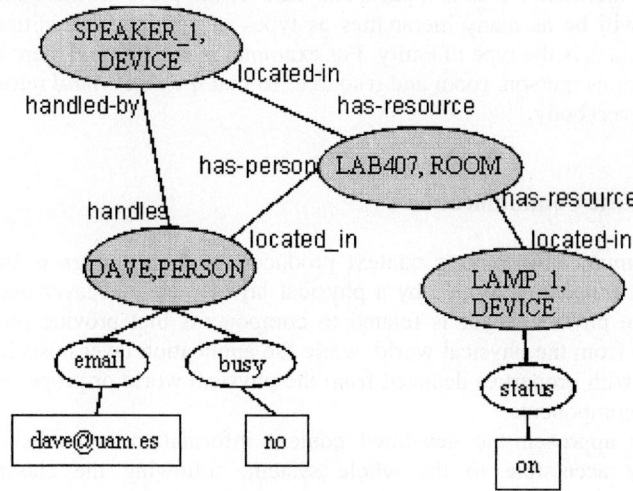

Fig. 3. Simplified blackboard graph

4.2 Name Space

Any node can be located, starting from any entity node and following the relationship path. This is called the node path. It is composed by a list of tokens separated by the slash character. Their order is determined as follows: the first token of the path is the word "name", the second one must be the entity name and the next tokens come as the result of concatenating the names of all the intermediate nodes until the target node. For instance, in the example showed in the figure 3, the lamp_1 status path is */name/lamp_1/status*. In addition, wildcards can be used to substitute one or several tokens. This allows referencing several nodes at the same time. For example, based on the Figure 1, */name/dave/** references all the properties and related entities of the entity *Dave*. As a result it gets the following list: the e-mail and busy property nodes and the Lab_407 and Speaker_1 entity nodes.

Two naming mechanisms are provided to improve the use of wildcards:

- Predefined hierarchy. This mechanism restricts the nodes that compose a path. It specifies how to go through the graph. To do this, each hierarchy defines a sequence of types of entities. For example, the first type of entity must be a room,

the second one a resource, etc... Therefore, when a wildcard is used, only the nodes that match with the expected type will be substituted. These hierarchies are called predefined because they are hard-wired. There is one of these hierarchies for each relationship between primary context entities (room-device, device-room, room-person, person-room, and so on). Following with the example of the figure 3, the path */roomdevice/lab407/*/status* is interpreted as follows: the initial token identifies the hierarchy *roomdevice*. This hierarchy establishes that the first type of entity must be a room followed by a resource. The other nodes remain unrestricted. Therefore, this path references the value of the status of all the devices located in lab407.
- Typed hierarchy. This is a particular case of the previous mechanism. By default, there will be as many hierarchies as types of entities. The initial token of these hierarchies is the type of entity. For example, in the figure 3 there are three default hierarchies: person, room and resource, so that */person/*/mail* retrieves the e-mails from everybody.

4.3 Context Communication

The communication among context producers and consumers is based on a three layered architecture, formed by a physical layer, a context layer and an application layer. The physical layer is related to components that provide properties directly measured from the physical world, while the application layer hosts intelligent agents that deal with properties deduced from the physical world or properties related to the software components.

In our approach the generated context information is published in a central repository accessible to the whole system, following the classical blackboard paradigm.

The blackboard provides standard procedures to request or modify node values, and to subscribe to context changes. Context agents can easily access to the properties of the entities in a transparent way. For example, one property of the context of a room may be the number of people in the room. Several sensors may be used to deduce such information. However, a single final value of the property is produced, and all the other devices and computational entities in the smart environment can use this information independently of the nature of the source.

The interaction process can be summarized as follows. Context producers (or interpreters) send their context changes to the blackboard, and consequently the blackboard modifies the context nodes. Context consumers (or interpreters) notice these changes either by polling the blackboard or by subscribing to blackboard changes. Thus, the blackboard acts as an intermediary, holding the context modifications. The components of the other two layers are responsible to process these changes and to react consequently.

Properties whose values are directly measured from a physical device are managed in a special way. In these cases, the property value is not stored in the blackboard: instead, the blackboard acts as a proxy. Whenever the value is requested, the blackboard asks to the physical device.

In addition to the above behavior, the blackboard provides a mechanism to add and remove relationships between entities.

Besides, the blackboard supports attaching and detaching new entities. When attaching an entity, its representation is sent to the blackboard and stored. The entity relationships must be established in separated operations. If detaching an entity, it and all its relations are automatically deleted from the blackboard. Consumer applications can subscribe to adding and removing relations and attaching and detaching entity events.

Finally, combining all these mechanisms, the required interaction is achieved. For example, if somebody enters an empty smart room, the presence agent notifies this event by adding an entity representing the new person, and establishing a relation among the room and the entity. A context-aware agent can be subscribed to this event and check the value of another node that indicates the current environment luminosity. If it is too dark, then the agent changes the node value that increases the intensity of the lights. Then the physical layer component reacts doing that the lights adjust to the required new state. The reciprocal operation is produced when the person leaves the room.

4.4 Command Heap

In the same way as Johanson and Fox [30] present an event heap to coordinate the interactions of applications, we propose a similar mechanism called command heap to manage conflict resolution. Command heaps are necessary when two or more applications want to change the same part of the blackboard model. For instance, two applications sending contradictory commands about the state of the lights. A command heap is a pre-emptive prioritized command queue. A command represents the desire of an application to change the value of a property or a relation in the blackboard. Each command is composed by an identifier, a priority, an expiration time and a sender's identification. Whenever a command arrives, it is stored in a command heap. If there is no command with higher priority, it will become the active command. Otherwise, it will be placed in the corresponding position of the heap. When a command is activated, the blackboard forwards it to the corresponding application. A sender can delete all its commands or all the commands whose identifiers match with a particular identifier. A command will remain active at the top of heap while its expiration time is valid. If this time expires or the sender explicitly removes the command from the heap, then the next highest priority command will become the active command. The expiration time is limited by an upper bound to avoid blocking a heap for too long. If the application needs more, it may resend the command. Finally, the command priority is chosen by each application and varies in a range of values.

4.5 Blackboard Implementation

Every blackboard is a server that can be accessed using client-server TCP/IP protocols. HTTP has been chosen as the transport protocol because it is simple and widely spread. To exchange information between the applications and a blackboard server an XML-compliant language is employed.

A blackboard provides, at least, the following basic operations:

- GetContext. The client supplies a node path and the blackboard, starting from this node, goes through the graph. For each node its value is obtained, either from the value stored in the blackboard or from a value requested to a physical device. The final result is a tree that is sent to the client. If some values are not available, the corresponding node is left empty, but the rest of the building process continues. Additionally, it is possible to use wildcards to get more than one entity at the same time.
- SetContext: the blackboard receives an order containing a node path pointing to a property and the desired changes. The order is stored in the order heap until it becomes active. Then, the new order is picked up and the value of the corresponding blackboard node is changed. This action may imply modifications outside the blackboard (in other blackboards, or in physical devices).
- SubscribeContext: for each node and each relation, the blackboard stores a list of its subscribed clients. Whenever a node changes, these clients are informed.
- UnsubscribeContext: a client requests that a subscription is cancelled.
- AddContext: this operation allows to dynamically add an XML representation of a new entity to the blackboard.
- RemoveContext: removes the referenced entities and the relationships associated to them.
- AddRelationship: this order establishes a relationship between two entities. It will be effective when the order is active.
- RemoveRelationship: the opposite order to the previously described.

Moreover, blackboard designers are provided with a tool that assists them in the construction of the blackboard. A compiler has been developed which produces a blackboard implementation from an XML file. This file specifies the node names, their initial values and their hierarchical structure. Finally, there is also an additional tool that processes the XML file to obtain comprehensible documentation.

4.6 Information Flows

We also find suitable the use of relationships to represent the flow of information among physical devices. The most interesting case is modelling how multimedia data (image, audio and video) flows through a room. For each multimedia resource, an entity is defined in the blackboard. When two multimedia resources have to be connected the corresponding relation is added to the blackboard. Then, both resources configure themselves to satisfy the new situation. A similar behaviour occurs when the relation is removed from the blackboard and the flow of multimedia information stops.

As an example, we have developed a context-aware application that changes the pictures showed in several flat-screens depending on the current occupants of the room. Following the interaction model depicts at figure 2, the application is decomposed in three modules: an image source, that acts as a producer, a manager, which plays the role of an interpreter, and one or more images sinks or consumers.

4.6.1 Image Source

This module decides which picture has to be displayed at each moment. A list of the room occupants is stored in a circular queue. Besides, for each occupant, there is another circular queue that holds the URLs of his or her favourite pictures. The URLs of the pictures that will be displayed are chosen following a two-phase selection procedure. Firstly, an occupant is selected from the occupant's queue, and secondly, an URL is picked up from his or her favourite picture URL queue. Both queues use a round-robin algorithm to select the next candidate. The selected URL is stored in the blackboard and broadcasted to every related sink.

Whenever a new person enters the room, the module is notified. This person is added to the occupant's queue, and a new circular queue is created to store his or her list of URLs. When an occupant leaves the room, his or her favourite picture URL queue is deleted, and the person is removed from the occupant's queue. If nobody is inside the room, a default queue storing two pictures is used.

At start up, the image source module stores in the blackboard: the URL of the first selected picture and the time that the selected URL remains valid.

4.6.2 Image Sink

Each image sink module manages a flat-screen. The image sink is idle until a relationship is established between an image source and itself. Then, the image sink consults the blackboard and retrieves the URL of the selected picture. The sink requests the picture using the HTTP protocol and displays it on the screen. This process is repeated whenever the image source selects a new URL, and keeps on until the relationship is removed from the blackboard.

4.6.3 Manager

A manager is any application capable of adding and removing relationships from the blackboard. Managers decide which sources are connected to which sinks creating a dynamically updated network of connections. The lists of sources and sinks are available in the blackboard and the manager reads them to set up the interface. The lists are updated when sources or sinks appear or disappear. The manager can also configure the refresh time of the sources.

We have developed a graphical interface tool that allows users to manually configure the connection network between sources and sinks. This tool can be easily adapted to manage other types of multimedia traffic, such as audio and video.

5 A Smart Room Prototype

A laboratory has been transformed into two rooms. The main room is equipped like the living room of a typical house and the adjacent one is equipped like an office. The context layer described above harmonizes the interaction between the components of these rooms. The laboratory is composed by a set of heterogeneous devices and applications. The context graph includes the representation of the installed devices and the associations among them.

Two physical networks have been deployed. For the connection of sensors (presence, temperature, luminosity, etc.) and actuators (switches, engine controllers, etc.) we utilize the European bus EIB. This bus tries to set a standard within the European Union for home automation. For the multimedia information flow (images, digital radio, ip-camara, etc.), we are using an Ethernet network. Each device can be connected to either network (or both), depending on its nature, and has access to the context blackboard through them. The access to the physical layer is uniformed by a SMNP (Simple Management Network Protocol) layer. This is described in [31].

The installed devices can be divided in three categories:

- **Home automation.** Composed of several independent systems: an automatic lock used to control the physical access, photoelectric sensors that inform when someone enters the room, a smart card system that identifies the users and several EIB devices, such as room lights, switching devices, an alphanumeric display, etc.
- **Audio-Video information.** It includes a digital radio, a TV set, two hi-fi speakers, a DVD player and several flat monitors that can be used alternatively as output devices for video or as system interfaces.
- **Voice interaction.** Wireless microphones that provide the users with free-movements.

We have developed several demonstrators that range from simple proof-of-concepts to release applications. Our purpose is to develop each demonstrator independently from the others. Furthermore, these demonstrators do not have to know either how the context information is generated or which context producers are involved.

These applications are grouped into three categories. The first two categories focus on different kinds of context changes. The first one deals with changes on context properties, while the second one studies the potential of the model of relationships. The third category includes two user interfaces that employ the context to customize their functionality. The three categories are:

- **Access applications.** They are interested in changes on the state of the main gate. There are two applications of this kind: the first one sends an e-mail to the room owner when the door is open for a long time and, if someone is inside the room, utilizes the voice synthesizer to notify him or her. The other prevents intruders. If an unauthorized person enters the room, it triggers a chain of events: the room lights turn on (if they were off), a web-cam takes a picture which is sent to the room owner via e-mail and, finally, an acoustic alarm goes off.
- **Person-identification applications.** They focus on services that depend on the identity of the people inside the room. Every time a relation between the room and a person is added or removed, these applications are notified. Besides, the number of people and their identifications can be retrieved from the blackboard at any time. We have developed several applications of this type: (a) The contextual picture application described at the Information Flow section. (b) A meeting-aware application. When it determines that a meeting is taking place it sends an e-mail to the rest of possible attendants. (c) A speech application that utilizes a voice synthesizer to make custom greetings when a user enters or leaves the room. The salutation is adapted to the user and to the time of the day. (d) A simple illumination module that turns the light on when the first user enters, and turns it off if nobody is inside it.

- **User interfaces**. Finally, two independent user interfaces have been integrated into the smart room: a web-based user interface [32] that permits to control the devices of the room and a spoken natural language dialogue system [33] that permits the user to interact with the environment. Both of them are dynamically set up using the blackboard information.

6 Current and Future Work

Our model relies on set of blackboard servers. Each server is associated to one environment, and provides a set of services to its computational devices. The representation of the mobile entities is attached or detached to the blackboard as they are carried in and out the rooms. The current blackboard implementation compels to send all the information related to the mobile entities. We are improving the current mechanism in order to allow sending a link that points to where the information is stored. This link is treated as another relationship, so that applications will continue perceiving a global view although its implementation is distributed.

The other research line, which is being explored, deals with how to apply semantic web technologies to our prototype. As we have explained in background section, there are several research groups that are integrating semantic web into pervasive computing, and they have obtained fruitful results in this area. Our work will aim to translate our current XML-compliant representation language to RDF or OWL. These languages exhibit interesting features that improve the representation model of entities and their relationships. Following this approach, we are developing a smart home ontology where the primary context model is refined and domain-dependent context information is added.

Finally, we are carrying on the implementation of a contextual broadcast audio player. This application uses the blackboard information to find out where the user is located and which speakers are available. This way, the sound can follow the user from room to room. The desired noise level of the user will be taken into account, as same as the preferences of another user in the room.

7 Conclusions

The present work addresses the interaction between ubiquitous computing devices. We have considered intelligent environments as a particular case of ubiquitous computing applications, and we have chosen a home environment as our framework. The problems that arise in an intelligent environment have been studied. In particular, those related to the deployment of heterogeneous technologies and the achievement of a natural user interaction. A common factor of these problems is that environment and its components produce highly dynamic context information.

We have proposed a context layer as the glue to achieve the required synergy among pervasive computing devices in order to constitute a smart environment. This context layer is based on a unified model view of the world shared by every computing devices and accessible using an asynchronous communication mechanism. This relies on a data-centric approach where the main goal is to publish the changes on the context in a common and structured repository independently of the source and how they are generated. Besides, a single interface, which abstracts from the communication details of the various computing devices, is also provided. An order heap is employed to solve conflicts between components that exchange the same information.

The context information is stored as graph and this is structured following a proposed context model. We have proposed that context can be represented by internal properties and by external relations between entities. Besides, we have followed Dey's approach to distinguish among primary and secondary context types. This classification guides the implementation of the model and aids developer and applications to find out the context information in the blackboard.

Several applications have implemented to demonstrate the utility of the relationships to model the context. In particular, we have explained how we utilize them to manage the flow information. Moreover, we have successfully developed two user interfaces that exploit the blackboard advantages. All of these applications have been tested in a real environment.

Acknowledgement. This paper has been funded by the Spanish Ministry of Science and Education, project number TIN2004-03140.

References

1. Weiser, M.: Some computer science issues in Ubiquitous Computing. Communications of ACM, 36(7). July (1993) 75-84
2. Satyanarayanan, M.: Pervasive Computing: Vision and Challenges. IEEE Personal Communications, 8(4). August (2001) 10-17
3. Want, R., Borriello, G., Pering, T., Farkas, K. I.: Disappering Hardware. IEEE Pervasive Computing, 1(1). January-March (2002) 36-47
4. Schilit, B. N.: Mega-Utilities Drive Invisible Technologies. IEEE Computer, 36(2). February (2003) 97-99
5. Pingali, G., Pinhanez, C., Levas, A., Kjeldsen, R., Podlaseck, M., Chen, H., Sukaviriya, N.: Steerable Interfaces for Pervasive Computing Spaces. In Proceedings of PerCom'03. March (2003)
6. Banavar, G., Beck, J., Gluzberg, E., Munson, J., Sussman, J., Zukowsk, D.: Challenges: An Application Model for Pervasive Computing. In Proceedings of Mobicom 2000. (2000) 266-274
7. Schilit, B., Adams, N., Want, R.: Context-Aware Computing Applications. IEEE Workshop on Mobile Computing Systems and Applications. (1994)
8. Pascoe, J.: Adding Generic Contextual Capabilities to Wearable Computers. In Proceedings of 2nd International Symposium on Wearable Computers. (1998) 92-99
9. Winograd, T.: Architectures for Context. Human-Computer Interaction, 16(2,3& 4). Lawrence Erlbaum Associates (2001) 401-419
10. Dey, A.: Understanding and using context. Personal and Ubiquitous Computing, 5(1) (2001)
11. Coutaz, J., Rey, G.: Foundations for a theory of contextors. Computer-Aided Design of User Interfaces III. Kluwer Academic Publishers. May (2002) 13-34

12. Henricksen, K., Indulska, J., Rakotonirainy, J.: Modeling Context Information in Pervasive Computing Systems. Pervasive Computing, First International Conference, Pervasive 2002. LNCS 2414. Springer-Verlag (2002) 167-180
13. Chen, H., Finin, T., Joshi, A.: Semantic Web in in the Context Broker Architecture. In Proceedings of PerCom 2004. March (2004)
14. Peters, S., Shrobe, H.: Using Semantic Network for Knowledge Representation in an Intelligent Environment. In Proceedings of PerCom'03. March (2003)
15. http://pervasive.semanticweb.org
16. Coen, M.: Design Principles for Intelligent Environments. Proceedings of the AAAI Spring Symposium on Intelligent Environments. (1998)
17. Kidd, C. K., Orr, R., Abowd, G. D., Atkenson, C. G., Essa, I. A., MacIntyre, B., Mynatt, E., Starner, T. E., Newstetter, W.: The Aware Home: A Living Laboratory for Ubiquitous Computing Research. In Proceedings of the Second International Workshop on Cooperative Buildings, CoBuild'99 (1999)
18. Coen, M.: Building Brains for Intelligents Environments. In Proceedings of the 1998 National Conference on Artificial Intelligence (AAAI98) (1998)
19. http://www.ai.mit.edu/projects/aire/
20. Johanson, B., Fox, A., Winograd, T.: The Interactive Workspaces Project: Experiences with Ubiquitous Computing Rooms. IEEE Pervasive Computing Magazine, 1(2). April-June (2002) 67 – 74
21. Tandler, P., Streitz, N. A., Prante, T.: Roomware-Moving Toward Ubiquitous Computers. IEEE Micro, 22(6). November-December (2002) 36-47
22. Le Gal, C., Martin, J., Lux, A., Crowley, J. L: SmartOffice: Design of an Intelligent Environment. IEEE Intelligent Systems, 16(4). July-August (2001) 60-66
23. Brumitt, B.L., Meyers, B., Krumm, J., Kern, A., Shafer, S. A.: EasyLiving: Technologies for Intelligent Environments. In Proceedings of Handheld and Ubiquitous Computing, 2nd Intl. Symposium. (2000) 12-27
24. Haya, P., Alamán, X., Montoro, G.: A Comparative Study of Communication Infrastructures for the Implementation of Ubiquitous Computing. UPGRADE 2(5) (2001)
25. Maglio, P., Campbell C.: Attentive Agents. Communications of the ACM, 46(3). July (2003) 47-51
26. Engelmore, R., Morgan, T.: Blackboard Systems. Addison-Wesley (1998)
27. Gelernter, D.: Generative communication in Linda. ACM Transactions on Programming Languages and Systems, 7(1). January (1985) 80-112
28. Wyckoff, P., McLaughry, S., Lehman, T., Ford, D.: TSpaces. IBM Systems Journal, 37(3) (1998) 454-474
29. Montoro, G., Alamán, X., Haya, P.: A plug and play spoken dialogue interface for smart environments. In Proceedings of CICLing'04. LNCS, Vol. 2945 (2004)
30. Johanson, B., Fox. A.: The EventHeap: A Coordination Infrastructure for Interactive Workspaces. In Proceedings of WMCSA 2002. (2002)
31. Martinez, A.E., Cabello, R., Gómez, F.J., Martínez, J.: Interact-DDM: A Solution for the Integration of Domestic Devices on Network Management Platforms. In Proceedings of IFIP/IEEE International Symposium on Integrated Network Management (2003)
32. Alamán, X., Cabello, R., Gómez-Arriba, F., Haya, P., Martínez, A., Martínez, J., Montoro, G.: Using context information to generate dynamic user interfaces. In Proceedings of 10th HCI International Conference (2003)
33. Montoro, G., Alamán, X., Haya, P.: Spoken interaction in intelligent environments: a working system. Advances in Pervasive Computing. (2004)

Trust-Aware Collaborative Filtering for Recommender Systems

Paolo Massa and Paolo Avesani

ITC-iRST
Via Sommarive 14 - I-38050 Povo (TN) - Italy
{massa,avesani}@itc.it

Abstract. Recommender Systems allow people to find the resources they need by making use of the experiences and opinions of their nearest neighbours. Costly annotations by experts are replaced by a distributed process where the users take the initiative. While the collaborative approach enables the collection of a vast amount of data, a new issue arises: the quality assessment. The elicitation of trust values among users, termed "web of trust", allows a twofold enhancement of Recommender Systems. Firstly, the filtering process can be informed by the reputation of users which can be computed by propagating trust. Secondly, the trust metrics can help to solve a problem associated with the usual method of similarity assessment, its reduced computability. An empirical evaluation on *Epinions.com* dataset shows that trust propagation can increase the coverage of Recommender Systems while preserving the quality of predictions. The greatest improvements are achieved for users who provided few ratings.

1 Introduction

Recommender Systems (RS) [12] are widely used online (e.g.: in *Amazon.com*) to suggest to users items they may like or find useful. Collaborative Filtering (CF) [4] is the most widely used technique for Recommender Systems. The biggest advantage of CF over content-based systems is that explicit content description is not required. Instead CF only relies on opinions expressed by users on items. Instead of calculating the similarity between an item description and a user profile as a content-based recommender would do, a CF system searches for similar users (neighbours) and then uses ratings from this set of users to predict items that will be liked by the current user.

In contrast with a centralized content-based recommender, the CF technique distributes the work load involved in evaluating and marking up the items in its data base. For this reason, it has obvious advantages over a content based system where the knowledge expense to annotate millions of items is very high.

However CF suffers some weaknesses: problems with new users (cold start), data sparseness and difficulty in spotting "malicious" or "unreliable" users.

We propose to extend RS with trust-awareness: users are allowed to also explicitly express their web of trust [5] (i.e., users they trust about ratings and opinions on items). Using a technique to propagate trust throughout the global trust network, Trust-aware Recommender Systems are able to overcome the previously mentioned weaknesses. In fact, trust allows us to base recommendations only on ratings given by users trusted directly by the current user or indirectly, for example trusted by another trusted user. In this way it is possible to cut out malicious users who are trying to influence recommendation accuracy. Moreover, in RSs users typically have rated only a small portion of the available items, but user similarity is computable only on the few users who have rated items in common. This fact greatly reduces the number of potential neighbours, whose ratings are combined to create recommendations for the current user. This problem is exacerbated for "cold start users", users who have just expressed a few ratings. Instead, by allowing a user to rate other users, the system can quickly make recommendations using the explicit neighbour set. This means the new user will soon receive good recommendations and so she has an incentive to keep using the system and to provide more ratings.

The contributions of this paper are three-fold:

- We identify specific problems with current Collaborative Filtering RSs and propose a new solution that addresses all of these problems.
- We precisely formalize the domain and the architecture of the proposed solution: namely Trust-Aware Recommender Systems.
- We conduct experiments on a large real dataset showing how our proposed solution increases the coverage (number of ratings that are predictable) while not reducing the accuracy (the error of predictions). This is especially true for users who have provided few ratings.

The rest of the paper is structured as follows: firstly we introduce Recommender Systems and their weaknesses (Section 2). In Section 3 we discuss trust from a computational point of view and we argue how trust-aware solutions can overcome the weaknesses described in the previous section. Section 4 is devoted to formalizing the environment in which Trust-aware Recommender Systems can operate while Section 5 describes the architecture of the framework and its components. Our experiments are presented in Section 6 and Section 7 provides a discussion of the results. Section 8 concludes the paper with a discussion of future work.

2 Motivation

Recommender Systems (RS) [12] suggest to users items they might like. Two main algorithmic techniques have been used to compute recommendations: Content-based and Collaborative Filtering.

The Content-based approach suggests items that are similar to the ones the current users has shown a preference for in the past. Content-based matching requires a representation of the items in terms of features. For machine-parsable items (such as news or papers), such a representation can be created automatically but for other kind of items (such as movies and songs), it must be manually inserted by human editors. This activity is expensive, time-consuming, error-prone and highly subjective. For this reason, content-based systems are not suitable for dynamic and very large environments, where items are millions and are inserted in the system frequently.

Collaborative Filtering (CF) [4], on the other hand, collects opinions from users in the form of ratings on items. The recommendations produced are based only on the opinions of users similar to the current user (neighbours). The advantage over content-based RS is that the algorithm doesn't need a representation of the items in terms of features but it is based only on the judgments of the user community.

Collaborative Filtering stresses the concept of community, where every user contributes with her ratings to the overall performances of the system. We will see in the following how this simple yet very powerful idea introduces a new concern about the "quality" and "reliability" of every single rating. In the rest of this paper we concentrate on RSs based on CF.

The traditional input to a CF algorithm is a matrix in which rows represents users and columns items. The entry at each element of the matrix is the user's rating of that item. Figure 1 shows such a matrix.

Table 1. The users × items matrix of ratings is the classic input of CF.

	Matrix Reloaded	Lord of the Rings 2	Titanic	La vita è bella
Alice	2	5		5
Bob	5		1	3
Carol		5		
Dean	2	5	5	4

In order to create recommendations for the current users, CF performs three steps:

- It compares the current user's ratings against every other user's ratings. CF computes a similarity value for every other user, where 1 means totally similar and -1 totally dissimilar. Usually the similarity measure is the Pearson correlation coefficient, but any other could be used [7]. The coefficient is computable only if there are items in common rated by both users. If this situation does not occur (as it is often the case), two users are not comparable.
- Based on the ratings of the most similar users (neighbours), it predicts the rating the current user would give to every item she has not yet rated.
- It suggests to the user the items with highest predicted rating.

The standard CF schema is simple but very effective, however it has some weaknesses which we discuss in the rest of the section.

RS are computationally expensive. The CF algorithm we have described is typical of a lazy, instance based learning algorithm. Such algorithms suffer can be computationally very expensive at query time, since they need search all the user profiles to find the best set of neighbours. This problem means that current RS cannot scale to large environments with millions of users and billions of items (for example, the envisioned Semantic Web [1]). This is also a very slow step, in the sense it may take several minutes to find neighbours of one user. For this reason, it is not feasible to do it when a recommendation request is made by the user and hence this should be done periodically offline. However this means that recommendations are not always up to date and that user ratings do not take effect immediately.

User similarity is computable only against few users. The first step suffers another problem. In order to be able to create good quality recommendations, RSs should be able to compare the current user against every other user with the goal of selecting the best neighbours with the more relevant item ratings. This step is mandatory and its accuracy affects the overall system accuracy: failing to find "good" neighbours will lead to poor quality recommendations. However, since the ratings matrix is usually very sparse because users tend to rate few of the millions of items, it is often the case that two user don't share the minimum number of items rated in common required by user similarity metrics for computing similarity. For this reason, the system is forced to choose neighbours in the small portion of comparable users and will miss other non-comparable but relevant users. This problem is not as serious for users with hundreds of ratings but for users with few ratings. However it can be argued that it is more important (and harder) for an RS to provide a good recommendation to a user with few ratings in order to invite her to provide more ratings and keep using the system than to a user with many ratings that is probably already using the system regularly.

Easy attacks by malicious insiders. Recommender Systems are often used in e-commerce sites (for example, in *Amazon.com*). In those contexts, being able to influence recommendations could be very attractive: for example, an author may want to "force" *Amazon.com* to always recommend the book she wrote. However, subverting standard CF techniques is very easy [10]. The simplest attack is the copy-profile attack: the attacker can copy the ratings of target user and the system will think the attacker is the most similar user to target user. In this way every additional item the attacker rates highly will probably be recommended to the target user. Since currently RSs are mainly centralized servers, creating a "fake" identity is a time-consuming activity and hence these attacks are not currently heavily carried on and studied. However we believe that, as soon as the publishing of ratings and opinions becomes more decentralized (for example, with Semantic Web formats such as RVW [2] or FOAF [3]), these types of attacks will become more and more an issue. Basically, creating such attacks will become as widespread as spam is today, or at least as easy.

3 Web of Trust

In decentralized environments where everyone is free to create content and there is no centralized quality control entity, evaluating the quality of this content becomes an important issue. This situation can be observed in online communities (for example, slashdot.org in which millions of users posts news and comments daily), in peer-to-peer networks (where peers can enter corrupted items), or in marketplace sites (such as *eBay.com*, where users can create "fake" auctions).

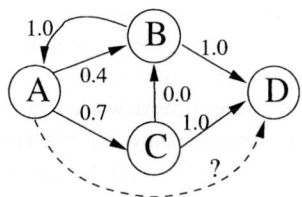

Fig. 1. Trust network. Nodes are users and edges are trust statements. The dotted edge is one of the undefined and predictable trust statements.

On these environments, it is often a good strategy to delegate the quality assessment task to users themselves. For example, by asking users to rate items, CF uses such a quality assessment approach.

Similarly, the system can ask the users to rate the other users: in this way, a user can express her level of trust in another user she has interacted with. For example, in Figure 1, user A has issued a trust statement in B (with value 0.4) and in C (with value 0.7); hence B and C are in the web of trust of A.

The webs of trust of all the users can then be aggregated in a global trust network, or social network (Figure 1), and a graph walking algorithm be used to predict the "importance" of a certain node of the network. This intuition is exploited, for example, by PageRank [11], one of the algorithm powering the search engine *Google.com*. According to this analysis, the Web is a network of content without a centralized quality control and PageRank tries to infer the authority of every single page by examining the structure of the network. PageRank follows a simple idea: if a link from page A to page B represents a positive vote issued by A about B, then the global rank of a page depends on the number (and quality) of the incoming links.

The same intuition can be extended from web pages to users: if users are allowed to cast trust values on other users, then these values can be used to predict the trustworthiness of unknown users. For example, the consumer opinion site *Epinions.com*, where users can express opinions and ratings on items, also allows users to express their degree of trust in other users. Precisely, the *epinions.com* FAQ suggests a user should add in her web of trust "reviewers whose reviews and ratings they have consistently found to be valuable"[1]

---

[1] From the Web of Trust FAQ (http://www.epinions.com/help/faq/?show=faq_wot)

Using explicit trust statements, it is possible to predict trust in unknown users by propagating trust; precisely, if A trusts B and B trusts D, it is possible to infer something about how much A could trust D (the dotted arrow in Figure 1). It is important to underline what is perhaps an obvious fact: trust is subjective, the same user can be trusted by someone and distrusted by someone else. In Figure 1, for example, we can see how B is trusted by A as 0.4 and by C as 0. It is important to take this into account when predicting trustworthiness. Another self-evident fact is that trust is not symmetric (see users A and B, for instance).

Trust metrics [3,14,8] have precisely the goal of predicting, given a certain user, trust in unknown users based on the complete trust network. For example, in Figure 1, a trust metric can predict the level of trust of A in D.

Trust metrics can be divided into local and global. Local Trust metrics take into account the very personal and subjective views of the users and end up predicting different values of trust in other users for every single user. Instead global trust metrics predict a global "reputation" value that approximates how the community as a whole considers a certain user. In this way, they don't take into account the subjective opinions of each user but average them across standardized global values. PageRank [11], for example, is a global metric. However, in general, local trust metrics are computationally more expensive because they must be computed for each user whereas global ones are just run once for all the community.

In the following, we argue that trust-awareness can overcome all the weaknesses introduced in Section 2. Evidence supporting this claim will be given in Section 6 and 7. Precisely, trust propagation allows us to compute a relevance measure, alternative to user similarity, that can be used as an additional or complementary weight when calculating recommendation predictions. In [9] we have shown how this *predicted trust* value, thanks to trust propagation, is computable on much more users than the *user similarity* value.

CF systems have problems scaling up because calculating the neighbours set requires computing User Similarity of current user against every other user. However, we can significantly reduce the number of users which RS has to consider by prefiltering users based on their "predicted trust" value. For example, it would be possible to consider only users at a small distance in social network from current user or considering only users with a predicted trust higher than a certain threshold.

Moreover, trust metrics can be attack-resistant [8], i.e. they can be used to spot malicious users and to only take into account "reliable" users and their ratings. It should be kept in mind, however, that there isn't a global view of which user is "reliable" or "trustworthy" so that, for example, a user can be considered trustworthy by one user and untrustworthy by another user.

In the process to identify malicious users, a very relevant role can play the concept of distrust. However, studying the meaning of distrust and how to computationally exploit it is very recent topic (we are aware of just one paper researching this [6]) and much work is needed in order to fully understand it.

Moreover the dataset we run experiments on (see Section 6) did not contain distrust information.

A more detailed description of RS weaknesses and how Trust-awareness can alleviate them can be found in the paper by Massa et al. [9].

4 Formal Domain Definition

In this section we precisely formalize the environment in which Trust-aware Recommender Systems can operate.

The environment is composed by:

- A set P of n uniquely identifiable peers.

$$P = \{p_1, p_2, p_3, ..., p_n\}$$

In this abstract domain definition, we use the term "peer" because the proposed framework can work for users of an online community but also for intelligent web servers (willing to trade and share resources), nodes of a peer-to-peer network, software agents or every possible conceivable independent entity able to perform some actions. A peer must be uniquely identifiable. For instance on the web, a reasonable unique identifier for peers could be an URI (Uniform Resource Identifier).

- A set I of m uniquely identifiable items.

$$I = \{i_1, i_2, i_3, ..., i_m\}$$

For items identifiers, we can think about globally agreed ones (such as ISBN for books, for instance) or we can use some hashing of the content, if digital, or of the item description to produce a unique id.

- n sets of Trust Statements. Every peer is allowed to express a trust value in every other peer. This should represent how much a peer consider valuable the ratings of another peer. Every peer's trust statements can be formalized in a trust function whose domain is P and whose codomain is $[0, 1]$ where 0 means total distrust and 1 total trust. A missing value (function not defined) represents the fact that the peer does not express a trust statement about that peer, probably because it didn't have a direct evidence for deciding about that peer's trustworthiness.

$$t_{p_i} : P \rightarrow [0, 1] \cup \perp \qquad \text{Trust function of peer } p_i$$

For example, $t_{p_1}(p_2) = 0.8$ means that peer p_1 issued a trust statement expressing its degree of trust in peer p_2 as 0.8, a high trust value.

In this model we do not consider the timing of trust statements, so that, for instance, if a peer expresses again another trust statement about the same user (probably updating the value based on last interactions), we just override the previous value.

- n sets of Ratings. Every peer is allowed to express a rating on every item. Every peer's ratings can be formalized in a rating function whose domain is I and the codomain is $[0,1]$ where 0 means total dislike and 1 maximum appreciation. A missing value (function not defined) means the user did not rate the item.

$$r_{p_i} : I \to [0,1] \cup \bot \qquad \text{Rating function of peer } p_i$$

For example, $r_{p_1}(i_1) = 0.1$ means that peer p_1 rated item i_1 as 0.1, a low rating expressing its partial dislike for the item.
In this case too, we simply consider the last rating given by one user to the same item.

Discrete ratings scales (for example the integers from 1 to 5) for trust statements and ratings can be easily mapped in the $[0,1]$ interval.

Similar models were proposed as Open Rating Systems [5] and in the context of Semantic Web Recommender Systems [13].

It is worth underlining how the trust and rating functions would always be very sparse (i.e., undefined for the largest part of the domain). This is so because no peer can reasonably experience and then rate all the items in the world (for example, all the books or songs). The same is true for trust: no peer can reasonably interact with every other peer (think of a community of 1 billion peers) and then issue a trust statement about them.

At present, this kind of environment has been created by some online companies, for example *epinions.com* or *amazon.com*. Likewise, many other environments are moving in this direction, for example, as we already mentioned, peer-to-peer networks, open marketplaces, and notably the Semantic Web [1] whose goal is to create a web of hyperlinked pages "understandable" automatically by machines. To this extend, two very interesting and promising semantic formats are FOAF [3] (for expressing friends and trusted users) and RVW [2] (for expressing reviews of items).

5 Trust-Aware Recommender Architecture

In this section we present the architecture of our proposed solution: Trust-aware Recommender Systems. Figure 2 shows the different modules (black boxes) as well as input and output matrices of each of them (white boxes).

The overall system takes as input the trust matrix (representing all the community trust statements) and the ratings matrix (representing all the ratings given by users to items) and produces, as output, a matrix of predicted ratings that the users would assign to the items. These matrix is used by the RS for recommending the most liked items to the user: precisely, the RS selects, from the row of predicted ratings relative to the user, the items with highest values. Of course, the final output matrix could be somehow sparse, i.e. having some cells with missing values, when the system is not able to predict the rating that the user would give to the item. Actually the quantity of predictable ratings is one of the possible evaluation strategies.

Let us now explain in detail every single module. First, we define the task of the module and then we describe the algorithm we chose for the experiments. However the architecture is modular and hence different algorithms can be plugged for the different modules.

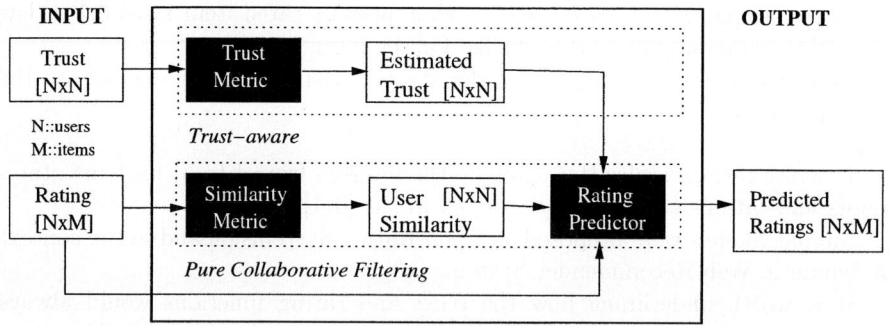

Fig. 2. Trust-Aware Recommender Systems Architecture.

Trust metric module. The Trust Metric Module takes as input the trust network (representable as a $N \times N$ trust matrix) and exploits trust propagation in order to predict, for every user, how much she could trust every other user. In this way, it produces an Estimated Trust matrix. The value in the cell i, j (if present) represents how much the metric predict peer p_i may trust peer p_j. This quantity can be used as a weight representing how much the user's ratings should be considered when creating a recommendation.

As already stated, trust metrics can be classified in local and global. In our framework, a global trust metric (for example, PageRank [11]) produces an Estimated Trust matrix with all the rows equal, meaning that the estimated trust in a certain user (column) is the same for every user (row).

While there are some attempts to propose trust metrics [3,14,8], this research topic is very recent and there aren't thorough analysis of which metrics perform better in different scenarios. Since the goal of this paper is to show that trust-awareness is useful in improving Recommender Systems, we use a simple trust metric in our experiments. More sophisticated ones can be deployed in our framework very easily.

We use the following local trust metric: given a source user, it assigns to every other user a predicted trust based on her minimum distance from the source user. Precisely, assuming trust is propagated up to the maximimum propagation distance d, a user at distance n from source user will have a predicted trust value of $(d - n + 1)/d$. Users that are not reachable within the maximum propagation distance have no predicted trust value (and cannot become neighbours). Our trust metric choice is guided also by the fact that the dataset we use for experiments does not have weighted trust statements but only full positive trust statement: we only have access to "peer p_i trusts p_j as 1" (see a description of dataset and experiments on Section 6). As an example, we analyze the trust network in Figure 1, but considering the trust statements values as 1. We predict trust values for user A and choose 4 as maximum propagation distance: in this case, our trust metric would assign to users at distance 1 (B and C) a predicted trust value of $(4-1+1)/4 = 1$ and to users at distance 2 (D) a predicted trust value of $(4-2+1)/4 = 0.75$. In this way, we adopt a linear decay in propagating trust: users closer in the trust network to the source user have higher predicted trust.

Similarity metric. Computing the similarity of current user against every other user is one of the standard steps of Collaborative Filtering techniques. Its task is to compute the correlation between two users (represented as vectors of ratings), producing the output $n \times n$ User Similarity matrix in which ith row contains the similarity values of ith user against every other user. The correlation value is used in next steps as a weight for the user ratings, according to the intuition that, if a user rates in a similar way to current user, then her ratings are useful for predicting the ratings of the current user. The most used technique is Pearson Correlation Coefficient [7].

$$w_{a,u} = \frac{\sum_{i=1}^{m}(r_{a,i}-\bar{r}_a)(r_{u,i}-\bar{r}_u)}{\sqrt{\sum_{i=1}^{m}(r_{a,i}-\bar{r}_a)^2 \sum_{i=1}^{m}(r_{u,i}-\bar{r}_u)^2}} \quad (1)$$

Note that this coefficient can be computed only on overlapping items. Moreover, if 2 users only have one item rated by both, then the coefficient is not meaningful. Hence, for a user, it is possible to compute the correlation coefficient only in users who share at least 2 co-rated items and this are usually a small portion as we described in [9]. In the experiments (see Section 6), we follow the most used strategy of keeping only positive similarities values because users with a negative correlation are dissimilar to current user and hence it is better to not consider their ratings.

Rating predictor. This step is the classical last step of Collaborative Filtering [7]. The predicted rating of item i for the current user a is the weighted sum of the ratings given to item i by the k neighbours of a.

$$p_{a,i} = \bar{r}_a + \frac{\sum_{u=1}^{k} w_{a,u}(r_{u,i}-\bar{r}_u)}{\sum_{u=1}^{k} w_{a,u}} \quad (2)$$

Neighbours can be taken from the User Similarity matrix or from the Estimated Trust matrix and the weights $w_{a,u}$ are the cells in the chosen matrix. For example, in the first case, the neighbours of user i are in the ith row of the User Similarity matrix.

Another option is to combine the two matrices in order to produce an output matrix that embeds both the information (user similarity and estimated trust). Usually, these matrices are very sparse so that this strategy could be useful in reducing sparseness and hence providing more neighbours for every single user. However, the goal of this paper is to evaluate separately the possible contributions of trust-awareness in RS and not to propose a combination technique that would require a dedicated evaluation.

In this section we have explained the architecture of Trust-aware Recommender Systems. In the following section, we present the experiments we have conducted and the dataset we have used.

6 Experiments

In this section we present experimental results that provide evidence supporting our claim that trust-awareness improve the performances of RSs.

The section is structured as follows: firstly we introduce details about the dataset we used, then we explain in detail the experiments we have run and discuss the chosen evaluation strategy.

We collected a dataset with the required features discussed in Section 4 from an online community, *epinions.com*. Epinions.com is a consumers opinion site where users can review items (such as cars, books, movies, software, ...) and also assign them numeric ratings in the range 1 (min) to 5 (max). Users can also express their *Web of Trust*, i.e. "reviewers whose reviews and ratings they have consistently found to be valuable"[2] and their *Block list*, i.e. a list of authors whose reviews they find consistently offensive, inaccurate, or not valuable. We collected the dataset by crawling the *epinions.com* site on November 2003. We stored, for every user, the rated items (with the numeric rating) and the trusted users (friends). Note that we could only access the publically available positive trust statements ($t_{p_i}(p_j) = 1$), and not the private Block lists.

The collected dataset consists of 49290 users who rated a total of 139738 different items at least once. 40169 users rated at least one item. The total number of reviews is 664824. The sparseness of the collected dataset is hence more than 99.99%. The total number of trust statements is 486985. More details about the dataset (with, for instance, standard deviations and distributions of rating and trust statements) and the way we collected it can be found in [9].

We should underline how the majority of users are what are termed "cold start users" [9], users who provided few ratings. For instance in our collected dataset more than half of the users (52.82%) provided less than 5 ratings. We will see in the following how it is precisely with these users that traditional CF systems tend to perform poorly. We will also see that a trust-aware solution is especially powerful for these users.

We now explain the different experiments we have run on the *epinions.com* dataset. We have instantiated the architecture presented in Figure 2 in order to compare the contributions of the trust metric and of the user similarity metric to the performances of the system. Hence we have run separately two techniques: a pure Collaborative Filtering strateg yand a Trust-aware one.

---

[2] From the Web of Trust FAQ (http://www.epinions.com/help/faq/?show=faq_wot)

For the Trust Metric technique, we have used the one introduced in Section 5. We performed different experiments with different maximum propagation distances, precisely 1, 2, 3 and 4. Choosing 1 as max propagation distance means considering, for every user, only the users explicitly inserted in the web of trust (friends, in the *epinions.com* vocabulary). Since the further away the user is from current user, the less reliable is the inferred trust value, we choose to run experiments propagating trust only up to distance 4. As expected, increasing the propagation distance implies that the technique is able to consider, on average, an increasing number of potential neighbours for every single user. Intuitively, the higher the propagation distance, the less sparse the resulting Predicted Trust matrix.

For the Similarity Metric technique, we have used the Pearson Correlation coefficient (Equation 1), the most commonly used similarity metric in RSs [7].

For the Rating Predictor module, we have used the standard CF technique (Equation 2). In one experiment we have generated the neighbourhood set using the User Similarity matrix, and in the others we used the Estimated Trust matrices.

In order to compare the performances of the two different approaches (pure CF and trust-aware), we need to choose a Recommender System evaluation technique. We use *leave-one-out* technique with Mean Absolute Error (MAE) as our error metric, since it is the most appropriate and useful for evaluating prediction accuracy in offline tests [7]. Leave one out involves hiding a rating and then trying to predict it. The predicted rating is then compared with the real rating and the difference (in absolute value) is the prediction error. Averaging this error over every prediction gives the overall MAE.

Another important way to discriminate between different recommender techniques is coverage. The RS may not be able to make predictions for every item. For this reason, it is important to evaluate also the portion of ratings that an RS is able to predict (*ratings coverage*).

However this quantity is not always informative about the quality of an RS. In fact, it is often the case that an RS is successful in predicting all the ratings for a user who provide many ratings and perform poorly for a user who has rated few items. For example, let us suppose that we consider one user with 100 ratings and 100 users with 1 rating. In this case, a probable situation is the following: the RS is able to predict all the 100 ratings given by the "heavy rater" and none of the other ones. So we have 100 predicted ratings over 200 possible ones, corresponding to 50% of the ratings, but we only have one "satisfied" user over 101 users, corresponding to less than 1%! For this reason, we also compute the *users coverage*, defined as the portion of users for which the RS is able to predict at least one rating.

A similar argument applies for Mean Absolute Error as well. Usually RSs produce small errors for "heavy raters" and higher ones for "cold start users". But, since heavy raters provide many ratings, in computing MAE, we are going to count these small errors many times, while the few big errors made for cold start users count few times. For this reason, we define another measure we call

Mean Absolute User Error (MAUE), for which we first compute the mean error for each user and then we average these user errors over all the users. In this way every user is taken into account once and a cold start user is influential as much as a heavy rater.

Since our argument is that trust-awareness is especially useful for cold start users, in the next section we will analyze the performances (coverage and error) of the different techniques, also focusing particularly on users who provided few ratings. This analysis is important because these users make up more than 50% of our dataset. In particular, we constructed three different views, considering only users who provided 2, 3 or 4 ratings.

In this section we discussed the dataset we use, our experiments and the chosen evaluation technique. In the next section, we will present and discuss the results.

7 Discussion of Results

The results of our experiments are summarized in Table 2. The rows of the table represent the evaluation measures we computed for the different techniques. The reader is referred to previous Section for an explanation of the different evaluation measures: ratings coverage, users coverage, MAE and MAUE. The different techniques we used in our experiments are *UserSim* and *Trust-x*. *UserSim* refers to the pure Collaborative Filtering strategy (bottom dotted box in Figure 2) while *Trust-x* refers to the trust-aware strategy (top dotted box), where x is the max propagation distance.

The columns of the table represent different views of the data. In the first column (labelled "ALL") we show the evaluation measures computed over all the users and this gives a picture of the average performances of the different techniques. Instead in the next columns we concentrate on cold start users (which are a large portion of the users). For example, in the second column (labelled "2"), only the users who expressed 2 ratings are considered. For every view of the data (i.e. column), we also indicate the number of users who satisfy the conditions on number of expressed ratings ("User Population Size"). For example, the users who expressed 2 ratings are 3937, almost 10% of the users. For every view of the data, we also present the mean number of users in the web of trust of the considered users. This is done in order to show the quantity of information available to the different techniques (number of ratings for *UserSim*, mean number of friends for *Trust-x*).

We now discuss results of experiments presented in Table 2.

User Similarity performs well with heavy raters and poorly with cold start users. As we have shown in [9], for the heavy raters (i.e. users who rated many items), the Pearson coefficient is computable on many other users that are potential neighbours. This means there is a high probability that some of these neighbours have rated the item under prediction. The opposite situation occurs with cold start users (users who rated few items). This is represented by the fact that

Table 2. Results of experiments. Rows represents different evaluation measures we collected for the different evaluated techniques. Columns represents different views of the data (e.g., in the column labelled "2", we present evaluation measures computed only on users who have rated exactly 2 items). For every column we also show the number of users in the specific view and the mean number of users in their webs of trust (friends).

# Expressed Ratings		ALL	2	3	4
User Population Size		40169	3937	2917	2317
Mean Web of Trust Size		9.88	2.54	3.15	3.64
Ratings	UserSim	**51%**	N/A	4%	8%
Coverage	Trust-1	28%	10%	11%	12%
	Trust-2	60%	23%	26%	31%
	Trust-3	74%	39%	45%	51%
	Trust-4	**77%**	45%	**53%**	59%
Users	UserSim	41%	N/A	6%	14%
Coverage	Trust-1	45%	17%	25%	32%
	Trust-2	56%	32%	43%	53%
	Trust-3	61%	46%	57%	64%
	Trust-4	**62%**	50%	**59%**	**66%**
MAE	UserSim	0.843	N/A	1.244	1.027
	Trust-1	0.837	0.929	**0.903**	0.840
	Trust-2	0.829	1.050	0.940	0.927
	Trust-3	0.811	1.046	0.940	0.918
	Trust-4	**0.805**	1.033	0.926	0.903
MAUE	UserSim	0.939	N/A	1.319	1.095
	Trust-1	0.853	0.942	0.891	0.847
	Trust-2	0.881	1.041	0.935	0.905
	Trust-3	0.862	1.033	0.942	0.915
	Trust-4	0.850	1.019	0.927	0.899

UserSim is able to cover 51% of the ratings (340906 out of 664824) but only 41% of the users (16378 out of 40169). The reason is that in the small percentage of users for which a prediction is possible, there are mainly heavy raters that provided a big percentage of the ratings. This is especially relevant if compared with *Trust-1* that has an opposite behaviour: in fact, it is able to cover only 28% of the ratings (187513 out of 664824) but 45% of the users (17897 out of 40169). This means *Trust-1* is able to predict at least one rating for many users but, for every user, it is able to predict a small portion of the ratings (on average, almost 10). We have already stated that, while predicting for heavy raters is reasonably easy, the real challenge for RS is in making recommendations to new users with few ratings so that they find useful the system and keep using it. *Trust-2*, *Trust-3*, *Trust-4* significantly increase both the users coverage and the ratings coverage.

Another fact confirming that *UserSim* works well with heavy raters and not with cold start users is the difference between MAE and MAUE. Averaging the prediction error over every rating gives a MAE of 0.843, while, considering the average error for every user, we obtain a MAUE of 0.939. This latter measure tells us that the error is higher on predictions for cold start users: in fact, they expressed few ratings and hence the high errors produced for their predictions contribute less to the overall Mean Absolute Error computed over every predictable rating. Instead, for *Trust-x*, MAE and MAUE values are in general close, meaning that errors (and performances) are more similar for every type of user and more uniformly distributed.

On average, Trust-x achieves better coverage without loss of accuracy. We now compare the global MAE for the different techniques over all the users (third row, first column of Table 2). The highest error is obtained in the experiment with *UserSim* (0.843). Instead every *Trust-x* technique has smaller error. Every additional allowed trust propagation step decreases the error, however the difference in error at different max propagation distances is small (the MAE of *Trust-4* is 0.805). Hence we can say that, even if *Trust-x* performs better than *UserSim*, the decrease in error is small. On the other hand, coverage is significantly higher for Trust-aware strategies; for example propagating trust up to distance 4 (*Trust-4*), we are able to cover 77% of the ratings and to make at least a prediction for 62% of the users. These values were, respectively, 51% and 41% for *UserSim* technique.

For cold start users, Trust-x achieves also better accuracy. As we have already argued, the most important and challenging users for an RS are the cold start users, users who provided few ratings. For this reason we analyze in detail the performances (both in term of coverage and error) of the different techniques only considering users who rated a small number of ratings.

For example, in the second column of Table 2, we consider only users who have rated 2 items. It is worth noting that there are 3937 out of 40169 users (10 %) who provided at least one rating and hence a significant portion. For users who have rated just 2 items, no prediction with *UserSim* is possible. In fact, since *leave-one-out* hides one rating, the Pearson Correlation coefficient is not computable and hence every user has zero neighbours.

It is important to note that, Trust-aware techniques and pure CF ones use different input (respectively, trust statements and ratings). However, we must compare their performances when they use comparable quantity of input information. Considering that *leave-one-out* hides one rating but does not affect the number of trust statements, we compare *UserSim* computed over users who expressed n ratings with *Trust-x* computed over users who expressed $n - 1$ trust statements (friends). In particular, in the following we compare the performances of *UserSim* over users with 4 ratings (because of leave one out, 3 ratings are used as input) with performances of *Trust-x* over users with 3 ratings (on average, 3.15 trust statements are available and used as input).

Considering coverage over ratings, *UserSim* is able to cover 8% of the ratings (750 out of 9268) and *Trust-1* 11% (976 out of 8751). A significant improvement in the ratings coverage is obtained increasing the trust propagation horizon, for example *Trust-4* is able to cover 53% of the ratings. Considering coverage over users, we observe a similar pattern with *UserSim* able to predict at least a rating for 14% of the users (318 out of 2317); the percentages are 25% (728 out of 2917) for *Trust-1* and 59% for *Trust-4*.

Also when considering the error on predictions, *Trust-x* techniques improve over *UserSim* technique. For example, *UserSim* produces a Mean Absolute Error (MAE) of 1.027 compared to a MAE of 0.903 for *Trust-1*. *Trust-4* presents a slight increase in MAE (0.926) if compared with *Trust-1*. This is so because *Trust-4* is able to predict much more ratings (4618 versus 976 of *Trust-1*), i.e. has a much higher ratings coverage, as already noted. These latter results are important: with a Trust-aware technique we are able to generate a prediction for more that half of the users with 3 ratings, while keeping the error low. Similar results can be observed for users who rated 2 and 4 items. Note that, as expected, for every technique, the average error for users with 2, 3 or 4 ratings is higher than the average error over all the users. This is because it is more difficult to predict ratings for users with small rating profiles.

In order to bootstrap the system for new users, it is better to promote the acquisition of few trust statements. Our experiments suggest that for cold start users (who are a sizeable portion of the dataset), a few trust statements (and the use of our trust metric) can achieve a much higher coverage and reduced error with respect to the comparable amount of rating information. For example, the last column of Table 2 shows that for users with 4 ratings (that have on average 3.64 friends), the best Trust-aware technique is able to make a prediction for 66% of the users while the technique based on User Similarity only to 14% and with a higher error. This fact suggests that, in order for an RS to be able to provide recommendations to a new user, collecting few trust statements is more effective, both in term of coverage and error, than collecting an equivalent number of ratings.

8 Conclusions and Future Work

The goal of this paper is to analyze the potential contribution of Trust Metrics in increasing the performances of Recommender Systems. We have argued how Trust-awareness can solve some of the traditional problems of RSs and we have proposed an architecture for Trust-aware Recommender Systems. We have shown, through a set of experiments on a large real dataset, that Trust Metrics increase the coverage (number of predictable ratings) and decrease the error when compared with traditional Collaborative Filtering RS. This effect is especially evident for new users who have rated few items. Hence, based on the experiments results, we are able to suggest a RS bootstrapping strategy for new users: collecting few trust statements is more effective than collecting an equivalent amount of ratings.

Our future work goes in several directions. We need to evaluate the performances of different trust metrics in RSs. In particular we are interested to test whether local trust metrics [3,14] performs better than global ones (for instance, PageRank [11]). Another direction deals with distrust [6], i.e. negative trust statements. We have recently obtained the complete and anonymized *epinions.com* dataset containing also the users' Block list. Considering distrust is a very recent topic and in our context it is especially useful in order to conduct a deep evaluation of possible RSs attacks [10] and to test wheter trust-aware solutions are able to detect malicious or not reliable users.

Our final goal is to create Trust-Aware Recommender Systems. In this paper we kept cleanly separated the technique using trust information (*Trust-x*) and the technique using rating information (*UserSim*) and conducted a comparative analysis. However in future we want to propose and study algorithms for combining trust and rating information, in order to take the advantages of both strategies. A specific analysis will be made also on understanding when this information are conflicting (for example, when a user predicted as trustable issues dissimilar ratings on the same items or viceversa).

References

1. T. Berners-Lee, J. Hendler, and O. Lassila. The semantic web. *Scientific American*, 2001.
2. A. Eaton. RVW module for syndicating and aggregating reviews, 2004. http://www.pmbrowser.info/rvw/0.2.
3. J. Golbeck, J. Hendler, and B. Parsia. Trust networks on the Semantic Web. In *Proceedings of Cooperative Intelligent Agents*, 2003.
4. D. Goldberg, D. Nichols, B.M. Oki, and D. Terry. Using collaborative filtering to weave an information tapestry. *Communications of the ACM*, 35(12):61–70, 1992.
5. R. Guha. Open rating systems. Technical report, Stanford University, CA, USA, 2003.
6. R. Guha, R. Kumar, P. Raghavan, and A. Tomkins. Propagation of trust and distrust. In *Proceedings of WWW2004*, 2004.
7. J. Herlocker, J. Konstan J., A. Borchers, and J. Riedl. An Algorithmic Framework for Performing Collaborative Filtering. In *Proceedings of the 1999 Conference on Research and Development in Information Retrieval*, 1999.
8. R. Levien. *Advogato Trust Metric*. PhD thesis, UC Berkeley, USA, 2003.
9. P. Massa and B. Bhattacharjee. Using trust in recommender systems: an experimental analysis. In *Proc. of 2nd Int. Conference on Trust Management*, 2004.
10. M. O'Mahony, N. Hurley, N. Kushmerick, and G. Silvestre. Collaborative recommendation: A robustness analysis. In *Proceedings of Int'l Semantic Web Conf. (ISWC-03)*, 2003.
11. L. Page, S. Brin, R. Motwani, and T. Winograd. The pagerank citation ranking: Bringing order to the web. Technical report, Stanford, USA, 1998.
12. P. Resnick and H.R. Varian. Recommender systems. *Communications of the ACM*, 40(3):56–58, 1997.
13. C. Ziegler. Semantic web recommender systems. In *Joint ICDE/EDBT Ph.D. Workshop*, 2004.
14. C. Ziegler and G. Lausen. Spreading activation models for trust propagation. In *IEEE International Conference on e-Technology, e-Commerce, and e-Service (EEE'04)*, 2004.

Service Graphs for Building Trust*

Pınar Yolum[1] and Munindar P. Singh[2]

[1] Department of Artificial Intelligence, Vrije Universiteit Amsterdam
De Boelelaan 1081a, 1081 HV Amsterdam, The Netherlands
pyolum@few.vu.nl
[2] Department of Computer Science, North Carolina State University
Raleigh, NC 27695-7535, USA
singh@ncsu.edu

Abstract. Information systems must establish trust to cooperate effectively in open environments. We are developing an agent-based approach for establishing trust, where information systems are modeled as agents that provide and consume services. Agents can help each other find trustworthy parties by providing referrals to those that they trust. We propose a graph-based representation of services for modeling the trustworthiness of agents. This representation captures natural relationships among service domains and provides a simple means to accommodate the accrual of trust placed in a given party. When interpreted as a lattice, it enables less important services (e.g., low-value transactions) to be used as gates to more important services (e.g., high-value transactions). We first show that, where applicable, this approach yields superior efficiency (needs fewer messages) and effectiveness (finds more providers) than a vector representation that does not capture the relationships between services. Next, we study trade-offs between various factors that affect the performance of this approach.

1 Introduction

We consider the problem of trust in large-scale, decentralized information systems that are represented by autonomous agents. In simple terms, the key problem is how an agent (or *trustor*) should trust another agent (or *trustee*). Trust is for a purpose. That is, a trustor would (or would not) trust a trustee for a particular service. For this reason and to relate our work to the recent interest on Web Services, we consider a setting wherein different agents consume and provide information services to one another [1]. The agents offer varying levels of trustworthiness to others and are potentially interested in finding trustworthy agents who provide the services that they need.

Trust can be established through three major means. *Institutional* trust or trust in authoritative institutions or organizations is common in the off-line world. People trust in the power of these institutions to stabilize their interactions [8, p. 26]. Current distributed trust management approaches can be thought of formalizing institutional trust, because they assume that digital certificates issued by various certificate authorities lead to trust [4].

---

* This research was supported by the National Science Foundation under grant ITR-0081742. An earlier version of this paper was presented at the AAMAS-03 Workshop on Trust, Fraud, Deception and Privacy.

That is, these approaches usually assume that trust is established merely through a chain of endorsements beginning with some trusted authority. However, only the most trivial level of trust can be established through such a mechanism. For example, knowing that a web-site carries a digital certificate issued by another known site does not guarantee that the web-site will act in a trustworthy manner.

For this reason, multiagent approaches seek to create trust based on *local* or *social* evidence. Social trust is built through information from others. This information could be testimonies from individual witnesses regarding the trustee, or from a reputation agency. The context in which the ratings were given as well as the evaluation of the services could vary by episode as well as by the parties that give the ratings. The credentials of the information sources (witnesses or reputation agencies) are crucial for interpreting this second-hand information correctly. Unless the agents that give the ratings are established to be trustworthy, their aggregate ranking would not be sufficient to create trust. That is, in order to create trust through second-hand information, the trustworthiness of the information sources must be established as well [15, p. 74]. A powerful way of ensuring that the sources themselves are trustworthy is by accessing them through *referrals* [14]. Local trust means considering previous direct interactions with a trustee, which often are the most valuable in creating trust for the following reasons. One, since the trustor itself evaluates the interactions, the results are more reliable. Two, the context in which the trustworthiness of the provider is evaluated is explicit and relevant to the trustor.

Previous agent approaches for trust emphasize either its local or its social aspects. By contrast, we develop an approach that takes a strong stance for both aspects. In our approach, the agents track each other's trustworthiness locally and can give and receive referrals to others. This approach naturally accommodates the above conceptualizations of trust: social because the agents give and receive referrals to other agents, and local because the agents maintain rich representations of each other and can reason about them to determine their trustworthiness. Further, the agents evaluate each other's ability to give referrals. Lastly, although this approach does not require centralized authorities, it can help agents evaluate the trustworthiness of any such authorities as well.

This approach enables us to address two properties of trust that are not adequately addressed by current approaches. One, trust often builds up over interactions. That is, you might trust a stranger for a low-value transaction, but would only trust a known party for a high-value transaction. Two, trust often flows across service types. That is, you might assume that a party who is trustworthy in one kind of dealings will also be trustworthy in related kinds of dealings.

Our main contributions are as follows. One, we introduce a graph-based representation of services, and show how it enables us to address the above two properties of trust. Two, we evaluate our graph-based representation by comparing it to a vector representation used in previous work, which is itself more advanced than a simple scalar representation. Graph representation enables trust to be propagated across service types, whereas vector representation does not capture the relation between services at all. Our results establish that the additional expressiveness of the graph representation helps: a graph-based representation enables trustworthy service providers to be found more effectively and efficiently. Three, we perform a sensitivity analysis of the graph-based representation to identify factors that affect its performance further.

The rest of this paper is organized as follows. Section 2 introduces a graph-based representation for agents to model services. Section 3 describes our referrals-based approach for trust and our experimental setup. Section 4 compares this graph-based representation with a vector representation in terms of efficiency and effectiveness. Section 5 discusses and experimentally evaluates factors related to the performance of our representation. Section 6 discusses the relevant literature and outlines some directions for further study.

2 Graph-Based Representation

We consider a setting with a fixed number of service types. Service providers offer one or more of these services. Some of these services may be related, i.e., being a good provider for one may imply being a good provider for another. Conversely, some services may be unrelated to each other.

One way of representing the set of services is through a vector space model, where each element in the vector corresponds to a different domain and the weight of the element denotes the fitness of the service for that domain [14]. This is similar to the vector descriptions of documents in information retrieval. The vector representation is simple and quite effective if the elements are independent, since a vector representation does not capture any relationships between vector elements.

The second way is to represent the services as a graph, whose nodes map to service types. The graph representation is more expressive in that it can capture relationships between service types that a vector representation cannot. For example, a service provider that has been found to be trustworthy for one type of service can be considered for another type of service based on how well the services relate.

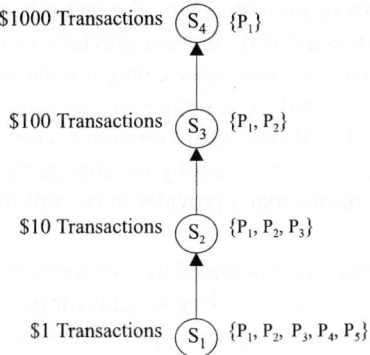

Fig. 1. A totally-ordered service graph

Figure 1 shows a simple graph. Here, each node represents transactions of different values. S_1 denotes transactions worth \$1, S_2 denotes transactions worth \$10, and so on. The list next to each node represents the trustworthy providers for that node. The agents trusted for a node are a subset of the agents trusted for the lower node. That is, if you trust someone for a $10 transaction, you trust him for a $1 transaction as well (e.g., P_3). The reverse need not hold. You might trust many for transactions of $1 but probably only a few for $1000 transactions (e.g., P_1).

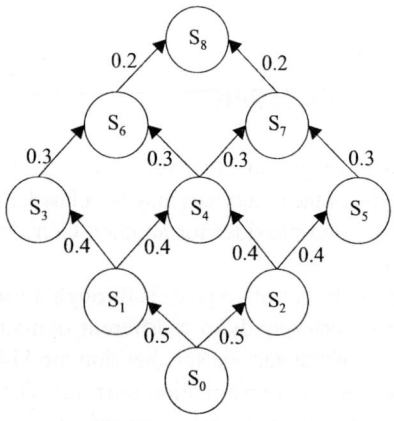

Fig. 2. An example service graph with weights

Figure 2 illustrates a setting with partially ordered services. Any two services that are related are joined by an edge. Here an edge $\langle s_i, s_j \rangle$ indicates that a provider who can perform s_i well may also be able to perform s_j well.

When an agent needs a provider for a service for which it knows of no providers, it can potentially ask others or *promote* a provider that it has used for another service. Promotions provide a systematic way to reuse previous experiences with the service providers. A provider is tried for a new service only if it has performed well for another service, and if performing well in the first service indicates that the provider may perform well for the second service. The likelihood of a service provider in a lower node to perform a service in the upper node is represented by weights on the edges. For example, the weight 0.5 from S_0 to S_1 means that a provider of S_0 will likely be providing S_1 half the time.

Notice that a service graph is maintained by each agent to autonomously capture its experiences. Thus agents may have differing weights for the same pair of services. The weights are adjusted independently by each agent. After delivering a service, a service provider is rated by the consumer. The rating reflects the satisfaction of the consumer. These ratings are used by the consumer to decide if this service provider will be used again or referred to other consumers. Service providers with low ratings are replaced with service providers that can potentially get higher ratings.

When promoting a provider from s_i to s_j, two factors are considered: how trustworthy the provider is for s_i and how related s_i and s_j are. We calculate the trustworthiness of the provider p at s_i (t_{pi}) through its ratings at s_i and the number of interactions (for s_i).

The strength of the relation between s_i and s_j are given by the edge weight, w_{ij}.

$$(w_{ij} \times t_{pi}) > \theta \qquad (1)$$

The product of the edge weight with the average ratings projects how much the agent can reproduce its ratings in s_j. If this projected value is greater than a promotion threshold θ, then the agent can be promoted to perform s_j.

Notice that in the extreme case, if $w_{ij} = 0$ (the services are not correlated), then the service provider is not expected to perform well in s_j even if it performs well in s_i. Conversely, if a provider is not trusted for s_i ($t_{pi} = 0$), then the provider will never be promoted to s_j irrespective of how correlated the two services are.

The weights that denote the relation between two services are estimated by each agent, which can update the weights in its graph based on its experiences. Hence, two agents can have different weights for the same edge. The graph weights are updated after promoting a provider and testing it for the higher service. The weights are tuned using a simple linear update mechanism. If a promotion from s_i to s_j is successful, i.e., if the provider gets a good rating in s_j as well, then w_{ij} is increased. Similarly, w_{ij} is decreased when a promoted provider gets a bad rating in s_j. The increase (or decrease) in the weight is proportional to the new rating of the service provider in s_j.

3 Experimental Setup

We investigate the properties of interest using agents who simulate requesting, providing, and evaluating services. The agents act in accordance with the following abstract protocol [17]. When an agent desires a service, it begins to look for a trustworthy provider for the specified service. The agent queries some other agents from among its *neighbors*, which are a small subset of the agent's acquaintances. A queried agent may either answer giving the identifier of a service provider who can potentially perform the desired service or may give referrals to other agents. The querying agent may accept a service offer, if any, and may pursue referrals, if any.

The agents are autonomous and may not respond to another agent. When an agent responds, there is no guarantee about the quality of the answer or the suitability of a referral. Likewise, no agent is necessarily trusted by others: an agent unilaterally decides how to rate another agent.

Each agent maintains models of its acquaintances, which describe their *expertise* (i.e., the quality of the answers they provide), and *sociability* (i.e., the quality of the referrals they provide). Each agent is initialized with the same model for each neighbor, but updates its models of its acquaintances based on interactions with them.

An agent that is generating a query follows Algorithm 1. Each agent starts by generating a query for a service (line 1). The distribution of requests for services captures the following intuition. In real life, we would expect most requests to be for services with intermediate risk rather than for services with little or too much risk. For this reason, we use a normal distribution to model the frequency of the incoming requests. As a result, the services S_0 and S_8 get the least number of requests, whereas services S_3, S_4, and S_5 get the most requests.

Algorithm 1 Find-Provider()

1: Generate query for service type j
2: promotedProviders = promoteLocally(j)
3: **if** (promotedProviders != null) **then**
4:    Add promotedProviders to *providerSet*
5: **else**
6:    Send query to matching neighbors
7:    **while** (!timeout) **do**
8:       Receive message
9:       **if** (message.type == referral) **then**
10:          Send query to referred agent
11:          Record referral
12:       **else**
13:          Add answer to *providerSet* {answer contains a provider id.}
14:       **end if**
15:    **end while**
16: **end if**
17: **for** $i = 1$ to $|providerSet|$ **do**
18:    Evaluate provider(i)
19:    Update agent models
20:    Update service graph
21: **end for**

The agent promotes all the service providers that qualify to be promoted to perform this new service (line 2). If there are no such providers, then the agent sends the query to a subset of its neighbors (line 6). The main factor here is to determine which of its neighbors would be likely to answer the query. An agent that receives a query can either answer by returning the identifier of a service provider or giving a referral to another agent who is likely know of a service provider for the requested service.

If an agent receives a referral to another agent, it sends its query to the referred agent (line 10) and records the referral link (line 11). Simply put, the referrals generated for each query are used to update acquaintance models based on the quality of the service that is ultimately received from the providers found. After an agent receives a provider identifier or promotes a provider within, it evaluates the provider (line 18). We simulate this evaluation by looking up an evaluation value from a predefined table.

After the answers are evaluated, the agent uses its *learning policy* to update the models of its neighbors (line 19). In the default learning policy, when a good answer comes in, the modeled expertise of the answering agent and the sociability of the agents that helped locate the answerer (through referrals) are increased. Similarly, when a bad answer comes in, these values are decreased. Hence, the agents that give answers as well as the agents that give referrals are rated. At certain intervals during the simulation, each agent has a chance to choose new neighbors from among its acquaintances based on its *neighbor selection policy*. Key factors include the expertise and the sociability of the agents [18].

The experiments use 100 service consumers and 32 service providers for nine types of services. Each agent has three randomly picked neighbors. Each agent generates 50

Algorithm 2 promoteLocally(j)

1: **for** $i = 1$ to $|nodes|$ **do**
2:     **for** $k = 1$ to $|providers(i)|$ **do**
3:         $p = providers(i)(k)$
4:         **if** ($t_{pi} \times w_{ij} > \theta$) **then**
5:             **if** (numberOfInteractions(p)$\geq \lambda$) **then**
6:                 Add p to promotedProviders
7:             **end if**
8:         **end if**
9:     **end for**
10: **end for**
11: return promotedProviders

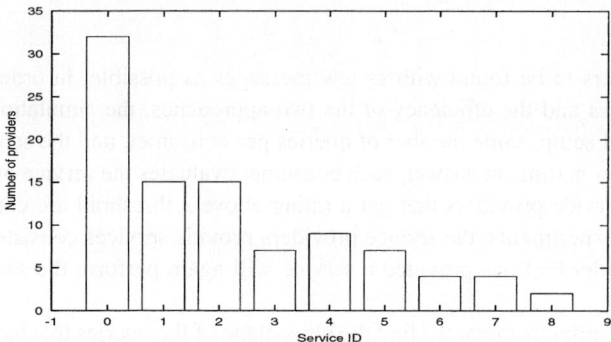

Fig. 3. Distributions of the service providers

queries and may change its neighbors after every 5 queries. Each query denotes the desired service type; e.g., S_0, S_1, and so on. Notice that not all 32 service providers offer all the services. The key property we want to capture in modeling the distribution of the service providers is that in real life, we would expect more service providers to offer easier services than harder ones. Hence, the number of providers would decrease as the service gets more specialized. With this intuition, the experiments are set up such that most of the 32 service providers can perform services that are lower down the graph, whereas only a few of them can perform harder services, say, S_8, the most specialized service. We capture this intuition by decreasing the number of providers approximately by half between two consecutive nodes. For example, while 15 service providers offer service S_1, only 7 of them provide S_3. The number of service providers for each type of service is given in Figure 3.

4 Comparison of Representations

Using this experimental setup, we compare the service graphs with the vector representation in terms of effectiveness and efficiency. A representation is effective if it allows agents to find the desired service providers. A representation is efficient if it allows the

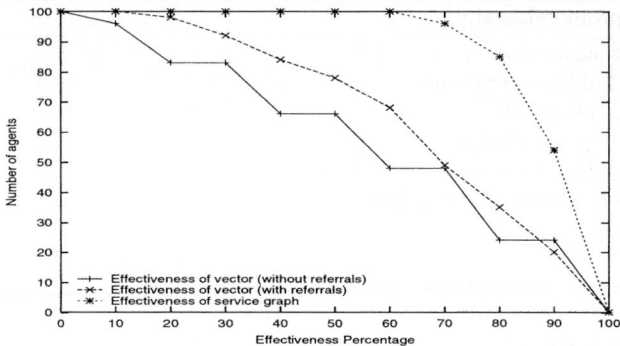

Fig. 4. The distribution of the agents for different values of effectiveness (After 10 queries)

service providers to be found with as few messages as possible. In order to compare the effectiveness and the efficiency of the two approaches, the simulation is run with the same initial setup, same number of queries per consumer, and the same number of neighbors. After getting an answer, each consumer evaluates the service provider in the answer. The service providers that get a rating above a threshold are considered useful. For these experiments, the service providers provide services consistently. That is, a service provider that has provided a service will again perform the same quality of service.

To measure effectiveness, we find the percentage of the queries that have resulted in finding a useful service provider. That is, the ratio of queries that lead to useful service providers to all the generated queries is calculated. We look at the effectiveness after every five queries for the graph-based representation and the vector representation. We look at two cases of the vector approach: one with referrals, two without referrals.

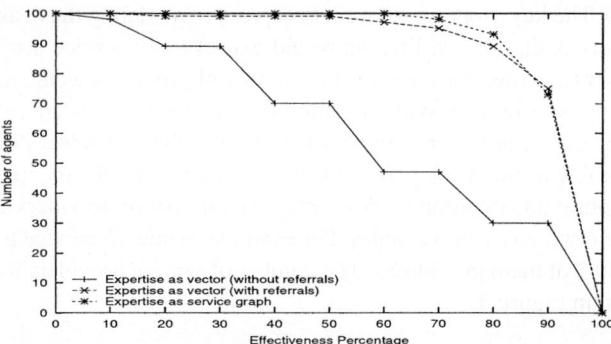

Fig. 5. The distribution of the agents for different values of effectiveness (After 20 queries)

Both in Figure 4 and in Figure 5, the x axis is the effectiveness percentage and the y axis is the number of agents. Both graphs plot the number of agents that achieve greater than or equal to the effectiveness percentage. The first graph shows the distributions after the 10th query and the second graph shows them after the 20th query.

In Figure 4, agents that employ service graphs achieve higher effectiveness than both of the vector approaches. The agents that use a vector with referrals generally do better than the agents without the referrals, except for one effectiveness value 90. That is, there are more agents that achieve at least 90 percent effectiveness in the vector approach without referrals, though the difference is minor.

The agents with the service graph achieve higher effectiveness rates in the second graph (Figure 5), too, though now the difference between the vector (with referrals) and the service graph approach is smaller. The performance of the vector approach increases as the agents learn about their neighbors and change their neighbors accordingly. After the 30th query, both approaches achieve an effectiveness rate of 99%, thus we do not show that in a different graph. However, when referrals are not employed, the effectiveness of the agents barely increases (Figures 4 and 5, solid lines). The average effectiveness for the no-referral case oscillates between 63% and 73%. Having no referrals causes two disadvantages to the agents. One, obviously they can pose their queries only to their neighbors, and incompetent neighbors cannot provide answers. Two, since there are no referrals, the agents interact with few other agents and learn only a small part of the society. Hence, when they change their neighbors, the set of agents they choose from is small and pseudo-random. Figure 6 plots the average effectiveness of all 100 agents after every five queries. We conclude that the consumers can locate trustworthy service providers more effectively with a graph-based representation than with a vector representation.

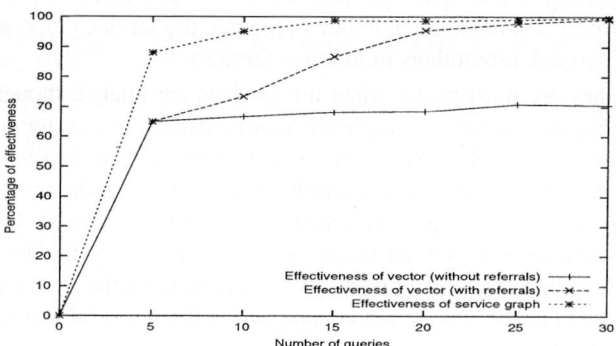

Fig. 6. Effectiveness of the representations

Next, we compare the average number of agents contacted per query (over 30 queries). Figure 7 plots this efficiency value for both approaches. The average value for the vector approach (with referrals) is 3.1, for the vector approach (without referrals) 2.81, and 0.45 for the service graph approach. In other words, the addition of referrals increases the number of contacted agents for the benefit of increased effectiveness. The service graph approach, on the other hand, yields a higher efficiency than both of the vector approaches as well as higher effectiveness.

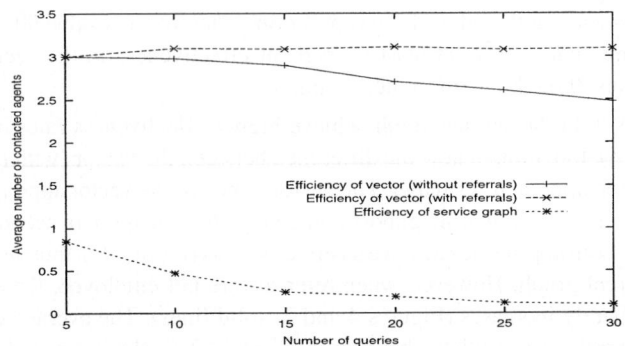

Fig. 7. Efficiency of the representations

Recall that initially, each agent knows of two service providers for possibly different services. For the results reported above, the initial distribution guaranteed that at least one agent in the system knows of a provider for each service. Consider a case, where none of the agents initially knew of a provider for S_8. In the vector approach, no matter how hard each agent searches for the provider through its neighbors, it will not be able to locate a provider for S_8. Whereas in the service graph approach, if an agent knows of a provider for S_6 or S_7, then it can promote the service provider to S_8. Thus, whereas the vector approach will definitely not find a provider, the service graph approach may find a provider through promotions from lower services.

Service graphs are most useful when the services are related, though even if the services are orthogonal the service graph would be equivalent to a vector representation. Thus, the service graph would in the worst case perform as well as the vector representation. There might only be one potential disadvantage. Following the previous scenario, assume that none of the service providers are trustworthy for service S_8. In this case, the service graph approach will promote service providers up only to find that they cannot fulfill S_8. Neither approaches will find a service provider, but the vector approach will use less time, whereas the service graph approach will try several providers (through promotions) and fail later.

5 Evaluation

We study how the initial setting, promotion threshold, and the number of previous interactions affect promotion accuracy and effectiveness of finding trustworthy service providers. For each experiment, we report averages from three simulation runs (additional runs yield similar results).

5.1 Control Variables

Initial Setting. The initial environments can differ in two main ways. The first factor is how much the neighbors can help each other in finding service providers, since providers can be found through referrals as well as through promotions. To study the performance of the service graph representation, we seek to reduce the effect of referrals and prior knowledge of an agent. Therefore, we use a setting where each agent only knows of two providers for service S_0, the lowest service. This setting forces agents to promote the providers and test them for higher services. In addition, at least in the beginning, agents cannot give well-targeted referrals for higher services, since none of them knows of a trustworthy provider for higher services.

The second factor is related to how much the agents are initially willing to try new service providers. This factor, termed *trust prejudice*, captures whether an agent is willing to trust newcomers [6]. We capture this intuition through the initial graph weights. For example, if initially all the weights are 1, then the agents are willing to try out all new service providers in all types of services. Conversely, when the weights are all 0, the agents have the prejudice that no agents can be trusted.

We evaluate our approach using three initial settings. In the *homogeneous* setting, each agent starts with the graph shown in Figure 2. In the *trusting* setting, the graph edges are the same but the weights are higher (meaning the agents trust others more). In the *heterogeneous* setting, each agent starts with random weights on random edges of its own.

Promotion Threshold. The estimated weight between two services is adjusted based on previous promotions between the two services. Intuitively, the promotion threshold denotes how much risk an agent is willing to take in its promotions. If the threshold for promoting up is low, then the agents will promote more providers, but might find out that more of these providers cannot perform the service. On the other hand, if the agents are reluctant to promote, then they might miss a chance to find a provider for a desired service. In Algorithm 2, θ refers to the promotion threshold.

Number of interactions. The overall rating of a provider at the previous service should be reliable. It is widely accepted that the number of previous interactions increases the accuracy of the trust assessment [5]. That is, the average rating may not be representative if the total number of interactions are few. In other words, a service provider with a ranking of 0.7 over three interactions might be trusted more than a provider with a ranking of 0.8 over one interaction. In our approach, agents use the number of interactions as a gating factor so that only those providers that have proved sufficiently trustworthy in another service, which is sufficiently closely related to the service under consideration, and such that the agent has interacted with these providers often enough to trust them adequately. In Algorithm 2, λ refers to the required number of interactions.

5.2 Results

Promotion Accuracy. Intuitively, high promotion accuracy captures the fact that only trustworthy service providers are promoted up the graph. Promotion errors are measured by the average number of wrong promotions performed by the agents.

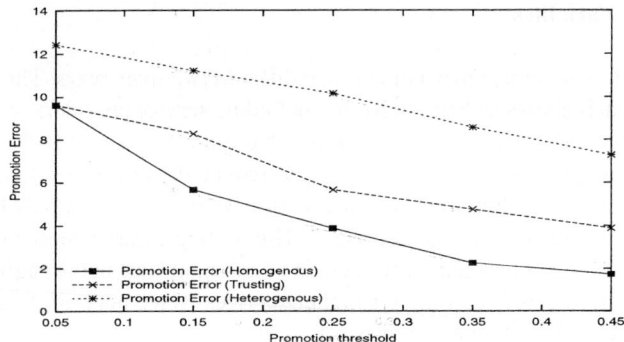

Fig. 8. Effect of initial setting

Figure 8 plots the promotion error for varying promotion thresholds. For all three curves, the error drops when the promotion threshold increases. That is, when agents take fewer risks, they make fewer mistakes. The heterogeneous setting has higher weights for more edges than the other two setups, and hence allows more promotions. For this reason, it is more prone to errors.

Next, we study the effect of number of interactions on promotion error. For each value of the promotion threshold, we plot the average promotion error. Figure 9 shows three plots for the homogeneous setting, corresponding to one, two, and three required interactions prior to promotion. The promotion error decreases with the number of previous interactions. For a threshold of 0.25, for example, when the required number of previous interactions is just one, the promotion error is almost 6. When the number of interactions is increased to two, the error drops below 4. When the number of interactions is further increased to three, the error becomes less than 2. In all three curves, increasing the promotion threshold decreases the promotion error, though the improvement is more significant for fewer interactions.

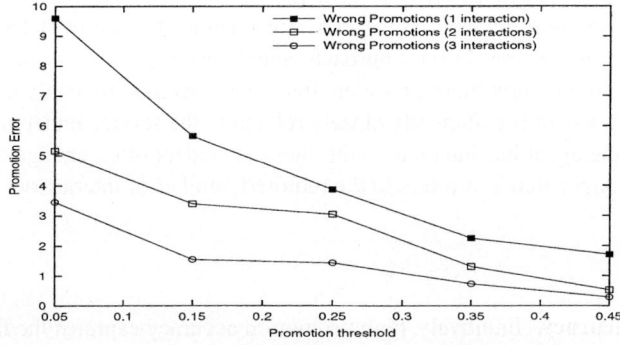

Fig. 9. Effect of previous interactions

Effectiveness. Recall that effectiveness measures how often consumers find trustworthy providers for the desired services. Thus, achieving a high promotion accuracy is not enough for good performance. The agents should also achieve high effectiveness.

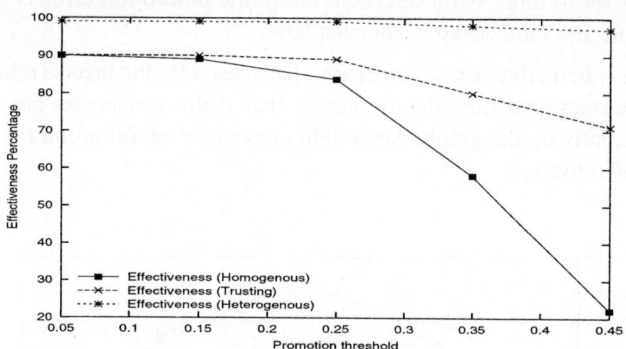

Fig. 10. Effect of initial setting

Again, we first look at the effect of initial setting on the effectiveness. Figure 10 plots three effectiveness curves for the three initial settings. This time the random setup achieves higher effectiveness than the other two setups. Since the random setup assigns weights to many edges, and hence allows more promotions, many providers—useful or not—are promoted and tested, resulting in almost always finding a provider.

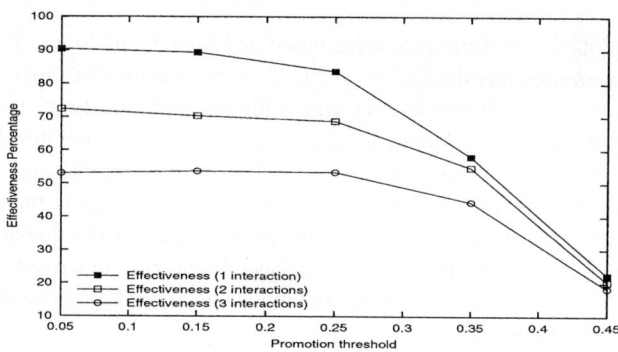

Fig. 11. Effect of the previous interactions on effectiveness

Figure 11 plots three effectiveness curves for varying values of the promotion threshold using homogeneous initial setting. Again, each curve corresponds to a case where different number of previous interactions is required. Independent of the number of interactions, if the threshold is high, the effectiveness is very low. Interestingly, for smaller values of the threshold, we see agents achieve a higher level of effectiveness (find more trustworthy agents to interact with) if the number of interactions are fewer. This is the opposite of the curves for the promotion accuracy, where we saw that the number of interactions decrease the promotion error. In other words, high promotion accuracy rarely coexists with high effectiveness. For example, in Figure 9 when the number of previous interactions is set to three (with threshold 0.35), the promotion error is below 1. But, effectiveness for the same setup is not even 50%.

Performance = Effectiveness × Accuracy. The reason for the inverse relation between promotion accuracy and the effectiveness is that if the consumers are cautious and promote reluctantly up the graph, they might miss many useful promotions, leading to sub-optimal effectiveness.

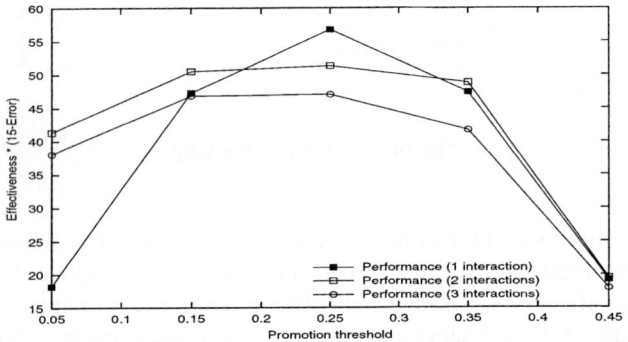

Fig. 12. Effectiveness and promotion error trade-off

Figure 12 plots this performance value based on Figure 9 and Figure 11. Neither extremes of the promotion threshold (0.05 and 0.45) achieve high performance. The lower threshold suffers from high promotion error, while the high thresholds lacks effectiveness. Optimal performance lies in the middle values of the promotion threshold. Among these, the performance is always better when the number of interactions is either 1 or 2. This suggests that the third interaction does not add much value to the performance. Among the 1 and 2 interaction cases, except for one value of the threshold (0.25), 2 interaction case outperforms the 1 interaction case. In general, this result suggests that it is better to be less cautious, trust more, and make some mistakes to be able to exploit a wider range of promotions.

6 Discussion

Lattice-based access control models have been used in computer security to regulate information flow [12]. Each node in the lattice denotes a different set of security privileges, called security classes. The more sensitive security classes are placed upper in the lattice. The information flow is only allowed from the lower security classes to the higher ones. Thus, even though the less confidential information from lower security classes can be carried to the upper security classes, no confidential information flows down. This is similar to how we handle service types. Providers that can perform services higher up the lattice can also perform lower services. In addition, we promote providers from lower service types to higher ones based on the providers performance on the lower services.

Wille use concept lattices for knowledge discovery in databases [16]. The data objects are classified into meaningful concepts based on common attributes. The concepts, then are arranged in a line diagram, which represents the concepts and the subconcept relationships among concepts. This representation is a structured way to visualize and analyze information.

Referrals capture the manner in which people normally help each other find trustworthy parties [9]. MINDS, based on the documents used by each user, was an early agent-based referral system [3]. Kautz *et al.* model social networks statically as graphs and study some properties of these graphs, e.g., how the accuracy of a referral to a specified individual relates to the distance of the referrer from that individual [7].

Yu and Singh [19] develop an approach for distributed reputation management where a reputation of an agent is computed based on testimonies of the witnesses using the Dempster-Shafer theory of evidence. They show how this model can be used to detect agents that are non-cooperative or agents that abuse their reputation by slowly decreasing their level of cooperativeness. Since the witnesses are found through referrals, Yu and Singh's approach captures social trust. Local evaluations are captured through belief functions, but relationships among service types are not captured.

Barber and Kim [2] propose an approach wherein agents use a belief revision algorithm to combine evidence they receive from other agents. In addition to providing evidence, each agent specifies its level of confidence in the evidence. Barber and Kim's approach captures social trust, but contrary to our approach, the trustworthiness of agents who provide evidence are not considered. Their approach does not consider local evidence, i.e., the previous interactions of the trustor with the trustee.

Pujol *et al.* [10] develop an algorithm to find the reputation of an agent based on its position in a social network. The Web pages of users are taken as a basis to come up with the social network. If an agent is pointed to by agents with high reputation, then the agent is also considered to have high reputation, similar to the notion of authority exploited in search engines such as Google. Pujol *et al.* use their approach to find the reputations of authors where the reputation of an author is defined as the number of citations received. Even though each agent can calculate its own reputation based only on local information (i.e., the agents that point at it), a central server is needed to access others' reputations. This approach does not capture local trust, since direct interactions are not taken into account. It captures social trust since the reputation of an agent is derived through how other agents have linked to it, but has no means to correct it based on local observations of an agent. In other words, the link structure is static and the positions of the agents do not change based on their interactions. In our approach, we allow agents to change neighbors using the neighbors' ability to give referrals as a heuristic. This allows us to rate the sources.

Sabater and Sierra [11] develop a system for reputation management where reputations are derived based on direct interactions as well as the social relations of the agents.

They use the number of interactions and the variance in ratings to derive the the trustworthiness of the agent through direct interactions. To assess the trustworthiness through indirect interactions, Sabater and Sierra use fuzzy inference to combine evidence from multiple witnesses. In this regard, their approach captures both social and local trust. On the other hand, Sabater and Sierra do not offer a mechanism to propagate trust across related services as we have done here.

Sen and Sajja [13] develop a reputation-based trust model used for selecting processor agents for processor tasks. Similar to our notion of service providers, each processor agent can offer varying performance. Agents are looking for trustworthy processor agents to interact with using only evidence from their peers. Sen and Sajja propose a probabilistic algorithm to find the number of agents to query to guarantee finding a trustworthy party. In our framework, we model the peers based on their prior performance and choose whom to ask for help based on these models. Thus, agents also decide the trustworthiness of the information source. However, in Sen and Sajja's framework, these models are not captured. All peers are treated the same independent of their previous behavior. This approach does not handle local trust, since previous interactions of an agent with processor agents are not taken into account.

The above approaches derive the trustworthiness of agents based on direct or indirect previous interactions. Our approach emphasizes the propagation of trust to related contexts as seen fit by an agent. In this respect, our graph-based representation complements the above approaches. Once the trustworthiness of an agent is derived, our approach can decide how this can be reused in other contexts.

7 Directions

Currently, we propagate trust based on a provider's trustworthiness for a single service. However, sometimes it would help to combine the trustworthiness of the provider in several services. For example, if a service is composed of several smaller services, the trustworthiness of the provider in all the subservices will affect the trustworthiness of the provider in the composed service. This problem is also acknowledged by Sabater and Sierra [11]. In future work, we plan to study such improvements to our model as well as evaluate our model with respect to different distributions for requesting and providing services.

References

1. A. Ankolekar, M. Burstein, J. R. Hobbs, O. Lassila, D. L. Martin, S. A. McIlraith, S. Narayanan, M. Paolucci, T. Payne, K. Sycara, and H. Zeng. DAML-S: Semantic markup for Web services. In *Proceedings of the International Semantic Web Working Symposium (SWWS)*, July 2001.
2. K. S. Barber and J. Kim. Belief revision process based on trust: Agents evaluating reputation of information sources. In R. Falcone, M. P. Singh, and Y.-H. Tan, editors, *Trust in Cybersocieties*, volume 2246 of *LNAI*, pages 73–82. Springer-Verlag, 2001.
3. R. Bonnell, M. Huhns, L. Stephens, and U. Mukhopadhyay. MINDS: Multiple intelligent node document servers. In *Proceedings of the 1st IEEE International Conference on Office Automation*, pages 125–136, 1984.

4. C. Castelfranchi and Y.-H. Tan. The role of trust and deception in virtual societies. In *Proceedings of the 34th Hawaii International Conference on System Sciences (HICSS 34)*, volume 7, pages 7011–7018. IEEE Computer Society Press, Jan. 2001.
5. R. Falcone and C. Castelfranchi. The socio-cognitive dynamics of trust: Does trust create trust? In R. Falcone, M. Singh, and Y.-H. Tan, editors, *Trust in Cyber-societies*, LNAI 2246, pages 55–72. Springer-Verlag, 2001.
6. C. M. Jonker and J. Treur. Formal analysis of models for the dynamics of trust based on experiences. In *Proceedings of the 9th European Workshop on Modelling Autonomous Agents in a Multi-Agent World, (MAAMAW)*, LNAI 1647, pages 221–232. Springer Verlag, 1999.
7. H. Kautz, B. Selman, and M. Shah. ReferralWeb: Combining social networks and collaborative filtering. *Communications of the ACM*, 40(3):63–65, Mar. 1997.
8. B. A. Misztal. *Trust in Modern Societies*. Blackwell Publishers, Cambridge, MA, 1996.
9. B. A. Nardi, S. Whittaker, and H. Schwarz. It's not what you know, it's who you know :Work in the information age. *First Monday*, 5(5), May 2000.
10. J. M. Pujol, R. Sangüesa, and J. Delgado. Extracting reputation in multi agent systems by means of social network topology. In *Proceedings of the 1st International Joint Conference on Autonomous Agents and Multiagent Systems (AAMAS)*, pages 467–474. ACM Press, July 2002.
11. J. Sabater and C. Sierra. Reputation and social network analysis in multi-agent systems. In *Proceedings of the 1st International Joint Conference on Autonomous Agents and Multiagent Systems (AAMAS)*, pages 475–482. ACM Press, July 2002.
12. R. S. Sandhu. Lattice-based access control models. *IEEE Computer*, pages 9–19, Nov. 1993.
13. S. Sen and N. Sajja. Robustness of reputation-based trust: Boolean case. In *Proceedings of the 1st International Joint Conference on Autonomous Agents and Multiagent Systems (AAMAS)*, pages 288–293. ACM Press, July 2002.
14. M. P. Singh, B. Yu, and M. Venkatraman. Community-based service location. *Communications of the ACM*, 44(4):49–54, Apr. 2001.
15. P. Sztompka. *Trust: A Sociological Theory*. Cambridge University Press, UK, 1999.
16. R. Wille. Why can concept lattices support knowledge discovery in databases? In *Proceedings of the International Workshop on Lattice-based theory, methods and tools for Knowledge Discovery in Databases*, pages 7–20, 2001.
17. P. Yolum and M. P. Singh. Emergent properties of referral systems. In *Proceedings of the 2nd International Joint Conference on Autonomous Agents and MultiAgent Systems (AAMAS)*, pages 592–599. ACM Press, July 2003.
18. P. Yolum and M. P. Singh. Self-organizing referral networks: A process view of trust and authority. In G. D. M. Serugendo, A. Karageorgos, O. F. Rana, and F. Zambonelli, editors, *Engineering Self-Organising Systems: Nature-Inspired Approaches to Software Engineering*, volume 2977, pages 195–211. Springer Verlag, 2004.
19. B. Yu and M. P. Singh. An evidential model of distributed reputation management. In *Proceedings of the 1st International Joint Conference on Autonomous Agents and MultiAgent Systems (AAMAS)*, pages 294–301. ACM Press, July 2002.

Detecting Violators of Multi-party Contracts

Lai Xu[1] and Manfred A. Jeusfeld[2]

[1] Free University, Department of Computer Science,
De Boelelaan 1081a, 1081 HV Amsterdam.
xu@few.vu.nl
[2] Tilburg University, CRISM/Infolab
5000 LE, Tilburg.
Manfred.Jeusfeld@uvt.nl

Abstract. In the business world, business coordinations are becoming global, execution of multi-party contracts has to be considered a vital point for successful business coordinations. The need for a new multi-party contract model is thus becoming evident. However, there is little known on how to formally model a multi-party contract. In this paper, we investigate how a contract involving multilateral parties can be modeled more easily for finding the contract responsible for given contract violations.

1 Introduction

In the business world, business coordinations are becoming global, execution of multi-party contracts has to be considered a vital point for successful business coordinations. The need for a new multi-party contract model is thus becoming evident. A two-party contract is not able to specify multilateral contractual relations. Most research [8], [5] on multi-party contracts tries to break down a multi-party contract into a number of bilateral contracts. A principle cause behind this is that current e-commerce environments only support bilateral executions. In some simple cases, the approach to supporting multi-party contract execution in current e-commerce environments, is to assume the whole business process goes correctly according to a number of bilateral contracts. However, in complicated multi-party relationships, this conversion results in information of relations being lost or hidden. Consequently this option to split the contracts up into several two-party agreements will not work for these complex multi-party contracts.

In a bilateral contract execution process it is easier to establish the responsible party for a given contract violation. In a multi-party business process, a contract violation can be as a result of a set of actions that did not occur. It can be caused by direct and indirect contractual parties. This thus raises the issue of finding all responsible partners for the aforementioned contract violation.

An agent-mediated e-commerce environment is regarded as one of the most suitable open environments for electronic marketplaces [15]. Agent-mediated e-marketplaces can lift the barrier of two-party e-commerce environments. As such the limits of more traditional e-commerce environments need no longer apply. Our research thus focuses on how to model multi-party contracts in a manner convenient detection of the parties responsible for a contract violation.

Various authors have proposed electronic contract models or languages based on different views. Kimbrough and Moore formalize and extend speech act theory as Formal Language for Business Communication (FLBC)[10] [13]. *Deontic logic* based contract models [21] [14] [12] [18] [22] describes obligations, permissions, and forbiddances for finishing a business process. CrossFlow [11] and E-ADOME[9] use contracts for inter-organizational workflow process integration. Contracts in CrossFlow and E-ADOME describe the agreed workflow interfaces as activities and transitions, based on WfMC's WPDL (Workflow Process Definition Language). Contracts also specify what data objects in the remote workflow are readable or updateable. Grosof discussed a rule-based approach [7] to representation business contracts, which also deal with exceptions. They are a side effect of business automations, and as for now do not address the multi-party situation and particularly do not looking into detecting contract violators. Although we presented a method to detect contract violators in paper [25], the concept of a role properties is not included. Therefore, the multi-party contract model in this paper is extended. The algorithm of detecting contract violators is changed consequently.

In this paper, we present a multi-party contract model and provide how to detect responsible parties for a multi-party contract violation by using our model. In Section 2 a standard multi-party car insurance case [16] is used to explain our model and to show that in a multi-partner contract it is more important and more difficult to find the responsible parties for a contract violation than in a bilateral contract. Section 3 introduces our multi-party contract model. A concept of contract violation, a detection method of a contract violation and some examples for using this method are presented in Section 4. The paper ends with conclusions and a short discussion of further work in Section 5.

2 Multi-party Contract Case

This case outlines the manner in which a car damage claim is handled by an insurance company (AGFIL). The contract parties work together to provide a service level which facilitates efficient claim settlement. The parties involved are called Euro Assist, Lee Consulting Services, Garages and Assessors. Euro Assist offers a 24-hour emergency call answering service to policyholders. Lee C.S. co-ordinates and manages the operation of the emergency service on a day-to-day level on behalf of AGFIL. Garages are responsible for car repair. Assessors conduct the physical inspections of damaged vehicles and agree upon repair figures with the garages.

The general process of a car insurance case is described as follows: the policyholder phones Euro Assist using a toll-free phone number to notify a new claim. Euro Assist will register the information, suggest an appropriate garage, and notify AGFIL, which will check whether the policy is valid and covers this claim. After AGFIL receives this claim, AGFIL sends the claim details to Lee C.S. AGFIL will send a letter to the policyholder for a completed claim form. Lee C.S. will agree upon repair costs if an assessor is not required for small damages; otherwise, an assessor will be assigned. The assessor will check the damaged vehicle and agree upon repair costs with the garage. After receiving an agreement for repairing the car from Lee C.S., the garage will then commence repairs. After finishing repairs, the garage will issue an invoice to Lee C.S., which will check the invoice against the original estimate. Lee C.S. returns all invoices to AGFIL. After AGFIL also receives the completed claim form from the policyholder, the payment is processed. In the whole process, if the claim is found invalid, all contractual parties will be contacted and the process will be stopped.

There are many potential contract violations in this case, for example, after sending invoices to Lee C.S., the garage does not get money back from AGFIL. It could be caused by

- Lee C.S., because Lee C.S. does not forward the invoices to AGFIL;
- policyholder, because the policyholder did not return the completed claim form to AGFIL;
- AGFIL, because AGFIL forgot to send the claim form to the policyholder or simply because AGFIL did not pay the garage in time.

or any combination from above.

The case study shows a rather complex business process between multiple parties. In particular, we provide an example that the contract violation could be caused by multiple parties.

3 Multi-party Contract Model

A contract is an agreement between two or more parties that is binding to those parties and that is based on mutual commitments [22]. Our multi-party contract model consists of three core components: actions, commitments and a commitment graph [26], [23], [25]. An *action* describes what each partner should do. A *commitment* in this paper is defined as a guarantee by one party towards another party that some action sequence shall be executed completely, and all involved parties fulfill their side of the transaction. A *commitment graph* is an overview of the commitments between parties, which shows commitment relationships in a contract. These components will be explained in turn in the next sections.

3.1 Actions

Contractual parties perform actions as an imposed requirement which often have restrictions on the contract. An action is an atom in our contract model. The contract is explained by a set of commitments, a contractual party can thus be involved in different commitments and play the different roles, we specify the roles of a party as $\mathcal{R}$. A set of total roles of a contract is denoted as $\mathbb{R}$.

Definition 1. *A party can act under different roles in different commitments. Let ID be a domain of identifier;* **roles of a party** $\mathcal{R}_x$ *is defined as*

$$\mathcal{R}_x \subseteq ID.$$

Let $\mathcal{P}$ *be a set of parties, the* **set of all roles** *is*

$$\mathbb{R} = \bigcup_{\forall x \in \mathcal{P}} \mathcal{R}_x.$$

The roles will form the nodes in commitment graphs.

Definition 2. *Let* $\mathbb{R}$ *be a set of all roles of all parties, ID be the domain ID, and* $\mathbb{T}$ *be the time. An* **action** *is specified as*

$$action = (name, sender, receiver, deadline),$$

where $name \in ID$, $sender, receiver \in \mathbb{R}$ *and* $deadline \in \mathbb{T}$. *We require all names of actions to be unique so they can be used as identifiers.*

A set of actions $\mathbb{A}$ *for a contract can be specified as*

$$\mathbb{A} = \bigcup_{\forall x \in \mathcal{P}} \{action\}.$$

The actions will form the edges in commitment graphs.

For example, action (A_agreeRepairCar,L,G",3.5) describes that Lee C.S. agrees the garage to repair the car during the car damage claim received 3.5 days. For the car insurance case, all actions are specified in [24]. Actions will form the edges in commitment graphs. Although only a single receiver of the action are specified in this car insurance case, a list of action receivers can be extend in this model.

We have explained that different contractual parties play different roles. Each role has a set of pre-determined properties, whose values are part of the contract. To specify the role properties in our contract model is a significant different with a multi-party contract model in paper [25]. The role property consists of three parts which are inputs, outputs and rules of the role property. The inputs and outputs of the role properties are domain related. The rules of the role properties are specified as the set of rules using predicate logic. The input of the role property determines the actions that a contractual party will take as a means of the fulfill its operations which have specified in the contract. The output of the role property determines the objects which are the results of the executing action. When the role attempts to execute an action, it first checks whether the input of the role property is satisfied, and subsequently generate the output of the role property.

Each role specifis values of input and output of the role property, e.g. input element *ClaimForm* indicates a empty claim form and input element *ClaimForm*$_{fi}$ illustrate a filled claim form with policyholder's data and signature. The rules of the role properties are specified as the set of rules using predicate logic. The conditions of the rules can be a conjection of the inputs of the role properties or a conjection of the inputs of the role properties and actions. For example, in the car insurance case, the garage (G') plays a repairer role in the repair service commitment C_dailyService. The input of the role property for G' is "$Car_{damaged}$" (i.e. G' receiving a damaged car). According to the rule $Car_{damaged} \rightarrow$ A_estimateRepairCost, the garage G' will fulfill the action A_estimateRepairCost after received the damaged car $Car_{damaged}$. According to the rule A_estimateRepairCost $\rightarrow estimatedRC$, the occurrence of A_estimateRepairCost will cause that the garage knows the estimated repair cost $estimatedRC$. All properties of the roles in the car insurance case are shown in Table 1.

A formal definition of the role property is specified as

Definition 3. *Let $\mathbb{R}$ be the set of all roles, $\mathbb{I}$ be the set of all information or objects involved in the contract. The condition of the rule is specified as*

$$condition = \cap \{input\} \cup \{action\}$$

where input $\in \mathbb{I}$; action $\in \mathbb{A}$. The result of the rule is specified as

$$result = \{action \wedge output\}$$

where action $\in \mathbb{A}$; output $\in \mathbb{I}$. The rule is specified as

$$rule = \bigcup_{\exists role \in \mathbb{R}, \forall input, output \in \mathbb{I}} \{(condition, result)\}$$

where role $\in \mathbb{R}$; input, output $\in \mathbb{I}$; action $\in \mathbb{A}$. The set of all rules $\mathbb{V}$ in the role properties is

$$\mathbb{V} = \bigcup_{\forall role \in \mathbb{R}} \{rule\}.$$

The role property is specified as

$$property = (role, input, output, rules)$$

where role $\in \mathbb{R}$; input, output $\in \mathbb{I}$; and rules $\in \mathbb{V}$.

A set of role properties $\mathbb{P}$ for a contract can be specified as

$$\mathbb{P} = \bigcup_{\forall role \in \mathbb{R}} \{property\}.$$

The next section specifies commitments that are the key part of contracts.

3.2 Commitments

In this paper, a commitment is a guarantee by one party towards another party that some action sequence shall be executed completely provided that some

Table 1. Role properties of the car insurance case

Role	Role Properties		
	Input	Output	Rules
P'	assignedG, Car_{fixed}.	Claim, Records1, $Car_{damaged}$.	$PS_1 \rightarrow$ Claim; $PS_2 \rightarrow$ Records1; assignedG $\wedge RS_1 \rightarrow Car_{damaged}$.
P''	ClaimForm	ClaimForm$_{fi}$	ClaimForm $\rightarrow PR_2(CF_3)$; $PR_2(CF_3) \rightarrow$ ClaimForm$_{fi}$.
E	Records1	assignedG, Records2	Records1 $\rightarrow PS_3$; $PS_3 \rightarrow$ assignedG; Recards1 $\wedge$ assignedG $\wedge PS_4(CF_1) \rightarrow$ Records2.
AG	Records2, ClaimForm$_{fi}$, Invoice.	Records3, ClaimForm, Payment.	Records2 $\rightarrow DS_1$; Records2 $\rightarrow CF_2$; $DS_1 \rightarrow$ Records3; $CF_2 \rightarrow$ ClaimForm; ClaimForm$_{fi} \wedge$ Invoice $\rightarrow PR_3$; $PR_3 \rightarrow$ Payment.

L	Records3, estimatedRC, NewRC, Invoice.	assignedA, agreeRepair(RC), Invoice.	Records3 $\rightarrow DS_2$;
			 if estimatedRC > 500 **then**
			 {estimatedRC $\rightarrow DS_4(IC_1)$;
			 $DS_4(IC_1) \rightarrow$ assignedA;
			 $NewRC \rightarrow DS_6(RS_3)_{RC=NewRC}$;
			 $DS_6(RS_3)_{RC=NewRC} \rightarrow$ agreeRepair(NewRC)}
			
			 if estimatedRC $\leq$ 500 **then**
			 { estimatedRC $\leq$ 500 $\rightarrow$
			 $DS_6(RS_3)_{RC=estimatedRC}$;
			 $DS_6(RS_3)_{RC=estimatedRC} \rightarrow$ agreeRepair(estimatedRC)}
			
			 Invoice $\rightarrow DS_9(PR_1)$;
			 $DS_9(PR_1) \rightarrow$ Invoice.

A	assignedA	NewRC	assignedA $\rightarrow IC_2$; $IC_2 \rightarrow$ NewRC.
G'	$Car_{damaged}$, agreeRepair$_{RC}$.	estimatedRC', Car_{fixed}	$Car_{damaged} \rightarrow RS_2$; $RS_2 \rightarrow$ estimatedRC'; agreeRepair(RC) $\rightarrow RS_4(DS_7)$; $RS_4(DS_7) \rightarrow Car_{fixed}$.
G''	estimatedRC'	Invoice, estimatedRC	estimatedRC' $\wedge DS_2 \rightarrow DS_3$; $DS_3 \rightarrow$ emtimatedRC $DS_8 \rightarrow$ Invoice .
G'''	Payment		

"trigger, involve, and finish" action happens, and all involved parties fulfill their side of the transaction. To finish a commitment, more than one party must finish relevant actions. From this point of view, the concept of our commitment is differ from the definition of a commitment in papers [20], [17], which a commitment only refers to two parties, a debtor and a creditor [20], or a vendor and customer [17]. The notion of commitment in this paper is not related to beliefs, desires, or intentions [2]. In Cohen and Levesque's research, commitments are related to establishing common beliefs about a certain state of the world. In our multi-party contract model, we do not reason about beliefs of the contractual parties involved, which Daskalopulu did in evidence-based contract performance monitoring research [4]. We also do not assess the of legal status and directives in business process automation [1].

A multi-party contract includes one or more commitments, a commitment includes some actions which could be performed by multi-parties. Those actions can trigger, involve, and finish the commitment. For example, in the car repair service commitment, the garage first needs to receive the policyholder's car as a trigger of this commitment. The actions included in a commitment thus have different attributes, which we specify as *trigger, involve and finish*. In a contract preparation stage, the actions with "trigger" attribute need to be paid attentions whether some "enforceable" or "compensable" clauses are required for smoothly fulfilling the contract. The actions with "finish" attribute eventually finish the commitment. A commitment is described by a commitment name, sender of the commitment, receiver of the commitment.

Definition 4. *Actions' attributes $\mathcal{U}$ can be specified as*

$$\mathcal{U} = \{tr, in, fi\}.$$

Let ID be the domain ID, $\mathcal{P}$ be a set of parties, $N = \{1, 2, 3, \ldots\}$, $\mathbb{A}$ be a set of actions. A **commitment** is specified as

$$commitment = (name, sender, receiver, n, \{(a_1, u_1), (a_2, u_2), \ldots, (a_n, u_n) :$$
$$a_i \in \mathbb{A}, u_i \in \mathcal{U}\}).$$

where name is an identifier, $name \in ID$; sender and receiver are the contract parties, $sender, receiver \in \mathcal{P}$; n denotes the total number of all actions involved, $n \in N$; $a_1, a_2, \ldots, a_n$ denotes all actions involved in the commitment and their attributes $u_1, u_2, \ldots, u_n$. We require all names of commitments to be unique so that they can be used as identifiers.

A set of commitments $\mathbb{M}$ can be specified as

$$\mathbb{M} = \bigcup_{\forall x \in \mathcal{P}} \{commitment\}.$$

Let $a_i \in \mathbb{A}$ and $m \in \mathbb{M}$, a sequence function $f_{position} : \mathbb{A} \times \mathbb{M} \to N$,

$$f_{position}(a_i, m) = \begin{cases} i & \text{iff } i \text{ is the sequence number} \\ & \text{of action } a_i \text{ in commitment } m. \\ undef & \text{otherwise.} \end{cases}$$

$f_{position}(a_i, m)$ denotes the position of action a_i in the commitment m.

For example, in commitment C_repairService, the garage will offer the repair service to the policyholder. After the policyholder sends his/her car to the garage (action A_sendCar has a trigger attribute), the garage estimates the repair cost (action A_estimateRepairCost has a finish attribute). After the garage receives an agreement from Lee C.S. about the repair cost (action A_agreeRepairCar has a trigger attribute), the garage repairs the car (action A_repairCar has a finish attribute). Commitment C_repairService is specified as

$$(\text{C\_repairService}, G, P, \{(\text{A\_sendCar}, tr), (\text{A\_estimateRepairCost}, fi), (\text{A\_agreeRepairCar}, tr), (\text{A\_repairCar}, fi)\})$$

For the car insurance case, all commitments are specified in [24]. The actions and commitments can be regard as a direct mapping from a paper contract to an e-contract. Information of the actions and commitments can compare with contents between "< $action$ >" and "< /$action$ >" in TPA(Trading Partner Agreement) [3] from ebXML. The difference is that we specify a multi-party contractual process using the commitment concept, and TPA only specifies bilateral business process.

3.3 Commitment Graph

Commitments are an even more important concept, though, to specify multi-party contracts. A commitment graph shows complex relationships among commitments. Commitment relationships are not only about a condition [19] or a chain [20] [17] relationship. For example, if a contractee first ships goods to a contractor, the contractor will pay the cost of goods later; the commitment of shipping goods is a condition to activate a commitment of payment.

Figure 1 shows the commitment graph for the car insurance case. Table 2 provides all abbreviations and labels used in this commitment graph. For all notes of this commitment graph, we use the following abbreviations: P' and P'' for a policyholder, AG for AGFIL, E for Euro Assist, L for Lee C.S., G', G'' and G''' for garage, and A for assessor. Each note represents a role that can be played by a contractual partner.

The abbreviations for the commitments can be found from Table 2. Each edge represents an action. Each action has one or more labels, where the first letter represents which commitments this action actually involves, the second number represents the order of a sequence actions within a commitment.

Being able to show how the commitment graph presents the complex commitment relationship, we give an example which shows a relationship between commitments C_repairService (repair service commitment) and C_dailyService (daily service commitment).

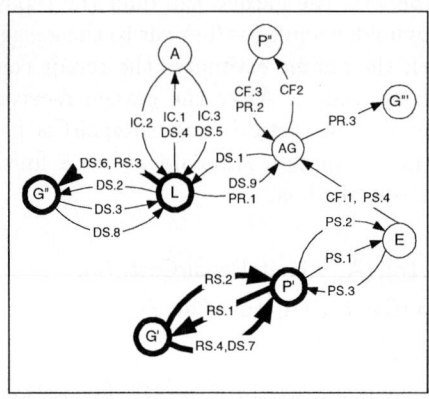 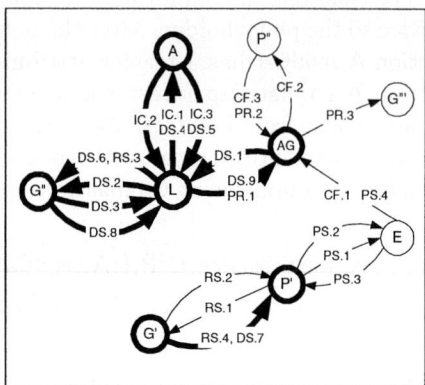

(a) Highlight repair service commitment C_repairService

(b) Highlight daily service commitment C_dailyService

Fig. 1. Commitment graphs

According to Section 3.2, C_repairService and C_dailyService are specified as follows:

(C_repairService, G, P, {(A_sendCar, tr), (A_estimateRepairCost, fi),

(⌊A_agreeRepairCar⌋, tr), (⌊A_repairCar⌋, fi)})

(C_dailyService, L, AG, {(A_forwardClaim, tr), (A_contactGarage, in),

(A_sendRepairCost, in), (A_assignAssessor, in),

(A_sendNewRepairCost, tr), (⌊A_agreeRepairCar⌋, fi),

(⌊A_repairCar⌋, tr), (A_sendInvoices, in),

(A_forwardInvoices, fi)}).

In Figure 1 (a) and (b), edge $RS3$ and $DS6$ both denote A_agreeRepairCar according Table 2. It means that A_agreeRepairCar is included in C_repairService as the third action ($R3$) and in C_dailyService as the sixth action ($DS6$). Another edge $RS4$ and $DS7$ both indicates A_repairCar. It means that A_agreeRepairCar is also included in C_repairService as the fourth action ($RS4$) and in C_dailyService as the seventh action ($DS7$).

The relationship between C_repairService and C_dailyService is a mixed relationship: after role L agrees with the repair costs in C_dailyService, the role G' can repair the car in C_repairService; after the role G' repairs the car and role G'' sends the invoice, C_dailyService will go on to execute its following actions. Commitments C_repairService and C_dailyService are mutually dependent on each other.

Table 2. Commitments, actions and action abbreviations

Commitment	Classification of Actions and Commitments			Labels
	Trigger	Involve	Finish	
C_phoneService (PS)	A_phoneClaim			PS.1
		A_receiveInfo		PS.2
			A_assignGarage	PS.3
			A_notifyClaim	PS.4, CF.1
C_repairService (RS)	A_sendCar			RS.1
		A_estimateRepairCost		RS.2
	A_agreeRepairCar			RS.3, DS.6
			A_repairCar	RS.4, DS.7
C_claimForm (CF)	A_notifyClaim			CF.1, PS.4
		A_sendClaimForm		CF.2
			A_returnClaimForm	CF.3, PR.2
C_dailyService (DS)	A_forwardClaim			DS.1
		A_contactGarage		DS.2
		A_sendRepairCost		DS.3
		A_assignAssessor		DS.4, IC.1
		A_sendNewRepairCost		DS.5, IC.3
			A_agreeRepairCar	DS.6, RS.3
	A_repairCar			DS.7, RS.4
		A_sendInvoices		DS.8
			A_forwardInvoices	DS.9, PR.1
C_inspectCar (IC)	A_assignAssessor			IC.1, DS.4
		A_inspectCar		IC.2
			A_sendNewRepairCost	IC.3, DS.5
C_payRepairCost (PR)	A_forwardInvoices			PR.1, DS.9
	A_returnClaimForm			PR.2, CF.3
			A_payRepairCost	PR.3

A commitment graph is a directed graph consisting of a set of nodes corresponding to all roles $\mathbb{R}$, a set of edges corresponding to actions and their labels, and commitment orders.

Definition 5. *Let $\mathbb{A}$ be a set of actions, $a \in \mathbb{A}$, $\mathbb{M}$ be a set of commitments, $m \in \mathbb{M}$, and $X = \{1, 2, \ldots\}$, a sequence function $f_{position}(a, m)$, an edge is specified as a relation from $\mathbb{A} \times \mathbb{M} \times X$*

$$edge = \bigcup_{\forall m \in \mathbb{M}, a \in \mathbb{A}} \{(a, m, f_{position}(a, m)) : a \in \mathbb{A}, m \in \mathbb{M}, f_{position}(a, m) \in X\},$$

a set of all edges is

$$\mathbb{E} = \bigcup_{\forall a \in \mathbb{A}} \{edge\}.$$

Definition 6. *Let $\mathbb{M}$ be a set of commitments. A commitment occurrence order is specified as a relation from $\mathbb{M} \times \mathbb{M}$:*

$$order\_commitment = \{(m_1 \cdot m_2) : m_1, m_2 \in \mathbb{M}, m_1 \neq m_2\}.$$

If $m_1 \cdot m_2$ is a commitment order, we interpret it as follows: commitment m_2 is only active when commitment m_1 has been finished.

Let $\mathcal{P}$ be a set of parties. A set of commitment orders lists all relationships in which a commitment occurs prior to another commitment, and is specified as follows:

$$\mathbb{O} = \bigcup_{\forall x \in \mathcal{P}} \{(m_1 \cdot m_2)\}.$$

For the car insurance case, examples of the commitment orders are presented in [24]. After specification of commitment graph notes, edges, and commitment occurrence orders, the commitment graph can be specified as follows:

Definition 7. *Let $\mathbb{R}$ be a set of nodes, $\mathbb{E}$ be a set of edges, and $\mathbb{O}$ be a set of commitment order list. The commitment graph is defined as follows*

$$G = (\mathbb{R}, \mathbb{E}, \mathbb{O}).$$

3.4 Multi-party Contract

Now that all elements of our multi-party contract model have been presented, a formal model is provided as follows:

Definition 8. *Let $\mathbb{A}$ be a set of actions, $\mathbb{M}$ be a set of commitments and G be a commitment graph of a contract. The multi-party contract is specified as*

$$Contract = \{\mathbb{A}, \mathbb{M}, G\}.$$

The next section will illustrate how to detect responsible parties after a contract violation.

4 Contract Violations and Detections

In the contract execution stage, detecting contract violations and figuring out the contract violators are the most important monitoring tasks. Section 4.1 discusses some special issues of contract violations in a multi-party relationship. The detection method is introduced in Section 4.2.

4.1 Contract Violations

Contract violations refer to break or fail to comply with a term of the contract by contractual parties. The contract violation can caused by more than one contractual parties in a contract execution, it thus becomes an essential problem for the contract automations. For example, in the car insurance case, the policyholder sent the car to the assigned garage. After the prescribed days, the policyholder find that his/her car did not fixed by the garage at all. Obviously the policyholder will directly complain to the garage. Actually, after sending an estimated repairing cost of the car to the Lee C.S., the garage maybe did not receive an agree-repair message from Lee C.S. Well, because the estimated repairing cost was too high, Lee C.S. have to send an assessor to check the car again. However, the assessor did not do his/her job properly. From the contract execution point of view, this contract violation is caused by the assessor, but Lee C.S. and the garage should take care of the deadline of repairing the car. In this example, the garage did not repair the car in time, which is directly caused by the assessor. In another scenario, after receiving an estimated repairing cost, Lee C.S. simple forget to send an agree repair information to the garage. The direct violator, in this scenario, is Lee C.S.

Normally the contract violations are found by any contractual parties or a contract monitor. Obviously inputs of role properties can missed in someway during the contract execution, e.g. Lee C.S. does not receive a forwarded record of the damaged car. Lee C.S. thus does not start its daily service commitment. More precisely, missing any input of role properties will become a potential contract violation at the particular contract.

4.2 Detecting Responsible Parties of the Contract Violation

The most common detection process is to retrieve all actions that should have already occurred [6]. Although it is a solution, this process is rather inefficient. Our approach is that use of a commitment graph and role properties to detect responsible parties for the contract violation.

After a contractual party finished a certain action, the party is waiting for a input of the role property. The process of detecting responsible partners of a contract violation has the following steps. The contractual party, who is playing a particular role, check this violation from the role property's input. If the violation is located at the role property's input, the outputs of other role properties, which have the same name as the input of the role property, need to be found. The action which actually causes this output of the role property need to be checked. If the action does not occur and the condition of rule to occur the action is true, the sender of the action is the responsible party. Using this input continues to follow the above steps until the known facts have met. The detecting responsible parties of the contract violation is presented in Algorithm 1. We use three typical scenarios to explain our algorithm.

First Scenario and Detecting Progress. In the car insurance case, after Lee C.S. contacted the garage, the garage did not send the estimated repair cost to Lee C.S.

Input: $Contract = \{\mathbb{A}, \mathbb{M}, G\}$
$action\_of\_missing$ =A_sendRepairCost (DS_3), which should be performed by role G'.
$action\_of\_done$ = A_contactGarage (DS_2), which is finished by the role L.

Initialization: $potential\_missing\_commitments = \emptyset$
$finished\_commitments = \emptyset$
$action\_need\_checked = \emptyset$

Algorithm 1 Detecting Responsible Parties of the Contract Violation

Input: $Contract = \{\mathbb{A}, \mathbb{M}, G\}$
$action\_of\_missing,$ ▷ an action which an contractual party fail to
▷ occur, $action\_of\_missing \in \mathbb{A}$.
$action\_of\_done$ ▷ $action\_of\_done \in \mathbb{A}$.

Initialization: $potential\_missing\_commitments = \emptyset$
$finished\_commitments = \emptyset$

Step 1:
▷ according to $action\_of\_done$, to identify which previous commitments
▷ belong to $potential\_missing\_commitment$ or $finished\_commitment$.
identify the $action\_of\_done$ involved in which commitments.
if there exists previous commitments (which before the $action\_of\_done'$ commitments) **then**
    if the previous commitments are completed **then**
        put the previous commitments into $finished\_commitments$.
    else
        put the previous commitments into $potential\_missing\_commitments$.
    end if
else if there exists mixed or embedded commitments (with the $action\_of\_done$'s commitment)s **then**
    if the mixed or embedded commitments are triggered **then**
        if the mixed or embedded commitments are completed **then**
            put the mixed or embedded commitments into $finished\_commitments$.
        end if
    else
        put the mixed or embedded commitments into $potential\_missing\_commitments$.
    end if
end if

Step2:
according to $action\_of\_missing$ and $finished\_commitments$,
update $potential\_missing\_commitments$.

Step3:
for each $potential\_missing\_commitments$ **do**
    for each involved role **do**
        if action a' (from this role) was occurred **then**
            check the role properties $(input, a')$
            if the $input$ has received **then**
                return(this roles as a violator)
            else
                check which role (r') is responsible for this input. $\{\exists r' \exists o, (r', o) \in property, o = input\}$
                according to the rule of the role property, identify the involved commitment and put it into $potential\_missing\_commitments$
            end if
        end if
    end for
end for

Step1:
Start with $action_of_done = $ A_contactGarage (DS_2).
In the commitment $\mathbb{M}$, we specify the commitment order $\mathbb{O}$,
(C_phoneService · C_dailyService) $\in \mathbb{O}$, and commitment C_phoneService is the only commitment before commitment C_repairService.
According to DS_1, the PS_4(action A_notifyClaim with "fi") is finished.
another action A_assignGarage with "fi" in the commitment C_phoneService is PS_3, which is not yet known whether or not have been performed.
thus PS_3(action A_assignGarage) need to keep in the set of $action\_need\_checked$, i.e. $action\_need\_checked = \{PS_3\}$
$finished\_commitment = \emptyset$
$potential\_missing\_commitments = \{$C_phoneService, C_dailyService$\}$

Step2:
$action\_of\_missing(DS_3)$ and $action\_of\_done(DS_2)$ involved in the same commitment C_dailyService

Step3:
Role G'' fails to perform action A_estimateRepairCost (DS_3), check the property of role G''', "estimatedRC'" did not received,
thus action RS_2(A_estimateRepairCost) is checked,
$potential\_missing\_commitments = \{$C_phoneService, C_repairService$\}$
for $\forall x, x \in potential\_missing\_commitments$ **do**
    if role G' has received the input "Car$_{damaged}$" **then**
        return(G' is a violator)
    else
        checking action RS_1 (A_sendCar)
        if role P' has received the input "assigned" $\wedge RS_1$ does not occur **then**
            return(P' is a violator)
        else
            checking action PS_3 (A_assignGarage)
            if role E has not performed this action **then**
                return(E is a violator)
            end if
        end if
    end if
end for

Second Scenario and Detecting Progress. In the car insurance case, the policyholder sent the car to the assigned garage. After the prescribed days, the policyholder finds that the garage did not repair his/her car at all.
    Input: $Contract = \{\mathbb{A}, \mathbb{M}, G\}$
                    $action_of_missing = $A_repairCar (RS_4/DS_7), which should be performed by role G'.
                    $action_of_done = $A_sendCar (RS_1), which is finished by the role P'.
    Initialization: $potential\_missing\_commitments = \emptyset$
                          $finished\_commitments = \emptyset$

Step1:
Start with $action_of_done = $ A_sendCar.
According to the label of action A_repairCar, the action involved in commtiments C_repairService and C_dailyService.
$pontential\_missing\_commitments = \{$C_repairService, C_dailyService$\}$
In the commitment $\mathbb{M}$, we specify the commitment order $\mathbb{O}$, (C_phoneService · C_repairService) $\in \mathbb{O}$, and commitment C_phoneService is the only commitment before commitment C_repairService.
According to RS_1, the PS_3(action A_assignGarage with "fi") is finished.
another action with "fi" in the commitment C_phoneService is PS_4, which is not yet known whether or not have been performed.
thus PS_4(action A_notifyClaim) need to keep in the set of $action\_need\_checked$, i.e. $action\_need\_checked = \{PS_4\}$
$finished\_commitment = \emptyset$
$potential\_missing\_commitments = \{$C_phoneService$\}$

Step2:
$action_of_missing = $ (A_repairCar)(RS_4/DS_7)
$potential\_missing\_commitments = \{$C_repairService, C_dailyService, C_phoneService$\}$

Step3:
In commitment C_repairService (G', P', L),
    for role G', checking action RS_2(A_estimateRepairCost)
    for role L, checking action RS_3/DS_6(A_agreeRepairCar)
In commitment C_dailyService (G'''', G'', L, A, P')
    for role G''', checking $none$
    for role G'''', checking action DS_3(A_sendRepairCost)
    for role L, checking action DS_2(A_contactGarage), DS_4(A_assignAssessor)
    (which will involved C_inspectCar into $potential\_missing\_commitments$)
    and DS_6(A_agreeRepairCar).
In commitment C_inspectCar (A, L),
    for role A, checking IC_2(A_inspectCar) and IC_3(A_sendNewRepairCost)

Third Scenario and Detecting Progress. In the car insurance case, the policyholder sent the car to the assigned garage. After the prescribed days, the policyholder finds that the garage did not repair his/her car at all.
    Input: $Contract = \{\mathbb{A}, \mathbb{M}, \mathbb{G}\}$
                $action_of_missing = $A_payRepairCost (PS_3), which should be performed by role AG.
                $action_of_done = $ A_sendInvoices (DS_8), which is finished by the role G'''.
    Initialization: $potential\_missing\_commitments = \emptyset$
                        $finished\_commitments = \emptyset$

Step1:
Start with $action_of_done = $ A_sendInvoices.
According to the labeling of actions in commitment C_dailyService,

A_sendNewRepairCost $DS_5(IC_3)$ should have done before (DS_8), thus commitment C_inspectCar has been finished; and A_repairCar $DS_7(RS_4)$ has been finished. According the commitment C_repairService, (C_phoneService · C_repairService) $\in \mathbb{O}$, commitment C_phoneService has been finished as well.
$finished\_commitment = \{$C_inspectCar, C_repairService, C_phoneService$\}$
$potential\_missing\_commitments = \emptyset$
Step2:
$action_of_missing = $ A_payRepairCost(PS_3), which involved in the
         commitment C_payRepairCost.
$potential_missing_commitments = $ C_payRepairCost
Step3:
In commitment C_payRepairCost,
    for role p'' checking action A_returnClaimForm $(PR_2(CF_3))$. Action A_returnClaimForm also belongs to another commitment C_claimForm
    for role L, checking action A_forwardInvoices $(DS_9(PS_1))$,
    for role AG, checking action A_payRepairCost (PS_3).
In commitment C_claimForm,
    for role AG, checking action A_notifyClaim $(CF_1(PS_4))$.

The section explained the concept of the contract violation and the detection process that makes it possible to detect the parties responsible for a contract violation. This approach uses the multi-party contract model, particularly the commitment graph, to improve the efficiency of the detection process.

5 Conclusions

This paper proposes an approach to formalizing multi-party electronic contracts for the purpose of detecting contractual violators. The multi-party contract model consists of three parts. The first part is formed by the so-called actions. The second part of the contract is the commitments which are essentially guarantees by one partner to another partner that some action sequence will occur. Finally, the commitment graph is used to specify the relationships between commitments. We provide a method using the commitment graph to trace back the commitments after a contract violation and to locate the partners who violated the commitments. This research also provides a foundation for representing and automating contractual deals on web services, so as to help search, select and compose them.

Further research has to be undertaken in the area of pre-calculating the costs of multi-party contract violations from one contractual party point of view. Because of the autonomous, reactive and proactive features of agents, they can act on behalf of their owners and use individual strategies to handle conflicts between multiple contract executions. Some agents may use a remedial mechanism which might return the business processes to a normal course of action after a contract violation. How to pre-calculate the cost of the contract violation and trying to reduce the potential costs are very important for a particular contractual party.

References

1. A. Abrahams. An asynchronous rule-based approach for business process automation using obligations. In *the 3rd ACM SIGPLAN Workshop on Rule-Based Programming*, Pittsburgh, USA, 2002.
2. Philip R. Cohen and Hector J. Levesque. Communicative actions for artificial agents. In Victor Lesser and Les Gasser, editors, *Proceedings of the First International Conference on Multi-Agent Systems*, pages 65–72, San Francisco, CA, USA, 1995. The MIT Press: Cambridge, MA, USA.
3. A. Dan, T. N . Nguyen, D. M. Dias, F. N. Parr, R. Kearney, M. W. Sachs, T. C. Lau, and H. H. Shaikh. Business-to-business intergration with tpaml and a business-to-business protocol framework. *IBM Systems Journal*, 40(1), 2001.
4. A. Daskalopulu, T. Dimitrako T, and T. Maibaum. Evidence-based electronic contract performance monitoring. *INFORMS Journal of Group Decision and Negotiation*, Special Issue: formal Modeling of Electronic Commerce, 2002.
5. Jean-Jacques Dubray. A new model for ebxml bpss multi-party collaborations and web services choreography, 2002. http://www.ebpml.org/ebpml.doc.
6. Paul Grefen, Jochem Vonk, and Peter Apers. Global transaction support for workflow management systems: from formal specification to practical implementation. *The VLDB Journal*, 2001.
7. B. Grosof and T. Poon. Sweetdeal: representing agent contracts with exceptions using xml rules, ontologies, and process descriptions, 2003.
8. Bob Haugen. Multi-party electronic business transactions, 2002. http://www.supplychainlinks.com/MultiPartyBusinessTransactions.PDF.
9. E. Kafeza, DKW. Chiu, and I. Kafeza. View-based contracts in an e-service cross-organizational workflow environment. In *the second International Workshop on Technologies for E-Service*, 2001.
10. S.O. Kimbrough and S.A. Moore. On automated message processing in electronic commerce and work support systems: Speech act theory and expressive felicity. *ACM Transactions on Information Systems*, 15(4):321–367, 1997. ACM Press. New York, NY.
11. M. Koetsier, P. Grefen, and Vonk. Contract model. Technical Report Deliverable D4b, Cross-Organisational/Workflow, Crossflow ESPRITE/28635, 1999.
12. Ron Lee. Towards open electronic contracting. *Electronic Markets*, 8(3), March 1998.
13. S.A. Moore. Kqml and flbc: Contrasting agent communication languages. *International Journal of Electronic Commerce*, 5(1), 2000.
14. T. J. Norman, C. Sierra, and N. R. Jennings. Rights and commitments in multi-agent agreements. In *Proceedings of the 3rd International Conference on Multi-Agent Systems (ICMAS-98)*, Paris, France, 1998.
15. Chris Preist. Agent mediated electronic commerce research at hewlett packard labs, bristol. *ACM SIGecom Exchanges*, 2001.
16. CrossFlow Project. Insurance requirements. Technical Report CrossFlow deliverable: D1.b, CrossFlow consortium, 1999.
17. R.Ervin. Chains of commitment software architecture. *ACM SIGecom Exchanges*, 3(1), 2002.
18. Y-H. Tan and W. Thoen. A logical model of directed obligations and permissions to support electronic contracting in electronic commerce. *International Journal of Electronic Commerce*, 3(2):87–104, 1999.

19. Mahadevan Venkatraman and Munindar P. Singh. Verifying compliance with commitment protocols: Enabling open web-based multiagent systems. *Autonomous Agents and Multi-Agent Systems*, 2(3), 1999.
20. M. Verdicchio and M. Colombetti. Commitments for agent-based supply chain management. *ACM SIGecom Exchanges*, 3(1), 2002.
21. H. Weigand, F. Dignum, and E. Verharen. Dynamic business models as a basis for interoperable transaction design. *Information Systems*, 1997.
22. Hans Weigand and Lai Xu. Contracts in e-commerce. In *9th IFIP 2.6 Working Conference on Database Semantic Issues in E-Commerce Systems (DS-9)*, 2001.
23. Lai Xu. Monitorable electronic contract. In *The 2003 IEEE Conference on E-Commerce (CEC'03)*. IEEE Computer Society Press, 2003.
24. Lai Xu. Appendix: all actions and commitments of a car insurance case, 2004. http://www.cs.vu.nl/$\sim$xu/appendix.pdf.
25. Lai Xu. A multi-party contract model. *ACM SIGecom Exchanges*, 5(1), 2004.
26. Lai Xu and Manfred A. Jeusfeld. Pro-active monitoring of electronic contracts. In *The 15th Conference On Advanced Information Systems Engineering in Lecture Notes of Computer Science*, volume 2681, pages 584–600. Springer-Verlag, 2003.

Leadership Maintenance in Group-Based Location Management Scheme*

Gary Hoi Kit Lam, Hong Va Leong, and Stephen Chi Fai Chan

Department of Computing, The Hong Kong Polytechnic University, Hong Kong
{cshklam, cshleong, csschan}@comp.polyu.edu.hk

Abstract. In a mobile environment, location management is fundamental in supporting location-dependent applications. It is crucial to reduce the communication overhead in location management, due significantly to the costly uplink traffic for mobile hosts reporting their location to the server. To reduce uplink traffic, the group-based location management scheme exploits the spatial locality of mobile hosts to generate an aggregated location update from a group leader for group members agglomerated through a dynamic clustering algorithm. Due to the mobility of group members, a leader may be decoupled from a group voluntarily or involuntarily. An intuitive approach to address leader departure is to re-execute the clustering algorithm among leaderless group members. However, system performance may suffer, due to the absence of a group leader for a period. In this paper, a leadership maintenance scheme is designed based on the notion of a *secondary leader*, which is ready for assuming the role of a primary leader. The *turnover activation policy* identifies endangered primary leader and triggers the *turnover procedure*, which involves host interaction in leadership handover from the primary to secondary leader. Simulation study shows that our leadership maintenance scheme is effective to further reduce the costly uplink traffic and aggregated cost in the group-based location management scheme.

1 Introduction

Location tracking and management is a fundamental service provided in a mobile computing environment in order to support higher level applications, including location-dependent applications. A mobile environment involves a set of mobile hosts moving around an area served by a base station or an infrastructure of base stations, interconnected by wired networks. Such a mobile environment focuses on the communication between the mobile hosts and the fixed server. Efficient utilization of the asymmetric bandwidth between the hosts and the server is often the key focus. Thus, client/server model is a popular approach in developing mobile services.

In traditional location management, the client/server model is assumed where the location server will maintain a moving object database [18] (or location database) to keep track of the location of mobile hosts, with each member reporting its own location information individually, as shown in Figure 1(a). We term this approach the *individual-based* approach. The server's load could be large in handling high volume of concurrent

---

* Research supported in part by the Research Grant Council and the Hong Kong Polytechnic University under grant numbers PolyU 5084/01E and H-ZJ86.

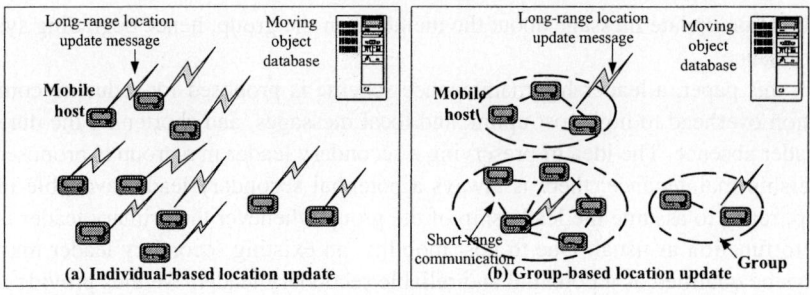

Fig. 1. Individual-based approach and group-based approach in location management

location updates from mobile hosts when the host population in the environment is large. With the emergence of short-range communication technologies like Bluetooth, mobile ad hoc networks can be established and mobile hosts can cooperate, in much a similar manner as a peer-to-peer (P2P) network. With the integration of mobile ad hoc network into traditional client/server communication environment, the strengths of mobile ad hoc communication paradigm and client/server paradigm complement each other. To capitalize on this integration, we proposed a *group-based location updating* scheme (GBL) [9] to reduce the volume of expensive wireless uplink traffic. In the GBL scheme, members in a group report their locations to the leader and the leader consolidates the reported locations as a single location update message to the location server on a fixed network. The number of location update messages from mobile hosts to server can be reduced by clustering mobile hosts with similar mobility into a set of groups. A single location report for the whole group is sent to the location server, as shown in Figure 1(b). A leader will be elected to perform location updating on behalf of the whole group to the moving object database. A direct and positive consequence is that mobile hosts no longer need to possess the communication capability with the remote server. In practical sense, this make a mobile system more robust to different kind of mobile devices, which do not always have long-range communication capability or available (e.g., PDA in outdoor environment). Location information can be reported via the group leader, thereby enhancing scalability.

Due to mobility of group members, a group leader may be decoupled from its group voluntarily or involuntarily. Leadership change among group members is unavoidable; it is important to develop an efficient scheme to deal with the issue. An intuitive approach in addressing the change of leadership is to re-execute a mobile ad hoc network clustering algorithm (either in a demand-driven or periodic manner). However, it is not a suitable approach in the group-based location management context because it could be costly in terms of communication cost if the clustering algorithm is re-executed, especially in large-sized groups. Message volume generated due to host interaction could be large. Additional uplink messages will be introduced for informing the server about the newly formed groups. The performance is also degraded because a leader is absent before the completion of the clustering algorithm. If the group leader fails, the location updating messages from members to the leader are wasted and members need to execute the leader election algorithm instead. During the election, the location server is not able to receive any location update message about the members in the group, hence degrading system performance.

In this paper, a leadership maintenance scheme is proposed for reducing communication overhead to high cost uplink and local messages, and shortening the duration of leader absence. The idea of preserving a secondary leader in a group is proposed for leadership maintenance: there is always a potential secondary leader available in the group, ready to assume the leadership of the group whenever the primary leader is not able to function as usual. Due to host mobility, an existing secondary leader may not always be qualified as a potential and reliable secondary leader. We thus provide a dynamic *secondary leader determination strategy* to appoint a potential secondary leader in the course of system execution. In order to properly trigger the takeover activity of a primary leader when an endangered primary leader is identified, a *turnover activation policy* is proposed. If such a takeover is deemed necessary, the *turnover procedure* is executed to effect the takeover.

This paper is organized as follows. Section 2 gives a survey on related research in location management and clustering in mobile ad hoc network, with also leader election. In Section 3, an overview of our group-based model and group-based location updating scheme (GBL) is described. Section 4 discusses the leadership maintenance scheme. We conduct a performance study on the proposed leadership maintenance scheme in the context of GBL in Section 5. Finally, we conclude this paper with a brief outline of our future work in Section 6.

2 Related Work

Location management [1,12,18] is concerned with efficient ways in keeping track of the location of mobile hosts and furnishing such information upon request. One important issue is location updating strategy, through which mobile hosts report to the location server about their current location. There are two major models with respect to location management in a centralized communication model. One is adopted in the personal communication network (PCS) [3] and the other is based on a moving object database residing on the fixed network. The PCS model is based on an infrastructure of cellular architecture, in which mobile hosts report eagerly to respective cells, whenever a cell boundary is crossed, or reporting lazily. Location management is concerned with location updating strategy to balance between the location update cost and the paging cost with varying location update condition. The precision is of the cellular granularity. In the moving object database model, it is often assumed that mobile hosts are equipped with location positioning system, e.g., GPS. Moving object databases, which are often realized with spatial databases [6], reside over the fixed network, maintaining the location information for the mobile hosts. Location information will be sent from the mobile hosts to the databases through uplink channels. Location updating strategy needs to consider the tradeoff between the location updating frequency and the location querying precision.

Regardless of the communication structure, the majority of traditional location updating strategies are based on the client/server communication model. Large volume of expensive uplink traffic will be generated for location reporting by a large host population to the fixed server. In [9], we have proposed a group-based location updating scheme (GBL), taking advantage of the cooperation between mobile hosts to reduce the uplink traffic and workload of servers. An overview for the system model and the GBL scheme will be presented in Section 3, while details of the scheme can be found in [9].

Mobile ad hoc mobile networks are established in an ad hoc manner and are self-organized among the mobile hosts. Research work on providing a relatively stable layer of network on top of flat ad hoc network routing forms a major research focus, and in the context of group-based paradigm, mobile host clustering in the ad hoc network into sets of groups. Popular schemes proposed include lowest-id and highest degree heuristics [4]. Clustering based on mobility prediction was also studied [15]. In addition, an on-demand distributed weighted-based clustering scheme [4] was designed. A mobility-based clustering algorithm [2] was developed in which the mobility of a mobile host is considered. A distributed sequential clustering algorithm was proposed in [17].

In mobile ad hoc network clustering, a leader may be elected among mobile hosts in each cluster, called *clusterhead*. For those clustering algorithms, leader election algorithm is always an integral part in the formation of clusters. On the other hand, there is little discussion on the issue of handing over the leadership to another host in a cluster when a leader departs its cluster in a voluntary or involuntary manner. An intuitive approach to deal with the problem is to repeat the clustering algorithm among the mobile hosts in the problem cluster periodically or adaptively. In [7], a data replication scheme, DRAM, was proposed. The scheme is done periodically according to the relocation period. DRAM consists of two major phases: the allocation unit construction phase and the replica allocation phases. Cluster maintenance tasks are collected in the allocation unit construction phase, including splitting groups, assigning leaders to newly split groups and forming group for the mobile hosts in the INITIAL state (i.e., not belonging to any group). Those maintenance tasks simply involve periodic execution of the clustering algorithm. In [4], the nodes will monitor the signal strength from the clusterhead. If a node finds that the signal strength falls below a threshold, it notifies the clusterhead while trying to move over to another cluster. If the node is not covered by any cluster, the clusterhead election algorithm is invoked.

Similar to clustering in mobile ad hoc network, virtual backbone formation [13] provides routing service in an ad hoc environment. A number of mobile hosts, termed virtual backbone nodes, participate in virtual backbone formation and maintenance. As with the role of a clusterhead in ad hoc routing, the virtual backbone nodes provide the routing service. As topology changes, structural and connectivity maintenance is required. Like leadership maintenance, mechanisms for generation or merging of virtual backbone nodes are required for handling mobility and failure of mobile hosts.

In both virtual backbone and clustering in mobile ad hoc network, failure in virtual backbone nodes and in clusterheads cause performance degradation in application or network services. The reason is that there is no leader for providing the necessary services during the period when the leader is absent. With a secondary leader in a group, the backup leader can stand by to take over the job from the primary leader, thus increasing system fault-tolerance.

Multi-hop leader election algorithms in mobile ad hoc network environment were proposed in [14], based on temporally ordered routing algorithm [16], which is in turn based on [5]. Two leader election algorithms were proposed. One is capable of handling a single topology change at a time, while the other handling multiple concurrent topology changes. Each node is assigned a unique "height". Links are directed from higher height to lower height. These directed links form a directed acyclic graph (DAG) so that the destination is the single sink. Each connected partition in the ad hoc networks is a DAG. The leader in a connected partition thus is the single sink in this partition. When a splitting or a merging of partitions is detected, the leader election algorithm is invoked. As a result, a single leader will be eventually elected in a connected partition. However, performance study of these leader election algorithms is lacking.

3 System Model and GBL Overview

This section provides an overview of the system model and the group-based location updating scheme. This paper is focused on the mechanism of maintaining leadership within groups, while further details about the group-based model and the group-based location updating mechanism taking into account of movement and update cost tradeoff can be found in [9].

3.1 System Model

In the GBL system model, each mobile host m is assumed to possess a unique ID and a GPS sensor for keeping track of its existing location and its movement information. The current location of m is denoted by $\langle x_m, y_m \rangle$, while the movement information is maintained and represented as a vector $\vec{v}_m = \langle v_{xm}, v_{ym} \rangle$, being resolved into the x and y components, as shown in Figure 2(a). Two mobile hosts are considered as *neighbors* if the Euclidean distance between them is smaller than their transmission range (i.e., they can communicate in an ad hoc mode). In addition to the conventional long-range wireless communication network, a mobile ad hoc network is also assumed in our model. In the mobile ad hoc network that connects most mobile hosts, each host maintains wireless links with one another within a transmission range of r, expressed as an Euclidean distance. Groups are formed by clustering together sets of nearby mobile hosts. In other words, the ad hoc network is conceptually split into potentially overlapping partitions. Each partition is called a *group*, each of which has a *leader* associated. The leader of a group is responsible for reporting the group location to the location server and managing group activities like *member join* and *member leave*. In particular, host interaction is required for a mobile host to find a suitable group to join. This could lead to high local communication overhead. A leader-filter join procedure was proposed in [10] to reduce the number of neighboring hosts participating in the process of finding a suitable group to join, hence reducing the number of messages.

In the GBL model, a group is a natural collection of mobile hosts that can communicate with one another and that move together in an aggregated manner. A leader can be elected from a group to act on behalf of the group. Thus, to qualify as a potential member to a group G, a mobile host m should be at most a distance of r away from the position of the group. The position of a group G refers to the center of the circle $\langle x_G, y_G \rangle$, where $x_G = \frac{1}{|G|} \sum_{m \in G} x_m$ and $y_G = \frac{1}{|G|} \sum_{m \in G} y_m$, and the movement of G is represented

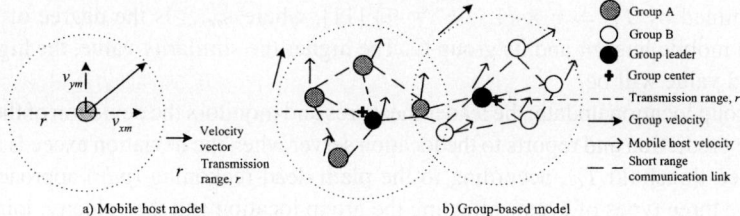

Fig. 2. The system model

as $\vec{v}_G = \langle v_{xG}, v_{yG} \rangle$, where $v_{xG} = \frac{1}{|G|} \sum_{m \in G} v_{xm}$ and $v_{yG} = \frac{1}{|G|} \sum_{m \in G} v_{ym}$. The network topology is illustrated in Figure 2(b), in which there are two groups **A** and **B** formed. The movement of the two groups, the group leaders and the individual group members are also shown. We call a group with only one member a *singleton group*, i.e., the sole member is the leader itself. The host in a singleton group will perform the group finding process periodically based on a predefined location sampling period, τ_s, until another group is found for joining or another host considers joining this singleton group. In order to maintain a more stable group, members within a group should be similar in term of mobility. We define a notion of *degree of affinity* to measure the movement similarity between mobile hosts or groups, which we term *mobile domains*. The value of degree of affinity between two mobile domains is contributed by the distance factor and movement factor, which measures the "normalized" distance between two mobile domains' locations and "normalized" difference between the two movement vectors of the mobile domains against their total length respectively. The degree of affinity, $s_{j,k}$, between two mobile domains, j and k, is defined by the equation:

$$s_{j,k} = \alpha(1 - \frac{dist(j,k)}{r}) + \beta(1 - \frac{\sqrt{(v_{xj} - v_{xk})^2 + (v_{yj} - v_{yk})^2}}{\sqrt{v_{xj}^2 + v_{yj}^2} + \sqrt{v_{xk}^2 + v_{yk}^2}}),$$

where $\alpha + \beta = 1$ and $dist(j,k)$ is the Euclidean distance between j and k.

3.2 Group-Based Location Updating

The group-based location updating scheme (GBL) is developed based on the model. In GBL, there are two levels of location update occurring. The first level, termed *local location update*, is about the strategy for reporting location and movement information to the leader of the group by its members. The second level, termed *group location update*, is about the strategy for reporting the group location information to the stationary location server via the uplink channel.

In local location update, a group member periodically samples its current location and velocity. Such information will then be compared with the predicted location according to its latest updated location and velocity. The derivation, in terms of the distance between the predicted location and the current location, will be measured. If the derivation is larger than a prescribed threshold T_L, an update message will be sent to the leader. The threshold value that will trigger an update is determined by the *degree of affinity* between a mobile host group member m and its group G. The next threshold value T_L

is determined by $T_L = r \times (1 - e^{-s_{m,G}})$ [11], where $s_{m,G}$ is the degree of affinity between mobile host m and its group G. The higher the similarity value, the higher the threshold value will be.

In group location update, the leader measures and monitors the deviation of the group from the prediction and reports to the location server when the deviation exceeds another prescribed threshold T_G, according to the plain dead-reckoning (*pdr*) approach [18]. There are three types of events affecting the group location and the velocity: join event, leave event and local location update event from group members. A group leader receives the relevant location information from its members. The group location and velocity will be refreshed. If the distance between the current location and predicted location of a group is larger than T_G, a location update message will be sent from the leader to the location server. In general, more sophisticated dead-reckoning approach, such as adaptive dead-reckoning (*adr*) [18], can be applied to group location updating. In the case of singleton group, individual-based plain dead-reckoning (*pdr*) will be applied, that is, the leader compares its current location with the predicted location from the latest location information updated to the server; if the derivation is larger than T_G, the leader will send a location update message to the server.

4 Leadership Maintenance Scheme

In order to maintain dynamic leadership within a group, we propose a leadership maintenance scheme with the aid of a secondary leader in the group. There are three major components in our leadership maintenance scheme, built on top of our group-based model and the GBL scheme. The first component is a *secondary leader determination* strategy, a strategy to determine who will be a potential secondary leader to take over the group leader's role when necessary. The second component, termed *turnover activation policy*, is a policy for identifying an endangered primary leader and making the proper decision on when to trigger the *turnover procedure*. The third component *turnover procedure* is triggered to really hand over the primary leader's duty to the secondary leader. This component consists of procedures for handling the turnover and notifying members about the change of primary leader. In general, there should always be a potential secondary leader in a group ready for assuming the leadership from the primary leader. We assume that there are occasional but infrequent message loss, as exhibited by most practical systems.

4.1 Secondary Leader Determination

To select a secondary leader responsible for taking over the activities of a primary leader after the primary leaves, the existing primary needs to gather the information required for secondary leader determination amongst members during system execution. Two pieces of information, namely, *member-neighbor connectivity*, $|N_m|$, and *degree of affinity*, $s_{m,G}$, between a member m and a group G, are maintained. Member-neighbor connectivity of m is the number of *member-neighbors* of m. The member-neighbors, N_m, of m are those neighbors of m belonging to G. The procedure can be illustrated with an example as shown in Figure 3.

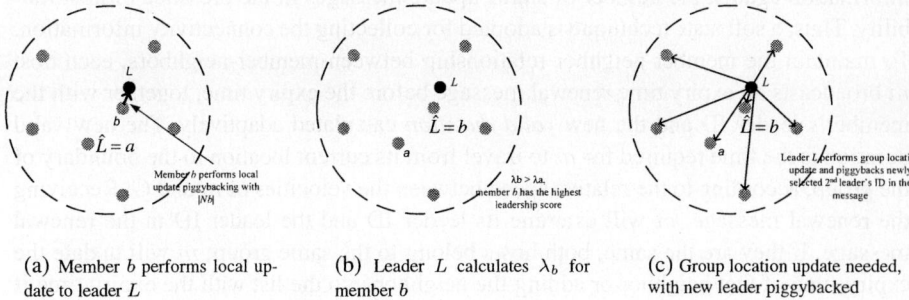

(a) Member b performs local update to leader L

(b) Leader L calculates λ_b for member b

(c) Group location update needed, with new leader piggybacked

Fig. 3. Secondary leader determination

The member-neighbor connectivity information will be piggybacked on local location update message, as depicted in Figure 3(a). The primary leader L obtains the degree of affinity between a member m and its group G by using the local location update information from m. The leadership score, λ_m, of m is defined as $\lambda_m = w_1 s_{m,G} + w_2 |N_m|$, where w_1 and w_2 are weights to the two factors, degree of affinity and member-neighbor connectivity, with $w_1 + w_2 = 1$. Whenever primary L receives a local location update message from a member m, the leadership score of m, λ_m, is calculated and stored, as exemplified in Figure 3(b). If a mobile host is not able to communicate with remote server, its member-neighbor connectivity will be set to negative infinity, making it ineligible for being appointed as a secondary leader. At the moment when a group location update is generated, the member with the highest leadership score is selected as the secondary leader $\hat{L}$, whose ID will be piggybacked on the group location update message, as in Figure 3(c). Due to dynamic host movement, the secondary leader $\hat{L}$ may leave the group. When $\hat{L}$ leaves the group, L removes the record of $\hat{L}$ from the member list. The next highest ranked member is then chosen to be the new secondary leader. L will also generate an intra-group location update to all members with information about the new secondary leader. Thus, members are kept informed of changes in secondary leader as soon as possible. This is beneficial in involuntary leader changing situation since the possibility of handing over the primary leader's job to a departed secondary leader is reduced. For intra-group location update, L will send a group location update message only to each member, but not to the server to reduce expensive uplink traffic. There is no change in the information stored in the leader about the latest updated location, velocity and update time. In each group location update message, the ID of the current secondary leader $\hat{L}$ is piggybacked. Primary leader L will also keep track of its own leadership score, λ_L, to monitor for possibility that secondary leader's score surpasses its own, thereby triggering the turnover procedure.

To determine the member-neighbor connectivity in group G, each member m maintains a *member-neighbor list*, storing the list of *member-neighbors* and *member-neighbor relationship expiry time* (or simply *expiry time*) of each member-neighbor. The member-neighbor relationship of a member to a neighbor is considered valid before its expiry time. The validity assumption serves as a tradeoff for the accuracy of member-neighbor information against the number of status update messages in the presence of host mobility. Thus, a soft state technique is adopted for collecting the connectivity information. To maintain the member-neighbor relationship between member-neighbors, each host m broadcasts an expiry time renewal message before the expiry time, together with the member's leader ID and the new *valid duration* calculated adaptively. The new valid duration is the time required for m to travel from its current location to the boundary of the group, according to the relative speed between the velocities of m and G. Receiving the renewal message, m will examine its leader ID and the leader ID in the renewal message. If they are the same, both hosts belong to the same group; m will update the expiry time of that neighbor or adding the neighbor into the list with the expiry time if it is a new neighbor. We adopt a lazy approach for the expired member in the member-neighbor list. The expired member-neighbors in the list will be removed only when the connectivity of the member is to be determined.

Although more accurate member-neighbor list can be maintained with a conservative approach in member-neighbor relationship renewal, this may induce high number of local messages. To improve system performance, a *relaxed* member-neighbor renewal strategy is employed to reduce the local communication overhead. The new valid duration is computed as the time required to travel from the current location to the boundary of the group *plus* its transmission range distance. To further reduce the number of local messages, *piggybacking* technique is adopted. Whenever there is a group location update or an intra-group location update, the primary leader calculates a new valid duration and embeds it in the group location update messages. Members of the group then update the group location information and renew the member-neighbor relationship of the primary with the message.

4.2 Turnover Activation Policy

Turnover activation policy is a mechanism for determining *when* the leader is required to turn over its current job to the secondary leader, that is, the primary has a high tendency to stay near the margin of a group and leave its group sooner or later, thus termed a *tend-to-leave* leader. Rather than waiting for a *tend-to-leave* leader leaving the group and reacting on demand, the policy identifies this kind of endangered leader proactively and triggers the turnover procedure. The reason is that it is desirable to have a leader often staying near the group center, rather than staying near the group margin. If it is discovered that the leader is often far away from the group center, it is better to hand over its job to another potential secondary leader, by invoking the turnover procedure.

Each group leader activates the *turnover activation policy* periodically. Figure 4 depicts the model employed in the turnover activation policy. An *inner circle* is introduced with radius r_i, centered at the group center. We define a *stayIndex* to indicate the tendency of a leader staying within the inner circle. The higher the value of the index, the higher tendency that the leader stays within the inner circle. The *stayIndex* is measured in each location sampling; it is incremented by one if the leader L is within the inner circle; otherwise, it will be divided by a *drop factor*, χ. The *drop factor* is adjusted adaptively according to the difference between the degree of affinity of the leader to the group in the previous and the current sampling periods, i.e., $s_{L,G}^{Prev}$ and $s_{L,G}$. *Drop factor* will be decreased when there is an increase in the current degree of affinity and vice versa, as

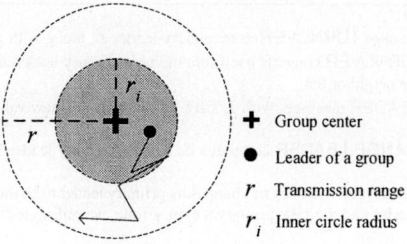

Fig. 4. Group-based model with the notion of inner circle

given by $\chi^{new} = \chi^{old}(1-(s_{L,G}-s_{L,G}^{Prev}))$, where two thresholds, χ_{min} and χ_{max}, are predefined to bound the drop factor, with $\chi_{min} > 1$ and $\chi_{max} > \chi_{min}$.

Figure 5 depicts the turnover activation policy. In short, the leader L executes the turnover activation policy in each location sampling period. *Drop factor* and *stayIndex* are evaluated. There is a predefined *turnover threshold*, *TurnThr* ($0 < TurnThr < 1$). If *stayIndex* < *TurnThr* and the leadership score $\lambda_L < \lambda_{\hat{L}}$, L is treated as a tend-to-leave leader and the turnover procedure will be invoked. Note that there is no need for the turnover activation policy for a group of size two, since the turnover will not achieve its desired goal for such a group.

Initial Condition:
1. stayIndex = 1

StayIndex Adjustment at L:
1. $\chi \leftarrow \chi(1-(s_{L,G}-s_{L,G}^{Prev}))$
2. if leader stays in the inner circle then
3. $stayIndex \leftarrow stayIndex + 1$
4. else
5. $stayIndex \leftarrow stayIndex/\chi$
6. end if

Turnover Activation Policy at L:
1. for each location sampling period do
2.   adjust $stayIndex$
3.   if ($stayIndex < TurnThr$ and $\lambda_L < \lambda_{\hat{L}}$) then
4.   turn over the job to $\hat{L}$ by invoking the voluntary turnover procedure
5.   revert L back to an ordinary member
6.   end if
7. end for

Fig. 5. Turnover activation policy

4.3 Turnover Procedure

Turnover should occur when the leader leaves the group (on demand), or when it is too risky to rely on the leader which has a strong tendency to stay near the margin of the group (anticipatory). There are three possible situations when a primary leader L is required to turn over its role. First, the turnover activation policy may identify L as a tend-to-leave leader. Second, voluntary leave event occurs when L moves out of the group range r, or L intends to power down or to disconnect itself. These two situations

---
Voluntary Turnover Procedure:
1. Primary leader L unicasts message TURNOVER to secondary leader $\hat{L}$, along with group information.
2. Secondary $\hat{L}$ that receives TURNOVER converts itself into the new primary leader and identifies an appropriate new secondary $\tilde{L}$ from its member-neighbor list.
   $\hat{L}$ broadcasts a CHANGE_LEADER message, with L's ID, $\tilde{L}$'s ID and $\hat{L}$'s new valid duration to all other members in the member list.
3. Member m that receives CHANGE_LEADER compares its current primary leader ID with the old leader ID in the message.
   If both IDs are equal, things are alright. Member m changes its primary leader to be the message sender. It also updates its record of the secondary leader and the new primary's expiry time, according to the information embedded in the message.
   Otherwise, m has changed group, a LEAVE message will be sent to the message sender to finish off with the group switching.

Fig. 6. Voluntary turnover procedure

are handled by the *voluntary turnover procedure*. Finally, involuntary leave event occurs when there is a sudden failure of L. The procedure in handling this situation is termed *involuntary leader changing procedure* (i.e., *involuntary turnover procedure*).

Voluntary Turnover Procedure. Figure 6 depicts the host interaction involved in the voluntary turnover procedure. To begin with, the existing primary leader L sends a TURNOVER message to the secondary leader $\hat{L}$. The TURNOVER message contains the group member list, the group location and velocity, and the latest update time, latest updated group location and velocity. If L initiates a voluntary leave, it will remove itself from the group member list before sending TURNOVER. After $\hat{L}$ receives TURNOVER, it considers itself the new primary leader and constructs a member list according to the message received. The new primary then identifies a new secondary based on its member-neighbor list, computes its valid duration, and broadcasts a CHANGE_LEADER message to all its members, with message content of previous leader ID, new secondary leader ID and its own new valid duration. After members receive CHANGE_LEADER, they update their own record about the new primary and secondary leader, and the expiry time of the new primary.

Owing to asynchrony of message passing and host mobility, a member m^* which has already departed group G for group G^* may receive a CHANGE_LEADER message from the new primary leader $\hat{L}$ of G. It occurs when the old primary leader L of G does not receive the LEAVE message from m^* before the voluntary turnover procedure is invoked by L. The new primary $\hat{L}$ would still consider this departed member m^* as a group member according to the member list it received and would send a CHANGE_LEADER message to m^*. When m^* receives CHANGE_LEADER, it should reply back a LEAVE message to $\hat{L}$ to remove itself from the member list of the latter, i.e., group G.

Owing to potential message loss, it may happen that a subset of members fail to receive the CHANGE_LEADER message. Upon timeout, those hosts would execute the *involuntary leader changing procedure* when they discover the loss of the existing primary and are unaware of the secondary becoming the new primary. This is a simplification to reuse an existing protocol in a slightly different but yet applicable context. Details in handling such a scenario will be discussed next.

Involuntary Leader Changing Procedure. In the involuntary leader changing procedure, each member utilizes the member-neighbor list and auxiliary information to detect the involuntary departure of the primary leader. We adopt a lazy approach in determining the necessity of involuntary leader turnover upon timeout. In other words, we only initiate the involuntary leader changing procedure when there is a need for a member to report its location via a local location update message. Involuntary leader changing is initiated with a *leader changing update* (CHANGE_UPDATE) message, on which a regular local location update message is piggybacked. The detail of the involuntary leader changing procedure is shown in Figure 7.

Before a member m issues a local location update, the expiry time of the primary leader L is checked. If it is valid, L is probably still around and a regular local location update message is sent to L. If it has expired, L may have disappeared from the view of m, which will then initiate the involuntary leader changing procedure, by sending a CHANGE_UPDATE message to its secondary leader $\hat{L}$. The latest group location update time stored in m and the primary leader L's ID are included in the message. The latest group location update time indicates the timestamp of leader L when L last issued a group location update to members.

When a member m initiates involuntary leader changing procedure to its secondary leader by a CHANGE_UPDATE message, the receiving secondary will re-confirm the existence of the primary leader by sending a probe (IS_ALIVE) message to check whether the primary has left the group. If the primary is still around, the involuntary leader changing procedure terminates with a REJECT message back to m, which updates its information. If the leader has departed from the group, the secondary declares itself as the new primary and broadcasts a CHANGE_LEADER message with the previous primary leader ID. This is slightly different from the CHANGE_LEADER message generated in voluntary turnover, without new secondary leader and primary leader's new expiry time information, since the new primary leader has only limited knowledge about the group and members within the group. Members of the group receiving CHANGE_LEADER will verify whether the change is legitimate, updating the new primary leader information, followed by a regular location update to the new primary.

In the presence of message loss, some members may not receive an expiry time renewal message from their leader. If this is the case, the primary leader's expiry time that they store will eventually expire. Upon expiry and when member m needs to report a local location update, the involuntary leader changing procedure is invoked. However, the primary leader still exists within the group and it is not necessary to change the leadership. To address this problem, the secondary leader that receives the CHANGE_UPDATE message will check the leader's expiry time. If it has not yet expired, the primary is still healthy and the secondary receiving the CHANGE_UPDATE message will reply with a REJECT message so that m will discontinue the leader changing procedure. It is also possible that the secondary leader missed the latest expiry time renewal messages from the primary leader, but the primary is still around. To guard against this, the secondary will confirm with the primary for its departure with a probe IS_ALIVE even if the expiry time is up. As with above, if there is no response, the secondary assumes the new leadership and broadcasts CHANGE_LEADER for the leadership turnover.

After the voluntary turnover procedure is finished, there may be some members failing to receive the CHANGE_LEADER message from the new primary leader. Before the expiration of leader's expiry time, those members may issue normal local location

---
Involuntary Leader Changing Procedure:
1. When a local update is to be issued by host m and the expiry time of primary L is up, m sends a CHANGE_UPDATE message to its secondary $\hat{L}$ with the latest group update time and its current leader ID.
2. Host h receives a CHANGE_UPDATE message from m.
   a. **case** h is a primary leader:
      // h has already become a primary leader triggered by other members but m does not know this
      h replies m with a CHANGE_LEADER message containing h's previous primary leader ID, current secondary leader ID and h's remaining valid duration
   b. **case** h is a secondary leader:
      if (h's leader ID == m's leader ID) then // m and h belong to the same group
         if leader L's expiry time is not up yet then // no change in leader
            h sends back a REJECT message to m
         else
            h probes L with an IS_ALIVE message
            if h receives before timeout a YES message from L then // no change in leader
               h sends back a REJECT message to m // primary leader is still healthy
            else // timeout and h becomes the new primary leader
               h broadcasts a CHANGE_LEADER message with L's ID only
   c. **case** host h is a member:
      if (h's leader ID == m's leader ID) then // m and h belong to the same group
         if leader L's expiry time is not up yet then // no change in leader
            h sends back a REJECT message to m // primary is healthy
         else if (latest group update time in h > latest group update time in CHANGE_UPDATE) then
            h sends another CHANGE_UPDATE message to h's secondary leader $\hat{L}$ and waits for reply
            if a REJECT message is received before timeout then // primary is healthy
               h sends back REJECT to m // propagate REJECT
            // else timeout, h cannot contact new leader, so it leaves the group
         else
            h probes L with an IS_ALIVE message
            if h receives before timeout a YES message from L then
               h sends back a REJECT message to m // primary leader is still healthy
            else // timeout and h becomes the new primary leader
               h broadcasts a CHANGE_LEADER message with L's ID only
3. Member m waits for the reply.
      if REJECT is received before timeout then // primary is healthy
         m sends location update to existing primary leader L
      else // timeout, m no longer belongs to the group
         m tries to find another group to join
4. Host n receives a CHANGE_LEADER message from host l.
      if (n's existing primary leader L's ID == previous leader ID in CHANGE_LEADER) then
         // change is ready for installation
         if CHANGE_LEADER contains new secondary's ID and primary's new expiry time then
            // (case in paragraph 2a)
            change primary leader to l
            update secondary leader and primary leader's expiry time
         else // (case in paragraph 2b or 2c)
            change primary leader to l
            send a regular local location update to l

Fig. 7. Involuntary leader changing procedure

update messages to the old leader. The old leader will simply discard the messages, even if it is still in the group. Thus this old leader behaves as if it were not in the group, thereby unifying the failure mode as observed by those negligent members. The old leader's expiry time will eventually be up at those negligent members, who will then send CHANGE_UPDATE messages to their secondary leader. At this moment, the secondary leader has already become the new primary leader. So, when this new primary receives a CHANGE_UPDATE message, it will reply a CHANGE_LEADER message to those negligent members only through unicast message passing. In this case, the group information is available and the CHANGE_LEADER message will contain information of the selected secondary leader ID and the primary leader's remaining valid duration.

Besides missing CHANGE_LEADER message from a new primary, there is a scenario that a member m misses a group location update message which indicates the change of secondary leadership. When a CHANGE_UPDATE message is issued by m, it is sent to its preferred secondary leader p, asking p to take over. Now p may be the secondary leader $\hat{L}$ or an old secondary leader. If p is an old secondary leader, it may still be a member of the group or may have become a member of another group with a different primary leader. Upon receiving a CHANGE_UPDATE message from m, p compares its current leader ID and the leader ID embedded in the local location update message. If p is still a member of the existing group (i.e., both IDs are the same), p will check for the expiration of primary leader's expiry time. If it has not yet expired, primary leader may still be valid and a REJECT message is replied to m. Otherwise, the latest group update time values stored in p and in the local update message are compared. If the update time stored in p is larger than that stored in the local update message, it will propagate the CHANGE_UPDATE message to the secondary leader p' that p prefers. Host p' will then execute the involuntary leader changing procedure. If the update time in p is less than that in the local update message, indicating that p missed a notification of secondary leader change, p then considers itself to be the new primary and broadcasts CHANGE_LEADER.

5 Performance Study

approaches in addressing the leadership maintenance problem. The first one is a straightforward extension of our clustering algorithm [9] for group formation, with re-execution (hereinafter referred to as re-run cluster algorithm). Whenever a leader departs from a group, all members become leaderless members, not belonging to any group. The clustering algorithm will then be invoked to form groups among those leaderless members. The second one is the leadership maintenance scheme as discussed in Section 4. In this approach, two different variants in maintaining member-neighbor connectivity are studied. The first variant is a straightforward realization of our proposed leadership maintenance scheme (called the basic scheme). The conservative member-neighbor renewal strategy is adopted and no renewal information is piggybacked in group location update messages. The second one is an improvement on the leader maintenance scheme, in which a relaxed member-neighbor renewal strategy is adopted and piggybacking technique is employed. This is called the improved scheme (see Section 4.1).

In the simulation, each mobile host moves freely according to the random waypoint movement model in a region of $100m$ by $100m$. We remove the assumption that a leader is allowed to move freely only around its group center from our previous works [9, 10]. Now, all mobile hosts can really move freely according to the random waypoint movement model [8], with speed from $0.1ms^{-1}$ to $5ms^{-1}$. Every host can interact with one another within a transmission range of $30m$. For simplicity, but without loss of generality, it is assumed that all mobile hosts possess the long-range communication ability. In other words, they can communicate with the location server and are eligible to act as a leader. Positioning system, e.g. GPS, is built in at each mobile host. Disconnection is assumed rare in the ad hoc network. Other parameter settings are as follows. The drop factor, χ, is initially set to 2.0. The drop factor bounds are $\chi_{max} = 5.0$ and $\chi_{min} = 1.25$. The inner circle radius r_i is 0.7 times of the group range r. The two factors in determining the degree of affinity carry equal weights, i.e., $\alpha = \beta = 0.5$. The leadership score is also computed with equal contributions from the degree of affinity and member-neighbor connectivity, i.e., $w_1 = w_2 = 0.5$.

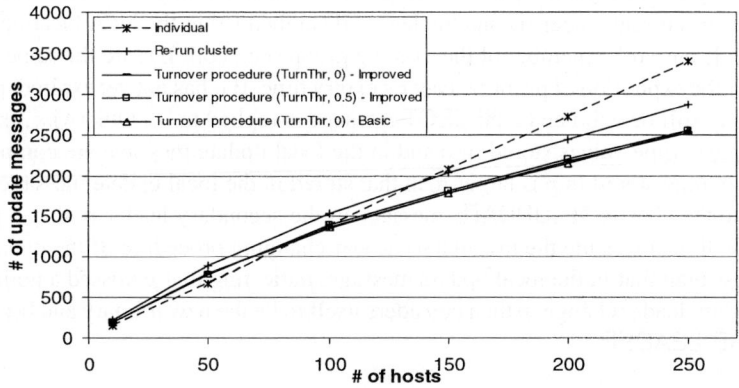

Fig. 8. Performance of GBL with leadership maintenance

We studied the impact on the number of expensive uplink group location update messages to server with two different approaches in leadership maintenance, when compared with the individual-based location updating scheme. As depicted in Figure 8, the GBL scheme with leader-filter join procedure [10], with filter threshold value 0.5, is experimented in these two approaches. This is because it was shown that it yields a best performance. In Figure 8, it is obvious that the GBL scheme with the two different leadership maintenance approaches are effective in reducing the number of group update messages to location server in medium to high host population environments. In particular, our proposed leader maintenance scheme and its variants outperform the individual-based scheme at a high population and they consistently outperform the re-run cluster approach. The reduction of update messages in our scheme stems from the fact that there are more groups formed with the re-run cluster approach, as depicted in Figure 9. Thus, more group location update messages are generated for conveying to the server information about the newly formed groups after the clustering algorithm has been executed. There are similar performance effects on the number of group location update messages to the server on the different variants of our leadership maintenance scheme. We also studied the performance effect of the proposed leadership maintenance scheme with the use of the turnover activation policy (*TurnThr* = 0.5) and without the policy (*TurnThr* = 0). As depicted in Figure 8, both experiments yield similar results.

Figure 9 shows the results of the average number of groups and average number of singleton groups with different host population densities. The average number of groups and singleton groups decrease with our proposed leader maintenance scheme. In other words, the group size increases with our proposed scheme. As the group size increases, the impact on the join or leave event from a mobile host is reduced, thus increasing the group stability. The re-run cluster approach induces more groups and more singleton groups because each member in a group suddenly becomes an individual leaderless host

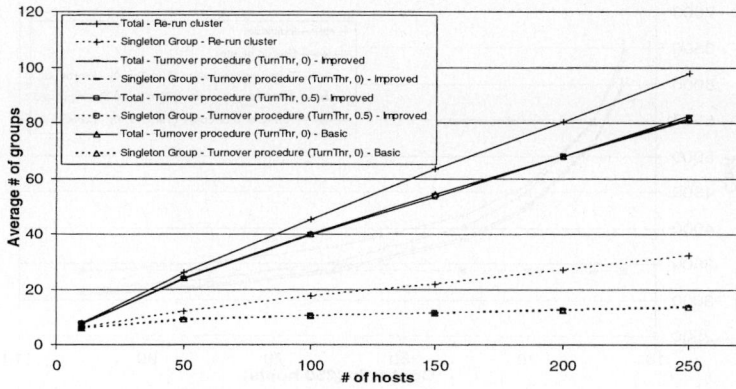

Fig. 9. Number of groups and singleton groups

after the group leader departs from the group. Meanwhile, fewer group location update messages are generated in our leader maintenance scheme, thereby alleviating the load of the server. Furthermore, with our leadership maintenance scheme, the duration of leader absence can be minimized. The GBL scheme is still functioning properly in the course of leadership changeover, without having to suspend location update activities to server for leadership maintenance through re-clustering. Thus, GBL scheme with our proposed leader maintenance approach has only a small impact on updating location information to the location server since there is less time spent for a primary leader handing over its job to a secondary, when compared with re-executing the clustering algorithm among those leaderless members.

From the result, there is little difference in average number of groups and singleton groups for different variants of our leadership maintenance scheme, except that the improved variant of leadership maintenance scheme with turnover activation policy performs slightly better in terms of average number of groups. Nevertheless, our scheme does exert a positive impact on the group stability. The group stability increases when the turnover activation policy is enabled under high population environments.

To study the performance of the GBL scheme from the collective view of all mobile hosts, both short-range and long-range communication costs should be taken into account, through an aggregated cost function defined as $C = c_s \times n_s + c_l \times n_l$, where c_s and c_l are the cost of a short-range message interaction in the ad hoc network and the cost of sending a long-range message through the uplink channel respectively, while n_s and n_l are the number of short-range messages and long-range messages respectively. It is assumed that $c_l > c_s$ and the cost in broadcasting a short-range message is the same as the cost in unicasting a short-range message. We define $\xi = \frac{c_l}{c_s}$ to be the global/local cost ratio. Thus, $C = c_l(\frac{n_s}{\xi} + n_l)$. Without loss of generality, we could assume that c_l is of unit cost, since it reflects the cost of standard individual-based location update scheme. The aggregated cost C at a client population of 250 with varying global/local cost ratio ξ is depicted in Figure 10.

From Figure 10, it is obvious that the cost for the individual-based scheme remains constant, since it involves no local message. However, the cost of all GBL schemes

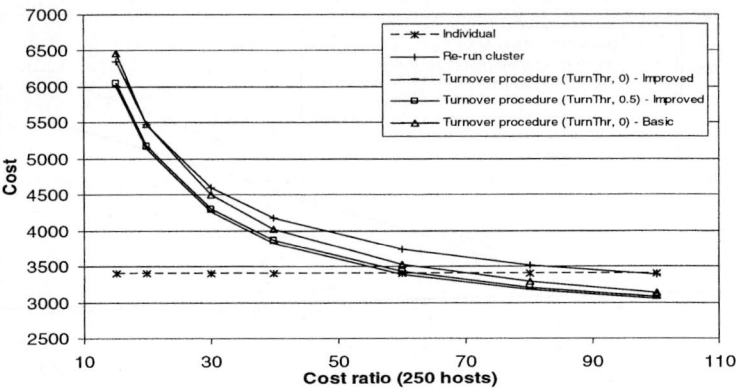

Fig. 10. Consolidated cost of GBL with leadership maintenance

decreases with increased host population, due to the increasing ease of group formation for the aggregated reporting effect. Thus, all GBL schemes are performing better than the individual-based scheme at a high cost ratio, but they worsen with lower cost ratio. It is interesting to note that only at the lowest cost ratio will the re-run cluster approach outperform the basic variant of the proposed leadership maintenance scheme, which is already the worst among other variants. This is because more message exchanges between mobile hosts are required in the clustering algorithm and more messages are generated for group location update. In executing clustering algorithm, host interaction is involved in electing a leader for a new group and joining the group by the members. However, in our approach, host interaction is reduced by embedding secondary leader selection information in both local location update and group location update messages, increasing leader's member-neighbor relationship renewal frequency by piggybacking new valid duration in the group location update messages. In addition, fewer message exchanges are required in the turnover procedure. The reduction in the group update message count to the server also contributes in reducing the aggregated cost. As a result, the straightforward approach of re-running clustering algorithm is not that effective, though it is still better than the individual-based scheme at high host population.

In comparison among the different variants of our leadership maintenance scheme, it can be observed that the basic variant is consistently the worst and the improved variant with turnover activation policy disabled performs marginally better than the improved variant with turnover activation policy enabled. The technique of piggybacking renewal messages in group location update messages and relaxing member-neighbor strategy does produce positive effect to our leadership maintenance scheme. However, there is a slight increase in aggregated cost when the turnover activation policy is enabled, though there is also a slight increase in group stability as depicted in Figure 9. This is a tradeoff to be considered between the group stability and the aggregated cost.

6 Conclusion

Group-based location updating scheme (GBL) provides a novel approach for location updating. Maintaining the leadership of a group properly is an important tactic in preserving the group stability and in enhancing the performance of group-based location updating scheme. We propose a leadership maintenance scheme by employing the notion of stand-by secondary leader. The secondary leader is dynamically selected in the course of system execution, and it will be able to take over the job of its primary counterpart as soon as possible when the primary departs from the group, by executing the *turnover procedure*. The turnover procedure can also be invoked when a tend-to-leave leader is identified by the *turnover activation policy*. Since there is always a secondary leader standing by, the duration of leader absence is basically eliminated. Simulation study of GBL scheme with different leadership maintenance approaches indicates that our leadership maintenance approach outperforms a straightforward approach under GBL, which re-executes the mobile ad hoc network clustering algorithm upon a leader departure event, in reducing the number of group location update messages, the average number of groups and the aggregated cost. An improved variant of our scheme can further reduce the aggregated cost.

By extending the notion of secondary leader, there could be a tertiary leader and so on, forming a chain. The secondary leader ranking could be re-evaluated periodically with new location information from local location updates. Viewing from another angle, location management can be treated as one mobile application that can take advantage of a group-based model. To further extend our work, a group-based framework could be developed for supporting a variety of applications. For example, mobile data accessing requests from group members could be consolidated within the group before sending to the servers. It is anticipated that the benefit of the group-based framework will become significant as more applications are being integrated into the framework.

References

1. P. K. Agarwal, L. Arge, and J. Erickson. Indexing moving points. In *Proceedings of ACM Symposium on Principles of Database Systems*, pages 175–186. ACM, 2000.
2. B. An and S. Papavassiliou. A mobility-based clustering approach to support mobility management and multicast routing in mobile ad-hoc wireless networks. *International Journal of Network Management*, 11(6):387–395, 2001.
3. E. Cayirci and I. F. Akyildiz. User mobility pattern scheme for location update and paging in wireless systems. *IEEE Transactions on Mobile Computing*, 1(3):236–247, 2002.
4. M. Chatterjee, S. K. Das, and D. Turgut. WCA: A weighted clustering algorithm for mobile ad hoc networks. *Journal of Cluster Computing (Special Issue on Mobile Ad hoc Networks)*, 5(2):193–204, 2002.
5. E. Gafni and D. Bertsekas. Distributed algorithms for generating loop-free routes in networks with frequently changing topology. *IEEE Transactions on Communications*, 29(1):11–15, 1981.
6. R. H. Güting. An introduction to spatial database systems. *The Very Large Data Bases Journal*, 3(4):357–399, 1994.
7. J.-L. Huang, M.-S. Chen, and W.-C. Peng. Exploring group mobility for replica data allocation in a mobile environment. In *Proceedings of the Twelfth International Conference on Information and Knowledge Management*, pages 161–168, 2003.

8. D. Johnson and D. Maltz. Dynamic source routing in ad hoc wireless networks. In Imielinski and Korth, editors, *Mobile Computing*. Kluwer Academic Publishers, 1996.
9. G. H. K. Lam, H. V. Leong, and S. C. F. Chan. GBL: Group-based location updating in mobile environment. In *Proceedings of the 9th International Conference on Database Systems for Advanced Applications*, pages 762–774, 2004.
10. G. H. K. Lam, H. V. Leong, and S. C. F. Chan. Reducing group management overhead in group-based location management. In *Proceedings of the 7th International Workshop on Mobility in Databases and Distributed Systems (DEXA Workshop)*, 2004.
11. K. Lam, O. Ulusoy, T. Lee, E. Chan, and G. Li. An efficient method for generating location updates for processing of location-dependent continuous queries. In *Proceedings of the 7th International Conference on Database Systems for Advanced Applications*, pages 218–225, 2001.
12. K. C. K. Lee, H. V. Leong, and A. Si. Approximating object location for moving object database. In *Proceedings of International Workshop on Mobile Distributed Computing (ICDCS Workshop)*, pages 402–407, 2003.
13. B. Liang and Z. J. Haas. Virtual backbone generation and maintenance for ad hoc network mobility management. In *Proceedings of 19th IEEE INFOCOM, vol. 3*, pages 1293–1302, 2000.
14. N. Malpani, J. L. Welch, and N. Vaidya. Leader election algorithms for mobile ad hoc networks. In *Proceedings of the 4th International Workshop on Discrete Algorithms and Methods for Mobile Computing and Communications*, pages 96–103, 2000.
15. A. B. McDonald and T. F. Znat. Mobility-based framework for adaptive clustering in wireless ad hoc networks. *IEEE Journal on Selected Areas in Communications*, 17(8):1466–1487, 1999.
16. V. D. Park and M. S. Corson. A highly adaptive distributed routing algorithm for mobile wireless networks. In *Proceedings of 16th IEEE INFOCOM, vol. 3*, pages 1405–1413, 1997.
17. K. H. Wang and B. Li. Efficient and guaranteed service coverage in partitionable mobile ad-hoc networks. In *Proceedings of 21st IEEE INFOCOM, vol. 2*, pages 1089–1098, 2002.
18. O. Wolfson, A. P. Sistla, S. Chamberlain, and Y. Yesha. Updating and querying databases that track mobile units. *Distributed and Parallel Databases Journal*, 7(3):257–387, 1999.

TLS: A Tree-Based DHT Lookup Service for Highly Dynamic Networks*

Francesco Buccafurri and Gianluca Lax

DIMET, Università "Mediterranea" di Reggio Calabria
Via Graziella, Località Feo di Vito, 89060 Reggio Calabria, Italy
bucca@unirc.it,lax@unirc.it
phone: +39 0965 875302, fax: +39 0965 875481

Abstract. The P2P paradigm is increasingly receiving attention in many contexts such as Cooperative Information Systems. In this paper we present a P2P lookup service based on a hash table distributed on a hierarchical data structure (a forest). The novelty of our proposal is that it provides a dynamically adapting (to the number of peers) routing load biasing for decreasing the cost of peer insertion and deletion w.r.t. the state of the art. This makes our system particularly suited to very dynamic environments.

1 Introduction

The P2P paradigm is increasingly receiving attention in various research (and application) contexts such as Cooperative Information Systems. Indeed, P2P applications are composed of a distributed collection of entities that cooperate and share information in order to perform some common task. In this scenario, there are a number of different research directions dealing with various aspects relating to P2P cooperation. Beside problems of data integration [5,10], arising from data source heterogeneity which occurs in P2P systems by nature, another relevant issue to be face is the *lookup* problem. It consists in the localization of peers storing a particular resource. Pure decentralized lookup services [14, 12,13,8,11] have been recently introduced for overcoming drawbacks of centralized ones, concerning the critical role of directory-server peers (super-peers) and the lack of scalability. There are many well known reasons invalidating the effectiveness of centralized directory services, but it is true that decentralization, compared with an *ideal* centralized solution, is worse w.r.t. the dynamic membership efficiency. Indeed, the existing techniques allow peer joining and leaving in time $O(\log^2 n)$, where n is the number of peers, due to the necessity of updating the distributed directory information.

---
* This work was partially funded by the Italian National Council Research under the "Reti Internet: efficienza, integrazione e sicurezza" project and by the European Union under the "SESTANTE - Strumenti Telematici per la Sicurezza e l'Efficienza Documentale della Catena Logistica di Porti e Interporti" Interreg III-B Mediterranee Occidentale project

Even though the polylogarithmic cost required for inserting and deleting peers ensures the feasibility of such operations, very dynamic P2P environments as well as large scale storage management systems [9,3,15], should rely on more efficient services.

Assumed that uniform routing load balancing intrinsically leads to polylogarithmic insertion/deletion costs, a way to face the above problem is renouncing the ambition of having *full* peer parity and going toward a solution embedding some form of load biasing. However, no solution giving to a (even large) number of peers extra routing load, may satisfy the essential property of scalability if such a number does not depend on the system size. On the other hand, arranging a lookup technique providing a dynamically adapting of peer roles is not a trivial task.

In this paper we propose a DHT (i.e., Distributed Hash Table) lookup P2P model, called TLS, which implements a non pure decentralized directory service based on a hash table distributed on a forest where peers receive a routing load depending on the position they occupy in the forest. The dynamics of such a hierarchy promotes peers toward higher levels by aging, in such a way that the more old and stable the peer, the higher the assigned routing load is. In other words, the protocol implements a sort of evolutionary selection in the peer population capturing real-life environments like Web services with P2P-based orchestration [4], where stability is always associated to high bandwidth capacity. The fraction of peers which the routing traffic is biased toward, is then depending on the total number of peers, and, as a consequence, the routing load biasing is designed in such a way that congestion of root peers is avoided, for every system size. We have theoretically proven the above claim by developing a probabilistic analysis of routing traffic. Thus, our approach allows us to overcome limits of the binary-tree-based approach where the root (as well as nodes close to the root) are overloaded, by providing an intermediate solution between the unfeasible full graph and the binary tree one. Under this perspective, our approach goes toward the same direction as [11], where the need of finding such a compromise represents the basic motivation.

Regarding traffic load biasing, we further observe that, in a practical implementation, additional optimizations, like caching used in hierarchical routing of DNS, can be anyway applied.

The strong advantage we obtain with our approach is to pull down the insertion/deletion cost from the state-of-the art $O(\log^2 n)$ to $O(\log n)$.

Performance of other operations locates our system on top of the main recent lookup proposals (see Section 2 for further details), as shown in the following table:

Technique	Join/Leave	Space	Hops
CHORD [14]	$O(\log^2 n)$	$O(\log n)$	$O(\log n)$
CAN [12]	$O(d)$	$O(nd)$	$O(dn^{1/d})$
Pastry [13]	$O(\log^2 n)$	$O(\log n)$	$O(n \log n)$
Tapestry [8]	$O(\log^2 n)$	$O(\log n)$	$O(\log n)$
This Paper (TLS)	$O(\log n)$	$O(\log n)$	$O(\log n)$

where the column *Join/Leave* reports costs of peer inserting/deleting, *Space* concerns to the storage information amount required for each peer, *Hops* is the routing cost per message, n is the number of peers in the system and d is the number of dimensional coordinates used in CAN [12].

Moreover, our model presents the following nice features:

- Control traffic generated by insertion and deletion is typically local. This increases the suitability of our protocol to dynamic environments.
- Our routing is based on the communication of each node with only its adjacent nodes in a tree. This allows us to effectively use routing traffic as a control information since the expected time for a node between two successive messages coming from a given node is not large.
- The system provides the on-line estimation of the number of peers occurring in a given instant.
- Broadcasting, which is recognized to be a non trivial task in P2P systems [8], is natively supported in our system in $O(\log n)$ time.

The plan of the paper is the following. Section 2 surveys the most important proposals in the field of information retrieval in P2P systems. In Section 3 we present the basic components of our system. In particular, Section 3.1 describes the LBT, that is the basic data structure which TLS relies on, Section 3.2 explains how item search is implemented, Section 3.3 describes our routing algorithm, Sections 3.4 and 3.5 deal with node joining and leaving, respectively, while, in Section 3.6, the problem of node failure is faced. The TLS service, in its complete form, is presented in Section 4 while experiments are reported in Section 5. We draw our conclusion in Section 6

2 Related Work

Information retrieval in P2P systems is a problem widely studied in the recent years. Some approaches are based on Distributed Hash Tables (DHT) [14,12,13,8,1]. In these systems the service key allows us to obtain the peer addressing to the peers providing the service itself. In particular, a random ID is assigned to each peer and an ID (derived from the hash of the service name) is assigned to each service. The peer with ID closest to the service ID stores the information about the peers providing such a service. The above indexing is dynamically maintained, according to the continuous joining and leaving of peers. In P-Grid system [1] a tree-like data structure is also employed. However, our approach is quite different, mainly because each node of our forest maps a peer in the system, we do not need routing tables, and, consequently our routing relies on very different strategies.

In [6] GIA, a Gnutella-like P2P system, that strives to avoid node overloading by explicitly accounting for their capacity constrains, is presented. The capacity of a node depends upon a number of factors including power, disk latency, and access bandwidth.

In [2] authors present some early measurements of a cluster-based architecture (CAP) for P2P systems decentralized, peer-to-peer content location and sharing system that uses network-aware clustering. Network-aware clustering is an effective technique to group clients that are topologically close and under common administrative control. The introduction of one more hierarchy is aimed at scaling up query lookup and forwarding. CAP also does not use hash functions to map objects to locations deterministically.

[16] proposes the Directed BFS technique, which relies on feedback mechanisms to intelligently choose which peer a message should be sent to. Neighbors that have provided quality results in the past will be chosen first, yet neighbors with high loads will be passed over, so that good peers do not become overloaded. The Iterative Deepening technique which allows the search to proceed incrementally until the user is satisfied with the results is also presented. These two simple techniques allow the search to be tuned on a per-query, per-user basis. Experiments over detailed query traces from the Gnutella network show that these techniques greatly reduce the cost of search, while maintaining good quality of results.

In [7], message routing is improved with "routing indices", compact summaries of the content that can be reached via a link. With routing indices, nodes can quickly route queries to the peers that can respond, without wasting the resources of many peers who cannot.

3 The TLS Framework

In this section we describe the basic features of the Tree-Based Lookup Service (TLS). In particular, we introduce the data structure the TLS relies on, peer joining and leaving, and key-based search. We assume that the underlying communication protocol is TCP/IP so that each peer is identified by the IP address. We stress that this section does not provide the description of the lookup service we propose, but only some basic features. Indeed, the TLS service, in its complete form, is presented in Section 4. Our remark here is to avoid that the reader might draw conclusions about performances and scalability of our technique on the basis of data structures here presented, which in fact are not those finally adopted in the system.

3.1 The Lookup Binary Tree

The basic data structure of TLS is a hash table distributed on a binary tree, which we denote by LBT (*Lookup Binary Tree*). In Section 3.2 we will describe how the distributed hash function works. Here we illustrate the LBT. There is a node in LBT for each peer in the system. As a consequence, throughout the paper, we use indifferently the terms peer and node. A given node N belonging to the level $x - 1$ of LBT is identified by the (usual) binary code (of length x) $\langle 1, b_2, \ldots, b_x \rangle$ such that, denoting by $C = \langle N_1, \ldots, N_x \rangle$ the path connecting the

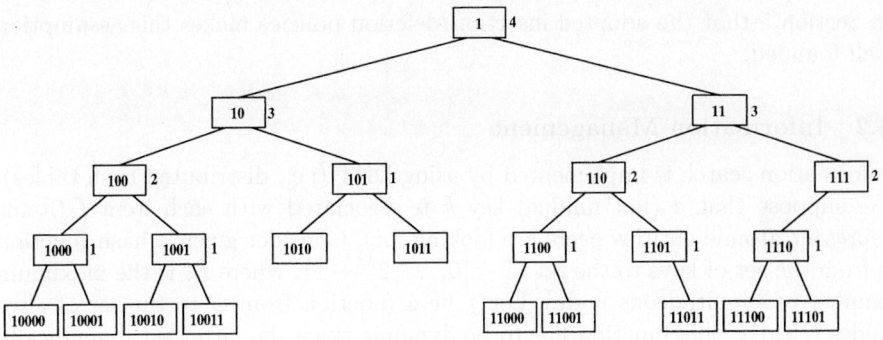

Fig. 1. Example of LBT

root to N, $b_i = 0$ if N_i is the left child of N_{i-1}, $b_i = 1$, otherwise, for each i such that $1 < i \leq x$. Let denote by $ID(N)$ the code of the node N.

We introduce now the notion of *depth* of a node corresponding to the standard notion of depth of the sub-tree rooted in this node. The depth of nodes will be used as a greedy criterion for inserting/deleting nodes into/from the tree respecting the tree balancing goal (see Sections 3.4 and 3.5).

The *depth* of a node N, denoted by *depth(N)*, is a non negative integer such that:

$$depth(N) = \begin{cases} 0 & \text{if } N \text{ is a leaf} \\ max_{M \in child(N)}\{depth(M)\} + 1 & \text{otherwise} \end{cases}$$

where $child(N)$ denotes the set of child nodes of N.

Example 1. In Figure 1 an example of LBT is reported. Each node is represented by a box. The root ID is $\langle 1 \rangle$, while the IDs of the left and right child nodes are $\langle 10 \rangle$ and $\langle 11 \rangle$, respectively. The depth of each node is reported on the right side of the box, except for leaves, whose depth is always 0.
□

LBT implements a logical network with tree topology allowing sharing information embedded into nodes. As usually, some connectivity redundancy is necessary in order to increase fault tolerance of the network. In our case, the minimum amount of information required for each node would be the IP addresses of the parent node and the two children nodes. However, we store in each node also the IP addresses of the sibling node and, furthermore, the addresses of all the ancestor nodes. We will explain in Section 3.6 how this additional information is exploited in case of node failure. Observe that the number of IPs stored in a node is at most logarithmic in the total number of nodes.

In the following sections we will deal with information search and LBT update (i.e., joining and leaving of peers). For the evaluation of the computational cost of all operations we will assume that LBT is balanced. We will show by simulation in Section 5 that the adopted insertion/deletion policies makes this assumption well founded.

3.2 Information Management

Information search is implemented by using DHT (i.e., distributed hash tables). We suppose that a (not unique) key k is associated with each item I (items represent atomic entities peers are looking for). Consider given a hash function h from the set of keys to the set $C = \{0, \ldots, 2^M - 1\}$, where M is the maximum number of simultaneous nodes. Let f be a function from C to the set of alive nodes (clearly, this function has to be dynamic since the latter set dynamically changes).

The composition function $f \circ h$ is used in order to map the key k to the alive node N containing the *goal* information. Such an information consists of all the links to the nodes of LBT where the items, with key k, are saved. Observe that N contains also all the links to the items with key k' which is *synonymous* w.r.t. h (i.e., $h(k) = h(k')$). Thus, when a node looks for an item i with key k, it submits the request to the node $f(h(k))$, and this node replies by sending the link to nodes containing i (if any). For h, any suitable consistent hash function may be used, like, for an instance, SHA-1. We define now how the dynamic function f is arranged. Recall that $h(k)$ is a number belonging to $\{0, \ldots, 2^M - 1\}$. Let $\hat{h}(k)$ be the M-size fix binary code of $h(k)$. Consider now LBT. Starting from the root, we go down along the tree by using the string $\hat{h}(k)$ for moving, at each step, either to the left child or to the right child (0 is associated to the former and 1 to the latter), until a leaf node is reached. Observe that, since the size of $\hat{h}(k)$ is M, that is the maximum number of simultaneous nodes, the above algorithm works also in the worst (very improbable) case of LBT completely unbalanced. Let denote by N the leaf node so identified. Then, the value returned by $f(h(k))$ is $ID(N)$, that identifies the peer *knowing* the location of peers storing items with key k (or synonymous of k w.r.t. h). We call such a peer *responsible* of the key k. Observe that the complexity of evaluating $f(h(k))$ is $O(\log n)$, where n is the number of peers in LBT and the computation of $h(k)$ is assumed to be $O(1)$.

The underlying assumption used above for ensuring the soundness of the above algorithm is that after a node N becomes responsible of a key, no change occurs in the tree. Indeed, the function f returns always a leaf node, but, due to changes (i.e., node joins and leaves), N could have been moved from its original position. Thus, we cannot guarantee in general the above condition.

To be more precise, consider the following argument. There is a moment t_k (corresponding to the join of a node containing the item with key k) when the node N, identified by $f(h(k))$, becomes responsible of the key k (this is called *spread* of k). Until N remains a leaf node, the algorithm above works as explained, so that the function $f(h(k))$ returns always the node N. However, due to changes in the LBT, in a successive time $t > t_k$, since the algorithm proceeds until a leaf node is reached, it may happen that $f(h(k))$, computed at time t, does not return the node N, since it is not a leaf node anymore.

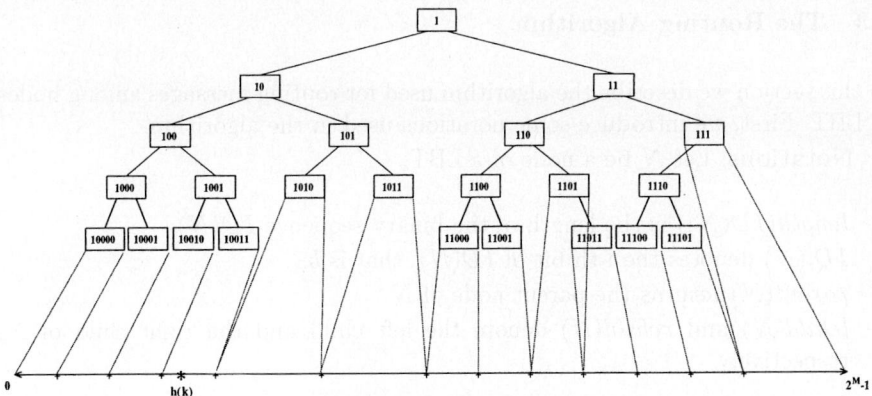

Fig. 2. Key spreading

The problem can be easily overcome by designing both node joining and node leaving algorithms (see Sections 3.4 and 3.5, resp.) in such a way that they guarantee the following invariant:

INVARIANT. Let N be a node in LBT responsible of a key k. Let t_k be the time when the node N becomes responsible of k. Then, at any time $t > t_k$, the node N, if alive, belongs to the path from $f(h(k))$ to the root.
□

Observe that the above solution has not overhead in terms of asymptotic computational cost, since, in order to find the node responsible of a given key k, it suffices to start from the node $f(h(k))$ and to go up toward the root. This requires at most $O(\log n)$ time.

Example 2. In Figure 2, an example of key spreading is reported. Therein, we suppose a new node N, sharing an item I with key k joins the system. The value $h(k)$ is displayed by the star symbol on a segment representing the domain $\{0, \ldots, 2^M - 1\}$. Observe that this domain can be viewed as the lowest level of a full binary tree with M levels. Thus, $h(k)$ identifies a leaf node of such a *virtual* tree.

At this point N has to assign the responsibility of the key k to the node $f(h(k))$. Therefore, this node has to be located. Once the ID of this node is computed, we only have to perform the routing algorithm (that we will introduce in Section 3.3). We have assumed that the binary representation of $h(k)$ is $\langle 0011011101\ldots\rangle$. Thus, the ID of the node responsible of k is $\langle 10011\rangle$. This node stores an information mapping the item I to the IP of N.
□

At this point, in order to complete the search, the routing strategy has to be applied. This is the matter of the next section.

3.3 The Routing Algorithm

In this section we describe the algorithm used for routing messages among nodes of LBT. First, we introduce some notations used in the algorithm.

Notations: Let N be a node of a LBT.

- $length(ID(N))$ is the length of the binary sequence $ID(N)$;
- $ID_i(N)$ denotes the i-th bit of $ID(N)$, that is b_i;
- $parent(N)$ returns the parent node of N;
- $lchild(N)$ and $rchild(N)$ denote the left child and the right child of N, respectively.

Denote by N_s the source node and by N_t the target node of a message in LBT. The algorithm is recursive. A message M is modeled as a tuple $\langle ID(N_s), ID(N_t), O \rangle$, where O denotes the content of M. Consider now the ID of the sender, i.e. $ID(N_s)$. If the string $ID(N_s)$ coincides with $ID(N_t)$ (i.e., sender and receiver coincide), the routing halts. Otherwise, if $ID(N_s)$ is a prefix of $ID(N_t)$, then N_t belongs to the sub-tree N_s. In particular, if $ID_i(N_t) = 0$ (resp. $ID_i(N_t) = 1$), where $i = length(ID(N_s)) + 1)$, N_t belongs to the sub-tree of the left (resp. right) child of N_s. The routing algorithm is recursively called with a new message $M_d = \langle ID(lchild(N_s)), ID(N_t), O \rangle$ (resp., $M_d = \langle ID(rchild(N_s)), ID(N_t), O \rangle$). In case $ID(N_s)$ is not a prefix of $ID(N_t)$, then the routing algorithm is recursively called with message $M_u = \langle ID(parent(N_s)), ID(N_t), O \rangle$. It is easy to see that the algorithm halts at most in 2·log n steps, where n is the number of nodes in LBT. The algorithm is clearly distributed. In particular, each call of the function *routing* is executed by a different peer (that belongs to the route from the source to the target).

The algorithm is reported in Figure 3.

In the next example we show how the routing algorithm works in the LBT of Figure 1.

Example 3. Suppose that a message M has to be sent from the node N_s with $ID = \langle 1000 \rangle$ to the node N_t having $ID = \langle 10010 \rangle$ in the LBT of Figure 1. First, N_s compares its ID with the ID of the message target, and detects that their first three values coincide; since $length(ID(N_s)) = 4$ (i.e., $ID(N_s)$ is not a prefix of $ID(N_t)$), N_s delivers the message to its parent, say N_p. At this point, since N_p is not the target node of the message, the routing algorithm is re-executed in the node N_p. Thus, the comparison between the ID of N_p and the ID of N_t is performed. This time, since $ID(N_p)$ is a prefix of $ID(N_t)$, and the first bit of $ID(N_t)$ following the prefix $ID(N_p)$ is 1, the message is delivered to the right child node of N_p, having $ID = \langle 1001 \rangle$. Let denote this node by N_r. As before, $ID(N_r)$ is a prefix of $ID(N_t)$ too. But, at this step, the first bit of $ID(N_t)$ following this prefix is 1, so that the message is delivered to the left child of N_r, which is the target node.

□

```
function routing (ID(N_s), ID(N_t), O)
  if ID(N_s) = ID(N_t) then
    exit
  else
    if ID(N_s) is a prefix of ID(N_t) then
      i := length(ID(N_s))
      if ID_{i+1}(N_t) = 0 then
        routing (ID(lchild(N_s)), ID(N_t), O)
        {M is sent to the left child node}
      else
        routing (ID(rchild(N_s)), ID(N_t), O)
        {M is sent to the right child node}
      end if
    else
      routing (ID(parent(N_s)), ID(N_t), O)
      {M is sent to the parent node}
    end if
  end if
```

Fig. 3. The Routing Algorithm

3.4 Node Joining

The knowledge of at least one IP of a peer belonging to the system is necessary for a new peer N joining the system.[1] Let S be a node *known* by N.

First, N initializes $ID(N)$ to the value of $ID(S)$. Then N, starting from S, proceeds downward in the tree until a non-full node L is reached. In particular, from a given intermediate full node I, the route goes to the child node having the lowest *depth* (see the definition given in Section 3.1). Clearly, in case of parity, a random choice is done. Each step toward a left (resp., right) child, appends the value 0 (resp., 1) to the sequence $ID(N)$. When a non-full node L is reached, N becomes the child of L, by randomly selecting among the empty positions.

It appears clear that in order to implement the above algorithm the information about its depth has to be store in each peer . As a consequence, such an information has to be updated after a node insertion in LBT (beside, clearly, the connectivity information described in Section 3.1 – this involves only the inserted node).

In particular, assumed the depth of the new node N is updated to the value 0, the algorithm proceeds recursively in the following fashion. Each node whose depth is updated (including N), send to the parent node the value of its new depth increased by 1. In addition, each node updates its depth with the received value (from a child node) only if such a value is greater than the old depth. Observe that the above algorithm requires at most $\log n$ time, where n is the number of nodes in LBT. However, it is easy to see that the amortized cost is

---

[1] In practice, such IPs can be obtained either by contacting a central server or by scanning a range of IP.

$O(1)$ (indeed, the logarithmic cost is produced only in case the insertion enforces the addition of a new level to the tree).

The above greedy criterion tries to maintain the tree as balanced as possible. Observe that, the same criterion has to be applied at the beginning stage, i.e., when the starting peer S is selected by the joining peer among the known peers. In particular, a peer with minimum ID length is chosen.

In Section 5 we will show by simulation that the greedy approach appears very satisfactory.

It is easy to verify that the overall worst-case complexity of the join of a node is $O(\log n)$, where n is the number of nodes in the system.

Observe that the node joining algorithm here illustrated, guarantees the Invariant introduced in Section 3.2. Moreover, the approach used for contrasting loss of balance, has not to compromise the Invariant, so that AVL trees cannot be employed.

An example of node joining to the LBT of Figure 1 is next reported.

Example 4. Suppose that the new node N obtains the IP of the node with $ID = \langle 10 \rangle$ as an "entry point". Following the greedy criterion, N traverses the tree through the path $\langle 1010 \rangle$, leading to the node $\langle 1010 \rangle$ (observe that the last node is chosen in randomly, solving, in this way, the ambiguity generated by the greedy criterion). N becomes the left child of the last node and, therefore, its ID results $\langle 10100 \rangle$.
□

3.5 Node Leaving

A node N may leave the system. Node failure is a different matter because it causes loss of information inside the system (this issue will be treated in the next section).

It is easy to see that node leaving, thanks to message passing, can be faced by a simple algorithm of node deletion in a binary tree.

In particular, the leaving node is replaced by the child with maximum depth (according to the greedy criterion), inducing a new (virtual) deletion of such a node. This deletion, recursively, is treated as above, until a leaf is reached. Also this algorithm is logarithmic in the number of nodes of the tree.

Clearly, depth of the involved nodes has to be updated.

Observe that, before leaving, the node send to its parent all information related to its key responsibility. This way, the parent node becomes responsible of every key the node were responsible of.

It is easy to verify that the node leaving algorithm preserves the Invariant introduced in Section 3.2.

The following example describes the leaving of the root of the LBT reported in Figure 1.

Example 5. Consider the LBT of Figure 1. Suppose the root leaves the system. Figure 4 shows how the shifting operation is cascaded. In this figure, an arrow

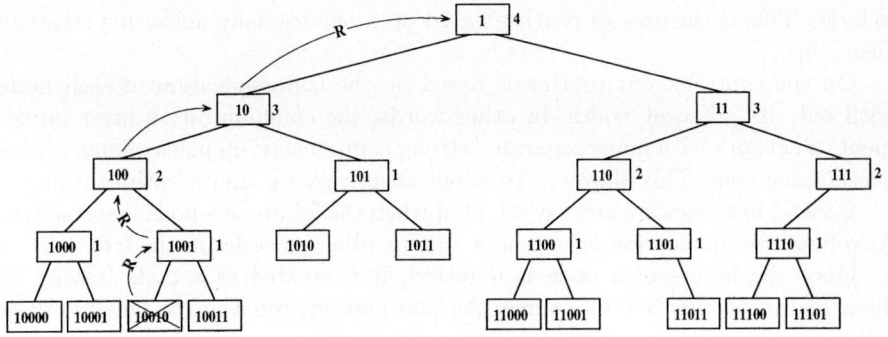

Fig. 4. Node shifting caused by the leaving of the root

from a node N_s to a node N_t, denotes that the replacement of N_t by N_s. Moreover, labeled arrows denote random choices (occurring in case of children with equal depth). Note that, after deletion, the leaf node with ID $\langle 10010 \rangle$ occurring in the original tree disappears.
□

REMARK. It is worth noting that the above mechanism implements an intrinsic measuring of information aging: if founding the node responsible of a key k requires too many steps, then, probably the searched node is *old* and, thus, maintains old information (potentially not valid anymore). On the basis of the above observation, it is thus possible to arrange some optimization technique for which the search halts after a suitable number of steps toward the root.
□

3.6 Node Failure

The failure of one or more nodes is an event that endangers the structure of the system and causes the loss of information stored in the failing nodes. The rapidity in detecting such an event becomes a crucial issue for guaranteeing the system consistence. Indeed in case of simultaneous failure of adjacent nodes, the actions to perform become dramatically more complex. Thus, the detection should be completed before the failure of other (possibly adjacent) nodes occurs.

In many systems, in order to detect node failure each node periodically sends control messages to other nodes, so that the prolonged absence of a control message from a node detects its failure [12]. It happens that a node is responsible of failure detection of a set of other nodes. The drawback of this technique is the overhead traffic.

One could think to use routing traffic as a control information. Indeed, incoming routing messages can be used as alive announcements for free. This optimization is always applicable. However it is not effective if, for a given node N, the expected time between two successive messages coming from a given node is large. This is the case of routing based on a one-to-many delivering strategy (like [14]).

On the contrary, our routing is based on the communication of each node with only its adjacent nodes. In other words, the communication layer implements a network with many separate "strong components" in place of many large overlapping ones. This allows us to adopt effectively the above optimization.

Control messages are anyway adopted when the failure of a node is suspected. Also here communication occurs only among adjacent nodes in the tree.

Once the failure of a node is detected, it is treated as a node leaving as described in Section 3.5. Of course, the information stored in the failed node is lost.

4 The TLS Service

In this section we describe the TLS service and give a probabilistic traffic analysis to theoretically prove the scalability of our system.

We start by analyzing how the total traffic, required for implementing routing in the model so far described, is distributed among nodes of the tree. Indeed, the suspect is that the hierarchical topology of the logical network may induce congestion problems involving nodes belonging to levels close to the root. Even though our goal is to have load biasing, we have to prevent node congestion.

This problem can be formally studied assuming both (1) uniform distribution messages among peers and (2) LBT full. For an LBT balanced but not full (the actual case, in general), the obtained results are asymptotically verified.

The next theorem gives the traffic probability of a LBT node. It results that such a probability depends only on the level of the node and decreases as the level increases.

Theorem 1. Let k be the number of levels of a LBT. Moreover, let I be a node belonging to the level i, where $0 \leq i \leq k-2$. Then, the probability that a routing message involves I is:

$$P_i = \frac{2\left((2^{k-i-2})^2 + (2^{k-i-1}) + (2^{k-i-1}+1)((2^k-1)-(2^{k-i-1}+1))\right)}{(2^k-1)(2^k-2)}$$

Proof (Sketch). First, observe that I is not a leaf node since $i \leq k-2$ and that (1) the system consists of $2^k - 1$ peers and (2) 2^{k-i-1} is the number of nodes descendent from I. The probability is computed by the fraction between the traffic involving I and the total traffic of the system. The traffic crossing I (represented by the numerator) consists of 3 components:

1. $2(2^{k-i-2})^2$ is the traffic between a nodes belonging to the left sub-tree having I as a root and a nodes belonging to the right one.
2. $2(2^{k-i-1})$ takes into account the traffic between I and a node descending from I.

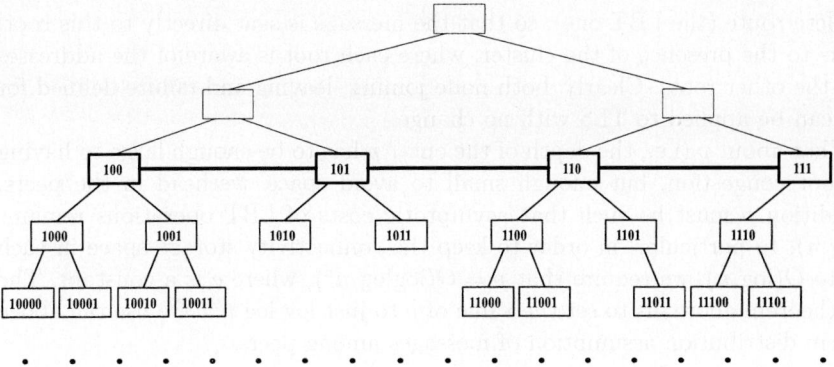

Fig. 5. Example of LBT-forest

3. $2(2^{k-i-1}+1)((2^k-1)-(2^{k-i-1}+1))$ models the traffic between a node descendent by I, plus I, and a remaining node of the system.

Finally, the denominator represents the number of possible messages between any pair of peers.

The above theorem makes evident a serious drawback of the *tout-court* tree-based approach. Indeed, it can be verified that for small i (i.e., for nodes close to the root), the value of P_i is considerably higher than lower nodes. Not surprisingly, the value of P_i (after a slight increase from $i=0$ to $i=1$ due to the absence for the root of traffic incoming from higher levels), decreases exponentially as i increases. Observe that P_i represents the fraction of traffic involving a node belonging to level i. Thus, the high concentration of probability in the highest levels, is not tolerable. This suggests us how to implement the tree-model in order to make TLS effective.

So far, we have assigned to each node of the LBT a peer of the system. Now we *cut* the head of the tree, by assigning to real peers only nodes below a given level, say p. p is not constant, but depends on the number of nodes in the system. This way we do not have a single LBT but a forest consisting of 2^{p-1} LBTs, built on the shape of the original LBT. We call this data structure LBT-*forest*. Observe that the hash indexing as well as peer encoding are global and corresponding to those defined in the original LBT. Figure 5 shows an example of LBT-forest. The black line connects the roots for denoting the cluster including them.

For increasing robustness we connect each other all the roots of these LBTs (producing a peer cluster). Observe that the routing algorithm described in Section 3.3 is preserved, modulo a slight change regarding the portion of the routes above the root cluster. Easily, once a route has reached a root of the forest, it can be trivially computed the other root of the forest involved in the complete route (the LBT one), so that the message is sent directly to this root, thanks to the presence of the cluster, where each root is aware of the addresses of all the other roots. Clearly, both node joining, leaving and failure defined for LBT can be applied to TLS with no change.

What about p (i.e., the depth of the cut)? p has to be enough large to having low root congestion, but enough small to avoid space overhead in the peers. In addition p must be such that asymptotic costs of LBT operations remains $O(\log n)$. In particular, in order to keep the connectivity storage space in each peer to $O(\log n)$, we require that $p = O(\mathrm{loglog}\, n^c)$, where c is a constant. The next theorem allows us to set the value of p to just $\log \log n^2$. We use the above uniform distribution assumption of messages among peers.

Theorem 2. Let R be a root of a LBT-forest obtained from a LBT with k levels by cutting the $p-1$ highest ones. Then, the probability that a routing message involves R is:

$$P_R = \frac{2(2^{k-p+1}-1)^2(2^{p-1}-1) + 2\frac{(2^{k-p+1}-2)^2}{4}}{2^{(p-1)}(2^{k-p+1}-1)(2^{(p-1)}(2^{k-p+1}-1)-1)} \simeq \frac{1}{2^{p-2}}$$

Proof (Sketch). The forest consists of 2^{p-1} tree, and each tree contains $(2^{k-p+1}-1)$ peers. The probability that R is involved in a routing message is computed as the fraction between the traffic involving R and the total traffic of the system. Moreover, the former can be traffic internal to the tree itself or cross traffic, i.e. traffic between two different trees. The numerator of the ratio consists of (1) the contribution of the traffic going from the tree, which R is the root of, toward any other node (among the $2^{p-1}-1$ trees), plus (2) the internal traffic crossing the two sub-trees of R. The denominator represents the number of possible messages between any pair of peers. The estimation probability is an upper bound of the real probability and is computed by suitably neglecting some small contributions of the formula.

By setting $p = \log \log n^2$, it results that $P_R = \frac{2}{\log n}$. Thus, the traffic fraction involving roots decreases as the number of peers increases in a heuristically acceptable measure.

The above solution implements a non uniform distribution of routing traffic by loading higher nodes more than lower ones in the LBT-forest. In this sense, TLS adopts a hybrid model (neither *pure* P2P nor *super-peer* based), where a sort of evolutionary selection in the peer population promotes the most stable peers (thus, belonging to high levels) as peers with the highest traffic load. This captures real-life environments like Web services, where stability is always associated to high bandwidth capacity.

As a further remark, we observe that the TLS model allows the dynamic change of the parameter p with no extra asymptotic cost. First, the system allows us to know an estimate of n by consulting the root depths of the LBT-forest, necessary for setting p. However, observe that the sensitivity of p w.r.t. changes of n is very low (recall that $p = \log \log n^2$). Anyway, the increase (resp.

decrease) of p can be easily implemented with $O(\log n)$ cost. Indeed, the increase is implemented simply by updating links of the new roots (in order to make the new cluster and to release parent nodes from the routing task) whereas the decrease is implemented by resuming parent nodes still alive and by producing a virtual failure of parent nodes not alive anymore. Another nice feature of TLS is that it supports broadcasting in $O(\log n)$ time by exploiting the tree structure.

We stress that the above traffic load biasing concerns only the routing traffic, that is dramatically smaller than the traffic involving centralized (even hierarchical) services commonly called *super-peers*, which are widely successfully used. Moreover, we observe that in a practical implementation of our approach a number of optimizations can be adopted, such as:

- Increasing the number of forests by setting p to higher values. In general, for $p = \log \log n^c$, where c is a positive integer constant, we have a probability that a routing message involves a root $P_R = \frac{\frac{4}{c}}{\log n}$. Thus, with only an overhead in terms of the exact cost (no overhead in terms of asymptotic cost is generated) of updating p (as well as the space required by each root for implementing the cluster in the top of the forest), we can set c to a suitable value depending on QoS requirements and performances of root nodes.
- A peer P may in each instant ask to one of its children to (partially) bypass routing in such a way that the traffic involving P is reduced. The price of this is storing in the child node the IPs of nodes which messages have to be forwarded to.
- Caching, similar to that employed in DNS, can be enabled.
- The shape of the top of the forest may differ from that considered in the probabilistic framework. In particular, it can be adapted to the actual traffic involving roots and to their capabilities, by going down (and thus splitting the job of a root) in case of congestion problems.

5 Simulation

In this section we perform a number of experiments by simulation with the purpose of analyzing both (1) LBT balancing, (2) joins and leaves control traffic and (3) routing performance. In the experiments n varies from 10^3 to 10^6. We consider a single LBT initially empty. Then we populate the LBT by performing n insertions and we simulate the dynamics of the system by executing n operations randomly chosen between insertion and deletion. Each operation involves a randomly chosen peer.

(1) In Figure 6 a graph displaying the number of levels versus n is reported. Experiments show that the greedy criterion used for node insertion/deletion allows us to evaluate costs of operation as in case of balanced LBT.

(2) In Figure 7 we display the average cost of insertion and deletion of a peer. As remarked earlier, being the depth management amortized cost $O(1)$, this operation has no impact on the overall cost displayed in figure. The behavior, as studied analytically, is logarithmic in the number of peers.

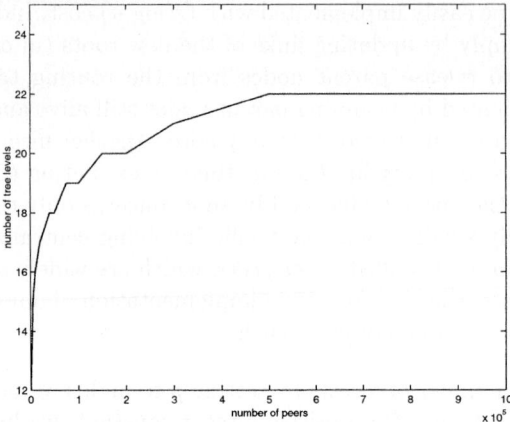

Fig. 6. Number of levels versus number of peers

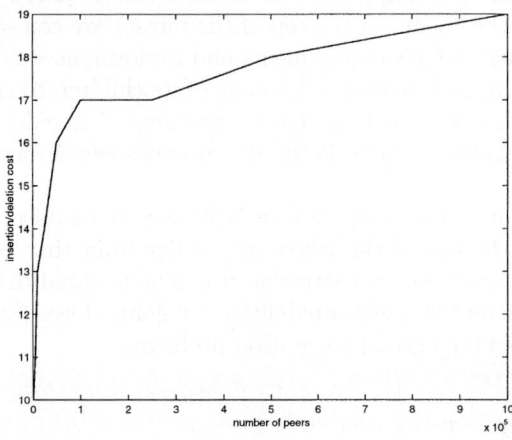

Fig. 7. Insertion/deletion cost versus number of peers

(3) Finally, in Figure 7 the number of hops versus number of peers is reported. This experiments measures the behavior of our routing protocol, confirming the result that message routing follows a logarithmic law in the number of peers.

6 Conclusion and Future Work

In this paper we have shown that renouncing to pure centralized lookup services may give sensible benefits in terms of joining/leaving efficiency without compromising other essential properties. This is done by distributing routing load in a non uniform way, consistent with a hierarchical organization of peers. Both theo-

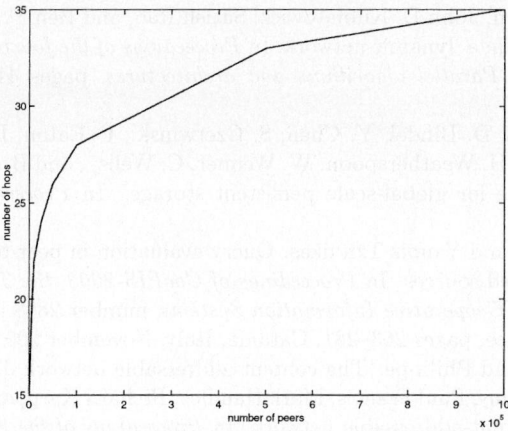

Fig. 8. Number of hops versus number of peers

retical and experimental results validate our proposal. As a future work we plan to perform and test some optimization techniques, analyzing security problems and improve the current prototype.

References

1. K. Aberer. P-grid: A self-organizing access structure for p2p information retrieval. In *Proceedings of the CoopIS*, pages 179–194, 2001.
2. Krishnamurthy B and Xie Y Wang J. Early measurements of a cluster-based architecture for p2p systems. In *Proceedings of the First ACM SIGCOMM Workshop on Internet Measurement*, pages 105–109. ACM Press, 2002.
3. W. Bolosky, J. Douceur, D. Ely, and M. Theimer. Feasibility of a serverless distributed file system deployed on an existing set of desktop pcs. In *Proceedings of SIGMETRICS*, 2000.
4. W.B. Bradley and D.P. Maher. The nemo p2p service orchestration framework. In *Proceedings of the 37th Annual Hawaii Int. Conf. on System Sciences*, 2004.
5. Diego Calvanese, Giuseppe De Giacomo, Maurizio Lenzerini, and Riccardo Rosati. Logical foundations of peer to peer data integration. In *Proceedings of the Twenty-third ACM SIGACT-SIGMOD-SIGART Symposium on Principles of Database Systems*, 2004.
6. Yatin Chawathe, Sylvia Ratnasamy, Lee Breslau, Nick Lanham, and Scott Shenker. Making gnutella-like p2p systems scalable. In *Proceedings of the 2003 conference on Applications, technologies, architectures, and protocols for computer communications*, pages 407–418. ACM Press, 2003.
7. A. Crespo and H. Garcia-Molina. Routing indices for peer-to-peer systems. In *Proceedings of the IEEE Int. Conf. on Distributed Computing Systems (ICDCS'02),*, 2002.

8. Kirsten Hildrum, John D. Kubiatowicz, Satish Rao, and Ben Y. Zhao. Distributed object location in a dynamic network. In *Proceedings of the fourteenth annual ACM symposium on Parallel algorithms and architectures*, pages 41–52. ACM Press, 2002.
9. J. Kubiatowicz, D. Bindel, Y. Chen, S. Czerwinski, P. Eaton, D. Geels, R. Gummadi, S. Rhea, H. Weatherspoon, W. Weimer, C. Wells, , and B. Zhao. Oceanstore: An architecture for global-scale persistent storage. In *Proceedings of ASPLOS*, 2000.
10. Carlo Meghini and Yannis Tzitzikas. Query evaluation in peer-to-peer networks of taxonomy- based sources. In *Proceedings of CooPIS-2003, the Tenth International Conference on Cooperative Information Systems*, number 2888 in Lecture notes in computer science, pages 263–281, Catania, Italy, November 2003. Springer Verlag.
11. Pierre Fraigniaud Philippe. The content-addressable network d2b, 2003.
12. Sylvia Ratnasamy, Paul Francis, Mark Handley, Richard Karp, and Scott Schenker. A scalable content-addressable network. In *Proceedings of the 2001 conference on Applications, technologies, architectures, and protocols for computer communications*, pages 161–172. ACM Press, 2001.
13. Antony I. T. Rowstron and Peter Druschel. Pastry: Scalable, decentralized object location, and routing for large-scale peer-to-peer systems. In *Proceedings of the IFIP/ACM International Conference on Distributed Systems Platforms Heidelberg*, pages 329–350. Springer-Verlag, 2001.
14. Ion Stoica, Robert Morris, David Karger, M. Frans Kaashoek, and Hari Balakrishnan. Chord: A scalable peer-to-peer lookup service for internet applications. In *Proceedings of the 2001 conference on Applications, technologies, architectures, and protocols for computer communications*, pages 149–160. ACM Press, 2001.
15. A. D. R. Marc Waldman and L. F. Cranor. Publius: A robust, tamper-evident, censorship-resistant, web publishing system. In *Proceedings of the 9th USENIX Security Symposium*, pages 59–72, 2000.
16. Beverly Yang and Hector Garcia-Molina. Improving search in peer-to-peer networks. In *Proceedings of the 22 nd International Conference on Distributed Computing Systems (ICDCS'02)*, page 5. IEEE Computer Society, 2002.

Minimizing the Network Distance in Distributed Web Crawling

Odysseas Papapetrou and George Samaras

University of Cyprus, Department of Computer Science,
75 Kallipoleos str., P.O. Box 20537, Nicosia, Cyprus
{cspapap, cssamara}@cs.ucy.ac.cy

Abstract. Distributed crawling has shown that it can overcome important limitations of the centralized crawling paradigm. However, the distributed nature of current distributed crawlers is currently not fully utilized. The optimal benefits of this approach are usually limited to the sites hosting the crawler. In this work we describe IPMicra, a distributed location aware web crawler that utilizes an IP address hierarchy and allows crawling of links in a near optimal location aware manner. The crawler outperforms earlier distributed crawling approaches without a significant overhead.

1 Introduction

The challenging task of indexing the web (usually referred as web-crawling) has been heavily addressed in research literature. However, due to the current size, increasing rate, and high change frequency of the web, no web crawling schema is able to pace with the web. While current web crawlers managed to index more than 3 billion documents [6], it is estimated that the maximum web coverage of each search engine is around 16% of the estimated web size [8].

Distributed crawling [10,11,9,1,3,4] was proposed to improve this situation. However, all the previous work was not taking full advantage of the distributed nature of the application. While some of the previously suggested systems were fully distributed over the Internet (many different locations), each web document was not necessarily crawled from the most near crawler but from a randomly selected crawler. While the distribution of the crawling function was efficiently reducing the network bottleneck from the search engine's site and significantly improving the quality of the results, the previous proposals were not at all optimized.

In this work, we describe a near-optimal, for the distributed crawlers, URL delegation methodology, so that each URL is crawled from the nearest crawler. The approach, called IPMicra, facilitates crawling of each URL from the nearest crawler (where nearness is defined in terms of network latency) without creating excessive load to the Internet infrastructure. Then, the crawled data is processed and compressed before sent to the centralized database, this way eliminating the network and processing bottleneck in the search engine's central database site. We use data from the four Regional Internet Registries (RIRs) to build a hierarchical clustering of IP addresses, which assists us to perform an efficient URL delegation to the migrating crawlers. In addition to location aware crawling, IPMicra, provides load balancing taking into consideration the crawler's capacity and configuration. Furthermore, it dynamically adjusts to the changing nature of the Internet infrastructure itself.

This short introduction is followed by a brief description on related work, giving emphasis to UCYMicra, a distributed crawling infrastructure which we extend to perform location aware web crawling. We then introduce and describe location aware web crawling. Section 4 describes and evaluates our approach toward location aware web crawling, called IPMicra. Section 5 summarizes the advantages of IPMicra. Conclusions and future work are presented in section 6.

2 Related Work

While the hardware bottleneck is easily (but not cheaply) handled in the modern web crawling systems with parallelization, the network bottleneck is not so easily eliminated. In order to eliminate the delay caused by the network latency (occurred mainly due to the network distance between the crawler and the target URLs), the modern crawlers issue many concurrent HTTP/GET requests. While this speeds up crawling, it does not optimize the utilization of the still limited network resources, and the overhead in hardware and network for keeping many threads open is very high. The network resources are not released (in order to be reused) as fast as possible. Furthermore, in most of the cases, the data is transmitted uncompressed (since most of the web-servers have compression disabled), and unprocessed to the central sink (the search engine), thus, its size is not reduced. Finally, the whole crawling process generates a big workload for the whole Internet infrastructure, since the network packets have to go through many routers (due to the big network distance of the crawler and the servers).

There were several proposals trying to eliminate the bottlenecks occurred in centralized crawling, such as [2,5]. However, in the authors' knowledge, none of them was able to solve the single-sink problem. All of the crawled data was transmitted to a single point, uncompressed, and unprocessed, thus, requiring great network bandwidth to perform the crawling function (the nature of centralized systems). Thus, realizing the limitations of centralized crawling, several distributed crawling approaches have been proposed [10,11,9,1,3,4]. The new approaches are based in the concept of having many crawlers distributed in the web, using different network and hardware resources, coordinated from the search engine, sharing the crawling workload. The crawlers sometimes run in the search engine's machines [3,4], sometimes in customers' machines [11,10], and sometimes in third parties (normal Internet users) [9]. The innovation in these approaches is that they mostly eliminate the network bottleneck in the search engine's site, since they reduce the size of the data transmitted to it (due to data processing, compression, and filtering before transmission). More exactly, while distribution introduces one more step - the step of transmitting the data from the distributed crawlers back to the central search engine database - distributed crawlers do eliminate the network and processing bottlenecks in the search engine's site, since they can significantly reduce the size of the data (due to filtering and compression), and prepare the data (using distributed resources) for integration in the database.

As in the centralized crawlers, distributed crawlers also issued many concurrent HTTP/GET requests to minimize the network latency. However, as in the centralized crawling case, this approach is not the optimal, neither for network utilization, nor for the Internet infrastructure. More specifically, the distributed crawlers are forced to open many concurrent threads in order to cover the network latency, thus, they require more hardware and network resources. Furthermore, the network resources cannot be reused as fast as possible, since they are not optimally released. Finally, increased load occurs in the Internet infrastructure since the HTTP/GETs and HTTP/HEADs results are transmitted from the web servers uncompressed, unprocessed, and unfiltered, over a long network distance, through many routers, until they arrive in the distributed crawling points, for filtering and compression. *To remedy all these*, we now propose a truly distributed location aware web crawling, which minimizes the network latency in distributed crawling (between the distributed crawlers and the web-pages), speeds up the web crawling process, and also enables efficient load balancing schemes.

2.1 The UCYMicra System

UCYMicra [10,11] was recently proposed as an alternative to distributed web crawling. Realizing the limitations of the centralized web crawling systems and several other distributed crawling systems we designed and developed an efficient distributed web crawling infrastructure, powered from mobile agents. The web crawlers were constructed as mobile agents, and dispatched to collaborating organizations and web servers, where they performed **downloading of web documents, processing and extraction of keywords, and, finally, compression and transmission** back to the central search engine. Then, the so-called migrating crawlers remained in the remote systems and performed constant monitoring of all the web documents assigned to them for changes.

More specifically, the original UCYMicra consists of three subsystems, (a) the Coordinator subsystem, (b) the Mobile Agents subsystem, and (c) a public Search Engine that executes user queries on the database maintained by the Coordinator subsystem.

The Coordinator subsystem resides at the Search Engine site and is responsible for administering the Mobile Agents subsystem (create, monitor, kill a migrating crawler), which is responsible for the crawling task. Furthermore, the coordinator is responsible for maintaining the search database with the crawling results that it gets from the migrating crawlers.

The Mobile Agents subsystem is divided into two categories of mobile agents; the Migrating Crawlers (or Mobile Crawlers) and the Data Carries. The former are responsible for on-site crawling and monitoring of remote Web servers. Furthermore, they process the crawled pages, and send the results back to the co-

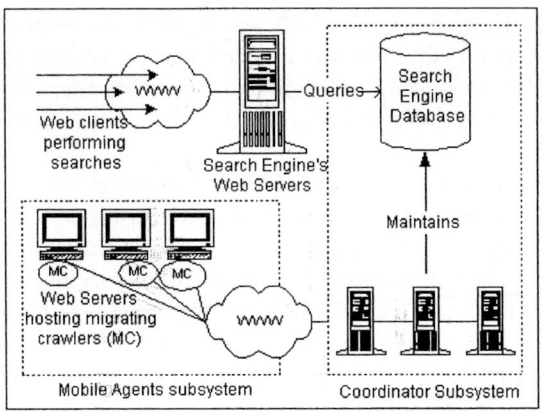

Fig. 1. UCYMicra basic components

ordinator subsystem for integration in the search engine's database. The latter are responsible for transferring the processed and compressed information from the Migrating Crawlers back to the Coordinator subsystem. Figure 1 illustrates the high-level architecture of UCYMicra.

The UCYMicra paradigm was easily received by the users, and was appreciated and tempting to the web server administrators, since it could offer a quality-controlled crawling service without security risks (they could easily and efficiently set security and resource usage constraints). Actually, the use of UCYMicra was twofold. Powered from the portability of the mobile agents' code, the UCYMicra crawlers could easily be deployed and remotely administered in an arbitrary number of collaborating machines and perform distributed crawling in machines' *idle time* (similar to the seti@home approach [12]. SETI users download and install a screensaver, which performs background processing while active, and sends the results back to the SETI team). Further on, the crawlers could be deployed in high-performance dedicated machines controlled from the search engine company, for performing efficient distributed crawling with very little communication overhead.

Due to its distribution, UCYMicra was able to outperform other centralized web crawling schemes, by requiring at least one order of magnitude less time for crawling the same set of web pages [11,10]. The processing and compression of the documents to the remote sites was also important, since this reduced the data transmitted through Internet back to the search engine site, and also eliminated the processing and network bottlenecks. Furthermore, UCYMicra not only respected the collaborating hosts (by working only when the resources were unused) but also offered quality crawling - almost like *live update* - to the servers hosted in the collaborating companies (a service usually purchased from the search engines).

3   Location Aware Web-Crawling

The concept behind **location aware web crawling** is simple. Location aware web crawling is distributed web crawling that facilitates the delegation of the web pages to the 'nearest' crawler (i.e. the crawler that would download the page the fastest). **Nearness** and **locality** are always in terms of network distance (latency) and not in terms of physical (geographical) distance. The purpose of finding the nearest crawler for each web-page is to minimize the time spent in crawling of the specific web-page, as well as the network and hardware resources required for the crawling function. This way, location aware web crawling can increase the performance of distributed web crawlers, promising a significant increase in web coverage.

Being distributed, the location aware web crawling approach introduces the load (small, compared to the gains of the approach) of transferring the filtered, compressed, and processed data from the distributed crawlers to the central database server. However, the search engine site's network is now released from the task of crawling the pages, which is now delegated in the distributed crawlers. This releases important network and hardware resources, significantly greater than the newly introduced load for transferring the data from the distributed crawlers back to the central search engine. Furthermore, optimization techniques, such as filtering, remote processing and compression, are enabled from the distributed crawlers and can be applied in the communication between the crawlers and the search engine, thus eliminating the network and processing bottlenecks in the search engine's site. In fact, distributed crawling, by combining filtering, processing, and finally compression, can reduce the size of the data transmitted to the search engine for integration in the database as much as one order of magnitude, without loosing any details useful for the search engine. Even further reduction in the size of data is available by adopting the distributed crawlers to the search engine's ranking algorithms.

In order to find the nearest crawler to a web server we use **probing**. Experiments showed that the traditional ICMP-ping tool, or the time that takes for a HTTP/HEAD request to be completed, are very suitable for probing. In the majority of our experiments, the crawler with the smallest probing time was the one that could download the web page the fastest. Thus, the migrating crawler having the smallest probing result to a web server is possibly the crawler most near to that web server.

Evaluating **location aware** web crawling, and comparing it with distributed **location unaware** web crawling (e.g. UCYMicra) was actually simple. UCYMicra was enhanced and, via probing, the URLs were optimally delegated to the available migrating crawlers. More specifically, each URL was probed from **all** the crawlers, and then delegated to the 'nearest' one. Location aware web crawling outperformed its opponent, the "unaware" UCYMicra, which delegated the various URL randomly, by requiring **one order of magnitude less time (1/10th)** to download the same set of pages, with the same set of migrating crawlers and under approximately the same network load.

4 The IPMicra System

While location-aware web crawling significantly reduces the download time, building a location aware web crawler is not trivial. In fact, the straight-forward approach toward location aware web crawling requires each URL to be probed (i.e. `ping`)from all the crawlers, in order to find the most near web crawler to handle it. Thus, extensive probing is required, making the approach impractical. The purpose of IPMicra is to eliminate this impracticality. IPMicra specifically aims in reducing the required probes for delegating a URL to the nearest crawler. We designed and built an efficient self-maintaining algorithm for domain delegation (not just a URL) with minimal network overhead by utilizing information collected from the Regional Internet Registries (RIRs).

Regional Internet Registries are non-profit organizations that are delegated the task of handling IP addresses to the clients. Currently, there are four regional Internet Registries covering in the world: APNIC, ARIN, LACNIC, and RIPE NCC. All the sub-networks (i.e. the companies' and the universities' sub-networks) are registered in their regional registries (through their Local Internet Registries) with their IP address ranges. Via the RIRs a hierarchy of IP ranges can be created. Consider the IP range starting from the complete range of IP addresses (from 0.0.0.0 to 255.255.255.255). The IP addresses are delegated to RIRs in large address blocks, which are then sub-divided to the LIRs (Local Internet Registries); lastly they are sub-divided to organizations, as IP ranges, called subnets.

The IPMicra system is architecturally divided in the same three subsystems that were introduced in the original UCYMicra: (a) the public search engine, (b) the coordinator subsystem, and (c) the mobile agents subsystem. Only the public search engine remains unchanged. The coordinator subsystem is enhanced for building the IP hierarchy tree and coordinating the delegation of the subnets, and the migrating crawlers are enhanced for probing the sites and reporting the results back to the coordinator.

4.1 The IP-Address Hierarchy and Crawlers Placement

The basic idea is the organizing of the IP addresses, and subsequently the URLs, in a hierarchical fashion. We use the WHOIS data collected from the RIRs to build and maintain a hierarchy with all the IP ranges (IP subnets) currently assigned to organizations (e.g., see figure 2). The data, apart from the IP subnets, contains the company that registers each subnet. Our experience shows that the expected maximum height of our hierarchy is 8. The required time for building the hierarchy is small, and it can be easily loaded in main memory in any average system. While the IP addresses hierarchy does not remain constant over time, we found out that it is sufficient to rebuild it every three months, and easy populate it with the old hierarchy's data.

Once the IP hierarchy is built, the migrating crawlers are sent to affiliate organizations. Since the IP address of the machine that will host the crawler is known, we can immediately assign that subnet to the new crawler(e.g., crawler X

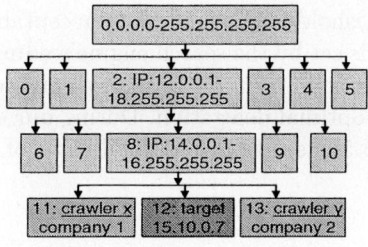

Fig. 2. A sample IP hierarchy. Subnets 11 and 13 belong to company 1 and company 2 respectively. Subnets 11 and 13 are assigned to crawlers X and Y respectively

is hosted by a machine belonging to subnet 11). In this way the various crawlers populate the hierarchy. The hierarchy can now be used to efficiently find the nearest crawler for every new URL, utilizing only a small number of probes. The populated hierarchy also enables calibrating and load-balancing algorithms (described later) to execute.

Updating the IP-address hierarchy is not difficult either. When we detect significant changes in the hierarchy data collected from the RIRs we rebuild the hierarchy from scratch (in our testing, rebuilding the hierarchy once a month was sufficient). Then, we pass the data from the old hierarchy to the updated one, in order to avoid re-delegations of already delegated URLs, and continue the algorithm execution normally. Any invalid re-delegations (i.e. important changes in the underlying connectivity of a web server or a web crawler), will be later detected, and the hierarchy will be calibrated (described later).

4.2 Probing

Since the introduction of classless IP addresses, the estimation of the network distance between two Internet peers, and subsequently, location aware web crawling, cannot be based in the IP addresses. For example, two subsequent IP addresses may reside in two distant parts of the planet, or, even worse, in the same part, but with very high network latency between. Therefore we needed an efficient function to estimate the network latency between the crawlers and the web-servers hosting the URLs.

Experiments showed that the traditional ICMP-ping tool, or the time that takes for a HTTP/HEAD request to be completed, are very suitable for probing. In the majority of our experiments (91% with ping and 92.5% when using HTTP/HEAD for probing), the crawler with the smallest probing time was the one that could download the web page the fastest. Thus, the migrating crawler having the smallest probing result to a web server is possibly the crawler most near to that web server.

Probing threshold: During the delegation procedure (described in detail in section 4.3) we consider a crawler to be suitable to get a URL if the probing result from that crawler to the URL is less than a threshold, called **probing**

threshold. Probing threshold is the maximum acceptable probing time from a crawler to a page and it is set by the search engine's administrator depending on the required system accuracy. In simple terms we can see the probing threshold as our tolerance on non-optimal delegation. During our experiments we found a probing threshold set to 50msec to give a good ratio of accuracy over required probes.

4.3 The URL Delegation Procedure

Based on the assumption that the sub-networks belonging to the same company or organization are logically (in terms of network distance) in the same area, we use the organization's name to delegate the different domains to the migrating crawlers. In fact, instead of delegating URLs to the distributed crawlers, we delegate subnets. This is done in a *lazy evaluation* manner, that is, we try to delegate a subnet only after we find one URL that belongs to that subnet.

We first find the **smallest** subnet from the IP hierarchy that includes the IP of the new URL, and check if that subnet is already delegated to a crawler. If so, the URL is handled from that migrating crawler. If not, we check whether there is another subnet that belongs to the same company and is already delegated to a migrating crawler (or more). If such a subnet exist, the new URL, and subsequently, the owning subnet, is delegated to this crawler. If there are more than one subnets of the same company delegated to multiple crawlers then the new subnet is probed from these crawlers and delegated to the fastest. In fact, we stop as soon as we find a crawler that satisfies the probing threshold(section 4.2).

Only if this search is unsuccessful, we probe the subnet with the migrating crawlers, in order to find the best one to take it over. We navigate the IP-address hierarchy bottom up, each time trying to find the most suitable crawler to take the subnet. We first discover the parent subnet and find all the subnets included in the parent subnet. Then, for all the sibling subnets that are already delegated, we sequentially ask their migrating crawlers, and the migrating crawlers of their children subnets to probe the target subnet, and if any of them has probing time less than a specific threshold (probing threshold), we delegate the target subnet to that crawler. If no probing satisfies the threshold, our search continues to higher levels of the subnets tree. In the rare case that none of the crawlers satisfies the probing threshold, the subnet is delegated to the crawler with the lower probing result.

The algorithm (see pseudo-code below) is executed in the coordinator subsystem.

```
for any newly discovered URL u {
  subnet s = smallestNonUnary(u);
  if (IsDelegated(s)){ // the subnet is delegated
    delegate u, s to the same migrating crawler;
    next u;
  }
  elseif (sameCompanySubnetDelegated(s.companyName)){
  // a subnet of the same company is delegated
```

```
      mc = migrating crawler that has the other subnet;
      mc.delegate(u, s) //the url and the subnet
    } else {
      while (s not delegated) {
        s = s.parent;
        if (IsDelegated(s)) { // check the parent
          mc = the migrating crawler that has subnet s;
          time = mc.probe(u);
          if (time<threshold)
            mc.delegate(u, s); //the url and the subnet
        }

        for every child of s until u is delegated {
          sch = s.child
          if (IsDelegated(sch)) { // check the child
            mc = migrating crawler that has subnet sch;
            time = mc.probe(u);
            if (time<threshold)
              mc.delegate(u, s)
          }
          if (allAvailableCrawlersProbed)
            delegate the subnet to the fastest crawler
        }
      }
    }
  }
}
```

A URL delegation example: For clarity purposes an example is in order. The example references the IP address hierarchy presented in figure 2.

Subnet 2 in figure 2 has an IP range from 12.0.0.1 to 18.255.255.255. Subnet 8 is included in subnet 2 with an IP range from 14.0.0.1 to 16.255.255.255. Subnet 12 is a unary subnet for IP 15.10.0.7. The scenario includes probing for a URL that resides to IP 15.10.0.7. Querying the IP addresses hierarchy, we discover that the smallest subnet including the target IP is subnet 12, which however is unary. Thus, according to our algorithm, we ignore subnet 12, and use subnet 8 instead. Subnet 8 is not delegated in any crawler, so we check to see if any other subnet belonging to the same company is already delegated to any crawler. Assuming that no other subnet of the same company is delegated (organization name is stored in every node in the hierarchy), we continue by checking for neighbouring subnets that are delegated. Looking again in our hierarchy, we discover that while subnet 8 is not delegated to any crawler yet, subnets 11 and 13 (its children) are delegated to two different crawlers, x and y respectively. Therefore, we ask these two crawlers to probe the new subnet. If probing in either of the two crawlers' results in time less than the probing threshold, we delegate the new subnet to that crawler, or else we proceed to higher levels of hierarchy. However, since in this scenario, subnet 12 is a unary subnet, we delegate both subnets 8 and 12 to the faster crawler. Since the subnets 11 and 13 are already delegated and are lower in the hierarchy than subnet 8, this does not affect them (their delegation supersedes the delegation of their father). Subnet 14, which is not yet delegated, stays un-delegated. If we need to delegate it in the future, we run the same algorithm until we find some crawler satisfying the probing threshold.

4.4 Load Balancing and Dynamic Calibration

Our algorithm performs dynamic calibration of the URLs in order to follow the vastly changing Internet infrastructure. More specifically, the time required for each network action for each URL (i.e. HTTP/GET) is compared with the previous counts/statistics for the same URL. If the time is sufficiently larger (a threshold defined from the search engine administrator) than the time demanded for the previous downloads of the same page, and if this repeats for more than one time continuously, then the subnet is re-delegated, so that a more suitable crawler is found. In this way, with negligible processing, and no extra network overhead, the algorithm dynamically detects changes and calibrates the URL delegations.

IPMicra also performs efficient load-balancing. Each crawler has a maximum capacity, the size of the assigned web-pages that the crawler has to check each day. In the case where a crawler gets overloaded, the coordinator removes the subnet(s) with the lower variance in their probing results (collected during their delegation, and stored in the coordinator), and delegates them to the next-best available crawler. Intuitively, small probing time variance implies that most of the probed crawlers have similar probing results, thus, we expect to be easily able to find a near optimal crawler to take over a page. This heuristic performs well, and was preferred over other studied approaches (i.e. linear programming) due to the simplicity in implementation. Our tests showed that this heuristic was performing optimal decisions in more than 2/3 of the cases. Furthermore, in all the rest cases the heuristic was able to find an acceptable solution. Unfortunately, due to space limitations we cannot present analytical results of our experiment here. While satisfied with this heuristic, part of our ongoing work is to apply and evaluate other load balancing algorithms.

4.5 Performance and Evaluation

The direct advantage and purpose of IPMicra is that it enables location-aware crawling in *distributed* crawling systems. As such, the evaluation of the new methodology must be focused in this exact point. In fact, what we need to compare is our distributed location-aware methodology with a representative of distributed crawling methodologies that does not account location during crawling. After all, distributed crawling *per-se* was already compared with centralized crawling [10,11,9,1,3,4], and was found significantly better.

The case of various crawling optimizations that exist in other crawling systems (distributed or not) such as in-memory lexicon [2], DNS caching [5] and hardware acceleration [7] do not affect our approach, and do not need to be taken into account to our experiments. As such, we only need to examine the effects of the proposed location-awareness in distributed web crawling. Thus, we compare the IPMicra approach with a typical representative of distributed crawlers, i.e.

UCYMicra. We selected UCYMicra over other distributed crawlers for two reasons: (i) we had the UCYMicra crawlers already up and running, in a network of collaborated universities and organizations, and (ii) IPMicra was built over UCYMicra, so, it was using the same code to download and process pages, with the same optimization functions. Namely, the only practical difference between the two approaches was location awareness, thus, our measurements would be as objective as possible. That is, any differences in performance between the two crawlers, the location-aware Vs the location-unaware crawler, would be only due to the location awareness.

Before proceeding to describing our experiments and results, we have to stress once more that our selection to compare IPMicra with UCYMicra and not other approaches is because we now want to evaluate only the location-aware web crawling schema, and not several other optimization techniques existing in other proposals (either for distributed or for centralized crawling). In fact, most of these techniques can be applied in any distributed crawler, and in IPMicra. Thus, such techniques can combine with IPMicra and improve IPMicra's performance even more. IPMicra *per se* is also applicable in any other distributed crawler, in order to perform location aware web crawling.

We performed a two-phase evaluation and repeated each experiment several times to get statistical significance.

The first evaluation phase involved three experiments, with four coordinating crawlers, hosted from affiliated universities in four distinct geographical locations(USA, Greece, Cyprus, and London). The experiments included distributed crawling of 1000 distinct domain names, using three different variations: (a) Location unaware distributed crawling i.e. UCYMicra, (b) Optimal location aware distributed crawling, and, (c) IPMicra. Location unaware distributed crawling was performed with an enhanced version of UCYMicra, which was performing a random delegation of the URLs to the crawlers. The optimal location aware distributed web crawling was performed from another version of UCYMicra, which probed (with HTTP/HEAD) each URL from all the crawlers prior each delegation, and delegated each URL to the most near crawler (this was approaching the theoretically optimal location aware delegation). IPMicra was also executed in the same setup, as described before. However, since IPMicra's performance depends on the probing threshold, we experimented with many different thresholds (25msec to 125msec). We found a threshold set to 50msec with HTTP/HEAD as the probing function to give a good ratio of (accuracy:#required probes). Setting the threshold to a lower value i.e. 25msec was resulting to much higher accuracy (more than 90% optimal delegations) but required more probes for each delegation.

We found that location aware web crawling required **one order of magnitude less time (average 1/10th)** in the downloading process from the location-unaware version. The case was very similar with IPMicra, which also required one order of magnitude less time (with probing threshold set to 50msec and using HTTP/HEAD for probing function) compared to location unaware web crawling. The evaluation results are illustrated in figure 3 (the worst-case scenario is the case where each URL is assigned to the farthest crawler). Note that even with only four crawlers the benefits are tremendous. In fact, as the number of crawlers increases the benefits increase as well. We expect the IP-address hierarchy to be instrumental in identifying the optimal number of crawlers for optimal location aware crawling.

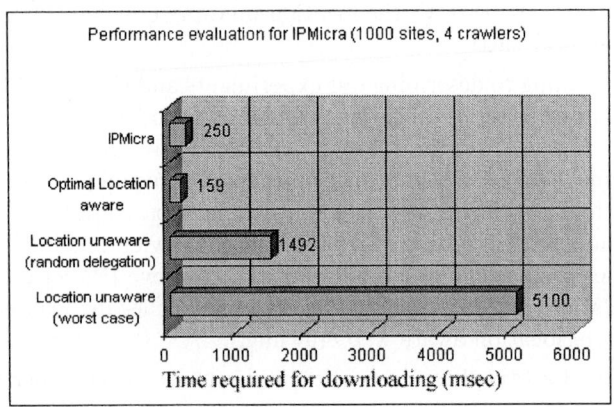

Fig. 3. IPMicra compared to the optimal location aware, the random, and the worst-case distributed crawling (1000 sites and 4 crawlers)

At the second evaluation phase, we included 12 crawlers (hosted in affiliated organizations and universities in USA, Europe and Australia) and 1000 randomly selected URLs - different than the previous. This experiment was to evaluate the accuracy of IPMicra in performing a location aware delegation, and the required probes for doing so. In this experiment, IPMicra was able to propose an optimal delegation in most of the URLs, by requiring very few probes. More specifically, with a probing threshold set to 50msec, IPMicra managed to perform the optimal delegation in 75% of the URLs, and required an average of only 3 probes per URL, compared to 12 needed for the brute-force approach presented in Section 3. With a probing threshold set to 25msec, IPMicra's accuracy was reaching to 90% accuracy (90% of the URLs were assigned in the nearest of the 12 crawlers), and required 6,5 probes for each URL. It is worth noting however that in all our experiments, the sub-optimal delegations were very near to the optimal ones, and always much better than a random delegation (from the delegation algorithm, one can realize that the maximum probing of any proposed non-optimal delegation was equal to the probing threshold, which however was significantly low in all cases). The effects of the probing threshold are illustrated in figure 4.

Due to practical difficulties (the difficulty of establishing controlled environment for our experiments in a number of distinct, world-distributed networks),

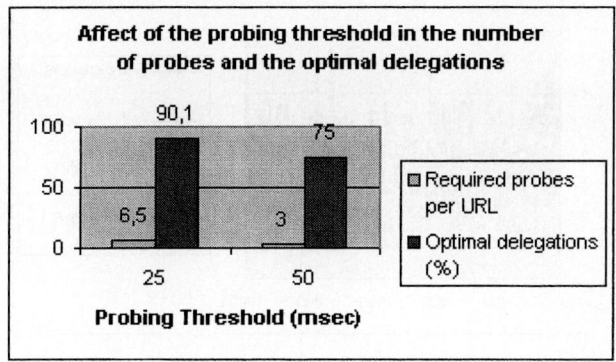

Fig. 4. Experimenting with probing threshold (25msec and 50msec), 12 crawlers and 1000 URLs

the two evaluations were made with a limited number of distributed crawlers and URLs. However, these crawlers were well distributed over the world (physically, and in network level), and they were significant for showing the advantages of the location-aware approach, and the effectiveness of IPMicra for performing location-oriented assignments of the IP subnets. Actually, we expect the approach to *react better with more collaborating crawlers*, since this will enable the algorithm to focus easier and faster to the most promising crawlers (without more probes). The crawlers populate in the hierarchy in a way that a number of IP subnets is automatically delegated (without probes) to them, and this knowledge is used for more effective future delegations. After all, the theoretical-ideal case of one IPMicra crawler in each subnet would result in 100% effectiveness of the approach - 100% optimal delegations, without any probing requirements (all the subnets would be optimally delegated to their own crawler). Furthermore, our experiments revealed an evolutionary nature of the approach (calibration in the course of time), promising more for the real-world deployment of the approach to hundreds of collaborated organizations, with the billions of URLs.

The adaptive/learning nature of IPMicra: In all our experiments, IPMicra was getting calibrated-optimized in the course of time, by facilitating *a priori* knowledge. For example, while the average number of probes for all the sites (phase 2 of the evaluation, with 12 crawlers) was 3 probes per URL, the average probing for the last 50 URLs was only 2.66 probes per URL. The fact that more delegations were performed in the IPMicra hierarchy - the hierarchy was getting *trained/calibrated* - was helping IPMicra to focus to the optimal crawler with less probes. The results of the previous experiment (with 6 and 12 crawlers) are also illustrated in graph 5. It is very important that the (linear) trendline in the graph is reducing, meaning that the required probes for each URL are also getting reduced in the course of time.

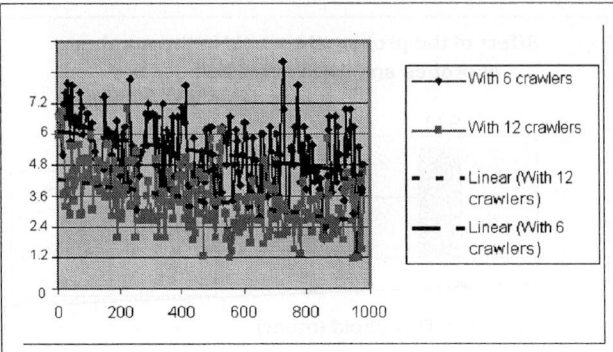

Fig. 5. The adaptive nature of IPMicra - Number of required probes per URL with probing threshold set to 50msec (for 1000 sites crawled from 6 and 12 crawlers)

5 Advantages of IPMicra

IPMicra has several advantages inherited from the mobile agents model, and its predecessor, UCYMicra. Furthermore, it supports load balancing and near optimal URL delegation. More specifically, IPMicra provides the following advantages:

1. Location aware crawling. It delegates the web sites to near migrating crawlers in order to take advantage of the lower network latency for faster crawling
2. IPMicra makes better use of the available bandwidth. While location unaware web crawlers (distributed or not) were trying to get over the network latency and increase the crawling rate by employing multiple crawling threads, the available bandwidth was not fully utilized and was always a bottleneck. Location aware web crawling needs less time to download a web document and releases network resources faster. Just by re-arranging the delegation of the URLs to the nearest web crawlers, we can complete the crawling function more efficient. Therefore, we expect to avoid the network bottleneck during crawling.
3. Load balancing. It uses an efficient load balancing scheme for URL delegation and re-delegation to alleviate bottlenecks in the migrating crawlers.
4. IPMicra eliminates the need of the traditional centralized web-crawlers, since the new crawling paradigm can follow newly found links and performs efficient load balancing.
5. IPMicra introduces less overall load in the Internet infrastructure, since importantly less data is transmitted uncompressed over the Internet. The distance that the uncompressed data has to be transmitted (between the web-servers and the distributed crawlers) is less or the two Internet points are connected with high bandwidth.
6. IPMicra has the important advantage of becoming dynamically calibrated in the course of time, for more focused (with less probes) searching for the

nearest crawler. Moreover, the system also detects important changes of the Internet's underlying network structure, and easily adjusts to them, to keep optimal delegations

Being distributed, IPMicra also inherits the advantages of distributed crawling. More specifically, not only it eliminates the enormous processing bottleneck from the search engine's site, by delegating the processing task to the migrating crawlers, but also it performs remote processing and compression (to the migrating crawlers) prior transmitting the results back to the search engine. The latter results to a significant reduction of the data transmitted back to the search engine's site (as in UCYMicra, we transmit **less than 1/20th** of the changed crawled data [10,11]), without loosing any search-useful information. Also, useless conditional GETs(If-Modified-Since headers) and HEAD requests do not any more occupy network resources from the search engine's site, but are executed distributed. Moreover, due to the flexibility of the mobile agents paradigm, the whole system is upgradeable at real time (the migrating crawlers' code can be upgraded *live*), and uses negligible network resources for coordination. At the end, it is very promising and easily acceptable from the users, due to the security constraints that can be set to the migrating crawlers, and since it can offer a fully configurable crawling service for the web server administrators(similar services are currently sold from commercial search engines).

6 Conclusions

In this work, we proposed IPMicra, an extension of UCYMicra, that allows, based on the notion of 'nearness', crawling of links in a near optimal location aware manner. The motivating power behind IPMicra is an IP address hierarchy tree, which is build using information from the four Regional Internet Registries. This hierarchy is used to delegate the web sites to near migrating crawlers in order to take advantage of the lower network latency for faster crawling.

IPMicra significantly improves the performance of distributed crawling by requiring one order of magnitude less time from a location unaware distributed crawler to crawl the same set of web pages. The performance is achieved just by re-arranging the URL delegations to the nearest crawlers. IPMicra also enables efficient load-balancing with negligible overhead.

This work can offer an efficient and generic solution to today's web indexing problem. We view this work as an important step toward a truly distributed and scalable web crawler, that will be able to catch up to the expanding and rapidly changing web. The location aware infrastructures developed in this work can be applied (as a framework) in any (fully or partially) distributed web crawler. The framework can even be applied in existing commercial approaches, like the Google Search Appliance or Grub. Furthermore, it can facilitate optimizations for distributed applications in the Internet in general. For example, this framework can efficiently enhance the load balancing schemes used from content delivery networks, such as Akamai.

References

1. C. Mic Bowman, Peter B. Danzig, Darren R. Hardy, Udi Manber, and Michael F. Schwartz. The Harvest information discovery and access system. *Computer Networks and ISDN Systems*, 28(1–2):119–125, 1995.
2. Sergey Brin and Lawrence Page. The anatomy of a large-scale hypertextual Web search engine. *Computer Networks and ISDN Systems*, 30(1–7):107–117, 1998.
3. Jan Fiedler and Joachim Hammer. Using the web efficiently: Mobile crawlers. In *Proceedings of the Seventeenth AoM/IAoM International Conference on Computer Science*, pages 324–329, San Diego CA, 1999. Maximilian Press Publishers.
4. Joachim Hammer and Jan Fiedler. Using mobile crawlers to search the web efficiently. *International Journal of Computer and Information Science*, 1(1):36–58, 2000.
5. Allan Heydon and Marc Najork. Mercator: A scalable, extensible web crawler. *World Wide Web*, 2(4):219–229, 1978.
6. Google Inc. Google, September 2003. http://www.google.com/.
7. Google Inc. Google search appliance, February 2004. http://www.google.com/appliance.
8. S. Lawrence and C. Lee Giles. Accessibility of information on the web. *Nature*, 400(6740):107–109, July 1999.
9. LookSmart Ltd. Grub distributed internet crawler, 2003. http://www.grub.org.
10. Odysseas Papapetrou, Stavros Papastavrou, and George Samaras. Distributed indexing of the web using migrating crawlers. In *Proceedings of the Twelfth International World Wide Web Conference (WWW)*, 2003.
11. Odysseas Papapetrou, Stavros Papastavrou, and George Samaras. Ucymicra: Distributed indexing of the web using migrating crawlers. In *Proceedings of the 7th East-European Conference on Advanced Databases and Information Systems*, Dresden, Germany, 2003.
12. SETI. Search for extra terrestrial intelligence, January 2004. http://setiathome.ssl.berkeley.edu/.

Ontologies, Databases, and Applications of Semantics (ODBASE) 2004 International Conference
PC Co-chairs' Message

Developing the Semantic Web is a key research challenge. The Conference on Ontologies, Databases, and Applications of Semantics for Large-Scale Information Systems (ODBASE 2004) provided a forum on ontologies and data semantics that included the many computing disciplines involved in such a challenge, such as ontology management, information mining, knowledge representation, information integration, Semantic Web services, and text processing. ODBASE 2004 also included research and interesting descriptions of real-life applications including scale issues in ontology management, information integration, and data mining, as well as papers that examine the information needs of various Web and knowledge applications, including medicine, e-science, history, e-government and manufacturing.

In order to draw a highly diverse body of researchers and practitioners, ODBASE 2004 was part of the Federated Symposium Event On the Move to Meaningful Internet Systems 2004 that co-located three conferences: Data and Web Semantics (ODBASE 2004); Distributed Objects, Infrastructure and Enabling Technology and Internet Computing (DOA 2004); and Workflow, Cooperation, and Interoperability (CoopIS 2004). All three conferences were hosted in Cyprus, October 25–29, 2004.

The ODBASE 2004 program mainly concentrated on techniques and tools to build and manage dynamic knowledge environments. In particular, the key areas covered included:

- Information integration and retrieval
  - Ontology pruning and alignment
  - Ontology merging
  - On-demand data integration
  - Distributed query answering
  - Multimedia retrieval
  - Natural language processing
- Information mining and discovery
  - Knowledge extraction
  - Text mining
  - Data and Web mining
  - Ontology learning
- Advances in information environments
  - Semantic Web services
  - XML, semantic interoperability
  - XML processing
  - Security and trust communities

This year, ODBASE received 122 original submissions from 27 countries. We were able to accept 31 full papers, and 8 poster papers. Each submitted paper was assigned for review by three program committee members. The accceptance rate for full papers was therefore approximately 25%. We hope that attendees found this program rich in research results, ideas and directions and that ODBASE provided them with opportunities to meet researchers from both academia and industry with whom to share their research perspectives.

Many people contributed to ODBASE. Clearly, first thanks go to the authors of all submitted papers. It is, after all, their work that became the conference program. The increased number of submissions, compared to the previous years, showed that ODBASE is increasingly attracting interest from many researchers involved in both basic and applied research. We are grateful for the dedication and hard work of all program committee members in making the review process both thorough and effective. We also thank the external referees for their important contribution to the review process.

In addition to those who contributed to the review process, there are others who helped to make the conference a success. Special thanks go to Kwong Yuen Lai for his invaluable help in the reviewing process and program preparation. We would like also to thank Robert Meersman and Zahir Tari – General Co-chairs of ODBASE – for their constant advice and support.

August 2004   Tiziana Catarci, Università di Roma "La Sapienza", Italy
                                Katia Sycara, Carnegie Mellon University, USA
                                (ODBASE 2004 Program Committee Co-chairs)

Helping People (and Machines) Understanding Each Other: The Role of Formal Ontology

Nicola Guarino

ISTC-CNR
Trento, Italy

Abstract. In scientific communication, we usually resort to formal theories - like algebra or first-order logic - to express our thoughts and intuitions in such a way they can be understood by our colleagues. I will argue that the tools of formal ontology (such as the notions of parthood, unity, dependence, identity) can play a similar role in ordinary communication, for instance during e-commerce transactions. I will briefly present what these tools are, and I will give examples concerning their role in facilitating mutual agreement, as well as recognizing and explaining disagreement.

Brief Speaker Bio

Nicola Guarino (1954) is a senior research scientist at the Institute of Cognitive Sciences and Technologies of the Italian National Research Council (ISTC-CNR), where he leads the Laboratory for Applied Ontology (LOA) in Trento. He graduated in Electrical Engineering at the University of Padova in 1978.

He has been active in the ontology field since 1991, developing a strongly interdisciplinary approach that combines together Computer Science, Philosophy, and Linguistics, and relies on Logic as a unifying paradigm. He has played a leading role in promoting a well-founded ontological approach within the Computer Science community, as testified by the successful series of conferences on Formal Ontology in Information Systems (FOIS), a long list of research papers, a number of special issues on international journals, and a series of invited talks and tutorials in different communities. His lab is currently involved in various ontology-related projects, and strong cooperation relationships exist with various national and international research institutes.

He is general chair of the FOIS conference series, associate editor of the International Journal of Human-Computer Studies and the Journal of Data Semantics, and editor-in-chief of the forthcoming Journal of Applied Ontology. He is a member of ACM, AAAI, and AI*IA.

Automatic Initiation of an Ontology

Marie-Laure Reinberger[1], Peter Spyns[2], A. Johannes Pretorius[2], and Walter Daelemans[1]

[1] University of Antwerp - CNTS,
Universiteitsplein 1, B-2610 Wilrijk - Belgium,
{Firstname.Lastname}@ua.ac.be
[2] Vrije Universiteit Brussel - STAR Lab,
Pleinlaan 2 Gebouw G-10, B-1050 Brussel - Belgium
{Firstname.Lastname}@vub.ac.be

Abstract. We report on an a set of experiments carried out in the context of the Flemish OntoBasis project. Our purpose is to extract semantic relations from text corpora in an unsupervised way and use the output as preprocessed material for the construction of ontologies from scratch. The experiments are evaluated in a quantitative and "impressionistic" manner.

We have worked on two corpora: a 13M words corpus composed of Medline abstracts related to proteins (SwissProt), and a small legal corpus (EU VAT directive) consisting of 43K words. Using a shallow parser, we select functional relations from the syntactic structure subject-verb-direct-object. Those functional relations correspond to what is a called a "lexon". The selection is done using prepositional structures and statistical measures in order to select the most relevant lexons. Therefore, the paper stresses the filtering carried out in order to discard automatically all irrelevant structures.

Domain experts have evaluated the precision of the outcomes on the SwissProt corpus. The global precision has been rated 55%, with a precision of 42% for the functional relations or lexons, and a precision of 76% for the prepositional relations. For the VAT corpus, a knowledge engineer has judged that the outcomes are useful to support and can speed up his modelling task. In addition, a quantitative scoring method (coverage and accuracy measures resulting in a 52.38% and 47.12% score respectively) has been applied.

Keywords: Machine learning, text mining, ontology creation, quantitative evaluation, clustering, selectional restriction, co-composition.

1 Introduction

A recent evolution in the areas of artificial intelligence, database semantics and information systems is the advent of the Semantic Web [5]. It evokes "futuristic" visions of intelligent and autonomous software agents including mobile devices, health-care, ubiquitous and wearable computing. An essential condition to the actual realisation and unlimited use of these smart devices and programs is the possibility for interconnection and interoperability, which is currently still lacking to a large extent. Exchange of meaningful messages is only possible when the intelligent devices or agents share a common conceptual system representing their "world"[1], as is the case for human communication. Meaning ambiguity should be, by preference, eliminated. Nowadays, a formal representation of such (partial) intensional definition of a conceptualisation of an application domain is called an ontology [26].

The development of ontology-driven applications is currently slowed down due to the knowledge acquisition bottleneck. Therefore, techniques applied in computational linguistics and information extraction (in particular machine learning) are used to create or grow ontologies in a period as limited as possible with a quality as high as possible. Sources can be of different kinds including databases and their schemas - e.g. [54], semi-structured data (XML, web pages), ontologies[2] and texts. Activities in the latter area are grouped under the label of Knowledge Discovery in Text (KDT), while the term "Text Mining" is reserved for the actual process of information extraction [29].

This paper wants to report on a joint research effort on the learning of ontologies from texts by VUB STAR Lab and UA CNTS during the Flemish IWT OntoBasis project[3]. The experiments concern the extraction and clustering of natural language terms into semantic sets standing for domain concepts as well as the detection of conceptual relationships. For this aim, the results of shallow parsing techniques are combined with unsupervised learning methods [45,46].

The remainder of this paper is organised as follows. The next section (2) gives an overview of research in the same vein (section 2.1). Methods and techniques including others than the ones applied for this paper are mentioned (section 2.2). In section 3, a short overview of the DOGMA ontology engineering framework is given as it is the intention that the experiments described in this paper lead to a less time consuming process to create DOGMA-inspired ontologies. The objectives are presented in section 4.1, while the methods and material (section 4.2) as well as the evaluation techniques (sections 5.2 and 5.3) are explained. The results are described in sections 6.1 and 6.2. Related work (section 7) is presented. Indications for future research are given in section 8, and some final remarks conclude (section 9) this paper.

2 Background

2.1 Overview of the Field

Several centres worldwide are actively researching on KDT for ontology development (building and/or updating). An overview of 18 methods and 18 tools for text mining with the aim of creating ontologies can be found in [23]. A complementary overview is provided in [34][4]. It is worth to mention that in France important work (mostly applied to the French language) is being done by members of the TIA ("Terminologie et Intelligence Artificielle") working group of the French Association for Artificial Intelligence (AFIA)[5]. TIA regroups several well known institutes and researchers included in

---
[1] See [52] for more details on the semantics of the Semantic Web.
[2] This is called ontology aligning and merging - e.g. [42]
[3] See http://wise.vub.ac.be/ontobasis
[4] We refer the interested reader to these overviews rather than repeating all the names of people and tools here.
[5] http://www.biomath.jussieu.fr/TIA

the overviews mentioned above and organises at a regular basis "Ontologies and Texts" (OLT) workshops linked to major AI-conferences (e.g., EKAW2000 [1], ECAI2002 [2]). Other important workshops on ontology learning were linked to IJCAI2001 [35], ECAI2000 [50] and ECAI2004 [12].

In addition to tools and researchers listed in the two overviews, there are the EU IST projects Parmenides[6] and MuchMore[7]. These projects have produced interesting state-of-the-art deliverables on KDT [28] - in particular section 3 - and related NLP technology [41]. The NLP groups of the University of Sheffield and UMIST (Manchester) are also active in this area [8,29]. A related tool is SOOKAT, which is designed for knowledge acquisition from texts and terminology management [40]. A specific corpus-based method for extracting semantic relationships between words is explained in [20]. Mining for semantic relationships is also - albeit in a rather exploratory way - addressed in the Parmenides project [47].

2.2 Overview of Methods

In essence, one can distinguish the following steps in the process of learning ontologies from texts (that are in some way or another common to the majority of methods reported):

1. collect, select and preprocess an appropriate corpus
2. discover sets of equivalent words and expressions
3. validate the sets (establish concepts) with the help of a domain expert
4. discover sets of semantic relations and extend the sets of equivalent words and expressions
5. validate the relations and extended concept definitions with the help of a domain expert
6. create a formal representation

Not only the terms, concepts and relationships are important, but equally the circumscription (gloss) and formalisation (axioms) of the meaning of a concept or relationship. On the question how to carry out these steps, a multitude of answers can be given. Many methods require a human intervention before the actual process can start (labelling seed terms - supervised learning, compilation/adaptation of a semantic dictionary or grammar rules for the domain ,...). Unsupervised methods don't need this preliminary step - however, the quality of their results is still worse. The corpus can preclude the use of some techniques: e.g., machine learning methods require a corpus to be sufficiently large - hence, some authors use the Internet as additional source [15]. Some methods require the corpus to be preprocessed (e.g., adding POS tags, identifying sentence ends, ...) or are language dependent (e.g., compound detection). Again, various ways of executing these tasks are possible (e.g., POS taggers can be based on handcrafted rules, machine-induced rules or probabilities). In short, many linguistic engineering tools can be put to use. To our knowledge no comparative study has been published yet on the efficiency and effectiveness of the various techniques applied to ontology learning.

---

[6] http://www.crim.co.umist.ac.uk/parmenides/
[7] http://muchmore.dfki.de/demos.htm

Selecting and grouping terms can be done by means of tools based on distributional analysis, statistics, machine learning techniques, neural networks, and others. To discover semantic relationships between concepts, one can rely on valency knowledge, already established semantic networks or ontologies, co-occurrence patterns, machine readable dictionaries, association patterns or combinations of all these. In [29] a concise overview is offered of commercially available tools that are useful for these purposes. Due to space restrictions, we will not discuss in this paper how the results can be transformed in a formal model (e.g., see [3] for an overview of ontology representation languages).

3 DOGMA

Before presenting the actual text mining experiments, we want to shortly discuss the framework for which the results of the experiments are meant to be used, i.e. the *VUB STAR Lab DOGMA* (Developing Ontology-Guided Mediation for Agents) ontology engineering approach[8]. Within the DOGMA approach, preference is given to texts as objective repositories of domain knowledge instead of referring to domain experts as exclusive knowledge sources[9]. Apparently, this preference is rather recent [1] and probably more popular in language engineering circles (see e.g. [11]).

Notice that also restrictions on a semantic relationship, e.g. indicating its mandatory aspect or its cardinality, should be mined from the corpus. These constraints serve to define more precisely the concepts and relations in the ontology. This is a step that should be added before the formal model is created, and that currently is hardly mentioned in the KDT literature. But one will easily agree that, e.g. when modelling a law text, there can be a huge difference between "must" and "may". This issue will not be further addressed in the present paper.

The results of the unsupervised mining phase are represented as *lexons*. These are binary fact types indicating which are the entities and the roles they assume in a semantic relationship [49].

Formally, a lexon is described as $< (\gamma, \lambda) : term_1 \; role \; co-role \; term_2 >$. For the sake of brevity, abstraction will be made of the context (γ) and language (λ) identifiers. For the full details, we refer to [6]. Informally we say that a lexon expresses that the $term_1$ (or head term) may plausibly have $term_2$ (or tail term) occur in an associating $role$ (with $co-role$ as its inverse) with it. The basic insights of DOGMA originate from database theory and model semantics [36].

In the near future, a strict distinction in the implementation of the DOGMA ontology server will be made between concept labels and natural language words or terms [6]. In many cases, "term" is interpreted in the ontology literature as "logical term" (or concept) of the ontology first order vocabulary and, at the same time, as a natural language term. Without going too much in detail here, we separate the conceptual level from the linguistic level (by using WordNet-like synsets - see also [21]), which has its impact on the KDT process, namely in step (3) mentioned in section 2.2. One of the rather rare KDT methods that also takes this distinction into account is described in [38]. It is easy to understand that the first step to initiate an ontology is situated on the linguistic level: lexons constitute

---

[8] See http://www.starlab.vub.ac.be/research/dogma
[9] This does not imply that texts will be the sole source of knowledge.

a necessary but intermediary step in the process of creating a (language-independent) conceptualisation and its corresponding implemented artefact, i.e. an ontology [26].

4 Unsupervised Text Mining

In the following sections, we will report on experiments with unsupervised machine learning techniques based on results of shallow parsing.

4.1 Objectives

Our purpose is to build a repository of lexical semantic information from text, ensuring evolvability and adaptability. This repository can be considered as a complex semantic network. We assume that the method of extraction and the organisation of this semantic information should depend not only on the available material, but also on the intended use of the knowledge structure. There are different ways of organising this knowledge, depending on its future use and on the specificity of the domain.

Currently, the focus is on the discovery of concepts and their conceptual relationships, although the ultimate aim is to discover semantic constraints as well. We have opted for extraction techniques based on unsupervised learning methods [45] since these do not require specific external domain knowledge such as thesauri and/or tagged corpora[10]. As a consequence, the portability of these techniques to new domains is expected to be much better [41, p.61].

4.2 Material and Methods

The *linguistic assumptions* underlying this approach are

1. the principle of selectional restrictions (syntactic structures provide relevant information about semantic content), and
2. the notion of co-composition [44] (if two elements are composed into an expression, each of them imposes semantic constraints on the other).

The fact that heads of phrases with a subject relation to the same verb share a semantic feature would be an application of the principle of *selectional restrictions*. The fact that the heads of phrases in a subject or object relation with a verb constrain that verb and vice versa would be an illustration of *co-composition*. In other words, each word in a noun-verb relation participates in building the meaning of the other word in this context [18,19]. If we consider the expression "write a book" for example, it appears that the verb "to write" triggers the informative feature of "book", more than on its physical feature. We make use of both principles in our use of clustering to extract semantic knowledge from syntactically analysed corpora.

In a specific domain, an important quantity of semantic information is carried by the nouns. At the same time, the noun-verb relations provide relevant information about the nouns, due to the semantic restrictions they impose. In order to extract this information

---

[10] Except the training corpus for the general purpose shallow parser.

automatically from our corpus, we used the ***memory-based shallow parser*** which is being developed at CNTS Antwerp and ILK Tilburg [9,10,14][11]. This shallow parser takes plain text as input, performs tokenisation, POS tagging, phrase boundary detection, and finally finds grammatical relations such as subject-verb and object-verb relations, which are particularly useful for us. The software was developed to be efficient and robust enough to allow shallow parsing of large amounts of text from various domains.

Different methods can be used for the ***extraction of semantic information*** from parsed text. Pattern matching [4] has proved to be a efficient way to extract semantic relations, but one drawback is that it involves the predefined choice of the semantic relations that will be extracted. On the other hand, clustering only requires a minimal amount of "manual semantic pre-processing" by the user. We rely on a large amount of data to get results using pattern matching and clustering algorithms on syntactic contexts in order to also extract previously unexpected relations. Clustering on terms can be performed by using different syntactic contexts, for example noun+modifier relations [13] or dependency triples [31]. As mentioned above, the shallow parser detects the subject-verb-object structures, which gives us the possibility to focus in a first step on the term-verb relations with the term appearing as the head of the object phrase. This type of structure features a functional relation between the verb and the term appearing in object position, and allows us to use a clustering method to build classes of terms sharing a functional relation. Next, we attempt to enhance those clusters and link them together, using information provided by prepositional structures.

The SwissProt corpus (see below) provides us with a huge number of those syntactic structures associating a verb to two nominal strings (NS), namely the subject nominal string (SNS) and the object nominal string (ONS). A nominal string is the string composed of nouns and adjectives appearing in a NP, the last element being the head noun of the NP.

However, we have to deal with the fact that the parser also produces some mistakes (f-score for objects is 80 to 90%), and that not all verb-object structures are statistically relevant. Therefore, we need to find a way to select the most reliable dependencies, before applying to them automatic techniques for the extraction of ontological relations. This step can be achieved with the help of pattern matching techniques and statistical measures.

Therefore, the stress is put in this experiment on the operation of filtering we are carrying out through pattern matching and statistical measures in order to discard automatically the irrelevant lexons. In a first step, we apply a pattern on the corpus in order to retrieve all the syntactic structures: NS-Preposition-NS. This structure has been chosen for its high frequency and because it generates few mistakes from the parser.

In a second step, the most relevant prepositional structures NS1-P-NS2 are selected, using a statistical measure. We want this measure to be high when the prepositional structure is coherent, or when NS1-P-NS2 appears more often than NS1-P and P-NS2. Therefore, it takes into account the probability of appearance of the whole prepositional structure (#NS1-P-NS2), as well as the probability of appearance of the two terms composing the whole structure (#NS1-P and #P-NS2):

---

[11] See http://ilk.kub.nl for a demo version.

$$\frac{\frac{\#NS1-P-NS2}{\min(\#NS1,\#NS2)}}{\frac{\#NS1-P}{\#NS1}+\frac{\#P-NS2}{\#NS2}}$$

The final step consist in the selection of the lexons. We consider the N prepositional structures with the highest rate, and we elect the relevant lexons or SNS-Verb-ONS structures by checking if the SNS and the ONS both appear among the N prepositional structures selected by the statistical measure.

We have worked with the 13M words *SwissProt **corpus*** composed of Medline abstracts related to genes and proteins. In a specific domain, an important quantity of semantic information is carried by the noun phrases (NP). At the same time, the NP-verb relations provide relevant information about the NPs, due to the semantic restrictions they impose. Therefore, we applied to this corpus the memory based shallow parser mentioned above. This shallow parser gives us the possibility to exploit the subject-verb-object dependencies. The selectional restrictions associated with this structure imply that the NPs co-occurring, as the head of the object, with a common set of verbs, share semantic information. This semantic information can be labeled as "functional", due to the semantic role of the verb, and therefore refers to the notion of "lexon" we have described in section 3. The smaller *VAT* corpus consists of 43K words. It constitutes the EU directive on VAT that has to be adopted and transformed into local legislation by every Member State. The VAT corpus has been chosen to validate the results of the unsupervised mining process on the SwissProt corpus.

5 Evaluation Criteria

5.1 Preliminary Remarks

The main research hypothesis in this paper is that lexons, representing the basic binary facts expressed in natural language about a domain, can be extracted from the available textual sources. Thus, a first step is the discovery and grouping of relevant terms. Using the lexons, a domain expert will, in a second step, distill concepts and determine which relationships hold between the various newly discovered concepts. Unambiguous definitions have to be provided. Note that the terms and lexons operate on the language level, while concepts and conceptual relationships are considered to be, at least in principle, language independent. The domain expert - together with the help of an ontology modeller - shapes the conceptualisation of a domain as it is encoded in the textual sources (taking synonymy into account). The second step will most probably be repeated several times before an adequate and shared domain model is commonly agreed upon (third step). Formalising the model is a subsequent step. The following sections discuss how the mining results will be evaluated.

5.2 The SwissProt Corpus

The results have been evaluated by experts of the biological domain. They were asked to consider a set of 261 relations corresponding to a subset of nominal strings appearing frequently in the corpus and including lexons as well as more general relations (spatial, part of...) issued from the prepositional relations. They had to rate each relation, regarding its relevance to the gene/protein domain as:

- false/irrelevant
- general information/weak relevance
- specific information/strong relevance

The subset of nominal strings considered for the evaluation contained every relation involving at least one of those keywords: DNA, cDNA, RNA, mRNA, protein, gene, ATP, polymerase, nucleotide, acid.

5.3 The EU VAT Directive Corpus

In this section, a more empirical evaluation method will be provided. Criteria for ontology evaluation have been put forward by Gruber [25, p.2] and taken over by Ushold and Grüninger [51]: clarity, coherence, extendibility, encoding bias and minimal ontological commitment. Gómez-Pérez [22, p.179] has proposed consistency, completeness and conciseness. Neither set of criteria are well suited to be applied in our case as the lexons produced by the unsupervised miner are merely "terminological combinations" (i.e. no explicit definition of the meaning of the terms and roles are provided not to mention any formal definition of the intended semantics). We have been mainly inspired by the criteria proposed by Guarino (coverage, precision and accuracy) [27, p.7], although there are problems to "compute" them in the current practice (unlike in information extraction evaluation exercises) as there are no "gold standards" available.

Qualitative method. Therefore, a human knowledge engineer has been asked to evaluate the practicality and usefulness of the results. A manually built lexon base is available, but this is a single person's work, which means that the "shared" and "commonly agreed" aspects - typical of an ontology - are lacking. Or stated in another way, a person - even an expert - maybe be wrong and therefore not the sole reference for a valid evaluation. Nevertheless, some questions have been formulated independently of the knowledge engineer/evaluator who is supposed to rely on his past experience. The evaluator/knowledge engineer was given a list of questions regarding the lexon bass as produced by the unsupervised miner.

- Do you think that w.r.t. the domain being modelled the lexon based produced is :
    - "covering" (are all the lexons there)
    - precise (are the lexons making sense for the domain)
    - accurate (are the lexons not too general but reflecting the important terms of the domain)
    - concise (are the lexons not redundant[12])
- Would you have produced (more or less) the same lexons (inter-modeller agreement)?
- Do you think that, using these lexons, ontology modelling happens faster (practicality)?

---
[12] This could be a tricky criterion as the terms and roles can have synonyms.

– Is it possible to create additional lexons from the original set to improve the coverage and accuracy while remaining precise ?

Note that this kind of evaluation implicitly requires an ontological commitment from the evaluator, i.e. he/she gives an intuitive understanding to the terms and roles of the lexons.

Quantitative method. In addition, for the coverage and accuracy criteria we have tried to define a quantitative measure and semi-automated evaluation procedure that will be explained subsequently. We don't define a computable precision measure here (see [45] for an earlier attempt). The underlying idea is inspired by Zipf's law [56]. It states that the frequency of the occurrence of a term is inversely proportional with its frequency class. Zipf has discovered experimentally that the more frequently a word is used, the less meaning it carries. E.g., the word "the" appears 3573 times and there is only 1 element in the frequency class 3573. "by-product" and "chargeability" occur only once, but there are 1155 words in the frequency class 1. Important for our purpose is the observation that the higher frequency classes contain mostly "empty" (also called function words). A corollary is that domain or topic specific vocabulary is to be looked for in the middle to lower frequency classes (see also [32,33]).

As the DOGMA lexons resulting from the unsupervised mining consist of three words[13] (two terms and one role[14]) extracted from the corpus, it is possible to investigate to what extent the produced lexons cover the corpus vocabulary, and more importantly how accurate they are. Note that the same technique can be applied to RDFS ontologies.

Coverage will be measured by comparing for each frequency class the number of terms from the lexons with the number of terms from the corpus. Accuracy will be estimated on basis of the coverage percentage for particular frequency classes. However, some caveats should be made from the on-set. It should be clear that a coverage of 100% is an illusion. Only terms in a V-O and S-O grammatical relation are selected and submitted subsequently to several selection thresholds (see section 4.2). Regarding the accuracy, determining exactly which frequency classes contain the terms most characteristic for the domain is still a rather impressionistic and intuitive entreprise. It should be kept in mind that no stopword list has been defined because lexons have been produced with a preposition assuming the role function.

6 Results

Evaluation typically has to do with avoiding all kinds of biases (e.g., the evaluator and developer is the same person, there is only one evaluator, evaluation is only done on machine produced output, etc. [17]). The results on the SwissProt and VAT corpus have been given to domain experts and a knowledge engineer for a qualitative evaluation. In addition, the quantitative measures (as defined in the previous section) have been applied on the VAT results. Below, the outcomes of the evaluation rounds are presented.

---

[13] In fact, the words have been lemmatised, i.e. reduced to their base forms. E.g., working, works, worked → work.

[14] Co-roles are not provided.

6.1 The SwissProt Corpus

Among the 261 relations that have been evaluated, we count 165 lexons and 96 other relations. What we obtain is a global precision of 55%, of which 47% have been evaluated as specific information, and 8% as general information. If we consider the lexons, we have a precision of 42%, with 35% of specific relations and 7% of general relations. Finally, considering the other relations, the precision is 76%, with 67% of specific relations and 9% of general relations.

Here are some examples of relations evaluated as specific information:

- DNA_damage induce transcription
- amino_acid_sequence reveal significant_homology
- fusion_protein with glutathione_S-transferase
- oligonucleotide_probe from N-terminal_amino_acid_sequence

And some examples of relations evaluated as general information:

- DNA contain human_chromosome
- amino_acid_sequence provide support
- uracil into DNA
- asparagine for aspartic_acid

6.2 The EU VAT Directive Corpus

Qualitative method. When applied to the VAT corpus, the unsupervised mining exercise outlined above resulted in the extraction of 817 subject-verb-object structures. These were analysed by a knowledge engineer using the LexoVis lexon visualisation tool [43]. This analysis was rather informal in the sense that the knowledge engineer was largely guided by his intuition, knowledge and experience with the manual extraction of lexons from the VAT legislature domain.

A first important aspect to consider is whether the domain (VAT legislature) is adequately described (or *covered*) by the set of extracted triples. In this regard, it soon became apparent that there is a significant amount of noise in the mining results; the triples need to be significantly cleaned up in order to get rid of inadequate (and often humorous) structures such as <*fishing, with, exception*>. The percentage of inadequate triples seems to fall in excess of 53%. According to this percentage, approximately 384 of the resulting 817 triples may be deemed usable. If this is compared to the number of lexons resulting from a manual extraction exercise on the same corpus of knowledge resources (approximately 900) there is doubt as to whether the domain is adequately covered by the results. As mentioned above, there is a significant portion of the unsupervised mining exercise results which are deemed inadequate. Firstly, this can be contributed to the fact that many resulting triples are not *precise* (intuitively, they do not make sense in the context of the VAT domain as the fishing example above illustrates). Furthermore, many of resulting triples were not considered *accurate* in the sense of describing important terms of the domain. In this respect, only the term VAT only occurs in three subject-verb-object structures, <*VAT, in, member*>, <*VAT, on, intra-Community_acquisition*> and <*VAT, to, hiring*> which are not considered appropriate to accurately describe the concept of VAT in the domain under consideration. In the same respect, there is only one mention of the term *Fraud*. In essence, the triples analysed form numerous disconnected graphs instead of one coherent and richly connected semantic network. The view is held that significant additions, in terms of roles, will need to be made in order to ensure that all applicable interrelationships in the domain are described. In this same vein, it is the case that no co-roles are defined. Clearly it would be a great advantage if this were the case. In Figure 1, the interpretation of the visual representation from left to right suggests that for any triplet $< t_i, r_{i-j}, t_j >$, the ontology engineer simply identifies t_j on the left arc, t_i on the right arc (or for a particular term in the object position, identify the same term in all subject positions). Consequently, r_{j-i} should then be presented. In this way, triplets may be combined to form lexons in which co-roles are also defined. However, as is evident from the symmetry of the visual representation in Figure 1, this is seldom the case [43].

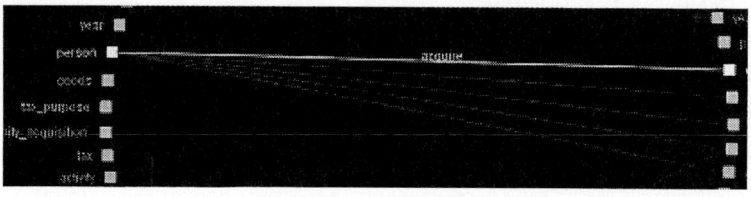

Fig. 1. Irreversibility

For instance, in the triplet <*person, acquire, goods*> exists, but there is no triplet of the form <*goods, acquire^{-1}, person*>, where *acquire^{-1}* signifies the inverse or co-role of *acquire* (see Figure1). This has the implication that in order to finalize the lexon base with which to describe the VAT domain, the knowledge engineer has to consider all machine extracted triplets in order to define co-roles, which could be quite an arduous task. However, a triplet such as <*person, acquire, goods*> does intuitively suggest a lexon of the form <*person, acquire, acquired_by, goods*> which should lessen the cognitive overhead required from the knowledge engineer. Furthermore, it is often the case that in the set of triples resulting from unsupervised mining of the VAT corpus, instances are identified rather than instance types. For example, the body of lexons includes the triplet <*Republic, of, Austria*>. Although this is clearly not satisfactory, such a triplet does suggest to the ontology engineer the inclusion of a lexon such as <*country, isA, isA, republic*>. It is striking that many roles take the form of prepositions. This includes triplets such as, <*application, of, exemption*>, <*adjustment, in, purchaser*>, <*agricultural_product, for, derogation*>, <*agricultural_product, of, agricultural_service*>, <*electronic_mean, to, data*>. Even though this might be conceptually correct, there exist many richer roles in a domain such as VAT legislature. One example might be <*agricultural_product, yields, agricultural_service*>, for instance.

Finally, the notion of *redundancy* is harder to evaluate, since terms and roles may have synonyms. However, the intuitive impression of the results was that redundancy was not a critical problem. In conclusion, the subject-verb-object structures resulting from unsupervised mining of the VAT corpus is not considered sufficient to represent the VAT domain. Even though the number of resulting triples approach the number manually extracted form the same texts, the impreciseness, inaccuracy and inconciseness results in many not being usable. However, the above analysis does have interesting methodological implications. Indeed, it suggests a *subtractive* approach to ontology engineering. That is, as opposed to an *additive* approach where the ontology engineer starts with an empty set of lexons to which he or she adds lexons to describe an universe of discourse.

Instead, the lexons resulting from a machine extraction exercise presents the ontology engineer with an initial corpus of lexons. These lexons are analysed, noise in the form of meaningless lexons removed or annotated, and new lexons added. In this regard, it is contended that through the analysis of such an initial body of lexons other lexons may be suggested to the ontology engineer and subsequently added to the resulting ontology base. Such an approach could significantly reduce the time investment needed from the knowledge engineer, since he or she does not have to start from scratch. It is further held that if unsupervised mining approaches such as those outlined in this paper can guarantee consistent results (that is, the same algorithm applied to the same corpus at different time instances results in similar results), then the knowledge engineer would be able to come up with an initial set of lexons by a process of elimination. Based on this set of lexons, the ontology engineer can then proceed to ensure that the domain is adequately described by considering this set.

Quantitative method. In order to produce illustrative graphics the highest frequency classes have been omitted (e.g., starting from class 300: member (336), which (343), article (369), taxable (399), person (410), tax (450), good (504), by (542), will (597), a (617), for (626), or (727), and (790), be (1110), in (1156), to (1260), of (2401), and the (3573)). At the other end, the classes 1 to 4 are also not displayed: class 1 containing 1165 lemmas, class 2 356, class 3 200 and class 4 has 132 members. Also some non-word tokens have been removed (e.g., 57.01.10, 6304, 7901nickel, 2(1, 8(1)(c, 2(2)). However, some of these non-word tokens have survived (which might influence the outcomes, especially in the lowest frequency classes).

The content of the frequency classes (FC) shows that they be can rated "contentwise" as follows:

- $FC < 3$: many non-words and/or too loosely related to the domain
- $3 < FC < 20$: domain related technical language
- $20 < FC < 50$: general language used in a technical sense
- $50 < FC < 300$: mixture of general language and domain technical language
- $300 < FC < 500$: general language and highly used domain terms
- $FC < 500$: function words and highly used general language terms

We determine the area with "resolving power of significant words" [33, p.16] to be the range of frequency classes 3 till 40. The range encompasses 596 terms that one would expect to be covered by the lexons. Figures 2 and 3 show that the coverage improves with the increasing rank of the frequency class. On average, the coverage ratio is 52.38%. The accuracy (i.e. the coverage percentage for the selected interval) ratio for the 3-40 interval is 47.31%.

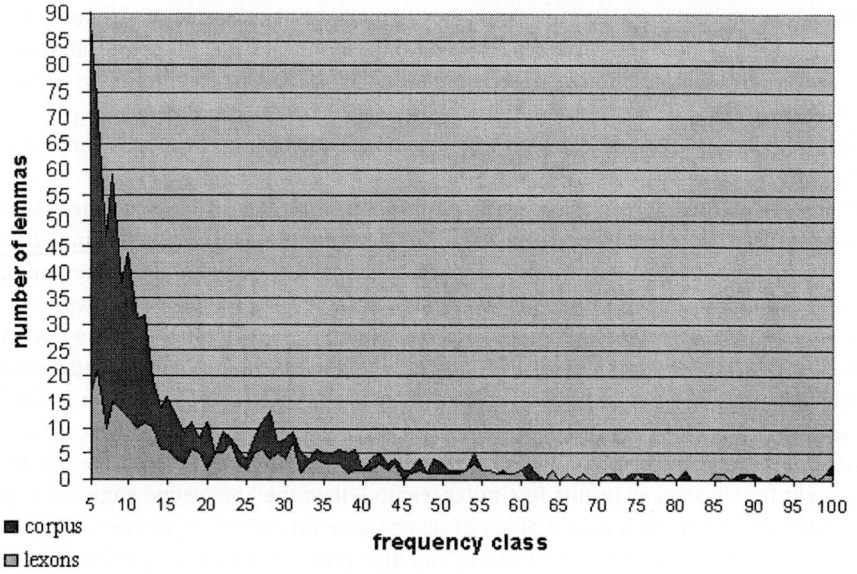

Fig. 2. Absolute coverage and accuracy of frequency classes by lexon terms

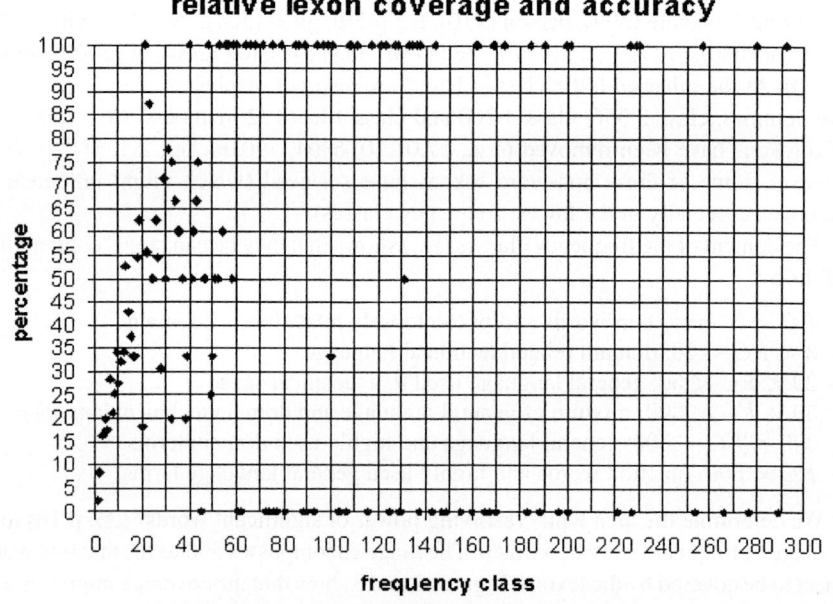

Fig. 3. Relative coverage of frequency classes by lexon terms

7 Discussion and Related Work

Unsupervised clustering allows us to build semantic classes. The main difficulty lies in the labelling of the relations for the construction of a semantic network. The ongoing work consists in part in improving the performance of the shallow parser by increasing its lexicon and training it on passive sentences taken from our corpus, and in part in refining the clustering. At the same time, we turn to pattern matching in order to label semantic relations. Unsupervised clustering is difficult to perform. Often, external help is required (expert, existing taxonomy...). However, using more data seems to increase the quality of the clusters ([31]). Clustering does not provide you with the relations between terms, hence the fact that it is more often used for terminology and thesaurus building than for ontology building.

Performing an automatic evaluation is another problem, and evaluation frequently implies a manual operation by an expert [7,16], or by the researchers themselves [24]. An automatic evaluation is nevertheless performed in [31], by comparison with existing thesauri like WordNet and Roget. Our attempt takes the corpus itself as reference and reduces the need for human intervention. Humans are still needed to clean the corpus (e.g. to choose the stopwords and to remove the non-words), but do not intervene in the evaluation process itself, except for setting the frequency class interval. Regression tests can be done. Currently, we estimate that the accuracy should be improved. Taking synonyms into account might help. On the other hand, more research should be done to determine the proportion of domain technical terms vs. general language terms in the "relevant" frequency class interval. If we look at it from a positive angle, we could argue that already half of the work of the domain specialist and/or terminographer to select the important domain terms is done. We were specifically (but happily) surprised by the fact that the different evaluation techniques performed in an independent way lead to similar conclusions.

8 Future Work

Some topics for future work can be easily sketched. From the work flow point of view, the lexons resulting from the unsupervised mining should be entered into an ontology modelling workbench that includes appropriate visualisation tools [43] and hooks to thesauri, controlled vocabularies and dictionaries, e.g. (Euro)WordNet [55,37]), on the one hand and (formal) upper ontologies, e.g. SUMO [39] or CyC [30] on the other. This workbench embodies the DOGMA ontology engineering methodology (see [48] for a limited illustration).

With respect to the quantitative evaluation of the outcomes of the unsupervised mining, insights from information science technology should be taken into account to answer some questions. E.g. does the length of a document influence the determination of the most meaningful frequency class interval ? Is it possible to establish a statistical formula that represents the distribution of meaningful words over documents ?

Once this interval can be reliably identified, one could apply the unsupervised learning algorithm only to sentences containing words belonging to frequency classes of the interval. This could be easily done after having made a concordance (keyword in context) for the corpus. We would like to carry out this experiment on a corpus of another domain, thereby also applying the domain relevance and domain consensus measures [53].

Part of the mistakes is due to the difficulty of parsing negative and passive forms. In the future, we are planning to increase the global number of structures, by considering also the verbal structures introducing a complement with a preposition. Also, spatial and part_of relationships should become more precise.

9 Conclusion

We have presented the results of an experiment on initiating an ontology by means of unsupervised learning. In addition, we have performed both a qualitative and quantitative evaluation of the outcomes of the mining algorithm applied to a protein and a financial corpus. The results can be judged as moderately satisfying. We feel that unsupervised semantic information extraction helps to engage the building process of a domain specific ontology. Thanks to the relatedness of a DOGMA lexon and an RDF triple, the methods proposed above can also be applied to ontologies represented in RDF(S).

Acknowledgments. The major part of this research was carried out in the context of the OntoBasis project (GBOU 2001 #10069), sponsored by the IWT (Institute for the Promotion of Innovation by Science and Technology in Flanders). Hannes Pretorius is supported by the EU IST FP5 FF Poirot project (IST-2001-38248).

References

1. Nathalie Aussenac-Gilles, Brigitte Biébow, and Sylvie Szulman, editors. *EKAW'00 Workshop on Ontologies and Texts*, volume http://CEUR-WS.org/Vol-51/. CEUR, 2000.
2. Nathalie Aussenac-Gilles and Alexander Maedche, editors. *ECAI 2002 Workshop on Machine Learning and Natural Language Processing for Ontology Engineering*, volume http://www.inria.fr/acacia/OLT2002, 2002.
3. Sean Bechhofer (ed.). Ontology language standardisation efforts. OntoWeb Deliverable #D4, UMIST - IMG, Manchester, 2002.
4. Matthew Berland and Eugene Charniak. Finfing parts in very large corpora. In *Proceedings ACL-99*, 1999.
5. T. Berners-Lee. *Weaving the Web*. Harper, 1999.
6. Jan De Bo and Peter Spyns. Creating a "dogmatic" multilingual ontology to support a semantic portal. In Z. Tari et al. R. Meersman, editor, *On the Move to Meaningful Internet Systems 2003: OTM 2003 Workshops*, volume 2889 of *LNCS*, pages 253 – 266. Springer Verlag, 2003.
7. Didier Bourigault and Christian Jacquemin. Term extraction + term clustering: An integrated platform for computer-aided terminology. In *Proceedings EACL-99*, 1999.
8. Christopher Brewster, Fabio Ciravegna, and Yorick Wilks. User centred ontology learning for knowledge management. In Birger Andersson, Maria Bergholtz, and Paul Johannesson, editors, *Natural Language Processing and Information Systems, 6th International Conference on Applications of Natural Language to Information Systems (NLDB 2002) - Revised Papers*, volume 2553 of *LNCS*, pages 203 – 207. Springer Verlag, 2002.
9. Sabine Buchholz. *Memory-Based Grammatical Relation Finding*. 1999.

10. Sabine Buchholz, Jorn Veenstra, and Walter Daelemans. Cascaded grammatical relation assignment. PrintPartners Ipskamp, 2002.
11. Paul Buitelaar, Daniel Olejnik, and Michael Sintek. A Protégé plug-in for ontology extraction from text based on linguistic analysis. In Frank Van Harmelen, Sheila McIlraith, and Dimitris Plexousakis, editors, *Proceedings of the Internal Semantic Web Conference 2004*, LNCS. Springer Verlag, 2004.
12. Paul Buitelaar, Siegfried Handschuh, and Bernardo Magnini, (eds.). *Proc. of the ECAI04 Workshop on Ontologies, Learning and Population*, 2004.
13. Sharon A. Caraballo and Eugene Charniak. Determining the specificity of nouns from text. In *Proceedings SIGDAT-99*, 1999.
14. Walter Daelemans, Sabine Buchholz, and Jorn Veenstra. Memory-based shallow parsing. In *Proceedings of CoNLL-99*, 1999.
15. A. Dingli, F. Ciravegna, David Guthrie, and Yorick Wilks. Mining web sites using adaptive information extraction. In *Proceedings of the 10th Conference of the EACL*, 2003.
16. David Faure and Claire Nédellec. Knowledge acquisition of predicate argument structures from technical texts using machine learning: The system ASIUM. In *Proceedings EKAW-99*, 1999.
17. C. Friedman and G. Hripcsak. Evalutating natural language processors in the clinical domain. *Methods of Information in Medicine*, 37:334 – 344, 1998.
18. Pablo Gamallo, Alexandre Agustini, and Gabriel P. Lopes. Selection restrictions acquisition from corpora. In *Proceedings EPIA-01*. Springer-Verlag, 2001.
19. Pablo Gamallo, Alexandre Agustini, and Gabriel P. Lopes. Using co-composition for acquiring syntactic and semantic subcategorisation. In *Proceedings of the Workshop SIGLEX-02 (ACL-02)*, 2002.
20. Pablo Gamallo, Marco Gonzalez, Alexandre Agustini, Gabriel Lopes, and Vera de Lima. Mapping syntactic dependencies onto semantic relations. In Nathalie Aussenac-Gilles and Alexander Maedche, editors, *ECAI 2002 Workshop on Machine Learning and Natural Language Processing for Ontology Engineering*, volume http://www.inria.fr/acacia/OLT2002, 2002.
21. Aldo Gangemi, Roberto Navigli, and Paola Velardi. The ontowordnet project: Extension and axiomatization of conceptual relations in wordnet. In Robert Meersman, Zahir Tari, and Douglas Schmidt et al. (eds.), editors, *On the Move to Meaningful Internet Systems 2003: CoopIS, DOA and ODBASE*, number 2888 in LNCS, pages 820 – 838, Berlin Heidelberg, 2003. Springer Verlag.
22. Asunción Gómez-Pérez, Mariano Fernández-López, and Oscar Corcho. *Ontological Engineering*. Advanced Information and Knowledge Processing. Springer Verlag, 2003.
23. Asunción Gómez-Pérez and David Manzano-Macho (eds.). A survey of ontology learning methods and techniques. OntoWeb Deliverable #D1.5, Universidad Politécnica de Madrid, 2003.
24. Ralph Grishman and John Sterling. Generalizing automatically generated selectional patterns. In *Proceedings of COLING-94*, 1994.
25. T. R. Gruber. A Translation Approach to Portable Ontology Specifications. *Knowledge Acquisition*, 6(2):199–221, 1993.
26. N. Guarino and P. Giaretta. Ontologies and knowledge bases: Towards a terminological clarification. In N. Mars, editor, *Towards Very Large Knowledge Bases: Knowledge Building and Knowledge Sharing*, pages 25 – 32, Amsterdam, 1995. IOS Press.
27. Nicola Guarino and Andreas Persidis. Evaluation framework for content standards. Technical Report OntoWeb Deliverable #3.5, Padova, 2003.
28. Haralampas Karanikas, Myra Spiliopolou, and Babis Theodoulidis. Parmenides system architecture and technical specification. Parmenides Deliverable #D22, UMIST, Manchester, 2003.

29. Haralampos Karanikas and Babis Theodoulidis. Knowledge discovery in text and text mining software. Technical report, UMIST - CRIM, Manchester, 2002.
30. D.B. Lenat and R. V. Guha. *Building Large Knowledge Based Systems*. Addison Wesley, Reading, Massachusetts, 1990.
31. Dekang Lin. Automatic retrieval and clustering of similar words. In *Proceedings of COLING-ACL-98*, 1998.
32. Robert Losee. Term dependence: A basis for luhn and zipf models. *Journal of the American Society for Information Science and Technology*, 52(12):1019 – 1025, 2001.
33. H. P. Luhn. The automatic creation of literature abstracts. *IBM Journal of Research and Development*, 2(2):159 – 195, 1958.
34. Alexander Maedche. *Ontology Learning for the Semantic Web*, volume 665 of *The Kluwer International Series in Engineering and Computer Science*. Kluwer International, 2003.
35. Alexander Maedche, Steffen Staab, Claire Nédellec, and Ed Hovy, editors. *IJCAI'01 Workshop on Ontology Learning*, volume http://CEUR-WS.org/Vol-38/. CEUR, 2001.
36. Robert Meersman. Ontologies and databases: More than a fleeting resemblance. In A. d'Atri and M. Missikoff, editors, *OES/SEO 2001 Rome Workshop*. Luiss Publications, 2001.
37. G. Miller. Wordnet: a lexical database for english. *Communications of the ACM*, 38(11):39 – 41, 1995.
38. Roberto Navigli, Paola Velardi, and Aldo Gangemi. Ontology learning and its application to automated terminology translation. *IEEE Intelligent Systems*, 18(1):22 – 31, 2002.
39. I. Niles and A. Pease. Towards a standard upper ontology. In Chris Welty and Barry Smith, editors, *Proceedings of the 2nd International Conference on Formal Ontology in Information Systems (FOIS-2001)*, 2001.
40. Päivikki Parpola. Managing terminology using statistical analyses, ontologies and a graphical ka tool. In Nathalie Aussenac-Gilles, Brigitte Biébow, and Sylvie Szulman, editors, *EKAW'00 Workshop on Ontologies and Texts*, volume http://CEUR-WS.org/Vol-51/. CEUR, 2000.
41. Stanley Peeters and Stefan Kaufner. State of the art in crosslingual information access for medical information. Technical report, CSLI, 2001.
42. H. Pinto, A. Gómez-Pérez, and J.P. Martins. Some issues on ontology integration. In R. Benjamins and A. Gómez-Pérez, editors, *Proceedings of the IJCAI'99 Workshop on Ontology and Problem-solving methods: lesson learned and future trends*, pages 7.1–7.11. CEUR, 1999.
43. A.Johannes Pretorius. Lexon visualization: visualizing binary fact types in ontology bases. In *Proceedings of the 8th international conference on information visualisation (IV04)*, London, 2004. IEEE Press. In press.
44. James Pustejovsky. *The Generative Lexicon*. MIT Press, 1995.
45. Marie-Laure Reinberger, Peter Spyns, Walter Daelemans, and Robert Meersman. Mining for lexons: Applying unsupervised learning methods to create ontology bases. In Robert Meersman, Zahir Tari, and Douglas Schmidt et al. (eds.), editors, *On the Move to Meaningful Internet Systems 2003: CoopIS, DOA and ODBASE*, number 2888 in LNCS, pages 803 – 819, Berlin Heidelberg, 2003. Springer Verlag.
46. Marie-Laure Reinberger and Peter Spyns. Discovering knowledge in texts for the learning of dogma-inspired ontologies. In Paul Buitelaar, Siegfried Handschuh, and Bernardo Magnini, editors, *Proceedings of the ECAI04 Workshop on Ontologies, Learning and Population*, 2004.
47. Fabio Rinaldi, Karel Kaljurand, James Dowdall, and Michael Hess. Breaking the deadlock. In Robert Meersman, Zahir Tari, and Douglas Schmidt et al. (eds.), editors, *On the Move to Meaningful Internet Systems 2003: CoopIS, DOA and ODBASE*, number 2888 in LNCS, pages 876 – 888, Berlin Heidelberg, 2003. Springer Verlag.
48. Peter Spyns, Sven Van Acker, Marleen Wynants, Mustafa Jarrar, and Andriy Lisovoy. Using a novel orm-based ontology modelling method to build an experimental innovation router. In Enrico Motta and Nigel Shadbollt, editors, *Proceedings of EKAW 2004*, LNAI. Springer Verlag, 2004. in press.

49. Peter Spyns, Robert Meersman, and Mustafa Jarrar. Data modelling versus ontology engineering. *SIGMOD Record Special Issue*, 31 (4): 12 - 17, 2002.
50. Steffen Staab, Alexander Maedche, Claire Nédellec, and Peter Wiemer-Hastings, editors. *Proceedings of the Workshop on Ontology Learning*, volume http://CEUR-WS.org/Vol-31/. CEUR, 2000.
51. M. Uschold and M. Gruninger. Ontologies: Principles, methods and applications. *Knowledge Sharing and Review*, 11(2), June 1996.
52. Michael Ushold. Where are the semantics in the semantic web? *AI Magazine*, 24(3):25 – 36, 2003.
53. Paola Velardi, Michele Missikoff, and Roberto Basili. Identification of relevant terms to support the construction of Domain Ontologies. In Maybury M., Bernsen N., and Krauwer S. (eds.)*Proc. of the ACL-EACL Workshop on Human Language Technologies*, 2001
54. R. Volz, S. Handschuh, S. Staab, L. Stojanovic, and N. Stojanovic. Unveiling the hidden bride: deep annotation for mapping and migrating legacy data to the semantic web. *Web Semantics: Science, Services and Agents on the World Wide Web*, 1:187 – 206, 2004.
55. P. Vossen, editor. *EuroWordNet: A Multilingual Database with Lexical Semantic Networks*. Kluwer Academic Publishers, Dordrecht, 1998.
56. George K. Zipf. *Human Behaviour and the Principle of Least-Effort*. Addison-Wesley, Cambridge MA, 1949.

Knowledge Extraction from Classification Schemas

Steffen Lamparter, Marc Ehrig, and Christoph Tempich

Institute of Applied Informatics and Formal Description Methods (AIFB),
University of Karlsruhe, Germany
http://www.aifb.uni-karlsruhe.de/WBS/
{sla,meh,cte}@aifb.uni-karlsruhe.de

Abstract. The availability of formal ontologies is crucial for the success of the Semantic Web. Manual construction of ontologies is a difficult and time-consuming task and easily causes a knowledge acquisition bottleneck. Semi-Automatic ontology generation eases that problem. This paper presents a method which allows semi-automatic knowledge extraction from underlying classification schemas such as folder structures or web directories. Explicit as well as implicit semantics contained in the classification schema have to be considered to create a formal ontology. The extraction process is composed of five main steps: Identification of concepts and instances, word sense disambiguation, taxonomy construction, identification of non-taxonomic relations, and ontology population. Finally the process is evaluated by using a prototypical implementation and a set of real world folder structures.

1 Introduction

The amount of digital information saved on hard disks all over the world is estimated from 403 to 1986 Terabyte and increased between 2000 and 2003 by 114%[1]. While search on the web now performs reasonable well, local information becomes increasingly unaccessible. In particular for virtual organizations, in which the stakeholder want to share their local information among each other, this obstructs collaboration. To make the information more accessible a systematical way to organize it is needed, which ontologies can provide. This view is supported by a case study which involved a virtual organization in the tourism domain where we deployed ontologies in a peer-to-peer knowledge sharing environment with promising results (cf. [1]). In the case study a common ontology was available to organize the information the participants wanted to share. Additionally they could extend the common ontology locally with concepts and relations. The participants used mainly the labels of their shared folders to create new ontological entities. Although the participants found it very useful to "customize" the ontology this manual engineering process is very time consuming and costly. In particular when it comes to changes in the folder structures the continuous updating of the "customized" ontology is not practical for the normal user.

To solve this *knowledge acquisition bottleneck* methods are needed that (semi-)automatically generate ontologies. In this context it is especially interesting how existing, legacy information can be used to generate explicit semantical descriptions of a domain. In our

---

[1] http://www.sims.berkeley.edu/research/projects/how-much-info-2003

case the available information are the local folder structures and existing thesauri/topic hierarchies which provide a vocabulary for the domain. More generally this information can be seen as classification schemas.

Following the ideas presented in [2] in the context of *Emergent Semantics* we have conceived a general process to learn ontologies from classification schemas as an extension of the ontology learning frame work described in [3]. Consequently we consider explicit as well as implicit semantics hidden in the structure of the schema and we combine methods from various different research domains such as natural language processing (NLP), web mining, machine learning, and knowledge representation to learn an ontology. In particular we introduce new methods to deduce concepts, relations and instances from the labels found in folder structures, relations from the arrangement of the schemas, and instantiated relations.

In the remainder of this paper the actual extraction process is presented. The process contains five steps: Identification of concepts and instances, word sense disambiguation, extracting taxonomic and non-taxonomic relations, and finally populating the ontology. Subsequently, we evaluate our process using a prototypical implementation and four real world folder structures. At the end we conclude with a short discussion and outlook.

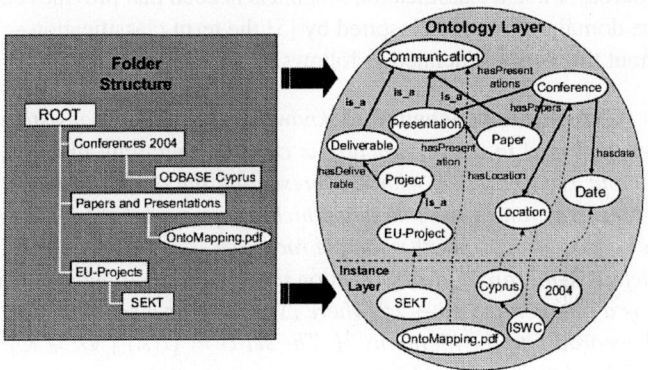

Fig. 1. Example

2 General Knowledge Extraction Process

In this section a general process is introduced that facilitates the creation of a formal and explicit description of semi-structured knowledge obtained from classification schemas (see Figure 2). The result of this method is entirely structured knowledge represented by an ontology.

Subsequently, we describe the input data our extraction process requires, the process steps we carry out, and the results we finally obtain. A more detailed description of this extraction process is presented in [4].

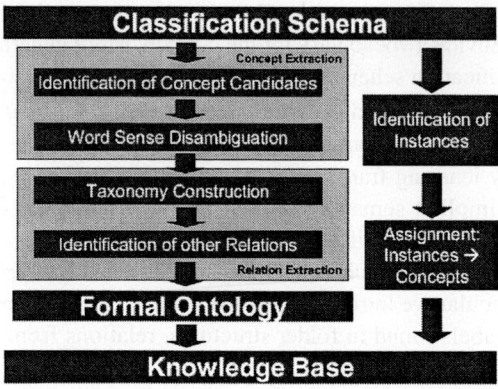

Fig. 2. Overview of the extraction process.

2.1 Definition of Input Data Structures

The extraction process presented in this paper is capable to use information from several knowledge sources. First, a classification schema is needed that provides basic information about the domain of interest. Inspired by [5] the term classification schema that is used throughout this paper is defined as follows.

Definition 1 (Classification Schema). *A knowledge structure consisting of a set of labeled nodes arranged in a tree-structure is called a* hierarchy *and can be formally defined as a tuple* $\mathcal{H} = (\mathcal{K}, \mathcal{E}, l)$ *with* $\mathcal{K}$ *representing the nodes,* $\mathcal{E}$ *the set of relations defining the hierarchy, and* l *the function which assigns a label* $l \in \mathcal{L}$ *to each node.* $(\mathcal{K}, \mathcal{E})$ *defines a tree-structure with a unique root.*

Having defined a hierarchy, a classification schema or hierarchical classification *can be regarded as a function* $\mu : \mathcal{K} \to 2^\Delta$ *where* Δ *represents a set of objects that have to be classified according to the hierarchy* $\mathcal{H}$. *The set* $\mathcal{B} = \{l(k) \mid \forall k \in \mathcal{K}\}$ *contains all node labels of the classification schema.*

Figure 1 shows on the left side an example for an classification schema. In this case the white rectangles are the nodes $\mathcal{K}$ and $\mathcal{B} = \{ROOT, Conferences\ 2004, ODBASE\ Cyprus, Papers\ and\ Presentations, EU\text{-}Projects, SEKT\}$ is the set of node labels. There is one classified object $\Delta = \{ontoMapping.pdf\}$. It is assigned to a node by the function $\mu(ontoMapping.pdf) =$ 'Papers and Presentations'.

In this context it is important to note that the relations in the set $\mathcal{E}$ do not necessarily have to be taxonomic, i.e. subclass/superclass relations. Hence, our notion of a classification schema covers a wide range of different structures. Classification schemas include for example folder structures on personal computers as well as web directories or product categories.

To extract semantically enriched information from a classification schema further background knowledge is needed. Therefore, a machine readable dictionary (MDR) such as WordNet provides the right means. It can be used to look up and stem words, to retrieve potential meanings of a word and to find taxonomic as well as non-taxonomic associations between these meanings. Additionally, already existing ontologies can be used in order to provide domain-specific knowledge to the extraction process. Ontologies are formally defined in the next section.

2.2 Definition of Output Data Structure

The objective of the process is to represent information found in a classification schema in a formal and explicit way. This is done by defining a knowledge base which includes an ontology together with concrete instances. The formal semantics of ontologies we use throughout this paper is described subsequently (cf. [6]).

Definition 2 (Ontology Layer). *An ontology is a tuple* $\mathcal{O} := (\mathcal{C}, \mathcal{P}, \mathcal{H}^\mathcal{C}, prop)$ *where the disjoint sets $\mathcal{C}$ and $\mathcal{P}$ contain concept and relation identifiers. $\mathcal{H}^\mathcal{C}$ defines taxonomic relations between concepts. I.e. $\mathcal{H}^\mathcal{C} \subseteq \mathcal{C} \times \mathcal{C}$. The function $prop : \mathcal{P} \to \mathcal{C} \times \mathcal{C}$ defines non-taxonomic relations between concepts.*

A *knowledge base* contains concepts as well as concrete instances of theses concepts. Therefore, an additional instance layer is needed.

Definition 3 (Instance Layer). *The instance layer of an ontology is defined by the tuple* $KB := (\mathcal{O}, \mathcal{I}, \mathcal{L}, inst)$. *$\mathcal{O}$ is the ontology the instance layer refers to. $\mathcal{I}$ is the set of instance identifiers and set $\mathcal{L}$ contains literals. The mapping between the ontology and instance level is done using the functions* $inst : \mathcal{C} \to 2^\mathcal{I}$.

On the right side of Figure 1 there is an example for a knowledge base. Here the set of concepts is defined by $\mathcal{C} = \{$*Communication, Conference, Paper,* ... $\}$ and taxonomic relations are represented by *isA*-Relations. That means, $\mathcal{H}^\mathcal{C} = \{$*(Communication, Presentation), (Paper, Communication),* ... $\}$. $\mathcal{P} = \{$*(Conference, Paper), (Paper, Presentation),* ... $\}$ specifies non-taxonomic relations. The set of instances $\mathcal{I} = \{$*SEKT, Cyprus, ODBASE, 2004, OntoMapping.pdf*$\}$ is mapped to corresponding concepts using the function $inst$. E.g. $inst(Cyprus) = $ '*Location*'.

2.3 Process Steps

The extraction process includes five major steps. First relevant concepts have to be identified. Therefore, node labels of the classification schema have to be analyzed with respect to a dictionary in order to find potential concept identifiers. This is done in the concept identification step. Then, these concept candidates have to be disambiguated to get the appropriate meanings in the given context. A concept identifier together with a concrete meaning defines a concept for the ontology.

Thereafter, explicit associations between the concepts are defined. First, a taxonomy is constructed. This has to be done from scratch, because hierarchies in classification schemas do not necessarily define a taxonomy in terms of *subClassOf*- or *isA*-relations, respectively. Furthermore, non-taxonomic relations between concepts have to be established.

Having an ontology, instances have to be assigned to get a complete knowledge base. Therefore, instances are identified in the classification schema by means of the dictionary. A further step is needed for the assignment of the instances to the corresponding concepts. In the next section methods that provide the functionalities mentioned above are described in detail.

3 Extraction Methods in Detail

Subsequently, methods for concept and instance identification, word sense disambiguation, taxonomy construction, identification of non-taxonomic relations, and assignment of instances are presented. Mostly these methods are supported by additional background knowledge in terms of dictionaries or domain-specific ontologies.

3.1 Identification of Concepts and Instances

In this step relevant concepts and instances are extracted from the classification schema. A basic problem is to draw the line between concepts and instances. Even for a human ontology engineer this can be a challenging issue.

All labels $\mathcal{B}$ of the classification schema are either classified into the set of concept candidates $\mathcal{B}_C$ or into the set of instances $\mathcal{B}_I$. Therefore, we assume $\mathcal{B}_C \cup \mathcal{B}_I = \mathcal{B}$ and $\mathcal{B}_C \cap \mathcal{B}_I = \emptyset$. This means all terms which are not concepts are instances and vice versa. In this work we use the assumption that general terms included in a dictionary are concepts and specific terms not contained in a dictionary are instances.

In the following we outline methods that identify potential concepts by analyzing all labels in $\mathcal{B}$. The first method distinguishes the labels in concept candidates $\mathcal{B}_C^{lex}$ and instances $\mathcal{B}_I^{lex}$. Thereafter, four methods are applied to revise this segmentation: (1) The sets are scanned for noun phrases, (2) the individual labels are decomposed, (3) entities are recognized by their names, (4) and concepts and instances are identified by domain-specific ontologies.

Due to the special properties of node labels in a classification schema compared to sentences in a normal NLP task, the following methods differ in some points from usual methods applied in NLP.

Lexical analysis of labels. In this step a solely syntactic analysis of the labels $b_j \in \mathcal{B}$ is performed. Therefore, special characters have to be replaced and the individual words have to be stemmed. A word is a set of letters separated form the rest of the label by space characters. In case all atomic words w_i of a label $b_j = w_{j1}, w_{j2}, \ldots, w_{ji}, \ldots, w_{jn}$ are contained in the dictionary as nouns the entire label b_j is a concept candidate. Otherwise b_j is an instance. Thus, if the set $\mathcal{W}_N$ contains only nouns from a dictionary the sets $\mathcal{B}_C^{lex}$ and $\mathcal{B}_I^{lex}$ will be defined as follows:

$$\mathcal{B}_C^{lex} = \{b_j \in \mathcal{B} \mid \forall i : w_{ij} \in \mathcal{W}_N\} \quad (1)$$

$$\mathcal{B}_I^{lex} = \{b_j \in \mathcal{B} \mid \exists i : w_{ij} \notin \mathcal{W}_N\} \quad (2)$$

In Figure 1 for instance, $b_3 = $ *'Papers and Presentations'* is assigned to $\mathcal{B}_I^{lex}$ and $b_4 = $ *'EU Projects'* to the set $\mathcal{B}_C^{lex}$.[2]

---

[2] Note that a consistent usage of characters and name conventions can improve the results of this step dramatically. If the labels of the nodes are very complex syntactic ambiguousness could arise. This is the case if particular nouns can also be used as adjectives for instance. The problem could be tackled by part-of-speech tagging [7,8]. For syntactic ambiguousness see also 3.2.

Knowledge Extraction from Classification Schemas   623

Recognizing noun phrases. Although concepts are mainly represented by one single noun it is also possible that a concept is represented by a whole expression, e.g. compounds (*'credit card'*), prepositional phrases (*'board of directors'*), and adjective-noun relation (*'Semantic Web'*). Such a group of words in a label behaves like a noun and is called *noun phrase*. Due to the fact that noun phrases can be included in both sets, $\mathcal{B}_C^{lex}$ and $\mathcal{B}_I^{lex}$, both sets have to be analyzed for noun phrases. A simple method for doing this is to look up a specific expression in the dictionary. But not all noun phrases should be regarded as concepts (e.g. *last week*). According to the assumption above a noun phrase is a concept candidate if it is contained in the dictionary.

Now, we consider an expression $b_j \in \mathcal{B}_C^{lex}$ containing a noun phrase a_{ji}. a_{ji} has to be marked as a noun phrase to support finding the correct sense in section 3.2. E.g. this would be the case for $b_j = a_{ji} =$ *'Computer Science'*. Here the term has to be marked and no further action is required, because the term is already classified as concept candidate.

Additionally, a_{ji} has to be included in the set $\mathcal{B}_C^{lex}$ as a separate concept candidate, if b_j contains other words beyond the noun phrase ($b_j \neq a_{ji}$). Consider a label $b_j =$ *'Lecture Computer Science'*. In this case the recognized noun phrase is still $a_{ji} =$ *'Computer Science'*. So a_{ji} has to be added as separate concept candidate. This scenario can be described by equation 3 (first line), whereas the set $\mathcal{W}_N$ contains all nouns (and noun phrases) of the dictionary.

In case a expression $b_j \in \mathcal{B}_I^{lex}$ is analyzed and a noun phrase a_{ji} is detected the expression has to be accepted as a concept candidate (see Equation 3, second line). If the label b_j doesn't contain other words beyond the noun phrase a_{ji} the whole label b_j can be removed from the set $\mathcal{B}_I$ (see Equation 4). For example, the phrase $b_j = a_{ji} =$ *'Artificial Intelligence'* can be removed from $\mathcal{B}_I^{lex}$, but $b_j =$ *'Applied Computer Science'* with $a_{ji} =$ *'Computer Science'* cannot be removed.

$$\mathcal{B}_C^{np} := \mathcal{B}_C^{lex} \cup \{a_{ji} \mid \exists i,j : b_j \in \mathcal{B}_C^{lex} \wedge a_{ji} \in \mathcal{W}_N \wedge b_j \neq a_{ji}\} \quad (3)$$
$$\cup \{a_{ji} \mid \exists i,j : b_j \in \mathcal{B}_I^{lex} \wedge a_{ji} \in \mathcal{W}_N\}$$

$$\mathcal{B}_I^{np} := \mathcal{B}_I^{lex} \setminus \{b_j \mid \exists j : b_j \in \mathcal{B}_I^{lex} \wedge a_{ji} \in \mathcal{W}_N \wedge b_j = a_{ji}\} \quad (4)$$

In the unusual case that node labels of the classification schema are very complex and similar to sentences in natural language, it is very hard to recognize proper concepts. The use of a chunk parser can be reasonable to solve this problem [9].

Lexical decomposition of labels. In the last two steps the labels $b_j \in \mathcal{B}$ are analyzed as a whole. Now, based on the lexical analysis done before the label is decomposed into the individual words $w_{j1}, \ldots, w_{ji}, \ldots w_{jn}$. To find out whether a subset of the entire label represents a concept candidate all words w_{ji} are looked up in a dictionary separately. If only one word w_{ji} is found as a noun in the dictionary this word can be accepted as a concept candidate (see Equation 5). For instance the concept $w_{11} =$ *'Conference'* can be extracted from the label $b_1 =$ *'Conferences 2004'*.

If more than one word of a label is found in the dictionary a method will be needed to decide whether these words should form one single multi-word concept c_{j1} or several different concepts c_{jr} with $r = 1, 2, \ldots, m$. Therefore, the non-substantival words between concept candidates can be used as indicator [5]. If two recognized concept candidates are connected by a space character or a preposition, they will be related by a logical 'and'-Relation. In this case objects $\delta \in \Delta$ classified under the label are belonging to both concept candidates. Thus, only one single concept candidate $c_{j1} \in \mathcal{B}_C^{decomp}$ should be composed. E.g. this is the case for $b_j = c_{j1} =$ 'EU Projects'. On the other hand, if two recognized concepts are connected by the word 'and' or a comma a logical 'or'-Relation is assumed. In this case classified objects belong to either the first or second part of the label and two different concept candidates $c_{j1}, c_{j2} \in \mathcal{B}_C^{decomp}$ are composed, consequently. The label $b_4 =$ 'Papers and Presentations' produces two separate concepts $c_{41} = w_{41} =$ 'Paper' and $c_{42} = w_{43} =$ 'Presentation'. In such a scenario maximal number of $n - 1$ concepts are extracted from one label ($m < n - 1$).

$$\mathcal{B}_C^{decomp} := \mathcal{B}_C^{np} \cup \{w_{ji} \mid \forall k \neq i : w_{ji} \in \mathcal{W}_N \land w_{jk} \notin \mathcal{W}_N\} \qquad (5)$$
$$\cup \{c_{jr} \mid \forall j : b_j \in \mathcal{B}_C^{np} \land \forall r : r \leq m\}$$

Named entity recognition. The task *named entity recognition* is about identifying certain entities as well as temporal and numeric expression by their name or format. That means, instances of generic concepts such as *Person, Location, Date* or *Time* are identified. Because dictionaries usually include very generic concepts as well as concrete named entities, both sets, B_C^{decomp} and B_I^{decomp}, have to be included in the named entity recognition process.

Named entity recognition can be regarded as a function $\gamma : \mathcal{N} \to \mathcal{C}_{NER}$ that assigns a concept $c \in \mathcal{C}_{NER}$ to each named entity $e \in \mathcal{N}$. In case a named entity $e_{ji} \in \mathcal{N}$ is found in the label $b_j \in \mathcal{B}_C^{decomp}$ the corresponding concept $c_{ji} = \gamma(e_{ji})$ has to be included in $\mathcal{B}_C^{name}$ (first line of Equation 6). E.g in the label $b_1 =$ 'Conferences 2004' the word $e_{11} =$ '2004' is recognized as date. In this case the concept $c_{11} =$ 'Date' can be added to the set $\mathcal{B}_C^{name}$.

If a named entity e_{ji} is identified in a label $b_j \in \mathcal{B}_C^{decomp}$ this named entity has to be deleted from concept candidates (second line of Equation 6) and moved to the set of instances $\mathcal{B}_I$ (Equation 7). Additionally, the concept $\gamma(e_{ji})$ has to be accepted as a concept candidate (first line of Equation 6).

$$\mathcal{B}_C^{name} := \mathcal{B}_C^{decomp} \cup \{\gamma(e_{ji}) \mid \exists j, i : e_{ji} = w_{ji} \land b_j \in \mathcal{B}_I^{decomp}\} \qquad (6)$$
$$\setminus \{e_{ji} \mid \exists j, i : e_{ji} = w_{ji} \land b_j \in \mathcal{B}_C^{decomp}\}$$

$$\mathcal{B}_I^{name} := \mathcal{B}_I^{decomp} \cup \{e_{ji} \mid \exists j, i : e_{ji} = w_{ji} \land b_j \in \mathcal{B}_C^{decomp}\} \qquad (7)$$

For instance a label $b_j =$ 'Cyprus' would be in the set $\mathcal{B}_C^{decomp}$ although it should be classified as instance. Therefore, *Cyprus* has to be deleted from the set of concept candidates $\mathcal{B}_C^{name}$ and added to the set of instances $\mathcal{B}_I^{name}$. Furthermore, the recognized concept *Location* has to be added to the set $\mathcal{B}_C^{name}$.

For sake of completeness we list some of the most prominent approaches for named entity recognition:

- Pattern-based approach: Context sensitive reduction-rules are defined statically and applied to the labels [10].
- Gazetteers-based approach: Already known entity names are saved in a lists (gazetteers) together with the concept they belong to. With this lists mapping between instances and concepts can be done easily.
- Automatic approaches: Theses are mostly statistical methods like the Hidden-Markow-Model [11] or the Maximum-Entropy-Model [12].

Often all three approaches are combined to achieve a better performance [13].

Mapping to a domain-specific ontology. In this step concept candidates which are not in the dictionary are identified by comparing words retrieved from the classification schema with concepts and instances of domains-specific ontologies. This method is based on the assumption that in a specific domain the same words always have the same meaning. Thus, it is possible to identify concepts simply by comparing the words w_{ij} of labels $b_j \in \mathcal{B}_I^{name}$ with the concepts $c_k \in \mathcal{C}_{domain}$ as well as with the instances $inst_{domain}(c_k)$ of a domain specific ontology. A word w_{ij} of a label classified as an instance $b_j \in \mathcal{B}_I^{name}$ that syntactically equals the label of a concept $c_k \in \mathcal{C}_{domian}$ is supposed to be a concept candidate (see Equation 9). E.g. there is a label b_j = 'Associate Professor' in the set $\mathcal{B}_I^{name}$ as well as a concept c_k = 'Associate Professor' in the domain-specific ontology $\mathcal{C}_{domain}$. In this case the concept label b_j could be added to the set $\mathcal{B}_C^{name}$.

If the label b_j only consists of the recognized concept candidate w_{ji} the label b_j can be deleted from the set of instances. In case of the label b_j = 'Associate Professor', b_j could be deleted from $\mathcal{B}_I^{name}$, because the label contains no other words.

$$\mathcal{B}_I^{onto} := \mathcal{B}_I^{name} \setminus \{b_j \mid b_j \in \mathcal{B}_I^{name} \land b_j = w_{ji}\} \tag{8}$$

If there is no match between w_{ji} and the concepts of the domain-specific ontology, w_{ji} is compared to the instances of this ontology $\mathcal{I}_{domain}$. If $w_{ji} \in \mathcal{I}_{domain}$ holds, w_{ji} will still be an instance, but the corresponding concept $c_k = inst_{domain}^{-1}(w_{ji})$ will be accepted as a concept candidate. Assuming the concept c_k = 'Topic' has an instance which matches the label b_j = 'Information Retrieval' with $b_j \in \mathcal{B}_I^{name}$. In this case c_k = 'Topic' can be added to $\mathcal{B}_C^{onto}$.

$$\mathcal{B}_C^{onto} := \mathcal{B}_C^{name} \cup \{w_{ji} \mid \exists j, i, k : w_{ji} = c_k \land c_k \in \mathcal{C}_{domain} \land b_j \in \mathcal{B}_I^{name}\} \tag{9}$$
$$\cup \{c_k \mid \exists i, j, k : w_{ji} = inst_{domain}(c_k)\}$$

For this method only domain-specific ontologies can be used which have at least the quality level that is claimed for the new ontology.

3.2 Word Sense Disambiguation

Lexical polysemy has been a hot topic since the earliest days of computer-based language processing in the 1950s [14]. Lexical polysemy either arises due to the fact that words can be used in different part-of-speeches (syntactical polysemy) or due to words that have varying meanings in different contexts (semantical polysemy). *Word sense disambiguation* is about solving semantical polysemy.

Having identified the concept candidates $\mathcal{B}_C$ word sense disambiguation algorithms are applied to assign appropriate meanings from the MRD to these concept candidates. Then, concept candidates and their distinct meaning are used as concepts $\mathcal{C}$ for the ontology. Having non-ambiguous concepts is necessary to define a correct taxonomy and to find valid non-taxonomic relations.

In [14] different approaches to word sense disambiguation are described. On the one hand there are global, context-independent approaches, which assign meanings retrieved form an external dictionary by applying special heuristics. E.g. a frequency-based approach where always the most frequently applied sense can be used. On the other hand there are context-sensitive approaches. This kind of methods uses the context of a word to disambiguate it. In our scenario the context is composed by other words in the label and by labels of the subordinated as well as superordinated nodes in the classification schema. For the disambiguation process knowledge-based, corpus-based and hybrid methods can be applied.

3.3 Taxonomy Construction

Having identified the concepts $\mathcal{C}$ of the ontology a taxonomic structure $\mathcal{H}_C \subseteq \mathcal{C} \times \mathcal{C}$ is needed. Therefore, the concepts have to be associated by irreflexive, acyclic, and transitive relations. The hierarchy already contained in the classification schema cannot be used for this purpose, because the relations in this hierarchy do not have to be taxonomic. There are already various algorithms available tackling the problem of building taxonomies. According to Maedche et. al. [15] they can be categorized in symbolic and statistical algorithms. Symbolic algorithms use pattern recognition to identify taxonomic relation between concepts. Due to the fact that in this scenario only node labels and not sentences are processed, lexico-syntactic patterns from a NLP-scenario can be reused only to a small extend. Alternatively, statistical methods can be applied. Here various kinds of clustering algorithms are available[15].

In the following two algorithms similar to [16] are outlined: One approach based on a semantic net such as WordNet and one symbolic, pattern-based algorithm.

Extracting taxonomic relations by pruning. Starting point for this process step are the individual concepts $\mathcal{C}$. In order to find taxonomic relations between these concepts we use the fact that all concepts are represented by a meaning in the machine readable dictionary. If the used machine readable dictionary defines also hyponym/hyperonym-relations between meanings (like WordNet does) it will easily be possible to find taxonomic relations between the concepts. This is done by comparing all concepts $c_i \in \mathcal{C}$ with the other concepts $c_j \in \mathcal{C}$ ($i \neq j$) to find out which concepts are directly taxonomic related, which have a common super-concept, and which are not taxonomic related at all. In case two concepts c_i and c_j are not directly connected, but they have common super-concepts, the most specific super-concept c_{ij} as well as two taxonomic relations have to be included in the ontology. In Figure 1, for instance, the concepts $c_1 = $ *'Presentation'* and $c_2 = $ *'Paper'* are not directly connected by a taxonomic relation, but they have the common super-concept c_{12} = *'Communication'*. In the following equations the operator '$\geq$' specifies taxonomic relations between two concepts. E.g. $c_1 \geq c_2$ states that c_2 is a subclass of c_1.

$$\mathcal{H}_\mathcal{C}^{new} := \mathcal{H}_\mathcal{C}^{old} \cup \{c_i \times c_j \mid \forall i,j : c_i \geq c_j \wedge i \neq j\} \quad (10)$$
$$\cup \{c_{ij} \times c_i, c_{ij} \times c_j \mid \forall i,j : i \neq j \wedge c_{ij} \geq c_i \wedge c_{ij} \geq c_j\}$$

$$\mathcal{C}^{new} := \mathcal{C}^{old} \cup \{c_{ij} \mid \forall i,j : c_i \not\geq c_j \wedge c_j \not\geq c_i \wedge c_{ij} \geq c_i \wedge c_{ij} \geq c_j\} \quad (11)$$

Iteratively, this step has to be repeated on bases of $\mathcal{C}^{new}$ until no super-concepts are included any more (i.e. $\mathcal{C}^{new} = \mathcal{C}^{old}$). Figure 3 shows an example for this iterative process.

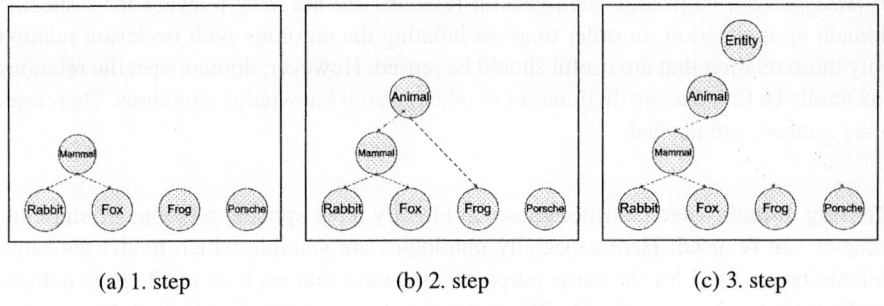

(a) 1. step   (b) 2. step   (c) 3. step

Fig. 3. Example for extracting taxonomic relations by pruning.

Pattern-based extraction of taxonomic relations. Additionally, a symbolic algorithm can be applied in order to generate taxonomic relations. [17] uses such a method for natural language processing and defines regular expressions that can be used to find relations between words. Designing such regular expressions for complex sentences is a cumbersome task and the results reached in the NLP-domain are not too promising. Nevertheless, for analyzing node labels a symbolic approach could be useful. Here, the label structure is much simpler than the structure of a natural language sentence. Therefore, finding regular expressions that indicate a taxonomic relation in a node label can be done more easily. For example the regular expression *[(NP)*NP]* indicates that the last noun phrase of a label is super-concept of the whole label. This is true, because in most cases the last word of a sequence determines the object type. E.g. *EU Project* is of type *Project*.

3.4 Identification of Non-taxonomic Relations

This section is about finding non-taxonomic relations $\mathcal{P} = \mathcal{C} \times \mathcal{C}$. Therefore, two tasks have to be performed. Firstly, we have to detect which concepts are related. And secondly, we have to figure out how these concepts are related. Thus, a name for the relation has to be found. For discovering taxonomic relations the second step was not necessary, because the name of the relation was already defined (*subClassOf, isA*).

There is a huge number of algorithms dealing with finding non taxonomic relations [18,19,20]. Mostly these approaches apply co-occurrences analysis in order to find out which concepts are related. Then, the label of the relation is generated using the predicate of the sentence. This is not possible in case of a classification schema, because node labels rarely contain predicates. But classification schemas also contain additional information compared to natural language texts. In the following we outline how this information can be exploited.

Identifying general relations by pruning. Due to the fact that concepts are represented by meanings of a dictionary relations contained in the dictionary can also be reused easily. These relations are mostly very general. E.g. *WordNet* contains relations such as *partOf* or *hasSynonym*. Normally, such general relations are not very relevant for a specific domain or application. In order to avoid inflating the ontology with irrelevant relation only those relation that are useful should be reused. However, domain-specific relations can hardly be found using dictionaries or other general knowledge structures. Therefore, other methods are needed.

Reusing domain-specific ontologies. To identify more specific relations existing ontologies can be used. Here especially ontologies are suitable which model the same domain or are used for the same purpose. Assuming that such an ontology is defined by the tuple $O_{domian} = (\mathcal{C}_d, \mathcal{P}_d, \mathcal{H}^\mathcal{C}, prop)$ the starting point $c_a^d \in \mathcal{C}_d$ and the endpoint $c_b^d \in \mathcal{C}_d$ of the relation $r_d \in \mathcal{P}_d$ has to match two concepts $c_a, c_b \in \mathcal{C}$. Then, a relation between c_a and c_b of type r_1^d can be included in the new ontology. Again, we assume that two concepts $c \in \mathcal{C}$ and $c_d \in \mathcal{C}_d$ will match if their labels are identical. E.g. there is a domain-specific ontology with the concepts $c_1^d = $ '*Conference*', $c_2^d = $ '*Presentation*', and a relation of type $r_1^d = $ '*hasPresentation*'. In this scenario the relation can be added to the new ontology.

Identifying relations using the classification hierarchy. A concept hierarchy – as mentioned above – is represented by a tuple $\mathcal{H} = (\mathcal{K}, \mathcal{E}, l)$. The set of relations $\mathcal{E}$ contains information about the human domain model underlying the classification schema. Although the relations define no real taxonomy and thus cannot be used for finding taxonomic relations, they are not meaningless. They indicate weather two concepts c_a, c_b are related in some way.

To show this we consider the set $\mathcal{E}' \subseteq \mathcal{E}$ that includes only relations between nodes $k \in \mathcal{K}$ which have corresponding concepts in $\mathcal{C}$. I.e. we will assume that two concepts c_a, c_b are related if the nodes k_a, k_b are also related by an association $r_{dom} \in \mathcal{E}'$. In Figure 1, for instance, *SEKT* is not in $\mathcal{E}'$, but $k_1 = $ '*Conference*' and $k_2 = $ '*Location*' are related since *ODBASE Cyprus* is a subfolder of *Conferences 2004*. In case two concepts are related by $r_{dom} \in \mathcal{E}'$ as well as by a general association $r_{general}$ found in the step before we assume r_{dom} is of type $r_{general}$ and include the relation in the ontology.

For the remaining relations $\mathcal{E}'^{new} = \mathcal{E}'^{old} \setminus \{r_{dom}\}$ the type of a relation $c_a \to c_b$ is generated by concatenating 'has' and the label of concept c_b. E.g. the type of the relation between *Conference* and *Location* would be *hasLocation*.

Pattern-based extraction of non-taxonomic relations. Information about relations between concepts is not only contained in the structure of the hierarchy but also in the labels of the nodes itself. If two concepts are extracted from the same node label they are related in some way. E.g. the label *Conferences 2004* includes the two concepts *Conference* and *Date*. Again, we know that there is an association between two concepts, but we do not know which. In the last section we used regular expressions to define patterns that indicate taxonomic relations. Now, we can extend this method to facilitate the discovery of non-taxonomic relations. Therefore, a list of regular expressions is needed together with the relation type they refer to. For instance, the regular expression [NP *within* NP] might indicate an *include*-relation. In order to find relations all node labels containing more than one concept have to be searched for the patterns defined in the list. The use of predicate-based patterns [21] seems to be not very promising due to the fact that predicates are rarely used in node labels. In case there are no additional words in the label that allow the use of pattern-based approaches we can adopt a method similar to that in the paragraph before. Again, we compose the relation type by concatenating *has* with the second concept. I.e. for example above a relation of type *hasDate* is introduced to connect *Conference* and *Date*.

3.5 Ontology Population

In order to populate the ontology $\mathcal{O} = (\mathcal{C}, \mathcal{H}^{\mathcal{C}}, \mathcal{P}, inst)$ the function $inst : \mathcal{C} \to 2^I$ has to be defined.

Reusing already extracted knowledge. During the generation process of the core ontology knowledge about the mapping between instances $\mathcal{B}_I$ and concept candidates $\mathcal{B}_C$ has already evolved. Now, this knowledge can be incorporated into the ontology population process.

In the concept identification step concepts are extracted from instances. We assume that a concept $c \in \mathcal{C}$ extracted from an instance $i \in \mathcal{B}_I$ represents the concept of this instance $(inst(i) = c)$. In this way all instances that produced a concept can be assigned to this concept. Other instances cannot be assigned by this method. E.g. named entity recognition discovers that *Cyprus* is an instance of *Location* and *2004* is an instance of *Date*.

A problem occurs if the mapping is not unique. If two concepts c_1, c_2 are extracted from one instance it will be not clear to which concept the instance has to be assigned. This is case for the file *OntoMapping.pdf*. The problem could be solved by assigning the instance to the most specific common super-class of c_1 and c_2. In this case some information contained in the classification schema is lost. For the file *OntoMapping.pdf* it is not possible to decide whether it is a *Presentation* or a *Paper*. Thus, it has to be assigned to *Communication*.

Populating by means of the classification schema. Now we consider all instances in the set B_I which have not been assigned in the last step. They are assigned by using the hierarchy of the classification schema. Therefore, we have to analyze the direct super-node of an instance. If a concept is extracted from this super-node the instance will be assigned to that concept. Otherwise the next superior node in the hierarchy has to be considered. If there is no node with a corresponding concept in the entire partial tree, the instance will be assigned to the root concept. In Figure 1 the instance *SEKT* will be assigned to the next superordinated concept. This would be *EU-Project* in this case.

Having described a process for representing knowledge obtained from a classification schema in an explicit and formal way, we will know evaluate this process using real world folder structures.

4 Evaluation

For evaluation purpose we used a prototypical implementation of the knowledge extraction method introduced in this paper. First we outline the architecture of this prototype. Then, the test data and the evaluation measures are introduced. Finally, the results automatically generated by the extraction method are evaluated.

Prototype. The prototype used for evaluation allows to extract an ontology from an underlying directory of a computer system. The extraction process comprises five steps, each including several algorithms. The prototype does not implement all algorithms introduced in the last sections, but it implements at least one for each process step. This guarantees a valid solution, but the performance of the prototype is only a base line for future enhancements.

The prototype includes the following algorithms:

Identification of concepts and instances. Lexical analysis and decomposition of node labels as well as reusing a domain-specific ontology is performed.
Word Sense Disambiguation. There are two alternative methods available. One global, context-independent algorithm, that assigns meanings based on the frequencies of their occurrence. The other method disambiguates words based on the context. The method combines the techniques of Magnini et. al. [5], Rada [22], and the frequency based approach mentioned above.
Taxonomy construction. In this step all algorithms suggested by the extraction method are implemented. Extracting relations by pruning and a pattern-based approach, where only the regular expression [(NP)*NP] is used.
Identification of non-taxonomic relations: A method for identifying non-taxonomic relations by using knowledge from the classification schema is implemented in this step.
Ontology Population: All algorithms for ontology population introduced in the extraction method are implemented.

For the concrete implementation the machine-readable dictionary *WordNet*[3] is used. The current version of this dictionary contains 152059 words and 115424 meanings

---
[3] http://www.cogsci.princeton.edu/$\sim$wn

that are expressed by synonym sets (*synsets*). These synsets are used internally for representing concepts of the ontology. Furthermore the ISWC-Ontology[4] is used which is highly relevant for the domain of the evaluation data set.

Evaluation data set. We use four real world folder structures to evaluate the prototypical implementation of the extraction method. The directories cover the domains university, project management, and Semantic Web technologies. All structures are working directories of employees of a research institute, which include academic as well as administrative data. We compared the automatically generated ontologies to one which we manually engineered. The 'reference' ontology contained only information which could directly be deduced from the folder structures with common sense.

The folder structures are serialized in RDF(S)-format according to the SWAP-Common ontology[5]. Table 4 contains statistical data about the used directories.

	# folders	# files	max. depth	avg. depth	$\frac{words}{label}$
Directory 1	293	493	15	5.9	1.44
Directory 2	548	1309	12	6.7	1.46
Directory 3	197	552	14	8.0	1.21
Directory 4	189	780	5	3.8	5.53

Fig. 4. Topology statistic of folder structures

Evaluation measures. To evaluate the extraction method we apply the standard measures *Recall* and *Precision* originally used in Information Retrieval. *Recall* shows how much of the existing knowledge is extracted.

$$Recall = \frac{\sharp \; correctly \; extracted \; entities}{\sharp \; entities} \quad (12)$$

To calculate the Recall values we count the number of correct extracted concepts, relations or instances, and divide it by the overall number contained the classification schema. Concepts will count as correct if they are contained in the 'reference' ontology. A relation will be correct if both concepts as well as the relation type is valid. To get a correct instance, the label and the assigned concept have to be correct.

Precision in contrast specifies to which extend the knowledge is extracted correctly. In this case we built the ratio between the correct extracted and the overall extracted concepts, relations, or instances.

$$Precision = \frac{\sharp \; correctly \; extracted \; entities}{\sharp \; exracted \; entities} \quad (13)$$

Since there are no preexisting ontologies for our evaluation data (Gold Standard), the Recall values can only be calculated for the concept and instance identification. In

---

[4] http://annotation.semanticweb.org/iswc/iswc.daml
[5] http://swap.semanticweb.org/2003/01/swap-common\#

these cases we were able to compare the results to the performance a human ontology engineer reaches based on the information contained in the classification schema. Of course, this measure cannot be completely objective.

Evaluation results. The overall Precision value for concepts, relations, and instances lies between 70% and 81% for the different directories. As mentioned above there is no Recall value for the overall process. Because errors in early process steps could cause cascading errors in the following steps we analyzed the five different steps separately.

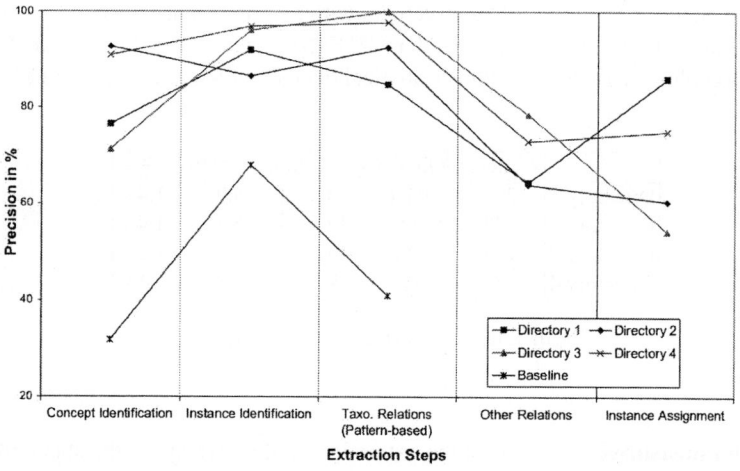

Fig. 5. Precision for each step

Concept and instance identification performs well for all directories (70%–93%). A major part of the errors are due to not recognized named entities. Another issue the prototype cannot handle are complex node labels. If labels similar to sentences are used, concept identification will fail quite often. In such cases NLP-techniques have to be introduced (POS-tagging, chunk-parsing, ...). We introduced a baseline where we assume that all labels of the classification schema are concepts (concept identification) or instances (instance identification), respectively. Here we achieve average Precision-values of 31% for concept identification and 61% for instance identification. That means our identification algorithms performs much better. Concept and instance identification achieves Recall values well above 80% .

In order to disambiguate the extracted concept candidates we evaluated two different algorithms. One context-sensitive algorithm based on the methods by Magnini et. al. [5] and Rada [22]. The second algorithm we apply is a simple frequency-based method. Except for one directory the frequency-based algorithm performs better than the context-sensitive one. Considering context improves the disambiguation result only in case of a very specific domain (directory 4). However, the difference between both approaches seems to be quite small.

In terms of Precision the extraction of taxonomic relations performs very well. This can be explained by the fact that the first method only reuses relations from WordNet. Thus, Precision of 100% can be reached if errors of earlier steps are neglected. The pattern-based approach achieves Precision values between 84,8% and 100%. Here we generated a baseline by interpreting the hierarchy of the classification schema as valid taxonomy and encountered a Precision value of about 40%.

Finding non-taxonomic relations is probably the most difficult task, because here not only the relation itself but also the label of the relation has to be extracted. The implemented approach based on the classification hierarchy achieves between 63,9% and 78,6% Precision. Errors are caused to the same extend by wrong relations identification and wrong assignment of labels.

The performance of the ontology population method depends highly on the previously generated ontology. I.e. an instance cannot be assigned correctly if the corresponding concept is not extracted. Thus, Precision between 55% and 85% is achieved. If errors that are caused by a wrong ontology are disregarded, we can achieve much better results. Especially the first method (using knowledge of the extraction process) performs very well with Precision values between 80% and 100%.

test directory	# concepts	# instances	# taxonomic relations	other relations	$\frac{concepts}{folder}$	max. depth	avg. depth	Precision
1	175	656	68	90	0.59	6	3.4	80.7%
2	299	1457	115	180	0.55	7	3.5	78.3%
3	262	624	52	14	1.33	6	3.8	80.1%
4	265	776	54	89	1.4	5	3.7	70.4%

Fig. 6. Topology statistic of generated ontologies

Figure 6 contains statistical data about the generated ontologies. It is obvious that the structure of the ontologies depend heavily on the properties of the underlying directories. Thus, the folder structures with shorter labels and a deeper tree structure (directory 1 and 3) achieve the best Precision values. Directory 4 has by far the longest labels and the shallowest tree structure and achieves the worst Precision result. The relative flat and coarse taxonomies of the ontologies are caused by the fact that the extraction of taxonomic relations is only executed once in the prototype. To get more complete taxonomies this algorithm has to be repeated iteratively until all super-concepts are introduced.

In general good results can be achieved although not all algorithms contained in the extraction process have been implemented yet.

5 Related Work

The extraction process depends heavily on the underlying data structures. One can distinguish between different ontology learning approaches: Learning from natural language texts, semi-structured schemas, dictionaries, knowledge bases and from entirely structured information such as relational schemas. Our work focuses on the area of ontology learning from semi-structured schemas. We used explicit as well as implicit semantics hidden in classification schemas in order to generate an ontology. Deitel et. al. [23] also use information in RDF-format to construct an ontology. They extract knowledge from RDF-annotations of Web-resources by applying graph theory techniques. Doan et. al. [24] use a machine learning approach to map between a semi-structured source file and a target ontology. First, mappings have to be defined manually and then the machine learning method tries to find new mapping based on the existing ones. [5] present methods for interpreting schema models on basis of the taxonomic relations as well as the linguistic material they contain. The main difference to our work is the fact that the schema models they build upon include already valid taxonomic relations.

Apart from the work done in the field of ontology learning there has been some effort to build ontologies from taxonomies manually. In [25] the authors describe a case study were they have engineered an ontology based on the Art and Architecture Thesaurus to describe architectonic images. Similarly in [26] the NCI thesaurus was used to model an ontology for medical domain. In contrast to our work they do not consider automated methods to build the ontology.

In [27] a method is presented to generate a global virtual view from database schemas. They use also WordNet as a common vocabulary. However, they do not learn new relations as we do from labels, but integrate different existing schemas.

6 Conclusion

In this paper we presented a method for automatic knowledge extraction from classification schemas. This extracted knowledge is represented by a formal ontology. The integration with methods based on other data structures is made possible by incorporating a generic ontology learning framework.

The extraction method we outlined above combines methods and algorithms from various research domains, which are usually treated separately in literature. Additionally, we introduced several heuristics that exploit the special semantics of classification schemas.

To evaluate this method we built an prototype for knowledge extraction from directories. This prototype implements the five steps of the extraction method and the majority of algorithms they include. Applying the method to real world folder structures we realize Precision values between 70% and 80%. In this scenario the entire method was executed automatically without human intervention. But the evaluation also made clear that there is a lot room for improvements. Especially the implementation of named entity recognition promises further improvement.

Certainly the prototype evaluated here is not suitable for entirely automatic ontology generation, but the results represent a good basis for a human ontology engineer. This enables more economical and efficient ontology engineering and thus saves time and money.

Acknowledgements. Research reported in this paper has been partially financed by the Graduate School for Information Management and Market Engineering (DFG grant no. GRK 895) and the EU in the IST projects SWAP (IST-2001-34103) and SEKT (IST-2003-506826).

References

1. Pinto, S., Staab, S., Sure, Y., Tempich, C.: OntoEdit empowering SWAP: a case study in supporting DIstributed, Loosely-controlled and evolvInG Engineering of oNTologies (DILIGENT). In Bussler, C., Davies, J., Fensel, D., Studer, R., eds.: First European Semantic Web Symposium, ESWS 2004. Volume 3053 of LNCS., Heraklion, Crete, Greece, Springer (2004) 16–30
2. Maedche, A.: Emergent semantics for ontologies - support by an explicit lexical layer and ontology learning. IEEE Intelligent Systems (2002)
3. Maedche, A., Staab, S.: Ontology learning for the semantic web. IEEE Intelligent Systems **16** (2001) 72–79
4. Lamparter, S.: (Semi-)Automatische Wissensextraktion aus Klassifikationsschemata. Master's thesis, Institute AIFB, University of Karlsruhe (TH) (2004)
5. Magnini, B., Serafini, L., Speranza, M.: Making explicit the semantics hidden in schema models. In: Proc. of the 2nd Int. Semantic Web Conference. (2003)
6. Hotho, A., Maedche, A., Staab, S., Zacharias, V.: On knowledgeable unsupervised text mining. In Franke, J., Nakhaeizadeh, G., Renz, I., eds.: Text Mining, Theoretical Aspects and Applications, Physica-Verlag (2003) 131–152
7. Brants, T.: TnT – a statistical part-of-speech tagger. In: Proc. of the 6th Applied Natural Language Processing Conference (ANLP), Seattle, WA (2000)
8. Brill, E.: Transformation-based error-driven learning and natural language processing: A case study in part of speech tagging. Computational Lingusitics **21** (1995) 543–565
9. Abney, S.P.: Parsing by chunks. In Berwick, R.C., Abney, S.P., Tenny, C., eds.: Principle-Based Parsing: Computation and Psycholinguistics. Kluwer, Dordrecht (1991) 257–278
10. Grishman, R.: The NYU system for MUC-6 or Where's the Syntax? In: Proc. of the 6th Message Understanding Conference (MUC-6, 1995), Morgan Kaufmann (1995)
11. Bikel, D.M., Miller, S., Schwartz, R., Weischedel, R.: Nymble: a high-performance learning name-finder. In: Proc. of 5th Conf. on Applied Natural Language Processing. (1997) 194–201
12. Borthwick, A.: A Maximum Entropy Approach to Named Entity Recognition. Ph.d. thesis, New York University (1999)
13. Mikheev, A., Moens, M., Grover, C.: Named entity recognition without gazetteers. In: In EACL'99, Bergen, Norway (1999) 1–8
14. Ide, N., Véronis, J.: Introduction to the special issue on word sense disambiguation: The state of the art. Computational Linguistics **24** (1998) 1–40
15. Maedche, A., Pekar, V., Staab, S. In: Ontology Learning Part One - On Discovering Taxonomic Relations from the Web. Springer Verlag (2002) 301–322
16. Missikoff, M., Navigli, R., Velardi, P.: The usable ontology: An environment for building and assessing a domain ontology. In: Proc. of 1st Int. Semantic Web Conference (ISWC 2002). Number 2342 in LNCS, Springer-Verlag, Berlin (2002) 39–53
17. Hearst, M.A.: Automatic acqusition of hyponyms from large text corpora. In: Proceedings of the 14th International Conference on Computational Linguistics, Nantes, France (1992)
18. Resnik, P.: Selection and Information: A Class-based Approach to Lexical Relationships. PhD thesis, University of Pennsylania (1993)
19. Maedche, A., Staab, S.: Discovering conceptual relations from text. In: Proceedings of ECAI 2000, IOS Press (2000)

20. Faure, D., Nedellec, C.: A corpus-based conceptual clustering method for verb frames and ontology acquisition. In: LREC-98 Workshop on Adapting Lexical and Corpus Resources to Sublanguages and Applications, Granada, Spain (1998)
21. Kavalec, M., Maedche, A., Svatek, V.: Discovery of lexical entries for non-taxonomic relations in ontology learning. In: SOFSEM – Theory and Practice of Computer Science, Springer LNCS 2932 (2004)
22. Rada, R., Mili, H., Bicknell, E., Blettner, M.: Development and application of a metric on semantic nets. IEEE Transactions on Systems, Man and Cybernetics **19** (1989) 17–30
23. Deitel, A., Faron, C., Dieng, R.: Learning ontologies from rdf annotations. In: Proc. of the IJCAI Workshop in Ontology Learning. (2001)
24. Doan, A., Domingos, P., Levy, A.: Learning source descriptions for data integration. In: Proc. of 3rd Int. Workshop on the Web and Databases, Dallas, Texas (2000) 81–86
25. Wielinga, B., Th, A., Wielemaker, S., Sandberg, J.: From thesaurus to ontology. In: Proc. of Int. Conf. on Knowledge Capture, New Yory, NY, USA, ACM Press (2001) 194–201
26. Golbeck, J., Fragoso, G., Hartel, F., Hendler, J., Parsia, B., Oberthaler, J.: The national cancer institute's thesaurus and ontology. Journal of Web Semantics **1** (2003)
27. Beneventano, D., Bergamaschi, S., Guerra, F., Vincini, M.: Synthesizing an integrated ontology. IEEE Internet Computing **XX** (2003) 42–51

Generation and Management of a Medical Ontology in a Semantic Web Retrieval System

Elena Paslaru Bontas[1], Sebastian Tietz[1], Robert Tolksdorf[1], and Thomas Schrader[2]

[1] Freie Universität Berlin
Institut für Informatik
AG Netzbasierte Informationssysteme
Takustr. 9, D-14195 Berlin, Germany
research@robert-tolksdorf.de
{paslaru, tietz}@inf.fu-berlin.de
[2] Institute for Pathology Charité
Rudolf-Virchow-Haus
Schumannstr. 20-21
D-10117 Berlin, Germany
thomas.schrader@charite.de

Abstract. Medicine is one of the best examples of application domains where ontologies have already been deployed at large scale and demonstrated their utility. However, most of the available medical ontologies, though containing huge amounts of valuable information, underlie different design principles as those required by Semantic Web applications and consequently can not be directly integrated and reused. In this paper we describe the generation, maintenance and evolution of a Semantic Web-based ontology in the context of an information system for pathology. The system combines Semantic Web and NLP techniques to support a content-based storage and retrieval of medical reports and digital images.

1 Introduction

Ontologies are generally accepted as a key technology for the realization of the Semantic Web vision. Their potential and usability has been analyzed in various application domains [7,11]. Medicine is one of the best examples of application domains where ontologies have already been deployed at large scale and have already demonstrated their utility [8,5,19,9]. The most prominent exponent of such approaches is UMLS, a medicine thesaurus integrating over 100 medical libraries in a common scheme [24]. Though containing a huge amount of domain information, the ambiguous and error-prone integration scheme and the heterogeneity of the libraries made the reuse of UMLS as information/knowledge source in applications as retrieval, annotation and text processing difficult [9,12,2,13, 20]. The task specificity of each UMLS library and the complexity of the complete thesarus could be managed only with powerful tools, which should allow a high quality customization of the information sources for concrete application needs. Besides tailoring the information sources to a application-relevant subset, the next problem, UMLS and most of the available medicine ontologies are confronted with, is the absence of a representation format which supports sharing and reuse. In this paper we address these issues by presenting the generation and management of a Semantic Web ontology for pathology. The ontology was generated on the basis of UMLS and will be used in a text and image retrieval system for lung pathology. In the rest of the paper we will briefly present the usage setting of the ontology and mainly address issues related to its engineering process.

2 The Project "A Semantic Web for Pathology"

The project "A Semantic Web for Pathology" aims to realize a retrieval system for pathology *based on Semantic Web technologies*. The core of the system is a knowledge base, consisting of an ontology library of domain and generic ontologies and a set of rules describing decision processes in routine pathology. The knowledge base can be used to improve the retrieval capabilities of the archive of pathology information items. We distinguish between two kinds of information items in our system:

- *pathology reports* in textual form, containing the observations of the domain experts (pathologists) w.r.t. medical cases.
- *digital histological slides*, i.e. digital images obtained through high-quality scanning of glass slides with tissue samples.

Every pathology report is de facto a textual representation of a set of histological slides corresponding to a specific medical case. This close relationship can be used to overcome the drawbacks of common retrieval systems for digital pathology and telepathology[1], which concentrate on image-based retrieval algorithms and ignore corresponding medical reports. Such analysis algorithms have the essential disadvantage that they operate exclusively on structural – or syntactical – image parameters such as color, texture and basic geometrical forms. They ignore the real content and the actual meaning of the pictures. Medical reports, however, contain much more than that since they are textual representations of the pictural represented *content* of the slides and are easier to analyze than the original image-based data. They capture *implicitly* the concrete semantics of what the picture graphically represent, for example "a tumor" in contrast to "a blob with the length of 15 mm" or "a co-located set of 1000 red colored pixels". In the project described in this paper, we understand the medical reports even as semantic meta data for the images prepared by an expert with high quality and make their content explicit using an ontology-driven NLP component.

---

[1] The main goal of digital pathology and telepathology is the extended usage of digital images for diagnostic support or educational purposes in anatomical or clinical pathology.

For the realization of the system we concentrate our efforts in two interrelated directions: 1) the construction of a *knowledge base* and, 2) the development of the *semantic representation* of medical reports and digital histological images. The knowledge base consists of a library of domain and generic ontologies, formalized using Semantic Web representation languages e.g. OWL and RDF(S) and a set of rules, formalized in RuleML and related languages. The domain ontologies use basically UMLS [24] as information source and adapt this information to the requirements of our concrete application domain "lung pathology". Generic ontologies capture common sense knowledge useful in knowledge intensive tasks like "differential diagnosis" (i.e. different medical findings with similar symptoms). The necessity of using this second category of ontologies has been emphasized in several similar projects, which analyzed the quality and usage challenges of UMLS in building knowledge bases [19,9]. Rules are intended to represent decision processes in diagnosis tasks and will be acquired in collaboration with domain experts. The role of the rules is also to extend the expressiveness of the ontological knowledge, by formalizing facts, which are not representable using OWL or RDF(S). The semantic representation of the medical reports is realized by a natural language component, which identifies domain specific phrases using the domain ontology. Every pathology report will be stored in the system in OWL. The NLP module uses the knowledge base to associate text expressions to ontology concepts and generates for every pathology report an OWL file containing instances of the recognized concepts (see Section 4 for details). In this paper we present our work so far for the realization of the knowledge base and focus on ontology engineering issues. The architecture of the system as well as a detailed description of the knowledge component and the NLP component is addressed in more detail in [23,16].

2.1 Motivation and Use Cases

The main goal of the project is to improve the retrieval capabilities of the pathology information items (text and images). Currently, enormous amounts of knowledge are lost by being stored in data bases, which are behaving as real data sinks. Reuse and retrieval of the information, once stored in the data base, is a very time-consuming operation which requires expert knowledge related to the query particularities of the storage system. Besides, the connection between image- and text-based data is lost, i.e. text data can not be used to improve the retrieval of digital images [23]. Furthermore, even if this connection would be available in a retrieval system, without a more powerful representation of the pathology reports, text retrieval could not exploit the real meaning of their content and is restricted to different flavors of string matching.

We foresee several valuable uses of the system in routine pathology: as an assistant tool for diagnosis and education tasks, as well as for quality assurance and control of the diagnosis decisions [23]. Finally, once the content of the pathology reports and the associated images is explicitly represented, this knowledge can be exchanged with external parties like other hospitals. This feature is also one of the goals of telepathology, whom main goal is exactly the realization and support of a networked infrastructure for diagnostic and educational purposes in pathology [6]. The representation within the system is already the communication format for information. Semantic Web technologies are by design open for the integration of knowledge that is relative to different ontologies and rules. Therefore we intend to use mainly such technologies for the realization of the retrieval system.

3 Building a Knowledge Base for Lung Pathology

Several methodologies have been published in the last decade to predefine the process of construction of a knowledge base or a knowledge-based system [26, 17,3]. For example in [3] the construction of a knowledge-based system should follow 8 steps:

- analysis of the application domain
- discovery of useful knowledge sources
- system design: discovery and design of useful knowledge structures and inference capabilities
- representation of the application knowledge using the selected knowledge representation language(s) (application ontology)
- implementation of a prototype
- prototype testing and refinement
- management of the knowledge base: evolution and maintenance

In our setting we identified the following subtasks, which will guide the implementation of the system:

- analysis of the application domain: during intensive collaboration with domain experts (pathologists) we identified the key features of the system: retrieval capabilities, integration in the current environment[2], quality assurance, statistics.
- knowledge sources, potentially relevant for the knowledge base: UMLS, domain knowledge of the experts.
- Semantic Web languages, especially OWL will be used for knowledge representation purposes. One of the goals of the system was to investigate the appropriateness and maturity of Semantic Web technology for a concrete knowledge-intensive application domain (medicine), in a often cited setting w.r.t. the Semantic Web: information retrieval.
- implementation, testing and refinement of a prototype: currently we realized a first domain ontology on the basis of UMLS and formalized additional

---

[2] The system should be integrated in the environment of the Digital Virtual Microscope, a tool realized by our project partners from the Charité hospital in Berlin, Germany. This tool allows web-based management and high-quality visualization of digital pathological slides.

application-relevant knowledge in OWL[3]. We also implemented a first prototype for the NLP component.
- knowledge base management: we are currently developing a tool for ontology engineering: populating the ontology is realized by the NLP component[4], which extracts valid ontology concepts from XML-formatted pathology reports [16]. Besides, the component reveals important information about the degree the current (domain) ontology covers the concrete knowledge and terminology formalized by the real users, which are also authors of the pathology reports.

In the following sections we will focus on the generation of the domain ontology and related engineering tasks.

4 Engineering the Ontology

4.1 Generating an Ontology for Lung Pathology

As input for the medical knowledge base we used UMLS, as the most complex medical thesaurus currently available [24]. UMLS as in the current release contains over 1,5 million concepts from over 100 medical libraries and is permanently growing. New sources and current versions of already integrated sources are mapped to the UMLS knowledge format. Due to the complexity of the thesaurus and the limitations of current Semantic Web tools we need to customize it w.r.t. to two important axes:

- 1) the *identification of relevant libraries and concepts* corresponding to "lung pathology" from UMLS and
- 2) their *adaptation* to the particularities of language and vocabulary of the case report archive.

This two-phase approach is justified by the application-oriented character of the system. We do not intend to build a general Semantic Web knowledge base for pathology, or even lung pathology, but one, which is tailored for and can be efficiently used in our application setting. Despite standards and tools for the main technologies, building concrete Semantic Web applications, their potential and acceptance at a larger scale is still a challenging issue for the Semantic Web research community. Besides, building the knowledge base implies also a subsequent adaptation of the content, performed by domain experts. Therefore they should be able to evaluate and modify the ontology. Apart from technical drawbacks, very large ontologies can not be used efficiently by humans as well.

---

[3] The domain ontologies can be found at
 "http://nbi.inf.fu-berlin.de/research/swpatho/owldata/"
[4] The natural language component is implemented at the Department of Linguistics at the University of Potsdam, Germany.

Identifying application-relevant knowledge in UMLS. The straightforward method to address this issue is to use the UMLS Knowledge Server [25], which provides the MetamorphoSys tool [24] and an additional API to tailor the thesaurus to specific application needs. However, both allow mainly syntactical filtering methods (e.g. exclude complete UMLS sources, exclude languages or term synonyms) and do not offer means to analyze the semantics of particular libraries or to use only relevant parts of them. In a "preselection" phase domain experts reduced the huge amount of medical information from UMLS to the domain "pathology". They identified potentially relevant UMLS libraries. The large number of partially overlapping libraries and the complexity of their interdepedencies made this process time-consuming and error-prone, so that the final goal of the "preselection" phase was to identify libraries, which are definitively irrelevant to our application domain.

Approximately 50 percent of the UMLS libraries were selected as *possibly* relevant for lung pathology, containing more than 500000 concepts. Managing an ontology of such dimensions with Semantic Web technologies is related to still unsolved issues w.r.t. to scalability and performance of the system. In the second step we used the case reports archive to identify concepts, which actually occur in medical reports. These concepts are really used by pathologists when putting down their observations and therefore will also occur as search parameters. We compared the vocabulary of the reports archive to the content of the preselected UMLS libraries by means of a retrieval engine. The result of this task was a list of 10 UMLS libraries, still containing approximately 350,000 different concepts.

The size of the concept set can be explained if we consider the fact that the UMLS knowledge is concentrated in few major libraries (e.g. MeSH [14], SNOMED98 [22]), which cover important parts of the complete thesaurus and therefore contain the most of the concepts in our lexicon. To differentiate among the concepts within the resulted 10 libraries, pathology experts selected 4 central concepts in lung anatomy (i.e. "lung", "pleura", "trachea" and "bronchia") and extracted similar or related concepts from UMLS libraries. They considered the list of all distinct concepts related through a relation of any kind[5] to the 4 initial concepts. The result was a set of approximately 1000 concepts describing the anatomy of the lung and lung diseases and served as initial input for the domain ontology.

Adapting the ontology to the application domain. The linguistic analysis of the patient report corpus evidenced the content-related limitations of UMLS w.r.t. the concrete vocabulary of the report archive. We modelled additional pathology-specific concepts, like the components and typical content of a medical

---

[5] The UMLS Metathesarus contains 7 important relations between concepts: parent, child, sibling, narrower, broader, related-other, source-synonymy.

report, and integrate them in the available ontology library. Besides content-related adaptation needs, the analysis of the generated ontology outlined several "syntactical" issues for further adaptations:

 – concept names in UMLS: concepts like "ARF-smaller-then-2", "RESECTION OF LUNG WITH RECONSTRUCTION OF CHEST WALL WITHOUT PROSTHESIS", "Unspecified injury of lung with open wound into thorax" are unlikely to be relevant to the retrieval of pathology reports. Besides, they should be modelled as concepts with corresponding properties and not directly as a single concept, whose name denotes its meaning.
 – the absence of concept names in German language: due to the predominance of English in denominating UMLS concepts and the predominance of German terms in the pathology report archive in our application setting one needs to translate the English terms in order to achieve an efficient retrieval.

The comparison of the vocabulary of the medical reports archive with the generated ontology also emphasized the need to extend the knowledge base with non-medical content. Especially part-whole and spatial relationships are often encountered in medical findings and are therefore included to the ontology library. Medical reports frequently contain ambiguous terms to describe the results of the examinations (e.g. terms like "high-grade", "low-grade", "slightly polymorphic"), which play an important role for the overall interpretation of the reports. The representation of such terms is still subject of future work.

OWL Representation. After identifying the relevant knowledge sources and the list of concepts which can be used as input for our application, we translated the UMLS data model to the OWL model and transformed the relevant data from one format to another. We implemented a Java-based module, which reads the UMLS data from a relational database and generates the corresponding OWL constructs using Jena2. The resulting ontologies are published server-side and can be accessed by all components in the system. The UMLS consists of two main parts [24]: the UMLS Semantic Network and the UMLS Metathesaurus. The Semantic Network contains generic medical categories and relationships (approximately 150 concepts, i.e. "semantic types" and 50 relations i.e. "semantic relations" in the current version). It is used as a "meta level" for the information of the Metathesaurus, which brings together the particular UMLS libraries. The Metathesaurus consists of a list of uniquely identified concepts and several generic relations. Every concept in the Metathesaurus references at least one semantic type and the relations between concepts are usually typed by means of the semantic relations from the Semantic Network.

A peculiarity of the UMLS data format is the meaning of the "relation attributes" used for some of the Metathesaurus relations. The relation attribute references a semantic relation from the Semantic Network, but its exact meaning in the context of the current concept pair depends on the associated Metathesaurus relation. E.g. the combination "associated_with" (a relation from the

Semantic Network) and "parent" (a relation from the Metathesaurus) means a *direct* relationship between the concepts, while the same attribute together with the Metathesaurus relation "broader" implies an indirect relationship between the concepts (i.e. something like a path of length greater than 1 between the concepts). The absence of a relation attribute reduces the Metathesaurus relations to their original meaning, e.g. a relation "child" with no attribute is interpreted as "subClassOf".

The list of application-relevant concepts is part of the Metathesaurus and therefore each of the concepts is subsumed by semantic types. First we translated the UMLS Semantic Network to OWL and created a taxonomy of semantic types as classes and a taxonomy of semantic relations as properties. A second ontology contains the UMLS concepts; every UMLS concept is transformed in an OWL class. The Metathesarus relations "parent" and "child" are formalized as OWL "subClassOf" constraints. The "narrower" and "broader" relations , which define indirect subsumption relations, are formalized as "ancestor" and "descendant" in the OWL ontology. These relations could also be ignored, since their meaning can be inferred from the ontology using a reasoner. Due to the fuzzy definition of the rest of the Metathesaurus relations, we merged them to a single "related_to" property. The connection between relations and relation attributes is also considered in the ontology. Since the relation attribute points to the semantics of a relationship between two concepts, we used this information if available. We considered the Metathesarus relations only for the case where a relation attribute was missing. We store for every concept the list of alternative names together with language specifications as rdfs:label and connect every concept to the corresponding UMLS libraries it is contained in. A list of all available UMLS libraries was also formalized in a separate ontology, which is imported by the core ontology.

After translating the UMLS data to OWL we checked the ontologies for consistency and analyzed the inferred classification hierarchy, which pointed out few differences compared to the original UMLS hierarchy. The UMLS contains several problematic modelling decisions which have been often described in research projects aiming to integrate it in knowledge-based applications. Still, a comprehensive analysis of the quality of UMLS in such a setting or especially for Semantic Web applications has not delivered an optimal solution to cope with this problem. A possible start point could be the Semantic Network, since every Metathesaurus concept is related to it. Besides, the Semantic Network is supposed to be independent of a particular area in medicine. [20] and [1] describe some of the deficiencies of the Semantic Network at an ontological level. [15] analyzes the same issue for the UMLS Metathesaurus. At this point it is not clear how important such issues are for the quality of our retrieval system, but we intend to extend the Semantic Network with a more detailed and coherent upper level ontology.

Representing medical knowledge using Description Logics is not a trivial task [4]. Although translating the UMLS data format to OWL was a straightforward procedure, the expressivity limitations of the language become clear after a detailed analysis of the semantics of the medical knowledge. Reasoning beyond subsumption hierarchies and an extended support for concrete domains are very important for an efficient semantic retrieval system.

4.2 Ontology Instantiation and Evolution

As outlined in the previous section the direct mapping of possible relevant concepts from UMLS is not enough for the realization of a high-quality medical ontology for our application domain. Possible evolution directions have also been discovered by comparing the real vocabulary of the text archive with the terminology used by UMLS and, implicitly by the core ontology. Due to the limitations of UMLS and the difficulties encountered by the identification of its application-relevant fragments, we need a precise approach for the evolution and extension of the ontology.

We are currently developing a tool to support a controlled ontology evolution process, which analyzes the textual pathology reports, recognizes possible concept names and maps these names against the current ontology. The NLP component is used to populate the ontology. The process and implementation details related to ontology evolution are represented in Figure 1. Every time a new pathology report is introduced to the system, it is parsed by the linguistic component. The implemented modules include a tokenizer, a tagger and a ontology-based phrase generator. The NLP component communicates with the ontology lookup Web Service. This services returns for parameters like concept names and attributes (basically nouns and adjectives) information whether such a concept is already part of the ontology and its properties. If both noun and adjective are submitted, the Web Service checks if a property with the name of the adjective is available in the ontology or if a compound name consisting of the two parameters is part of it. Another Web Services addresses the task of recognizing concepts by their properties. For this purpose, the Web service receives names of relations or attributes and returns the name of the concepts having these properties in the ontology or checks if some concept could possess a certain property. A second Web Service was implemented to make suggestions for ontology extensions. Once a term is not available in the ontology, the NLP component attends to categorize it as medical or non-medical, using an embedded lexicon and makes suggestions to the ontology manager, which in turn propose an extension of the domain or generic ontologies to the ontology engineer. The ontology evolution is guided by domain experts.

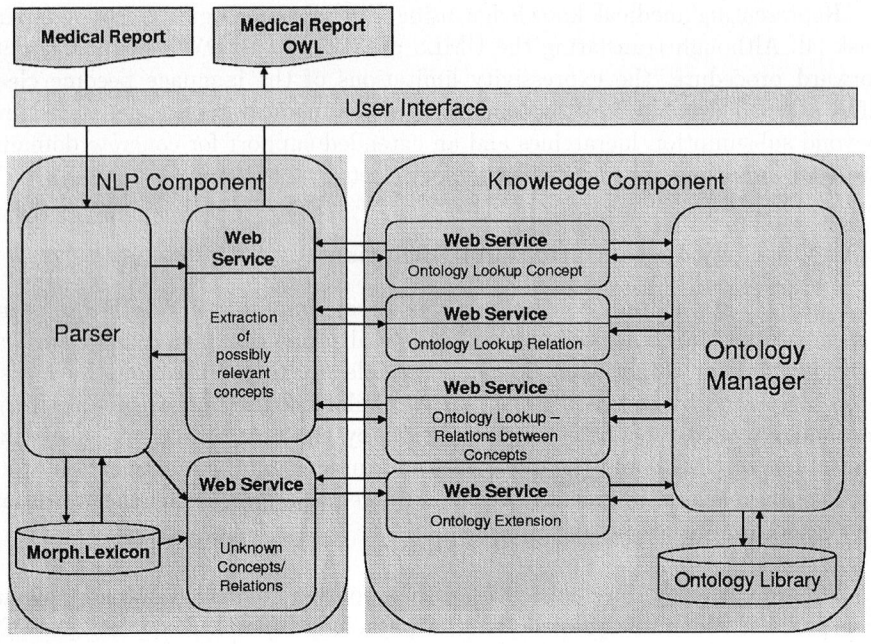

Fig. 1. Ontology Instantiation and Evolution

The result of these procedures is an intermediate logical representation (Figure 3 presents a fragment of the intermediate representation of the XML pathology report in German in Figure 2). The logical forms produced by the parser are transformed by the linguistic component into OWL-compliant representations. The process is fairly straightforward as should be clear from comparing the intermediate representation in Figure 3 with the OWL representation in Figure 4.

- unique identifiers for the instances of concepts have to be created, and
- in cases of plural entities ("two cylinder" → $card(x, 2) AND.cylinder(x)$), several separate instances have to be created.
- Appropriateness conditions for properties are applied: if a property is not defined for a certain type of entity, the analysis is rejected.

Note that this also handles potential syntactic ambiguity, since it might filter out analyzes on the grounds because they specify inconsistent information.

4.3 Ontology Storage

As outlined in Section 2 the knowledge base contains a library of domain and generic ontologies. The storage problem arises when considering the core ontology describing the anatomy of the lung and the typical diseases. Generally there

```
<section><caption>Befund</caption>
  <section><caption>Makroskopie</caption>
    <paragraph><content>[1]Zwei Gewebszylinder von 15 und 4 mm Laenge[1].
    </content></paragraph>
  </section>
  <section><caption>Mikroskopie</caption>
    <paragraph><content>[2]Stanzbiopsate aus Lungengewebe mit
    deutlicher Stoerung der alveolaren  Textur, soweit noch
    nachweisbar deutlich Verbreiterung der Alveolarsepten,
    stellenweise Nachweis von Bronchialepithelregeneraten[2].
    [3]Restliche Alveolarlumina z.T. durch Fibroblastenproliferate
    verlegt[3].[4]Im Interstitium ein gemischt entzuendliches
    Infiltrat, bestehend aus Plasmazellen und Lymphozyten[4].
    [5]Darunter relativ viele CD3-positive kleine und mittelgrosse
    T-Lymphozyten und CD68-positive Makrophagen[5].</content></paragraph>
  </section>
  <section><caption>Kritischer_Bericht</caption>
      <paragraph><content>[6]Stanzbiopsate aus der Lunge mit Zeichen
      der organisierenden Pneumonie (klin. Mittellappen)[6].</content>
      </paragraph>
  </section>
</section>
```

Fig. 2. Input of the transformation component

are two storage choices, either as a file or in a database. Since the complete knowledge base (or even the domain ontology) is too large to be maintained in the server's memory permanently at execution time, we analyzed different possibilities for the persistent storage of OWL data.

The storage of Semantic Web information, especially ontologies and their instantiations has already been subject of several research projects. However most of the current proposals are not directly intended to store OWL (DL) data and focus on RDF(S) or propose a deductive database storage e.g. based on F-Logic. Finding an appropriate storage system for OWL data which allows acceptable retrieval performance and reasoning capabilities is still an unsolved issue. At this moment the most cited systems for this purpose are Jena2[6] and Sesame[7]. Sesame is an open source RDF database covering RDF Schema inferencing and querying, which supports expressive querying of RDF data and Schema information using the RQL query language. Jena2 offers a variety of tools for the management of RDF/OWL ontologies, including reasoning for RDFS and OWL Lite. The persistent storage back-end uses a relational database, which can be queried using the RDQL query language. The integration of a extended reasoner to support OWL DL is not covered by any of the systems available.

---

[6] Jena2: www.hpl.hp.com/semweb/jena.htm
[7] Sesame Database System: http://www.openrdf.org/

```
[1]card(x1, 2) AND cylinder(x1) AND length(x1, [15, 14])
[2]unspec_plur_det(x2) AND punch_biopsat(x2)AND from_rel(x2, x3)
AND unspec_plur_det(x3) AND lung_tissue(x3)AND with_rel(x3, x4)
AND def_det(x4) AND disturbance(x4, x5) AND def_det(x5) AND texture(x5)
AND alveolar(x5)
unspec_det(x6) AND extension(x6, x7) AND def_det_plur(x7)AND
aleveolar_septum(x7) AND unspec_det(x8) AND evidence(x8, x9)
AND indef_det(x9) AND epithelial(x9) AND bronchial(x9)
AND regenerates(x9)
[3]def_det(x10) AND alveolarlumina(x10)
unspec_det_plur(x11) AND fibrolastial_proliferate(x11)
[4]def_det(x12) AND interstitium(x12)
indef_det(x13) AND inflammatory(x13) AND infiltrate(x13)AND
consisting_of_rel(x13, x14) AND unspec_det_plur(x14) AND konj(x14, x15, x16)
AND plasma_cell(x15) AND lymphocyte(x16)
[5]indef_det_plur(x17) AND konj(x17, x18, x19) AND t_lymphocyte(x18)
AND cd68_positive(x19) AND macrophagus(x19)
[6]indef_det_plur(x20) AND punch_biopsate(x20) AND from_rel(x20, x21)
AND def_det(x21) AND lung(x21) AND with_rel(x20, x22) AND evidence(x22, x23)
AND def_det(x23)AND organising(x23) AND pneumonia(x23)
```

Fig. 3. Intermediate output of the transformation component

Currently we store the ontology in a Sesame database and use RQL to retrieve ontological information used in the ontology instantiation and evolution processes.

5 Using the Ontology in the Retrieval System

Besides guiding the instantiation process, the medical ontology will be intensively used in every application scenario. Retrieval of pathology reports and the associated digital images is the main application of the designed system. We identified following retrieval scenarios:

- the user (pathologist) searches reports with certain characteristics. In this case it is important that the ontology goes beyond the string matching or synonym extension capability and retrieves relevant content. For example if the user needs reports about a certain kind of tumor, the system would not return reports where the string "Kein Tumor" ("no tumor") is specified. At this point we assigned parts of the pathology reports as being probably interesting for a user: morphology of the tissue sample, diagnosis and patient data. For this reason, we will offer advanced search capabilities for queries focusing on these features(e.g. reports with a certain diagnosis or reports concerning a male patient of age 60-65).
- the user compares several medical reports. In this case we differentiate among the scenario where the user wants to find diagnosis decisions of reports with similar patient data and tissue samples or the one of the differential diagnosis, where the user needs different diagnosis for similar appearances.
- the user searches similar reports w.r.t. to a given one, he/she is currently editing or analyzing. In this case we need a matching function to compare pathology reports.

```xml
<?xml version="1.0" encoding="UTF-8" ?>
<rdf:RDF
    xmlns:sources="http://nbi.inf.fu-berlin.de/.../umlssources.owl#"
    xmlns:bb="http://nbi.inf.fu-berlin.de/.../befundbericht.owl#"
    xmlns:rdfs="http://www.w3.org/2000/01/rdf-schema#"
    xmlns:owl="http://www.w3.org/2002/07/owl#"
    xmlns:swpatho="http://nbi.inf.fu-berlin.de/.../swpatho1.owl#"
    xmlns:sn="http://nbi.inf.fu-berlin.de/.../umlssn.owl#"
    xmlns:rdf="http://www.w3.org/1999/02/22-rdf-syntax-ns#"
    xmlns:umlsmeta="http://nbi.inf.fu-berlin.de/.../umlsmeta.owl#"
    xml:base="http://a.com/ontology">
  <owl:Ontology rdf:about="">
    <owl:imports rdf:resource="http://.../umlssources.owl#"/>
    <owl:imports rdf:resource="http://.../umlssn.owl#"/>
    <owl:imports rdf:resource="http://.../befundbericht.owl#"/>
    <owl:imports rdf:resource="http://.../umlsmeta.owl#"/>
  </owl:Ontology>
  <swpatho:Plasma_Cell rdf:ID="plasma_cell-1"/>
  <bb:Infiltrat rdf:ID="infiltrat-1">
    <sn:has_location>
      <Interstitium rdf:ID="interstitium-1"/>
    </sn:has_location>
    <sn:consists_of><swpatho:Lymphocyt rdf:ID="lymphozyt-1">
      <sn:part_of_T33 rdf:resource="#infiltrat-1"/>
    </swpatho:Lymphocyt></sn:consists_of>
    <sn:consists_of><swpatho:Lymphocyt rdf:ID="lymphozyt-2">
      <sn:part_of_T33 rdf:resource="#infiltrat-1"/>
    </swpatho:Lymphocyt></sn:consists_of>
    <sn:consists_of><swpatho:Makrophage rdf:ID="makrophage-1">
      <sn:part_of_T33 rdf:resource="#infiltrat-1"/>
    </swpatho:Makrophage></sn:consists_of>
    <sn:consists_of><swpatho:Makrophage rdf:ID="makrophage-2">
      <sn:part_of_T33 rdf:resource="#infiltrat-1"/>
    </swpatho:Makrophage></sn:consists_of>
  </bb:Infiltrat>
  <sn:Cylinder rdf:ID="cylinder-1">
    <sn:length rdf:datatype="http://www.w3.org/2001/XMLSchema#float">
    15.0</length>
  </sn:Cylinder>
    <swpatho:Pneumonia_C0032285 rdf:ID="pneumonia_C0032285-1">
    <sn:related_with>
      <swpatho:Middle_lobe rdf:ID="middle_lobe-1">
        <sn:part_of_T33>
          <swpatho:Lung rdf:ID="lung-1">
            <sn:consists_of>
              <swpatho:Tissue_of_lung rdf:ID="tissue_of_lung-1">
              <sn:hasTexture>
                <swpatho:alveolare_Textur rdf:ID="alveolare_Textur-1"/>
              </sn:hasTexture>
              </swpatho:Tissue_of_lung>
            </sn:consists_of>
          </swpatho:Lung>
        </sn:part_of_T33>
        <sn:related_with rdf:resource="#pneumonia_C0032285-1"/>
      </swpatho:Middle_lobe_of_lung_NOS_C0225757>
    </sn:related_with>
  </swpatho:Pneumonia_C0032285>
  <swpatho:Alveolarlumen rdf:ID="alveolarlumen-1">
    <sn:related_with rdf:resource="#lung-1"/>
  </swpatho:Alveolarlumen>
  <bb:Biopsy_Material rdf:ID="biopsy_material-2">
    <sn:part_of_T33 rdf:resource="#tissue_of_lung-1"/>
    <bb:hasShape rdf:resource="#cylinder-1"/>
  </bb:Biopsy_Material>
```

Fig. 4. OWL Representation of the pathology report

```xml
<swpatho:CD68_positive_Makrophage rdf:ID="cd68_pos_makrophage-1">
  <sn:part_of_T33 rdf:resource="#makrophage-1"/>
  <sn:part_of_T33 rdf:resource="#makrophage-2"/>
</swpatho:CD68_positive_Makrophage>
<swpatho:Fibroblastenproliferat rdf:ID="fibroblastenprolif-1">
  <sn:related_with><swpatho:Alveolarlumen rdf:ID="alveolarlum-2"/>
  </sn:related_with><sn:related_with rdf:resource="#alveolarlumen-1"/>
</swpatho:Fibroblastenproliferat>
<swpatho:Fibroblastenproliferat rdf:ID="fibroblastenproliferat-2">
  <sn:related_with rdf:resource="#alveolarlumen-2"/>
  <sn:related_with rdf:resource="#alveolarlumen-1"/>
</swpatho:Fibroblastenproliferat>
<swpatho:CD68_positive_Makrophage rdf:ID="cd68_pos_makrophage-2">
  <sn:part_of_T33 rdf:resource="#infiltrat-1"/>
</swpatho:CD68_positive_Makrophage>
<bb:Punch_Biopsy rdf:ID="punch_biopsy-1">
  <bb:hasShape rdf:resource="#cylinder-1"/>
  <sn:part_of_T33 rdf:resource="#tissue_of_lung-1"/>
</bb:Punch_Biopsy>
<swpatho:CD3_positive_T-Lymphocyt rdf:ID="cd3_positive_t-lymphocyt-1"/>
<bb:Punch_Biopsy rdf:ID="punch_biopsy-2">
  <bb:hasShape rdf:resource="#cylinder-1"/>
  <sn:part_of_T33 rdf:resource="#tissue_of_lung-1"/>
</bb:Punch_Biopsy>
<swpatho:Bronchialepithelregenerat rdf:ID="bronchialepithelreg-1"/>
<swpatho:T-Zell-Lymphom rdf:ID="t-zell-lymphom-1"/>
<swpatho:T-Lymphocyt rdf:ID="t-lymphozyt-1">
  <sn:part_of_T33 rdf:resource="#lymphozyt.-1"/>
</swpatho:T-Lymphocyt>
<bb:Biopsy_Material rdf:ID="biopsy_material-1">
  <sn:part_of_T33 rdf:resource="#tissue_of_lung-1"/>
  <bb:hasShape rdf:resource="#cylinder-1"/>
</bb:Biopsy_Material>
<swpatho:Alveolarseptum rdf:ID="alveolarseptum-2"/>
</rdf:RDF>
```

Fig. 4. continued

Due to the fixed structure of the pathology reports and the precise characterization of the retrieval-relevant features we can focus our search strategy on these issues. This means on one hand, that the NLP component extracts and recognizes information about tissue morphology and diagnosis from the text, since these are the most important features playing a role in the ranking algorithms.

On the other hand since every pathology report contains four syntactic parts (macroscopy, microscopy, diagnosis and comments) [23] with very precise content, this structure provides valuable information about what type of knowledge is contained (implicitly) in every part of the report. E.g. the macroscopy part describes the external features of the tissue sample, like the body part the tissue comes from, its size, form, color etc. The microscopy part describes the tissue at a microscopical level, e.g. internal distinguishing features. The diagnosis part refers to the presence or absence of a disease. Since every report is formalized in XML on the basis of an XML schema which distinguishes among these categories, the NLP component can be optimized to try to identify only specific concepts (actually concept instances) of the ontology.

6 Related Work

Due to the knowledge-intensive character of its processes, medicine is one of the most cited use cases for Semantic Web technologies. Medicine ontologies have already been developed and used in different application settings: GeneOntology [5], NCI-Ontology [10], GALEN [8], LinKBase [4] and finally UMLS [24]. Though their modelling principles or ontological commitment have often been subject of research [21,15,20], there is no generally accepted methodology how these knowledge sources could be embedded in real Semantic Web applications. This issue is extremely important if we consider the size of an ontology like UMLS, which has to be customized for specific application needs. The project GALEN ([8]) develops a special representation language, tailored for the particularities of the (English) medical vocabulary. However, the usage of a proprietary representation makes the ontological knowledge difficult to be extended by third parties or exchanged in a Semantic Web. In ONIONS [9] the authors aimed to develop a generic framework for ontology merging and used UMLS as an example to apply their methodology. Therefore they needed a detailed analysis of the ontological properties of UMLS and used the Loom language as formalization basis. The project MEDSYNDIKATE [18] is also confronted with the ontological commitment beyond UMLS in order to use it in text processing algorithms for knowledge discovery. UMLS serves in this case as an annotation vocabulary for medical texts. Both projects offer valuable experiences and facts concerning UMLS and medical ontologies generally, but they do not use Semantic Web technologies to facilitate knowledge share and reuse, which is the crucial feature of ontologies. Besides modelling principles, none of the projects addresses the topic of customization, which is in our opinion essential for most of the concrete applications, which focus on a specific area of medicine and therefore need a coherent fragment of UMLS, manageable both by (Semantic Web) tools and by human experts.

7 Summary and Future Work

In this paper we presented our experiences in building and managing an ontology for lung pathology. We presented the application setting of the ontology, which is a Semantic Web-based retrieval system for text and image information and outlined the main issues we have been confronted with during the process of developing and adapting this domain ontology on the basis of UMLS. Currently we have implemented an Ontology Manager, a module for the generation of the domain ontology for lung pathology using UMLS as input and modelled additional domain knowledge, not covered by UMLS. We also developed a prototypical NLP module for the instantiation of the domain ontology. The communication between the modules is realized using Web Services, which offer information about the ontology or detect instances or new concepts to be added to it. We are currently working on a first version of the search functionality and analyze possibilities for an efficient storage with reasoning capabilities.

Acknowledgment. The project "Semantic Web in the Pathology" is funded by the Deutsche Forschungsgemeinschaft, as a cooperation among the Charité Institute of Pathology, the Institute for Computer Science at the FU Berlin and the Department of Linguistics at the University of Potsdam, Germany.

References

1. A. Burgun and O.Bodenreider. Mapping the UMLS Semantic Network into General Ontologies. In *Proc. of the AMIA Symposium*, 2001.
2. G. Carenini and J. Moore. Using the UMLS Semantic Network as a Basis for Constructing a Terminological Knowledge Base: A Preliminary Report. In *Proceedings of 17th Symposium on Computer Applications in Medical Care (SCAMC '93)*, 1993.
3. E. Castillo, J.M. Gutierrez, and A.S. Hadi. *Expert systems and probabilistic network models*. Springer Verlag, 1997.
4. W. Ceusters, B. Smith, and J. Flanagan. Ontology and Medical Terminology: Why Description Logics are Not Enough. In *Proc. Towards An Electronic Patient Record, TEPR2003*, 2003.
5. The Gene Ontology Consortium. Gene Ontology: tool for the unification of biology. *Nature Genetics*, 25:25–30, 2000.
6. F. Demichellis, V. Della Mea, S. Forti, P. Dalla Palma, and C.A. Beltrami. "Digital storage of glass slide for quality assurance in histopathology and cytopathology". *Telemed Telecare*, 8(3):138–42, 2002.
7. D. Fensel. *Ontologies: A Silver Bullet for Knowledge Management and Electronic Commerce*. Springer Verlag, 2001.
8. Ontology GALEN. http://www.opengalen.org, 2001.
9. A. Gangemi, D. M. Pisanelli, and G. Steve. An Overview of the ONIONS Project: Applying Ontologies to the Integration of Medical Terminologies. *Data Knowledge Engineering*, 31(2):183–220, 1999.
10. J. Golbeck, G. Fragoso, F. Hartel, J. Hendler, B. Parsia, and J. Oberthaler. The National Cancer Institute's Thesaurus and Ontology. *Journal of Web Semantics*, 1(1), 2003.
11. Thomas R. Gruber. Toward principles for the design of ontologies used for knowledge sharing. *Int. J. Hum.-Comput. Stud.*, 43(5-6):907–928, 1995.
12. H. Gu, Y. Perl, J. Geller, M. Halper, L. Liu, and J. Cimino. Representing the UMLS as an OODB: Modeling issues and advantages, 2000.
13. U. Hahn, M.Romacker, and K. Schnattinger. Automatic knowledge acquisition from medical text. In *Proc. of the 1996 AMIA Annual Symposium*, pages 383 – 387, 1996.
14. Medical Subject Headings. http://www.nlm.nih.gov/mesh/meshhome.html, 2003.
15. D.M. Pisanelli, A. Gangemi, and G. Steve. Ontological Analysis of the UMLS Metathesaurus. *JAMIA*, 5:810 – 814, 1998.
16. D. Schlangen, M. Stede, and E. Paslaru Bontas. Feeding OWL: Extracting and Representing the Content of Pathology Reports. In *to appear in Proc. NLPXML 2004*, 2004.
17. A.T. Schreiber, B.J. Wielinga, R. de Hoog, H. Akkermans, and W. van de Velde. CommonKADS: A Comprehensive Methodology for KBS Development. *IEEE Expert*, pages 28–37, December 1994.

18. S. Schulz and U. Hahn. Medical knowledge reegineering - converting major portions of the UMLS into a terminological knowledge base. *International Journal of Medical Informatics*, 2001.
19. S. Schulz, M. Romacker, and U. Hahn. Knowledge engineering the UMLS. *Stud Health Technol Inform*, 77:701–5, 2000.
20. S. Schulze-Kremer, B. Smith, and A. Kumar. Revising the UMLS Semantic Network. In *Proc. Medinfo 2004*, 2004.
21. B. Smith, J. Williams, and S. Schulze-Kremer. The Ontology of GeneOntology. In *Proceedings of the AMIA*, 2003.
22. Snomed International. http://www.snomed.org, 1998.
23. R. Tolksdorf and E. Paslaru Bontas. Organizing Knowledge in a Semantic Web for Pathology. In *to appear in Proc. NetObjectDays 2004*, 2004.
24. Unified Medical Language System. http://www.nlm.nih.gov/research/umls, 2002.
25. UMLS Knowledge Source Server. http://umlsks.nlm.nih.gov, 2003.
26. G. van Heijst, A. Schreiber, and B.J. Wielinga. Using explicit ontologies in KBS development. *International Journal of Human Computer Studies*, 46(2):183–292, February 1997.

Semantic Web Based Content Enrichment and Knowledge Reuse in E-science

Feng Tao[1], Liming Chen[1], Nigel Shadbolt[1], Fenglian Xu[2], Simon Cox[2], Colin Puleston[3], and Carole Goble[3]

[1] Department of Electronics and Computer Science, University of Southampton,
Southampton, U.K.
{ft, lc, nrs}@ecs.soton.ac.uk

[2] e-Science Centre, School of Engineering Science, University of Southampton,
Southampton, U.K.
{flx, s.j.cox}@soton.ac.uk

[3] Department of Computer Science, University of Manchester, Oxford Road, Manchester, U.K.
{carole, colin.puleston}@cs.man.ac.uk

Abstract. We address the life cycle of semantic web based knowledge management from ontology modelling to instance generation and reuse. We illustrate through a semantic web based knowledge management approach the potential of applying semantic web technologies in GEODISE, an e-Science pilot project in the domain of Engineering Design Search and Optimization (EDSO). In particular, we show how ontologies and semantically enriched instances are acquired through knowledge acquisition and resource annotation. This is illustrated not only in Protégé with an OWL plug-in, but also in a light weight function annotator customized for resource providers to semantically describe their own resources to be published. In terms of reuse, advice mechanisms, in particular a knowledge advisor based on semantic matching, are designed to consume the semantic information and facilitate service discovery, assembly and configuration in a real problem solving environment. An implementation has demonstrated the integration of the advisor in a text mode domain script editor and a GUI mode workflow composition environment. Our research work shows the potential of using semantic web technology to manage and reuse knowledge in e-Science.

1 Introduction

The GEODISE (Grid Enabled Optimisation and Design Search for Engineering) project [3] aims to provide a Problem Solving Environment (PSE) that couples together Grid middleware, engineering design packages, a database and a knowledge base to help engineers conduct large-scale distributed simulation of design search and optimisation in a virtual organization.

The Grid [2] has provided an operational infrastructure that enables distributed scientific computing and resource sharing in e-Science, yet it has become increasingly important that resources are consistently and semantically enriched to enable process automation and knowledge reuse within a distributed e-Science community. The Semantic Web technology promises to make Web content machine understandable, enabling software agents to process it and produce value-added knowledge to end users. The Semantic Grid[1] [10,] addresses this issue by applying Semantic Web technologies in Grid computing to enable easy-to-use and seamless automation towards the full richness of e-Science vision of future large-scale science over the Internet where the sharing and coordinated use of diverse resources in dynamic, distributed virtual organization is commonplace.

In order to achieve this vision, we proposed a Semantic Web based knowledge management approach in GEODISE. Knowledge acquisition is carried out through ontology modelling and semantic annotation. An ontology forms the conceptual structure of the knowledge base, and the semantic annotation populates the knowledge base with semantic instances. Knowledge reuse is then achieved through consuming these instances to generate knowledge driven decisions. In e-Science practice, it is common that the activities of generating and reusing the instances are conducted by different parties (e.g. human experts, beginner users, or computers), in different locations, time and environments. For example, in GEODISE, various Grid services and domain software components are used, such as the Java Cog [20] in Globus toolkit and the OPTIONS design exploration package [21] for EDSO. They are wrapped as Matlab functions which form our key resource in Grid enabled engineering problem solving. Semantic instances of these resources can be generated by knowledge engineers using knowledge acquisition tools such as Protégé, or by resource providers themselves using annotation tools such as the Function Annotator [14]. Semantics acquired in either way can be represented in the Web Ontology Language (OWL), which is a W3C standard that aims to help machines to understand data. Third-party programs can be used to process the instances in the knowledge base for different knowledge reuse purposes. This potentially allows for the knowledge to be used outside the awareness of its providers. In GEODISE, the purpose of knowledge support is to help engineers exploit reusable resources. We use the Jena semantic toolkit [13] to process the semantic information of these existing resources and formulate advice on activities during domain script editing and workflow assembly that require appropriate manipulation on these resources.

The rest of the paper is organized as follows. In the next section, we describe the knowledge management approach with respect to the life cycle of semantic web based knowledge management in GEODISE. In section 3, our experience of knowledge modeling is described in the context of GEODISE. This includes knowledge acquisition in regard to building ontologies and generating semantic annotations as instances in a knowledge base. We then describe in section 4 knowledge reuse issues, in particularly the workflow advisor that consumes the instances of semantic annotation in

---

[1] http://www.semanticgrid.org

the knowledge base and provides value-add outputs to end users in suitable forms. In section 5, implementations are given to demonstrate the knowledge advisor and its integration with a domain script editor and the workflow composer in regards to the knowledge reuse. We finally give related work in section 6 and conclude in section 7.

2 Semantic Web Based Knowledge Management Approach

A Semantic Web based knowledge management approach is proposed in order to semantically enrich the content of resources and extract actionable knowledge for reuse in an e-Science application. Fig. 1, shows our approach, whereby we integrate various knowledge tools and e-Science applications covering the three key phases of the knowledge life cycle – knowledge acquisition, semantic storage and processing, and the (re)use of knowledge in semantic driven applications.

The knowledge acquisition aims to collect necessary information, build an ontology to represent the domain conceptualization and use the ontology to annotate Grid resources. The ontological information is collected by interviewing domain experts and studying domain manuals. Various tools, such as PC-PACK, Protégé [8] and OilEd [5] have been used to facilitate this building process. The ontological information extracted from the resources is used again to annotate these resources.

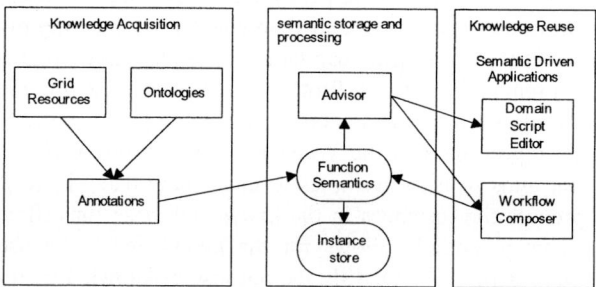

Fig. 1. Semantic web based knowledge management approach in GEODISE

The result of the annotations is a set of semantically enriched content represented as instances that conform to the ontology used in the annotation process. These instances are stored in a flat file or database repository so that they can be accessed later. Sophisticated semantic matching and reasoning can be carried out on these instances to deduce knowledgeable decisions. The advisor is designed for this purpose. It retrieves relevant semantic information from the instance repository and processes it in order to provide context-sensitive advice according to the requests from the application side.

The last phase of the life cycle addresses knowledge reuse. In GEODISE, editing domain scripts and building workflows are two frequent tasks. A domain script editor has been developed to help editing domain scripts in a more efficient way. With the advisor integrated, it is capable of yielding contextual advice from processing semantic instances pre-acquired. The advisor has been also integrated into the workflow composition environment (WCE) for the same purpose.

3 Knowledge Modeling

GEODISE makes available a suite of grid-enabled functions [4] that allows design engineers to exploit grid resources when carrying out computational intensive EDSO processes in their favorite PSE (in our case: Matlab). The toolkit can be viewed as a powerful yet flexible script-based environment for grid computing. Components built on it can be used either separately or assembled together, invoked with certain configurations, conforming to best practice, to solve a particular engineering problem. Therefore we choose these grid-enabled Matlab functions and high level components (Fig. 2) as the resources to be semantically enriched for knowledge reuse.

The task of knowledge modeling can be broken down into ontology modeling and instance generation.

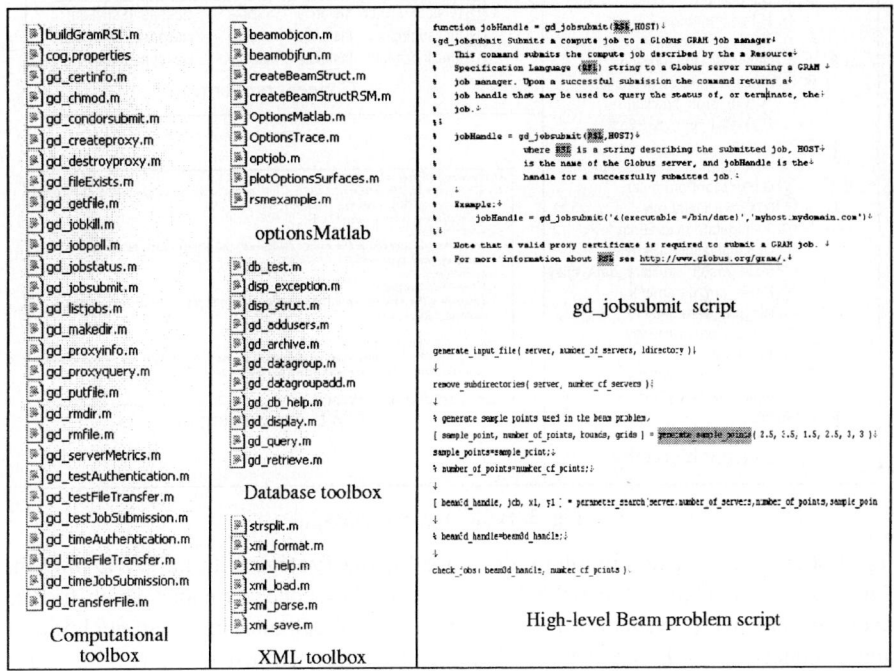

Fig. 2. Grid-enabled Matlab functions and scripts

3.1 Building Ontologies

An ontology is a specification of conceptualization [6]. It explicitly defines the domain concepts and their relationships. It is similar to a dictionary or glossary, but with richer structure, relationship and axioms that describe a domain of interest more precisely. Many languages have been designed to express the ontology and semantic information. Among them, the most recent is the Web Ontology Language (OWL), which is built on top of RDF to provide more expressive power [24]. RDF is a graph model (or sets of triple statements) which is designed for describing and searching resources on the Web. DAML+OIL is a schema language that adds constraints on properties to assist machine reasoning. For example when "daml:TransitiveProperty" is added as a constraint on the property "P1:older_than" of a RDF model, if we have A1:P1:A2 and A2:P1:A3, then A1:P1:A3 can be inferred. This is useful for reasoning and inferring new knowledge that has not been directly stated. DAML+OIL also uses subProperty to describe relationship at different granularities.

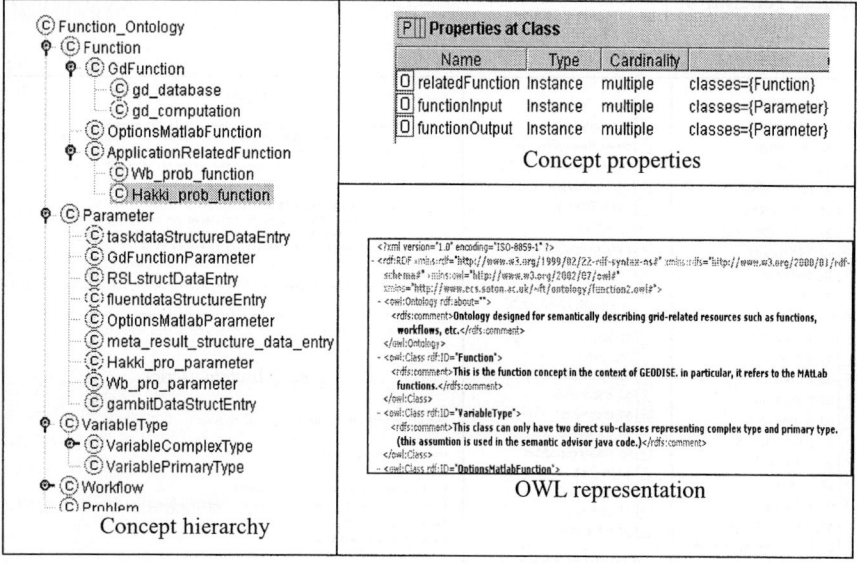

Fig. 3. Building Ontologies

Fig. 3 shows our function ontology developed using Protégé with an OWL plug-in. "Function", "Parameter", "VariableType", etc. are key concepts under which further taxonomy are made available to express hierarchical relationships (parent/children) among concepts. Each concept also has its properties defined to express the subject/predicate relationship (who uses who). The ontological information is saved in OWL format for content enrichment through instance generation.

3.2 Instance Generation

Whilst an ontology is important in specifying the conceptual structure and a constrained vocabulary set, instances are treated as the concrete content in a semantic knowledge base. Generating the instances involves annotating the raw data source using pre-defined ontologies. In this paper, two methods are used to generate instances. Based on their operational mechanism, they are called "Ontology Instantiation" and "Resource Annotation" respectively.

1) Ontology Instantiation

Protégé 2000 [8] is an ontology building and knowledge acquisition tool that has been frequently used for knowledge modelling purposes [15]. It allows knowledge engineers to focus on modelling without worrying about the underlying language and syntax. The modeling work can be saved in various formats including RDF and OWL.

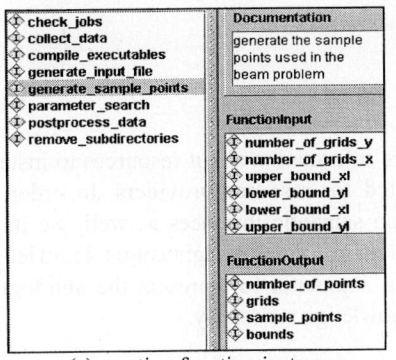
(a) creating function instances

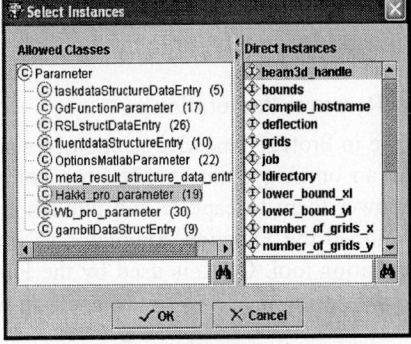
(b) selecting parameter instances

Fig. 4. Generating semantic instances in Protégé

As illustrated in Fig. 4-a, to create function instances relevant information in the function source (Fig. 2) is used to instantiate its corresponding ontology classes, such as "Function", "Parameter" and "VariableType", as defined in the function ontology in Fig. 3. Each instance in the left column of Fig. 4-a represents a function. Its properties ("FunctionInput", "FunctionOutput" as defined in the ontology) are also filled with object instances, the class of which is constrained by class properties defined in the ontology. The object instances can be created on the fly or selected from previously generated instances.

Instances generated in this way can be exported from Protégé (with the OWL plug-in) as is illustrated in Fig. 5, where the instances are represented using RDF as well as OWL enhancements for extra semantics. The RDF can be also interpreted as N-Triples for efficient machine processing.

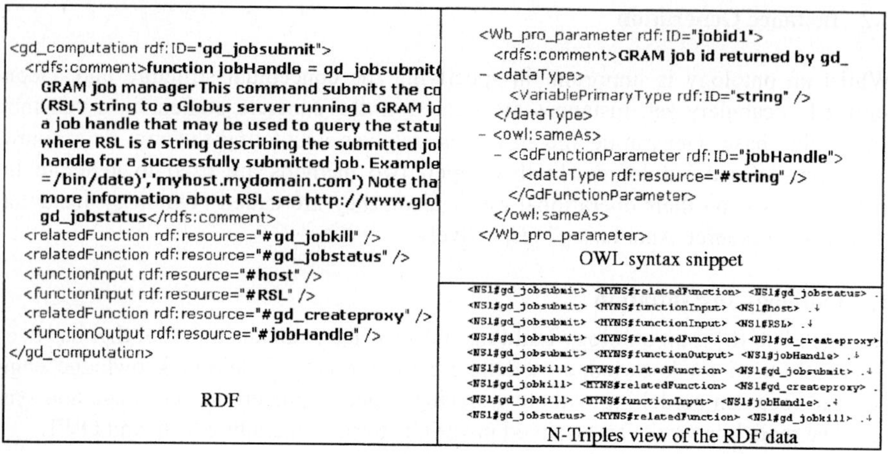

``
<gd_computation rdf:ID='gd_jobsubmit'>
  <rdfs:comment>function jobHandle = gd_jobsubmit(
  GRAM job manager This command submits the co
  (RSL) string to a Globus server running a GRAM jo
  a job handle that may be used to query the statu
  where RSL is a string describing the submitted jo
  handle for a successfully submitted job. Example
  =/bin/date)','myhost.mydomain.com') Note tha
  more information about RSL see http://www.glo
  gd_jobstatus</rdfs:comment>
  <relatedFunction rdf:resource="#gd_jobkill" />
  <relatedFunction rdf:resource="#gd_jobstatus" />
  <functionInput rdf:resource="#host" />
  <functionInput rdf:resource="#RSL" />
  <relatedFunction rdf:resource="#gd_createproxy" />
  <functionOutput rdf:resource="#jobHandle" />
</gd_computation>
``
	``
	<Wb_pro_parameter rdf:ID="jobid1">
	  <rdfs:comment>GRAM job id returned by gd_
	  - <dataType>
	    <VariablePrimaryType rdf:ID="string" />
	  </dataType>
	  - <owl:sameAs>
	    - <GdFunctionParameter rdf:ID="jobHandle">
	      <dataType rdf:resource="#string" />
	    </GdFunctionParameter>
	  </owl:sameAs>
	</Wb_pro_parameter>
	``

	OWL syntax snippet

	`<NS1#gd_jobsubmit> <MYNS#relatedFunction> <NS1#gd_jobstatus>`
	`<NS1#gd_jobsubmit> <MYNS#functionInput> <NS1#host>`
	`<NS1#gd_jobsubmit> <MYNS#functionInput> <NS1#RSL>`
	`<NS1#gd_jobsubmit> <MYNS#relatedFunction> <NS1#gd_createproxy>`
	`<NS1#gd_jobsubmit> <MYNS#functionOutput> <NS1#jobHandle>`
	`<NS1#gd_jobkill> <MYNS#relatedFunction> <NS1#gd_jobsubmit>`
	`<NS1#gd_jobkill> <MYNS#relatedFunction> <NS1#gd_createproxy>`
	`<NS1#gd_jobkill> <MYNS#functionInput> <NS1#jobHandle>`
	`<NS1#gd_jobstatus> <MYNS#relatedFunction> <NS1#gd_jobkill>`

RDF	N-Triples view of the RDF data

Fig. 5. Function semantic instances

2) Resource Annotation

While in Protégé, knowledge engineers acquire information about resources to instantiate an ontology, this is often too complicated for resource providers. In order to empower them to capture and publish function semantic instances as well, we have developed the Function Annotator as illustrated in Fig. 6, a lightweight knowledge acquisition tool. OWL is used by the Function Annotator to represent the ontologies and for storing the semantic instances in the knowledge repository.

Once function sources are loaded into the source panel (right bottom), they are parsed for potential semantic information listed in the function browser (right top). According to the content to be annotated, users can establish an annotation panel (middle) automatically generated from a particular selected ontology (left). The annotation is carried out by dragging relevant information from the function browser, dropping it into the annotation panel and filling out relevant fields.

The generated function semantic annotations contain the same information as the function semantic instances. Details can be found in [14].

4 Knowledge Reuse

Once semantic instances are made available, it is possible to access and process these instances for the purpose of knowledge reuse. Since instances are represented in standard OWL language, any OWL compliant API can be used, for example, the Wonder Web OWL API [7] and the Jena ontology API [13]. We use Jena in this work.

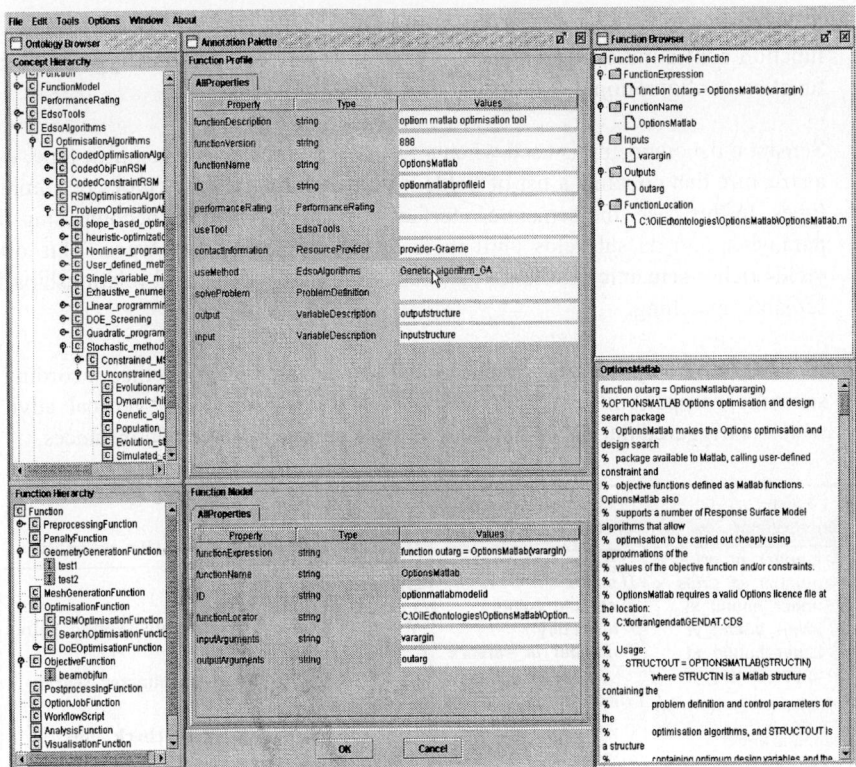

Fig. 6. Function Annotator

4.1 Reusing Semantic Instances to Advise Engineers

Functions can only be assembled together if their interfaces semantically match each other to some extent, i.e. a function's input semantically consumes the output of another function. Workflow builders, especially beginners, often are not clear about the semantic interfaces of the functions. However, suggestions can be deduced through semantic interface matching. This is especially useful when the function repository is dynamically updated or the number of functions is large, which is the case in our engineering e-Science community.

Each function can be viewed as a domain specific service which must be configured correctly and composed with other services to form a problem solving workflow. The granularity of the services varies from low level atomic functions (usually generic) to high level workflow building blocks (often more problem specific) that are made up of low level functions.

There are two types of advice:

1. *Function configuration advice* - this provides automatically generated advice on function configuration. We call this "horizontal advice" as it is triggered during function configuration, i.e., horizontal scripting.

   Semantic decomposing is used when a function parameter is a complex type, e.g., a structure that contains a list of fields which are either primary types or complex types. In this case, the semantic interface can be expanded by decomposing this parameter and its subfields until there are no more complex types. This often yields richer semantic interfaces that contain more concepts and relationships for semantic matching.

2. *Function assembly advice* – functions that can be assembled together according to semantic compatibility of their interfaces. This is named as "vertical advice" which is triggered during vertical assembly of configured function instances.

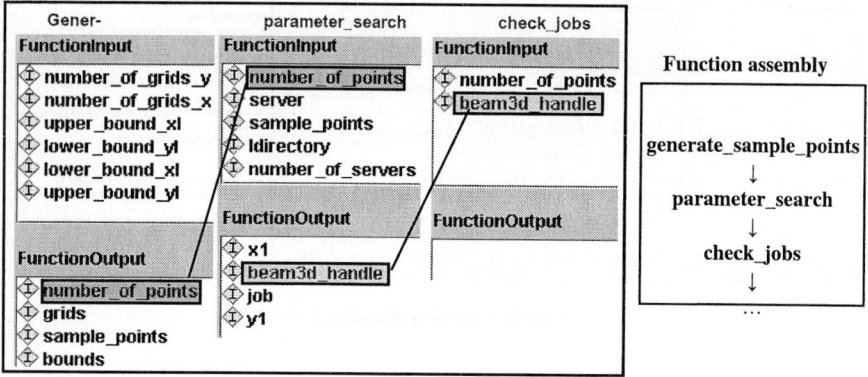

Fig. 7. Semantic matching for function assembly

The function assembly advice is base on matching functions, there are two types of elements in the function interface that can be used for matching:

i. Primary data type: two functions can be assembled together only if the second function gets its input interface satisfied. Primary data types such as "string" or "integer" used in function interfaces can be used to consider function compatibility when suggesting the next function to use after a currently deployed function.

ii. Semantic data type: this refers to the "ArgumentType" instances (beam3d_handle, number_of_points, etc.) used as function semantic interface. They are used in semantic matching functions for advice on workflow assembly. This is demonstrated in Figure 7 where semantic interfaces of three functions have been listed and the matches (represented as links) implicates a valid function assembly as shown in the right.

Although this is useful in suggesting compatible functions in terms of workflow assembly, there are often occasions where very few or no match exists because the semantic interface of the target function is too restricted. To solve this problem, OWL expressions such as "SameAs" (in Fig. 5) are used to map equivalent concepts and therefore relax the semantic matching.

5 Implementations and Applications

5.1 Knowledge Advisor

The advisor module is based on an API capable of retrieving and post-processing semantic instances expressed in OWL. The process operations include ontology interpretation, semantic matching and reasoning/inference. The advisor is implemented using Jena OWL ontology API [19].

A tutorial Java class demonstrates how the API is used to provide semantic support and advice. Figure 8 shows usage cases related to semantic consumption and advice based on it.

1	List all classes – (all classes defined in the ontology)
2	List subclass of a given class (as defined in the ontology)
3	List all individuals of a class (instances under of particular class, either direct or indirect)
4	List properties of a given individual (declared properties of a particular instance)
5	Expose semantic interface of a given individual function (an example of case 4 on function)
6	**Suggest contextual functions in a workflow**
7	**Expose in/output parameter individual of a given individual function**
8	**Decompose a particular parameter individual**
9	Documentation (provide human readable comment on any semantic resources)
10	Individual exists? (Check instance existence)

Fig. 8. Advisor functions on processing semantic instances

We can also use the tutorial class to demonstrate key functionalities of using the semantic advisor API. In Figure 8, numbers 1 to 4, 9 and 10 are generic usage of ontology interpretation and semantic consumption. The rest of the cases are domain specific cases that use the generic API and provide further functionality such as exposing the semantic interface of a particular function individual, advising function candidates for workflow assembly, etc. Some example output of the tutorial class can be seen in Figure 9.

```
Expose semantic interface
generate_sample_points

   Semantic Interface is: [http://www.ecs.soton.ac.uk/~ft/ontology/function2.owl#number_of_points,
http://www.ecs.soton.ac.uk/~ft/ontology/function2.owl#grids,
http://www.ecs.soton.ac.uk/~ft/ontology/function2.owl#number_of_grids_y,
http://www.ecs.soton.ac.uk/~ft/ontology/function2.owl#lower_bound_yl,

   Decompose a particular parameter individual
optionsMatlabInputStru

   RDF type is: http://www.ecs.soton.ac.uk/~ft/ontology/function2.owl#OptionsMatlabParameter
   Direct decomposed parameter individuals are: [
   org.geodise.knowledge.semanticweb.ParameterIndividual
<http://www.ecs.soton.ac.uk/~ft/ontology/function2.owl#OLEVEL> , integer,
   org. geodise.knowledge.semanticweb.ParameterIndividual
<http://www.ecs.soton.ac.uk/~ft/ontology/function2.owl#VNAM> , Vector,

   Advice on contextual component (workflow assembling advice based on semantic interface matching)
parameter_search

   its pre-contextual functions are: [
   org. geodise.knowledge.semanticweb.FunctionIndividual
<http://www.ecs.soton.ac.uk/~ft/ontology/function2.owl#generate_sample_points>]
   its post-contextual functions are: [
   org.geodise.knowledge.semanticweb.FunctionIndividual
<http://www.ecs.soton.ac.uk/~ft/ontology/function2.owl#postprocess_data>,
   org. geodise.knowledge.semanticweb.FunctionIndividual
<http://www.ecs.soton.ac.uk/~ft/ontology/function2.owl#check_jobs>,
   org. geodise.knowledge.semanticweb.FunctionIndividual
<http://www.ecs.soton.ac.uk/~ft/ontology/function2.owl#collect_data>]
```

Fig. 9. Example output of the tutorial class

5.2 Using the Knowledge Advisor

There are two applications in which the advisor can be integrated. In both case, semantic based knowledge can be reused in GEODISE.

a) Workflow Composition Environment (WCE)

The workflow composer in GEODISE is a GUI based application which allows engineers to visually select tasks from a function hierarchy, configure and assemble them into a workflow for e-science problem solving.

The purpose of integrating the semantic based advisor in the GUI based WCE is to make use of the rich semantic content and help the users choose suitable functions and make appropriate configuration during workflow assembly.

As illustrated in Figure 10, each function (in the left hand side panel) that has been previously semantically enriched, the workflow advisor can be called to deduce its contextual functions (as listed in the left bottom panel in Figure 10) that can be deployed before/after. This is achieved by semantically processing the semantic instances as described in section 4.1. In this way, the users can focus on compatible functions can be of use to further assemble the workflow without tediously investigating the semantic interface of all irrelevant functions. It then generates a Matlab script and submits it to a Matlab server for execution. It also takes care of the workflow management, monitoring and execution, but this is outside the scope of the current paper: interested readers can refer to [12] for further information.

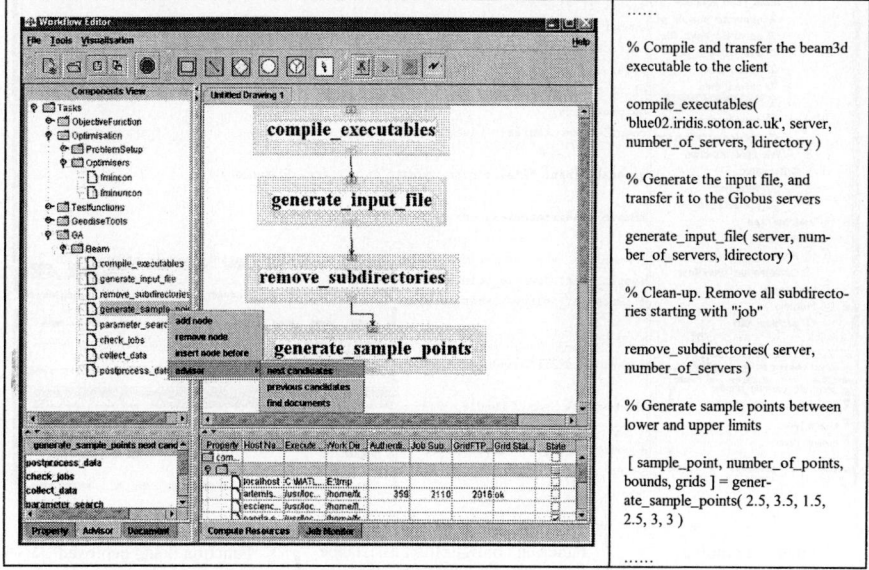

Fig. 10. Advisor integrated in the WCE and the generated scripts

b) Domain Script Editor (DSE)

Quite often, engineers need to edit domain related scripts in addition to GUI based design tools, such as the WCE. But manipulating plain texts is painful and tedious. In GEODISE, Matlab is the script language that glues EDSO and grid computing resources together. This motivated the design of a domain script editor with the advisor integrated.

Key features include:
- Component based - It can be delivered as a Java swing GUI component that can be used in any Java application (e.g., in the GUI based workflow composer as an alternative view of the workflow).
- Generic – The DSE is Ontology/Semantic powered meaning that it can be used to advise on different domain scripts when loaded with corresponding semantic annotations. E.g., Gambit scripts, gd_xxx functions including GEODISE computation toolbox and database toolbox, problem specific function scripts in Matlab, etc.

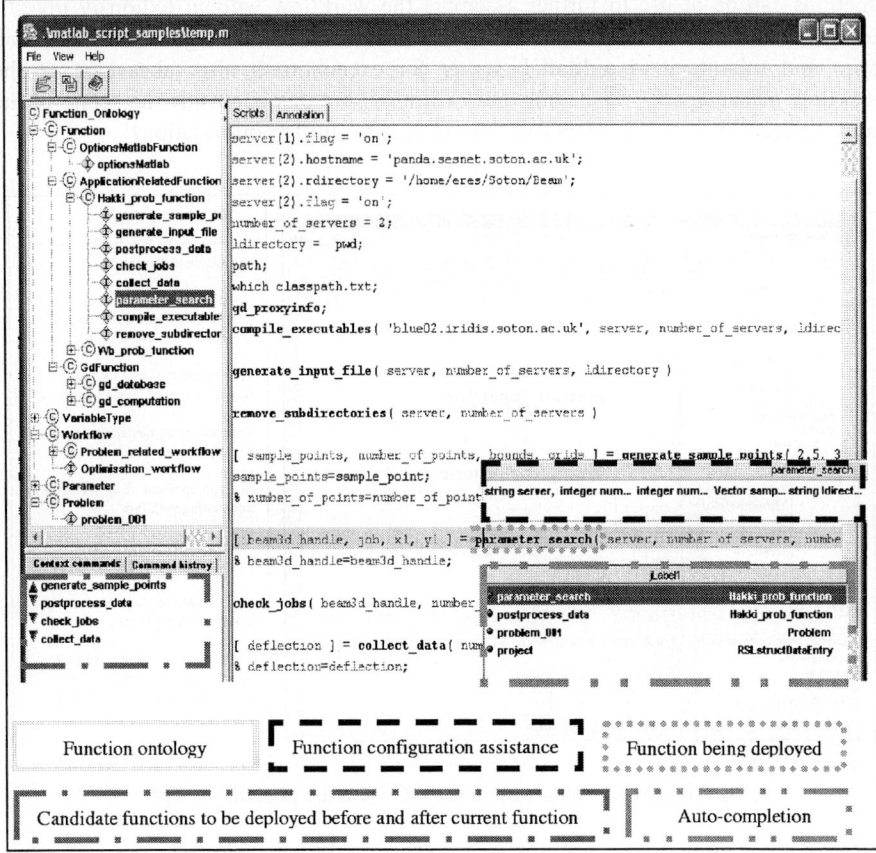

Fig. 11. Domain script editor integrated with the advisor

- De-centralized - Semantic instances are collected (in Protégé with OWL plug-in and in the function annotator) separately from their use, i.e., advisor integrated in domain applications.
- Horizontal advice on component configuration – exposing semantic interfaces, tool-tipping semantic annotations, auto-completions, etc, as shown in popping up windows in Figure 11.
- Vertical advice on component assembly – semantic interface matching and reasoning for contextual component recommendation as shown in the left bottom panel in Figure 11, where the blue arrow represents for a pre-contextual candidate and the red one for a consequence candidate.

6 Related Work

There are many projects that address the life cycle of knowledge management. Amongst them the Advanced Knowledge Technologies project (AKT) tackles the problems which arise during from knowledge acquisition, through modelling to publication and reuse. In particular, the AKT triple store [17] focuses on knowledge retrieval of RDF triples: the example cited in [17] is populated over an OWL ontology of UK computer science research expertise. Our approach is similar to this in that we construct an EDSO and function ontology based on which semantic annotations of GEODISE functions and related resources are generated and stored in a semantic repository. Instances in the AKT triple store are reused for query and semantic web browsing while the semantic annotated functions in GEODISE are reused for service discovery (function query) and workflow assembly through semantic matching.

The Ontobroker project uses ontologies to annotate and wrap Web documents and provides an ontology-based answering service to enhance the accessibility of their web documents [16]. COHSE Mozilla Annotator [25] and OntoMat-Annotizer [26] are two of the annotators to enrich web page with ontological information.

Pre-defined rules in a JESS rule base were used in [9] to advice on workflow assembly, but this is limited with regard to scalability and has high overhead cost when the rules increase. It is also difficult to elicit rules consistently.

Efforts have been made to locate services by semantically matching the requirements to the service descriptions. In [23], a semantic matching approach is proposed to match between service requests and advertisements described using DAML-S. It aims to extend the representation capabilities of registries such as UDDI and languages such as WDSL so that semantically enriched web services can be discovered through semantic marching. Here we adopt a similar approach but aim to provide advice on service assembly, in particular what can be deployed as a pre/post contextual task. The difference is that as long as there is service already deployed, the user does not need to describe their service request, the semantic matching can be carried out to find compatible services to the deployed one. The users only need to browse the returned services that are semantically compatible and select one of them for service assembly.

7 Summary and Conclusion

We describe the life cycle of semantic web based knowledge management from ontology modelling, instance generation to reuse. Resources in the GEODISE project such as grid-enabled functions and workflow building components have been targeted for ontological modelling and semantic instance generation using Protégé with OWL plug-in and our own Function Annotator. We show that semantic instances generated can be consumed to deduce advice. In particular, we use semantic decomposition and semantic matching mechanisms to generate advice on function configuration and assembly. These have been demonstrated through the knowledge advisor suggesting semantically compatible function candidates and their possible configuration. We have also integrated the advisor into the domain text editing and workflow composition developed for the GEODISE project. The examples we have used demonstrate that the approach proposed is feasible and helpful. We intend to support further aspects of the knowledge life-cycle in further work and improve integration of knowledge technologies into users' Problem Solving Environments.

References

1. Tao, F, Cox, S.J, Chen, L, Shadbolt, N.R, Xu, F, Puleston, C, Goble, C, and Song,W. "Towards the Semantic Grid: Enriching Content for Management and Reuse", Proceedings of UK e-Science All Hands Conference 2003, pp. 695-702
2. Ian Foster , Carl Kesselman, "The Grid: Blueprint for a New Computing Infrastructure", 2nd Edition, Morgan Kaufmann, 2004. ISBN: 1-55860-933-4
3. GEODISE project, http://www.GEODISE.org
4. Eres, M.H, Pound, G.E, Jiao, Z, Wason, J, Xu, F, Keane, A.J, and Cox, S.J, "Implementation of a Grid-enabled Problem Solving Environment in Matlab", Proceedings of the International Conference on Computer Science (ICCS 2003), Part IV, Lecture Notes in Computer Science, pp. 420-429
5. Sean Bechhofer, Ian Horrocks, Carole Goble, Robert Stevens. "OilEd: a Reason-able Ontology Editor for the Semantic Web", Proceedings of KI2001, Joint German/Austrian conference on Artificial Intelligence, September 19-21, Vienna. Springer-Verlag LNAI Vol. 2174, pp 396--408. 2001
6. T. R. Gruber. "A translation approach to portable ontologies", Knowledge Acquisition, 5(2):199-220, 1993. http://ksl-web.stanford.edu/KSL_Abstracts/KSL-92-71.html
7. WonderWeb API, http://owl.man.ac.uk/api.shtml
8. The Protégé homepage, http://protege.stanford.edu/index.html
9. Tao, F, Chen, L, Shadbolt, N,R. Pound, G, Cox, S.J., "Towards The Semantic Grid: Putting Knowledge To Work In Design Optimisation", Proceedings of I-KNOW '03, 3rd International Conference of Knowledge Management, p.p. 555-566.
10. Carole Goble and David De Roure The Semantic Grid: Building Bridges and Busting-Myths, 16th European conference on Artificial Intelligence ECAI 2004, Valencia, Spain, 23-27 July 2004.
11. De Roure, D. Hendler, J.A., "E-science: the grid and the semantic web", Intelligent Systems, IEEE, Vol. 19, Issue 1, 2004, p.p. 65-71. http://ieeexplore.ieee.org/xpl/abs_free.jsp?arNumber=1265888
12. Xu, F and Cox, S.J. "Workflow Tool for Engineers in a Grid-Enabled Matlab Environment", Proceedings of UK e-Science All Hands Meeting 2003, pp. 212-215
13. HP Labs Semantic Web Research, http://www.hpl.hp.com/semweb/
14. Chen L., Shadbolt N.R., Tao F., Puleston C., Goble C., Cox S.J. "Empower Resource Providers to Build the Semantic Grid", submitted to the IEEE/WIC/ACM International Conference on Web Intelligence 2004 (WI'04)
15. Holger Knublauch , An AI tool for the real world: Knowledge modeling with Protégé , http://www.javaworld.com/javaworld/jw-06-2003/jw-0620-protege.html, 2003
16. OntoBroker project. http://ontobroker.aifb.uni-karlsruhe.de/index_ob.html

17. AKT triple store, http://triplestore.aktors.org/
18. Qian, Cheng Yuan, Charles, An Integrated Process of CFD Analysis and Design Optimization with Underhood Thermal Application, SAE Paper 2001-01-0637 SAE 2001 World Congress, Detroit, MI, Mar 5-8, 2001..
19. Jena, a semantic web framework, http://www.hpl.hp.com/semweb/jena.htm
20. Gregor von Laszewski, Ian Foster, Jarek Gawor, and Peter Lane, "A Java Commodity Grid Kit," Concurrency and Computation: Practice and Experience, vol. 13, no. 8-9, pp. 643-662, 2001, http:/www.cogkits.org/
21. Keane, AJ. OPTIONS Design Exploration System http://www.soton.ac.uk/~ajk/options/welcome.html
22. M. H. Eres, G. E. Pound, Z. Jiao, J. L. Wason, F. Xu, A. J. Keane, and S. J. Cox. (2003) Implementation and utilisation of a Grid-enabled Problem Solving Environment in Matlab, Journal of Future Generation Computer Systems, in press.
23. Massimo Paolucci, Takahiro Kawamura, Terry R. Payne, Katia Sycara; "Semantic Matching of Web Services Capabilities." In Proceedings of the 1st International Semantic Web Conference (ISWC2002)
24. Ian Horrocks, Peter F. Patel-Schneider, and Frank van Harmelen. From SHIQ and RDF to OWL: The making of a web ontology language. *Journal of Web Semantics*, 1(1):7-26, 2003.
25. Cohse Mozilla Annotator , http://cohse.semanticweb.org/mozilla/annotation/
26. OntoMat-Annotizer , http://annotation.semanticweb.org/ontomat/index.html

The Role of Foundational Ontologies in Manufacturing Domain Applications

Stefano Borgo[1] and Paulo Leitão[2]

[1] Laboratory for Applied Ontology, ISTC-CNR, via Solteri 38,
38100 Trento, Italy
borgo@loa-cnr.it
[2] Polytechnic Institute of Bragança, Quinta Sta Apolónia, Apartado 1134,
5301-857 Bragança, Portugal
pleitao@ipb.pt

Abstract. Although ontology has gained wide attention in the area of information systems, a criticism typical of the early days is still rehearsed here and there. Roughly, this criticism says: general ontologies are not suited for real applications. We believe this is the result of a misunderstanding of the role of general ontologies since, we claim, even foundational ontologies (the most general and formal ontologies) have a crucial role in building reusable, adaptable and transparent application systems. We support this view by showing how foundational ontologies can be used in the manufacturing control area. Our approach (partially presented here through an example) provides a domain-specific ontology which is explicitly designed for applications, theoretically organized by a foundational ontology, driven by the application field for all intents and purposes, suitable for communication across different applications.

1 Introduction

In information science, ontology stands for a knowledge engineering artifact constituted by an interpreted language plus a set of explicit assumptions; its goal is to describe a certain reality of interest [1]. Taking the degree of semantic precision as basic metric, ontologies form a spectrum with simple glossaries and thesauri on one side and rich logical theories on the other. Ontologies resembling glossaries and thesauri, like WordNet [2], are helpful in organizing databases and protocols where only terminological services are needed. When sophisticated knowledge structures become necessary, much richer systems should be applied, e.g. those described in the Library of Foundational Ontologies [3]. Since these rich ontologies do not enjoy nice computational properties, to maintain effective computability one separates representation

---

* The first author has been partially supported by the Provincia Autonoma di Trento. The authors would like to thank Claudio Masolo and the anonymous referees for their comments.

and reasoning issues by adopting two types of ontology: a foundational ontology that provides the full system and is applied at development-time, and a lightweight ontology (a simplified version of the previous) that furnishes an efficient, although minimal, system used at run-time. Adopting this distinction, we concentrate on foundational ontologies and show their role in generating reliable representation systems.

Ontologies are nowadays quite common in information systems[1], however in the literature one hardly finds real applications developed on top of foundational ontologies. There are several reasons for this; foundational ontologies are relatively new and only in the last few years well axiomatised and justified systems have been proposed. Moreover, the development of application systems based on these ontologies is demanding so that few projects have undertaken this challenge [4]. More often, researchers focus on goals that seem to be just pieces of the process we envision [5]. Our hope is that a consistent deployment of foundational ontologies in a traditional and well established area like the manufacturing domain will foster a better understanding of these theoretical tools and of the advantages of systems based on them.

The majority of the ontologies so far developed in Artificial Intelligence express simple relationships among terms (primarily taxonomies) perhaps with some set of formal constraints (formal ontologies). Foundational ontologies stand out as specialized logical theories (a subclass of formal ontologies) not limited to particular domains and developed with the intention of characterizing explicitly a viewpoint on the "reality": the aim is to *capture formally the (intended) meaning of the adopted language*. Among the advantages in applying these, they drastically reduce misinterpretation of the knowledge base (semantic explicitness) and make information sharing reliable even in communication among untrained users and software agents (conceptual transparency). However, these ontologies are trustworthy only if based on a careful and detailed ontological analysis of (a viewpoint of) reality, a lengthy and time-consuming process which must be coupled with a rigorous logical characterization. Furthermore, they must guarantee the coverage of general and disparate concepts, allow for subtle distinctions, and make space for the specific interests of potential users. Indeed, the primitive notions of the ontology and the constraints stated to characterize them form a richly structured framework where entities, concepts, and relations of the domain at stake must find a place. In other terms, in deploying a foundational ontology one assumes that this system covers (perhaps only implicitly) all possible concepts and relations of interest. Furthermore, one accepts the view that any element in the domain can be captured in logical terms within this framework and that any expression means whatever the formal semantics states. Some researchers maintain that these assumptions are too strong and that no ontology can deliver such a characterization of the language. Consequently, they prefer to use weak terminological ontologies claiming that foundational ontologies are too brittle theoretical tools and, as such, not suited for application domains [6].

We disagree with this general standpoint. We believe this criticism is the result of a misunderstanding of the significance of foundational ontologies in application domains. It is widely recognized that foundational ontologies furnish an important tool

---

[1] http://www.semanticweb.org/

for establishing links and comparisons among domain ontologies, especially when the focus is on communication and standardization. Indeed, they make explicit the philosophical, cognitive, and linguistic commitments the different systems have. However, this is not the only role such ontologies can play. On the contrary, we claim that foundational ontologies are crucial for the very development of domain-specific ontologies and, as such, they are profitable in applications. The case we present corroborates this view by applying foundational ontologies in modelling problems, by showing the role of foundational ontologies in building applicative systems, and by highlighting their relevance. For this, we chose to work in a domain (manufacturing enterprise) that has proven to be quite successful in modelling production processes but that shows some weakness in the area of information integration and management.

Organization of the paper. Section 2 gives an overview of the manufacturing domain and section 3 concentrates on the ADACOR architecture with its terminological system. In section 4, we discuss interoperability issues and briefly look at different foundational ontologies available in the literature motivating our choice to adopt the DOLCE ontology. The next section begins with an introduction to DOLCE and proceeds with the alignment of ADACOR to this ontology. Then, we show how to formalize (a part of) a crucial example. Section 6 concludes with some general remarks.

2 Manufacturing Problem Description

This study applies to manufacturing control systems. We look at a manufacturing enterprise that produces discrete items, and model (part of) the factory plant components as well as aspects of the scheduling, monitoring, and execution processes.

2.1 Manufacturing System Description

The manufacturing enterprises produce products that are offered to the market. The products are described by the product model, which contains all technical data and describes the constitution of a product, and by the process model, which defines how to produce the product. The process model specifies the process plan, that is, a list of operations and related information like estimated processing time and requirements necessary to produce the part. An operation is a job to execute and involves one of the following main functions: processing, assembly, storage, transportation, manipulation, maintenance or inspection. Each operation has aggregated a set of services.

A customer interacts with a company to order one of the available products or a new product. This order, known as customer order, involves the reference to a product, a quantity, a deliver date and a price. Additionally, it is necessary to create forecast orders to anticipate the market demands. The manufacturing planning convert the customer and forecast orders into production orders, aggregating if possible several customer orders into a production order, to obtain volume and transport advantages. The production orders must specify a quantity, a delivery date and a cost. A production order is indexed to a product object and comprises a list of work orders. A work order is a job that should be executed by a resource.

The shop floor consists of a group of resources (such as movers, transporters, drilling, milling, and turning machines) with different characteristics (spindle speed, list of tools and grippers, tool length compensation, payload, time autonomy, etc.), which have to be carefully described in the factory model. Each resource is an entity that can execute a certain range of jobs, when it is available, as long as its capacity is not exceeded. The availability of a resource is represented by an agenda that indicates the list of orders allocated to the resource over the time. The agenda comprises also time slots where the resource is: free, allocated to execute orders, temporarily out of service (due for example to maintenance) and out of service.

2.2 Manufacturing Control Description

The main functions required by a manufacturing control system are process planning, resource allocation planning, plan execution, and pathological state handling.

The production of a product involves the execution of several steps, according to a precedence diagram, defined in the process plan. At the process planning level, the manufacturing orders are launched to the shop floor, associated to a process plan that defines the required sequence of operations and the required machine type for each operation. Based on the available resources, it is possible to create alternative process sequences, each one indicating the exact resource that should execute each operation.

The resource allocation planning schedules the necessary operations to produce the parts, including processing, transport, maintenance and set-up operations, taking into account the process plans, the constraints and resources capacity, in order to produce the products, minimizing the costs and increasing the productivity, and organizing the production unit to react to any modification in demand or machine failure.

The plan execution functions deals with the physical implementation of the schedule into the factory through the dispatching of the scheduled orders to the manufacturing process, and with the production progress monitoring. The reaction to disturbances is initially taken by the execution plan level, and may imply the need of rescheduling of the operations with the aim of minimizing the effects of the disturbance.

2.3 Towards a Manufacturing Ontology

In order to improve agility and flexibility, nowadays one uses distributed approaches in developing manufacturing control applications. These are built upon autonomous and cooperative entities, such as those based on multi-agent and holonic systems.

In the communication between distributed and autonomous entities, besides the issues related to interfaces and protocols, it is important to verify that the semantic content is preserved during the exchange of messages. These distributed entities need to have a common understanding of the concepts of their domain knowledge, which is given by a domain (or core) ontology [7]. The inter-operability in distributed and different multi-agent or holonic platforms increases the need for shared ontologies, in order to allow the exchange of knowledge between those distributed platforms.

3 ADACOR Holonic Control Architecture

Our work concentrates on an application domain where several different approaches are implemented and improved continuously. To ground the discussion, we must first select one architecture and one foundational ontology and then provide an ontological assessment of the concepts adopted by the first through the knowledge structure provided by the latter. Once the notions of this architecture have been ontologically analyzed and classified, we can use the resulting system as a core ontology in the manufacturing domain, perhaps including new concepts from other architectures.

One of the proposed architecture for the manufacturing control is ADACOR (ADAptive holonic COntrol aRchitecture for distributed manufacturing systems) [8], which addresses the agile reaction to disturbances at the shop floor level, increasing the agility and flexibility of the enterprise, when it works in volatile environments, characterized by the frequent occurrence of unexpected disturbances. In the following sections, we introduce this system and clarify its ontological stand.

3.1 Overview of ADACOR Manufacturing Control System

The ADACOR architecture is based in the Holonic Manufacturing Systems (HMS) paradigm[2], and it is built upon a set of autonomous and cooperative holons, each one being a representation of a manufacturing component, i.e., a physical resource (numerical control machines, robots, etc.) or a logic entity (orders, etc.). A generic ADACOR holon comprises the Logical Control Device (LCD) and the physical resource capable of performing the manufacturing tasks, if it exists. The LCD device is responsible for regulating the logic activities related to the holon and comprises three main components: decision, communication and physical interface components [8].

The ADACOR architecture groups the manufacturing holons into product, task, operational and supervisor holon classes. Each available product to be produced in the factory plant is represented by a product holon that contains all knowledge related to the product and is responsible for the short-term process planning. Each production order launched to the shop floor in order to execute a product (or sub-product) is represented by a task holon, which is responsible to manage the execution, containing the dynamic information about the production order. Operational holons represent the

---

[2] HMS (http://hms.ifw.uni-hannover.de/) translates to the manufacturing world the concepts developed by Arthur Koestler for living organisms and social organizations [9]. Holonic manufacturing is characterized by holarchies of holons (i.e., autonomous and cooperative entities), which represent the entire range of manufacturing entities. A holon, as Koestler devised the term, is a part of a (manufacturing) system that has a unique identifier, may be made up of sub-ordinate parts and, in turn, can be part of a larger whole.

physical resources available in the shop floor, such as operators, robots and numerical control machines, managing their behaviors according to the resource goals and skills. The supervisor holon introduces coordination and global optimization in decentralized control approaches and is responsible for the group formation and coordination.

The ADACOR adaptive production control balances between a more centralized and a more flat approach, due to the self-organization associated to each ADACOR holon, translated in the autonomy factor and in the propagation mechanisms.

3.2 The ADACOR Manufacturing Ontology

ADACOR defines its own manufacturing ontology, expressed in an object-oriented frame-based manner as recommended in the FIPA Ontology Service Recommendations [10]. Thus, the architecture uses classes to describe concepts and predicates and fixes them as part of the application ontology. This allows for a practical and fast way of creating an ontology with an immediate underlying implementation.

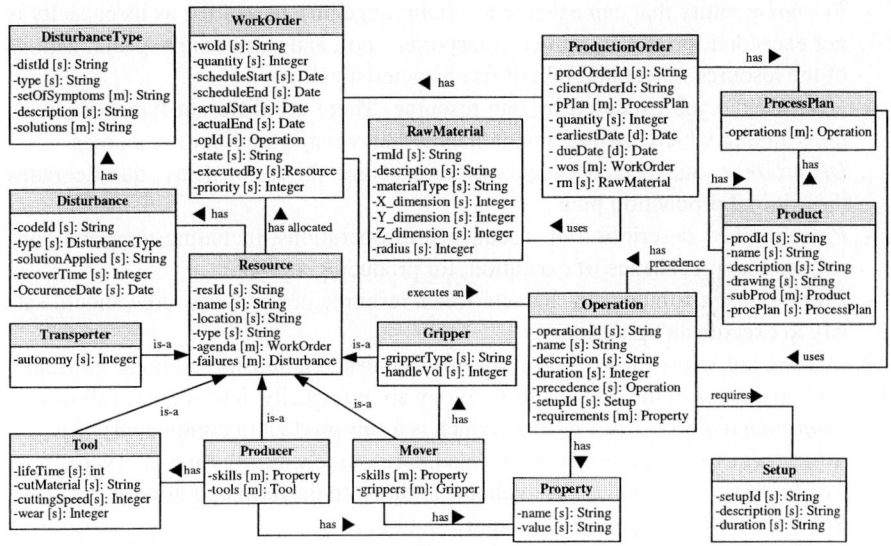

Fig. 1. Manufacturing Ontology Developed in the ADACOR Architecture

The manufacturing ontology used in ADACOR is developed through the definition of a taxonomy of manufacturing components, which contributes to the analysis and formalization of the manufacturing problem (these components are mapped into a set of objects, illustrated in the UML-like diagram of Figure 1). For this, one must fix the vocabulary used by the distributed entities over the ADACOR platform, isolate the ADACOR-concepts, the ADACOR-predicates and -relations, the ADACOR-attributes of the classes, and the meaning of each term. Note that not all ADACOR concepts find a place in Figure 1. The diagram is restricted to the relationships between simple manufacturing components used by the manufacturing control system. For example, since a production order may index one customer order or an aggregation of these, this relationship and the latter concept are not shown.

ADACOR-concepts are expressions that hold for complex entities whose structure can be defined in terms of classes or objects. The main concepts in the ADACOR architecture (see Figure 1) are informally described as follows:
- *Product*: entity produced by the enterprise (it includes sub-products).
- *Raw-material*: entity acquired outside the enterprise and used during the production process, e.g. blocks of steel, nuts and bolds (unless produced internally).
- *Customer order*: entity that the enterprise receives from a customer that requests some products.
- *Production order*: entity obtained by converting the customer and forecast orders (it may result from the aggregation of several customer orders).
- *Work order*: entity generated by the enterprise in order to describe the production of a product. The work order lists one or more operations including their processing time, participants (e.g. name and number of resources involved in the execution), priority, scheduled dates, state and quantity.
- *Resource*: entity that can execute a certain range of jobs as long as its capacity is not exceeded. Producer, mover, transporter, tool, and gripper are specializations of the resource object and inherit its characteristics[3].
- *Operation*: a job executed by one resource. There are different types of operations among which drilling, maintenance, and reconfiguration of resources.
- *Disturbance*: unexpected event, such as machine failure or delay, that degrades the original production plan.
- *Process Plan*: description of a sequence of operations, including temporal constraints like precedence of execution, for producing a product.
- *Property*: an attribute that characterizes a resource or that a resource should satisfy to execute an operation.

Predicates are expressions that allow to establish relationships among concepts. The main predicates in the ADACOR ontology are informally described as follows:
- *SubproductOf(x,y)*: x is a product which is a sub-product (a component) of y.
- *Allocated(x,y,i)*: operation x is allocated to resource y during time interval i.
- *Available(x,y,t)*: resource x is available at time t to perform operation y.
- *RequiresTool(x,y)*: operation x requires tool y.
- *HasTool(x,y,t)*: resource x has tool y available in its tool magazine at time t.
- *RequiresSkill(x,y)*: execution of operation x requires property (skill) y.
- *HasSkill(x,y)*: resource x has property (skill) y.
- *HasFailure(x,y,t)*: a disturbance x occurred in resource y at time t.
- *Proposal(x,y,w,z,u)*: the entity x proposes to the entity y the execution of the work order w with location u and charging the price z.

---

[3] Here we do not consider human operators which, for completeness, should be listed among the resources of the system. Indeed, sometimes operations like maintenance or reconfiguring must be executed by human operators.

4 Interoperability in Manufacturing Control Applications

The ontologies currently used in the manufacturing domain are the result of non-coordinated efforts and relinquish the interoperability with other agents communities. As seen in section 3.2, in the ADACOR architecture a basic and proprietary manufacturing ontology has been developed to support the inter-operability between ADACOR holons. However, the lack of inter-operability between different agent-based or holonic manufacturing control platforms pushes for a common manufacturing ontology capable of merging (or at least of communicating adequately with) these.

Lately, several efforts to develop standard mechanisms for the unambiguous exchange of information within the manufacturing domain have been undertaken. The International Organization for Standardization (ISO) developed STEP (Standard for the Exchange of Product Model Data) that defines a standard data format for exchanging a complete product specification (e.g. geometry and production process) between heterogeneous CAD/CAM systems. However, STEP refers to the product information only and does not cover the process and enterprise engineering information. A set of initiatives seeks to fulfill this gap. The Process Specification Language (PSL) project [11] aims to develop general ontology for representing manufacturing processes to serve as an interlingua to integrate multiple process-related applications throughout the manufacturing life cycle. A Language for Process Specification (ALPS) [12] identifies information models to facilitate process specification and to transfer this information to process control. The Toronto Virtual Enterprise (TOVE) [13] defines a domain-specific ontology for enterprise modelling. The Enterprise Ontology provides "a collection of terms and definitions relevant to business enterprises to enable coping with a fast changing environment through improved business planning, greater flexibility, more effective communication and integration" [14]. The goal of the Process Interchange Format (PIF) project [15] is to support the exchange of business process models across different formats and schemas. We conclude with the Plinius project [16], whose goal is to define a domain-specific ontology for mechanical properties of ceramic material. Of course, this list of projects is far from complete, it is provided just to show the variety of approaches and standardization initiatives in this area.

In spite of the referred efforts to develop ontologies in areas related to manufacturing, as of today no formal ontology is available in the manufacturing domain. The application of foundational ontologies to support the interoperability between agent-based and holonic manufacturing control applications provides a feasible and reliable way to solve this problematic situation. Also, the ongoing activity of the holonic manufacturing community within FIPA (Foundation for Intelligent Physical Agents) to adequate the FIPA specifications to the manufacturing requirements would benefit as well from the adoption of well-justified and organized formal ontologies, that is, ontologies furnished with a deep logical characterization.

Just a few foundational ontologies have been developed and motivated to a satisfactory level in the literature, in particular DOLCE (the Descriptive Ontology for Linguistic and Cognitive Engineering, http://www.loa-cnr.it/Ontologies.html), GFO (the General Formal Ontology [17], http://www.onto-med.de), OCHRE (the Object-Centered High-level Reference Ontology, developed by L. Schneider [3]), OpenCyc (http://www.opencyc.com), SUMO (the Suggested Upper Merged Ontology [18], http://www.ontologyportal.org) and, although only partially formalized, BFO (the Basic Formal Ontology. developed at IFOMIS [3], http://www.ifomis.uni-leipzig.de).

Since foundational ontologies are complex systems, there are two crucial elements that should be considered in choosing an ontology: the ontology has to provide a rich set of conceptual distinctions (at least relatively to the domain of application), and all the features that one deems relevant should be clearly characterized (or characterizable) within the ontology. In our case, the chosen foundational ontology is the DOLCE ontology because it distinguishes between objects (like products) and events (like operations), it includes a useful differentiation among individual qualities, quality types, quality spaces, and quality values, it allows for fine descriptions of properties and capacities, and it relies on a very expressive language, namely first-order modal logic[4]; all features crucial in modelling physical objects, agents, and processes. Even more so, DOLCE let the user define the qualities needed in the application, allowing in this way a great level of freedom while facilitating update and maintenance. Finally, as said in the introduction, the application of a foundational ontology should be coupled with a lightweight version of that very ontology: lightweight versions of DOLCE are available in LOOM, DAML+OIL, RDFS, DIG, and OWL.

5 Formalization of the ADACOR Ontology in DOLCE

DOLCE, the foundational ontology developed at the Laboratory for Applied Ontology (ISTC-CNR, http://www.loa-cnr.it), is mainly an ontology of particulars in the sense that it focuses on this class of entities. Universals (predicates) are considered in so far as they help in the classification of particulars. This ontology adopts the multiplicative approach, that is, it assumes that different entities can be co-located in the same space-time. Co-located entities differ because they enjoy incompatible properties, for example, a drilling machine does not survive a radical shape deformation while its amount of matter does, therefore the machine and the amount of matter are different entities in DOLCE, yet co-located. An important aspect of DOLCE is the treatment of qualities. Endurants (objects like a gripper, a person) and perdurants (events like making a hole, moving a steel block) come with a bunch of qualities, e.g. shape, weight, duration, velocity, etc. Qualities may be specific to a subclass of entity, for instance weight is a quality of physical endurants only. An entity like Hammer_#123 has its own individual qualities: its shape, its weight, its color, etc. that exist as long as that hammer does. These individual qualities are elements in DOLCE so that one can refer to them directly in formal expressions. For each quality, there exists a quality space: the quality space of shape, the quality space of weight, etc. Each individual quality of an entity (say, its weight-quality) is associated to a position

---

[4] This should not be surprising. Foundational ontologies are used to structure the knowledge base and are not applied at run-time when computability and effectiveness issues are crucial.

in the corresponding quality space (the weight-space) and this position is called its quale. This allows us to make important distinctions and comparisons even *before* introducing measurement. Indeed, measures depend on units of measurement and methodologies, thus are obtained only once these elements have been fixed. Independently of the measurement, at each point in time the hammer weight-quale is a precise position in the weight quality space. Two hammers that have the same weight-quale, must have the same weight-measure, no matter how we assign measures to positions in the space.

On a different level, the DOLCE ontology has been compared to other foundational ontologies (e.g. OCHRE and BFO in [3]) and it is included in other merging initiatives [19]. This is important to our project: it is generally granted that interoperability is obtained through the compliance with ontologies thus, if DOLCE is included in merging initiatives, our core ontology is likely to be easily linked to other manufacturing ontologies, at least those developed for interoperability.

The taxonomy of the most basic categories of particulars in DOLCE is depicted in Figure 2. An informal (and partial) description of the main predicates is given next. We refer the reader to [3] for the formal characterization of these predicates and a throughout discussion of the DOLCE assumptions.

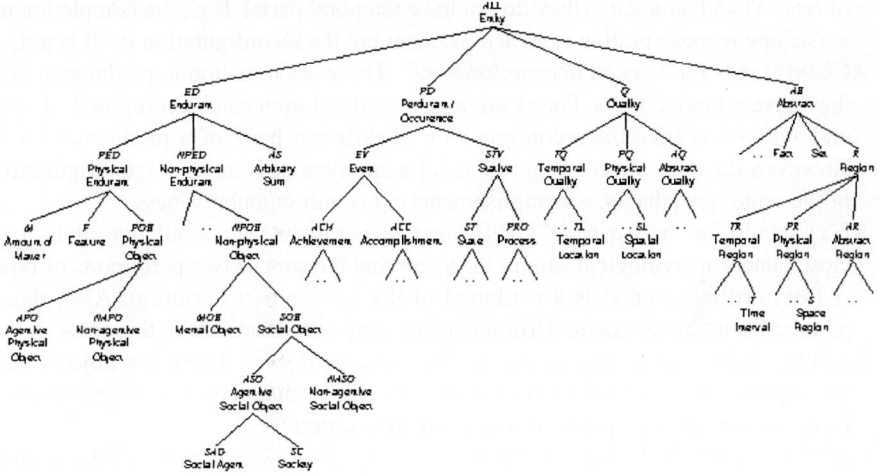

Fig. 2. Taxonomy of DOLCE basic categories [3]

ED(x), PED(x) stand for "*x is an endurant*" and "*x is a physical endurant*", respectively. An endurant is an entity that is *wholly* present at any time it is present. It is physical if located in space and time: a hammer, a mover machine, an amount of plastic. See the predicate NASO below for examples of non-physical endurants.

PD(x) stands for "*x is a perdurant or event*", i.e., an entity that is only partially present at any time it is present. For instance, consider the perdurant "producing an item of type #234" that consists in attaching two metal pieces together with screws and painting the resulting piece. While the painting goes on, the (temporal) part corresponding to attaching the two pieces is not present anymore and when this is present, the painting is not yet. Perdurants can have spatial parts as well. Note that objects are not parts of perdurants, rather objects participate in them. Perdurants form four sub-classes: achievements, accomplishments, states, and processes.

In the manufacturing domain, one needs to refer to a wide variety of operations. Some of these, like turning, are said to be homeomeric, i.e., every part of a turning is a turning itself. In other terms, if one divides a turning operation with temporal interval t in two parts, one initial operation with interval t_1, and one final operation with interval t_2 (such that t_1 and t_2 partition t), then both the initial and the final operations have all the characteristics of a turning operation. This does not happen with, say, a setup operation. It is necessary for a setup to reach a specific state since it is the achievement of such a state that justifies its classification as a setup. Thus, if we divide a setup operation in two temporal parts, only one of the two sub-operations (if any) can be considered a setup operation. This and similar distinctions will drive the ontological classification of the ADACOR notions and are captured by the DOLCE predicates below.

ACH(x) stands for "*x is an achievement*". These perdurants are characterized by anti-cumulativeness (the sum of two achievements of, say, type A is not an event of type A) and atomicity (they do not have temporal parts). E.g., the completion of a machine reconfiguration is an achievement but the reconfiguration itself is not.

ACC(x) stands for "*x is an accomplishment*". These are non-atomic perdurants, i.e., they have temporal parts. For example, a reconfiguration can be composed of several sub-events (like the reconfiguration of different parts of a production line). However, the sum of reconfigurations of some type A is never a reconfiguration of the same type, that is, accomplishments enjoy anti-cumulativeness.

ST(x) stands for "*x is a state*". This class of perdurants is cumulative, thus it is closed under mereological sum in the sense that the sum of two perdurants of type A (say, drilling events) is a perdurant of the same type (a drilling). Also, these perdurants are homeomeric. Drilling and moving perdurants are in this class.

NAPO(x) stands for "*x is a non-agentive physical object*". These are objects that have spatial and temporal location but to which one cannot ascribe intentions, believes, or desires; e.g., products and production orders.

NASO(x) stands for "*x is a non-agentive social object*". These objects have neither (direct) spatial or temporal location nor intentions, believes, or desires. They depend generically on societies like laws and plans.

qt(q,x) stands for "*q is a quality of x*". Qualities are basic 'properties' of entities. They can be perceived or measured. In this sense, they represent partial characterizations of an entity and depend existentially on it. Every endurant (perdurant) comes with its physical (temporal) qualities.

ql(r, q), ql(r,q,t) stand for "*r is the quale of the perdurant's quality q*", "*r is the quale of the endurant's quality q during time t*", respectively. The quale is the position of an individual quality in the corresponding quality space. If a quality space is poor, then there are few different positions in it and it is likely that corresponding individual qualities (of different entities) are associated to the same quale. Rich quality spaces allow for finer distinctions among qualities. Two entities with individual qualities associated to the same quale (in their quality space) are undistinguishable regarding to the corresponding quality.

5.1 Alignment of ADACOR with DOLCE

DOLCE provides a natural way to classify entities in the ADACOR architecture. Beside the basic distinction between endurants and perdurants, descriptions can be modelled explicitly as a type of objects, and properties are simply qualities. Below, we present the classification of some entities of section 3 according to our work.

Products, resources and orders[5] are physical, non-agentive objects (NAPO)

$(Product(x) \lor Resource(x) \lor Order(x)) \rightarrow NAPO(x)$

In ADACOR, raw-material refers to objects and to amounts of matter as well, thus we classify raw-material as generic physical endurants (PED)

$Raw\_material(x) \rightarrow PED(x)$

At this point, we constrain the meaning of the terms "Order" and "Resource" in ADACOR, that is, we formalize the predicates of ADACOR that are new in DOLCE,

$Order(x) \leftrightarrow (Production\_order(x) \lor Customer\_order(x) \lor Work\_order(x))$

$Resource(x) \leftrightarrow (Producer(x) \lor Mover(x) \lor Transporter(x) \lor Gripper(x) \lor Tool(x))$

The remaining entities of section 3 are perdurants (PD) since they identify activities or states. DOLCE makes a clear-cut distinction between achievements (ACH), accomplishments (ACC), states (ST), and processes (PRO). We found this partition of perdurants very helpful and it is used systematically in the system. Note that "Operation" and "Disturbance" are disjoint top classes of ADACOR perdurants[6].

$Operation(x) \rightarrow PD(x)$

$Disturbance(x) \rightarrow ACH(x)$

$\neg (Operation(x) \land Disturbance(x))$

$Completion(x) \rightarrow ACH(x)$

$(Setup(x) \lor Reconfiguration(x) \lor Inspection(x) \lor Maintenance(x) \lor Assembly(x) \lor Production(x)) \rightarrow ACC(x)$

$(Transportation(x) \lor Turning(x) \lor Drilling(x) \lor Milling(x)) \rightarrow ST(x)$

Most notably, in our limited list we find no instance of the DOLCE notion of process. Consider, for instance, transportation: since all the temporal parts of transportation are

---

[5] The notions of resource and agent are related. Section 5.3 discusses these in the manufacturing domain. Also, note that we distinguish between orders and order-descriptions.
[6] In principle, one can consider disturbances as operations. However, this seems unnatural to people working in manufacturing. For this reason, disturbances and operations are presented as disjoint classes.

transportation as well, this type of event is stative (ST). A similar argument holds for turning, drilling, and milling.

As done for the endurants, we must characterize the meaning of the general terms "Operation", "Disturbance", "Completion" and "Reconfiguration" in our formalization. The constraints are given below.

Operation(x) ↔ (Completion(x) ∨ Reconfiguration(x) ∨ Inspection(x) ∨ Setup(x) ∨ Maintenance(x) ∨ Assembly(x) ∨ Production(x) ∨ Milling(x) ∨ Transportation(x) ∨ Turning(x) ∨ Drilling(x))

Disturbance(x) ↔ (Failure(x) ∨ Delay(x))

Completion(x) ↔ (Completion_of_setup(x) ∨ Completion_of_inspection(x) ∨ Completion_of_assembly(x) ∨ Completion_of_reconfiguration(x) ∨ Completion_of_maintenance(x) ∨ Completion_of_production(x))

Reconfiguration(x) ↔ (Addition_of_new_resource(x) ∨ Change_of_layout(x) ∨ Removal_of_resource(x) ∨ Change_of_resource_capability (x))

There is a misalignment between the notion of Setup as an operation (above) and the concept of Setup in Figure 1. Some operations may have a Setup operation as requirement and this is the reason to show Setup as a separate entry in Figure 1.

The notions of Delay, Disturbance, and Failure are related concepts and their formalization require some caution. A disturbance is an unexpected event: machine failure or machine delay are the only examples of disturbances we consider. These are crucial since they affect the scheduled production plan. When an operation is being executed, we can expect several different scenarios: (1) the resource finishes the execution of the operation within the estimated time interval, (2) the resource fails and it cannot finish the operation (a failure has occurred) or (3) the operation is delayed (a delay has occurred). Thus, failures and delays are perdurants and machines participate in them. Clearly, Failure is a kind of accomplishment. However, the classification of Delay is less obvious: a delay occurs when the need of rescheduling is officially established, thus it is an atomic event. Also, the sum of two delays is not a delay since the sum does not correspond to a single rescheduling requirement. Thus, Delay is taken to be an accomplishment as well.

As mentioned in the manufacturing description, a "Process Plan" is a description of a sequence of operations (plus related properties and interconnections). Then, a Process Plan is a non-agentive social object (NASO), which implies that it is non–physical. Indeed, we distinguish the description (a non–physical object) from the document that contains the description (a physical object)[7]. Here it suffices to consider the first:

Process_plan(x) → NASO(x)

In the terminology of DOLCE, skills are qualities of objects. For each type of skill we must include a quality space and, for each object that has that skill, an individual

---

[7] This distinction raises in different forms and it is pervasive. For instance, one should distinguish between order and order-description, operation and operation-description, and so on. This issue is related to the notion of role. See [20] for a treatment of roles in DOLCE.

quality specific to that object. It is crucial to note that we inherit from DOLCE the distinction between individual qualities (stating that the object at stake has that skill) and the corresponding quale (roughly, a classification of the object's skill). The quale shows the characteristic of that object with respect to the given skill. For example, consider "Autonomy" to be an individual quality[8] enjoyed by *any* resource. It characterizes for how long a resource can work without the need to re-fill its batteries (assuming a way of measuring this skill is given). If AutL is the class of autonomy-qualities, then the following constraint states that "Autonomy" is a quality defined for resources only

$$\text{AutL}(q) \rightarrow \exists x \, (qt(q,x) \land \text{Resource}(x))$$

The specific relations "q is the autonomy of resource x" and "resource x has autonomy d at time t" are not part of the language but can be defined in it as follows

$$\text{Autonomy}(q,x) =_{def} \text{Resource}(x) \land \text{AutL}(q) \land qt(q,x)$$

$$\text{Autonomy}(d,x,t) =_{def} \text{Resource}(x) \land \exists q \, (\text{Autonomy}(q,x) \land ql(d,q,t))$$

Every resource must be explicitly associated to a (finite) set of qualities or skills that capture its characteristics, e.g. Autonomy, Magazine_capacity, Max_feed_rate. If $QL_1,\ldots,QL_n$ are the skills of resource A_i, then we set the following constraint

$$\exists q_1,\ldots,q_n (QL_1(q_1,A_i) \land \ldots \land QL_n(q_n,A_i))$$

Then, by using skill indices in the argument we can define the relation Has_skill

$$\text{Has\_skill}(y,j) =_{def} \text{Resource}(y) \land \exists q \, QL_j(q,y)$$

Sometimes we must be able to state some general condition (like "resource *x* has tool *y* available") or to select resources that not only have a given skill but that can perform it in a certain way. These cases are captured through the notion of "Requirement", that is, through relations like "Has_drilling_feed_speed_rate", "Has_tool", etc., that describe some general properties. These relations are often defined by complex logical expressions so here some of them are presented with a minimal characterization only (below we use QL_d for a quality related to drilling, this is not characterized further; f-s-r stands for 'feed speed rate')

$$\text{Executes}(x,y,t) \rightarrow (\text{Resource}(x) \land \text{Operation}(y) \land T(t))$$
(resource x executes operation y at time t)

$$\text{Has\_tool}(x,y,t) \rightarrow (\text{Resource}(x) \land \text{Tool}(y) \land T(t))$$
(resource x has tool y available at time t)

$$\text{Has\_drilling\_feed\_speed\_rate}(x,t,a,b) =_{def} (\text{Resource}(x) \land \exists q \, (QL_d(q,x) \land \forall y \, ql(y,q,t) \rightarrow a \leq y \leq b))$$
(resource x has drilling f-s-r between a and b at t)

$$\text{Requires\_skill}(x,j) =_{def} (\text{Operation}(x) \land \forall y,t \, (\text{Executes}(y,x,t) \rightarrow \text{Has\_skill}(y,j)))$$
(operation x requires skill y to be executed)

---

[8] One could take 'Autonomy' to be reducible to other simpler qualities. This alternative view is compatible with the characterization we provide.

Setup_requires_tool(x,y) $=_{def}$ (Setup(x) ∧ ∀z,t (Executes(z,x,t) →
Has_tool(z,y,t))) (setup x requires tool y to be performed)

Milling_requires_autonomy(x,t,y) $=_{def}$ (Milling(x) ∧ ∀z,d (Executes(z,x,t) ∧
Autonomy(d,z,t) → d≥y)) (milling x at time t requires autonomy at least y)

5.2 An Example: Bidding for a Job Task

We concentrate on a specific example, an instance of a task allocation interaction, and show how the ontology shapes its formalization in the system. Here, we limit ourselves to the language fragment introduced in sections 3 and 5.

The agent **t1** (contractor) has a job task that comprises two different operations, "mach-piece" and "drill-holes". The first operation has precedence over the second, that is, the "drill-holes" operation can start only once the first operation has been completed. The "mach-piece" operation for this job must be executed by a resource with the following characteristics: it should be a milling machine with feed speed 1000. For the second operation the following is needed: it should be executed by a drilling machine with the feed speed 700. Agent **t1** sends a message to all agents connected to the system. The message announces an operation and the requirements for it. For example, the message for the operation "drill-holes" is:

```
(Cfp
 :sender (agent-identifier :name t1)
 :receiver (agent-identifier :name mach-a, mach-b)
 :language FIPA-SL0
 :ontology Adacor-ontology
 :protocol FIPA-Contract-Net
 :content ((ONLY-OPERATION (OPERATION :name drill-holes
     :exectime 55 :rawmaterial steel-100 :precedence mach-piece
     :properties (set (PROPERTY :name mach_type :value drilling)
     (PROPERTY :name speed :value 700)) :quantity 100 :state
     NOT-ALLOCATED :earlieststart 094248884 :duedate 094316884))
)
```

The message contains several fields where the language, ontology and protocol used in the message construction are reported. The content of the message stores the information that the contractor wants to send to the contractees. In this case the content has information formatted using the "Operation" concept.

Without entering into the details of the message configuration and exchange protocols, our ontological assessment of the terminology allows us to share information with a clear meaning (through the formal semantics of the DOLCE ontology) by including logical expressions in the message. Let us write "DrillH1" for this specific operation, then the entry content is explicitly characterized by the following[9]:

Bidder(x,DrillH1,t) →

(Resource(x) ∧

---

[9] This is only a partial charactcrization limited to the adopted language fragment.

$\exists y$ (Has_tool(x,y,t) $\wedge$ Drilling_tool(y)) $\wedge$ Available(x,DrillH1,t) $\wedge$

$\forall j$ (Requires_skill(DrillH1,j) $\rightarrow$ Has_skill(x,j)) $\wedge$

$\forall a,b$ (Has_drilling_feed_speed_range(x,t,a,b) $\rightarrow$ a$\leq$700$\leq$b) $\wedge$

Autonomy(d,x,t) $\wedge$ d$\geq$55)

where "Bidder(x,DrillH1,t)" stands for "*x bids to perform operation DrillH1 at time t*", and "Drilling_tool(y)" is a specialization of "Tool(y)".

With the alignment of ADACOR to DOLCE, the above logical expression states formally (in an explicit and ontologically sound setting) that if an entity x bids for the job DrillH1 at a time t, then x has the following (now unambiguous) characteristics:

- x is a resource
- a tool to execute drilling operations is available to x at time t
- x is available at time t to execute the drilling operation DrillH1
- x has all the skills required by the drilling operation DrillH1
- x has capacity to drill at 700 feed speed rate at time t
- x is autonomous for at least 55 time-units

Each resource agent verifies its capabilities to execute the operation (both in terms of skills and calendar) and, if it finds a time t such that the conditions above are satisfied, it answers the call for operation DrillH1 and time t.

If agent **mach-a** wants to bid the announcement, it produces this message:

```
(Propose
 :sender (agent-identifier :name mach-a)
 :receiver (agent-identifier :name t1)
 :language FIPA-SL0
 :ontology Adacor-ontology
 :protocol FIPA-Contract-Net
 :content ((OP-PROPOSE (OPERATION :name drill-holes :exectime
    55 :rawmaterial steel-100 :precedence mach-piece :properties
    (set (PROPERTY :name mach_type :value drilling) (PROPERTY
    :name speed :value 700)) :quantity 100 :state NOT-ALLOCATED
    :earlieststart 094248884 :duedate 094316884)(PROPOSAL
    :name mach-a :price 100 :location IDIT)))
)
```

The bid message is similar to the first one but now the content of the message contains different information, translated with the relation between the "Operation" and the "Proposal" concepts. The proposal data structure comprises the name of the entity that is sending the proposal, its physical location and the price proposed to execute the operation. In particular, if the system is formalized according to the alignment to the DOLCE ontology, agent **mach**-a can send a logical expression stating that this agent can execute the operation DrillH1, that it satisfies all the constraints (this part is obtained easily from the one given above), and other relevant information like restrictions in the operational skills that may interfere with the job execution. Furthermore, the message will include a new piece of information[10]

---

[10] For the sake of the example, here we assume that a single operation can play the role of a work order.

Proposal(**mach-a,t1**,DrillH1,100,IDIT)

where the predicate "Proposal", being ontologically characterized, is now a formal concept with clear meaning and implications (obligations, responsibilities, legal rights) even for the new entities not previously connected to the system.

5.3 Issues in Modelling the Manufacturing Domain

If the need to distinguish between values (essentially, numbers) and value ranges can be taken for granted in the manufacturing domain, subtler distinctions are not. We find helpful to distinguish a skill of a machine (for instance, being able to execute a particular job like drilling a hole) from qualitative and quantitative aspects of that skill (the way the hole is obtained, the speed of execution and so on). Indeed, being able to execute a particular operation is a necessary condition to answer a bid for a work order independently of qualitative and quantitative aspects. On the other hand, these aspects are necessary for any rescheduling process. Similar distinctions arise in dealing with time. Talking of the expected duration of an operation, one may need to refer to the precise event (the operation executed by a given resource at a given time), the duration of that event (the time is spans), and the length of a temporal interval.

A different set of problems raises from the different conceptualization of the entities in the domain. For instance, the notion of agent in the manufacturing community is often application-dependent, that is, the very same entity might (or might not) play the role of an agent in a manufacturing process depending on the application we are considering. However, in other cases the notion of agent is used in absolute terms, that is, an agent is any entity that has the capacity to initiate actions (perhaps in a proactive and rational way). An analogous argument holds for the notion of resource as used in this paper. These views appear to be incompatible since in the first case simple tools (like a hammer) might be considered on a par with machines (complex floor resources) while in the latter case such tools are ontologically distinct from agents. In order to be transparent across different ontologies, the modeller must take this different conceptualizations seriously. For instance, one can classify these entities as (generic) physical objects and allow the application specifications to introduce further differentiations among the entities (with corresponding ontological properties attached to them). This issue could be solved within DOLCE exploiting the use of quality spaces or introducing roles explicitly.

Other entities seem hard to formalize because we point to different aspects in different contexts. An example is the notion of raw-material. Consider a company that produces clothes and that buys buttons from another producer. For the company, the buttons are classified as raw-material. Indeed, this company conceptualizes buttons as "components" of the items it produces and not as "products" themselves. However, the very same items are products for the button producer. This discrepancy is only apparent since ontologically the items we refer to (talking of raw-material or product) have the same properties in all contexts; they are physical objects with well defined characteristics. The real problem is that raw-material is not an ontological distinction and thus it collects things of different ontological types like amounts of matter (sand, water, steel and the like) and complex artefacts (buttons, pipes, hammers). This is the reason we classify them as generic (physical) endurants. Further characterizations have to take into account the specific items one is talking about.

6 Conclusions

Our work, here presented only in part, aims at a domain-specific ontology (core ontology) for the manufacturing production field. Once completed, the resulting ontology will be well-founded, in particular because driven by a foundational ontology. Also, it inherits the advantages of a richly characterized ontology making it suitable for information communication and sharing. On the other hand, it is modelled by the subject field because specific applicative concerns have driven the alignment and refinement of the initial vocabulary. In short, the combination of a foundational ontology and an application architecture to produce a core ontology has the advantage of mixing bottom-up and top-down strategies maintaining crucial characteristics of both.

As of today, the concrete application of foundational ontologies is rather limited. We believe this situation is due more to structural than to scientific reasons. The development of foundational ontologies requires highly interdisciplinary efforts and involves expertise in a variety of areas (logic, philosophy, linguistics, conceptual modelling, information systems). There are only a few research groups that cover adequately these areas and that are active in ontology for information science. Unfortunately, application domains (enterprise management, medicine, law, and the like) differ considerably so that the application of general ontologies to these domain is necessarily the result of specific collaboration efforts with domain experts. This explains the actual shortage of concrete examples, although recently we have observed increasing interests in the exploitation and comparison of application experiences centred upon foundational ontologies[11]. We believe that when foundational ontologies become available with clear documentation and supporting tools for the non-trained user, we will notice an increasing application of these ontologies and, consequently, an improvement of the average domain-specific ontologies available on the market.

References

1. N. Guarino, Formal Ontology and Information Systems, FOIS 1998, Trento, Italy, pp 3-15.
2. C. Fellbaum (ed.), WordNet An Electronic Lexical Database, Bradford Book, 2000.
3. C. Masolo, S. Borgo, A. Gangemi, N. Guarino, A. Oltramari, Ontology Library (WonderWeb Deliverable D18), http://wonderweb.semanticweb.org/deliverables/documents/D18.pdf

---

[11] This is one motivation for the workshop on "Core Ontologies in Ontology Engineering" which is held at EKAW 2004, http://www.loa-cnr.it/core_onto.html

4. D.M. Pisanelli, A. Gangemi, G. Steve, Ontologies and Information Systems: the Marriage of the Century?, Proceedings of Lyee Workshop, Paris 2002.
5. P. Bertolazzi, C. Krusich, M. Missikoff, An Approach to the Definition of a Core Enterprise Ontology: CEO, OES-SEO '01, Rome, 2001.
6. Y. Wilks, Ontotherapy: or how to stop worrying about what there is, 2003/8/6 http://www.racai.ro/EUROLAN-2003/html/presentations/SheffieldWilksBrewsterDingli/Ontotherapy_YWilks.ppt
7. A. Gangemi, N. Guarino, C. Masolo, A. Oltramari, Understanding Top-Level Ontological Distinctions, Workshop on Ontologies and Information Sharing, IJCAI 2001.
8. P. Leitão and F. Restivo, Holonic Adaptive Production Control Systems, Proceedings of the 28th Annual Conference of the IEEE Industrial Electronics Society, 2002, pp 2968-2973.
9. A. Koestler, The Ghost in the Machine, Arkana Books, London, 1969.
10. Foundation for Intelligent Physical Agents, http://www.fipa.org/ (June 2003).
11. C. Schlenoff, A. Knutilla, S. Ray, Unified Process Specification Language: Requirements for Modelling Process, NIST, Interagency Report 5910, Gaithersburg MD, September 1996.
12. B. Catron, S. Ray, ALPS: A Language for Process Specification, International Journal of Computer Integrated Manufacturing, Vol. 4, No. 2, 105-113, 1991.
13. F. Fadel, M. Fox and M. Gruninger, A Generic Enterprise Resource Ontology, 3rd IEEE Workshop on Enabling Technologies: Infrastructures for Collaborative Enterprises, 1994.
14. M. Uschold, M. King, S. Moralee, Y. Zorgios, The Enterprise Ontology, The Knowledge Engineering Review, 13(1), Special Issue on Putting Ontologies to Use, pp. 31-89, 1998.
15. J. Lee, M. Gruninger, Y. Jin, T. Malone, A. Tate, G. Yost and the PIF WG, The PIF Process Interchange Format and Framework, Know. Eng. Rev. 13(1), pp.91-120, 1998.
16. P. van der Vet, P.-H. Speel, N. Mars, The PLINIUS Ontology of Ceramic Materials. ECAI'94, Workshop on Comparison of Implemented Ontologies, 1994.
17. B. Heller, H. Herre, Ontological Categories in GOL, Axiomathes (14):1 pp 57-76.
18. I. Niles and A. Pease, Toward a Standard Upper Ontology, FOIS 2001, pp. 2-9
19. P. Martin, Correction and Extension of WordNet 1.7, LNAI 2746, pp 160-173.
20. Masolo, C., Vieu, L., Bottazzi, E., Catenacci, C., Ferrario, R., Gangemi, A., Guarino, N., Social Roles and their Descriptions, KR 2004, pp. 267-277

Intellectual Property Rights Management Using a Semantic Web Information System

Roberto García, Rosa Gil, and Jaime Delgado

Universitat Pompeu Fabra (UPF), Departament de Tecnologia,
Pg. Circumval·lació 8, E-08003 Barcelona, Spain
{jaime.delgado, roberto.garcia, rosa.gil}@upf.edu

Abstract. IPR (Intellectual Property Rights) Management is a complex domain. The IPR field is structured by evolving regulations, practises, business models,... Therefore, DRMS (Digital Rights Management Systems) are very difficult to develop and maintain.
The NewMARS DRMS is our contribution to this field. A knowledge oriented approach has been chosen in order to make this development capable of dealing with this complicated domain. This requirement and the objective of easy Web integration have made the Semantic Web technologies the best choice.
NewMARS is a semantics enabled metadata managing system. Metadata is associated to IPs (Intellectual Properties) using URIs and it is structured using web ontologies. There are descriptive, rights and e-commerce ontologies for the different views on IPs. Semantic enabled metadata is then used to facilitate content providers to publish intellectual properties offers and customers to find and automatically negotiate purchase conditions.
All NewMARS modules are interrelated using the ontologies shared semantics. This has allowed developing very flexible project infrastructures that facilitates easy adaptation to new IP e-commerce scenarios.

1 Introduction

This research tries to make a contribution to the Intellectual Property Rights (IPR) Management field. IPR Management has been strongly affected by the digital era changes. Even now, all the new situations related to the Intellectual Property arisen from digitalisation and the Internet have not been satisfactorily resolved yet.

Some of these problems are faced by current initiatives trying to solve interoperability between Digital Rights Management (DRM) systems. They are systems responsible for managing digital rights like digital content IPR. DRM systems started from isolated and proprietary initiatives. However, they are lately moving to a web-broad application domain due to the World Wide Web effect on the digital content market.

One of the main initiatives is MPEG-21[1], a MPEG standardisation framework for digital contents management. MPEG-21's IPR modelling part is divided into the Rights Expression Language (REL) [2] and the Rights Data Dictionary (RDD) [3].

There are many other initiatives but, basically, all have one thing in common, they work at the syntactic level. Their approach is to make a formalisation of some XML DTDs and Schemas [4] that define a rights expression language (REL). In some cases, the semantics of these languages, the meaning of the expressions, are also provided but formalised separately as rights data dictionaries (RDD). Rights dictionaries list terms definitions in natural language, intended for human consumption and not easily automatable.

However, this kind of syntactic approaches are not solving the problem as a whole. They do not scale well in really wide and open domains like the Internet. Therefore, the interoperability problems are reappearing as it is very difficult to establish one "fit all requirements" standard. For instance, the OMA (Organisation for Mobile Applications) has tried a REL different from MPEG-21 one. For OMA the choice is ODRL that has been proposed to W3C [5].

Most probably, we are not going to see a clear winner in the REL battlefield, at least in the short time range. However, automatic processing means for the huge and heterogeneous amounts of metadata produced by DRM are required. The syntax is not enough when unforeseen expressions are met. Here is where machine understandable semantics come to help metadata interpretation to achieve interoperability.

Our idea is to facilitate the automation and interoperability of IPR frameworks integrating both parts, the Rights Expression Language and the Rights Data Dictionary. These objectives can be accomplished using ontologies, which provide the required definitions for the right expression language terms in a machine-readable form. Thus, from the automatic processing point of view, a more complete vision of the application domain is available and more sophisticated processing can be carried out.

We have taken the Semantic Web approach [6] because it is naturally prepared for the Internet domain and thus we use web ontologies [7]. The modularity of web ontologies allows their easy extension and adaptation to meet evolvability and interoperability.

Once we chose the Semantic Web approach we proceeded to develop an IPR Ontology, IPROnto [8,9,10]. However, the ontology is only a formalisation without utility if it is not put into practice. This has been the objective of the NewMARS project: to build an IPR Management utility that takes profit from the advantages of the IPROnto formalisation, which will facilitate the implementation of digital content e-commerce solutions.

2 Application Domain

In order to effectively put NewMARS into practice, what has been done first is to analyse the IPR business model. This business model defines the environment where NewMARS will fit, the actors with which it will interact and the interaction rules. The business model we have considered is presented in subsection 2.1.

The NewMARS Project planning has been guided by the idea to make a knowledge guided development, from a computer point of view. This implies transferring a great amount of the development effort from the functional model to the domain knowledge model.

Consequently, the number of application functions is reduced to some basic ones in charge of message interchange among the application parts. A user actions diagram detailing actors and functions is detailed in subsection 2.2. Therefore, the focus is placed on the semantics of these messages.

As it has been introduced before, IPROnto is used as the basis of the knowledge model. Therefore, a great part of this effort has been already done and it is reused in NewMARS. There are only some small extensions to the knowledge model derived from the practical aspects of the project. More details about this are given in subsection 2.3.

2.1 Business Model

The e-commerce of IPR is guided by a business model that has emerged from the associated regulations framework, the commercial activity and the electronic means that have influenced it.

In order to build NewMARS upon a quite generic and flexible business model, the one defined as a result of the detailed work carried out in the IMPRIMATUR Project [11] has been the foundation. The NewMARS Business Model identifies a set of basic roles and interactions among them. These basic roles of the IPR activity are shown in Fig. 1. They constitute the value chain.

In parallel, some support services have been also identified. They constitute the basic services that facilitate the IPR e-commerce activity. They are shown in Fig. 1 around the roles to which they give support along the whole value chain.

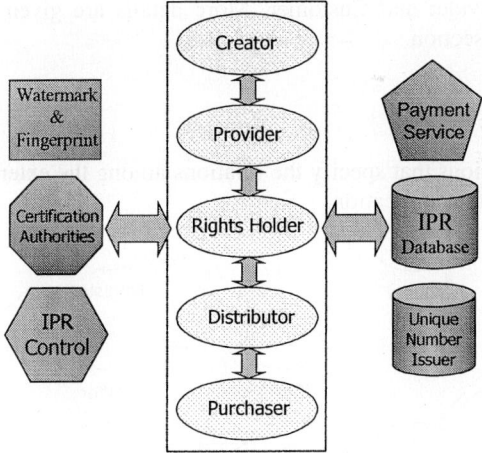

Fig. 1. Generic IPR Business Model

To facilitate the implementation of this model, it has been combined with a broker-based e-commerce model that has been extensively tested in previous research [12,13,14]. The final broker-based business model implemented in NewMARS is shown in Fig. 2.

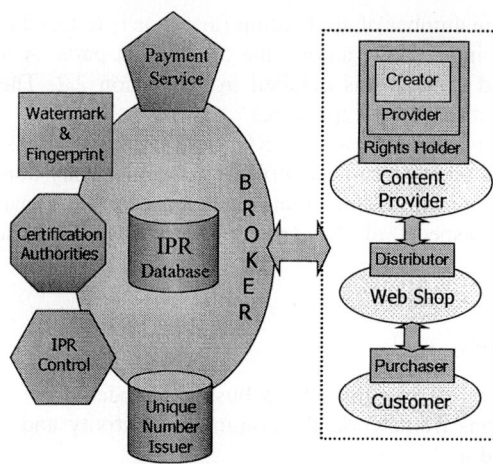

Fig. 2. NewMARS Broker-based IPR Business Model

The broker facilitates value chain actors access to the IPR e-commerce services. Moreover, in the NewMARS scenario, actors have been simplified to three, each one playing one or more roles: Content Provider (it can play Creator, Provider and Rights Holder roles), Web Shop (it plays Distributor role) and Customer (it plays Purchaser role).

In addition to the broker, the NewMARS project is also going to implement the Distributor role through a web shop. Consequently, there will be only two external actors: Content Provider and Customer. More details are given in the user actions analysis in the next section.

2.2 User Actions Analysis

Fig. 3 shows the actions that specify the relations among the external actors that have been identified and the application.

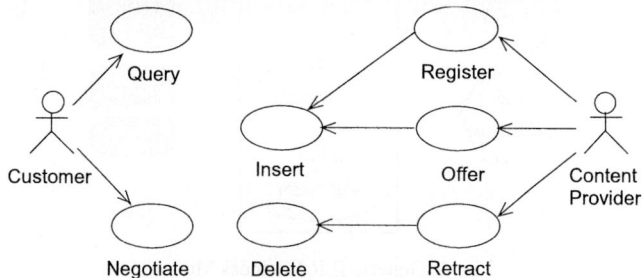

Fig. 3. User actions diagram

The user actions are detailed below:
- **Insert**: this is an "internal" action that is not directly accessible to external actors. Its functionality is accessed from other actions. Basically, what this action does is to store information about a resource into the NewMARS system. Due to the

knowledge-oriented approach this action can be viewed as the assertion making one.
- **Delete**: it is also "internal" but it is the counterpart of the previous action. It is responsible for un-asserting facts.
- **Register**: content providers use this to add new information about the intellectual properties (IPs) they manage. The information chunks are sets of assertions describing the IPs and their rights situation.
- **Offer**: this action is accessed by the Content Provider to add e-commerce information about an IP.
- **Retract**: content providers can delete information chunks about IPs they have previously inserted in NewMARS. This includes descriptive, rights and e-commerce information.
- **Query**: customers can use this action to look for desired IPs. The queries submitted by the customer are matched against descriptive, rights and e-commerce information stored in NewMARS. In return, the customer receives all the registries associated to the resources that have matched the criteria.
- **Negotiate**: once e-commerce information has been retrieved, if it does not completely satisfy the customer it can be negotiated. When a satisfactory offer is achieved the customer can accept it, then it is fulfilled.

2.3 Metadata

The IPs information that is managed by NewMARS is modelled as metadata associated to resources. There is also a set of ontologies that provide the required semantics. As it has been introduced before, IPROnto is used as the foundation for rights and e-commerce metadata.

However, descriptive metadata depends on the particular IPs that are managed. Due to project requirements, NewMARS was planned considering digital multimedia content. Therefore, ontologies about descriptive metadata for this kind of content where considered.

The MPEG-7 standard [15] was taken as the source for the descriptive ontology due to its coverage and relevance. First of all, an RDF Schema modelling MPEG-7 characterisation of multimedia content types [16] was reused. However, it only covered a small part of MPEG-7. Then, it was complemented with a 350 genres ontology generated automatically from some MPEG-7 multimedia description schemes [17].

The previous descriptive ontologies provide a quite satisfactory framework for multimedia content description. Finally, the multimedia specific aspects are complemented with the generic ones provided by Dublin Core [18]. An example of RDF metadata description is shown in Table 1.

Another key element about metadata in NewMARS is that it is expected to come from many different sources, i.e. metadata stores. Therefore, it is required that the metadata management processes implemented support this feature. However, from the outside, the users should experience an integral view of metadata so the metadata must be merged transparently.

Table 1. IP metadata example including descriptive, rights and e-commerce information

```
<!DOCTYPE rdf:RDF [...
    <!ENTITY mp7 'http://metadata.net/harmony/MPEG7/MPEG7.rdfs#'>
    <!ENTITY mp7g http://dmag.upf.edu/ontologies/2003/03/MPEG7Genres.rdfs#'>
    <!ENTITY ipr 'http://dmag.upf.edu/ontologies/2003/12/ipronto.owl#'>
    <!ENTITY cur 'http://www.daml.ecs.soton.ac.uk/ont/currency.daml#'>
    <!ENTITY nms 'http://dmag.upf.edu/ontologies/2003/05/NewMARS.rdfs#'>
]>
<rdf:RDF xmlns:rdf="&rdf;" xmlns:rdfs="&rdfs;" xmlns:dc="&dc;" xmlns:mp7="&mp7;"
xmlns:mp7g="&mp7g;" xmlns:ipr="&ipr;" xmlns:cur="&cur;" xmlns:nms="&nms;">
<mp7:Video rdf:about="urn:newmars:30m-USAP">
    <rdf:type rdf:resource="&mp7g;Documentary"/>
    <dc:title xml:lang="ca">També més que un club</dc:title>
    <dc:description xml:lang="es">Seguimiento de...</dc:description>
    <dc:language>ca</dc:language>
    <dc:date rdf:datatype="&xsd;date">1999-05-16</dc:date>
    <dc:format>video/mpeg</dc:format>
    <dc:creator><rdf:Bag>
        <rdf:li>Guardia, Carles</rdf:li><rdf:li>Pou, Francesc</rdf:li>
    </rdf:Bag></dc:creator>
    <dc:publisher rdf:resource="http://www.tvcatalunya.com"/>
</mp7:Video>
<ipr:Offer rdf:about="http://dmag.upf.es/newmars/offer19990611-103520">
    <ipr:offerer>NewMARSSeller@dmag.upf.es:1099/JADE</ipr:offerer>
    <ipr:time rdf:datatype="&xsd;date">1999-06-11</ipr:time>
    <ipr:patient>
        <ipr:PurchaseLicense>
            <ipr:licenser rdf:resource="http://www.tvcatalunya.com"/>
            <ipr:permission><ipr:Access>
                <ipr:place rdf:resource="http://www.tvcatalunya.com/online/30m-USAP"/>
                <ipr:patient rdf:resource="urn:newmars:30m-USAP"/>
                <ipr:timeFrom rdf:datatype="&xsd;date">1999-07-01</ipr:timeFrom>
                <ipr:timeTo rdf:datatype="&xsd;date">2004-07-01</ipr:timeTo>
            </ipr:Access></ipr:permission>
            <ipr:obligation><ipr:Compensation>
                <ipr:payee rdf:resource="http://www.tvcatalunya.com"/>
                <ipr:input>
                    <ipr:CurrencyMeasure rdf:value="1">
                        <nms:currencyUnit rdf:resource="&cur;EUR"/>
                    </ipr:CurrencyMeasure>
                </ipr:input>
            </ipr:Compensation></ipr:obligation>
        </ipr:PurchaseLicense></ipr:patient>
</ipr:Offer></rdf:RDF>
```

In order to implement this feature, the best option is to use RDF metadata through all the NewMARS information flows. Therefore, NewMARS receives RDF metadata as input, manages it and also produces RDF metadata as output. When RDF metadata coming from different sources must be combined, the RDF graph model facilitates metadata integration that is reduced to a process of graph merging. Once integrated, the metadata graph can be serialized and sent to the output. More details about how this is implemented are shown in section 3.1.3.

3 Development

Once the application domain has been introduced, this section details how the application has been developed. The driving force has been knowledge orientation. This has been materialised by prioritising application modules decoupling and basing module interrelation in shared semantics.

Web technologies, and more concretely Semantic Web tools, have been chosen as the more appropriate ones considering these requirements. First of all the following technological choices have been realised:

- Message transport: SOAP [19].
- Message encoding: RDF [20].
- Message semantics: ACL [21].
- Ontology language: OWL [22].
- User interface: HTML.
- Negotiation: JADE+JESS [23,24].

From the combination of requirements, design principles and technological choices, the architecture shown in Fig. 4 has emerged.

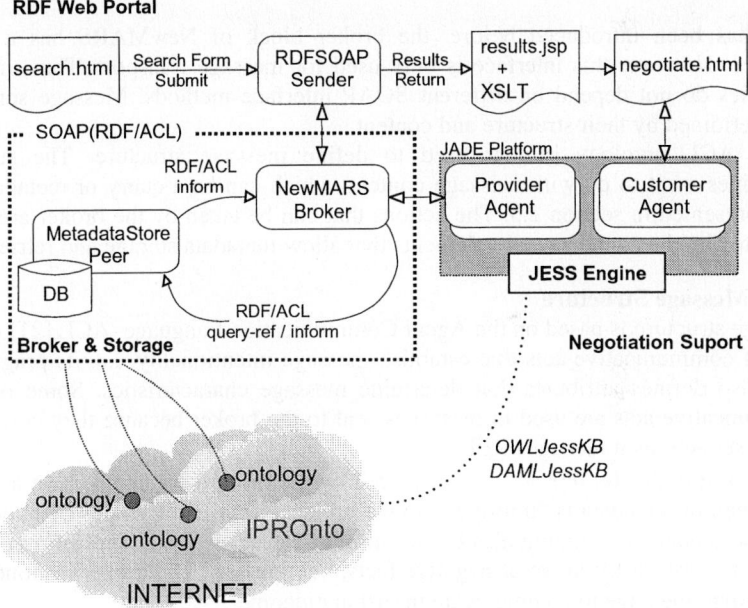

Fig. 4. NewMARS architecture

The architecture defines three main blocks:
1. **Broker and Storage**: this block is in charge of the main NewMARS responsibilities, i.e. all actions apart from "Negotiate". The broker offers a SOAP interface through which it interchanges SOAP messages. These messages are encoded using RDF and then structured using a web ontology that models FIPA ACL (Agent Communication Language) in order to provide message semantics. Message semantics define which messages are queries, facts assertions or facts removals. In each case, independent metadata stores are accessed for metadata retrieval, insertion or deletion. More details in section 3.1.

2. **Web Portal**: this block is the front-end that interacts with external users. The objective of this block is to provide an easy and common user interface, so HTML has been selected. In order to interact with the broker the RDFSOAPSender has been developed. First, RDFSOAPSender facilitates sending messages to the broker: it encapsulates HTML forms submissions as RDF/ACL messages and sends them using SOAP to the broker. Second, it manages messages responses: it processes the return messages in order to transform their RDF content to HTML that can be shown to the user. This block is detailed in section 3.2.
3. **Negotiation Support**: this block is responsible of giving service to the "Negotiate" action. The objective is to offer automatic or semiautomatic negotiation support to users. Agents' technology is used to perform this. We have chosen JADE as the multi-agent platform because it provides agent technology building-blocks and implements FIPA standards. Agents' decision support is managed by the JESS expert system. More details are given in section 3.1.3.

3.1 Broker and Storage

As it has been introduced before, the broker block of NewMARS has a SOAP interface. However this interface is only used for message transport. Thus, message semantics do not depend on different SOAP interface methods. Message semantics are determined by their structure and content.

The ACL ontology [25] is used to define message structure. The structure determines what to do with message content, which can be a query or metadata like those presented in section 2.3. The actions that can be taken by the broker are at last supported by the metadata store elements that allow metadata storage and retrieval.

3.1.1 Message Structure

Message structure is based on the Agent Communication Language. ACL [21] defines a set of communicative acts that establish message intentionality, i.e. its pragmatics. ACL also defines attributes that determine message characteristics. Some of these communicative acts are used in messages sent to the broker because they correspond to the user actions it manages:REF

- **Insert and Delete**: this action is captured by the **inform** communicative act when a chunk of metadata is "informed" to the broker. When a reference (URI) pointing to the metadata is communicated the **inform-ref** act is used. The **inform** can be used to assert affirmative or negative facts, i.e. unassert. The broker responds with a **inform** message to communicate insertion outcome.
- **Query**: this action corresponds to the **query-ref** act. It is a query by reference, where the reference is the pattern encoded by the query sentence. There are many RDF query languages so the language attribute is used to tell the broker which one is used. The broker responds to the query with an **inform** message.

The message semantics defined by ACL are used by the broker to route them to the appropriate metadata store peer as detailed next. The appropriate store is determined by the broker, for instance by considering the message language attribute.

3.1.2 Metadata Storage

The different broker actions end up with an access to the metadata storage system. As it has been shown in the architecture, it has been separated from the broker in different independent modules. Communication between the broker and the selected metadata storage peer is also performed by means of ACL structured messages.

The message communicative act tells the store peer how it has to interpret it. The content of inform messages is inserted or deleted and query-ref messages content is interpreted as query sentences.

The store peer is supported by a RDF store that is in charge of really storing the metadata or retrieving the stored metadata corresponding to the pattern determined by the query sentence. The store peers make the broker and all the application independent from the particular RDF store used. Therefore, they show the same behaviour. They receive RDF metadata as input of Insert and Delete actions.

MetadataStore Peers are not only responsible for making the NewMARS system independent from the different metadata store particularities. Moreover, they are also responsible for converting metadata query results from the common table-like result sets to RDF metadata as it is detailed next.

3.1.3 Metadata Retrieval

As has been shown in the previous section, the Broker receives RDF metadata as input. This is a common behaviour of RDF stores so, in this case, little work has to be done.

On the other hand, as it has been stated during the application domain analysis, it is also very interesting to get RDF metadata as output from RDF stores so the whole information flow is done in RDF form. This has been justified as it facilitates the integration of metadata coming from different sources.

Moreover, if the web portal receiving the output from the NewMARS broker gets RDF metadata instead of table-like result sets, more information would be available in order to render this metadata to the user. In other words, the stored metadata semantics would not be lost in the query output and would arrive intact until the last information processing step.

In this case there is some work to do as producing RDF metadata as query output is a very uncommon behaviour of RDF metadata stores. Query sentences are augmented by the NewMARS Broker with a special construct "graph(*sentence, depth*)". When this construct is sent to a store peer, it indicates that the store peer has to construct one or more RDF graphs from the resources selected with the query sentence.

This is done by retrieving RDF triples from the selected resource to the maximum depth specified. However, blank nodes are not considered when computing this depth; i.e. triples with blank node resources are always added if they are directly connected to selected resources or indirectly through a chain of blank resources.

For an example see Fig. 5. From a query that selects the resource "urn:newmars:30m-USAP", the graph construction algorithm is applied with depth equal to one. All the grey filled resources and literals and the solid line properties are retrieved. The Bag anonymous resource is ignored in order to compute depth so its members and its type are also retrieved. On the other hand, the metadata attached to the Video and Documentary types, the white filled resources and literals and the dotted line properties, are not retrieved as they are at a greater depth.

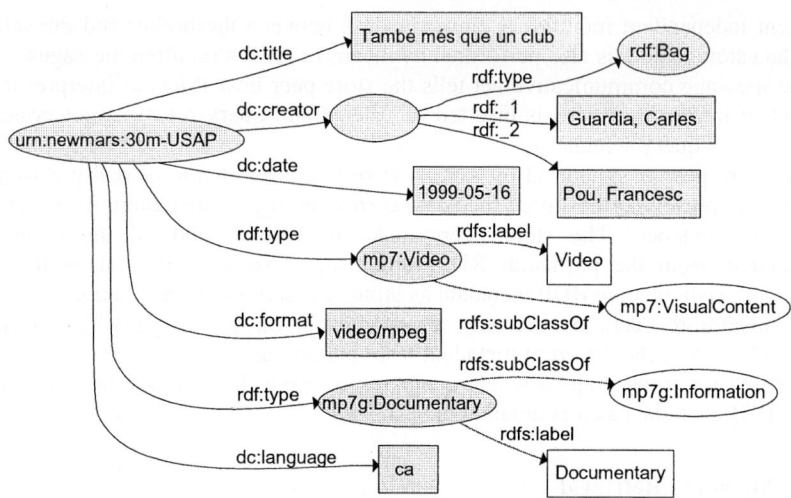

Fig. 5. Graph construction example for metadata retrieval

Once the query response graph or graphs have been constructed, they are serialised as RDF/XML and encapsulated in the response messages. They are structured as inform messages containing the response metadata.

As it has been shown in this and the previous section, store peers allow a great independence from the concrete RDF stores used. Currently two RDF stores have been integrated: RDF Suite [26] and Sesame [27].

3.2 Web Portal

The web portal has been developed as the user interface to the NewMARS functionality. The application has been developed based on the interchange of RDF messages with SOAP transport. Therefore, the portal must have a mechanism to encapsulate user interactions as RDF/ACL messages and send them to the broker by SOAP. Moreover, the responses to user interactions are made visible to the user by translating them to HTML. The web portal functionality is detailed in the next subsections.

3.2.1 RDFSOAPSender

This is the module responsible for the interaction between the portal and the broker. It is a servlet that receives user commands encoded as HTML form submissions. The form parameters are transformed into RDF triples, one for each parameter. All the triples have the same resource that identifies the current command. The properties are the parameter names and the resources their values.

The triples are serialised as RDFXML that is inserted into a new SOAP message in order to be sent, as shown in Table 2. The RDF content of the messages is built from the parameters received from the HTML forms through which the users interact with the system. Three basic forms can be identified: Query, Register/Offer and Retract.

Table 2. Example of SOAP envelope used to transport RDF/ACL messages

```
<SOAP-ENV:Envelope xmlns:... >
  <SOAP-ENV:Body>
    <rdf:RDF ... >...</rdf:RDF>
  </SOAP-ENV:Body>
</SOAP-ENV:Envelope>
```

3.2.2 Query Form

This form is composed by a set of fields relative to the attributes that finally will compose the RDF/ACL message that the RDFSOAPSender is going to generate. The available fields in the Query form are:

- **Sender**: the form web page URL or the identifier with which the user has identified himself in the web portal.
- **Receiver**: the broker URL where the SOAP message will be sent.
- **Reply-to**: the URL where the results will be sent in order to show them.
- **Content**: the query sentence.
- **Language**: the query language. Current RDF stores (RDF Suite and Sesame) use RQL. However, other possibilities can be easily incorporated.
- **Performative**: it indicates the message communicative act. For the query form it is fixed to the query-ref act.

Table 3 shows an example of RDF/ACL message built from a query form submission. It is an RQL query that retrieves metadata associated to offers that allow access to multimedia contents. The response is redirected to a web page that will format the output RDF metadata as HTML.

Table 3. Example RDF/ACL message built by RDFSOAPSender for a query form submission

```
<rdf:RDF  xmlns:acl="http://daml.umbc.edu/acldaml" ...>
<acl:query-ref>
    <acl:sender>http://dmag.upf.edu/newmars/search.html</acl:sender>
    <acl:receiver>http://dmag.upf.edu/newmars/broker</acl:receiver>
    <acl:language>RQL</acl:language>
    <acl:content parseType=Literal>
graph(select X,Y from {X;Offer}permission{;Access}.patient{Y;AudioVisual})
    </acl:content>
    <acl:reply-to>http://dmag.upf.edu/newmars/results.jsp</acl:reply-to>
</acl:query-ref>
```

3.2.3 Register/Offer Form

This form is used to tell the broker the IP descriptive, rights or e-commerce metadata to be inserted in the system. It is like the previous form. The only changes are performative, inform or inform-ref, and language that now is RDF/XML in order to reflex that the content is RDF metadata.

3.2.4 Metadata Web Rendering

The result web pages use XSL style sheets in order to transform the RDF metadata form response messages into HTML that can be shown by the web portal. There is a basic style sheet responsible for transforming each RDF description in the response metadata into an HTML table. Each row corresponds to one property directly associated to the description. The first column is the property id and the second column is the property value. If the value is another resource, a sub-table is recursively inserted and the whole table construction process is repeated.

This basic XSL style sheet is then combined with particular ones that complete HTML layout in order to particularise output to the special needs required. An example of complete HTML layout of a RDF encoded offer is shown in Fig. 6.

		http://dmag.upf.edu/newmars/offer19990611-103520		
type	Offer			
time	1999-06-11			
offerer	NewMARSSeller@dmag.upf.edu:1099/JADE			
patient	type	PurchaseLicense		
	permission	type	Access	
		timeFrom	1999-07-01	
		timeTo	2004-07-01	
		patient	urn:newmars:30m-USAP	
		place	http://www.tvcatalunya.com/online/30m-USAP	
	obligation	type	Compensation	
		input	type	CurrencyMeasure
			value	1
			currencyUnit	http://www.daml...uk/ont/currency.daml#EUR
		payee	http://www.tvcatalunya.com	
	licenser	http://www.tvcatalunya.com		

Fig. 6. HTML after the XSL transformation of the RDF-encoded Offer presented in Table 1

As has been shown in section 3.1.3, the metadata that is rendered is collected by building graphs from the selected resources to a given depth, commonly with depth one. In many cases this produces bunches of metadata with the relevant information for the posed query. However, sometimes it is necessary to get deeper in the graph and retrieve more metadata.

In order to facilitate metadata navigation, the XSL style sheet also produces HTML links for all the resource URLs. This links correspond to queries to the NewMARS broker for metadata about the clicked resource. Then, a pop-up window is opened showing the new metadata detail. The same XSL style sheet is applied to it so new HTML links are generated and they allow continuing the RDF metadata browsing experience through HTML. It can be tested on-line in the NewMARS web site [28].

3.3 Negotiation Support

Agents technology is used to perform negotiation. Negotiation is the last customer action. It is performed once the customer has located the desired content and the corresponding offer that is going to be negotiated. Offers can be directly accepted, rejected or negotiated.

We have chosen the JADE multiagent platform. In order to reason about facts coming from messages, JESS (Java Expert System Shell) [24] has been used because of its easy interoperability with JADE.

If the customer wants to negotiate the offer, he can choose a personal agent that will intermediate between the customer and the content provider agent. Customer and content provider agents are JADE agents controlled by the expert system. They negotiate the license offers.

The negotiation protocol is controlled by JESS and this allows a dynamic negotiation between the agents, making offers and counteroffers and processing licenses. There are two main phases in the negotiation that are only introduced in the next subsections. More details about the negotiation support are given in other publications from our group especially devoted to this issue [29,30].

3.3.1 First Phase

Once the customer has chosen his representative agent, it is created and all the necessary data is loaded in the expert system. The metadata that models the negotiated offer and its context is loaded together with all the ontologies that define the concepts used by the metadata.

As has been already shown, all is expressed in RDF and OWL. In order to operate with JESS, all the metadata and ontologies are imported using OWLJessKB [1]. After that, the negotiation protocol and policies are also loaded. They are modeled as a set of rules in JESS format, i.e. CLIPS.

The protocol rules govern the timing of the different negotiation phases. On the other hand, the policy rules support the decision process of the agent. For instance, buy or sell only when a condition about price or duration is achieved.

This is an important feature because it allows us to flexibly determine important contract parameters as duration, prices and so on. Thus, we get a dynamic negotiation mechanism because negotiation policies can be easily changed and configured.

3.3.2 Second Phase

In this phase the negotiation is finally carried out. The customer agent contacts the agent that is in charge of the offer negotiation. This is done using the information captured in the initial offer. There is the "offerer" property that identifies the corresponding agent using a JADE identifier, see Table 1.

The content provider agent that is responsible for negotiating the offer is the representative of the content provider that made the offer. It is ready to handle negotiations and pre-configured with the desired negotiation policy.

When it is contacted, it retrieves the negotiated offer from the NewMARS broker. It is loaded together with the received counteroffer and the required ontologies in the JESS engine that governs its behaviour.

The customer will then use the customer agent as the intermediary between him and the content provider agent. The customer agent can be more or less interactive, i.e. more or less autonomous. On the other hand, the content provider agent is totally autonomous and thus it takes decisions completely on its own, as specified in its negotiation policy.

The negotiation process goes on through the corresponding protocol as a series of offers and counteroffers. The final outcome can be an agreement if both parts agree on the offer conditions. These conditions will then constitute the license that is digitally signed by both parts. On the other hand, the negotiation process can fail if any part leaves the process.

4 Conclusions and Future Work

The main conclusion from the NewMARS development has been the great benefits that can be obtained from a knowledge oriented application. A high module independence based on the particular semantics has been achieved. This allows employing the same techniques for different domains by only adapting the conceptual framework, i.e. the ontologies that define the metadata structure.

For instance, in order to check NewMARS semantic capabilities, it has been also used with third party metadata. Concretely, it has been fed with RDF metadata from the MusicBrainz [2] project. This project has its own ontology for the music domain, i.e. album, track, artist,... The only effort necessary in order to make NewMARS manage resources annotated with MusicBrainz metadata has been to connect its ontology with the NewMARS ontological framework.

This has been easy thanks to the foundation of NewMARS ontological framework in IPROnto, a quite generic conceptualisation. Therefore, NewMARS can be easily configured to manage rights for any kind of intellectual property.

Our future plans include extending the NewMARS functionality in order to cope with a greater range of IP e-commerce scenarios. This can be reduced, thanks to the NewMARS knowledge oriented infrastructure, to ontologies modelling and negotiation policies definition. Moreover, NewMARS can deal with even more distant domains if the whole ontological support is properly adapted.

Finally, we are aligning NewMARS with MPEG-21 IPR management standardisation efforts. To achieve this, we are developing MPEG-21 compliant ontologies [3,4] that would allow NewMARS to manage standard IPR metadata.

Acknowledgements. NewMARS is part of the Agent Web project, partly supported by the Spanish administration TIC 2002-01336 (http://dmag.upf.edu/newmars). The final part of the work presented was developed within VISNET, a European Network of Excellence (http://www.visnet-noe.org), funded under the European Commission IST FP6 program.

References

1. Bormans, J. and Hill, K. (eds.): "MPEG-21 Overview". ISO/IEC JTC1/SC29/WG11/N5231, 2002
   http://www.chiariglione.org/mpeg/standards/mpeg-21/mpeg-21.htm
2. ISO/IEC FDIS 21000-5, MPEG-21 Rights Expression Language (REL), ISO/IEC JTC 1/SC 29/WG 11/N5839, July 2003
3. ISO/IEC FDIS 21000-6, MPEG-21 Rights Data Dictionary (RDD), ISO/IEC JTC 1/SC 29/WG 11/N5842, July 2003

4. Bray, T.; Paoli, J.; Sperberg-McQueen, C. M. and Maler, E. (eds.): "Extensible Markup Language (XML) 1.0 (Second Edition)". W3C Recommendation 6 October 2000 http://www.w3.org/TR/REC-xml
5. Iannella, R.: Open Digital Rights Language (ODRL) Version 1.1. W3C Note, 2002 http://www.w3.org/TR/odrl
6. Berners-Lee, T.; Hendler J. and Lassila O.: "The Semantic Web". Scientific American, May 2001, http://www.sciam.com/article.cfm?articleID=00048144-10D2-1C70-84A9809EC588EF21
7. Hendler, J. "Agents on the Semantic Web". IEEE Intelligent Systems, Vol. 16, No. 2, March-April 2001, http://www.ai.mit.edu/people/jimmylin/papers/Hendler01.pdf
8. Intellectual Property Rights ONTOlogy, http://dmag.upf.edu/ontologies/ipronto
9. Delgado, J.; Gallego, I.; Llorente, S. and García, R.: "Regulatory Ontologies: An Intellectual Property Rights approach". Workshop on Regulatory ontologies and the modeling of complaint regulations, WORM Core. LNCS, Vol. 2889, pp 621-634, 2003
10. Delgado, J.; Gallego, I.; Llorente, S. and García, R.: "IPROnto: An Ontology for Digital Rights Management". 16th Conference on Legal Knowledge and Information Systems, JURIX. Frontiers in Artificial Intelligence and Applications, Vol. 106, IOS Press, 2003
11. "The IMPRIMATUR Business Model, Version 2.1". IMPRIMATUR Project (Esprit 20676), WP4, 1999. http://www.imprimatur.net/IMP_FTP/BMv2.pdf
12. Gallego, I.; Delgado, J. and Acebron, J.J.: "Distributed models for brokerage on electronic commerce". In Trends in distributed systems for electronic commerce, 1998
13. Delgado, J., Gallego, I., Polo, J. "Electronic commerce of multimedia services", in MultiMedia Modeling, World Scientific Publishing, pp. 97-110, 1999
14. García, R.; Delgado, J.: "Brokerage of Intellectual Property Rights in the Semantic Web". 1st Semantic Web Working Symposium (SWWS-1), Stanford, CA, 2001
15. Martinez, J. "Overview of the MPEG-7 Standard". MPEG Document ISO/IEC JTC1/SC29/WG11 N4509, 2001 http://www.chiariglione.org/mpeg/standards/mpeg-7/mpeg-7.htm
16. Hunter, J. "An RDF Schema/DAML+OIL Representation of MPEG-7 Semantics". MPEG Document ISO/IEC JTC1/SC29/WG11 W7807, 2001
17. ISO/IEC 15938-5 FDIS Information Technology. "Multimedia Content Description Interface - Part 5: Multimedia Description Schemes". ISO/IEC JTC1/SC29/WG11 Document W4242, 2001
18. Hunter, J. "An Application Profile which combines Dublin Core and MPEG-7 Metadata Terms for Simple Video Description". Harmony Project Draft, 2002 http://metadata.net/harmony/video_appln_profile.html
19. Mitra, N. (ed.) "SOAP Version 1.2 Part 0: Primer". W3C Working Draft, W3C XML Protocol Working Group, 2002 http://www.w3.org/TR/soap12-part
20. Lassila, O. and Swick, R.R. (eds.): "Resource Description Framework (RDF)". Model and Syntax Specification. W3C Recommendation 22 February 1999 http://www.w3.org/TR/REC-rdf-syntax
21. "FIPA ACL Message Structure Specification". FIPA Agent Communication Language Specifications, Document Id. XC00061, 2002 http://www.fipa.org/specs/fipa00061
22. Dean, M. and Schreiber, G. (eds.): "OWL Web Ontology Language Reference". W3C Proposed Recommendation, Web Ontology Working Group, 2003 http://www.w3.org/TR/owl-ref
23. Bellifemine, F. ; Caire, G. ; Poggi, A.; Rimassa, G. : "JADE - A White Paper". Telecom Italia Lab, EXP Online, Vol. 3. n. 3, 2003 http://exp.telecomitalialab.com/upload/issues/v3n3.pdf
24. Friedman-Hill, E.: "Jess in Action: Rule-Based Systems in Java". Manning Publications Co., 2003
25. ACL DAML Ontology, http://www.cs.umbc.edu/~yzou1/daml/acl.daml
26. ICS-FORTH RDF Suite, http://www.ics.forth.gr/proj/isst/RDF

27. Sesame, http://www.openrdf.org
28. NewMARS Web Site, http://dmag.upf.edu/newmars
29. Gil, R.; García, R. and Delgado, J.: "Delivery context negotiated by mobile agents using CC/PP". Int. Conference on Mobile Agents for Telecommunication Applications, MATA'03. LNCS, Vol. 2881, pp 99-110. Springer-Verlarg, 2003
30. Delgado, J.; Gallego, I.; García, R.; Gil, R.: "An architecture for negotiation with mobile agents". Int. Conference on Mobile Agents for Telecommunication Applications, MATA'02. LNCS, Vol. 2521, pp 21-31. Springer-Verlarg, 2002
31. Kopena, J. and Regli, W.: "DAMLJessKB: A Tool for Reasoning with the Semantic Web". IEEE Intelligent Systems, Vol. 18, No. 3, pp. 74-77, 2003
32. MusicBrainz, http://www.musicbrainz.org
33. García, R.; Delgado, J.; Rodríguez, E.; Llorente, S. and Gallego, I.: "RDDOnto, Rights Data Dictionary Ontology Version 2". ISO/IECJTC1/SC29/WG11/M10423, 2003
34. Delgado, J.; Gallego, I.; García, R.: "Use of Semantic Tools for a Digital Rights Dictionary". Accepted in EC-WEB'04 conference. To be published in LNCS, 2004

Intelligent Retrieval of Digital Resources by Exploiting Their Semantic Context[*]

Gábor M. Surányi, Gábor Nagypál, and Andreas Schmidt

FZI Research Center for Information Technologies at the University of Karlsruhe
Haid-und-Neu-Str. 10–14
D-76131 Karlsruhe, Germany
{suranyi, nagypal, aschmidt}@fzi.de

Abstract. Although the first digital archives storing a huge number of resources came into existence years ago, they still lack effective retrieval methods. The most obvious example is the World Wide Web: search engines are improved constantly, however, their hits are still unsatisfactory apart from simplest queries. Most prosperous solutions employ user contexts to estimate the user's information demand and use this information to deliver more adequate results. In the current paper we introduce the idea of resource context-based information retrieval. In this approach, semantic context description is assigned to each digital resource known to the system and this semantic metadata are exploited by each step during an intelligent search process. Our solution is implemented and evaluated in the VICODI project, as part of a web portal for European history.

Keywords: Information retrieval, resource context, ontology, web-based information system

1 Introduction

It has always been the purpose of archives to make available collected resources to authorised users in order to fulfil their information need. Digital archives, leveraging on the benefit of digital content, additionally aim at

- storing more information and/or
- serving significantly more people and/or
- providing more efficient access to the resources.

Unfortunately, the former two goals turn out to be contradictory to the third one to some extent. On the one hand, with broadening the audience, not only domain experts, but also more casual users are beginning to access the archive. On the other hand, with increasing the volume of information, the scope of such archives purposefully widens into multiple disciplines. Both the users' lack

---

[*] This work was partially supported by the EU in the framework of the VICODI project (EU-IST-2001-37534).

of profound domain knowledge and the multidisciplinary character of digital archives make specialised search interfaces practically impossible. But general tools usually make it difficult to formulate precise (and thus selective) queries.

Additionally, efficient access from a user's perspective also includes the ease of query formulation. Instead of precise queries expressed via a powerful search interface, users usually prefer starting with simple queries, refining, modifying and discarding them in favour of alternatives in subsequent iterations. In many cases, a search result is only a starting point for exploring the archive along its organisation (e.g. taxonomy).

The mission of the Visual Contextualization of Digital Content (VICODI)[1] project in which 7 partners from 6 countries of the European Union co-operate is to enhance people's comprehension of digital content on the Internet. We achieve that goal by semi-automatically contextualising digital resources, i.e. by creating semantic metadata to put them in context. The purpose of semantic metadata is twofold: to facilitate the understanding of the resource's content, and to facilitate the retrieval of resources. With the help of the metadata the context of a resource can be visualised later, thus the users can better re-construct the context of the information, which raises it to the knowledge level. (We refer to the metaphor well known in knowledge management which states that knowledge is information in context.) In the perspective of the current paper it is more important, however, that resource contexts may also assist the users in information retrieval.

During the VICODI project we use the European history as the showcase domain and develop a web portal[2] which demonstrates the idea of setup and application of context of historical resources (articles, pictures, videos etc.) stored in our digital archive. Although the project's target users have solid knowledge of historical notions, terms etc., when specifying a search condition they do not really go into details, just like a naive user. It is therefore a challenging task to implement an easy-to-use and efficient information retrieval method with well-known technologies.

Our approach to the problem is to implement an *intelligent search process*. Its key ideas are as follows.

1. The digital archive should not leave the user alone when he explores resources starting from a list of search results, but it should rather accumulate information on his trail and offer better hits based on it at each step of the retrieval process.
2. When the user navigates from a resource to another in order to fulfil his information need, he automatically identifies himself with the resource context, i.e. he is interested in the target resource from the point of view of the current resource. Its context gives a better description of the user's information need than a user context established at the beginning of the search process.

---

[1] http://www.vicodi.org
[2] http://www.eurohistory.net

Based on these ideas, the users of VICODI follow the *context-aware browsing* workflow depicted in Fig. 1 during retrieval. Generally speaking, they obtain an initial resource from the archive (e.g. via the traditional full text search) or provide such a resource themselves. Queries which are inserted as links into the document by the system or presented next to the resource serve as primary means of expressing interest. If a link is selected, a copy of the context of the original document is altered to place an emphasis on the link's underlying unit of knowledge. The modified context is eventually used to search for potential link targets. This means that, based on an initial entry point to the document space, users can refine their search result based on a simple 'click on a link and pick the next document' workflow.

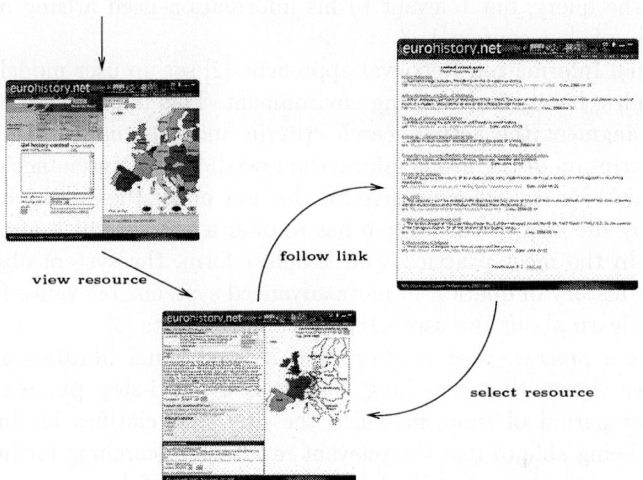

Fig. 1. User-system interaction in the intelligent search process in VICODI

In this paper we present this intelligent search process, which has been implemented and successfully evaluated in the VICODI project. We raise the overall description, however, to a more general level in the next section, as the solution can be applied to any digital archive. Section 3 gives an overview of the system architecture of VICODI and illustrates how it supports the efficient information retrieval from its archive. We describe the management of resource contexts including their creation and application in Section 4. Section 5 is about the evaluation of VICODI. Related work is summarised in Section 6. At the end of the paper, conclusion is drawn.

2 The Role of Context in the Search Process

2.1 Context and the Search Process

Context matters. It has become an important insight that the trade-off between ease of query formulation and high selectivity of queries can be overcome if the user's interaction with the system is not limited to the query-response paradigm. The user usually specifies only part of what characterises his information need. This corresponds to inter-human communication in which the communication partners also build upon a shared communication context. So in order to enrich the interaction, the system has to consider *implicit* assumptions of the user. But how can we capture these implicit assumptions, how can we capture the real-world situation in which the user issues queries and expect results not only relevant to the query, but relevant to his information need arising out of that situation (i.e. of that context[1])?

Traditional Information Retrieval approaches[2] set up user models with the user's attitudes, habits and working environment. This information can in turn be used to augment the actual search criteria and eventually to give a more detailed description of the user's information need. The maintenance of the user context is, however, rather expensive for the user or for the system as it has to be entered by the user or the system has to offer a service which automatically acquires it. In the most practical and simplest form, the system observes and analyzes the history of queries, in more advanced systems, relevance feedback is employed to learn about the user's relevance judgements [3].

Search is a process. User studies both in traditional libraries and digital archives have shown that searching usually is a multi-step process [3], often over a longer period of time, in which the user first clarifies his information need before being able to find the relevant results [4]. Searching for information can be most adequately described by the metaphor of *berry-picking*[5] or as *orienteering*[6]. In contrast to the view that there is a single relevant result, these process models emphasise that the user rather goes from here to there and collects bits of information from different sources which can be put together to satisfy the information need. This implies that

- searching in digital archives is predominantly exploratory, and
- there is a process context that interconnects individual query-response steps.

At this point, we have to consider a second question for context-aware information retrieval systems: how do we use the information about the user's context in order to improve the efficiency of retrieval from a digital archive? In general, there are two possible approaches: augmenting queries or providing navigational support. The first approach has been studied in various settings in Information Retrieval, also considering the multi-step anatomy of search[3]. The second approach is taken by adaptive hypermedia systems[7], especially by the technique of link adaptation. Information Retrieval methods are usually biased towards descriptive searches, whereas adaptive hypermedia approaches usually assume that hyperlink structures are modelled explicitly and the system adapt the selection and order of links to the individual user.

On the one hand, in VICODI we assume that resources can be added to a digital archive independently, so there is no uniform hyperlink structure from which we can deduce possible links. On the other hand, we did not want to restrict ourselves to descriptive queries, as this does not reflect the way digital archives are supposed to be used. So we have combined the two approaches by presenting navigational elements, which generate user context-aware queries to the archive once activated, along with digital resources. The primary source of the query context is the resource currently viewed by the user. For instance, if the user has just read an article about *World War I* and requests more information about *Serbia*, then we can assume that he is not interested in the *Kosovo conflict*, but in information about Serbia at the beginning of the 20th century.

2.2 Anatomy of Resource Contexts

It must be realised that the notion of context has eluded philosophers and computer scientists alike, and thus, it would be unrealistic to propose a 'solution' through a research or a technology project. However, the work to date is sufficient to experiment with smaller subsets of these theories. Work in computational semantics in the early 90s has led to systems that allow the specification of contexts with features [8]. Wurman's LATCH (Location, Alphabetic order, Time, Category and Hierarchy) properties[9] were used in identifying structural mechanisms for storage, retrieval, presentation and navigation.

More recently, the notions of context and contextualisation have become very fashionable in web-based information systems. Typically, the term 'context' is here used to describe formal models for expressing the whereabouts of users (mobile and ubiquitous computing), the users' goals and interests (adaptive hypermedia and personalised information systems) and semantic indices for resources and knowledge spaces (semantic web technologies). So in general we can roughly resolve the status quo of the term context into 'user models, user profiles and semantic indices'.

For context representation we have chosen a pragmatic approach which follows the semantic indices view of context and we based our context definition on [10]. Our contexts are basically sets of weighted elements from a suitable set of domain concepts. Because time plays an important role in history, we also represent time in contexts.[3] A possible (partial) context of a document describing the causes and consequences of the *Russian revolution* could be the following:

$$\{\langle Lenin, 1.0\rangle, \langle 1919\text{-}1924, 1.0\rangle, \langle Russia, 0.8\rangle, \langle Russian\ revolution, 1.0\rangle\}$$

where *Lenin*, *Russia* and *Russian revolution* are historical concepts, 1919-1924 is a temporal interval and the second element of the pairs is the relevancy weight. More formally, our VICODI resource context consists of two sets defining the *conceptual part* and the *temporal part*. The conceptual part is a set of weighted ontology elements, the temporal part is a set of weighted time intervals. We use

---
[3] But time specifications are time intervals and not ontology instances for technical reasons.

float weights between 0.0 and 1.0, and time has year granularity. For visualisation purposes the part of the context which specifies the L, T and C components of the LATCH approach mentioned above is particularly interesting for us. We term that part of the context *LATCH context*.

2.3 Resource Context Operations

Three operations on resource contexts are identifiable in a digital archive supporting the intelligent search process.

Context generation: Resource contexts have to be established. Clearly, in archives storing more than a few resources the application of an automated method is a must.

Dynamic generation of navigational elements: Based on the resource context, navigational elements have to be displayed along with each resource. Their function is to initiate context-based queries when the user activates them.

Context-based search: After a navigational element is activated, all resources which have a context relevant to the current one should be returned.

Obviously, the first and the third operations must be aware of domain knowledge. For instance, considering history, whenever a location is mentioned all its parts are also referred to. This background knowledge can be represented as an ontology, i.e. the set of its elements is the domain of the elements of the conceptual part of resource contexts and there can be relationships defined between the ontology elements.

The way in which concepts and properties among them are modelled in the historical ontology of VICODI is depicted in Fig. 2. The root of the concept hierarchy is `VicodiOI`. The name stands for VICODI ontology instance. Any instance is either a temporal interval called `Time` or a `Time Dependent`. Instances of `Time Dependent` may have an existence time modelled by the `exists` property. There are four other special properties, two of which together with instances of the `PartRelation` concept describe part-container relationship between instances of `Locations`. The other two properties are `hasRole` and `playedAt`, which designate where a `Flavour` instance plays its `Role`. Most historical concepts are instances of subconcepts of `Flavour`, such as `Events`, `Individuals` and `Organisations`. Any instance may be `related` to any number of other instances and it denotes a general relationship between them, for example between two `Individuals` or `Events`, or between `Events` and its participants.

Although in this paper we concentrate on the problems of context-based search, we briefly discuss the issues concerning the other two operations as well.

3 The VICODI System

3.1 System Architecture

The system architecture comprises the following components.

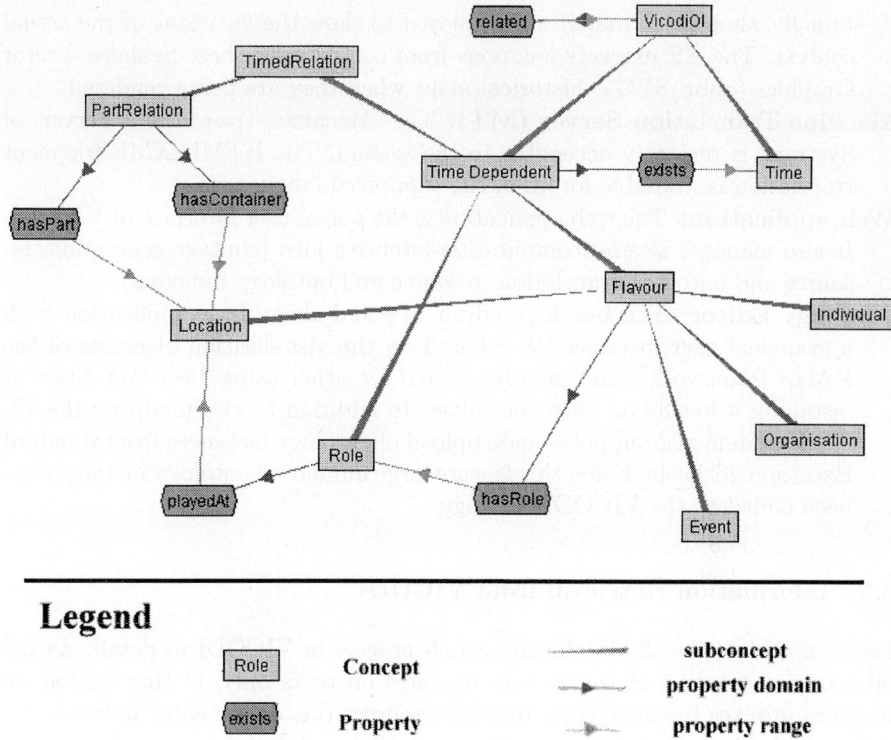

Fig. 2. Concepts and properties in the ontology of VICODI

Management System of Knowledge Space (MSKS): This component consists of three subcomponents: Ontology, Resource and Search. The interface of the Ontology module hides the details of the underlying open-source KAON framework[11], which manages the VICODI ontology stored in a database. The Resource module provides access to the resources stored in the repository and their metadata including their context information. The Search module provides two types of search: context-based search and ordinary full text search. The context-based search heavily relies on the CE component described next.

Contextualisation Engine (CE): This component is made up of the client CE Engine (JCE) and the remote Computational CE server (CCE). One task of the CE module is to automatically generate context data of resources newly submitted to the system. Another function of this module is to support the context search by providing various methods to calculate pairwise context similarity.

Transformation Engine (TE): The Transformation Engine implements the core of the text transformation functions for visualisation purposes. Additionally, choropleth maps[4] are employed to show the locations of the actual context. The TE extracts locations from contexts for these Scalable Vector Graphics (abbr. SVG)[5] historical maps when they are being rendered.

Machine Translation Server (MT): The Machine Translation Server of Systran[6] is remotely accessible to the system. The HTML/XML fragment translation is available for all of the supported languages.

Web application: The web application is the portal user interface of VICODI. It also manages several computation-intensive jobs (context generation, resource and ontology translation, resource and ontology indexing).

Ontology Editor: The ontology editor is stand-alone Java application with a graphical user interface. It is based on the visualisation elements of the KAON framework[7], and may be started by either using Java Web Start or installing it locally on client machines. In addition to visual editing the VICODI system also supports mass upload of ontology instances from standard Excel spreadsheets. Using this feature large number of ontology instances has been added to the VICODI ontology.

3.2 Information Retrieval from VICODI

Let us now describe the intelligent search process in VICODI in detail. As the pilot implementation of the archive operates on texts only, in this section we restrict ourselves to considering textual resources (i.e. documents, articles).

At the beginning, the user specifies the initial context by pasting the text (or the URL) of a document found on the Internet or wrote himself. By recognising certain parameters (keywords, years, names etc.), the system generates an appropriate context for the whole article. Context generation makes use of the already contextualised resources stored in the VICODI document repository and the ontology encoding domain (in our case: historical) knowledge. Alternatively the user can specify the initial LATCH context visually by selecting a time period and clicking on category icons, and countries on the map (cf. Fig. 3). If he chooses this way to enter the system, he is provided with a list of already stored and relevant resources to that LATCH context. Power users can also construct an arbitrary context by browsing the ontology and adding specific elements to the context.

Now we assume that the user submits a document and receives its contextualised version. Then the screen looks similar to the one depicted in Fig. 4. On the left side, elements of the resource context which have been found in the document text are displayed as hyperlinks. A separate hyperlink list of context elements which do not occur in the text is also presented. On the right side of the web page a map is shown. Countries which are part of the context are painted

---

[4] http://www.personal.psu.edu/faculty/c/a/cab38/GEOG321/05_choro02/choro1_02.html
[5] http://www.w3.org/Graphics/SVG/
[6] http://www.systransoft.com/Technology/WhitePapers.html
[7] http://kaon.semanticweb.org

in red in the map. The brightness of the colour increases with the weight of the location in the document context.

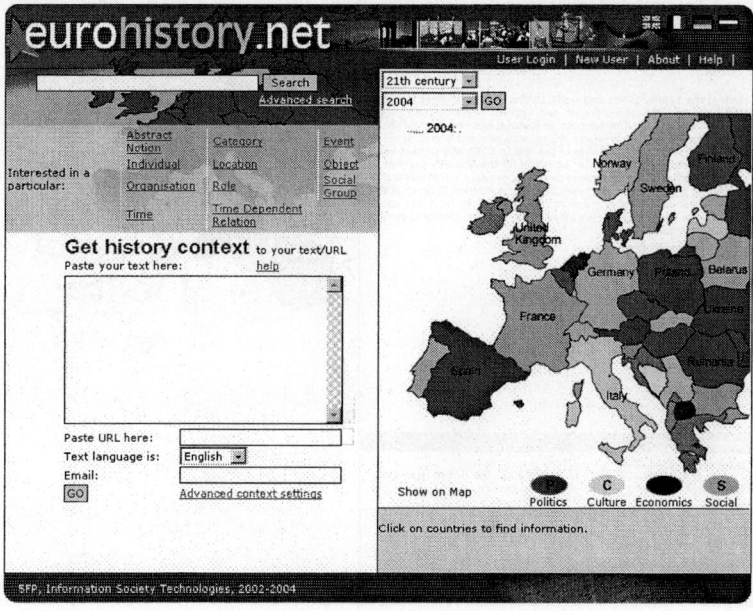

Fig. 3. The initial screen of the VICODI portal

If the user selects a hyperlink of a domain concept, a new context-based query will be initiated. All elements of the conceptual part of current document's context go into the new query context, however their weight is lowered except for the selected domain concept, which is emphasised. The currently selected temporal interval, i.e. the year 1805 forms the temporal part of the query context. An advanced search interface is also provided. It operates on the actual context, which originally equals to the context of the current resource, i.e. *The Battle of Trafalgar*. Having clicked on Set different context, the user can freely modify the actual context by adding or removing time intervals, ontology concepts and instances. Moreover, time- and location-based queries can be initiated in an intuitive way by using the map on the right side.

Alternatively, if the user realises that the current document is of no interest concerning his information need, he can use his browser's back button to return to the previous web page, to the previous step in the search process.

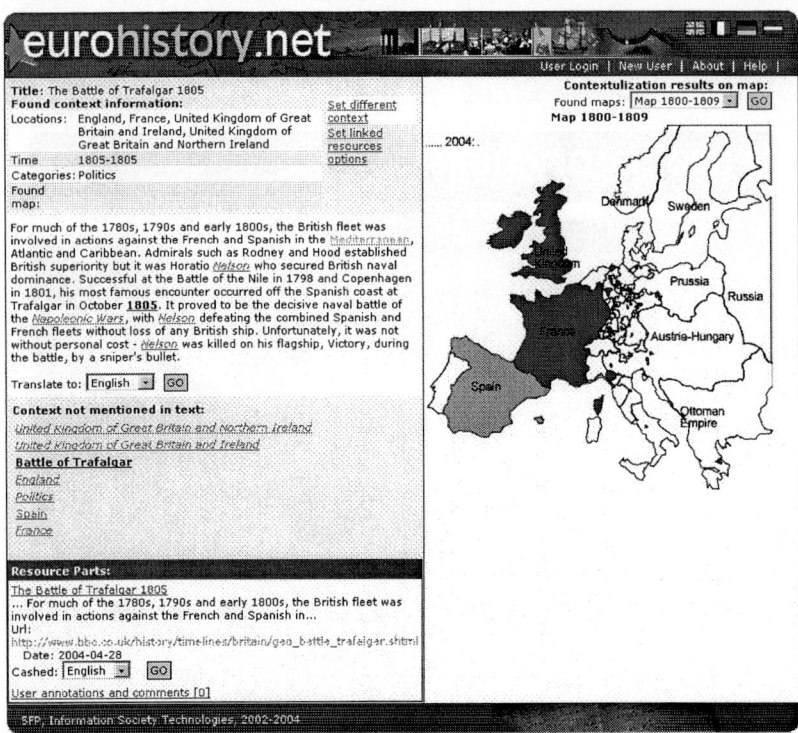

Fig. 4. The web page of VICODI with a document and its visualised context

4 Resource Contexts and Queries

4.1 Resource Context Generation

Context generation is semi-automated in VICODI, i.e. for textual resources the CE can establish a resource context by examining the document. Of course, these resource contexts can be later manually fine adjusted.

Automated context generation may seem trivial in the case of textual resources since the document context can be estimated by ontology entities found in the text (e.g. matching the string **Lenin** with the ontology instance labelled *V. I. Lenin* by means of named entity recognition). Although it is a good starting point, it does usually not suffice to get high quality results. Firstly, there can be matched ontology elements which are negligible parts of the document context. For instance, a document describing the political background of the medieval crusades cites a present-day politician. This politician may be defined in the ontology but should be excluded from *this* context. Secondly, there can be ontology entities which are part of the context but are not mentioned explicitly in the document. For example, a newspaper article on the *Kosovo conflict* probably does not mention this event explicitly. Consequently, the context and the set of ontology elements quoted in the text differ in general.

Thirdly, natural languages are inherently ambiguous, which makes label matching in a document a non-trivial task. For instance, the string **the king** refers to *Elvis* in a document on Rock'n'Roll and to *King Richard, the Lionheart* in a text on the crusades. And lastly, not only context elements but their significance (their weight in the context) are important as well. Basically, it can be simply estimated by the occurrence numbers but there can be significant context elements which do not occur in the text at all.

The technique applied by the CE to generate the conceptual part of the initial document context is based on a weighted 1-to-N classification method[12]. It represents the documents as bags of words and makes use of the cross-correlation values of calculated by the classifier from the training data (i.e. annotated class relevance values).[8] This enables the CE to identify domain concepts explicitly not mentioned in the document text and also turns out to be useful to resolve ambiguous domain concept matches.

It is much easier to generate the temporal part of the document context. The CE simply looks for dates and temporal intervals in the text. Then compares them to the existence times of the elements included in the conceptual part. Several adequate comparison operators are conceivable, see e.g. [13] for an overview. Whenever the CE recognises a constructive 'interference' between the sets of dates, a large weight is assigned to it, otherwise it gets a low weight. Destructive 'interferences' are quite frequent because most documents contain a date of publication or similar. It would not be correct, however, to treat them as significant parts of the document context.

4.2 Presenting Navigational Elements

Navigational elements are, as outlined in Section 2, the key components of the user interface in the intelligent search process. They correspond to elements of both the conceptual and the temporal part of the current resource context and initiate the next context-based query in the digital archive.

VICODI organises the navigational elements in two groups. The first group resides in the textual representation of the resource (if exists) and highlights all the domain concepts which occur in the text. It is based on the generated context of the resource text, when each mentioned domain concept is recognised. Then the weight and the actual position(s) of each context element in the text are passed to the TE (Transformation Engine), which constructs the hyperlinked version of the document. The transformed text is stored in the archive for caching purposes so that it does not have to be re-generated each time the document is displayed. The original text and its URL (if any) are also archived and displayed upon request so that copyright is not infringed.

The other group of navigational elements lists all elements of the conceptual part of the resource context which are not mentioned in the resource text. These elements as well as elements of the first group are all rendered according to their

---

[8] Further details on the CE algorithms will be published separately because of their complexity and space limits of this paper.

weight in the current resource context, i.e. absolute relevance is indicated by a bold font, strong by an italic one and slight by underlining.

4.3 Searching for Relevant Contexts

Although a resource context captures well what the resource is about, the selection of relevant contexts to a query context is a challenging task because a simple syntactical comparison does not suffice. For example, if we look for resources on *Trocki*'s role in the *Russian revolution*, a resource on *Lenin* and *Russia* may contain some relevant information. As a consequence, a sophisticated method which also takes into account the semantics of context elements has to be employed and such a method requires one-by-one processing of resource contexts. The temporal part of different contexts does not impose such problems as they are comparable with minor difficulties (see e.g. [13] for modelling issues).

The semantic comparison of the conceptual part of two contexts is straightforward if several important points in the space of domain concepts are identified by means of a clustering algorithm in advance. This is possible as the background knowledge is provided as an ontology. Then the relative position of the conceptual part of the context to these points can be determined and the distance between the contexts can be calculated. This is what exactly the CE does.

Despite the facts that this method runs quickly and scales well (its complexity is linear in terms of the size of the contexts), it has to be repeated for millions of resources in huge archives and it would therefore deliver the most relevant contexts in several minutes, which is simply unacceptable. Consequently, we must significantly reduce the number of resource contexts to which the query context is compared in each query. This step is called *filtering* and executed as a part of each query processing. Clearly, it cannot rely on similarity results, but it should yet exhibit good precision and recall characteristics. That is it should not filter out any potentially interesting contexts but it should remove any non-interesting resources hence reducing the size of the candidate context set.

Our filtering method is based on the insight that the elements of a context of a relevant resource must lie close to the elements of the query context. We thus *extend* the conceptual part of the query context to the ontology elements which are semantically close to it based on the temporal part of the query context. Which concepts are considered semantically close highly depends on the properties in the ontology since one may indicate stronger connection than the other. Figure 5 depicts the steps of query processing and their interaction.

To justify why properties have to be distinguished during query extension consider for example a location. Referring to this location, usually all its parts are also referred to (as already pointed out in Section 2.3) but not necessarily a role which is played at that location. Locations also explain why the query context is extended each time for filtering and not the resource contexts only once. The temporal part of the query context is not known when resource contexts are created, and it is a necessary condition for resource contexts in order to be returned in the result set of a query that they contain the same *geographical*

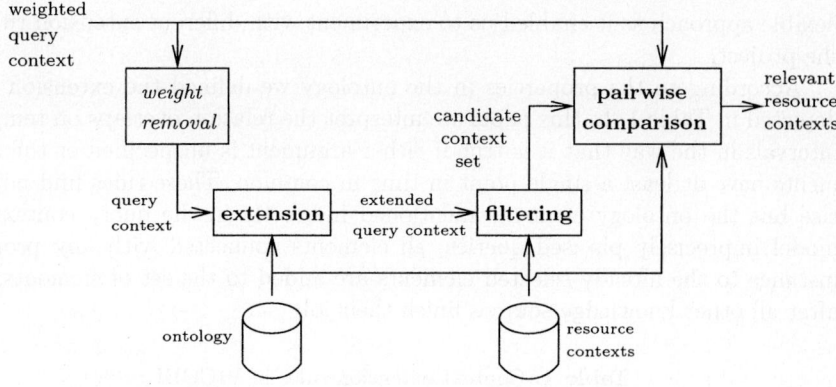

Fig. 5. Finding relevant resource contexts to a query context

location as the query context but at the time specified in the query. Location entities corresponding to given location entities at a given time can be retrieved by following the time-annotated container-part property instances in the presence of the target time period, i.e. the temporal part of the query context.

The task of query extension is carried out by a blackboard system[14,15] in VICODI. In this blackboard architecture, which is depicted in Fig. 6, the blackboard stores the actual extended query context, and is initialised with the original query context received from the user interface. Then each knowledge source is responsible for ensuring that the blackboard is closed under its own extension rule. They accomplish their task by continuously examining the blackboard's content and adding further entities to it if required. We have no separate control shell, i.e. the extension phase completes as soon as the blackboard is found closed under the extension rules by all the knowledge sources. The finiteness of ontology guarantees the termination of the loop.

Fig. 6. Blackboard architecture for query context extension in VICODI

Query extension is a highly data-driven and complex task, as the inclusion of an entity may imply further entities' inclusion in the extended query. However, the use of a blackboard system for this purpose successfully decouples the functionality from the data. It means that only the knowledge sources have to be replaced in order to implement filtering for other application domains. Moreover, if properties change in the VICODI ontology, only the 'data', i.e. the extension rules within the knowledge sources have to be modified accordingly. It is also a flexible approach as it enabled us to experiment with different extension rules in the project.

According to the properties in the ontology we defined the extension rules depicted in Table 1. In this paper we interpret the relation *overlaps* on temporal intervals in the way that it is true if either argument is unspecified or the arguments have at least a single point in time in common. These rules find nothing else but the ontology elements mentioned indirectly in the query context. To model imprecisely phrased queries, all elements connected with *any* property instance to the already selected elements are added to the set of elements, too, after all other knowledge sources finish their job.

Table 1. Context extension rules in VICODI

NAME OF RULE	DESCRIPTION
related	includes all instances of Time Dependent which are related to another Time Dependent instance contained in the blackboard and whose existence time overlaps the temporal part of the query context
hasRole	includes all instances of Role which is played by any Flavour instance contained in the blackboard if the existence time of the Role instance overlaps the temporal part of the query context, also includes all instances of Flavour which have a Role instance contained in the blackboard and whose existence time overlaps the temporal part of the query context
Location–Location	includes all parts and containers of all locations contained in the blackboard if existence time of the PartRelation instance overlaps the temporal part of the query context
playedAt	includes all instances of Role which are playedAt a Location contained in the blackboard if the existence time of the Role instance overlaps the temporal part of the query context, also includes all instances of Location where any Role contained in the blackboard is played and whose existence time overlaps the temporal part of the query context

The actual output of the filtering phase contains only the resource contexts whose conceptual part contains at least one element of the extended set of domain concepts *and* whose temporal part overlaps the temporal part of the query context.

The goal of filtering is to speed up the query evaluation process by reducing the number of resource contexts to be checked so that the user gets the results within a reasonable time frame. The question naturally arises: does this blackboard architecture, which realises a more complex algorithm than the original context comparison method, meet this requirement?

Indeed, filtering is relatively slow. Instead of calculating the extended query context, thousands pairs of contexts could be compared by the CE with the same effort. It should be noted, however, that in contrast to the pairwise context comparison the complexity of filtering does not depend on the number of resources in the archive, which makes it beneficial to use in huge digital archives.

In the current configuration of VICODI, with approximately 5000 historical concepts and 10000 property instances filtering runs within 20 seconds even for the most complex queries and usually $\frac{1}{10}$ of the resource contexts are eventually compared to the query context one by one during query processing. The latter ratio is not notably good but in the current, pilot implementation documents focus on certain episodes of the European history. When the whole historical timeline is covered in a more uniform manner, a better ratio is expected.

5 User Evaluation

Although VICODI prototype portal is still under development, the system was recently tested by a group of history lecturers. Since the project is not yet finished the user testing and evaluation is still in its first phase, which is meant to tease out the design flaws of the portal interface, the ontology, contextualisation and retrieval systems. A second evaluation phase will take place right before the end of the project.

To test the site scenario-based evaluation techniques were used. We modified Erskine et al.'s approach to scenario-based design[16] for this purpose. On the contrary to the original approach, we not only tested the design but also the functions of the portal including the value of the content as well as the ontology.

The user evaluation process started by identifying classes of intended users: students and educators, historians and other professionals, interested public. We chose Education as our evaluation domain, because we had contact with that user group during the project.

After a guided walk-through of the design elements (artefacts), functions and tools including the contextualisation process, information retrieval and the ontology, all the testers were given the same scenario consisting of a series of tasks and they were ask to complete an evaluation form during solving the tasks. These tasks included a series of operations intended to simulate the use of primary sources for seminar/tutorial based group teaching as well as research for essays. The lecturers were asked to retrieve certain documents and consider the contextualisation results. During retrieval they had to use all of the navigation aids described in Section 3.2. In addition testers were asked to put certain texts into the system, contextualise them and judge the results.

The initial response of the evaluators was that the strong visual aspect greatly aids in data presentation and that the maps are a tremendous asset. All testers agreed that maps provide a positive reinforcement tool for teaching purposes. The combination of maps and chronology offers a new way of searching that is potentially pedagogically useful. Most testers found that the highlighted (contextualised) links would encourage students to explore wider contexts, to use more documents and that it would make visible how historical resources relate to each other. This was in fact regarded as the most significant feature of the VICODI system. It can be concluded therefore that user evaluation showed the value of our visual contextualisation approach.

There were also some critical notes during the evaluation, however. Most of them were concerned with the quality and coverage of documents which were added to the system at the time of the evaluation. Our evaluators who had a strong historical background found both average document quality and historical coverage not adequate from a historical point of view. It is not a surprise, however, as the goal of the project is not to develop a full-fledged history portal, but to demonstrate the feasibility of the approach. The prototype portal will be available publicly, however, even after the project end, and therefore it has also the potential to evolve into a comprehensive history portal, as a side effect of our work.

Perhaps the only serious criticism over the context-centric resource management itself referred to the speed of the context generation and search processes. Our users felt that in the digital age it is a significant flaw not getting real-time results. This criticism shows that significant improvements have to be yet made in the speed of context generation and search processes without sacrificing the quality of automatic context estimation and retrieval. This task is subject to future research.

As a conclusion it can be said that while users found the idea of visual contextualisation and context-based search interesting and useful, a high quality resource archive is needed to fully exploit the potential of this new technology.

6 Related Work

As stated in Section 2, retrieval system of VICODI is basically the combination of the adaptive hypermedia approaches with a predefined hyperlink structure and descriptive querying approaches in Information Retrieval.

The incorporation of implicit query conditions has a long tradition in Information Retrieval. The initial efforts concentrated on previous queries and/or relevance feedback of the user. This allowed the system for constructing a user model, which was in turn used for query augmentation. The last years show a clear evolution in the direction of context-awareness. However, all of them rely on external monitoring of the user. This can yield much more powerful contextual capabilities, but usually constitutes a considerable barrier for casual users. Furthermore, all approaches requiring to store information about the user over a longer period of time raise privacy issues, i.e. the user must be aware of the information stored about him and the system must guarantee the protection of this data.

In adaptive hypermedia, most approaches also require explicit user models, which the user has to provide by specifying his interests in some way. There are several approaches trying to determine the context automatically, like electronic tourist guides[17] taking location as a context information. Another approach described in [18] takes the page referrer as a source for narrowing down the context of the user. Because VICODI exploits domain knowledge (in contrast to other adaptive hypermedia systems), appropriate navigation targets can be deduced from the resource content alone.

There are already several systems available, which follow similar goals as our system. Sites following the Wiki idea[9] also generate hyperlinks in new documents automatically, allowing an easier navigation within the document space. There, however, links are generated on a purely syntactic base, and only 1-to-1 connection is possible. Other systems, like HyperNietzsche[19], SRFG LATCH-Browser[10] or COHSE[20] also have a notion of context, which is, however, specified in those systems only manually. Finally, information extraction applications – most of them are based on the open-source GATE framework[21] – try to achieve what we do in the context generation step. They mostly work only on the syntactical level, although some of them (like the Armadillo system[22], which employs ontologies to infer relevant locations) begin to realise the advantages of using semantic information during this process. Novel information extraction algorithms can be integrated into our system in the future to improve the quality of the automatically generated context estimation.

7 Conclusion

Making retrieval from digital archives efficient for users continues to be a challenging problem, gaining importance with the increase in the volume of available information and the scope of the audience. The traditional query-response paradigm has proven inadequate because it neglects the predominant exploratory search tactics of users and the fact that searching is a learning process. Awareness of the usage context has become the most promising approach to support the user by incorporating information about his situation as implicit assumptions into the interaction with the system. However, acquiring such context information is very difficult.

In this paper, we have presented the VICODI approach, which allows for context-aware browsing through the archive content. To each resource in the archive is automatically assigned a resource context, consisting of temporal information and entities from a domain ontology. When the user views a certain resource, its context becomes part of the user's context. The system generates navigational elements for entities or time periods, which represent context-dependent queries to the archive. These queries themselves are constructed as modifications of the resource context. Traditional retrieval methods have been replaced by more sophisticated context matching algorithms exploiting the semantics expressed in the domain ontology. The required context similarity calculation is, however, computationally rather expensive. In order to retain scalability and short response times, we have presented a filtering framework, which implements query extension heuristics based on semantical relationships in the ontology.

---

[9] e.g. http://en.wikipedia.org/wiki/History
[10] http://suntrec.salzburgresearch.at/projects/LATCHBrowser/

Evaluation sessions with end users in the domain of European history have shown that – despite the limited amount of documents in the prototypical archive – the VICODI approach is considered to provide valuable help for exploring digital archives.

The VICODI approach is domain-neutral. Required domain knowledge and query extension rules can be easily plugged in so that it is open to other application domains. We are currently exploring the potential of VICODI in the e-learning domain, and we plan to integrate this approach with context-aware support of learning processes (like [23]). This would enhance self-steered learning capabilities and also increase the learning efficiency by making suggested learning material more relevant to learners. By combining the resource context-based approach of VICODI with personalization techniques, this can be supported even better.

Acknowledgements. We would like to thank Bob Mulrenin and Tobias Berka at Salzburg Research, who provided invaluable help in describing the CE component. We would also like to thank Jan Oosthoek at the University of Newcastle and Richard Deswarte at University of East Anglia, who provided material on user evaluation.

References

1. Dey, A.: Understanding and using context. Personal and Ubiqutous Computing Journal **1** (2001) 4–7
2. Baeza-Yates, R., Ribeiro-Neto, B.: Modern Information Retrieval. Addison-Wesley (1999)
3. Rolker, C., Kramer, R.: Quality of service transferred to information retrieval: The adaptive information retrieval system. In: Proceedings of the 1999 International Conference on Information and Knowledge Management, ACM (1999) 399–404
4. Kuhlthau, C.: Seeking Meaning: A Process Approach to Library and Information Services. Ablex Publishing (1993)
5. Bates, M.: The design of browsing and berrypicking techniques for the on-line search interface. Online Review **13** (1989) 407–431
6. O'Day, V., Jeffries, R.: Orienteering in an information landscape: How information seekers get from here to there. In: INTERCHI 93, Amsterdam, The Netherlands (1993)
7. Brusilovsky, P.: Adaptive hypermedia. User Modeling and User Adapted Interaction **11** (2001) 87–110
8. Tin, E., Akman, V.: Situations and computation: An overview of recent research. In Griffith, J., Hinrichs, E.W., Nakazawa, T., eds.: Proceedings of Topics in Constraint Grammar Formalism for Computational Linguistics: Papers Presented at the Workshop on Grammar Formalisms for Natural Language Processing held at ESSLLI-94, Copenhagen, Denmark (1995) 77–106
9. Wurman, R.S., Sume, D., Leifer, L.: Information Anxiety 2. Que (2000)
10. Jurišica, I.: How to retrieve relevant information? In Greiner, R., ed.: Proceedings of the AAAI Fall Symposium Series on Relevance, New Orleans, Louisiana (1994) 101–104

11. Motik, B., Maedche, A., Volz, R.: A conceptual modeling approach for semantics-driven enterprise applications. In Meersman, R., Tari, Z., eds.: CoopIS/DOA/ODBASE. Volume 2519 of Lecture Notes in Computer Science., Springer (2002) 1082–1099
12. Mladenic, D.: Text-learning and related intelligent agents. IEEE Expert Special Issue on Applications of Intelligent Information Retrieval (1999)
13. Nagypál, G., Motik, B.: A fuzzy model for representing uncertain, subjective, and vague temporal knowledge in ontologies. In Meersman, R., Tari, Z., Schmidt, D.C., eds.: CoopIS/DOA/ODBASE. Volume 2888 of Lecture Notes in Computer Science., Springer (2003) 906–923
14. Craig, I.: Blackboard Systems. Ablex Publishing Corporation, Norwood, New Jersey (1995)
15. Corkill, D.D.: Collaborating software: Blackboard and multi-agent systems & the future. In: Proceedings of the International Lisp Conference, New York, New York (2003)
16. Erskine, L.E., Carter-Tod, D.R.N., Burton, J.K.: Dialogical techniques for the design of web sites. International Journal of Human-Computer Studies **47** (1997) 169–195
17. Cheverst, K., Mitchell, K., Davies, N.: The role of adaptive hypermedia in a context-aware tourist guide. Communications of the ACM **45** (2002) 47–51
18. Kushmerick, N., McKee, J., Toolan, F.: Towards zero-input personalization: Referrer-based page prediction. In: International Conference on Adaptive Hypermedia (AH '00). (2000)
19. D'Iorio, P.: HyperNietzsche. Presses Universitaire de France (2000)
20. Bechhofer, S., Goble, C., Carr, L., Kampa, S.: COHSE: Semantic web gives a better deal for the whole web. Poster presentation at ISWC International Semantic Web Conference (2002)
21. Bontcheva, K., D.Maynard, Tablan, V., Cunningham, H.: GATE: A unicode-based infrastructure supporting multilingual information extraction. In: Workshop on Information Extraction for Slavonic and other Central and Eastern European Languages. (2003)
22. Fabio Ciravegna, Alexiei Dingli, D.G., Wilks, Y.: Integrating information to bootstrap information extraction from web sites. In: Workshop on Information Integration on the Web, 18th International Joint Conference on Artificial Intelligence (IJCAI 2003). (2003)
23. Schmidt, A.: Context-steered learning: The learning in process approach. In: IEEE International Conference on Advanced Learning Technologies (ICALT '04), Joensuu, Finland (2004)

The Chrysostom Knowledge Base: An Ontology of Historical Interactions

Dan Corbett[1] and Wendy Mayer[2]

[1] Intelligent Systems Laboratory
School of Computer and Information Science
University of South Australia
Adelaide, South Australia 5095
[2] Centre for Early Christian Studies
Australian Catholic University
Brisbane, Queensland
Australia

Abstract. The semantics of order-sorted type hierarchies are fundamental both to the retrieval of knowledge from large real-world-size knowledge bases and to the next generation of web technology. The Chrysostom web knowledge-base project provides an interesting case for furthering this research. An attempt to model the social world of the late Roman Empire, this knowledge base rests upon an ontology which uses the knowledge found in a very large body of documents associated with the cities of Antioch in ancient Syria and Constantinople (modern Istanbul) in the fourth and fifth centuries. We describe the knowledge base and its use, as well as the ontology that was created (and continues to develop) to support it.

Keywords: Knowledge retrieval, ontology, knowledge servers

1 Introduction

With the large amount of information (and knowledge) available through the Internet, users are starting to look for effective ways to filter through the information, to find only the information relevant to their work. Instead of using the web to provide documents and raw data, users will instead use a knowledge server to filter and combine the retrieved knowledge to the user's specific purposes.

It has been widely acknowledged that the semantics of order-sorted type hierarchies are fundamental both to the retrieval of knowledge from large real-world-size knowledge bases and to the next generation of web technology [1-3]. The Chrysostom web knowledge-base project provides an interesting case for furthering this research.

The Chrysostom project is an attempt to model the social world of the late Roman Empire. The underlying ontology captures the knowledge found in a very large body of documents associated with the cities of Antioch in ancient Syria and Constantinople (modern Istanbul) in the fourth and fifth centuries. The initial idea behind the Chrysostom Knowledge Base (CKB) was to capture all of the speeches of the fourth-century orator and bishop John Chrysostom in one, easily accessible location.

The point of capturing the knowledge found in the speeches is that they contain a wealth of information about everyday life. Capturing this information in a knowledge base is a significant first step in creating a model of fourth-century society, and also helps to make that information more accessible.

2 Background

Until now, scholars have dipped into these orations selectively, getting bits and pieces of unrelated information. Our research shows that a user can get a distorted picture when not looking across the entire corpus [4]. Hence, the need for an ontology was twofold: to try to enforce responsible use of the data on scholars, and to provide a uniform framework for the knowledge contained in the speeches.

The Chrysostom knowledge base which runs on top of this ontology makes it possible to search and get every single instance of a piece of knowledge. But because the search is not directly expressed as keywords (due to the nature of the rhetoric, use of broad categories, allusions, etc) the user needs more than the standard keyword search mechanism.

The intent of the project which implements this knowledge base is to extract all information about how society functioned in fourth-century Near-Eastern Helenic cultures. The breadth and variety of the coverage of topics common to the everyday lives of the people of these regions makes this knowledge an extremely valuable resource for researchers of social history.

The original design called for phrases and passages from Chrysostom's speeches to be placed into categories which would then be keyword searchable in an online database. The designers of the CKB soon discovered problems with this design. For example, a historian may want to look for competing uses of public spaces. In a keyword search, this would involve a combination of searches including marketplace, street system, religious building, civic building, plaza, parade, ceremony, and so on. Even then, many concepts would be lost to the user. It is necessary to give the user the ability to find the combination of these *concepts*, not merely a conjunction of the keywords. Furthermore, the commonality among all of these concepts may not have been specifically implemented by the database designer, which would necessitate the creation of new intersections of concepts in the knowledge base.

Similarly, ideas and concepts may not be directly represented literally in the database. The user may want to find all mention of beggars and begging, for example, but must also search topics related to poverty and homelessness. Concepts may not be directly searchable. For example, the keywords of „psychology", „superstitious behavior" and „value systems" are all unsearchable in the raw database, but all of these concepts appear in the form of other words or phrases.

As the process of design always forces the designers to re-examine what they want and what they can do, developing the CKB has shaped what the users and designers want to do with it. The original intent was to capture the ideas contained in Chrysostom's orations, but they found that what they really wanted was to make something that was concept-based, and not just data-based.

The intent was to make all of the speeches (more than 1,000 of them exist in text form) available to any web user. The texts already exist in an accessible form, thanks to the Thesaurus Lingua Graeca Project (TLG), which has been working for more than two decades to put Greek speeches into an electronic form. This combination of concepts and raw text would make a highly useful database of fourth-century life in these cultures. The database was to contains all of the concepts expressed in the speeches, and they would be searchable and indexable. Since the database is so large, including many concepts, many types and categories, and many text passages, our problem was to discover how to best handle the size and complexity of this knowledge base?

Therefore, the aims of the Chrysostom Knowledge Base are:

To capture every piece of information which might have relevance to daily life
To index that knowledge so that it enables semantic as well as keyword searches
To direct the user from the search results to the original text in the TLG
To make the knowledge base available as widely as possible via the web

In this paper, we will show portions of the Chrysostom knowledge base, to demonstrate the size and complexity of the ontology. We will then show how lattice techniques have already improved the performance and accessibility of the knowledge base. We conclude with discussion on how our techniques will further improve this knowledge base, and how the techniques developed for this project will benefit knowledge representation, knowledge retrieval and the semantic web.

3 The Chrysostom Knowledge Base

3.1 Ontology and Knowledge Base

An ontology, in the Knowledge Engineering and Artificial Intelligence sense, is a framework for the domain knowledge of an intelligent system. An ontology structures the knowledge, and acts as a container for the knowledge. We base our formal definition of ontology on the Conceptual Graph (CG) Theory definition of canon, as defined in [5, 6] and others.

A canon in the sense discussed here is the set of all CGs which are well-formed, and meaningful in their domain. A complete discussion and formalization of CG concepts can be found in [6] and [7], but briefly, canonical formation rules specify how ontologies can be legally built and guarantee that the resulting graphs satisfy „sensibility constraints," called the Canonical Basis. The canonical basis is a set of rules in the domain which specifies how the relations can be legally used, for example that the concept *eats* must have a theme which is *food*.

A type hierarchy can then be established for both the concepts and the relations within a canon. A type hierarchy is based on the intuition that some types subsume other types. For example, every instance of *cat* would also have all the properties of *mammal*. This hierarchy is expressed by a subsumption or generalization order on types. Since not all types are comparable in this way, the hierarchy represents a partial order. We now depart from general discussions of ontology and knowledge systems in order to discuss our knowledge base. While we choose to describe the implemented system in this paper, the interested reader can find discussions of the formalization of some of these ideas in our previous work [8].

3.2 An Ontology of Historical Interactions

Given the stated goal of creating a knowledge base of fourth century society, the obvious direction to take was first to define an ontology of the domain, including terminology, relations and concept types. The historical researchers on our team then „filled in" the ontology with the passages from Chrysostom's orations (translated into English) by attaching short passages to the concepts that represent them. Thus, the ontology is populated by the text-based data to create the Chrysostom Knowledge Base. The work of completing the knowledge base continues, as more than a thousand of Chrysostom's works exist, but the knowledge base is implemented and functioning.

The ontology represents the interactions among the concepts in the domain. That is, not just interactions between people, or business transactions, but interactions between, for example, travel and shipping, sea and ship, tools and agriculture, etc. Figure 1 shows a portion of the Chrysostom ontology, including the top of the hierarchy and some of the highest-level types. When complete, the CKB will contain about 65,000 individual text entries spread among more than 1,500 types. At its deepest paths, there are nine layers of subsumption between the top and bottom elements.

It can be seen in Fig. 1 that the highest level types express very broad categories of the things that Chrysostom discusses in his orations. It is possible for any type to have a specialization in common with any other type (this is called a „join" in the terminology of concept type hierarchies). For example, the concept „travel" has a join with the concept of „the sea", which is „shipping". The concepts of „plants," „tools," and „occupation" are joined at the concept of „farmer" and „farming."

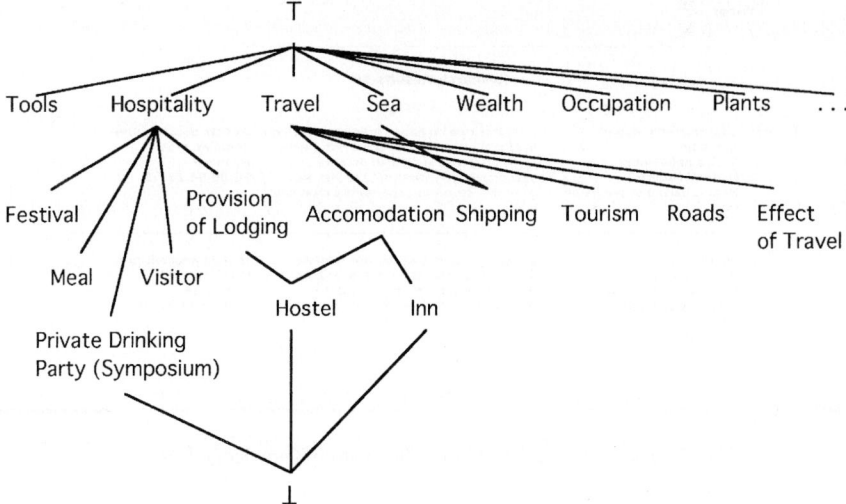

Fig. 1. A portion of the Chrysostom ontology.

4 Examples

4.1 Search on Concrete Concepts

The user interface is implemented as a web-based interface, and there are several ways in which a user can interact with the knowledge base. In our first example, the user is looking for any mention of lodgings for travelers. This user decides to start by entering „hospitality" as a search query. The CKB will respond by showing the subsumed types under hospitality (which is a high-level type). The subsumed types include *festival, meal, visitor* and *provision of lodging*, as shown in Fig. 1. The user interface showing these results is shown in Fig. 2. Our user follows the hierarchy to *provision of lodging* to find two categories, which are two different types of hostels. However, the user can see from the texts mentioned that these words refer to hostels set up for the poor, or for political refugees. The user sees that *hostel* is a join between *provision of lodging* and *accommodation*, and decides to explore *accommodation* as a promising category. *Accommodation* subsumes two types, *hostel* and *inn*, and it is this latter category that contains the texts that the user is looking for.

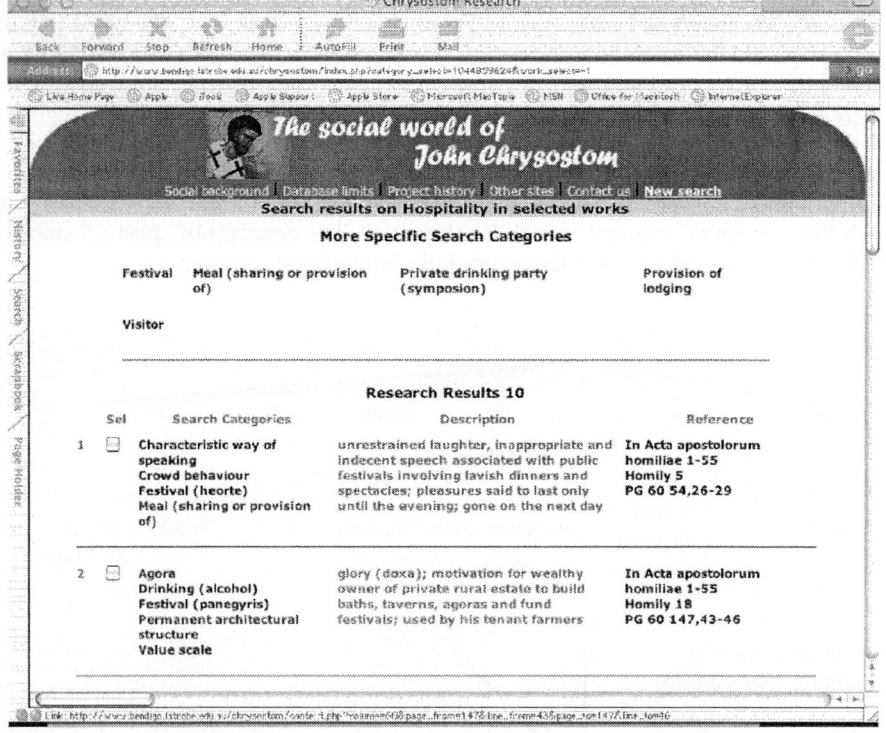

Fig. 2. The user interface to the Chrysostom Knowledge Base.

Another example is illustrated by the partial CKB hierarchy shown in Fig. 3. (Note that in order to save space, we leave out most of the lattice, such as the explicit top and bottom and other concepts related to the concepts shown here.) Here, our user is interested in finding out about shipping in the ancient world. She searches on the term „shipping" and finds, not surprisingly, that the concept of *shipping* is a join formed between the concepts of *Travel* and *The Sea*. Further, the user finds that there are several categories under shipping that may be of interest, including *personal travel, ship/boat, shipwreck, shipping personnel* and *shipping of goods*. The user navigates through *shipping of goods*, and finds that *trading* also subsumes *shipping of goods*. She then finds text passages of interest under the categories of *import* and *export*.

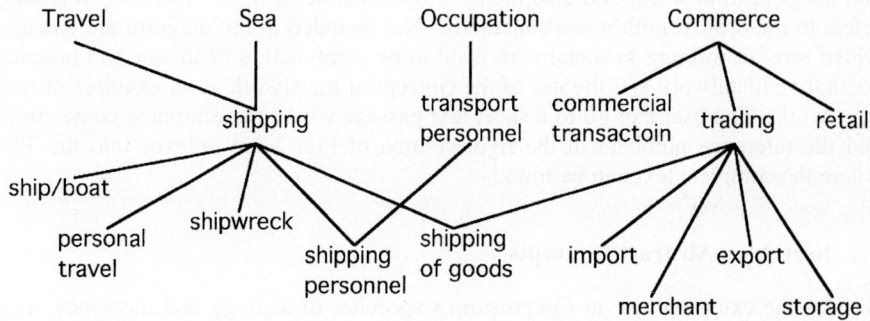

Fig. 3. A portion of the Chrysostom ontology showing shipping and commerce.

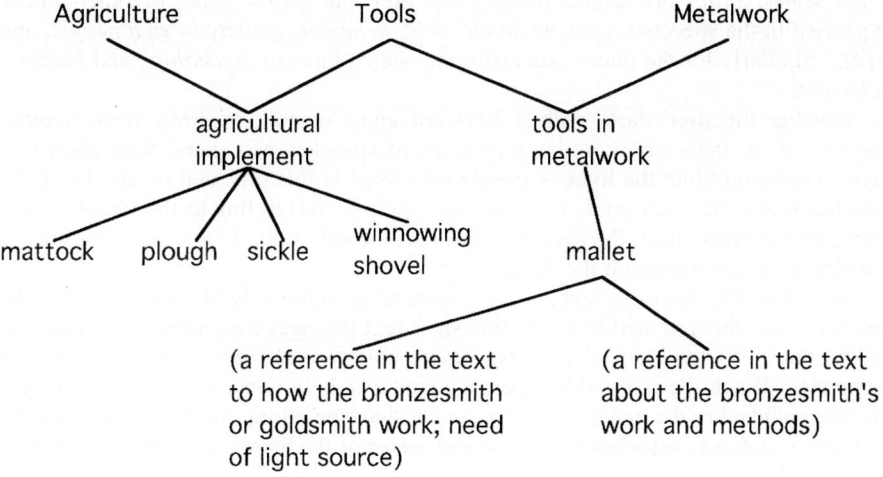

Fig. 4. Another portion of the Chrysostom ontology showing tools.

At any given point in a search, not only is the text that is associated with that concept available, but also the user can click on any of the categories of that text. For example, under *shipwreck*, the user can click on *disaster, captain, crew* or *doctor*.

Here, the user did not ask for the join of *disaster* and *personnel* to get *captain*, but the concept of *captain* existed there already, as a join of other concepts. This linking of implied joins (that the user was not searching for) allows greater search and expression of the query.

As a further example, a user is interested in reading about the work methods or environment of the bronzesmith. The user may enter the query as „bronzesmith," „metalwork," or even „mallet." As shown in Fig. 4, these queries will yield results which discuss the work practices of metalworkers.

Fig. 4 also includes brief summaries of some of the result passages discovered here, showing that in one case the passage is a reference to how both the bronzesmith and the goldsmith work, and also the need for a source of light. The second passage refers to the bronzesmith's work methods. Not included in the diagram are passages which refer to training in metalwork (said to be combination of theory and practice) decorative metalwork and the use of the concept of metalwork as an example of truly hard work. The user can go to a short text passage where the reference comes from, and the reference numbers in the right column of Fig. 2 are indexes into the TLG where the complete text can be found.

4.2 Search on Abstract Concepts

Besides the extensive use in Chrysostom's speeches of analogy and metaphor, users will want to be able to search on abstract concepts. As mentioned earlier, the user can now search for psychology, values, superstitious behavior and other abstract notions. For example, the query „value" will yield many passages associated with values and value scales. From this point, though, the user can follow links to other values expressed in the speeches, such as *honor, debt, behavior, activity of rich people*, and so on. Similarly for the query „superstition," which links to *psychology* and *habitual behavior*.

Whether the user starts with a keyword entry or follows links from another concept, all of these concepts have portions of speeches associated with them that give some insight into the lives of people who lived in this time and place. Once the user has found the appropriate concept type, she only has to link to the Greek text to read a short section from the speech. Note that the entire text is not available online, but can be obtained through the TLG.

Note also, that there are text passages associated with nearly all of the types in the ontology. So, the user will not only find short text passages associated with mallet or sickle, but also with *agricultural implement, commercial transaction,* or *transport personnel*. When the original text passage contains these concepts as a general idea, the text is linked to the general concept, rather than something more specific. So, the text data is not only associated with the leaf nodes of the hierarchy, but with nodes at every level.

5 Lattice Operators

One major result of our previous work in Knowledge Representation and Reasoning has been a unification tool for conceptual graphs [8, 9]. The knowledge and information in the knowledge base can be described in conceptual graphs, and the conceptual graphs tools of type hierarchies, subsumption and unification can be exploited to index the knowledge. We have demonstrated the use of type hierarchies and subsumption in this paper, but we haven't yet explored how to use these techniques or unification to retrieve concepts which are hidden in the text because those concepts haven't been made explicit in the type hierarchy.

The problem is that it's not always possible to find a join in a straightforward manner. For example, *heatstroke* can be found as a join between *summer* and *medical treatment*. However, that join is not explicit in our ontology, and so is not a searchable term. The user must follow links from either *medicine* or *season* down to the reference on heatstroke.

Our work has now brought us to the point where it will be necessary to create new join terms on the fly. The *heatstroke* example illustrates the direction of the project. In the event of finding a term which may need to be referred to again, there needs to be a mechanism which will create this new concept and place it on the hierarchy. In this case, there will be issues of the subsumption ordering, and how the information is retrieved and indexed.

Exactly how case retrieval and the subsumption ordering, introduced by the unification tool, interact is to be determined. However, the emphasis will be on constructing indices based on the classification of conceptual graph terms into hierarchies complementing the structure of the explored knowledge space. This means that it will be essential to have the knowledge organized into a hierarchical structure which in itself contains much of the semantics for understanding the knowledge, as we have done with the Chrysostom Knowledge Base.

When generating new states the expressiveness of the representation acts to restrict the possibilities requiring consideration. Constraints in the partially elaborated problem statement (ie query) and in the specificity of the corresponding partial solution filter the matching passages. Together with the operation of ordered types in unification, these constraints help to eliminate results which are inappropriate to the state under consideration. Given a computationally efficient implementation of the type system, which is the subject of our future work, a unification tool over conceptual graphs will help to efficiently match appropriate solutions to the partial fragment (or query, keyword, semantic fragment, partial graph) under consideration. In this sense, a unification tool will not only make it easier to create domain rules, but also aid in the retrieval of the solution to the query by making it faster and easier to find appropriate types.

The strength of the system lies in generating formal representations to be indexed by classification techniques. The current thinking in conceptual graph theory is that, once the conceptual graph has been classified into a hierarchy, the hierarchy can be encoded into boolean strings, and lattice operations like inclusion, least upper bound and greatest lower bound can be used to perform inference operations by bit string manipulations on compact codes [10]. While this sort of approach was proposed over a decade ago, the supporting theory (and indeed technology) has not been sufficiently developed to support this sort of lattice operation.

These lattice methods are domain and representation independent and are based on an abstract data type for partially ordered sets. For a given object domain, a partial order over objects serves as an index to that domain. For example, building designs can be ordered in terms of spatial symmetries, software specification can be ordered by generalization of behavior and social history can be ordered by social role or value systems. The effect is that case retrieval efficiency can be dramatically enhanced.

The knowledge-base which is the subject of our work is unique in that there is no single definition for subsumption, or a „more specific" concept. In fact, it is this feature of a natural database which forces us to enhance the theory behind the semantics of subsumption and type hierarchy, as opposed to the ordering which naturally accompanies databases of artifacts, such as architecture or software constructs.

The point in building a unification tool for conceptual graphs is that conceptual structure term unification is more computationally efficient than standard constraint processing. In our future tool, when a user constrains a query to the database (for example, by specifying dates, people involved, particular events, etc.) those constraints don't need to be resolved immediately, as in standard constraint satisfaction tools. Using the computational power of the indexing system, constraints in the query can be unified with the knowledge-base to produce a result which is very specific to the query. Fewer constraints are solved because constraints are already stored in the hierarchy of the lattice as classifications. This is similar to existing approaches to constraint solving (for example, Baader and Siekmann [11]) with the exception that conceptual graphs have the additional semantic power of being a typed and order-sorted structure. Constraints are used, then, to help select appropriate indices and to refine the search result generated by the user's queries.

6 Future Directions

We are still left with several open questions which we hope to address in this project. These questions include the semantic and theoretical support and the implementation techniques of the lattice operators, the efficiency considerations of the indexes and the construction of the lattices. However, these issues are intimately related to the indexing mechanism that we propose to explore. In general, we need to find a conceptual graph solution that helps this historical knowledge-base run in an efficient way when the solutions are many and varied. These issues are directly related to engineering an indexing tool.

Our goal is to automatically create an index into the knowledge base as the query is being formed. The new index item will precisely target the knowledge the user wants to locate, ignoring knowledge that is semantically unrelated, and therefore irrelevant. We achieve this by expanding theory first developed for lattice theory and conceptual graphs to create partially-ordered subsumption hierarchies to index the knowledge. This solution has implications for knowledge merging over multiple ontologies.

An example of the use of this sort of indexing of the knowledge can be illustrated by considering a query regarding the travel time between two cities in that time. Ultimately, we want to give the capability to the user to make hypothetical queries that are not explicit in the texts, but can be answered by putting together facts found in the knowledge base. For example, a user may want to query the knowledge base as to whether it would be possible to travel from Constantinople to Antioch in less than ten days. Chrysostom is never explicit on this point, but certain facts about travel do appear in his orations. He discusses military movements, travel by land and by sea, and messengers sent between various cities. Given the time and patience, a researcher in social history could find the answer to the query by reading many speeches, and piecing together the scraps of information they contain.

Our Chrysostom Knowledge Base of the future would allow this sort of query, by matching on the concepts of travel contained in these texts, by performing constraint processing automatically, and by a little use of the knowledge indexing. The new and improved CKB would tell the user that it was possible to travel between those two cities in less than ten days, if the traveler moved by ship.

As stated earlier, the current CKB is based on concepts from Conceptual Graph Theory, and we expect the project to continue in that direction. We anticipate that both the text in the knowledge base and the queries will be expressed as conceptual graphs. A possible conceptual graph for the query discussed previously is shown in Figure 5. This graph illustrates that concepts can match in general terms (so that *travel* can match more specific types of travel, such as *travel by sea*). It also shows that the user can make some constraints explicit (< 10 days) while others are not important (the asterisks in the agent concept are used in Conceptual Graph Theory to illustrate a match with any concept).

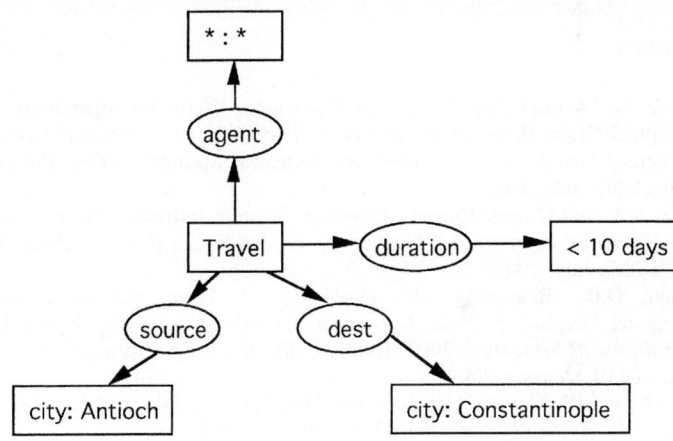

Fig. 5. A conceptual graph query for the CKB.

7 Conclusions

We have designed and implemented the Chrysostom Knowledge Base, which contains knowledge of the social history of fourth-century Helenic cultures. The significance of the knowledge is that it contains facts and information about the everyday lives of the people who lived at the time. As such, it is a very valuable resource for researchers studying that time and place. The further significance of this knowledge base is that it is a working implementation of an ontology constructed using concept type hierarchies. The resulting knowledge structure is an ontology of fourth-century social history.

When complete, the concept type hierarchy will consist of more than 70,000 entries. While lattice techniques are currently employed to link the knowledge to over

1,500 types, this indexing solution is inadequate for the types of search queries that the user is likely to employ. In particular, at present users aren't always able to locate concepts closely related semantically to their search.

Ultimately, we would like to see the knowledge base instantiated by representing all text passages as conceptual graphs, so that search and indexing is made easier, but we have anecdotal evidence from users that the knowledge base has made research easier because of the lattice structure of the hierarchy. We also see the knowledge base surpassing its original intent of a knowledge base of Chrysostom's work to become an ontology for historical research.

8 An Invitation

The authors welcome feedback on the Chrysostom Knowledge Base, and invite readers to explore the knowledge base, and its underlying ontology. The CKB can be accessed at: http://www.cecs.acu.edu.au/chrysostom/

References

1. Mineau, G. "A First Step Toward the Knowledge Web: Interoperability Issues Among Conceptual Graph Based Software Agents, Part I". in *Proc. International Conference on Conceptual Structures.* 2002. Borovets, Bulgaria: Springer-Verlag. Published as LNAI volume 2393. July, 2002.
2. Arara, A.A. and D. Benslimane. "Ontology Concept Extraction from Terminologies". in *Proc. Eleventh International Conference on Intelligent Systems.* 2002. Boston, Mass, USA: ISCA. July, 2002.
3. Corbett, D.R. "Reasoning with Ontologies by Using Knowledge Conjunction in Conceptual Graphs". in *Proc. International Conference on Ontologies, Databases and Applications of Semantics.* 2002. Irvine, California, USA: Springer. Published as LNCS volume 2419. October, 2002.
4. Allen, P. and W. Mayer, "Computer and Homily: Accessing the Everyday Life of Early Christians". *Vigiliae Christianae.* **47**: p. 260-280, 1993.
5. Mugnier, M.-L. and M. Chein, "Représenter des Connaissances et Raisonner avec des Graphes". *Revue d'Intelligence Artificielle.* **10**(6): p. 7-56, 1996.
6. Corbett, D.R., *Reasoning and Unification over Conceptual Graphs.* 2003, New York: Kluwer Academic Publishers.
7. Chein, M. and M.-L. Mugnier, "Conceptual Graphs: Fundamental Notions". *Revue d'Intelligence Artificielle.* **6**(4): p. 365-406, 1992.
8. Corbett, D. "Comparing and Merging Ontologies: A Concept Type Hierarchy Approach". in *Proc. Fourteenth International Symposium on Methodologies for Intelligent Systems.* 2003. Maebashi, Japan: Springer-Verlag. October, 2003.
9. Corbett, D.R. and A.L. Burrow. "Knowledge Reuse in SEED Exploiting Conceptual Graphs". in *Proc. Supplemental Proceedings of the Fourth International Conference on Conceptual Structures.* 1996. Sydney, NSW, Australia: UNSW Press. August, 1996.
10. Aït-Kaci, H., R. Boyer, P. Lincoln, and R. Nasr, "Efficient Implementation of Lattice Operations". *ACM Transactions on Programming Languages and Systems.* **11**(1): p. 115-146, 1989.
11. Baader, F. and J. Siekmann, "Unification Theory," in *Handbook of Logic in Artificial Intelligence and Logic Programming*, D.M. Gabbay, C.J. Hogger, and J.A. Robinson, Editors. 1994, Clarendon Press: Oxford. p. 41-126.

Text Simplification for Information-Seeking Applications

Beata Beigman Klebanov[1], Kevin Knight[2], and Daniel Marcu[2]

[1] The Hebrew University, Jerusalem, 91904, Israel
beata@cs.huji.ac.il,
http://www.cs.huji.ac.il/~beata
[2] Information Science Institute, University of Southern California
90292 Marina Del Rey, CA, USA
{knight,marcu}@isi.edu
http://www.isi.edu/{~marcu, ~knight}

Abstract. This paper addresses the issue of simplifying natural language texts in order to ease the task of accessing factual information contained in them. We define the notion of Easy Access Sentence - a unit of text from which the information it contains can be retrieved by a system with modest text-analysis capabilities, able to process single verb sentences with named entities as constituents. We present an algorithm that constructs Easy Access Sentences from the input text, with a small-scale evaluation. Challenges and further research directions are then discussed.

1 Introduction

It has been argued previously that complicated sentences are a stumbling block for systems that rely on natural language data; applications like machine translation, information retrieval and text summarization were cited as potential benefactors of text simplification [5][6]. However, what exactly makes a sentence simple for computers has not yet been made clear.

Possible dimensions of complexity are numerous. Long sentences, conjoined sentences, embedded clauses, passives, non-canonical word order [4], use of low-frequency words [7] were all proposed as aspects of sentence complexity for language-impaired humans. Are the same things difficult for computers? Why?

The crucial question is what language technology applications use texts for. Taggers and parsers of various sorts perform *linguistic analysis of the text* and are hence pre-processors for applications that make use of the (analyzed) text, usually for *finding information in it*. This goal statement pertains information retrieval and extraction, to question answering and summarization. Machine translation systems might also have an information-seeking component if translation is viewed as a task of conveying the same message in a different language, rather than transforming the structures of one language to those of the other.

In this paper, we address the question of what makes finding information in a text easy for a computer and how to transform texts to comply with these requirements.

2 Easy Access Sentences

Intuitively, a simple sentence is a sentence from which it is easy to retrieve the information it contains. For example, consider the following sentences that all convey the fact that Bill Clinton married Hillary Rodham in 1975.

1. Bill Clinton married Hillary Rodham in 1975.
2. Bill Clinton graduated from Yale in 1973 and married Hillary Rodham in 1975.
3. After marrying Hillary Rodham in 1975, Bill Clinton started a career as a politician.
4. Bill Clinton met Hillary Rodham in Yale, and married her in 1975.
5. Bill Clinton met Hillary Rodham in the early 1970s; their wedding took place in 1975.
6. Bill Clinton was introduced to the Rodhams in the early 1970s, and married their daughter Hillary in 1975.

Consider the processes involved in retrieving the information "Bill Clinton married Hillary Rodham in 1975". Example (1) states just this in a concise and explicit fashion. To get the information from (2), one needs to retrieve the subject of the verb "married" from elsewhere in the sentence; (3) requires in addition assigning tense to "marrying"; (4) needs subject retrieval and resolution of the anaphor "her" to Hillary Clinton. To handle example (5), the system should also possess some lexical knowledge (having a wedding is equivalent to getting married); example (6) assumes world-knowledge based inference (a daughter's family name is usually the same as her parents'). While the exact degree of difficulty depends on the information-seeking system's having the appropriate knowledge sources and skills, (1) is clearly the least demanding case. Our model example being (1), we define:

Easy Access Sentence. *EAS* based on a text *T* satisfies the following requirements:
Sentence. *EAS* is a grammatical sentence;
Single Verb. *EAS* has one finite[1] verb;
Information Maintenance. *EAS* does not make any claims that were not present, explicitly or implicitly, in *T*;
Named Entities. The more Named Entities a sentence satisfying the previous three requirements contains, the better *EAS* it is.

The first requirement ensures that sub-sentential entities are excluded; thus, *married Hillary Clinton* is not an EAS.

---
[1] A finite verb is a verb in some tense - present, past, future.

The Single Verb requirement eliminates the need to assign tense to the verb (*Bill Clinton marrying Hillary Clinton* is not an EAS) and to retrieve a dependent[2] of a verb from the dependency structure of another verb.

Information Maintenance ensures that when representing a text as a set of EASes based on it, we do not introduce information that was not in the text. For example, if an information-seeking system resolves *her* in example (4) above to Yale, it could produce a putative EAS *Bill Clinton married Yale in 1975*, which would fail the Information Maintenance requirement.

The drive towards Named Entities encodes preference of sentences with full names of entities to sentences with partial or indirect references to the entities which need to be resolved, like pronouns (*he, she*), partial names (*Mr Clinton*), definite noun phrases (*the former president of the United States*).

3 Text Based EASes

To exemplify the notion of EASes based on a text, let us consider a stretch of text converted by hand into a set of Easy Access Sentences. The example is adapted from a biography of Harriet Beecher Stowe:

> Harriet Beecher Stowe is a writer. She was born in Litchfield, Connecticut, USA, the daughter of Lyman Beecher. Raised by her severe Calvinist father, she was educated and then taught at the Hartford Female Seminary (founded by her sister Catherine Beecher). Moving to Cincinnati with her father (1832), she began to write short fiction, and after her marriage (1836) persevered in her writing while raising seven children.

Had we been able to rewrite the text into the following set of sentences, applications that are looking for information about this 19th century writer would have found it easily.

- Harriet Beecher Stowe is a writer.
- Harriet Beecher Stowe was born in Litchfield, Connecticut, USA.
- Harriet Beecher Stowe is the daughter of Lyman Beecher.
- Harriet Beecher Stowe was raised by her severe Calvinist father.
- Harriet Beecher Stowe was raised by Lyman Beecher.
- Lyman Beecher is Harriet Beecher Stowe's father.
- Harriet Beecher Stowe was educated at the Hartford Female Seminary.
- Harriet Beecher Stowe taught at the Hartford Female Seminary.
- Catherine Beecher founded the Hartford Female Seminary.
- Catherine Beecher is Harriet Beecher Stowe's sister.
- Harriet Beecher Stowe moved to Cincinnati with her father in 1832.
- Harriet Beecher Stowe moved to Cincinnati with Lyman Beecher in 1832.
- Harriet Beecher Stowe wrote short fiction.
- Harriet Beecher Stowe married in 1836.
- Harriet Beecher Stowe raised seven children.

---

[2] Verb dependents are subject, direct and indirect objects, modifiers.

All of the above sentences comply with the EAS requirements - each is a grammatical sentence with one tensed verb reporting a piece of information explicitly or implicitly present in the original text (for example, the fact that Lyman Beecher is Harriet Beecher Stowe's father is not stated explicitly, but is a correct inference from the text). Pronouns and some other anaphoric elements (like *her severe Calvinist father*) are substituted with the appropriate names. Now pieces of factual information about Harriet Beecher Stowe, like date of marriage, father's name, birth place, number of children can all be retrieved using relatively simple tools.

Our aim is automatic construction of EASes from a text. It can be argued that if it is possible to construct them automatically, this could as well be done by the information-seeking application itself, using the very same tools and methods we will be using.

We note that information-seeking applications are usually quite complex systems that have to worry about many things other than those involved in EAS-construction, like query formulation, search algorithm and validation of the answer (in question answering and information retrieval), lexicon translation and text generation in another language (for a machine translation system), database maintenance and employment (for applications that mine data for future use). Thus, it would be useful to outsource a part of text analysis to a specially designed mechanism that produces a representation from which the information contained in the text can be easily accessed.

In addition, many state-of-the-art language processing systems [9] operate on phrase or word level; hence information scattered across a number of phrases or even sentences is difficult to pinpoint and consolidate. Information dispersion, however, is quite abundant; the resolution of an anaphor can be a number of sentences back; the correct tense of the verb needs to be inferred by looking at the governing verb and possibly other things; the implicit subject of a verb in a relative clause resides somewhere in the area of the main clause of the sentence. Thus, bringing related pieces of information closer together and structuring them in a certain pre-defined way might help increase the accuracy and coverage of these systems.

Finally, as sentences containing a single verb and its dependents, EASes lend themselves to coding into databases that can later be re-used as external knowledge sources for various applications.

4 Constructing EASes

In this section, we present an algorithm for constructing EASes from a given text, and discuss our implementation of the key issues.

4.1 Main Algorithm

We first identify the person names in a text using BBN's Identifinder [2] and derive dependency structures for its sentences using MINIPAR [8]. We then proceed verb-wise, trying to construct an EAS with this verb as its single finite verb. Hence, for every verb V:

1. Check if an EAS with V is in a semantically problematic environment (see section 4.2 for details). If it is, skip V and proceed to the next verb.
2. If V is not finite, assign tense (section 4.3).
3. Collect V's dependents $Deps$ (section 4.4).
4. Try to increase the number of Named Entities among $Deps$ (section 4.5).
5. Output an EAS containing V and $Deps$.

Appositions are treated as if they were dependents of the verb *is*. Hence, an apposition like *George Bush, the president of the US...* is turned into *George Bush is the president of the US*. We use MINIPAR to detect appositions, and currently process only those that mention a person name.

MINIPAR's output eliminates lexical realizations of conjunctions; hence there is no way to differentiate between *and* and *or*. When outputting EASes, we substitute *and* for every conjunction node. While this is an error-prone procedure (for example, *The benchmark tumbled 301.24 points, or 1.06 percent* turns into *The benchmark tumbled 301.24 points and 1.06 percent*), we have not yet implemented a device to track down the original lexical realization of the conjunction.

4.2 Semantically Problematic Environments

Certain constructions do not contain factual information, and thus are not amenable to transformation into EAS. Consider:

– If Jane *arrives* early, John will be happy.
– I did not see John *coming*.
– George believes that Helen *died* yesterday.

For all the italicized verbs, there is no simple tense we can put them into such that an EAS centered around them would pass Information Maintenance test: none of *Jane arrives early, Jane arrived early, Jane will arrive early* represents information contained in the original sentence. Similarly, we can't derive any definite statement about John's coming or Helen's death.

One can envision an implementation where both *Jane will possibly leave early* and *Jane will possibly not leave early* are generated; however, the value of these EASes for information-seeking applications is doubtful. The current implementation uses lists of conditional markers, negation, verbs not presupposing their sentential, gerundive and infinitival complements[3] to detect governors[4] of these kinds, and avoids extraction of EASes from their domains.

Modality is another semantically problematic environment. Although *IBM started laying off employees* means that *IBM lays off employees*, once modality is applied, the inference does not hold anymore. Hence, *IBM*

---

[3] We used lexical units from *attempt, cogitation, desiring, request* and other frames of FrameNet [1] to help construct these verb lists.
[4] A governor of a node N is a node within the transitive closure of the is-a-dependent-of relation, starting from N.

might/should/would/must start laying off employees does not yield *IBM lays off employees*. The current implementation does not build any EASes from sentences with modals; further research is needed to see whether a definite negative statement can be produced: *IBM might start laying off people* means that *IBN does not lay off people*.

Checking 123 putative EASes generated by our system from 10 subsequent newswire articles from a random TREC-2002 [11] document (henceforth TestSet), we found 5 cases of erroneous extraction from a semantically problematic environment. 4 were due to the non-presupposing governor missing from our list; 3 were due to parser errors where the governor was mis-identified[5].

4.3 Tense Assignment

To assign tense to an infinitival or a gerundive verb, we go up the dependency structure and assign the tense of the closest tensed governor. Hence, *Jane continued writing* would yield *Jane wrote*. In the TestSet, there were 26 cases of tense assignment, out of which 17 were correct (65.4%).

Wrong tense assignment means a mistake in building the tense (ex. *helded* as past tense of *held*), or non-compliance with Information Maintenance. As an example of the latter, consider inferring *The squad prepared for next year's internationals* and *Next year's internationals included the World Cup* from the following sentence: *John Hart named a 42-man squad to prepare for next year's internationals, including the World Cup*. In both cases the past tense was taken from that of *named*, instead of the correct present tense.

4.4 Collecting Verb's Dependents

The dependency information is given in the output of MINIPAR. We recursively collect dependents of the verb ignoring verb-level conjunctions, relative clauses[6] and the surface subject (marked *s*).

When the deep subject of the verb (marked *subj*) is an empty string, we follow the antecedence links provided by MINIPAR to retrieve the subject. If this does not help, we default to the subject of the clause to which the current clause is attached[7]. In the TestSet, 33 cases needed subject retrieval, 17 of which were treated correctly. 13 mistakes were due to MINIPAR's incorrect antecedence links, 1 - to a mistake in the dependency structure returned by MINIPAR, 1 - to our procedure of substituting *and* for conjunctions, and in one case our default subject retrieval algorithm produced an incorrect result.

Out of the 123 sentences in the TestSet, 26 contained mistakes in verb's dependents other than the subject. 18 of those were due to MINIPAR's misparsing the clause, 7 were due to the conjunction substitution procedure and

---

[5] In 2 of the 5 cases both failures happened - the parser mis-identified the non-presupposing governor, but even had it been identified correctly, the EAS-construction software would have erred, since this governor was missing from the list.
[6] to comply with the Single Verb requirement
[7] See Clinton-Rodham examples 2 and 3 in section 2.

one was due to dropping the relative clause which turned out to be a restrictive one, hence the resulting general meaning was not supported: we produced *The selling weighed on the broader Tokyo Stock Price Index of all issues* from *The selling weighed on the broader Tokyo Stock Price Index of all issues listed on the first section*.

4.5 Getting More Named Entities

There is a certain tension between the drive towards Named Entities and Information Maintenance: a sure way to fail the latter is to perform a resolution of an anaphoric expression to a wrong Named Entity.

The current implementation is rather conservative, attempting resolution of just *he, his, him, her, she* to antecedents that are Named Entities. This task was shown to be within reach of a shallow resolution method with a success rate of almost 80% [3], as opposed to lower than 50% success rates for *it*.

We implement salience based anaphora resolution, maintaining two stacks of person names found in the text, one for each gender. The stacks are updated when a person is mentioned – by a full name, a partial name or a pronoun; Appendix A describes the algorithm.

Out of the 20 such pronouns in the TestSet sentences, 16 were resolved correctly. 3 mistakes were due to the missed reference with a common noun (ex. *his* in *The king wanted to convey his wishes ...* was resolved to a proper name from the previous sentence, rather than to *the king*). One mistake was due to our algorithm: *his* is resolved to *Andre Agassi* in *... Agassi said, congratulating Kroslak for his performance in the match ....*

The EAS-construction algorithm also substitutes partial names with full names; this occurred 5 times in the 123 TestSet EASes, all of which were correct.

4.6 Example

As an example of EAS construction, let us consider a sentence from the extract from Harriet Beecher Stowe's biography presented earlier (section 3). This name is the top one on the female names stack when we get to this sentence.

Example Sentence. Moving to Cincinnati with her father in 1832, she began to write short fiction.

Figure 1 presents MINIPAR's analysis of this sentence. Solid arcs represent dependency links; dashed ones - antecedence (*same-entity-as*) links. Labels on the solid arcs correspond to the dependency relations (for example, *subj, obj, aux, mod*). Every node consists of: the lexical string, including () for the empty string; base form (*move, begin*) and syntactic category information (*V(erb), N(oun), fin(ite) C(lause), A(djective)*); semantic information (tense).

From the sentence above, we automatically construct the following EASes:

1. Harriet Beecher Stowe moved to Cincinnati with her father in 1832.
2. Harriet Beecher Stowe began to write short fiction.
3. Harriet Beecher Stowe wrote short fiction.

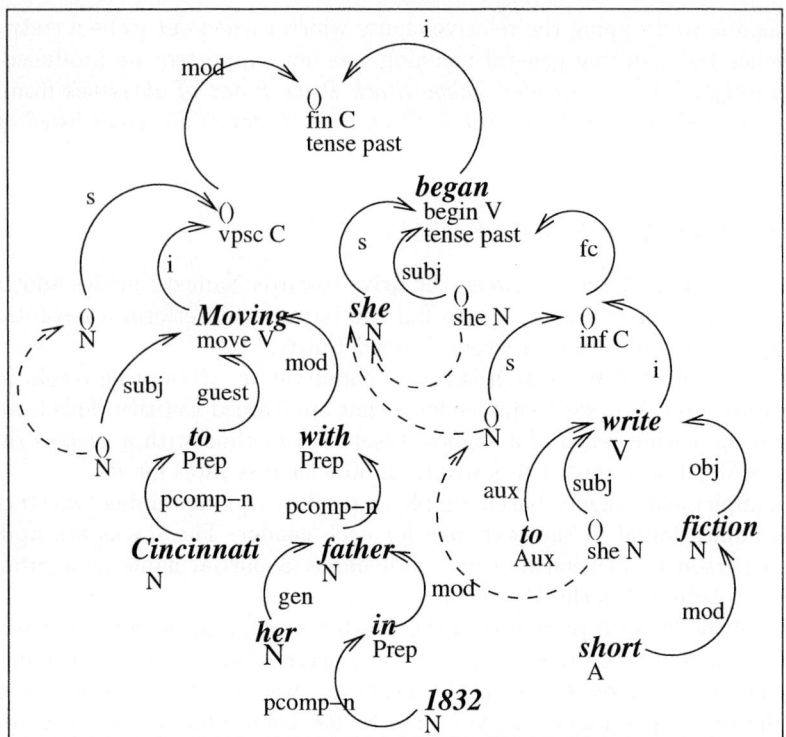

Fig. 1. MINIPAR's analysis of the source sentence

To generate (1), we determine that *moving* is not in a semantically problematic environment. It gets assigned the tense of its closest tensed governor, which is the past tense of the clause with the head *began* (the topmost node in Figure 1). Since the antecedence links for the subject of *moving* do not lead to any lexically realized string, we default to the subject of the clause of which the current clause is a modifier (see the left topmost dependency link labeled *mod* in Figure 1), which yields *she*. We then resolve the pronoun to the top of the stack. Getting to the pronoun *her*, we check the configuration and see that it is a possessor entity modifying a dependent of the main verb[8]. Since the subject of the verb is resolved to the same entity, we do not substitute the full name for *her*, as the corresponding Named Entity already appears in the clause.

In (2), *began* passes the semantic check. Since it is already tensed, no tense assignment is performed. Dependents are collected from the dependency structure, and the pronoun is resolved to the topmost element in the female names stack.

During the construction of (3), *write* is submitted to the semantic test. Since the governor *began* is not in the list of verbs that do not presuppose their complements, the test is successful[9]. Tense is again taken from *began*, and the an-

---

[8] Here dependence is mediated by the preposition *with*.
[9] The test would have failed had the sentence had *wanted* instead of *began*.

Table 1. Precision of EAS construction algorithm

Requirement	Met (%)
S-level Entity	112 (91%)
Single Verb	118 (96%)
Info-Maintenance	69 (56%)
1-3 together	68 (55%)

Table 2. Split of Information Maintenance Mistakes

Mistake	Made by (%)
Wrong verb	8 (6.5%)
Wrong tense of the right verb	10 (8.1%)
Comes from a bad sem. environment	5 (4%)
Wrong subject of the verb	16 (13%)
Wrong other dependent of the verb	26 (21.1%)
Wrong pronoun resolution	1 (0.8%)

tecedence links provided by the parser help us identify the subject, which is resolved to Harriet Beecher Stowe.

5 Testing the Algorithm

We use TestSet to evaluate the precision of the EAS construction algorithm. Out of the 123 sentences, 68 passed EAS requirements 1-3 (55%). Table 1 shows the detailed breakdown, with absolute numbers and percentages of EASes meeting the relevant criterion.

Table 2 shows the breakdown of Information Maintenance mistakes. For each mistake, the number and percentage of EASes that committed it are shown; if a certain EAS contained two different mistakes, it was counted twice.

We note that only one EAS actually had a wrong name substituted for a pronoun. The evaluation of the pronoun resolution algorithm reported in section 4.5 was performed running the system in the mode that just resolves pronouns. Hence, it tried to resolve all the relevant pronouns[10] in the texts, even if, when run in the EAS-construction mode, no EAS would have been produced from a certain sentence with a pronoun, or the pronoun would not have been substituted in an EAS (ex. *her* is not substituted in *Jane loves her mother* if the resolution is *Jane*).

To estimate the recall of our system, we asked 5 people to generate single verb sentence from an extract from Bertrand Russell's biography (the text and the exact wording of the instructions we gave to the examinees can be found in Appendices B and C, respectively). Our EAS-construction software and the 5 humans cumulatively produced 121 candidate EASes from the 7-sentence text. We then asked two other humans to judge whether each of these 121 can be inferred from the text.

---

[10] His, him, he, she, her

Next we identified 31 EASes that were produced by at least 3 humans; all of these were marked correct by both judges. We consider this set to be the gold standard set, since some of the EASes produced by just two humans were rejected as incorrect inference by one of the judges. Appendix D reproduces these 31 sentences.

Out of these, our EAS-construction software produced 10 (see Appendix D). It produced one additional EAS that was generated by two humans and marked correct. It also constructed 3 EASes that were not generated by any human but considered correct by both judges. Finally, 4 sentences were produced just by the software and marked as incorrect by both judges.

6 Discussion and Future Work

In this paper, we defined the notion of Easy Access Sentence - a unit of text from which the information it contains can be retrieved by relatively simple means, built to process single verb sentences with named entities. This is an attempt to mediate between the information-rich natural language data and applications that are designed to ensure the effective use of canonically structured and organized information, which is, however, hard to obtain without extensive human intervention.

We identified challenges in producing such middleware, the most difficult being the requirement to maintain the factual information encoded in the original text. This means both not to over-produce (avoiding non-factual constructions, like conditionals and domains of belief and desire verbs) and not to miss information (trying to consolidate into one fragment information that is dispersed in the original text, by resolving anaphora and retrieving covert subjects of verbs).

The small-scale evaluation of our implementation of EAS-production suggests that precision and recall figures are not yet satisfactory, estimated at 50% and 30%, respectively. While this might already turn out to be useful for some applications, our first objective is improving the performance of the algorithm. Error analysis showed that many mistakes are due to the dependency parser we employed (MINIPAR); using additional parsers and combining their analyses by a weighted vote might improve the reliability of the parse. In addition, whereas some disambiguation procedures we employed work well (anaphora resolution, name substitution), others need further analysis from the lexical semantic perspective - for example, the tense assignment procedure does not take into account the semantic behavior of the governor, and produces the correct result only in 65% of the cases. Finding conservative procedures for resolving definite noun phrases to named entities would also improve the EAS-hood of the system's output.

Acknowledgements. We would like to thank Lara Taylor and Jerry Hobbs for useful suggestions; Franz Josef Och, Dragos Stefan Munteanu, Eric Melz, Hal Daume, Mark Sprangen, Jonathan Graehl for their help in evaluating the system's performance.

References

1. Collin F. Baker, Charles J. Fillmore and John B. Lowe. 1998. The Berkeley FrameNet project. *Proceedings of COLING/ACL'98.* http://www.icsi.berkeley.edu/framenet/
2. Daniel M. Bikel, Richard Schwartz and Ralph M. Weischedel. 1999. An Algorithm that learns What's in a Name. *Machine Learning*, 34:211-231.
3. Kalina Bontcheva, Marin Dimitrov, Diana Maynard, Valentin Tablan and Hamish Cunningham. 2002. Shallow Methods for Named Entity Coreference Resolution. *Proceedings of TALN'02.*
4. John Carroll, Guido Minnen, Darren Pearce, Yvonne Canning, Siobhan Devlin and John Tait. 1999. Simplifying Text for Langauge-Impaired Readers. *Proceedings of EACL'99.*
5. R. Chandrasekar, Christine Doran and B. Srivinas. 1996. Motivations and Methods for Text Simplification. *Proceedings of COLING'96.*
6. R. Chandrasekar and B. Srivinas. 1997. Automatic Induction of Rules for Text Simplification. *Knowledge-Based Systems*, 10:183-190.
7. Siobhan Devlin. 1999. Simplifying natural lanauge text for aphasic readers. *PhD dissertation.* University of Sunderland, UK.
8. Dekang Lin. 1998. Dependency-based Evaluation of MINIPAR. *Workshop on the Evaluation of Parsing Systems.*
9. Franz Josef Och, Daniel Gildea, Sanjeev Khudanpur, Anoop Sarkar, Kenji Yamada, Alex Fraser, Shankar Kumar, Libin Shen, David Smith, Katherine Eng, Viren Jain, Zhen Jin and Dragomir Radev. 2004. A Smorgasbord of Features for Statistical Machine Translation. *Proceedings of HLT/NAACL 2004.*
10. Joel Tetrault. 2001. A corpus-based evaluation of centering and pronoun resolution. *Computational Linguistics*, 27(4):507-520.
11. E. M. Voorhees and Lori P. Buckland (Eds) 2002. *Proceedings of the 11th Text REtrieval Conference.*

A Anaphora Resolution

Two gender stacks of Named Entities are maintained and reset for every text. We approximate the grammatical roles hierarchy (subject > object > indirect object > modifier) by the linear order of the constituents[11]. We proceed as follows:

- Upon hitting a name N
    - If N repeats[12] a name already in one of the stacks, extract it from the relevant stack unless the previous mention was in the same sentence. If so, do nothing more.
    - If N repeats a name, push N underneath names last mentioned in the current sentence that are also repeated names, but on top of new names in the current sentence and names last mentioned in the previous sentences.

---

[11] Tetrault's Left-to-Right Centering [10] performed very similarly with syntax-based and surface-based ordering - see comparison of LRCsurf and LRC therein.

[12] Just surname or just first name repeat a full name, unless there are different names with the same surname in both gender stacks - then the surname is rendered ambiguous and no substitution is performed.

- If N is new, push N underneath names last mentioned in the current sentence, but on top of names last mentioned in the previous sentences.
- If the gender of N is unknown[13], push to both stacks.
− Upon hitting a pronoun P
  - Resolve P to the *target name*, which is the top of the gender matching stack, unless P is accusative (him, her), and the subject of the verb is same-gender pronoun or a proper name; then *target name* is second in stack.
  - Update mention of *target name* with the current sentence number.
  - If *target name* is second in stack and the subject was a proper name, move *target name* to the top of the stack[14].
  - If *target name* appears in both stacks, extract if from the opposite gender stack.

B Bertrand Russell's Biography

Bertrand Russel, a philosopher and mathematician, was born in Trelleck, Monmounthshire, in 1872. He studied in Cambridge, where he became a fellow of Trinity College in 1895. Concerned to defend the objectivity of mathematics, he pointed out a contradiction in Frege's system, published his own Principles of Mathematics (1903), and collaborated with A N Whitehead in Principia Mathematica (1910-3). In 1907 he offered himself as a Liberal candidate, but was turned down for his "free-thinking". In 1916 his pacifism lost him his fellowship (restored in 1944), and in 1918 he served six months in prison. From the 1920s he lived by lecturing and journalism, and became increasingly controversial. One of the most important influences on 20th century analytic philosophy, he was awarded the Nobel Prize for Literature in 1950, and wrote an Autobiography (1967–69) remarkable for its openess and objectivity.

C Instructions to Human Generators

We have lately been working on software to make natural language texts simpler and more explicit. Our system currenly performs rewrites of the original sentences into sets of "factoids": subject-verb-object (possibly with some modifiers) assertions that the sentence makes.

We would like to ask for your help in evaluating the system. We would provide you with a text, and ask you to write down, for each sentence, the simple SVO factoids that you believe to be explicitly and implicitly asserted in the sentence. We are interested in generating factoids that depart as little as possible from the wording of the original texts. That is, we are interested in factoids that can be obtained from sentences via word/phrase deletions and some minimal rewriting. We are not after generating "Close the window" from "It is cold

---

[13] Lists of male and female first names are maintained; we thank Ulf Hermjakob for making these available to us.
[14] Pronominalization is a stronger salience marker than subject mention.

here". The rewrites below may help you internalize at the intuitive level the factoid definition we are after[15].

D Gold Standard Rewrites

Bertrand Russell was born in 1872 (5)[16]. Bertrand Russell was born in Trelleck, Monmountshire (4). Bertrand Russell was born in Trelleck (3). Bertrand Russell was born in Trelleck in 1872 (3). Bertrand Russell was born in Trelleck, Monmountshire, in 1872 (3). Bertrand Russell studied in Cambridge (5*). Bertrand Russell became a fellow of Trinity College in 1895 (5*). Bertrand Russell became a fellow of Trinity College (4). Bertrand Russell was concerned to defend the objectivity of mathematics (5). Bertrand Russell pointed out a contradiction in Frege's system (5). Bertrand Russell published Principles of Mathematics (5). Bertrand Russell collaborated with A N Whitehead in Principia Mathematica in 1910-3 (5). Bertrand Russell published Principles of Mathematics in 1903 (4). Bertrand Russell collaborated with A N Whitehead (4). Bertrand Russell collaborated with A N Whitehead in Principia Mathematica (3*). Bertrand Russell offered himself as a Liberal candidate in 1907 (4*). Bertrand Russell offered himself as a Liberal candidate (4*). Bertrand Russell's fellowship was restored in 1944 (5). Bertrand Russell served six months in prison (4*). Bertrand Russell served six months in prison in 1918 (4*). Bertrand Russell was pacifist (3). Bertrand Russell lost his fellowship (3). Bertrand Russell lived by lecturing and journalism from the 1920s (5*). Bertrand Russell became increasingly controversial from the 1920s (5*). Bertrand Russell was one of the most important influences on 20th century analytic philosophy (5). Bertrand Russell was awarded the Nobel Prize for Literature in 1950 (5*). Bertrand Russell was awarded the Nobel Prize for Literature (5). Bertrand Russell wrote an Autobiography from 1967 to 1969 (5). Bertrand Russell's autobiography is remarkable for its openness and objectivity (5). Bertrand Russell was awarded the Nobel Prize (3). Bertrand Russell was awarded the Nobel Prize in 1950 (3). Bertrand Russell wrote an Autobiography (3). Bertrand Russell's autobiography is remarkable for its openness (3). Bertrand Russell's autobiography is remarkable for its objectivity (3).

---

[15] There followed an example with EASes generated by one of us from the biography of Harriet Beecher Stowe.
[16] The numbers in brackets show the number of humans who generated the sentence. An asterisk marks sentences generated by the software.

Integration of Integrity Constraints in Federated Schemata Based on Tight Constraining

Herman Balsters and Engbert O. de Brock

University of Groningen
Faculty of Management and Organization
P.O. Box 800 9700 AV Groningen,
The Netherlands
{h.balsters,e.o.de.brock}@bdk.rug.nl

Abstract. A database federation provides for tight coupling of a collection of heterogeneous legacy databases into a global integrated system. A large problem regarding information quality in database federations concerns achieving and maintaining consistency of the data on the global level of the federation. Integrity constraints are an essential part of any database schema and are aimed at maintaining data consistency in an arbitrary database state. Data inconsistency problems in database federations resulting from the integration of integrity constraints can basically occur in two situations. The first situation pertains to the integration of existing local integrity constraints occurring within component legacy databases into a single global federated schema, whereas the second situation pertains to the introduction of newly-defined additional integrity constraints on the global level of the federation. These situations gives rise to problems in so-called global and local understandability of updates in database federations. We shall describe a semantic framework for specification of federated database schemas based on the UML/OCL data model; UML/OCL will be shown to provide a high-level, coherent, and precise framework in which to specify and analyze integrity constraints in database federations. This paper will tackle the problem of global and local understandability by introducing a new algorithm describing the integration of integrity constraints occurring in local databases. Our algorithm is based on the principle of tight constraining; i.e., integration of local integrity constraints into a single global federated schema takes place without any loss of constraint information. Our algorithm will improve existing algorithms in three aspects: it offers a considerable reduction in complexity; it applies to a larger category of local integrity constraints; and it will result in a global federated schema with a clear maintenance strategy for update operations.

1 Introduction

Modern information systems are often distributed in nature; data and services are spread over different component systems wishing to cooperate in an integrated setting. Information integration is a very complex problem, and is relevant in several fields, such as data re-engineering, data warehousing, Web information systems, E-commerce, scientific databases, and B2B applications. Information systems involving integration of cooperating component systems are called *federated information systems*; if the component systems are all databases then we speak of a *federated database system* [29]. In this paper we will address the situation where the component systems are so-called legacy systems; i.e. systems that are given beforehand and which are to interoperate in an integrated single framework in which the legacy systems are to maintain as much as possible their respective autonomy.

Data integration systems are characterized by an architecture based on a global schema and a set of local schemas. There are generally three situations in which the data integration problem occurs. The first is known as global-as-view (GAV) in which the global schema is defined directly in terms of the source schemas. GAV systems typically arise in the context where the local schemas are given, and the global schema is derived from the local schemas. The second situation is known local-as-view (LAV) in which the relation between the global schema and the sources is established by defining every source as a view over the global schema. LAV systems typically arise in the context where the global schema is given beforehand and the local schemas are derived in terms of the global schema. The third situation is known as *data exchange*, characterized by the situation that the local source schemas as well as the global schema are given beforehand; the data integration problem then exists in trying to find a suitable mapping between the given global schema and the given set of local schemas [22]. An overview of data integration concentrating on LAV and GAV can be found in [21]; papers [1,17,18] concentrate on LAV, and [12,31,32] concentrate on GAV. Our paper focuses on a specific legacy problem pertaining to constraint integration in database federations in the context of GAV.

A major problem in data integration is that of so-called *semantic* heterogeneity [11,18,32]. Semantic heterogeneity refers to disagreement on (and differences in) meaning, interpretation, or intended use of related data. The process of creation of uniform representations of data is known as *data extraction*, whereas *data reconciliation* is concerned with resolving data inconsistencies. A specific example of the data reconciliation problem is the integration of local integrity constraints on the global level of the federation. Detection and handling of conflicts due to integrity constraints occurring in local database schemas is essential for correct schema integration. On the global level of the federation it is also possible to introduce newly defined integrity constraints pertaining to the federation as a whole. These so-called federation constraints can also cause conflicts with respect to the local databases occurring in the federation. Our paper more or less abstracts from the data extraction problem, and concentrates on the topic of constraint integration as part of the data reconciliation problem in database federations.

Examples of papers concentrating on GAV as a means to tackle semantic heterogeneity in database federations are found in [5,6,7,12,20,31,32]. A large part of the literature on the subject of (semantically-oriented) data integration, however, refrains from treating integration of integrity constraints [16,19,23,24,30]. There are some approaches that do treat the problem of integrating integrity constraints in a federated setting [3,5,6,7,12,27,28,31,32] by providing a method for adding global integrity constraints to the federated schema. With the exception of [6,7,31], however, the above-mentioned papers refrain from treating the integration of local integrity constraints on the global level of the federation. Conflicts between local integrity constraints and federation conflicts on the global level of the federation are therefore still possible.

This paper looks in detail at the correspondence between local integrity constraints and federation constraints on the global level of the federation. This paper is largely based on the results offered in [6,7,31]; it generalizes the results offered in [6,7] by offering an algorithm and a theory for constraint integration, and it offers an improvement and generalization of the algorithm offered in [31]. Our approach is based on the principle of tight constraining, and uses so-called exact views to realize tight constraining in the context of database federations.

As in [31] we shall abstract from problems concerning data extraction by assuming that these problems have been resolved beforehand (i.e. before the actual mapping from local to global is investigated), and concentrate solely on the constraint integration problem.

We will focus on the UML/OCL data model to tackle the problem of semantic heterogeneity in data integration. The Object Constraint Language OCL [25,33] offers a textual means to enhance UML diagrams, offering formal precision in combination with high expressiveness. In particular [4] has shown that OCL has a query facility that is at least as expressive as SQL. Also, UML is the *de facto* standard language for analysis and design in object-oriented frameworks, and is being employed more and more for analysis and design of information systems, in particular information systems based on databases and their applications. By abstracting from the typical restrictions imposed by standard database models (such as the relational model), we can now concentrate on the actual modeling issues. Subsequently, papers [10,13,14] offer descriptions of methods and tools in which a transformation from our model to the relational data model could take place.

One of the central notions in database modeling is the notion of a *database view*, which closely corresponds to the notion of derived class in UML. In [4] it is demonstrated that in the context of UML/OCL the notion of derived class can be given a formal basis, and that derived classes in OCL have the expressive power of the relational algebra. We will employ OCL and the notion of derived class as a means to treat database constraints and database views in a federated context. Using the concept of *exact view* [1,2,12], we will establish that only when we construct a specific *isomorphic* mapping from the local sources to the global schema, that we will obtain no information loss due to integrity constraints.

The organization of this paper is as follows. First we will explain the problems of inconsistency and incompleteness that can occur in the data integration process. We will then offer a solution in a UML/OCL-framework based on exact views, by first explaining how the integration can take place without constraints, and then subsequently showing how to gradually introduce constraints to the global level of the federation. Finally, we describe an algorithm constructing the federated schema, and end in discussing the properties of this algorithm.

2 The Problem: Inconsistency and Incompleteness

As pointed out in [24], schema integration has to satisfy certain completeness and consistency requirements in order to reflect correct semantics of the different local schemata on the global integrated level. These requirements can be summarized as follows: each object on the local level should correspond to exactly one object on the global federated level, and each object on the global level should correspond to exactly one combination of objects on the various local component levels. Both requirements can only be satisfied if there exists an adequate mapping from the global federated database states to the component database states. In this paper, we will coin such a mapping from the collection of local database states to the collection of global federated states as a ψ-map.

Constructing a ψ-map can be a very challenging task. First of all there are certain matters concerning inconsistency stemming from the problem area of *data extraction*. The process of data extraction [7] can give rise to various inconsistencies due to matters pertaining to the *ontologies* [26] of the different component databases. Ontology deals with the connection between syntax and semantics, and how to classify and resolve difficulties and classification between syntactical representations on the one hand, and semantics providing interpretations on the other hand. Matters such as naming conflicts (e.g. homonyms and synonyms), conflicts due to different underlying data types of attributes and/or scaling, and missing attributes all deal with differences in structure and semantics of the different local databases. Careful analysis of these problems usually reveal that these conflicts are not real inconsistencies, but rather that by employing techniques such as renaming, conversion functions, default values, and addition of suitable extra attributes can result in the construction of a common data model in which these (quasi-) inconsistencies are resolved. Since these techniques are well known and rather standard, we will abstract from such data extraction problems, and assume that there already exists some common uniform data model to start with, in which we can represent the various component database schemata.

A ψ-map, however, also has to capture the requirement that local integrity constraints restrict the set of correct database states, and also has to capture the requirement that global integrity constraints on the federated level restrict the set of correct federated database states. Hence, a ψ-map has to deal with the *data reconciliation* problem pertaining to the real inconsistencies due to conflicting integrity constraints. We will explain these inconsistencies following [31] using the terms local and global understandability.

In databases, *transparency* means that users do not see the internals of a database, e.g. the location of data on a disk. In the context of federated schemata, *global transparency* requires that global users do not see the local schemata, and also that the local users do not see the global schema. At the global level, *global understandability* demands that global transactions (updates, queries) are not rejected whenever they satisfy the global integrity constraints. *Local understandability*, on the other hand, demands that local transactions are not rejected whenever the local integrity constraints are satisfied in the corresponding local component database.

The problem of global understandability arises when a global update operation that satisfies the global integrity constraints is rejected without an obvious reason to the global user. This can occur when the local integrity constraints are not reflected in the federated schema; due to global transparency, the global user does not see the local constraints which are possibly not satisfied. On the other hand, the problem of local understandability arises when a local update operation satisfies the local integrity constraints, but is rejected without an obvious reason to the local user. The latter situation can occur when the local update gives rise to a conflict with an integrity constraint defined in the federated schema. Again, due to global transparency, the local user does not see this conflicting constraint on the global level.

Both problems of global and local understandability deal with the fact that any update on the global level is propagated to a corresponding update (or combination of updates) on the local level, and vice versa. This is due to the fact that a federated database is not materialized, and only exists in a virtual sense in terms of a certain view defined on the local databases. Ideally, both global and local understandability should be satisfied [31], meaning that

1. Local integrity constraints of the component schemata must be reflected in the federated schema in order to avoid the problem of global understandability
2. Global integrity constraints on the federation level, such as pure federation constraints defined by the database integrator, must be reflected in the component schemata in order to avoid the problem of local understandability.

In this paper we will demonstrate that global understandability is indeed always feasible. Local understandability, however, is generally not feasible due to the general character that federation constraints can have. Should there be no extra purely federated constraints on the global level, then we can ensure local understandability. These two conditions, one in full strength and the other weakened, together constitute a criterion that we will coin as the *criterion of preservation of system integrity*, or psi-criterion (ψ-criterion). When this ψ-criterion is met, will there be a completeness result in the sense that

1. each correct global update will correspond to exactly one combination of correct local updates, and
2. each correct local update, without the presence of purely federated constraints on the global level, will correspond to exactly one correct global update

This does not mean, however, that we have nothing to say about (full-strength) local understandability (i.e., in the presence of purely federated constraints on the global level). In Section 9 we will devote a discussion to this topic and show how to develop a maintenance strategy that in practice can deal with this matter.

In the sequel of this paper we will show that given an arbitrary collection of component database schema, how to construct a corresponding federated schema and a ψ-map linking the collection of local schemas and the federated schema.

3 Tight Constraining and Exact Views

Papers [2,3,12,27,28,31,32] have all investigated the problem of integrity constraint integration, and each (with exception of [31]), fall short in coming up with a satisfactory solution, in the sense that all constraint information offered on the local level is precisely (consistently and completely) represented on the global level of the integration. The approach adopted in these papers (with exception of [31]) basically boils down to so-called *loose constraining*, meaning that at least one of the contradicting integrity constraints is logically weakened on the global level. As we have seen in the previous section, this solution strategy does not solve the problem of global understandability. In contrast, we propose an approach based on so-called *tight constraining*, meaning that we faithfully (consistently and completely) represent all local constraint information on the global level of the federation. We will do so by employing so-called *exact views*; this in contrast with sound views [12], which more or less comply to the approach based on loose constraining. We will develop an algorithm that will calculate the appropriate exact view representing the (virtual) federated database state, given a collection of local database states. We will consider a so-called *component frame* of a collection of local databases, and define a derived attribute within this component frame in order to calculate the accompanying federated database state. This derived attribute will correspond to a view defined on top of the collection of local databases.

A component frame is a structure consisting of a collection of local databases, as depicted below

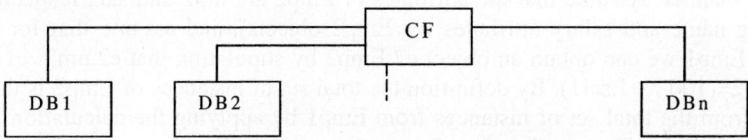

We will offer a definition in terms of UML and OCL [4,33] of both the component frame and the exact view corresponding to the federated database that we are targeting for. The reason for employing UML/OCL as a data modeling language for representing federated databases is two-fold. In the first place, UML is the de facto standard language for analysis and design in object-oriented frameworks, and is being employed more and more for analysis and design of information systems, in particular information systems based on databases and their applications. By abstracting from the typical restrictions imposed by standard database models (such as the relational model), we can now concentrate on the actual modelling issues. Subsequently, papers [10,13,14] offer descriptions of methods and tools in which a transformation from our model to the relational data model could take place. The second reason for using UML/OCL, is that the Object Constraint Language OCL [25,33] offers a textual means to enhance UML diagrams, offering formal precision in combination with high expressiveness. One of the central notions in database modelling is the notion of a *database view*, which closely corresponds to the notion of derived class in UML. In [4] it is demonstrated that in the context of UML/OCL the notion of derived class can be given a formal basis, and that derived classes in OCL have the expressive power of the relational algebra, thus making OCL suitable for defining general views on database. We will employ OCL and the notion of derived class as a means to treat database constraints and database views in a federated context.

In the next section we will offer a description of how to define databases and views in UML/OCL. We will then proceed by offering a description of a component frame in terms of UML, and in particular show how to define a federated database on this component by means of a so-called exact view.

4 Databases and Views in UML/OCL

Let's consider the case that we have a class called Emp1 with attributes nm1 and sal1, indicating the name and salary (in euros) of an employee object belonging to class Emp1

```
Emp1
-------
nm1: String
sal1: Integer
```

Now consider the case where we want to add a class, say Emp2, which is defined as a class whose objects are completely derivable from objects coming from class Emp1, but with the salaries expressed in cents. The calculation is performed in the following manner. Assume that the attributes of Emp2 are nm2 and sal2 respectively (indicating name and salary attributes for Emp2 objects), and assume that for each object e1:Emp1 we can obtain an object e2:Emp2 by stipulating that e2.nm2=e1.nm1 and e2.sal2=(100 * e1.sal1). By definition the total set of instances of Emp2 is the set obtained from the total set of instances from Emp1 by applying the calculation rules as described above. Hence, class Emp2 is a *view* of class Emp1, in accordance with the concept of a view as known from the relational database literature. In UML terminology [10], we can say that Emp2 is a *derived class*, since it is completely derivable from other already existing class elements in the model description containing model type Emp1.

We will now show how to faithfully describe Emp2 as a derived class in UML/OCL [33] in such a way that it satisfies the requirements of a (relational) view. First of all, we must satisfy the requirement that the set of instances of class Emp2 is the result of a calculation applied to the set of instances of class Emp1. The basic idea is that we introduce a class called DB that has an association to class Emp1, and that we define within the context of the database DB an attribute called Emp2. A database object will reflect the actual state of the database, and the system class DB will only consist out of one object in any of its states. Hence the variable *self* in the context of the class DB will always denote the actual state of the database that we are considering. In the context of this database class we can then define the calculation obtaining the set of instances of Emp2 by taking the set of instances of Emp1 as input.

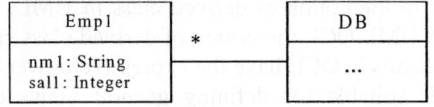

```
context   DB
def:  Emp2: Set(Tupletype{nm2:String, sal2: Integer}) =
          (self.emp1-> collect(e:Emp1 |
           Tuple{nm2=e.nm1, sal2=(100*e.sal1)}))-> asSet
```

In this way, we specify Emp2 as the result of a calculation performed on base class Emp1. Graphically, Emp2 could be represented as follows (figure (1) below)

DB
/Emp2: Set(Tupletype{nm2:String, sal2: Integer})

(1)

where the slash-prefix of Emp2 indicates that Emp2 is a derived attribute. Since in practice such a graphical representation could give rise to rather large box diagrams (due to lengthy type definitions), we will use the following (slightly abused) graphical notation (indicated by the figure (2) below) to indicate this derived class

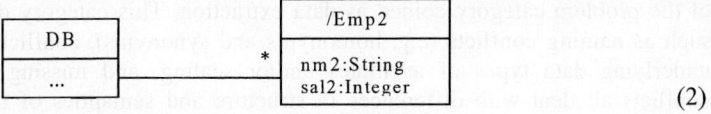

(2)

The intention is that these two graphical representations are to be considered equivalent; i.e., graphical representation (2) is offered as a diagrammatical convention with the sole purpose that it be formally equivalent (*translatable*) to graphical representation (1). Note that we have introduced a root class DB as an aid to represent the derived class Emp2. Since in OCL, we only have the possibility to define attributes and operations within the context of a certain class, and class Emp1 is clearly not sufficient to offer the right context for the definition of such a derived construct as derived class Emp2, we had to move up one level in abstraction towards a class such as DB. A derived class then becomes a derived attribute on the level of the root class DB.

5 Component Frames

A component frame can be modelled as a root class with relations to the respective local databases. Each database, in turn, is modelled as a root class with relations to the associated database tables (modelled as classes). Hence, if there are n local databases to be considered in the component frame, then a component-frame state consists of one object with a collection of n relations, each to a database object; each database object has a number of relations, each to a class representing a table of objects. For example, consider a component frame CF consisting of two databases (DB1 and DB2), and consider the situation that DB1 has a class C1 (a.o.) representing one of its tables, and that DB2 has a class C2 (a.o.) representing one of its tables. This can be depicted as follows

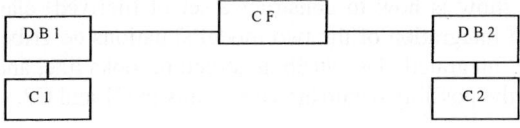

(3)

Hence, a state of CF consists of two database states, one for DB1 and one DB2, and each database state consists of a collection of tables, where a table is represented as the set of current object instances of a certain class. Let us consider the situation that we wish to integrate databases DB1 and DB2, and that classes C1 and Emp2 are related in the sense that they might have some characteristics in common. We will proceed by offering a general methodology to integrate these two classes Emp1 and Emp2, resulting in a collection of classes on the global level of a database federation.

But before we do so, we first have to make explicit a number of assumptions to describe the context of our approach.

Basically, we wish to concentrate in this paper on *constraint integration*, and therefore wish to abstract from other features that in themselves are possibly very relevant in the context of integration. In an earlier part of this paper, we made mention of the problem category coined as data extraction. This category deals with matters such as naming conflicts (e.g. homonyms and synonyms), conflicts due to different underlying data types of attributes and/or scaling, and missing attributes. These conflicts all deal with differences in structure and semantics of the different local databases. By employing techniques such as renaming, conversion functions, default values, and addition of suitable extra attributes, one can construct a common data model in which these (quasi-) inconsistencies are resolved. Since these techniques are well known and rather standard, we will abstract from such *data extraction* problems, and assume that there exists a common uniform data model in which to represent the various component database schemata. The problem category we will focus on is coined as *data reconciliation*, and in particular we will concentrate on problems concerning constraint integration in order to tackle the problems of global and local understandability.

Consider the situation that C1 and C2 have a collection of attributes in common, and that this (maximal) collection is denoted by α. Assume that β (resp. γ) is that set of attributes in C1 (resp. C2), not common to the set of attributes in C2 (resp. C1). Furthermore, assume that C1 has a subclass S with a specific set of attributes (denoted by σ), and assume that C2 has a relation with a class D with a specific set of attributes denoted by δ. This situation gives a general account of the problems that can occur when trying to integrate two classes such as C1 and C2. This situation can be depicted as follows

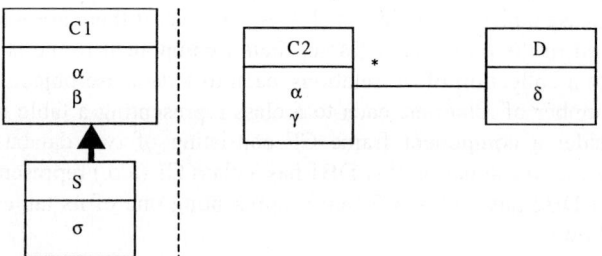

(4)

What we will now show is how to construct a set of (derived) classes that, as a whole, are the result of integration of the two model situations described above. First we will show what the integrated class-attribute structure looks like, and then we will show how to integrate the possibly occurring constraints in C1 and C2.

Consider the following diagram

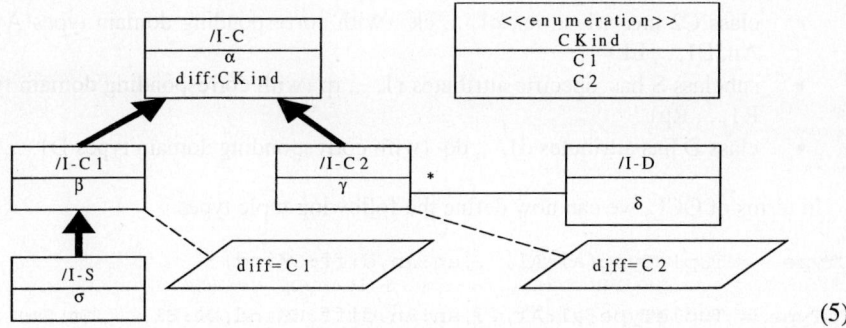

(5)

The slashes prefixing the class names in this model diagram indicate that we are dealing with derived classes (as discussed in section 4). This diagram will serve as a visual aid to show the result on the global level of the integration of classes C1 and C2. Basically, we have introduced a common super class I-C consisting of an attribute section that is common to both C1 and C2. We then introduce two subclasses I-C1 and I-C2, with attribute sections that are specific as possible differentiating them from the common class I-C. In order to differentiate between C1 and C2, we have introduced an enumeration class CKind. Class I-C1 is added with a constraint stating "diff=C1", and class I-C2 is added with the constraint "diff=C2".

The next section deals with two important matters. The first matter concerns the formal definition of the integrated database, which is given in terms of a derived attribute /FDB within the context of the component frame class CF. The second matter concerns the correspondence between the set of local databases, consisting of DB1 and DB2, with the integrated database FDB. In particular, we have the obligation to show that there exists a ψ-map connecting these local databases and the federated database FDB. In section 7 we will tackle the eventual problem of integrating local integrity constraints on the level of the federated database FDB.

6 Federations as Exact Views

In this section we will show how to define a federated database, in terms of the UML/OCL data model, as an exact view on the set of local databases. Formally, this will amount to defining the federated database as a special kind of derived attribute /FDB within the context of the component frame class CF. Once that has been established we will show that FDB satisfies the ψ-criterion, informally meaning that
- every global update τ on FDB, corresponds to exactly one local update τ' on CF
- every local update τ on CF corresponds to exactly one global update τ' on FDB

We assume that in the original model diagram classes C1, C2, S, and D have the following attributes and domain types
- class C1 has attributes a1, .., an, b1, .., bm (with corresponding domain types A1, .., An, B1, .., Bm)

- class C2 has a1, .., an, c1, .., ck (with corresponding domain types A1, .., An, E1, .., Ek)
- subclass S has specific attributes r1, .., rp (with corresponding domain types R1, .., Rp)
- class D has attributes d1, .., dq (with corresponding domain types D1, .., Dq)

In terms of OCL, we can now define the following tuple types

```
CType   = TupleType{a1:A1,..,an:An,diff:CKind}

C1Type  = TupleType{a1:A1,..,an:An,diff:CKind,b1:B1,..,bm:Bm)

C2Type  = TupleType{a1:A1,..,an:An,diff:CKind,c1:E1,..,ck:Ek,
          d:DType}

SType   = TupleType{a1:A1,..,an:An,diff:CKind,b1:B1,..,bm:Bm,
          r1:R1,..,rp:Rp}

DType   = TupleType{d1:D1,..,dq:Dq}
```

Within the context of the original model diagram classes C1, C2, S, and D, we now define functions converting objects from these classes to corresponding tuples related to the OCL-types defined above

```
context C1
def: convertToI-C1: C1Type =
Tuple{a1=self.a1,..,an=self.an,b1=self.b1,..,bm=self.bm,diff=C1}
def:convertToI-C:Ctype = Tuple{a1=self.a1,..,an=self.an,diff=C1}

context D
def: convertToI-D: DType = Tuple{d1=self.d1,..,dq=self.dq}

context C2
def: convertToI-C2: C2Type =
Tuple{a1=self.a1,..,an=self.an,c1=self.c1,..,ck=self.ck,diff=C2,
      dep=(self.d).convertToI-D}
def:convertToI-C:Ctype = Tuple{a1=self.a1,..,an=self.an,diff=C2}

context S
def: convertToI-S: SType =
Tuple{a1=self.a1,..,an=self.an,diff=C1}
def:convertToI-C1: C1Type =
Tuple{a1=self.a1,..,an=self.an,b1=self.b1,..,bm=self.bm,diff=C1}
def: convertToI-S: Stype = Tuple{a1=self.a1,..,an=self.an,
b1=self.b1,..,bm=self.bm,r1=self.r1,..,rp=self.rp,diff=C1}
```

We can now define the underlying type of the database federation
```
FDBTYPE = TupleType{
I-C:Set(CType),
I-C1:Set(C1Type),
I-C2:Set(C2Type),
```

```
I-S:Set(SType),
I-D:Set(DType)}
```

Using FDBTYPE we can define the federated database as a derived attribute within the class CF.

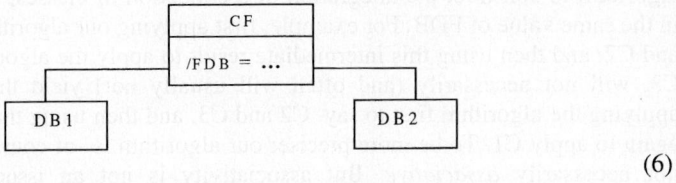

(6)

We note that CF is a class with two relations to the classes DB1 and DB2, respectively. Hence, a formula like `CF.self.DB1.C1.allInstances` is the OCL-expression denoting the set of all object instances of the class C1 residing in the component frame. The derived attribute /FDB in the class CF can now be defined by:

```
context CF
def: FDB : FDBType =
Tuple{
I-C1:self.DB1.C1.allInstances->
collect(o1| o1.convertToI-C1)-> asSet
I-C2: self.DB2.C2.allInstances->
collect(o2| o2.convertToI-C2)-> asSet
I-S: self.DB1.S.allInstances->
collect(s| s.convertToI-S)-> asSet,
I-D: self.DB2.D.allInstances->
collect(d| d.convertToI-D)-> asSet,
I-C= ((self.DB1.C1.allInstances->
collect(o1| o1.convertToI-C))->
union((self.DB2.C2.allInstances->
collect(o2|o2.convertToI-C))-> asSet }
```

It is now easily seen that
- each CF-state results in exactly one value of FDB, and
- each of the conversion functions is injective, and hence
- each existing value of FDB corresponds to exactly one state of CF

This means that the derived attribute /FDB also has a unique inverse; this shows that /FDB constitutes an exact view on our component frame, and –hence- also establishes the fact that the ψ-criterion for the database federation is satisfied. We note that up to now, we have not yet treated the question of integrating constraints, but only the question of how to integrate data structures. In section 7 we will treat the addition of constraints and its effects on FDB.

We still have to say something about the generality of applicability of our approach. Our approach deals with the structural integration of two classes such as C1 and C2, which are completely arbitrary except for the fact that they contain overlapping attributes (both in syntax and semantics). C1 is furthermore provided with a possible subclass (such as S), and C2 is provided with a possible relation to another class (such as D). Should C1, for example, also have a relation with some class, the same treatment as with D applies in constructing a corresponding value of FDB. The same holds if C2 has a subclass, or if C2 has more classes with which it has relations. Our construction can just be applied again in the same manner. This does not mean, however, that applying a different *order* of the various steps of the algorithm to construct the integration of a collection of classes, will in general result in the same value of FDB. For example, first applying our algorithm to two classes C1 and C2, and then using this intermediate result to apply the algorithm again to a class C3, will not necessarily (and often will usually not) yield the same result when applying the algorithm first to say C2 and C3, and then using that intermediate result again to apply C1. To be more precise: our algorithm is -of course- symmetric, but is not necessarily *associative*. But associativity is not an issue here; this can be compared to normalization algorithms in relational database theory, which are also not associative, but do always yield a result that satisfies a certain join criterion. In our case, the resulting value of the federated database FDB has to satisfy the ψ-criterion, which always is the case, since the conversion functions as described above are required to be injective.

Another matter that we still have to deal with, however, is the integration of local integrity constraints in DB1 and DB2 on the global level of the federation; i.e., how these local constraints are handled with respect to FDB. In the next section, we will demonstrate how to deal with integration of local constraints, and also how to handle newly introduced integrity constraints on the level of the federation, thus treating global and local understandability in the context of our example component frame. We will then show how our approach to constraint integration generalizes to an arbitrary component frame. Our algorithm computing the federated database (including local and global integrity constraints) as an exact view, will turn out to be of $O(n)$ complexity and will not produce any unwanted or-branches as the result of integrating local integrity constraints on the global level of the federation. These results will therefore be an improvement on the algorithm offered in [31].

7 Adding the Constraints

This section concerns the second step in the integration process; once we have constructed a common underlying data structure for FDB as described in the previous section, we have to add the local and global integrity constraints. First we will offer a categorization of the various constraints, and then show one by one how each category of constraints obtains its place on the level of FDB.

We will discern between five categories of constraints [8,9], and subsequently show how each category is integrated on the level of FDB. We will first do so by some specific examples, and then treat constraint integration in more general terms.

– Attribute constraints

Such a constraint deals solely with a restriction on possible values of one attribute inside a class. As an example consider the following constraint specification

```
context Emp
inv    attrcons: age>30
```

where we have assumed that an employee class Emp has an attribute called age and that each age value is required to be larger than 30.

– Object constraints
Such a constraint deals solely with a restriction on possible values of a combination of attributes on the level of an arbitrary object within a class. As an example consider

```
context Emp
inv   objcons: age>30 implies sal>5000
```

stating that each employee older than 30 earns a salary higher than 5000.

– Class constraints
Such a constraint pertains to the set of all instances of a class in an arbitrary database state. As an example consider

```
context Emp
inv   classcons: (Emp.allInstances-> size)<1000
```

stating that the number of instances of the Emp-class is always less than 1000.

– Database constraints
Such a constraint states an invariant property between different classes inside one database. As an example consider

```
context DB
inv   dbcons:
(emp.allInstances-> size) > 10*(man.allInstances-> size)
```

stating that in some database DB, the number of managers (Man is a subclass of Emp) is always less than 10% of the total number of employees.

– Federation constraints
Such a constraint is imposed on the collection of local databases participating in the federation; hence, it is an integrity constraint pertaining to the component frame, and it obtains its final representation within the derived class /FDB. As an example consider

```
context CF
inv   fedcons:
(DB1.emp.allInstances-> size) < (DB2.man.allInstances-> size)
```

stating that he number of employees of the Emp class in database DB1 is always smaller than the number of managers in the Man class of database DB2.
We will now show how to tackle the problem of global understandability within the context of our representation of FDB. We will offer a general algorithm for treating the constraints as described above per category. We then proceed by offering

a general approach to including federation constraints on the global level, and treat the problem of local understandability.

The Context
Consider the situation as depicted in our component frame (figures 3, 4, and 6). What we want is to describe the integration of local constraints occurring in classes C1 and C2. That is, we want to represent the integration as a set of constraints that will be placed somewhere in classes /I-C, /I-C1, /I-C2, /I-S, /I-D, and possibly also /FDB (cf. figures 5 and 6).

The Algorithm
We will define our algorithm per constraint category, and show how to represent local integrity constraints within FDB.

– Attribute constraints
Suppose that the attribute in question is a and that $\varphi(a)$ denotes the constraint in the local class Ci (i=1,2). On the global level, this constraint is now represented by the following prescription:

If attribute $a \in \alpha$ then the constraint moves up to class I-C and is changed to "if diff=Ci then $\varphi(a)$" else the constraint remains unchanged and is placed in I-Ci

Remark: Note that attribute constraints are inherited by subclasses

– Object constraints
Denote the set of attributes involved in the object constraint by attr. If the object constraint in question pertains to class Ci (I=1,2) and is denoted by $\varphi(attr)$ then the following prescription applies:
If attribute set $attr \subseteq \alpha$ then the constraint moves up to class I-C and is changed to "if diff=Ci then $\varphi(attr)$" else the constraint remains unchanged and is placed in I-Ci

Remark: Note that object constraints are inherited by subclasses

– Class constraints
Suppose that the class constraint in question pertains to class Ci (I=1,2); denote this constraint by $\varphi(Ci)$ and let attr denote the set of attributes involved in $\varphi(Ci)$, then the following prescription applies:

If attribute set $attr \subseteq \alpha$ then the constraint moves up to class I-C and I-C is constrained by $\varphi((o \in /I\text{-}C \mid o.diff=Ci))$, else the constraint remains unchanged and is placed in I-Ci

Remark: Note that class constraints are, in general, **not** always inherited by subclasses [8].

– *Database constraints*

These constraints remain unchanged, except for being applied to the I-prefixed versions of the classes involved in the database constraint in question.

– *Federation constraints*

Such a constraint is actually not really available before integration of a set of local databases. Once one has agreed to integrate, then possible federation constraints can arrive on the scene. The proper place to include them is on the global level of FDB. An example of a federation constraint is that class C1 always has less instances than class C2. Such a constraint could be represented in FDB as follows

```
context CF
inv  fedcons:
(FDB.I-C1.allInstances-> size) < (FDB.I-C2.allInstances-> size)
```

being an attribute (!) constraint (namely on the attribute FDB) within the component frame class CF.

In summary, what we have done, is shown how to lift local constraints to the integrated level of FDB by giving them suitable new classes to which they apply. The context of FDB can now be depicted by

C F
/FDB = ...
λ
φ

where λ denotes the set of local integrity constraints pertaining to FDB, and φ denotes the set of pure federation constraints pertaining to FDB.

The next section concerns a discussion on properties of our algorithm.

8 Properties of the Algorithm Computing the Database Federation

We will now discuss consistency and completeness results, and show that our algorithm when applied correctly always results in a federated database satisfying the ψ-criterion.

Our algorithm has the following properties:
  i)   The algorithm applies to all possible categories of constraints
  ii) The integrated database FDB as the result of our algorithm satisfies the ψ-criterion
  iii) Algorithm complexity is of order O(n), where n denotes the number of local constraints
  iv) The resulting FDB does not contain indeterminate or-branches in order to integrate local constraints

These four properties are an improvement over the algorithm offered in [31]: the latter algorithm applies only to very specific (so-called *decidable*) local constraint sets; its complexity is of exponential order; and it introduces a possibly large number of indeterminate or-branches on the global level in order to integrate local constraints. Also, our ψ-criterion offers a sharper correctness criterion, offering a clear maintenance strategy when dealing with updates subjected to constraints on the federated level. We proceed by offering a discussion pertaining to these four properties.

Ad i) As seen in section 7, we have covered all possible kinds of (ad-hoc) constraints that are applicable to database situations. We have covered constraints on the attribute-, object-, class, database-, and federation levels.

Ad ii) Close inspection of our construction of the data-structural part of FDB (cf. results at the end of Section 6), and the careful differentiation technique applied in Section 7 when lifting local constraints to the global level of FDB show that, indeed,
- each correct CF-state results in exactly one correct value of FDB, and
- each existing correct value of FDB corresponds to exactly one correct state of CF

This means that the derived attribute /FDB also has a unique inverse, in the sense that each possible correct value of FDB corresponds to exactly one (combination of) objects in the component frame. This property is attributed to the property that each of the local conversion functions mapping local objects to a tuple element of FDB is injective. This shows that /FDB constitutes an exact view on our component frame, and –hence- also establishes the fact that the ψ-criterion for the database federation is satisfied.

Ad iii) The order magnitude of our algorithm is clearly $O(n)$, where n denotes the number of local integrity constraints; this in contrast with [31], where only an order $O(2^n)$ magnitude can be guaranteed.

Ad iv) In [31] the global level of the federation is burdened by indeterminate or-branches in order to integrate local constraints. Our representation, in contrast, has an explicit and deterministic correspondent for each local constraint on the global level of the federation.

As mentioned earlier, our algorithm is symmetric (of course), but not necessarily associative; i.e., first applying our algorithm to two classes C1 and C2, and then using this intermediate result to apply the algorithm again to a class C3, will not necessarily (and often will usually not) yield the same result when applying the algorithm first to say C2 and C3, and then using that intermediate result again to apply to C1. Associativity, however, is not an issue here; since the computation of our federated database (no matter how it arises) always satisfies the desired ψ-criterion.

We now treat the remaining question of how to deal with issues of local understandability.

9 Local Understandability and Maintenance Strategies

Local understandability is hard to realize when additional purely federated constraints are introduced on the global level of the federation. The problem is that this latter type of constraint cannot be represented on the local level. We shall therefore adopt the following maintenance strategy when dealing with local understandability: each update on a local database will redirected to the global level of the federation, and subsequently we shall treat that update as an update on the federation. This is special kind of updatability through views; the view being the database federation computed along the lines of the algorithm described in previous sections of this paper.

This maintenance strategy has the following implications
- all local constraints pertaining to this update are indeed checked, as also would have been the case in the original database, since we have taken care to represent these local constraints faithfully on the global level of the federation
- possible violations of newly introduced purely federated constraints are also identified

A local user will therefore possibly receive a signal that his update has not been accepted, due to violation of a purely federated constraint; also, this same user will not be able to interpret failure of the update in question. Hence, pure local understandability will not be fully achieved, but at least federated constraints will in this case be respected.

In summary, we can formulate the following strategy in getting the local databases to successfully work together in a federation:
1. Use the algorithm described in Sections 5,6, and 7 to compute the *initial* state of the federated database; let FDB_0 denote this initial state. Our algorithm will guarantee that FDB_0 is correct with respect to all integrity constraints (especially the new class of federation constraints)
2. Each *global* user of the database federation can then directly pose his update to FDB
3. Each *local* user will have his update redirected from the local database to FDB (as described earlier in this section)

Following this strategy we can guarantee that the federation
- is always in a consistent state (*full local and global consistency*)
- satisfies full global understandability (*full global completeness*)
- satisfies local understandability, with the exception of update rejections due to violations of purely federated constraints on the global level of the federation (*partial local completeness*)

10 Conclusion

A large problem regarding information quality in database federations concerns achieving and maintaining consistency of the data on the global level of the federation. Data inconsistency problems in database federations resulting from the integration of integrity constraints can basically occur in two situations. The first situation pertains to the integration of existing local integrity constraints occurring within component legacy databases into a single global federated schema, whereas the second situation pertains to the introduction of newly defined additional integrity constraints on the global level of the federation. These situations gives rise to problems in so-called global and local understandability of updates in database federations. We have described a semantic framework for specification of federated database schemas based on the UML/OCL data model; UML/OCL has been shown to provide a high-level, coherent, and precise framework in which to specify and analyze integrity constraints in database federations. Problems of global and local understandability are tackled by introducing a new algorithm describing the integration of integrity constraints occurring in local databases. Our algorithm is based on the principle of tight constraining; i.e., integration of local integrity constraints into a single global federated schema takes place without any loss of constraint information. Our algorithm improves existing algorithms in three aspects: it offers a considerable reduction in complexity; it applies to a larger category of local integrity constraints; and it results in a global federated schema with a clear maintenance strategy for update operations.

References

1. Abiteboul, S., Douschka, O.; Complexity of answering queries using materialize views ACM PODS'98, ACM Press, 1998
2. Abiteboul, S., Hull, R., Vianu, V.; Foundations of Databases; Addison Wesley, 1995
3. Alzahrani, R.M.; Qutaishat, M.A.; Fiddia, N.HJ.; Gray, W.A.; Integrity merging in an object-oriented federated database environment; Int. Conf. BNCOD; LNCS 940, 1995
4. Balsters, H. ; Modeling Database Views with Derived Classes in the UML/OCL framework;«UML» 2003 6th Int. Conf.; LNCS 2863, Springer, 2003
5. Balsters, H., de Brock, E.O.; An object-oriented framework for managing cooperating legacy databases; 9th Int. Conf. Object- Oriented Information Systems, LNCS 2817, Springer, 2003
6. Balsters, H.; de Brock, E.O.; Integration of Integrity Constraints in Database Federations;6th IFIP TC-11 WG 11.5 Conference on Integrity and Internal Control in Information Systems, Kluwer Academic Press, 2003
7. Balsters, H., de Brock, E.O.; An object-oriented framework for reconciliation and extraction in heterogeneous data federations; Proc. 3rd Int. Conf. ADVIS2004, Advances in Information Systems, Izmir, Turkey, October 2004
8. Balsters, H., de By, R.A., Zicari, R.; Sets and constraints in an object-oriented data model; Proc. 7th ECOOP, LNCS 707, Springer 1993.
9. Balsters, H., Spelt, D.; Automatic verification of transactions on an object-oriented database, 6th Int. Workshop on Database Programming Languages, LNCS 1369, Springer, 1998.
10. Blaha, M., Premerlani, W.; Object-oriented modeling and design for database applications; Prentice Hall, 1998
11. Bouzeghoub,M., Lenzerini, M; Introduction to: data extraction, cleaning, and reconciliation, Special issue; Information Systems 26 ; Elsevier Science, 2001
12. Cali, A., Calvanese, D., De Giacomo, G., Lenzerini, M.; Data integration under intergrity constraints; CAISE 2002, LNCS 2348, Springer, 2002
13. Demuth, B., Hussmann, H.; Using UML/OCL constraints for relational database design; «UML»'99: 2nd Int. Conf., LNCS 1723, Springer, 1999
14. Demuth, B., Hussmann, H., Loecher, S.; OCL as a specification language for business rules in database applications; «UML» 2001, 4th Int. Conf., LNCS 2185, Springer, 2001
15. Grahne, G., Mendelzon, A.O.; Tableau techniques for querying information sources through global schemas; ICDT'99, LNCS 1540, Springer, 1999

16. Garcia-Solaca, M., Saltor, F., Castellanos, M.; Semantic heterogeneity in multi-database systems; Object-oriented multi-database systems (eds. Elmagarid, Bukhres); Prentice Hall, 1996
17. Halevy, A.Y.; Answering queries using views: A survey; VLDB Journal 10; 2001
18. Hull, R.; Managing Semantic Heterogeneity in Databases; ACM PODS'97, ACM Press 1997.
19. Josifoski, V., Risch, T; Integrating heterogeneous overlapping databases through object-oriented transformations; 25th Int. Conf. VLDB, Morgan Kaufmann, 1999
20. Kashyap, V; Sheth, A.; Semantic and schematic similarities between database objects: a context-based approach; VLDB Journal (1996) 5; Springer Verlag, 1996
21. Lenzerini, M.; Data integration: a theoretical perspective; ACM PODS'02, ACM Press 2002
22. Miller, R.J., Haas, L.M., Hernandez, M.A.; Schema mapping as query discovery; Proc. 26th VLDB Conf.; Morgan Kaufmann, 2000
23. Mannino, M.V., Navathe, S.B., Effelsberg, W.; A rule-based approach for merging generalization hierarchies; Information Systems 13(3):257-272, 1988
24. Navathe, S.B., Elmasri, R,, Larson, J.A.; Integrating user views in database design; IEEE Computer 19(1):50-62, 1986
25. Response to the UML 2.0 OCL RfP, Revised Submission, Version 1.6, January 6, 2003
26. Rahm, E, Bernstein, P.A.; A survey of approaches to automatic schema matching; VLDB (10):334-350, 2001
27. Reddy, M.P., Prasad, B.P., Gupta, A.; Formulating global integrity constraints during derivation of global schemas; Data & Knowledge Engineering 16(4):241-268, 1995
28. Ramesh, V., Ram, S.; Integrity constraint integration in heterogeneous databases; Information Systems 22(8):423-446, 1997
29. Sheth, A.P., Larson, J.A.; Federated database systems for managing distributed heterogeneous and autonomous databases; ACM Computing Surveys 22, 1990
30. Spaccapietra, S., Parent, C., Dupont, Y.; Model independent assertions for integration of heterogeneous schemas; VLDB Journal 1(1):81-126, 1992
31. Türker, C., Saake, G.; Global extensional assertions and local integrity constraints in federated schemata; Information Systems, Vol. 25, No.8, 2000
32. Vermeer, M., Apers, P.G.M.; The role of integrity constraints in database interoperation; Proc. 22nd VLDB Conf.; Morgan Kaufmann, 1996
33. Warmer, J.B., Kleppe, A.G.; The object constraint language (2nd ed.); Addison Wesley, 2003

Modal Query Language for Databases with Partial Orders

Zoran Majkić

Dipartimento di Informatica e Sistemistica, University of Roma "La Sapienza"
Via Salaria 113, I-00198 Rome, Italy
majkic@dis.uniroma1.it
http://www.dis.uniroma1.it/ ∼ majkic/

Abstract. The data integration of a number of local heterogeneous databases, with possible conflicting, *mutually inconsistent*, information, coming from different places, is an increasingly important issue. In order to avoid such inconsistency, a number of current in-practice developed database systems are based on different software and architectural paradigms, and are specified a number of embedded ad-hoc algorithms for a kind of preferred query-answering w.r.t. some preordering. The query-answering to conjunctive queries is usually performed in two consecutive steps: first are obtained certain answers from the underlying DBMS system, and successively is applied a filtering software, based on particular user-written algorithms, in order to obtain a 'best subset' of answers. Thus, the obtained resulting answers does not correspond to the original user's query: to which kind of logic formula the obtained answers correspond was an open problem. In this paper we show that such bivalent database/software-algorithm paradigm can be unified in an equivalent Abstract Object Type (AOT) database with a partial order, and that the query formula which returns with the same answers, as the answers to a conjunctive query of the original database/software-algorithm, is a modal logic formula.

1 Introduction

The enormous amount of information even more dispersed over many data sources, often stored in different heterogeneous formats, had boosted in recent years the interest for Data Integration Systems. A data integration system [22] is the problem of providing users with a unified view of heterogeneous sources, called global schema (with integrity constraints also). It provides transparent access to the data, and relieves the user from the burden of having to identify the relevant data source for a query, accessing each of them separately, and combining the individual results into the global view of the data. Doing so provides a natural framework for the semantic understanding of logic programs, used in order to define such data integration, that are distributed over several sites, with possible conflicting, thus *mutually inconsistent* w.r.t a subset of integrity constraint, information coming from different places. As classical logic semantics decrees that inconsistent theories have no models, classical 2-valued logic is not the appropriate formalism for reasoning about inconsistent databases: certain inconsistences should not be allowed to significantly alter the intended meaning of such databases.

A number of different approaches to overcome this difficulty is provided:
1. By replacing the classical 2-valued logic by a many-valued logic: *Signed* logics [8, 24,1], *Annotated* logic programming [7,20,21], and *Bilattice-based* logics, [19,17,16, 15].
2. By some kind of 'minimal' repairing of database strategies [6,5].
3. By elimination of all integrity constraints which is causae for such inconsistency, and replacing them with some kind of *partial orders*, $\preceq$, (usually realized by some filtering algorithms, as for example in the Cooperative Information Systems (CISs), where the quality of data is a *necessary* requirement. *CISs need data quality* and also Record matching algorithms.
In the rest of this paper we will consider this approach.

1.1 Technical Database Preliminaries

In this section we illustrate the formalization of a database system, extended by data quality information, specified in some data definition language $\mathcal{L}$. Such language may be choused for semistructured XML data or relational data or other (description logic, object-oriented, etc..) to define logical schema of the database system.
In such model, predicate symbols are used to denote the concepts in the database, whereas constant symbols denote the values stored in records. We assume to have a fixed (infinite) alphabet Γ of constants, and, if not specified otherwise, we will consider only databases over such an alphabet. In such a setting, the UNA *unique name assumption* (that is, to assume that different constants denote different objects) is implicit.
A *database schema* (or simply *schema*) is constituted by:
1. An *alphabet* $\mathcal{A}$ of concept (or predicate) symbols, each one with the associated arity. i.e., the number of arguments of the predicate (or, attributes of the concept).
2. A set $\Sigma_{\mathcal{G}}$ of *integrity constraints*, i.e., generally first-order logic assertions on the symbols of the alphabet $\mathcal{A}$ that express conditions that are intended to be satisfied in every database coherent with the schema.
The *logic theory* for a database systems, $\mathcal{L}_{DB}$, is composed by its schema (intensional database) and a finite number of ground facts (records in source, or local, databases).
We consider that from the set $\Sigma_{\mathcal{G}}$ are eliminated all constraints which become inconsistent for a given set of ground facts of this database, and that instead of them we have an embedded software module for a filtering algorithm, m_{alg}.
What follows is related to the standard 2-valued (true, false) logic semantics.
A *database* $\mathcal{DB}$ for a schema $\mathcal{G}$ is a set of database concepts defined in $\mathcal{L}$, with constants as atomic values, and with one set of records $r^{\mathcal{DB}}$ of arity n for each concept symbol r of arity n in the alphabet $\mathcal{A}$: the set of records $r^{\mathcal{DB}}$ is the interpretation in $\mathcal{DB}$ of the concept symbol r, in the sense that it contains the set of records that satisfy the concept r in $\mathcal{DB}$.
A *query* is a formula in a given language $\mathcal{L}_Q$ of all *finite conjunctive* queries over a database $\mathcal{DB}$ for $\mathcal{G}$, that specifies a set of records to be retrieved from a database. The *certain answer* (i.e., known answer [23]) to a query $q(\mathbf{x})$ of arity n over a database $\mathcal{DB}$ for $\mathcal{G}$, denoted $q(\mathbf{x})^{\mathcal{DB}}$, is the set of n-records of constants $(c_1, \ldots, c_n)$, such that, when substituting each c_i for x_i, the formula $q(c_1, \ldots, c_n)$ evaluates to true in $\mathcal{DB}$ for *every*

model of this database (we consider the general case when the data base has a number of different minimal Herbrand models, caused by incomplete information).
We define the set of all views, Υ_{DB}, and the set of all tuples, X, which can be obtained from a database $\mathcal{DB}$, as follows:
$\Upsilon_{DB} = \{q(\mathbf{x})^{\mathcal{DB}} \mid q(\mathbf{x}) \in \mathcal{L}_Q\}$, $X = \bigcup_{w \in \Upsilon_{DB}} w$.
We consider that the algorithm $m_{alg} : \Upsilon_{DB} \to \Upsilon_{DB}$ is coherent with the partial order in a database, as follows: $t_1 \preceq t_2$ iff $m_{alg}(\{t_1, t_2\}) = \{t_2\}$, so that for any $w \in \Upsilon_{DB}$, $m_{alg}(w) = \{t \in w \mid \forall t' \in w . t \preceq t' \Rightarrow t' \preceq t\} \subseteq w$.
Intuitively, if $\preceq$ is the 'best' preorder between tuples which are considered mutually inconsistent by *user* (we recall the fact that Σ_G remain consistent for such tuples), then the algorithm returns only with the maximal 'best' subset of certain answers in w.

1.2 Categorial Preliminaries

We shall be using a particular collection of functors (on a category *Set* with sets as objects and functions between them as arrows), $T : Set \to Set$, as interfaces of coalgebras. These so-called Kripke polynomial functors are built up inductively from the identity and constants, using products, coproducts (disjoint unions), exponents (with constants) and powersets. Products of sets S_1, S_2, written as $S_1 \times S_2$, have two projections $\pi_i : S_1 \times S_2 \to S_i$ (for $i = 1, 2$). Coproducts, $S_1 + S_2$, come with injective functions $\kappa_i : S_i \to S_1 + S_2$ (for $i = 1, 2$). The collection of functions from a set X to Y is denoted by Y^X with an evaluation mapping $ev : Y^X \times X \to Y$. For a function $f : Y \to Z$ there is an associated function $f^X : Y^X \to Z^X$ by $g \mapsto f \circ g$, where $\circ$ is a composition of functions. The covariant powerset functor $\mathcal{P} : Set \to Set$ sends a set Y to the set of its subsets $\mathcal{P}(Y) = \{S \mid S \subseteq Y\}$, and a function $f : Y \to Z$ to the function $\mathcal{P}(f) : \mathcal{P}(Y) \to \mathcal{P}(Z)$ given by image: $S \mapsto f(S) = \{f(y) \mid y \in S\}$.

Definition 1. *The collection of Kripke polynomial functors (KPFs) is defined as follows:*
1. The identity functor $I_d : Set \to Set$ is a KPF.
2. For each non-empty finite set D, the constant functor $D : Set \to Set$, given by $X \mapsto D$ and $(f : Y \to Z) \mapsto id_D$, is a KPF.
3. The product $X \mapsto T_1(X) \times T_2(X)$ of two KPFs T_1, T_2 is a KPF.
4. The coproduct $X \mapsto T_1(X) + T_2(X)$ of two KPFs T_1, T_2 is a KPF.
5. For a KPF T, and an arbitrary non-empty set D the exponent functor $X \mapsto T(X)^D$ is a KPF.
6. For a KPF T, the functor $X \mapsto \mathcal{P}(T(X)))$ is a KPF.

The collection of finite KPFs is constructed in the same way, except that in the last point the finite powerset $\mathcal{P}_{fin}$ is used, instead of the ordinary one.
A *coalgebra* of a KPF, $T : Set \to Set$, consists of a set X, usually called the state space or set of states, together with a function $c : X \to T(X)$, giving the operations of the coalgebra. A homomorphism of coalgebras from $c : X \to T(X)$ to $d : Y \to T(Y)$ is a function $f : X \to Y$ between the underlying state spaces which commutes with operations: $d \circ f = T(f) \circ c$.
Abstract Object Type (AOT) for databases: The *coagebraic specification* of a class of systems, i.e., Abstract Object Types (AOT), is characterized by a set of operations (destructors) which tell us what can be *observed* out of a system-*state* (i.c., an element of

the carrier), and how can a state be transformed to successor state. Recently [12], the coalgebraic semantics is extended to the logic programming, thus to the specification of database ontologies.

We start introducing the class of coalgebras for database query-answering systems [13]. They are presented in an algebraic style, by providing a co-signature. In particular, sorts include one single "hidden sort", corresponding to the carrier of the coalgebra, and other "visible" sorts for inputs and outputs, which are given a fixed interpretation. Visible sorts will be interpreted as sets without any algebraic structure defined on them. Input sorts are considered as the set $\mathcal{L}_Q$ of conjunctive queries, $q(\mathbf{x})$, while output sorts are "valuations", that is, the set $\varUpsilon$ of a resulting views.

Definition 2. *A co-signature for Database query-answering system is a triple $\mathcal{D}_\Sigma = (S, OP, [\_])$, where S, the sorts, OP, the operators, and $[\_]$ the interpretation of visible sorts are as follows:*

1. $S = (W_A, \mathcal{L}_Q, \varUpsilon)$, where W_A is the hidden sort (a set of states of a database A), $\mathcal{L}_Q$ is an input sort (set of all finite conjunctive queries), and $\varUpsilon$ is an output sort (set of all views of all databases, $\varUpsilon = \bigcup \varUpsilon_{DB}$).

2. OP is set of operations: a method $Next_q : W_A \times \mathcal{L}_Q \to W_A$, which corresponds to an execution of a next query $q(\mathbf{x}) \in \mathcal{L}_Q$ in a current state of a database A, such that a database A pass to the next state; and $Out_Q : W_A \times \mathcal{L}_Q \to \varUpsilon$ is an attribute which returns with an obtained view of a database for a given query $q(\mathbf{x}) \in \mathcal{L}_Q$.

3. $[\_]$ is a function mapping each visible sort to a non-empty set.

The Abstract Object Type for a query-answering system is given by a coalgebra

$< \lambda Next_Q, \lambda Out_Q >: W_A \to W_A^{\mathcal{L}_Q} \times \varUpsilon^{\mathcal{L}_Q}$, of the polynomial endofunctor $(\_)^{\mathcal{L}_Q} \times \varUpsilon^{\mathcal{L}_Q} : Set \to Set$, where λ denotes the lambda abstraction for functions of two variables into functions of one variable (Z^Y denotes a set of all functions from Y to Z).

1.3 Predicate Lifting

In this subsection we will consider [3,4] the unfolding and structural properties of Kripke Polynomial Functors (KPFs), $T : Set \to Set$, such that $T = ...S...$ is a composition of its KPFs subcomponents S. We shall make such occurences explicit by defining how such an S can be reached via a path p inside T, denoted by a relation $p : T \leadsto S$. The path p is a finite set of symbols (see paragraph for KPF) $\pi_1, \pi_2, \kappa_1, \kappa_2, ev(d)$, for elements $d \in D$ of sets D occurring as exponents in T.

Definition 3. *The relation $p : T \leadsto S$, for any two KPFs, is the least relation defoined as follows:*

1. $\langle \rangle : T \leadsto T$, where $\langle \rangle$ is the empty list.
2. $\pi_1 \cdot p : T_1 \times T_2 \leadsto T$ for $p : T_1 \leadsto S$, and $\pi_2 \cdot p : T_1 \times T_2 \leadsto T$ for $p : T_2 \leadsto S$.
3. $\kappa_1 \cdot p : T_1 + T_2 \leadsto T$ for $p : T_1 \leadsto S$, and $\kappa_2 \cdot p : T_1 + T_2 \leadsto T$ for $p : T_2 \leadsto S$.
4. $ev(d) \cdot p : T^D \leadsto S$ for all $d \in D$ and $p : T \leadsto S$.
5. $\mathcal{P} \cdot p : \mathcal{P}(T) \leadsto S$ for all $p : T \leadsto S$.

We define the set of (global) nextime-modal operators $Op(T)$ of the KPF T as:
$Op(T) = \{p \mid p : T \leadsto Id\}$.

It is easy to see that these paths can be composed (via concatenation of lists): if $p : T_1 \leadsto T_2$ and $q : T_2 \leadsto T_3$, then $p \cdot q : T_1 \leadsto T_3$.

Basically we are only interested in the paths having identity functors as targets, but for a generality we introduce the following general concept of a "predicate lifting" [3,4]:

Definition 4. *For a path $p : T \leadsto S$ and an arbitrary set X there is a "predicate lifting" function $(\_)^p : \mathcal{P}(S(X)) \to \mathcal{P}(T(X))$ defined on $Y \subseteq S(X)$ by induction on p:*
1. $Y^{\langle\rangle} = Y$.
2. $Y^{\pi_i \cdot p} = \{z \mid \pi_i(z) \in Y^p\}$, for $i = 1, 2$.
3. $Y^{\kappa_i \cdot p} = \{z \mid \forall y. z = \kappa_i(y) \Rightarrow y \in Y^p\}$, for $i = 1, 2$.
4. $Y^{ev(d) \cdot p} = \{f \mid f(d) \in Y^p\}$.
5. $Y^{\mathcal{P} \cdot p} = \{Z \mid Z \subseteq Y^p\}$.

For a coalgebra $c : X \to T(X)$ we define for a modal operator $(p : T \leadsto Id) \in Ob(T)$ an interpretation function $[p] : \mathcal{P}(X) \to \mathcal{P}(X)$, by, for any $Y \in \mathcal{P}(X)$, $[p](Y) = c^{-1}(Y^p) = \{x \in X \mid c(x) \in Y^p\}$, thus $[p] = c^{-1} \circ (\_)^p$.

Example 1: The frame $(X, R_{\preceq})$ can be represented by the coalgebra $\gamma : X \to \mathcal{P}(X)$, and for any $t \in X$, $\gamma(t)$ is the set of all successors of the point t (i.e., the set of all t' such that $(t, t') \in R_{\preceq}$, or, equivalently, $t' \preceq t$).
Let us consider the unique modal operator $p = \mathcal{P} : T \leadsto Id$ for the functor $T = \mathcal{P}$. Thus we obtain its interpretation function $[\mathcal{P}]$ such that for any $Y \subseteq X$
$[\mathcal{P}](Y) = \gamma^{-1}((Y)^{\mathcal{P}}) = \gamma^{-1}(\{Z \mid Z \subseteq Y\}) = \{x \in X \mid \gamma(x) \in \{Z \mid Z \subseteq Y\}\} = \{x \in X \mid \gamma(x) \subseteq Y\}$, i.e., this modal operator is the standard universal modal operator □.

The plan of this paper is the following: In Section 2 we present one example for databases with partial orders based on a data quality database requirements. Section 3 defines the Abstract Object Types (AOTs) for a database A with external filtering algorithm, and for, equivalent to it, the database A with a partial order (obtained by embedding of this algorithm into a database theory). This definition is given by two coalgebras α and β, for polynomial functors with conjunctive query language $\mathcal{L}_Q$ and modified query language $\mathcal{L}_{mQ}$, respectively. The behavioral equivalence of these two AOTs is defined by an isomorphism between coalgebras (for a coalgebra α) w.r.t. the functor with the conjunctive query language $\mathcal{L}_Q$. In Section 4 we present the formal semantics for the modal operator of the modal language $\mathcal{L}_{mQ}$, based on predicate lifting: first we define the frame derived from the structure of the partial order of a database, then we define a coalgebra for a partial-bounded set of successors for this frame which captures the meaning of the modal operator under consideration. Then we present the dual formalization for the equivalence of AOTs (defined in precedence), based on an isomorphism between coalgebras (for a coalgebra β) w.r.t. the functor with the modal query language $\mathcal{L}_{mQ}$.

2 Case Study: Partial Orders in a Database Quality Environment

The case study for partial orders in databases will be considered in the following example of the Data Quality in CIS (DaQuinCIS)[18]. It is a platform for exchanging and improving data quality in cooperative information systems, such that includes a data integration system that allows to access data and quality 'dimensions' (meta-data): the structure of such auxiliary information is expressed in the same definition language of the ordinary data integration system, so it is able to elaborate these meta-data as ordinary data and to process the complex conjunctive queries over both data and their meta-data. The *formal framework* [14] for DaQuinCIS is that of data integration system,$\mathcal{I}_Q$, is a triple $\mathcal{I}_Q = \langle \mathcal{G}_Q, \mathcal{S}_Q, \mathcal{M}_Q \rangle$, where $\mathcal{G}_Q$ is the *global schema*, an extension of ordinary data schema by quality 'dimensions' concepts, $\mathcal{S}_Q$ is the *source schema*, an extension of ordinary source schema by quality 'dimensions' concepts, and $\mathcal{M}_Q$ is the *mapping* between $\mathcal{G}_Q$ and $\mathcal{S}_Q$, an extension of ordinary Global/Local as-view mappings between source data and global schema by mappings between 'dimension' concepts.

The $\mathcal{I}_Q$ denotes a *logic theory* which defines this quality-data integration system also. The *certain answers* to user *conjunctive query* $q(\mathbf{x})$ in a data integration system, denoted by $q^{\mathcal{I}_Q}(\mathbf{x})$ must be true in all models of such logic theory $\mathcal{I}_Q$.

Generally speaking, when data are considered locally, they must satisfy only the integrity constraints specified in the source to which they belong, but they are not required to satisfy the fundamental integrity constraint for the global schema: the *real world entity* must be represented by the unique record of the corresponding concept in the global schema. This requirement is often unsatisfied: different records from local (source) databases, which corresponds to the same real world entity, are mapped to the concept in global schema. Thus, while integrating data coming from different sources, it often happens that the global database, which is constructed in the integration process, is *inconsistent* with such fundamental integrity constraint. In that case the *record matching algorithm* has to provide the unique record (with the best quality) to the user. Thus, this matching algorithm, is an alternative 'external-to-DBtheory' way (w.r.t. the explicit 'internal' integrity constraint over database) to guarantee the satisfaction of this fundamental user implicit requirement. If we denote by $\leq_Q$ the quality preorder between tuples of certain answers, and by $\approx$ the equivalence relation between tuples of certain answers, obtained by record matching algorithm [14] (tuples $t_1 \approx t_2$ are equivalent if they represent the same real world entity), then the partial order is defined by:
$t_1 \preceq t_2$ iff $t_1 \approx t_2$ and $t_1 \leq_Q t_2$ □.

In the rest of this Section we will consider these properties in a more detailed and formal way [14].

As we have explained, the elimination of formal integrity constraints over a global schema in DaQuinCIS database systems, in order to avoid 2-valued inconsistent databases, needs, as counterpart, the Record matching algorithms during the query answering processing, in order to select (for each cluster of certain answers to a query) at maximum one record for a real world entity underlined in the query.

The certain answers $q^{\mathcal{I}_Q}(\mathbf{x})$ defined in precedence will be called pre-answers also: such set of records has to be successively filtered in order to avoid to have more records associated *by user* to the same real world entity.

Thus, all DaQuinCIS database systems hide some part of model-theoretic certain pre-answers, $q^{\mathcal{I}_Q}(\mathbf{x})$, in order to satisfy the implicit (user's) real world identity constraint. If we consider such constraint at epistemic (user's) meta-level, the following two logic principles must be satisfied:

1. *Epistemic consistency*: at maximum one record for a real world entity can be contained in the answer.
2. *Epistemic completeness*: the filtered answers has to contain a record for every real world entity referred by model-theoretic certain answers.

Let us try now to give a general logical/mathematical framework for the semantics of query-answering which satisfies also the epistemic principles defined in precedence.

Let denote by $|\mathbf{x}|$ the number of variables (attributes) of the query $q(\mathbf{x})$, and the set $S_k = \{i \mid 1 \leq i \leq k\}$, so that $S_{|\mathbf{x}|} = \{1, 2, .., |\mathbf{x}|\}$. Thus we introduce the functional space, $2_{space} = \{\{0,1\}^{S_k} \mid k = 1, 2, ...\}$, such that each element $f \in 2_{space}$ is a function $f : S_k \to \{0, 1\}$ for some $k \geq 1$. Thus we can define the Choice of the matching key algorithm, Ψ_{mkey}, such that for any given pre-answer $q^{\mathcal{I}_Q}(\mathbf{x})$ returns with the matching key set of attributes $\mathbf{x}_{ID}$, as follows:

Definition 5. *Let $\mathcal{L}_Q$ denote the set of all conjunctive queries, $\mathcal{D}_I^Q$ the set of all DaQuin-CIS systems, and $\mathcal{P}(V)$ the powerset of all variables in $\mathcal{L}_Q$. Then the Choice of the matching key algorithm can be defined as the function:* $\Psi_{mkey} : \mathcal{L}_Q \times \mathcal{D}_I^Q \to \mathcal{P}(V)$, *such that for any query $q(\mathbf{x}) \in \mathcal{L}_Q$ and DaQuinCIS system $\mathcal{I}_Q \in \mathcal{D}_I^Q$,*
$\mathbf{x}_{ID} = \Psi_{mkey}(q(\mathbf{x}), \mathcal{I}_Q) = \Psi_{mkey}(q^{\mathcal{I}_Q}(\mathbf{x}), \mathcal{I}_Q) \subseteq \mathbf{x}$,
where $\mathbf{x}_{ID}$ is the obtained matching key, thus a subset of all attributes $\mathbf{x}$ of the query. We define also the function $\Phi : \mathcal{P}(V) \times \mathcal{P}(V) \to 2_{space}$, such that for any $(\mathbf{x}, \mathbf{y}) \in \mathcal{P}(V) \times \mathcal{P}(V)$,
$\Phi(\mathbf{x}, \mathbf{y}) = f : S_{|\mathbf{y}|} \to \{0, 1\}$, where for any $1 \leq i \leq |\mathbf{y}|$, $\mathbf{y} = \{y_1, y_2, ..., y_{|\mathbf{y}|}\}$, holds $f(i) = 1$, if $y_i \in \mathbf{x}$; 0 otherwise.

Notice that in the case when in a data integration system $\mathcal{I}$ are defined ID-attributes for their concepts in global and local schemas (for example, when global schema is defined as the Universal relation [11]), the function Ψ_{mkey} does not depend by the second argument, i.e., its λ-abstraction, function $\lambda \Psi_{mkey} : \mathcal{D}_I^Q \to \mathcal{P}(V)^{\mathcal{L}_Q}$ is a constant mapping. In this case the matching key is defined directly from ID-attributes used in the query $q(\mathbf{x})$.

Example 2: In [2] is proposed to exploit quality data exported by each cooperating organization in order to automatically choose the matching key. The idea is to choose a high "quality" key. Let us consider as an example the choice of a key with a low completeness value; after a sorting on the basis of such a key, the potential matching records can be not close to each other, due to null values. Similar considerations can be made also in the case of low accuracy or low consistency of the chosen key; a low accurate or low consistent key does not allow to have potential matching records close to each other. Therefore, we evaluate the quality of the matching key in terms of accuracy, consistency and completeness. Besides quality of data, the other element influencing the choice of the key is the *identification power*.

The *Identification Power* IP_j *of the field j* is defined as:

$$\frac{Number\ of\ eq_j\ Classes}{Total\ Number\ of\ Records}$$

where eq_j Classes are the equivalence classes originated by the relation eq_j applied to the totality of records (Given two records r_1 and r_2, and given a field j of the two records, we define the equivalence relation eq_j such that: $r_1 eq_j r_1\ iff\ r_1.j = r_2.j$, i.e.

the value of the field j of the record r_1 is equal to the value of the field j of the record r_2). The data quality parameter called Data Quality of the field j (DQ_j) represents an overall quality value for the field j and can be calculated in different ways. As an example, in [2], we calculate (DQ_j) as a linear combination of accuracy, consistency and completeness values for the field j, where the coefficients were experimentally determined.

Given the overall quality value DQ_j and the identification power IP_j, we introduce the function K_j, such that: $K_j = DQ_j * IP_j$.

Let us consider all the fields j of records, the steps to calculate the matching key are the following ones:

- Computation of the Data Quality of the field j.
- Computation of the Identification Power of the field j.
- Computation of the function K_j.
- Selection of the matching key as $max\{K_j\}$.

The selection of a set of fields to construct the key is also possible and the computation of the Data Quality and the Identification Power can be easily extended to such cases.
□

From the definition above, given any query over a DaQuinCIS system, $(q(\mathbf{x}), \mathcal{I}_Q) \in \mathcal{L}_Q \times \mathcal{D}_I^Q$ we obtain a function $f = \Theta(q(\mathbf{x}), \mathcal{I}_Q) \in 2_{space}$, where
$\Theta = \Phi \circ (Var \times \Psi) \circ ass \circ (\Delta \times id_D) : \mathcal{L}_Q \times \mathcal{D}_I^Q \to 2_{space}$, with
$Var : \mathcal{L}_Q \to \mathcal{P}(V)$, is a function which for any query returns its free variables,
$ass : (\mathcal{L}_Q \times \mathcal{L}_Q) \times \mathcal{D}_I^Q \simeq \mathcal{L}_Q \times (\mathcal{L}_Q \times \mathcal{D}_I^Q)$ is associativity isomorphism,
$\Delta : \mathcal{L}_Q \to \mathcal{L}_Q \times \mathcal{L}_Q$ is a diagonal function, and $id_D : \mathcal{D}_I^Q \to \mathcal{D}_I^Q$ is identity function.
It is easy to verify that for any query $q(\mathbf{x})$ the obtained matching key sattisfy
$\mathbf{x}_{ID} = \{x_i \mid x_i \in \mathbf{x} \text{ and } \Theta(q(\mathbf{x}), \mathcal{I}_Q)(i) = 1\}$.

When we obtain matching key for a given query $q(\mathbf{x})$ over DaQuinCIS database system, we are ready to consider matching method in order to obtain a partition of records (set of *clusters*), each one consisting of records referring to the same world entity.

Example 3: Usually a matching decision is based on a specific edit distance function; string or edit distance functions consider the amount of difference between strings of symbols. We can chose the Levenshtein distance [9], which is a well known early edit distance where the difference between two text strings is simply the number of insertions, deletions, or substitutions of letters to transform one string into another.

The function we use for deciding if two strings S_1 and S_2 are the same is also dependent from the lengths of the two strings as follows:

$f(S_1, S_2) = \frac{max(length(S_1), length(S_2)) - LD(S_1, S_2)}{max(length(S_1), length(S_2))}$

According to such a function, we normalize the value of the Levenshtein distance by the maximum between the lengths of the two strings, i.e. the function f is 0 if the strings are completely different, 1 if the strings are completely equal.

The procedure we propose to decide if two records match each other is the following:

- the function f is applied to the values of a same field in the two records. If the result is greater than a fixed threshold T_1, the two values are considered equal; we call T_1 *field similarity threshold*. It is fixed experimentally.

- If the number of equal pairs of values in the two records is greater than a threshold T_2, then the two records are considered as match; we call T_2 *record similarity threshold*.It is fixed experimentally.

□

Let now try to give an abstract definition for matching algorithm:

Definition 6. *The matching algorithm can be given by the following function:*
$Match : \sum_{i \leq \omega} \{0,1\}^{S_i} \times \Gamma^i \times \Gamma^i \to \{0,1\}$, *such that for a given matching key (or, equivalently, the function $f \in \{0,1\}^{S_i}$), and any two records $t_1, t_2 \in \Gamma^i$, if $t_1 \approx t_2$ (i.e. they refer the same real world entity) then $Match(f, t_1, t_2) = 1$; otherwise, if not $t_1 \approx t_2$ then $Match(f, t_1, t_2) = 0$.*

In this definition the symbol $\sum_{i \leq \omega}$ represents the disjoint union for matching functions over records wit arity equal to i. Thus we can write
$Match =< Match_1, Match_2, ... >$, where $Match_i : \{0,1\}^{S_i} \times \Gamma^i \times \Gamma^i \to \{0,1\}$ is i-th projection of $Match$, i.e., $Match_i = \pi_i(Match)$.
By λ-abstraction we obtain the function $\lambda(Match_i) : \{0,1\}^{S_i} \to \{0,1\}^{\Gamma^i \times \Gamma^i}$, so that for a given matching key (or, equivalently, the function $f \in \{0,1\}^{S_i}$) we obtain the derived matching function
$\lambda(Match_i)(f) : \Gamma^i \times \Gamma^i \to \{0,1\}$.
The meaning of this abstraction is that $\lambda(Match_i)(f) = \lambda(\pi_i Match)(\Theta(q(\mathbf{x}), \mathcal{I}_Q))$ explicitly contains all data quality 'dimensions' (meta-data), necessary to compare any two records $t_1, t_2 \in \Gamma^i \times \Gamma^i$ in order to decide if they are referred to the same real-world entity. Formally, only this functional abstractions deal with meta-data knowledge of DaQuinCIS database systems, their *semantics* represent the meta-data of DaQuinCIS, i.e. we may consider that the *meta-data are encapsulated* into such functional abstractions. So, for any given query $q(\mathbf{x})$ over DaQuinCIS database system, we obtain that the matching function may be given by: $\lambda(\pi_i Match)(\Theta(q(\mathbf{x}), \mathcal{I}_Q)) : \Gamma^i \times \Gamma^i \to \{0,1\}$, where $i = |Val(q(\mathbf{x}))|$, such that for any two records in the certain answer, $t_1, t_2 \in q^{\mathcal{I}_Q}(\mathbf{x}) \subseteq \Gamma^i$, they are in the same cluster, $t_1 \approx t_2$ if $\lambda(\pi_i Match)(\Theta(q(\mathbf{x}), \mathcal{I}_Q))(t_1, t_2) = 1$.
In the simplest case when the functional abstraction
$\lambda(\pi_i Match)(\Theta(q(\mathbf{x}), \mathcal{I}_Q))$ does not depend of the meta-data (quality dimensions), than it is the characteristic function of the equality $|t_1|_{\mathbf{x}_{ID}} = |t_2|_{\mathbf{x}_{ID}}$, $t_1, t_2 \in \Gamma^i$, where $|t|_{\mathbf{x}_{ID}}$ denotes a projection of the record t on attributes in $\mathbf{x}_{ID}$.

Definition 7. *We define the quality function, Qual, and the database partial order, $\preceq$, as follows*
$Qual : \mathcal{D}_I^Q \times \sum_{i \leq \omega} \Gamma^i \to \mathcal{R}$, *where $\mathcal{R}$ is a set of real numbers, such that given any two records $t_1, t_2 \in q^{\mathcal{I}_Q}(\mathbf{x})$, the $Qual(\mathcal{I}_Q, t_1) \leq_Q Qual(\mathcal{I}_Q, t_2)$ means that t_2 has better quality than t_1.*
Then the partial order is defined by: $\quad t_1 \preceq t_2 \quad iff \quad t_1 \approx t_2$ and $t_1 \leq_Q t_2$.

3 Abstract Object Types for Databases with Filtering Algorithms

The Abstract Object Type for a query-answering system of a database A together with the *external algorithm* $m_{alg} : \Upsilon \to \Upsilon$, can be represented by the following coalgebra (see the Def.2):
$$\alpha = <\lambda Next_Q, m_{alg} \circ \lambda Out_Q>: W_A \to W_A^{\mathcal{L}_Q} \times \Upsilon^{\mathcal{L}_Q}$$
Such database with external software (algorithm m_{alg}) can be equivalently represented as an AOT for a *database with a partial order* $\preceq$ (obtained by *embedding* of the algorithm m_{alg} into a database logic theory), denoted by $A+\preceq$, given by a following coalgebra:
$$\beta = <\lambda Next_{mQ}, \lambda Out_{mQ}>: W_{A+\preceq} \to W_{A+\preceq}^{\mathcal{L}_{mQ}} \times \Upsilon^{\mathcal{L}_{mQ}}$$
of the polynomial endofunctor $(\_)^{\mathcal{L}_{mQ}} \times \Upsilon^{\mathcal{L}_{mQ}} : Set \to Set$, where $\mathcal{L}_{mQ}$ is the set of all *modified* conjunctive queries, $\mathcal{L}_{mQ} = \{\triangledown q(\mathbf{x}) \mid q(\mathbf{x}) \in \mathcal{L}_Q\}$, so that $\triangledown q(\mathbf{x})^{\mathcal{DB}}$ denotes the set of certain answers equal to $m_{alg}(q(\mathbf{x})^{\mathcal{DB}})$. The set of internal states of this AOT is defined by $W_{A+\preceq} = \{s \bigcup R_{\preceq} \mid s \in W_A\}$, where $R_{\preceq}$ denotes the partial ordered set ($(t_1, t_2) \in R_{\preceq}$ iff $t_2 \preceq t_1$), which is an *invariance* (i.e., holds in all internal states of AOT system). We denote by $\varphi : W_A \to W_{A+\preceq}$ this bijection between these two sets of states.

The idea is to obtain the behavioral equivalence of these two AOT's: that is, the original database A, for a given conjunctive query $q(\mathbf{x})$ in the first step computes certain answer $q(\mathbf{x})^{\mathcal{DB}}$, and successively filtered answer $m_{alg}(q(\mathbf{x})^{\mathcal{DB}})$, while, the AOT of a database $A+\preceq$ computes the (equivalent) answer to the modified logic formula $\triangledown q(\mathbf{x})$.

Example 2: It is easy to verify [14] that, for the Example 1, $\triangledown q(\mathbf{x})$ is equivalent to the modified query formula $q(\mathbf{x}) \wedge \forall \mathbf{x}'.((q(\mathbf{x}') \wedge \mathbf{x} \preceq \mathbf{x}') \Rightarrow \mathbf{x}' \preceq \mathbf{x})$, so that the semantics of the operator $\triangledown$ corresponds to the mapping m_{alg}, that is $[\triangledown] = m_{alg}$. □

Proposition 1. *The following commutative diagrams represent the behavioral equivalence for AOT's of a database A with external and embedded algorithm m_{alg}, respectively*

$$
\begin{array}{ccc}
W_A \times \mathcal{L}_Q \xrightarrow{<Next_Q, Out_Q>} W_A \times \Upsilon & \quad & (W_A \xrightarrow{\alpha} W_A^{\mathcal{L}_Q} \times \Upsilon^{\mathcal{L}_Q}) \\
\varphi \times \triangledown \downarrow \quad\quad\quad\quad \varphi \times m_{alg} \downarrow & & \varphi \downarrow \quad\quad \phi \downarrow \\
W_{A+\preceq} \times \mathcal{L}_{mQ} \xrightarrow{<Next_{mQ}, Out_{mQ}>} W_{A+\preceq} \times \Upsilon & & (W_{A+\preceq} \xrightarrow{\beta} W_{A+\preceq}^{\mathcal{L}_{mQ}} \times \Upsilon^{\mathcal{L}_{mQ}})
\end{array}
$$

where $\phi = (\varphi^{-1} \circ \_ \circ \triangledown) \times (\_ \circ \triangledown)$, such that for each pair of functions, $s_1 : \mathcal{L}_{mQ} \to W_{A+\preceq}$, $f_1 : \mathcal{L}_{mQ} \to \Upsilon$, we obtain $(s, f) = \phi(s_1, f_1) \in W_A^{\mathcal{L}_Q} \times \Upsilon^{\mathcal{L}_Q}$, where $s = \varphi^{-1} \circ s_1 \circ \triangledown : \mathcal{L}_Q \to W_A$ and $f = f_1 \circ \triangledown : \mathcal{L}_Q \to \Upsilon$.
The commutative diagrams above can be represented by the behavior-equivalence isomorphism $\varphi : (W_A, \alpha) \simeq (W_{A+\preceq}, \delta)$, where $\delta = T_c(\varphi) \circ \phi \circ \beta$, *of the polynomial functor* $T_c = (\_)^{\mathcal{L}_Q} \times \Upsilon^{\mathcal{L}_Q} : Set \to Set$, *for the language of conjunctive queries* $\mathcal{L}_Q$.

Notice that in the right commutative diagram, the horizontal arrows α and β represents these two equivalent AOT's, for database with external algorithm and the 'encapsulated' database with embedded algorithm, respectively, such that for any state of database $w \in W_A$, and the conjunctive query $q(\mathbf{x}) \in \mathcal{L}_Q$, we obtain that for a two bisimilar states (w, w_1), that is $w_1 = \varphi(w)$:

$w'_1 = \varphi(w')$, where $w' = Next_Q(w, q(\mathbf{x})) = \lambda Next_Q(w)(q(\mathbf{x}))$ and $w'_1 = Next_{mQ}(w_1, \triangledown q(\mathbf{x})) = \lambda Next_{mQ}(w_1)(\triangledown q(\mathbf{x}))$ are two next (bisimilar) states of these two AOT's, and
$m_{alg}(Out_Q(w, q(\mathbf{x}))) = m_{alg}(\lambda Out_Q(w)(q(\mathbf{x}))) = Out_{mQ}(w_1, \triangledown q(\mathbf{x})) = \lambda Out_{mQ}(w_1)(\triangledown q(\mathbf{x}))$ are identical observations (i.e., answers to user queries).

Let verify the second part of the proposition. The right commutative diagram can be equivalently represented by the following commutative diagram

$$\begin{array}{ccccc}
W_A \times \mathcal{L}_Q & \xrightarrow{<Next_Q, Out_Q>} & W_A \times \Upsilon & \xrightarrow{id \times m_{alg}} & W_A \times \Upsilon \\
\varphi \times id \downarrow & & & & \downarrow \varphi \times id \\
W_{A+\preceq} \times \mathcal{L}_Q & \xrightarrow{id \times \triangledown} & W_{A+\preceq} \times \mathcal{L}_{mQ} & \xrightarrow{<Next_{mQ}, Out_{mQ}>} & W_{A+\preceq} \times \Upsilon
\end{array}$$

The horizontal arrow above corresponds to the T_c-coalgebra of the original database A and represents the two step query computation: first computes certain answer to the conjunctive query and then is applied the filtering algorithm m_{alg}; while the horizontal arrow below corresponds to the T_c-coalgebra of the database $A+ \preceq$ and represents the two step computation: first rewrites the original user's conjunctive query and then computes the certain answer to this modified query w.r.t. the database A with the partial order.

From this diagram, by λ-abstraction (curring) we obtain the following commutative diagram

$$\begin{array}{ccc}
W_A & \xrightarrow{\alpha} & W_A^{\mathcal{L}_Q} \times \Upsilon^{\mathcal{L}_Q} = T_c(W_A) \\
\varphi \downarrow & & \downarrow T_c(\varphi) \\
W_{A+\preceq} & \xrightarrow{\delta} & W_{A+\preceq}^{\mathcal{L}_Q} \times \Upsilon^{\mathcal{L}_Q} = T_c(W_{A+\preceq})
\end{array} \quad \begin{array}{c} (W_A, \alpha) \\ \\ \downarrow \varphi (\simeq) \\ \\ (W_{A+\preceq}, \delta) \end{array}$$

where $T_c(\varphi) = (\varphi \circ \_) \times id$. This diagram is the isomorphism (bijective homomorphism) $\varphi : (W_A, \alpha) \to (W_{A+\preceq}, \delta)$, where $\delta = T_c(\varphi) \circ \phi \circ \beta =< \lambda(Next_{mQ} \circ (id \times \triangledown)), \lambda(Out_{mQ} \circ (id \times \triangledown)) >$, of the polynomial functor $T_c = (\_)^{\mathcal{L}_Q} \times \Upsilon^{\mathcal{L}_Q} : Set \to Set$.

Thus, the database $A+ \preceq$ with a partial order, obtained by embedding of the algorithm, can be considered as a preorder-enrichment of a database A: for each minimal Herbrand model M of a database A, we have a minimal model $M \bigcup R_{\preceq}^M$ of a database $A+ \preceq$, where $R_{\preceq}^M$ is the restriction of the preorder relation $R_{\preceq}$ to ground atoms in M; that is, $R_{\preceq}^M = \{(t_1, t_2) \mid (t_1, t_2) \in R_{\preceq} \text{ and } t_1, t_2 \in M\}$.

4 Modal Query Language for Databases with a Partial Order

From the fact that the 'best answering' w.r.t. the given partial order $\preceq$ and user defined conjunctive query $q(\mathbf{x})$ is the set of tuples:

$\triangledown q(\mathbf{x})^{\mathcal{DB}} = m_{alg}(q(\mathbf{x})^{\mathcal{DB}}) = \{\mathbf{t} \mid q_L(\mathbf{t})$ is true in all models of database $A+ \preceq\}$
where q_L is a lifted by $\preceq$ predicate q, that is
$q_L(\mathbf{x}) \Leftrightarrow q(\mathbf{x}) \wedge \forall \mathbf{x}'.((q(\mathbf{x}') \wedge \mathbf{x} \preceq \mathbf{x}') \Rightarrow \mathbf{x}' \preceq \mathbf{x}).$
Now we will show that the semantics of the syntax symbol $\triangledown$ corresponds to the modal logic operator, so that $\mathcal{L}_{mQ}$ is the modal query language.
We begin from the fact that for any given database A with $\Upsilon_{\mathcal{DB}} = \{q(\mathbf{x})^{\mathcal{DB}} \mid q(\mathbf{x}) \in \mathcal{L}_Q\}$, and $X = \bigcup_{w \in \Upsilon_{\mathcal{DB}}} w$, the couple $(X, R_\preceq)$ corresponds to the frame with X the set of points, and partial order $R_\preceq$ its accessibility relation.

Definition 8. *The frame* $(X, R_\preceq)$ *can be represented by the coalgebra* $\gamma : X \to \mathcal{P}(X)$, *where* $\mathcal{P}$ *is a powerset operation (moreover, it is powerset functor* $\mathcal{P} : Set \to Set$) *and for any* $t \in X$, $\gamma(t)$ *is the set of all successors of the point* t (*i.e., the set of all* t' *such that* $(t, t') \in R_\preceq$, *or, equivalently,* $t' \preceq t$).

For any subset $Y \subseteq X$ of the partially ordered set (poset) X, we denote by $\bigvee Y$ the subset of all Least Upper Bounds (lub's) in Y.

Example 3: It is easy to verify that for any conjunctive query $q(\mathbf{x})$ for $Y = q(\mathbf{x})^{\mathcal{DB}} \subseteq X$, we have that $\bigvee Y = \bigvee q(\mathbf{x})^{\mathcal{DB}} = m_{alg}(q(\mathbf{x})^{\mathcal{DB}})$.
That is, in our framework the 'best answers' filtering algorithm m_{alg} is an operation which extracts only lub's of the answer to the conjunctive query. □

The idea that the functor of a coalgebra determines a certain modal logic was first put forward by Moss [10]. He developed it for very general functors, namely those which admit the existence of the initial algebra, however it is lack of abstract syntax. Here we will use the other approach [3,4] based on Kripke Polynomial Functors: Multi-modal logic for coalgebras which utilize *predicate lifting* to interpret modalities (interested reader can find a short overview in the Appendix of this paper).

Definition 9. *We define a* partial-bounded *set of successors for a frame* $(X, R_\preceq)$ *by the following mapping:* $l : X \times \Upsilon_{\mathcal{DB}} \to \mathcal{P}(X)$
such that for any point $t \in X$ *and the set* $Y \in \Upsilon_{\mathcal{DB}} \subseteq \mathcal{P}(X)$, (*thus* $Y \subseteq X$), *holds:*
$l(t, Y) = \gamma(t) \bigcap Y$ *if* $t \in \bigvee Y$; X, *otherwise.*
We denote by λl *its* $\lambda -$ *abstraction (curring),* $\lambda l : X \to \mathcal{P}(X)^{\Upsilon_{\mathcal{DB}}}$. *It is a coalgebra* $(X, \lambda l)$ *with a carrier set* X, *of the functor* $T = \mathcal{P}(\_)^{\Upsilon_{\mathcal{DB}}} : Set \to Set$.

Proposition 2. *The operator* $\triangledown$ *is a nextime modal operator defined for any conjunctive query* $q(\mathbf{x})$, *and* $w = q(\mathbf{x})^{\mathcal{DB}}$ *by the path* $p = ev(w) \cdot \mathcal{P} : \mathcal{P}(\_)^{\Upsilon_{\mathcal{DB}}} \rightsquigarrow Id$, *so that holds* $[ev(w) \cdot \mathcal{P}](w) = (\lambda l)^{-1} \circ (\_)^{ev(w) \cdot \mathcal{P}})(w) = m_{alg}(w)$.
Thus, by generalization, we obtain the interpretation of the modal operator $\triangledown$, *restricted to a subset* $\Upsilon_{\mathcal{DB}} \subseteq \mathcal{P}(X)$, *given by*
$[\triangledown] = (\lambda l)^{-1} \circ (\_)^{ev(\_) \cdot \mathcal{P}} : \Upsilon_{\mathcal{DB}} \to \mathcal{P}(X)$.

Proof. For any $w \in \Upsilon_{\mathcal{DB}}$, thus, $w \subset X$, we have that
$[ev(w) \cdot \mathcal{P}](w) = (\lambda l)^{-1} \circ (\_)^{ev(w) \cdot \mathcal{P}})(w) = (\lambda l)^{-1}((w)^{ev(w) \cdot \mathcal{P}}) =$
$= (\lambda l)^{-1}(\mathcal{P}(w))^{ev(w)} = (\lambda l)^{-1}(\{f \mid f(w) \in \mathcal{P}(w)\})$
$= \{x \mid \lambda l(x) \in \{f \mid f(w) \in \mathcal{P}(w)\}\}$
$= \bigvee w$, from the fact that $x \notin \bigvee w$ iff $\lambda l(x)(w) = l(x, w) = X \notin \mathcal{P}(w)$
$= m_{alg}(w)$.

Corollary 1. *The query formulae for a databases enriched with partial order (by an embedded best-answer filtering algorithm) are the modal logic formulae obtained by predicate lifting of original conjunctive queries. The answer to such lifted query is equal to the (by algorithm) filtered answer to the original conjunctive query.*

Now, from the fact that $\triangledown$ is the syntax of the (surjective) modal operation $\triangledown : \mathcal{L}_Q \to \mathcal{L}_{mQ}$, where the set of modified conjunctive queries, $\mathcal{L}_{mQ}$ is the image of this mapping, we can introduce its inverse mapping, denoted by $\triangledown^{-1}$, such that for any $\triangledown q(\mathbf{x}) \in \mathcal{L}_{mQ}$, we obtain that $\triangledown^{-1}(\triangledown q(\mathbf{x})) = q(\mathbf{x}) \in \mathcal{L}_Q$). Thus the T_c-coalgebra isomorphism $\varphi : (W_A, \alpha) \to (W_{A+\preceq}, \delta)$, of the polynomial functor $T_c = (\_)^{\mathcal{L}_Q} \times \Upsilon^{\mathcal{L}_Q} : Set \to Set$ for the language $\mathcal{L}_Q$ of finite conjunctive queries, can be, equivalently, represented by the coalgebra isomorphism $\varphi^{-1} : (W_{A+\preceq}, \beta) \to (W_A, \delta_1)$, of the 'modal' endofunctor $T_m = (\_)^{\mathcal{L}_{mQ}} \times \Upsilon^{\mathcal{L}_{mQ}} : Set \to Set$ for the modal language $\mathcal{L}_{mQ}$. That is, the following commutative diagram holds

$$W_A \times \mathcal{L}_{mQ} \xrightarrow{id \times \triangledown^{-1}} W_A \times \mathcal{L}_Q \xrightarrow{<Next_Q, m_{alg} \circ Out_Q>} W_A \times \Upsilon$$

$$\varphi^{-1} \times id \uparrow \qquad\qquad\qquad \varphi^{-1} \times id \uparrow$$

$$W_{A+\preceq} \times \mathcal{L}_{mQ} \xrightarrow{<Next_{mQ}, Out_{mQ}>} W_{A+\preceq} \times \Upsilon$$

Where the horizontal arrow above corresponds to the three steps computation: for a given modal formula first step reduce it to the conjunctive query, then it is computed a certain answer for this query on a database A and, it is filtered by the algorithm m_{alg}. From this diagram, by λ-abstraction (curring) we obtain the following commutative diagram

$$W_A \xrightarrow{\delta_1} W_A^{\mathcal{L}_{mQ}} \times \Upsilon^{\mathcal{L}_{mQ}} = T_m(W_A) \qquad (W_A, \delta_1)$$

$$\varphi^{-1} \uparrow \qquad\qquad T_m(\varphi^{-1}) \uparrow \qquad\qquad \varphi^{-1}(\simeq) \uparrow$$

$$W_{A+\preceq} \xrightarrow{\beta} W_{A+\preceq}^{\mathcal{L}_{mQ}} \times \Upsilon^{\mathcal{L}_{mQ}} = T_m(W_{A+\preceq}) \qquad (W_{A+\preceq}, \beta)$$

where $T_m(\varphi) = (\varphi^{-1} \circ \_) \times id$ and $\delta_1 = < \lambda(Next_Q \circ (id \times \triangledown^{-1})), \lambda(m_{alg} \circ Out_Q \circ (id \times \triangledown^{-1})) >$, so that $\phi = ((\_ \circ \triangledown) \times (\_ \circ \triangledown)) \circ T_m(\varphi)$.
These two isomorphisms, $\varphi : (W_A, \alpha) \to (W_{A+\preceq}, \delta)$, and $\varphi^{-1} : (W_{A+\preceq}, \beta) \to (W_A, \delta_1)$, represent the behavioural equivalence of these two AOTs: AOT for a original database A with the external-to-database algorithm m_{alg} w.r.t. the conjunctive query language $\mathcal{L}_Q$, and the AOT for a database $A+ \preceq$ (with algorithm embedded into a database A) w.r.t. this modal language $\mathcal{L}_{mQ}$, respectively.

5 Conclusion

We have proposed a novel formal logic method to the well known and important, yet frequently ignored problem of considering the query-answering semantics in information integration with also filtering algorithms which restricts the answers to conjunctive queries in a subset of 'best consistent' answers. This problem has not, to our best knowledge, been adequately addressed before: the developed in practice software systems are mainly focused in formalization and implementation of their filtering algorithms, considering that such software systems implicitly support their particular *operational* semantics, by a particular developed algorithm, for a query answering of the whole system.

But such discrepancy in the formal logic theory of the database and, external to it, the software which implements filtering algorithm needs to be overcomed by the logic- theoretical considerations in order to provide a model theoretic (denotational) semantics for query answering.

Moreover, we generalize such mixed database/external-software-module into equivalent to it, database with partial order (obtained by embedding the algorithm into a database logic theory), which can be applied in other in practice developed systems also.

The query formula to such poset-enriched database is a modal formula, such that certain answers (true in all models for such poset-enriched database) to such query formula is equal to the algorithm-filtering of the set of certain answers to the original conjunctive query of the (non enriched) database.

The formalization of query-answering database systems by mean of Abstract Object Types is useful for embedding other procedural database features also. Such abstraction, together with the concept of behavior equivalence for query answering is a good framework to analyze the model theoretic properties of the whole system, but also to define the specification for mappings, based on views, between different database systems, as for example in complex P2P database systems, where each peer can be considered as an AOT which possibly encapsulate a database system (thus all internal structure and application embedded algorithms, of a database peer, are hidden).

Acknowledgments. This research is partially supported by the project NoE INTEROP-IST-508011 and the project SEWASIE-IST-2001-3425. The author wishes to thank Tiziana Catarci and Maurizio Lenzerini for their support.

References

1. B.Beckert, R.Hanhle, and F.Manyá. Transformations between signed and classical clause logic. *In Proc. 29th Int.Symposium on Multiple-Valued Logics, Freiburg,Germany*, pages 248–255, 1999.
2. P. Bertolazzi, L. D. Santis, and M. Scannapieco. Automatic Record Matching in Cooperative Information Systems. In *Proceedings of the ICDT'03 International Workshop on Data Quality in Cooperative Information Systems (DQCIS'03)*, Siena, Italy, 2003.
3. B.Jacobs. Towards a duality result in coalgebraic modal logic. *In H.Reichel, editor, Coalgebraic Methods in computer science, Vol.33 of Elec.Notes in Theor. Comp. Sci.*, 2000.
4. B.Jacobs. Many-sorted coalgebraic modal logic: a model-theoretic study. *Theoretical Informatics and Applications, 35(1)*, pages 31–59, 2001.
5. D.Lembo, M.Lenzerini, and R.Rosati. Source inconsistency and incompleteness in data integration. *In Proc. of the 9th Int.Workshop on Knowledge Representation meets Databases (KRDB 2002) CEUR*, 2002.

6. G.Greco, S.Greco, and E.Zampano. A logic programming approach to the integration, repairing and querying of inconsistent databases. *In Proc. of the 17th Int. Conf. on Logic Programming*, 2237:348–364, 2001.
7. H.A.Blair and V.S.Subrahmanian. Paraconsistent logic programming. *Theoretical Computer Science,68*, pages 135–154, 1989.
8. G. Imaz and F.Manyá. The satisfiability problem for multiple-valued horn formulae. *In Proc. International Symposium on Multiple-Valued Logics (ISMVL), Boston, IEEE Press, Los Alamitos*, pages 250–256, 1994.
9. V. I. Levenshtein. Binary codes capable of correcting deletions, insertions and reversals. *Doklady Akademii Nauk SSSR*, 10(8), 1966.
10. L.S.Moss. Coalgebraic logic. *Annals of Pure and Applied Logic*, 96:277–317, 1999.
11. D. Maier, J. D. Ullman, and M. Y. Vardi. On the foundations of the universal relation model. *ACM Trans. Database Syst.*, 9:283–308, 1984.
12. Z. Majkić. Coalgebraic semantics for logic programming. *18th Worshop on (Constraint) Logic Programming, WLP 2004, March 04-06, Berlin, Germany*, 2004.
13. Z. Majkić. Database mappings and partial trees derived from abstract object type. *Notes in http://www.dis.uniroma1.it/ ~ majkic/*, 2004.
14. Z. Majkić. General framework for query answering in data quality cooperative information systems. *International Workshop on Information Quality in Information Systems (IQIS), June 18, Paris, France*, 2004.
15. Z. Majkić. Meta many-valued logic programming for incomplete and locally inconsistent databases. *8th International Database Engineering and Application Symposium (IDEAS),July 7-9, Coimbra, Portugal*, 2004.
16. Z. Majkić. Ontological encapsulation of many-valued logic. *19th Italian Symposium of Computational Logic (CILC04),June 16-17, Parma, Italy*, 2004.
17. M.C.Fitting. Billatices and the semantics of logic programming. *Journal of Logic Programming,11*, pages 91–116, 1991.
18. M. Mecella, M. Scannapieco, A. Virgillito, R. Baldoni, T. Catarci, and C. Batini. Managing Data Quality in Cooperative Information Systems. *Journal of Data Semantics*, (to appear) 2003.
19. M.Ginsberg. Multivalued logics: A uniform approach to reasoning in artificial intelligence. *Computational Intelligence, vol.4*, pages 265–316, 1988.
20. M.Kifer and E.L.Lozinskii. A logic for reasoning with inconsistency. *Journal of Automated reasoning 9(2)*, pages 179–215, 1992.
21. M.Kifer and V.S.Subrahmanian. Theory of generalized annotated logic programming and its applications. *Journal of Logic Programming 12(4)*, pages 335–368, 1992.
22. M.Lenzerini. Data integration:a theoretical perspective. pages 233–246, 2002.
23. R. Reiter. What should a database know? *Journal of Logic Programming*, 14:127–153, 1990.
24. R.Hahnle. Automated deduction in multiple-valued logics. *Oxford University Press*, 1994.

Composing Mappings Between Schemas Using a Reference Ontology

Eduard Dragut and Ramon Lawrence

IDEA Lab, Department of Computer Science, University of Iowa
Iowa City, IA, USA, 52242
{eduard-dragut, ramon-lawrence}@uiowa.edu
http://www.cs.uiowa.edu/~rlawrenc/

Abstract. Large-scale database integration requires a significant cost in developing a global schema and finding mappings between the global and local schemas. Developing the global schema requires matching and merging the concepts in the data sources and is a bottleneck in the process. In this paper we propose a strategy for computing the mapping between schemas by performing a composition of the mappings between individual schemas and a reference ontology. Our premise is that many organizations have standard ontologies that, although they may not be suitable as a global schema, are useful in providing standard terminology and naming conventions for concepts and relationships. It is valuable to leverage these existing ontological resources to help automate the construction of a global schema and mappings between schemas. Our system semi-automates the matching between local schemas and a reference ontology then automatically composes the matchings to build mappings between schemas. Using these mappings, we use model management techniques to compute a global schema. A major advantage of this approach is that human intervention in validating matchings mostly occurs during the matching between schema and ontology. A problem is that matching schemas to ontologies is challenging because the ontology may only contain a subset of the concepts in the schema or may be more general than the schema. Further, the more complicated ontological graph structure limits the effectiveness of some matchers. Our contribution is showing how schema-to-ontology matchings can be used to compose mappings between schemas with high accuracy by adapting the COMA schema matching system to work with ontologies.

1 Introduction

Database integration is a challenging problem that has been extensively studied [1,2] for many years. Automating integration has proven difficult because schemas do not always capture the necessary semantics to identify related concepts. Schema matching systems [3] are used to build mappings between schemas that are then used to construct an integrated view. Although good accuracy has been achieved by schema matching techniques, validating matches is difficult because a user must understand the semantics of both schemas. Further, if many schemas are matched together, this validation must be performed for each pairwise matching. In an integration scenario, it is hard for a global integrator to understand the semantics of each schema to be integrated in order to validate matches. It is also difficult to define and maintain a global schema as it requires identifying all concepts in all databases.

Many organizations, especially biomedical organizations such as the National Cancer Institute (NCI) and National Institutes of Health (NIH), have been developing standard ontologies for their domains. These ontologies are not suitable as global schemas because they are more general than the domain being modeled or do not contain all the concepts required. However, they are useful in the matching process as they can be used as a reference ontology. The idea is to match each source to the domain ontology, and each schema-to-ontology match is validated by the database administrator. The advantage of this approach is that the administrator only needs to understand the semantics of their schema when validating matches. Schema-to-ontology matches can be used to build mappings to any schema that is also matched to the ontology by composing the schema-to-ontology matchings. The goal of this work is to use these pre-existing ontologies to automate schema matching and global view construction.

The challenge is that an existing ontology may not cover the domain exactly. Schema concepts that are not in the ontology will not be discovered during matching. The ontology may be more general and have many more concepts which reduces the matching accuracy. The more complicated ontological structure reduces the effectiveness of some matchers, specifically those that use names and paths. Our overall contribution is demonstrating how existing schema matching systems can be adapted for discovering schema-to-ontology matchings useful for ontology-based integration. The contributions of this work are:

- An algorithm for mapping ontologies into schema graphs for use with automatic schema matching systems such as COMA [4].
- A method for composing schema-to-ontology matchings to produce mappings between schemas.
- A model management [5] methodology for producing an integrated view using schema-to-ontology matchings. The integrated view is a federated view in the sense that it can be dynamically constructed from any number of schemas and may be site specific.
- An experimental evaluation demonstrating that schema-to-ontology matching can be achieved with good accuracy and that schema-to-schema mappings derived from these matchings can have similar accuracy to direct, pair-wise schema matching.

This work is different than other ontology-based integration approaches [6,7, 8] as the schema-to-ontology matchings are generated semi-automatically. Generation of these matchings is a bottleneck to integration using ontologies. The schema matching on ontologies is different than other schema matching systems [3,4,9] that either perform schema-to-schema matching or ontology-to-ontology matching. Ontological matching has distinctive features that have received less attention in schema matching systems such as IS-A relationships, complex hierarchies, limited or no data instances, and no explicit keys and identifiers. Thus, schema-to-ontology matching deserves special attention as many existing matchers have poor performance in this environment.

The organization of this paper is as follows. Section 2 provides a brief discussion on related work on database integration and schema matching. The problem domain and overall approach is covered in Section 3. In Section 4, we describe how the COMA matching system [4] is used to match ontologies with schemas. Once schemas are individually matched to an ontology, composition is used to build mappings between schemas. Composing mappings from schema-to-ontology matchings is discussed in Section 5. Constructing a global view using model management techniques and schema-to-ontology matchings is covered in Section 6. The approach allows each client to produce its own "global view" by composing only the schema-to-ontology matchings for the sources required. Detailed performance experiments on the accuracy of schema-to-ontology matchings and mapping composition are discussed in Section 7. The paper closes with future work and conclusions.

2 Related Work

Ontologies have been used in various roles for database integration [1,2]. An ontology may be used instead of a global schema such as in the Carnot project [7] that used the Cyc ontology [10]. The Carnot system required administrators to manually map their schema into the global ontology. Global queries were then posed on the ontology. The MOMIS system [6] semi-automates the construction of the global view by extracting and manually annotating schema using WordNet [11] as a shared lexical database. Using WordNet allows the system to detect lexicon relationships as well as structural relationships in the schemas. The challenge with using a large ontology like WordNet is that it is not specific to the domain and does not model relationships between entities. For example, although the concepts *Order* and *Date* will be in WordNet, the complex concept *OrderDate* (representing that an order has a date) will not. This forces the designer to map a schema element to many WordNet terms. There are other systems that use ontologies for integration [12] including ONTOBROKER [13] and OBSERVER [8]. OBSERVER performs integration using multiple existing ontologies by translating vocabulary that conflicts in different ontologies. The common challenge in these approaches is that the mappings must be *manually* determined between ontology and schema. The deployment of ontology-based integration approaches would be greatly aided by more automated mapping discovery techniques as discussed in this paper.

Ontologies are also used to improve the accuracy of schema matching. Several systems [4,14] use WordNet or thesauri to detect synonym relationships and related concepts. Xu and Embley [15] used custom constructed ontologies to detect concepts by matching their data values to expected data values using regular expressions. In these systems, the ontology serves a supporting role in the matching, but is not directly involved in the process. There has also been work on matching ontologies [9] using algorithms similar to matching schemas [16]. Methods for merging ontologies given manual matchings [17] have also been performed. The PROMPT system [18] semi-automatically guides a user in merging ontologies. OntoBuilder [19] can merge ontologies extracted from web search interfaces. Ontologies have been used in the SCROL project [20] to detect semantic conflicts given manually specified mappings between the schemas and federated schema. There has been limited work on matching schemas to ontologies, where the reference ontology is an intermediary in the integration process (without being the entire global view).

Model management [5,21] and schema matching [3] have been proposed to semi-automate database integration. The idea is to semi-automatically match schemas and then use these mappings to manipulate schemas using higher-level operators. A *match* is a correspondence between schema elements. A *mapping* between two schema elements is an expression that relates the two elements. A schema matching system will detect matchings between elements, but may not determine the mapping expression between them. Schema matching systems [4,16,14] use schema and instance level matchers to determine when elements in different schemas represent the same concept. The matchers may use linguistic information such as names and comments, schema information such as paths and constraints, and data instances. Most systems combine matchers into hybrid or composite matchers to improve the accuracy compared to individual matchers. Schema matchers that use data instances are not applicable for schema-to-ontology matching as discussed in this paper as the reference schemas are assumed to have no data instances. COMA [4] is a schema matching system that contains many matchers and is a flexible system for adding and combining matchers. COMA supports re-use of matches to improve matching accuracy.

Corpus-based matching [22] also re-uses matches and is similar in spirit to our proposed approach. In corpus-based matching, previous matches are archived into a Mapping Knowledge Base (MKB) that functions as a universal schema. When a concept is matched, it is matched to an existing concept in the universal schema or added to the schema. When two schemas are to be matched, each schema element is matched to the concepts in the MKB. If two elements from different schemas, match to the same MKB concept, they are predicted to match to each other. The MKB functions as an intermediary for the matching and learns classifiers for each universal schema element. Our approach using a reference ontology is similar as the ontology acts as a given (incomplete) universal schema of the domain. The difference is that the ontology is an accepted reference ontology available to the user during matching. The MKB is a hidden construct used by the system for matching. Our system allows the user control over the schema-to-ontology matching process and is more suitable to environments where users map to shared ontologies.

Overall, ontology-based integration systems can benefit from semi-automatic schema-to-ontology mapping algorithms and from an approach to build a global view using a reference ontology that may not model the domain perfectly.

3   System Architecture

The goal is to use a *pre-existing* reference ontology to semi-automate the construction of mappings between schemas. The reference ontology contains some of the concepts in the schemas, but may be incomplete or more general than the schemas. We assume that the ontology is more than a taxonomy as it should contain containment and general relationships between concepts. The ontology does not have instances, and thus should not be considered as a schema. Source schemas have an overlapping set of concepts, but are not identical in their modeling of the domain. Constructing a global view of these schemas is accomplished in a three step process:

- Independent matching of each schema to the ontology.
- Composing schema-to-ontology matches to produce schema-to-schema mappings.
- Merging the schemas to build a global view using the mappings.

It is useful to consider how the approach would be performed manually before examining how to automate it. First, a database administrator would match schema elements to ontological concepts. A schema element may not be in the ontology or may not match perfectly if it is more general or more specific than an ontological concept. Each schema element matches to zero or more ontological concepts. Since the administrator understands the schema, producing and validating matchings to the ontology is reasonable, although it does require the administrator to understand the pre-existing reference ontology. Composing the schema-to-ontology matchings produced independently by two administrators is straightforward. It is assumed that two schema elements match if they both map to the same ontological concept. Finally, given the schema mappings, applying a *Merge* operator as defined in the model management approach can be used to build the global view. Even with an entirely manual approach, matching to a reference ontology has the benefit that administrators only have to understand the semantics of their own schema and must only perform and validate one matching. The manual matching approach has been used in previous ontology-based integration systems where it is assumed that the ontology serves as an all-encompassing global view. It is not common for an ontology to model all domain concepts in a form suitable for use as a global view, but it is very common for pre-existing, shared, standard ontologies to be available for many domains.

Several complexities arise when automating the global view construction. It is valuable to re-use existing schema matching algorithms (such as COMA [4]), but this requires converting an ontology into a suitable form (Section 4). The matching algorithms will be less accurate as the ontology does not completely cover the domain and will model it in a different form. The composition to produce schema-to-schema mappings (Section 5) may create false matches or may miss matches when elements map to different ontological concepts or do not have any correspondences within the ontology. Merging schemas, even with mappings, is not fully automatic as the mappings are often imperfect and require user intervention [21]. We discuss these issues in the following sections.

4 Ontological Matching

Given the reference ontology, the first step is to convert it into a form suitable for schema matching. We use the COMA [4] schema matching system that models a schema as a rooted directed acyclic graph. A schema consists of a set of elements, such as relational tables and columns or XML elements and attributes. In COMA schema elements are represented by graph nodes connected by directed links of different types, such as containment and referential relationships.

We map ontologies that consist of collections of taxonomies and properties. The native format of the ontologies are ASCII files containing the concept definitions in OWL or DAML format. The translation into graphs is performed using an import filter that understands the definitions of concepts and properties in OWL or DAML specification. The ontology is converted to COMA graph format using an import tool developed using the *JENA* ontology parser[1]. Schemas and an ontology in the order domain are used as examples. The reference ontology is in Figure 1.

During the import, each ontology concept (class) becomes a node in the graph. For the properties (attributes) of each class, add a node to the graph and connect it to its class. Each class property has associated information such as a data type and cardinality that is stored as additional information with the node. This information is used by many schema matching algorithms. Properties that have both domain and range as concepts in the ontology (i.e. *shipTo*) are represented as nodes in the graph. Each of these nodes has a parent node that represents the class that is its domain and a child node that represents the class that is its range. A directed edge from the parent (domain) node to the new node is added to the graph as well as a directed edge from the new node to its child (range) node. In the current implementation we do not support properties that have a domain or range specified as intersection or union of concepts. IS_A relationships in the ontology are inserted as directed edges from the subclass node to the superclass node. In Figure 2 is an example of converting the ontological relationship *shipTo* between *PurchaseOrder* and *Organization* into a *shipTo* node and two directed edges.

After all the relationships (edges) are in the graph, a graph traversal is performed along IS_A links to make IS_A relationships explicit. COMA does not handle IS_A relationships, so these relationships are made explicit by having each subclass contain the properties of its superclasses. In the final step, top nodes are identified that are not contained in any other node. If there are multiple top nodes, then a new root node is added and all top nodes become its children. In Figure 3 is an example of making superclass properties (*Phone, Email, Fax*) explicit in the subclasses *Person* and *Organization*.

Once the ontology is converted into a schema graph, the COMA system will *automatically* match the schema to the ontology. The result is a schema-to-ontology matching. We define two approaches to generating these schema-to-ontology matchings and extend the COMA system to support them. The first

---

[1] http://jena.sourceforge.net/

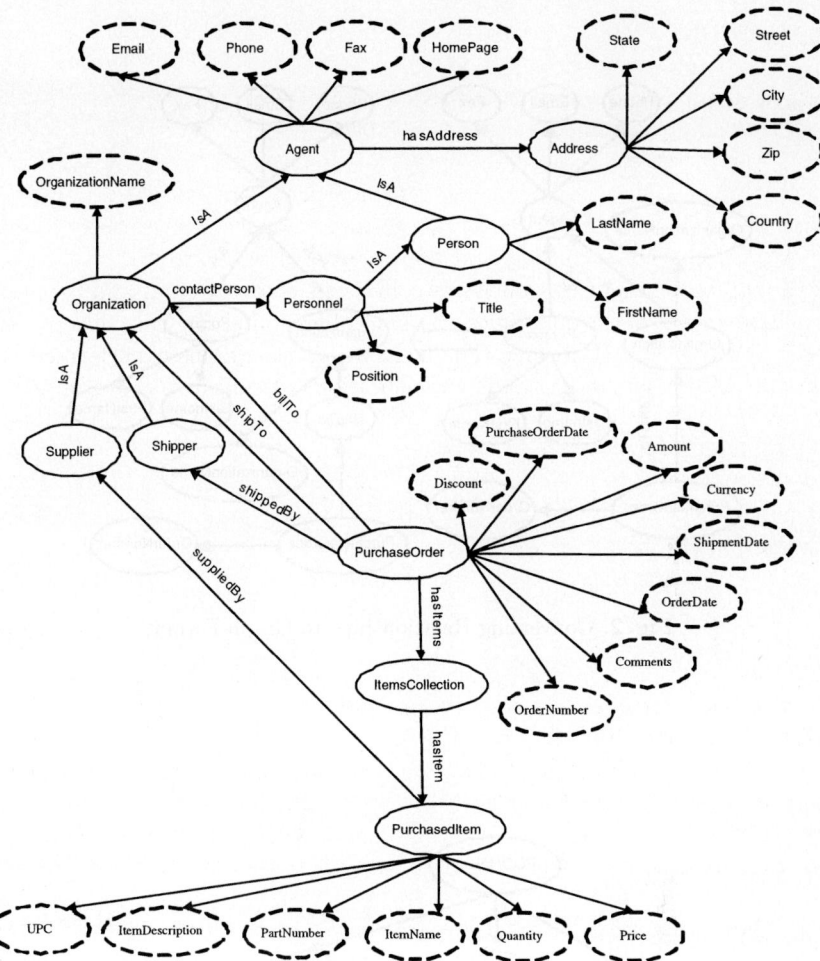

Fig. 1. Order Ontology

approach called Max generates up to one match between a schema element and its best matching ontological concept. A schema element may not have a match if the similarity is below a threshold. This may occur if the schema element concept is not in the ontology. The Max approach is good if the user will validate and improve matchings as it will generate only one match per schema element. Unfortunately, it will often miss matches where a schema element should map to two or more ontological concepts (such as *full name* matching to *first name* and *last name*) and may not always select the correct concept.

The second approach, called noMax, generates a variable number of matchings for each schema element. The advantage of noMax is that it allows a schema element to map to multiple ontological concepts and may allow mappings to be

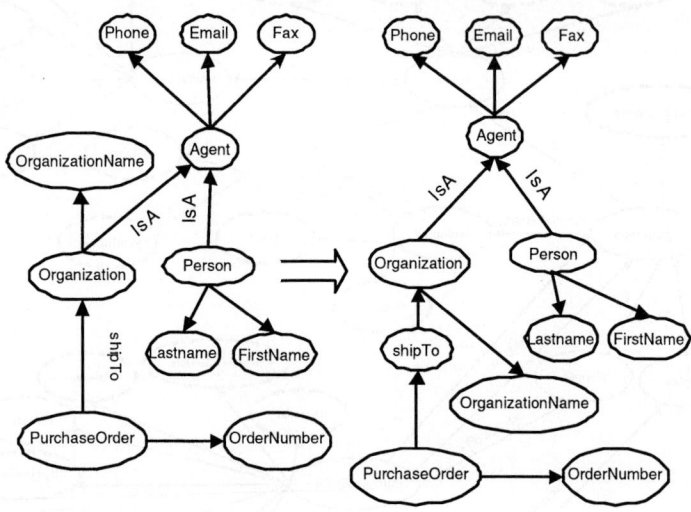

Fig. 2. Converting Relationships to Graph Format

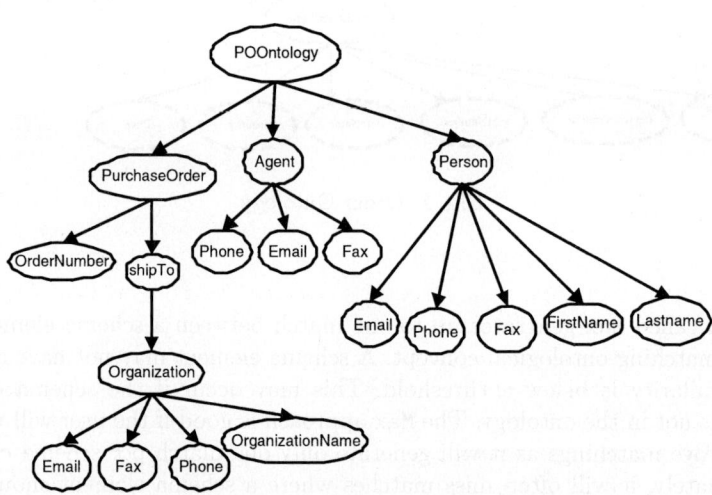

Fig. 3. Making IS-A Relationships Explicit

discovered that would have been discarded using Max. The problem with noMax is that it generates many incorrect mappings. An administrator seeking to create a "perfect" schema-to-ontology mapping would then spend a fair amount of time removing these invalid matches. If these invalid matches are left in the schema-to-ontology matching, the composition must then filter them out for the schema-to-schema mapping to be accurate.

The result after this stage is *automatically* constructed schema-to-ontology matchings. This is an improvement over previous ontology-based integration systems that required manual matching with the ontology. Except for the instance level matchers, we have used all the matchers included with COMA (e.g. Name, DataType, and NamePath). More details on how COMA automatically constructs matchings can be found in [4]. Our modifications include the algorithm to convert an ontology into a directed acyclic graph supported by COMA, and the Max and noMax approaches to filter ontological matches.

5 Composing Mappings

Mapping composition has been used in schema matching systems to reuse previous match results. In COMA [4], the *Compose* operation is used to build matchers that reuse previous match results. Re-using previous match results was shown to significantly improve the matching accuracy. In our system, the *Compose* operation is used to construct mappings between schemas by composing schema-to-ontology matchings. Two schema elements are assumed to be identical if they match the same ontological concept. Therefore we assume a transitive nature of the similarity relation between elements of schemas and the referenced ontology, i.e. if an element a of one schema is similar to an element o of the ontology and o is similar to an element b of the other schema, then a is also similar to b. If the schema-to-ontology matching is "perfect", then the schema-to-schema mapping will be very accurate. However, the schema-to-schema mapping will always miss matchings where an element in a schema does not have a matching ontological concept. The composition may also generate false matches if two or more schema elements map to the same ontological concept, but are not identical concepts.

In this paper, mappings are binary relations over the sets of elements of schemas and ontology, i.e. if $map : S \rightarrow O$ then map is a set of pairs $< l, r >$, where $l \in S$ and $r \in O$. This representation of mappings does not convey any semantics. Given two mappings map_1 that relates schema S_1 and the referenced ontology O and map_2 between schema S_2 and O, the *Compose* operation, denoted by $*$, produces a mapping map between the two schemas, as follows: $map = map_1 * map_2^{-1}$. That is given an element x of S_1, $(map_1 * map_2^{-1})(x) = (map_1(map_2^{-1}))(x)$ is an element in S_2, where map_2^{-1} denotes the inverse of map_2. The operation also computes the transitive similarity of schema elements. We adopt the COMA strategy of computing transitive similarity by taking the average of the two similarity values. For example, if <postalCode, Zip, 0.8> and <Zip, postCode, 0.7> *Compose* will produce <postalCode, postCode, 0.75>.

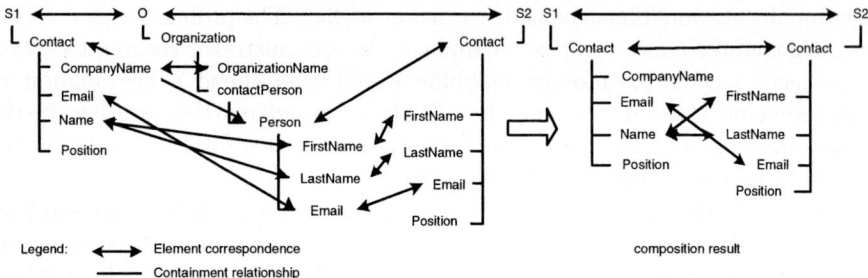

Fig. 4. Composition example

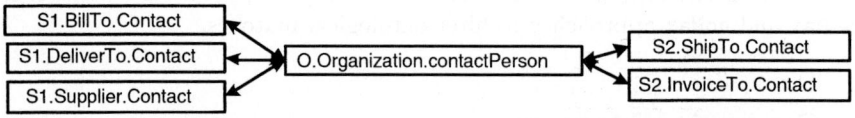

Fig. 5. Composition example with undesirable m:n matches

Figure 4 shows the general approach of deriving the match $S1 \leftrightarrow S2$ from composing the two match results $map_1 : S1 \leftrightarrow O$ and $map_2 : S2 \leftrightarrow O$. Since match results are binary relationships with similarity values, the *Compose* operator is defined as the natural join of two match results, yielding another match. The composition inherently filters out some of the bad schema-to-ontology matches. If the transitive similarity is below a threshold, the mapping produced is discarded. Thus, the difference between Max and noMax schema-to-ontology matching approaches is that the composition will discard fewer matches in the Max approach.

The example in Figure 4 illustrates some of the common problems of the *Compose* operation. Match composition may miss some correspondences, such as between *Position* of $S1$ and $S2$, due to the absence of a match counterpart in the ontology. In addition, composition may introduce unwanted correspondences when elements of the referenced ontology are related to several elements of the schemas. For example, in Figure 5, several contacts of schema $S1$ and $S2$ are matched to a generic contact person in the ontology. The composition result is six matches when only two are correct: S1.Billto.Contact=S2.InvoiceTo.Contact and S1.DeliverTo.Contact=S2.ShipTo.Contact.

6 Global View Construction

In this section is an algorithm, called *GlobalView*, for computing the global view. The goal is to create a schema that represents all of the information expressed in n database schemas, $S_i, i = 1..n$. The algorithm is formulated using model

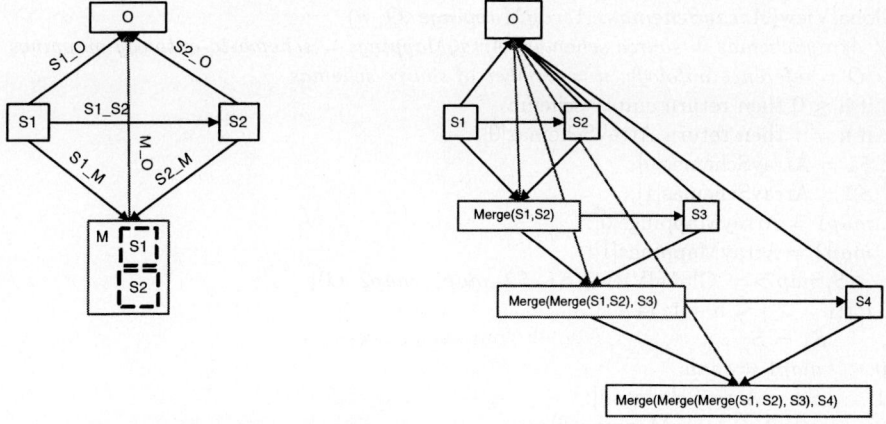

Fig. 6. Constructing a Global View using Model Management Operations

management primitives and is initially described for two schemas and then generalized for n schemas. Model management is an approach to metadata-intensive applications that proposes a higher level of abstraction than current techniques [5]. Its main abstractions are models (e.g. schemas, interface definitions) and mappings between models. It offers such operators as Match, Merge, Extract, Delete, and Compose.

Consider a reference ontology O, two schemas $S1$ and $S2$, a mapping $S1\_O$ between $S1$ and O, and a mapping $S2\_O$ between $S2$ and O. The global view can be computed by:

1. Detecting similar objects in $S1$ and $S2$ using the *Compose* operator to compute a mapping between $S1$ and $S2$, called $S1\_S2$.
2. Given the mapping $S1\_S2$ computed in the previous step, using *Merge* operator to produce the integrated schema M and the mappings $S1\_M$ and $S2\_M$.
3. Using the *Compose* operator to compute a mapping between the newly created schema M and reference ontology O.

On the left-hand side of Figure 6 is a schematic representation of the process, where the rectangles denote schemas (e.g. the rectangles labeled S1, S2, M, and O) and the arcs between rectangles represent mappings between the schemas (e.g. the mapping between S1 and S2 is depicted as the labeled arc $S1\_S2$). The sequence of model management operations applied are:

operator GlobalView2($S1$, $S2$, O, $S1\_O$, $S2\_O$)
1. $S1\_S2 = S1\_O * \text{Invert}(S2\_O)$;
2. $< M, S1\_M, S2\_M > = \text{Merge}(S1, S2, S1\_S2)$;
3. $M\_O = \text{Invert}(S1\_M) * S1\_O + \text{Invert}(S2\_M) * S2\_O$;
4. return $< M, M\_O >$;

GlobalView(*ArraySchemas, ArrayMappings ,O, n*)
// *ArraySchemas* = source schemas, *ArrayMappings* = schema-to-ontology mappings
// *O* = reference ontology, *n* = number of source schemas
1. if n ≤ 0 then return empty schema;
2. if n = 1 then return ArraySchemas[0];
3. $S1$ = ArraySchemas[0];
4. $S2$ = ArraySchemas[1];
5. $map1$ = ArrayMappings[0];
6. $map2$ = ArrayMappings[1];
7. $< S, map >$ = GlobalView2($S1, S2, map1, map2, O$);
8. for(i = 2; i ≤ n − 1; i++)
9. $S1 = S$;
10. $map1 = map$;
11. $S2$ = ArraySchemas[i];
12. $map2$ = ArrayMappings[i];
13. $< S, map >$ = GlobalView2($S1, S2, map1, map2, O$);
14. end for;
15. return $< S, map >$;

Fig. 7. Global View Construction Algorithm

The merging of two schemas is driven by the mapping $S1\_S2$ computed using composition in Line 1. Observe that for the composition to be correct, $S2\_O$ needs to be inverted (i.e. the domain and range of the mapping has to be swapped.) The global schema M is computed using the *Merge* operator that also produces two mappings $S1\_M$ and $S2\_M$ that relate M to the two original schemas. In Line 3, the mapping M_O is computed so that *GlobalView2* can be used in further merge operations. The output of the algorithm consists of pair $< M, M\_O >$, where M is the global schema over $S1$ and $S2$, and M_O is the mapping between new schema M and the referenced ontology O. The steps above are encapsulated as a new operator, called *GlobalView2*, that is re-used to compute the global view for N schemas. The general global schema composition algorithm for N sources is given in Figure 7. The iterative process of the computation of the global view using a reference ontology is depicted on the right-hand side of Figure 6 for $n = 4$.

Note that the integrated view construction algorithm is not a fully automated solution to the problem. Designer intervention may be required, especially when the intermediate output of the operations is only an approximate one. For example, with the current implementations of *Compose* operator it is very probable that false matches are suggested and that not all the correct matches are outputted. Merging is a semi-automatic process that requires human intervention and validation.

7 Experimental Study

We performed an experimental study to demonstrate the effectiveness of the approach. The five sample XML order schemas: CIDR, Excel, Noris, Paragon, and Apertum from www.biztalk.org used to evaluate COMA [4] were tested. These schemas are assigned numbers 1, 2, 3, 4, and 5 respectively. We constructed a reference order ontology (Figure 1) that models the order domain. This ontology has different structure than the schemas. For instance, the ontology uses IS-A whereas none of the sample schemas have IS-A relationships. The ontology does not have all concepts used in the schemas such as *unitOfMeasure*, *count*, and *VAT* information. Further, the ontology contains no ids or keys and does not model the order amounts, tax issues, and street addresses in as much detail as some schemas. We have used the correct mappings as given by COMA as ground-truth. As always there are some mappings that are open to interpretation which affect the results.

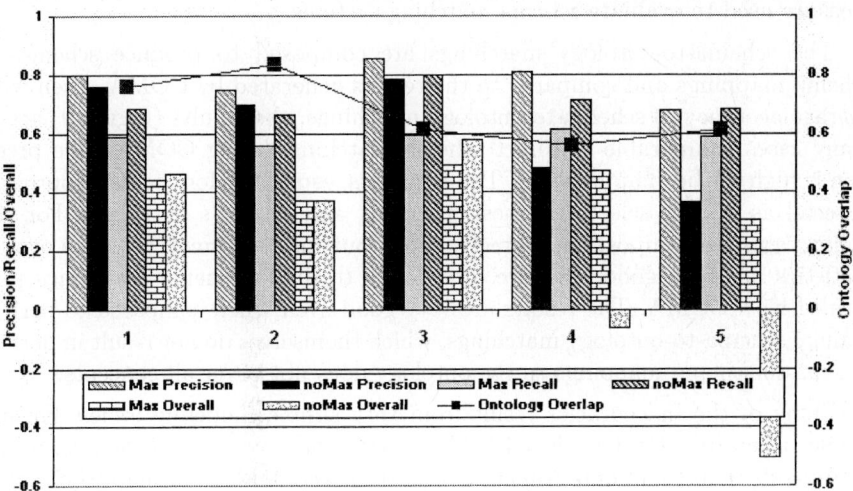

Fig. 8. Schema-to-Ontology Matching

The first experiment is to determine the accuracy of the schema-to-ontology matching using both Max and noMax. The results are in Figure 8. The accuracy of schema-to-ontology matching is quite good. Max has precision of 75-80% and recall around 60%. Recall is lower as it misses some matchings that are not evaluated as the best. noMax has slightly better recall than Max but loses some precision as it generates many matchings where only one is correct. The overall is always positive for Max indicating that it saves effort over manual matching. For noMax the matching with schema 5 results in a negative overall because the schema contains the concept *Buyer* which is not in the ontology and gets incorrectly matched to several higher-level concepts in the ontology such as *Agent* and *Person*. Without the improvements such as expanding IS-A, the accuracy is very bad. Fortunately, we are willing to accept less accuracy in this case as the matching process will only be performed once and the administrator has full understanding of the semantics of their schema to detect and resolve mismatches. It is also important to note that perfect matching is not possible since the ontology may not cover the schema concepts exactly. The fraction of schema elements that can be manually matched to the ontology is also shown in Figure 8. This fraction represents the schema overlap with the ontology and is the best possible match performance that can be achieved. A schema element is considered to match to the ontology even if it is not a perfect match. The last three schemas have relatively poor matching with the ontology (about 60% of the concepts are present in the ontology in some form). For example, approximately 60% of the elements in schema 4 can be matched to the ontology. noMax has a recall of 70%, so it finds ontological matches for 42% of all elements in schema 4. The statistic Overall is defined as $Recall * (2 - 1/Precision)$, and is a common measure used to evaluate schema matching systems.

The schema-to-ontology matchings are composed to produce schema-to-schema mappings and compared to the results generated by COMA. Even with average accuracy of schema-to-ontology matchings, the results (Figure 9) are in many cases comparable to direct schema matchings using COMA. The precision is high for both approaches. The weakness, especially for the Max approach, is recall as it only selects the best matching and discards all others. For the noMax case, the composition correctly filters out many mismatches. The overall statistics are very good, and are often close to direct schema matchings performed with COMA. The results are very good even when compared to perfect manual schema-to-ontology matchings, which themselves do not result in perfect schema-to-schema mappings as the ontology does not cover all concepts.

Many of the inaccuracies result from very simple modeling issues. For example, when one database has 4 fields: *Street1, Street2, Street3, Street4*, do all these fields map to an ontological concept of *Street*? If they all map to *Street* in the ontology, then the composition will generate one correct and numerous incorrect matches with two schemas that represent street in this way as discussed in Section 5. This is the reason for the poor performance between schemas 1 and 2. Matchings involving schemas 3, 4, and 5 have lower accuracy due to their relative poor overlap with the ontology. However, the performance is still very good and sometimes is as good or better than COMA. Mapping schemas 4 to 5 is poor because the concept of *Buyer* in schema 5 is not in the ontology and gets incorrectly mapped to concepts in schema 4. This results in many false matchings after composition.

The matching accuracy can be further improved by using the schema-to-schema mappings generated as existing matches that are re-used when directly matching the schemas. The matches missed during composition because the concepts were not in the ontology can be correctly matched when the schemas

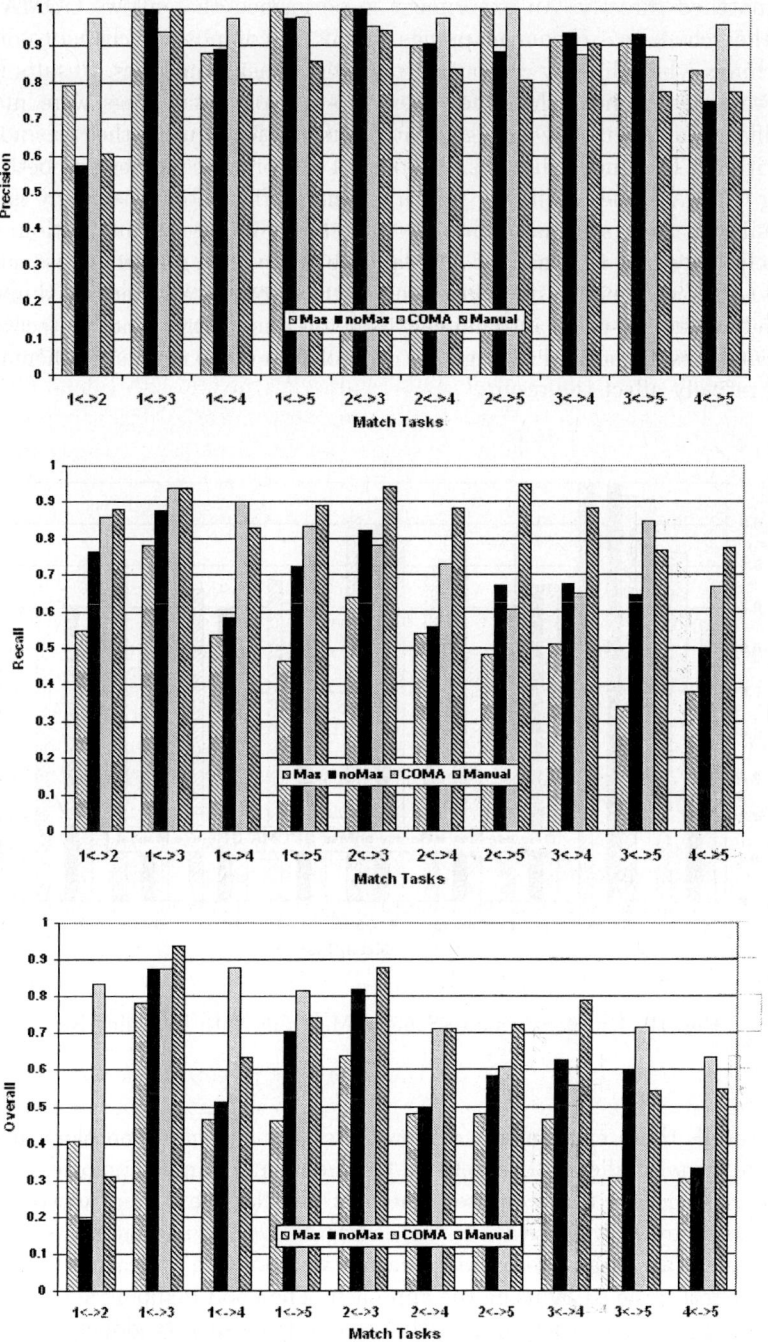

Fig. 9. Schema-to-Schema Mapping Statistics

are matched directly. An experiment is performed that allows COMA to reuse the schema-to-schema mappings found by composing schema-to-ontology matchings when directly computing pair-wise schema matches. Results (Figure 10) were determined when the schema-to-ontology matchings were manually specified, and when they were generated automatically using the Max and noMax algorithms. In almost all cases, the overall performance is near or better than using COMA alone to directly match schemas. This shows that there is benefit to building these schema-to-ontology matchings for use in integration as they are relatively easy to construct and validate and can be re-used across matching tasks. Although manual mappings are better, automatically generated mappings also add value. Re-using automatically generated mappings is not perfect because false matches introduced through the composition (as in matching schemas 1 and 2) negatively affect the result.

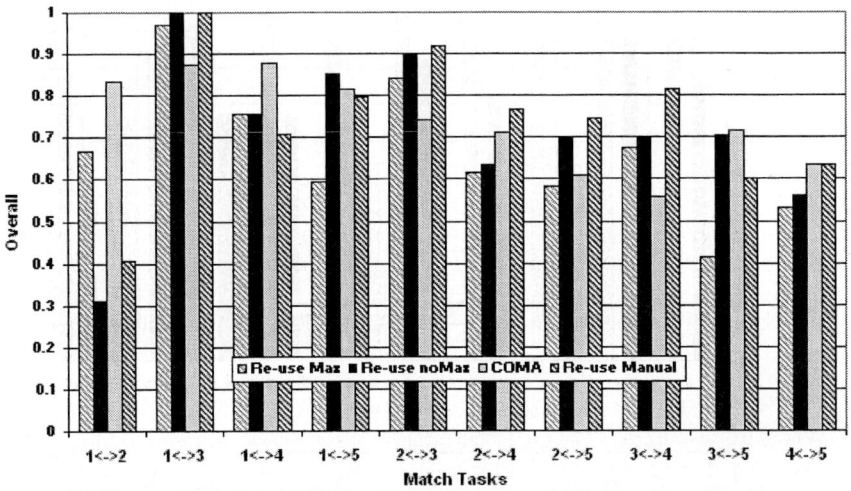

Fig. 10. Direct Schema-to-Schema Matching with Matching Re-use

Overall, these experiments demonstrate that schema-to-ontology matching has additional challenges over schema-to-schema matching. Ontologies have more complex structure that confuses matchers like NamePath, and existing match algorithms are very sensitive to the degree of overlap and similar structure of schemas. In all cases, the overall measure was positive indicating that manual match effort is saved by using the approach. The good mapping accuracy allows the global view construction algorithm to construct quality global schemas with limited user input. This results in significant savings in designer effort in building the global schema for integrated systems.

8 Future Work and Conclusions

In this work we have provided algorithms for automatically constructing global views for integrated systems using schema-to-ontology matchings. These algorithms are useful for previous ontology-based integration approaches that had to manually generate such matchings and required the global ontology to completely model the entire domain. The experimental results demonstrate that the ontology does not have to perfectly overlap the integration domain for it to be useful in schema matching and global view construction. This allows pre-existing ontologies to be used for integration. By using semi-automatic matching techniques developed for relational schemas, the overhead of manual matching to the ontology is avoided. We have shown how ontologies can be converted into a form suitable for use with existing relational matchers and demonstrated how the approach achieves high accuracy in finding schema-to-schema mappings.

Future work involves improving the composition to handle mismatches due to multiple matches to the same ontological concept or to different concepts in a IS-A hierarchy. This may involve using more sophisticated matches such as sub-concept and super-concept matches.

References

1. Batini, C., Lenzerini, M., Navathe, S.: A Comparative Analysis of Methodologies for Database Schema Integration. ACM Computing Surveys **18** (1986) 323–364
2. Sheth, A., Larson, J.: Federated Database Systems for Managing Distributed, Heterogenous and Autonomous Databases. ACM Computing Surveys **22** (1990) 183–236
3. Rahm, E., Bernstein, P.: A survey of approaches to automatic schema matching. VLDB Journal **10** (2001) 334–350
4. Do, H.H., Rahm, E.: COMA - A System for Flexible Combination of Schema Matching Approaches. In: VLDB. (2002) 610–621
5. Bernstein, P.: Applying Model Management to Classical Meta Data Problems. In: CIDR. (2003)
6. Beneventano, D., Bergamaschi, S., Guerra, F., Vincini, M.: Synthesizing an Integrated Ontology. IEEE Internet Computing **7** (2003) 42–51
7. Collet, C., Huhns, M., Shen, W.M.: Resource Integration Using a Large Knowledge Base in Carnot. IEEE Computer **24** (1991) 55–62
8. Mena, E., Illarramendi, A., Kashyap, V., Sheth, A.: OBSERVER: An Approach for Query Processing in Global Information Systems based on Interoperation across Pre-existing Ontologies. Distributed and Parallel Databases **8** (2000) 223–271
9. Doan, A., Madhavan, J., Domingos, P., Halevy, A.: Learning to Map between Ontologies on the Semantic Web. In: Proceedings of the 11th International Conference on the World Wide Web. (2002) 662–673
10. Lenat, D., Guha, R., Pittman, K., Pratt, D., Shepherd, M.: Cyc: Towards programs with common sense. Communications of the ACM **33** (1990) 30–49
11. Miller, G., Beckwith, R., Fellbaum, C., Gross, D., Miller, K.: Five Papers on WordNet. Technical Report CSL Report 43, Cognitive Systems Laboratory, Princeton University (1990)

12. Tzitzikas, Y., Constantopoulos, P., Spyratos, N.: Mediators over Ontology-Based Information Sources. In: WISE. (2001) 31–40
13. Decker, S., Erdmann, M., Studer, R.: ONTOBROKER: Ontology based access to distributed and semi-structured information. In: Database Semantics - Semantic Issues in Multimedia Systems. Volume 138 of IFIP Conference Proceedings., Kluwer (1998)
14. Madhavan, J., Bernstein, P., Rahm, E.: Generic Schema Matching with Cupid. In: VLDB. (2001) 49–58
15. Xu, L., Embley, D.: Discovering Direct and Indirect Matches for Schema Elements. In: DASFAA. (2003) 39–46
16. Doan, A., Domingos, P., Halevy, A.: Reconciling schemas of disparate data sources: a machine-learning approach . In: Proceedings of the ACM SIGMOD Conference on Management of Data. (2001) 509–520
17. Pottinger, R., Bernstein, P.: Merging Models Based on Given Correspondences. In: VLDB. (2003) 826–873
18. Noy, N., Musen, M.: PROMPT: Algorithm and Tool for Automated Ontology Merging and Alignment. In: AAAI/IAAI. (2000) 450–455
19. Gal, A., Modica, G., Jamil, H.: OntoBuilder: Fully Automatic Extraction and Consolidation of Ontologies from Web Sources. In: ICDE. (2004) 853
20. Ram, S., Park, J.: Semantic Conflict Resolution Ontology (SCROL): An Ontology for Detecting and Resolving Data and Schema-Level Semantic Conflicts. IEEE Trans. Knowl. Data Eng. **16** (2004) 189–202
21. Melnik, S., Rahm, E., Bernstein, P.: Rondo: A Programming Platform for Generic Model Management. In: SIGMOD. (2003) 193–204
22. Madhavan, J., Bernstein, P., Chen, K., Halvey, A., Shenoy, P.: Corpus-based Schema Matching. In: Workshop on Information Integration on the Web (IJCAI03). (2003)

Assisting Ontology Integration with Existing Thesauri

Jan De Bo, Peter Spyns, and Robert Meersman

Vrije Universiteit Brussel - STAR Lab
Pleinlaan 2, Gebouw G-10, B-1050 Brussels, Belgium
{jdebo,Peter.Spyns,meersman}@vub.ac.be
http://www.starlab.vub.ac.be

Abstract. In this paper a stepwise methodology for ontology alignment and merging is proposed. The knowledge model underlying this methodology is based on an extended version of the initial Dogma framework that is a database inspired approach to ontology engineering. The methodology we propose in this paper encompasses several techniques and algorithms that can be used and combined in order to assist the user with the integration of ontologies. We explain how some of these algorithms make use of already existing thesauri in order to provide the user with useful suggestions. The implementation of these algorithms has resulted in a tool that clearly visualises the overall ontology integration process.

1 Introduction

Through the (recent) years, research groups have been developing an increasing number of ontologies, mostly independently from each other. There is a growing need to *integrate* these seperate ontologies. Over time, the term "ontology integration" has been assigned different meanings. In [8] the authors identify three meanings for ontology integration:

1. Building a new ontology reusing other available ontologies.
2. Merging different ontologies into a single one that *unifies* all of them.
3. Integration of ontologies into applications.

In this paper we refer to this second definition when we talk about *integration*. We consider alignment as the weakest form of integration. Integration of ontologies is always performed over the intersection of their respective domains. By aligning ontologies, we try to establish links or mappings between them while the ontologies themselves persist autonomously. By merging, we try to create one coherent ontology that is a merged version of the source ontologies. We consider alignment as an important preceding step in the process of merging ontologies. Experience shows that integrating ontologies without any tool support is an extremely tedious and time-consuming process. However, human interaction will always remain indispensable. Therefore, our aim is to develop a semi-automatic tool that guides the user in the process of aligning and merging. In this paper we want to present its underlying methodology.

The next section of this paper contains a description of the DOGMA framework and some of its extensions in view of ontology integration (section 2). In section 3 we present two example ontologies that will be used throughout the paper to illustrate the proposed integration methodology. The main part of the paper describes the algorithms of alignment and merging (section 4). In section 5 we present an ontological mediator framework in order to enable semantic interoperability between heterogeneous datasources. Sections on related (section 6) and future work (section 7) precede the conclusions (section 8).

2 DOGMA and Ontology Integration

Within the framework of DOGMA, we adopt Gruber's definition of an ontology being an *explicit, formal specification of a shared conceptualisation of a certain domain* [7]. A DOGMA inspired ontology is based on the principle of a double articulation: an ontology is decomposed into an *ontology base*, also called lexon base, which holds (multiple) intuitive conceptualisation(s) of a domain and a layer of *ontological commitments*, where each commitment holds a set of domain rules to define a partial semantic account of an intended conceptualisation.

2.1 DOGMA Ontology Base

Currently, the ontology base consists of sets of intuitively plausible conceptualisations of a real world domain where each is a set of context-specific "representationless" binary facts types, called *lexons*, formally described as $< \gamma\ term_1\ role\ co-role\ term_2 >$, where γ denotes the context, used to group lexons that are logically related to each other in the conceptualisation of the domain [19]. E.g., *"bookstore: book is_identified_by/identifies ISBN"* is a lexon, with "bookstore"=γ, "book"= $term_1$, "ISBN"= $term_2$, "is_identified"= role and "identifies" = co-role.

2.2 DOGMA Commitment Layer

The commitment layer, mediating between the ontology base and applications, is organised as a set of ontological commitments, each being an explicit instance of an (intensional) first-order interpretation of a task in terms of the ontology base. A commitment is a consistent set of rules (or axioms) in a given syntax that specify which lexons of the ontology base are visible (*partial account*) for usage in this commitment and that semantically constrain this view (i.e. the visible lexons). The rules that constrain the relations between the concepts (*semantic account*) of the ontology base are specific to an application (*intended conceptualisation*) using the ontology. Experience shows that agreement on the domain rules is much harder to reach than on the conceptualisation.

2.3 Context

Contexts were incorporated in DOGMA to disambiguate the lexical meaning of terms inside a lexon. A context is represented by a symbol $\gamma_i \in \Gamma$, where Γ is the context space of the domain to be modelled. Initially, γ_i was a mere label that refered in a non formal way to a source (e.g., a document that contains and "explains" how the various terms are used in that particular context). In [11] we refined the notion of context $\gamma_i \in \Gamma$, being a semantic cluster of concepts that are logically and meaningfully related. To establish a relationship between terms and concepts in a given context γ_i, we define a *context mapping* ψ_i, from a domain T (the set of terms) to a range C (the set of concepts within that particular context γ_i), formally noted as $\psi_i : T \to C$, so that $range(\psi_i) = \gamma_i$.

2.4 The Concept Definition Server

As already pointed out in section 2.3 we make a clear separation between lexical terms and concepts.[1] According to the DOGMA approach, terms are part of a *lexon* and are represented by natural language *words* in the ontology base. To define the semantics of these terms in a computer understandable way we link terms to concepts of existing semantic networks like WordNet [3], CIDOC CRM [13], UMLS [1] etc.. To make this possible we have created a *concept definition server* where all these lexical resources are represented in a common format. It is clear that if we want to take benefit of these existing knowledge bases we will have to align our terms in a very precise and consequent manner to the adequate concepts on the concept definition server.

Because ontology engineering often concerns rather specific domains (e.g. cultural heritage, medical domain) to be modelled, we cannot only rely on Wordnet's vocabulary since it exclusively includes the 95.000 most common English words and lacks very specific or technical terms. In case we are building a medical ontology we will align the terms inside a lexon to the UMLS dictionary and if we are building an ontology about cultural heritage we will likely align our terminology with the dictionary of CIDOC CRM[2]. If possible however we will always try to align our terms to the WordNet vocabulary since this allows us to make use of the research that has been done regarding similarity measures between WordNet synsets.

If it is not possible to map certain terms to predefined concepts at the concept definition server we have to define new concepts to link these terms to. To describe a concept we propose to associate with each concept a set of semantically equivalent terms.

---

[1] To avoid ambiguity between terms and concepts we adopt the notational convention that terms are noted between single quotes and concepts are noted between double quotes starting with a capital letter.

[2] The CIDOC Conceptual Reference Model (CRM) provides definitions and a formal structure for describing the implicit and explicit concepts and relationships used in cultural heritage documentation

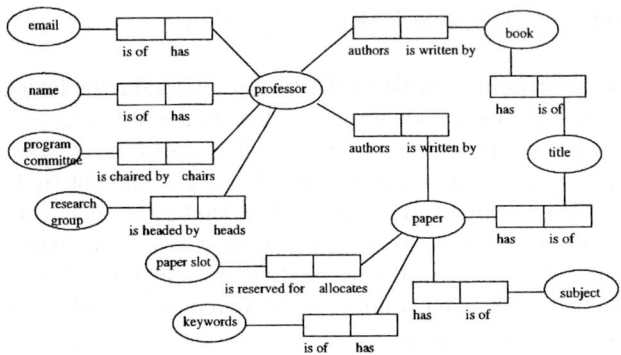

Fig. 1. Excerpt of the source ontology (Ω_s)

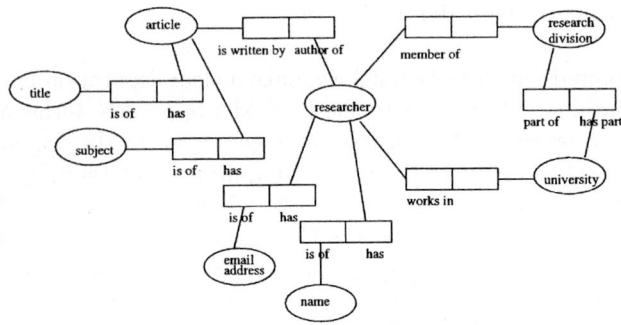

Fig. 2. Excerpt of the target ontology (Ω_t)

Formally, by using the equivalence sign " $\equiv$ ", we state that: $\psi_i(t) = c \equiv \{t, t', t'', t'''\}$, where $t, t', t'', t''' \in T$ and $c \in \gamma_i$. This specification allows a machine to retrieve, compare etc. concepts. These unique combinations of synonymous terms describe the logical vocabulary we use to model a given domain.

3 An Example

In order to introduce the reader to the main features and problems of ontology integration we present an example. In figure 1 and 2 we have depicted parts of the ontologies that represent conceptual knowledge about how *universities* are structured. These ontologies were modeled independently from each other. We adopt the graphical representation of ORM (Object Role Modelling) to visualize lexons. Ellipses depict the terms and rectangular boxes depict the role and co-role of a lexon. In the next section we present a stepwise methodology for ontology integration. The different steps in this methodology will be applied to the example ontologies which are presented here.

4 A Methodology for Ontology Integration

Independently of the integration strategy adopted[3], ontology integration is divided into several methodological steps: relating the different components of ontologies, finding and resolving conflicts in the representation of the same real world concepts, and eventually merging the conformed ontologies into one global ontology. We adopt for ontology integration the same methodological steps that were singled out in database schema integration [2]:
1. preintegration
2. comparison of ontologies (*ontology alignment*)
3. conforming of the alignment
4. ontology merging and restructuring

4.1 Preintegration

Preintegration consists of an analysis of the ontologies to decide the general integration policy: choosing the ontologies to be integrated, choosing the strategy of integration, deciding the order of integration, and possibly assigning preferences to entire ontologies or portions thereof. All these decisions have to be made by humans. We adopt the *binary ladder strategy* to integrate ontologies [2].

4.2 Comparison of Ontologies: Ontology Alignment

Ontology comparison consists of an analysis phase to determine correlations among concepts of different ontologies. Inter ontology relations are typically discovered during this phase. In general, comparison of ontologies is synonym for *ontology alignment*. In this section we present a stepwise methodology for ontology alignment.

Formally we define *an alignment* between two Dogma inspired ontologies as a commitment (i.e. an interpretation) of the source ontology's lexon base in terms of the target ontology's lexon base. A commitment consists of a set of *commitment rules*, here (for ontology integration purposes) also called *mapping rules*. We discuss these mapping rules in more detail in the sections that follow.

Find overlapping region(s) of both domains. The first thing we have to deal with while comparing two ontologies is to specify both parts of the ontologies that correspond to the intersection of their respective domains. In section 3 we have only visualised those parts of the example ontologies that are related to the intersection of their domains.

Detecting similar concepts and identifying inter ontology relations. The fundamental activity in this step consists of detecting and resolving several kinds of heterogeneities like semantically equivalent concepts that are denoted

---
[3] Due to space restrictions, we make abstraction of ontology language mismatches and how to cope with them.

by means of different terms in both ontologies and identifying inter ontology relationships between concepts of different ontologies.

Identifying equivalent concepts: Because ontology mismatches often occur through ambiguity of terms, miss-spelled terms, usage of different terminology to denote the same concept etc., we will always consider concepts in the comparison phase instead of the term labels that represent them. The degree of similarity between two concepts c_1 and c_2 is measured by means of a *similarity score*, formally stated as: $\mathbf{sc(c_1, c_2)} : \mathbf{C} \times \mathbf{C} \rightarrow [\mathbf{0}, \mathbf{1}]$. The way this similarity score is computed depends on how the concepts are defined. This is discussed next.

In case the concepts are WordNet synsets we can make use of the freely available software package, called *WordNet::Similarity*[4][21], to measure the semantic similarity and relatedness between a pair of concepts. This software package provides six measures of similarity and three measures of relatedness, all of which are based on the structure and content of WordNet. *Measures of similarity* use information found in an *is-a* hierarchy of concepts (or synsets), and indicate how much a concept is like (or is similar to) an other concept. *Measures of relatedness* on the other hand make use of information found in WordNet relations like *part-of* in order to determine how much concepts are related to each other.

In the next example we apply the *lin* measure, also available in the software package WordNet::Similarity, to calculate the degree of similarity between the synsets of *paper* and *article*(paper#n#4 denotes the synset that corresponds to the fourth sense of the noun *'paper'*). The result (0.91) justifies our intuition that both concepts are very similar to each other. Note that similarity measures that only encounter syntactic differences between concepts would result in a low similarity score if applied on this example. Syntactic differences are typically discovered by rules like Porter Stemmer, Levenshtein, Substring and Prefix/Suffix. These rules are explained in detail in the following paragraphs.

```
similarity.pl --type WordNet::Similarity::lin paper#n article#n
Loading WordNet... done.
Loading Module... done.
paper#n#4   article#n#1   0.914941563572112
```

In case the concepts cannot be identified with existing WordNet synsets we compute the similarity score between two concepts $c_1 \equiv t_1^1, \ldots, t_n^1$ en $c_2 \equiv t_1^2, \ldots, t_m^2$ by calculating the similarity score between all possible pairs of terms where the two terms in a pair come from different concepts. The full algorithm is denoted below in pseudo code.

- initialize *similaritylist* to null;
- for each term t_i^1 in c_1 until $i = n$
  - for each term t_j^2 in c_2 until $j = m$
    * compute the similarity score, $sc(t_i^1, t_j^2)$;
    * add $(t_i^1, t_j^2, sc(t_i^1, t_j^2))$ to the *similaritylist*;

---

[4] WordNet::Similarity is a sourceforge project and can be found at http://sourceforge.net/projects/wn-similarity

- * $j++$;
  - $i++$;
- sort *similaritylist* on descending similarity score
- initialize *termlist* to null;
- similarity_score = 0;
- for each element $(t_i^1, t_j^2, sc(t_i^1, t_j^2))$ in the *similaritylist*
  - if t_i^1 or t_j^2 in *termlist* then continue
  - else {
  - similarity_score = similarity_score + $sc(t_i^1, t_j^2)$;
  - add t_i^1 and t_j^2 to *termlist* }
- similarity_score = similarity_score / $\min(n, m)$

If the similarity score is above a given treshold then the concepts are considered to be equivalent. The treshold can be modified by the expert performing the alignment.

As mentioned above computing the similarity score between two concepts boils down to calculating the similarity scores between natural language terms. We will now introduce a list of natural language processing techniques that are applied in order to determine the degree of similarity between terms. All these techniques are based on syntactic differences between terms and do not take any semantic value of them into consideration. Therefore we have to be very critical with the interpretation of these results.

- **Porter Stemmer.** We have implemented the Porter stemming algorithm that removes the morphological and inflexional endings from words in English. Its main use is as part of a term normalisation process that is usually done when setting up Information Retrieval systems. The most practical use of this algorithm for our purposes is that it reduces the plural form of a word to its singular base form. E.g. 'papers' → 'paper', 'researchers' → 'researcher', etc. The '→' symbol indicates how the word before the arrow transforms after stemming.
- **Levenshtein Distance (LD).** This measure is also called *Edit Distance*. The Levenshtein distance is a measure of the similarity between two terms, which we will refer to as the source term (s) and the target term (t). The distance is the number of deletions, insertions, or substitutions required to transform s into t. The greater the Levenshtein distance, the more different the terms are. Therefore we propose the following similarity score between terms s and t:

$$sc(s,t) = \frac{max\_transitions - LD}{max\_transitions}$$

where *max_transitions* is the maximum number of transitions to transform s into t and is equal to $\max(\text{length}(s), \text{length}(t))$. An example illustrates that measures which only take the syntax of terms into account sometimes perform very poor. For instance, the terms 'prof' and 'professor' are both synonyms of each other but have a rather low similarity score: $sc = \frac{9-5}{9} = \frac{4}{9}$. In this example the LD is 5 because we have to add 5 letters to 'prof' in order to transform it to 'professor'.

- **Longest common prefix/suffix.** Calculating the longest common prefix or suffix between terms can also give a good indication of the degree of similarity that holds between terms. The similarity score between two terms s and t should increase with the length of the longest common prefix or suffix. It is defined like:

$$sc(s,t) = \frac{length\ longest\ common\ prefix\ (s,t)}{\min(length(s), length(t))}$$

  We recall the same example of the Levenshtein Distance. Since the longest common prefix of 'prof' and 'professor' is 4 this results in a perfect similarity score, namely 1.

- **Longest common substring.** The longest common substring of s and t is the longest run of characters that appears in order inside both s and t. The algorithm we have implemented is a simplified version of the *Levenshtein Distance* algorithm implementation. Since the longest common substring of the terms 'research department' and 'research deptmnt' is the latter term itself this results in a perfect similarity score ($= 1$) if we define the score as:

$$sc(s,t) = \frac{length\ longest\ common\ substring\ (s,t)}{\min(length(s), length(t))}$$

- **Metaphone Algorithm.** Another manner to relate terms is based on the assumption that sometimes terms are phonetically equivalent. The Metaphone algorithm[12] is an improved version of Soundex and reduces each input string to a Metaphone character code using relatively simple phonetic rules. Some examples: 'university' and 'universities' transform to the respective character codes 'UNFRST' and 'UNFRSTS' and both 'faculty' and 'faculties' are converted into 'FKLT'. The similarity score we propose here between two terms s and t is given by:

$$sc(s,t) = \frac{lcs(MC(s), MC(t))}{\min(MC(s), MC(t))}$$

  where MC stands for Metaphone Code and lcs stands for longest common substring.

The total similarity score between two terms is the weighted sum of all similarity measures listed above on the condition that these similarity measures are greater than a given treshold value, $\alpha \in [0,1]$. So if $sc_i(s,t) < \alpha$ then $w_i = 0$.

$$sc(s,t) = \sum_{i=1}^{n} w_i\ f(sc_i(s,t)) \quad with \sum_{i}^{n} w_i = 1$$

The weight values w_i determine how the different similarity scores are combined with each another. In order to emphasize high similarity scores we assign high weight values to high scores and low weights to low scores with respect to the equality $\sum_{i=1}^{n} w_i = 1$.

Up to now we have taken the syntax and semantics of concepts into account in order to find equivalent concepts. We will now show that in some cases a lot of valuable information for integration purposes can be derived from the ontologies themselves. The technique we propose to apply in order to retrieve equivalent lexons is based on a linguistic theory called *distributionalism* [22]. The underlying idea is that terms appearing in the same formal linguistic context (i.e. distribution) are semantically related. We say that these terms belong to the same pragmatic class.

Formally stated, for a given context γ_i, we have:

$$\left. \begin{array}{l} \gamma_i \quad t_1 \ r \ co-r \ t_2 \\ \gamma_i \quad t_1 \ r \ co-r \ t_3 \end{array} \right\} \Longrightarrow t_2 \sim t_3$$

The presence of the co-role label in the lexon model of Dogma imposes an additional constraint to conclude that two terms are similar in a given context. For instance, in the example above both the role label and the co-role label have to be equal to conclude that t_2 and t_3 are similar terms. However, this rule is not always applied succesfully. We advise not to apply the distributional approach in case the co-role label is not given or if the role is not meaningfully labeled. The reason for the latter issue is that role and co-role labels like *has* and *is_of* cause the negative side effect that too many related concepts will be found. On the other hand the *has* role is often followed by properties that characterize a certain concept. If two concepts have a set of properties in common we interpret this as an indication that both concepts are equivalent. Since both terms 'article' and 'paper' have properties like 'subject' and 'title' in common we can conclude that they represent equivalent concepts.

The detection of equivalent concepts leads to a first type of mapping rule, which is formalized by:

$$< c_{id}, \underbrace{\Omega_s.\psi_a(t_i)}_{c_i}, R, \underbrace{\Omega_t.\psi_b(t_j)}_{c_j}, sc >$$

whereby c_{id} stands for a commitment-id that uniquely identifies the mapping rule. The relation in the mapping rule R is either "*equivalence*" or "*equality*". sc is the similarity score between the concept c_i ($= \psi_a(t_i)$) of the source ontology Ω_s and the concept c_j ($= \psi_b(t_j)$) of the target ontology Ω_t. In the case of equal ($sc = 1$) or equivalent ($0 < sc < 1$) concepts the *domains* of both concepts are more or less identical.

Identifying inter ontology relationships: In order to identify inter ontology relationships between concepts of different ontologies we have to define the exact semantics of these relationships. We distinguish the following set of relationships with predefined semantics:

- **SubClassOf**: This relationship holds between concepts that have subsuming domains.[5]

---

[5] We define the domain of a concept as the set of all possible instances that can be associated with that concept

- **Generalize**: This relationship generalizes two concepts by a new concept and typically occurs between concepts that have overlapping domains.
- **PartOf**: This relationship indicates that a concept is part of another concept. This type of relation occurs frequently between concepts that have disjoint domains.
- **InstanceOf**: This relationship indicates that an object is an instance of a concept.

We will now present a methodology that allows to automate the task of finding inter ontology relationships between concepts. This methodology uses a formal upper level ontology, called SUMO (Suggested Upper Merged Ontology), which has been proposed as the initial version of an eventual Standard Upper Ontology (SUO).[6] The methodology works as follows:

- Each concept used in the ontology is aligned with an appropriate SUMO concept. In the case of WordNet concepts we do not have to establish the alignment mappings ourselves because we can use predefined mappings from WordNet 1.6 to SUMO concepts. These mappings are available in plain text format on the website of SUMO (http://ontology.teknowledge.com). We had to spent some additional effort in converting the unique synset identifiers from WordNet 1.6 to WordNet 2.0. For this we made use of the mappings that are made available at http://www.lsi.upc.es/ nlp/tools/mapping.html. Thanks to these conversions we managed to align part of WordNet 2.0 (the part covered by WordNet 1.6) with the SUMO upper level ontology.
- The mapping of WordNet to the SUMO upper level ontology is described in [10]. In this mapping methodology a WordNet synset is considered to be an instance of, a subclass of or a synonym of a SUMO concept. Since these relationships form a subset of the mapping rules that we distinguish we consider the mapping from WordNet to SUMO as a special alignment case.
- Since SUMO is a formal upper level ontology we can make use of its axioms to derive relations that hold between SUMO concepts to the ontology level. We demonstrate this in the examples that follow.

We will now apply the methodology presented in the previous paragraph to automatically detect inter ontology relations like *SubClassOf* and *Generalize* between concepts of the example ontologies in section3.

SubClassOf: The WordNet concepts "Professor" and "Researcher" are aligned with the SUMO concepts *Position* and *OccupationalRole*. In the hierarchy of the SUMO ontology holds that, *Position SubClassOf OccupationalRole*. Therefore we are able to derive the lexon, *"Professor" SubClassOf "Researcher"*, at the ontology level. We formulate this derivation mechanism by the following rule:

---

[6] The SUMO ontology can be browsed online (http://ontology.teknowledge.com) and source files for all of the versions of the ontology can be freely downloaded (http://ontology.teknowledge.com/cgi-bin/cvsweb.cgi/SUO/)

IF ($c \mapsto$ SumoConcept) **AND** ($c' \mapsto$ SumoConcept') **AND** (SumoConcept **SubClassOf** SumoConcept') **THEN** c **SubClassOf** c'
where c and c' are concepts and the symbol $\mapsto$ denotes the alignment. SumoConcept and SumoConcept' denote arbitrary Sumo concepts.

The mapping rule that corresponds to this observation is of the form:

$$< c_{id}, \Omega_s.\psi_a(t_1), R, \Omega_t.\psi_b(t_2) >$$

where R represents the *SubClassOf* relation. Therefore, the semantics of this mapping rule is often referred to as "specialisation" and is denoted by $R =\subset$. Furthermore, it holds that $\psi_a(t_1)$ denotes the concept labeled by the term 'professor' and that $\psi_b(t_2)$ denotes the concept labeled by the term 'researcher' in our example.

Generalize: The WordNet concepts "Book" and "Article" are aligned with the SUMO concepts of the same name, namely *Book* and *Article*. Since in the SUMO ontology holds that, *Book SubClassOf Text* and *Article SubClassOf Text*, we conclude that the ontological concepts "Book" and "Article" are generalized by a concept that is mapped to the SUMO concept *Text*. "Publication" is a good candidate concept. From this example it is obvious that we cannot automatically conclude that the concept "Publication" generalizes "Book" and "Article" because we have the choice between the entire set of concepts that are mapped to the SUMO concept *Text*. Therefore manually assistance will be needed to complete this step.

We formulate this rule as follows:

IF ($c \mapsto$ SumoConcept) **AND** ($c' \mapsto$ SumoConcept') **AND** (SumoConcept **SubClassOf** SumoConcept") **AND** (SumoConcept' **SubClassOf** SumoConcept") **THEN** (c **SubClassOf** c'') **AND** (c' **SubClassOf** c'') $\forall c'' \mapsto$ SumoConcept"
whereby c, c' and $c'' \in C$.

The mapping rule that is associated with this type of inter ontology relation is defined as:

$$< c_{id}, \Omega_1.\psi_a(t_1), R, \Omega_2.\psi_b(t_2), c >$$

with R standing for "generalization" and denoted by $\bigcup$. The association between the concepts $\psi_a(t_1)$="Article" and $\psi_b(t_2)$="Book" is given by a concept c which is a generalization of the former two concepts.

The same heuristics can be applied to discover the other relations like *InstanceOf* and *PartOf*. In our example however, these relations do not occur.

4.3 Conforming of the Alignment: Instant Validation

Conforming of an alignment is in fact checking its consistency 'on the fly'. Each time an alignment rule is proposed by the system or the user the rule is instantly checked if it conflicts with other rules which have already been added to the alignment rule repository. We propose the following heuristics in order to validate te alignment rules:

- **Cycles [9]:** A cycle is created when concepts c_{s1} and c_{s2} of the source ontologies are aligned with concepts c_{t1} and c_{t2} of the target ontologies but while c_{s2} is subclass of c_{s1}, c_{t1} is subclass of c_{t2}. Cycles are considered to be the result of an incorrect alignment.
- **Conflicting Situations through Misalignments:** If a concept c_s is aligned with a concept c_t and one of the superconcepts/subconcepts of c_t on its turn is aligned with some concept of the source ontology that is not a superconcept respective a subconcept of c_s we say that a conflict has arisen through a misalignment of c_s with c_t.
- More elementary validation heuristics involve the lookup procedure for a concept to check if it has already been aligned to some other concept and for the proposed alignment rule to look if it already exists.

4.4 Ontology Merging and Restructuring

During this activity the (source) ontologies are superimposed, thus obtaining a global ontology. The merge process is essentially based upon the mapping rules established in the comparison phase 4.2. We discuss the merge methodology by defining an ontology algebra for it.

Merge operator. Equivalent concepts are considered as candidates for merging. Merging two concepts involves the following steps: i) creating a concept name for the merged concept in the merged ontology ii) lexons related to equivalent concepts are compared with each other and in case they are considered equivalent they are copied to the merged concept. If a lexon is not equivalent and also has no inter ontology relationship with another one it is copied to the merged concept as well.

The dotted line in figure 3 simulates the creation of the merged concept. 'paper' and 'article' are both terms that refer to the same underlying concept. Therefore they are merged into one concept "Paper" during the merge phase. The lexons 'paper has/is_of title' and 'paper has/is_of subject' in the source ontology are equivalent with 'article has/is_of title' and 'article has/is_of subject' in the target ontology and are copied once in the merged ontology. The lexons 'paper allocates/is_reserved_for paper slot' and 'paper has/is_of keywords' are not aligned and are therefore integral copied to the merged ontology.

The corresponding operator in our ontology merge algebra is *merge*. It takes two concepts as arguments and is more formally defined as: $merge(c_1, c_2)$, where $c_1, c_2 \in C$. This operator implements the two functionalities mentioned.

Specialize operator. The alignment rule corresponding to $R = specialization = \subset$ is associated with the *specialize* operator in the ontology merge algebra. Formally this operator is defined as $specialize(c_1, c_2)$, where $c_1, c_2 \in C$. The result of applying this operator is 'c_1 SubClassOf c_2'. Recall that during the alignment phase we have automatically discovered the *SubClassOf* relationship between "Professor" and "Researcher" with the aid of the SUMO upper level ontology.

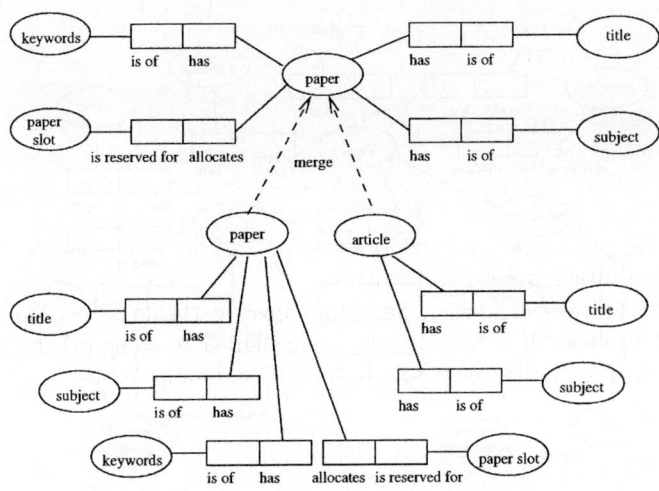

Fig. 3. The merge operation

This is illustrated in figure 4. The interpretation we give to the SubClassOf relation is one of non-monotonic inheritance, which means that one can modify certain inherited properties (a property is the part of a lexon without head term (t_1) and context (γ)). An example of this is: the lexon 'professor heads/is_headed_by research group' overrides 'researcher member_of research group'. Since the concept of "Professor" is considered to be more specific than "Researcher" it can have properties, like 'professor chairs/is_chaired_by program committee', which are not inherited from "Researcher". In general, properties which are specific to the subconcept "Professor" and properties which override inherited properties from the superconcept "Researcher" have to be written down explicitly. All the properties of the superconcept "Researcher" that are not explicitly modified by the subconcept are inherited implicitly.

Generalize operator. The alignment rule corresponding to $R = generalization = \bigcup$ stands for a *generalize* operator. It is formally defined as *generalize(c_1, c_2)*, where $c_1, c_2 \in C$. The operator generalizes the concepts c_1 and c_2 by creating a new concept c, such that "c_1 *is_a* c" and "c_2 *is_a* c". During the alignment phase we generalized the concepts "Book" and "Article" by a new concept, namely "Publication". Since the *merge* operator has merged "Article" and "Paper" into the shared concept of "Paper", the concepts "Paper" and "Book" in the merged ontology are now generalized by the concept "Publication". Common properties of "Paper" and "Book" like for instance, 'has title', are now moved to the generalized concept "Publication". The result of merging both example ontologies, introduced in section 3, is depicted in figure 4.

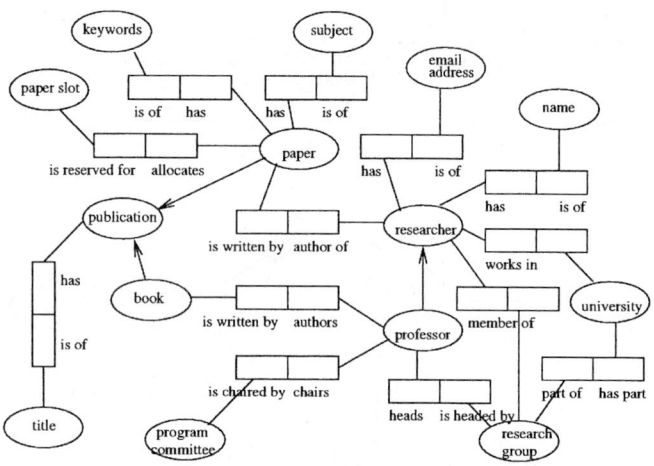

Fig. 4. The merge result of the two example ontologies Ω_s and Ω_t

4.5 Schematic Overview of the Methodology

We now give a schematic overview of the integration methodology proposed in this paper. The double sided arrow between step 2 and 3 denotes a loop. An alignment rule is suggested in step 2 and step 3 checks if it would cause inconsistencies when approved and stored in the alignment rule repository.

Step 1   Step2   Step3   Step4
Preintegration $\longrightarrow$ Alignment $\longleftrightarrow$ Conforming $\longrightarrow$ Merging and Restructuring

5 Semantic Interoperability Through Ontology Integration

Often, it will be very unlikely that a user's information needs will be satisfied by accessing the data repositories accessible through mappings associated with a single ontology. In order to enable semantic interoperation between datasources that are committed to different ontologies one solution is to align these ontologies with each other. The OBSERVER framework [5] proposes an approach to use the inter ontology relationships to translate the original query from terms of the source ontology into terms of another component, also referred to as a target ontology. This kind of query rewriting does not always occur without loss of information. The *Interontology Relationship Manager (IRM)* in the Observer system serves as a pool where all interontology relationships between the different ontologies are made available. The ONION methodology[17] captures the semantic bridges between two ontologies using *articulation rules*. These rules express the relationship between two or more concepts belonging to ontologies that seek to interoperate. Like the OBSERVER methodology ONION also believes that due to the complexity of achieving and maintaining global semantic integration the merging approach is not scalable. Therefore both methodologies

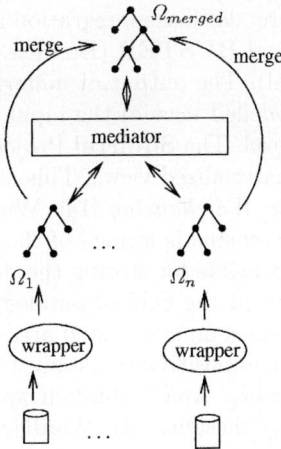

Fig. 5. Mediator approach for data integration

are based on a distributed approach which allows the sources to be updated and maintained independent of each other. One of the drawbacks of this interoperation mechanism is that to integrate n ontologies one has to compute $\frac{n(n-1)}{2}$ sets of interontology relationships. To minimize this effort we have chosen for a *mediator inspired framework*. It is our goal to develop a framework for data integration that is easy to maintain and to extend. Therefore we have chosen to merge the source ontologies into one global ontology. In a binary merging strategy this requires only $n-1$ alignments [2]. The only additional steps to be performed are to check for conflicts and to integrate the separate ontologies into a global ontology. The mediator then decomposes the global query into a union of queries on the underlying source ontologies and unifies all resultsets into a global result. The mediator is made up of a mapping table which enlists the mappings from the concepts in the source ontology to the concepts of the global ontology. The framework is depicted in figure5.

Each time our framework is extended with a new ontology we only have to merge this ontology with the global ontology and adjust the mediator accordingly. It is obvious that this is less time consuming than having to perform alignments with all present ontologies.

6 Related Work

Ontology merging clearly has links with the research field of data integration. A short classification of various approaches to data integration from heterogeneous sources is given below - see also [14]. *Schema integration* is often referred to as *view integration* in the database research community. A stepwise methodology for schema integration is given in [2]. *Virtual data integration* provides global and unified access to the sources. The data are kept only in the sources. Examples of virtual data integration are: database integration in distributed databases environments, **MOMIS** [18] and **BUSTER** (Bremen University Semantic Translator for Enhanced Retrieval). The output of *materialized data integration* is a data set representing a reconciled view of the input sources, both at the intentional and the extensional level. The **Squirrel** Project provides a framework for data integration based on materialized views. This kind of integration is the one most closely related to *Data Warehousing* [14]. With the aid of wrappers and mediators a data warehouse schema is formed of the local source schemata. The data warehouse itself is responsible for storing the data of the local sources.

Some summaries on work in the field of ontology integration are available. Mitra and Wiederhold developed an automated articulation generator (ArtGen) for the **ONION** (ONtology compositION) system [17]. They have also presented an ontology composition algebra. Apart from our approach, ONION is the only approach that takes external thesauri, like WordNet, into account in order to assist the linguistic matching of terms.

Chimaera is a browser-based ontology *merging* and *diagnosis* tool. It finds semantically identical terms in different ontologies and merge them into a single one in the resulting ontology. The tool also identifies terms that should be related by subsumption, disjointness and provide support for introducing these relationships [4]. **SMART and PROMPT** are both algorithms for semi-automatic ontology alignment and merging [15]. The tool starts by automatically creating a list of suggestions based on linguistic class name similarity. Subsequently, for each operation invoked by a user, the tool makes suggestions to guide the user, checks for conflicts and proposes solutions to these conflicts. The **PROMPT** algorithm has been extended to **Anchor-PROMPT** [16]. The central observation behind Anchor-Prompt is that if two pairs of terms from the source ontologies are similar (i.e. **anchors**) and there are paths (of the same length) connecting the terms, then the elements in those paths, occuring at the same positions, are often similar as well. We also mention the **FCA-Merge** [6] method for merging ontologies which makes use of the principles of Formal Concept Analysis.

Tools like Chimaera and PROMPT help significantly automate the process. However, these tools do not contain a component that identifies concept names that are linguistically similar automatically and use that knowledge as the basis for further alignment of ontologies. These approaches require manual construction of alignment rules. Our approach provides a greater degree of automation and at the same time we give human experts the chance to intervene in the integration process if conflicts need to be resolved or if certain suggestions could not be found automatically by the system.

7 Future Work

In order to evaluate the performance of our implemented algorithms we should calculate the *precision* and *recall*. *Precision* is the proportion of the number of relevant suggestions that were automatically found by the application to the total number of suggestions proposed by the application. *Recall* is the proportion of the number of relevant suggestions that were automatically found by the application to the real number of alignment rules that are effectively necessary in order to align two ontologies. We are currently implementing a framework to automatically calculate these measures. We plan to present detailed evaluation results at a later stage. In addition, we will continue to elaborate on the framework, presented in section5, to integrate various heterogenous datasources. Thanks to a Flemish IWT project, SCOP, we have already gained some experience in coupling medical databases to a medical ontology Linkbase©[20], which will facilitate our endeavour.

8 Conclusion

In this paper we have adopted the methodological framework for database schema integration proposed by [2]. One of the novel aspect of our approach is the formal separation between terms and concepts (cfr. *concept definition server*) that allows for a more precise detection of equivalent concepts and semantic relationships than is the case in the approaches discussed earlier (see section 6). We have also constructed an external reference framework based on the exisiting upper level ontology of SUMO that helps to automatically establish inter ontology relations.

Acknowledgments. This work has been funded by the IWT (Institute for the Promotion of Innovation by Science and Technology in Flanders): Jan De Bo has received an IWT PhD grant (IWT SB 2002 #21304) while Peter Spyns is supported in the context of the OntoBasis project (IWT GBOU 2001 #10069).

References

1. Humphreys B. and Lindberg D. The umls project: Making the conceptual connection between users and the information they need. *Bulletin of the Medical Library Association*, 81(2), 1993.
2. Batini C., Lenzerini M., and Navathe S. A comparative analysis of methodologies for database schema integration. *ACM Computing Surveys*, 18(4):323–364, 1986.
3. Fellbaum C. *Wordnet: An Electronic Lexical Database*. Cambridge, US: The MIT Press, 1998.
4. McGuinness D., Fikes R. Rice R., and Wilder S. An environment for merging and testing large ontologies. In Cohn A., Guinchiglia F., and Selman B, editors, *In Proc of the 7th International Conference on Principles of Knowledge Representation and Reasoning (KR2000)*, pages 483–493. Morgan Kaufmann, 2000.
5. Mena E., Kashyap V., Illaramendi A., and Sheth A. Domain specific ontologies for semantic information brokering on the global information infrastructure. In Nicola Guarino, editor, *In Proceedings of the First International Conference on Formal Ontology in Information Systems, (FOIS'98)*, pages 269–283, 1998.
6. Stumme G. and Maedche A. Fca-merge: Bottom-up merging of ontologies. In *In Proc of IJCAI 2001*, pages 225–234, 2001.
7. Tom Gruber. A translation approach to portable ontology specifications. *Knowledge Acquisition*, 5(2), 1993.

8. Pinto H., Gómez-Pérez A., and Martins J. Some issues on ontology integration. In *In Proc of the Workshop on Ontologies and Problem Solving Methods*, 1999.
9. E. Hovy. Combining and standardizing largescale, practical ontologies for machine translation and other uses. In *In Proc of First International Conference on Language Resources and Evaluation (LREC)*, pages 535–542, 1998.
10. Niles I. and Pease A. Linking lexicons and ontologies: Mapping wordnet to the suggested upper merged ontology. In *In Proc of the 2003 International Conference on Information and Knowledge Engineering (IKE ?03)*, 2003.
11. De Bo Jan, Peter Spyns, and Robert Meersman. Creating a dogmatic multilingual ontology infrastructure to support a semantic portal. In Zahir Tari et al. Robert Meersman, editor, *In Proc of On The Move 2003 Workshops*, volume 2889 of *LNCS*, pages 253–266. Springer, 2003.
12. Philips Lawrence. Hanging on the metaphone. *Computer Language*, 7(12):39–43, 1990.
13. Doerr M. The cidoc crm - an ontological approach to semantic interoperability of metadata. *AI Magazine, Special Issue on Ontologies*, 2002.
14. Jarke M., Lenzerini M., Vassiliou Y., and Vassiliadis Y. *Fundamentals of Data Warehouses*. Springer-Verlag, 1999.
15. Fridman Noy N. *Handbook on Ontologies, International Handbooks on Information Systems*, chapter Tools for Mapping and Merging Ontologies, pages 365–384. Springer, 2003.
16. Fridman Noy N. and Musen M. Anchor-prompt: Using non-local context for semantic matching. In *in Proc of the Workshop on Ontologies and Information Sharing at the International Joint Conference on Artificial Intelligence (IJCAI)*, 2001.
17. Mitra P. and Wiederhold G. Resolving terminological heterogeneity in ontologies. In *Workshop on Ontologies and Semantic Interoperability at the 15th European Conference on Artificial Intelligence (ECAI)*, 2002.
18. Bergamaschi S., Castano S., De Capitani di Vimercati S., Montanari S., and Vincini M. An intelligent approach to information integration. In Nicola Guarino, editor, *In Proc of Formal Ontology in Information Systems (FOIS'98)*, pages 253–268, 1998.
19. Peter Spyns, Robert Meersman, and Mustafa Jarrar. Data modelling versus ontology engineering. *SIGMOD Record Special Issue on Semantic Web, Database Management and Information Systems*, 31(4), 2002.
20. Deray T. and Verheyden P. Towards a semantic integration of medical relational databases by using ontologies: a case study. In Zahir Tari et al. Robert Meersman, editor, *In Proc of On The Move 2003 Workshops*, volume 2889 of *LNCS*, pages 137–150. Springer, 2003.
21. Pedersen T., Patwardhan S., and Michelizzi J. Wordnet::similarity - measuring the relatedness of concepts. In *Appears in the Proceedings of the Nineteenth National Conference on Artificial Intelligence (AAAI-04)*, 2004.
22. Harris Z. *Methods in Structural Linguistics*. Chicago: University of Chicago Press, 1951.

Author Index

Aagedal, Jan Øyvind II-1190
Abdellatif, Takoua II-1571
Abecker, Andreas II-1080
Aberer, Karl II-859
Adamus, Radosław II-823
Alamán, Xavier I-477
Albani, Antonia I-408
Alchieri, Eduardo Adílio Pelinson II-1395
Analyti, Anastasia II-873
Anceaume, Emmanuelle II-1445
Antoniadis, George I-422
Antunes, Pedro I-37
Avesani, Paolo I-492

Babaoğlu, Özalp II-1413
Bacarin, Evandro I-319
Bailey, James I-245
Baldoni, Roberto II-1558
Balsters, Herman I-748
Barbi, Emanuela II-1558
Barthelmess, P. II-1427
Bartoli, Alberto II-1413
Beigman Klebanov, Beata I-735
Bernard, Guy II-1322
Bhiri, Sami I-3
Bhowmick, Sourav II-927
Bitsaki, Marina I-422
Bittner, Sven I-301
Blair, Gordon II-1463
Böhm, Klemens I-337
Borgo, Stefano I-670
Braun, Peter II-1358
Brena, Ramon II-999
Buccafurri, Francesco I-563
Buchmann, Erik I-337
Businger, Dominik I-355
Bussler, Christoph I-1

Cahill, Vinny II-1123
Cai, Wei II-1463
Caragea, Doina II-963
Carrillo-Ramos, Angela I-264
Cart, Michelle I-155
Catarci, Tiziana I-597

Cazalens, Sylvie I-19
Ceballos, Hector II-999
Cecchet, Emmanuel II-1571
Cerqueira, Renato II-1285
Chan, Stephen Chi Fai I-544
Chan, Syin II-1050
Chaudhry, Eric II-927
Chaudron, Michel II-1225
Chen, Liming I-654
Cheng, Betty H.C. II-1243
Chia, Liang-Tien II-1050
Chimaris, Avraam II-1173
Cimmino, Stefano II-1558
Coelho, Jorge II-1098
Conan, Denis II-1322
Conesa, Jordi II-981
Cooper, Chris II-1463
Corbett, Dan I-724
Coulson, Geoff II-1463
Cox, Simon I-654
Cudré-Mauroux, Philippe II-859

Dadam, Peter I-101
Daelemans, Walter I-600
da Silva Fraga, Joni II-1395
Davis, Joseph II-1012
Dayal, Umeshwar I-2
De Bo, Jan I-801
de Brock, Engbert O. I-748
Dehnert, Juliane I-139
Delgado, Jaime I-689
De Meo, Pasquale I-209
de Souza, Kleber Xavier Sampaio II-1012
Deters, Ralph II-1125
Dietz, Jan L.G. I-85
Dittrich, Klaus R. I-355
Dragut, Eduard I-783
Dramitinos, Manos I-422
Duce, David II-1463
Duzan, Gary II-1208

Ehrig, Marc I-618
Ellis, C.A. II-1427
Emmerich, Wolfgang II-1303

Fensch, Christian II-1358
Ferrié, Jean I-155
Florido, Mário II-1098
Friedman, Roy II-1445

Gaaloul, Walid I-3
Gal, Avigdor I-1
Gançarski, Stéphane I-174
García, Roberto I-689
Geihs, Kurt II-1538
Geist, Ingolf I-227
Gellersen, Hans II-1124
Gensel, Jérôme I-264
Gil, Rosa I-689
Gill, Chris II-1520
Goble, Carole I-654
Godart, Claude I-3
Grace, Paul II-1463
Gradinariu, Maria II-1445
Gray, W. Alex I-442
Guarino, Nicola I-599

Habing, Nathalie I-I-85
Halepovic, Emir II-1125
Han, Zhongming I-55, II-1113
Harmon, Trevor II-1155
Hauser, Rainer I-121
Haya, Pablo A. I-477
Heineman, George T. II-1208
Herrero, Pilar I-391
Hinze, Annika I-283, I-301
Hodel, Thomas B. I-355
Honavar, Vasant G. II-963
Huemer, Christian I-66

Issarny, Valérie II-1608
Ivins, Wendy K. I-442

Jeusfeld, Manfred A. I-526
Jin, Beihong I-373
Jung, Doris I-283

Kemme, Bettina II-1376
Kern, Steffen II-1358
Kim, Ja-Hee I-66
Kirchhof, Michael I-460
Klefstad, Raymond II-1155
Knight, Kevin I-735
Koehler, Jana I-121
Koeller, Andreas II-891

Kon, Fabio II-1590
Kouici, Nabil II-1322
Kuhn, Werner II-1062
Kvilekval, Kristian II-1340

Lachaize, Renaud II-1571
Lam, Gary Hoi Kit I-544
Lamarre, Philippe I-19
Lamparter, Steffen I-618
Lawrence, Dave R. I-194
Lawrence, Ramon I-783
Lax, Gianluca I-563
Le, Jiajin I-55, II-1113
Leitão, Paulo I-670
Lemp, Sandra I-19
Leong, Hong Va I-544
Le Pape, Cécile I-174
Li, Jing I-373
Li, Jun II-1482
Liu, Song II-1050
Loyall, Joseph P. II-1208
Lung, Lau Cheuk II-1395
Lutz, Michael II-1062

Madeira, Edmundo I-319
Madria, Sanjay II-927
Maia, Renato II-1285
Majkić, Zoran I-768
Marchetti, Carlo II-1558
Marcu, Daniel I-735
Maréchal, Olivier II-1502
Martin, Hervé I-264
Mascolo, Cecilia II-1303
Massa, Paolo I-492
Mathy, Laurent II-1463
Maverick, Vance II-1376, II-1413
Mayer, Wendy I-724
McKinley, Philip K. II-1243
Medeiros, Claudia B. I-319
Meersman, Robert I-801
Meghini, Carlo II-945
Miles, John C. I-442
Momeni, Hossein II-1143
Montoro, Germán I-477
Moore, Keith II-1482
Mourão, Hernâni I-37
Mühl, Gero II-1538
Mukherjee, Saikat II-909

Nagypál, Gábor I-705
Neves Bessani, Alysson II-1395

Author Index

Norbisrath, Ulrich I-460

Oldevik, Jon II-1190
Olivé, Antoni II-981

Papa, Paolo II-1558
Papadopoulos, George A. II-1173
Papapetrou, Odysseas I-581
Paslaru Bontas, Elena I-637
Passi, Kalpdrum II-927
Patarin, Simon II-1413
Pathak, Jyotishman II-963
Poizat, Pascal II-1502
Pretorius, A. Johannes I-600
Probst, Florian II-1062
Puleston, Colin I-654

Quattrone, Giovanni I-209
Querzoni, Leonardo II-1558

Rafe, Vahid II-1143
Rahmani, Adel Torkaman II-1143
Ramakrishnan, I.V. II-909
Ramamohanarao, Kotagiri I-245
Reichert, Manfred I-101
Reinberger, Marie-Laure I-600
Rinderle, Stefanie I-101
Rodriguez, Noemi II-1285
Rossak, Wilhelm II-1358
Roy, Matthieu II-1445
Royer, Jean-Claude II-1502
Rundensteiner, Elke A. II-891
Russello, Giovanni II-1225
Ryan, Caspar II-1262

Sadjadi, S. Masoud II-1243
Sahlmann, Arnd II-1062
Samaras, George I-581
Sattler, Kai-Uwe I-227
Schade, Sven II-1062
Schallehn, Eike I-227
Schantz, Richard E. II-1208
Schanzenberger, Anja I-194
Schirner, Gunar II-1155
Schmidt, Andreas I-705
Schmidt, Douglas C. II-1520
Schrader, Thomas I-637
Shadbolt, Nigel I-654
Shapiro, Richard II-1208
Sharifi, Mohsen II-1143

Sharma, Praveen K. II-1208
Singh, Ambuj II-1340
Singh, Munindar P. I-509
Skrzypczyk, Christof I-460
Solberg, Arnor II-1190
Speicys Cardoso, Roberto II-1590
Spyns, Peter I-600, I-801
Stamoulis, George D. I-422
Stirewalt, R.E. Kurt II-1243
Stojanovic, Ljiljana II-1080
Stojanovic, Nenad II-1080
Studer, Rudi II-1080
Subieta, Kazimierz II-823
Subramonian, Venkita II-1520
Surányi, Gábor M. I-705
Sycara, Katia I-597

Tao, Feng I-654
Tempich, Christoph I-618
Terracina, Giorgio I-209
Tietz, Sebastian I-637
Tolksdorf, Robert I-637
Traversat, Bernard II-1125
Turowski, Klaus I-408
Tzitzikas, Yannis II-873, II-945

Ulbrich, Andreas II-1538
Unruh, Amy I-245
Ursino, Domenico I-209

Valduriez, Patrick I-19, I-174
van der Aalst, Wil I-1
van Steen, Maarten II-1225
Vassiliadis, Panos II-1608
Venkatasubramanian, Nalini II-1626
Vidot, Nicolas I-155
Villanova-Oliver, Marlène I-264
Vinoski, Steve II-1123
Vogels, Werner II-1123
Vučković, Jakša II-1413

Wang, Jinling I-373
Wang, Nanbor II-1520
Wei, Jun I-373
Weis, Torben II-1538
Westermann, Utz II-1030
Westhorpe, Christopher II-1262
Wickramasuriya, Jehan II-1626
Winiwarter, Werner II-1030
Winnewisser, Christian I-408
Wu, Huaigu II-1376, II-1413

Xu, Fenglian I-654
Xu, Lai I-526

Yeung, Wai Kit II-1463
Yolum, Pınar I-509
Yu, Shoujian I-55, II-1113

Zachariadis, Stefanos II-1303
Zarras, Apostolos II-1608
Ziegler, Cai-Nicolas II-840
Zillner, Sonja II-1030
Zimmermann, Armin I-139

Lecture Notes in Computer Science

For information about Vols. 1–3192

please contact your bookseller or Springer

Vol. 3305: P.M.A. Sloot, B. Chopard, A.G. Hoekstra (Eds.), Cellular Automata. XV, 883 pages. 2004.

Vol. 3293: C.-H. Chi, M. van Steen, C. Wills (Eds.), Web Content Caching and Distribution. IX, 283 pages. 2004.

Vol. 3292: R. Meersman, Z. Tari, A. Corsaro et al. (Eds.), On the Move to Meaningful Internet Systems 2004: OTM 2004 Workshops. XXIII, 885 pages. 2004.

Vol. 3291: R. Meersman, Z. Tari et al. (Eds.), On the Move to Meaningful Internet Systems 2004: CoopIS, DOA, and ODBASE. Part II. XXV, 824 pages. 2004.

Vol. 3290: R. Meersman, Z. Tari et al. (Eds.), On the Move to Meaningful Internet Systems 2004: CoopIS, DOA, and ODBASE. Part I. XXV, 823 pages. 2004.

Vol. 3287: A. Sanfeliu, J.F.M. Trinidad, J.A. Carrasco Ochoa (Eds.), Progress in Pattern Recognition, Image Analysis and Applications. XVII, 703 pages. 2004.

Vol. 3286: G. Karsai, E. Visser (Eds.), Generative Programming and Component Engineering. XIII, 491 pages. 2004.

Vol. 3284: A. Karmouch, L. Korba, E.R.M. Madeira (Eds.), Mobility Aware Technologies and Applications. XII, 382 pages. 2004.

Vol. 3280: C. Aykanat, T. Dayar, İ. Körpeoğlu (Eds.), Computer and Information Sciences - ISCIS 2004. XVIII, 1009 pages. 2004.

Vol. 3274: R. Guerraoui (Ed.), Distributed Computing. XIII, 465 pages. 2004.

Vol. 3273: T. Baar, A. Strohmeier, A. Moreira, S.J. Mellor (Eds.), <<UML>> 2004 - The Unified Modelling Language. XIII, 454 pages. 2004.

Vol. 3271: J. Vicente, D. Hutchison (Eds.), Management of Multimedia Networks and Services. XIII, 335 pages. 2004.

Vol. 3270: M. Jeckle, R. Kowalczyk, P. Braun (Eds.), Grid Services Engineering and Management. X, 165 pages. 2004.

Vol. 3269: J. López, S. Qing, E. Okamoto (Eds.), Information and Communications Security. XI, 564 pages. 2004.

Vol. 3266: J. Solé-Pareta, M. Smirnov, P.V. Mieghem, J. Domingo-Pascual, E. Monteiro, P. Reichl, B. Stiller, R.J. Gibbens (Eds.), Quality of Service in the Emerging Networking Panorama. XVI, 390 pages. 2004.

Vol. 3265: R.E. Frederking, K.B. Taylor (Eds.), Machine Translation: From Real Users to Research. XI, 392 pages. 2004. (Subseries LNAI).

Vol. 3264: G. Paliouras, Y. Sakakibara (Eds.), Grammatical Inference: Algorithms and Applications. XI, 291 pages. 2004. (Subseries LNAI).

Vol. 3263: M. Weske, P. Liggesmeyer (Eds.), Object-Oriented and Internet-Based Technologies. XII, 239 pages. 2004.

Vol. 3262: M.M. Freire, P. Chemouil, P. Lorenz, A. Gravey (Eds.), Universal Multiservice Networks. XIII, 556 pages. 2004.

Vol. 3261: T. Yakhno (Ed.), Advances in Information Systems. XIV, 617 pages. 2004.

Vol. 3260: I.G.M.M. Niemegeers, S.H. de Groot (Eds.), Personal Wireless Communications. XIV, 478 pages. 2004.

Vol. 3258: M. Wallace (Ed.), Principles and Practice of Constraint Programming – CP 2004. XVII, 822 pages. 2004.

Vol. 3257: E. Motta, N.R. Shadbolt, A. Stutt, N. Gibbins (Eds.), Engineering Knowledge in the Age of the Semantic Web. XVII, 517 pages. 2004. (Subseries LNAI).

Vol. 3256: H. Ehrig, G. Engels, F. Parisi-Presicce, G. Rozenberg (Eds.), Graph Transformations. XII, 451 pages. 2004.

Vol. 3255: A. Benczúr, J. Demetrovics, G. Gottlob (Eds.), Advances in Databases and Information Systems. XI, 423 pages. 2004.

Vol. 3254: E. Macii, V. Paliouras, O. Koufopavlou (Eds.), Integrated Circuit and System Design. XVI, 910 pages. 2004.

Vol. 3253: Y. Lakhnech, S. Yovine (Eds.), Formal Techniques, Modelling and Analysis of Timed and Fault-Tolerant Systems. X, 397 pages. 2004.

Vol. 3252: H. Jin, Y. Pan, N. Xiao, J. Sun (Eds.), Grid and Cooperative Computing - GCC 2004 Workshops. XVIII, 785 pages. 2004.

Vol. 3251: H. Jin, Y. Pan, N. Xiao, J. Sun (Eds.), Grid and Cooperative Computing - GCC 2004. XXII, 1025 pages. 2004.

Vol. 3250: L.-J. (LJ) Zhang, M. Jeckle (Eds.), Web Services. X, 301 pages. 2004.

Vol. 3249: B. Buchberger, J.A. Campbell (Eds.), Artificial Intelligence and Symbolic Computation. X, 285 pages. 2004. (Subseries LNAI).

Vol. 3246: A. Apostolico, M. Melucci (Eds.), String Processing and Information Retrieval. XIV, 332 pages. 2004.

Vol. 3245: E. Suzuki, S. Arikawa (Eds.), Discovery Science. XIV, 430 pages. 2004. (Subseries LNAI).

Vol. 3244: S. Ben-David, J. Case, A. Maruoka (Eds.), Algorithmic Learning Theory. XIV, 505 pages. 2004. (Subseries LNAI).

Vol. 3243: S. Leonardi (Ed.), Algorithms and Models for the Web-Graph. VIII, 189 pages. 2004.

Vol. 3239: G. Nicosia, V. Cutello, P.J. Bentley, J. Timmis (Eds.), Artificial Immune Systems. XII, 444 pages. 2004.

Vol. 3238: S. Biundo, T. Frühwirth, G. Palm (Eds.), KI 2004: Advances in Artificial Intelligence. XI, 467 pages. 2004. (Subseries LNAI).

Vol. 3236: M. Núñez, Z. Maamar, F.L. Pelayo, K. Pousttchi, F. Rubio (Eds.), Applying Formal Methods: Testing, Performance, and M/E-Commerce. XI, 381 pages. 2004.

Vol. 3235: D. de Frutos-Escrig, M. Nunez (Eds.), Formal Techniques for Networked and Distributed Systems – FORTE 2004. X, 377 pages. 2004.

Vol. 3232: R. Heery, L. Lyon (Eds.), Research and Advanced Technology for Digital Libraries. XV, 528 pages. 2004.

Vol. 3231: H.-A. Jacobsen (Ed.), Middleware 2004. XV, 514 pages. 2004.

Vol. 3230: J.L. Vicedo, P. Martínez-Barco, R. Muñoz, M. Saiz Noeda (Eds.), Advances in Natural Language Processing. XII, 488 pages. 2004. (Subseries LNAI).

Vol. 3229: J.J. Alferes, J. Leite (Eds.), Logics in Artificial Intelligence. XIV, 744 pages. 2004. (Subseries LNAI).

Vol. 3226: M. Bouzeghoub, C. Goble, V. Kashyap, S. Spaccapietra (Eds.), Semantics for Grid Databases. XIII, 326 pages. 2004.

Vol. 3225: K. Zhang, Y. Zheng (Eds.), Information Security. XII, 442 pages. 2004.

Vol. 3224: E. Jonsson, A. Valdes, M. Almgren (Eds.), Recent Advances in Intrusion Detection. XII, 315 pages. 2004.

Vol. 3223: K. Slind, A. Bunker, G. Gopalakrishnan (Eds.), Theorem Proving in Higher Order Logics. VIII, 337 pages. 2004.

Vol. 3222: H. Jin, G.R. Gao, Z. Xu, H. Chen (Eds.), Network and Parallel Computing. XX, 694 pages. 2004.

Vol. 3221: S. Albers, T. Radzik (Eds.), Algorithms – ESA 2004. XVIII, 836 pages. 2004.

Vol. 3220: J.C. Lester, R.M. Vicari, F. Paraguaçu (Eds.), Intelligent Tutoring Systems. XXI, 920 pages. 2004.

Vol. 3219: M. Heisel, P. Liggesmeyer, S. Wittmann (Eds.), Computer Safety, Reliability, and Security. XI, 339 pages. 2004.

Vol. 3217: C. Barillot, D.R. Haynor, P. Hellier (Eds.), Medical Image Computing and Computer-Assisted Intervention – MICCAI 2004. XXXVIII, 1114 pages. 2004.

Vol. 3216: C. Barillot, D.R. Haynor, P. Hellier (Eds.), Medical Image Computing and Computer-Assisted Intervention – MICCAI 2004. XXXVIII, 930 pages. 2004.

Vol. 3215: M.G.. Negoita, R.J. Howlett, L.C. Jain (Eds.), Knowledge-Based Intelligent Information and Engineering Systems. LVII, 906 pages. 2004. (Subseries LNAI).

Vol. 3214: M.G.. Negoita, R.J. Howlett, L.C. Jain (Eds.), Knowledge-Based Intelligent Information and Engineering Systems. LVIII, 1302 pages. 2004. (Subseries LNAI).

Vol. 3213: M.G.. Negoita, R.J. Howlett, L.C. Jain (Eds.), Knowledge-Based Intelligent Information and Engineering Systems. LVIII, 1280 pages. 2004. (Subseries LNAI).

Vol. 3212: A. Campilho, M. Kamel (Eds.), Image Analysis and Recognition. XXIX, 862 pages. 2004.

Vol. 3211: A. Campilho, M. Kamel (Eds.), Image Analysis and Recognition. XXIX, 880 pages. 2004.

Vol. 3210: J. Marcinkowski, A. Tarlecki (Eds.), Computer Science Logic. XI, 520 pages. 2004.

Vol. 3209: B. Berendt, A. Hotho, D. Mladenic, M. van Someren, M. Spiliopoulou, G. Stumme (Eds.), Web Mining: From Web to Semantic Web. IX, 201 pages. 2004. (Subseries LNAI).

Vol. 3208: H.J. Ohlbach, S. Schaffert (Eds.), Principles and Practice of Semantic Web Reasoning. VII, 165 pages. 2004.

Vol. 3207: L.T. Yang, M. Guo, G.R. Gao, N.K. Jha (Eds.), Embedded and Ubiquitous Computing. XX, 1116 pages. 2004.

Vol. 3206: P. Sojka, I. Kopecek, K. Pala (Eds.), Text, Speech and Dialogue. XIII, 667 pages. 2004. (Subseries LNAI).

Vol. 3205: N. Davies, E. Mynatt, I. Siio (Eds.), UbiComp 2004: Ubiquitous Computing. XVI, 452 pages. 2004.

Vol. 3204: C.A. Peña Reyes, Coevolutionary Fuzzy Modeling. XIII, 129 pages. 2004.

Vol. 3203: J. Becker, M. Platzner, S. Vernalde (Eds.), Field Programmable Logic and Application. XXX, 1198 pages. 2004.

Vol. 3202: J.-F. Boulicaut, F. Esposito, F. Giannotti, D. Pedreschi (Eds.), Knowledge Discovery in Databases: PKDD 2004. XIX, 560 pages. 2004. (Subseries LNAI).

Vol. 3201: J.-F. Boulicaut, F. Esposito, F. Giannotti, D. Pedreschi (Eds.), Machine Learning: ECML 2004. XVIII, 580 pages. 2004. (Subseries LNAI).

Vol. 3199: H. Schepers (Ed.), Software and Compilers for Embedded Systems. X, 259 pages. 2004.

Vol. 3198: G.-J. de Vreede, L.A. Guerrero, G. Marín Raventós (Eds.), Groupware: Design, Implementation and Use. XI, 378 pages. 2004.

Vol. 3196: C. Stary, C. Stephanidis (Eds.), User-Centered Interaction Paradigms for Universal Access in the Information Society. XII, 488 pages. 2004.

Vol. 3195: C.G. Puntonet, A. Prieto (Eds.), Independent Component Analysis and Blind Signal Separation. XXIII, 1266 pages. 2004.

Vol. 3194: R. Camacho, R. King, A. Srinivasan (Eds.), Inductive Logic Programming. XI, 361 pages. 2004. (Subseries LNAI).

Vol. 3193: P. Samarati, P. Ryan, D. Gollmann, R. Molva (Eds.), Computer Security – ESORICS 2004. X, 457 pages. 2004.

Vol. 3192: C. Bussler, D. Fensel (Eds.), Artificial Intelligence: Methodology, Systems, and Applications. XIII, 522 pages. 2004. (Subseries LNAI).

Vol. 3191: M. Klusch, S. Ossowski, V. Kashyap, R. Unland (Eds.), Cooperative Information Agents VIII. XI, 303 pages. 2004. (Subseries LNAI).

Vol. 3190: Y. Luo (Ed.), Cooperative Design, Visualization, and Engineering. IX, 248 pages. 2004.

Vol. 3189: P.-C. Yew, J. Xue (Eds.), Advances in Computer Systems Architecture. XVII, 598 pages. 2004.